**W9-AJR-622**

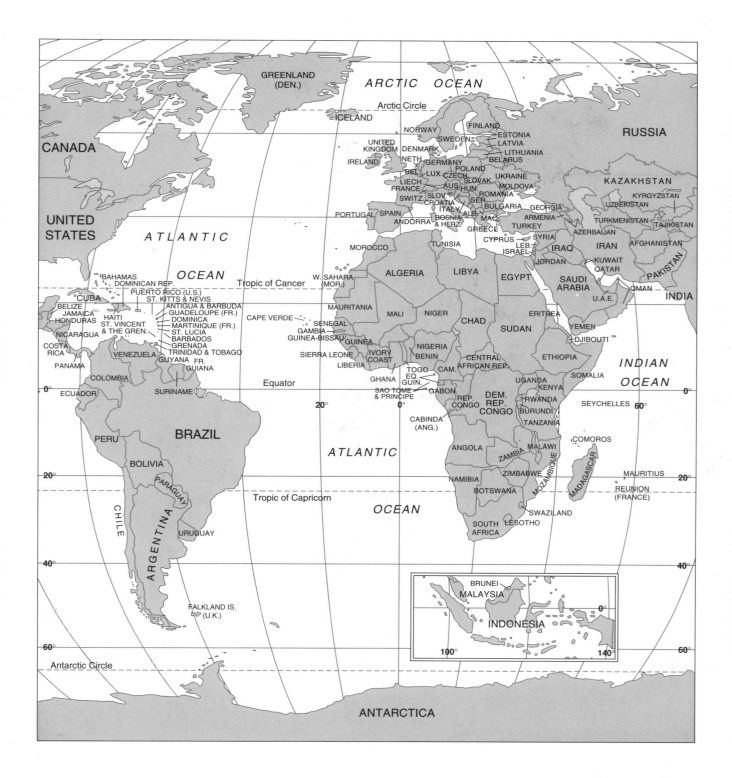

GREENLAND
(DEN.)

ARCTIC OCEAN

Arctic Circle

ICELAND

CANADA

NORWAY   FINLAND
         SWEDEN   ESTONIA
UNITED   DENMARK   LATVIA
KINGDOM           LITHUANIA
IRELAND  NETH.   GERMANY   BELARUS
         BEL.   POLAND
         LUX. CZECH   UKRAINE
         LIECH.   SLOVAK
FRANCE   AUS. HUN.   MOLDOVA
         SLOV.   ROMANIA
SWITZ.   CROATIA   SER.
         ITALY   BULGARIA   GEORGIA
PORTUGAL  SPAIN   BOSNIA   ALB.   ARMENIA
         ANDORRA  & HERZ.   MAC.   TURKEY   AZERBAIJAN
                  GREECE

RUSSIA

KAZAKHSTAN
                  KYRGYZSTAN
         UZBEKISTAN
                  TAJIKISTAN
TURKMENISTAN
         AFGHANISTAN

UNITED
STATES

ATLANTIC

OCEAN

BAHAMAS
DOMINICAN REP.
CUBA
PUERTO RICO (U.S.)
ST. KITTS & NEVIS
BELIZE
JAMAICA
HONDURAS
HAITI
ST. VINCENT
& THE GREN.
NICARAGUA
COSTA
RICA
PANAMA
VENEZUELA
COLOMBIA

ANTIGUA & BARBUDA
GUADELOUPE (FR.)
DOMINICA
MARTINIQUE (FR.)
ST. LUCIA
BARBADOS
GRENADA
TRINIDAD & TOBAGO
GUYANA   FR.
         GUIANA
SURINAME

Tropic of Cancer

W. SAHARA
(MOR.)

MOROCCO

TUNISIA

CYPRUS   SYRIA
LEB.
ISRAEL

IRAQ   IRAN
JORDAN   KUWAIT
         QATAR
SAUDI   U.A.E.   OMAN
ARABIA

PAKISTAN

INDIA

ALGERIA   LIBYA   EGYPT

MAURITANIA
         MALI   NIGER   CHAD
CAPE VERDE
SENEGAL
GAMBIA
GUINEA-BISSAU   GUINEA
         SIERRA LEONE   IVORY   NIGERIA
                  COAST   BENIN
         LIBERIA
GHANA   TOGO
         EQ.   CAM.
         GUIN.
SAO TOME   GABON
& PRINCIPE   0°

SUDAN
         ERITREA
                  YEMEN
                  DJIBOUTI
ETHIOPIA
         SOMALIA
CENTRAL
AFRICAN REP.
UGANDA   KENYA
REP.   DEM.   RWANDA
CONGO   REP.   BURUNDI
CABINDA   CONGO   TANZANIA
(ANG.)

SEYCHELLES

INDIAN

OCEAN

Equator

20°      0°   60°

PERU

BRAZIL

BOLIVIA

PARAGUAY

CHILE

ARGENTINA

URUGUAY

ATLANTIC

OCEAN

ANGOLA   ZAMBIA   MALAWI
NAMIBIA   ZIMBABWE   MOZAMBIQUE
         BOTSWANA
                  SWAZILAND
SOUTH   LESOTHO
AFRICA

COMOROS

MADAGASCAR

MAURITIUS
REUNION
(FRANCE)

Tropic of Capricorn

FALKLAND IS.
(U.K.)

BRUNEI
MALAYSIA

INDONESIA

100°      140°

0°

Antarctic Circle

ANTARCTICA

# International Business Law and Its Environment

*Fourth Edition*

**Richard Schaffer**

Walker College of Business
Appalachian State University

**Beverley Earle**

Bentley College

**Filiberto Agusti**

Steptoe & Johnson, Attorneys at Law

*with contributions from*
**F. William McCarty**
Western Michigan University
*and*
**Erika M. Brown**
Boston College

**WEST**

WEST EDUCATIONAL PUBLISHING COMPANY

*An International Thomson Publishing Company*

PUBLISHER/TEAM DIRECTOR: Jack W. Calhoun
SENIOR ACQUISTIONS EDITOR: Rob Dewey
ACQUISITIONS EDITOR: Scott D. Person
DEVELOPMENTAL EDITOR: Susanna C. Smart
PRODUCTION EDITOR: Kara ZumBahlen
MARKETING MANAGER: Michael Worls
MANUFACTURING COORDINATOR: Georgina Calderon
PRODUCTION HOUSE: BookMasters, Inc.
COMPOSITION: BookMasters, Inc.
INTERIOR DESIGN: Jennifer Lynne Martin
COVER DESIGN: Barbara M. Libby Book Design and Illustration, Cincinnati

**COPYRIGHT © 1999**
by West Educational Publishing
Cincinnati, Ohio
*An International Thomson Publishing Company*

**Library of Congress Cataloging-in-Publication Data**

Schaffer, Richard.
    International business law & its environment/Richard Schaffer, Beverley Earle,
    Filiberto Agusti. — 4th ed.
      p.  cm.
    Includes bibliographical references and index.
    ISBN 0-538-88483-5 (alk. paper)
    1. Commercial law.  2. International business enterprises—Law and
    legislation.  3. Export sales contracts.  4. Foreign trade regulation.  I.
    Earle, Beverley.  II. Agusti, Filiberto.  III. Title.  IV. Title: International
    business law and its environment.
  K1005.4.S33  1999
  341.7′53—DC21                                  98-3008
                                                        CIP

3 4 5 6 7 8 9  D1  7 6 5 4 3 2 1 0 9

Printed in the United States of America

I(T)P®

International Thomson Publishing
West Educational Publishing is an ITP Company.
The ITP trademark is used under license.

R. S.

*To my children, Anna Elizabeth and David Harris.*

B. E.

*To my husband, John, and our daughter, Molly,*
*for their love and support.*

F. A.

*To my father, Filiberto, and my mother, Maria Luisa,*
*who sacrificed so much that I might be free to write and read as I wish;*
*and to my wife Susan and our daughters, Caroline,*
*Olivia, and Jordan, for their patience.*

# About the Authors

RICHARD SCHAFFER is Professor of Business Law, Department of Finance, Walker College of Business, Appalachian State University. His primary teaching responsibilities have been in the area of business law, international business transactions, and the law of international trade and investment. Schaffer received his J.D. from the University of Mississippi and his LL.M. from New York University. A former practicing attorney, he has served as visiting consultant to the United Nations Department of International Economic and Social Affairs (CSDHA/CRIMP), New York, San Jose, and Vienna, on projects related to multinational corporations, corrupt practices, and socioeconomic development and as an expert member and *rapporteur* of international working groups on international economic criminality.

Schaffer has acted as Director for Education of the 1,000-industry-member North Carolina World Trade Association. He also has served as consultant to business schools on the interntionalization of the curriculum. He consults regularly with industry on topics related to the international home-textile industry.

BEVERLEY EARLE is an associate professor in the Law Department at Bentley College, where she has been on the faculty since 1983. She currently teaches the legal environment of business and international business law. She graduated with a B.A. from the University of Pennsylvania and a J.D. from Boston University and was admitted to practice in Massachusetts. Professor Earle taught law at Yunnan University in Kunming, China, on a U.S.I.A. grant during May and June of 1990 and in Strasbourg, France, in 1992; she studied in Paris on a sabbatical in 1993 and 1994. She has presented papers on various international law topics at professional meetings and has published papers in law journals. Professor Earle is the president of the International Section of the Academy of Legal Studies in Business.

FILIBERTO AGUSTI is a partner in the Washington, D.C., law firm of Steptoe & Johnson LLP, where he has practiced law since 1978. He represents major business lenders, governments, equity investors, and other participants in complex international commercial financing and corporate acquisition transactions. These representations have included negotiation, structuring, and legal drafting in international project finance and privatization transactions, cross-border corporate acquisitions, international joint ventures, and financing facilities. Mr. Agusti has authored several articles for the *Harvard Law Review* and other legal publications in the corporate arena. He also is a frequent speaker on corporate and commercial finance issues at professional and industry seminars in the United States and abroad.

Mr. Agusti was law clerk to Judge William H. Timbers, U.S. Court of Appeals for the Second Circuit, 1977–78. He is a 1977 graduate of the Harvard Law School, where he was a senior editor of the *Harvard Law Review*. He graduated summa cum laude with a B.A. from the University of Illinois in 1974.

# Contents in Brief

# Contents

# List of Frequently Used Acronyms

**As Used by the United States Trade Representative**

APEC . . . . . . . . . Asia Pacific Economic Cooperation

ASEAN . . . . . . . . Association of Southeast Asian Nations

BIT . . . . . . . . . . Bilateral Investment Treaty

CACM . . . . . . . . Central American Common Market

CARICOM . . . . . Caribbean Common Market

CFTA . . . . . . . . Canada Free Trade Agreement

EU . . . . . . . . . . European Union

EFTA . . . . . . . . European Free Trade Association

GATS . . . . . . . . General Agreement on Trade in Services

GATT . . . . . . . . General Agreement on Tariffs and Trade

GCC . . . . . . . . . Gulf Cooperation Council

GDP . . . . . . . . . Gross Domestic Product

GSP . . . . . . . . . Generalized System of Preferences

IPR . . . . . . . . . . Intellectual Property Rights

ITA . . . . . . . . . . Information Technology Agreement

MAI . . . . . . . . . Multilateral Agreement on Investment

MERCOSUR . . . . Southern Common Market

MFA . . . . . . . . . Multifiber Arrangement

MOSS . . . . . . . . Market-Oriented-Sector-Selective

MOU . . . . . . . . . Memorandum of Understanding

MRA . . . . . . . . . Mutual Recognition Agreement

NAFTA . . . . . . . North American Free Trade Agreement

NIS . . . . . . . . . . Newly Independent States

OECD . . . . . . . . Organization for Economic Cooperation and Development

SADC . . . . . . . . Southern African Development Community

TRIPs . . . . . . . . Trade-Related Aspects of Intellectual Property Rights

TRIMs . . . . . . . Trade-Related Investment Measures

USDA . . . . . . . . U.S. Department of Agriculture

USITC . . . . . . . U.S. International Trade Commission

USTR . . . . . . . . United States Trade Representative

WTO . . . . . . . . World Trade Organization

# Table of Cases

The principal cases are in bold type. Cases cited or discussed in the text are roman type. References are to pages. Cases cited in principal cases are within other quoted materials are not included.

# Preface

It has been said that America's interest in international education has peaked and ebbed with the changing tide of the American political climate, rising in times of economic expansion and ebbing during periods of political isolation or economic protectionism. Perhaps however, the cycle has finally been broken, and industry leaders, government policymakers, and educators alike have come to understand the importance of making a permanent commitment to international education. During the last two decades America has been faced with an increasingly competitive global marketplace and a mounting trade deficit. As a result, the nation has realized the necessity of competing more aggressively with foreign firms, both here and abroad. More significantly, new trade and investment opportunities abroad have been spurred by the opening of markets in the developing countries and by the decline of communism. The outcome has been perhaps the greatest renewal of interest in international business education in our history—a renewal sure to last well into the next century.

These changes are broadly reflected in higher education in general and in business school curricula in particular. They have originated from stricter accreditation requirements, the needs of American industry, increased funding for international business research and travel, increased study-abroad opportunities for students, and a higher level of awareness by business faculty and administrators. These changes include the internationalization of the core curricula and the introduction of specialized courses in international business. This text is designed for use in courses in International Business Law, International Business Transactions, or the Law of International Trade and Investment. The authors have attempted to provide a fairly comprehensive treatment of the three primary forms of international business: the laws of international trade, the licensing of intellectual property, and foreign investment. Our approach is to present these three market-entry methods beginning with trade, which involves the least penetration into the foreign market, and concluding with foreign investment, which immerses the firm completely in the social, cultural, and legal systems of its host country.

Most readers will be familiar with textbooks written for courses in the Legal Environment of Business or the more traditional Business Law. While the format of *International Business Law* is similar to those other texts (particularly in the blending of text and edited cases), the content and the approach to the subject matter are very different.

**Environmental vs. Traditional Approach Balanced.** This text covers both the international aspects of traditional business law subjects (sales, commercial paper, corporate law, agency, etc.) and those subjects generally considered more "environmental" in nature (antitrust law, administrative law, ethics, trade regulation, employment law, crimes, environmental law and others).

**Emphasis on Private Law.** In keeping with the needs of the intended audience, this text emphasizes the law as it affects international business transaction, whether it be in the area of trade, licensing, or investment. Of course, in-depth treatment also is given to the public law of international trade, investment restrictions, technology transfer laws, and other political controls over international business. General principles of international law, such as the law of treaties and the role of international and intergovernmental organizations, are presented to provide the fundamentals needed for study.

**International/Comparative Approach.** No text can attempt to teach the business law of every nation in which a firm might do business. As a result, discussions of foreign law are often intended simply to illustrate trends in the law in different regions of the world or within certain legal or economic systems. This comparative approach will be used throughout the text, in such areas as sales law, negotiable instruments law, advertising law, and antitrust law. Of course, U.S. law and relevant international treaties and conventions are treated in greater detail.

**A Business/Managerial Approach.** Where appropriate, the text focuses on management decision making for the business person. This approach is reflected in two important aspects of the text's organization. First, the discussion progresses from forms of international business that require the least involvement and commitment in foreign markets to forms that require the greatest penetration and risk—that is, from trade (exporting and importing) through the licensing of patents, copyrights, and trademarks to investment in overseas plants and factories. Second, it is often said that the management of international business is the management of risk. Chapter 1 is designed to introduce the reader to the risks of international business and to how they differ from the risks of doing business at home. A study of these subjects in subsequent chapters then should reveal to the reader the importance of planning to avoid, shift, or reduce these risks.

Where appropriate, the text links international business law to the development of a firm's international business strategy. For example, Chapter 13, on imports, customs, and tariff law, does not view importing as an isolated transaction but rather stresses the importance of customs and tariff law on business decision making by the global firm (e.g., the use of Mexican *maquiladora* assembly plants by U.S. or Japanese manufacturing firms).

**Cultural, Political, and Economic Aspects.** Discussion of the cultural, political, and economic aspects of international business has been integrated throughout the text. For instance, political risk is introduced early in the first chapter but then is covered in more detail in later discussions of such topics as the risks of foreign investment, the impact of the 1979 Iranian crisis on American firms, or the impact of the 1956 closing of the Suez Canal on international shipping. Similarly, the cultural aspects of doing business in foreign cultures are discussed within the context of the legal problems of employing local sales or buying agents. Only through such integration can a coordinated approach to the subject be managed. Excerpted articles on the cultural and economic environments of international business, however, are included to provide varying perspectives.

**Ethics.** Because ethical questions can arise in varying contexts, the discussion of ethics and social responsibility also has been integrated throughout the text. The great influence of political, economic, and social forces on international business requires an even broader discussion of ethics than normally would be undertaken in a legal environment course. These questions are pursued in many contexts, including bribery and corrupt practices, export controls, investment in developing countries (e.g., the Bhopal case), and technology transfer. Many of the case problems at the end of the chapters present ethical issues for discussion.

**Developing and Nonmarket-Economy Countries and Privatization.** In any international business text, a thorough treatment of these topics is essential. Here again, however, we have chosen to integrate our discussions throughout the text. The decision was made to address the legal problems of doing business in the developing countries of Africa, Asia, Latin America, and the Caribbean, or in countries with economies in transition (including many formerly communist countries of Russia and

Eastern Europe), within the context of the three forms of international business on which the book is based: trade, licensing, and investment. This context seems most in keeping with the format of the book and the nature of international business.

The most difficult aspect of preparing this book has been the need to update the content on an almost daily basis. Political changes during the past few years have had a great impact on trade and investment law. We can only trust that the diligent student will make every effort to follow current events and to consider this text in that light.

**Key Revisions.** Since the publication of the third edition of *International Business Law and Its Environment,* many political and economic changes have taken place around the world. These changes are addressed in this new edition.

## Part One: The Legal Environment of International Business

- Political and economic changes in the republics of the former Soviet Union and Eastern Europe and their impact on firms trading and investing there are addressed.
- Updated trade and economic data, including new charts and graphs.
- Expanded coverage of the principles of international law and the importance of international organizations.
- Expanded coverage of the recent changes in the European Union.
- A revised chapter on the resolution of disputes.

## Part Two: International Sales, Credits, and the Commercial Transaction

- Revised treatment of international sales law and new case selections, including choice of law clauses; requirements of a contract; international battle of the forms; warranties; *force majeure;* and a comparative analysis of U.S., Chinese, and international contract law.
- Thorough analysis of Incoterms 1990.

- New material on the liability of air carriers under the Warsaw Convention and a new U.S. Supreme Court case on maritime bills of lading.
- Inclusion of a new *Uniform Customs and Practices 500* and its new rules for handling letters of credit.

## Part Three: International and U.S. Trade Law

- Thorough coverage of the new GATT 1994 and World Trade Organization agreements and the *North American Free Trade Agreement.*
- An updated chapter on GATT 1994 and its basic principles, including WTO dispute settlement cases.
- A chapter on *Laws Governing Access to Foreign Markets,* including technical barriers to trade, ISO standards, important licensing, government procurement, trade in agriculture and textiles, and intellectual property.
- Updated discussion of U.S. Section 301.
- Updated sections on unfair import laws, with new discussion on Chinese prison labor.
- A chapter on *North American Free Trade Laws,* including trade and tariff provisions, Mexican import regulations, rules of origin, cross-border issues, environmental and labor issues, and dispute settlement.
- Updated material on doing business in Mexico.
- U.S. export control material updated to reflect political changes of the 1990s.

## Part Four: Regulations of the International Marketplace

- A chapter devoted to laws regulating the protection of labor and employment discrimination outside the United States and extraterritorial application of U.S. law.
- A chapter on environmental law, including regulations for the export of hazardous material and marine pollution.
- A chapter on privatization—the sale of state-owned property to private interests—and on legal aspects of economic restructuring in Latin America, Eastern Europe, and the republics of the former Soviet Union.
- Updated treatment of foreign investment regulations in developing countries.

- Expanded and updated sections on international protection of patents, trademarks, and copyrights.

## Pedagogical Features of the Fourth Edition

- Revised case selection, reflecting recent legal changes.
- New sample documents and forms.
- Up-to-date regional maps.
- Issues boxes providing real-world examples.
- Increased discussion of cultural and ethical issues.
- Detailed subject-matter index.
- Internet addresses to direct students to relevant international sites.

# Acknowledgments

The authors wish to express their gratitude to the following reviewers for their help in preparing the past two editions:

Mark B. Baker
University of Texas-Austin

Joan T. A. Gabel
Georgia State University

Larry A. Di Matteo
University of Miami

David P. Hanson
Duquesne University

Sandra L. Linda
University of Delaware

F. William McCarty
Western Michigan University

Carol J. Miller
Southwest Missouri State University

Fred Naffziger
Indiana University at South Bend

Gregory T. Naples
Marquette University

Lynda J. Oswald
University of Michigan

Bruce L. Rockwood
Bloomsburg University

John C. Ruhnka
University of Colorado-Denver

Clyde D. Stoltenberg
University of Kansas

Alan R. Thiele
University of Houston

Susan M. Vance
St. Mary's College

Peter C. Ward
Millsaps College

John Wrieden
Florida International University

Beverley Earle would like to thank Professor Elliot Mossman, Director of the Center for Soviet and East European Studies and Chairman of the Slavic Languages Department, University of Pennsylvania, for steering her towards law and teaching.

Filiberto Agusti would like to thank Maureen O'Keefe Ward, Wolfram Anders, Gennady Pilch, Mark D. Davis, Robert W. Fleishman, Stanley Smilack, Edward J. Krauland, and Betty Ann Smith.

Each of us would like to thank Jay A. Erstling and Susan J. Marsnik of St. Thomas University for preparing the instructor's manual. We also wish to express our sincere appreciation to our editors at West Educational Publishing Company—Rob Dewey, Scott Person, Susan Smart, and Kara ZumBahlen—for their continued advice, support, and encouragement throughout the revision of this book.

Richard Schaffer
Beverley Earle
Filiberto Agusti

# International Business Law and Its Environment

# Part One

# The Legal Environment of International Business

P art One of *International Business Law* provides a framework for understanding both international business and the legal environment in which it operates. The chapters focus on how economic, social, and political forces influence the development of the law and legal institutions. Chapter One provides a conceptual framework for studying international business. The chapter explains the three major forms of international business: trade (importing and exporting); licensing agreements for the transfer of patents, copyrights, trademarks, and other intellectual property (including franchising); and active foreign investment (particularly in facilities of production) through mergers, acquisitions, and joint ventures.

In Chapter One the reader is also asked to consider how the risks of international business differ from the risks of doing business at home. How does a firm deal with the added risks of doing business over great distances, the risks of language and cultural barriers, the risks of miscommunications, currency fluctuations, international hostilities and political interference, the risks of trade controls or restrictions on investment, the risks of foreign litigation, or the risks of nonpayment or breach of contract? By raising these questions, this chapter illustrates that the management of an international business transaction is, in large part, the management of risk. The remainder of the book provides the opportunity for

the thoughtful reader to consider how careful business and legal planning can help to avoid or reduce these risks or shift them to another party to the transaction.

Many readers will have little familiarity with either international business or international legal principles. Chapter Two explains the nature and sources of international business law, which includes both internationally agreed-upon legal principles, such as those embodied in a treaty, convention, or other international agreement, and the rules and decisions found in the domestic law of individual nations (e.g., statutes passed by a national legislature).

In turn, each of these bodies of law can be classified as either public law or private law. If the rule of law affects a private (often commercial) transaction between two parties, such as between buyer and seller or shipper and ocean carrier, it is considered private law. If the rule of law determines the rights and responsibilities of nations in relation to one another, or places public controls on an otherwise private transaction (e.g., criminal penalties for making a false customs declaration), the law is considered public law. Chapter Two lays a foundation for understanding these basic principles.

The reader must also understand the role of intergovernmental organizations. Many international business problems can be resolved only through international or regional cooperation.

Whether the problem is related to the laundering of drug money through the international banking system, setting standards for the protection of the environment from oil spills, using restrictions on business or trade with countries such as Iraq for political purposes, or developing uniform rules for international sales contracts, international organizations can be useful in bringing individual nations to agreement on difficult issues. These organizations are introduced in Chapter Two.

Customs unions and other free trade areas are groups of countries, or trading blocs, that are economically and legally united to enhance trade and to improve economic and business conditions. Free trade areas have reduced barriers to trade and led to great economic and societal changes. These trading blocs exist in all regions of the world, but the two best known are the *European Union* (sometimes still referred to as the European Community) and the *North American Free Trade Agreement*. Chapter Three looks at the legal relationships among countries within these areas and the impact of economic integration on business.

Chapter Four discusses how disputes are settled in an international business transaction, including litigation and arbitration. It addresses issues of jurisdiction and procedural rules for litigating international cases. For instance, the chapter attempts to answer such questions as: If a company does business in a foreign country, can the company be sued there? If a buyer purchases goods from a foreign firm that does not regularly do business in the United States, under what circumstances can the buyer sue that firm in U.S. courts? If a product that is produced in one nation injures a consumer in another nation, where should the injured party's claim be heard? If a firm obtains a court judgment in one country, can the firm enforce it against the defendant's assets held in another country? Since the costs and risks of foreign litigation are substantial, what can the parties do in advance to provide an alternative to litigation should a dispute result?

## Chapter One

# Introduction to International Business

## Economic Interdependence

Many economists and business experts believe that no business can be purely domestic. The realities of the modern world make all business international. No longer can an economic or political change in one country occur without causing reverberations throughout the world's markets. The effects of the Persian Gulf War were reflected on international stock exchanges. A civil war on the African continent affects the price of commodities in London and New York. A change in interest rates in Germany affects investment flows and currency exchange rates in the United States. The European Monetary Union could have great impact on exchange rates and cost of doing business. A deterioration in trade relations between the United States and China can affect a manufacturing plant in Canada or Australia. The world today is more economically interdependent than at any other time in history, which has led to the globalization of product, service, and capital markets.

Economic interdependence is the result of many factors. Precious natural resources and raw materials are located around the world. Technological advances in travel and communications have brought people closer together. Nations have moved away from protectionism and increasingly toward free trade; thus markets for goods and services that were once closed to foreign competition are now open. The world has seen a steady movement toward economic integration and the development of free trade areas and "common markets" among nations. Greater political stability in the developing countries has led to increased foreign investment, industrial-

ization, and the integration of those nations into the world economy. Economic interdependence also can be attributed to the sharing of technology and know-how, with patents, copyrights, and trademarks now licensed for use around the globe as freely as goods and services are sold. The interrelatedness of financial markets, the worldwide flow of capital, and the coordination of economic policies between nations have had a tremendous impact on the global economy.

Political changes in the last decade also increased countries' interdependence. Throughout the world, countries are moving toward greater political freedom and democracy. The breakup of the Soviet Union in 1991 into independent republics, the largest of which is Russia, opened those countries to opportunities for investment by western companies. It also freed much of Eastern and Central Europe from communist oppression, leaving them open for foreign investment. This process of converting from closed communist-dominated governments to a free market economic system based on private enterprise has allowed these nations to become more economically integrated with the rest of the world. A similar phenomenon is occurring in Latin America and Asia as well. Many of these countries that were once ruled by military dictatorships have moved toward democracy. This new freedom opens them up to foreign investors and helps to integrate them into the world's economic community.

This greater economic interdependence has required nations to reach agreement on important legal issues. Thus the global economy has been affected by the development of widely accepted legal norms and conventions, which provide a stable and consistent legal environment for firms operating on a global scale. In summary, the factors that yet hold the greatest promise for change are the growth of democracy, the resurgence of market-oriented economies, and the decline of socialism.

## The Global Marketplace

Economic interdependence has caused many changes in the global marketplace. The impact on American firms has been dramatic. New competitive forces created by the emergence of economic powerhouses in Europe and Asia have transformed the modern business world. The European Union is forming a single market, with a reunified Germany emerging as the continent's economic giant. The Asian countries have become increasingly industrialized and powerful. Goods from countries such as Japan and South Korea, once known only for their low cost, are now known for their quality and workmanship. Tokyo and Hong Kong now rival New York as world financial centers.

Many countries are now capable of wielding the tremendous economic clout they derive from their rich supplies of natural resources, such as bauxite, copper, and rubber. Middle Eastern nations, rich with oil, have moved from the biblical age to the industrialized age in a single generation. Mexico and the countries of Latin America possess not only precious natural resources, but also an abundant supply of labor. And the economies of Eastern Europe, Russia, and the other newly independent republics of the former Soviet Union, now in need of economic assistance, may some day themselves become competitive players in the global marketplace.

**The U.S. Experience.** Americans have long been active in all aspects of international business. U.S. history is rich with stories of the "Yankee trader"—from the colonial period to the present. U.S.–owned trademarks, such as Coca Cola and McDonald's, are recognized in every culture and in every language. U.S. firms have built factories around the globe and shared their technology, know-how, and management capabilities with their investment partners.

U.S. involvement in international business has come chiefly from its largest companies. Small and medium-sized manufacturing firms traditionally shied away from involvement overseas due to a provincial attitude, rooted in America's westward expansion and based on the idea that business could expand infinitely merely by tapping domestic markets. The country had a vast supply of natural resources, and domestic demand exceeded supply, so businesses felt little need to sell products overseas. The presence of vast oceans separating the nation from its trading partners made foreign trade seem even more bothersome. Furthermore, the United States was preoccupied with other matters. First came the movement westward, then the political isolationism and economic protectionism spawned by the first World War. The new European immigrants quickly sought to forget their pasts, preferring to become Americans and to adopt the language and customs of their new country.

At the close of World War II, the United States was in a preeminent political and economic position relative to the war-devastated nations of Europe and the Far East. The factories of Europe and Japan lay in rubble, with North America having virtually the only functioning industrialized economy in the world. The United States, to its credit, quickly recognized its responsibility to pull the world out of the ravages of war. It succeeded, in large part, through the creation of a massive industrial economy based on consumer goods that stimulated and strengthened the redevelopment of once-industrial Europe and Japan. In the process, however, many U.S. companies never viewed themselves as a part of a world marketplace and did not structure their market objectives or economic goals accordingly. Indeed, not until the 1980s, when the effect of mounting U.S. deficits began to be felt, and when foreign firms gained a greater share of U.S. domestic markets, did U.S. companies realize that oceans could no longer insulate them from foreign competition.

**The Education of U.S. Managers.** U.S. companies have learned about international business the hard way. Unlike their Dutch and Swiss counterparts, U.S. managers did not have a wealth of experience to draw upon. The Dutch, for instance, have always depended on trade for the very existence of their small country. Americans learned through trial and error, and, in the process, made many mistakes. A number of infamous marketing blunders and cultural *faux pas* committed by naive U.S. managers are now a part of marketing folklore.

Many U.S. firms simply lacked the commitment to international business. Some companies, for instance, viewed exporting as essential only when domestic market cycles turned downward. As a result, many ventures failed. During the time needed to gear up for the export process (e.g., identifying foreign market potential, developing a marketing plan, identifying potential buyers, participating in foreign trade shows, finding foreign sales representatives and establishing channels of distribution, arranging for trade finance, etc.), the domestic cycles would turn again, and U.S. companies would soon lose their new-found interest in selling overseas. These same firms would ship products abroad with no thought given to the problems of marketing in foreign cultures or to how they would supply parts or service for the products they sold. Without a long-term commitment, these firms were viewed by foreign buyers as unreliable suppliers. Companies that tried to find foreign buyers or investment partners soon learned that entering international markets required much patience, time, and commitment.

Recently, U.S. managers have undergone a difficult and arduous retraining process. They have had to be retrained to negotiate, sell, manage, and compete with their foreign counterparts in foreign environments. They now recognize that cultural and ethnic differences will influence their business dealings overseas. They are aware, for example, of the influence of religion on business in the Middle East, of the impact of the reunification of a once-divided Germany on the German people, and of their image as arrogant, rich Yankees when doing business in Panama or Mexico. U.S. managers are learning to be sensitive to labor issues in Haiti and southern Africa and to the feelings of some Canadians who seek to preserve the use of the French language in Quebec.

U.S. managers are also keenly aware of the necessity of keeping abreast of the day-to-day changes in the world's economic and political events. U.S. multinational corporations, international banks and brokerage houses, insurance companies, air and ocean carriers, international architectural and construction firms, overseas branches of U.S. law firms, trading companies, and many others all feel the impact of world events. Morning television now gives nearly instantaneous foreign exchange quotations and the results of opening trading on stock exchanges around the world. International managers must scrutinize political events carefully, and their impact on business is evaluated continually. War in the Persian Gulf can disrupt shipping, an oil spill in foreign waters means negotiations with foreign governments, and the toppling of a communist government can mean great political instability—or it can mean great opportunity. The experienced international manager is continually reassessing these global economic and political situations to gauge their impact on the firm's operations.

## Forms of International Business

This text classifies international business into three categories: (1) trade, (2) international licensing of technology and intellectual property (trademarks, patents, and copyrights), and (3) foreign direct investment. To the marketer, these broad categories describe three important methods for entering a foreign market. To the lawyer, they also represent the form of doing business in a foreign country and the legal relationship between parties to a business transaction. Each method brings a different set of problems to the firm, because the level of *foreign penetration* and entanglement in each country is different. Trade usually represents the least entanglement, and thus the least political, economic, and legal risk, especially if the exporting firm is not soliciting business overseas or maintaining sales agents or inventories there. An investment in a plant and operations overseas usually represents the greatest market penetration and thus the greatest risk to the firm.

Considerable overlap occurs among these different forms of doing business. A business plan for the production and marketing of a single product may contain elements of each form. To illustrate, a U.S. firm might purchase the rights to a trademark for use on an article of high-fashion clothing made from fabric exported from China and assembled in offshore plants in the Caribbean for shipment to the United States and Europe. Here, a business strategy encompasses elements of trade, licensing, and investment. For firms just entering a new foreign market, the method of entry might depend on a host of considerations, including the sophistication of the firm, its overseas experience, the nature of its product or services, its commitment of capital resources, and the amount of risk it is willing to bear.

## Trade

Trade consists of the import and export of goods and services. *Exporting* is the term generally used to refer to the process of sending goods out of a country, and *importing* is used to denote when goods are brought into a country. However, a more accurate definition is that *exporting is the shipment of goods or the rendering of services to a foreign buyer located in a foreign country. Importing* is then defined as *the process of buying goods from a foreign supplier and entering them into the customs territory of a different country.* Every export entails an import, and vice versa.

Trade is as old as the oldest civilization. Throughout history, countries traded to obtain needed items that were not readily available in their country. The marketplaces of Europe, Africa, Asia, and the Middle East had been the scene of trade for hundreds of years before seaborne trade became established. By the sixteenth century, the first international sea trade routes were established by the Europeans. With the advent of great naval power, Portugal and Spain opened the Americas, India, and the Pacific to trade. Portuguese was the language of the ocean traders. Portugal purchased textiles from India and China with gold taken from Africa. They traded Chinese porcelain to Spain for gold that Spain had taken from Mexico. By the eighteenth century the Dutch had created a great trading empire based on pepper and spices, and England relied on America for tobacco, corn, and cotton. And for more than three hundred years, trade in horses, weapons, and slaves thrived.

**Comparative Advantage.** Today the products are different, but the economic concepts are the same. In theoretical terms, the concept of *absolute advantage* states that nations should concentrate their efforts on producing those goods that they can make most efficiently, with a minimum of effort and waste. Any surplus of goods left over after domestic consumption is then traded for goods that another nation has produced under the same circumstances. David Ricardo, a nineteenth century British economist, stated that a country can gain from trading goods even though it may not have an absolute advantage in producing those goods. This notion formed the basis for the theory of *comparative advantage.* Comparative advantage exists if the costs of production and price received for the goods allow the goods to be sold for a higher price in a foreign country than at home. When countries specialize in producing goods over which they have a comparative advantage, all countries will produce more, consume more, and wealth and employment will increase. An example from the early trading days illustrates how this concept works.

By the sixteenth century, Portugal had already established outposts for trading silk, cloth, and spices throughout the Indian Ocean. The Portuguese had also found ways of trading with faraway China. Portuguese traders discovered that although they could get silk most easily from their outposts in Persia or India, it would be to their benefit to obtain these products from China. China had greater resources and more effective production methods, which made their products less costly and of a better quality than anything that Portugal could obtain elsewhere. China, on the other hand, had a great appetite for the pepper that Portugal could obtain readily from Indian outposts. China could produce its own pepper, but not of the same quantity or quality that the Portuguese traders could provide. Although Portugal had its own source of silk, and China its own pepper, their advantage came from obtaining these goods from one another. Thus, Portugal had a comparative advantage in pepper and China in silk. By focusing their capital and labor on doing what they did best, each country could produce and consume more of both products.

It is important to emphasize that this transaction was not regulated by today's barrage of tariffs, government subsidies to producers, politics, historical events, or other complicating factors. Michael Porter, in *The Competitive Advantage of Nations,* introduced a modification of this earlier concept, advocating that a nation's advantage is determined by the ability of its companies to increase productivity and continuously innovate. In today's world, the politics of protectionism or free trade could turn an economic model inside out. But world trade has developed and become the major commercial activity that it is today based upon this principle of comparative advantage.

**Recent Trends in U.S. Trade.**   Since the 1970s, U.S. imports have increased dramatically, outpacing the growth in exports. This has led to a growing trade deficit for the nation. In the early 1980s, the trade deficit was blamed on the high value of the U.S. dollar, which made U.S. goods expensive for export to foreign buyers (who had to exchange their currencies for dollars in order to buy U.S. goods). The decade of the 1980s, however, saw intense international efforts, coordinated by central banks in the United States, Japan, and Europe, to bring the value of the dollar down (to the chagrin of U.S. tourists abroad). By 1995 the U.S. dollar had sunk to record lows against most major foreign currencies (which boosted exports, but prompted fears of inflation due to the high cost of imported goods). The U.S. government initiated a large-scale incentive and public awareness program to encourage small and medium-sized manufacturers and service companies to enter foreign markets. During the 1980s reports showed that a mere 250 of the largest U.S. multinational corporations accounted for 85 percent of U.S. exports. The U.S. Department of Commerce believed that a great number of smaller U.S. firms had products suitable for export markets if they would only make the commitment needed to tap those potential customers. To assist these "new-to-export" companies, the Department of Commerce spearheaded a national effort to introduce small firms to the how-to's of exporting. By the end of the decade, many of these new-to-export companies were contributing significantly to the U.S. export

base. Furthermore, foreign firms that had invested heavily in U.S. factories were turning their attention to exporting their U.S.-made products. Honda Motor Company, for example, exports sizeable numbers of automobiles from its U.S. plants to many countries, including Japan. A recent study of one state, North Carolina, showed that a large percentage—more than 50 percent—of foreign-owned firms operating in that state were exporting their products abroad. In the 1990s, as U.S. firms became more competitive, and as economic growth in Europe and in the developing countries provided markets for U.S. goods and services, U.S. exports continued to increase.

The U.S. economic recovery begun in the early 1990s continues. The U.S. dollar has appreciated in 1996–1997 and combined with low inflation and price competitiveness, the economy remains strong. In 1995, the U.S. led the world in exporting with 11.6 percent of merchandise and 16.1 percent of world services.

During the last ten years, the U.S. share of world merchandise exports remained fairly constant, at about 12 percent. The U.S. is the world's largest exporter, with Germany and Japan just behind. The U.S.'s largest trading partners are Canada and Japan. But in terms of the U.S. balance of trade in goods with its major trading partners, the U.S. maintained a surplus of exports over imports only with Mexico. U.S. consumers purchased far more from Canada, Europe, Asia, Japan, and China than was sold in return. The U.S. suffered its worst trade deficits with Japan (about one-half of which was in automobile imports) and China. Some of the best prospects for future export growth are predicted to be in the emerging markets of developing countries.

The importance of trade to the U.S. economy cannot be overstressed. According to the U.S. Department of Commerce, U.S. exports of goods and services accounted for 37 percent of real gross domestic product growth from 1986 to 1993. This has been especially important during recessionary periods, when exports continued to fuel growth in the economy. Estimates are that during this period exports accounted for 51 percent of the new jobs in the United States, and for virtually all of the increase in manufacturing jobs. The Office of the United States Trade Representative estimates that wages paid to U.S. workers in export manu-

**EXHIBIT 1.1  World, Regional, and Country Growth: 1987–98: The World Economic Expansion Continues in 1997**

| Item | Average 1987–91 | 1992 | 1993 | 1994 | 1995 | 1996 | 1997 Forecast (Low/High) | 1998 Forecast (Low/High) |
|---|---|---|---|---|---|---|---|---|
| **World** | **3.3** | **2.4** | **2.4** | **3.7** | **3.5** | **3.8** | **3.8/4.2** | **3.7/4.3** |
| **Industrial Countries** | **2.9** | **1.7** | **0.8** | **2.8** | **2.1** | **2.3** | **2.2/2.6** | **2.2/2.8** |
| United States | 2.1 | 2.7 | 2.3 | 3.5 | 2.0 | 2.4 | 2.2/2.4 | 1.8/2.0 |
| Canada | 1.9 | 0.8 | 2.2 | 4.1 | 2.3 | 1.5 | 2.9/3.3 | 2.5/2.9 |
| Japan | 4.8 | 1.1 | 0.1 | 0.5 | 0.9 | 3.6 | 1.6/2.0 | 2.5/3.0 |
| European Union | 3.0 | 1.1 | (0.5) | 2.8 | 2.5 | 1.6 | 2.2/2.6 | 2.4/3.0 |
| Germany[1] | 3.6 | 2.2 | (1.1) | 2.9 | 1.9 | 1.3 | 2.2/2.6 | 2.3/2.9 |
| France | 2.9 | 1.2 | (1.3) | 2.8 | 2.2 | 1.1 | 2.0/2.4 | 2.6/3.4 |
| Australia | 2.6 | 2.3 | 4.0 | 4.9 | 3.2 | 4.1 | 3.0/3.4 | 3.0/3.6 |
| **Developing Countries** | **5.0** | **6.4** | **6.3** | **6.6** | **5.9** | **6.3** | **5.8/6.5** | **5.8/6.6** |
| By Region: | | | | | | | | |
| Africa | 2.5 | 0.8 | 0.9 | 2.9 | 3.0 | 5.0 | 4.7/5.3 | 4.5/5.5 |
| Sub-Saharan Africa | 2.2 | 0.9 | 1.7 | 2.8 | 4.4 | 5.3 | 5.3/5.8 | 4.5/5.5 |
| Asia | 7.3 | 8.8 | 8.7 | 9.1 | 8.6 | 8.0 | 7.8/8.4 | 7.2/7.8 |
| NICs[2] | 8.6 | 5.8 | 6.3 | 7.6 | 7.5 | 6.5 | 6.4/7.0 | 6.0/6.8 |
| China | 7.9 | 14.2 | 13.5 | 12.6 | 10.2 | 9.7 | 9.0/10.0 | 9.0/10.0 |
| ASEAN[3] | 8.3 | 6.6 | 7.2 | 7.8 | 8.1 | 7.4 | 7.2/7.6 | 7.2/8.0 |
| Middle East and Europe[4] | 3.3 | 6.2 | 4.2 | 0.5 | 3.6 | 3.9 | 3.0/3.6 | 4.0/5.0 |
| Western Hemisphere | 2.1 | 2.8 | 3.2 | 4.7 | 0.9 | 3.0 | 3.5/4.5 | 4.3/5.3 |
| Mexico | 2.9 | 2.8 | 0.6 | 3.5 | (6.9) | 5.1 | 3.5/4.5 | 4.0/5.0 |
| **East Europe & Former USSR** | **(1.3)** | **(14.7)** | **(8.5)** | **(8.8)** | **(1.3)** | **0.4** | **3.7/4.3** | **4.0/5.0** |
| Central and Eastern Europe | N.A. | (9.9) | (4.9) | (2.9) | 1.2 | 1.6 | 3.8/4.6 | 4.0/5.0 |
| Russia | N.A. | (19.0) | (12.0) | (12.6) | (4.0) | (4.0) | 1.0/3.0 | 2.0/4.0 |
| **World Trade Volume** | **6.2** | **4.7** | **3.9** | **8.8** | **8.9** | **6.7** | **6.8/7.4** | **6.3/7.7** |

[1]Data prior to 1990 refer to West Germany only.
[2]NICs—Newly Industrialized Countries (e.g., Hong Kong, Singapore, South Korea, Taiwan).
[3]ASEAN—Indonesia, Malaysia, Philippines, Thailand, Singapore, Brunei, and Vietnam.
[4]Developing countries in Europe are Turkey, Cyprus, and Malta.
SOURCES:  IMF World Economic Outlook (October 1996); U.N. Project LINK (November 14, 1996), OECD Economic Outlook (December 1996), and official country publications.
Forecasts by U.S. Department of Commerce, International Trade Administration.
Negative figures are shown in parentheses.
SOURCE:  *Business America*, September 1997, p. 25.

## EXHIBIT 1.2   Key International Comparisons

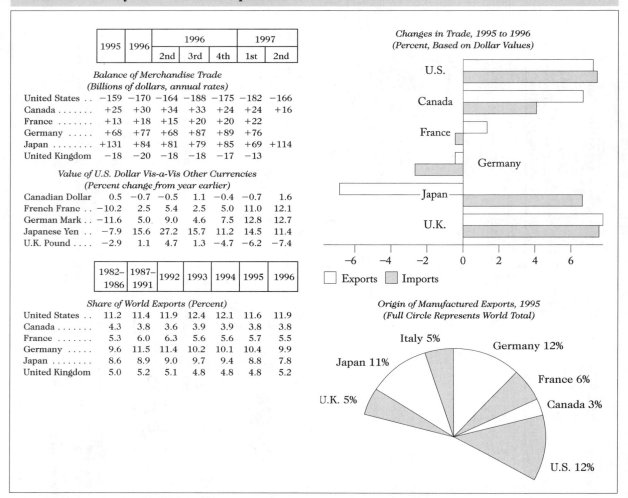

|  | 1995 | 1996 | 1996 | | | 1997 | |
|---|---|---|---|---|---|---|---|
|  |  |  | 2nd | 3rd | 4th | 1st | 2nd |

**Balance of Merchandise Trade**
*(Billions of dollars, annual rates)*

| | 1995 | 1996 | 2nd | 3rd | 4th | 1st | 2nd |
|---|---|---|---|---|---|---|---|
| United States .. | −159 | −170 | −164 | −188 | −175 | −182 | −166 |
| Canada ....... | +25 | +30 | +34 | +33 | +24 | +24 | +16 |
| France ....... | +13 | +18 | +15 | +20 | +20 | +22 | |
| Germany ..... | +68 | +77 | +68 | +87 | +89 | +76 | |
| Japan ........ | +131 | +84 | +81 | +79 | +85 | +69 | +114 |
| United Kingdom | −18 | −20 | −18 | −18 | −17 | −13 | |

**Value of U.S. Dollar Vis-a-Vis Other Currencies**
*(Percent change from year earlier)*

| | 1995 | 1996 | 2nd | 3rd | 4th | 1st | 2nd |
|---|---|---|---|---|---|---|---|
| Canadian Dollar | 0.5 | −0.7 | −0.5 | 1.1 | −0.4 | −0.7 | 1.6 |
| French Franc .. | −10.2 | 2.5 | 5.4 | 2.5 | 5.0 | 11.0 | 12.1 |
| German Mark .. | −11.6 | 5.0 | 9.0 | 4.6 | 7.5 | 12.8 | 12.7 |
| Japanese Yen .. | −7.9 | 15.6 | 27.2 | 15.7 | 11.2 | 14.5 | 11.4 |
| U.K. Pound .... | −2.9 | 1.1 | 4.7 | 1.3 | −4.7 | −6.2 | −7.4 |

| | 1982–1986 | 1987–1991 | 1992 | 1993 | 1994 | 1995 | 1996 |
|---|---|---|---|---|---|---|---|

**Share of World Exports (Percent)**

| | 1982–1986 | 1987–1991 | 1992 | 1993 | 1994 | 1995 | 1996 |
|---|---|---|---|---|---|---|---|
| United States .. | 11.2 | 11.4 | 11.9 | 12.4 | 12.1 | 11.6 | 11.9 |
| Canada ....... | 4.3 | 3.8 | 3.6 | 3.9 | 3.9 | 3.8 | 3.8 |
| France ....... | 5.3 | 6.0 | 6.3 | 5.6 | 5.6 | 5.7 | 5.5 |
| Germany ..... | 9.6 | 11.5 | 11.4 | 10.2 | 10.1 | 10.4 | 9.9 |
| Japan ........ | 8.6 | 8.9 | 9.0 | 9.7 | 9.4 | 8.8 | 7.8 |
| United Kingdom | 5.0 | 5.2 | 5.1 | 4.8 | 4.8 | 4.8 | 5.2 |

*Changes in Trade, 1995 to 1996*
*(Percent, Based on Dollar Values)*

U.S.   Canada   France   Germany   Japan   U.K.

−6   −4   −2   0   2   4   6

☐ Exports   ▨ Imports

*Origin of Manufactured Exports, 1995*
*(Full Circle Represents World Total)*

Italy 5%   Germany 12%   France 6%   Canada 3%   U.S. 12%   U.K. 5%   Japan 11%

SOURCE: *Business America,* September 1997, p. 24.

facturing industries are about 17 percent higher than average. The leading U.S. exporting states were California, New York, and Texas.

**http://www.stat-usa.gov/BEN/subject/trade.html**
The "stat-usa/Internet" is a subscription service of the U.S. Department of Commerce. It provides "the most extensive government-sponsored business, economic, and trade information databases in the world today." ($150 per year) This address is for their Export and International Trade databases.

**Trade in Services.**   Trade in services includes business services such as travel, banking, insurance and securities brokerage. It also includes professional services such as law, accounting, or architecture, and technical services such as waste management, industrial and environmental engineering, software development, and management consulting. In the developed countries of Europe, Japan, Canada, and the United States, business services have actually accounted for the majority of the gross domestic product, jobs, and job growth in recent years. Cross-border trade in services account for over 20 percent of world trade. Exports of services by the U.S. have

**EXHIBIT 1.3   U.S. Exports and Imports (Billions of dollars, annual rates)**

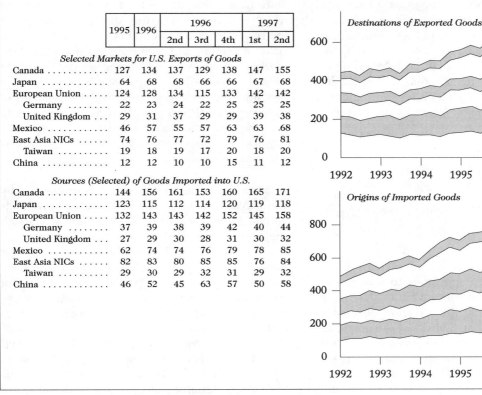

| | 1995 | 1996 | 1996 2nd | 1996 3rd | 1996 4th | 1997 1st | 1997 2nd |
|---|---|---|---|---|---|---|---|
| *Selected Markets for U.S. Exports of Goods* | | | | | | | |
| Canada . . . . . . . . . . . | 127 | 134 | 137 | 129 | 138 | 147 | 155 |
| Japan . . . . . . . . . . . . | 64 | 68 | 68 | 66 | 66 | 67 | 68 |
| European Union . . . . . | 124 | 128 | 134 | 115 | 133 | 142 | 142 |
| Germany . . . . . . . . | 22 | 23 | 24 | 22 | 25 | 25 | 25 |
| United Kingdom . . . | 29 | 31 | 37 | 29 | 29 | 39 | 38 |
| Mexico . . . . . . . . . . . | 46 | 57 | 55 | 57 | 63 | 63 | .68 |
| East Asia NICs . . . . . . | 74 | 76 | 77 | 72 | 79 | 76 | 81 |
| Taiwan . . . . . . . . . | 19 | 18 | 19 | 17 | 20 | 18 | 20 |
| China . . . . . . . . . . . . | 12 | 12 | 10 | 10 | 15 | 11 | 12 |
| *Sources (Selected) of Goods Imported into U.S.* | | | | | | | |
| Canada . . . . . . . . . . . | 144 | 156 | 161 | 153 | 160 | 165 | 171 |
| Japan . . . . . . . . . . . . | 123 | 115 | 112 | 114 | 120 | 119 | 118 |
| European Union . . . . . | 132 | 143 | 143 | 142 | 152 | 145 | 158 |
| Germany . . . . . . . . | 37 | 39 | 38 | 39 | 42 | 40 | 44 |
| United Kingdom . . . | 27 | 29 | 30 | 28 | 31 | 30 | 32 |
| Mexico . . . . . . . . . . . | 62 | 74 | 74 | 76 | 79 | 78 | 85 |
| East Asia NICs . . . . . . | 82 | 83 | 80 | 85 | 85 | 76 | 84 |
| Taiwan . . . . . . . . . | 29 | 30 | 29 | 32 | 31 | 29 | 32 |
| China . . . . . . . . . . . . | 46 | 52 | 45 | 63 | 57 | 50 | 58 |

SOURCE: *Business America,* September 1997, p. 25.

been rising steadily ($247 billion in 1996), leaving the U.S. with a 1996 trade surplus in services of $88 billion.

## Exporting

Trade is often a firm's first step into international business. Compared to the other forms of international business (licensing and investment) trade is relatively uncomplicated. It provides the inexperienced or smaller firm with an opportunity to penetrate a new market, or at least to explore foreign market potential, without significant capital investment and the risks of becoming a full-fledged player (i.e., citizen) in the foreign country. For many larger firms, including multinational corporations, exporting may be an important portion of their business operations. The U.S. aircraft industry, for example, relies heavily on exports for significant revenues.

Firms that have not done business overseas before should first prepare an export plan, which may mean assembling an export team, composed possibly of management and outside advisors and trade specialists. Their plan should include the assessment of the firm's readiness for exporting, the export potential of its products or services, the firm's willingness to allocate resources (including financial, production output, and human resources), and the selection of its channels of distribution. The firm may need to modify products, design new packaging and foreign language labeling, and meet foreign standards for product performance or quality assurance. The firm must also gauge the extent to which it can perform export functions in-house or whether these functions should best be handled indirectly through an independent export company. Export functions include foreign marketing, sales and distribution, shipping, and handling international transfers of money.

Firms accept varying levels of responsibility for moving goods and money and for other export functions. The more experienced exporters can take greater responsibility for themselves and are more likely to export directly to their foreign customers. Firms that choose to accept less responsibility in dealing with foreign customers, or in making arrangements for shipping, for example, must delegate many export functions to someone else. As such, exporting is generally divided into two types: direct and indirect.

**http://www.ita.doc.gov/**
The home page for the International Trade Administration, with links to many relevant sites, including countries, industries, export assistance, and trade statistics.

**Direct Exporting.**    At first glance, *direct exporting* seems similar to selling goods to a domestic buyer. A prospective foreign customer may have seen a firm's products at a trade show, located a particular company in an industrial directory, or been recommended by another customer. A firm that receives a request for product and pricing information from a foreign customer may be able to handle it routinely and export directly to the buyer. With some assistance a firm can overcome most hurdles, get the goods properly packaged and shipped, and receive payment as anticipated. While many of these one-time sales are turned into long-term business success stories, many more are not. A firm hopes to develop a regular business relationship with its new foreign customer. However, the problems that can be encountered even in direct exporting are considerable.

Many firms engaged in direct exporting on a regular basis reach the point at which they must hire their own full-time export managers and international sales specialists. These people participate in making export marketing decisions, including product development, pricing, packaging, and labeling for export. They should take primary responsibility for dealing with foreign buyers, for attending foreign trade shows, for complying with government export and import regulations, for shipping, and for handling the movement of goods and money in the transaction. Direct exporting is often done through *foreign sales agents* who work on commission. It also can be done by selling directly to *foreign distributors.* Foreign distributors are independent firms, usually located in the country to which a firm is exporting, that purchase goods for resale to their customers. They assume the risks of buying and warehousing goods in their market and provide additional product support services. The distributor usually services the products they sell, thus relieving the exporter of that responsibility. They often train end users to use the product, extend credit to their customers, and bear responsibility for local advertising and promotion.

**Indirect Exporting.**    *Indirect exporting* is used by companies seeking to minimize their involvement abroad. Lacking experience, personnel, or capital, they may be unable to locate foreign buyers or are not yet ready to be handling the mechanics of a transaction on their own. There are several different types of indirect exporting. *Export trading companies,* commonly called ETCs, are companies that market the products of other manufacturers in foreign markets. They have extensive sales contacts overseas and experience in air and sea shipping. They often operate with the assistance and financial backing of large banks, thus making the resources and international contacts of the bank's foreign branches available to the manufacturers whose products they market. Since the mid-1980s, ETCs have been able to apply for and receive a certificate from the U.S. Department of Justice that waives the application of U.S. antitrust laws to their export activities. This waiver makes it lawful for many manufacturers to cooperate in exporting to foreign markets, when such collusion might otherwise be illegal under the antitrust laws of the United States. Many of the world's largest export trading companies, even those that export U.S.-made products, are Japanese owned.

*Export management companies,* or EMCs, on the other hand, are really consultants that advise manufacturers and other exporters. They are used by firms that cannot justify their own in-house export managers. They engage in foreign market research, identify overseas sales agents, exhibit goods at foreign trade shows, prepare documentation for export, and handle language translations and shipping arrangements. As in direct exporting, all forms of indirect exporting can involve sales through agents or to distributors.

## Importing and Global Sourcing

When reading this text, the reader should keep in mind that importing is not to be viewed in the isolated context of a single transaction. True, many importers do import only on a limited or one-time basis. However, in this book importing is presented from the perspective of the global firm for which importing is a regular and necessary part of their business. *Global sourcing* is the term commonly used to describe the process by which a firm attempts to locate and purchase goods or services on a worldwide basis. These goods may include, for example, raw materials for manufacturing, component parts for assembly operations, commodities such as agricultural products or minerals, or merchandise for resale.

## Government Controls over Trade: Tariffs and Nontariff Barriers

Importing and exporting is governed by the laws and regulations of the countries through which goods or services pass. A central portion of this text will be devoted to understanding why and how nations regulate trade, known as *international trade law.* Nations regulate trade in many ways. The most common methods are *tariffs* and *nontariff barriers.* Tariffs are import duties or taxes imposed on goods entering the customs territory of a nation. Tariffs are imposed for many reasons, including (1) the collection of revenue, (2) the protection of domestic industries from foreign competition, and (3) political control (e.g., to provide incentives to import products from politically friendly countries and to discourage importing products from unfriendly countries).

**Nontariff Barriers to Trade.** Nontariff barriers are *all barriers to importing or exporting other than tariffs.* Nontariff barriers are generally a greater barrier to trade than are tariffs, because they are more insidious. Unlike tariffs, which are published and easily understood, nontariff barriers are often disguised in the form of government rules or industry regulations and are often not understood by foreign companies. Countries impose nontariff barriers to protect their national economic, social, and political interests. Imports might be banned for health and safety reasons. Imported goods usually have to be marked with the country-of-origin and labeled in the local language so that consumers know what they are buying. One form of nontariff barrier is the *technical barrier to trade,* or *product standard.* Examples of product standards, include safety standards, electrical standards, and environmental standards (e.g., German cars meeting U.S. emission standards not mandated in Europe). A *quota* is a restriction imposed by law on the numbers or quantities of goods, or of a particular type of good, allowed to be imported. Unlike tariffs, quotas are not internationally accepted as a lawful means of regulating trade except in some special cases. An *embargo* is a total or near total ban on trade with a particular country, sometimes enforced by military action and usually imposed for political purposes. An internationally orchestrated embargo was used against Iraq after its invasion of Kuwait in 1990. A *boycott* is a refusal to trade or do business with certain firms, usually from a particular country, on political or other grounds.

Tariffs and nontariff barriers have a tremendous influence on how firms make their trade and investment decisions. These decisions, in turn, are reflected in the patterns of world trade and the flows of investment capital. Consider this illustration. In 1992 the European nations lowered trade barriers between themselves. In the years prior to this event, companies from the United States, Canada, and Japan invested heavily in Europe. They purchased ongoing firms there and established new ones. If they had stayed on "outside" and remained contented to export to Europe, they would have lost competitiveness to European firms who could take advantage of the new lowered trade barriers. But by manufacturing there, they could sell within Europe on the same basis as other European firms. Similar capital investment flows occurred in Mexico in the early 1990s as a result of Mexico's closer trade ties to the United States and Canada. For example, when Japanese firms learned that Mexican-made products could be traded in North America with lowered tariffs and nontariff barriers, companies from Japan quickly sought to establish manufacturing facilities in Mexico to take advantage of changes in trade laws.

**Export Restrictions.**   Another type of control over trade is the export restriction. An *export restriction* limits the type of product that may be shipped to any particular country. They are usually imposed for economic or political purposes. For instance, high-tech computers might not be allowed to be shipped from the United States or Canada to another country without a license from the U.S. or Canadian government. Before signing a contract for the sale of certain products or technical know-how to a foreign customer, U.S. exporters must consider whether they will be able to obtain U.S. licensing for the shipment.

## Intellectual Property Rights and International Licensing Agreements

*Intellectual property rights* are a grant from a government to an individual or firm of the exclusive legal right to use a copyright, patent, or trademark for a specified time. *Copyrights* are legal rights to artistic or written works, including books, software, films, music, or to such works as the layout design of a computer chip. *Trademarks* include the legal right to use a name or symbol that identifies a firm or its product. *Patents* are governmental grants to inventors assuring them of the exclusive legal right to produce and sell their inventions for a period of years. Copyrights, trademarks, and patents compose substantial assets of many domestic and international firms. As valuable assets, intellectual property can be sold or licensed for use to others through a licensing agreement.

*International licensing agreements* are contracts by which the holder of intellectual property will grant certain rights in that property to a foreign firm under specified conditions and for a specified time. Licensing agreements represent an important foreign market entry method for firms with marketable intellectual property. For example, a firm might license the right to manufacture and distribute a certain type of computer chip or the right to use a trademark on apparel such as bluejeans or designer clothing. It might license the right to distribute Hollywood movies or to reproduce and market word-processing software in a foreign market, or it might license its patent rights to produce and sell a high-tech product or pharmaceutical. U.S. firms have extensively licensed their property around the world, and in recent years have purchased the technology rights of Japanese and other foreign firms.

A firm may choose licensing as its market entry method because licensing can provide a greater entrée to the foreign market than is possible through exporting. A firm may realize many advantages in having a foreign company produce and sell products based on its intellectual property instead of simply shipping finished goods to that market. When exporting to a foreign market, the firm must overcome obstacles such as long-distance shipping and the resulting delay in filling orders. Exporting requires a familiarity with the local culture. Redesign of products or technology for the foreign market may be necessary. Importantly, an exporter may have to overcome trade restrictions such as quotas or tariffs set by the foreign government. Licensing to a foreign firm allows the licensor to circumvent trade restrictions by having the products produced locally, and it allows entrance to the foreign market with minimal initial start-up costs. In return the licensor might choose to receive a guaranteed return based on a percentage of gross revenues. This arrangement insures payment to the licensor whether or not the licensee earns a profit. Even though licensing agreements give the licensor some control over how the licensee utilizes its intellectual property, problems can arise. For instance, the licensor may find that it cannot police the licensee's manufacturing or quality control process. Protecting itself from the unauthorized use or "piracy" of its copyrights, patents, or trademarks by unscrupulous persons not party to the licensing agreement is also a serious concern for the licensor. The following case illustrates what can happen to a firm that fails to take proper legal steps to protect its trademark rights in a foreign country. Notice how this firm's strategy involved both exporting and licensing.

**Protecting Intellectual Property Rights.**   Rights in property can be rendered worthless if those rights cannot be protected by law. The protection of intellectual property is a matter of national

First Flight
Associates v.
Professional
Golf
Company, Inc.
*527 F.2d 931 (1975)*
*United States Court of*
*Appeals (6th Cir.)*

## BACKGROUND AND FACTS

Pro Golf, a U.S. company, manufactured and sold golf equipment under the brand name "First Flight," which had been registered in the United States and certain other foreign countries. In 1961 Pro Golf negotiated with Robert Wynn to act as their foreign sales representative in Japan. Wynn incorporated First Flight Associates, Inc. (FFA) under Japanese law for the purposes of selling Pro Golf's products there. No formal agency or distributorship agreement was ever entered into by the parties. In 1967 the parties entered into a trademark agreement, whereby FFA was permitted to use Pro Golf's "First Flight" trademark on golf soft goods, such as golf bags and clothing, in return for the payment of a royalty. FFA attempted to sublicense the trademark to another Japanese company, Teito, for a royalty much larger than that paid to Pro Golf. When Pro Golf objected, the company learned that its attempt to register the trademark in Japan had not been completely successful, but that third parties had obtained the right to use the trademark in Japan in marketing certain types of soft goods. Pro Golf terminated the agency agreement with FFA, and FFA brought this action for breach of contract.

## MARKEY, CHIEF JUDGE

The issue on appeal is whether the district court erred in finding that . . . Pro Golf was entitled to terminate the sales representation contract; . . . and that FFA was not liable under the counterclaims for royalties received from Teito or for Pro Golf's expenditures relating to its trademark rights in Japan. . . .

As to the initial 1961 contract for Japanese sales representation on clubs and balls, we agree with the district court that Pro Golf effectively and lawfully terminated FFA as its representative, the termination being effective as of the end of July 1973. That termination did not breach the contract. . . .

The contract was clearly therefore one for an indefinite period of time. Contracts silent on time of termination are generally terminable at will by either party with reasonable notice. . . .

It is unnecessary to discuss the conduct of Wynn or FFA under the trademark license contract or whether "satisfactory business" was being done under the sales representation contract. The latter contract being terminable at will, Pro Golf was clearly within its rights in terminating it.

Pro Golf contends that royalties paid to FFA by Teito should have been passed through to Pro Golf. That contention is based on Pro Golf's fundamentally unsound characterization of FFA as its agent in entering into the Teito contract. As we have indicated, that contract is a trademark sub-license, wherein FFA conveyed to Teito some or all of its rights to use "First Flight" in Japan as a trademark on "soft goods," which rights FFA had under its license from Pro Golf. Nothing in FFA's trademark license contract with Pro Golf prohibited FFA from granting sub-licenses to others or required FFA to pass along to Pro Golf any royalties FFA might receive from such sub-licenses.

Pro Golf also counterclaimed for damages equal to its expenditures incurred in attempting to perfect its Japanese rights in "First Flight" as applied to certain golf soft goods. Pro Golf's difficulties stemmed from its own failure to obtain complete registration in Japan of "First Flight" in all of the relevant classes of goods. Under Japanese trademark law, rights are acquired through registration and not through use in commerce as in the United States. Although Pro Golf had exclusive rights in "First Flight" when applied to clubs and balls and to some of the classes of soft goods on which the trademark was being used by FFA, third parties had obtained Japanese registrations of "First Flight" for use on other classes of goods, including other golf soft goods. Pro Golf found it necessary to deal with those third-party registrants in seeking to acquire exclusive rights in "First Flight" as a trademark in Japan for the entire spectrum of golf soft goods. We fully agree with the district court that FFA is not liable for expenditures incurred by reason of Pro Golf's own failure to properly register its trademark in Japan.

*(continued)*

*(continued)*

Accordingly, the decision of the district court is in all respects affirmed.

**Decision.** Pro Golf was permitted to terminate its Japanese sales agency relationship with FFA be-cause, under U.S. law, sales agency contracts are terminable at will. However, Pro Golf was not en-titled to royalties earned by FFA on soft goods bearing the "First Flight" trademark because Pro Golf had failed to perfect its rights to the use of that trademark under Japanese law.

---

law (as in the United States where it is protected primarily under federal statutes). However, intel-lectual property rights granted in one nation are not legally recognized and enforceable in an-other, unless the owner takes certain legal steps to protect those rights under the laws of that for-eign country. Most developed countries such as Canada, Western Europe, and Japan, have laws that protect the owners of intellectual property, and they enforce those laws. However, copyrights, patents, and trademarks are widely pirated in the developing countries of Asia, Latin America, Africa, Russia, Eastern Europe, and the Middle East, whose protection laws are either nonexistent or not enforced. Indeed, some developing coun-tries encourage piracy because of the perceived fi-nancial gains to their economies. Some products deemed indispensable to the public, such as phar-maceuticals and chemicals, are often not covered by patent laws at all in these countries.

Lost profits and lost royalties to U.S. firms now amount to billions of dollars each year in counter-feited goods sold overseas. But international ef-forts are being made to rectify the problem. At the behest of U.S. movie and record producers, phar-maceutical manufacturers, software makers, and publishers, the United States has encouraged these countries to pass legislation protecting in-tellectual property and to insure the enforcement of these laws. For instance, in 1991 the People's Republic of China acted to avert a trade war with the United States by agreeing to bring its intellec-tual property laws in line with those in other de-veloping countries. The United States had been losing an estimated $700 million per year in China due to piracy. The United States threatened to im-pose punitive tariffs on Chinese goods (toys, games, footwear, clothing, and textiles). China an-nounced stricter enforcement efforts and a new copyright law, and a major trade war was averted. Today, the protection of property rights abroad is a principal objective of U.S. trade policy.

**Technology Transfer.** The exchange of technol-ogy and manufacturing know-how between firms in different countries through arrangements such as licensing agreements is known as *technology transfer.* Transfers of technology and know-how are regulated by government control in some countries. This control is common when the li-censor is from a highly industrialized country such as the United States and the licensee is lo-cated in a developing country such as those in Latin America, the Middle East, or Asia. In their efforts to industrialize, modernize, and develop a self-sufficiency in technology and production methods, these countries often restrict the terms of licensing agreements in a manner benefiting their own country. For instance, government reg-ulation might require that the licensor introduce its most modern technology to the developing countries or train workers in its use.

**International Franchising.** Franchising is a form of licensing that is gaining in popularity worldwide. The most common form of franchis-ing is known as a *business operations franchise,* usually used in retailing. Under a typical fran-chising agreement, the franchisee is allowed to use a trade name or trademark in offering goods or services to the public in return for a royalty based on a percentage of sales or other fee struc-ture. The franchisee will usually obtain the fran-chiser's know-how in operating and managing a profitable business and its other "secrets of suc-cess" (ranging from a "secret recipe," to store de-sign, to accounting methods). Franchising in the United States accounts for a large proportion of total retail sales. In foreign markets as well, fran-chising has been successful in fast-food retailing, hotels, video rentals, convenience stores, photo-copying services, and real estate services, to name but a few. U.S. firms have excelled in fran-chising overseas, making up the majority of new franchise operations worldwide. The prospects for future growth in foreign markets are enormous, especially in developing countries such as in Latin America. For instance, American fast-food and retail franchises are common throughout Mexico City. Brazil now offers one of the best opportunities for franchising, with some 25,000 franchise outlets already in operation. In 1994 two U.S. firms, Subway and Blockbuster Video, announced that they had concluded franchise agreements in Brazil and that each were hoping to have more than 200 locations within a few years. By 1994 franchising had extended into the countries of Eastern Europe and the former Soviet Union as a method of introducing private enterprise to their formerly communist-dictated economies.

**Some Legal Aspects of Franchising.**  Franchising is a good vehicle for entering a foreign market because the local franchisee provides capital investment, entrepreneurial commitment, and on-site management to deal with local customs and labor problems. However, many legal requirements affect franchising. Franchising in the United States is regulated primarily by the Federal Trade Commission at the federal level. The agency requires the filing of extensive disclosure statements to protect prospective investors. Other countries have

also enacted new franchise disclosure laws. Some developing countries have restrictions on the amount of money that can be removed from the country by the franchiser. Moreover, some countries such as China also require government approval for franchise operations. Other countries might have restrictions on importing supplies (ketchup, bed linens, paper products, or whatever) for the operation of the business, to protect local companies. However, more progressive developing countries are now abandoning these strict regulations because they want to welcome franchisers, their high quality consumer products, and their managerial talent to their markets. Because of this more receptive attitude toward foreign firms, Mexico and Brazil have become home to many profitable new franchise operations.

The *Raymond Dayan v. McDonald's* case illustrates the difficulty in supervising the operations of a franchisee in a distant foreign country. Consider how any U.S. franchiser will allow its franchisees to adapt to the cultural environment in a foreign country while still providing the same consistent quality and service that is expected whenever anyone patronizes one of their establishments anywhere in the world.

For a discussion of other problems faced by franchisers, see the following article.

---

### Raymond Dayan v. McDonald's Corp.
*125 Ill. App.3d 972, 466 N.E.2d 958 (1984)*
*Appellate Court of Illinois*

BACKGROUND AND FACTS
In 1971, Dayan, the plaintiff, received an exclusive franchise to operate McDonald's restaurants in Paris, France. The franchise agreement required that the franchise meet all quality, service, and cleanliness (QSC) standards set by McDonald's. Dayan acknowledged his familiarity with the McDonald's system and with the need for maintaining McDonald's quality standards and controls. The franchise agreement stated that the rationale for maintaining QSC standards was that a "departure of restaurants anywhere in the world from these standards impedes the successful operation of restaurants throughout the world, and injures the value of its [McDonald's] patents, trade-marks, tradename, and property." Dayan agreed to "maintain these standards as they presently existed" and to ob-

serve subsequent improvements McDonald's may initiate. Dayan also agreed not to vary from QSC standards without prior written approval. After several years of quality and cleanliness violations, McDonald's sought to terminate the franchise. Dayan brought this action to enjoin the termination. The lower court found that good cause existed for the termination and Dayan appealed.

BUCKLEY, PRESIDING JUSTICE
Dayan also argues that McDonald's was obligated to provide him with the operational assistance necessary to enable him to meet the QSC standards.

*(continued)*

*(continued)*

. . . Dayan verbally asked Sollars (a McDonald's manager) for a French-speaking operations person to work in the market for six months. Sollars testified that he told Dayan it would be difficult to find someone with the appropriate background that spoke French but that McDonald's could immediately send him an English-speaking operations man. Sollars further testified that this idea was summarily rejected by Dayan as unworkable even though he had informed Dayan that sending operations personnel who did not speak the language to a foreign country was very common and very successful in McDonald's international system. Nonetheless, Sollars agreed to attempt to locate a qualified person with the requisite language skills for Dayan.

Through Sollar's efforts, Dayan was put in contact with Michael Maycock, a person with McDonald's managerial and operational experience who spoke French. Dayan testified that he hired Maycock some time in October 1977 and placed him in charge of training, operations, quality control, and equipment.

As the trial court correctly realized: "It does not take a McDonald's-trained French-speaking operational man to know that grease dripping from the vents must be stopped and not merely collected in a cup hung from the ceiling, that dogs are not permitted to defecate where food is stored, that insecticide is not blended with chicken breading; that past-dated products should be discarded; that

a potato peeler should be somewhat cleaner than a tire-vulcanizer; and that shortening should not look like crank case oil."

Clearly, Maycock satisfied Dayan's request for a French-speaking operations man to run his training program. . . . The finding that Dayan refused non-French-speaking operational assistance and that McDonald's fulfilled Dayan's limited request for a French-speaking operational employee is well supported by the record. To suggest, as plaintiff does, that an opposite conclusion is clearly evident is totally without merit. Accordingly, we find McDonald's fulfilled its contractual obligation to provide requested operational assistance to Dayan.

In view of the foregoing reasons, the judgment of the trial court denying plaintiff's request for a permanent injunction and finding that McDonald's properly terminated the franchise agreement is affirmed.

**Decision.**   Judgment was affirmed for McDonald's. McDonald's had fulfilled all of its responsibility under the agreement to assist the plaintiff in complying with the provisions of the license. The plaintiff had violated the provisions of the agreement by not complying with the QSC standards. The plaintiff is permitted to continue operation of his restaurants, but without use of the McDonald's trademarks or name.

**Comment.**   McDonald's has recovered in France from this public relations fiasco.

---

*Foreign Accents*

# Johannesburgers and Fries

**McDonald's efforts to break into South Africa suggest that multinationals can rely too heavily on their powerful brands. Local brands, and tastes, matter too.**

If the managers of any food brand could be forgiven for arrogance, it would be those at McDonald's. Last year, the burger-chain's trademark was rated the world's top brand by Interbrand, a consultancy, beating Coca-Cola into second place. McDonald's operates over 21,000 fast-food restaurants in 104 countries. Its golden arches overlook piazzas and shopping malls from Moscow to Manila.

In recent years, faced with greater competition in the United States, the company has increasingly relied on overseas markets as a source of profits . . . . Managers at McDonald's pride them-

*(continued)*

*(continued)*

selves on knowing how to adapt the Big Mac to local markets (the firm serves terriyaki burgers in Tokyo), whilst promoting the same basic idea: good, fast food served in clean surroundings by a company with a strong family brand

In 1995, as part of this overseas empire-building, McDonald's made its first venture into sub-Saharan Africa, the last frontier of emerging markets. . . .

Like many American multinationals, McDonald's had long had its eye on the South African market, but waited until the end of apartheid before it felt ready to enter. During the 1980s, the strong anti-apartheid lobby in America, combined with federal, state and local trade sanctions, made the prospect of investing in South Africa a big public-relations risk. Under such pressure, several American companies already trading there had left the country. Others, including McDonald's, stayed well away.

But McDonald's was only biding its time. It had registered its world-famous trademark in South Africa as early as 1968. In 1993, a year before South Africa's first non-racial general election, McDonald's finally decided to press ahead with an investment in the country.

However, by the time the first McDonald's restaurant opened in 1995, it was clear that the American giant was entering a rather unusual market. Its forays into other emerging markets around the world had generally been successful. But South Africa did not fit the typical formula: it had already developed a first-world consumer industry in almost complete commercial isolation, behind the shelter of sanctions and its own protective tariffs. Thus cosseted, South Africa's fast-food companies had built up several strong home-grown brands, specifically catering to South African tastes. Nobody at McDonald's realised how difficult it would be to break in.

### McDonald's v MacDonalds

The first sign that South Africa might give McDonald's some indigestion came in mid-1993, when the company discovered that a local trader had applied both to register the "McDonald's" trademark for his own use, and to have the American company's rights to the trademark withdrawn (its trademark registration had technically expired). McDonald's instantly filed a case against the trader, and applied to re-register the trademark for itself.

At the time, the company's managers did not expect the lawsuit to be too much of a bother. As one of the world's leading brands, by then running fast-food restaurants in dozens of countries worldwide, McDonald's was plainly associated with the trademark around the globe and could reasonably expect the South African courts to protect it from looka-likes. Although its trademark registration had expired in the country, there were good reasons for this. McDonald's argued, under a clause in South African law, that "special circumstances" had prevented it entering the market: namely, trade sanctions against South Africa and pressure from the anti-apartheid lobby in America.

When the case came to the Supreme Court, in October 1995, things did not turn out quite the way McDonald's had expected. Three cases, in fact, were heard at the same time. Two were brought by South African traders, Joburgers Drive-Inn Restaurant and Dax Prop, each of which already ran a fast-food restaurant under the name "MacDonalds" and each of which wanted to deprive McDonald's of the right to trade under that name. The third case was brought by McDonald's, which was suing the other companies for using and imitating its brand.

The cases rested on two questions. The first was whether McDonald's was a "well-known mark". If it was, then the company would be instantly entitled to protection from imitation by local traders, and the impostors would have to pack up shop. The second was whether McDonald's claim of "special circumstances" could be justified.

For McDonald's managers, the answer to the first question was self-evident. Though they recognised that South Africa had a relatively sophisticated fast-food industry of its own, with many brands of beef- and chicken-burgers, the idea that such a famous global brand might not be well-known on the southern tip of African seemed preposterous.

As part of its defence, McDonald's presented the results of two market-research surveys conducted in South Africa to show that the brand was well-known. Both confirmed that a large majority of those interviewed had at least heard of the name, and over half were both aware of the brand and could recognise the McDonald's logo. Which was all very well, said the judge presiding in the Supreme

*(continued)*

*(continued)*

Court case, but the surveys were conducted among whites living in posh suburbs and could "by no stretch of the imagination be regarded as representative of the entire South African population," 76% of which is black. The judge took an equally dim view of other evidence presented by McDonald's, and threw its case out.

What of the second question, concerning the firm's claim that "special circumstances" had kept it out of South Africa's market? McDonald's had first registered its trademark in South Africa in 1968, and then renewed it at regular intervals until 1985. Under South African law as it stood at the time, a company lost its right to the trademark if it languished unused on the books for five years, unless there was a good reason.

Again, the judge was unconvinced. He did not believe that "special circumstances"—pressure from anti-apartheid groups and sanctions—were the real reasons that McDonald's had left its trademarks unused for so long: "there is no explanation for the failure to commence business in South Africa," he declared, "other than the fact that South Africa simply did not rank on McDonald's list of priorities."

These legal setbacks were embarrassing but temporary. McDonald's was allowed to press ahead with opening restaurants whilst it prepared its case for the Appeal Court. In 1996 the American burger chain won this second battle: the Appeal Court, in essence, applied a less strict test of what it meant to be well-known in South Africa, and accepted the evidence in the two surveys because it thought that whites represented McDonald's target market.

Although the direct financial effect of the first court decision was negligible, the case was a harbinger of the sort of trouble that McDonald's was to encounter throughout South Africa. It was also the first inkling that South Africans might not regard the Big Mac with the same reverence that Americans do. . . .

McDonald's experience in South Africa shows how even the strongest brands from developed countries cannot expect to trample all before them in developing ones—particularly when consumers can choose established local alternatives. McDonald's has also run into trouble in the Philippines, where a popular local fast-food firm, called Jollibee, has so far trounced it with a distinctively Asian menu that includes burgers and rice.

Many observers would bet that, through the sheer power of its marketing, McDonald's will eventually barge into South Africa and other emerging markets. But given that the owner of "the world's leading brand" has had such trouble, western companies with a less recognisable trademark might think twice before following its example.

## Foreign Direct Investment

In this text the term *foreign investment,* or *foreign direct investment,* refers to the ownership and active control of ongoing business concerns, including investment in manufacturing, mining, farming, assembly operations, and other facilities of production. Throughout the text, a distinction is made between the home and host countries of the firms involved. The *home country* refers to that country under whose laws the investing corporation was created or is headquartered. For example, the United States is home to multinational corporations such as Ford, Exxon, and IBM, to name a few, but they operate in *host countries* throughout every region of the world. Of the three forms of international business, foreign investment provides the firm with the most involvement, and perhaps the greatest risk, abroad. Investment in a foreign plant is often a result of having had successful experiences in exporting or licensing, and of the search for ways to overcome the disadvantages of those other entry methods. For example, by producing its product in a foreign country, instead of exporting, a firm can avoid quotas and tariffs on imported goods, avoid currency fluctuations on the traded goods, provide better product service and spare parts, and more quickly adapt products to local tastes and market trends. Manufacturing overseas for foreign markets can mean taking advantage of local natural resources, labor, and manufacturing economies of scale.

## Multinational Corporations

*Multinational corporations* are firms with significant foreign direct investment assets. They are characterized by their ability to derive and transfer capital resources worldwide and to operate facilities of production and penetrate markets in more than one country, usually on a global scale. Over the past twenty years, many writers have argued over the best name to use in referring to these companies. *Multinational enterprise* has been a popular term because it reflects the fact that many global firms are not, technically speaking, "corporations." The terms *transnational corporation* and *supranational corporation* are often used within the United Nations system, in which many internationalists argue that the operations and interests of the modern corporation "transcend" national boundaries. This text makes no play on words, and places no special meaning on any of the terms used to describe these companies.

One significant trend in business during the last half of the twentieth century has been the globalization of multinational corporations. At one time multinational corporations were simply large domestic companies with foreign operations. Today they are global companies. They typically make decisions and enter strategic alliances with each other without regard to national boundaries. They move factories, technology, and capital to those countries with the most hospitable laws, the lowest tax rates, the most qualified workforce, or abundant natural resources. They see market share and company performance in global terms. Foreign sales and operations are extremely profitable for many multinationals. As an example, Gillette, Colgate, IBM, Coca-Cola, and many of the 500 largest U.S. corporations collected over 50 percent of their revenues from products sold outside the United States. Switzerland's Nestle Corporation garnered over 95 percent of its revenues from outside Switzerland.

Multinational corporations have a noticeable impact on the world's economy. According to the *World Investment Report* issued by the United Nations Conference on Trade and Development in 1994, multinational corporations account for about one-third of the world's production of goods and services, with over 70 million employees and annual sales at almost $5 trillion.

**Subsidiaries, Joint Ventures, and Acquisitions.** Multinational corporations wishing to enter a foreign market through direct investment can structure their business arrangements in many different ways. Their options and eventual course of action may depend on many factors, including industry and market conditions, capitalization of the firm and financing, and legal considerations. Some of these options include the start-up of a new foreign subsidiary company, the formation of a joint venture with an existing foreign company, or the acquisition of an existing foreign company by stock purchase. These arrangements are discussed in detail in Part Four of this book. For now, keep in mind that multinational corporations are usually not a single legal entity. They are global enterprises that consist of any number of interrelated corporate entities, connected through extremely complex chains of stock ownership. Stock ownership gives the investing corporation tremendous flexibility when investing abroad.

The *wholly owned foreign subsidiary* is a "foreign" corporation organized under the laws of a foreign host country, but owned and controlled by the parent corporation in the home country. Because the parent company controls all of the stock in the subsidiary it can control management and financial decision making.

The *joint venture* is a cooperative business arrangement between two or more companies for profit. A joint venture may take the form of a partnership or corporation. Typically, one party will contribute expertise and another the capital, each bringing its own special resources to the venture. Joint ventures exist in all regions of the world and in all types of industries. Where the laws of a host country require local ownership or that investing foreign firms have a local partner, the joint venture is an appropriate investment vehicle. *Local participation* refers to the requirement that a share of the business be owned by nationals of the host country. These requirements are gradually being reduced in most countries who, in an effort to attract more investment, are permitting wholly owned subsidiaries. Many American companies do not favor the joint venture as an investment vehicle because they do not want to share technology, expertise, and profits with another company.

Another method of investing abroad is to purchase an ongoing firm. This option has appeal because it requires less know-how than does a new start-up and can be concluded without disruption of business activity.

### U.S. Foreign Direct Investment

The United States supports open investment policies worldwide. In its negotiations with foreign nations, notably Japan, Mexico, and Canada, the United States has pressed for a reduction of barriers to investment by U.S. firms. At the end of 1993 foreign direct investment by U.S. firms reached almost $550 billion.

Similarly, the policy of the United States encourages foreign investment in this country. This policy is based on the principle of *national treatment*—that foreign investors will be treated the same as domestic firms. There are some limitations to the rule, however. For example, under the *Exon-Florio Amendments* to the Defense Production Act, the president can prohibit foreign investment in such industries as atomic energy, transportation, and telecommunications, or in cases involving a potential threat to national security. Unless a specific statute limits foreign investment, the courts have generally not been willing to restrict the purchase of U.S. firms.

In the past, foreign direct investment in the United States has resulted mainly from foreign firms creating their own U.S. subsidiaries. Today, it results in large part from foreign firms acquiring or merging with existing firms, many of which are publicly owned companies. Total foreign investment in the United States, or *reverse investment,* as it is often called, has risen to more than $440 billion in 1993 from $160 billion in 1984. Most investment is in manufacturing, and has come from firms in the United Kingdom, Japan, the Netherlands, and Canada. Foreign firms have acquired everything from office buildings and movie studios to factories and supermarkets. Some of the best-known companies in the United

States are foreign owned, and their impact on the U.S. economy has been significant. (By 1995, economic conditions coupled with a declining dollar value caused a sell-off of U.S. assets by many Japanese investors, often at a loss. For many Japanese real estate companies and banks, their foray into the U.S. real estate market in the 1980s proved a disaster.)

## Conducting Business in Developing Countries

Most of the more than 190 nations in the world have not reached the same state of economic advance as have the *industrialized countries,* which include the United States, Canada, Japan, and Western Europe. Rather, most countries could be classified as having economies that are either (1) developing, (2) less developed, or (3) newly industrialized. For the purposes of our discussion, a fourth category includes the newly independent republics of the former Soviet Union and Eastern Europe. These groups of countries differ in culture, geography, language, religions, and in their economic, political, and legal systems as well. Two-thirds of the world's population is located in the less-developed countries—in Africa, Latin America, the Caribbean, parts of Asia and the Pacific Rim, and the Middle East.

*http://ciber.bus.msu.edu/publicat/ mktptind.htm*
*Provides information on market potential indicators for emerging markets worldwide.*

### The Developing Countries

The *developing countries* are located in every region of the world. Examples in the Americas include Mexico and Brazil, with Brazil having the tenth largest economy in the world. In Asia, examples include the People's Republic of China (referred to as China), as well as India and Pakistan. Malaysia, Indonesia, and the Philippines in the Pacific Rim are developing countries. The oil-producing countries of the Middle East, such as Saudi Arabia and Kuwait, are also included despite their tremendous wealth, because they are only in the early stages of industrialization.

The "typical" developing country is impossible to describe. Most have a large agrarian population, densely populated cities, and a plentiful supply of unskilled labor. Many support high-tech industries. While some are rich in natural resources, such as Brazil, many others have depleted their natural resources. The protection of the environment has often taken a back seat to industrialization and economic "progress," and so pollution chokes their air and water. Toxic waste dumps threaten entire communities. Crimes such as smuggling, hijacking, robberies, organized crime, and illicit drug production are major problems. Sanitation and water systems are often inadequate. Poor communication and transportation systems make business difficult. Inadequate distribution systems make it costly to get goods to market. Floods and natural disasters, exacerbated by inappropriate agricultural and industrial policies, have disrupted entire populations. Overpopulation, homelessness, malnutrition, and disease are still common. One example of how disease can affect business is the epidemic of plague that struck India in 1994. It caused workers to flee industrial communities in fear and forced the closing of many factories. A wide disparity in social and economic classes exists in many countries, with great inequality in income between the rich and poor. Political systems differ widely in developing countries. Some developing countries have stable, democratic governments; others do not. For instance, Costa Rica has the oldest continuing democracy in Central America, dating back to 1948. Other Central and South American countries have not been stable at all and have experienced varying degrees of freedom, from parliamentary rule to military dictatorship.

## The Economic Environment in Developing Countries

Students of economics know that the economies of the developing countries have trailed those of the industrialized countries for many complex reasons, including basic geography, political instability and civil wars, ethnic and religious rivalries, a lack of an educated middle class, government corruption, and for some, the consequences of cold war clashes between the United States and the Soviet Union. Perhaps the most

important factor has been government policies unfavorable to trade and investment. Governments often imposed high import duties and import licensing requirements to protect local industries from the competition of more efficient foreign firms. This protection allowed local companies to sell inferior products at higher costs than they could have if they had not been insulated from foreign competition. Developing countries also put strict controls over the inflow of capital and technology. These policies were based on the notion that government could best direct how capital and technology should be used, instead of leaving it up to free market forces. In many cases, socialist policies led to government ownership of businesses and industry. These policies forced many multinational corporations and other investors to stay away.

Latin America is a good example. During the 1970s and 1980s, the region suffered from increased unemployment, declining personal income, financial instability, the flight of capital, low rates of savings, and high rates of inflation. Inflation was caused partly by the printing of money to cover government spending, and by automatic indexing of wage and price increases. For example, during the 1970s and 1980s Brazil and Argentina suffered from what has been called *hyperinflation*—several thousand percent per year—that wore away the value of its currency, destroyed the buying power of its consumers, frightened investors, and damaged public confidence in the government's ability to manage its own economy. Governments were forced to cut basic services such as health care, water, and sewage. Multinational corporations pulled their capital out of the region. Investment in factories, plants, roads, and other infrastructure fell by 30 percent during the 1980s. The inflation was so severe in Latin America that, according to the U.S. International Trade Commission and the reports of international agencies, the region's economic growth rate and living standards during the 1980s actually declined. By the late 1980s, 38 percent of households were living in poverty.

The economy of Latin America began to improve only when extreme fiscal controls were instituted in the early 1990s. By 1994, inflation was down considerably. In Brazil and Venezuela inflation was down to around 40–50 percent annually (still outrageous by U.S. standards). In Argentina and several other Latin American countries inflation was running between 5 percent and 10 percent, or even lower. Of course, economic instability still exists. In 1995, for example, the value of Mexico's *peso* declined precipitously, causing widespread concern for Mexico's economy.

**Availability of Foreign Exchange in Developing Countries.** Developing countries also lack a ready reserve of foreign exchange. Keep in mind that their currencies are not generally accepted for trade around the world as are the dollar, pound sterling, mark, or yen. A developing country's only access to foreign exchange comes from either receiving foreign payments for the export of locally made products, foreign direct investment, or foreign aid from the United States or international community. Thus they often cannot afford to purchase the products or technologies they need, or to undertake public construction projects in roads, sewage, hospitals, and ports. Government banking restrictions have been designed to keep as much foreign exchange as possible in the country's central bank. Thus, local companies wanting to import foreign products often have to apply to their central bank for authority to make an overseas transfer of money to their supplier. Historically, their requests were often turned down, particularly when the import was a luxury or consumer good. These restrictions made entering into foreign contracts especially risky, because the money might not be available to pay one's foreign suppliers.

## Controls on Trade and Licensing in Developing Countries

The protectionist policies of developing countries have been implemented by restrictions on imports and on licensing, including high tariffs and other barriers to imported products that competed with locally made goods, and barriers to goods that did not contribute to the economic goals set out in national development plans. For instance, a developing country trying to industrialize might have allowed the import of tractors, hydroelectric generators, or machine tools, but not hair dryers, cosmetics, or luxury goods. Imports of foods and pharmaceuticals have been restricted in many countries to protect local producers. Even the content of foreign television shows and advertising has been restricted. For instance, India still has some of the most severe restrictions in the world. They have high tariffs and quotas on imports, import licensing requirements, a ban on the import of practically all consumer goods, and strict control over the import of commodities. Like many other developing countries, India also has many restrictions on trade in services. Foreign lawyers cannot practice in Indian courts, and foreigners cannot own a seat on an Indian stock exchange. The banking and insurance sectors are not open to foreign firms. Licensing agreements are also restricted. During the 1970s, Coca-Cola abandoned its efforts to negotiate a licensing agreement for a bottling operation in India after the Indian government insisted that the company disclose its secret formula for making Coke and required that at least 60 percent of Coke's bottling operations there be Indian owned. Other developing countries with strict barriers to imports include China, Egypt, Indonesia, Malaysia, Pakistan, and the Philippines. They severely limit trade in both goods and services. A few countries, such as newly industrialized Singapore, have a very open trade environment. Latin America is also opening its doors rapidly.

## Controls on Investment in Developing Countries

Developing countries have also maintained strict controls over investment by foreign firms. Restrictions on investment have included *local participation* requirements whereby a foreign firm would have to include local investors in any new factory or business venture; a foreign firm might be allowed to own only a portion of the stock of a business, with the remainder owned by local investors. These restrictions are most severe in petroleum and energy industries, utilities, agriculture, and transportation. For example, ocean and air freight or package delivery services are often not open to foreign companies. In many countries, broadcasting companies cannot be foreign owned. In India insurance companies and banks are still government owned.

A foreign firm that wants to open a factory in a host developing country might face many restrictions and disincentives to investment. It might be required to employ local managers, build water treatment and sewage facilities, or pay excessive taxes on earnings or property, or export a percentage of its finished goods to other countries for foreign currency. The firm might be restricted in its *repatriation of profits;* it might be required to reinvest profits in the host country instead of removing, or repatriating, them to its stockholders in its home country. As a condition of entering into a joint venture with a local firm, a foreign investor might be required to transfer its most advanced technology and products to the joint venture partner in the host country. An extreme example of government control occurs when a country seizes the property of a foreign company, such as factories, farms, mines, or oil refineries, and takes it for its own use. This type of activity is called *nationalization* or *expropriation.* Such harsh actions resulted from the socialist-inspired belief that the seized assets could best be operated by the government itself for the benefit of the country, rather than for private profit. Nationalization and expropriation were a greater problem twenty, thirty, or forty years ago than they are today.

Doing business in a foreign country may mean subjecting one's company to foreign laws and possibly foreign courts, and carries many risks, especially in developing countries. In the following case, *In re Union Carbide Corporation Gas Plant Disaster at Bhopal,* a U.S. corporation owned the majority of stock in an Indian corporation that operated a chemical plant in Bhopal, India. The company, Union Carbide, delegated responsibility for operating the plant to local managers. The escape of poisonous chemicals resulted in the deaths of thousands of people living near the plant—the worst industrial disaster in history. Union Carbide was placed in the position of defending itself in India. As you read, consider the legal responsibility of a corporation for negligent acts committed by its subsidiaries abroad. Also, consider the risks of a multinational corporation operating in a far-off developing country.

---

### In re Union Carbide Corporation Gas Plant Disaster at Bhopal

*809 F.2d 195 (1987)*
*United States Court of Appeals (2d.Cir.)*

BACKGROUND AND FACTS

This case arose out of what has been considered the most devastating industrial disaster in history—the deaths of thousands of persons (estimates range from 2000 to 4000) and injuries of several hundred thousand caused by the release of a lethal gas known as methyl isocyanate from a chemical plant operated by Union Carbide India Limited (UCIL) in Bhopal, India, in 1984. The accident occurred on the night of December 2, 1984, when winds blew the deadly gas from the plant operated by UCIL into densely occupied parts of the city of Bhopal. UCIL is incorporated under the laws of India. Fifty-one percent of its stock is owned by Union Carbide Corporation (UCC), a U.S. corporation, 22 percent is owned or controlled by the government of India, and the balance is held by approximately 23,500 Indian citizens. The stock is publicly traded on the Bombay Stock Exchange. The company is engaged in the manufacture of a variety of products, including chemicals, plastics, fertilizers, and insecticides, at 14 plants in India and employs more than 9,000 Indian citizens. Approximately 650 people are employed at the Bhopal plant. It is managed and operated entirely by Indian citizens. All products produced at Bhopal are sold in India. The operations of the plant were regulated by more than two dozen Indian governmental agencies.

Four days after the accident, the first of some 145 actions in federal district courts in the United States was commenced on behalf of victims. In the meantime, India enacted the *Bhopal Gas Leak Disaster Act,* granting to its government (the Union of India [UOI]), the exclusive right to represent the victims in India or elsewhere. In April

*(continued*

*(continued)*

1985, the Indian government filed a complaint in the Southern District of New York on behalf of all of the victims. India's decision to bring suit in the United States was attributed to the fact that although nearly 6,500 lawsuits had been instituted by victims in India against UCIL, the Indian courts did not have jurisdiction over UCC, the parent company. UCC contended that the actions are properly tried in the courts of India on the doctrine of *forum non conveniens.* The district court dismissed the action on the condition that UCC submit to the jurisdiction of the Indian courts and that UCC agree to satisfy any judgment taken against it in the courts of India.

MANSFIELD, CIRCUIT JUDGE

The plaintiffs seek to prove that the accident was caused by negligence on the part of UCC in originally contributing to the design of the plant and its provision for storage of excessive amounts of the gas at the plant. As Judge Keenan found, however, UCC's participation was limited, and its involvement in plant operations terminated long before the accident. . . . The preliminary process design information furnished by UCC could not have been used to construct the plant. Construction required the detailed process design and engineering data prepared by hundreds of Indian engineers, process designers, and subcontractors. During the ten years spent constructing the plant, its design and configuration underwent many changes.

The vital parts of the Bhopal plant, including its storage tank, monitoring instrumentation, and vent gas scrubber, were manufactured by Indians in India. Although some 40 UCIL employees were given some safety training at UCC's plant in West Virginia, they represented a small fraction of the Bhopal plant's employees. The vast majority of plant employees were selected and trained by UCIL in Bhopal. The manual for start-up of the Bhopal plant was prepared by Indians employed by UCIL.

In short, the plant has been constructed and managed by Indians in India. No Americans were employed at the plant at the time of the accident. In the five years from 1980 to 1984, although more than 1,000 Indians were employed at the plant, only one American was employed there and he left in 1982. No Americans visited the plant for more than one year prior to the accident, and during the five-year period before the accident the communications between the plant and the United States were almost nonexistent.

The vast majority of material witnesses and documentary proof bearing on causation of and liability for the accident is located in India, not the United States, and would be more accessible to an Indian court than to a United States court. The records are almost entirely in Hindi or other Indian languages, understandable to an Indian court without translation. The witnesses for the most part do not speak English but Indian languages understood by an Indian court but not by an American court. These witnesses could be required to appear in an Indian court but not in a court of the United States. Although witnesses in the United States could not be subpoenaed to appear in India, they are comparatively few in number and most are employed by UCC, which, as a party, would produce them in India, with lower overall transportation costs than if the parties were to attempt to bring hundreds of Indian witnesses to the United States. Lastly, Judge Keenan properly concluded that an Indian court would be in a better position to direct and supervise a viewing of the Bhopal plant, which was sealed after the accident. Such a viewing could be of help to a court in determining liability issues.

After a thorough review, the district court concluded that the public interest concerns, like the private ones, also weigh heavily in favor of India as the situs for trial and disposition of the cases. The accident and all relevant events occurred in India. The victims, over 200,000 in number, are citizens of India and located there. The witnesses are almost entirely Indian citizens. The Union of India has a greater interest than does the United States in facilitating the trial and adjudication of the victims' claims.

India's interest is increased by the fact that it has for years treated UCIL as an Indian national, subjecting it to intensive regulations and governmental supervision of the construction, development, and operation of the Bhopal plant, its emissions, water and air pollution, and safety precautions. Numerous Indian government officials have regularly conducted on-site inspections of the plant and approved its machinery and equipment, including its facilities for storage of the lethal methyl isocyanate gas that

*(continued)*

*(continued)*

escaped and caused the disaster giving rise to the claims. Thus India has considered the plant to be an Indian one and the disaster to be an Indian problem. It therefore has a deep interest in ensuring compliance with its safety standards. Moreover, plaintiffs have conceded that in view of India's strong interest and its greater contacts with the plant, its operations, its employees, and the victims of the accident, the law of India, as the place where the tort occurred, will undoubtedly govern.

**Decision.** The district court's dismissal of the actions against Union Carbide Corporation is upheld. The doctrine of *forum non conveniens* is a rule of U.S. law, which states that where a case is properly heard in more than one court, it should be heard by the one that is most convenient. Given the facts of this case, the courts of India are the more convenient forum.

**Comment.** In 1989 the Supreme Court of India approved a settlement fund of $470 million to compensate the victims of the disaster.

## The Road to Free Markets, Consumer-Based Economics, and Private Ownership

In the late 1980s, the more progressive developing countries, particularly in Latin America, began to give up their isolationist policies and to loosen controls over trade and investment. Today they are trying to attract large sources of new capital for investment, new technologies, new manufacturing techniques and business know-how, improved training for their labor force, and organizational and managerial expertise. For example, developing countries are reducing tariffs on most imported products. They are gradually ending burdensome import licensing schemes and making it easier for local companies and investors to obtain foreign currency. They are reducing many kinds of taxes on business. Some countries are lowering taxes on royalties paid to foreign companies under licensing agreements for modern technology and technical assistance. China, Argentina, and other countries are lifting controls over prices and wages, allowing market mechanisms to work. Gradually, developing countries are passing new, more progressive laws—protection of intellectual property, protection of the environment, protection of consumers from fraud and abuse, protection of workers, securities laws to protect investors and increase investment opportunities, and many more. Even accounting standards are changing so that investors will be given more information about a company and can better understand its financial health. Government "red tape" is being cut, allowing a faster and easier flow of paper-

work through government bureaucracies, which speeds up the application process for investment and eases the way for importers to bring goods into the country. Government agencies are applying laws and regulations to foreign firms in a fairer and more consistent manner.

**Capital Investment.** Several important forces allow the developing countries to find new sources of capital investment—the globalization of financial markets, the lifting of restrictions over cross-border capital flows, and the return of once state-owned industries to private owners. Although a discussion of the globalization of financial markets is beyond the scope of this book, readers should note that many large investors already seek to maximize their investment, commensurate with risk, on a global basis. Using computers and modern communications systems, investors can quickly move money, stocks, bonds, and other financial instruments almost anywhere in the world. Advanced communications have facilitated international flows of capital into all regions of the world, including developing countries. Next, developing countries that compete in these global financial markets for sources of investment find that they must give up many of their severe restrictions on investors to get it. Multinational corporations are turning to the option of building plants or entering joint ventures with local firms. Locally owned companies are also finding greater access to foreign capital. U.S. mutual funds are already heavily invested in Latin American and Asian stocks and bonds. Stock markets, such as the Mexican

*Bolsa,* are attracting more and more investors. Personal savings rates are increasing. One major source of capital—the pension funds of employees in developing countries that were once only invested in state-owned companies—is now beginning to be invested in private companies. This tremendous infusion of capital into developing countries is spurring the growth of modern, competitive factories, new technologies, and increased productivity. Indeed, some economists believe that most of the growth in the world's economy in the next fifty years will be in the developing countries. Capital investment flows into developing countries have increased from about $30 billion in 1986 to as much as $200 billion by 1995. Nearly 70 percent of foreign investment by the developed countries worldwide is now taking place in the developing countries.

Developing countries have also instituted new, more prudent fiscal policies. Latin American countries have reduced government borrowing and spending. Several countries, notably Brazil and Argentina, have enacted new regulations to stabilize their exchange rates. For example, Brazil adopted a new currency effective July 1, 1994, called the *real,* that is tied to the value of the U.S. dollar. These efforts are bringing inflation under control and returning consumer and investor confidence.

**Privatization.**   An important development in these countries is the movement toward privatization. *Privatization* refers to the process by which a government sells or transfers government-owned industries or other assets to the private sector. Privatization is happening in the developing countries and throughout the world, including Great Britain and Western and Eastern Europe. The selling of state-owned assets to private investors has caused an infusion of new capital investment, managerial know-how, technological innovation, and entrepreneurial spirit. These issues will be discussed in greater depth in Part Four of this book.

**The Results of Reform.**   The developing countries will continue to experience economic instability for many years to come. Financial stability and economic growth, however, are beginning to return after years of decline. Jobs and personal incomes are rising. Modern factories are increasing productivity and turning out products of greater quality. As the quality of products improves, those products are more in demand in world markets, thus increasing export earnings and access to foreign exchange. As the economies of these countries improve, they present important emerging markets for foreign products—industrial equipment, computer and telecommunications technologies, health care, and new agricultural and environmental technologies and chemicals. The developing countries are also vast untapped consumer markets. For instance, in Brazil fewer than one out of ten people own a telephone. The market for telecommunications products ranging from fiber-optic cable to cellular phones is tremendous. Indeed, the United States is Latin America's leading trading partner, with exports to that region more than doubling between 1986 and 1994.

Doing business in developing countries is still not like doing business in the United States or Canada, however. They have a long way to go in opening up their product and financial markets. Investors have no guarantee that inflation will not skyrocket again, nor that the value of foreign currencies will not plummet again. Most developing countries are still experiencing considerable political instability. They are far behind in education, infrastructure, and public health; however, as the last half of the 1990s approaches, the prospects for business in the developing countries look good.

**The People's Republic of China.**   China has one-quarter of the world's population and one of the world's largest economies despite its communist-dominated government and centrally planned economy. As a communist player in many world markets, China represents a special area of interest to those studying international business. In the modern period, it was not until the 1970s that China began to open its doors to outside trade and investment. Since that time, China has made many changes in its economic system necessary to doing business with the West. It has opened up opportunities for collectively and privately owned enterprises, and made it easier to set up joint ventures with foreign companies. China also has undertaken legal reform needed to attract foreign companies. However, China has almost constantly, over the last decade, been at the verge of one "trade war" or another with the United States. One area of dispute is China's failure to stop the infringement of U.S.-owned copyrights and trademarks (for instance, the piracy of U.S.-developed and copyrighted computer software). Another area is U.S.-imposed quotas on imports of Chinese textiles and apparel. Attempts by Chinese firms to get around these quotas have consistently led to threats of retaliation by the United States. The United States has also threatened to increase duties on Chinese products for political reasons, such as imprisonment of dissidents, the use of prison labor to manufacture consumer goods, and the sale of missiles to hostile countries. Nevertheless, in 1994 the Clinton administration signaled that it would not link U.S.–Chinese trade relations to politics. This pragmatic policy had two ostensible reasons: to keep China's markets open to U.S. products and services, and to attempt to influence China's policies for the better. U.S. businesspeople view China both as a future market of incredible potential as well as a powerful competitor. Many businesspeople also believe China may become the world's "economic powerhouse" of the next century.

## The Newly Industrialized Countries

The *newly industrialized countries,* primarily in southeast Asia, have made tremendous economic progress in recent years due to a highly motivated work force and a stable climate for foreign investment. These countries export a broad mix of high-quality products, from computers to steel, attracting a reserve of foreign exchange. Their success has led to a dramatic rise in per capita gross domestic product and to improvements in jobs, wages, education, health care, living accommodations, and the overall quality of life. Most notable among these countries are the four "Asian Tigers": Hong Kong, Singapore, Taiwan, and South Korea. Hong Kong is one of the largest banking centers in the world. In 1997–1998, many Asian countries were rocked by an economic and currency crisis. Hong Kong also reverted to Chinese control. These developments merit close attention in the future.

## The Less-Developed Countries

The prospects for business in the *less-developed countries* are not as good as in those regions already discussed. The less-developed countries are located primarily in sub-Saharan Africa. Examples might be Rwanda, Ethiopia, or Somalia in Africa, Haiti in the Caribbean, or countries of Central Asia. They lack many of the basic resources needed for development and require vast amounts of foreign aid from the wealthier nations. Many of these countries have inadequate roads and bridges, inadequate public utilities and telephone systems, poor educational and health care facilities, a lack of plentiful drinking water, unstable governments, little or no technological base, illiteracy, high infant mortality, AIDS and other diseases, rampant crime, excessive armaments, ethnic and tribal warfare, and weak or nonexistent financial institutions. Their economies are often based on agriculture, mining, some assembly operations, and some manufacturing. Their reserves of foreign exchange are limited. Most of these countries lack a market-based economy that characterizes the developed world. Business opportunities for trade in consumer goods and for the products and services of most western companies are limited. Less-developed countries are in need of investment and products that will help them in dealing with these basic problems.

# The Business Environment in Eastern Europe, Russia, and the Newly Independent Republics of the Former Soviet Union

Until its breakup in 1991, the Soviet Union extended from Eastern Europe on the west, across two continents to the Pacific Ocean, and from China and Central Asia on the south to the Arctic Ocean on the north. It was the third most populated nation in the world, after China and India, comprising more than 100 different ethnic groups. It consisted of the Slavic republics of Russia, Byelorussia, and the Ukraine; the Baltic States of Latvia, Estonia, and Lithuania; the Caucasus that includes Armenia and Georgia; and the largely Moslem Central Asian republics that extend geographically from the Caspian Sea to the Mongolian border. When the Soviet Union collapsed in 1991, it changed the political and economic landscape of Europe and much of Asia. The Soviet republics gained independence. Russia emerged as the largest of these, called the *Russian Federation.* Eastern Europe, which borders the Soviet Union, was freed from Soviet and communist domination. Poland, Hungary, Bulgaria, East Germany, Romania, and Czechoslovakia experienced political and economic reform. The Berlin Wall fell, and communist East Germany was reunited with democratic West Germany (the Federal Republic of Germany).

## The Transition from Communism to Free Markets and Private Enterprise

These countries are striving to free their economies from years of communist control by liberalizing controls over trade and investment. They are rapidly privatizing their industries, turning formerly state-owned properties over to private ownership and management. New investors from the United States, Germany, Japan, and other countries are entering joint ventures with Russian and Eastern European firms. Russian citizens are investing in their own companies. Inefficient plants are closing. Russia represents an enormous potential market for modern consumer goods, housing, and industrial equipment. Russia has a highly trained technical workforce, including superb engineers, scientists, and technicians. Russians and Eastern European managers are attending business schools in the United States for management training. International economic aid is pouring into the region. Their governments are hoping for closer ties to the United States and Western Europe.

For more than seventy years these countries operated under an economic and political system in which the state owned all natural resources, factories, farms, and other means of production. The allocation of resources, as well as production and pricing decisions, were dictated by government agencies based on their central economic plans. Because production and the supply of goods were not dictated by demand forces, consumer tastes and preferences became irrelevant. Consumer industries were totally neglected, operating with inefficient, antiquated machinery. The economy was based on military and defense industries. Illegal "black markets" provided some western consumer goods to those few who could obtain much sought-after foreign currency.

Today, the newly emerging nations of the former Soviet Union are suffering from the results of seventy years of economic neglect. Many roads, bridges, and railroads are near collapse. Transportation systems are in disrepair. Power plants are deteriorating, and the risk of a serious nuclear disaster is high. Years of communist rule have caused damaging pollution of the land, air, and waters. Toxic waste has been abandoned near populated communities, causing terrible epidemics of disease and death. Oil spills, far worse than the Alaskan oil spill of the *Exxon Valdez,* have been reported. Food shortages exist because no distribution system exists to harvest the food and bring it to market. The state-owned industries provide no worker incentive and therefore experience low productivity. Many workers do not show for work at all. Alcoholism is a severe problem. Machinery and equipment are antiquated. Many factories have simply ceased to operate because of a lack of raw materials, constant breakdowns, and an absence of spare parts. To complicate matters, in the transition from a state-owned and state-run system, people are confused as to who is really in charge of the factories and farms. After so many years of communism, most workers lack managerial skills and the understanding of how to run a company in a free market.

The economies of these countries, especially Russia, are plagued by fraud and corruption. Criminals have preyed on unsuspecting and inexperienced foreign investors and on Russian citizens unaccustomed to doing business in a free market economy. Organized crime and gangs extort "protection money." In what some reporters have described as a "Wild West atmosphere," private businesses have resorted to armed guards to protect their assets. Laws affecting business and commercial transactions are often contradictory and unreasonably burdensome. Government agencies often "make up" rules when they feel the need to do so. Even though laws have been passed to protect intellectual property, the government has virtually no way to enforce them. Pirated brandname goods are sold in stores and on street corners with impunity. Taxes are often imposed arbitrarily, and are so high that they discourage investment. The banking system is almost unworkable. The Russian currency, the *ruble,* has been unstable, and inflation high. This instability is making trade and investment difficult, and threatens to hold up Russia's entrance into important international economic organizations. Many western business ventures are not profitable and are losing money. In the political realm, civil unrest among ethnic minorities in the Central Asian republics threatens to ignite the region in war. Perhaps the greatest threat to economic liberalization is that Russia is still undergoing tremendous political instability, despite democratic elections. Many people are still hostile to the United States and private enterprise and would like to return Russia to a Soviet empire. As of 1997, economic reforms were still proceeding but no one could yet predict whether they would succeed.

## Managing the Risks of International Business

Readers need to keep one particular truism in mind throughout this text: *The management of international business is the management of risk.* No manager can make a strategic business decision or enter into an important business transaction without a full evaluation of the risks involved. Many of the best business plans have been ruined by a miscalculation, a mistake, or an error in judgment that could have been avoided with proper planning. This textbook is full of such cases:

- An importer of "camping tents" who thought they would be dutied at the same rate as "sporting goods," but found out too late that the U.S. Customs service considered them to be textile products and imposed a much higher import duty.
- The owner of a yacht shipped aboard an ocean carrier from Asia, who failed to declare its real value on the shipping documents, found that when the yacht was destroyed on loading, international law allowed the yacht's owner to collect a mere $500.

- The multinational corporation that invested millions in a foreign country only to lose it amidst a revolution.
- The U.S. exporter whose goods were stranded at a foreign port, thousands of miles away, when the buyer refused to pay for them.

Advance planning could have reduced the risk in these cases. The importer of tents could have sought and received an advance ruling from U.S. customs prior to importing them and avoided an unexpected surprise in determining the tariff rate after they were already in the country. A better understanding of the risks of shipping goods on the high seas would have induced the yacht owner to take greater precautions in making the shipping arrangements. Had the multinational corporation evaluated the political risk in its host country, it would have been better prepared to protect its investment there. A U.S. exporter who understood the problems in collecting a debt in a foreign country would have made different arrangements for payment.

If the risk cannot be reduced through advance planning and careful execution, perhaps it can be shifted to some other party to the transaction. For example, can a seller of goods who does not want to bear the risk that the goods might be lost at sea "shift the risk" to the buyer in the process of contract negotiations? If a U.S. exporter is fearful that it may not get paid for selling merchandise to a buyer in, say, Venezuela, can it shift the transaction risk to the buyer by requiring a letter of credit from the buyer's bank? After all, in both of these cases, the parties can negotiate which one of them will bear the risk of loss to the goods, or the risk of not getting paid. Risks become a point of negotiations between parties to a transaction, be it a sale of goods contract, a patent or trademark agreement, or a joint venture contract to build a factory.

If the risk cannot be shifted to another party to the transaction, it might be shifted to an insurance company. Many types of risks can be insured against, including the risk of damage to goods at sea, the risk of losing an investment in a developing country, and many others. Finally, a company must assess whether, after having tried to manage the risks as best as possible, the potential profits will be adequate to compensate for the risks that remain.

## Risk Assessment and the Firm's Foreign Market Entry Strategy

When a firm is considering its entry or expansion in a foreign market, it must weigh all options and decide on a course of action commensurate with its objectives, capabilities, and its willingness to assume risk. As stated earlier, trade generally entails less penetration into a foreign market than licensing, and licensing less than foreign investment. To say it another way, selling to a customer in another country results in less risk to the firm than licensing patents, trademarks, and copyrights there. Licensing usually requires less risk than forming a joint venture with a foreign firm to build a factory together in China or India, for instance. A firm's global business strategy must take into account the amount of risk that the firm is willing to bear in entering the foreign market.

Consider this actual real-life example. A U.S. manufacturer of industrial equipment exported products to Europe, but faced growing competition from European firms, higher ocean freight rates, and increased European import restrictions. Moreover, the company experienced some difficulty in servicing its equipment from the United States as well as maintaining a ready supply of spare parts for Europe. It evaluated its options for overcoming the problems of exporting and for expanding its presence in the European market through a country-by-country analysis of the business climate in Europe. On the basis of labor, tax, and other factors, it determined that its best course of action was to enter the European market through Spain. Prominent in its decision was the presence of an existing firm in Spain that, with the financial and technical assistance of the U.S. firm, would have seemed to make an appropriate joint venture partner. During negotiations, the two firms preliminarily agreed that the U.S. company would take a 40 percent minority interest in the new business venture, sharing profits with their partner. The Americans had done all of the usual background checks, reviewed credit reports, and made inquiries of others with whom the Spanish company had dealt. Although everything proved to be in order, and despite many trips abroad by management, the U.S. firm wanted their auditors to visit the Spanish company and review their books. During their visit to Spain the auditors were asked "which set of

books and numbers" they wanted to review—the real financial records of the Spanish company or those used to report to Spanish tax authorities. The U.S. company became uneasy about their potential exposure as a minority partner in a foreign investment with this company. Not only were they fearful that they could be misled by their "partner," but they feared liability to Spanish legal and tax authorities for the conduct of their partner over which they had little or no control. As a result, they decided not to share ownership of a joint venture with the Spanish company, but instead decided to license their technology and know-how to the Spanish firm. They would obtain patent rights to their products in Europe, license those rights to the Spanish company, provide technical assistance, and in return receive an upfront cash payment and future royalties based on sales. This arrangement would give them the access to the European customers that they needed, without the capital costs and risks of building a plant there. This text will present many such examples of how the risks of international business will affect a firm's strategy for entering a foreign market.

## Managing Distance and Communications

The risks of doing business in a foreign country are different from those encountered at home. A Texas firm, for example, will find doing business in Japan, or even neighboring Mexico, to be different from doing business in Oklahoma. The Texas firm will find Oklahoma City hardly different at all from Austin. Texas and Oklahoma share a common language and customs, a common currency, uniform commercial laws, a seamlessly networked communications system, and so on. The Texas firm would not find these similarities in a foreign country. It would encounter greater distances; problems in communications; language and cultural barriers; differences in ethical, moral, and religious codes; exposure to strange foreign laws and government regulations; and different currencies. All these factors affect the risks of doing business abroad.

**Selling Face-to-Face.**    Parties to an international transaction must find ways of reducing the distance between them. Even though the advent of satellite communications, video teleconferencing, and fax machines have brought businesspeople closer to each other than ever before, no one has discovered a substitute for face-to-face meetings. Doing business in Asia may require many trips there and many years of ongoing negotiations in order for the parties to develop trust between them. Face-to-face meetings are essential to negotiations because they enable the parties to better describe their needs, their capabilities, and their products and services. They are better able to communicate and explain their positions, and most importantly, to gauge each others intentions, attitudes, and integrity. These benefits of face-to-face meetings apply in banking, as well as in other industries. International bankers often travel abroad to meet foreign bankers, foreign government representatives, and foreign customers so they can personally evaluate the risks of lending money or doing other banking business.

Ask any international sales manager about the importance of face-to-face meetings, and he or she will tell you that you cannot sell your product abroad from the confines of your office. A successful sales director from a European textile firm once claimed that he had established a policy of not selling to any foreign firm that he had not visited, nor to anyone he had not met. He thus participated in every U.S. textile trade show and made semiannual trips across the United States to visit his customers. This policy was not just because he found it easier to sell face-to-face, but because he learned more about his customer's needs for new products, styles, and colors. He was also better able to evaluate the customer's creditworthiness and the potential for a long-term business relationship.

**Attendance at International Trade Shows.** One opportunity for identifying new customers, renewing old business relationships, and expanding contacts in a given industry is to attend an international trade show, or trade fair. Most industries have these regularly scheduled exhibitions—computer and software, home textiles, restaurant products, aircraft, boats, sporting goods, clothing and apparel, paper, and industrial equipment. They are often organized by industry trade associations or convention centers. These shows give sellers from around the world the opportu-

nity to exhibit their products and services, meet prospective buyers and write orders.

## Language and Cultural Differences

As the world's economy moves toward greater globalization, languages and cultural differences become less of a barrier to international business. Even though English is widely used in business all over the world, the language of a given transaction still depends on the type of business one is doing and on the region of the world. In the case of importing and exporting, some truth can be found in the saying that if you're the buyer, the seller will find a way to speak your language; but if you're the seller, you should find a way to communicate with your customer. One corporate CEO argued that he could not possibly know all the languages of all the countries in which he does business. That argument may not be so valid, however, for an international sales manager who does business in one or two primary foreign markets. Some positions require an even greater level of foreign language competency. For certain types of selling or contract negotiations, a mastery of a foreign language will be essential. As a firm moves toward a greater penetration of the foreign market, for instance, negotiating a licensing or investment contract, the use of native speakers or nationals of the host country becomes crucial. Contracts such as these will often be written in the languages of both parties, and so the use of foreign lawyers becomes necessary. In other cases, only social conventions are needed: to make introductions, to be courteous, and to show you took the time to learn something about their language and culture. An appreciation for the cultural environment and religious beliefs of a host is absolutely essential. In selling in a foreign country, the use of local sales agents and distributors will ease the language and cultural problems. They will also give good advice on handling the cultural differences you might face in their countries. Moreover, many countries are moving toward the use of uniform laws—laws and legal codes that are commonly agreed on and adopted by many countries (and written and made available in many languages). The following case, *Gaskin v. Stumm Handel,* illustrates what can happen by not being able to read and understand a foreign language contract.

## Gaskin v. Stumm Handel GMBH
*390 F.Supp. 361 (1975)*
*United States District*
*Court (S.D. N.Y.)*

### BACKGROUND AND FACTS

The plaintiff, a U.S. citizen, entered into an employment contract with the German firm of Stumm Handel, the defendant. The contract presented to the plaintiff was written entirely in German. Without being able to speak or read German, the plaintiff signed the contract. He never received an English language version. At the time of the signing of the contract, however, the terms of the contract were explained to him in English. One of the terms of the contract, known as a "forum selection clause" provided that any disputes that might arise between the parties would be settled in the courts of Germany. Later, when the parties reached a disagreement, the plaintiff brought this action against the defendant in the United States, contending that his failure to understand German rendered the forum selection clause invalid.

### CANNELLA, DISTRICT JUDGE

With regard to such translation, Gaskin asserts that "I was never informed that by executing the (contract), I was consenting to the Republic of West Germany as the forum within which I must submit all controversies" and that "had I known this, I would not have agreed to the same, as such an obligation is onerous and unconscionable, and a deterrent to bringing any actions whatsoever." . . . We find that in making the foregoing assertions, Gaskin flies in the face of well-settled contract law principles and has failed to sustain his burden.

It is a settled proposition of contract law in this state and nation that "the signer of a deed or other instrument, expressive of a jural act, is conclusively bound thereby. That his mind never gave assent to the terms expressed is not material. If the signer could read the instrument, not to have read it was gross negligence; if he could not read it, not to procure it to be read was equally negligent; in either case the writing binds him." (citations omitted) . . .

While Mr. Gaskin's apparent "blissful ignorance" with regard to the contract under which he was to render his labors to the defendant strikes us as highly incredible as a matter of common sense, we take note of certain facts which are relevant to the disposition of this matter. It must be remembered that Mr. Gaskin is not an ignorant consumer, unlearned in the language of the contract, who has become entangled in the web of a contract of adhesion through the overreaching or other unconscionable practices of the defendant. The contract at bar does not involve the credit sale of a refrigerator or color television set, but rather compensation of some $36,000 per annum for Mr. Gaskin's services as the manager in charge of the defendant's New York operations which were to be conducted under the name Stumm Trading Company. His office (Park Avenue, New York City) is not located in an area which would have precluded his easy access to a competent translation of the involved document. There existed no emergency condition or other exceptional circumstances at the time plaintiff entered into this contract; conditions which might now serve to excuse his present plight. . . .

Thus, we find that the instant transaction was a commercial arrangement of a nature which warranted the exercise of care by Mr. Gaskin before his entry into it and that his conduct with regard to this undertaking can only be characterized as negligent, the consequences of which he must now bear. . . .

We, therefore, decline to exercise our jurisdiction over this cause in deference to the contractual forum. An order dismissing this action will be entered.

**Decision.** The court dismissed the plaintiff's action, holding that the plaintiff's failure to speak or read German was not grounds for invalidating any of the provisions of the contract.

## Managing Currency and Exchange Rate Risks

*Currency risk* is risk a firm is exposed to as a result of buying, selling, or holding a foreign currency, or transacting business in a foreign currency. Currency risk includes (1) exchange rate risk and (2) currency control risk. (Other risks such as inflation risk and interest rate risk are not the subject of this book.) Most international business transactions involve the use or transfer of foreign currency. Currency risk exists when a firm must convert one currency to the currency of another country before it can be used.

**Exchange Rate Risk.** *Exchange rate risk* results from the fluctuations in the relative values of foreign currencies against each other when they are bought and sold on international financial markets. Virtually every international business transaction is affected by exchange rate risk. Take a simple example. Assume that a company based in the United States sells goods to a firm in France. In an export/import transaction, one of the parties will be dealing in the currency of the other. The one that deals in the other party's currency will bear the exchange rate risk. If the contract calls for payment in U.S. dollars upon shipment of the goods in sixty days, then the French importer bears the risk during the intervening period. If the French firm does not have a source of income in dollars, it must buy dollars from a French bank at the prevailing rate for dollars at the time it makes the purchase. If the value of the French franc declines vis-à-vis the dollar during the same period, then more francs are needed to purchase the same number of dollars to pay the U.S. firm. Similarly, if the franc appreciates in value against the dollar, then the French firm will find the goods "cheaper" than it had expected. Whichever way the currencies fluctuate, the U.S. exporter will have shifted the exchange rate risk to the French side. The U.S. firm spends dollars to pay labor, utilities, taxes, and other expenses, and it will receive dollars for the goods sold to France. (Of course, even when dealing in one's own currency, a company still faces "opportunity risk"—if it had sold goods for francs, and the franc had appreciated, then the company might have reaped a windfall profit on the exchange to dollars.) On the other hand, if the U.S. firm prices its goods in francs at the request of its customer (which an exporter often must do for its customers), it will bear the exchange rate risk. As one can see from this example, currency exchange rates can have a tremendous effect on trade and investment decisions made by firms, and thus affect the flow of money in and out of all countries.

**Floating and Fixed Exchange Rates.** Floating or "hard" currencies are those currencies of the western countries and Japan freely traded on world markets. A currency's value (or price) is determined by what buyers and sellers will pay for it at any given time. Currency values can also be affected by the action of central banks (government intervention), by interest rates, or by other market factors.

Currencies with a *fixed exchange rate* are also called "soft" currencies. The Russian *ruble,* Indian *rupee,* or Chinese *renminbi* are examples of soft currencies and can only be purchased at the fixed rate established by the government.

**Methods of Managing Exchange Rate Risk.** Most international bankers claim that predicting currency fluctuations is more difficult than predicting the stock market. The ability of a firm to manage its currency risk depends on the size, sophistication, and global resources of the firm. The small domestic company might "buy forward" or hedge. A firm *hedges* when it enters into a contract, usually with a bank, for the purchase of a foreign currency to be delivered at a future date at a price agreed upon in the contract. Multinational corporations have many more complex and sophisticated options for managing exchange risk. For instance, a multinational corporation's subsidiary units in foreign countries may have excess local currency derived from revenues there. These assets can be transferred to affiliated units owned by the parent company for use anywhere in the world.

Some companies engage in speculative trading of foreign currencies. These risky transactions require experience, skill, and, as traders know, "iron nerves." The following case, *Bank Brussels Lambert v. Intermetals Corporation,* illustrates the risks of currency trading.

## Bank Brussels Lambert v. Intermetals Corporation

779 F.Supp. 741 (1991)
United States District
Court (S.D.N.Y.)

### BACKGROUND AND FACTS

Intermetals Corporation (IM), a New Jersey corporation, engaged in the international trading of steel and other metals. Its president, Traub, had some experience in "hedging" foreign exchange contracts with Bank Brussels Lambert (BBL), a Belgium bank with a branch office in New York City. Traub began discussing other more speculative foreign exchange transactions with representatives of the bank. IM opened an account for speculative foreign exchange trading with BBL, to be managed by BBL foreign exchange traders. The trading was done on the "spot market"—at the current market price for currency—not the futures market. Spot transactions in foreign currencies call for settlement within two days. The trader purchases or sells foreign currency for IM at an agreed U.S. dollar price, to be paid for at settlement in two days. A purchase of a foreign currency would be made to speculate that, before settlement, the U.S. dollar would weaken against that foreign currency. A sale of the foreign currency would effect a speculation that, in the intervening two days, the U.S. dollar would gain against that foreign currency. When such contracts would come due in two days, the trader would either take the gain or loss of U.S. dollars or would "rollover" into another speculative position. BBL immediately notified IM of every trade by telephone and confirmed it in writing. Profits were credited to IM's bank account. IM had no control over the trading decisions. Losses would be charged to IM's account. If losses exceeded gains, this meant that BBL was extending credit to IM. After a year of trading, IM's losses exceeded $1.5 million. BBL demanded reimbursement from IM. IM declined responsibility. BBL brought this action to recover the deficit.

### LEVAL, DISTRICT JUDGE

IM's principal claim is that it had a contractual agreement with BBL that its losses would be limited to $50,000. I find as a matter of fact that there was no such contractual understanding. . . . IM was intimately aware on a daily basis of the results of all of the trading done for its account. In the first period of trading through June 1989, the losses in its account exceeded the alleged loss limit by more than six times. IM nonetheless continued the trading program placing many millions of dollars at risk and sometimes realizing losses far in excess of the alleged limit on a single day. IM therefore cannot have thought it was operating under a loss limit unless it believed that the bank was absorbing all the losses itself. Furthermore, the notion that the bank was offering its customer that it would trade speculatively in large volumes of foreign currencies under the understanding that profits would belong to the customer and that losses would be absorbed by the bank is so unlikely as to be preposterous.

IM makes numerous allegations of fraud and breach of fiduciary duty. It contends that BBL overstated the skill and expertise of its traders, failed to disclose the risks of foreign exchange trading, failed to disclose its fee and compensation structure, and failed to disclose that it was acting as a principal counterparty to IM in many of IM's trades. With respect to the expertise of the traders, IM has shown nothing worse than permissible puffing.

As to failure to disclose the risks of such speculation, there are at least two deficiencies in IM's argument. First, it has not shown that BBL was under a duty to advise IM of risks. Second, the evidence shows that IM was well aware of the risks. Traub was an experienced businessman. Although he had no experience in foreign exchange trading before February 1988, he was aware of the risk of fluctuations in foreign currency well before he began this speculative trading. Indeed, his first foreign exchange transaction with BBL, a hedge transaction, was motivated by Traub's desire to avoid that risk. IM had earned a $300,000 profit, payable in the future in Deutsche marks. . . . The trading it undertook thereafter was equally motivated by awareness of the risks of fluctuation of foreign currencies but now seeking to profit from that risk. From February to June 1989, IM lost $237,000 in foreign exchange trading. From June to November 1989, it made profits of over $500,000 in speculative foreign exchange trading. It can have been no secret to him that where one can earn $500,000 in speculative trading, one can

*(continued)*

*(continued)*

as easily lose it. IM's withdrawal of more than $200,000 of such trading profits eloquently punctuated its awareness of the speculative nature of its activity. By the time IM entered the disastrous phase of its foreign exchange trading, it had already experienced nearly a year of active trading in which it had experienced big losses and had pocketed big profits. It was well educated in the risks. When IM was risking $50,000,000 positions in foreign currency fluctuation, it needed no instruction from the bank to know that the results could be bad.

IM claims that BBL acted negligently in carrying and supervising the trading activity done for its account. Although that it is true without question that BBL had a duty to exercise reasonable skill and care in carrying out its activities for its cus-

tomer, IM has failed to show a breach of the requirements of reasonable care and skill. There is, of course, no obligation under law to be successful in speculation.

The court finds that plaintiff, Bank Brussels Lambert, S.A., has shown entitlement to judgment (in the amount of approximately $1,500,000 plus interest) for the credit it extended to defendant, Intermetals Corporation, to finance the losses incurred in Intermetals' foreign exchange trading.

**Decision.**   Judgment for the bank. The bank committed no breach of contract, fraud, or negligence in engaging in speculative foreign currency trading on behalf of its customer, Intermetals Corporation. Speculative trading is inherently risky, and a company like Intermetals is deemed to understand the risks involved.

---

**Currency Control Risk.**   Some countries, particularly developing countries in which access to ready foreign reserves is limited, put restrictions on currency transactions. In order to preserve the little foreign exchange that is available for international transactions, such as importing merchandise, these countries restrict the amount of foreign currency that they will sell to private companies. This limitation can cause problems for a U.S. exporter waiting for payment from its foreign customer who cannot obtain the dollars needed to pay for the goods. (The creative exporter may have to weigh alternative methods of payment in these countries, such as bartering.) The most severe form of currency restriction is the *blocked currency.* Blocked currencies, used by the former Soviet bloc countries of Eastern Europe under communism, could not legally be removed from the issuing country at all.

A multinational corporation with income earned in a country with a restricted currency, may find restrictions on its freedom to remove, or repatriate, the earnings to its home country. Repatriation of profits or dividends may be limited to a small portion of earnings or taxed at discouragingly high levels. Working in this environment presents one of the greatest creative challenges to a multinational corporation's financial managers. Industrialized countries have only

rarely instituted austere currency controls in the past, and then only in times of a national monetary crisis.

## Special Transaction Risks in Contracts for the Sale of Goods

A major portion of this book focuses on the special risks inherent in international transactions for the purchase and sale of goods. These transactions present special risks to both parties because the process of shipping goods and receiving payment between distant countries is riskier than when done within a single country. Because they are of special importance to international firms, these risks are described here.

**Payment or Credit Risk.**   The risk that a buyer will default on a sales contract and fail to pay for the goods is known as *payment risk,* often called *credit risk.* The consequences of a buyer defaulting on an international contract can be potentially disastrous. Because a company generally incurs greater expense in selling overseas, a failed contract can mean a large loss. Selling overseas adds the costs of travel, foreign marketing and advertising, procuring foreign licenses, retaining counsel overseas, distributor's fees and agent's commissions, packaging and insuring for international shipment, communications expenses, and freight forwarder's fees. One of the major consideration is the expense of international air or ocean freight. Freight costs for ocean cargo, for example, are determined by the greater of weight or volume. Thus, heavy, bulky cargo that cannot be disassembled or have its volume reduced by the removal of air or water during shipment is quite expensive to ship. In some cases the freight costs can equal the value of replacing the goods themselves. One export manager, unable to locate a substitute buyer in a foreign country, had to abandon goods at a foreign port rather than incur the costs of bringing them home! The buyer's nonpayment or default can occur in a sales transaction for a variety of reasons. Perhaps the buyer found the goods cheaper from another source. Perhaps currency fluctuations have destroyed the buyer's anticipated profits on the purchase. Perhaps the buyer has become insolvent. Whatever the reason, a seller must plan for these potential risks. If sellers were not able to do so, all world trading would soon come to a grinding halt.

**Delivery Risk.**   The risk that a buyer will not receive the goods called for under a contract is called *delivery risk.* It can result from a late shipment, or no shipment at all, or from shipment of goods that do not conform to the contract specifications. It can result from adverse business conditions, labor strikes, disasters at sea, or the actions of an unscrupulous seller. Whatever the cause, buyers must assess the risk of dealing with their foreign suppliers. Business credit reports, trade references, product samples, and visits to their factory are all important in evaluating a vendor. In the words of one experienced purchasing manager for an international firm, "There is no substitute for knowing your seller."

**Property or Marine Risk.**   One special form of delivery risk, known as *property risk* or *marine risk,* is the potential for loss or damage to cargo or freight while in transit over great distances. Between the time that the parties initially enter their agreement and the time that the goods arrive at their destination, any number of unexpected events may cause one or more parties to incur losses under the contract. For example,

goods can be damaged by the sea or salt air, ships can sink, planes can crash, refrigeration units in containers can break, food can spoil, grain can become infested with insects, and labor strikes can delay the departure of a vessel. Some of the risks can be quite surprising. Assume that an exporter is shipping goods on an ocean vessel. The ship damages its hull on rocks in the harbor because the captain had negligently left the deck. Imagine the exporter's surprise when it finds out that, not only can it not recover from the carrier, but that it must contribute to the ship's owner for the costs of towing the ship to safety, for rescuing the crew, and even for saving cargo that belonged to other shippers!

**Pilferage and Containerized Freight.**   Pilferage and theft has been a problem for international shippers for many years. During the days of *break-bulk* freight, when goods were loaded and unloaded on pallets or in boxes, cargo was relatively easy to steal. However, in the past 20–30 years shipping has changed dramatically. Today nearly all merchandise is transported in large containers sealed by the shipper and opened only by the buyer or by customs officials. This practice has helped reduce damage and pilferage to shipments. Of course, pilferage is still a tremendous problem, especially in the ports of developing countries. One U.S. shipper of cellular phones to Latin America recently said that his firm could not mark the contents on the outside of the shipping boxes or crates because if they did the phones never reached their destinations.

## Managing Political Risk

*Political risk* is generally defined as the risk to a firm's business interests resulting from political instability or political change in a country in which the firm is doing business. By definition, it exists in all countries and all regions regardless of political or economic system. Political risk includes risk derived from potentially adverse actions of governments of the foreign countries in which one is doing business or to whose laws and regulations one is subject. It also includes laws and government policies instituted by the firm's home country, which adversely affect the firms that do business in a foreign country. Political risk can take many forms—from war and revolution to changes in law or policy. It can affect all aspects of international business—the right to ship goods to a country or to own and operate a factory there. Although almost any adverse law or regulation of a government could be considered political risk, including restrictions on trade or currencies, this text examines political risk in more general terms.

**Causes of Political Risk.** One cause of political risk is political or economic instability in a country and exposure to that country's laws or regulations, which create a hostile environment for business dealings. Instability is a particular problem in countries that experience rapid changes in government—be they democracies or less-than-democratic developing countries. As governments change, so might their trade, investment, tax, and other economic policies. When the changes result from democratic elections, the impact on business is usually gradual. Italy has undergone a succession of democratically elected governments since World War II, and firms there have had to adjust to changing economic policies. The potential for faster, more dramatic change is greater in the developing countries. Even though foreign business interests may have been welcomed under one government, its successor may take a different view. For many years, a nation may welcome foreign investment, consumer products, and Western culture, and then virtually overnight turn to resent any foreign influence at all. Cuba, Libya, Iran, and Iraq are examples. For most of U.S. history, U.S. firms have had friendly relationships and extensive investments in these countries. Yet after political upheaval, each of these countries became hostile to Americans there.

A change in government can occur as a result of a popular revolution or military takeover, a *coup d'etat*. In the 1950s, communist-inspired revolutions forced sudden changes in some governments. Fidel Castro's takeover of Cuba is a good example. U.S. companies in Cuba experienced the seizure of their assets and expulsion from the island. Changes in some countries have been inspired by religious fundamentalism. The Islamic Revolution in Iran in the late 1970s and the ouster of the Shah of Iran, a dictator himself, resulted in tremendous political instability and economic uncertainty for firms that had done business there for many years. The new Islamic government retaliated against the United States for its support of the Shah of Iran. It seized the U.S. embassy in Tehran, held U.S. citizens hostage, cancelled contracts with U.S. firms, and confiscated the assets of firms operating there. The taking of privately owned assets, such as a farm or factory, by a government is called *expropriation*. The taking of ownership of a firm or of an entire industry that had been operated privately, as a part of a plan to restructure a national economy, is called *nationalization*. U.S. and western firms have faced the risk of expropriation and nationalization all over the world, and they have been a risk of international business since time immemorial.

**The Impact on Trade Relations.** The text provides repeated examples of how trade relationships between nations are linked to their political relationships. Indeed, many nations control trade—the right to import or export goods to or from another country—as a political tool. Thus, a firm that trades with companies in a foreign country must consider the possibility of being caught up in a "trade war." Earlier, the chapter described how this has happened to U.S. firms doing business in China. Take another example: Imagine that a firm is operating in a country whose dictator decides to invade a neighboring country. If the United States and the world community take action against the invader, such as imposing economic sanctions, then the firm will be caught in the middle—and subject to those sanctions. U.S. firms have had to comply with U.S. embargoes of other countries on many occasions—Iraq after its invasion of Kuwait, Cuba, Nicaragua, Haiti, countries in southern Africa, and innumerable more. Many of these cases are discussed in this text.

**The Risk of International Hostilities.** Even the best laid business plans can be upset when transportation and communications are disrupted by war or revolution. Consider what happened when Egypt blocked the Suez Canal to international shipping during its 1956 war with Israel. Because this important waterway was closed, cargo ships were diverted around the Cape of Good Hope on the southern tip of the African continent, a costly journey of many thousands of miles. The loss fell upon companies that used the canal. These events present risks that the prudent businessperson must be aware of and minimize to avoid potential losses.

**Handling Political Risk.**    Handling political risk requires planning and vigilance. First, the firm must have an understanding of the domestic affairs of a country. Typical questions might include: Is the country politically stable? Will democracy prevail? Is the country subject to religious or ethnic strife? How are minority groups treated, and how will their treatment be viewed by the more democratic countries of the world? What is the country's economic situation? The firm must also understand regional politics. Is the region stable? Are neighboring countries in the region hostile? Are border conflicts likely to erupt? These considerations might be especially important in the Middle East. Finally, international affairs must be considered. Is the country abiding by international human rights standards? Is it a member of international organizations? Does it abide by international law?

At a minimum, international managers are well advised to keep abreast of all political affairs that could affect their operations and interests worldwide. Access to the latest information is critical. Good sources include newspapers such as *The Journal of Commerce* or *The Wall Street Journal,* and even cable news channels. Beyond that, the firm can obtain more sophisticated assessments of the political environment in a foreign country through the process known as *political risk analysis.* Professionally prepared political risk analysis reports are available, giving current assessments and forecasts of future stability. Other resources include political risk consulting firms, insurance industry reports, reports of U.S. government agencies, and informal discussions with experienced international bankers and shipping company representatives. In some cases, *political risk insurance* is available for firms making investments in foreign countries where their exposure is great. Importantly, strategic corporate planning should take this information into consideration in developing its global business strategy and in transacting business.

## Risks of Foreign Laws and Courts

Settling disputes between companies can be much more difficult in international business than in domestic business. Litigation of a case in a court in a foreign country is both costly and time consuming. In addition, the laws of a foreign country can differ greatly from those laws one is accustomed to at home. Countries may exhibit vast differences in the law of contracts, crimes, torts, intellectual property, securities and investment, and more. People cannot possibly know all the laws of their own country, let alone those of every foreign country in which they do business. Language and logistical issues can be problems as well. A firm may need representation by attorneys in their own country *and* in the country of litigation. Frequent court appearances could require great travel expense. International cases also involve complex procedural problems: What country's courts should hear the case? What country's laws should apply? How does a court compel the testimony of witnesses or the production of business records not found in that country? Should the case be submitted to arbitration—perhaps in some "neutral" country? When a firm is negotiating an agreement with a foreign party, such as a contract to sell goods or to franchise a business, both parties will usually want to reach an agreement on these issues, and so the advice of an attorney at this stage in a transaction is extremely important.

*http://www.state.gov/www/about_state/ business/*
*http://www.ita.doc.gov/ita_home/ itacnreg.html*
Two U.S. government sites with information necessary for country-specific risk analysis.

## Ethical Issues in International Business

Just as laws differ from county to country, so does the definition of ethical behavior. In international business, *"the law is a floor for our behavior, but ethical codes and personal values call on us to exceed that which is required by law."* When called on to evaluate a course of action according to a code of ethics or personal value system, one must consider the decision in the cultural context. In other words, what is considered appropriate behavior in one culture may not be so in another. Readers of the situations and cases presented in this book should keep in mind, as they study international business, that managers often must evaluate their actions according to ethical codes or personal values that may or may not be commonly accepted in the country in which they are operating. The following examples serve as preparation in the consideration of ethical issues throughout this text.

**Example A:** You have been negotiating with a representative of the Portuguese government to sell products to them for a new state building project. He arrives at your company's offices with a blank purchase order in hand. After negotiating a fixed price and delivery, he "suggests" that you prepare a price quotation on a "pro forma invoice"—at double the negotiated price. His government will pay the full amount shown on the invoice through a Portuguese bank, and your firm will pay him the difference as a "commission" in U.S. dollars deposited to his bank account in New York. He convincingly argues that this practice is customary in his country. The temptation for you might be great; the deal would be a profitable one. But would it be legal or ethical? Certainly, laws and ethical standards vary from country to country. In this example, you would have to consider the laws and ethical codes of both Portugal and the United States. Even though bribery is more common in certain other countries, this transaction would clearly be illegal under U.S. law, and you would be subject to criminal prosecution, fines, and possible imprisonment.

**Example B:** Imagine that your firm enters into a contract to sell drilling equipment to a Korean company. The contract is closed while the Korean company president is visiting the U.S. plant. After closing, the Korean executive points out that all imports to Korea must be channeled through a registered "local agent." He quickly suggests that a wholly owned trading company *that he owns* could handle all of the paperwork—for a fee. Compare this with the first example. Should you comply with his request? Is it legal? If it is, is it ethical? The prudent manager will avoid potential legal liability and will also attempt to conform to what he or she deems to be ethical.

**Example C:** Your company intends to locate a plant in Mexico for the assembly of automobile engines. If the plant were in the United States, the laws require considerable expenditures for environmental controls such as antipollution equipment. U.S. law also mandates expensive safeguards to protect the health and safety of U.S. workers, as well as the added cost of minimum wage rules, social security contributions, health care, and other employee benefits. Assume that Mexican law is not so strict and that operating costs there are less as a result. To what extent should you conform to the legal standards applicable in the United States? Is it ethical not to? Indeed, should any firm operating in a host country carry with it the ethical codes of its home country? How does the international manager justify decisions in cross-cultural situations?

**Example D:** You are an international manager for an U.S. apparel designer that sells to major U.S. department stores and retailers. Several years ago your firm decided to have clothing sewn in India and Pakistan, which resulted in tremendous cost savings as opposed to having the work done in the United States. In making the decision, the firm considered its impact on U.S. families who depend on the income from these jobs. It opted for the cost savings, seeing its responsibility to produce a profit for shareholders as more important than providing jobs in the United States. Now, however, it finds that its contractor in India is overworking and abusing child labor in violation of internationally accepted standards for the treatment of children in the workplace. The Indian government shows little interest in policing its own labor practices. The sad story of the Indian children is run on national television and appears in the national press. If you decide to discontinue working with sewing contractors in India, would you do so to protect Indian children or because of the adverse publicity in the United States, or both? Consider the company's course of action and how you should react now.

## Receiving Professional Assistance in Going International

International managers must often rely on advice and assistance from individuals and agencies outside their own firm. Various professionals provide these necessary services: attorneys, bankers, and customs brokers. (For a *Survey of U.S. Government Services and Information* useful to firms entering foreign markets, see Exhibit 1.4.)

**EXHIBIT 1.4   A Survey of U.S. Government Services and Information**

| Program | Description or Service Available |
| --- | --- |
| *General Information*<br>Trade Information Center | A comprehensive resource for locating government information on trade, advice on exporting, and foreign market information. Trade specialists available. Provides access to the computerized *National Trade Data Bank.* |
| National Trade Data Bank | A computerized CD-ROM database with information on U.S. imports and exports, the *CIA World Factbook,* current market research reports, the *Foreign Traders Index,* the *Export Yellow Pages,* the *Report on Foreign Trade Barriers,* and the *Export Promotion Calendar.* |
| *Counseling*<br>U.S. Export Assistance Centers | Pilot projects in four U.S. cities that provide one-on-one counseling to firms to aid them in identifying foreign markets and developing export strategies. |
| International Trade Administration (ITA) | A unit of the U.S. Department of Commerce that includes the U.S. and Foreign Commercial Service, the Country Desk Officers, and the Trade Development Industry Officers. (See separate headings.) |
| U.S. Foreign and Commercial Service | Part of the ITA. An international network of government trade specialists in 69 U.S. cities and 69 countries worldwide. They provide information on foreign markets, locating foreign agents and distributors, trade leads, and counseling. |
| Country Desk Officers | Part of the ITA. Individual specialists who provide a firm with information and advice on selling to specific countries, including trade information, foreign laws and regulations, tariffs business practices, and assessments of potential for U.S. products. |
| Trade Development Industry Officers | Part of the ITA. Industry specialists who provide export assistance to U.S. firms and conduct trade fairs and executive trade missions abroad. |
| Office of Export Trading Company Affairs | Provides information on using export trading companies as intermediaries for exporting. |
| Export Legal Assistance Network | Nationwide network of attorneys who provide free initial consultations to small businesses on exporting. |
| Small Business Administration | Provides management counseling, fee-based training for exporting, and advice on financing exports. |
| *Country and Market Information*<br>Business Information Service for the Newly Independent States | Information on commercial and investment opportunities in the former Soviet Union, trade contacts, and sources of financing. |
| Eastern Europe Business Information Center | Information on doing business in Eastern Europe, potential partners, trade and investment regulations, and trade events. |
| Japan Export Information Center | Assists U.S. companies in exporting to Japan, counseling, market data, information on customs, procedures, tariffs, and barriers to entry of U.S. products. |
| *General Information*<br>Latin America/Caribbean Business Development Center | Promotes U.S. business in the region. Publications offer trade opportunities and information. Counseling service available. |

*(continued)*

## EXHIBIT 1.4  A Survey of U.S. Government Services and Information—(continued)

| Program | Description or Service Available |
|---|---|
| National Institute of Standards Technology | Assists U.S. exporters in identifying and complying with and European standards for products to be marketed in Europe. |
| *Trade Contacts and Services* Agent/Distributor Service | Assistance in locating foreign sales agents or distributors for U.S. exporters. |
| World Traders Data Report | A service for checking the credit, financial, and other detailed trade information on foreign firms. |
| Trade Opportunities Program | Provides current sales leads by listing names of foreign firms seeking to buy specific products. |
| Export Yellow Pages | A directory of U.S. manufacturers, banks, service companies, and export trading companies. |
| Trade Fairs and Missions Programs | ITA-sponsored programs designed to encourage and assist U.S. exporters to participate in foreign trade fairs and industry exhibitions. ITA also leads U.S. companies on foreign trade missions to call on potential foreign customers. |
| *Specialized Financing and Insurance* Eximbank Hotline | Information on Eximbank programs that provide export credit insurance and financing for U.S. exports, including loans and guarantees to foreign buyers of U.S. products or services. |
| Overseas Private Investment Corporation (OPIC) Hotline | Information on OPIC programs to encourage U.S. businesses to invest in developing countries, insurance against currency control risk, loss from expropriation of property, and loss from political risk such as war or revolution, etc. |

SOURCE:  Trade Information Center established by the Trade Promotion Coordinating Committee of the U.S. Department of Commerce.

**The International Attorney.**   Lawyers who practice in international business can be in either private practice or employed as in-house counsel to a multinational corporation. Their work might include import/export law, customs and tariff law, immigration and nationality law, admiralty law, the licensing of intellectual property, foreign investment contracts, and other legal issues. Private practice attorneys who specialize in these areas are usually located in the larger cities and have associations with other lawyers in foreign countries. Attorneys who are employees of multinational corporations practice in these areas as well as in immigration and nationality law, tax law, and international antitrust law. They advise management on trade, licensing, and foreign investment matters; draft documents; develop internal corporate polices; work on external government relations at home and abroad; supervise litigation abroad; and coordinate the work of foreign counsel.

**Freight Forwarder/Customs Broker.**   The function of the freight forwarder or customs broker is to expedite the physical transportation of goods and the preparation of the shipping or customs documents. The documentation, or paperwork, required in an export or import shipment is quite extensive. Even though any businessperson needs to understand the legal nature and significance of all documents used to sell goods and transfer money in an international transaction, much of the paperwork is done by the forwarder. Freight forwarders act as the shipper's (the seller) agent for exporting. In doing so, they help consolidate cargo, arrange for marine insurance policies, book the least costly freight space with a carrier, and occasionally prepare the bank collection documents an exporter needs in order to be paid. When these agents represent U.S. importers they are called customs brokers. A power of attorney is usually required for them to perform their services and to act for the importer or exporter.

Customs brokerage firms are licensed and bonded under the rules of the Federal Maritime Commission and the U.S. Customs Service.

**The International Banker.**   This text devotes considerable study to the role of international banks in all international business transactions. A later chapter, for example, describes how banks move money and shipping documents and thus make the international sales contract work. They not only provide important financing, but they also offer a range of specialized international banking services necessary to any firm going abroad. Some international bankers possess a great wealth of expertise and foreign contacts, and are therefore able to play an advisory role in international business.

# Chapter Summary

The business environment of the 1990s has changed dramatically since the end of World War II. To be competitive in world markets today, the international manager or world trader needs to be familiar with economics, culture, politics, and law. Multinational firms have adopted business strategies that see the world, and profits, in global terms. Even small and medium-sized manufac-

turing and service firms are important competitors in international markets, and will become even more important in the future.

The three basic forms of international business—trade, licensing, and investment—are methods of entering foreign markets. They are not mutually exclusive. One joint venture agreement, for instance, can have provisions for the building of a plant and the manufacture of goods, for the licensing of trademarks or patents to the joint venture for a determined period, and for the export or import of those products to other countries of distribution. The methods employed to enter a foreign market must be tailored to the type and size of firm, the nature of its product or service, and its experience and goals.

The process of managing an international business transaction is the process of managing risk. Nowhere is that risk greater than in the rapidly changing developing world, in Eastern Europe, or in the newly independent republics of the former Soviet Union. The economic and social problems in those regions make experience and caution a prerequisite to tapping the new opportunities that wait there. Through the study of international business law, one can better prepare to identify potential risks and problems and to plan business strategies accordingly.

---

## QUESTIONS AND CASE PROBLEMS

1. What factors have influenced the globalization of business?
2. Describe the "investment risk" that a multinational corporation might face in establishing a plant overseas. What were the risks faced by Union Carbide, a Connecticut-based multinational, in the ownership and operation of its plant in Bhopal, India? At the time the investment was being planned, the government of India had made its restrictions clear: Union Carbide's Indian plant would have to have Indian joint ownership, Indian engineers and contractors would be responsible for construction, and Indian citizens would manage and operate the plant. For instance, although Union Carbide provided the basic design for the plant, India insisted that its own firms build it. From 1972 to 1980 the construction was supervised by Indian engineers. During that time the design was changed many

times. Labor and employment polices were set by the Indian government. As the court stated, "more than 1,000 Indians were employed at the plant; only one American was employed there and he left in 1982." The court also notes that plant operations were supervised by more than two dozen Indian government agencies. Evaluate India's policies in this case. Why did they set such strict conditions? Could Indian policies have contributed to the disaster, or was Union Carbide entirely at fault? Why do you think Union Carbide agreed to the terms of the Indian government?

3. How does international business differ from domestic business? What are the risks of entering foreign markets?
4. Undertake a study of one country or one region of the world and evaluate its business climate, its attitude toward trade and foreign investment, and the level of political risk. Where would you go for sources of information? How has the breakup of the

former Soviet Union affected the business climate in that region?

5. Who are the members of a firm's "export team"? Describe each of their functions.

6. Plaintiff, a Swiss corporation, entered into contracts to purchase chicken from B.N.S. International Sales Corporation. Defendant was a New York corporation. The English language contracts called for the delivery of "chicken" of various weights. When the birds were shipped to Switzerland, the two-pound sizes were not young broiling chickens as the plaintiff had expected, but mature stewing chickens or fowl. The plaintiff protested, claiming that in German the term *chicken* referred to young broiling chicken. The question for the court was what kind of chicken did the plaintiff order. Was it "broiling chicken" as the plaintiff argued, or any chickens weighing two pound as the defendant argued? *Frigaliment Importing Co., Ltd. v. B.N.S. International Sales Corp.,* 190 F.Supp 116 (S.D.N.Y. 1960). What could the parties have done to avoid this misunderstanding?

7. Successful international managers agree that success in entering a foreign market comes from planning and commitment. What does this mean? What kind of commitment do you think they are referring to? It is also often said that exporting is not an "elixir" for a company that is failing in its home market and is looking for new sales elsewhere. Evaluate this statement. Do you think it is true?

8. What industries in your state are the leading exporters? Who are the leading export firms? What do you think is the impact of exports on your state's economy? Where would you go for information? What role does your state government play in promoting exports?

9. U.S. firms have been very successful in foreign franchising, particularly in fast food and other retail businesses and service companies. How do you account for this success? Where do you think the best opportunities and hottest markets are for foreign franchising?

10. Multinational corporations and other firms must abide by the laws and regulations of their host countries. They must also understand the unwritten or informal rules of doing business there—rules based on culture, religious codes, and societal constraints. Sometimes these laws and rules can be very different from those in the firm's home country, or in other countries in which it operates. Pollution may be a crime in one country, and tolerated in another; bribery may be a crime in one country, and customary in another; and so on. How does the multinational manager reconcile differences like these? What is the appropriate standard of ethical conduct for a multinational manager—and how is it influenced by the laws, unwritten rules, and cultural values of the host country? How does the multinational manager balance his or her social responsibility to the people of the host country with the company's overall objective of maximizing shareholder profit? What can a multinational corporation do to aid its managers in the development of a personal ethical value system that is in keeping with the legal and cultural values of their host countries?

## MANAGERIAL IMPLICATIONS

Your firm, SewTex., Inc., manufactures consumer and industrial sewing machinery. The consumer machines retail for $350 to $1,000 and are sold in the United States through department stores, discount stores, and home sewing stores. The industrial machines range in price from $5,000 to $50,000. The machines contain a unique computer chip that allows them to embroider words and designs on fabric in a choice of four scripts. The firm owns the patent on the machines in the United States. Currently the industrial machines are made in the United States from components made in the U.S. and Taiwan. The consumer machines are assembled at plants in Texas and in the Caribbean from parts made in Taiwan. The computer chip is manufactured for SewTex by a California firm.

Currently SewTex exports about 5 percent of its production of industrial machines. Of the total exported, the most sophisticated machines went to German and Swiss textile firms. A few earlier generation models were shipped to India, Pakistan, and Brazil, although market prospects there look excellent.

The president of SewTex is concerned about the decline of the U.S. textile industry. She has asked your opinion on whether the company should consider increasing sales in foreign markets. She feels that some board members might caution against "getting involved overseas," and even she anticipates the U.S. textile market will pick up if the U.S. Congress places higher tariffs on textile imports. But she would like your thoughts. She has asked you to prepare a memorandum on the subject, and requests that you address some of the following issues.

1. She feels that she must have the support of the directors for any major overseas venture. What arguments can she offer to explain why SewTex should become active in international markets? She understands that making a commitment is important, but what does that really mean?

2. If SewTex were to consider increasing its export base, what problems might it encounter? What are the advantages and disadvantages in exporting products to Europe? Should it consider direct or indirect exporting in view of its product? If it chooses to continue exporting, how can it offer a repair service and a supply of spare parts to its customers?

3. Should SewTex consider licensing its technology to one of the other textile machinery manufacturers in Europe? Compare the advantages and disadvantages of this method of market entry to exporting.

4. The company president would like to know the options available for investment in the European market. Would this be preferable to the other market entry alternatives?

5. The company president recently read that Volkswagen and Mercedes have negotiated the purchase of automobile plants in the Czech Republic. She wonders whether the Czech government might be offering significant incentives to operate one of their mills. She knows that this country split from the Slovak Republic, in what had been Czechoslovakia, and that tension has existed between them over the years. She is concerned about the stability of a democratic government there. What sources can she turn to for more information on investment in the Czech Republic and Eastern Europe? What are the risks inherent in taking over operations there? What are the advantages?

6. SewTex's president is interested in knowing more about its market potential in Latin America for both types of machines. Can you advise her on the best methods for SewTex to penetrate that market. How would your plans for entry into the Latin American market affect SewTex's assembly operations and sales efforts worldwide?

7. Finally, can you advise SewTex on copyright, patent, and trademark issues related to its penetration of foreign markets? What are the major issues and concerns?

# Chapter Two

# International Law and Organizations

Most people are familiar with local, state, and federal law as it applies to their personal conduct and business behavior. For example, U.S. federal securities laws will affect the manner in which securities are traded within the United States. If the transaction crosses national borders, however, two nations' laws may apply to the transaction. Wouldn't it be simpler if once a business transaction crossed a nation's border, some international law automatically applied to the transaction? What about international law? Is there law that transcends national boundaries or is "supranational"? Unfortunately, no single body of law or comprehensive code called "international law" governs activities in the way that German law, Japanese law, or Massachusetts law does. Although some philosophers may dream of an orderly system in which the planet is governed by one legal and political system, given the diverse cultures, political philosophies, and values, such a system is certainly not imminent.

The development of international law can be studied through treaties, custom, and national law. In addition, international organizations such as the World Trade Organization (WTO), the United Nations, and the World Bank, to name only a few, have a direct impact on the conduct of transnational business. This chapter grapples with the question of what is international law. It also looks at the increasing importance of international organizations and their effect on business.

> **http://www.wto.org**
> The home page for the World Trade Organization.

## Public International Law

International law does exist. It has been defined as a "rule . . . that has been accepted as such [law] by the international community." The legal scholars who wrote the *Restatement of the Law, 3rd, Foreign Relations,* define it as shown in Exhibit 2.1.

Although this definition provides guidance, it also raises many questions. For example, at what point has a "rule" been accepted by the international community of states? What is a customary law? Where does one find general principles common to major legal systems? Scholars wrote the *Restatement* in an attempt, to summarize general principles of law. Remember that it is only evidence of what scholars think of the law and has not been adopted in its entirety by any country.

When the term *international law* is used, people most often think of public international law. Public international law involves relationships between states (meaning nations or countries) and applies "norms regarded as binding on all members of the international community," which may be reflected in treaties, conventions, or the charters of international organizations such as the United Nations (U.N.). Some issues related to public international law include the following: When is it appropriate or legal for a nation to use force? How should prisoners taken pursuant to a war be treated? Is torture of prisoners ever justified? Questions of international law are typically raised in national courts.

A famous U.S. Supreme Court case, *Paquette Habana,* illustrates how the Court discerned what was the applicable international law. The Court discusses the necessity of resorting to "customs and usage" to ascertain international law.

**EXHIBIT 2.1    Sec. 102 Sources of International Law**

1. A rule of international law is one that has been accepted as such by the international community of states
   a. in the form of customary law;
   b. by international agreement; or
   c. by derivation from general principles common to the major legal systems of the world.
2. Customary international law results from a general and consistent practice of states followed by them from a sense of legal obligation.
3. International agreements create law for the states parties thereto and may lead to the creation of customary international law when such agreements are intended for adherence by states generally and are in fact widely accepted.
4. General principles common to the major legal systems, even if not incorporated or reflected in customary law or international agreements, may be invoked as supplementary rules of international law where appropriate.

SOURCE:   ©1988 by the American Law Institute. Reprinted with permission.

Although no uniform codified set of laws exists at the international level, conventions and treaties are a step toward this. Public international law was formerly defined as the laws governing relations between states; this definition, however, has been expanded, and now public international law is more commonly thought of as "rules and principles of general application dealing with the conduct of states and of international organizations and with their relations inter se [among themselves] as well as with some of their relations with persons, whether natural or juridical."[1]

## The Law of Treaties

The *Vienna Convention on the Law of Treaties,* adopted in 1969, entered into force in 1980. Legal scholars view it as a summary statement of existing law, even though not all countries are signatories. The convention covers such issues as when treaties enter into force, their interpretation, amendment, termination, and the rights and duties of countries party to a treaty. This statement has ramifications for business because treaties affect trade between parties from countries that are signatories to various conventions.

The *Vienna Convention* codified some customary international law. For example, Article

---

## The Paquette Habana
### 175 U.S. 677 (1900)
### United States Supreme Court

BACKGROUND AND FACTS
Two vessels, sailing under Spanish flags and owned by a Spanish citizen living in Cuba, were used to fish and sell the catch. The owner had no ammunition and was unaware of the hostilities with Spain nor of the 1898 blockade of Cuba. The United States seized the ship. The Spanish owner sued for damages.

The Federal District for the Southern District of Florida upheld the United States' condemnation of the vessels as prizes of war. The owner appealed to the United States Supreme Court.

JUSTICE GRAY
These are two appeals from decrees of the district court of the United States for the southern district of Florida condemning two fishing vessels and their cargoes as prize of war. . . .

We are then brought to the consideration of the question whether, upon the facts appearing in these records, the fishing smacks were subject to capture by the armed vessels of the United States during the recent war with Spain.

By an ancient usage among civilized nations, beginning centuries ago, and gradually ripening into a rule of international law, coast fishing vessels, pursuing their vocation of catching and bringing in fresh fish, have been recognized as exempt, with their cargoes and crews, from capture as prize of war. . . .

The doctrine which exempts coast fishermen, with their vessels and cargoes, from capture as prize of war, has been familiar to the United States from the time of the War of Independence. . . .

Since the United States became a nation, the only serious interruptions, so far as we are informed, of the general recognition of the exemp-

*(continued)*

*(continued)*

tion of coast fishing vessels from hostile capture, arose out of the mutual suspicions and recriminations of England and France during the wars of the French Revolution. . . .

In the war with Mexico, in 1846, the United States recognized the exemption of coast fishing boats from capture. . . .

International law is part of our law, and must be ascertained and administered by the courts of justice of appropriate jurisdiction as often as questions of right depending upon it are duly presented for their determination. For this purpose, where there is no treaty and no controlling executive or legislative act or judicial decision, resort must be had to the customs and usages of civilized nations, and, as evidence of these, to the works of jurists and commentators who by years of labor, research, and experience have made themselves peculiarly well acquainted with the subjects of which they treat. Such works are resorted to by judicial tribunals, not for the speculations of their authors concerning what the law ought to be, but for trustworthy evidence of what the law really is. . . .

This review of the precedents and authorities of the subject appears to us abundantly to demonstrate that at the present day, by the general consent of the civilized nations of the world, and independently of any express treaty or other public act, it is an established rule of international law, founded on consideration of humanity to a poor and industrious order of men, and of the mutual convenience of belligerent states, that coast fishing vessels, with their implements and supplies, cargoes and crews, unarmed and honestly pursuing their peaceful calling of catching and bringing in fresh fish, are exempt from capture as prize of war. . . .

This rule of international law is one which prize courts administering the law of nations are bound to take judicial notice of, and to give effect to, in the absence of any treaty or other public act of their own government in relation to the matter. . . .

**Decision.** The Supreme Court reversed the holding of the district court and said that under an established rule of international law, peaceful fishermen are exempt from capture as prizes of war. The Court ordered that the owner receive payment for the loss of the ship, along with damages and costs. The Court acknowledged that it was "bound" to take judicial notice of international law.

26, titled *"Pacta sunt servanda,"* states that "Every treaty in force is binding upon the parties to it and must be performed by them in good faith." The Convention also provides for the occasion in which a "Fundamental change in circumstance" has occurred, under Article 62 stipulating the circumstances that constitute grounds for termination of the treaty. The test is two pronged: (1) "the existence of those circumstances constituted an essential basis of the consent of the parties to be bound by the treaty" and (2) "the effect of the change is radically to transform the extent of obligations still to be transformed under the treaty" The Convention provides another basis for termination; if the treaty violates a "peremptory norm of general international law" (*ius cogens*), the treaty becomes void (articles 53 and 64). The Convention lays out a procedure that countries may follow in the event of termination. Treaties may be multilateral (involving many parties), may focus on a particular subject area, or be bilateral. An example of a recent bilateral treaty that has significant import to business is the U.S.–Poland Treaty

signed March 21, 1990. An example of a recent multilateral convention is the Chemical Weapons Convention which prohibits the development, stockpiling, and use of chemical weapons as well as deals with their destruction. The U.S. recently signed it and it entered into force in April 1997, despite initial fierce opposition. The Anti-Land Mine Treaty was not signed by the U.S. because of concerns about Korea and leaving U.S. troops without sufficient protections.

In a relatively recent U.S. case, the Supreme Court addressed the issue of international law as evidenced by both treaty provisions and general principles of international law and whether an abduction of a Mexican to stand trial in the United States was a basis of an objection to jurisdiction by the U.S. court.

*http://www.tufts.edu/departments/ fletcher/multi/chrono.html*
*Makes available the texts of international multilateral conventions and other instruments, including the Vienna Convention.*

### United States v. Alvarez-Machain
### 504 U.S. 655 (1992)

**BACKGROUND AND FACTS**

Alvarez-Machain was a citizen and resident of Mexico. He was kidnapped from home and flown by private plane to Texas where he was arrested for participation in the kidnapping, torture, and murder of a U.S. Drug Enforcement Agent (DEA) and the agent's pilot. Although the DEA agents did not themselves abduct Alvarez-Machain, the Court concluded that they were responsible. The torture and murder had been videotaped, and the agent had been given drugs by the accused to prolong his consciousness during torture. Mexico protested a violation in the extradition treaty with the United States. The district court dismissed the indictment based on the conclusion that the abduction violated the extradition treaty and ordered the accused be returned to Mexico. The court of appeals affirmed. The Supreme Court granted certiorari.

REHNQUIST, CHIEF JUSTICE

The issue in this case is whether a criminal defendant abducted to the United States from a nation with which it has an extradition treaty thereby acquires a defense to the jurisdiction of this country's courts. We hold that he does not and that he may be tried in federal district court for violations of criminal of the United States. . . .

[O]ur first inquiry must be whether the abduction of Alvarez from Mexico violated the extradition treaty. . . . In construing a treaty as in construing a statute we first look to its terms to determine its meaning. . . . The Treaty says nothing about the obligations of the United States and Mexico to refrain from forcible abductions of people. In the absence of an extradition treaty, nations are under no obligation to surrender those in their country to foreign authorities for prosecution. . . . Extradition treaties exist so as to impose mutual obligations to surrender individuals in certain defined sets of circumstances, following established procedures. [The Treaty thus provides a mechanism which would not otherwise exist, requiring, under certain circumstances, the United States and Mexico to extradite individuals to the other country, and establishing the procedures to be followed when the Treaty is invoked.]

The history of negotiation and practice under the Treaty also fails to show that abductions outside of the Treaty constitute a violation of the Treaty. . . .

Thus, the language of the Treaty, in the context of its history, does not support the proposition that the Treaty prohibits abductions outside of its terms. The remaining question, therefore, is whether the Treaty should be interpreted so as to include an implied term prohibiting prosecution where the defendant's presence is obtained by means other than those established by the Treaty.

Respondent contends that the Treaty must be interpreted against the backdrop of customary international law, and that international abductions are "so clearly prohibited in international law" that there was no reason to include such a clause in the Treaty itself. The international censure of international abductions is further evidenced, according to respondent, by the United Nations Charter and the Charter of the Organization of American States. Respondent does not argue that these sources of international law provide an independent basis for the right respondent asserts not to be tried in the United States, but rather that they should inform the interpretation of the Treaty terms. . . .

Respondent would have us find that the Treaty acts as a prohibition against a violation of the general principle of international law that one government may not "exercise its police power in the territory of another state." There are many actions which could be taken by a nation that would violate this principle, including waging war, but it cannot seriously be contended an invasion of the United States by Mexico would violate the terms of the extradition treaty between the two nations.

In sum, to infer from this Treaty and its terms that it prohibits all means of gaining the presence of an individual outside of its terms goes beyond established precedent and practice. . . . By contrast, to imply from the terms of this Treaty that it prohibits obtaining the presence of an individual by means outside of the procedures the Treaty establishes requires a much larger inferential leap, with only the most general of international law principles to support it. The general principles cited by respondent simply fail to persuade us that we should imply in the United States-Mexico Extradition Treaty a term prohibiting international abductions.

*(continued)*

*(continued)*

The judgment of the Court of Appeals is therefore reversed, and the case is remanded for further proceedings consistent with this opinion.

STEVENS, BLACKMUN, AND O'CONNOR, JUSTICES DISSENTING

The Court's admittedly "shocking" disdain for customary and conventional international law principles, is thus entirely unsupported by case law and commentary.

As the Court observes at the outset of its opinion, there is reason to believe that respondent participated in an especially brutal murder of an American law enforcement agent. That fact, if true, may explain the Executive's intense interest in punishing respondent in our courts. Such an explanation, however, provides no justification for disregarding the Rule of Law that this Court has a duty to uphold. That the Executive may wish to reinterpret the Treaty to allow for an action that the Treaty in no way authorizes should not influence this Court's interpretation. Indeed, the desire for revenge exerts "a kind of hydraulic pressure . . . before which even well-settled principles of law will bend," but it is precisely at such moments that we should remember and be guided by our duty "to render judgment evenly and dispassionately according to law, as each is given understanding to ascertain and apply it." . . . I suspect most courts throughout the civilized world will be deeply disturbed by the "monstrous" decision the Court announces today. For every Nation that has an interest in preserving the Rule of Law is affected, directly or indirectly, by a decision of this character. As Thomas Paine warned, an "avidity to punish is always dangerous to liberty" because it leads a Nation "to stretch, to misinterpret, and to misapply even the best of laws." To counter that tendency, he reminds us: "He that would make his own liberty secure must guard even his enemy from oppression; for if he violates this duty he establishes a precedent that will reach to himself."

**Decision.** The court held the defendant did not have a basis to object to jurisdiction. Thus, he could be tried by the lower court.

**Comment.** The Alvarez case addressed the problem of interpretation of a treaty. Although this particular case may be a good example of the adage that hard cases make bad law, understanding of the law of treaties is important. Mr. Alvarez, after almost three years in custody, was acquitted at trial and he returned to Mexico. The American Civil Liberties Union is currently pressing a $20 million civil lawsuit on his behalf.

## The Impact of Treaties on Business

Treaties can have significant impact on private individuals' rights.

Tax treaties are part of international law and can have a dramatic impact on business. For example, the United States and Mexico negotiated a tax treaty that went into effect on January 1, 1994. The Senate approved this treaty along with the NAFTA agreement. The treaty was an attempt to remedy problems of double taxation as well as the evasion of taxes, including a unilateral lowering of withholding rates by Mexico and a commitment to nondiscrimination vis-à-vis the tax treatment of residents of either country. Dramatic tax reductions were also announced by Mexico. For example, patent and trademark royalty was lowered from 35 percent to 10 percent, equipment rentals from 21 percent to 10 percent, interest to banks from 15 percent to 4.9 percent, and investment interest from 35 percent to 4.9 percent, to mention a few.

Another example is the Chemical Weapons Convention, which bans the production of chemical warfare materials and imposes significant reporting requirements on private industry including data declarations and on-site inspections to monitor enforcement of the convention. This ban recently went into effect on April 29, 1997.

A last example of the role of international treaties and their effect on business can be seen in the Law of the Sea Convention. The Convention had been the subject of long and bitter debate between developing countries and the developed countries. The wealthier countries saw it as a measure to redistribute the wealth of nations. Presidents Reagan and Bush had been opposed to the treaty. Language recognizing oceans as "a common heritage of Mankind" that would be part of a "just and equitable order" was problematic. President Clinton successfully sought amendments to allay some of these concerns including dropping both the fee required to explore for minerals on the ocean floor as well as the extraction of royalties to fund the oversight agency, the International Seabed Authority, in Jamaica. The advantages the treaty offered were numerous. The treaty clarified the right of passage through straits, sovereignty over 12 miles off shore, and control of fishing oil and gas rights within 200 miles off shore. The treaty had 61 country ratifications and took effect in November of 1994. Although Clinton has signed it, the U.S. Senate has not ratified the treaty.

## International Court of Justice

Some public international law disputes may be heard by the World Court. The International Court of Justice or ICJ (also known as the World Court) was formed in 1945 with its statute attached to the United Nations charter. Its precursor, called the Permanent Court of Justice, was established in 1920 as part of the League of Nations. The World Court has 15 judges who are elected by the United Nations General Assembly and the Security Council for a term of nine years. If a state is a party to a dispute before the Court and no judge of that nationality is sitting on the Court, a sixteenth and possibly seventeenth judge will be temporarily elected. The Court sits in The Hague, The Netherlands, and bases its decisions on the Statute of the International Court of Justice. (See Exhibit 2.2). The ICJ also uses three to five member chambers to hear some cases. This practice allows for a quicker, less cumbersome process.

---

**EXHIBIT 2.2    Statute of the International Court of Justice**

**Article 36**

1. The jurisdiction of the Court comprises all cases which the parties refer to it and all matters specially provided for in the Charter of the United Nations or in treaties and conventions in force.
2. The states parties to the present Statute may at any time declare that they recognize as compulsory *ipso facto* and without special agreement, in relation to any other state accepting the same obligation, the jurisdiction of the Court in all legal disputes concerning;
   a. the interpretation of a treaty;
   b. any question of international law;
   c. the existence of any fact which, if established, would constitute a breach of an international obligation; and
   d. the nature or extent of the reparation to be made for the breach of an international obligation.
3. The declarations referred to above may be made unconditionally or on condition of reciprocity on the part of several or certain states, or for a certain time.
4. Such declarations shall be deposited with the Secretary-General of the United Nations, who shall transmit copies thereof to the parties to the Statute and to the Registrar of the Court.
5. Declarations made under Article 36 of the Statute of the Permanent Court of International Justice and which are still in force shall be deemed, as between the parties to the present Statute, to be acceptance of the compulsory jurisdiction of the International Court of Justice for the period which they still have to run and in accordance with their terms.
6. In the event of a dispute as to whether the Court has jurisdiction, the matter shall be settled by the decision of the Court.

**Article 38**

1. The Court, whose function is to decide in accordance with international law such disputes as are submitted to it, shall apply:
   a. international conventions, whether general or particular, establishing rules expressly recognized by the contesting states;
   b. international custom, as evidence of a general practice accepted as law;
   c. the general principles of law recognized by civilized nations;
   d. subject to the provisions of Article 59, judicial decisions and the teachings of the most highly qualified publicists of the various nations, as subsidiary means for the determination of rules of law.
2. This provision shall not prejudice the power of the Court to decide a case *ex aequo et bono* if the parties agree thereto.

**Problems of Jurisdiction.** The World Court has not been a major force in settling world disputes, particularly commercial ones, for several reasons. First, only states can be parties before the Court, although a state may bring an action before the Court on behalf of an individual or individuals, alleging that some infringement of an individual's right is an infringement against the sovereign state. Secondly, decisions are binding only on the parties involved; however, some unofficial case precedent has been developed through the evolution of general principles of law. Third, before a nation can be brought before the Court, it must accept jurisdiction of the Court, because no compulsory process forces a state to come before the Court. Many communist countries have not accepted the jurisdiction of the Court by filing declarations of acceptance with the Court; thus, they preserve their right to pick and choose when they will consent to the jurisdiction of the court on matters related to them. This selective acceptance of jurisdiction limits the World Court's ability to assume as prominent a role as it otherwise could. Lastly, the enforcement powers of the Court, although detailed in the statute as well as in the United Nations charter, rely in large part on good faith compliance of the parties.

The following case examines the first problem—that only states may be parties—and how the Court may address individual or corporate injury despite this limitation.

---

BACKGROUND AND FACTS
Nottebohm was born in Germany in 1881. He moved to Guatemala for business reasons in 1905 and lived there until 1943 except for business trips and visits to his brother in Liechtenstein.

In 1939, Germany attacked Poland. Visiting Liechtenstein that year, Nottebohm applied to be naturalized as a citizen and asked Liechtenstein to waive the three-year residency requirement. He paid taxes to Liechtenstein and filed the requisite forms, and in 1939 Liechtenstein waived the required time period, swore him in as a citizen, and issued him a passport.

In 1943 Guatemala entered World War II, siding with the United States. Guatemala seized Nottebohm as a German enemy, turned him over to the United States for internment, and seized his property for the government. Nottebohm was released in 1946, but his property was not returned.

Liechtenstein filed a "memorial," as it is called, before the International Court of Justice (ICJ), claiming that Guatemala had violated international law and was obligated to pay damages.

Guatemala has referred to a well-established principle of international law, which it expressed in Counter-Memorial, where it is stated that "it is

## Liechtenstein v. Guatemala
(Nottebohm Case)
I.C.J. REP.4 (1955)
International Court of Justice

the bond of nationality between the State and the individual which alone confers upon the State the right of diplomatic protection."

. . . Counsel for Liechtenstein said: "The essential question is whether Mr. Nottebohm, having acquired the nationality of Liechtenstein, that acquisition of nationality is one which must be recognized by other States."

The Court does not propose to go beyond the limited scope of the question which it has to decide, namely, whether the nationality conferred on Nottebohm can be relied upon as against Guatemala in justification of the proceedings instituted before the Court. It must decide this question on the basis of international law.

International arbitrators have . . . given their preference to the real and effective nationality, that which accorded with the facts, that based on stronger factual ties between the person concerned and one of the States whose nationality is involved.

The character thus recognized on the international level as pertaining to nationality is in no way inconsistent with the fact that international law leaves it to each State to lay down the rules governing the grant of its own nationality.

*(continued)*

*(continued)*

At the time of his naturalization, does Nottebohm appear to have been more closely attached by his tradition, his establishment, his interests, his activities, his family ties, his intentions for the near future to Liechtenstein than to any other State?

Naturalization was asked for not so much for the purpose of obtaining a legal recognition of Nottebohm's membership in fact in the population of Liechtenstein, as it was to enable him to substitute for his status as a national of a belligerent State that of a national of a neutral State, with the sole aim of thus coming within the protection of Liechtenstein but not of becoming wedded to its traditions, its interests, its way of life or of assuming the obligations—other than fiscal obligations—and exercising the rights pertaining to the status thus acquired.

Guatemala is under no obligation to recognize a nationality granted in such circumstances. Liechtenstein consequently is not entitled to extend its protection to Nottebohm vis-à-vis Guatemala, and its claim must, for this reason, be held to be inadmissible.

**Decision.** The World Court held that the claim was inadmissible because Guatemala was not required to recognize the citizenship granted by Liechtenstein in a way that did not follow well-established principles of international law.

---

Although only a state can be a party before the Court, sometimes a state will itself take up the cause of a person or company, often only after attempts to resolve the matter through diplomatic channels have failed. The *Nottebohm* case illustrates this point.

As noted in preceding case, a state must accept the jurisdiction of the Court before a case can be brought before the Court. Many communist countries have not accepted the jurisdiction of the Court, and many other nations, particularly Western ones, have filed declarations accepting the Court's jurisdiction with various limitations. For example, France, Norway, and the United States filed statements accepting the jurisdiction of the ICJ. The United States stated that the declaration did not apply to

a. disputes the solution of which the parties shall entrust to other tribunals by virtue of agreements already in existence or which may be concluded in the future; or

b. disputes with regard to matters which are essentially within the domestic jurisdiction of the United States of America as determined by the United States of America; or

c. disputes arising under a multilateral treaty, unless (1) all parties to the treaty affected by the decision are also parties to the case before the Court, or (2) the United States of America specially agrees to jurisdiction.

Because of hostilities and philosophical differences between the United States and Nicaragua, on April 6, 1984, the United States amended its declaration to exempt matters dealing with Central America. The declaration stated in part that the aforesaid declaration shall not apply to disputes with any Central American State or arising out of or related to events in Central America, any of which disputes shall be settled in such manner as the parties to them may agree.

Notwithstanding the terms of the aforesaid declaration, this proviso shall take effect immediately and shall remain in force for two years, so as to foster the continuing regional dispute settlement process which seeks a negotiated solution to the interrelated political, economic and security problems of Central America.

Three days later, Nicaragua filed an action with the ICJ, claiming that the United States had mined Nicaraguan harbors and committed other covert acts designed to destabilize the government of Nicaragua.

The United States claimed on the basis of its amended declaration that the Court did not have jurisdiction. The Court did not agree with the United States, because the previous declaration had contained a six months notice provision, and issued a decision stating that it had jurisdiction and would proceed to hear arguments in the case. The United States withdrew and refused to participate in the hearings on the merits. The United States noted that nine of the fifteen judges came from states that did not accept compulsory jurisdiction. The Court proceeded to hear the case in the absence of the United States, but tried to anticipate and address arguments that the United States might have raised had it participated. Not surprisingly, the Court voted in 1986 that the United States had not acted in self-defense, that it had breached "customary international law not to intervene in the affairs of another state" by arming the "contra forces," and that it violated the sovereignty of another state. The Court ordered the United States to cease all acts that constituted a breach of international law and to make reparation to Nicaragua for any injury caused. The decision included sixteen separate findings in which the judges' votes ranged from 11–4 to 14–1. In the latter case, only the United States' judge voted against the finding. Only the final finding, "to seek a solution to their disputes by peaceful means in accordance with international law," was unanimous.

The near-unanimous sentiment expressed by the judges, with the exception of the U.S. and British judges, underscores how differently other nationalities view the United States's interpretation of actions permissible under international law, particularly in Central America.

It also underscores how "politicized" the Court had become. The future of the Court was in question, because the United States, a long-time proponent of the Court, now questioned its purpose and utility. Due to a political change in Nicaragua from the Sandinista regime to an elected government, the U.S. Republican administration began negotiations about the resumption of financial aid. Following these discussions, Nicaragua asked the ICJ to discontinue the proceedings and the Court on September 26, 1991, entered such an order.

**Developments Since the Nicaragua Case.**    The United States has signaled a subtle shift in policy since it amended its declaration and walked out on the *Nicaragua* case proceeding in the World Court. Thereafter, the United States agreed to submit a case involving the expropriation (or taking over by a state) of a Raytheon subsidiary, ELSI, in Italy to five agreed-upon judges, illustrating the use of a chamber proceeding. In 1987 Italy and the United States agreed to go forward with the case. Nevertheless, the United States lost the case. States have continued to bring matters to the World Court. In 1997, the Court handed down a decision concluding that both Hungary and Slovakia had violated a bilateral treaty. In 1998, Saddam Hussein reportedly is considering bringing to the court the matter of access to Iraq by the U.N. weapons inspection team.

# The Role of the United Nations in the Public International Law

The original fifty-one founding states' purpose for establishing the United Nations is stated in the Charter, as shown in Exhibit 2.3. Since the fall of the Berlin Wall and the demise of communism, the member countries have been able to use the United Nations more as its founders originally envisioned.

Currently, the United Nations has 185 members. Most countries, both communist and democratic, are members; Switzerland, which is prohibited from joining international organizations by its constitution, does not belong.

**http://www.law.cornell.edu/icj/unchart.htm**
*Provides the full text of the Charter of the United Nations.*

## The General Assembly and the Security Council

The United Nations is structured with a General Assembly, the Security Council, and the Secretary General, who tries to lead both of them. Each member nation sends a delegate to the General Assembly and has one vote. In the General Assembly, all countries have equal votes; thus, the United States, the United Kingdom, and Japan share the same position as the Republic of Burkina Faso.

The Security Council is composed of fifteen member states with five permanent members. The People's Republic of China, France, the United Kingdom, the USSR (now Russia), and the United States each have a permanent representative, and ten nonpermanent members are elected by the General Assembly every two years.

Japan seeks a seat as a permanent member of the Security Council in recognition of its economic strength and its role as a world power. A number of nations have pledged their support for the enlargement. India has indicated its desire for a permanent seat as well as Germany. Their inclusion offers certain cost-sharing advantages for the wealthier nations and would bring an end to the arrangement of power determined by the

---

**EXHIBIT 2.3    Charter of the United Nations**

**We the Peoples of the United Nations Determined**

- to save succeeding generations from the scourge of war, which twice in our lifetime has brought untold sorrow to mankind, and
- to reaffirm faith in fundamental human rights, in the dignity and worth of the human person, in the equal rights of men and women and of nations large and small, and
- to establish conditions under which justice and respect for the obligations arising from treaties and other sources of international law can be maintained, and
- to promote social progress and better standards of life in larger freedom,

**and For These Ends**

- to practice tolerance and live together in peace with one another as good neighbours, and
- to unite our strength to maintain international peace and security, and to ensure, by the acceptance of principles and the institution of methods, that armed force shall not be used, save in the common interest, and
- to employ international machinery for the promotion of the economic and social advancement of all peoples,

**Have Resolved to Combine Our Efforts to Accomplish These Aims**

Accordingly, our respective Governments, through representatives assembled in the city of San Francisco, who have exhibited their full powers found to be in good and due form, have agreed to the present Charter of the United Nations and do hereby establish an international organization to be known as the United Nations.

**Chapter I. Purposes and Principles**

*Article 1*
The purposes of the United Nations are:

1. To maintain international peace and security, and to that end: to take effective collective measures for the prevention and removal of threats to the peace, and for the suppression of acts of aggression or other breaches of the peace, and to bring about by peaceful means, and in conformity with the principles of justice and international law, adjustment or settlement of international disputes or situations which might lead to a breach of the peace;
2. To develop friendly relations among nations based on respect for the principle of equal rights and self-determination of peoples, and to take other appropriate measures to strengthen universal peace;
3. To achieve international cooperation in solving international problems of an economic, social, cultural, or humanitarian character, and in promoting and encouraging respect for human rights and for fundamental freedoms for all without distinction as to race, sex, language, or religion; and
4. To be a centre for harmonizing the actions of nations in the attainment of these common ends.

SOURCE:   59 STAT. 1031, T.S. 933, 3 BEVANS 1153.

---

victors of World War II. Developing nations are also interested in playing an expanded role. Some have suggested the Council could expand to 20 or 25 members. Others question whether such a large council could be effective. Regardless of which proposal for expansion comes forward, however, it would need to be ratified by a two-thirds majority of the General Assembly and then be approved by national parliaments, which is not likely to happen in the near future.

Permanent members of the Security Council have a veto over nonprocedural issues, thereby ensuring that a superpower can block an action proposed by the Security Council. The use of the veto exercised by the former Soviet Union or the United States had effectively rendered the Security Council impotent and unable to take any action. This impasse had shifted the focus from the Security Council to the General Assembly. For example, the General Assembly voted to move its site to Switzerland so that Yassar Arafat could address the group, thus obviating the problem of the United States's refusal to issue him a visa in 1988. The superpowers are not dominant in the General Assembly. With one country representing one vote, the Assembly level is not subject to a comparable superpower control. Even countries that receive substantial foreign aid do not always support the developed countries' positions.

The United Nations Charter delineates the powers of the Security Council, which include the severance of diplomatic relations, and military action via blockades or air, sea, and land operations. For example, the Security Council acted unanimously in 1990 and passed a resolution concerning the annexation of Kuwait by Iraq, stating that it had "no legal validity and is declared null and void." This move was significant because Yemen, a Security Council member, had not participated in an earlier resolution condemning the invasion, and Cuba and Yemen had abstained on the vote to impose economic sanctions. Note how the abstentions of the nonpermanent members does not impair the ability of the council to act. During the successive months, the Security Council passed resolutions giving increasing power to the coalition forces to act. For example, the August 25, 1990, Resolution granted "member states cooperating with the government of Kuwait which are deploying maritime forces to the area use [of] such measures commensurate to the specific circumstances as may be necessary." Subsequently, on November 29, 1990, the Security Council passed Resolution 678, which "authorizes member states cooperating with the government of Kuwait unless Iraq on or before January 15, 1991, fully implements the foregoing resolutions, to use all necessary means to uphold and implement the Security Council resolutions and to restore international peace and security to the area." This resolution was the basis of the war in the Gulf to expel Iraq from Kuwait. The coalition partners including the United States touted the resolution as the legal basis for their actions. However, as the U.S. ambassador commented in reference to Iraqi troops' threatening moves towards Kuwait: "We recognize this area as vital to U.S. national interests, and we will behave with others multilaterally when we can and unilaterally when we must." She signaled the pragmatic view that countries like to operate in conformance with the law, but if conformance is not possible then national interest may suffice.

Similarly the Security Council was used as a basis of intervention in Haiti in 1994. The May 6, 1994, Resolution 917 listed the conditions necessary to the lifting of economic sanctions. On July 31, 1994, the Council adopted Resolution 940, which "authorizes Member states to form a multinational force under unified command and control and in this framework, to use all necessary means to facilitate the departure from Haiti of the military leadership . . . the prompt return of the legitimately elected President and the restoration of the legitimate authorities." The peaceful landing of the US forces under the UN resolution and the restoration of President Aristide demonstrates the successful operation of the Security Council. Whether democracy will work in Haiti is an entirely separate question. The Security Council is not able to resolve all problems. The quagmire in Bosnia grows with no clear solution in sight.

The end of the Cold War and the establishment of trade relations with China has enabled the permanent five members to move forward together or at the very least not blocking one another in the resolution under law of international disputes.

The Secretary General functions as the chief administrative officer within a Secretariat designed to provide an apolitical supranational civil service. In practice, this has not always been the case. The Secretary General is recommended by the Security Council and elected by the General Assembly. Historically, the Secretaries General have tried to exercise a leadership role in achieving the United Nations' goal of international peace.

## The Decade of International Law

Clearly, a major change in the attitudes of countries, including the United States, came as a result of the Iraqi invasion of Kuwait in August 1990 and the United Nations' response to the crisis. The United States along with other members of the Security Council invoked international law, first as a basis of sanctions and then as the basis of war. Thus, the United States, having placed great weight on international law in 1990, would now have a more difficult time taking the same position it did in the *Nicaragua* case. As a result, the 1990s were dubbed the "decade of international law" to signal the new-found acceptance of these important principles and *modus operandi*.

In 1989, the United States and the former Soviet Union agreed to accept the jurisdiction of the

ICJ regarding a number of treaties. A record number of cases are pending before it, suggesting a new, enhanced role for the Court.

Some people have suggested a need for and, in fact, drafted a statute for a world criminal court to address global issues of terrorism. Because of the implications for a nation's sovereignty, these proposals have moved forward slowly until recently. Progress has been made, and a conference in 1998 may result in a treaty. The tribunals created to deal with alleged war crimes in the Balkans and Rwanda have offered encouragement to the international community about the prospect of enforcing international law. A federal judge commenting on the Balkan tribunal noted:

We . . . brought together 11 judges all from different systems in different countries and we were able to draft rules of procedure and evidence. . . . We basically created an international code of criminal procedure. . . . The only flaw in the system is that the present tribunals lack the power to order or make arrests, slowing the judicial process.

One stumbling block to the prospect of a permanent world criminal court is that only the U.S. wants the Security Council to determine which cases would go to the new court. This would preserve the superpower's veto power. Other concerns focus on jurisdiction over terrorism and whether women's rights would be included. A U.S. spokesman noted:

Our military forces are often called upon to engage overseas in conflict situations for purposes of humanitarian intervention to rescue hostages, to bring out American citizens from threatening environments, to deal with terrorists. We have to be careful that this proposal does not limit the capacity of our armed forces to legitimately operate internationally. We have to be careful that it does not open up opportunities for endless frivolous complaints to be lodged against the United States as a global military power.

While there is no longer euphoria about the "decade of international law," a realistic hope remains that the countries will be able to continue to work toward a coexistence based on adherence to certain principles and a mechanism to resolve breaches of international law.

# Private International Law

Up to this point, our discussion has focused on public international law and not specifically on international business law. Scholars and practitioners often divide international law into two categories: public international law and private international law. *Private international law,* defined as the laws applying to private parties in international transactions, is sometimes described as *conflict of laws* or the "domain of rights, duties, and disputes between and among persons from different places," and often involves commercial transactions.[2] In other words, private international law concerns how a nation's courts deal with a different nation's laws. Different national legal systems may compete for jurisdiction, and the laws they choose conflict.

Private international law is a misnomer in that it suggests that a separate body of law governs private transactions. Just as in public international law, private international law has no uniform codified set of accepted law. The field of conflict of laws consists of three areas: choice of law (which law applies to the transaction), choice of forum (who has jurisdiction or the power to hear the case), and recognition and enforcement of judgments. Private international law is also affected by multilateral conventions that provide a base for initial unification of substantive law.

Examples of these conventions include the Recognition and Enforcement of Foreign Arbitral Awards, June 10, 1958; Service Abroad of Judicial and Extra-Judicial Documents, November 15, 1965; Taking of Evidence Abroad; 1975 Inter-American Convention on Letters Rogatory; 1980 Hague Convention on International Child Abduction; and the Convention on the International Sale of Goods.

Through these conventions, some progress has been made in securing national agreement that arbitration awards should be honored and that foreign courts should be assisted by national courts in collecting evidence, although not necessarily in exact compliance with the requesting legal system. In other words, although France might assist a party in a dispute in New York to gather evidence in France, it will not necessarily comply with every deposition, interrogatory, or motion to produce documents that would be honored in the United States.

Historically, law evolved to deal with the growth of trade. Early regional attempts at codification of mercantile law include the Sea Law of Rhodes, adopted in 300 B.C., and the Amalfitan Table, adopted after the First Crusade by the Republic of Amalfi. The expansion of agriculture and the rise of cities in the twelfth and thirteenth centuries led to the development of special courts for merchants, which were familiar with their business practices. The noted thirteenth-century English judge and legal scholar Henry de Bracton noted that such courts were essential for merchants because they had special requirements, such as a need for speedy justice, which could be aided by a reduced time to answer a summons. The law administered by these courts, the "Law Merchant" or *Lex Mercatoria,* derived from ancient codes developed among merchants, some of which can be traced back to the Chaldeans in Mesopotamia (Iraq) and to the Babylonian king Hammurabi, who issued a code of laws around 2,000 B.C. The *Lex Mercatoria* represents the earliest form of private international law.

These special mercantile courts disappeared in England by the eighteenth century (although they lingered on in France, Germany, and Switzerland), and thereafter merchants were forced to prove the *Lex Mercatoria* as if it were some foreign law such as Turkish or French law in regular courts. In English and U.S. courts, the Law Merchant has been absorbed into the common law.

In his *Commentaries,* the great eighteenth-century English jurist Sir William Blackstone said of the law merchant:

The affairs of commerce are regulated by a law of their own called the law merchant or *lex mercatoria,* which all nations agree in and take notice of, and it is particularly held to be part of the law of England which decides the causes of merchants by the general rules which obtain in all commercial countries, and that often even in matters relating to domestic trade, as for instance, in the drawing acceptance and the transfer of Bills of Exchange.

Another English jurist, Lord Mansfield, noted:

Mercantile law is not the law of a particular country, but the law of all nations.

Lord Blackburn, another English jurist, observed:

The general law merchant for many years has in all countries caused bills of exchange to be negotiable; there are in some cases differences and peculiarities which by the municipal law of each country are grafted on it.

National law is a major factor in private international law, because in dealing with conflicts of law problems (e.g., which state's law applies), the national legal system takes center stage.

## Comparison of National Legal Systems

For the student who is not widely traveled, the great differences among national legal systems may come as a surprise. These systems may be classified in many ways: for example, by origin, cultural similarity, or political ideology. For the purposes of this text, they are classified as follows:

- *Civil law countries:* France, Germany, and Japan. Communist and Islamic legal systems are also based upon a code, but because of their unique national aspects, they will be treated separately.
- *Common law countries:* United States, Canada, Great Britain, and Nigeria.

An example of national differences can be seen in the types of cases that are filed. (See the accompanying news article about French law and the aftermath of the crash in which Princess Diana was killed.) One should be cognizant of the limits of generalizations, however, because the legal environment of any country is continually evolving. In Japan, companies are not subjected to the same volume of product liability and negligence law suits and subsequent punitive damage awards as they are in the United States. However, there are small signs that change is coming to Japan, as heretofore unheard of plaintiff victories, albeit with small monetary awards, have been recorded. Recently, a Japanese district court reportedly awarded a woman employee approximately $12,000 for the sexual harassment inflicted upon her by her boss. The harassment was repetitive, lewd comments and sexually derogatory statements about her. Thus, even though one can fairly say that Japan has less litigation than the United States, and that this type of suit is not common in Japan, their legal environments show emerging similarities.

# Ins and Outs of French Law

## Hotel Could Be Charged in Diana's Death

PARIS, Sept. 14—Consider the legal position of Mohamed al-Fayed. He is the owner of the Ritz Hotel; employer of Henri Paul, the driver in the crash that killed Diana, Princess of Wales, and father of Diana's escort on the fatal ride.

Under French law, his lawyers stand alongside the prosecutors, pressing the investigation of photographers who were chasing the Princess's car when it crashed two weeks ago.

But now, after three separate blood tests, it seems beyond doubt that the driver, Mr. Paul, was drunk and under the influence of drugs used to counter depression and the effects of alcoholism. So the focus of the investigation may quickly shift. Mr. Fayed's position is shifting too.

Last week, Mr. Fayed's lawyer, Bernard Dartevelle, hinted at a new legal position: primary responsibility for the crash still lies with the photographers, but perhaps there is also "secondary responsibility" on Mr. Paul's part. But even if that is so, no fault lies with the hotel. . . .

The quick shift of strategies illustrates the subtlety of French law, which is still based on the Napoleonic Code, and how it is likely to influence the progress of the case. Victims and their representatives can become parties to an investigation, while the prosecuting authorities are especially powerful in determining the outcome of the case.

As the father of Diana's escort—Emad Mohamed al-Fayed, nick-named Dodi—Mr. Fayed was entitled to become a civil party to the criminal investigation that two French investigating judges began into the actions of nine photographers and a motorcycle driver.

### The Judges' Scope: Virtually Unlimited

But the Napoleonic Code gives the investigating judges almost unlimited scope to follow the facts wherever the fault seems to lie. And the law gives other people who have suffered from the accident—the family of the injured British bodyguard, for instance—the same incentive to push for criminal prosecution that Mr. Fayed had.

Only by becoming civil parties to the proceedings can they eventually hope to collect damages from those responsible, and so they, like Princess Diana's sisters, are civil parties just like Mr. Fayed.

This complicated system could eventually pit the civil parties against one another. Last week, lawyers for Mr. Fayed and for the photographers say, investigators were swarming all over a possible new target: the management and staff of Mr. Fayed's Ritz Hotel.

French law, lawyers say, exposes the Ritz to the risk of criminal prosecution for negligence if it knowingly allowed Mr. Paul, the hotel's assistant security director, to take the wheel not only drunk but also unqualified to drive the rented Mercedes S-280 limousine that night. According to the Paris police, Mr. Paul did not have a limousine chauffeur's license.

"The driver is dead, and so under French law he can't be charged with being criminally responsible for their deaths," said Aram J. Kevorkian, an American lawyer with a longstanding practice in France. "But the investigating judges are free to interrogate people at the Ritz about why they allowed him to drive a car the hotel had hired, from a rental agency that night, and name them as suspects in an investigation if they see fit.". . .

Whether the senior Mr. Fayed, an Egyptian citizen who lives in London, could risk prosecution or an expensive lawsuit seems doubtful, legal experts say. The Ritz is owned by a London corporation. Mr. Fayed is listed as a director but not an officer, and lawyers say that only the corporation and its officers can be charged criminally or sued under French law.

Mr. Dartevelle said the Ritz and Mr. Fayed were fully covered by liability insurance, and all liability policies in France, by law, have unlimited coverage. The agency that rented the Mercedes to the Ritz has also said it was fully covered.

*(continued)*

*(continued)*

### Anglo-Saxon Law Has No Equivalent

After the Emperor himself, Napoleon said two centuries ago, the most powerful person in France is an investigating judge. There is no equivalent in Anglo-Saxon law.

There are two in this case, Hervé Stéphan and Marie-Christine Devidal, who can place suspects under investigation and charge them with specific crimes or free them of suspicion.

So far, they have placed nine photographers and a motorcycle driver who was working with one of them under investigation, all on suspicion of the crimes of contributing to the causes of the crash by recklessly pursuing the Mercedes and of failing to summon aid or impeding the actions of emergency crews.

If the judges decide to prosecute they will define the charges at the end of their investigation, which is expected to take months. . . .

### Possible Liability of the Hotel

French law allows companies and their officers to be charged with crimes and sued, but Mr. Kevorkian and other lawyers here say officers are more often charged than corporations are.

The Ritz is legally owned by a company called The Ritz Hotel Ltd., based in London, according to documents on file in France. Dun & Bradstreet International lists Franz Josef Klein, a German citizen, as the chief executive of the company in France.

Mr. Klein and another member of the Ritz management here, Franke Mora, have been interrogated by prosecutors, lawyers say. But lawyers said they believed that the Ritz might have more to worry about from a civil suit for damages than for criminal prosecution.

In practical terms, that probably means pursuing an insurance settlement. But, according to Mr. Kevorkian, "damage awards are not very high in France, almost always less than a million dollars."

In any case, nobody would be in a position to sue for damages under French law without bringing a complaint and becoming a civil party to the criminal proceedings. So far, Mr. Fayed, the family of Mr. Paul (who was a bachelor), and the Princess's family in England—but not her two sons—have done so.

### Royal Family Plans No Role in the Case

Prince Charles, as legal guardian of the two princes, could wait until the end of a criminal trial in France before doing the same, but spokesmen for the royal family in London said last week that at this point it had no intention of becoming a civil party to the French criminal proceedings.

The lawyers for those who have are entitled, as attorneys for the defendants are, to see investigation files as the case develops.

There are potential grounds, Mr. Kevorkian says, for suing the city of Paris in an administrative court contending that the tunnel where the accident occurred was unsafe.

If any of the criminal charges mentioned are brought against any defendants, they would be misdemeanors, not felonies, under French law. The trial would take place in the Correctional Court, without a jury, before a panel of three judges, all of them ready to give the benefit of the doubt to the case made by the investigating judge.

"In many cases," Mr. Kevorkian said, "the presiding judge will start off by asking the defendant, 'Do you recognize the facts in the case, clearly considering that the facts are the way the investigating judge has laid them out?'"

Trials in France hear witnesses and go over evidence, but without a daily transcript of the proceedings to help the lawyers. And, in contrast to the United States, the prosecutor can appeal to a higher court to reverse an acquittal.

*Craig R. Whitney*

## Common and Civil Law

To start at a basic level, the civil law system established in continental Europe is based on a comprehensive code, whereas the common law system, established in England and carried on in its former colonies, evolves through case precedent. One author summarized the difference as follows:

If we may generalize, the European is given to making plans, to regulating things in advance and therefore in terms of drawing up rules and systematizing them. He approaches life with fixed ideas and operates deductively. The Englishman improvises, never making a decision until he has to . . . and so he is not given to abstract rules of law. . . . But recently the attitudes of common law and continental [civil] law have been drawing closer. On the continent statute law is losing something of its primacy; lawyers no longer see decision-making as a merely technical and automatic process, but accept the comprehensive principles laid down by statute call for broad interpretation. . . . At the same time, the need for large scale planning and ordering of social affairs has forced Anglo American law into using abstract norms.[3]

Civil law came from the Roman tradition and was codified in the sixth century in the Justinian Code. In the eighteenth century, France codified the law into a civil, commercial, penal, civil procedure, and criminal procedure code. Other European countries such as Germany and Switzerland followed with a codification of their law. The colonization of Africa, Asia, and Latin America spread the civil law system. However, some countries such as Japan and Taiwan simply adopted law based upon the civil law model.

This explanation could be amplified by contrasting the role of judge and lawyer in civil and common law systems. The judge in a civil law system takes on many of the functions of the lawyer in deciding what evidence needs to be developed and/or produced. In a common law jurisdiction, the judge is more neutral and rules more on requests by the parties' lawyers. Thus, in a common law system the person one hires as a lawyer arguably plays a more critical role in the outcome. However, this difference should not be interpreted in the extreme, because in civil law states, lawyers are still important. One commentator noted that

there [Germany] as here [United States], the lawyers advance partisan positions from first pleadings to final arguments. German litigators suggest legal theories and lines of factual inquiry, they superintend and supplement judicial examination of witnesses, they urge inferences from fact, they discuss and distinguish precedent, they interpret statutes, and they formulate views of law that further the interests of their clients.[4]

Among nations, differences occur within a single category, such as common law. For example, the use of "contingency fees" (the attorney takes the case and is paid a percentage that has been negotiated in advance), which is common in the United States, is prohibited in England. Likewise, the English principle that the loser pays the legal fees is quite rare in the United States, although there are some statutory provisions for attorney's fees, such as in civil rights actions.

The jury in both criminal and civil cases in the United States, a common law country, is not used comparably in civil law countries. In some civil law countries, the citizens assist the judge in criminal cases in determining guilt and imposing sentence.

Legislative proposals in the U.S. Congress to reform civil litigation by adopting a version of "loser pays" did not pass, leaving reform to the states.

## Socialist Law

Socialist law is based upon a code, so it can be classified as civil law, but its ideological basis produces some fundamental differences. One cannot conclude, however, that all socialist legal systems are the same; both the People's Republic of China and Cuba could be classified as socialist, yet they differ in significant ways.

The political and economic philosophy of a communist society, in which the state traditionally owns and controls the means of production, is reflected in its legal system. These countries exhibit no great need for commercial law because any dispute can be solved bureaucratically or politically. Until recently, private ownership ran counter to established principles of law in both the former Soviet Union and China. Hungary led the experiment by passing legislation to encourage foreign investment and provide a legal framework that would encourage business people. China followed suit in 1978, and the former Soviet Union, approximately ten years later, passed a law authorizing the establishment of joint ventures as well as privately owned cooperatives. The nagging concern from a noncommunist perspective is whether reform is temporary, an idiosyncrasy that might be eradicated as quickly as it was implemented, or whether it will endure and provide a secure legal environment for lasting economic partnerships.

Law under communist rule serves a different function than in a democracy. Initially, the individual's rights are of less concern in a communist country because the emphasis is on the collective or society. Likewise, the concept of law as a limit on governmental power is not embraced, but, rather, the state is permitted to limit even rights it has granted, for example, speech or the right to assemble.

The dramatic changes in Eastern Europe and the breakup of the Soviet Union demonstrate that changes in the law follow political transformation. These countries are now struggling with the universal issues, such as states' rights, freedom, rights of property owners, taxation, and price control.

## Islamic Law

Too often, students, and professors as well, look at a problem or issue through an exclusively Western perspective. The power and importance of nations adhering to Islam compel other countries to have some basic understanding of this different system. Many Persian Gulf countries are adopting new commercial codes, in the civil law tradition, to encourage business, but they are to be interpreted in harmony with Shari'a (or God's rules) and the Koran. The Koran is not a code of law, but the expression of the Islamic ethic; it contains general injunctions to honor agreements and to observe good faith in commercial dealings. Shari'a describes the Islamic legal system, and the Koran is based on the Sunnah (sayings or decisions of the prophet Muhammad). Tenth century scholars concluded that the early scholars had interpreted the divine law sufficiently and "ijtihad" or independent reasoning was finished. Therefore, harmonizing commer-

cial reality and Shari'a can be a mine field because so many developments have occurred since the tenth century and yet theoretically, new law is not needed. Moral conduct is the preeminent concern. For example, because Shari'a embraces a concept called "riba," which prohibits "unearned or unjustified profits," interest on loans can be problematic. Some countries acknowledge that interest can be legitimate and have found ways to comply with the scripture and still secure financing. "Mudaraba" allows the bank to buy shares in the enterprise and receive a portion of the profits or share the loss. Through Mudaraba the bank loans money to purchase assets and could be paid in a year or two, not with interest, but with an additional payment to show thanks and appreciation. Although it sounds like interest, according to the country legal experts it is not. Similarly, "gharar" prohibits any gain that is not clearly outlined at the time of the contract because it is likened to gambling. Many countries have adopted civil codes that define contracts and cover commercial transactions. Business can still be conducted in these countries, but only with sensitivity to and ingenuity in dealing with the national legal systems.[5] Even countries that adhere to Shari'a are changing; for example, the Sudan reportedly modified the sentences of several convicted criminals, deleting the mandatory limb amputation for stealing. One should be aware of the differences among countries that adhere to the teachings of Islam. Iran's and Saudi Arabia's legal systems are not identical. Before doing business in any one country, one should familiarize oneself with the particular characteristics of that country's system.

## Comparative Law

Comparative law is the name of the discipline that examines differences between legal systems. (Chapter 4 continues this discussion, particularly with regard to litigation.) Within national systems, international legal principles and standards can be noted. For example, the Zimbabwe Supreme Court in 1989 found that a sentence of whipping a juvenile violated both the Zimbabwean constitutional provision of "inhuman or degrading punishment" and international human rights norms. The youth convicted of assault had been sentenced to "receive a moderate correction of four cuts with a light cane, which was to be administered in private by a prison officer." The court noted that

> the courts of this country are free to import into the interpretation of section 15(1) (of the Constitution) interpretation of similar provisions in international and regional human rights instruments such as, among others, the International Bill of Human Rights, the European Convention for the Protection of Human Rights and Fundamental Freedoms, and the InterAmerican Convention on Human Rights. In the end International Human Rights norms will become a part of our domestic Human Rights law. In this way our domestic human rights jurisdiction is enriched.[6]

The comparison of foreign criminal law is of increasing concern to businesspeople who find themselves under the control of a foreign government, accused of crimes. For example, a businesswoman was arrested in Nigeria for selling oil without a license. The penalty (changed after she was arrested) was death. She was tried and ultimately acquitted. This acquittal, however, occurred in part because of active intervention by Counsel and the United States congressional representatives. In another case, a furniture importer was arrested in Taiwan when he complained about the quality of the goods. When he arrived in Taiwan, he was charged with fraud and placed under house arrest for a year. More severe

was the outcome for a business consultant named Flynn who was assisting a U.S. printing company that was unable to comply with the contract terms with a Mexican company. Flynn flew to Mexico to resolve the matter and was arrested and sentenced to six years in prison. After three years in prison, the conviction was overturned because he had not been a party to the contract. Perhaps illustrative of the principle that one cannot generalize from one's own experiences is the case of the man in Greece who bought jewelry worth $300 on his VISA® card. He was arrested and placed in jail because the purchase had gone over his credit limit. He faced up to twelve years in prison. He asked the authorities to try confirming the purchase once more and it worked. He later tried to sue VISA® in the United States. The U.S. Court of Appeals noted:

> It is elementary that a person who purchases goods without paying for them (whether a rubber check, a forged instrument, or a credit card without enough credit available) risks civil and criminal penalties whether in the United States or Greece.

Bonstingh v. Maryland Bank N.A. et al. 841 F. 2d 1122 (4th Cir. 1988), aff'g, 662 F. Supp. 882 (D. 1987).

Even two common law countries can have differences in the law. In the following case, a U.S. court denied enforcement of a British judgment because of the differences in libel law.

---

### Vladimir Matusevitch v. Vladimir Ivanovich Telnikoff

*United States District Court, District of Columbia*
*877 F.Supp.1 (D.D.C. 1995)*

**BACKGROUND AND FACTS**
Mr. Telnikoff and Mr. Matusevitch are both Russian emigrants. Mr. Telnikoff wrote an opinion editorial for a London newspaper criticizing the BBC for hiring Russian "minorities." Mr. Matusevitch, a U.S. citizen, wrote a letter to the editor of the London paper stating that the use of "minority" in conjunction with Russian was anti-Semitic because it referred to Jewish people in the Russian context. Mr. Telnikoff sued for libel and was awarded $416,000 by a London court. He sought to enforce the judgment in the United States where Mr. Matusevitch had assets. Mr. Matusevitch asked the U.S. court to declare the

British libel law judgment unenforceable because it violated the First and Fourteenth Amendments of the U.S. Constitution.

**URBINA, DISTRICT JUDGE**
British law on libel differs from U.S. law. In the United Kingdom, the defendant bears the burden of proving allegedly defamatory statements true and the plaintiff is not required to prove malice on the part of the libel defendant. . . . As a result, a libel defendant would be held liable for statements the defendant honestly believed to be true and published without any negligence. In contrast, the law in the

*(continued)*

*(continued)*

United States requires the plaintiff to prove that the statements were false and looks to the defendant's state of mind and intentions. In light of the different standards, this court concludes that recognition and enforcement of the foreign judgment in this case would deprive the plaintiff of his constitutional rights.

Speech similar to the plaintiff's statements have received protection under the First Amendment to the Constitution and are thereby unactionable in U.S. courts. . . . The Supreme Court held that hyperbole is not actionable. Plaintiff contends that his statements were plainly hyperbolic because they were stated in an attempt to portray defendant's extremist position.

In addition, in the United States, courts look to the context in which the statements appeared when determining a First Amendment question. . . .

In the case at hand, the court notes that the British judgment was based on jury instructions which asked the jury to ignore context. Therefore, this court finds that if the statements were read in context to the original article or statement and in reference to the location of the statements in the newspaper, a reader would reasonably be alerted to the statements' function as opinion and not as an assertion of fact.

The defendant in this case has described himself as a prominent activist for Human Rights in the Soviet Union since 1955. Therefore, for purposes of his article about the composition of Russian personnel hired by Radio Free Europe/Radio Liberty, the court finds that the defendant was a limited public figure. In light of defendant's status as a limited public figure, the plaintiff is entitled to all the constitutional safeguards concerning speech used against public figures.

For the reasons stated herein, the court grants summary judgment in favor of the Plaintiff.

**Decision.** The court refused to recognize the English judgment because it would deprive the plaintiff of his constitutional rights.

The legal environment of the country is an important part of any businessperson's briefing before assignment. Looking at legal systems out of socio-cultural context can be a mistake, however. For example, U.S. businesspeople may successfully adopt an aggressive litigation strategy in the United States, but find this tactic not only unworkable but actually detrimental in Germany or Japan. Therefore, simply knowing the law is not enough.

## Foreign Investment Codes

Foreign investment law is another area of law that can be compared. Many countries, including Eastern European, Latin, and South American ones, have been changing their laws to attract foreign investment, including laws on government approval for foreign investment and technology transfer agreements. One example is the recently enacted Ukraine Protection of Foreign Investment adopted September 10, 1990. It offers protection against state intervention and the ability to repatriate profits. Jamaica, to encourage foreign investment, removed restrictions on foreign currency exchange, allowing the movement of capital in and out of the country. Similarly, Russia announced plans to make the ruble convertible by August 1, 1992, and to allow the repatriation of profits without restriction. These changes in national laws profoundly affect the business climate of a country. In another example, Mexico, to further encourage private investment, issued new regulations in 1989 that allowed more companies to be owned 100 percent by foreign interests. The government also lowered tax rates as an additional business incentive. These codes are an important factor in inducing investment in a country. The Mexican Foreign Investment Act of 1993, shown in Exhibit 2.4, stipulated new percentages for foreign participation in Mexico. Because of these tremendous differences among countries, codes should be reviewed carefully.

Each country, depending upon its stage of development as well as past experience with foreign investment, will develop unique investment codes. Assumptions about what is permissible for business in a particular country are dangerous, because while one country allows wholly owned foreign companies, other countries may require some level of local participation.

---

**EXHIBIT 2.4    Mexican Foreign Investment Act of 1993**

**Chapter III Activities and Acquisitions with Specific Regulations**

*ARTICLE 7.*

In the economic activities and corporations herein mentioned, foreign investment may participate in the following percentages:

   I. Up to 10% in:
      Cooperatives (i.e.: Sociedades cooperativas de producción);
  II. Up to 25% in:
      a.  National air transportation;
      b.  Air taxi transportation; and
      c.  Specialized air transport.
 III. Up to 30% in:
      a.  Corporations that control financial groupings;
      b.  Credit institutions of multiple banking services;
      c.  Stockmarket offices; and
      d.  Stockmarket experts.
  IV. Up to 49% in:
      a.  Insurance institutions;
      b.  Bond institutions;
      c.  Money exchange houses;
      d.  General deposit warehouses;
      e.  Financial leasing offices;
      f.  Financial factoring corporations;
      g.  Financial corporations of a limited purpose referred to in Article 103, paragraph IV, of the General Credit Institutions Act (*i.e.: Ley de Instituciones de Crédito*);
      h.  Corporations referred to in Article 12 Bis of the Stockmarket Act (*i.e.: Ley del Mercado de Valores*);
      i.  Representative shares of fixed capital of investment corporations and operating corporations of investment corporations;
      j.  Manufacturing and commercialization of explosives, firearms, cartridges, ammunition and fireworks, not including the acquisition and utilization of explosives for industrial and extractive activities, nor the manufacturing of explosive mixtures for the use in said activities;
      k.  Printing and publication of newspapers to be circulated within the national territory exclusively;
      l.  Series "T" shares of corporations holding property in agricultural, livestock and forestry lands;
      m.  Cable television;
      n.  Basic telephone services;
      o.  Freshwater and coastal fishing and fishing in the exclusive economic zone, not including aquaculture;
      p.  Comprehensive port management; and
      q.  Pilotage port services for vessels engaged in inland navigation, in accordance with the applicable Act.

SOURCE:   Reproduced with permission from 33 I.L.M. 207 (1994). Translation by Jorge A. Vargas, Professor, University of San Diego School of Law. The original Spanish text appears in the Mexican *Diarlo Official de le Federación* of December 27, 1993, First Section, pp. 92–99. © The American Society of International Law.

# International Organizations

International organizations, both governmental and nongovernmental (NGO) play an increasingly important role in today's global society as forums for legal, political, and economic issues. The remainder of this chapter examines the structures and functions of several of these organizations, and pays particular attention to how they impact on international business.

## Organizations Affiliated With the United Nations

The United Nations is an important organization that has been discussed in a previous section. A number of organizations affiliated with the United Nations undertake activities affecting the international business environment. The United Nations Economic and Social Council consists of members elected by the General Assembly for three-year terms and coordinates the efforts of all specialized agencies "established by Governmental agreement and having wide international responsibilities . . . in economic, social, cultural, educational, health, and related fields."

The following list provides a sense of the types of work many of the agencies perform:

- Food and Agriculture Organization
- International Labor Organization
- IBRD (World Bank)
- IMF (International Monetary Fund)
- UNESCO (United Nations Educational, Scientific, and Cultural Organization)
- World Health Organization (WHO)
- WIPO (World International Property Organization)

Numerous commissions have also been established to deal with special issues. For example, the United Nations Conference on Trade and Development (UNCTAD) promotes trade, particularly of developing countries. UNCTAD fosters the signing of multilateral trade agreements and the systematizing of trade law and policy. For example, UNCTAD drafted a Transfer of Technology Code (TOT-Code), which has not yet been implemented. It has also developed a Restrictive Business Practices Code (RBP-Code), but it too is not operative.

The objective of the United Nations Commission on International Trade Law (UNCITRAL) is to promote international trade through the harmonization of trade law among nations. This agency includes members from many nations. One of its major achievements has been the entry into force of the Convention on Contracts for the International Sale of Goods (CISG, which is discussed in Chapter 5). The United Nations Convention on the Carriage of Goods by Sea of 1978 was initiated by UNCITRAL and addresses international bills of lading used in the shipment of goods. In 1976, UNCITRAL adopted arbitration rules, which have been widely used. Other projects involve the drafting of model laws to be used by countries, such as the model law on Electronic Funds Transfer. Two other organizations are complementary to UNCITRAL in that they also strive to unify international law: the Hague Conference on Private International Law and the International Institute for the Unification of Private Law (UNIDROIT).

The United Nations Industrial Development Organization (UNIDO) works with UNCTAD to assist in the industrial development of less-developed countries.

The United Nations Commission on Transnational Corporations developed a Draft Code of Conduct on Transnational Corporations. This code, however, has not been accepted by many countries, including the United States.

> **http://www.un.org/MoreInfo/ngolink/ partners.htm**
> Lists and describes the roles of non-governmental organizations (NGOs) in partnership with the U.N.

## History and Development of the "Bretton Woods" Institutions

After World War I, a confluence of economic conditions resulted in many countries facing dramatically similar problems, including inflation, high unemployment, and currency fluctuations. Many nations turned toward protectionism as a way to deal with these problems. Although these measures were largely unsuccessful, the onset of World War II absorbed the world's attention. While World War II was still in progress, several major meetings were held laying the groundwork to prevent future economic and military catastrophes. A multinational conference was convened at Bretton Woods, New Hampshire, in 1944 to focus on short-term financial problems, ways to promote free trade, and the creation of a bank that would help finance the necessary rebuilding after the war. The conference culminated in the creation of the International Monetary Fund (IMF) and the International Bank for Reconstruction and Development (World Bank).

## International Monetary Fund

In general, the objectives of the IMF are "to promote international monetary cooperation, to facilitate the expansion and balanced growth of international trade and to promote stability in foreign exchange." The fund lends money to developing countries to assist them with fundamental problems blocking development, such as high interest rates and inflated oil prices. The fund works closely with commercial banks in this process.

Membership in the IMF (currently 181 states) obliges a nation to adhere to the initial goals of Bretton Woods as reflected in the articles. Members must act in a way that promotes stable exchange rates and must pursue economic and fiscal policies that foster growth in an orderly way. The purpose here is to avoid the chaos of the 1930s. Members must also be careful not to pursue policies with another member that may discriminate against a third member. The fund headquarters are located in Washington, D.C.

## The IMF and the World Bank

Many people have difficulty distinguishing the IMF from the World Bank. This difficulty is understandable because these international organizations do have much in common. Both institutions were created at the Bretton Woods Conference of 1944, have the same membership, and are concerned with international economic issues. In addition, the two organizations, although distinct entities, work together in close cooperation and hold joint annual meetings.

Despite their similarities, the IMF and the World Bank are separate entities. The IMF, as noted, oversees the international monetary system and promotes exchange stability and orderly exchange relations among its members. The IMF assists all members, rich or poor, that have balance of payments difficulties. On the other hand, the World Bank seeks to promote economic development of poorer countries and is concerned with assisting developing countries through the financing of specific development projects and programs.

> **http://www.worldbank.org/**
> The home page of the World Bank Group.

## International Bank for Reconstruction and Development

The name "World Bank" encompasses two institutions, the International Bank for Reconstruction and Development (IBRD) and the International Development Association (IDA). These institutions should not be confused with EBRD (European Bank for Reconstruction and Development). The IBRD was established in 1945, but due to the beginning of the Cold War (the postwar tension between the Soviet Union and the United States), when it opened in 1946, the USSR did not join.

The IBRD does not make high-risk loans, and the loans it makes are generally at market terms. Thus, it cannot achieve its goals as much as it might hope. The IDA was created in 1960 to bridge this gap between IBRD objectives and reality. The IDA makes loans to poor countries with average per capita GNP of less than $410 on more favorable terms than the IBRD. (To put this into perspective, the United Arab Emirates has a per capita GNP of $30,000.) Loans can be made only to governments, however, which stifles some private initiatives. The IDA and the IBRD share staffs.

A separate entity, the International Finance Corporation (IFC), was created in 1956 to address the issue of loans to private enterprises in developing countries. The IFC works jointly with commercial banks and also advises countries on developing capital markets. The IFC does not have the backing of a governmental guarantee when it borrows.

The idea behind the IBRD and the IDA is that countries should "graduate," moving first from the assistance of the IDA to the assistance of the IBRD and then eventually becoming a contributor to the IBRD. Japan is the sterling example of a country that has "graduated" from borrower to contributor.

## GATT and WTO

In the aftermath of World War II, many nations reflected on recent history and tried to devise ways to avoid repeating past mistakes. The 1930s had brought a wave of protectionism and high tariff rates to keep foreign goods out. The United States joined this trend by passing the Smoot Hawley Tariff Act of 1930, thereby exacerbating the Depression. As part of the postwar examination, in 1947–48, fifty-three nations negotiated the Havana Charter, which established the International Trade Organization (ITO). The United States, although a participant in the conference, changed its mind about signing as a result of ensuing Cold War tensions. The GATT (General Agreement on Tariffs and Trade) was signed January 1, 1948, as a temporary measure to salvage some of the principles of the ITO.

The purpose of GATT was to commit member countries to the principles of nondiscrimination and reciprocity, meaning that if a bilateral trade treaty is negotiated between two GATT members, those provisions will be extended to other members. Countries that are members are granted "most favored nation" (MFN) status. All member nations must harmonize their laws with GATT or face sanctions. (For a complete history of GATT, see Chapter 10.) Currently, GATT has approximately 100 members. China has applied for membership, as have many states of the Commonwealth of Independent States (CIS) and other Eastern European nations.

GATT members bargain in multiyear rounds of discussion on tariff reduction, quantitative restrictions, and settlement of disputes. Thus, bilateral trade talks are replaced (though not entirely) with talks with all contracting parties participating. Countries designated as LDCs (less-developed countries) receive additional breaks. The group offices are headquartered in Geneva. A council made up of member representatives is responsible for enforcement and dispute settlement. The GATT process has been criticized for its leisurely pace and, indeed, the group has been said to be so slow to agree that it should be called the "gentlemen's agreement to talk and talk." GATT has delivered dramatic reductions in tariffs, however, and subsequent rounds of negotiation, though less dramatic, have netted results. The organization became the World Trade Organization (WTO) and will be discussed in Chapter 10.

## OECD

The Organization for European Economic Cooperation (OEEC), born out of General Marshall's plan to aid recovery of Europe after World War II, was formed in 1948 by the Western European nations, with the United States and Canada as associate members. The Organization for Economic Cooperation and Development (OECD) replaced the OEEC in 1961 and added the United States, Canada, and Japan as full members. The goals remained the same but included coordinating efforts to aid less-developed countries.

In 1976 the OECD issued a "Declaration on International Investment and Multinational Enterprises" and "Guidelines for Multinational Enterprises." The purposes of the declaration were to establish the principle of "national treatment" for corporations, meaning treatment consistent with international law and no less favorable than domestic corporations receive. The guidelines, without being mandatory, alert multinational corporations (MNC) to take into account the policies and objectives of the country within which they are operating. Other principles include disclosure of information, competition policy, financing (balances of payment and credit policies), taxation, employment and industrial relations, support of trade unions, nondiscrimination, and the goal of utilizing "reasonable terms" when transferring technology.

These OECD documents present problems: (1) They are not binding, and (2) developing and developed countries disagree about their interpretation. After all, "reasonable terms" is in the eye of the beholder.

*http://www.oecd.org/*
*The home page of the Organization for European Economic Cooperation.*

## International Chamber of Commerce

The International Chamber of Commerce (ICC) is a worldwide organization that draws its members from all sectors of the business community. The basic purposes of the organization are stated in its brochure:

1. Permanently represent business vis-à-vis the major intergovernmental institutions and conferences.
2. Harmonize, codify, and standardize international business practices.

3. Provide practical services for its members and for the international business community.
4. Provide a link between countries with different economic systems, or a meeting place for sectors of economic activity with different interests.

The ICC can point to many achievements that have facilitated the development of multinational business. It developed the Uniform Customs and Practice for Documentary Credits, which are used in financing, and Incoterms, the uniform definitions used in trade. The ICC also created a forum for the settlement of disputes, the International Court of Arbitration. The ICC serves as a liaison with the United Nations and its agencies to help advocate the views of the private sector.

## Other Organizations

Numerous other organizations with countries as members impact on business. For example, the International Whaling Commission, based in Cambridge, England, was established in 1946. It has 36 country members dedicated to regulating whaling to promote conservation. The commission helps to fund studies and compiles statistics regarding the whale populations.

Private organizations also play a significant role in international business. For example, professional groups can be involved in standard-setting for a particular industry, thus having far-reaching impact on business.

# International Codes of Conduct and the Ethical Dimension

Codes of conduct for corporations have been in existence for years but without widespread support. Both the U.N.–affiliated Center for Transnational Corporations and the OECD have promulgated codes of conduct for corporations in host countries in an attempt to set ethical standards for behavior. The developing countries were a major impetus in developing the codes because of the concern that they were often taken advantage of by multinational enterprises (MNE). MNEs often achieved a position of dominance within the host country without providing generous compensation to or sharing the technology with the host country.

OECD in 1994 promulgated an antibribery recommendation hoping to get more nations to support through national legislation a commitment to eradicate bribery in international business. Unfortunately, the immediate likelihood of nations embracing such a measure is scarce since the United States passed the Foreign Corrupt Practices Act in 1977 with no perceptible move on other countries' part with the exception of Sweden.

More recently in the United States, companies have shown a greater interest in ethics codes because under the U.S. Federal Sentencing Guidelines, if the corporation institutes a code of conduct and compliance program to reduce the likelihood of criminal conduct, it can then use the code as a basis to argue for a reduced fine in the event of a corporate crime. Thus corporations have inaugurated ethics programs and compliance officers to demonstrate their intent to comply with the law and to mitigate any fine in the event of a corporate transgression.

Two other interesting examples of codes dealing with the environment are the CERES Principles (formerly the Valdez Principles) and Responsible Care, a chemical industry self-generated code.

The Valdez Principles were amended in 1992 and renamed the Coalition for Environmentally Responsible Economies, or CERES Principles. The following text shows the differences between the two versions and explains why the latter is more attractive to businesses.

**CERES Principles**
[Note that deletions are indicated by ( ) parentheses and insertions by italicized sections.]

1. Protection of the Biosphere. We will (minimize and strive) *reduce and make continual progress* to eliminate the release of any (pollutant) *substance* that may cause environmental damage to the air, water or earth and its inhabitants. We will safeguard *all* habitats *affected by our operations and will protect open spaces and wilderness while preserving biodiversity* (in rivers, lakes, wetlands, coastal zones and oceans and will minimize contributing to the greenhouse effect, depletion of ozone layer, acid rain or smog.)

2. Sustainable Use of Natural Resources. We will make sustainable use of renewable natural resources, such as water, soils and forests. We will conserve nonrenewable natural resources through efficient use and careful planning. (We will protect wildlife habitat, open spaces and wilderness while protecting biodiversity.)

3. Reduction and Disposal of Waste. We will (minimize the creation of) reduce and where possible eliminate waste (especially hazardous waste and wherever possible recycle materials) through source reduction and recycling. (We will dispose of all wastes through safe and responsible methods.) *All waste will be handled and disposed of through safe and responsible methods.*

4. (Wise Use of Energy) *Energy Conservation. We will conserve energy and improve the energy efficiency of our internal operations and of the goods and services we sell.* We will make every effort to use environmentally safe and sustainable energy sources (to meet our needs). (We will invest in improved energy efficiency and conservation in our operations. We will maximize the energy efficiency of products we produce or sell.)

5. Risk Reduction. We will minimize the environmental, health and safety risks to our employees and the communities in which we operate (by employing) through safe technologies, *facilities* and operating procedures and by being (constantly) prepared for emergencies.

6. (Marketing of) Safe Products and Services. (We will sell products or services that minimize adverse environmental impacts and that are safe as consumers commonly use them.) *We will reduce and where possible eliminate the use, manufacture or sale of products and services that cause environmental damage or health and safety hazards.* We will inform consumers of environmental impacts of our products or services *and try to correct unsafe use.*

7. (Damage Compensation) *Environmental Restoration.* (We will take responsibility for any harm we cause the environment by making every effort to fully restore the environment and to compensate those persons who are adversely affected.) *We will promptly and responsibly correct conditions we have caused that endanger health, safety or the environment. To the extent feasible, we will redress injuries we have caused to persons or damage to the environment and will restore the environment.*

8. (Disclosure) *Informing the Public.* (We will disclose to our employees and to the public incidents relating to our operations that cause environmental harm or pose health or safety hazards. We will disclose potential environmental, health or safety hazards posed by our operations, and we will not take any action against employees who report any condition that creates a danger or poses health and safety hazards.) *We will inform in a timely manner everyone who may be affected by conditions caused by our company that might endanger health, safety or the environment. We will regularly seek advice and counsel through dialogue with persons in communities near our facilities. We will not take action against employees for reporting dangerous incidents or conditions to management or to appropriate authorities.*

9. (Environmental Directors and Managers) *Management Commitment.* (At least one member of the Board of Directors will be a person qualified to present environmental interests. We will commit management resources to implement these Principles, including the funding of an office of vice president for environmental affairs or an equivalent executive position, reporting directly to the CEO, to monitor and report upon our implementation efforts.) *We will implement these Principles and sustain a process that ensures that the Board of Directors and Chief Executive Officer are fully informed about pertinent environmental issues and are fully responsible for environmental policy. In selecting our Board of Directors, we will consider demonstrated environmental commitment as a factor.*

10. (Assessment and Annual Audit) *Audits and Reports.* We will conduct (and make public) an annual self-evaluation of our progress in implementing these Principles (and in complying with all applicable laws and regulations throughout our worldwide operations.) We (will work toward) *support* the timely creation of (independent) *generally accepted*

environmental audit procedures (which we will complete annually and make available to the public.) *We will annually complete the CERES Report, which will be made available to the public.*

*DISCLAIMER*
*These Principles establish an environmental ethic with criteria by which investors and others can assess the environmental performance of companies. Companies that sign these Principles pledge to voluntarily go beyond the requirements of the law. These Principles are not intended to create new legal liabilities, expand existing rights or obligations, waive legal defenses or otherwise affect the legal position of any signatory company and are not intended to be used against a signatory in any legal proceeding for any purpose.*

The major difference between the two versions is the dilution of the 1989 language thus facilitating commitment to the Principles by corporations. Perhaps the 1992 disclaimer states the difference best: a pledge to CERES should not be used against the company in a subsequent court proceeding by an environmental group.

A detailed exegesis of the CERES and Valdez Principles reveals other important changes. In number 2, the deletion of specific guarantees of protection to "wildlife, habitat, open space and wilderness" leaves much more room for the corporation to make decisions which balance environmental and business growth factors rather than place the environment above all other considerations. The term *hazardous waste* is removed in its entirety from number 3. Number 4 deletes the commitment of "investment" in energy conservation. Here again, the 1992 version limits the specific guarantee of measurable outcomes. Number 7 retracts the specific commitment to "compensate persons," thus closing the door on any consent by the signatory to automatic payment to neighbors who claim injury. The rewording of number 8 retrenches from the commitment to disclose potential environmental, health, or safety hazards. The new language in number 8 is substantially narrower in scope. The most dramatic change appears in number 9, where the commitment to the creation of a vice

president for environmental affairs, an environmental "seat" on the board of directors, and the mention of financial resources are conspicuously absent. Lastly, in number 10, the 1992 version embraces "generally accepted audit procedures" rather than the pledge to institute an independent environmental audit.

This new approach has achieved its objective of garnering more industry support. As of April 1993, 52 companies signed the CERES pledge, including Ben & Jerry's, The Body Shop, Smith and Hawken, and the Sun Company.

The chemical industry charted a different course in developing its own code. The Chemical Manufacturers' Association response to pressing environmental issues was to adopt a program called "Responsible Care®." The cornerstone of the program was a voluntary commitment of the manufacturers for "performance improvement." There are ten guiding principles which range from simple statements of "operate plants safely" to "work with others to resolve past problems."

### RESPONSIBLE CARE®: GUIDING PRINCIPLES

1. To recognize and respond to community concerns about chemicals and our operations.
2. To develop and produce chemicals that can be manufactured, transported, used and disposed of safely.
3. To make health, safety and environmental considerations a priority in our planning for all existing and new products and processes.
4. To report promptly to officials, employees, customers and the public, information on chemical-related health or environmental hazards and to recommend protective measures.
5. To counsel customers on the safe use, transportation and disposal of chemical products.
6. To operate our plants and facilities in a manner that protects the environment and the health and safety of our employees and the public.
7. To extend knowledge by conducting or supporting research on the health, safety and

environmental effects of our products, processes and waste materials.

8. To work with others to resolve problems created by past handling and disposal of hazardous substances.

9. To participate with government and others in creating responsible laws, regulations and standards to safeguard the community, workplace and the environment.

10. To promote the principles and practices of Responsible Care® by sharing experiences and offering assistance to others who produce, handle, use, transport or dispose of chemicals.

The anonymous public advisory panel, which gives feedback, and self-evaluation will contribute to the Code's effectiveness. Companies committed to using "First World standards in Third World countries" will improve the industry's performance and reduce the risks to the surrounding population and the global village, which recognizes no environmental boundaries. Sanctions are apparently absent, however, for the Chemical Manufacturers Association seems to be relying instead on the companies' own good will and good faith compliance.

Why would Responsible Care® be more palatable than the Valdez Principles to some companies? Basically the cornerstone of the program is compliance with the law coupled with a public relations effort. For example, Responsible Care® pledges to "recognize and respond to community concerns." This commitment is to a process, not to outcomes. The commitment of Responsible Care® to "work with others to resolve problems" is infinitely more acceptable than the outcome commitment in the Valdez Principles to compensate individuals and to restore the environment. However, the transformation from the Valdez to the CERES Principles has narrowed the differences between the latter and Responsible Care®. Essentially, both are statements of the signatory's commitment to go beyond the letter of the law and to pledge to "strive" toward as high a standard as possible. Nevertheless, the CERES Principles have more specificity despite the modifications and require more of a company commitment than Responsible Care®.[7]

The codes do help a corporation to better understand a developing country's perspective and may alert a company to foreseeable problems with the host country. Negotiating the best financial deal may look good in the short run, but companies that want the relationship with the host country to be a long-lasting one should take into account the ramifications of the deal within the context of social responsibility as interpreted by these codes. Individual companies may choose to develop their own codes as well. Levi Strauss illustrates this practice.

## Cultural and Ethical Environment

Levi Strauss uses more than 400 subcontractors overseas. They recently discovered that 25 percent or more of those subcontractors abuse employees in some fashion. One plant in Bangladesh uses child labor. (This practice is not uncommon in parts of the world, as documented in *By the Sweat and Toil of Children: The Use of Child Labor in American Imports,* a monograph published by the U.S. Department of Labor, July 15, 1994.) Levi Strauss stopped this practice. Also Levi Strauss, despite local law, adopted a standard that no worker may work more than sixty hours a week. This example raises several issues. Is complying with the local law sufficient? Is setting a standard higher than local law but lower than U.S. law sufficient? How does one define *sufficient*? What is the difference between legally sufficient and ethically defensible? Can a company realistically commit to "First World" standards for labor and the environment in the Third World? Does it benefit the children when a company fires its workers below a certain age? These are all difficult questions. Levi Strauss recently announced its Global Sourcing Guidelines. See the following feature outlining these guidelines.[8]

Companies can face problems with overseas subcontractors even when they don't control them. The subcontractors' treatment of workers can pose ethical dilemmas as well as public relations nightmares. Nike, faced with accusations of abuse of workers by overseas contractors, decided to hire a distinguished former a U.N. ambassador, Andrew Young, to investigate

# Levi Strauss & Co. Global Sourcing and Operating Guidelines

## Business Partner Terms of Engagement

The Terms of Engagement are tools that help protect Levi Strauss & Co.'s corporate reputation and, therefore, its commercial success. They assist us in selecting business partners* that follow work place standards and business practices consistent with our Company's policies. As a set of guiding principles, they also help identify potential problems so that we can work with our business partners to address issues of concern as they arise.

Specifically, we expect our business partners to operate work places where the following standards and practices are followed:

1. ETHICAL STANDARDS
   We will seek to identify and utilize business partners who aspire as individuals and in the conduct of all their businesses to a set of ethical standards not incompatible with our own.
2. LEGAL REQUIREMENTS
   We expect our business partners to be law abiding as individuals and to comply with legal requirements relevant to the conduct of all their businesses.
3. ENVIRONMENTAL REQUIREMENTS
   We will only do business with partners who share our commitment to the environment and who conduct their business in a way that is consistent with Levi Strauss & Co.'s Environmental Philosophy and Guiding Principles.
4. COMMUNITY INVOLVEMENT
   We will favor business partners who share our commitment to contribute to the betterment of community conditions.
5. EMPLOYMENT STANDARDS
   We only do business with partners whose workers are in all cases present voluntarily, not put at

*Business partners are contractors and subcontractors who manufacture or finish our products and suppliers who provide raw materials used in the production of our products. We have begun applying the *Terms of Engagement* to business partners involved in manufacturing and finishing and plan to extend their application to suppliers.

risk of physical harm, fairly compensated, allowed the right of free association and not exploited in any way. In addition, the following specific guidelines will be followed.

- WAGES AND BENEFITS
  We will only do business with partners who provide wages and benefits that comply with any applicable law and match the prevailing local manufacturing or finishing industry practices.
- WORKING HOURS
  While permitting flexibility in scheduling, we will identify prevailing local work hours and seek business partners who do not exceed them except for appropriately compensated overtime. While we favor partners who utilize less than sixty-hour work weeks, we will not use contractors who, on a regular basis, require in excess of a sixty-hour week. Employees should be allowed at least one day off in seven.
- CHILD LABOR
  Use of child labor is not permissible. Workers can be no less than 14 years of age and not younger than the compulsory age to be in school. We will not utilize partners who use child labor in any of their facilities. We support the development of legitimate workplace apprenticeship programs for the educational benefit of younger people.
- PRISON LABOR/FORCED LABOR
  We will not utilize prison or forced labor in contracting relationships in the manufacture and finishing of our products. We will not utilize or purchase materials from business partners utilizing prison or forced labor.
- HEALTH & SAFETY
  We will only utilize business partners who provide workers with a safe and healthy work environment. Business partners who provide

*(continued)*

*(continued)*

residential facilities for their workers must provide safe and healthy facilities.

- DISCRIMINATION

  While we recognize and respect cultural differences, we believe that workers should be employed on the basis of their ability to do the job, rather than on the basis of personal characteristics or beliefs. We will favor business partners who share this value.

- DISCIPLINARY PRACTICES

  We will not utilize business partners who use corporal punishment or other forms of mental or physical coercion.

## Country Assessment Guidelines

The diverse cultural, social, political, and economic circumstances of the various countries where Levi Strauss & Co. has existing or future business interests raise issues that could subject our corporate reputation and therefore, our business success, to potential harm. The Country Assessment Guidelines are intended to help us assess these issues. The Guidelines are tools that assist us in making practical and principled business decisions as we balance the potential risks and opportunities associated with conducting business in a particular country.

In making these decisions, we consider the degree to which our global corporate reputation and commercial success may be exposed to unreasonable risk. Specifically, we assess whether the:

1. BRAND IMAGE

   would be adversely affected by a country's perception or image among our customers and/or consumers;

2. HEALTH AND SAFETY

   of our employees and their families, or our Company representatives would be exposed to unreasonable risk;

3. HUMAN RIGHTS ENVIRONMENT

   would prevent us from conducting business activities in a manner that is consistent with the Global Sourcing Guidelines and other Company policies;

4. LEGAL SYSTEM

   would prevent us from adequately protecting our trademarks, investments or other commercial interests, or from implementing the Global Sourcing Guidelines and other Company Policies; and

5. POLITICAL, ECONOMIC AND SOCIAL ENVIRONMENT

   would threaten the Company's reputation and/or commercial interests.

In making these assessments, we take into account the various types of business activities and objectives proposed (e.g., procurement of fabric and sundries, sourcing, licensing, direct investments in subsidiaries) and, thus, the accompanying level of risk involved.

Levi Strauss & Co. is committed to continuous improvement in the implementation of its Global Sourcing & Operating Guidelines. As we apply these standards throughout the world, we will acquire greater experience. As has always been our practice, we will continue to take into consideration all pertinent information that helps us better address issues of concern, meet new challenges and update our Guidelines.

and make a public report. Young recently released a report exonerating Nike of responsibility, but exhorted them to strive for continuous improvement.

In the future, each business must decide to adopt its own code and what method of enforcement to utilize. Codes are not laws. (See article on Nike.)

The U.S. government recently issued Model Business Principles to encourage businesses to adhere to human rights standards overseas and to issue codes similar to Levi Strauss. This was the Clinton administration's attempt to broaden the discussion of human rights beyond China. (See Exhibit 2.5.)

Whether this code is embraced by many companies or has any significant impact on business practice must be answered sometime in the future.

# Can't Just Do It Anymore
## Nike's Recent Success Turns Spotlight on Firm—for Better or Worse

BEAVERTON, ORE.—Wearing jeans and, of course, Nikes, Robin Carr-Locke says sometimes public relations for the world's largest sneaker company is easy, like the groove of an early-morning jog.

Then again, she says, sometimes it feels a lot like running in place.

When Nike Inc. signed golfer Tiger Woods, he became her full-time job. She now spends her days—and nights—responding to interview requests ranging from "Inside Edition" to Swedish television. She also gets calls from the general public complaining about Woods's "Hello World" commercial, which says there still are courses where he is not welcome because of the color of his skin.

"It's hard to find adoring media," Carr-Locke said, conceding that she knows she has it easier than most in the 12-person public relations department at Nike's campus here.

Take last week, for example.

On Tuesday, former UN Ambassador Andrew Young issued a report—which was immediately criticized by human rights groups—on Nike's Asian factories. At about the same hour, the company announced a recall of 38,000 sneakers after Muslims said the flame-shaped logo resembled the Arabic word for Allah.

By Wednesday, Nike had placed a full-page ad in The New York Times regarding the Young report, Bloomberg business wire had released nine headlines on Nike, and Garry Trudeau had churned out yet another derogatory Doonesbury strip about Nike's labor practices.

For Nike—whose total revenue has nearly doubled over the past two years to $9 billion—it seems no image is harder to cultivate than its own. . . .

"Nike is the player that everyone wants to talk about. If you have an issue to pick, you want to pick it with the biggest player. You go straight to the top. The reason why we see it so much now is because they're so big," said Brett Barakett, an analyst for Salomon Brothers.

By contrast, officials at Stoughton, Mass.-based Reebok International Ltd.—with $3.5 billion in revenue—faced media criticism several years ago for its own practices at Asian factories.

But, for better or worse, Reebok—the world's No. 2 sneaker maker—is able to go about its business more quietly. . . .

So far, Madkour added, Reebok is holding its own in the market-place, even though many in the industry are comparing its advertising push to Nike's Just Do It Campaign.

Nike news can cannibalize its own messages, too.

After trying for more than a year to swat down reports that its overseas manufacturing facilities mistreated workers and watching the comic strip Doonesbury regularly attack the company on that point, Nike hired Young to visit its Far East plants.

Young said upon his return: "It is my sincere belief that Nike is doing a good job in the application of its code of conduct, but Nike can and should do better."

Reaction to Young's remarks was swift.

Medea Benjamin, president of the San Francisco-based human rights group Global Exchange, said, "Nike has spent millions of dollars buying off major athletes. Now it's bought off Andrew Young."

Yesterday, it was announced that a floor manager at a Taiwanese-owned factory that makes shoes for Nike was sentenced to six months in prison for physically abusing workers. The manager—the second foreign manager brought up on charges of mistreating workers—was accused of making 56 female workers at the Nike plant, just outside Ho Chi Minh City, run laps as punishment for not wearing regulation shoes, according to a labor rights activist.

How does Kathryn Reith compete with that?

One month into her job in the Nike public relations department in charge of women's sports, she is bleary-eyed, just back from a late night in Los Angeles partying with the likes of Queen Latifah to kick off the LA Sparks WNBA game and introduce player Lisa Leslie's signature basketball sneaker.

Nightline and CNN-SI were at NikeTown to record the event. Reith was not there to sip chardonnay.

*(continued)*

*(continued)*

One of the priorities of her job is to try to change a few stereotypes in order to sell more sneakers.

So amid the klieg lights and Hollywood stars, and amid talks of offensive shoes and questionable labor practices in Asia, Reith was selling Nike, telling reporters—mostly male—that yes, women's sports were here to stay and their sneakers are no longer inferior to men's.

While they may seem to be incongruous issues, Reith, back in Beaverton, is still wearily shaking her head over the difficulty the company is having with those two points, at such a crucial time. . . .

*Tina Cassidy*
*Boston Globe*, June 28, 1997.
Reprinted courtesy of the *Boston Globe*.

---

**EXHIBIT 2.5   United States Model Business Principles**

Recognizing the positive role of U.S. business in upholding and promoting adherence to universal standards of human rights, the Administration encourages all businesses to adopt and implement voluntary codes of conduct for doing business around the world that cover at least the following areas:

1. Provision of a safe and healthy workplace.
2. Fair employment practices, including avoidance of child and forced labor and avoidance of discrimination based on race, gender, national origin or religious beliefs; and respect for the right of association and the right to organize and bargain collectively.
3. Responsible environmental protection and environmental practices.
4. Compliance with U.S. and local laws promoting good business practices, including laws prohibiting illicit payments and ensuring fair competition.
5. Maintenance, through leadership at all levels, of a corporate culture that respects free expression consistent with legitimate business concerns, and does not condone political coercion in the workplace; that encourages good corporate citizenship and makes a positive contribution to the communities in which the company operates; and where ethical conduct is recognized, valued and exemplified by all employees.

In adopting voluntary codes of conduct that reflect these principles, U.S. companies should serve as models, encouraging similar behavior by their partners, suppliers, and subcontractors.

Adoption of codes of conduct reflecting these principles is voluntary. Companies are encouraged to develop their own codes of conduct appropriate to their particular circumstances. Many companies already apply statements or codes that incorporate these principles. Companies should find appropriate means to inform their shareholders and the public of actions undertaken in connection with these principles. Nothing in the principles is intended to require a company to act in violation of host country or U.S. laws. This statement of principles is not intended for legislation.

---

# Chapter Summary

Doing business internationally requires an understanding of international (public and private) law, national law, and organizations. Trade between entrepreneurs from different countries can never be totally divorced from the relationships of the home countries of the businesspeople. Political allegiances shift and trade is affected. For example, just as trade between the former Soviet Union and the

United States increased during the late 1970s, the Soviet incursion into Afghanistan and President Jimmy Carter's consequent grain embargo chilled all business ventures. A businessperson must be able to assess astutely the environment and formulate an effective business plan. Knowledge of the host country's legal system and its ramifications for business is essential.

International business law draws from both public and private law as they relate to business transactions. Some of the distinction between public and private international law has been blurred, however, as organizations such as the United Nations, WTO, and various treaties have expanded their effect on business transactions. Treaties such as bilateral tax treaties or multilateral conventions (Convention on the International Sale of Goods, or CISG) create obligations for private parties. Similarly, national law, such as investment codes, can play a substantial role in business decisions. All of these issues together then are considered international business law.

---

## QUESTIONS AND CASE PROBLEMS

1. Where does one look for international law?
2. What is international business law?
3. What role does the World Court play in settling disputes between countries? What are some of its limitations?
4. Does the World Court serve any function in the settlement of disputes involving individuals or business?
5. What impact do national legal systems have on the outcome of business disputes?
6. What is meant by the phrase *the decade of international law?* Is a person unduly optimistic to believe that the rule of international law has been universally accepted?
7. Atlas Corporation, located in the country of Oz, establishes a wholly owned subsidiary in the country of Rogo. Oz and Rogo have entered into a Friendship, Commerce, and Navigation Treaty. After a revolution in Rogo, the new leader nationalizes Atlas and jails its executives (Ozian citizens), alleging that they are "running dogs who have engineered the economic rape of Rogo." What recourse does Atlas have? Assume that Oz and Rogo are both members of the United Nations.
8. What enforcement mechanisms are present in international law?
9. Professor Jones is visiting Singapore for a semester and decides to write a column for the *International Herald Tribune*. He criticized the country's leader, Lee Kuan Yew, as a "liar." Does Professor Jones have any cause for concern given that the United States Constitution offers broad protection for freedom of speech and of the press?
10. What power does the Security Council have to enforce its resolutions? Give examples in which the Council has been utilized successfully. Given its limited success, should the Security Council be expanded? How?

## MANAGERIAL IMPLICATIONS

1. As a CEO of a large chemical company with sites all over the world, do you have any concerns about the impact of a world criminal court on your business? How and to whom will you convey your concerns?
2. Your company, Cool Duds, Inc. manufactures clothes and sells them all over the world. You have several plants located in Third World countries. When you visited the plant in LeBOP, you discover 13 year old children running the machinery. Do you have any concerns about this? Legal concerns? Ethical concerns? Your board has asked for a memo outlining your plan of action.
   a. Does the U.S. code of Model Business Principles help you?
   b. What position, if any, should the United Nations take on this issue?

## NOTES

1. Restatement of the Law, 3rd Foreign Relations, Sect. 101, Copyright 1987 by the American Law Institute. Reprinted with permission of the American Law Institute.
2. David D. Siegel, *Conflicts* p. 2 (West, 1986).
3. Copyright Elsevier Science Publishers, Physical Sciences and Engineering Division, Amsterdam, The Netherlands. Reprinted with Permission.
4. Langvein, "The German Advantage in Civil Procedure," 52 *University of Chicago Law Review* 823, 824 (1985).
5. For additional reading on one example of a legal system, see Nabil Saleh, "The Law Governing Contracts in Arabia" 38 Int. Comp. Law Quarterly 761, 775, 788 (1989).
6. *Juvenile v. State* 64/69, Crim App. No 156/88 Supr. Ct. Zimbabwe 3/22. 6/19 1989. Discussion in 84 *Am. Society of Int. Law* 768 (1990).
7. Reprinted with permission from Earle, Integrating Ethics into an International Business Law Course; 12 Journal of Legal Studies Education 44 (Winter/Spring 1994).
8. Ibid.

# Chapter Three

# The European Union and the Development of Trade Areas

A significant trend in the post–World War II period has been the development of regional economic alliances to facilitate trade. These regional agreements have significant impact on the conduct of business. Historical precedents for economic integration can be traced back as far as Charlemagne; however, the devastation of Europe by World War II and efforts to rebuild were the major forces in bringing the original six European countries—Belgium, West Germany (now called Germany), France, Italy, Luxembourg, and The Netherlands—together to form the Common Market or European Community, the forerunner of the European Union (EU). The European Union, numbering 15 countries with 11 countries hoping to join, is preparing to move toward the ambitious goal of European Monetary Union (EMU) in 1999. The single currency is designed to continue the reforms begun in 1957 and to spur economic growth. This chapter examines the structure and operation of the EU and the ramifications for business. It also looks at the development of other trade areas in the world. The North American Free Trade Agreement (NAFTA) and its precursor, the United States–Canadian Free Trade Agreement (CFTA), are discussed in detail in Chapter 14 on trade.

> **http://europa.eu.int/index.htm**
> See for policies, institutions, and other information on the EU.

## The Philosophy of Economic Integration

Of the numerous paradigms of economic integration, some involve more comprehensive economic and political integration, while others are more limited in scope. The United States of America offers a good starting point for analysis.

### Federal Model

The U.S. model of federalism involves 50 states cooperating and agreeing to have one currency, army, and foreign policy managed by the federal executive branch. The states have autonomy on other matters. The president is the Commander in Chief of the Armed Forces and state law is subordinated to federal law under the Supremacy Clause of the U.S. Constitution. Remember, when the Constitution was drafted, many states were concerned about losing their independence and being subsumed by a national identity. The smaller states were concerned about being overpowered by a large federal nation state as well as the larger former colonies. The Tenth Amendment, adopted in 1791 as part of the Bill of Rights, addressed this concern. It states, "The powers not delegated to the United States by the Constitution, nor prohibited to it by the States are reserved to the States respectively, or to the people." In the vernacular, this statement is called the "states' rights" clause.

The U.S. Constitution is a remarkable document; it managed to allay many concerns by creating a balance of power between the branches of government as well as between federal government and the states. Each state has two senators regardless of its size, while representation in the House of Representatives is based on population. Thus more populated states have more representatives.

Article I, Section 8 of the Constitution states that Congress shall have the power "to make all laws which shall be necessary and proper for carrying into execution the foregoing." In return, the states agreed to one currency, free movement of people between states, the principle of nondiscrimination among states, as well as federal courts to deal with conflict between states, and ceded the power to Congress to regulate commerce. The individual states have also given their authority over international trade to Congress. For purposes of foreign policy, the country acts as one unit. For example, Massachusetts would not send troops to Rwanda without authorization from the federal government. Despite political differences, the states within the country act as one nation.

The U.S. experiment is now over 200 years old and is unquestionably a success; however, this system is not for every constellation of countries. The U.S. model took recently settled colonies, often no more than 100 years old, and politically united them, laying the foundation for future economic cooperation. Other models start from quite the opposite direction, beginning with economic cooperation and moving into political cooperation and possible unification (see Exhibit 3.1).

## Free Trade Area

In contrast to the federal model, a Free Trade Area (FTA) develops when two or more countries agree to eliminate or phase out duties and other barriers to trade among the member countries. The FTA does not attempt to control relations of

**EXHIBIT 3.1  Models of Economic and Political Union**

| Political Union | ⟶ | Economic Union |
|---|---|---|
| Economic Union | ⟶ | Political Union |

member countries to third countries. Thus a country can be a member of an FTA and still have separate bilateral relations with other countries. FTAs vary greatly and have different approaches in handling intercountry disputes. A good dispute settlement mechanism is critical to the success of a FTA. An FTA and a federal system represent the two distinct ends on the continuum of integration.

## Customs Union

A *customs union* is more ambitious in scope than an FTA. Not only does it reduce tariffs between member countries, but the customs union members also agree to deal similarly with nonmembers. The goal is to encourage trade between members just as in the FTA; however, the customs union begins to exhibit fortress-like characteristics that could lead to the erection of barriers to entry for companies and products from nonmember countries.

## Common Market

A *common market* or *economic community* goes further than a customs union by trying to make uniform standards and laws among the member countries. The goal of a common market is the free movement of people, goods, services, and capital within the market. A court with jurisdiction and power to enforce its rulings is a critical element in the effectiveness of the members compliance with the standards and laws. Without effective enforcement, each member state can continue to operate its own protectionist barriers.

## Compatibility of Trade Areas With GATT

At first glance, the principles underlying the formation of trade areas seem to contradict the basic principles of GATT, which require nondiscrimination and reciprocity among all members. How can members of an FTA or customs union treat those members more favorably than other GATT members? Article XXIV of the GATT agreement cryptically states

Accordingly, the provisions of this Agreement shall not prevent, as between the territories of contracting parties, the formation of a customs union or of a free-trade area or the adoption of an interim agreement necessary for the formation of a customs union or of a free-trade area; Provided that: (a) with respect to a customs union, or an interim agreement leading to the formation of a customs union, the duties and other regulations of commerce imposed at the institution of any such union or interim agreement in respect of trade with contracting parties not parties to such union or agreement shall not on the whole be higher or more restrictive than the general incidence of the duties and regulations of commerce applicable in the constituent territories prior to the formation of such union or the adoption of such interim agreement, as the case may be.

This section has been used to lower the rates of external tariffs within a trade area for the benefit of non-FTA, GATT members. This achieves the goals of GATT for the benefit of GATT members.

The following section looks at the example of the EU and its movement from a customs union to common market to European Union and the current uncertainty about future integration efforts.

# European Union

The European Union of today did not spring forth fully developed in its current form. Rather, it developed over a period of years and with successive modifications. Understanding the present issues requires an examination of the Union's past history.

## History

Winston Churchill, former prime minister of Great Britain, stated in 1946 that postwar Europe needed a

. . . Sovereign remedy . . . to recreate the European family, or as much of it as we can, and provide it with a structure under which it can dwell in peace and safety and freedom. We must build a kind of United States of Europe.

Jean Monnet, who held a number of different positions in the French government and is credited as the founding father of the EU, said that "the states of Europe must form a federation." George

Marshall, Secretary of State for the United States, supported this concept as a way to rebuild Europe after World War II and to enable the United States to work with both the victors and the vanquished in Europe as strong strategic allies. They hoped this type of partnership would obviate the possibility of a third world war.

The EU was preceded by several earlier and less ambitious attempts at regional cooperation. The European Coal and Steel Community (ECSC), established in 1952, included the six founding countries and centered on combined price and output controls, investment subsidies, tariff protection, and competition rules. Many of the European coal and steel industries were and are government owned. The ECSC and the respective governments were instrumental in rebuilding the industries after the war and in protecting those industries from competition.

**Treaty of Rome.** The European Community (EC as it was called) was formed by the signing of the Treaty of Rome on March 25, 1957, which created the Common Market. The six member countries (Belgium, West Germany, France, Italy, Luxembourg, and The Netherlands) hoped to build on the success of the ECSC and use the organization to advance all of the countries economically without sacrificing their individuality, culture, or sovereignty.

The Treaty of Rome stated the original objectives of the Community (see Exhibit 3.2).

These principles were based on the creation of a customs union that would both eradicate the internal tariffs and restrictions and create a uniform external tariff for nonmembers. The Community committed to achieving the free movement of people, goods, services, and capital; and to eradicating the barriers to the establishment of business by establishing a single, integrated common market. The goals of the community are often stated as a commitment to the "Four Freedoms"—that is, to the free movement of capital, goods, people, and services.

In the following case, the Treaty of Rome was interpreted to provide rights to individuals from member countries and to have *direct effect*.

In 1965, the Merger Treaty, integrated the ECSC and the EURATOM (European Atomic

---

**EXHIBIT 3.2    Treaty of Rome**

### Article 2

The Community shall have as its task, by establishing a common market and progressively approximating the economic policies of Member States, to promote throughout the Community a harmonious development of economic activities, a continuous and balanced expansion, an increase in stability, an accelerated raising of the standard of living, and closer relations between the States belonging to it.

### Article 3

For the purposes set out in Article 2, the activities of the Community shall include, as provided in this Treaty and in accordance with the timetable set out therein.

A. the elimination, as between Member States, of customs duties and of quantitative restrictions on the import and export of goods, and of the other measures having equivalent effect;
B. the establishment of a common customs tariff and of a common commercial policy towards third countries;
C. the abolition, as between Member States, of obstacles to freedom of movement for persons, services, and capital;
D. the adoption of a common policy in the sphere of agriculture;
E. the adoption of a common policy in the sphere of transport;
F. the institution of a system ensuring that competition in the common market is not distorted;
G. the application of procedures by which the economic policies of Member States can be coordinated and disequilibria in their balances of payments remedied;
H. the approximation of the laws of Member States to the extent required for the proper functioning of the common market;
I. the creation of a European Social Fund in order to improve employment opportunities for workers and to contribute to the raising of their standard of living;
J. the establishment of a European Investment Bank to facilitate the economic expansion of the Community by opening up fresh resources;
K. the association of the overseas countries and territories in order to increase trade and to promote jointly economic and social development.

---

BACKGROUND AND FACTS

On 9 September 1960 the company Van Gend & Loos imported into the Netherlands from the Federal Republic of Germany a quantity of ureaformaldehyde. . . .

Instead of applying, in respect of intra-Community trade, an import duty of 3% uniformly to all products, import duty was fixed at 8%. . . .

The first question is whether Article 12 of the Treaty has direct application in national law in the sense that nationals of Member States may on the basis of this Article lay claim to rights which the national court must protect.

The objective of the EEC Treaty, which is to establish a Common Market, the functioning of which is of direct concern to interested parties in

*N.V. Algeme Transport-en Expedite on-Derneming Van Gend & Loos v. Netherlands Fiscal Administration*

Case No. 26162, February 5, 1963
[1963] E.C.R. 1.
Court of Justice of the
European Communities

the Community, implies that this Treaty is more than an agreement which merely creates mutual obligations between the contracting states. This view is confirmed by the preamble to the Treaty which refers not only to governments but to peoples. It is also confirmed more specifically by the establishment of institutions endowed with sovereign rights, the exercise of which affects Member States and also their citizens. Furthermore, it must be noted that the nationals of the states brought together in the Community are called upon to cooperate in the functioning of this Community through the intermediary of the European Parliament and the Economic and Social Committee.

*(continued)*

*(continued)*

In addition the task assigned to the Court of Justice under Article 177, the object of which is to secure uniform interpretation of the Treaty by national courts and tribunals, confirms that the states have acknowledged that Community law has an authority which can be invoked by their nationals before those courts and tribunals. . . .

[T]he real meaning of the question is whether, in law, an effective increase in customs duties charged on a given product as a result not of an increase in the rate but of a new classification of the product arising from a change of its tariff description contravenes the prohibition in Article 12 of the Treaty. . . .

The vigilance of individuals concerned to protect their rights amounts to an effective supervision in addition to the supervision entrusted by Articles 169 and 170 to the diligence of the Commission and of the Member States.

It follows from the foregoing considerations that, according to the spirit, the general scheme and the wording of the Treaty, Article 12 must be interpreted as producing direct effects and creating individual rights which national courts must protect.

## THE COURT

**Decision.**   In answer to the questions referred to it for a preliminary ruling by the Tariefcommissie by decision of 16 August 1962, [the Court] hereby rules:

1. Article 12 of the Treaty establishing the European Economic Community produces direct effects and creates individual rights which national courts must protect.
2. In order to ascertain whether customs duties or charges having equivalent effect have been increased contrary to the prohibition contained in Article 12 of the Treaty, regard must be had to the duties and charges actually applied by the Member State in question at the date of the entry into force of the Treaty.

Such an increase can arise both from a rearrangement of the tariff resulting in the classification of the product under a more highly taxed heading and from an increase in the rate of customs duty applied.

---

Energy Commission, which was dedicated to the peaceful development and application of nuclear energy) into the organizational structure of the EC. Denmark, Ireland, and the United Kingdom joined in 1973, Greece in 1981, Portugal and Spain in 1986, and Austria, Sweden, and Finland in 1995.

**1992 and the Single European Act.**   The ensuing years saw some progress towards the ambitious goals stated in the Treaty of Rome, but the dream of free movement of capital, goods, people, and services was not a reality between the member countries. Even today, fewer than two percent of the EU population lives outside of the country of their birth.

In the 1980s, the members of the EC realized that because of their growth in membership and strong national allegiances and the accompanying protectionism, they had not achieved the goals of the Treaty of Rome. In 1985, the members called "for the abolition of barriers of all kinds, harmonization of rules, approximation of legislation and tax structures, strengthening of monetary cooperation, and the necessary . . . measures to encourage European firms to work

together." The members acknowledged the need to eliminate physical barriers—such as custom checks at borders, veterinary and plant checks, technical standards and building codes, and services and professional standards—and to revamp VAT (Value Added Tax) collection. As a result of this realization and the promise of increased competitiveness upon the elimination of these barriers, the twelve existing members enacted the Single European Act (SEA), effective July 1, 1987. The purpose of the SEA was to strengthen the EC institutions and enable them to act and thus to achieve the goals of the Treaty of Rome. The SEA also set the deadline December 31, 1992, to achieve economic integration.

The Single European Act signalled a dramatic move away from business as usual. The members abandoned the requirement of unanimous consent to move forward and adopted the concept of qualified majority voting. This change meant that for proposals related to the internal market all the countries did not have to agree—the community could make decisions in spite of some objection.

**Maastricht and the Monetary Union.**   After the passage of the SEA, the pace of change within the

Community quickened. Members began to think and discuss the next steps of integration including a single currency, central bank, a unified foreign and security policy at meetings in 1989 and 1990. The leaders were divided in their vision of Europe. Britain, as voiced by former Prime Minister Margaret Thatcher, saw a limited role for the Community and zealously guarded the autonomy of members. Other countries, notably Germany, pressed for a more unified Europe. Part of the conflict centered around the vision of a federal Europe or how far toward a United States of Europe the Community would move. Students in the United States are familiar with the division of power and allocation by the Constitution between state and federal government. For the British, however, *federal* was a dirty word, signaling a loss of control over domestic matters.

The recession had been slower to hit Europe than the United States, and so the buoyancy of an expanding economy led to optimism about the future. Also, the sheer enormity of incorporating East Germany into Germany after the 1989 fall of the Berlin Wall had not been absorbed. Nor did European nations fully appreciate the growing pressures of nationalism that were set free along with the crumbling of communism.

In December 1991, the twelve leaders met in Maastricht, the Netherlands, and hammered out the historic agreement known as *Maastricht Treaty*. The Treaty needed ratification by the member states and in 1993 the European Union was born. Ratification was not a simple process, nor one whose outcome was guaranteed. Several referendums had narrow margins supporting ratification and the Danish voters rejected the Treaty in the first instance. National legal issues were also brought to the courts. For example, in Germany a number of challenges to the Treaty were raised. The most serious issue was that it transferred power to the new Union, which had been guaranteed to German citizens under Article 38 of the German Basic Law. The following case shows the discussion of the issues and the decision that ushered in the beginning of the EU on November 1, 1993. (See Exhibit 3.3 for members.)

---

## Germany Federal Constitutional Court Decision Concerning the Maastricht Treaty

### 33 I.L.M. 388 (1994)
### Federal Constitutional Court of Germany[1]

**BACKGROUND AND FACTS**

The case was brought as a result of constitutional complaints filed by two classes of complainants, the first being a group of politicians and professors, including a prominent former official of the EEC, and the second being several German members of the European Parliament belonging to the "Green" Party. The complaints challenged the constitutionality of the Maastricht Treaty, which was signed at Maastricht on February 7, 1992. Under the Treaty, the Member States of the former European Communities amended the various treaties and legal instruments establishing the European Communities in order to achieve further integration on the social, monetary, and political levels. . . .

Article N of the Maastricht Treaty states that it shall come into force "after being ratified by all the Member States in accordance with their respective constitutional requirements." Under Article 59(2) of the German Basic Law, parliamentary ratification is required for most treaties entered into by the Federal Republic of Germany. On December 2, 1992, the Federal Parliament *(Bundestag)* adopted a law approving the Maastricht Treaty by a vote of 543 to 25, and on December 18, 1992, the Federal Council *(Bundesrat)* approved this law unanimously. The law was then promulgated on December 30, 1992, and entered into force on December 31, 1992. However, it was still necessary for the Federal President *(Bundespräsident)* to sign the Instrument of Ratification, and before this happened constitutional complaints were filed as mentioned above with the Federal Constitutional Court. The Federal President then stated that he would not sign the Instrument of Ratification until the Federal Constitutional Court had reached a decision in the case. Oral hearings were held by the Court on July 1 and 2, 1993, and on October 12, 1993, the Court announced its decision.

*(continued)*

*(continued)*

## THE FEDERAL CONSTITUTIONAL COURT

The complainants alleged that the German Act of Accession to the Maastricht Treaty and the Act Amending the Basic Law, which had been adopted earlier, would violate their constitutional rights as follows:

1. Article F, paragraph 3 of the Treaty grants the European Union an exclusive competence for jurisdictional conflicts which it can use to assume any further responsibilities it may require, thereby violating the German peoples' right of representation by their elected representatives;

2. The European Union evidences a lack of democracy, in that real decisions are reached by the heads of government, rather than the ostensibly-democratic institutions such as the European Parliament;

3. The fact that citizens of other Member States will be granted the right to vote and to stand as candidates in elections in Germany violates the rights of German citizens to vote and to stand as candidates in elections;

4. The Maastricht Treaty reduces the protection of basic rights by the Federal Constitutional Court by transferring some of the responsibility for their protection to the institutions of the European Union;

5. The entry into a monetary union will eventually result in the adoption of a common European currency, thereby eliminating the right to pay and be paid in Deutsche Marks;

6. The Maastricht Treaty transfers various sovereign rights from Germany to the European Union in a way which is unconstitutional, and which will result in elimination of the constitutional order set forth in the Basic Law;

7. The expansion of the powers of the European Union will mean that in many cases laws will be adopted not by the legislator, but by the executive branch that has the responsibility for enforcing them;

8. Entry into the European Union will eventually threaten the existence of Germany as an independent, sovereign state, and therefore will infringe upon rights which are supposed to be inviolable under the Basic Law;

9. There is a basic right to hold a referendum on the Maastricht Treaty, which has not been observed.

In ruling on constitutional complaints, the Federal Constitutional Court first determines if they are admissible *(zulässig),* and if so, whether they are well-founded *(begründet).* In this case, the Court found that one of the complaints regarding a diminution of democracy in the European Union was admissible, but that none of them were well-founded. Its decision on the one admissible constitutional complaint was based on the fact that, under the principle of democracy which underlies the Basic Law, the Federal Government may not assign the duties and rights of the Federal Parliament to the European Union to such an extent that the minimum requirements of democratic legitimation would be violated. That is, while the principle of democracy does not prevent Germany from becoming a member of an "intergovernmental community" such as the European Union, there must be some minimum amount of democracy which remains vested with the national authorities of the Member States. However, after examining both German constitutional law and the structure and history of the Maastricht Treaty, the Court found that no such violation had occurred in this case, since the German constitutional order evidences a favorable attitude toward European integration, and the institutions of the European Union are sufficiently democratic to survive constitutional challenge.

The Court rejected all the other constitutional complaints. It found that previous amendments to the *Grundgesetz* providing for a transfer of some competencies of the German Central Bank to the European Union meant that the German Basic Law recognized the development of the European Monetary Union. Moreover, the Court noted, it was not necessarily true that the Deutsche Mark would automatically be replaced by the ECU someday. With regard to basic rights, the Federal Constitutional Court found that it would continue to oversee the protection of basic rights sufficiently, and that such rights would also be protected by the European Court of Justice and other institutions of the European Union.

**Comment.**  The Court's emphasis on protecting basic rights under the national laws of the Member States, rather than under the international law of human rights applicable within the European Union, leaves the reader with the distinct impression that it has less than total confidence in the ability of the Union to protect basic rights. The Court is also determined to ensure that any
*(continued)*

*(continued)*

interpretation of the Union's powers is kept within strict limits, even stating that an interpretation which exceeds such powers would have no binding effect in Germany. This conclusion could introduce a good deal of uncertainty into the German legal system, since there is no central authority for determining when the entities of the Communities have exceeded their powers.

One of the complaints brought against the Maastricht Treaty was that it allows the executive to allocate powers to the European Union, which properly belong to the legislative branch. While the Court did not fully accept this argument, the limits the Court set on the transfer of sovereignty from the Federal Republic of Germany may lead to strains in Germany's constitutional structure in the future if the German parliament is faced with approving a further expansion of the Union's powers.

In regard to the only one of the constitutional complaints the Federal Constitutional Court held to be admissible, the Court found that Article 38, paragraphs 1 and 2, of the Basic Law grants to German citizens not only a formal right to vote, but also a guarantee to participate in the legitimation of the organs of government and to influence the implementation of state power. These findings may have far-reaching consequences since they leave open the possibility of constitutional claims being brought by German citizens based upon the assertion that the competencies of the German Federal Parliament are being infringed by the European Union.

---

**EXHIBIT 3.3    Current Members of the European Union (372 million people):**

| | |
|---|---|
| ORIGINAL | Belgium<br>Germany<br>France<br>Italy<br>Luxembourg<br>The Netherlands |
| 1973 | Denmark<br>Ireland<br>United Kingdom |
| 1981 | Greece |
| 1986 | Portugal<br>Spain |
| 1995 | Austria<br>Finland |

Potential New Members:
Lithuania, Latvia, Estonia, Czech Republic, Slovenia, Bulgaria, Hungary, Slovakia, Romania, Poland, Cyprus, and Turkey (unlikely)

---

The Maastricht Treaty commits the EU countries to monetary union by 1999. The European Central Bank in Frankfort, Germany, newly created, will set interest rates and impose certain criteria. Monetary union offers member countries both the hope of Europe becoming more competitive and the fear of losing national control over something so critical to a country's destiny as fiscal policy. Before a country can join the single currency, it must meet several criteria. In May 1998, leaders of the EU countries will meet to determine which countries meet the criteria.

Britain had negotiated an "opt out" from the agreement to go forward on monetary union, but recently the Blair government has signaled an interest in joining the single currency sometime after its inauguration in 1999. This represents a sea change in attitude, and the news bodes well for the EMU. Denmark and Sweden have voiced reservations to the plan for monetary union.

The Maastricht criteria focus on trying to move countries together to "sustainable convergence." The criteria are listed below:

- *Budget deficit* no greater than 3 percent of GDP. GDP is defined as gross domestic product, which includes consumer spending, business investment, government purchases, and net exports.
- *Public debt* no more than 60 percent of GDP.
- *Price stability*—inflation within 1.5 percent of three best countries.
- *Long-term interest rates* within 2 percent of three best countries.
- *Exchange rate stability*—2 years within the band of the Exchange Rate Mechanism (ERM).

Why are these criteria so important? It is reported that 60 percent of EU trade is among EU nations. The Euro, the future currency unit, will make this trade easier. The Euro will also be a boon to businesspeople from outside the EU who want to enter the single market. The common currency, however, will indubitably increase and intensify competition.

The danger of monetary union for EU countries is that if a recession hits one country, it will no longer be able to individually lower interest rates or devalue its currency—only the central bank could do that. The coping mechanism for people in the United States facing a recession in one part of the country is to move to another section of the country—for example, Texas or California—which may be prospering economically. This strategy will not be attractive to Europeans, who are not as mobile and who do not see Italy and Sweden as fungible environments. The EU countries must believe that this recession danger is offset by the overall gains of increased investment and stimulation of economic growth.

The following timetable is set by the Maastricht Treaty:

May 1998: determination of which countries meet criteria; exchange rates set.

January 1, 1999: Euro-single currency is born;

1999–2002: National currencies continue to exist until 2002, work in parallel.

The Maastricht Treaty has three so called "pillars." The first, monetary union, has received the most press. The second pillar is a common foreign and security policy; since 1991, however, there has been little progress on this front, and it is stated only as a goal. One need but look at the Bosnia fiasco to know that Europe does not speak with one voice. The EU does not appear to have momentum to move in this arena. The third pillar addresses justice and home affairs concerning asylum, immigration, terrorism, and drugs. An example of progress under this third pillar is the Schengen Agreement. Thirteen countries have signed the agreement and seven are full members. The goal is free travel without the necessity of showing passports within the member countries. Britain has been opposed to this agreement because of concerns about terrorists and drug traffic.

The entire unification process has been complicated by the fears that member countries will lose autonomy, but the principle of "subsidiarity" enshrined in the Maastricht Treaty assuages some of these concerns. *Subsidiarity* means that the EU will only take action in those areas that are particularly appropriate for community-level action and that whenever possible the individual country will be able to address the issue itself.

The Treaty "marks a new stage in the process of creating an ever closer union among peoples in Europe in which decisions are taken as closely as possible to the citizen." The goals are stated in Title I, article B, shown in Exhibit 3.4. Maastricht also increases the use of qualified majority voting, which limits the ability of countries to deadlock the Union.

---

**EXHIBIT 3.4  Goals of the Maastricht Treaty**

**Title I**

*Common Provisions*
The Union shall set itself the following objectives:

- to promote economic and social progress which is balanced and sustainable, in particular through the creation of an area without internal frontiers, through the strengthening of economic and social cohesion and through the establishment of economic and monetary union, ultimately including a single currency in accordance with the provisions of this Treaty.
- to assert its identity on the international scene, in particular through the implementation of a common foreign and security policy including the eventual framing of a common defense policy, which might in time lead to a common defense.
- to strengthen the protection of the rights and interests of the nationals of its Member States through the introduction of a citizenship of the Union.
- to develop close cooperation on justice and home affairs.
- to maintain in full the "acquis communautaire" and build on it with a view to considering, through the procedure referred to in Article N(2), to what extent the policies and forms of cooperation introduced by this Treaty may need to be revised with the aim of ensuring the effectiveness of the mechanisms and the institutions of the Community.

The objectives of the Union shall be achieved as provided in this Treaty and in accordance with the conditions and the timetable set out therein while respecting the principle of subsidiarity as defined in Article 3b of the Treaty establishing the European Community.

The Treaty commits to a phase in process for the monetary union. The first phase is the continuation of fiscal tax policies and the freeing of movement of capital between countries. During the second stage, a European Monetary Institute, created by 1994, lays the groundwork for the creation of a European central bank and a European system of central banks. The third stage begins on January 1, 1999, unless another date is set, and then follows the "rapid introduction" of the Euro as the single currency.

---

*http://europa.eu.int/en/record/mt/top.html*
*This is the site of the text and provisions of the Maastricht Treaty.*

---

## Structure of the European Union

The Treaty of Rome allocated power between the Council of Ministers, the Commission, the Assembly or Parliament, and the Court of Justice. This structure was not disturbed by the Maastricht Treaty; however, new members changed the seats allocated to each country.

**The Council.**   The Council is located in Brussels, Belgium. It is composed of one representative of each member state. The position of president of the Council rotates among the membership every six months. The purpose of the Council is to coordinate economic policies of member states and "to make decisions," which includes approving legislation and international agreements.

With the accession of Finland, Austria, and Sweden the votes were changed to the following:

| | |
|---|---|
| Belgium | 5 |
| Denmark | 3 |
| Germany | 10 |
| Greece | 5 |
| Spain | 8 |
| France | 10 |
| Ireland | 3 |
| Italy | 10 |
| Luxembourg | 2 |
| The Netherlands | 5 |
| Austria | 4 |
| Portugal | 5 |
| Finland | 3 |
| Sweden | 4 |
| United Kingdom | 10 |
| TOTAL | 87 |

Qualified majority voting was introduced by the SEA. A qualified majority requires 62 votes (71 percent). The number of votes needed to block legislation equals 26 votes. However, the members have agreed that if 23–25 votes are cast against a measure, the measure will be delayed so "a satisfactory solution could be adopted by at least 65 votes." This measure was called the "Ioannina compromise" crafted by the Council president to address British and Spanish objections to increasing the difficulty of blocking a Council action. As a practical matter, two larger countries and a smaller country can block EU action.

**The Commission.**   The Commission consists of 20 members who theoretically represent the Community rather than specific national interests. The 20 seats are apportioned as

| | |
|---|---|
| France | 2 |
| Spain | 2 |
| Germany | 2 |
| Italy | 2 |
| United Kingdom | 2 |
| Denmark | 1 |
| Ireland | 1 |
| Greece | 1 |
| Portugal | 1 |
| Belgium | 1 |
| The Netherlands | 1 |
| Luxembourg | 1 |
| Finland | 1 |
| Austria | 1 |
| Sweden | 1 |

Each member, appointed by the Council, serves a four-year term and may be reappointed. The Commission is the most ambitious attempt to become supranational and to forge a Community identity. The Commission elects a president from among its members. The president must be approved by the Parliament. Each commissioner is in charge of a special area based in part on the country's interest. The commissioners head up the directorates and are staffed by the cabinets.

The commissioners are named to coordinate such areas as agriculture, competition, single-market, and common-trade policies; transport; and the various geographic regions themselves. The directorates serve as support to the commissioners. Much of the work of the Commission is done in the directorates, where policies are developed. The Commission proposes regulations to the Council.

**The Court of Justice.** The European Court of Justice (ECJ) in Luxembourg functions as the final arbiter of EU law. Fifteen justices are appointed by the Council for a term of six years; one justice is appointed from each country. The Court is fashioned in the civil law tradition because most of the judges come from civil, rather than common law, jurisdictions. The Court's procedure reflects civil law influences. More specifically, unlike the United Kingdom or Ireland, the Court itself calls witnesses, demands the production of documents, and hires necessary experts. The Court recently has allowed limited cross-examination by the parties. (See Exhibit 3.5.)

Several other features serve to distinguish this court. First the decisions of the Court are issued without any dissenting opinions. This practice does not indicate total agreement among the justices; however, the public is not privy to it as in the United States where the public, press, and legal scholars examine dissenting opinions to divine the theoretical differences between the judges and to predict future outcomes on different cases. This EU process helps to protect the national judges from pressure within their state, an issue about which U.S. Supreme Court judges, appointed for life, do not have to worry.

---

**EXHIBIT 3.5  Court of Justice Jurisdiction**

**Court of Justice Jurisdiction Includes**

Proceedings for

- Failure to meet an obligation.
- Annulment of community legislation.
- Failure to act by community institution.
- Action for damages by community institution.
- Appeals.
- Preliminary ruling—clarification of community law.

---

The Court also has positions of advocates general, a position unfamiliar in the United States or Britain, but found in France, for example. Both the parties, as well as the Advocate General, submit their positions on the case to the Court. Often, although not required, the Court bases its opinion on the material from the Advocate General.

National courts are obligated to follow Community law and the ECJ decisions. An English Court recognized this authority in a famous opinion noting the difference between English and Community law, but nonetheless followed the controlling Community law. Lord Denning in *Bulmer v. Bollinger* (1974) stated

The (EC) Treaty is quite unlike any of the enactments to which we have become accustomed. . . . It lays down general principles. It expresses its aims and purposes. All in sentences of moderate length and commendable style. But it lacks precision. It uses words and phrases without defining what they mean. An English lawyer would look for an interpretation clause, but he would look in vain. There is none. All the way through the Treaty there are gaps and lacunae. These have to be filled in by the judges, or by the regulations or directives. It is the European way. . . . Seeing these differences, what are the English courts to do when they are faced with a problem of interpretation? They must follow the European pattern. No longer must they argue about the precise grammatical sense. They must divine the spirit of the Treaty and gain inspiration from it. If they find a gap, they must fill it as best they can. . . . These are the principles as I understand it, on which the European Court acts.

The Court of Justice must also interpret Community law and is the ultimate authority for these conflicts. A famous case, called the *Cassis de Dijon Case,* illustrates how the Court addressed a conflict between German law and the Treaty of Rome.

The Court of the First Instance was established and went into operation in September 1989 to help reduce the workload of the European Court of Justice. It has jurisdiction over appeals of the Commission's decisions on mergers and acquisitions, as well as penalties imposed for price fixing and other actions taken by the Commission. It will also hear cases between EU institutions and their respective employees. If this court functions

## BACKGROUND AND FACTS

Rewe, a limited liability company with an office in Cologne, Germany, imports goods from member countries. On September 14, 1976, Rewe applied to the defendant, the Federal Monopoly for Spirits (a German agency) for permission to import certain spirits. The defendant responded that authorization was not necessary but that only spirits with at least 32 percent alcohol could be marketed in Germany according to German law. Cassis de Dijon had only 15–20 percent spirit content and thus could not be imported. The German court referred the case to the Court of Justice to deal with conflicts between German law and Articles 30 and 37 of the EC treaty.

The plaintiff takes the view that the fixing by the German rules of a minimum alcohol content leads to the result that well-known spirits products from other Member States of the Community cannot be sold in the Federal Republic of Germany and that the said provision therefore constitutes a restriction on the free movement of goods between Member States which exceeds the bounds of the trade rules reserved to them. In its view, it is a measure having an effect equivalent to a quantitative restriction on imports, contrary to Article 30 of the ECC Treaty. Since, furthermore, it is a measure adopted within the context of the management of the spirits monopoly, the plaintiff considers that there is also an infringement of Article 37. . . .

The Government of the Federal Republic of Germany, intervening in the proceedings, put forward various arguments which, in its view, justify the application of provisions relating to the minimum alcohol content of alcoholic beverages, adducing considerations relating on the one hand to the protection of public health and on the other to the protection of the consumer against unfair commercial practices.

As regards the protection of public health, the German Government states that the purpose of the fixing of minimum alcohol content by national legislation is to avoid the proliferation of alcoholic beverages on the national market, in particular alcoholic beverages with low alcohol content, since, in its view, such products may more easily induce a tolerance toward alcohol than more highly alcoholic beverages.

Such considerations are not decisive since the consumer can obtain on the market an extremely

## Rewe-Zentral AG, Bundesmono-Polverwaltung fur Branntwein, (Cassis de Dijon Case)

Case No. 120/78,
February 20, 1979
In CCH 8542 p. 7778
Court of Justice of the
European Communities

wide range of weakly or moderately alcoholic products, and furthermore a large proportion of alcoholic beverages with a high alcohol content freely sold on the German market is generally consumed in a diluted form.

The German Government also claims that the fixing of a lower limit for the alcohol content of certain liqueurs is designed to protect the consumer against unfair practices on the part of producers and distributors of alcoholic beverages. This argument is based on the consideration that the lowering of the alcohol content secures a competitive advantage in relation to beverages with a higher alcohol content, since alcohol is by far the most expensive constituent of beverages by reason for the high rate of tax to which it is subject. Furthermore, according to the German Government, to allow alcoholic products into free circulation wherever, as regards their alcohol content, they comply with the rules laid down in the country of production would have the effect of imposing as a common standard within the Community the lowest alcohol content permitted in any of the Member States, and even of rendering any requirements in this field inoperative since a lower limit of this nature is foreign to the rules of several Member States.

It therefore appears that the unilateral requirement imposed by the rules of a Member State of a minimum alcohol content for the purposes of the sale of alcoholic beverages is an obstacle to trade which is incompatible with the provision of Article 30 of the Treaty. There is therefore no valid reason why, provided that they have been lawfully produced and marketed in one of the Member States, alcoholic beverages should not be introduced into any other Member State; the sale of such products may not be subject to a legal prohibition on the marketing of beverages with an alcohol content lower than the limit set by the national rules.

**Decision.** The Court found that the minimum alcohol requirement effectively excluded products from other member states and was not for a purpose in the general interest that would "take precedence over the requirements of the free movement of goods." Therefore, it struck down Germany's attempt to restrict the products' entry into the country.[2]

well, its jurisdiction may be expanded in the future to include certain trade disputes, much as the Court of International Trade functions in the United States. As of 1995 there are 15 judges. The first women judges to this court were appointed in 1995 by Finland and Sweden.

> **http://europa.eu.int/cj/en/index.htm**
> The home page for the Court of Justice of the EC.

**The Parliament.** The Parliament is served by elected representatives from each state. Originally the members were each appointed for a five-year term but now they are elected directly by the people for terms set by state law. The current number of representatives has increased to 626 because of additional seats added by the inclusion of the former East Germany into Germany. The accession of Finland, Austria, and Sweden added 16, 21, and 22 seats, respectively.

| | |
|---|---|
| Belgium | 25 |
| Denmark | 16 |
| Germany | 99 |
| Greece | 25 |
| Spain | 64 |
| France | 87 |
| Ireland | 15 |
| Italy | 87 |
| Luxembourg | 6 |
| The Netherlands | 31 |
| Austria | 21 |
| Portugal | 25 |
| Finland | 16 |
| Sweden | 22 |
| United Kingdom | 87 |

The Parliament is divided among political factions that create alliances across national boundaries including the Socialists, Christian Democrats, European Democrat Alliance, Communists, Rainbow Group, Rightist, and Unaligned. The Parliament elects a president as well. Originally the powers of the Parliament were limited to a general consultative role but with the power to censure the commission and force their resignation by a two-thirds majority vote. They have never used this power. They also had the power to reject the budget.

The Maastricht Treaty significantly strengthened the role of Parliament. The Parliament now approves the appointment of members of the European Commission. It must approve international agreements. It has new co-decision powers with the Council of Ministers on measures dealing with the single market and other significant areas such as consumer protection, the environment, health, education, and culture. Exhibit 3.6 summarizes the relationship of the European Union institutions.

**Distinction Between Institutions.** Non-Europeans have some difficulty following developments in the EU because of lack of clarity about the institutions. The Council of Ministers can be confused with the Council of Europe, or the Conseil de l'Europe. The latter is separate from the European Union, but it meets in the same building as the Parliament in Strasbourg, France, called the Palais de l'Europe. The Council has all the EU members plus a number of other countries, including Switzerland. To be a member, a country must be a parliamentary democracy and recognize human rights. The Council has a European Court of Human Rights that hears complaints about violations of the European Convention on Human Rights and the Anti-Torture Convention. The Council works to support democracy and human rights and to address the issues facing Europe. Russia was recently rejected as a member because it did not meet the criteria for membership at this stage in its development.

Similarly one should not confuse the Court of Justice in Luxembourg with the International Court of Justice (annexed by statute to the United Nations Charter) or the European Court of Human Rights. The Luxembourg Court, an EU institution, hears cases dealing with the interpretation of the Treaty of Rome, Maastricht Treaty, or EU legislation and with conflicts between EU and national law.

## Harmonization: Directives and Regulations

Much of the work of achieving the goal of a barrier free internal market is accomplished through the process of harmonization or approximation of laws. In other words, the member countries strive to make their laws similar in order to have

**EXHIBIT 3.6  European Union Institutions**

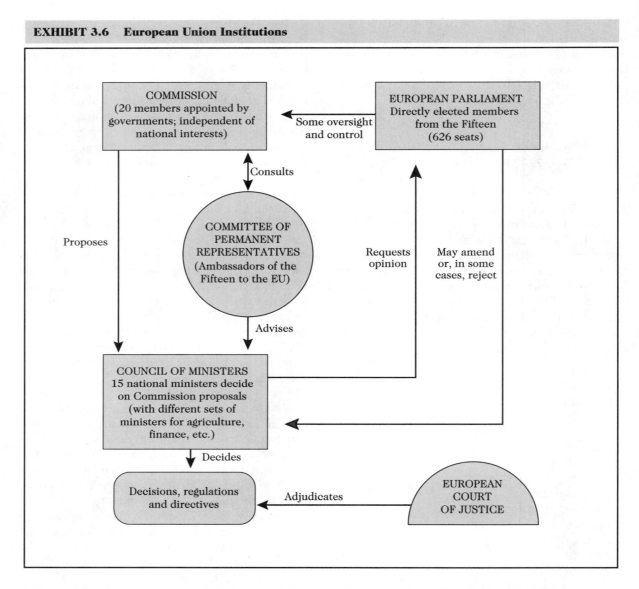

a common legal environment. Article 189 of the Treaty of Rome states that

- A regulation shall have general application. It shall be binding in its entirety and directly applicable in all member states.
- A directive shall be binding as to the result to be achieved upon each member state to which it is addressed but shall leave to the national authorities the choice of form and methods.
- A decision shall be binding in its entirety upon those to whom it is addressed.
- Recommendations and Opinions shall have no binding force.

Thus, the Council, Commission, and Parliament have several avenues open to them. Regulations having direct effect on the states, without the necessity of passing national legislation, have been used in the agriculture and competition areas and most recently in the area of merger regulations. Directives, in contrast to regulations, require that members bring their laws into harmony with the standard stated in the directive. This approach has been used in the environmental and products liability areas, to mention two. Politically, directives allow members more autonomy to implement the legislative program. Frequently directives allow a country three years to implement the required measures. The problem attendant with a directive, however, is that national legislation may not comply with the directive, forcing the Commission to initiate action (in the Court of Justice) to force compliance of the member state. One EU lawyer commented that this part of implementation was like "slogging through mud," trying to bring the member nations into compliance on a number of issues. A European Commission study reports that as of April 1994, 85 percent of the necessary national legislation had been implemented to achieve the single market. However, at the same time, only 119 of the 230 identified measures have been implemented in all twelve states. Surprisingly the Danes and the Portuguese have been the most efficient in implementing national legislation, whereas Germany, Greece, and Ireland have been the slowest to bring their national law into compliance.

The famous "beer" case illustrates that problems still arise within the member states. The Germans' thinly veiled concern about competition in the 1987 case is still present over ten years later. American beer imports containing maize and rice, which are very popular with Germany's young people, continue their onslaught on the competition and continue to offend beer purists. (See the article.)

The court reached a contrary result in the Mirepoix case, but the relevant Community rule had not previously addressed the pesticide at issue.

---

### BACKGROUND AND FACTS

German law, dating back to Bavaria in 1516, in the *Biersteuergesetz* [Law on Beer Duty], has prohibited additives in the manufacture of beer. Although certain additives are permitted in other food, according to German foodstuffs law, they are prohibited in beer.

The Community, in its efforts to harmonize laws, issued four Council directives on additives. The Commission notified Germany on February 12, 1982, that its beer law created barriers to importing member states' products and thus violated Articles 30 and 36 of the Treaty, which state:

### ARTICLE 30

Quantitative restrictions on imports and all measures having equivalent effect shall without prejudice to the following provisions be prohibited between the member states.

### ARTICLE 36

The provisions of Article 30–34 shall not preclude prohibitions or restrictions on imports, exports, or goods in transit justified on the grounds of public morality, public policy, or public security; the protection of life of humans, animals, or plants. . . . Such prohibitions or re-

**Commission of European Communities v. Federal Republic of Germany**

Case No. 178/84
March 12, 1987
Court of Justice of the European Communities

strictions shall not, however, constitute a means of arbitrary discrimination or a disguised restriction on trade between member states.

Germany defended its action on several grounds, including that it would mislead consumers to label such a drink with additives (substitutes for malted barley) as "bier" and cause a public health concern. The government cited a survey that "beer" meant a beverage produced exclusively from malted barley and containing no additives.

### THE COURT

Firstly, consumers' conceptions which vary from one Member State to the other are also likely to evolve in the course of time within a Member State. The establishment of the Common Market is, it should be added, one of the factors that may play a major contributory role in that development. Whereas rules protecting consumers against misleading practices enable such a development to be taken into account, legislation of the kind contained in Paragraph 10 of the Biersteuergesetz prevents it from taking place. As the Court of Justice has already held in another context (judgment of February 27, 1980, in Case No. 170/78, Commission v. United Kingdom [1980] E.C.R. 417 [8651]), the

*(continued)*

*(continued)*

legislation of the kind contained in Paragraph 10 of the Biersteuergesetz prevents it from taking place. As the Court of Justice has already held in another context (judgment of February 27, 1980, in Case No. 170/78, Commission v. United Kingdom [1980] E.C.R. 417 [8651]), the legislation of a Member State must not "crystallize given consumer habits so as to consolidate an advantage acquired by the national industries concerned to comply with them." . . .

The German designation 'Bier' and its equivalents in the languages of the other Member States of the Community may therefore not be restricted to beers manufactured in accordance with the rules in force in the Federal Republic of Germany. . . .

By indicating the raw materials utilized in the manufacture of beer "such a course would enable the consumer to make his choice in full knowledge of the facts, and would guarantee transparency in trading and in offers to the public." It must be added that such a system of mandatory consumer information must not entail negative assessments for beers not complying with the requirements of Paragraph 9 of the Biersteuergesetz. . . .

In the Commission's opinion, the absolute ban on the marketing of beers containing additives cannot be justified on public-health grounds. It maintains that the other Member States control very strictly the utilization of additives in foodstuffs and do not authorize the use of any given additive until thorough tests have established that it is harmless. In the Commission's view, there should be a presumption that beers manufactured in other Member States which contain additives authorized there represent no danger to public health.

In view of the foregoing considerations, it must be held that by prohibiting the marketing of beers lawfully manufactured or marketed in another Member State if they do not comply with Paragraphs 9 and 10 of the Biersteuergesetz, the Federal Republic of Germany has failed to fulfill its obligations under Article 30 of the EEC Treaty.

**Decision.**   The Court found that Germany's regulations violated Article 30 and ordered Germany to pay costs. The opinion made reference to the earlier *Rewe* opinion and said that this decision was consistent with the earlier decision.[3]

---

*Foreign Accents*

# American Beer in Germany

## Brew-ha-ha

At this year's Oktoberfest in Munich, the capital of Bavaria, Germany's *Braumeisters* have a lot to swallow. It is bad enough that in the past six years worries about health and fitness have helped push annual beer consumption down from 142 litres (250 pints) to 131.7 litres per person in Germany, a country with 1,230 breweries. But now the brewers have to face a cheeky American challenge as well.

In invading Germany, the two biggest American brewers, Anheuser-Busch of St Louis and Miller of Milwaukee, espy a niche market. Nicholas Crossley, a general manager for Miller's operations in continental Europe, says: "Our target consumer in Germany is 18–25 years old, upwardly mobile, part of the contemporary scene, brand conscious, into sports, into Levi's—very aware of American influence."

So strong is the American influence that Germany's youngsters consider it fashionable to be seen drinking bottles of Miller Genuine Draft or Anheuser-Busch's "B" beer at German clubs and discos. At $DM_5$ to $DM_7$ ($2.80 to $4) a bottle, Miller Genuine Draft costs twice as much as high quality German beer, but this seems to worry them not at all. They are only too willing to pay extra for the American image and status.

The fact that the founders of Miller and Anheuser-Busch, Frederick Miller and Adolphus Busch, were German-born does not seem to make the brew any less exotic to today's young trend-seeking guzzlers. It does, however, have Anheuser-Busch executives a bit peeved at having to market their world-famous Budweiser brand as "B" beer in

*(continued)*

*(continued)*
its ancestral homeland; Budweiser Budvar, a rival from the neighbouring Czech Republic, is Germany's top imported beer and holds trademark protection there.

"It is a hindrance," admits Mark Danner, a top Anheuser-Busch executive for Europe. "But we're doing what we can to market the 'B' brand, and it's working."

German brewers are not amused. "It is true that American beer is fashionable with youth now," sniffs Bech & Co's Jurgen Anfang. "But how long will that last?" Less callow Germans, he notes, find it

hard to take seriously beer that does not comply with the *Reinheitsgebot*. This German purity law has been in effect since 1516 and demands that German beer be made only from water, hops, malt (traditionally barley or wheat) and yeast. As Miller beer contains maize and Anheuser-Busch's contains rice as well, these beverages are seen by German brewers and many older drinkers as ersatz substitutes for native brews.

© 1997 The Economist Newspaper Group, Inc. Reprinted with permission. Further reproduction prohibited.

---

## Ministere Public v. Xavier Mirepoix

ECR 1067, 1987
2 Cm. Mkt. L.R. 44 Case
54/88 March 13, 1986
Court of Justice of the
European Communities

### BACKGROUND AND FACTS

Mirepoix was charged with importing into France, from the Netherlands, onions treated with a pesticide, maleic hydrazide, which was not permitted in France. The French court referred the case to the Court of Justice to determine whether French law amounted to a restriction on imports in violation of Articles 30 and 36 of the Treaty, which deal with the free movement of goods.

### MANCINI, ADVOCATE GENERAL

To begin with, it should be noted that the use of the pesticide at issue in this case is not regulated either by Council Directive 76/895 of 23 November 1976 relating to the fixing of maximum levels of pesticide residues in and on fruit and vegetables [1976] OJ L340/26 or by Council Directive 76/117 of 21 December 1978 prohibiting the placing on the market and use of plant protection products containing certain active substances [1978] OJ L33/36.

The imposition by a Member State of a total ban on the use of maleic hydrazide for treating crops and the resulting ban on the importation of any products treated with that substance are capable of affecting imports from other Member States in which treatment involving the use of that substance is permitted either wholly or in part. Accordingly, rules imposing such a ban constitute a measure having an effect equivalent to a quantitative restriction. . . .

In the absence of harmonisation in this field it is therefore for the Member States, pursuant to Article 36, to determine the level of protection which should be given to human health and life, whilst taking account of the requirements of the free

movement of goods as laid down by the Treaty and, in particular, by the last sentence of Article 36.

Thus, insofar as the relevant Community rules do not cover certain pesticides, the Member States may regulate the presence of residues of those pesticides on foodstuffs in a way which varies from one country to another according to the climatic conditions, the normal diet of the population, and their state of health.

The answer to the question submitted must therefore be that, as Community legislation on foodstuffs treated with pesticides stands at present, neither Articles 30 and 36 of the Treaty nor any other provisions of Community law preclude a Member State from applying to fruit and vegetables imported from another Member State its own rules prohibiting the marketing of those products if they have been treated with maleic hydrazide.

As Community legislation on foodstuffs treated with pesticides stands at present, neither Articles 30 and 36 of the Treaty nor any other provisions of Community law preclude a Member State from applying to fruit and vegetables imported from another Member State its own rules prohibiting the marketing of those products if they have been treated with maleic hydrazide.

**Decision.** The Court found that because there were no EC standards, the country could set levels to protect health and life while considering the free-movement-of-goods requirement of Article 36. This result could change if the EC imposes uniform pesticide standards.[4]

**The Common Agricultural Policy.** The Community is committed to the establishment of a Common Agricultural Policy (CAP). It utilizes several means, such as government price supports and support for agricultural production, that are not uncommon in many countries. Figures from 1990 compare national agricultural support:

| | |
|---|---|
| European Union | $133.4 billion |
| United States | 74 billion |
| Japan | 59 billion |

It is estimated that slightly under 50 percent of the EU budget is earmarked for this program.

The CAP has been divisive within the Community because the financial burden falls heaviest on countries that it does not directly benefit, specifically the United Kingdom and Germany.

While the CAP has helped to provide food to the Community at consistent prices, its cost has been the resultant surpluses, and in spite of increased support, farm income has continued to decline. Because their way of life is threatened by any change in the CAP, increasingly militant farmers are resorting to creative demonstrations (unloading sheep to clog roads). Another example of the limits of planning was the "butter mountain." In 1987, the EC had one million tons of butter stockpiled. Ironically, a portion of the CAP must pay for storage of these surpluses.

In 1992, another effort was made to reform the CAP by shifting to direct income subsidies and taking a portion of the land out of production.

The GATT agreement in 1994 affected agriculture and was one of the most difficult parts of the negotiations. The system of fixed import tariffs replacing nontariff import charges was extended. Tariffs will be reduced 36 percent over a six-year period for advanced countries and 24 percent for developing countries over a 10-year period. Advanced countries, like the European Union and the United States agreed to reduce the amount of exports that are subsidized by 21 percent. The countries also agreed to a "peace clause" whereby members would show "due restraint" in filing complaints about subsidies until 2003.

The CAP poses a long-term problem for the expansion of the European Union to include Eastern European countries because their inexpensive agricultural products could disrupt the CAP.

## The Business Implications of the European Union

Businesses hoping to penetrate or to grow in the European market are dramatically affected by the developments in the European Union. As harmonization and standardization continues, companies can more easily gain access to separate markets such as Italy and Portugal. A company can centralize or at least regionalize offices rather than having a separate office for each country. Obviously, national and cultural, and linguistic, differences must still be respected. As regulations become more uniform, they benefit both Europeans and non-Europeans who want to do business there. Clearly, the most significant development will be the implementation of the European Monetary Union. This offers tremendous opportunities to non-European business as well.

Companies need to follow EU developments closely and to be aware of how to effectively influence the process. Lobbying American style, or aggressive lobbying efforts, have been disastrous according to reports in *The Wall Street Journal*. A U.S. executive stated, "The most important lessons we've learned so far are for American interests to get in early; get in a European way; and demonstrate from the start that American interests are compatible and consistent with European interests." The article noted that the European way "implies a lower key, lower pressure lobbying approach stressing persuasion through polite explanation."

Clearly, many companies concerned that Europe was becoming a fortress tried to gain a foothold prior to 1993. Even now, however, many industries report the opportunities are just beginning. For example, the liberalization of the telecommunications field and the gradual increasing competition within phone systems offers great new markets in Europe.

The accession of Finland, Austria, and Sweden in 1995 caused some tariffs on goods to rise for non-EU nations. Currently the European Union, United States, Japan, Canada, Australia, and other countries are negotiating this issue. The EU officials counter that despite the tariff increases, the three countries have reduced their protection of their own agricultural sectors. The countries have negotiated a temporary solution through which items are allowed in at the old tariff rates until the matter can be resolved. This situation is reminiscent of a trade war narrowly averted in 1986, when Spain and Portugal joined.

While Britain has been a cautious member, the change in government has led to other policy changes that will reverberate in the EU and in international business. (See the following article.)

# U.K. To Sign On to EU Labor Law Pact
## Social Charter Adherence to Boost Business Cost

LONDON—While business has welcomed New Labor's ending of 18 years of Conservative rule in Britain, both U.K. companies and foreign subsidiaries operating here are concerned about the impact the party's social policies could have on profits, sales and investment.

One of the first policy declarations the Labor administration made was that it would haul Britain back into the cut and thrust of Europe, particularly where employment law and social policy are concerned. The first tangible product of this is scheduled to be witnessed in Amsterdam. The Netherlands, June 16 and 17, when Britain formally ends its opt-out to the part of its 1991 political union treaty that deals with labor laws and social policy, the so-called Social Charter.

Directors, managers and investors are concerned that subscribing to the Social Charter—and thus to the social and employment legislation emanating from Brussels—will not only drive up costs and create an inflexible labor market, but also may deter investors from the United States and the Far East from choosing management-friendly Britain as their foothold in Europe.

"We don't like measures which lead to the over-regulation of the labor market," said Tracy-Jane Malthouse, a policy spokeswoman for the Institute of Directors, Britain's foremost association of top management.

The Social Charter of the 1991 Maastricht Treaty, which is formally a protocol that members had the option of signing, is not so much a catalog of labor market laws as a framework through which directives from Brussels are transposed onto law in European Union member states. Despite dire warnings about an avalanche of costly new laws, such as a higher minimum wage, only two directives have actually passed through the Social Charter conduit.

The first, the European Works Council Directive, came into force in September 1994; it obliges all multinational companies with more than 1,000 employees and all national enterprises with at least 150 employees in two member states to establish councils for consultations on key management decisions, such as mergers or downsizings. The second, the Parental and Family Leave Directive of June 1996, gives employees the right to a minimum period of three months' unpaid leave on the birth or adoption of a child.

"The actual impact of these directives in the U.K. isn't going to be all that drastic," said Deborah France, head of international social policy at the Confederation of British Industry, an employers group. "The Social Chapter won't close down U.K. industry tomorrow, but we must make sure the existing flexibilities are drafted into U.K. law."

The Labor government has stressed as much, arguing that scores of multinationals have already voluntarily complied with the provisions of the works council directive even though it has not yet been transposed onto British law. It has also contended that legislation such as the parental leave directive, which increases the benefits of the work force, can only have a positive effect on worker morale and boost the commitment and effectiveness of the active work force as a whole.

Moreover, the government has stressed that while determined to establish a new constructive engagement in Europe, it will oppose measures that it feels would place excessive burdens on business, thereby hampering competitiveness, or impose unacceptable rigidness on the labor market.

*(continued)*

*(continued)*

But this is where the debate opens up. Business argues that it is not the two measures that have been passed that should be cause for concern, but the possibility of a whole raft of further legislation that could be foisted on Social Chapter participants under its majority-rules procedure, thereby saddling Britain with an increasingly inflexible labor market and uncompetitive economy.

"The idea that workers have to be paternalistically protected is out of date," said Geoffrey Wood, professor of economics at London's City University Business School. "There is scope for many other measures to come in through the chapter, including working hours, health and safety and the minimum wage."

Specifically, other measures include three possible pieces of legislation already in the pipeline. The first would extend terms and conditions enjoyed by full-time workers to part-time and temporary workers whose numbers have burgeoned in Britain in the past decade. The second and third are aimed at combating sexual discrimination and harassment by making it easier for workers to prove their allegations.

Further down the line, the Institute of Directors sees possible legislation to extend the scope of works councils to smaller businesses and catalogs other directives that could extend sick pay benefits and home worker protection as well as requiring compulsory collective bargaining, a labor market tool familiar to France and Germany, but anathema in Britain.

"Even companies in the U.K. don't realize what's about to happen, but it's quite clear that over the next six months we're going to see a renewed attempt by the European Commission to bring forward a number of directives, including part-time workers rights, information and consultation in national companies which will affect U.S. investors," said the CBI's Ms. France.

**Mark Rice-Oxley**
Special to the National Law Journal

## Other Economically Integrated Trade Areas

The United States and the European Union are not the only countries that have experimented with economically integrated trade areas. However, they are the most fully integrated as of this writing. The U.S.–Canada Free Trade Agreement and the North American Free Trade Agreement are discussed in a later chapter.

Canada itself comprises ten provinces and is attempting to reduce its own internal barriers inhibiting the free movement of goods, capital, and people. For example, Quebec bans construction workers from out of the province. Other rules require that construction materials for public works projects be locally obtained. The Canadian Trade Minister has identified 500 internal barriers to be eliminated in much the same way as in the European Union has done.

Other countries, spurred on by the European Union and wanting to stimulate development and investment in their own regions, are accelerating their own integration efforts. The next section looks briefly at some of these other examples.

## MERCOSUR: Southern Common Market

Argentina, Brazil, Paraguay, and Uruguay agreed to form the Southern Common Market in 1991. This area encompasses 215 million people today and is predicted to have 240 million by 2001. The countries were committed to both opening their markets as well as pushing exports dubbed "open regionalism." In 1994 they committed further to pushing integration toward a customs union model with a common external tariff. Some hope eventually for the free movement of labor and capital as well. A common market group forms the executive branch. Notably absent, however, is a court, an integral part of the European Union and the United States. Annex III of the Agreement outlines how disputes will be handled. The first step is direct negotiation between the states. Second is referral to the common market group. Third, if no solution can be reached, the council should propose a settlement. Without a final authority to issue binding rulings, the thorny problems of regional integration and national autonomy will not be solved easily.

This common market has been successful and experienced a 250 percent increase in trade since 1990.

On January 1, 1995, tariffs on approximately 95 percent of goods traded among the four countries were ended. They created a customs union by enacting a common tariff of 12 percent on goods coming from a nonmember. Trade has tripled since the inception of the pact. Brazil, formerly an enemy, is now Argentina's largest trading partner. Bilateral agreements have been negotiated with Chile. Although the countries are moving toward the goal of free trade in goods, little progress has been made on the issues of services or labor. Brazil recently imposed a quota on the number of cars that can be imported into Brazil. Argentina has reacted strongly because of its reliance on auto exports. These disputes underscore the difficulties of successful implementation of any trade agreement.

## Andean Common Market

The Andean Common Market (ANCOM) or Andean Group includes Bolivia, Venezuela, Colombia, Ecuador, and Peru. It was founded in 1969 by the Cartagena Agreement and involves 100 million people. Venezuela joined in 1973; Chile withdrew in 1977. Peru temporarily suspended its membership in 1992 but has since rejoined.

Its legal structures include the Commission, Junta, Andean Development Bank and Reserve Fund, and the Andean Court of Justice. Initially the countries hoped to exclude the other countries' products and to buy only from one another. This exclusionary practice meant that the population was paying a lot for goods.

ANCOM has moved toward integration, but national interests have kept these countries from moving as far on the continuum as the European Union.

The Commission (one representative from each country) functions as an executive branch, makes policy, appoints Junta members, approves and vetoes legislation, and ensures compliance with the Agreement. The Junta (three members) supervises and implements the Commission's decisions. The Bank assists in financial development spurred both by members' contributions and foreign capital. It also assists with balance of payments problems. The Court of Justice Treaty (drafted in 1979; ratified in 1983) created the Court, which sits in Quito, Ecuador. The Andean Court, unlike the EU Court, has the power only to hear cases involving ANCOM law that "may be referred"; it has no mandatory jurisdiction. Accordingly, it must rely on countries to voluntarily allow the Court to review a matter. Since this acquiescence involves giving up some national interests, most countries are reluctant to do so.

The Andean Parliament (in Lima, Peru) plans to have direct regional elections, but has not done so to date. This format parallels the European Union, which only recently adopted this reform. The Parliament issues recommendations to achieve the goals of the Cartagena Agreement; thus, its power is limited.

In 1987, as evidenced by the Quito Protocol, the countries stepped backward in terms of integration by letting individual countries enter into bilateral agreements dealing with trade, licensing, and investment. One of the most interesting recent developments in ANCOM was the repeal of the 1970 Commission Decision 24, the Foreign Investment and Transfer of Technology Code. The Code had been an attempt to establish uniform policies and practices within the member countries and to control foreign investment and technology in a way that would reap maximum benefits while retaining control. Not all member states implemented the Code at a national level, however. Therefore, they encountered problems with consistency. Bowing to reality, the Commission issued Decision 220, on May 11, 1987, repealing No. 24. Since 1989, at least one country, Venezuela, has dropped its tariffs substantially as a way of encouraging investment within its borders.

## Free Trade in the Americas Area (FTAA)

In December 1994, 34 countries agreed to work toward the creation of a Western hemisphere agreement creating a free trade area by 2005. The countries, including the United States, talked about reducing tariffs and dealing with bribery, drug trafficking, and the liberalization of capital markets.

The initial euphoria of the prospect of such a large regional organization has been dimmed by the recent lack of momentum. President Clinton was denied authority (see Chapter 9) to negotiate such an agreement during the 1996 election campaign. The President will try again in 1998 to secure Congressional approval, and the talks are scheduled in 1998.

> **http://www.iep.doc.gov/ftaa2005**
> *This site provides brief information on the FTAA, with several links, including the FTAA home page in English, French, Portuguese, and Spanish, at http://www.alca-ftaa.org/.*

## Colombia-Venezuela Free Trade Pact

This pact, signed in 1992, is designed to end smuggling across borders, to reduce both countries' imports from third countries, and to ease trade restrictions on a number of items. Since the signing of the pact, trade has grown dramatically between the countries.

## Central American Common Market

Guatemala, El Salvador, Costa Rica, Nicaragua, Honduras, and Panama signed a new agreement October 1993 to create a common market, but the efforts to implement a uniform tariff have been unsuccessful as individual countries seek to implement separate tariffs to address domestic problems.

## African Trade Areas

The development of Africa in the next century will be critically important. Ravaged by civil wars and famine after the end of the colonial occupation, many countries are trying to rebuild their economies. Just as many south American countries realized that centralized planning did not work and have moved toward restructuring internally and free trade models, so too will many African states. In 1990, 12.1 percent of world population was African. If the trend continues, by 2150, 25 percent of world population will be African and another 25 percent will be Chinese.

**African Economic Community.** This proposed 51-member group contemplates a six-phase implementation of an African common market over a 20-year period. The official languages will be English, French, and Portuguese. The agreement will enter into effect after two-thirds of the members ratify the Agreement.

**COMESA: Common Market for Eastern and Southern Africa.** This 1982 treaty involves 23 African states. The trade area encompasses 220 million people. The group recently set a five- to seven-year goal to achieve the common market. To date they have created "standard customs documents and a dispute tribunal," but not with the powers of the EU Court of Justice.

> **http://www.ita.doc.gov/mena/econof.html**
> *Select Country Commercial Guides for executive summaries on African countries.*
>
> **http://www.stat-usa.gov/bems/bemssoaf/bemssoaf.html**
> *The site for South Africa as a big emerging market.*

**Southern African Development Community.** The SADC, formed on August 17, 1992, involves Angola, Botswana, Lesotho, Malawi, Mozambique, Namibia, Swaziland, Tanzania, Zambia, Zimbabwe, Mauritius, and South Africa, representing 135 million people. The group sees itself working in concert with the African Economic Community to develop "regional economic communities," building blocks for the continental community. Although in embryo stage, the agreement sketches cooperation on human resources, science and technology, food, security, natural resources, environment, infrastructure and services, finance, investment, trade, peace, and security. To date, however, they have issued a statement of purpose but have no structure and power necessary to develop and implement law and policy.

The major change in Africa centers around the transformation of South Africa and the end of Apartheid. Privatization in some countries has spurred a GDP growth of 6 percent. Many hope that these regional agreements will assist Africa's economic development in the way it has benefited Europe and South America. Before free trade can exist, however, there must be an infrastructure (i.e., roads, telecommunications systems, and education) to support development.

## U.S.–Israel Free Trade Agreement

The United States has agreement with Israel as well as with the European Union. Even though Israel has had a free trade agreement with the European Union since 1975, which became operational in 1989, the United States and Israel signed a Free Trade Agreement in 1985. This agreement was the first such attempt for the United States, although prior to this, Israel enjoyed beneficial trading privileges with the United States. The pact offered continued access to the U.S. market for Israel and allowed the United States to compete with the European Union for access to Israel's markets. Politically, it was also advantageous because if free trade stabilized Israel, it would be less dependent on U.S. aid. The agreement can be terminated on twelve month's notice. The Gulf War delayed and perhaps cooled temporarily interest in using Israel as an intermediary trader between the European Union and the United States.

## APEC: Asia Pacific Economic Cooperation Group

The current 18-member group, including the United States, Japan, Australia, Canada, South Korea, China, and Indonesia, issued the Bogor Declaration (named after a town in Indonesia), to achieve "free and open trade and investment" by the year 2020 and in industrialized nations by 2010. This agreement is historic—though without powers of enforcement—in that half the world has agreed to be tariff free by 2020. The tariff schedules are to be finished by 2000.

The definition of free trade and whether it includes services, however, have not yet been spelled out. Nevertheless, the implications for business are enormous. If the tariffs on autos in some countries were dropped just a bit from their high of 30–60 percent (compared to 2.5 percent in the United States), significant new market access would be created. A secretariat was formed in 1991 and a yearly meeting is scheduled to move the group toward the stated objectives. The agreement contains no enforcement mechanisms to deal with recalcitrant members.

## CARICOM

This alliance comprises 13 English-speaking Caribbean countries with a total of six million people. The Caribbean Community, or CARICOM, was created to form a single market. Barbados, Jamaica, and Trinidad already have cross-trading on their stock exchanges. Mebers agreed to reduce its common external tariff on imports to 20 percent from 45 percent by 1998.

## ASEAN

The Association of South East Asian Nations (ASEAN) was formed in 1967 by Indonesia, Malaysia, the Philippines, Singapore, Thailand, and Brunei (joined in 1984) with the Bangkok Declaration. In May 1997 Myanmar, Laos, and Cambodia were admitted. Unlike the EU and ANCOM, the Declaration does not set up a legal mechanism to enforce its goals of economic growth and development through trade and industry. On a continuum, as shown in Exhibit 3.7, ASEAN would fall closer to the less integrated end than any of the groups previously discussed. The structures within ASEAN are less formal too. It has a standing committee of ministers from each state. In 1976, a secretariat was formed, seated in Jakarta, Indonesia, which functions as an organizational center. The group has sponsored

**EXHIBIT 3.7    Trade Alliance Continuum**

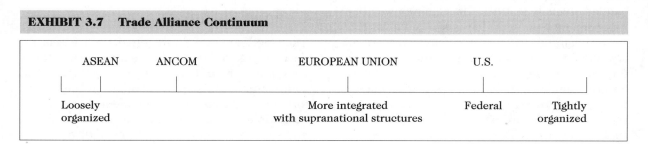

industrial development projects with the help of Japanese funding. Tariff reductions among member states are one achievement. ASEAN has also represented its members in dealing with other groups such as the European Union. Significantly, however, it has no court or legislature.

Two developments are worth noting: In spite of the lack of integration and supranational structures, ASEAN has advocated for associations such as the ASEAN Federation of Cement Manufacturers to create "complementation schemes," in which barriers are reduced and manufacturers use all ASEAN components wherever possible. The ministers met in 1994 and agreed to set 2003 rather than 2008 as a deadline for achieving a free trade area. The ministers also agreed to include agriculture. Tariffs will be brought down to under 5 percent. Because of the crisis in Asia, tariffs may be reduced even more quickly on some items.

Although it is not a member, Japan plays a significant role in ASEAN by buying 21 percent of ASEAN exports, providing 64 percent of foreign aid, and investing significantly in all ASEAN countries except Brunei and the Philippines.

> **http://infoserv2.ita.doc.gov/apweb.nsf**
> *This address will link you to sites for APEC, ASEAN, Australia, Bangladesh, Bhutan, and Brunei.*

## COMECON

The Council for Mutual Economic Assistance, or Comecon (also called CMEA), consisted of the USSR, Hungary, Poland, Romania, Bulgaria, East Germany, Cuba, Czechoslovakia, Mongolia, and Vietnam. Founded in 1949, Comecon served as the association of Soviet-aligned countries that negotiated annual and long-term trade agreements and dealt with balance of trade problems caused by currencies (rubles, zlotys) that were not freely traded or convertible. The group disbanded officially in 1991. The Commonwealth of Independent States, which is struggling with issues of common currency, defense, foreign policy, and economic survival after the break-up of the Soviet Union, will be interesting to follow. Several republics, including the Slavic ones of Russia, Byelorussia, and Ukraine, have signed an agreement to "coordinate domestic and foreign trade policy as well as joint activity in customs and migration policies, and the development of transport and communications systems." These republics have 70 percent of the former USSR's population, but are not centers for agricultural production. The religious and ethnic differences in the diverse land of the former Soviet Union may ultimately precipitate the balkanization of the republics, thus dissolving the single currency and the foreign policy and economic cooperation that Europe is ironically trying to achieve. However, the former Soviet model was built on military and political coercion, not cooperation. Also, some of the former Soviet republics have applied for membership in the European Union.

## Gulf Cooperation Council

Saudi Arabia, Kuwait, Bahrain, Qatar, the United Arab Emirates, and Oman formed the Gulf Cooperation Council (GCC) in 1981. The GCC focuses on standardizing subsidies, unifying rates for eliminating trade barriers, and negotiating with other regional groups like the European Union to achieve favorable treatment.

## Arab League

The Arab League was founded in 1945 and currently has 22 members (Algeria, Bahrain, Djibouti, Egypt, Iraq, Jordan, Kuwait, Lebanon, Libya, Mauritania, Morocco, Oman, Palestine, Qatar, Yemen, Saudi Arabia, Somalia, Sudan, Syria, Tunisia, the United Arab Emirates, and the Yemen Arab Republic). The League focuses on maintaining peace and security and on advancing cooperation in other areas (e.g., economic). Obviously, the Gulf War was evidence of its ineffectiveness, as demonstrated by members of the League splitting and fighting against one of its own, Iraq.

## Chapter Summary

The development of integrated trade areas reflects an age-old desire to maximize each country's strength and to grow and prosper. The United States is a successful model of such an effort. The more recent developments in the European Union have been more difficult to initiate and sustain because of centuries of distinct language, culture, and history, as well as currencies and legal systems. Regional trading blocs raise issues about regional protectionism and the conflict with the GATT and WTO. Members are acutely aware of both benefits as well threats of integration, but are driven by the need to compete internationally.

In reaction to EU unification, other countries have been stimulated to consider cooperative efforts to reduce trade barriers as a counterbalance to the threat of "Fortress Europe."

States are motivated to form trade areas to improve their own economic position and to secure the future. Numerous forms of alliances are possible but the conflicts perennially remain. The persistent question is how to subordinate state interests so as to achieve unity. What national interests can be deferred, and what are the tradeoffs?

New technology also offers new opportunities for trade. President Clinton announced in 1997 plans to make the Internet a "global free trade zone" and to negotiate an international agreement. Internet trade in the U.S. is expected to value over $200 billion by the year 2000.

Only a little over 130 years ago the United States was ripped apart by the Civil War. Although the United States has been reunified, one cannot forget how regional differences may place a great stress on unity. The regional groups discussed here have strived to form lasting alliances despite major differences in ideology, culture, and language.

These regional efforts should be watched closely to see how they progress towards economic and possibly political integration. The divisive issue of nationalism will hinder some groups' efforts. The delicate balance between promoting trade and economic growth and protectionism may either prompt great trade rivalries between "mega" associations or open the way to truly free trade for all nations.

---

## QUESTIONS AND CASE PROBLEMS

1. What role does the European Court of Justice play in the European Union? Compare and contrast the European Court of Justice with the United States Supreme Court. How does the legal structure of the EU differ from other economically integrated trade areas?

2. What legal strategies might U.S. and Japanese companies adopt to deal with the threat of "Fortress Europe"?

3. What are the implications of EMU for businesspeople thinking about expanding into Europe? What are some Europeans afraid of from EMU?

4. Do customs unions violate the GATT principles of nondiscrimination and reciprocity?

5. In the Maastricht Treaty, Denmark has a restriction on the purchase of second homes in Denmark by non-Danish people. Does this violate the Treaty of Rome? Explain you answer from both a legal and a political perspective.

6. The Culture minister in France, Jacques Toubon, sponsored a French law that required 3,000 English words used in France to be replaced by the new French equivalents in all media—TV, print, and academic—commercial as well as governmental. For example, sports announcers could not say "corner" in soccer games but only "jet de coin." Prime-time would be "heures de grande ecoute." Do conflicts arise between this French government interest in eradicating Franglais and the rights of Europeans as enunciated in the various treaties?

7. After the EC (now EU) passed a law, Italy passed a national law that contradicted the EU law. Which prevails and why? *Costa v. ENEL* case 6/64 (1964) 3 ECR 585.

8. Can the EU Court of Justice require part-time workers to be covered under a company's pension plan? Can it require the pension plan to have retroactive effect? What remedy does a state have that believes 18 years of retroactivity is too much?

9. Is a Turkish worker who was entitled by an Association Agreement with Turkey to free access to Germany to seek employment after 4 years of legal employment entitled to a residence permit to seek employment after he voluntarily terminated his employment?

10. Irish students distributed information about where one could obtain an abortion outside of Ireland, because abortions are illegal in Ireland. The students were forbidden to distribute such information. The case went to the EU Court of Justice. Was the restriction on the students a legitimate exercise of an individual state's autonomy, or did it constitute an unlawful restriction of the freedom to provide services across state borders in contravention of Article 59?

## MANAGERIAL IMPLICATIONS

1. You are President of HIGRO W, Inc., a chemical manufacturing facility. You are considering establishing a European and an African site. What concerns do you have, if any, about the new Works Council Directive? How will you address these? How will regional trade groups affect your decision on placement in Africa?
2. Your board has asked you to prepare a memo to explain the impact of EMU on your proposed plan in Europe. Prepare a two-page memo targeting U.K. and German operations.

## NOTES

1. Reproduced with permission from 33 I.L.M. 388 (1994), Introductory Note and Translation by Gerhard Wegen and Christopher Kuner of Gleiss Lutz Hirsch & Partners (Stuttgart/Berlin/Frankfort/Brussels/Prague) © The American Society of International Law.
2. Reproduced with permission from Common Market Reports published and copyrighted by Commerce Clearing House, Inc., 4025 W. Peterson Ave., Chicago, Illinois, 60646.
3. Reproduced with permission from Common Market Reports published and copyrighted by Commerce Clearing House, Inc., 4025 W. Peterson Ave., Chicago, Illinois, 60646.
4. Reproduced with permission from Common Market Reports published and copyrighted by Commerce Clearing House, Inc., 4025 W. Peterson Ave., Chicago, Illinois, 60646.

# Chapter Four

# The Resolution of International Disputes

## Methods of Resolution

The resolution of disputes among people who are citizens of different countries, with business deals that span continents and cultures, can be fraught with difficulty and uncertainty. Distance can also make resolution more time-consuming and costly. For example, consider a domestic dispute in which a New York supplier tries to sue a Texas distributor. This situation raises several questions that must always be answered in any dispute:

1. Should the parties settle, litigate, mediate, or arbitrate?
2. Where should the dispute be settled? In which forum, New York or Houston? Federal or state court?
3. Which law applies to the transaction? New York law? Texas law? Some other law?
4. If a resolution (a settlement, a verdict, or a judgment) is reached, how will it be enforced?

Changing the parties to a New York supplier and a Japanese distributor adds several dimensions, both legally and culturally, to the resolution of a business dispute. The same four questions that were relevant to a domestic dispute are equally relevant to an international dispute. This chapter examines these questions and decision points as they apply to disputes in international business.

The threshold question focuses on whether the parties will settle the matter through discussion, mediation, arbitration, or litigation. Parties must agree to mediate or arbitrate; one cannot force a party to arbitrate in the absence of an agreement. Mediation is a voluntary dispute-resolution process that is not binding on the parties, while binding arbitration is a more formal-ized voluntary process whereby a neutral third party or parties listen to the evidence and render a judgment by which the parties agree to abide. A number of organizations provide a framework for arbitration; these groups are discussed later in the chapter.

Litigation is used more frequently as a means of settling business disputes in the United States than in virtually any other country. For example, Japan has one lawyer for every 9,300 people, compared to the United States, which has one per 360. Not surprisingly, Japan has substantially less litigation and lower liability insurance costs. A recent joke circulating, credited to Russell Baker, suggests that the United States could cure the trade imbalance with Japan by exporting one lawyer for every Japanese car imported. Joking aside, the number of lawyers is not the only difference between these countries' legal environments. Both countries exhibit major differences in host country law that directly affects litigation.

Many societies view litigation negatively, as evidence of personal failure by the parties. Thus, in these societies, even parties with fundamental disagreements are motivated to seek an accord.

Even in societies such as the United States that have developed a business culture of litigation, if parties desire to continue their business relationship, they will be interested in resolving their disputes outside of court. However, litigation, though costly, may still be the best option in some cases.

## Litigation

A lawsuit will not proceed if the court does not have *jurisdiction*. Jurisdiction means the "power to hear," the "legal right by which judges exercise their authority" or "competence," as it is referred to in Japan.

**http://itl.irv.uit.no/trade_law/**
*Provides a subject index through the International Trade Law Monitor with links to various legal topics on international trade.*

## Jurisdiction and Venue

Jurisdiction is defined by the U.S. Constitution, as well as by various statutes.

*Venue* is sometimes confused with jurisdiction, but it means the appropriate geographical location of the court with jurisdiction. For example, several federal district courts may have jurisdiction over a suit, but venue might be proper in only one of them. A federal statute addresses the issue of venue generally.

A civil action wherein jurisdiction is founded on diversity of citizenship may except as otherwise provided by law, be brought only in the judicial district where all plaintiffs or all defendants reside, or in which the claim arose.

Counsel may ask the court to change the venue or to move the site of trial "[f]or the convenience of the parties and witnesses in the interest of justice . . . " (28 U.S.C. 1404). Jurisdiction and venue are the focus of initial maneuvering by lawyers, and part of the overall legal strategy of any case. In an international dispute, both nations' courts may assert jurisdiction over the matter.

## Forum Non Conveniens

The legal doctrine of *forum non conveniens* (inconvenient forum) may be used to prevent a court from taking jurisdiction and proceeding to hear a case. This doctrine is applicable in the United States as well as many other countries. The Bhopal case (also discussed in Chapter One) exemplifies its application.

**Bhopal.** The chemical disaster in Bhopal, India, prompted litigation on two continents. The Union Carbide subsidiary was owned 50.9 per-

cent by the parent company, headquartered in Danbury, Connecticut; however, the plant was controlled by the Indians, who owned 49.1 percent. A number of lawyers representing Indian citizens filed suit in Federal District Court for the Southern District of New York, the district covering Manhattan, but the judge dismissed the case stating that it was *forum non conveniens* and that the case should be tried in India. The court noted factors such as the cost of transporting witnesses, as well as translation problems. The judge also stated that "to retain litigation in this forum [the United States] would be another example of imperialism, another situation in which an established sovereign inflicted its rules, its standards and values on a developing nation." The case was settled in India in 1989 prior to trial. Union Carbide Corporation, the parent company, agreed to pay $470 million in compensation.

While the Gandhi government had approved this settlement in 1989, the new Indian government alleged that Union Carbide was criminally responsible for the leak. The Indian Supreme Court in October 1991 affirmed the civil settlement of $470 million, but opened the possibility of criminal prosecution of the chairman, Warren Anderson, thus reversing a grant of immunity from criminal prosecution. The Indian court ordered Mr. Anderson's assets attached and ordered him to appear in India. The company denies that either it or the former chairman are subject to the Indian court's criminal jurisdiction. To complicate matters, the United States and India have an extradition treaty, but to date the U.S. government has not agreed to extradite Mr. Anderson.

The cost of the Bhopal disaster in human and economic terms has stirred many companies to reconsider their foreign operations and subsidiaries. The fact that the Indians had control of the plant did not insulate Union Carbide, the parent company, from liability. Even the plant's compliance with local law was not sufficient. The training and supervision of the workers was also an element in the accident. A multinational enterprise (MNE) such as Union Carbide faced a difficult problem—on the one hand, it was not allowed to control the Indian company; yet, in the instance of this disaster, the officers concluded that it was advisable to settle the matter rather than risk litigation.

The uncertainties of litigation in a foreign judicial system compound the risks. The accident in Bhopal has many ramifications. First, companies may no longer be willing to go along with the lower safety standards required in many developing countries, despite their initial attractiveness in terms of short-term cost savings. Second, an MNE may insist on more careful monitoring of the company's training and safety practices in an effort to avoid incidents like Bhopal in the future. Third, a forum selection clause would not have helped in this situation in which the plaintiffs are third parties. A company can try to manage the risks, but it can't eliminate them.

**Forum Non Conveniens: Another Approach.** Another example of the application of *forum non conveniens* with a different result is the case *Dow Chemical v. Domingo Castro Alfaro,* which follows. In this case, the court found that the doctrine did not bar the lawsuit. The plaintiff's attorneys were anxious to find a U.S. forum because any recovery in Costa Rica would be low—only about $1,800 a person, based on one lawyer's prediction.

---

## Dow Chemical v. Domingo Castro Alfaro
786 S.W.2d 674
(Tex. 1990) Reh. Den.
Supreme Court of Texas
Cert den 498 U.S. 1024 (1991)

BACKGROUND AND FACTS
A Costa Rican employee of Standard Fruit Company and 81 other employees brought suit against Dow and Shell for the injuries they suffered, including sterility, as a result of exposure to DBCP, a pesticide. The Texas trial court dismissed for *forum non conveniens.* The court of appeals reversed. The defendants appealed to the Texas Supreme Court.

JUSTICE RAY
At issue in this cause is whether the statutory right to enforce a personal injury or wrongful death claim in the Texas courts precludes a trial court from dismissing the claim on the ground of *forum non conveniens.* The court of appeals held that Texas courts lack the authority to dismiss on the grounds of *forum non conveniens.* Because we conclude that the legislature has statutorily abolished the doctrine of *forum non conveniens* in suits brought under section 71.031 of the Texas Civil Practice and Remedies Code, we affirm the judgment of the court of appeals.

Section 71.031 of the Civil Practice and Remedies Code provides:

a. An action for damages for the death or personal injury of a citizen of this state, of the United States, or of a foreign country may be enforced in the courts of this state, although the wrongful act, neglect, or default causing the death or injury takes place in a foreign state or country, if:
1. a law of the foreign state or country or of this state gives a right to maintain an action for damages for the death or injury;
2. the action is begun in this state within the time provided by the laws of this state for beginning the action; and
3. in the case of a citizen of a foreign country, the country has equal treaty rights with the United States on behalf of its citizens.[1]
b. All matters pertaining to procedure in the prosecution or maintenance of the action in the courts of this state are governed by the law of this state.
c. The court shall apply the rules of substantive law that are appropriate under the facts of the case.

Tex.Civ.Prac. & Rem.Code Ann. § 71.031 (Vernon 1986). At issue is whether the language of Section 71.031(a) permits a trial court to relinquish jurisdiction under the doctrine of *forum non conveniens.*

Dow and Shell argued before this Court that the legislature did not intend to make section 71.031 a guarantee of an absolute right to enforce a suit in Texas brought under that provision. . . .

The doctrine of *forum non conveniens* arose from the doctrine of *forum non competens* in Scottish cases. The Scottish courts recognized that the plea of *forum non competens* applied when to hear the case was not expedient for the administration of justice. In *Longworth v. Hope,* 3 Sess.Cas. (3d ser.) 1049, 1053 (1865), the court stated:

The next question is the question of *forum non competens.* Now the plea usually thus expressed does not mean that the forum is one in which it is wholly incompetent to deal with the

*(continued)*

*(continued)*

question. The plea has received a wide signification, and is frequently stated in reference to cases in which the Court may consider it more proper for the ends of justice that the parties should seek their remedy in another forum.

By the end of the nineteenth century, English courts had "accepted the doctrine of *forum non conveniens* as a means of preventing abuse of the court's process when the plaintiff's choice of forum is vexatious and works unnecessary hardship on the defendant."

In 1929, Paxton Blair, a Wall Street lawyer, brought the term "forum non conveniens" into American law with his article entitled, *The Doctrine of Forum Non Conveniens in Anglo-American Law.* Although Blair found only three or four cases in which the American courts had used the term, he concluded:

> Upon an examination of the American decisions illustrative of the doctrine of *forum non conveniens,* it becomes apparent that the courts of this country have been for years applying the doctrine with such little consciousness of what they were doing as to remind one of Molière's M. Jourdain, who found he had been speaking prose all his life without knowing it.

Blair cited hundreds of cases dismissing suits for the same reasons now employed under the doctrine of *forum non conveniens.* . . .

We therefore must determine whether the legislature in 1913 statutorily abolished the doctrine of *forum non conveniens* in suits brought under article 4678 [now section 71.031].

We conclude that the legislature has statutorily abolished the doctrine of *forum non conveniens* in suits brought under section 71.031. Accordingly, we affirm the judgment of the court of appeals, remanding the cause to the trial court for further proceedings.

### JUSTICE GONZALEZ, DISSENTING

Under the guise of statutory construction, the court today abolishes the doctrine of *forum non conveniens* in suits brought pursuant to section 71.031 of the Civil Practice and Remedies Code. This decision makes us one of the few states in the Union without such a procedural tool,[2] and if the legislature fails to reinstate this doctrine, Texas will become an irresistible forum for all mass dis-

aster lawsuits. *See generally,* Note, *Foreign Plaintiffs and Forum Non Conveniens: Going Beyond Reyno,* 64 Tex.L.Rev. 193 (1985). "Bhopal"-type litigation, with little or no connection to Texas will *add* to our already crowded dockets, forcing our residents to wait in the corridors of our courthouses while foreign causes of action are tried.[3] I would hold that section 71.031 of the Texas Civil Practice and Remedies Code *does not* confer upon foreign litigants an *absolute right* to bring suit in Texas. Because I believe that trial courts have the inherent power to apply *forum non conveniens* in appropriate cases, I would provide guidelines and set parameters for its use. I would thus modify the judgment of the court of appeals and remand the cause to the trial court for further proceedings.

This cause of action arose in Costa Rica where certain Costa Rican agricultural workers suffered injuries allegedly as a result of exposure to a pesticide manufactured by the defendants. The injured workers are seeking to enforce in Texas courts claims for personal injuries that occurred in Costa Rica. Several suits involving many of the same plaintiffs and essentially the same defendants have previously been filed in the United States and then dismissed on *forum non conveniens* grounds.

### JUSTICE COOK, DISSENTING

Like turn-of-the-century wildcatters, the plaintiffs in this case searched all across the nation for a place to make their claims. Through three courts they moved, filing their lawsuits on one coast and then on the other. By each of those courts the plaintiffs were rejected, and so they continued their search for a more willing forum. Their efforts are finally rewarded. Today they hit pay dirt in Texas.

No reason exists, in law or in policy, to support their presence in this state. The legislature adopted within the statute the phrase "may be enforced" to permit plaintiffs to sue in Texas, irrespective of where they live or where the cause of action arose. The legislature did not adopt this statute, however, to remove from our courts all discretion to dismiss. To use the statute to sweep away, completely and finally, a common law doctrine painstakingly developed over the years is to infuse the statute with a power not contained in the words.

**Comment.**    Texas's Republican governor pledged to rewrite the state law to limit jurisdiction in these types of cases. The law was changed and applies to cases filed on or after September 1, 1993.

## Minimum Contacts

The Due Process Clause of the U.S. Constitution requires that before a person or company can be brought before a court in the United States, it must have had *minimum contacts* with the forum. This requirement is based on the premise that bringing an individual or corporation before a court when that "person" had never had "legal" contact with that place would be unfair. This concept has important implications as to when a company has had sufficient contacts that it can be brought before a particular court on a tort, contract, or statutory claim.

**Domestic Context.**  In a domestic context, the Due Process Clause of the Fourteenth Amendment limits the power of the court to impose judgment on a defendant who does not live in the state. The courts have generally looked to see whether they can reasonably or fairly force the nonresident to come to the particular state. Through case law, this interpretation questions whether the defendant has "contacts" within the state and the reasonableness of forcing the defendant to come to the state. Courts have looked at several factors including the burden on the defendant, the state's interest, and the plaintiff's interest. Additional factors as stated by the Supreme Court include

[t]he interstate judicial systems' interest in obtaining the most efficient resolution of controversies; and the shared interest of the states in furthering fundamental substantive social policies.

In numerous cases on this issue the courts have looked at all the circumstances and determined that the court has jurisdiction. The courts have reached the opposite conclusion, too. For example in the *Worldwide Volkswagen Corp. v. Woodson* case, the Supreme Court stated that a New York automobile retailer and distributor was not required to appear in Oklahoma in a product liability lawsuit based on a sale of an Audi in New York that was involved in a serious car accident in Oklahoma. The facts are important because if the defendant has an office or sales reps in the state, that fact could be sufficient to establish minimum contacts and thus jurisdiction.

**The International Dimension.**  Another recent Supreme Court case illustrates the international ramifications of the concept of due process and minimum contacts for doing business as a prerequisite for jurisdiction.

These cases have left open a number of issues. Therefore, corporate counsel cannot predict with absolute certainty the outcome of a particular question. For example, just placing a product into "the stream of commerce" as Asahi (the Japanese corporation) did was not enough to warrant jurisdiction; however, four justices in the *Asahi* dissent objected to this reading. Currently, the courts show no unanimity on this issue. Advertising or some other deliberate entry into the forum might be sufficient to trigger an exercise of jurisdiction. Future decisions will have to further delineate the remaining questions about jurisdiction.

---

### *Asahi Metal Ind. v. Superior Court of California, Solano*
107 S.Ct. 1026 (1987)
United States
Supreme Court

BACKGROUND AND FACTS
Asahi Metal, a Japanese corporation, manufactured valve assemblies in Japan and sold them to tire manufacturers including Cheng Shin (a Taiwanese corporation) from 1978 to 1982. Cheng Shin sold tires all over the world, including in California. On September 23, 1978, in Solano County, California, Gary Zurcher was injured riding his motorcycle. His wife was killed. He filed a product liability action against Cheng Shin (Taiwan), the manufacturer of his motorcycle tire, alleging that the tire was defective. Cheng Shin filed a cross-complaint seeking indemnification from Asahi Metal Industry. Cheng Shin settled with Zurcher. However, Cheng Shin (Taiwan) pressed its action against Asahi (Japan), and Asahi petitioned for certiorari to the United States Supreme Court. The case presented the question of whether a dispute between a Taiwanese company and a Japanese

*(continued)*

*(continued)*

company with the preceding relationship to California should be heard by the California courts. In other words, did the California court have jurisdiction over the matter?

JUSTICE O'CONNOR

. . . The Due Process Clause of the Fourteenth Amendment limits the power of a state court to exert personal jurisdiction over a nonresident defendant. "[T]he constitutional touchstone" of the determination whether an exercise of personal jurisdiction comports with due process "remains whether the defendant purposefully established 'minimum contacts' in the forum State." *Burger King Corp. v. Rudzewicz,* 471 U.S. 462, 474, 105 S.Ct. 2174, 2183, 85 L.Ed.2d 528 (1985), quoting *International Shoe Co. v. Washington,* 325 U.S. 310, 316 66 S.Ct. 154, 138, 90 L.Ed. 95 (1945). Most recently we have reaffirmed the oft-quoted reasoning of *Hanson v. Denckla,* 357 U.S. 235, 253, 78 S.Ct. 1228, 1239, 2 L.Ed.2d 1283 (1958), that minimum contacts must have a basis in "some act by which the defendant purposefully avails itself of the privilege of conducting activities within the forum State, thus invoking the benefits and proportions of its laws." *Burger King,* 471 U.S., at 475, 105 S.Ct., at 2183. "Jurisdiction is proper . . . where the contacts proximately result from actions by the defendant *himself* that create a substantial connection with the forum State." Ibid., quoting *McGee v. International Life Insurance Co.,* 355 U.S. 220, 223, 78 S.Ct., 199, 201, 2 L.Ed.2d 223 (1957) (emphasis in original). . . .

The placement of a product into the stream of commerce, without more, is not an act of the defendant purposefully directed toward the forum State. Additional conduct of the defendant may indicate an intent or purpose to serve the market in the forum State, for example, designing the product for the market in the forum State, advertising in the forum State, establishing channels for providing regular advice to customers in the forum State, or marketing the product through a distributor who has agreed to serve as the sales agent in the forum State. But a defendant's awareness that the stream of commerce may or will sweep the product into the forum State does not convert the mere act of placing the product into the stream into an act purposefully directed toward the forum State.

Assuming, arguendo, that respondents have established Asahi's awareness that some of the valves sold to Cheng Shin would be incorporated into tire tubes sold in California, respondents have not demonstrated any action by Asahi to purposefully avail itself of the California market. It has no office, agents, employees, or property in California. It does not advertise or otherwise solicit business in California. It did not create, control, or employ the distribution system that brought its valves to California. Cf. *Hicks v. Kawasaki Heavy Industries,* 452 F.Supp. 130 (1978). There is no evidence that Asahi designed its product in anticipation of sales in California. Cf. *Rockwell International Corp. v. Costruzioni Aeronautiche Giovanni Agusta,* 553 F.Supp. 328 (ED Pa.1982). On the basis of these facts, the exertion of personal jurisdiction over Asahi by the Superior Court of California exceeds the limits of Due Process.

The strictures of the Due Process Clause forbid a state court from exercising personal jurisdiction over Asahi under circumstances that would offend "traditional notions of fair play and substantial justice." *International Shoe Co. v. Washington,* 326 U.S., at 316, 66 S.Ct., at 158; quoting *Milliken v. Meyer,* 311 U.S., at 463, 61 S.Ct., at 342.

We have previously explained that the determination of the reasonableness of the exercise of jurisdiction in each case will depend on an evaluation of several factors. . . .

Certainly the burden on the defendant in this case is severe. Asahi has been commanded by the Supreme Court of California not only to traverse the distance between Asahi's headquarters in Japan and the Superior Court of California in and for the County of Solano, but also to submit its dispute with Cheng Shin to a foreign nation's judicial system. The unique burdens placed upon one who must defend oneself in a foreign legal system should have significant weight in assessing the reasonableness of stretching the long arm of personal jurisdiction over national borders.

When minimum contacts have been established, often the interests of the plaintiff and the forum in the exercise of jurisdiction will justify even the serious burdens placed on the alien defendant. In the present case, however, the interests of the plaintiff and the forum in California's assertion of jurisdiction over Asahi are slight. All that remains is a claim for indemnification asserted by Cheng Shin, a Taiwanese corporation, against Asahi. The transaction on which the indemnification claim is based took place in Taiwan; Asahi's components were shipped from Japan to

*(continued)*

*(continued)*

Taiwan. Cheng Shin has not demonstrated that it is more convenient for it to litigate its indemnification claim against Asahi in California rather than in Taiwan or Japan.

Because the plaintiff is not a California resident, California's legitimate interests in the dispute have considerably diminished. The Supreme Court of California argued that the State had an interest in "protecting its consumers by ensuring that foreign manufacturers comply with the state's safety standards." . . . The State Supreme Court's definition of California's interest, however, was overly broad. The dispute between Cheng Shin and Asahi is primarily about indemnification rather than safety. Moreover, it is not at all clear at this point that California law should govern the question whether a Japanese corporation should indemnify a Taiwanese corporation on the basis of a sale made in Taiwan and a shipment of goods from Japan to Taiwan.

Considering the international context, the heavy burden on the alien defendant, and the slight interests of the plaintiff and the forum State, the exercise of personal jurisdiction by a California court over Asahi in this instance would be unreasonable and unfair.

Because the facts of this case do not establish minimum contacts such that the exercise of personal jurisdiction is consistent with fair play and substantial justice, the judgment of Supreme Court of California is reversed, and the case is remanded for further proceedings not inconsistent with this opinion.

It is so ordered.

**Decision.** Reversed and remanded. The United States Supreme Court found that there was no jurisdiction, reversing the California Supreme Court. This Supreme Court case is significant because it lists several factors that will be taken into account in determining whether the court will take jurisdiction.

Many cases raising jurisdiction issues have been product liability actions in which the plaintiff was an injured consumer. Such questions are less likely to be raised between two business people because they are more likely to try to control where a matter will be litigated before a dispute even arises, most often through a contract that contains a *choice of law and forum* clause. A contract is critical to fixing some of the uncertainty that exists in transnational disputes.

## Choice of Law and Forum

Historically, any attempt by private parties to control jurisdiction was viewed with hostility by the courts as an effort to usurp their authority. The realities of the international marketplace, however, and the recognition of the importance of reducing uncertainty, and thereby lessening risk and cost, have persuaded many courts to accept choice of law and forum clauses. Choice of forum clauses fix in advance where the case will be heard, thus reducing the forum shopping by parties' lawyers. Choice of law clauses stipulate in advance what law the parties have selected to apply to this transaction. The *Bremen* case illustrates the U.S. Supreme Court's view of a forum clause.

A more recent case illustrates how a foreign corporation can become ensnared in a court's jurisdiction. The court addresses the issues of minimum contacts, forum selection, and *forum non conveniens*.

Choice of law clauses are another way parties attempt to fix in advance and control the laws that are applied to the dispute. In general, at common law and in many civil law jurisdictions, the choice of law is upheld as long as "a reasonable relation" between the transaction and the jurisdiction can be made.

For example, a Japanese manufacturer and a New York buyer who agree to have California law apply to their contract, sign the contract in California, and both have offices in San Francisco, California, provide a reasonable nexus between the transaction and the law. The *Convention on the International Sale of Goods (CISG)* has broadened this right for subscribing countries, allowing the parties to choose any law. The EU directives also support this move. The only cautionary note is that in some instances the international law concept of "Ius Cogens" (preemptory norms) may intercede; in this instance, the nation's court may deem something to be a law or fundamental public policy that cannot be altered, and the court will then abrogate the parties' choice.

**The Bremen
v. Zapata
Off-Shore Co.**
407 U.S. 1 (1972)
United States Supreme
Court

## BACKGROUND AND FACTS

In 1967, Zapata, a Houston-based corporation, entered into a contract with Unterweser, a German corporation, to tow Zapata's drilling rig from Louisiana to Ravenna, Italy. The contract the parties signed contained the clause "Any dispute arising must be heard before the London Court of Justice." During a storm, the rig was damaged, and Zapata instructed Unterweser's tug, the *Bremen,* to tow instead to Tampa, Florida, the nearest port. Immediately thereafter, Zapata filed suit in federal district court in Tampa, Florida, on the basis of admiralty jurisdiction seeking $3,500,000 damages in personam against Unterweser and in rem against the *Bremen.* Unterweser moved to dismiss for:

1. Lack of jurisdiction on the basis of the forum clause
2. *Forum non conveniens* (not a convenient forum)
3. A stay of action pending resolution in the London Court of Justice

Unterweser filed suit in London for breach of contract. The U.S. District Court and Court of Appeals had denied the motion to stay, thus allowing the case to proceed in U.S. court despite the forum selection clause. Unterweser filed a petition of certiorari to the Supreme Court.

## CHIEF JUSTICE BURGER

We hold, with the six dissenting members of the Court of Appeals, that far too little weight and effect were given to the forum clause in resolving this controversy. For at least two decades we have witnessed an expansion of overseas commercial activities by business enterprises based in the United States. The barrier of distance that once tended to confine a business concern to a modest territory no longer does so. Here we see an American company with special expertise contracting with a foreign company to tow a complex machine thousands of miles across seas and oceans. The expansion of American business and industry will hardly be encouraged if, notwithstanding solemn contracts, we insist on a parochial concept that all disputes must be resolved under our laws and in our courts. Absent a contract forum, the consider-ations relied on by the Court of Appeals would be persuasive reasons for holding an American forum convenient in the traditional sense, but in an era of expanding world trade and commerce, the absolute aspects of the doctrine of the Carbon Black case have little place and would be a heavy hand indeed on the future development of international commercial dealings by Americans. We cannot have trade and commerce in world markets and international waters exclusively on our terms, governed by our laws, and resolved in our courts.

Forum-selection clauses have historically not been favored by American courts. Many courts, federal and state, have declined to enforce such clauses on the ground that they were "contrary to public policy," or that their effect was to "oust the jurisdiction" of the court. Although this view apparently still has considerable acceptance, other courts are tending to adopt a more hospitable attitude toward forum-selection clauses. This view, advanced in the well-reasoned dissenting opinion in the instant case, is that such clauses are prima facie valid and should be enforced unless enforcement is shown by the resisting party to be "unreasonable" under the circumstances. We believe this is the correct doctrine to be followed by federal district courts sitting in admirality. . . .

This approach is substantially what followed in other common-law countries including England. It is the view advanced by noted scholars and that adopted by the Restatement of the Conflict of Laws. It accords with ancient concepts of freedom of contract and reflects an appreciation of the expanding horizons of American contractors who seek business in all parts of the world. . . . The choice of that forum was made in an arm's length negotiation by experienced and sophisticated businessmen, and absent some compelling and countervailing reason it should be honored by the parties and enforced by the courts.

The elimination of all such uncertainties by agreeing in advance on a forum acceptable to both parties is an indispensable element in international trade, commerce, and contracting. There is strong evidence that the forum clause was a vital part of the agreement, and it would be unrealistic to think that the parties did not conduct their

*(continued)*

*(continued)*

negotiations, including fixing the monetary terms, with the consequences of the forum clause figuring prominently in their calculations.

Thus, in the light of present-day commercial realities and expanding international trade we conclude that the forum clause should control absent a strong showing that it should be set aside. Although their opinions are not altogether explicit, it seems reasonably clear that the District Court and the Court of Appeals placed the burden on Unterweser to show that London would be a more convenient forum than Tampa, although the contract expressly resolved that issue. The correct approach would have been to enforce the forum clause specifically unless Zapata could clearly show that enforcement would be unreasonable and unjust, or that the clause was invalid for such reasons as fraud or overreaching. Accordingly, the case must be remanded for reconsideration.

**Decision.** Vacated and remanded for proceedings consistent with the opinion. The Court vacated the Court of Appeals judgment stating, "Thus in light of present-day commercial realities and expanding international trade we conclude that the forum clause should control absent a strong showing that it should be set aside."

**Comment.** The Court noted the possible reasons that a forum selection clause could be unenforceable: (1) if it contravenes strong public policy and (2) if the forum is seriously inconvenient. These reasons still hold today. Other reasons forum selection clauses may be ignored by the courts are because parties are of unequal bargaining power, counsel was not consulted, the clause was written in a foreign language, the clause violates federal law, changed circumstances (where the forum is the site of a revolution hostile to one party's country—for example, a forum selection of Iran after the Iranian revolution could be held invalid). Many other countries also support the validity of forum selection clauses, including Austria, England, France, Germany, Italy, and many Latin American and Scandinavian countries.

## Revlon, Inc., Plaintiff v. United Overseas Limited Defendant

93 Civ. 0863 (SS), 1994 WL 9657 (S.D.N.Y.) Decided Jan. 7, 1994

BACKGROUND AND FACTS

Revlon, a Delaware corporation headquartered in New York, is engaged in the manufacture and distribution of consumer products. UOL is a corporation organized and existing under the laws of the United Kingdom, with its corporate headquarters in Peterborough, England. UOL purchases manufacturers' "close-outs" of various consumer products for resale in Europe and in the Middle East.

On or about April 1, 1992, and again in September 1992, Revlon and UOL entered into a contract, whereby Revlon agreed to sell UOL certain specially manufactured shampoos for a purchase purchase price of over four million dollars. Revlon maintains that in each instance UOL breached the contract by failing to pay for the goods, and as a result, has caused Revlon to suffer substantial damages.

UOL has moved to dismiss the complaint for lack of personal jurisdiction based on a forum selection clause allegedly vesting jurisdiction over disputes arising out of the April 1992 contract in English courts. Alternatively, UOL argues that Revlon's complaint should be dismissed on *forum non conveniens* grounds. Revlon asserts that personal jurisdiction over UOL is proper under New York Law. Revlon further claims that the proffered forum selection clause is not controlling, and that the doctrine of *forum non conveniens* does not justify dismissal of its complaint.

JUSTICE SOTOMAYOR

2 CPLR s 301 provides that a "court may exercise such jurisdiction over persons, property, or status as might have been exercised heretofore." Section 301 preserves case law holding that a foreign corporation "doing business" in New York is subject to personal jurisdiction in New York with respect to

*(continued)*

*(continued)*

any cause of action, related or unrelated to its contacts with the state. *Rolls-Royce Motors, Inc. v. Charles Schmitt & Co.*, 657 F.Supp. 1040, 1044 (S.D.N.Y. 1987). To satisfy the "doing business" test of Section 301, the defendant must be present in New York not merely "occasionally or casually, but with a fair measure of permanence and continuity." Although this test is highly fact-sensitive, New York courts typically have focused on the following factors in determining whether a nonresident corporation is "doing business" in New York: "the existence of an office in New York; the solicitation of business in New York; the presence of bank accounts or other property in New York; and the presence of employees or agents in New York." *Landoil Resources Co. v. Alexander & Alexander Serv., Inc.*, 918 F.2d 1039, 1043 (2d Cir.1990).

Revlon claims that UOL is "doing business" in New York because it either has maintained an office here or has held itself out as having a New York office. Based on the affidavit of Jay Knox, who solicited business in New York on UOL's behalf, Revlon asserts that (1) a UOL sign was displayed at the entrance to the New York office of UniTrade Marketing Group, Inc., a New York company in which UOL has a 50 percent ownership interest; (2) an executive officer of UOL represented to customers that this office was UOL's New York office; (3) Knox used stationery listing UniTrade's office as UOL's "New York office;" (4) Knox solicited business for UOL from this office and (5) UOL executive officers used this office to conduct business when in New York. . . .

Indeed, even if a foreign corporation does not actually maintain an office in New York, if it holds itself out to the public as having one, such corporation will be deemed "doing business" in New York for jurisdictional purposes . . .

Accordingly, I conclude that Revlon has made out a prima facie showing of jurisdiction, and thus, deny UOL's motion to dismiss Revlon's complaint.

UOL asserts that this Court lacks subject matter jurisdiction over this dispute based on a forum selection clause written on the reverse side of the April 1992 purchase orders, numbered 001312 and 001313. This clause provides that the parties "hereby agree to submit to the jurisdiction of the English Courts" disputes arising out of the contract. UOL claims that it sent the purchase orders to Revlon both by fax and by mail, and that the mailed originals contained the disputed forum selection clause "on their reverse side." Revlon acknowledges receiving the faxed purchase orders but denies receipt or knowledge of the mailed forum selection clause.

Thus, I must accept Revlon's version of the facts on this issue, and accordingly, conclude that enforcement of the proffered forum selection clause would be unjust and unreasonable since Revlon never knew nor received that portion of the purchase orders containing this clause (forum selection clauses should be enforced absent clear showing that "enforcement would be unreasonable and unjust," or that such clauses are "invalid for such reasons as fraud or overreaching").

However, even assuming that Revlon had received the mailed forum selection clause, it still would not control disputes arising out of the April 1992 transaction because this clause constitutes a material alteration, which Revlon never accepted, to a pre-existing contract. Revlon alleges, and UOL does not dispute, that a binding contract was formed when UOL faxed the purchase orders to it on April 1, 1992. Hence, the contract terms to which the parties allegedly agreed are limited to those contained on that portion of the purchase orders which UOL faxed to Revlon on April 1, 1992. Purchase order 001313 on its face contains a list of six conditions to the agreement, none of which included or made mention of a forum selection clause. Hence, by UOL's own admission, Revlon could not have considered or agreed to the alleged forum selection clause contained on the reverse side of Purchase Order 001313 until it received the completed purchases orders in the mail—some time after the alleged formation of the April 1992 contract.

That Revlon is headquartered in New York, the preliminary negotiations took place in New York, and the contracts were to be performed in New York further suggest that New York, rather than English, law may apply here. New York choice-of-law principles call for the application of "the law of the jurisdiction having the greatest interest in the litigation" and these factors demonstrate New York's substantial interest in this litigation.

Yet, even assuming English law were to govern this case, applying this foreign law would not unduly burden the court, given the common history of the English and American legal systems, and the shared language of our two nations.

**Decision.** For the reasons stated, the defendant's [UOL] motion to dismiss the complaint is *denied.*

So ordered.

## Collection of Evidence

Countries have their own rules governing which materials or evidence the parties to a lawsuit may access. In the United States, the Federal Rules of Civil Procedure governs. The process of evidence-gathering before trial is called discovery.

Discovery provides broad access, which some have called a fishing expedition. Some attorneys have used discovery requests that are burdensome as a tactic in the lawsuit. Numerous other problems may arise in international litigation. For example, how does one collect evidence from a French corporate party? The 1970 *Hague Convention on the Taking of Evidence Abroad in Civil or Commercial Matters* provides a method to collect evidence through (1) letters of request, (2) a diplomatic consular officer, or (3) a specially appointed commissioner; however, fewer than 25 countries are signatories. The Hague Convention may not provide a party with as much evidence as it could obtain under the Federal Rules of Civil Procedure had the litigation occurred in the United States. Many countries do not have such broad discovery rules as the United States; their courts look with disfavor upon the United States's burdensome, exhaustive discovery procedures; nor are all countries signatories to the convention, either.

Japan's system of discovery is quite different from that of the United States. The scope of evidence collected is limited and controlled by the court. Japan is not a signatory to the Hague Evidence Convention, but is a signatory to the *Hague Convention on the Service Abroad of Judicial and Extrajudicial Documents in Civil or Commercial Matters*. In a recent case a U.S. court found that mail service on a Japanese company in Japan violated the Hague Convention. Bilateral conventions between countries may also be a source of authority as in the U.S.–Japan Consular Convention. When a U.S. court tries to enforce its discovery process on an individual in Japan, it may find the system uncooperative. In order to complete discovery, the U.S. court requests via a letter rogatory; however, the Japanese government may tell the Japanese company not to comply with the request.[4]

The Hague Convention is useful to parties outside the United States as well. In a British case, *In Re State of Norway*, the court ordered the witnesses in England to comply with the Norwegian request despite their protests that the discovery was a "fishing expedition," and that it was not a "civil or commercial matter" within the Hague Convention. In a recent industrial espionage case pitting General Motors against Volkswagen AG, however, the German government had not responded in 5 months to GM's request for documents and diskettes, as well as fingerprints. GM alleges that a former employee took proprietary information with him to Germany. The case is proceeding slowly, and German cooperation is by no means assured.

## Management of Litigation

Transnational litigation increases the expense and risk of the process. Businesses can reduce the uncertainty and the cost of litigation by the inclusion of choice of law and forum clauses in contracts; however, these clauses are of no assistance in suits initiated by third parties as in the Bhopal case. A business believing its position justifiable may nevertheless make the hard decision to settle a matter in order to fix the cost of the loss and move forward. Even if a business wins a court case, it may lose if the cost of winning (lawyers fees and expenses) was high. A manager must be able to assess the risks and manage the cost of litigation working closely with the company lawyers. For a look at McDonald's experience with litigation in Britain, see the following article.

## Enforcement of Foreign Judgments

Once a judgment is secured, how will it be enforced? Suppose that Down Pillow, Inc., and Eiderhoff, GmbH, negotiate a contract with a forum selection clause (Federal District Court, Atlanta, Georgia) and choice of law clause (Georgia law). A dispute arises, the matter is litigated, and Down Pillow obtains a judgment in its favor. If Down Pillow finds that Eiderhoff has no assets within the reach of the court to satisfy the judgment, Down Pillow would try to reach Eiderhoff's assets in Germany and would look to a German court to enforce the judgment. What occurs next depends upon how the German court views the U.S. District Court's judgment.

*http://itl.irv.uit.no/trade_law/nav/enforce.html*
*Provides the text for the U.N. Conventions on Arbitral Recognition and Enforcement.*

# Golden Arches Are Victorious, But Bloodied, in a British Court

LONDON, June 19—McDonald's has had more than its fair share of grief lately: hamburger sales are down, hackers are spreading nasty sales through the Internet, and the company's 55-cent burger campaign in its native United States fell flat.

Today the company had some good news. After the longest trial in British history, a judge in a libel case ruled that McDonald's does not destroy the world's rain forests, discriminate against employees or poison its customers.

But the $96,000 judgment the judge issued, after the company had spent millions in legal fees to defend its reputation, was a decidedly Pyrrhic victory.

After two and a half years of testimony, the judge agreed with the claim of two anti-McDonald's activists that the company is cruel to animals, that it exploited children in its advertising and that its low wages in Britain tended to depress salaries in the fast-food industry.

The case, which came to be known as the McLibel trial, was undoubtedly something of a nadir in the hamburger chain's public relations history.

The defendants, Helen Steel and Dave Morris, were respectively a part-time bartender and an unemployed ex-mailman, and the sight of the multibillion dollar corporation hauling them into court provoked innumerable stories about Goliath taking on David.

Ms. Steel and Mr. Morris were sued for libel after they helped distribute a detailed pamphlet attacking McDonald's some eight years ago.

In summarizing his exhaustive decision, which filled three hefty volumes, Justice Rodger Bell said that while some of the defendants' assertions—touching on everything from the sorry living conditions of the company's future Chicken McNuggets to the fat and salt content of a Big Mac and fries—were true, the preponderance were, in fact, false.

Accordingly, he said, Mr. Morris and Ms. Steel had harmed the reputation of the McDonald's chain and were liable for the damages.

McDonald's said today that it was "broadly satisfied" with the judgment.

"For the sake of our employees and our customers, we wanted to show these serious allegations to be false, and I am pleased that we have done so," said Paul Preston, chairman and chief executive of McDonald's in Britain.

But Michael Mansfield, a lawyer who has been advising Ms. Steel and Mr. Morris, called the result "a major victory" for the defendants, who are known in the anti-McDonald's movement as the McLibel 2.

"They have dared to tread where no others have dared to tread, where those with resources have not dared to go, to raise issues that matter to us all," Mr. Mansfield said, speaking of Mr. Morris and Ms. Steel at a raucous news conference attended by many people waving signs saying things like "We will not be silenced."

The case dates to the late 1980's, when Ms. Steel joined London Greenpeace, an informal group that campaigns for a range of social issues and is not connected to the international Greenpeace organization. In 1989 and 1990, London Greenpeace distributed the pamphlet in question, "What's Wrong with McDonald's," which made seven broad charges against the company.

McDonald's, which is well-known for being fiercely protective of its reputation, was decidedly displeased and sued five members of the group for libel. Three said they were sorry and would not do it again; Mr. Morris and Ms. Steel decided to fight on.

The trial began in June 1994, with McDonald's represented by a top-drawer lawyer in wig and gown, and Mr. Morris and Ms. Steel representing themselves, in jeans and sweat shirts.

Under British law, the burden of proof is on the defendants to show that their statements are true. This meant that Mr. Morris and Ms. Steel had to call

*(continued)*

*(continued)*

experts in nutrition, in deforestation and in employment practices, among other things, in an effort to prove the veracity of even the most far-reaching generalizations in their pamphlet.

With no legal experience and no free time, the defendants held strategy meetings on the subway each day and turned to a motley group of vegetarians, environmentalists, libertarians and animal-rights campaigners around the world for both moral and substantive support.

An anti-McDonald's site was set up on the World Wide Web, so that an expanded version of the pamphlet that so upset McDonald's became available to anyone with a computer and a modem.

By the end of the case, the court had heard from 180 witnesses, sat for 313 days over two and a half years and generated 60,000 pages of transcripts and other documents.

At a news conference, Mr. Preston said that McDonald's had "no intention of bankrupting" Mr. Morris or Ms. Steel by demanding the $96,000 if the two could not afford to pay it. And, when asked whether he thought McDonald's reputation had been hurt by the case and the attendant publicity, Mr. Preston said he did not.

"I think our reputation is valuable," he said, "and it is something you must be willing to stand up and protect."

***Sarah Lyall***
**The New York Times INTERNATIONAL, June 20, 1997.**

Copyright © 1997 by the New York Times Company. Reprinted with permission.

## The U.S. View

In early 1895, the U.S. Supreme Court examined the issue of the enforcement of foreign judgments in the *Hilton* case.

Even though *Hilton* is still good law, many of these issues may be dealt with by state courts, which, in following state law, may find the foreign judgment binding upon the parties. For example Massachusetts General Law states in part

A foreign judgment meeting the requirements of section 2 is conclusive between the parties to the extent that it grants or denies recovery of a sum of money. The foreign judgment is enforceable in the same manner as the judgment of a sister state which is entitled to full faith and credit.

### *Hilton v. Guyot*
### 159 U.S. 113 (1895)
### United States Supreme Court

**BACKGROUND AND FACTS**

Guyot, a citizen of France, who was a liquidator of Fortin Co., brought an action at law in France (on behalf of several individuals) against two U.S. citizens, Hilton and Libby, partners who were doing business in New York and Paris under the name AT Stewart and Company. Fortin had supplied Stewart with shipments of gloves. A French court found that roughly one million francs or $195,000 was owed to Guyot. However, no property in France would satisfy the judgment. Guyot filed suit in U.S. District Court. Hilton and Libby (Americans) claim that the French judgment should not be enforced.

**JUSTICE GRAY**

. . . It appears, therefore, that there is hardly a civilized nation on either continent, which, by its general law, allows conclusive effect to an executory foreign judgment for the recovery of money. In France, and in a few smaller States—Norway, Portugal, Greece, Monaco, and Haiti—the merits of the controversy are reviewed, as of course, allowing to the foreign judgment, at the most, no more effect than of being prima facie evidence of the justice of the claim. In the great majority of the countries on the continent of Europe—in Belgium, Holland, Denmark,

*(continued)*

*(continued)*

Sweden, Germany, in many cantons of Switzerland, in Russia and Poland, in Roumania, in Austria and Hungary, (perhaps in Italy) and in Spain—as well as in Egypt, in Mexico, and in a great part of South America, the judgment rendered in a foreign country is allowed the same effect only as the courts of that country allow to the judgments of the country in which the judgment in question is sought to be executed.

The prediction of Mr. Justice Story (in 618 of his Commentaries on the Conflict of Laws, already cited), has thus been fulfilled, and the rule of reciprocity has worked itself firmly into the structure of international jurisprudence.

The reasonable, if not the necessary, conclusion appears to us to be that judgments rendered in France, or in any other foreign country, by the laws of which our own judgments are reviewable upon the merits, are not entitled to full credit and conclusive effect when sued upon in this country, but are prima facie evidence only of the justice of the plaintiffs' claims.

In holding such a judgment, for want of reciprocity, not to be conclusive evidence of the merits of the claim, we do not proceed upon any theory of retaliation upon one person by reason of injustice done to another; but upon the broad ground that international law is founded upon mutuality and reciprocity, and that by the principles of international law recognized in most civilized nations, and by the comity of our own country, which it is our judicial duty to know and to declare, the judgment is not entitled to be considered conclusive.

By our law, at the time of the adoption of the Constitution, a foreign judgment was considered as prima facie evidence, and not conclusive. There is no statute of the United States, and no treaty of the United States with France, or with any other nation, which has changed that law, or has made any provision upon the subject. It is not to be supposed that, if any statute or treaty had been or

should be made, it would recognize as conclusive the judgments of any country, which did not give like effect to our own judgments. In the absence of statute or treaty, it appears to us equally unwarrantable to assume that the comity of the United States requires anything more.

If we should hold this judgment to be conclusive, we should allow it an effect to which, supposing the defendants' offers to be sustained by actual proof, it would, in the absence of a special treaty, be entitled in hardly any other country in Christendom, except the country in which it was rendered. If the judgment had been rendered in this country, or in any other outside of the jurisdiction of France, the French courts would not have executed or enforced it, except after examining into its merits. The very judgment now sued on would be held inconclusive in almost any other country than France. In England, and in the Colonies subject to the law of England, the fraud alleged in its procurement would be a sufficient ground for disregarding it. In the courts of nearly every other nation, it would be subject to reexamination, either merely because it was a foreign judgment, or because judgments of that nation would be reexamined in the courts of France.

**Decision.** Reversed and remanded for a new trial.

**Comment.** The Court concluded that foreign judgments were "prima facie evidence" only, not conclusive proof entitled to automatic enforcement. The Court examined the notion of "comity," defining it as " . . . the recognition which one nation allows within its territory to the legislative, executive, or judicial acts of another nation having due regard both to international duty and convenience and to the rights of its own citizens or of other persons who are under protection of its laws." The Court found that the fatal defect, however, was that there was no "mutuality and reciprocity": France would not enforce a U.S. judgment.

Grounds for nonrecognition are included in the statute, such as lack of due process, fraud, violation of public policy, lack of jurisdiction over the parties, lack of notice, original forum was seriously inconvenient, and the original proceeding contravened a predispute agreement, to mention a few.

The question of the enforcement of foreign judgments may be confusing to the student who is familiar with the domestic problem of whether a New York court will honor a Texas court judgment. Article IV, Section I, of the U.S. Constitution states that "Full Faith and Credit shall be given in each State to the Public Acts, Records, and judicial proceedings of every other state." Thus, a New York court, absent fraud or lack of notice, should enforce a Georgia court's decision. Note that the Full Faith and Credit Clause does *not* apply to foreign court judgments, however.

The Restatement (third) of Foreign Relations Law of the United States summarized the basis for nonrecognition of a judgment:

1. Except as provided in § 482, a final judgment of a court of a foreign State granting or denying recovery of a sum of money, establishing or confirming the status of a person, or determining interests in property, is conclusive between the parties, and is entitled to recognition in courts in the United States.

2. A judgment entitled to recognition under Subsection (1) may be enforced by any party or its successor or assigns against any other party, its successors or assigns, in accordance with the procedure for enforcement of judgments applicable where enforcement is sought.
§ 482,
1. A court in the United States may not recognize a judgment of the court of a foreign State if:

   a. the judgment was rendered under a judicial system that does not provide impartial tribunals or procedures compatible with due process of law; or
   b. the court that rendered the judgment did not have jurisdiction over the defendant in accordance with the law of the rendering state and with the rules set forth in Section 421.

2. A court in the United States need not recognize a judgment of the court of a foreign State if:

   a. the court that rendered the judgment did not have jurisdiction of the subject matter of the action;
   b. the defendant did not receive notice of the proceedings in sufficient time to enable him to defend;
   c. the judgment was obtained by fraud;
   d. the cause of action on which the judgment was based, or the judgment itself, is repugnant to the public policy of the United States or of the State where recognition is sought;
   e. the judgment conflicts with another final judgment that is entitled to recognition; or
   f. the proceeding in the foreign court was contrary to an agreement between the parties to submit the controversy on which the judgment is based to another forum.[5]

An example of this doctrine is seen in *Stiftung v. V.E.B. Carl Zeiss* in which a U.S. court refused to enforce an East German judgment because, in the judge's view, of a lack of fair procedure, and that the East German judiciary "orient their judgments according to the wishes of the leaders of the Socialist State." *Carl Zeiss Stiftung v. V.E.B. Carl Zeiss, Jena,* 293 F. Supp. 892 (S.D.N.Y. 1968), 433 F. 2d. 686 (2d Cir. 1970), *cert. den.* 403 U.S. 905 (1971).

Another example in which a court refused to enforce a foreign judgment (although from a country with a legal system on which the United States system is modeled) is a libel case against India Abroad Publications. The plaintiff sought enforcement in New York of an award of $70,000. The paper had printed a story connecting the plaintiff to a weapons deal involving a Swedish company. The New York court would not enforce the judgment against the N.Y.-based company and its assets because the British court used a less strict standard than is used in the U.S. (under the First Amendment), thus making it easier for a plaintiff to win such a lawsuit in Britain. One distinguished professor, in summarizing this confusing area of the law, said that many states would enforce a foreign judgment unless "it is inconsistent with our nation's most basic notions of morality and justice."

In 1948, the Uniform Enforcement of Foreign Judgments Act was proposed by a group trying to standardize U.S. state law, but few states adopted it. Subsequently, the same group proposed the Uniform Recognition of Foreign Money Judgments Act, which 18 states have implemented.

The following case illustrates how a state court deals with the dual problem of both a foreign judgment and the problem of the date of conversion from pounds to dollars. Note that the outcome is different from *Hilton v. Guyot.*

## Other Countries' Views

Japan provides an additional example of how another country deals with the enforcement of a

## Manches & Co.
## v. Suzanne Gilby
## & Another

*419 Mass. 414*
*Decided Feb. 6, 1995*
*Supreme Judicial Court*
*of Massachusetts*

### BACKGROUND AND FACTS

On August 20, 1992, the Queen's Bench Division of the High Court of Justice in London entered a default judgment in favor of Manches & Co., a London firm of solicitors, against Suzanne Gilbey and Peter Thorton totaling £30,138.35. On November 9, 1992, Manches commenced this action in the Superior Court in Barnstable County to enforce the foreign judgment pursuant to G.L. c. 235, § 23A (1992 ed.), the Uniform Foreign Money—Judgments Recognition Act. Manches's underlying claim was that the defendants were liable for legal services rendered to Gilbey in England following the death of her father.

The principal issue in this appeal concerns the amount of the judgment that should have been entered in Massachusetts in view of changes in the exchange rate between the British pound and the American dollar. It appears that on August 20, 1992, the date that judgment was entered in London, approximately $58,450 equaled the amount stated in pounds in the English judgment (£30,138.35). On December 13, 1993, the date on which summary judgment was granted in favor of Manches in Barnstable Superior Court, approximately $45,130 would have purchased £30,138.35. Thus, because of the decline in the British pound in relation to the American dollar, the defendants could satisfy their obligation to Manches, expressed in pounds, by paying out considerably fewer dollars in late 1993 than they could have sixteen months earlier when the English default judgment was entered.

### JUSTICE WILKINS

Because the motion judge entered judgment in dollars using the latter exchange rate (the one more beneficial to the defendants), Manches has appealed. Because the motion judge entered judgment in favor of Manches, the defendants have appealed, arguing that, for various reasons, the English judgment is not worthy of enforcement in Massachusetts. We transferred the cross appeals to this court on our own motion. If the defendants are correct in their claim that the English judgment is unenforceable, the question of the proper amount of any judgment that should be entered in favor of

Manches in Massachusetts is unimportant. Therefore, we shall discuss the defendants' appeal first. We conclude that the English judgment is enforceable in Massachusetts and that the appropriate judgment is one that reflects the exchange rate at the time of the payment of the judgment.

None of the defendants' arguments in opposition to the enforcement of the English judgment has merit. The defendants rely on grounds set forth in G.L. c. 235, § 23A, that, if they exist, would deny enforcement of a foreign judgment: lack of jurisdiction over them in England, denial of due process in the English justice system, and a form of *forum non conveniens*.

The English court had jurisdiction over the defendants. Manches received court permission to serve the defendants outside the jurisdiction. The contract for legal services to be rendered in England was governed by English law, and thus under English law the court there had jurisdiction over the parties.

There is no showing that the English system lacked "procedures compatible with the requirements of due process" or that the defendants were denied due process in their attempt to claim an appeal from the default judgment. England was not a "seriously inconvenient forum" and that statutory basis for denial of enforcement of a foreign judgment has no application in any event, because it applied when, unlike this case, jurisdiction in the foreign court was based "only on personal service."

The obligation to pay pounds, expressed in the English judgment, should be enforced by a judgment that orders the defendants at their option either (a) to pay £30,138.35 (with interest) or (b) to pay the equivalent in dollars of £30,138.35 (with interest), determined by the exchange rate in effect on the day of payment (or the day before payment). Manches is entitled to be restored to the position in which it would have been if the defendants had paid their obligations, but it is not entitled to more. The so-called payment day rule achieves this result.

There is no guiding Massachusetts law on this point. The decided cases in this country have

*(continued)*

*(continued)*

adopted various positions. Some have followed the breach day rule, the one Manches advocates, in which the conversion of foreign obligations is made as of the date of breach of the obligation. Others have used the judgment day rule, converting the foreign obligation into dollars based on the exchange rate on the date the judgment is entered. We prefer a third option, the payment day rule.

The Restatement (Third) of Foreign Relations Law advises that the conversion to dollars should be "made at such rate as to make the creditor whole and to avoid rewarding a debtor who has delayed in carrying out the obligation." The Restatement becomes more specific and tentatively adopts the breach day rule if, as here, the foreign currency has depreciated since the breach, and, if the foreign currency has appreciated since the breach, it adopts the exchange rate on the date of judgment or the date of payment. "The court is free, however, to depart from those guidelines when the interests of justice require it."

The Uniform Foreign–Money Claims Act, which has been enacted in eighteen American jurisdictions (but not in Massachusetts), adopts the payment day rule. It is this rule that, for the circumstances of this case, we apply as a matter of common law. That rule will award Manches in pounds (or the equivalent in dollars on or near the day of payment) the amount it would have re-covered had it been able to collect on the judgment in Great Britain. Satisfaction of the judgment in present day pounds will make Manches whole. In entering judgments, courts do not normally reflect changes in the purchasing power of local currency between the date of a breach and the date of the award of judgment. As the prefatory note to the Uniform Act states: "The principle of the Act is to restore the aggrieved party to the economic position it would have been in had the wrong not occurred. . . . Courts should enter judgments in the money customarily used by the injured person." Manches incurred its expenses in England, expected to be compensated in pounds, and sustained its loss in pounds. The payment day rule is fair in this case because its application meets the reasonable expectations of the parties in this case.

**Decision.** Judgment shall be entered ordering that Manches & Co. shall recover from the defendants, at the defendants' option, either (a) the amount of the English judgment (£30,138.35) or (b) the equivalent in dollars of the English judgment determined at the exchange rate in effect on the day or or the day before payment, with interest on that amount (in each instance), payable in pounds or dollars, at the Massachusetts rate of interest from the date of entry of the action until the date of payment.

*So ordered.*

---

foreign court's judgment. Article 200 of the Japanese Code of Civil Procedure establishes five conditions that must exist before a foreign judgment will be found to be valid and thus enforceable:

1. Jurisdiction did not contravene Japanese statutes, treaties, and the like.
2. Proper notice was given.
3. The judgment does not violate Japanese policy or morals.
4. The foreign court would recognize a Japanese judgment, or operates under a commitment to reciprocity.
5. It was a final, not an interlocutory, judgment.

Also, for Japan to enforce a judgment, it must be a civil one—not criminal. Thus, some treble damage awards construed as criminal would not be enforced.

On the basis of Article 200, a Japanese court denied enforcement in Japan of a judgment won in a U.S. state court by a U.S. plaintiff who was injured in the United States by a machine made by a Japanese manufacturer.[6]

Eighteen European countries signed a Convention on Jurisdiction and Enforcement of Judgments on Civil and Commercial Matters, sometimes referred to as the Lugano Convention, on September 16, 1988. (See Exhibit 4.1.)

In other countries, national laws and the courts' interpretation of those laws determine to what extent a foreign judgment will be enforced. For example, in Germany, foreign judgments are generally honored subject to several exceptions involving whether the German entity received proper service of notice, whether the judgment violates German law, or whether the foreign court would grant reciprocity to a German judgment.

The German Federal Supreme Court refused to recognize in its entirety a California judgment

**EXHIBIT 4.1    Selections from the Lugano Convention**

### Section 1: Recognition

*Article 26*

A judgment given in a Contracting State shall be recognized in the other Contracting States without any special procedure being required.

Any interested party who raises the recognition of a judgment as the principal issue in a dispute may, in accordance with the procedures provided for in Section 2 and 3 of this Title, apply for a decision that the judgment be recognized.

If the outcome of proceedings in a court of a Contracting State depends on the determination of an incidental question of recognition that court shall have jurisdiction over that question.

*Article 27*

A judgment shall not be recognized:

1. if such recognition is contrary to public policy in the State in which recognition is sought;
2. where it was given in default of appearance, if the defendant was not duly served with the document which instituted the proceedings or with an equivalent document in sufficient time to enable him to arrange for his defence;
3. if the judgment is irreconcilable with a judgment given in a dispute between the same parties in the State in which recognition is sought;
4. if the court of the State of origin, in order to arrive at its judgment, has decided a preliminary question concerning the status or legal capacity of natural persons, rights in property arising out of a matrimonial relationship, wills, or succession in a way that conflicts with a rule of the private international law of the State in which the recognition is sought, unless the same result would have been reached by the application of the rules of private international law of that State;
5. if the judgment is irreconcilable with an earlier judgment given in a noncontracting State involving the same cause of action and between the same parties, provided that this latter judgment fulfils the conditions necessary for its recognition in the State addressed.

SOURCE:    Reprinted with permission from 28 I.L.M. 620 (1989), © The American Society of International Law.

awarding punitive damages. A U.S. citizen sought to enforce a California judgment against a dual U.S.–German citizen in Germany. The defendant had previously had homosexual relations with the plaintiff who was a minor at the time. The court awarded $750,260 in damages, which was broken down as $260 for medical treatment, $150,000 for psychiatric treatment, $200,000 for pain and suffering, and $400,000 for punitive damages. The German Supreme Court found the award enforceable up to $350,260, but not for the punitive damages, because the purpose of German law was merely to compensate not to punish or deter. The court also noted that the actions took place when both parties lived in California and under California laws. The ruling did not deal with a product liability case, a matter in which Germany might have a stronger national interest.

The English express a similar distaste for U.S. law and punitive damages. Lord Denning sums up the European view:

As a moth drawn to the light, so is a litigant drawn to the United States. If he can only get his case into their courts, he stands to win a fortune. At no cost to himself; and at no risk of having to pay anything to the other side. . . . The lawyers will charge the litigant nothing for their services but instead they will take 40 percent of the damages. . . . If they lose, the litigant will have nothing to pay to the other side. The courts in the United States have no such cost deterrents as we have. There is also in the United States a right to trial by jury. These are prone to award fabulous damages. They are notoriously sympathetic and know that the lawyers will take their 40 percent before the plaintiff gets anything. All this means that the defendant can be readily forced onto a settlement.
*Smith Kline and French Lab. Ltd. v. Bloch* (1983), 1 W.L.R. 730, 733-4 (Eng. C.A. 1982)

Despite this antipathy, however, British law is changing. (See previous Foreign Accents box, on page 116.)

Within the EU, the Lugano Convention sets a standard for uniformity. But since the United

States is not a party to multilateral or bilateral convention on the enforcement of judgments in Europe, a U.S. litigant must use national law. Just as the young man in the previous case discovered, the foreign court may see the case differently. In France, courts will as a general rule enforce private civil judgments with some safeguards such as conforming with French public policy and principles of a fair process. For an example of the French criminal process, see the article below.

The Convention on the Recognition and Enforcement of Foreign Judgments in Civil and Commercial Matters (1966) was not ratified. It is now being revisited by the Hague Convention on International Law. Clearly, an international treaty would be of assistance in this matter.

---

*Foreign Accents*

---

# A French White-Collar Trial
## Quelle Différence!

**M**y colleague at Aix-en-Provence, where I teach every year, is a distinguished French advocate and professor of criminal law. He told me of a complex white-collar case he would try during my visit.

"How long," I asked.

"Perhaps three days," he said, and added in explanation, "There are six defendants."

"And in your Oklahoma case," he asked, "how long will the first trial take?"

"The prosecutors and defense estimate four months."

Maitre DiMarino rolled his eyes in amazement, and wondered aloud how with such long trials the system can work. There must, he thought, be a terrible backlog of cases.

I reminded him of the plea bargain, that uniquely American method of sweeping the docket. In France, one cannot simply plead guilty to a serious offense. Even if, after the police and magistrate investigation, one wishes to "acknowledge the facts," a trial will be held to determine appropriate punishment.

At this trial, the three robed judges sat on the dais. The prosecutor sat off to their right. Six defense counsel, in their robes, sat along one wall. The accused sat on a bench before the judges. Ranged behind were lawyers for the insurance company. They had joined the case as civil parties to request that any judgment of conviction include an order to pay damages.

At 8:30 a.m., Mme. President (the presiding judge) read the formal accusation: M. Starckman, on behalf of his company, placed an order for 15 million francs worth of computer equipment, to be sent to Vietnam.

The computers were designed to operate with the Cyrillic alphabet. Another defendant, M. Tran, arranged financing for the deal through a Vietnamese bank.

M. DeFalques supplied the goods and arranged to insure them.

### Disappearing Goods
As the shipment was being trucked to the Marseille port, the truck driver was intercepted at a truck stop by several armed men, who have yet to be caught. He was told to park his truck near the port and leave it overnight. He did so, and when he returned in the morning, the shipment was gone.

Messrs. Starckman and DeFalques were accused of masterminding the theft—M. DeFalques was to receive the insurance proceeds; M. Starckman was to get the computer equipment, which (although the proof was hazy) he could sell in Russia for ready cash.

M. Starckman is an international arms trader operating through a series of shell corporations in several countries, including the United States. The police never found the computers, so their eventual resting place was open to argument.

The accusation detailed the role of minor defendants, such as young M. Laurence, who had actually offloaded the goods.

At 9 a.m., the judge had each defendant stand while she read their life histories from the thick file in front of her. The thickness of the file evokes the major difference between American and French criminal procedure.

*(continued)*

*(continued)*

In this country, a white-collar grand jury investigation spanning several continents could well take several years. Most of the action would be in the grand jury room, and by lawyer and FBI investigation. In France, the same type of investigation begins with the police, but is quickly turned over to a juge d'instruction. This magistrate takes statements from witnesses and supervises preparation of a dossier. Defense lawyers may try to influence the instruction process, and may find their clients detained during all or part of it. But once that file is finished, it becomes the basis for formal charges and a trial.

At 9:30, the contents of the thick file became the center of attention. The hijacked truck driver testified briefly; he was the only live witness.

When the truck driver left the courtroom, Mme. President turned to M. Laurence.

He admitted offloading the computers, and said M. DeFalques had paid him by check. M. DeFalques stood and began to explain that he had paid M. Laurence for some innocent purpose. The president turned to and quoted from a statement from M. DeFalques' accountant that contradicted the story. M. DeFalques' lawyer, pulled out a document and approached the bench to offer "clarification and detail." On the way, he gave M. DeFalques a fierce look, to signal that he should not antagonize the court.

The president started the story from the time the computer order was placed, reciting facts from the file and calling on each defendant to stand and respond to questions. If one defendant accused another, the two of them would be on their feet trading versions. The lawyers interrupted to suggest a question now and again, or to point to a significant document.

By 11:30, the main outlines and the defendants' differing versions, had begun to appear. M. DeFalques was clearly in trouble, because M. Laurence was pointing at him.

M. Tran had made damaging statements to the police, but claimed he had been pressured. M. Starckman could not explain why Cyrillic alphabet computers would be of use in Vietnam, and his complex financial dealings looked suspicious. In the afternoon, he would claim that Gaullist politicians had a grudge against him.

Defense counsel trooped out with their clients to lunch and confer. After lunch, the president probed into the financial evidence, and the lawyers were more active. They pointed to documents. They raised questions. The president, with an occasional question from the other judges, focused on the shadowy nature of the financing, suggesting that the deal was an insurance scam from the start.

After two days of trial, the lawyers made their arguments, each taking about an hour. Their mastery of the file was evident. This was the moment for which they had waited.

The long instruction had built the record. The trial was to clear up details and to judge the legal effect of proven facts. Then the judges retired to prepare their judgment.

The lawyers' role was therefore more classically rhetorical—to impose on the record a theme that served their clients' interests, and to argue in mitigation.

In the French system, the person claiming innocence is best advised to present that argument during the instruction. Once formal charges are lodged, the judges are inclined to think that proof beyond a reasonable doubt (or conviction in time) will lurk in the file. On the other hand, the French system helps to guarantee that each accused has a hearing before disposition, something that our plea bargain system denies to the great majority of defendants.

*Michael E. Tigar*

# Arbitration

As the preceding section pointed out, litigation as a means of settling disputes presents a number of problems at both the domestic and international levels. Consequently, many parties are turning to other ways of resolving problems; these methods are known collectively as *alternate dispute resolution* (ADR). One of the most popular forms of ADR is *arbitration,* which can be defined as "the submission for determination of the disputed matter to private unofficial person(s) selected in a manner provided by law or agreement." Many factors must be considered in choosing binding arbitration:

1. Cost-arbitration may be cheaper than litigation.
2. Pretrial discovery is more limited and less expensive in arbitration.
3. Speed-arbitration is faster than litigation.
4. The rules on the admissibility of evidence are more flexible in arbitration.
5. An arbitration decision is more enforceable than a court judgment.
6. The forum is more likely to be neutral in arbitration.
7. Arbitration proceedings may be more private.
8. Arbitration proceedings are less adversarial than a court.
9. A party's rights of appeal are limited in arbitration.

Arbitration has become popular in both domestic and international business agreements. For example, an arbitration clause may be inserted in an employment contract, credit card agreement, cruise ship ticket, bank account application as well as in multimillion dollar contracts.

Arbitration is not cheap. Under some arbitral organizations' procedures, if ten million dollars were at stake, the organization would receive $30,000, the arbitrator $20,000–$80,000, and the lawyers an hourly fee. On the other hand, arbitration is growing in popularity, particularly in the intellectual property and licensing area. In addition, countries previously hostile to arbitration have changed their attitudes: Brazil recently enacted a new law endorsing arbitration, the signal of a historic change.

For a number of years, international construction contracts have been in the forefront of change, including an arbitration clause as a dispute settlement mechanism. Arbitration, however, can be expensive and even lengthy, despite its reputation as the quicker and cheaper alternative to litigation. In a construction project, time is money so any delay can be quite costly. Experts have noted a new trend toward the inclusion of a resolution mechanism for immediate problems, in addition to arbitration including a neutral advisor or special dispute panel.

*http://itl.irv.uit.no/trade_law/nav/*
*arbitration.html*
*Will link you to numerous international arbitration, conciliation, and mediation sites.*

## IBM and Fujitsu Example

An example of major multinational companies choosing arbitration involved IBM and Fujitsu, which selected arbitration to settle their dispute even after litigation had already begun. On September 15, 1987, the two companies settled a four-year legal battle by a final order of two arbitrators from the American Arbitration Association. (The companies had each selected an arbitrator; one was a computer specialist and the other a law professor from Stanford University.) The dispute focused on the operating system software for IBM computers and whether Fujitsu was infringing on IBM's rights. Fujitsu believed IBM was engaging in legal maneuvers largely to discourage Fujitsu's competition. The uncertainty of the law was a major factor in persuading both parties to agree to arbitration. The arbitrators awarded IBM $833.2 million and gave Fujitsu access to the operating systems without fear of future suits.

The decision in the IBM-Fujitsu case presented a unique solution to a complex problem, but it has been somewhat controversial. Some commentators have praised it for providing a quick and final settlement, but others have expressed concerns about the fact that the parties gave up the right to appeal.

## Enforcement of Arbitration Judgments

Once an arbitration judgment is made, how can you enforce it? Recall that we faced the same problem with regard to a court judgment. One advantage of arbitration is that such awards are recognized by signatories to the 1958 United Nations Convention on the Recognition and Enforcement of Foreign Arbitral Awards, known as the New York Convention. This agreement makes enforcement in countries that are signatories to the convention perfunctory. More than 100 countries have signed the New York Convention, including the United States, Canada, China, Germany, and the former Soviet Union, to name only a few.

Many Latin American countries are signatories to the InterAmerican Convention on International Commercial Arbitration. Note also that the U.S. Congress passed the Federal Arbitration Act, which went into effect in 1926. The FAA acknowledged that arbitration was like any other contract provision, one that parties could agree to subject to certain constraints. Despite this Convention and law, parties were still willing to attempt to use the old judicial hostility to forum selection clauses as a means to block the commencement of an arbitration.

The U.S. case *Scherk v. Alberto-Culver*, tested the waters on the enforceability of an arbitration agreement.

Despite the *Scherk* case, many businesspeople continued to believe that certain antitrust claims were so unique that they were not arbitrable and

---

### Scherk v. Alberto-Culver
417 U.S. 506, 94 S.Ct. 2449,
41 L.Ed.2d 270 (1974)
United States
Supreme Court

### BACKGROUND AND FACTS

Alberto-Culver Co., a Delaware Corporation with its principal office in Illinois, manufactures toiletries and hair products in the United States and abroad. In February 1969, Alberto-Culver signed in Austria a contract to purchase three businesses of Fritz Scherk (a German citizen) that were organized under German and Liechtenstein law, as well as the trademarks to related cosmetics. In the contract, Scherk warranted that he had the sole and unencumbered ownership of these trademarks. The contract also contained a clause that provided that "any controversy or claim [that] shall arise out of this agreement or the breach thereof would be referred to arbitration before the International Chamber of Commerce in Paris, France, and that the laws of Illinois shall govern." One year after the closing, Alberto-Culver discovered that others had claims to Scherk's trademarks. Alberto-Culver tried to rescind the contract; Scherk refused, and Alberto-Culver filed suit in Illinois Federal District Court claiming that the misrepresentations violated the Securities and Exchange Act, sec. 10(b) and the SEC rule 10b-5. Scherk moved to dismiss or to stay the action pending arbitration. In the U.S. District Court, the motion to dismiss was denied and arbitration was enjoined. The Court of Appeals affirmed. The Supreme Court granted certiorari.

### JUSTICE STEWART

The United States Arbitration Act, now 9 U.S.C. 1 et seq., reversing centuries of judicial hostility to arbitration agreements, was designed to allow parties to avoid "the costliness and delays of litigation," and to place arbitration agreements "upon the same footing as other contracts. . . . "

Alberto-Culver's contract to purchase the business entities belonging to Scherk was a truly international agreement. Alberto-Culver is an American corporation with its principal place of business and the vast bulk of its activity in this country, while Scherk is a citizen of Germany whose companies were organized under the laws of Germany and Liechtenstein. The negotiations leading to the signing of the contract in Austria and to the closing in Switzerland took place in the United States, England, and Germany, and involved consultations with legal and trademark experts from each of those countries and from Liechtenstein. Finally, and most significantly, the subject matter of the contract concerned the sale of business enterprises organized under the laws of and primarily situated in European countries, whose activities were largely, if not entirely, directed to European markets.

Such a contract involves considerations and policies significantly different from those found controlling in *Wilko.* In *Wilko,* quite apart from the arbitration provision, there was no question but that the laws of the United States generally, and the federal securities laws in particular, would govern disputes arising out of the stock-purchase agreement. The parties, the negotiations, and the subject matter of the contract were all situated in this country, and no credible claim could have been entertained that any international conflict-of-laws problems would arise. In this case, by contrast, in the absence of the arbitration provision considerable uncertainty existed at the time of the agreement, and still exists, concerning the law applicable to the resolutions of disputes arising out of the contract.

Such uncertainty will almost inevitably exist with respect to any contract touching two or more countries, each with its own substantive laws and conflict-of-laws rules. A contractual provision specifying in advance the forum in which disputes shall be litigated and the law to be applied is, therefore, an almost indispensable precondition

*(continued)*

*(continued)*

to achievement of the orderliness and predictability essential to any international business transaction. Furthermore, such a provision obviates the danger that a dispute under the agreement might be submitted to a forum hostile to the interests of one of the parties or unfamiliar with the problem involved.

A parochial refusal by the courts of one country to enforce an international arbitration agreement would not only frustrate these purposes, but would invite unseemly and mutually destructive jockeying by the parties to secure tactical litigation advantages. In the present case, for example, it is not inconceivable that if Scherk had anticipated that Alberto-Culver would be able in this country to enjoin resort to arbitration he might have sought an order in France or some other country enjoining Alberto-Culver from proceeding with its litigation in the United States. Whatever recognition the courts of this country might ultimately have granted to the order of the foreign court, the

dicey atmosphere of such a legal no-man's-land would surely damage the fabric of international commerce and trade, and imperil the willingness and ability of businessmen to enter into international commercial agreements. . . .

For all these reasons we hold that the agreement of the parties in this case to arbitrate any dispute arising out of their international commercial transaction is to be respected and enforced by the federal courts in accord with the explicit provisions of the Arbitration Act.

**Decision.** Reversed and remanded.

**Comment.** The Court understood that an arbitration agreement was the ultimate type of forum selection clause. The Court made reference to national legislation that indicated an acceptance of arbitration (the Arbitration Act, 9 U.S.C 1 et. seq.). Other countries have similar national legislation or are signatories to the New York Convention and/or the European Convention on International Arbitration.

could be addressed only by a court. The question in the *Mitsubishi* case focused on the enforceability of the arbitration clause between a Japanese–U.S. joint venture and a Puerto Rican corporation.

Except in cases of exigent circumstances, arbitration clauses will be enforced particularly in dealing with international business contracts. Despite this trend, parties continue to use dilatory

## Mitsubishi Motors v. Soler Chrysler-Plymouth
### 473 U.S. 614, 105 S.Ct. 3345 (1985)
### United States Supreme Court

BACKGROUND AND FACTS
In 1979, Soler Chrysler-Plymouth, Inc., became a distributor for CISA, a Swiss subsidiary of Chrysler. Soler was to sell Plymouth cars in Puerto Rico. Mitsubishi Motors was a joint venture between CISA and Mitsubishi Heavy Industries, Inc. CISA, Soler, and Mitsubishi Motors entered into an agreement that contained the following clause:

Arbitration of Certain Matters. All disputes, controversies, or differences which may arise between MMC and buyer (Soler) . . . Shall be finally settled by arbitration in Japan in accordance with the rules and regulations of the Japan Commercial Arbitration Association.

The agreement worked for several years until during a slowdown Mitsubishi filed a request

for arbitration in Tokyo and also filed an action in Federal District Court to compel arbitration. Soler claimed that antitrust as well as other violations were involved that should not be addressed by arbitration. The District Court ordered arbitration: The Court of Appeals reversed the part of the order submitting Soler's antitrust claim to arbitration. The Supreme Court granted certiorari.

JUSTICE BLACKMUN
. . . We also reject the proposition that an arbitration panel will pose too great a danger of innate hostility to the constraints on business conduct that antitrust

*(continued)*

*(continued)*

law imposes. International arbitrators frequently are drawn from the legal as well as the business community; where the dispute has an important legal component, the parties and the arbitral body with whose assistance they have agreed to settle their dispute can be expected to select arbitrators accordingly. We decline to indulge the presumption that the parties and arbitral body conducting a proceeding will be unable or unwilling to retain competent, conscientious, and impartial arbitrators. . . .

There is no reason to assume at the outset of the dispute that international arbitration will not provide an adequate mechanism. To be sure, the international arbitral tribunal owes no prior allegiance to the legal norms of particular states; hence, it has no direct obligation to vindicate their statutory dictates. The tribunal, however, is bound to effectuate the intentions of the parties. Where the parties have agreed that the arbitral body is to decide a defined set of claims which includes, as in these cases, those arising from the application of American antitrust law, the tribunal therefore should be bound to decide that dispute in accord with the national law giving rise to the claim. . . .

Having permitted the arbitration to go forward, the national courts of the United States will have the opportunity at the award-enforcement stage to ensure that the legitimate interest in the enforcement of the antitrust laws has been addressed. The Convention reserves to each signatory country the right to refuse enforcement of an award where the "recognition or enforcement of the award would be contrary to the public policy of that country.". . . While the efficacy of the arbitral process requires that substantive review at the award-enforcement stage remain minimal, it would not require intrusive

inquiry to ascertain that the tribunal took cognizance of the antitrust claims and actually decided them.

As international trade has expanded in recent decades, so too has the use of international arbitration to resolve disputes arising in the course of that trade. The controversies that international arbitral institutions are called upon to resolve have increased in diversity as well as in complexity. Yet the potential of these tribunals for efficient disposition of legal disagreements arising from commercial relations has not yet been tested. If they are to take a central place in the international legal order, national courts will need to "shake off the old judicial hostility to arbitration," *Kulukundis Shipping Co. v. Amtorg Trading Corp.,* 126 F.2d 978, 985 (CA2 1942), and also their customary and understandable unwillingness to cede jurisdiction of a claim arising under domestic law to a foreign or transnational tribunal. To this extent, at least, it will be necessary for national courts to subordinate domestic notions of arbitrability to the international policy favoring commercial arbitration.

**Decision.** Affirmed in part, reversed in part, and remanded.

**Comment.** The Supreme Court reversed the Court of Appeals and ordered submission of the antitrust claim to arbitration. Another recent Supreme Court opinion, *Shearson/American Express v. McMahon* (1987), reinforced the enforceability of predispute arbitration agreements. The Court in *Soler* acknowledged the unique, complex, and diverse nature of disputes between transnational parties and reiterated that, especially for these business ventures, arbitration provides a certainty of resolution.

and jurisdictional objections to arbitration enforcement. In the recent case, Terrain Vehicles, a Delaware corporation, objected to the confirmation in a U.S. court of a Japanese Commercial Arbitration Association award. The action commenced in 1986 in state court. Ultimately, however, the Japanese Commercial Arbitration Association (JCAA) issued a decision in favor of Daihatsu in 1992. Daihatsu sought judicial confirmation in the United States. It was granted on

December 17, 1993, and affirmed on January 12, 1994. Arbitration is not always swift.

When, if ever, will a court *not* enforce an arbitration agreement? The New York Convention lists several reasons for not enforcing an arbitration judgment, including the following:

• The parties were incapacitated.
• The agreement was not valid under law (e.g., fraud).

- No notice was given.
- The matter was not within the scope of the arbitration clause.
- The arbitration did not follow the agreement.
- The judgment violates public policy.

## Different Arbitration Bodies

If an arbitration clause is going to be included in a contract, the parties must decide what body they want to control the process. Some possibilities include the following:

- International Chamber of Commerce (ICC) (Paris)
- International Center for the Settlement of Investment Disputes (World Bank Affiliated)
- American Arbitration Association
- London Court of International Arbitration
- Arbitration Institute of the Stockholm Chamber of Commerce
- Euro-Arab Chamber of Commerce
- United Nations Commission for International Trade Law (UNCITRAL)

Each of these organizations has different characteristics, particularly with regard to rules, structure, payment, and power. For example, the ICC requires the parties to submit *terms of reference,* defined as "a summary of the parties' respective claims and a definition of the issues to be determined." The terms of reference help the ICC deal with all the claims and counterclaims, as well as the differences between parties coming from differing legal systems (common law, civil law, Islamic law). The terms of reference may also help in certain jurisdictions (some Arab and Latin American countries) that do not recognize an arbitration clause that relates to some unknown future dispute. The ICC sets the fees for the arbitrators in advance.

Arbitration clauses may differ in their wording. The American Arbitration Association recommends the following standard clause for commercial contracts:

Any controversy or claim arising out of or relating to this contract, or the breach thereof, shall be settled by arbitration in accordance with the Commercial Arbitration Rules of the American Arbitration Association, and judgment upon the award rendered by the Arbitrator(s) may be entered in any Court having jurisdiction thereof.[7]

Another sample clause, drawn from the Stockholm Chamber of Commerce, states:

Any dispute, controversy, or claim arising out of or in connection with this contract, or the breach, termination, or invalidity thereof, shall be settled by arbitration in accordance with the Rules of the Arbitration Institute of the Stockholm Chamber of Commerce.[8]

These clauses are by way of example and should be reviewed with counsel before the selection is made.

The UNCITRAL rules have been used in the Iran-United States Claim Tribunal since 1981 with modification. Several countries have recently enacted statutes specifically authorizing arbitration. Switzerland enacted the Private International Law Act. This act allows parties to agree to any procedure. Any challenge to a final award goes directly to the high court, and this right also can be waived.

Several states within the United States have adopted international commercial arbitration acts. North Carolina adopted one in 1991 based on the UNCITRAL rules.

In an arbitration agreement, the parties should consider having choice of law and forum clauses, because otherwise the arbitrator will decide these matters. The parties may choose to restrict the arbitrator's powers or to let the arbitrator decide what is *ex aequo et bono* (equitable and good). In the IBM–Fujitsu case, the arbitrators used neither U.S. nor Japanese law, but made up their own principles, which made sense in that instance because of the lack of clarity currently surrounding software/computer law. Allowing arbitrators to do this adds certain risks, however. The agreement could also make reference to *lex mercatoria* or the Law Merchant.

## Disadvantages of Arbitration

In summary, what are the disadvantages of arbitration? The limited discovery and the limited rights to appeal any decision are the main problems for those used to the Federal Rules of Procedure. If either IBM or Fujitsu is dissatisfied with the outcome of the arbitration, it has limited opportunity to appeal. Nevertheless, because litigation between parties of different countries is so difficult and often involves the problems of concurrent and overlapping jurisdiction (where both countries' courts take jurisdiction in the absence of choice of law and forum clauses), arbitration is increasingly the option of choice.

## Mediation

Mediation, another form of ADR, occurs when the third party tries to bring the two or more parties in conflict to a mutually satisfactory solution. Mediation, however, is successful only if the parties are persuaded to agree and settle the matter. The parties retain a high degree of control over the process because each step requires their cooperation. Thus, all legal rights are preserved, obviating some of the drawbacks of arbitration. The parties may at any point initiate litigation or agree to submit the dispute to arbitration.

## Commercial Disputes with Nations

Up until now, the text has focused on disputes between private parties, but international disputes may also be between a businessperson and a state. The International Center for the Settlement of Investment Disputes (ICSID), created under the auspices of the International Bank for Reconstruction and Development (World Bank), was established to settle "investment disputes" between individuals and "contracting states" or those states that are signatories to the Washington Convention establishing ICSID. More than 92 parties have signed this convention.

Since 1965, few arbitrations have taken place, however, so it is a vehicle of limited assistance.

This topic is also addressed in Chapter 19.

> **http://www.worldbank.org/**
> The World Bank home page, which provides links with the ICSID and the IBRD.

## Chapter Summary

Some multinational business ventures, whether trade, licensing, or investment matters, will inevitably culminate in a dispute between the parties. This chapter reviewed the legal problems encountered in settling such disputes, from litigation and enforcement of foreign judgments to alternate dispute resolution.

Through the contract, parties can exercise control by including choice of law and choice of forum (and even arbitration) clauses. Concurrently, national courts will continue to address the issues raised by jurisdiction questions. Nations will also continue to look for ways, by treaty or agreements, to find a neutral common ground that will reduce unresolved disputes in transnational trade, licensing, and investment. A global economy cannot function effectively unless businesspeople can count on timely adjudication of disputes.

---

QUESTIONS AND CASE PROBLEMS

1. Explain the concepts of jurisdiction and minimum contacts. What applications do they have in international disputes?

2. Samuels bought a BMW in Texas. According to his complaint on December 3, 1978, "the carburetor stuck, causing him to lose control and turn the car over." He was severely injured and his passenger died. Samuels brought suit in Texas against Bayerische Motoren Werke, AG, and BMW of North America, a wholly owned subsidiary, under the theory of strict liability. Bayerische objects to the jurisdiction, but BMW of North America does not. Samuels argues that by a Texas "longarm jurisdictional statute," any foreign entity that "engages in business in the state" may be brought before a Texas court; Samuels contends this statute therefore applies to Bayerische. Under state statute, doing business includes "committing a tort within the

State." Will the court include Bayerische as a defendant party? See *Samuels v. BMW (North America) and Bayerische Motoren Werke, A.G.* 554 F. Supp. 1191 (E.D. Tex. 1983).

3. Petitioner, Helicopteros Nacionales de Colombia, S.A., (Heli), a Colombian corporation, made a contract to provide transportation during the construction of a Peruvian pipeline. Heli negotiated the contract in Texas with the Consortium, was paid by a Texas bank check, purchased helicopters in Texas, and sent staff to Texas to be trained by the manufacturer. A helicopter crashed in Peru, killing U.S. citizens employed by the Consortium. Wrongful death actions were filed in Texas against the Texas manufacturer, the Consortium, and Heli. Does the Texas court have personal jurisdiction over the Colombian corporation? See *Helicopteros Nacionales de Colombia v. Hall,* 466 U.S. 408 (1984).

4. What are the risks associated with arbitration? Why might a company prefer to settle disputes by litigation? What are the advantages of arbitration?

5. How would a choice of law clause and a clause clearly delineating the power of the arbitrator help to address some of a party's concerns?

6. Petrocks, Inc., an Igoan corporation, and Volcoproducts, a Mabuan corporation, have begun to litigate a dispute in the Igoan court about the supply of volcanic rocks, as stipulated by the contract terms. Before the trial started, one CEO turns to the other and suggests that a revered monk hear the dispute instead. May the parties change the forum after they have written a choice of forum clause in a previously signed contract?

7. Arbitration has been thought to be private. If one party to an arbitration decided it wanted to publicize the dispute, could the other party stop it? *Esso/Australia Resources Ltd. v. Plowman* (1995 A.L.R. 391).

8. Partners in Italy provided that disputes will be settled by arbitration. An arbitrator ruled that the partners had passed a resolution to force out one of the partners illegitimately. The other partners appealed to the court. What was the result? Decision no. 2657 of March 7, 1995, Supreme Court of Cassation, *Massero v. Putto Gnerro* (Italy).

9. Discuss the international law principles of comity and jurisdiction that require a U.S. court to refuse to hear a case in which antitrust violations are alleged against British insurers based upon activities legal in Britain but that have an effect in the United States.

10. What can a party do to compel a foreign country to assist in gathering evidence related to a case in the party's country?

## MANAGERIAL IMPLICATIONS

You are CEO of a large publicly traded company called Microtech. You are negotiating several contracts with foreign governments in Vietnam, India, and Brazil to provide hardware and software to government agencies. Are you interested in including an arbitration clause in the contract? What are the plusses and minuses of such a clause? What alternatives do you have?

How does your plan change, if at all, if you are dealing with a corporation in the same countries? What about a corporation in England and one in New York? Discuss how these variables may affect your decision.

## NOTES

1. The United States and Costa Rica agreed to the following:

   The citizens of the high contracting parties shall reciprocally receive and enjoy full and perfect protection for their persons and property, and shall have free and open access to the courts of justice in the said countries respectively, for the prosecution and defense of their just rights; and they shall be at liberty to employ, in all cases, the advocates, attorneys, or agents of whatever description, whom they may think proper, and they shall enjoy in this respect the same rights and privileges therein as native citizens.

   Treaty of Friendship, Commerce, and Navigation, July 10, 1851, United States—Costa Rica, art. VII, para. 2, 10 Stat. 916, 920, T.S. No. 62. Subsection (a)(3) requires the existence of similar treaty provisions before an action by a citizen of a foreign country may be maintained under Section 71.031.

2. *See Chambers v. Merrell-Dow Pharmaceuticals,* 35 Ohio St.3d 123, 519 N.E.2d 370, 373, n. 3 (1988).

3. For example, in July 1988, there was an oil rig disaster in Scotland. A Texas lawyer went to Scotland, held a press conference, and wrote letters to victims or their families. He advised them that they had a good chance of trying their cases in Texas where awards would be much higher than elsewhere. Houston Post, July 18, 1988, at 13A, col. 1; *The Times* (London), July 18, 1988, at 20A, col. 1; *Texas Lawyer,* Sept. 26, 1988 at 3.

4. For additional reading, see Ohara "Judicial Assistance to be Afforded by Japan for Proceedings in the United States" 23 International Lawyer 10, 27 (1989).

5. Copyright © 1987 by the American Law Institute. Reprinted with permission of the American Law Institute.

6. For additional reading on this topic see Takao Sawaki, "Recognition and Enforcement of Foreign Judgments in Japan," *International Lawyer* 23 (Spring 1989): 29.

7. Reprinted with permission of the AAA.

8. Reprinted with permission of the Secretary General, Arbitration Institute of the Stockholm Chamber of Commerce.

# Part Two

# International Sales, Credits, and the Commercial Transaction

In Part Two of *International Business Law* we turn our attention to more traditional commercial law topics: the rights of buyer and seller under a contract for the international sale of goods, the legal mechanism for transferring title to the goods sold and for allocating the risk of loss or damage to the goods between buyer and seller, the methods of financing the sale and assuring payment for the goods, the rights and responsibilities of the ocean carrier, and the methods for resolving international commercial disputes.

In this area of study the law is derived primarily from the domestic law of individual nations, including statutes and court decisions. However, the impact of international law is still quite great, since many of the domestic laws are derived from international conventions, codes, or agreements. For instance, international sales law in the United States, as well as U.S. statutes governing the rights and responsibilities of air and ocean carriers, is largely based on international conventions to which many nations of the world subscribe. There are also many court decisions affecting international commercial law. These are particularly relevant to our study in the field of contracts, negotiable instruments, documents of title, and letters of credit. Some of the decisions are rooted in those of the English Law Merchant of hundreds of years ago, although none in this text is so old. The decisions appearing in the following chapters, whether English or American cases, are composed of both classic, or "landmark," cases offered to explain long-standing principles of commercial law, and illustrative cases designed to demonstrate common day-to-day problems faced by merchants and other international traders.

In Chapter Five we will study basic principles of international sales law as they are illustrated by the provisions of the *United Nations Convention on Contracts for the International Sale of Goods.* While this is not the applicable law for all international sales, it does provide us with the opportunity to study the first widely accepted body of international sales law. It also provides many opportunities to engage in a comparative analysis of sales law, so as to see how different legal systems might address the same legal problem in different ways.

In many international sales, the movement of the goods and the exchange of money are inextricably connected to the transfer of the document of title and other shipping documents. This is easily explained. Since the risks of buying or selling goods across great distances are considerable, a special mechanism has developed in the law to assure the maximum protection to both parties. As a result, ownership and control over the goods passes from the seller to the buyer only upon some assurance that the seller will receive payment. Similarly, the exchange of money, from

the buyer to the seller, will be conditional upon some assurance that delivery of the goods is imminent. These topics are discussed in Chapter Six.

Chapter Seven deals with the liability of ocean and air carriers for damage or loss to cargo. It also covers some interesting problems of maritime and marine insurance law. No area of international business has engendered as much litigation in the courts as has the carriage of goods. Goods are subjected to a wide range of risks during international shipment—from storms to piracy at sea. This is a fascinating and important area of study.

In Chapter Eight we begin with a discussion of how international payments are handled in a transaction for the sale of goods. From there we will look generally at the law of letters of credit and at the role that banks play in international commercial transactions. Many exporters find that they are successful in selling to foreign customers not because they necessarily offered the best product at the best price, but because they provided trade finance to the customer to make the sale possible. Thus, Chapter Eight looks at trade finance alternatives in the banking industry and the legal relationship between the parties to the transaction.

# Chapter Five

# Sales Contracts and Excuses for Nonperformance

## The Development of International Law

In the twelfth century, medieval Europe experienced a renaissance of trade and commerce. Merchants from the cities, many traveling by caravan, met at trade fairs and city markets to exchange goods such as wool, salted fish, cotton cloth, wine, fruit, and oils. Trade routes to the East were opening, with access to silk and new spices. Rudimentary banking systems were founded so that money could be used as payment in long-distance transactions. New legal instruments—the forerunners of today's bank checks—were created. Over time the merchants developed a set of customs for exchanging goods—an unwritten code of how to bargain, barter, and sell goods at market. For instance, merchants decided that if one bought goods at a city market and later discovered that the goods had been stolen, then the innocent buyer took ownership of the goods anyway. By relying on custom, they knew what was expected of both parties to a transaction and how to avoid or resolve a disagreement. These customs of the marketplace became known as the *lex mercatoria* or *law merchant,* and they were "enforced" by the merchants themselves. Similar customs were developing in the maritime trade. In the centuries to follow, the local courts recognized the *law merchant* and used juries made up of other merchants to decide cases. As trade spanned greater distances, and nations created colonies, merchants took on greater risks, and transactions required more complex legal rules. In England, by the eighteenth century, the law merchant became a part of the *common law* of England when a famous English judge, Lord Mansfield, ruled that it was up to the English courts to say what the law merchant was and not merely what merchants thought it to be.

More than 100 years later, in 1894, England enacted its *Sale of Goods Act* that codified many rules for merchants, thus adapting the common law to business needs of the time. In Europe, the law merchant gave way to stricter legal codes enacted by local lawmakers and legislatures, based on legal concepts dating to the Roman period. In 1906, in the United States the *Uniform Sales Act* (although no longer in effect) was passed in many states codifying the law of sales. The result, by the dawn of the twentieth century, was that nations had developed very different commercial codes. As the business world became more complex, and with the dawn of air travel and worldwide communications, there was a need for a clearer set of modern rules, and for more uniformity in the application of commercial laws around the world. Virtually all trading nations of the world today have modern commercial codes governing the sale of goods.

## Modern Sales Law in the United States: The UCC and CISG

In 1951 a new commercial law was proposed in the United States. Known as the *Uniform Commercial Code* (UCC), it is the primary body of commercial law for domestic transactions in the United States. The purposes of the UCC are

1. To simplify, clarify, and modernize the law governing commercial transactions.

2. To permit the continued expansion of commercial practices through custom, usage, and agreement of the parties.
3. To make uniform the law among the various jurisdictions (states). UCC 1-102.

The UCC has been adopted in all fifty states (only partially in Louisiana). It covers many areas of commercial law, ranging from bank deposits to secured transactions. It does not, however, cover the sale of real estate or services, insurance, intellectual property, bankruptcy, or many other areas. Many subjects covered in the UCC are traditional areas of study in college courses in Business Law. For instance, Article 2 of the UCC applies to "transactions in goods"—*sales* and *contracts of sale*. A contract of sale includes both the present sale of goods and contracts to sell goods at a future time. Contracts not governed by the UCC or other code are governed by the common law, and where the UCC is silent, the common law of contracts applies to the transaction. Many early principles of the law merchant are still found in Article 2 in a modern, codified form.

For international transactions, the UCC is gradually being supplanted by a new law, the *United Nations Convention on Contracts for the International Sale of Goods* (CISG). The CISG is the uniform international sales law in countries that account for over two-thirds of all world trade. It was drafted under an effort led by the United Nations and has been adopted as law by countries from five continents. Its purpose is to unify the law of sales between nations. The process of making laws more uniform between countries is known as the *harmonization* of laws. The CISG, adopted by a diplomatic conference in 1980, became effective in the United States in 1988. It now applies to many international sales when buyer or seller are located in countries that have adopted the convention. Many provisions of the UCC and the CISG are similar, but many are different. This chapter discusses international contracts for the sale of goods with an eye toward comparing these two laws.

**http://www.law.cornell.edu/ucc/ ucc.table.html**
The site of the UCC Articles.

## Conflicts of Law

The sales contract is universally recognized as the legal mechanism for conducting trade in goods. It is essential to trade because an international agreement to buy and sell goods, like many domestic agreements, takes time to perform. If buyer and seller could fully perform the contract at the moment the agreement was reached, or if every seller handed over the goods when the purchase price was paid, they would not need binding agreements. But few merchants or traders, from any country, would enter a potentially risky long-term transaction without a contract. Thus the contract's importance stems from its embodiment of the agreement of the parties, which provides assurances that each party will perform its part of the bargain. If the agreement breaks down, and a court must resolve a dispute, the rights and obligations of the parties will be based on the law applicable to the case. In an international transaction, at least one party is likely to have its rights decided under the law of a foreign country. Thus, when a firm enters a contract governed by foreign law, it is undertaking an added risk. The interpretation of the terms of the contract under that law or a firm's rights and obligations according to the contract may be surprising.

To know what law applies to a contract, courts will resort to *conflict of law* rules. Should the applicable law be that of the country in which the contract was made, in which it was to be performed, or in another country with a close connection to the contract? Consider the following example. Assume a French subsidiary of a U.S. company enters into a contract with a company from Zaire for the purchase of copper. The contract is negotiated and signed in Switzerland and calls for the copper to be shipped from Zaire to the parent company in the United States. If the copper is impure or of the wrong grade—where will the case be heard? Once the case does go to court, which country's law will decide the buyer's damages? This uncertainty and lack of predictability over how the case will be resolved increases the risk of an international sale.

**Choice of Law Clauses.** Many international contracts designate the parties' choice of law that is to apply in case of dispute. The laws of most countries, within limits, allow this designation. The choice of law that they agree upon may depend on the relative bargaining position of the parties and on each party's ability to extract this choice as a concession from the other side. The following case, *General Electric Co. v. G. Siem-* *pelkamp GmbH & Co.*, contains both a forum selection clause (one in which the parties indicate where contract disputes are to be resolved) and a choice of law clause. It also illustrates how a U.S. court applies the law of a foreign country to resolve a contract dispute.

---

## General Electric Co. v. G. Siempelkamp GmbH & Co.

### 29 F. 3d 1095 (1994)
### United States Court of Appeals
### Sixth Circuit

**BACKGROUND AND FACTS**

General Electric (G.E.) contacted an American subsidiary of Siempelkamp, a German manufacturer of heavy machinery, and expressed interest in Siempelkamp's "Conti Roll" presses built for the production of industrial laminates. The presses were to be used at a G.E. plant in Ohio that manufacturers copper-clad technical laminates for the computer circuit industry. The negotiations took place between G.E. and Siempelkamp's German headquarters. G.E. issued a standard-form purchase order for one press. Siempelkamp then issued an order confirmation for the press. At Siempelkamp's German headquarters, two days later, the G.E. representative and a Siempelkamp agent signed under the words "accepted" on Siempelkamp's order confirmation. The G.E. agent also initialed each page of the 60 page document. The order confirmation contained the following forum selection and choice of law clauses:

> Place of jurisdiction for all disputes arising in connection with the contract shall be at the principal place of business of the supplier. This shall also apply for claims in summary procedures on bills of exchange, promissory notes or cheques. The supplier is also entitled to file suit at the principal place of business of the purchaser.

> All matters under this contract and any disputes arising hereunder shall be exclusively governed by the law of the Federal Republic of Germany.

G.E. filed suit in U.S. district court alleging breach of contract, violation of the Uniform Commercial Code, misrepresentation and breach of warranty in connection with the installation of the Siempelkamp press. The district court, relying on the forum selection clause of the contract, granted summary judgment for Siempelkamp (The dismissal was without prejudice so that the case could be heard in another jurisdiction). G.E. appealed, as follows.

**NATHAN R. JONES, CIRCUIT JUDGE**

The occurrences here appear straightforward. G.E. made an offer to Siempelkamp in a purchase order. Siempelkamp then submitted a counteroffer, in the form of an order confirmation that contained terms very different from the purchase order. G.E. signed and thereby accepted that counteroffer, creating a binding contract. Both parties are therefore bound by the terms of the contract, including the forum selection clause in the counteroffer.

G.E. argues [here] that even if the forum selection clause applies, it is not exclusive or mandatory. Because the clause states that "all" disputes "shall" be at Siempelkamp's principal place of business, it selects German court jurisdiction exclusively and is mandatory. . . . The clause is clear and should be enforced according to its terms.

Finally, G.E. claims that it would be unreasonable to enforce the clause here. It is true that we may refuse to enforce even an unambiguous, bargained-for form selection clause if a party can "clearly show that enforcement would be unreasonable and unjust, or that the clause [is] invalid for such reasons as fraud or overreaching. . . ."

In this case, we take judicial notice that G.E. is a sophisticated party that is used to dealing with complex international business transactions. We see no evidence that G.E. was exploited or unfairly treated in this transaction. . . . With regard to G.E.'s implication that Ohio is the reasonable

*(continued)*

---

*(continued)*

venue for this suit, we note that Germany also has significant contacts with actions arising out of the agreement: the deal was negotiated and signed in Germany, much of the contract was performed in Germany, the presses were manufactured primarily in Germany, and witnesses presumably would be located in Germany, as well as the United States. Application of the forum selection clause is not unreasonable here.

**Decision.** Enforcement of the forum selection clause providing for resolution of the dispute in a German forum is not unreasonable. Affirmed.

---

Note that the contracting parties in the G.E. case provided for where any disputes were to be heard "at the principal place of business of the supplier" and which law was controlling "all matters . . . and any disputes . . . shall be exclusively governed by the law of the Federal Republic of Germany." Usually when business parties specify the choice of forum and the choice of law, courts and tribunals in most countries will require the parties to honor their contractual commitments.

## Development of the CISG

The CISG was drafted to avoid two of the major problems associated with the conflict of laws—uncertainty and unpredictability. Companies doing business throughout the world can benefit from knowing what their rights will be under a sales contract. And lawyers can more easily advise their clients when laws are uniform. But the task of producing one international sales law to satisfy the needs and interests of every country was enormous. The many differences between national laws had to be resolved. Some differences date back to the time when the law merchant was incorporated into English common law, while the European countries moved toward Roman civil law. Even greater differences occurred in those countries whose legal codes were based on Islamic religious beliefs or on socialist principles derived from Marxist ideology. As a result, the function and nature of sales law are viewed differently in different legal systems. Each system has its individual rules for deciding the validity of a contract, for interpreting its terms, and for defining the remedies available to a party upon a breach. As the European Union (EU) moves toward greater economic integration, it is also seeking to standardize those principles that are used to interpret contracts and to determine appropriate remedies for nonperformance by a party. Somewhat akin to the *Restatement of the Law of Contracts* in the United States, the *Principles of European Contract Law* have been drafted by lawyers from each of the EU member countries. Exhibit 5.1 provides some general information about this recent statement regarding contract law in Europe. The following sections look at contract law from the perspective of socialistic countries, the People's Republic of China, and in developing countries.

> *http://www.cisg.law.pace.edu*
> or
> *http://itl.irv.uit.no/trade_law/doc/Hague.*
> *Applicable.Law.SOG.Convention.1986.html*
> Sites of the CISG articles.

## Contract Law in Socialist Countries

Many countries contributed to the development of the CISG, including the socialist and communist countries of the time. Today most of these countries have abandoned communism and have moved toward greater democracy, private enterprise, and free markets. Despite these vast changes, as socialist principles remain influential in many countries, socialist legal principles exert a profound impact on the development of international law.

Socialist contract law serves primarily to protect national interests, to achieve state goals for the production and distribution of goods to individuals, and to regulate foreign trade contracts with outside companies. Socialist countries conduct foreign trade through state trading organizations instead of through private companies. State trading organizations, such as those in the

| EXHIBIT 5.1   European Contract Law |
|---|

**The Principles of European Contract Law 1997**

In response to the expanding volume of laws regulating specific types of contracts in the European Union (the Community), a body of lawyers drawn from all of the 15 Member States have prepared a document that presents a Community-wide infrastructure of contract law. The lawyers who have prepared the Principles are known as the *Commission on European Contract Law.* The Principles are intended to be applied as general rules of contract law in the European Communities. The Principles apply when contracting parties have agreed to incorporate them into their contracts or have specified that their contract is to be governed by them.

The official publication of the text was published at the end of 1997. It contains nine chapters dealing with topics ranging from the Scope of the Principles (Chapter 1 includes sections on the freedom of contract, usages and practices, and the good faith obligation) to the Formation of Contracts (Chapter 2) and Remedies for Nonperformance (Chapters 8 and 9).

The provisions of *The Principles of European Contract Law* may be viewed by visiting the web site at: *http://itl.irv.uit.no.trade_law/doc/EU.Contract.Principles.1997.*

People's Republic of China (PRC), are heavily bureaucratic. Because of their strict organizational structure, state trading organizations seek as much certainty and predictability in the law as possible. As a result, sales law in socialist countries differs greatly from sales law in Western countries. Generally speaking, socialist law is more mechanical and far more cumbersome than law in western countries. For instance, while many western countries do not require that contracts for the sale of goods be in writing, the socialist countries do. Where the West might favor a law that would allow courts to "fill the gaps" in a contract by looking to the customs and usages of the trade, the socialist countries do not do so. Where Western countries do not require that the parties specify the exact price to be paid for the goods, provided that a reasonable price could later be ascertained (i.e., a "market price"), the socialist countries generally do insist that the parties specify the price by writing it into the contract.

## Contract Law in the People's Republic of China: An Illustration

Contract law in China has evolved from both its ancient history and the dictates of socialist principles.[1] Today, the PRC has two codes of contract law. The first, known as the 1981 *Economic Contract Law,* is applicable only to domestic transactions. The second, the 1985 *Foreign Economic Contract Law,* applies to foreign sales contracts. In China, as the opinions of judges in deciding specific cases are not publicly reported, there is no case law. The law is found in the codes, and the judge's role is to apply the codes as written to each case being reviewed.

Although economic reforms have been made in recent years, the Chinese economic system has changed little in 40 years. In 1952 China adopted a system of centrally controlled state planning similar to that in effect in the Soviet Union at that time. There is, to this day, strong central planning of most economic activity, with few market mechanisms for regulating the factors of production or pricing. State policy, and not consumer demand, dictates how much and what kinds of goods are to be produced. In this system there is little need for private contracts, for a body of contract law to protect private rights. Contracts serve only to implement government policy. In other words, domestic contract law ensures that state doctrine is followed and that commitments made to and among state agencies are upheld. Interestingly enough, in sharp contrast to what lawyers in the West are accustomed to, "breach of contract" actions more closely resemble quasi-criminal prosecutions for breaching one's obligation to the state. This difference is reflected in the remedies most commonly used. In the West, when a party breaches a contract, a court typically awards damages to the nonbreaching party as a form of compensation. In China, the focus is on protecting the interests of the state through legal rules that compel a breaching party to do what it had promised. Penalties and other forms of punishment are also routinely used.

As China opened its doors to trade with the rest of the world, its legal codes needed modernizing. The 1985 *Foreign Economic Contract Law,* which applies to transactions between Chinese and foreign firms, differs from the domestic code in that it is more modern and more western. (Parts of this

Chinese law appear as Exhibits in this chapter so that you can compare them to the CISG, which you will soon study in detail. Readers familiar with the Uniform Commercial Code, the contract law of the U.S., may want to compare and contrast the Chinese law with this code as well. (See Exhibit 5.2.) This updating of its foreign contract law was done in order to attract more western buyers for Chinese goods and more investment in the country. The foreign-trade law provides more suitable remedies in case a party breaches an agreement. Like Western laws, these remedies are intended to return the parties to the position they would have been in had the contract been completed. Thus, the code recognizes damages instead of penalties, including damages for lost profits. The code embodies many other legal concepts found in the West, concepts that would sound remarkably familiar to a Western-trained lawyer. The *Foreign Economic Contract Law* of China applies not only to contracts for the sale of goods, but to other types of contracts as well. Its applicability to many contracts for the *international* sale of goods has been superseded by the CISG, which China has adopted.

## Contract Law in the Developing Countries

The developing countries' concern over the governing of contracts stems directly from their economic position relative to the industrialized countries. Although all developing countries cannot be lumped into the same category, and they are not all in the same state of development or industrialization, developing countries have long faced three related problems in their business relationships with the wealthier industrialized nations. First, they often do not have a cadre of trained professionals, such as economists, engineers, lawyers, or business managers, to help their governments in contract negotiations. Consequently, some developing countries have been at a negotiating and bargaining disadvantage in dealing with experienced representatives of Western multinational corporations. Secondly, these countries have often found themselves in desperate need of hard currency to fund their socioeconomic development programs, such as health care, education, irrigation, or foreign debt repayment. As a result, they have lacked

---

**EXHIBIT 5.2    Applicability of Chinese Domestic Law to Contract Cases**

**The People's Republic of China Foreign Economic Contract Law of 1985**

**Article 1.** This law is enacted to protect the legitimate rights and interests of parties to economic contracts for deals involving foreign businesses, and to promote our country's foreign economic relations.

**Article 2.** This law applies to economic contracts (hereinafter referred to as contracts) between enterprises, or other economic institutions, of the PRC and their foreign counterparts or individuals. However, international transport contracts shall be excluded.

**Article 3.** In making contracts, the principle of equality and mutual benefit, and of reaching unanimity through consultation shall be followed.

**Article 4.** In making contracts, the laws of the PRC shall be observed, and its social and public welfare shall not be harmed.

**Article 5.** The parties to a contract may seek settlement to disputes in accordance with laws of their choosing applicable to such disputes. If the parties make no such choice, the law of the country most closely related to the contract shall apply. Contracts for joint ventures, cooperative management, and cooperative prospecting and development of natural resources, operating within the boundaries of the PRC, are subject to the laws of the PRC.

   In the absence of relevant stipulations in the laws of the PRC, international norms shall apply.

**Article 6.** If the relevant laws of the PRC conflict with international treaties to which the PRC is a signatory or a party, the international treaty stipulations shall apply. However, articles to which the PRC has declared reservations shall be excluded.

SOURCE:    Reprinted with permission from 24 I.L.M. 797 (1985). Copyright © 1985 by The American Society of International Law, Washington, D.C. The English translation of the law originally appeared in the May 1985 issue of *East Asian Executive Reports* and is reprinted with permission.

the economic bargaining power of their trading partners in carrying out contract negotiations.

Representatives of developing countries are quick to point out that many contract provisions were forced on them even though the provisions were not in their best interest. For instance, the developing countries contend that they have often been victims of unconscionable contracts. They point to cases in which they were sold shoddy equipment, tainted foods, or goods unsuitable for sale or banned in Western countries, such as expired pharmaceuticals. They also point to contracts for the sale of inappropriate technology and equipment. They argue that for many years their development funds were squandered on needless weaponry purchased by local political officials who had been willing to accept the cash bribes of Western companies. Consider this dramatic example from 1992. It was disclosed that an American firm had contracted to export needed chemicals to an African country, whose purchase received financial backing from the U.S. Agency for International Development. When the drums which were to contain the chemicals arrived, the buyers discovered, incredibly, that they were victims of a fraud. Instead of the needed chemicals, they had been sent a shipment of toxic waste for which the owners could not find a dumping site in the United States.

A third problem in contract negotiations, particularly in southern Africa, is that in the past many developing countries simply did not have the sophisticated legal system for dealing with contract disputes, such as those needed to enforce a buyer's rights against a seller of defective equipment. These developing countries were eager for an international agreement that would modernize and strengthen their sales laws and make them more attractive for foreign investment.

## The Convention on Contracts for the International Sale of Goods

Early attempts at constructing an international law of sales actually began in the late 1920s with the work of the *International Institute for the Unification of Private Law,* or UNIDROIT, an organization of European lawyers that was working closely with the League of Nations. It successfully developed two conventions in 1964. However, the effort was primarily a European one (the United States and many other countries did not participate in drafting these documents), and the conventions never received wide acceptance.

In 1966 the United Nations created the *U.N. Commission on International Trade Law,* or UNCITRAL. UNCITRAL consists of 36 representatives from nations in every region of the world. Supported by a highly respected staff of lawyers, it is headquartered at the U.N. Vienna International Centre in Austria. UNCITRAL has drafted several widely accepted legal codes for international business, including the *Convention on Contracts for the International Sale of Goods* (CISG). Unlike many other U.N. codes that are not binding, the CISG is a convention or agreement among nations that is binding once the legislature of a country adopts it. It then becomes a part of the country's domestic law. In the United States, a convention must be ratified by the Senate. The CISG received Senate ratification in 1986 and became U.S. law on January 1, 1988.

Now, if a U.S. buyer or seller contracts for the sale of goods with a company whose place of business is in a country that has also ratified the convention, then the CISG will determine their rights under the contract. Treaties prevail over state statutes. To say it another way, if a U.S. buyer brings an action for the delivery of defective merchandise purchased from a seller in France or China, or if the seller brings an action for nonpayment, their rights will be determined in court by the CISG—and not the *Uniform Commercial Code* (UCC) or French or Chinese law—regardless of the country in which the case is heard.

A similar situation would result in China, which has adopted the CISG. In a case involving the sale of goods between a Chinese firm and a party whose place of business is in another country that has adopted the CISG, the CISG would apply. Therefore, the Chinese *Foreign Economic Contract Law,* discussed in the last section, would govern other kinds of contracts, such as employment contracts. (Of course, sales contracts between Chinese parties and parties *whose place of business is in a country that has not* adopted the CISG could be decided under the *Foreign Economic Contract Law* according to conflicts of law rules.)

The CISG has already been adopted by 51 countries and is being considered by still others. Exhibit 5.3 shows those countries that have adopted the CISG. Translations are available in Arabic, Chinese,

## EXHIBIT 5.3  Countries that Have Ratified or Acceded to the CISG

| | |
|---|---|
| Argentina | Latvia |
| Australia | Lesotho |
| Austria | Lithuania |
| Belarus | Luxembourg |
| Belgium | Mexico |
| Bosnia and | The Netherlands |
| Herzegovina | New Zealand |
| Bulgaria | Norway |
| Canada | Poland |
| Chile | Republic of Moldova |
| China | Romania |
| Cuba | Russian Federation |
| Czech Republic | Singapore |
| Denmark | Slovakia |
| Ecuador | Slovenia |
| Egypt | Spain |
| Estonia | Sweden |
| Finland | Switzerland |
| France | Syrian Arab Republic |
| Georgia | Uganda |
| Germany | Ukraine |
| Ghana | United States |
| Guinea | Uzbekistan |
| Hungary | Venezuela |
| Iraq | Yugoslavia |
| Italy | Zambia |

English, French, Russian, and Spanish. A copy of the CISG appears in the appendix, and students are encouraged to refer to it often in this chapter.

This chapter examines the following aspects of the CISG: (1) the applicability of the CISG to international sales, (2) its general provisions, including the rules for interpreting and forming contracts, (3) provisions related to the warranty of goods, (4) provisions regarding performance of the contract and remedies available to the injured party on breach, and (5) excuses for nonperformance of a contract.

> **http://itl.irv.uit.no/trade_law/papers/
> unidroit.html**
> The site of UNIDROIT.

> **http://www.un.org.at/uncitral/index.html**
> *and*
> **http://itl.irv.uit.no/trade_law/papers
> /UNCITRAL.html**
> Both sites for UNCITRAL.

## Applicability of the CISG to International Transactions

In the United States, UCC Article II applies to purely domestic sales of goods. The CISG, however, applies if the following three conditions are met:

1. The contract is for the commercial sale of goods.
2. It is between parties whose places of business are in different countries (nationality or citizenship of individuals is not a determining factor).
3. The places of business are located in countries that have ratified the convention.

**Place of Business Requirement.**  In the case of buyers or sellers with places of business in more than one country, such as a multinational corporation, its "place of business" would be considered to be in the country that has the closest relationship to the contract and where it will be performed. This could mean that if two American companies negotiated a contract entirely within the United States, but one of them had a place of business outside of the United States and the contract was to be *performed outside* the United States (e.g., the contract calls for delivery of the goods to a point outside the United States), then the CISG might govern the transaction.

**Sales Excluded from the CISG.**  The following types of sales have been specifically excluded from the convention:

1. Consumer goods sold for personal, family, or household use.
2. Goods bought at auction.
3. Stocks, securities, negotiable instruments, or money.
4. Ships, vessels, or aircraft.
5. Electricity.
6. Assembly contracts for the supply of goods to be manufactured or produced wherein the buyer provides a "substantial part of the materials necessary for such manufacture or production."
7. Contracts that are in "preponderant part" for the supply of labor or other services.
8. Liability of the seller for death or personal injury caused by the goods.
9. Contracts where the parties specifically agree to "opt out" of the convention or where they choose to be bound by some other law.

# Negotiating International Business Transactions
## An International Lawyer's Look at Contract Negotiations

### Importance of Procedure

It may be, and often is, that the procedure employed in international business negotiations is the single most important cause of their success or failure. The careful lawyer will make advance inquiry about whether contracts preliminary to the negotiation are advisable and about which locations may be preferable for conducting negotiations. Procedures calculated to facilitate the building of personal relationships increase prospects for a successful negotiation, especially in Asia. In tough moments during a negotiation, courtesy alone may keep a consensus momentum going; enduring courtesy is the essential lubricant of international negotiations.

A negotiating opposite may not want to admit that an apparent unwillingness to agree to a suggested point is caused by bureaucratic foot-dragging, lack of coordination, lack of technical understanding, or simple confusion on its side. Procedures that are flexible enough to allow time to work out such problems may cultivate ego, avoid a loss of "face," and continue participation in the negotiations. For example, a negotiating opposite may be unwilling to let you know that failure to reach quick agreement is due to the fact that he or she, despite having a lofty-sounding title or other credentials, does not have authority to make a final agreement or will not assume personal responsibility for the consequences of an agreement. The latter case occurs frequently in Japan. Some nations find it prudent to advertise publicly that only certain government agencies are authorized to carry out sales or purchases.

Procedures which cause surprise are intimidating and can engender hostility and distrust. Obvious examples include emotional displays used as smokescreens, changing the agreed agenda for negotiation, unannounced or late arrivals and departures of negotiating personnel, and retreating from agreements already made.

### Importance of Culture

Cultural and language differences between negotiating opposites accentuate the importance attached to procedure in international negotiations. Self-praise is deprecated in virtually all cultures. Story is told of one MNE investor in Africa who inserted certain "whereas" clauses into a negotiated agreement to the effect that the local government was unable to perform a task and that the investor possessed worldwide management and technical success at the same task. An African newspaper published those "whereas" clauses as evidence of "imperialist attitudes."

Although giving gifts of modest value is appreciated in virtually all cultures, it is an expected occurrence between negotiating opposites in some countries. Certain gifts, such as books depicting the natural beauty of the investor's home area, are generally appreciated, while more specialized gifts may be preferred in a particular country. For example, Johnny Walker Black Label Scotch is appreciated in Japan, but Red Label is valued in Thailand and Burma.

There is an almost universal cultural importance attached to sharing a meal with a negotiating opposite. Meal time affords a good opportunity for an investor to show an interest in and sensitivity about the host's culture. But in some cultures talking about business matters during a meal is considered impolite and may be counterproductive.

There is considerable cultural diversity about the meaning in international negotiations of silence and delay. The common law rule that, under appropriate circumstances, "silence is acceptance" is not shared widely in many countries. In some countries silence may mean "no," while in other countries periods of silence are an acceptable and common occasion during which thoughts are arranged and re-arranged. For example, an investor in Indonesia brought the final draft of a completely negotiated agreement to a counterpart for signature and, following some pleasant conversation, placed the agreement on the desk. In complete silence, the counterpart simply returned the document, un-

*(continued)*

*(continued)*

signed, to the investor who the next day learned that the previous day was not considered propitious in Indonesia for signing one's name. The agreement was signed that next day. Delays of days or even of months may not be signs that a negotiation is in difficulty or represent attempts at increasing one party's cost of negotiating. Such delays may simply be the minimum time period in which a necessary consensus or authority is being achieved within a negotiating opposite's team. . . .

### The Language of Negotiations

Differences in language skills between negotiating opposites raise some peril in every international business transaction. Each negotiating party prefers quite naturally to use the language whose nuances are best known. Words that have a clear and culturally acceptable meaning in one language may be unclear or culturally offensive in another tongue; the converse may be true as well. For example, the French word "detente" does not translate easily into the English language. The consequences of this transaction difficulty have worldwide importance. Because some hand gestures and body movements are acceptable in one culture yet deeply offensive in another culture, they are rarely an appropriate communications aid in international negotiations. For example, raising an open hand in the direction of another party can mean in North Africa that you hope that person will lose all five senses.

The use of interpreters substantially slows the pace of negotiations and may spawn further difficulties because the interpreter is one more fallible person taking part in the negotiations. Interpreting is exhausting work and rarely exact. During an international commercial arbitration in Los Angeles, a witness testified in German alongside a skilled interpreter whose job it was to translate the testimony into English. While the arbitrators waited, it required the interpreter's efforts, the efforts of a United States lawyer fluent in German, and the efforts of a German lawyer fluent in English to produce an oral translation which all agreed was sufficiently accurate. Even assuming the availability of a literate oral translation, a Japanese person saying "yes" in answer to a question may not be signifying agreement but may mean only "Yes, I understand the question."

The peril or language difficulty can be equally acute in negotiations between a lawyer from the United States and a negotiating opposite who speaks the English language. Each party may be embarrassed to raise a language question. For example, in the middle of a telephone conversation between a lawyer from the United States and a negotiator in England, a London operator interrupted to ask if the lawyer was "through." Not wishing to terminate the conversation, the American answered, "No, I am not through"; the operator disconnected the circuit, apologized, and once again dialed to get the call "through." A few minutes later the London operator came on the line again, interrupting the parties' conversation, to ask again if the United States caller was "through." Desiring to continue the conversation without further interruption, the American lawyer this time said "Yes, thank you," and the operator left the line connected. . . .

Even exceptionally able interpreters may have difficulty if a United States lawyer uses American slang in communications during an international negotiation. The American penchant for using "ball park" figures may not be shared or understood in countries where baseball is not a popular sport. Slow and distinct patterns of speech combined with simple declarative sentences will always facilitate international business negotiations.

**Folsom, Gordon, & Spanogle**
*International Business Transactions in a Nutshell,* 5th edition (1996), pp. 27–33.

© West Publishing Company. Reprinted with permission.

In the United States, Article II of the UCC applies to both consumer and commercial transactions. Consumer sales were excluded from the CISG because consumer protection laws are so specific to every country that it would have been very difficult to harmonize them. Further, consumer sales are usually domestic in nature.

The parties to a sales contract are free to negotiate other terms that might differ from the CISG. If they feel unsure about the code, they may "opt out" entirely, simply by specifying that the UCC (or the law of some other nation) will apply. Article 6 of the CISG states, "The parties may exclude the application of this Convention or . . . derogate from or vary the effect of any of its provisions."

## Validity and Formation of International Sales Contracts

Under the common law, a *valid contract* is an agreement that contains all of the essential elements of a contract. As students of business law well know, a contract contains a number of elements.

1. It is an agreement between the parties entered into by their mutual assent (e.g., an offer and acceptance of the contract's material terms).
2. The contract must be supported by legally sufficient consideration (e.g., the exchange in the contract as bargained for by the parties).
3. The parties must have legal capacity (e.g., that the parties are not minors, legally incompetent, or under the influence of drugs or alcohol).

4. The contract must not be for illegal purposes or to carry on an activity that is illegal or contrary to public policy.

If a contract is missing any one of these essential elements, it is a *void contract*. It will not be enforced by the courts. The CISG only governs the forming of a contract and the rights and obligations of the seller and buyer. The Convention does not provide rules for determining whether a contract is valid, for determining whether a party to a contract is legally competent, nor for determining whether a party is guilty of fraud or misrepresentation. These rules are left to individual state or national laws. For an example, see the specific articles of PRC's Foreign Economic Contract Law noted in Exhibit 5.4.

## Enforcement of Illegal Contracts

A generally recognized principle of contract law is that, in all legal systems, contracts that violate the laws of a state or nation are void. A void con-

---

**EXHIBIT 5.4    Formation and Validity of a Contract under Chinese Domestic Law**

**The People's Republic of China Foreign Economic Contract Law of 1985**

**Article 7.** A contract will be established when the parties reach agreement on the articles in writing and sign their names. If an agreement is reached through letters, cables, or telexes, the contract will be established only when a letter of affirmation is signed, provided a party to the contract requests the signing of such a letter.

A contract will be established only when it is approved by the government of the PRC if such an approval is required by the laws or administrative decrees of the PRC.

**Article 9.** A contract that contradicts the laws of the PRC or its social or public welfare is invalid.

**Article 10.** A contract is invalid if it is established by means of deception or coercion.

**Article 11.** A party to a contract responsible for the invalidation of the contract has the obligation to compensate the other party for the losses resulting from the invalidation of the contract.

**Article 12.** In general, a contract shall contain the following provisions: 1) Titles or names, nationalities, and addresses of main offices or residences of the parties involved; 2) date and place the contract was signed; 3) type of contract, and category and scope of the contract objectives; 4) technical terms, quality, standards, specifications, and number of contract objectives; 5) time limit, place, and method for fulfilling the contract; 6) price conditions, sum of payment, payment method, and various additional expenses; 7) transferability of the contract and conditions for transfer; 8) compensation and other responsibilities for violating the contract; 9) ways for solving contract disputes; and 10) the language used in the contract and its effectiveness.

**Article 13.** The parties to a contract must agree on a limit to the risks that are involved in fulfilling the contract objectives. When necessary, they should agree on the scope of insurance for the contract objectives.

SOURCE:    Reprinted with permission from 24 I.L.M. 797 (1985). Copyright © 1985 by The American Society of International Law, Washington, D.C. The English translation of the law originally appeared in the May 1985 issue of *East Asian Executive Reports* and is reprinted with permission.

tract is of no legal effect and will not be enforced by a court. As you read the following case, *Tarbert Trading, Ltd. v. Cometals, Inc.*, consider both the legality of the sales contract in question and the ethical behavior of the parties.

## The Writing Requirement

The laws of many nations differ as to whether contracts for the sale of goods must be in writing. Under the UCC, American law requires that contracts for the sale of goods of $500 or more must be in writing. Such writing requirements in common law countries date back to an act of the English Parliament in 1677. Today, however, the many exceptions to this UCC rule make most oral sales contracts quite enforceable. In 1954 Great Britain repealed its law. Civil law countries for the most part never had any writing requirement at all. Under the CISG, contracts for the sale of

### Tarbert Trading, LTD. v. Cometals, Inc.
#### 663 F.Supp. 561 (1987)
#### United States District Court (S.D.N.Y.)

BACKGROUND AND FACTS

Cometals purchased Kenyan red beans from Tarbert Trading, an English commodities trading company. Agrimen, a South African company engaged in commodities trading, acted as an agent for Tarbert in connection with the sale. The beans were held in a warehouse in Rotterdam, the Netherlands. Cometals had purchased the beans for resale to a buyer in Columbia. Columbia would only allow the beans to be imported if the seller could provide a certificate of origin (issued by a Chamber of Commerce) proving the beans were a product of a country in the European Economic Community (EEC). Cometals requested that Tarbert supply such a certificate and Tarbert agreed. Both parties understood that it was impossible to honestly furnish the certificate since the Kenyan red beans originated in Africa. Later, the defendant refused the beans claiming that they were of poor quality and the plaintiff sued. Defendant also maintains that the agreement should be declared void and unenforceable because plaintiff could not, except through fraud, supply defendant with an EEC certificate of origin for the beans.

NEWMAN, SENIOR JUDGE

We first address the issue concerning conflict of laws. As to that matter, the court agrees with the contention of Tarbert that the law of New York is applicable in this case rather than the law of the Netherlands, as urged by Cometals. The court has considered various facts: Cometals resides in New York; negotiations took place between Cometals in New York and Agrimen in South Africa; the formal letter agreement was prepared by Cometals in New York; and the physical location of the beans in

Rotterdam was not a significant factor in the parties' transaction. . . . However, in view of the result reached in this case, it is immaterial whether the law of the Netherlands or of New York is applied.

Under the law of the Netherlands a contract that calls for the doing of an illegal or tortious act is absolutely void and unenforceable. See Martindale-Hubbell, *Netherlands Law Digest,* p. 5 (1985).

Insofar as New York law is concerned: *Stone v. Freeman,* 298 N.Y. 268, 271, 82 N.E.2d 571, 572 (1948),

it is the settled law of this State (and probably of every other State) that a party to an illegal contract cannot ask a court of law to help him carry out his illegal object, nor can such a person plead or prove in any court a case in which he, as a basis for his claim, must show forth his illegal purpose. . . . For no court should be required to serve as paymaster of the wages of crime, or referee between thieves. Therefore, the law "will not extend its aid to either of the parties" or "listen to their complaints against each other, but will leave them where their own acts have placed them."

Concededly, both Tarbert and Cometals were cognizant of the fact that an EEC certificate of origin stating that the Kenyan beans were of the origin of an EEC member would be false and would be shown to third persons. Simply put, [Cometals] intended to deceive the Colombian customs officials with a false certificate as to the beans' country of origin so that they would allow the importation of the beans by Cometals' customer. . . .

*(continued)*

*(continued)*

Irrespective of the rather incredible explanations of [Tarbert's employees] as to what they understood to be the purport of the requested certificate of origin, they finally and grudgingly conceded that an EEC certificate stating that the goods were of the origin of an EEC member would be understood by anyone reading it to mean that the beans were grown in an EEC country and not simply shipped from such country. Consequently, it is completely understandable why [Agrimen's employees] expressed shock, dismay and disapproval of the oral agreement concerning the EEC certificate between [Cometals and Tarbert]. . . . The fact that the agreement drafted by Cometals duplicitously described the subject commodity simply as "Small red beans, 1982 crop," . . . does not avoid the illegality of the contract inasmuch as both parties understood from the prior communications and intended that the Kenyan beans stored in [a Rotterdam] warehouse were the subject of the contract.

It is evident from the Kenyan origin of the beans that it would have been impossible for Tarbert to honestly obtain from a Chamber of Commerce and furnish Cometals with a bona fide EEC certificate of origin stating that the goods were of the origin of a member of the EEC since concededly Kenya is not an EEC member. Thus, the only way in which Tarbert could have complied with the agreement would have been to convince an of-ficial of a Chamber of Commerce to issue a fraudulent certificate or to obtain a forged certificate. Both acts are obviously illegal.

No one shall be permitted to profit by his own fraud, or take advantage of his own wrong, or to found any claim upon his own iniquity, or to acquire property by his own crime. These maxims are dictated by public policy, have their foundation in universal law administered in all civilized countries, and have nowhere been superseded by statutes. Plaintiff maintains that the furnishing of the EEC certificate of origin was a non-essential and separable part of the bargain, and that therefore the court may hold only that portion of the agreement unenforceable. However, the court finds that the illegality is inseparable from and goes to an essential ingredient of the bargain between the parties, because Cometals insisted upon the EEC certificate in the requested form with an eye to its . . . surreptitious importation of the beans into Colombia. Plainly, enforcement of the agreement for either party would be contrary to public policy. . . . [T]he complaint and counterclaim are dismissed.

**Decision.**   Contracts that violate the law are void and will not be enforced by a court. In this case, a contract calling for the delivery of a fraudulent certificate of origin is illegal and contrary to public policy.

---

goods need not be in writing. The code states what is probably obvious, that the contract may be proven by any means, including witnesses, which is in keeping with modern trends toward flexibility in contracting and the necessity of speed in modern commercial transactions. Several countries including Russia have elected to omit this provision from its version of the CISG. China too has maintained its writing requirement for foreign trade contracts; (see Article 7 in Exhibit 5.4 for the Chinese code's requirement).

## Problems of Interpretation

No contract can be written in such precise terms that its meaning will never be in question. The best lawyers cannot possibly craft a written contract in such perfect form, especially when language barriers affect the negotiation and drafting of an international contract. Oral agreements can have even more ambiguity.

**The Parol Evidence Rule.**   The *parol evidence rule* states that where the parties have entered into a written sales contract that is intended to be the final expression of the parties' agreement, the written agreement may not be contradicted by any prior agreement or contemporaneous oral agreement (parol evidence). Parol or extrinsic evidence may be introduced to clarify an ambiguity, to prove additional terms of the agreement not covered in the written contract, or to prove fraud. The CISG allows a court, when considering the intent of the parties to a contract, to consider "all relevant circumstances of the case, including the negotiations, any practices which the parties have established between themselves, usages, and any subsequent conduct of the parties." Courts apparently have wide leeway in using parol evidence.

**Customs, Practices, and Trade Usages.** The courts of the United States and many other common law countries will often look to the past dealings of the parties and to *trade usages* for guidance in interpreting contracts or filling the gaps. Trade usages are derived from the customs of an industry, the practices of merchants in their past dealings, and the usages of trade terminology and language. For example, the Tampa Cigar Co. contracts to buy an ocean container of "Sumatra tobacco" from an independent broker in Mexico City. Tampa Cigar, and indeed most of the industry, believes that Sumatra tobacco is grown on the island of Sumatra. Unless agreed otherwise, this term becomes a part of the contract. If the broker delivers tobacco grown in Honduras from Sumatra seed, he may be in breach of contract if the law recognizes "Sumatra tobacco" as a valid trade usage.

Take another example of a trade usage. Suppose that a buyer sues a seller for delivery of defective goods. The seller points to a guarantee in the contract that the goods "will be of average and acceptable quality for the kind and type of goods sold in the trade." How would a court interpret this provision? It could look to testimony and evidence attesting to what the trade considers "average and acceptable."

Courts, lawyers, and trade negotiators in some developing countries do not rely on trade usages to interpret contracts, because of their widespread belief that many customs and trade usages were derived from the practices of European trading nations and colonial powers. In the early history of international trade, they were able to establish mercantile practices that favored the English, Dutch, and other colonial traders. A good example might be the cocoa trade, which was dominated by London merchants. When they traded in Africa, the Mediterranean, or the Caribbean, these merchants established their trade usages and practices there. Some developing countries still believe that a trade usage derived from European traders and in use by modern Western firms could only be to their disadvantage.

**Trade Usages under the CISG.** The CISG provisions of Article 9 more closely resemble the

way trade usages are handled under American law. The only trade usages that can be used to interpret or fill in the gaps in a contract are (1) those to which the parties agree to be bound or that derive from their past dealings, or (2) those usages of which the parties knew or ought to have known and that are regularly observed in the industry or trade involved.

> *http://www.cisg.law.pace.edu/cisg/text/ e-text-09.html*
> *or*
> *http://itl.irv.uit.no/trade_law/doc/ UN.Contracts.International.Sale.of.Goods. Convention.1980.html#NR12*
> See for Article 9.

## Entering the Agreement: The Offer

The contract laws of all countries require that the parties reach a mutual agreement and understanding about the essential terms of a contract. This agreement is reached through the bargaining process, between offeror and offeree. The offeror, by making the offer, creates in the offeree the power of acceptance, or the power to form a contract.

**The Intention to be Bound.** Under Article 14 of the CISG, a communication between the parties is considered an offer when (1) it is a proposal for concluding a contract, and (2) it is "sufficiently definite and indicates the intention of the offeror to be bound." An offer is considered sufficiently definite if it (1) indicates or describes the goods, (2) expressly or implicitly specifies the quantity, and (3) expressly or implicitly specifies the price for the goods.

However, one should not think that the presence of these three terms always indicates a contract. In many international contracts involving a great deal lot of money, no firm would make a commitment without reaching an agreement on many other terms, such as methods of payment, delivery dates, quality standards, etc. Take the following example. Buyer and seller are negotiating the sale of ten industrial knitting machines for five million Deutsche marks. The buyer states, "Everything seems agreeable. I'll take the machines." The agreement probably is not a contract even though it seems "sufficiently definite" under the CISG. The lack of any agreement on other matters indicates that the parties might not as yet have demonstrated their intention to be bound to a contract. However, if the court does find that the parties had the intention to be bound, it can supply many of the missing terms by looking at the past dealings of the parties, and at customs in the trade or industry, or by referring to the applicable provisions of the CISG.

**Public Offers.**  The laws of some nations hold that an offer must be addressed to one or more specific persons. In those countries, an advertisement can never create the power of acceptance in a member of the public who reads the ad. In Germany, for instance, advertisements addressed to the public in general are mere invitations to deal. Other countries, such as the United States, while treating most advertisements as mere invitations to deal, do recognize that specific advertisements that describe the goods, their quantity, and price may be considered an offer. The CISG takes a middle position by creating a presumption that an advertisement or circular is not an offer "unless the contrary is clearly indicated by the person making the proposal." Consequently, a seller may want to include in all of its price sheets and literature a notice that the material does not constitute an offer.

**Open Price Terms.**  Merchants often fail to include price terms in the chain of correspondence or communications making up a contract. Perhaps they were relying on some external market factor or course of dealings to determine price. A contract may even make reference to a market price on a date, months or even years away. If the price is left "open," is the parties' understanding sufficiently definite to constitute a valid contract? In the U.S. most state UCC laws provide that if price is not specified, a "reasonable price" will be presumed. Under this flexible approach, the contract does not fail. On the other hand, such a provision would not be found in a socialist legal system in which prices are dictated by government central planning. Open price terms are not favored in developing countries either, because they are major exporters of agricultural commodities, minerals, and other raw materials subject to a highly fluctuating market. Even in most civil law nations, such as France, a sales

price must be sufficiently definite in order for a contract to be valid.

Although some conflict stems from the language of the CISG regarding open price terms (see Articles 14 and 55), the CISG provisions seem similar to those of U.S. state law. Article 55, found under the section on the obligations of the buyer, states that where price is not fixed, the price will be that charged "for such goods sold under comparable circumstances in the trade concerned." Accordingly, if the buyer and seller fail to specify the price of the goods, a court might look to the trade to make its own determination of price, and the contract and all its other provisions will remain in effect.

**Firm Offers.**  As a general rule, an offer may be revoked at any time prior to acceptance. Under the UCC, as between merchants, an offer may not be revoked if it is made in a signed writing that gives assurance that it will remain open for a stated period of time, not to exceed three months. Under the CISG, firm offers are valid even if they are not in writing. Moreover, an offer may not be revoked if the offeree reasonably relies on the offer as being irrevocable and the offeree has acted in reliance on the offer. Consider a buyer who states to a supplier, "Within the next month I will be placing an order for 100 computers, so please give me your best price." The supplier responds, making no reference as to whether the offer will remain open. If the buyer then quotes a price on the computers for resale to a customer, the offer will be irrevocable during that month. Some civil law countries, such as Germany, France, Italy, and Japan, go even further in limiting the offeror's power to revoke. In civil law countries, the offeror may not revoke during the period of time normally needed for the offeree's acceptance to arrive.

## Entering the Agreement: The Acceptance

A contract is not formed until the offer is accepted by the offeree. The acceptance is the offeree's manifestation of the intention to be bound to the terms of the offer. In all legal systems, the offeree may accept at any time until the offer is revoked by the offeror, until the offer expires due to the passage of time, until it is rejected by the offeree, until the offeree makes a counteroffer, or until termination in some other manner. Under the CISG, an acceptance may take the form of a statement or *any other conduct* by the offeree that indicates the offeree's intention to be bound to the contract.

> **http://itl.irv.uit.no/trade_law/doc/**
> **UN.Contracts.International.Sale.of.Goods.**
> **Convention.1980.html#NR17**
> *See for the Articles in Part II: Formation of the Contract.*

**Silence as Acceptance.** The rule in most countries is that the offeree's silence should not be interpreted as an acceptance. This interpretation does not take into account, however, the realities of modern commercial trade practices. One exception, therefore, occurs when the parties' previous dealings indicate that the rule should not be followed. Consider this case: For the past five years, company A regularly ordered quantities of soda ash from company B that were to be shipped within three months of placing the order. At first, B confirmed all orders. Soon, B stopped sending written confirmations of orders and just shipped. This time, A placed the order and B never responded and never shipped. A can sue for breach of contract on the basis that the established practice of the parties presumes B's acceptance of A's order.

**Valid Acceptance.** The time differences between buyers and sellers located across the globe increase the importance of knowing with some certainty when their correspondence or telecommunications form a contract (or, in terms of contract law, when the acceptance of the offeror's terms is effective).

Under the common law, a contract is formed when the acceptance is dispatched by the offeree. In the case of an acceptance by letter, the time of dispatch is the time the letter is put into the hands of the postal authorities. This rule assumes that the correct mode of transmission is used, i.e., one that the offeror specifies or, if none, one that is reasonable under the circumstances. This assumption makes sense, for if a fax arrives offering to sell fresh roses sitting on the tarmac in Columbia, one does not accept by letter and expect a contract to be formed on dispatch. Hence, if a

buyer submits a purchase order to a seller, a contract is formed upon the dispatch of the seller's order confirmation. The buyer's power to withdraw the purchase order ended at that time. Furthermore, the effect of this rule is that the seller is also bound to the contract upon dispatch and may no longer withdraw the offer after that time.

The CISG follows a somewhat different approach. Under Article 18, an acceptance is not effective upon dispatch, but is effective when it reaches the offeror. Article 16 protects the offeree by stating that the dispatch of an acceptance cuts off the offeror's right to revoke the offer. Thus, an acceptance may possibly be withdrawn if the withdrawal reaches the offeror before or at the same time as the acceptance does (Article 22). Recall that under the common law the offeree would not have had the same right, because the contract would have been formed at the moment of dispatch.

**The Mirror Image Rule.** Most countries of the world follow the *mirror image rule.* The rule requires that an offeree respond to an offer with an acceptance that is definite and unconditional, and that matches the terms of the offer exactly and unequivocally. Under these laws, a purported acceptance that contains different or additional terms is considered a counteroffer and thus a rejection of the original offer.

## The Manner of Offer and Acceptance: Buyer's and Seller's Forms

In the real world, the chain of correspondence or exchange of documents between buyer and seller often makes it difficult to tell which one is the offer and which one is the acceptance. When an agreement is put into one document, signed by both parties, it is easier to tell. But this one-document agreement is not always the practice. In reality, the offer might come from either buyer or seller. The only way to tell which is the offer and which is the acceptance is to understand basic contract rules. A correspondence can be an offer if it is "sufficiently definite and indicates the intention of the offeror to be bound" (Article 14). The other party's response might be an acceptance, or if it contradicts the terms of the offer, it might be a counteroffer. For instance, a buyer might have looked at the seller's catalogs and samples. On that basis, he or she requests a price quote from the seller. If the price quote is sufficiently definite in its terms, then the seller has made an offer, and the buyer may accept or reject. Formal price quotes used in international trade are often done in the form of a sellers' *pro forma invoice,* as shown in Exhibit 5.5. In another case, a buyer might have enough price and product information at hand to send a *purchase order* to the seller. If it is sufficiently definite in its terms then it would be the offer, and the seller's reply, via an *order confirmation,* would be the acceptance (assuming it meets the legal requirements for an acceptance and is not a counteroffer).

**The Pro Forma Invoice.** One common method of offering products for sale to a foreign buyer is through the pro forma invoice. It is a formal written offer to a specified buyer to sell the products described. It sets out the price for the goods in

---

**EXHIBIT 5.5** **Pro Forma Invoice**

**DownPillow International, Inc.**
**Pro Forma Invoice**
**Boone, North Carolina, U.S.A.**

| Invoice to: | Japanese Retailer | Date of pro forma invoice: |
| | Osaka, Japan | Oct. 12, 1997 |
| Ship/Consign to: | as per buyer's instructions | This pro forma no. 000044372 |
| Shipment via: | U.S. port to destination Kobe | Terms of Payment: |
| Notify Party: | Buyer to advise | Cash against documents, |
| Country of Origin: | U.S.A. | irrevocable LC payable in |
| | | U.S. dollars |
| Total weight (est.): | 9405 lbs/4266 kg. | Shipment Date |
| Shipping volume (est.): | 3000 cu.ft./85 cu.m. | 15 days after receipt of LC |

| Quantity | Item Code | Description | Price | Amount |
|---|---|---|---|---|
| 5000 | 5WGD-1 | Bed pillows of white goose down total fill weight 26oz./0.74kg, contents sterilized shell: 100% cotton, with piping size 26″ × 26″, 66cm × 66cm | $32.00 | $160,000 |
| | | PRICE F.O.B. BOONE | | $160,000 |
| | | Export packing/vacuum pack charges | | 850 |
| | | Cartage/Inland freight charge | | 1250 |
| | | Pier delivery charge | | 150 |
| | | Freight forwarder's fees | | 200 |
| | | PRICE F.A.S. NC PORT | | $162,450 |
| | | Ocean freight charges port to port | | $3355 |
| | | Container rental charge | | 450 |
| | | Marine insurance charges | | 640 |
| | | PRICE C.I.F. Port of KOBE, Japan | | $166,895 |

DownPillow International, Inc.

_____     _____
by, Export Sales Manager                      Authorized buyer's signature

| SEE OTHER SIDE FOR ADDITIONAL TERMS AND CONDITIONS (*not reproduced herein*) |
| --- |

the currency stated, plus any additional charges payable by the buyer's account, including the cost of packing and crating; the cost of inland freight; the cost of ocean or air freight, freight forwarders fees, and pier delivery charges; wharfage and warehouse charges; and insurance. (Most exporters rely heavily on their freight forwarders to obtain this cost information and, later, to make these shipping arrangements.) The pro forma invoice specifies the mode of shipment, the method of payment, the length of time for which the quoted terms will be valid, and any and all other terms required by the seller as a condition of sale. Sellers usually require the buyer to accept the offer by signing it and returning it to them before shipment. In other cases, a buyer might accept by sending their own purchase order form. Pro forma invoices are often required by the customs authority in the buyer's country prior to importation of the goods so that import licenses can be issued in advance. Pro forma invoices are used in all types of industries, manufacturing firms in particular. The pro forma invoice should not be confused with the *commercial invoice,* which is the final bill for the goods that accompanies the request for payment.

## Contract Terms and Conditions and the "Battle of the Forms"

The mirror image rule requires that an acceptance be unconditional and that it not attempt to change any of the terms proposed in the offer. These requirements present special problems when both parties, buyer and seller, negotiate back and forth via "standard" business forms. The seller might quote prices by letter or by formal pro forma invoice. The buyer might use a preprinted purchase order form to place orders with all vendors. The seller might rely on an order confirmation form or sales acknowledgement form. Typically, these forms leave room on the front so the parties may insert important contract terms—those that they "bargained for," such as price, quality, or ship date. The reverse side often contains detailed "fine-print" provisions or standard clauses, often called *terms and conditions,* or *general conditions of sale,* as shown in Exhibit 5.6.

Their use is common in international trade. They are often drafted by attorneys to protect

their client's rights, placing greater liability on the other party. Often they are adapted from recommended standard clauses provided by industry or trade associations. For instance, one set of standard clauses might be utilized by the steel industry, another by grain merchants, and yet another by the chemical industry. The parties may not even be aware of the legal significance of these seldom read fine-print provisions. For the most part, a seller would only read the most crucial provisions on the front page of a buyer's purchase order to see what was ordered. A buyer may only glance at the key provisions of the seller's confirmation to see when the goods will be shipped. Usually the preprinted terms on these forms differ, sometimes in significant ways. Here are several examples of how they might differ

- Buyer's purchase order allows the buyer to bring suit for consequential damages if the seller breaches the contract. Seller's confirmation specifically excludes consequential damages.
- Buyer's purchase order calls for disputes to be resolved in the buyer's country. Seller's confirmation calls for disputes to be heard in the courts of the seller's country.
- Buyer's purchase order requires shipment by a certain date named in the order. Seller's confirmation allows a grace period for late shipping or provides for excuses for late shipment.
- Buyer's purchase order is silent about whether the buyer has to notify the seller in the event of problems with the merchandise. Seller's confirmation requires buyer to notify the seller of any problems in the order within seven days.

The potential for conflict is almost endless. When this occurs, lawyers call it a *battle of the forms.* In the following sections, assume that the buyer is the offeror and that the buyer's purchase order is the offer. Assume also that the seller is the offeree and that the seller's confirmation of that order is the (attempted) acceptance. The assumptions serve to simplify the discussion for understanding. Keep in mind that the seller could possibly make an offer first, such as in pro forma invoice, in which case the buyer's purchase order might actually be an attempted acceptance.

---

**EXHIBIT 5.6    Terms and Conditions of Sale**

---

**(Seller's Order Confirmation - Reverse Side)**
**TERMS AND CONDITIONS OF SALE**

*1. Acceptance*

This constitutes acceptance by Seller of Buyer's purchase order. This acceptance is expressly made conditional upon Buyer's assent, express or implied, to the terms and conditions set forth herein without modification or addition. Buyer's acceptance of these terms and conditions shall be indicated by any part of the following, whichever first occurs: (a) Buyer's written acknowledgment hereof; (b) Buyer's acceptance of shipment of the goods herein described; (c) Buyer's failure to acknowledge or reject these terms and conditions in writing within five business days after delivery; or (d) any other act or expression of acceptance by the Buyer. Seller's silence or failure to respond to any such subsequent term, condition or proposal shall not be deemed to be Seller's acceptance or approval thereof.

*2. Price and Delivery*

The quoted price for the goods may be varied by additions upwards by the Seller according to market conditions at the date of shipment and the Buyer shall pay such additions in addition to the quoted price, including but not limited to increases in the cost of labor, material, operations, and/or transport. Delivery and payment terms shall be made according to this order confirmation. Trade formulas used herein (e.g., CIF, CPT, FAS or FOB) shall be interpreted according to INCOTERMS (1990). Payment in the currency and at the conditions of this confirmation.

*3. Force Majeure*

Seller shall not be liable for loss or damage due to delay in manufacture, shipment, or delivery resulting from any cause beyond Seller's direct control or due to compliance with any regulations, orders, acts, instructions, or priority requests of any government authority, acts of God, acts or omissions of the purchaser, fires, floods, epidemics, weather, strikes, factory shutdowns, embargoes, wars, riots, delays in transportation, delay in receiving materials from Seller's usual sources, and any delay resulting from any such cause shall extend shipment or delivery date to the extent caused thereby and Seller shall be reimbursed its additional expenses resulting from such delay. In the case of delay lasting more than eight weeks, Seller has the right to cancel contract. Receipt of merchandise by the Buyer shall constitute a waiver of any claims for delay.

*4. Warranties*

The Seller makes no representations or warranties with respect to the goods herein. Seller hereby disclaims warranties, express or implied, as to the products, including but not limited to, any implied warranty of quality or merchantability or fitness for any particular purpose, and the Buyer takes the goods on the Buyer's own judgment. Seller not liable for any damage or loss for a breach of warranty.

*5. Limitation of Liability*

Seller is not liable for any special, consequential, or incidental damages arising out of this agreement or the goods sold hereunder, including but no limited to damages for lost profits, loss of use or any damages or sums paid by Buyer to third parties, even if Seller has been advised of the possibility of such damages.

*6. Governing Law*

In respect of any standard, test, mode of inspection, measurement, or weight, the practice governing the same adopted for use in Hong Kong shall prevail. This agreement shall be governed by the Laws of Hong Kong and in the event of any dispute arising whether touching on the interpretation hereof or otherwise, the same shall be referred to a single arbitrator to be appointed by the President of the Chartered Institute of Arbitrations or failing him by the President of the Law Society of Hong Kong in accordance with the Arbitration Ordinance, whose decision shall be final.

---

**The Battle of the Forms under the Common Law and Civil Law.** If a seller sends a confirmation in response to a buyer's purchase order, and the seller's form contains differing or additional terms, no matter how minor, then no contract would exist. The mirror image rule has been violated. Each form or correspondence between them is considered a counteroffer, canceling the previous one. If the parties do not perform (e.g., the seller does not ship the goods), then no contract is formed. Indeed, the buyer cannot force the seller to ship because no contract exists. If the parties do perform—the seller ships the goods—then that action is an acceptance of the terms on the other party's last form. The result usually is that the form sent last in time will prevail as the contract. Consider the following two examples:

- Suppose that a U.S. company, DownPillow International, Inc., sends a purchase order to Federhaus, a German supplier of feathers. Federhaus replies with a confirmation stating that the buyer has only ten days to notify the seller in the event of a problem with the shipment. DownPillow faxes back that it must have thirty days. With no more said, Federhaus ships. This action is an acceptance—and the contract terms are those in DownPillow's last correspondence. DownPillow has thirty days. If the ten-day provision was important to Federhaus, it should have gotten an affirmative response from DownPillow before shipping.

- Now assume that Federhaus's confirmation states that a charge of one percent per month will be applied to outstanding balances if the account is not paid within thirty days. Down-Pillow does nothing more. If the seller ships, it might not have recourse against DownPillow for refusing the goods—the new term was not a mirror image of the buyer's order, and thus no contract was formed to protect the seller. On the other hand, if DownPillow accepts the feathers and then fails to pay within thirty days, it will be liable for the interest penalty because the confirmation was a counteroffer that DownPillow accepted by receiving the merchandise. These determinations would be the result if the case were heard in a court that applied the common law or civil law rules. These results are not the case in the United States today.

**The Battle of the Forms and Mirror Image Rule under the UCC.** In the United States the mirror image rule has been modified by statute to deal with modern business practices and to avoid the problems in the preceding examples. Under UCC 2-207:

1. "A written confirmation which is sent within a reasonable time operates as an acceptance even though it states terms additional to or different from those" in the purchase order, unless the confirmation "is expressly made conditional on assent to the additional or different terms." UCC 2-207 (1)

2. If both parties are merchants, any additional terms contained in the seller's confirmation automatically become a part of the contract *unless:*

   a. The buyer's purchase order "expressly limits acceptance" to the terms in that order;

   b. The additional terms in the confirmation "materially alter" the terms of the order; or

   c. The buyer notifies the seller of an objection to the additional terms within a reasonable time after receiving the confirmation containing the new terms. UCC 2-207 (2)

A careful reading of UCC 2-207 shows that the UCC attempts to uphold the intentions of the parties by keeping the contract in existence where there are only *minor differences* between the forms used by the parties. The UCC states that, between merchants, an acceptance by confirmation that contains additional terms that reflect only minor changes from the buyer's order will be effective to produce a contract, and the minor terms become a part of it (unless the buyer notifies the seller of an objection to the new term). A minor term might be one that is in *usual and customary usage* in the trade. Adding a provision which calls for an interest penalty for late payment is an example of a minor term (such penalties are common in sales contacts).

Now reconsider our example under the UCC. DownPillow faxes its purchase order for feathers; its order does not expressly limit the acceptance to the terms of the order. All the "bargained" terms such as price, quality, and ship date are agreed upon. Seller Federhaus's confirmation states, however, that a charge of one percent per month will be applied to outstanding balances if the account is not paid within thirty days. Down-Pillow does nothing more. This time, under the UCC, a contract is formed. The seller is safe in shipping and DownPillow will have breached it if it refuses delivery of the goods. Moreover, if DownPillow is late in paying, interest will run on its open account. DownPillow could have objected to the inclusion of the late payment fee term, but it did not.

The situation is different in the case of new terms in the acceptance that attempt to *materially alter* the offer. A material term is generally considered to be one that is not commonly accepted in the trade and that would result in *surprise hardship* to one party if unilaterally included in the contract by the party. Such new terms do not become a part of the contract unless accepted by the other party. Suppose that DownPillow sends a purchase order to Federhaus in Germany. The order does not expressly limit an acceptance to the terms of the order. The confirmation is identical as to price, quality, ship date, and other bargained terms. However, the standard clause on the reverse side of the confirmation from Federhaus states that "all disputes are to be resolved in arbitration before the International Chamber of Commerce in Paris." A term that affects the rights of the parties in the event of a breach, such as an arbitration clause like this, is a material term. A contract will be formed without Federhaus' new terms. *Sellers who wish to be assured that their order confirmation will comprise the entire agreement, should request that the buyer show its acceptance of the new terms by signing the confirmation and returning the completed contract to them.*

**Confirmation Notices—German Law and the CISG.** As stated earlier, these determinations would not be the result under the civil codes of European countries that strictly follow the mirror image rule. However, some special rules in effect in some European countries take into account the special formalities and formal business practices of the European firms. In Germany, for example, manufacturing firms regularly confirm purchase orders with their *Auftragsbestätigung,* or "order confirmation." These documents are given special treatment under German law. If this formal confirmation alters the terms of a buyer's purchase order, the terms of the confirmation prevail unless the buyer specifically rejects them in a prompt and timely fashion. However, while Germany applies this law in contracts between parties in Germany, a German court has held that the confirmation notice principle does not apply under the CISG. Thus, the failure to respond to a confirmation note has no effect if a contract with a German firm is governed by the CISG.[2]

**The Battle of the Forms under the CISG.** The CISG rules fall somewhere between the rules set out by the common and civil law and the UCC. In an international sales transaction governed by the CISG, an acceptance containing new terms that do not materially alter the terms of the offer becomes a part of the contract, *unless the offeror promptly objects to the change.* However, a purported acceptance that contains additional or different terms that do materially alter the terms of the offer *would constitute a rejection of the offer and a counteroffer.* No contract would arise at all unless the offeror in return accepts all of the terms of the counteroffer (recall that under the UCC a contract would arise, albeit without the new terms). Continuing the previous example, no contract would be formed between DownPillow and Federhaus under the CISG, and Federhaus's new material terms would amount to no more than a counteroffer.

In the following case, *Filanto v. Chilewich International Corporation,* a U.S. court discussed the battle of the forms under the CISG. As you read, consider the importance of knowing the rules for forming a contract if you are a businessperson. Also consider the need for the parties to communicate clearly during the negotiating process and to object to contract proposals that they do not want to be a part of their agreement.

Under the CISG, an acceptance of the counteroffer may arise by assent or *by performance.* In other words, if the original offeror takes some steps toward performing the contract, after having received a counteroffer, the offeror will be deemed to have accepted the counteroffer and a contract will be created on the new terms. So, if DownPillow remits payment for the feathers without having read the fine-print provisions of Federhaus's confirmation (a counteroffer), it implies acceptance of Federhaus's terms, including the arbitration terms. By way of example, a draft commentary to Article 19 states:

## Filanto v. Chilewich International Corporation
### 789 F.Supp. 1229 (1992)
### United States District Court
### (S.D.N.Y.)

**BACKGROUND AND FACTS**

Chilewich, a New York company, entered a contract for the sale of shoes to Raznoexport, a foreign trade agency of the Soviet Union. The contract provided that all disputes were to be settled by arbitration in Moscow. Chilewich then negotiated with Filanto, an Italian company that manufactures footwear, offering to purchase the boots needed to fulfill its contract with Raznoexport. In March 1990, Chilewich prepared and sent to Filanto a signed "Memorandum Agreement" for signature by Filanto. It contained price, payment, and delivery terms. It called for Chilewich to open a letter of credit at its bank to assure payment to Filanto. This offer also incorporated the arbitration agreement of the original Russian contract. Filanto did not sign and return this memo at this time. In May, Chilewich had its bank issue the letter of credit to Filanto. Some boots were shipped and paid for. In August, Filanto signed and returned the memo. It appended a cover letter stating that although it agreed to supply the boots, it excluded the arbitration clause. Chilewich never accepted the balance of the boots it had ordered. Filanto brought this action to enforce the balance of the contract. Defendant Chilewich claims that the case must be arbitrated in Moscow.

**BRIEANT, CHIEF JUDGE**

. . . [A]s plaintiff correctly notes, the "general principles of contract law" relevant to this action, do not include the Uniform Commercial Code; rather, the "federal law of contracts" to be applied in this case is found in the United Nations Convention on Contracts for the International Sale of Goods (the "Sale of Goods Convention"). . . .

Defendant Chilwich contends that the Memorandum Agreement dated March which it signed and sent to Filanto was an offer. It then argues that Filanto's retention of the letter, along with its subsequent acceptance of Chilewich's performance under the Agreement—the furnishing of the letter of credit—estops it from denying its acceptance of the contract . . . [T]his is . . . an acceptance by conduct argument, e.g., that in light of the parties' course of dealing, Filanto had a duty timely to inform Chilewich that it objected to the incorporation by reference of all the terms of the Russian Contract. Under this view, the return of the Memorandum Agreement along with the covering letter purporting to exclude parts of the Russian contract, was ineffective as a matter of law as a rejection of the March offer, because this occurred some five months after Filanto received the Memorandum Agreement and two months after Chilewich furnished the Letter of Credit. Instead, in Chilewich's view, this action was a proposal for modification of the March Agreement. Chilewich rejected this proposal. . . . Accordingly, Filanto under this interpretation is bound by the written terms of the March Memorandum Agreement; since that agreement incorporates by reference the Russian Contract containing the arbitration provision, Filanto is bound to arbitrate. . . .

The Court is satisfied on this record that there was indeed an agreement to arbitrate between these parties. There is simply no satisfactory explanation as to why Filanto failed to object to the incorporation by reference of the Russian Contract in a timely fashion. As noted above, Chilewich had in the meantime commenced its performance under the Agreement, and the Letter of Credit it furnished Filanto on May 11 itself mentioned the Russian Contract. An offeree who, knowing that the offeror has commenced performance, fails to notify the offeror of its objection to the terms of the contract within a reasonable time will, under certain circumstances, be deemed to have assented to those terms. The *Sale of Goods Convention* itself recognizes this rule: *Article 18(1)*, provides that "A statement made by or other conduct of the offeree indicating assent to an offer is an acceptance." Although mere "silence or inactivity" does not constitute acceptance, *Sale of Goods Convention Article 18(1)*, the Court may consider previous relations between the parties in assessing whether a party's conduct constituted acceptance, *Sale of Goods Convention Article 8(3)*. In this case, in light of the extensive course of prior dealing between these parties, Filanto was certainly under a duty to alert Chilewich in timely fashion to its objections to the terms of the March Memorandum Agreement—particularly since Chilewich had repeatedly referred it to the Russian

*(continued)*

*(continued)*

Contract and Filanto had had a copy of that document for some time. . . .

Lastly, the plaintiff contends that if this Court does order arbitration, the Court should take judicial notice of the unsettled conditions in Moscow and order arbitration to proceed in this judicial district. . . . These parties, though, did agree to arbitrate their disputes in Moscow. Whatever the applicability of these cases in the arbitration context, the chosen forum in this case does have a reasonable relation to the contract at issue, as the ultimate purchaser of the boots was a Russian concern and the Russian Contract was incorporated by reference into Filanto's Memorandum Agreement with Chilewich. Furthermore, though conditions in the Republic of Russia are unsettled, they continue to improve and there is no reason to believe that the Chamber of Commerce in Moscow cannot provide fair and impartial justice to these litigants.

**Decision.**  Judgment for the defendant, Chilewich. The parties were referred to arbitration in Moscow. According to the CISG, Filanto's failure to object to the arbitration term in Chilewich's offer in a timely fashion, and its willingness to accept Chilewich's performance, amounted to an acceptance. Filanto was under a duty to alert Chilewich in a timely fashion to its objections to the terms of the Memorandum Agreement.

For example, an offeree might reply to an offer stating that the offeror has fifty tractors available for sale at a certain price by sending a telegram that accepts the offer but adds "ship immediately." . . .

. . . [T]he additional or different terms contained in [this] reply would constitute material alteration since the terms "ship immediately" would change the time of delivery (since no shipping date had been specified, a "reasonable time" for shipment would have been presumed under the CISG). . . .

If the reply contains a material alteration, the reply would not constitute an acceptance but would constitute a counteroffer. If the original offeror responds to this reply by shipping the goods . . . a contract may eventually be formed by notice to the original offeree of the shipment. . . .

Unlike the UCC, the CISG states those key elements of a contract that will materially alter a contract: *price, payment, quality and quantity of goods, place and time of delivery, extent of one party's liability to the other, and settlement of disputes.* This list is so broad that almost any term could conceivably be interpreted as "material." Thus, under the CISG, almost any new or different term in the acceptance could constitute a counteroffer. The effect is that many businesspeople may believe that they are "under contract" when they really are not. Consequently, those businesspeople negotiating an international contract must make certain that all material terms of the contract are understood and agreed upon by the parties.

## Warranty Provisions

Product warranties are contractual terms that define a product's design and performance characteristics, quality, and workmanship. These terms need to be spelled out clearly so that no confusion arises over what the seller is responsible for doing. A misunderstanding here can permanently injure the long-term relationship between the parties. Consequently, warranties are often subject to intensive bargaining. Typically, sellers will want to limit the scope of their liability, place a ceiling on the amount of damages for which they can be liable, and place a limit on the time that the warranty will run. Buyers will want to negotiate the broadest provisions and gain the most legal protection.

Sometimes the parties might not realize that they are negotiating warranty terms. International contracts for the sale of goods are often not embodied in formal written documents carefully drafted by experienced lawyers. Due to the great distances involved in international business, contracts often arise through a chain of correspondence and catalogs sent through the mail, by telex, or by facsimile over the telephone wires. Plagued with potential language problems and the possibility of a misunderstanding, international companies and experienced traders tend to place greater reliance on the use of models, diagrams, spec sheets, and samples to explain their product's quality, packaging, and ability to perform. Each communication might contain some warranty about the product which also becomes an important part of the bargain between the parties.

## Implied Warranties

Implied warranties are those warranties that are not expressly given by the seller but are "read into the contract" by the law. In the United States, the law governing express and implied warranties is found in the UCC. The provisions of the CISG are similar to those in the UCC. Under CISG Article 35, the seller must deliver goods that are of the quantity, quality, and description required by the contract, and that

1. Are fit for the purposes for which goods of the same description would ordinarily be used.
2. Are fit for any particular purpose expressly or implied made known to the seller at the time of the conclusion of the contract.
3. Possess the qualities of goods which the seller has held out to the buyer as a sample or model.

4. Are contained or packaged in the manner usual for such goods or, where there is no such manner, in a manner adequate to preserve and protect the goods.

Clearly, items 3 and 4 reflect two important features of international business—the greater use of samples and models and the greater need for packaging that protects goods during ocean shipment.

*Nonconforming goods* are those that do not conform to the express or implied terms of a contract. In *United Trade Associates Limited v. Dickens & Matson,* a U.S. court decided a case involving a breach of warranty for nonconforming telephones shipped from the United States to Russia. A choice of law provision in the contract called for it to be governed by the law of England. After you read, compare and contrast the meaning of *merchantablility* under English law with that found in the CISG and the UCC of the United States.

Trade usages and custom are also used by courts to determine whether a product is merchantable

---

### United Trade Associates Limited v. Dickens & Matson

848 F.Supp. 751 (1994)
United States District Court
(E.D. Mich.)

**BACKGROUND AND FACTS**
UTAL is an international trading company based in the Ukraine, with offices in London. It trades goods to the republics of the former Soviet Union. In light of the rapid changes there, UTAL believed that the demand for telephones would increase. They purchased used telephones from Dickens & Matson, a mail order company, for resale in the Ukraine. UTAL specified that the phones had to be "two-piece push button phones with necessary cords, in good working and operating condition" and that they had to comply with the guidelines of the Ukrainian telephone commission. Dickens & Matson arranged to buy the phones from Telparts, with whom it had dealt in the past. Dickens & Matson provided UTAL with samples that matched the types of phones that it had previously sold in Russia. A representative of Dickens & Matson testified that he had watched the phones being loaded into ocean containers at Telparts' warehouse in Florida and had "spot checked" to see that the phones conformed to the contract. UTAL's bank paid Dickens & Matson for the phones upon shipment. When the phones were unloaded in the Ukraine, UTAL discovered that the boxes contained cracked, smashed, and tangled telephone parts and no working phones. UTAL notified Dickens & Matson by fax that it was rejecting the shipment. UTAL sued for breach of contract. The contract specified that it should be interpreted according to the Law of England.

**ANNA DIGGS TAYLOR, DISTRICT JUDGE**
According to the English law of contract, it is the duty of the seller to deliver goods in accordance with the terms of the contract of sale. *English Sale of Goods Act of 1979 § 27.* If a term in a contract constitutes a substantial ingredient in identifying the thing sold, it is a "condition." The effect of breaching a condition expressed in the contract or implied by statute is that the innocent party can rescind the contract. Thus the innocent party is excused from performance and can sue for damages. In contrast, when a party breaches

*(continued)*

*(continued)*

a term in the contract that is relatively unimportant, English courts label the action a breach of warranty. A breach of a warranty entitles the innocent party to maintain an action for damages, but the innocent party is not excused from performance. The test to determine whether a breach of a term in a contract amounts to a breach of a condition rather than a breach of a warranty is whether the innocent party is deprived of the benefit it bargained for when it entered into the contract.

The shipment of nonconforming goods by Dickens & Matson clearly breached the contract. Furthermore, Dickens & Matson's action of shipping unusable and damaged phone parts amounted to a breach of an express condition of the contract. UTAL's purpose for entering into the contract was to sell phones that could function in the Ukraine. Based on the evidence of record, the goods that arrived in the Ukraine did not work. When confronted with this evidence, even Dickens & Matson admitted that the telephone parts displayed in the photographs did not conform with the specifications of the contract. They also conceded that the description of the goods offered in the customs report did not match with the description of the goods contained in the contract. UTAL was deprived of the benefit it sought when it entered into the contract. Thus, Dickens & Matson's actions amounted to a breach of an express condition of the contract.

In addition to breaching an express condition of the contract, Dickens & Matson is liable for breaching the implied conditions of the contract. By shipping broken telephone parts rather than two-piece push button telephones, Dickens & Matson clearly breached the implied condition of correspondence with description. The goods shipped differed from the description included in the contract and the letter of credit so extensively that customs officials refused to release the goods.

Furthermore, Dickens & Matson breached the implied condition of merchantability because, based on the description of the goods offered in the contract, it is a reasonable expectation that the telephones would work. Finally, Dickens & Matson breached the implied condition of fitness for a particular purpose because UTAL informed Dickens & Matson of its purpose to sell working telephones in the Ukraine, and the goods shipped were not fit for that purpose. *Sale of Goods Act 1979 § 14(2,3)*.

**Decision.**    Judgment for the plaintiff for $135,000, the amount paid under the contract. The defendant breached both express and implied conditions in the contract, including the implied condition of merchantability as defined under English law.

**Comment.**    In the case, no evidence clearly indicates whether intentional fraud was committed against UTAL, or whether it was done by Dickens & Matson, Telparts, or both. Do you think this case involved fraud? What could UTAL have done to have protected itself in either case?

---

under a contract. *T. J. Stevenson v. 81,193 Bags of Flour*, 629 F.2d 338 (1980), is a U.S. case decided under the UCC (see Exhibit 5.7 for applicable UCC provisions). In the case, the court looked to trade usages and custom in the agricultural commodities business to determine whether flour that was infested with beetles was *merchantable and fit for human consumption*. The court stated,

. . . [W]e observe that finding what the parties meant by "merchantability" requires some evaluation of standards in the commercial market and the state of the art in flour manufacturing. The merchantability of infested flour to be sold to consumers is a question of degree and kind. We have often recognized that no food is completely pure. The FDA has long permitted very small amounts of insect fragments and other dead infestation in food products. To declare that any contamination of flour—even by small amounts of insect fragment—renders the flour unmerchantable would no doubt be out of step with commercial reality and would wreak havoc on food manufacturers and distributors while affording little or no additional protection to the consumer. What this case involves, however, is significant amounts of live infestation, by flour beetle eggs, larvae, pupae, and adults. Here the question is: How much live infestation renders consumer-destined flour unfit for the ordinary purposes for which it is used?

Judicial interpretation, trade usage, and course of dealing point to but one conclusion as to flour

**EXHIBIT 5.7   UCC Implied Warranties, Merchantability, and Usage of Trade**

§2-314(2)   Goods to be merchantable must be at least such as
  (a) pass without objection in the trade under the contract description; and
  (b) in the case of fungible goods, are of fair average quality within the description; and
  (c) are fit for the ordinary purposes for which such goods are used; and
  (d) run, within the variations permitted by the agreement, of even kind, quality, and quantity within each unit and among all units involved; and
  (e) are adequately contained, packaged, and labeled as the agreement may require; and
  (f) conform to the promises or affirmations of fact made on the container or label if any.

§2-314(3)   (a) Unless excluded or modified other implied warranties may arise from course of dealing or usage of trade.

infested with significant amounts of live flour beetles: although the flour may be "fit for human consumption" in the sense that it can be eaten without causing sickness, it is nonetheless not of merchantable quality. Such flour is not what is normally expected in the trade.

*http://www.cisg.law.pace.edu/cisg/text/ e-text-35.html*
*or*
*http://itl.irv.uit.no/trade_law/doc/ UN.Contracts.International.Sale.of.Goods. Convention.1980.html#NR44*
*See for Article 35 of the CISG.*

**Disclaiming Implied Warranties.**   One notable difference between the UCC and the CISG is that U.S. law places restrictions on the parties' ability to limit the implied warranties of the UCC. For instance, under the UCC, a seller may "disclaim" an implied warranty only by using conspicuous, or specified, language to that effect, such as the words "as is." However, the CISG contains no pro-

visions limiting disclaimers for several reasons: International sales contracts take place between more sophisticated and experienced buyers and sellers; the CISG does not apply to consumer sales, where the greatest chance of fraud and abuse might occur; and the nations participating in the drafting of the CISG wanted to preserve as much freedom of contract as possible for the merchants or companies involved. As such, any form of disclaimer will suffice under the CISG.

## Notice of Nonconforming Goods

If the shipment is nonconforming, or if the goods that are delivered are in some way deficient in quality, quantity, description, packaging, or warranties, both parties must understand what is expected of them and what their alternative courses of action may be. Most legal systems require that notice be given by a buyer to a seller in the event of a breach. In many European countries, that period is fairly short, often a year or less.

During the drafting of the CISG, the developing countries objected to such a short period. Many products imported by developing countries might contain defects that are not readily discoverable, such as with mechanical equipment or pharmaceuticals. They usually required some time to obtain technical assistance from abroad in order to test the imported products for quality or performance. In some cases, products might remain aboard ship, perhaps anchored offshore, for months or years waiting for a strike to be settled or for government red tape to clear before delivery becomes possible.

The CISG reflects the concerns of developing countries and requires that the buyer examine the goods "within as short a period as is practicable" after they are received. Unless some reasonable excuse prevents doing so, the buyer must give notice of a nonconformity or defect in the goods within a reasonable time after it is discovered or should have been discovered. In any event, however, notice must be given within two years from the date on which the goods were "handed over" to the buyer. If the buyer fails to give proper notice, the results are clear: the buyer loses the right to assert the breach against the seller.

The German "mussels" case discusses both the fitness of the goods and the buyer's duty to give notice of a claim of nonconformity within a reasonable time period.

*Decision of March 8, 1995 on New Zealand Mussels*
Federal Supreme Court
(Bundesgerichtshof),
Decision of March 8, 1995

German Courts do not identify the parties to a case.

### BACKGROUND AND FACTS

A German fish importer purchased 1,750 kilograms (kg) of New Zealand mussels for U.S. $3.70 per kg from a seller residing in Switzerland. The seller delivered the goods to a storage facility belonging to the buyer. When the mussels were inspected by a governmental agency while at the buyer's storage facility, they were found to have a high cadmium content.

The German buyer then sent a fax to the seller stating that it planned to return the mussels since they were "not harmless" due to their cadmium content. The seller said it would not accept the returned goods. The seller sued, claiming the mussels were suitable for consumption because, while the cadmium level was higher than recommended, the cadmium content did not exceed the permitted level. The seller also claimed the buyer had not given timely notice of the defects. The buyer claimed the mussels were defective because the cadmium level exceeded the guidelines.

### OPINION

The *U.N. Convention on Contracts for the International Sale of Goods* (CISG) applies [here]. It is true that a delivery of goods that does not conform with the contract can be a fundamental breach of contract within the meaning of CISG; in case of a lack of express agreement, CISG governs the question whether the goods conform with the contract. The question whether only goods of average quality are suitable for ordinary use or whether it is sufficient that the goods are "marketable" may be left open. The delivered mussels are not of inferior quality even if their cadmium content exceeds the examination results known so far. The reason for this is that the standard for cadmium content in fish, in contrast to the standard for meat, does not have a legally binding character but only an administratively guiding character. . . . There is no evidence that the parties implicitly agreed to comply with [German standards]. . . . The mere fact that the mussels were to be delivered to the storage facility in Germany does not necessarily constitute an agreement regarding the compliance with certain public law provisions on which the resalability may depend.

Where the parties have not agreed on anything, the goods do not conform with the contract if they are unsuitable for the ordinary use or for a specific purpose expressly or impliedly made known to the seller. . . . In the examination of whether the goods were suitable for ordinary use, the Court of Appeals rightly left open the question—controversial in the legal literature—whether this requires generic goods of average quality or whether merely "marketable" goods are sufficient. . . .

According to the absolutely prevailing opinion in the legal literature, which this Court follows, the compliance with specialized public law provisions of the buyer's country or the country of use cannot be expected.

The appeal wrongly requests that [seller] submit a statement that New Zealand mussels usually have such a high cadmium contamination. After taking delivery without giving notice of the lack of conformity, the buyer must allege and prove that the goods do not conform with the contract and the seller does not have to allege and prove that they do conform with the contract. . . .

[In addition,] the buyer lost any right to rely on the lack of conformity and to declare the contract avoided because it waited almost two months before it notified the seller about the nonconformity. As the goods were perishable food items, one month after delivery would be a "generous" period of time, but obviously acceptable as a "reasonable time" for providing notice as specified in CISG.

**Decision.** The German Supreme Court held that the high cadmium concentration in the mussels delivered by the Swiss seller did constitute a lack of conformity of the mussels, but found the mussels were still edible even though the cadmium concentration exceeded the limit recommended by the German health authority. There was no obligation on the seller to supply goods conforming to public provisions in force in the import state unless the same provisions also exist in the export state, or the buyer informs the seller about such a provision. The court also stated that the buyer's notice of the nonconformity was not given in a reasonable time period. It had to examine them within as short a time period as practicable under the circumstances. Judgment for the seller.

# Remedies for Breach of Contract

The remedies available to a buyer or seller under the CISG are drawn from both common law and civil law systems. They are intended to give the parties the benefit of their bargain and to put the parties into the economic position they would have been in had the breach not occurred. The remedies outlined in the CISG include (1) avoidance of the contract, (2) sellers right to remedy or cure, (3) seller's additional time to perform, (4) price reduction, (5) money damages, and (6) specific performance.

> http://itl.irv.uit.no/trade_law/doc/
> UN.Contracts.International.Sale.of.Goods.
> Convention.1980.html
> *See Part III, Sale of Goods, for Articles 45–52 and 61–65 on breach of contract.*

## Avoidance and the Fundamental Breach

Both the UCC and the CISG have provisions that allow the buyer to refuse deliveries of nonconforming or defective goods, or to return them once the defects are discovered. Under the UCC, these remedies are called "rejection" and "revocation of acceptance," and under the CISG they are referred to as *avoidance of the contract.* The term refers to a party's right to cancel the contract.

**Fundamental Breach.**  A buyer's right of rejection of defective goods under the UCC is somewhat broader than a buyer's right of avoidance under the CISG. Under the "perfect tender" provisions of the UCC, the buyer has greater rights in rejecting a shipment for minor nonconformities. Thus, if the seller is under an obligation to deliver 25 computer chips, and one or two are defective, the buyer may reject the entire lot. Once the delivery is accepted, the buyer may reject only if the goods show substantial nonconformity.

The CISG goes further to keep the parties in their bargain. In the case of a dispute under the CISG, a buyer can avoid the contract only in the case of a *fundamental breach* by the seller. The CISG distinguishes between a serious or fundamental breach of the contract and one that is minor or less than fundamental. Article 25 de-

fines a fundamental breach as one that will "substantially deprive him of what he is entitled to expect under the contract." The seller's shipment of seriously defective goods that cannot be repaired, or that have no value to the buyer under the contract, is probably a fundamental breach. So too would be the seller's failure and refusal to ship at all. A partial shipment may also amount to a fundamental breach if it presents a serious problem for the buyer and one that cannot quickly be remedied. Any further interpretation of fundamental breach will have to be left up to the courts.

**Buyer's Right to Avoidance.**  If the breach is fundamental, the buyer need not take delivery nor pay for the goods, nor find a buyer to take them. A buyer may simply cancel the contract by notifying the seller of avoidance of the contract, take care that the goods are temporarily protected and preserved, and return them for a full refund of monies already paid. When the goods can rapidly deteriorate or decay, such as with certain foods, the buyer may notify the seller and then take steps to sell them. These rights are especially important to a buyer in an international transaction because of the hardships associated with having to accept delivery and then reselling or disposing of imported goods in a foreign (i.e., the buyer's) market. A buyer who avoids a contract may still sue the seller for damages resulting from the seller's breach.

**Notice of Avoidance.**  The buyer's avoidance rights are not effective until the seller is given notice. A buyer who has already accepted the goods, and then discovers their nonconformity, loses the right to avoid the contract, if the buyer does not notify the seller of the intention to avoid, within a reasonable time after the buyer knew or should have known of the breach. Thus, if the defect can be discovered only upon use, the buyer has a reasonable period from then on to notify the seller. In the case of goods that have been delivered late, so that they no longer have any value to the buyer (i.e., a fundamental breach), the buyer can lose the right to avoid the contract, unless the buyer does so within a reasonable time after becoming aware of the late delivery.

## Seller's Right to Remedy

A seller who has delivered some goods to the buyer prior to the delivery date, even if the goods are nonconforming or the shipment is not complete, has the chance to remedy (also called *cure*), or correct the problem in the shipment. The seller maintains this right to cure, and the buyer may not avoid, until the time for performance expires. Thus, if the buyer receives a defective shipment, or missing parts, or a quantity less than what was ordered, the seller has the right to cure by sending substitute or replacement goods if it can be done by the date for performance called for in the contract. Article 37 states that the seller may exercise this right only if it does not cause unreasonable inconvenience or expense to the buyer.

Unless the parties specify otherwise, the "date for delivery" under the contract (and for the purposes of determining the seller's right to cure), is the date the seller hands the goods over directly to the first carrier (truck, rail, air, or ocean carrier). Consider the following example: Down-Pillow, Inc., enters a contract to buy 4,000 pounds of feathers from Federhaus, GmbH. The contract calls for delivery by October 1. Federhaus ships 3,000 pounds on September 1 that arrive on October 15. Federhaus also ships 1,000 pounds on September 30, one day prior to the delivery date. This shipment does not arrive until November 15. Federhaus has successfully remedied the short shipment of September 1 by delivering the remaining 1,000 pounds to a carrier before the October 1 date. If the contract did not permit two shipments, then Federhaus could cure the defect only if the second shipment does not cause unreasonable inconvenience or expense to Down-Pillow. This example should serve as a warning to all international buyers. Businesses that require the goods to be in their hands by a certain date had better clearly specify an arrival date as well as a shipment date in the contract.

## Seller's Additional Time to Perform

Both the UCC and the CISG allow the seller to cure a nonconforming shipment if it can be done within the time for performance called for in the contract. Unlike the UCC, however, civil law systems traditionally grant an additional period of time, *beyond the date called for* in the contract, within which the parties may perform. This grace period is often referred to in French civil law as *mise en demeur* and in German law as *nachfrist*, meaning "the period after." The CISG adopts the civil law rule. In the event that the seller has failed to deliver the goods, and the time for their shipment or delivery has passed, the buyer may grant the seller extra time to do so. During this time, the buyer may not avoid the contract or resort to a breach of contract action. If the seller does not perform within the *nachfrist* period, the buyer may avoid the contract whether or not the breach was fundamental.

Article 48 contains a provision entitling the seller to invoke a *nachfrist* period, which allows a seller who fails to perform on time, or who delivers nonconforming goods, to cure performance if it does not cause the buyer "unreasonable delay" or "unreasonable inconvenience." If a seller asks a buyer to agree to an extension of time for delivery and the buyer fails to respond within a reasonable time, the seller may perform within the time requested.

These provisions of the CISG attempt to encourage the parties to stay in their contract rather than to repudiate it in the event of a dispute. The parties will be more likely to negotiate, and where commercially reasonable, resolve their disputes in a manner that will keep the contract together and give each of them the benefit of their bargain. The CISG goes far beyond the UCC in achieving this goal.

**Seller's Avoidance.**   The seller also may avoid a contract. A seller may avoid a contract if a buyer either fails to take delivery, pay the purchase price, or otherwise commits a fundamental breach (Article 64). The effect of avoidance is that the seller is released from the contract, need not deliver the goods still in the seller's possession, and may claim their return if they have already been delivered. The seller also may seek damages under Article 74.

## Price Reduction

One solution for the buyer in the event that the seller makes only a partial shipment, or if the goods are nonconforming, is that of *price reduc-*

*tion.* A buyer who would like to retain the goods may (unilaterally and without notice to the seller) adjust the amount paid by withholding a proportionate part of the purchase price in order to offset the shortage or to reflect the reduced value of the nonconforming goods. If the buyer can repair the goods, or bring them up to contract specifications, the buyer may adjust the price paid accordingly. If the goods have already been paid for, the buyer may ask that the seller return a portion of the amount paid. Obviously, the amount of price reduction is far easier to calculate when the seller delivers less than the quantity promised, than if the goods are damaged or are of inferior quality. The amount of reduction, then, is within the discretion of the buyer. A seller who disputes the buyer's calculation can only resort to legal action.

The remedy of price reduction may be used by the buyer whether or not the seller's breach has been fundamental. In the case of fundamental breach, price reduction is an alternative to the buyer's other remedies. In the case of a minor breach (one not fundamental), price reduction is often the buyer's best remedy because the parties can more easily come to an amicable solution. Assume a contract for the sale of 4,000 pounds of white goose down at $60 per pound. If the seller commits a fundamental breach by delivering only 1,000 pounds, the buyer may avoid the contract entirely. But if the seller delivers only 3,800 pounds, the buyer probably will want to deduct $12,000 (200 pounds x $60) and keep the delivered goods. Price reduction is not available if the seller has already delivered substitute goods or if the buyer has refused to accept the seller's attempt to remedy or cure the breach.

## Money Damages

In breach of contract cases, the usual remedy granted by common law courts is the legal remedy of money damages. The CISG provides that a breaching party shall be liable for damages in an amount sufficient to make the injured party whole in the event of a breach. Article 74 states that damages to an injured party shall consist of a "sum equal to the loss."

The method of measuring money damages depends on whether the buyer has been able to pur-

chase substitute goods from another supplier. If the seller fails to perform and the buyer does purchase substitute goods, the buyer may claim damages if the substitute goods cost more than the contract price. If the buyer has not purchased substitute goods, damages are measured by the difference between the contract price and the current market price. As under the UCC, damages under the CISG may also include an amount for *lost profits* and other *consequential damages* arising as a "reasonably foreseeable" consequence of the breach. These consequential damages are limited under Article 74 to those that the parties "foresaw or ought to have foreseen at the time of the conclusion of the contract." For the wording or remedies for breach of contract in the CISG and several other codes, see Exhibit 5.8. Note that the UCC provisions are more detailed and specific than the Chinese FECL and the CISG articles.

In the following case, *Delchi Carrier v. Rotorex,* the buyer incurred many expenses as a result of the seller's delivery of nonconforming goods: repair expenses, storage expenses, assembly line down-time, sourcing substitute merchandise, and lost profits. As you read, consider how the court determines which expenditures are consequential damages and which are not.

The power to avoid a contract is even more important in a fluctuating market for the goods. If the buyer chooses to accept the goods and sues for damages for the seller's breach of contract, the money damages the buyer could collect would be equal to the difference between the value of the nonconforming goods and the contract price. However, if a buyer avoids the contract under Article 49, and refuses to take delivery at all, *and the value of the goods falls greatly in the marketplace,* the buyer may be able to purchase the goods for much less than the amount agreed to under the contract. Alternatively, *if the value of the goods increases in the marketplace,* the buyer may still sue for the difference between the contract price and the higher market price at which it purchased substitute goods.

**Foreign Money Judgments.** In the event that a party to an international contract is successful in its damage claim against another party, the question remains as to whether the court may award

---

**EXHIBIT 5.8    Comparison of Consequential Damage Provisions of the CISG, the UCC, and the FECL**

**Convention on Contracts for the International Sale of Goods**

**Article 74.** Damages for breach of contract by one party consist of a sum equal to the loss, including loss of profit, suffered by the other party as a consequence of the breach. Such damages may not exceed the loss which the party in breach foresaw or ought to have foreseen at the time of the conclusion of the contract, in the light of the facts and matters of which he then knew or ought to have known, as a possible consequence of the breach of contract.

**Uniform Commercial Code §2-715**
**Buyer's Incidental and Consequential Damages**

1.  Incidental damages resulting from the seller's breach include expenses reasonably incurred in inspection, receipt, transportation and care and custody of goods rightfully rejected, and commercially reasonable charges, expenses or commissions in connection with effecting cover and any other reasonable expense incident to the delay or other breach.

2.  Consequential damages resulting from the seller's breach include
    a.  any loss resulting from general or particular requirements and needs of which the seller at the time of contracting had reason to know and which could not reasonable be prevented by cover or otherwise; and
    b.  injury to person or property proximately resulting from any breach of warranty.

**People's Republic of China**
**Foreign Economic Contract of Law of 1985**

**Article 18.** When one party fails to fulfill a contract or fails to meet the conditions agreed on for fulfilling a contract, it will have violated the contract, and the other party will have the right to ask the former to compensate for the loss suffered or to take other remedial measures. If the remedial measures are not sufficient to compensate for the loss suffered by the other party, the other party may ask for a further compensation for its loss.

**Article 19.** The compensation made by the party that violates a contract should equal the loss suffered by the other party, but should not exceed the possible loss anticipated at the time the contract was signed should one party violate the contract.

SOURCE:   Reprinted with permission from 24 I.L.M 797 (1985). Copyright © 1985 by The American Society of International Law, Washington, D.C. The English translation of the law originally appeared in the May 1985 issue of *East Asian Executive Reports* and is reprinted with permission.

---

### Delchi Carrier, Spa v. Rotorex Corporation
1994 WL 495787 (1994)
United States District Court
(N.D.N.Y.)

BACKGROUND AND FACTS

Rotorex, a New York corporation, agreed to sell air compressors to Delchi, an Italian company. The compressors were for use in producing Ariele air conditioners. The first shipment reached Delchi, and Delchi paid $188,000. In preparation Delchi had spent 39 million *lire* for special tooling, and 27 million *lire* for special insulation and tubing for use in making Arieles. Delchi expended 18 million *lire* in shipping and customs duties. Delchi then paid $130,000 to Rotorex for a second shipment. While the second shipment was en route, Delchi discovered that the first lot was nonconforming. It rejected the compressors and canceled the contract. Delchi spent several million *lire* to replace problem grommets, inspect, repair, and retest the compressors in an effort to make them usable. During this time, Delchi's assembly line shut down incurring unproductive assembly worker wages. Delchi was able to obtain some substitute compressors from other sources in time for the selling season, which it had to adapt for Ariele units at additional expense. It arranged to have a shipment of Sanyo compressors, which it has previously ordered, sent to it by air freight

*(continued)*

*(continued)*

so that it could fill some orders. Delchi was also unable to fill some orders, amounting to millions of *lire* in lost profit. Delchi brought this action for damages.

MUNSON, SENIOR DISTRICT JUDGE

The governing law of the instant case is the United Nations Convention on Contracts for the International Sale of Goods ("CISG").

\* \* \*

Rotorex breached its contract with Delchi by failing to supply 10,800 conforming compressors. Under CISG Delchi is entitled to collect monetary damages for Rotorex's breach in "a sum equal to the loss, including loss of profit," although not in excess of the amount reasonably envisioned by the parties. (CISG, article 74). This provision seeks to provide the injured party with the benefit of the bargain, including both its expectation interest and its reliance expenditure.

CONSEQUENTIAL DAMAGES

**i. Plaintiff's Attempts to Remedy Nonconformity** Delchi is entitled to recover damages incurred as a result of its attempts to remedy the nonconformity of Rotorex's compressors. These were not anticipated costs of production, but were costs that would not have been incurred without Rotorex's breach. Further, such damages were a foreseeable result of Rotorex's breach. Hence Delchi is entitled to recover for unreimbursed expenses [for repairing the units], . . . for labor costs relating to replacing original, problematic grommets with substitutes, . . . for extraordinary reinspection and texting or units after [repair].

**ii. Expedited Shipment of Sanyo Compressors** Once Delchi's attempts to remedy the nonconformity failed, it was entitled to expedite shipment of previously ordered Sanyo compressors to mitigate its damages. Indeed, CISG requires such mitigation. CISG, article 77 ("A party who relies on a breach of contract must take such measures as are reasonable in the circumstances to mitigate the loss"). The shipment of previously ordered Sanyo compressors did not constitute cover under CISG article 75, because the Sanyo units were previously ordered, and hence cannot be said to have replaced the nonconforming Rotorex compressors. Nonetheless, Delchi's action in expediting shipment of Sanyo compressors was both com-

mercially reasonable and reasonably foreseeable, and therefore Delchi is entitled to recover . . . the net cost of early delivery of Sanyo compressors [the cost of air shipment less the expected cost for ocean shipment].

**iii. Handling and Storage of Rejected Compressors** Delchi is further entitled to collect costs incurred for handling and storage of nonconforming compressors. . . .

**iv. Lost Profits** CISG permits recovery of lost profit resulting from a diminished volume of sales. In conformity with the common law, to recover a claim for lost profit under CISG, a party must provide the finder of fact with sufficient evidence to estimate the amount of damages with reasonable certainty. Delchi proved with sufficient certainty that it incurred, as a foreseeable and direct result of Rotorex's breach, . . . a total of 546,377,612 lire in lost profit in Italy. Delchi did not prove with sufficient certainty any lost sales from "indicated [anticipated] orders" in Italy. Delchi's claim of 4,000 additional lost sales in Italy is supported only by the speculative testimony of Italian sales agents who averred that they would have ordered more Arieles had they been available. . . . Delchi provides no documentation of additional lost sales in Italy, and no evidence that if any such lost sales did exist, that Delchi's inability to fill those orders was directly attributable to Rotorex's breach. Delchi can not recover on its claim for additional lost profits in Italy because the amount of damages, if any, cannot be established with reasonable certainty.

COST OF PRODUCTION

Delchi is not entitled to recover expenses related to the anticipated cost of production of Ariele units with Rotorex compressors, because those costs are accounted for in Delchi's recovery on its lost profits claim. Those fixed costs for which Delchi may not recover include: . . . expenses incurred by Delchi in shipping, customs and incidentals relating to the first . . . (and second) . . . shipment of Rotorex compressors; . . . production line employees' down time, . . . obsolete insulation materials and tubing purchased for use with only Rotorex compressors; . . . obsolete tooling purchased exclusively for production of units with Rotorex compressors. Delchi is not entitled to recover . . . for modification of electrical panels for

*(continued)*

*(continued)*

use with substitute Sanyo compressors. Delchi failed to prove that this cost was directly attributable to Rotorex's breach, and that the cost was notpart of the regular cost of production of units with Sanyo compressors.

**Decision.** The plaintiff was awarded compensatory damages for those expenses incurred in repairing the nonconforming goods, obtaining substitution goods and for lost profits. Lost profits does not include profits which may arise from anticipated sales which cannot be established by reasonable certainty.

[On appeal, the Court of Appeals concluded: "We affirm the award of damages. We reverse in part the denial of incidental and consequential damages. We remand for further proceedings in accord with this opinion." These conclusions were based on the governance of CISG provisions.

The circuit court upheld the district court's decision regarding breach of contract, and " . . . held that 'there is no question that [Rotorex's] compressors did not conform to the terms of the contract between the parties. . . .'"

Further, the circuit court agreed with the district court's award of damages for lost profits, but did not agree with the denial of incidental and consequential damages. In its cross-appeal, Delchi disputed the district court's denial of reimbursement for shipping and customs costs for two returned shipments, obsolete material and tooling, and labor costs. The circuit court said these were legitimate consequential damages that did not duplicate lost profits damages, that to deny reimbursement would cut into the lost profits award, and that the reimbursement "furthers the purpose of giving the injured party damages 'equal to the loss,'" based on the CISG.]

the damages in the currency of the contract. If so, then the injured party can most easily be made whole. The parties pay and receive what they had bargained for. Since 1921, however, courts in the United States have not been willing to award judgments in foreign currencies. This rule is rooted in English law dating back several hundred years. Thus, if the contract called for payment in, say, Deutsche marks, and the judgment is awarded in dollars, the parties may not be receiving an amount equal to what they had bargained for under the contract. One party may be greatly disadvantaged and the other may receive a windfall profit. And if many years have passed while the case progressed through the courts, the risk of a fluctuating exchange rate increased. In the *Teca-Print* case a New York court wrestles with this problem.

**EXHIBIT 5.9   U.S. Courts and the CISG**

**U.S. Courts and the CISG: An Example of Ethnocentricity?**

Although the CISG entered into a force ten years ago, as of 1997 only two cases interpreting the Convention have arisen in courts of the United States. Those two cases are the *Delchi* case extracted on page 166 and the *Filanto* case which appears on page 157. The Delchi case was subsequently appealed and the decision of the Court of Appeals is the first decision on the CISG for a federal appellate court.

As V. Susanne Cook notes in an article in the *Journal of Law and Commerce*,[3] "this is a stunning result considering the broad scope of the Convention's application." Cook, a Pittsburgh attorney, finds the Circuit Court's decision in the Delchi case "encouragingly insightful, yet ultimately disappointing at the same time."

The encouraging portion of the Court's opinion is found in its clear recognition of the international character of the CISG. The Circuit Court's opinion in the Delchi appeal stated: "the instant matter is governed by the CISG, a self-executing agreement between the United States and other signatories, including Italy. Because there is no case law under the Convention, we look to its language and to the 'general principles' upon which it was based." The Convention directs that its interpretation be informed by its "international character and . . . the need to promote uniformity in its application and the observance of good faith in international trade."

The disappointment occurs because the Court did not examine the language of the Convention's Article 74 when it had an opportunity and indeed an obligation to do so. Cook also takes the Court to task for its failure to examine the interpretations of Articles 25 and 74 made by foreign courts. While its observation that "there is virtually no case law under the Convention" is correct in so far as U.S. case law is concerned, she notes "numerous decisions interpreting Articles 25 and 74 of the Convention have been made by European Courts." The failure to consult these other sources, exemplifies the ethnocentric view of the world, which she notes, is common to most U.S. citizens.

## Teca-Print A.G. v. Amacoil Machinery, Inc.
### 525 N.Y.S.2d 535 (1988)
### Supreme Court, New York County

### BACKGROUND AND FACTS

Plaintiff is a Swiss manufacturer of machinery. It bills foreign sales in Swiss francs because its own expenses are incurred in that currency. As a relatively small company, it has no desire to engage in foreign exchange speculation and wants to ensure that its purchasers remit an agreed-upon price to cover plaintiff's labor costs, manufacturing expenses, etc., plus a reasonable profit. The plaintiff made nine shipments to the defendant between 1982 and 1983, which remained unpaid. As of November 30, 1983, the date of breach, the defendant owed the plaintiff a total of 71,224 Swiss francs. On that date, the Swiss franc had a value of approximately U.S. $0.45. As of December 2, 1986, the date of plaintiff's judgment against the defendant, the value of the Swiss franc was U.S. $0.6085. The Swiss plaintiff contends that the date for conversion from Swiss francs to United States dollars for purposes of the judgment must be the date of the judgment. The defendant contends that the currency exchange rate should be based on the date of the breach.

### KRISTIN BOOTH GLEN, JUSTICE

It is generally unquestioned that there is no power in the state and federal courts to award judgments in a foreign currency. No cases have been found in which judgments were granted in a foreign currency, regardless of whether the claim was denominated in a foreign currency or based on a judgment of a foreign court rendered in its own currency. Whatever the origin of this rule, it has come under attack. . . .

The desire to make an award which will be "accurate" in the currency of the party suffering loss, as well as consistent with general principles of the law of damages, has resulted in a change in British law. In Great Britain, foreign currency judgments, totally unavailable before 1975, are now permissible under a number of circumstances. . . .

The instant case is a classic example of the problems which exist under the "dollars only" rule. A judgment in Swiss francs, the currency designated by plaintiff, contracted for by defendant and used by plaintiff in its own commercial and internal transaction would best make plaintiff "whole" without creating either a windfall or an unfair burden. Since, however, such an award is presently unavailable in New York or anywhere in the U.S., variations on the currency-conversion rules must be considered to produce a result as similar as possible to that which would occur were a foreign currency judgment possible.

Many of the problems which flow from the unavailability of foreign money judgments are actually a result of worldwide currency fluctuations over which the courts have no control. . . . As *The New York Times* recently noted, U.S. economic decline and the loss of U.S. political hegemony has created a situation in which "[T]he dollar and other major currencies [may] go on fluctuating dramatically in value, perhaps into the 21st century, because none of the industrial nations can agree on fair exchange rates and the United States lacks the clout to impose standards, as it once did.

In cases where, because of devaluations, plaintiffs would reap an unfair windfall through application of the breach day rule, New York courts have not hesitated to reject that rule in favor of judgment date in order to achieve an equitable result. See e.g., *John S. Metcalf Co., Ltd. v. Mayer, et al.,* 213 App.Div. 607, 211 N.Y.S. 53 (1st Dept. 1925); In *Metcalf* the court wrote

The purchase price of the goods in question was not payable in American dollars. . . . It was payable in French francs, and merely by bringing action in this jurisdiction, the plaintiff, I apprehend, acquired no right to a more favorable judgment than she could have obtained had the action been brought in France. . . . It follows that the time of the application of the rate of exchange is at the time of the rendition of the judgment.

Careful reading of the New York cases demonstrates that there has never been a strict rule requiring use of the breach date in currency conversions. Instead, the courts have consistently looked at the surrounding circumstances to reach a just and equitable result. . . . Unless and until courts are empowered to award judgments in the foreign currency denominated by the parties,

*(continued)*

*(continued)*

courts will be required to choose a date for conversion which, under the particular circumstances of the case, affords a fair and equitable result. In the instant case, that date, because of the continuing fluctuation of the U.S. dollar against the Swiss franc, must be the date of judgment.

**Decision.** To achieve equity and fairness, the plaintiff's judgment against the defendant in Swiss francs should be based on the conversion rate to U.S. dollars on the date of judgment. Most courts that have considered the problem have recognized the only equitable result comes from se-

lecting the conversion rate that will "make the parties whole."

**Comment.** Many other countries historically have allowed foreign currency judgments. The CISG does not authorize foreign money judgments. In an attempt to reach an equitable solution, the National Conference on Uniform State Laws has approved for enactment in the United States, the *Uniform Foreign Money Claims Act*. This draft statute, if enacted by U.S. state legislatures, would give state courts the authority for issuing judgments in foreign currency. The draft, however, does not have universal support in the United States. See New York's law in Exhibit 5.10.

---

**EXHIBIT 5.10    Computation of Judgments and Accounts**

**Judiciary Law of New York**
**Chapter 30**

*Article 2—General Provisions Relating to Courts and Judges*
**§ 27.**

a. Except as provided in subdivision (b) of this section, judgments and accounts must be computed in dollars and cents. In all judgments or decrees rendered by any court for any debt, damages or costs, in all executions issued thereupon, and in all accounts arising from proceedings in courts the amount shall be computed, as near as may be, in dollars and cents, rejecting lesser fractions; and no judgment, or other proceeding, shall be considered erroneous for such omissions.

b. In any case in which the cause of action is based upon an obligation denominated in a currency other than currency of the United States, a court shall render or enter a judgment or decree in the foreign currency of the underlying obligation. Such judgment or decree shall be converted into currency of the United States at the rate of exchange prevailing on the date of entry of the judgment or decree.

SOURCE:   As amended L. 1987, c. 326, s 1.

## Specific Performance in Common Law and Civil Law Systems

The usual legal remedy in contract cases in common law countries is an award for money damages. The usual remedy in civil law countries, on the other hand, is that of *specific performance*.

Specific performance is used when a court requires a party to the contract to perform, or carry out its part of the bargain. To be sure, courts in the United States and other common law countries hesitate to require parties to specifically perform. It is considered a harsh remedy to be used only where money damages cannot be calculated or are inadequate, which may occur when the subject matter of the contract is unique. For example, in a dispute over the sale of a prized race horse, or a famous work of art, a common law court may specifically require a seller to deliver the item to the buyer because of the "unique" nature of the goods. Money damages would not have been sufficient to remedy the buyer in such a case; the buyer wants the goods contracted for. But in civil law countries, the use of specific performance is not only more common, it is preferred.

**Specific Performance under the CISG.**  The CISG draws strongly on the civil law's acceptance of specific performance as a remedy in contract cases. This is based on the idea that the buyer wants what was ordered and not just the right to sue for those injuries that the seller's nondelivery may have caused. Under Article 46, a court may grant specific performance only if all of the following conditions are met: (1) the buyer had not resorted to another remedy, such as avoidance or price reduction; (2) the seller had failed to deliver or, in the case of nonconforming goods, the nonconformity was so serious that it constituted a fundamental breach; (3) the buyer gave timely notice to the seller that the goods were nonconforming; and (4) the buyer had made a timely request that the seller provide substitute goods. As in the civil law nations, the court may grant specific performance without regard to whether money damages are inadequate.

The provisions of the CISG probably will not have much effect on the law in common law countries. Article 28 places a limit on the buyer's right to specific performance by providing that a court need not grant specific performance unless "it would do so under its own law." Thus, the CISG will have little effect on the use of specific performance in the United States.

## Anticipatory Breach

*Anticipatory breach* occurs when one party clearly sees that the other party to the contract either will not perform a substantial part of its obligations or that it will commit a fundamental breach. The breach may occur as a result of one party repudiating the contract and notifying the other that it will not perform, or it may be determined from the conduct of the breaching party.

**Right to Suspend Performance.** Either party may *suspend performance* under a contract if one party realizes that the other party will not perform a "substantial part" of its obligations. A buyer may suspend payment when aware of evidence that the seller cannot or will not ship. A seller may suspend shipment when the buyer obviously cannot pay or take delivery of the goods. A seller who has already shipped may stop the goods in transit. The right to suspend performance ends when the other party provides adequate assurance that it will perform. If adequate assurance becomes impossible, the other party may then avoid the contract entirely.

Consider this example: Assume that seller is required to deliver goods by March 15. Seller learns that buyer is insolvent and about to declare bankruptcy. On February 1, seller suspends performance and halts shipment. On March 1, buyer provides bank guarantees to seller that it can pay for the goods. The market price of the goods has risen significantly and seller refuses to ship. Seller is correct in suspending performance,

but commits a breach of contract by not accepting buyer's assurance of performance.

**Right to Avoidance.** If one of the parties is likely to commit a fundamental breach, the other party may avoid the contract. In contrast to the right to suspend, just discussed, avoidance is allowed where one party will *never* be able to perform. For instance, if the seller's plant burns down, or if an embargo in the seller's country makes it legally impossible to ship the contracted goods, then the buyer may avoid the contract.

**Avoidance of Installment Contracts.** When a contract calls for the delivery of goods by installments, the rules of avoidance apply to each individual delivery. Therefore, a single nonconforming shipment may be refused by a buyer if the seller has committed a fundamental breach. Assume that buyer and seller have a contract for 160,000 pounds of peanuts, to be shipped from Georgia to Denmark in 20 shipments over a five-year period. One shipment arrives in Denmark and is unfit for human consumption. In terms of the entire contract, the one shipment may not amount to a fundamental breach, but because it is an installment contract, the buyer may avoid the contract with respect to this shipment.

Where the breach of one installment indicates strong grounds that a party will breach future installments, the nonbreaching party may declare the contract avoided if done within a reasonable time. So if a buyer refuses to pay for one or two installments, the seller may avoid the remainder of the contract.

## Events Beyond the Control of the Parties: Excuses for Nonperformance

Occasionally, a party will find that circumstances make carrying out its part of the contract difficult, unprofitable, or even impossible. As a defense to an action for breach of contract, it may claim that it has been excused because intervening events beyond its control have made performance impossible or financially impracticable. But it will have a difficult time convincing a court. Courts generally do not allow a party to escape contractual obligations merely because it becomes unable to perform, even though inability to perform was through no fault of its own. When a seller's employees go on strike, when suppliers fail to deliver raw materials on time, when equipment breaks down, when crops are destroyed due to bad weather, or when a party simply becomes financially distressed, its failure to deliver on time will generally not be excused. This common ruling is in keeping with generally accepted legal principles, which hold that contracts are binding. After all, when parties enter into agreements, do they not weigh these contingencies in setting their prices and establishing their terms? Yet, in the real world in which international transactions are conducted, the parties are liable to find many roadblocks in their path to performance.

Whether an intervening event will cause a party to be excused and discharged from its contractual promise depends on the reasoning used by the court. Some courts reason that a party's performance is excused (1) if performance of the contract has been rendered physically or legally impossible; (2) if the underlying purposes of the contract no longer exist; or (3) if a change in circumstances has rendered the contract commercially or financially impracticable.

## Impossibility of Performance

Under English law, a court may excuse a party's nonperformance where it becomes *objectively impossible* for it to perform. The courts hold that it must be impossible for *anyone* to perform, not just this particular party, and that the parties did not expressly assume such risk. Impossibility would therefore excuse nonperformance in cases involving the death of one of the parties, the destruction of the specific subject matter of the contract, or when performance of the contract has been rendered illegal or made impossible due to the fault of the other party. Impossibility is usually recognized only where performance becomes a physical impossibility. The inability to pay money is usually never accepted as an excuse.

**Supervening Illegality.** A contract becomes impossible to perform and the parties excused when performance becomes illegal. For instance, suppose that a U.S. company is under contract to

ship computers to Iraq. After Iraq's invasion of Kuwait, the U.S. government declared that conducting business with Iraq or shipping goods there was illegal. Since the contract has been rendered illegal, performance is discharged.

## Frustration of Purpose

Under the English common law, a party's performance could be excused if some unforeseen event occurred that frustrated the purposes of the contract. This event, called *frustration of purpose,* would have to destroy totally the value of the contract to the party relying on the excuse. Moreover, both parties must have known what the purposes of the contract were. To understand, one might ask the question, "Had this event existed at the time of the contract, would the parties have gone through with it?" In a leading English Case, *Knell v. Henry,* 2 K.B. 740 (1903), a party leased a room overlooking the coronation route of the king. When the king took ill and the coronation canceled, the court ruled that the party was excused form paying rent on the room, because the coronation was essential to the purposes of the contract. Although it had been *possible* to perform, the party would have realized *no value* in doing so. Frustration of purpose is not widely recognized in the United States today.

## Commercial Impracticability

A party to a contract that is prevented from performing may attempt to be excused under the doctrine of *commercial impracticability.* This modern doctrine is used in the United States today. It dates back to 1916 when a court stated, "A thing is impossible in legal contemplation when it is not practicable; and a thing is impracticable when it can be done only at an excessive and unreasonable cost." Today, impracticability in the United States has been codified in the UCC (see Exhibit 5.11) and in Article 79 of the CISG (found in the appendix). Remember, courts hesitate to excuse parties from contracts. Accordingly, the breaching party will be excused only if performance would result in extreme hardship, difficulty, or unreasonable expense as a result of an unforeseen event.

---

**EXHIBIT 5.11    Excuse by Failure of Presupposed Conditions**

**Uniform Commercial Code**

**§ 2-615.**  Except so far as a seller may have assumed a greater obligation and subject to the preceding section on substituted performance:

a. Delay in delivery or nondelivery in whole or in part by a seller who complies with paragraphs (b) and (c) is not a breach of his duty under a contract for sale if performance as agreed has been made impracticable by the occurrence of a contingency the nonoccurrence of which was a basic assumption on which the contract was made or by compliance in good faith with any applicable foreign or domestic governmental regulation or order whether or not it later proves to be invalid.

b. Where the causes mentioned in paragraph (a) affect only a part of the seller's capacity to perform, he must allocate production and deliveries among his customers but may at his option include regular customers not then under contract as well as his own requirements for further manufacture. He may so allocate in any manner which is fair and reasonable.

c. The seller must notify the buyer seasonably that there will be delay or nondelivery and, when allocation is required under paragraph (b), of the estimated quota thus made available for the buyer.

---

**Extreme Hardship, Difficulty, or an Unreasonable Expense.**   The courts have experienced some difficulty in determining what is a "hardship" and how much additional cost is "unreasonable." If the cost of performing the contract becomes so excessive that performance is rendered unrealistic and senseless, and threatens the viability of the business itself, performance may be excused. Of course, what is a lot of money to one company, may be a drop in the bucket to another. Thus, if a large multinational corporation contracts to deliver goods at a contract price, and discovers that wage increases or an increase in the price of raw materials will cause it to lose millions of dollars on the deal, the courts still may not release the company from its obligation.

**Unforeseen Events.**   Courts also look to see whether the party claiming the excuse should have foreseen the likelihood of its occurrence. If the event was foreseeable, the nonperforming party will not be released from its obligations, which does not mean that the parties had to foresee the *specific event* that actually occurred. Rather, the parties *should have* foreseen that an event *of this kind* could occur. Thus, if a party is a sophisticated business, experienced and familiar with the risks of entering into this kind of contract, they might have difficulty in proving that they should not have foreseen a particular risk. Consider the following examples:

- A mining company should foresee the possibility of a cave-in.
- A farming conglomerate should foresee the possibility of bad weather.
- An oil company should foresee the possibility of oil price increases in the Middle East.

The courts generally feel that if a particular risk was foreseeable, then the parties would have provided in their contract to be excused if it occurs—if they did not provide for the excuse in the contract, then they must have intended to bear this risk. In the *Transatlantic* case that follows, the court was unwilling to excuse an ocean carrier from a contract to haul freight at the contract price because the company should have foreseen that a war could block the Suez Canal to shipping and that a longer, more expensive trip around Africa might be required.

**Shortages and Market Price Fluctuations.**   For the most part, shortages, inflation, and even dramatic fluctuations in market prices are to be anticipated by parties to a contract. Such a result is illustrated by *Eastern Air Lines, Inc. v. Gulf Oil Corporation,* 415 F. Supp. 429 (S.D. Fla. 1975), a case arising out of the oil price increases caused by the Arab oil embargo in 1973. In 1972, Eastern Air lines contracted with Gulf Oil Corporation for a supply of jet aviation fuel. In the following year, the Middle East war and Arab oil embargo of the United States resulted in a 400 percent increase in the price of crude oil. These events caused Gulf to demand a price increase from Eastern and to

## Transatlantic Financing Corporation v. United States

363 F.2d 312 (1966)
U.S. Court of Appeals
(D.C. Cir.)

### BACKGROUND AND FACTS

The United States contracted with Transatlantic Financing, operator of a steamship, under a voyage charter to ship a cargo of wheat from Texas to Iran in 1956. Six days after Transatlantic's ship sailed from Texas, the government of Egypt was at war with Israel and had blocked the Suez Canal to shipping. As a result, the ship had to sail around the Cape of Good Hope on the tip of the African continent. Transatlantic sued for the added expense of the longer journey, claiming that it had contracted only to travel the "usual and customary" route to Iran. The lower court ruled in favor of the United States and the plaintiff appealed.

### JUDGE SKELLY WRIGHT

. . . If anything, the circumstances surrounding this contract indicate that the risk of the Canal's closure may be deemed to have been allocated to Transatlantic. We know or may safely assume that the parties were aware, as were most commercial men with interest affected by the Suez situation that the Canal might become a dangerous area. No doubt the tension affected freight rates, and it is arguable that the risk of closure became part of the dickered terms. We do not deem the risk of closure so allocated, however. Foreseeability or even recognition of a risk does not necessarily prove its allocation. Parties to a contract are not always able to provide for all the possibilities of which they are aware, sometimes because they cannot agree, often simply because they are too busy. Moreover, that some abnormal risk was contemplated is probative but does not necessarily establish an allocation of the risk of the contingency which actually occurs. In this case, for example, nationalization by Egypt of the Canal Corporation and formation of the Suez Users Group did not necessarily indicate that the Canal would be blocked even if a confrontation resulted. The surrounding circumstances do indicate, however, a willingness by Transatlantic to assume abnormal risks, and this fact should legitimately cause us to judge the impracticability of performance by an alternative route in stricter terms than we would were the contingency unforeseen.

We turn then to the question whether occurrence of the contingency rendered performance commercially impracticable under the circumstances of this case. The goods shipped were not subject to harm from the longer, less temperate Southern route. The vessel and crew were fit to proceed around the Cape. Transatlantic was no less able than the United States to purchase insurance to cover the contingency's occurrence. If anything, it is more reasonable to expect owner-operators of vessels to insure against the hazards of war. They are in the best position to calculate the cost of performance by alternative routes (and therefore to estimate the amount of insurance required), and are undoubtedly sensitive to international troubles which uniquely affect the demand for and cost of their services. The only factor operating here in appellant's favor is the added expense, allegedly $43,972.00 above and beyond the contract price of $305,842.92, of extending a 10,000 mile voyage by approximately 3,000 miles. While it may be an overstatement to say that increased cost and difficulty of performance never constitute impracticability, to justify relief there must be more of a variation between expected cost and the cost of performing by an available alternative than is present in this case, where the promisor can legitimately be presumed to have accepted some degree of abnormal risk, and where impracticability is urged on the basis of added expense along.

We conclude, therefore, as have most other courts considering related issues arising out of the Suez closure, that performance of this contract was not rendered legally impossible.

**Decision.** The judgment was affirmed for the United States. Under a voyage charter, the risks of the journey are on the shipowner, and an increase in expense due to a change in routes did not excuse its performance under the contract.

threaten a cutoff in supply. Eastern brought an action under the UCC to insure its supply of oil at the contract price. Gulf claimed that the contract as it had been negotiated was commercially impracticable. The court disagreed, noting that not only had Gulf not suffered a sufficient hardship to claim impracticability, but that the actions of the OPEC oil cartel and the resulting energy crisis were reasonably foreseeable by a multinational oil company such as Gulf.

## The CISG Exemptions for Impediments Beyond Control

CISG Article 79 provides that a party is not liable for a failure to perform any obligations if (1) it was due to an *impediment beyond control;* (2) the impediment was not reasonably foreseeable at the time the contract was concluded; (3) the impediment was unavoidable or beyond his control; and (4) notice was given to the other party of the impediment and of its effect on the contract. An impediment does not entirely excuse performance, but merely suspends it during the time that the impediment exists.

> **http://www.cisg.law.pace.edu/cisg/ text/e-text-79.html**
> This is the site of UN Contracts and International Sale of Goods. See Section IV, Article 79, Exemptions.

### *Force Majeure* Clauses

Courts do not like to release parties from a contract on the basis of an excuse. Under the rule of commercial impracticability, a party will not be excused if the risk was foreseeable, because the party is assumed to have provided for that excuse in the contract itself. As a result, lawyers frequently advise their clients to incorporate a *force majeure* clause into a contract.

The term *force majeure* means "superior force." A force majeure clause in a contract is an exculpatory clause. It excuses a party from failing to perform on the occurrence of an event specified in the clause itself—a force majeure. These clauses usually list, specifically, those events that will excuse nonperformance. These events might include war, blockades, fire, acts of governments,

inability to obtain export licenses, acts of God, acts of public enemies, failure of transportation, quarantine restrictions, strikes, and others. (For an example of a force majeure clause, see the *Terms and Conditions of Sale,* Exhibit 5.6.)

Lawyers advise that force majeure clauses should not just provide for standard contingencies such as those listed, but should be tailored to the special nature of the contract and the type of businesses involved. Force majeure clauses for the mining industry would not be the same as for the steel or textile industries, for example. A clause in a shipping contract issued by an ocean carrier would be different too because the risks differ. In major contracts, the drafting of a force majeure clause requires skilled lawyers. Language that is too narrow may not provide sufficient protection, and language that is too broad may leave too many outs in the contract.

In practice, most force majeure clauses do not excuse a party's nonperformance entirely, but only suspend it for the duration of the force majeure. Another special type of force majeure clause, is the *government approval* clause. Because government permission is often needed to transact business across national borders, many companies include a provision in their contract stating that the contract is subject to obtaining government approval or licenses. The following case illustrates the operation of a force majeure clause.

## Cultural Influences on Contract Negotiations

Lawyers and businesspeople in different countries treat their approach to negotiating and drafting contracts quite differently. First, Americans tend to approach contract negotiations in an aggressive, adversarial manner. They often view contracting as a win–lose proposition, taking pride in having driven the hardest bargain. This attitude leads them to attempt to gain legal and business advantages over the other party. Similarly, U.S. lawyers, who are accustomed to practicing in a highly litigious society, press for every legal advantage. They draft their contracts in calculated, technical, and detailed language, setting forth exactly how the parties are to perform and what their legal rights are if the deal falls apart.

## Harriscom Svenska, AB v. Harris Corporation
### 3 F.3d 576 (1993)
### United States Court of Appeals (2nd Cir.)

BACKGROUND AND FACTS
RF Systems, a division of Harris Corporation, manufactures radio communications products in New York. It appointed Harriscom, a Swedish firm, as its exclusive distributor to the Islamic Republic of Iran. The contract contained a force majeure clause. In 1985 the U.S. Customs Service detained a shipment of radios ordered by Harriscom and bound for Iran. The government prohibited all sales to Iran of goods it categorized as military equipment. In 1986 RF Systems negotiated a compromise under which it agreed to "voluntarily withdraw from all further sales to the Iranian market." Harriscom brought this action for a breach of contract against RF Systems. The District Court granted judgment for the defendants on the basis of commercial impracticability and force majeure, and the plaintiff appealed.

CARDAMONE, CIRCUIT JUDGE
One of the issues before us is whether the manufacturer's refusal to ship the spare parts was a voluntary act on its part, subjecting it to liability to its distributor for damages for breach of contract. We think it a foregone conclusion that a government bureaucracy determined to prevent what it considers military goods from leaving this country and with the will to compel compliance with its directives is an irresistible force, one that cannot reasonably be controlled. The government in these circumstances may be likened to the wife of "Rumpole of the Bailey," John Mortimer's fictional barrister, who describes his wife as "she who must be obeyed." . . .

What appellant ignores is the overwhelming and uncontradicted evidence that the government would not allow RF Systems to continue sales to Iran. RF Systems established the affirmative defense of commercial impracticability because it compiled in good faith with the government's informal requirements. Further, for RF Systems to have failed to comply would have been unusually foolhardy and recalcitrant, for the government had undoubted power to compel compliance. Like commercial impracticability, a force majeure clause in a contract excuses nonperformance when circumstances beyond the control of the parties prevent performance. The contracts between these parties specifically contained force majeure clauses to excuse RF Systems' performance under the present circumstances, namely, "governmental interference."

**Decision.**   Summary judgment affirmed for the defendant, RF Systems. The force majeure clause in the distributorship agreement excused the manufacturer from performance on the grounds of "government interference."

## Negotiating Contracts in Japan

By contrast, contract negotiations in many countries take a much different form. Japan presents perhaps the best example. The role of a contract in Japanese society is influenced tremendously by three aspects of Japanese culture and ancient Confucian thinking.[4] First, every person must strive to maintain harmony and accord in society. From childhood, individuals are taught to avoid disputes and acrimony in their personal and business relationships with others. Second, the maintenance of harmony and the importance placed on personal dignity stress the importance of not causing others to "lose face" or become embarrassed. The considerable social pressure to avoid dishonor works in all aspects of life, including negotiating contracts and resolving contract disputes. Third, the Japanese attach the utmost importance to the social group to which one belongs, particularly to one's school or company. Thus, Japanese businesspeople may be characterized by their group loyalty and their desire for group harmony and consensus.

These attributes make doing business in Japan, and indeed throughout Asia, different from doing business anywhere else. They also affect the way the Japanese view contractual relationships. A contract is a relationship, and as

# When West Meets East
## Cultural Aspects of Doing Business in Asia

Unbelievable miscommunication and misunderstandings can occur when cultures cross, even in countries that share a common heritage and language. For peoples with different traditions and languages, the possibilities for culture-clash multiply. Although many Asians speak English, the language that culturally conditions their life is not English. And the religious beliefs, the ethical systems, and rules of interpersonal relationships and behavior that define Asian societies are most definitely not Western. The potential for miscommunication with Westerners is enormous.

Americans who contemplate doing business with Asians are well advised to study these cultural differences in detail in the many good books available on these subjects. This article will focus on those aspects of Oriental culture that are most important for Western businesspeople to keep in mind when in Asia. The single most important concept is face.

### Save Face
Pride and dignity are important to all human beings, but nowhere in the world are they so culturally protected as in Asia. To speak or act in a way that causes an Asian person to "lose face" is tantamount to physical assault in the West. Asians go to great extremes to save their own face and everyone else's. This causes problems for the Westerner, who may not get a straight answer to a straightforward question.

"Can you tell me the way to the nearest post office?" If Asians know, it would not be unusual for them to escort you there, even though it may be far out of their way. If they do not know, they probably will point and say "that way." To be seen not to know is to lose face.

"Can you make this piece of furniture that I have designed?" Yes, they can. And they will, even though they know it will collapse almost immediately because the design is poor. To suggest a flaw in your design is to cause you to lose face.

The solution to these problems lies in the way the question is asked. "Do you know someone who might help me find a post office?" "I've designed a piece of furniture, but I would appreciate any suggestions you might have for improvement."

Americans pride themselves on their frankness and honesty. Asians also are honest people, but honesty is mediated by the demands of face. For this reason, "frankness" in Asia is almost always rudeness.

It's possible for self-assured Americans in Asia to leave wide paths of resentment and never know that they have offended anyone. No one will tell them. Or, if anyone does, the message will be delivered so obliquely that it probably will not be received. Such Americans will find that life becomes "difficult," that no one seems very cooperative. More than likely they will not blame themselves nor examine their actions and words. They may well conclude that the people are lazy and stupid and dismiss them with the thought, "I can't wait to get back to the good old U.S.A. where people can understand plain English."

### Preserve Your Own Dignity
Class and caste are realities of Asia. If Americans, who supposedly (and admirably) believe in the equality of all, cannot accept those realities of Asia, they may encounter problems. This is not to suggest that the lower classes of Asia should be treated with disrespect. But if American businesspeople in Asia wish to be respected, they must conduct themselves with dignity.

Above all, never show anger, even if you feel it. No matter how high your official position, the public display of strong emotion will label you a "peasant."

### Establish Trust
Asians do business on the basis of personal relationships with people they have come to trust. This remark may seem trite, but it is much truer of Asia than of the West, where faith is placed in legal contracts.

Asians are not so legalistic. Contracts are often renegotiated, as an act of faith in the relationship,

*(continued)*

*(continued)*

when things go badly for one of the parties or unforeseen difficulties arise. The primary objective is to cement the long-term relationship and to establish enduring mutual trust and goodwill. From the beginning, it is assumed that both parties are acting in good faith. In fact, if a great deal of mutual trust had not already been achieved, it is doubtful that a business arrangement ever would have been agreed upon.

Establishing trust takes time. The fact that many Americans are not willing to invest the time to develop the necessary interpersonal trust has sabotaged many a budding business opportunity. The American desire to "get down to business" interferes with the relaxed development of the social relationship that is itself the true cornerstone of an Asian business agreement.

### Be Sincere

In doing business in Asia, as in the West, the word *sincerity* means demonstrating a genuine intention to come to terms and carry out your part of the bargain. But, in Asia, it carries additional meaning and significance connected to the preference for personal and long-term relationships. When a potential business opportunity turns sour, Asians often say that the other party failed to show "sincerity." Generally, what is meant is either arrogance or tightfistedness or both.

In Asia, both parties to a potential business deal will, in the early stages of negotiations, go out of their way to entertain each other, usually through expensive dinners or banquets. Thoughtful gifts are given. Small favors are done. Time is given. Failure to appreciate the importance of such things shows a lack of "sincerity."

Americans who do business in Asia, particularly in the initial stages, must often work through intermediaries, people who know the culture, who can monitor events and help smooth out difficulties, who have a relationship with the Asian businesspeople. A failure to show "sincerity" to the intermediary will be just as detrimental to business prospects as a failure to show it to the other party. An attempt to "bypass" the intermediary or an attitude of arrogance ("I know what I'm doing so you stay out of it") will prove to be a dead-end street.

### Be Patient

Business in Asia cannot be rushed. The first meeting between parties most probably will be in a restaurant or nightclub, and the subject of business is not likely to arise. And as the guest, you should not be the one to bring up the subject.

The appearance of being in a rush, and the tenseness and closed-mindedness that it brings, can in itself result in a loss of dignity for the person in a hurry. It is also an affront to the "face" of the other person or persons present. After all, how can you think them important people if you don't seem to want to spend time with them socially? Your impetuosity is also interpreted as a sign that you do not understand the importance of personal relationships; therefore, you probably are not to be trusted.

Delays and "wasted time" must be expected in Asia for many reasons. In China, everything is difficult and time-consuming because of the bureaucracy; for all practical purposes, the whole country is one gigantic organization. In Japan, everyone even remotely affected by a business decision must first be consulted. In most Asian countries, delays arise because of a combination of both bureaucratic red tape and the need for broad consultation. Because a show of impatience will only complicate matters further, Americans are well advised to relax and try to enjoy the slower pace of life.

Perhaps even more crucial than short-term patience is patience for the long-term. Asians look primarily for business relationships that promise to be rewarding over the years. They are much more willing to endure low returns or none at all in the initial months of a business venture than are most Americans.

The American preoccupation with the monthly profit and loss statement (as a means of judging corporate, divisional, and individual performance) is one of the greatest barriers to the establishment of successful business relationships with Asians. American focus on the short-run is detrimental to the development of ventures and relationships with high promise for long-run economic success—exactly those things that most interest Asian businesspeople.

### Be Flexible

In some Asian countries, appointments are kept on time; in some, they are not. In some, little advance

*(continued)*

*(continued)*

warning will be given of meetings, banquets, events. A knock on your door: "Can you be ready to talk with [Mr. X] and his advisors in fifteen minutes?" You must maintain the utmost flexibility in planning your time. In fact, it's better not to plan time very closely.

Minimize preconceived notions, and let your Asian hosts suggest the flow of events. In terms of business negotiations, let them suggest how things should proceed and what the terms might be. Asia is different from the West, and Asians know what will work there and what will not. They know their own country in a way that a foreigner never will. American society is relatively open. Asian societies are not.

This is not to suggest that you must be "easy." You must be prepared to bargain. Most Asians enjoy bargaining, and they are good at it. Don't immediately put all your cards on the table; they won't. Be willing to compromise, but don't give up more than you should. A persistent firmness, combined with

flexibility and the willingness to explore all possible alternatives, will earn respect. A calm and relaxed stubbornness is advised, with calm and relaxed the key words. Be firm, but avoid obstinacy and rudeness. Be persuasive in a gentle way, a way that saves everyone's face.

After a bargain is reached, giving a little extra to show goodwill should prove, in the long-run, to be worth far more than the price of the "little extra." You will be on your way toward genuine friendship and mutual respect, the ultimate basis for most successful business ventures in Asia. If difficulties arise later, don't insist on following the contract to the letter. With understanding, patience, and empathy, you will establish a long-term working relationship that will prove to be invaluable, even in terms of money.

*John Reeder, Ph.D.*
Reprinted from *Business Horizons*, 30, no. 6 (November-December 1987).

Copyright 1987 by the Foundation for the School of Business at Indiana University. Used with permission.

much a social one as a business one. Therefore, the desire to maintain harmony in society has a dramatic effect on how the Japanese view their business contracts. Instead of the combative approach of U.S. lawyers, Japanese lawyers view the contract as an expression of a common goal and of a desire for a long-lasting business relationship.

These cultural and societal influences affect the manner in which contracts are negotiated and drafted. Because lawyers must do all they can to protect their own clients' interests, they are necessarily adversarial. Japanese firms normally prefer that lawyers not be involved in negotiating, because they feel that lawyers interfere with the parties' concentrating on their mutual business interests. Western negotiators also must remember that they must never put the other parties in a situation in which losing face is the only out. One must be careful not to create embarrassment by making demands without offering something in exchange. By avoiding a loss of face, the parties strengthen their business relationships and reduce the likelihood of misunderstanding and contract disputes.

In addition, a Western company must be prepared to carry out negotiations for an extended period of time. In many cases, the Japanese firm requires a long period of time to reach a group consensus before a decision can be made. Many U.S. senior managers have gone abroad to negotiate a contract only to face frustration at the other party's apparent refusal or unwillingness to conclude an agreement. The U.S. managers simply may not realize that, while they have the authority to bind their firms to the agreement, the foreign party does not. The foreign negotiator may require approval from superiors or from a working group. In doing business in Asia, the watchwords are not only "trust" and "respect," but "patience" as well.

When the contract is finally put into writing, it is typically short and written in little detail. The Japanese consider this necessary because a long-term relationship requires a flexible agreement, and one that the parties can easily modify in the future. Many U.S. lawyers are unaccustomed to this Japanese practice.

The desire to maintain social harmony and to avoid the embarrassment of litigation also affects the manner in which contract disputes are resolved. Unlike contracts between Americans, contracts with the Japanese might state that, in the event of a dispute, "the parties will resolve their disagreement harmoniously and in mutual consultation with each other." If the contract breaks down and the parties disagree over an issue, they are more likely to want to settle the matter through private conciliation. Litigation, while on the increase in Japan as elsewhere, is still to be avoided if at all possible.

Another factor that U.S. contract negotiators should be aware of is that foreign firms, more so than U.S. firms, rely on technical experts during contract negotiations. More than one U.S. company has failed to obtain an important order because its negotiating team did not include the necessary engineers, specialists, or technicians. This aspect of who is on a negotiating team is true not only in Japan, but also in many European countries and much of the rest of the world.

**http://www.ita.doc.gov/region/japan/
japan.html**
*Information on doing business in Japan.*

## Chapter Summary

All commerce and trade require a stable and predictable legal environment in which to prosper. In recent years, the international community has agreed on a common body of international sales law, the U.N. *Convention on the International Sale of Goods.* The CISG is important not only because it governs transactions for the trade in goods between parties in those nations that have adopted it, but also because it represents internationally accepted legal principles of sales law.

The CISG was drafted under the aegis of the United Nations by skilled lawyers representing countries with diverse political, economic, and legal systems. It has already achieved wide international acceptance, and more countries are expected to adopt it in the years to come.

This chapter does not purport to cover all aspects of international sales law. For example, the actual mechanics of the transaction to see how the contract is carried out by the parties is yet to be discussed. The next two chapters look at how goods are shipped, paid for, and what happens if the goods are lost at sea. These chapters also examine the responsibility of the carrier for transporting the goods, and the carrier's relationship to buyer and seller.

---

### QUESTIONS AND CASE PROBLEMS

1. Bende had a contract to sell boots to the government of Ghana for $158,500. Bende promised to deliver the boots "as soon as possible." Bende then contracted with Kiffe who agreed to make the boots in Korea and to deliver them in Ghana within 60 to 90 days at a price of $95,000. The contract contained no force majeure clause. Kiffe knew that Bende was going to resell the boots. Kiffe failed to deliver the boots on the agreed date because a train had derailed carrying the boots in Nebraska. Bende brought this action against Kiffe for breach of contract. *Bende and Sons, Inc. v. Crown Recreation and Kiffe Products,* 548 F. Supp 1018 (E.D.N.Y. 1982).

   a. Bende and Kiffe are both U.S. companies. The contract was entered into in the United States. Assuming that the parties did not have a choice of law provision in the contract, does the UCC or the CISG apply?

   b. Kiffe claims that the contract had been rendered commercially impracticable and that performance was excused. Do you agree? Why or why not? Was the train wreck foreseeable or unforeseeable?

   c. What could Kiffe have done in negotiating the contract to protect itself from this contingency?

   d. If Bende would have incurred an additional $18,815 in freight charges and miscellaneous costs had the breach not occurred, what would be its measure of damages? Is Bende entitled to lost profits? How are damages measured in a case such as this?

   e. In this case, the risk of damage or loss to the boots while in transit remained with the seller, Kiffe. How would the case differ if the parties had agreed that Kiffe would merely ship the goods by a certain date (instead of deliver) and that Kiffe would bear the risk of loss during transit? (You may have to wait until the next chapter to answer this one.)

2. The defendant purchased sewing machines from a Swiss manufacturer in Swiss francs. The machines were imported into the United States for sale through distributors. The importer's contract with a distributor contained an "open-price term" that allowed it to pass cost increases in the machines to the distributor. The open-price term worked well until fluctuation in the exchange rate between the U.S. dollar and the Swiss franc became extreme. When the Swiss franc rose in value against the dollar, the importer's profit margin was cut in half. The importer then imposed a 10 percent surcharge to protect itself. The distributor did not feel that this additional "cost" fell under the term used in the contract. The importer believed that increased costs due to currency fluctuations were covered by the open-price term, and further, that the exchange risk had rendered performance under the contract commercially impracticable. The distributor brought this action to have the contract enforced at its original price. Judgment for whom, and why? *Bernina Distributors v. Bernina Sewing Machine Co.*, 646 F.2d 434 (1981).

3. The CISG contains no provisions that a contract for the sale of goods be supported by consideration. Further, the CISG does not address questions related to the validity of the contract, including legality, mistake, fraud, duress, or undue influence. How will national courts handle these issues in cases that they might be called upon to decide under the CISG? In common law countries? In civil law countries of Europe? How has this been addressed by courts in the United States?

4. CISG Articles 71–73 contain legal rules on anticipatory breach. Article 77 contains rules on the mitigation of damages. These articles can be found in the appendix. Consider the following case: Contract provides that Mexicana Fabricators, S.A., deliver 1,000 personal computer housings by December 1 to AES Computer, Inc., in Austin, Texas, for a total price of $50,000. On July 1, Mexicana faxed AES that due to a rise in prices they could not deliver for less than $60,000. AES replied that it would insist that Mexicana deliver at the $50,000 price. From July 1 through September, AES could have bought the housings from other suppliers for $55,000 for December 1 delivery. On December 1, AES covered and purchased the housings for $64,000 for delivery on February 1. Because of the delay until February 1 AES Computer suffered additional damages of $2,000. What is the measure of AES's damages? Was AES under any duty to mitigate damages? Why or why not?

5. An importer of children's toys, Fun 'N Games, Inc., receives a price quotation from a German toy maker offering toy train sets: "KBG train sets. Locomotive. Four cars. Transformers. Thirty pieces of track. Minimum order thirty sets. $7,500 C.I.F. Baltimore." Fun 'N Games, Inc., sends an order stating: "Ship 30 KGB train sets: to include locomotive, four cars, transformer, forty pieces of track," along with a check for $7,500. Was the price quotation from the German toy maker an offer? If it was, how does Fun 'N Games change in terms—"forty pieces of track"—affect acceptance? If the German toy maker ships the thirty sets with "thirty pieces of track," does a contract exist? Decide the case under the common law, the UCC, and the CISG.

6. A computer printer distributor in Argentina receives an offer by mail from Epson, a U.S. company, in reply to an inquiry. The offer arrives in Argentina on June 2. On June 12, the Argentinean company sends its acceptance by mail. On June 8, Epson sends a revocation of its offer that was received on June 13 in Argentina. The acceptance from Argentina arrives in the United States on June 17. Did a valid contract arise? When was the offer valid? When was the acceptance valid? When was the revocation valid? Decide the case under the common law and under the CISG.

7. Your company, Acme Widgets, sells its widgets worldwide. Acme has a contract for 250,000 widgets to be shipped to the Czech Republic. The price stated in the offer and acceptance is $1 per widget, C.I.F. Prague. During the production of the widgets, the price of one component increases 250 percent due to a shortage. In addition these widgets are due for shipment on June 15 and arrival in Prague no later than July 1. On June 15, a stevedores' strike begins, which lasts for 60 days. Are either or both of these factors—material price increase and the stevedores' strike—an excuse for Acme's nonperformance? What legal theory might Acme use under U.S. common law as an excuse? Under the CISG?

8. A German seller brought a claim against a Russian buyer because the buyer failed to pay for the equipment supplied to the buyer pursuant to their contract. The buyer acknowledged it had received the goods but said its non-payment should be excused as it was due to the failure of the bank responsible for buyer's foreign currency transactions to make payment to the seller. The buyer claimed the fact it lacked the available currency resources should be regarded as a *force majeure*, discharging it from liability for non-payment to the buyer. The contract did include a *force majeure* clause but it did not refer to the buyer's lack of foreign currency. Do you agree with the buyer?

*Tribunal of International Commercial Arbitration at the Russian Federation Chamber of Commerce and Industry 17 October 1995.* (See case law on UNICTRAL texts Abstract No. 142; it is reproduced with permission on Pace University's CISG website found on p. 175 of this chapter.)

9. Henri Ramel, A French wine merchant, contracted to purchase Italian wine from Sacovini, a firm which a place of business in Italy. The wine delivered by Sacovini became chaptalized (it turned to vinegar) and the French buyer sought to avoid the contract claiming the wine it received was not of merchantable quality. The seller said it did deliver the wine specified so it did not breach its contract obligation. The CISG applies to the contract and the buyer claims article 35 requires the seller to deliver goods conforming to the contract (wine the buyer could sell as drinking wine). Did the seller's delivery of chaptalized wine meet the requirements of the CISG Article 35? *Societe Sacovini v. Societe Les fil de Henri Ramel 23 January 1996 Cour de Cassation (French Supreme Court).* (The Abstract of this case found in the UNICTRAL case Abstracts, No. 150. Consult the Pace University CISG website listed on p. 175 of the chapter for information about this case.)

10. An Austrian buyer brought a claim against a Ukrainian seller for damages resulting from the seller's refusal to deliver a certain quantity of goods. The seller claimed it never reached a contract with the buyer. The seller had sent a telex to the buyer regarding the nature of the goods, their quantity, and period for delivery. The telex stated the price could be agreed to ten days prior to the new year.

   The buyer confirmed the contents of the telex but said nothing regarding the price. The parties did not subsequently agree as to the price. Did the lack of agreement on an established price prevent the parties from reaching a valid contract under the CISG? (The CISG controlled because the parties elected Austrian law and that law referred to the CISG for international sales contracts.) *Tribunal of International Commercial Arbitration at the Russian Federation Chamber of Commerce and Industry 3 March 1995.* (The Abstract of this case is found in the UNICTRAL case Abstracts. Consult the Pace University CISG website listed on p. 175 of the chapter for information about this case.)

## MANAGERIAL IMPLICATIONS

You are the vice president of sales for DownPillow International, Inc., a U.S. manufacturer of bed pillows. The raw materials needed for making pillows are all sourced from suppliers overseas. Your firm purchases feathers from exporters in China who maintain large flocks of geese and ducks for breeding. Cotton ticking and other textiles are purchased from mills in Germany. Every year you show your products at the International Bed Show in New York. This year, a delegation of Japanese buyers, representing several well-known Toyko stores, showed interest in your best quality pillows. The president of your firm expressed interest in these contacts because while Americans use the same old cruddy pillow forever, the Japanese are fastidious about their bedding. You followed up with samples, product, and pricing information. After several discussions and months of correspondence, you now expect to be receiving your first overseas orders.

You are to meet with legal counsel next week to discuss this opportunity. What questions might you want to ask about entering a sales contract with a Japanese buyer? If a buyer shows interest in purchasing large quantities, should you consider a visit to their Toyko office? What would you accomplish? Should your attorney conduct negotiations there for you? If you and your buyer agree to put your agreement in writing, what terms might the document contain? Your customers want assurances that their pillows will be made of the finest white goose down, with less than ten percent feathers. What assurance will you be able to give them regarding product quality and specifications? What factors might influence the selection of a choice of law clause? Do you think your lawyer will insist on a force majeure clause? Can you suggest some of the things DownPillow might want in its clause?

If you anticipate that you may have several accounts in Japan, and each of them will be sending in purchase orders for each order, will you need a confirmation form? Will your attorney recommend that you develop a standard form to use for confirming all export orders? How will this form differ from the form you use for domestic shipments? What kind of provisions should it have?

How might negotiating your supply contracts with the Chinese differ from dealing with the German textile mills? You have some concern about making sure that the quality of the down from China remains consistent? How can you be assured that you will receive goose down and not duck down? What other precautions should you take? The German mill has asked that your orders be mailed in or faxed. Your lawyer recommends that certain terms be put into your purchase order form. What might they be? Your purchase order states that the seller is liable for consequential damages for late shipment. The mill's confirmation states that "the liability of the seller is limited to the replacement of returned goods." In the event of a dispute, which will prevail under U.S. law? Under German law? Under the CISG?

Your contract with the Japanese buyer specifies that the CISG is to govern the transaction. Your pillows arrive in Japan and the buyer discovers that they contain only 13 oz. of down instead of the full 16 oz. of down as promised. You goofed and want to resolve the problem. But, the buyer has just been offered the same quality pillow at considerably lower prices from a firm in Taiwan and wants out. Discuss the rights of each of the parties under the CISG.

## NOTES

1. *See* Yuqing and McLean, "China's Foreign Economic Contract Law: Its Significance and Analysis," 8 *NW. J. Int'l. L. Bus.*, 120 (1987).

2. *See* Martin Karollus, "Judicial Interpretation and Applications of the CISG in Germany 1988–1994," in *Cornell Review of the Convention of Contracts for the International Sales of Goods* (1995). Karollus cites a case from Cologne (Köln), Judgment of Feb. 22, 1994 OLG Koln, 1994 RIW at 973, as authority for a German court's treatment of such a provision in a contract governed by the CISG.

3. V. Susanne Cook, "The UN Convention on Contracts for the International Sale of Goods: A Mandate to Abandon Ethnocentricity," *Journal of Law and Commerce* 16, pp. 257–263 (1997).

4. For an excellent discussion of this topic, see Hahn, "Negotiating Contracts with the Japanese," 14 *Case W. Res. J. Int.L.* 377 (1982); Przeracki, "Working it Out: A Japanese Alternative to Fighting it Out," 37 *Clev. St. L. Rev.* 149 (1989).

# Chapter Six
# The Documentary Sale and Terms of Trade

Chapter Five discussed how the contract represents the agreement of the parties to an international sale. Their agreement typically includes the description and price of the goods, warranties, and other essential terms. The contract also can specify other important terms and conditions of sale, including the conditions of payment, the shipping and insurance terms, and the responsibility for damage to the goods while in transit. These terms are important for the parties because they determine how much risk each party bears in the transaction.

The first part of this chapter looks at how the parties use secure payment terms that provide assurance that the seller will be paid and that the buyer will receive the goods. This assurance helps them to manage significant transaction risks. The discussion provides the opportunity to study the documentary sale and the law of negotiable bills of lading.

Next, the text examines how to allocate, to either the buyer or seller, the risk of damage to the goods while in transit. Despite the importance of air transport today, the greatest volume of cargo is still carried by sea. While all forms of transportation put cargo at risk, ocean cargo can be imperiled by time, moisture, storms, shipwrecks, and, even today, piracy. Both parties want to know exactly when the risk of loss to the goods passes from the seller to the buyer.

The text also discusses how the parties can allocate the responsibility for shipping arrangements and charges. In international trade, the shipping terms are an integral part of the price terms. Because of the high cost of freight, the parties typically negotiate the invoice price for the goods and the shipping terms as a package deal.

A seller may then offer the goods for one price at the factory, another at a seaport, and yet another for the goods delivered to the buyer's warehouse. This chapter describes how the parties negotiate these terms as a part of the terms of sale.

## Payment and Delivery Risk

The discussion begins by looking at how seller and buyer might manage both payment and delivery risk in an international sale. The risk that the buyer will fail to pay is called the seller's *payment risk* (often called *credit risk*). The risk that the buyer will fail to receive the goods is called the buyer's *delivery risk.* The buyer will want assurance that the goods will be shipped on time, properly packaged, and adequately insured.

No seller would want to ship goods overseas and place them into the hands of a foreign buyer without some assurance of payment. Once the goods leave the seller's control, any remedies to recover from the buyer can be costly and time-consuming. If the buyer fails or refuses to pay, the seller might have to resort to litigation in the buyer's country in order to recover the money owed. Even then, recovery might become impossible, such as where the buyer becomes insolvent or bankrupt.

Ideally, if they could have their way, sellers would like to have *cash in advance* from foreign buyers before the goods leave their hands. On the other hand, few buyers would part with their money merely in the hope that the goods they ordered would ever arrive. Once the seller has the cash, what motivation would induce the seller to ship conforming goods, or goods that are not defective, or any goods at all? The seller may have no long-term interest in exporting to a foreign market, or may just be dishonest. Cultural and language barriers might make it especially hard to gauge a seller's honesty or intentions. So this payment option, cash in advance, usually will not serve to bring buyer and seller together.

On the other hand, all buyers would like to be able to buy on open credit terms, or on *open account.* In domestic sales, for the seller who has had an opportunity to learn the creditworthiness of the buyer, sales are often made on, say, 30-day open account terms. However, few sellers would risk shipping their goods to a foreign market, giving up possession, control, and even ownership of the goods, to a buyer so far away. Perhaps after a long relationship has developed between them, they may agree to do business this way; but an open account sale is usually not secure enough for most larger international transactions. In addition, a seller who quotes on open account in a foreign currency bears considerable currency risk during the open credit period. Thus, if cash in advance or open account were the only payment options, buyer and seller would be at an impasse. To bring them together, some other method of assuring that the seller will ship and the buyer will pay as promised are required. One method that provides such assurance is the documentary sale.[1]

# The Documentary Sale

The *documentary sale* is a type of contract for the sale of goods in which the buyer is required to pay upon the presentation of a negotiable document of title by the seller (see Exhibit 6.1). It serves to reduce the transaction risks between a buyer and a seller who are great distances apart by assuring that if one releases the title to the goods the other will release the money.

The documentary sale is a unique method of exchange devised by early traders as their sailing vessels traveled medieval trade routes. The method spread by custom and practice, and eventually became recognized in early English law—in the modern common law countries and in the civil law countries of Europe. Today the documentary sale is a common type of contract for the sale of goods.

## The Document of Title

The key to understanding the documentary sale is understanding the nature of a *document of title.* Documents of title are legal instruments that evidence the ownership of goods. Common documents of title include dock receipts, warehouse receipts, and bills of lading. They are issued by a party (known as the *bailee*) in receipt for goods taken into its possession from a *bailor.* Documents of title may be either negotiable or non-negotiable. A *negotiable document* is one that can legally be transferred from one party to another in return for value or payment. Negotiable documents of title are used to transfer ownership of goods from one party to another without the necessity of transferring physical possession of the goods themselves. The property can stay in the possession of the bailee, while the owner can safely trade, barter, pledge, or deal with it in the commercial world.

## The Bill of Lading

A *bill of lading* is a document of title issued by a *carrier* to a shipper upon receiving goods for transport (see Exhibit 6.2). Having first been used in the sixteenth century, the bill of lading has played a vital role in international trade. It serves three purposes:

1. A receipt for the goods from the carrier, indicating any damage to the goods that was visible at the time of loading.
2. The contract of carriage between the shipper and the carrier (i.e., a *transport document*).
3. The document of title to the goods described in it.

Other types of transport documents will serve as a contract of carriage, but do not act as a document of title.

**Order and Bearer Documents.**   Only negotiable bills of lading are used in documentary sales. To be negotiable, they must state that the goods are to be delivered "to the bearer" or "to the order of" a named person. Negotiable bearer documents can be transferred to another party by mere delivery of the document. Because of the danger that they might fall into the wrong hands, bearer documents are not used for foreign trade.

**EXHIBIT 6.1   The Documentary Sale**

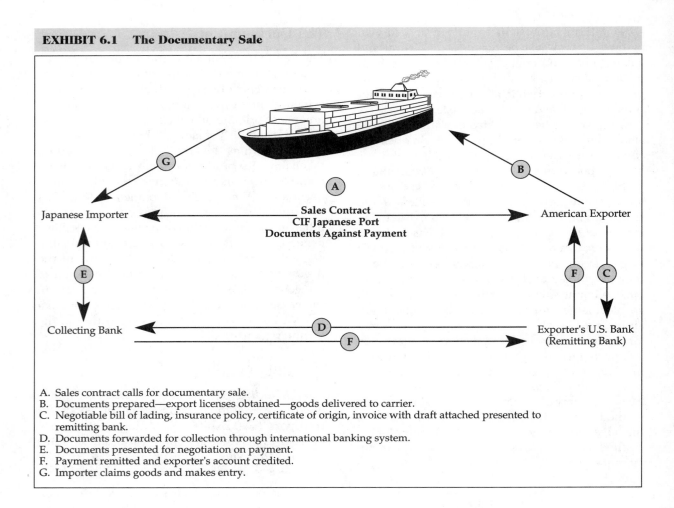

A. Sales contract calls for documentary sale.
B. Documents prepared—export licenses obtained—goods delivered to carrier.
C. Negotiable bill of lading, insurance policy, certificate of origin, invoice with draft attached presented to remitting bank.
D. Documents forwarded for collection through international banking system.
E. Documents presented for negotiation on payment.
F. Payment remitted and exporter's account credited.
G. Importer claims goods and makes entry.

Because of the protection they provide to the seller, order bills of lading are the most common type of bill used in international transactions. Once a carrier issues a bill of lading, the carrier may surrender the goods only to the holder of the bill. If the carrier delivers to anyone else, it will be liable to the holder for *misdelivery of the goods.*

Since the carrier is required to deliver the goods only to the holder of the bill of lading, the seller may make the bill payable to its own order so that the buyer is prevented from gaining possession of the goods before payment is made. After receiving payment, the seller then endorses the bill of lading to the order of the buyer or the bank that is financing the transaction. Unfortunately, however, mistakes may prevent the process of exporting from running smoothly. An

article follows on p. 188 which discusses how a small trading company copes with mistakes that affect its first shipment to Panama.

In the United States, the laws governing the negotiability of bills of lading are the Federal Bills of Lading Act (for bills originating in the United States for export shipments) and the Uniform Commercial Code.

**Importance of Negotiability to Trade.**   The negotiability of the bill of lading is what makes it so important to trade. As the document is bought and sold, so too are the goods it represents. Negotiability permits merchants to trade in cargo while it is still afloat. With a bill of lading, goods can be bought and sold, time and again, while they are still on the high seas, with the bill of lading circling the globe from one buyer to the next. This

**EXHIBIT 6.2  Ocean Bill of Lading**

OCEAN BILL OF LADING

| Shipper/Exporter | Export References |
|---|---|
| Shipper's name<br>Address | Invoice or order number<br>(Not negotiable unless consigned to order) |

| Consignee: (Complete Name and Address)<br>To the order of:<br><br>Shipper | Forwarding Agent – References<br><br>Shippers Freight Forwarder |
|---|---|

| | Forwarding Agent – References<br>U.S.A. | Forwarding Agent – References |
|---|---|---|

| Notify Party (Complete Name and Address)<br><br>Buyer or buyer's import agent | Domestic Routing/Export Instructions Pre-carriage<br>These commodities licensed by U.S. for ultimate destination Japan and for resale to any destination except North Korea, Iraq, Cambodia, or Cuba. |
|---|---|

| Pier | Onward Inland Routing | Place of delivery |
|---|---|---|

| Ocean Vessel | Flag | Port of Loading | | |
|---|---|---|---|---|
| Port of Discharge | | For Transshipment To | | |

Carrier's Receipt | Particulars Furnished By Shipper

| Marks and Numbers | No. of Cont. or Other Pkgs. | Description of Goods | Gross Weight | Measurement |
|---|---|---|---|---|
| Container No.<br>UP 362459<br>Seal # 2398112 | 95 | 1 x 40' container said to contain down pillows on invoices to be as per proforma invoices nos. 2368714, 2368715 dated April 15, 1990. | | |
| Shipping Marks:  Down Bedding | | "Shipper Load, Stuff & Count" | 1,550 Kg (Net) | |
| | | Clean Shipped on board<br>5/10/90 | | |
| | | "Freight Prepaid"<br>House to port basis | | |
| | | Signed _____ *Nury*<br>Title of Company Official | | |

ON BOARD

Received in apparent good order and condition except as otherwise noted hereon the goods, containers, or other packages, or units mentioned above for transportation from the place of receipt if named above or (if not named) the port of loading to the port of discharge or place of delivery (as the case may be) subject to exceptions, limitations, conditions and liberties hereof and there to be delivered to the consignee or his or their assigns.

**(TERMS OF THIS BILL OF LADING CONTINUED ON REVERSE SIDE HEREOF)**

| Freight Charges | Prepaid | Collect |
|---|---|---|
| Land Charges | | |
| Port Charges | | |
| Ocean Charges | | |
| Container Rental | | |
| | | |
| | | |
| Total | 4850.00 | |

IN WITNESS WHEREOF, The Master or Agent of said vessel has affirmed to THREE (3) _____ Bills of Lading, all of this tenor and date, one of which being accomplished, the others stand void.

Carrier        TAMPA BAY STEAMSHIP
               JACKSONVILLE, FLA.

By _____ *Shry*
   Agent (for the Master) TBS

| Dated at<br>Port of<br>Shipment | Mo.<br>5 | Day<br>10 | Yr.<br>90 |
|---|---|---|---|

B/L No.

# Late-Summer Lapses in Judgment Often Trigger a Variety of Shipping Mishaps

Strange things happen in August. All Western Europe goes on vacation. Even the Japanese take some time off. Brazil, I am told, goes absolutely crazy. UPS goes on strike. Those of us who continue working go brain dead.

A series of almost comical errors caused World War I to break out, in August.

Strange things happen in August.

Even at my small trading company. The company has two forwarders, reflecting our product breakdown. One is highly specialized in pleasure boats. The other, less specialized but better organized, handles all our other exports.

We fight like steers to keep our forwarders in control of our shipments, a point I have harped on often in this column. However, there are times when we must yield to customer preference. We are, after all, only a small trading company.

Late last July we received a very nice first order from Panama. The buyer insisted that we use his designated Miami forwarder. . . .

The buyer's credit checked out so well that we agreed to extend 30- and 60-day draft payment terms, something we seldom do with new customers.

Since we decided to trust the buyer, we reluctantly agreed to use his forwarder as well.

**Going Through Checklist to Minimize the Risk**

We have a procedure to prequalify customer-designated forwarders. . . .

As a start, we ask the forwarder to send us a Shipper's Letter of Instruction (SLI), which spells out any particular shipping steps the forwarder wants us to follow. Most forwarders are happy to oblige. We really wonder about those that do not have any such form.

Next, for ocean shipments, we ask whether the forwarder has a license from the Federal Maritime Commission. A few don't know what we are talking about and this really raises a red flag. One or two claim to have one, but decline to give us the num-

ber, raising an even larger red flag. This one not only had a license, but actually took it off the wall and faxed us a copy. Point made.

Sure enough, when the documents came, the ocean bill of lading was consigned directly to the buyer—not good at all for us, but certainly an advantage for the buyer. (I have NEVER seen a situation where a customer-designated forwarder made an error in seller's favor!)

It is essential that negotiable ocean bills of lading be used for ocean shipments when payment terms involve drafts. Such a bill of lading shows the phrase "order of shipper" in the consignee field.

Carriers will not release shipments covered by negotiable bills of lading unless the original is surrendered. The seller sends the original to a bank in the buyer's country with instructions that it be given to the buyer only when the draft(s) is (are) paid or accepted as the payment terms indicate.

However, if the ocean bill of lading shows the buyer's name in the consignee field, the carrier will not insist upon surrender of the original ocean bill of lading. Therefore, the buyer would not need to deal with the bank in order to get the shipment.

Back to our story. The forwarder was able to have replacement bills of lading issued quickly, so no harm was done. However, if we had instructed the forwarder to bank the documents, as we sometimes do with our own forwarder, we would have lost our payment protection.

Moral: NEVER allow a customer-designated forwarder to bank your documents.

Just to prove that all their errors do not necessarily work in favor of the importer that appointed them, the same forwarder made another mistake that benefitted no one.

**Goofs Aren't Limited to Buyer's Own Forwarder**

We ship under the AERP program, an automated export documentation system that allows us to file our

*(continued)*

*(continued)*

Shippers' Export Declarations (SEDs) electronically each month.

Since most forwarders routinely file paper SEDs, we print in large Gothic type NO SED REQUIRED, SEC. 30.39 FTSR, on our commercial invoices and the SLIs we give the forwarders. Sure enough, just about every time we use a buyer-designated forwarder, we get a copy of the paper SED they filed contrary to our instructions (usually bearing incorrect Schedule B numbers).

So much for buyer-designated forwarders. Our own didn't do much better last month. It is a real source of embarrassment when we convince our reluctant customers to use one of our designated forwarders, only to have to apologize later for forwarding errors. This happened often enough to make us very aware that it was August.

Next time we'll look at ways to minimize the harm these forwarders cause.

*Frank Reynolds*

*The Journal of Commerce,* September 17, 1997.
© 1997 *The Journal of Commerce.* Reprinted by permission.

---

practice is, in fact, quite common. Persian Gulf oil can change hands 20 or 30 times in the six weeks that it takes a tanker to reach U.S. waters.

The negotiability of bills of lading was recognized in most European trading centers at least as early as the sixteenth century. Early records of them have been found in many languages. In 1883, Lord Justice Bowen described the bill of lading in this time-honored description from *Sanders Brothers v. Maclean & Co.* 11 Q.B.D. 327 at 341 (1883).

The law as to the indorsement of bills of lading is as clear as in my opinion the practice of all European merchants is thoroughly understood. A cargo at sea while in the hands of the carrier is necessarily incapable of physical delivery. During this period of transit and voyage, the bill of lading by the law merchant is universally recognized as its symbol, and the indorsement and delivery of the bill of lading operates as a symbolical delivery of the cargo. Property in the goods passes by such indorsement and delivery of the bill of lading, whenever it is the intention of the parties that the property should pass, just as under similar circumstances the property would pass by an actual delivery of the goods. And for the purpose of passing such property in the goods and completing the title of the indorsee to full possession thereof, the bill of lading, until complete delivery of the cargo has been made on shore to some one rightfully claiming under it, remains in force as a symbol, and carries with it not only the full ownership of the goods, but also all rights created by the contract of carriage between the shipper and the shipowner. It is a key which in the hands of a rightful owner is intended to unlock the door of the warehouse, floating or fixed, in which the goods may chance to be.

As the vessel bearing the goods proceeds out of the harbor and onto the open ocean, the seller safely retains the title to the merchandise, literally held in hand. The seller can sell the goods as planned by sending the bill of lading ahead to the buyer, divert the shipment to another buyer around the globe, pledge it for a loan, or bring it home. This unique flexibility has made the documentary sale essential to world trade and the international economy.

## Documentary Collections

The *documentary collection* is the process by which banking institutions serve as intermediaries between seller and buyer to handle the exchange of the bill of lading for payment. The documentary collection is an integral part of the documentary sale. It provides a safer alternative for payment than either cash in advance or sale on open account. The parties might indicate their desire for a documentary collection by specifying in the contract that payment terms are "cash against documents" or "documents against payment." Such an indication is not always essential, because the collection process is implied in most documentary sales contracts.

Typically, the documentary collection works like this: Seller places the goods in the hands of a carrier and receives a bill of lading in return. Seller indorses the bill of lading and presents it to the bank for collection. Along with the bill of lading, the seller will include other essential documents, such as a *marine insurance* policy on the goods covering the risks of the ocean voyage. A *certificate of origin* (see Exhibit 6.3) may be required by customs regulations in the buyer's country. The seller's *commercial invoice* describing the goods and showing the price to be paid is always required. Finally, a *documentary draft* will be needed to expedite the exchange of money. The draft is a negotiable instrument used to make payment for the invoice and for the bill of lading. As described in a later chapter, the draft is a negotiable "order to pay" made out by the seller, drawn on the buyer for collection, and payable to the order of the seller. Its purpose is to tell the parties how much to pay when purchasing the bill of lading. The draft will also be needed by the bank if financing is to be provided for the sale. Other documents may be required, as well, depending on the needs of the parties or the export-import regulations of their countries.

The seller's bank forwards the draft and documents to a *collecting bank* in the buyer's country, with instructions that the documents can be released to the buyer only upon payment of the draft. The collecting bank negotiates the documents to the buyer upon payment of the draft, and remits the money back to the seller's bank. In addition to the many variations of the collection process, banks offer a range of *trade finance* services to help finance the deal between buyer and seller.

## Rights of Purchasers of Bills of Lading

While some readers may be familiar with the rights of parties that purchase *negotiable istruments,* such as checks and promissory notes, the law regarding the transfer and sale of negotiable *documents* is somewhat different because their functions are different. Negotiable instruments serve as a substitute for money, while negotiable documents are used to move goods.

**Good Faith Purchasers of Bills of Lading.**   In order for documents of title to be freely accepted in commerce and trade, the law gives special protection to purchasers of bills of lading (and

other documents of title as well). Purchasers take their documents free from the adverse claims of other parties to the goods. The rights of the purchaser of a document depends on whether the case is governed in the United States by Article 7 of the Uniform Commercial Code, or by the Federal Bills of Lading Act. This discussion generally applies to both laws. Under the UCC, special protection is accorded to holders by due negotiation, also called good-faith purchasers.

A *holder by due negotiation* or a *good faith purchaser* is one who purchases the document (1) for value (and not in settlement of a past debt), (2) in good faith and without any notice of any adverse claim against it, and (3) in the ordinary course of business or financing. If it is an order instrument, then the *good faith purchaser* must take it by indorsement. When a buyer, bank, or other party takes a document as a good faith purchaser, it acquires even greater rights in the document than the one from which it had been negotiated. In other words, the good faith purchaser takes the document free from any claims that other parties might have against either the document or the goods.

Consider the following case: A entrusts goods to B for storage. B delivers the goods to a carrier, obtains a bill of lading, negotiates the document to C and absconds with the money. C, who is a good faith purchaser, takes title to both the document and the goods. A may not reclaim them because C takes *paramount title.* C's rights are paramount even to the original owner because B had been entrusted with the goods and then wrongfully sold them. There are many cases where the good faith purchaser takes greater rights than the transferor of the document had. But in other instances, a good faith purchaser would not enjoy greater rights. For instance, when a thief steals goods and obtains a bill of lading, a purchaser of the document does not obtain paramount title over the original owner.

Different rules apply to transferees of *nonnegotiable* bills of lading and to transferees of negotiable bills of lading who did not take them by due negotiation or as good faith purchasers. In these cases, the holder receives only those rights that the transferor had, or which the transferor had the actual authority to convey, and no more. Recall the example in which A entrusted goods to B for storage. Here, B transfers a nonnegotiable

**EXHIBIT 6.3  Certificate of Origin for U.S. Export Sale**

# CERTIFICATE OF ORIGIN

| SHIPPER/EXPORTER | DOCUMENT NO. |
|---|---|
| ABC Company<br>123 Elm St.<br>Anytown, NC 12345 | EXPORT REFERENCES<br><br>Shipper Ref: PO# 0001 |

| CONSIGNEE | FORWARDING AGENT – REFERENCES |
|---|---|
| XYZ Corporation<br>456 Wind St.<br>Anycity, France | Smith Forwarders/REF 10001 |
| | POINT AND COUNTRY OF ORIGIN<br>NC, USA |

| NOTIFY PARTY | DOMESTIC ROUTING/EXPORT INSTRUCTIONS |
|---|---|
| Foreign Custom Broker<br>1001 Maple Ave.<br>Anycity, France | |

| PIER OR AIRPORT<br>Charlotte | |
|---|---|

| EXPORTING CARRIER (Vessel/Airline)<br>US Air | PORT OF LOADING<br>Charlotte | ONWARD INLAND ROUTING |
|---|---|---|
| AIR/SEA PORT OF DISCHARGE<br>Paris | FOR TRANSHIPMENT TO<br>Anycity | |

### PARTICULARS FURNISHED BY SHIPPER

| MARKS AND NUMBERS | NO. OF PKGS. | ONWARD INLAND ROUTING | NET KILOS OR POUNDS | GROSS KILOS | GROSS POUNDS |
|---|---|---|---|---|---|
| MKD:<br>AS ADDR<br>PO# 0001 | 10 | Cartons Leather Aprons | 97 KG | 109 | 240 |

The undersigned _ ABC Company _ _ _ _ (Owner or Agent), does hereby declare for the above named shipper, the goods as described above were shipped on the above date and consigned as indicated and are products of the United States of America.

Dated at _ _ _ _ _ _ Anytown, NC _ _ _ _ _ _ _ _ on the _ 01 _ day of _ _ _ _ _ _ June _ _ _ _ _ _ _ _ 19 92 _ .

Sworn to before me this _ 01 _ day of _ _ _ _ June _ _ _ _ _ _ _ _ 19 92 _ .

_ _ _ _ _ _ _ _ _ _ _ _ _ _ _ _ _ _ _ _ _ _ _ _     _ _ _ _ _ _ _ _ _ _ _ _ _ _ _ _ _ _ _ _ _ _ _ _ _ _ _ _ _ _ _

SIGNATURE OF OWNER OR AGENT

The _ _ _ _ _ _ _ _ _ Anytown Chamber of Commerce _ _ _ _ _ _ _ _ _ _ _ _ _ _ _ _ _ _ , a recognized Chamber of Commerce under the laws of the State of _ _ _ _ North Carolina _ _ _ _ , has examined the manufacturer's invoice or shipper's affidavit concerning the origin of the merchandise, and, according to the best of its knowledge and belief, finds that the products named originated in the United States of America.

Secretary _ _ _ _ _ _ _ _ _ _ _ _ _ _ _ _ _ _ _ _ _ _ _ _ _ _ _ _ _ _ _ bill of lading to C and absconds with the money. A can reclaim the goods from C.

**Carrier's Misdelivery.** The carrier may deliver the goods only to the holder of an original bill of lading. Assume that A entrusts a shipment of animal skins to an ocean carrier and obtains a bill of lading. The carrier delivers the goods to B without asking B to produce the document. Without knowledge of what has occurred, A sells the bill to C, who takes it for value and in good faith. C is the good faith purchaser and the owner of the goods, and may bring an action to reclaim the goods from B. C also has a cause of action against the carrier for misdelivery of the goods, because the carrier violated the terms of the contract of carriage. The *Kanematsu* case, involves a suit by the holder of the bill of lading against the carrier for misdelivery.

---

### *Kanematsu (Hong Kong) v. Eurasia Express Line*
*September 18, 1997*
*Court of Appeal (Civil Division)*

BACKGROUND AND FACTS

Eurasia Express Line, a carrier, issued a bill of lading covering a cargo of steel which was shipped from Russia to China on the "Prosperity." Billiongold claimed title to the goods but did not present a bill of lading. Eurasia Express released the goods to Billiongold upon receiving from Billiongold a written guarantee that it had title to the goods. Kanematsu, the true holders of the bill of lading, sued Eurasia Express for misdelivery and were awarded $2,133,316 in damages.

EVANS, JUDGE

In essence, the defendants say that they performed their obligations under the bill of lading by discharging the goods into the custody of the agents and that they are not liable for the subsequent misdelivery. They are free from liability, they say, because the clauses say so. In particular, the first sentence of clause 6(2) and the last sentence of clause 14. Those sentences say in summary that the carrier is not to be liable for mishaps occurring after discharge from the vessel.

The learned judge rejected the clause 6(2) argument, relying upon a statement of the law by Clarke J in "the Ines" [1995] 2 Lloyd's Rep. 144. He quoted a passage beginning on page 152 which I will read because in my view it expresses admirably what the law is on this topic:

> One of the key provisions of the bill of lading, so far as the shipper is concerned, is the promise not to deliver the cargo other than in return for an original bill of lading. That principle protects the shipper from fraud. It also protects the ship-owner. The parties would not in my judgment be likely to have contracted out of it. Thus clear words would be required for them to be held to have done so. The clause should be construed so as to enable effect to be given to one of the main objects and intents of the contract, namely that the goods will only be delivered to the holder of an original bill of lading.

It is an implied if not express term of a bill of lading contract that the goods will be delivered at the discharging port only to or to order of the holder of the bill of lading which must be duly presented by him. . . . I would say that in the present case it is quite impossible to suggest that this court would hold that the clauses relied on here have the effect of qualifying the ship-owner's obligation not to deliver the goods except against production of the bill of lading.

It is true that the undertaking printed on the face of the bill of lading refers expressly to the clauses printed overleaf and does not say in terms that the goods will not be delivered except against production of the bill of lading. . . . However if the appellants' [Eurasia Express] submissions were correct, this document although masquerading as a bill of lading, would not give to its holder or to third parties that deal with them the security which it leads them to expect. On the true construction of this document it is, in my judgment, what it purports to be, that is a bill of lading contract which cannot be accomplished except by delivery against presentation of the bill of lading itself.

Appeal denied.

**Decision.** According to the court, unless the contract states otherwise, the carrier's duty under the bill of lading is not to deliver goods unless the original bill of lading is produced. Failure to do so constitutes misdelivery and the carrier will be held liable.

**Carrier's Lien.** All carriers have a lien on the cargo covered by the bill of lading, while it is in their possession, to cover the payment of freight, storage, or other fees. If the carrier is not paid for these expenses, it may, if necessary, sell the cargo at auction and remit any balance to the holder of the bill of lading.

> **http://www.silkweb.bc.ca/portview/k_7.htm**
> See for a sample bill of lading.

## Responsibilities of Buyer and Seller in a Documentary Sale

Now that the documentary collection process has been explained, the next area to examine is exactly what is expected of the buyer and seller in fulfilling their responsibilities under the contract.

The exact responsibilities of buyer and seller depend on their agreement. In many documen-tary sales, the seller must not only tender a bill of lading to the buyer for payment, but also must provide marine insurance on the goods and must prepay the freight to the foreign port. These contracts are called *CIF contracts,* standing for "cost, insurance, and freight." This and other *trade terms* are discussed later in the chapter. In the following case involving a CIF contract, the seller in San Francisco tendered the documents to the buyer in London even before the goods were shipped. Wanting to inspect the merchandise first, the buyer refused to pay until delivery was made. The seller claimed that payment was due upon presentation of the documents alone.

The Kennedy dissent in *Biddell Brothers* represents a virtually universal view of CIF and other documentary sales contracts today. This rule has been adopted by both the Uniform Commercial Code and the U.N. Convention on Contracts for the International Sale of Goods, and it has long been recognized by courts in the United States.

---

### Biddell Brothers v. E. Clemens Horst Co.
*1 King's Bench 934 (1911)*
*Court of Appeal*

**BACKGROUND AND FACTS**

The defendant entered into a contract to sell hops to the plaintiff in London, as follows:

> . . . one hundred bales, equal to or better than choice brewing Pacific Coast hops of each of the crops of the years 1905 to 1912 inclusive. The said hops to be shipped to Sunderland. The [buyer] shall pay for the said hops at the rate of ninety shillings sterling per 112 lbs. CIF to London, Liverpool, or Hull. Terms net cash.

The seller wrote to the buyer stating that they were ready to ship and that they expected payment upon presentation of a negotiable bill of lading. The buyer replied that it was prepared to take delivery, but insisted that the seller either submit samples for prior inspection or that it be permitted to inspect each bale prior to payment. The buyer was unwilling to accept a certificate of inspection from the San Francisco Merchant's exchange as assurance of quality. The seller refused to ship and the buyer brought this action. The seller counter-claimed for the buyer's refusal to pay on the documents. The lower court ruled in favor of the defendant buyer. The Court of Appeals affirmed, with Kennedy, L.J., dissenting. On appeal to the House of Lords, the judgment was reversed in favor of the seller.

**LORD JUSTICE KENNEDY, DISSENTING**

The plaintiffs' case is that the price was not to be paid until they had been given an opportunity of inspecting the shipment, which could not be given until after its arrival in this country. The defendants contend that the plaintiffs' obligation was to pay for the hops, whether they arrived or not, against tender of the shipping documents. The Court, therefore, has in the present case to decide what are the true conditions of the right of the seller to payment under a CIF contract, if that commercial contract is to be performed strictly according to its tenor.

Let us see, step by step, how according to those principles and rules the transactions as in such a CIF contract as that before us is and, I think, must be carried out in order to fulfill its terms.

*(continued)*

*(continued)*

At the port of shipment—in this case San Francisco—the vendor ships the goods intended for the purchaser under the contract. Under the Sale of Goods Act, 1893, s. 18, by such shipment the goods are appropriated by the vendor to the fulfillment of the contract, and by virtue of s. 32 the delivery of the goods to the carrier—whether named by the purchaser or not—for the purpose of transmission to the purchaser is prima facie to be deemed to be a delivery of the goods to the purchaser. Two further legal results arise out of the shipment. The goods are at risk of the purchaser, against which he has protected himself by the stipulation in his CIF contract that the vendor shall, at his own cost, provide him with a proper policy of marine insurance intended to protect the buyer's interest, and available for his use, if the goods should be lost in transit. How is such a tender to be made of goods afloat under a CIF contract? By tender of the bill of lading, accompanied in case the goods have been lost in transit by the policy of insurance. The bill of lading in law and in fact represents the goods. Possession of the bill of lading places the goods at the disposal of the purchaser. . . . But then I understand it to be objected on behalf of the plaintiffs: "Granted that the purchaser might, if he pleased, take this constructive delivery and pay against it the price of the goods; what is there in the 'cost freight and insurance' contract which compels him to do so? Why may he not insist on an option of waiting for a tender of delivery of the goods themselves after having had an opportunity of examining them after their arrival?"

There are, I think, several sufficient answers to such a proposition. In the first place, an option of a time of payment is not a term which can be inferred, where the contract itself is silent. So far as I am aware, there is no authority for the inference of an option as to times of payment to be found either in the law books or in the Sale of Goods Act. Secondly, if there is a duty on the vendor to tender the bill of lading, there must, it seems to me, be a corresponding duty on the part of the purchaser to pay when such tender is made. For thereunder, as the bill of lading with its accompanying documents comes forward by mail, the purchaser obtains the privilege and absolute power of profitably dealing with the goods days or weeks, or, perhaps, in the case of shipments from a distant port, months, before the arrival of the goods themselves. This is, indeed, the essential and peculiar advantage which the buyer of imported goods intends to gain under the CIF contract according to the construction which I put upon it.

Finally, let me test the soundness of the plaintiffs' contention that according to the true meaning of this contract their obligation to pay arises only when delivery of the goods has been tendered to them after they have an opportunity of examination, in this way. Suppose the goods to have been shipped, the bill of lading taken, and the insurance for the benefit of the buyer duly effected by the seller, as expressly stipulated in the contract. Suppose the goods then during the ocean transit to have been lost by the perils of the sea. The vendor tenders the bill of lading, with the insurance policy and the other shipping documents (if any) to the purchaser, to whom from the moment of shipment the property has passed, and at whose risk, covered by the insurance, the goods were at the time of loss. Is it, I ask myself, arguable that the purchaser could be heard to say, "I will not pay because I cannot have delivery of and an examination of the goods?" But it is just this which is necessarily involved in the contention of these plaintiffs. The seller's answer, and I think conclusive answer, is, "You have the bill of lading and the policy of insurance."

In my judgment, the judgment of Hamilton, J., was right, and this appeal, so far as relates to the plaintiffs' claim, should be dismissed.

**Decision.**   Under a CIF sales contract the buyer has no right to inspect the goods, but is obligated to pay upon the presentation of the proper documents.

## Seller's Duty to Tender Documents

If the documents are in good order, then the collection process normally works smoothly, with buyer and seller each getting what had been bargained for in the contract. The process may not be so smooth, however, if the documents tendered to the buyer contain one or more obvious defects. If the documents appear improper, the buyer may reject them. For instance, if the documents show that the goods were shipped later than the date called for in the contract, or on an improper vessel, or if they are improperly or inadequately insured, or if the documents on their face appear fraudulent, the buyer may have grounds for refusal. The buyer's refusal could come as quite a surprise to the seller, who, in good faith shipped and tendered documents to the buyer, only to find that they have been rejected and the draft unpaid, due to some "technicality." Of course, the point of contention may be more than just a technicality from the buyer's point of view, who may feel the rejection was based on good cause. But the effect is to leave the seller with a good deal of exposure while goods remain in a distant foreign port. Learning to manage these risks will have to wait for a later chapter, however.

## Seller's Additional Risk of Nonpayment

Although the documentary sale considerably reduces the seller's payment risk in an international sale, the possibility remains that the buyer may simply become insolvent or may find the goods cheaper from another source, and refuse to pay for the documents when they arrive. Even though the seller can control the goods through the bill of lading, the seller may still be burdened with getting rid of unneeded goods. For protection against these circumstances, the seller may require in the contract, as a precondition of ship-

ment, that the buyer's bank irrevocably promise to buy the documents when presented to it.

## Certificates of Inspection or Analysis

The documentary sales transaction serves to protect not only the seller, but also the buyer. The bill of lading assures that the goods have been loaded aboard ship for transport on the date shown, and the insurance policy serves to protect against covered marine losses. However, is not the buyer taking the description of the goods in the bill of lading, and in the invoice that usually accompanies it, at face value? If the goods are nonconforming or defective, the buyer's only remedy may be an action for breach of contract. In many industries, buyers will require that bills of lading be accompanied by a *certificate of inspection,* a *certificate of weight,* or perhaps a *certificate of analysis* from a reputable inspection company, usually located in the seller's country. While inspections are common in the chemical, extraction, and commodities business, they are also common throughout international trade. For instance, even major apparel retailers in the United States have garments inspected for defects in Hong Kong before they are shipped from the Orient.

In the *Basse* case, the buyer claimed that its bank should have been more diligent in accepting an inspection certificate that the seller had obtained from a chemist by fraud and trickery.

---

### Basse and Selve v. Bank of Australasia
90 Law Times 618 (1904)
King's Bench

BACKGROUND AND FACTS
The plaintiff had purchased ore from Oppenheimer. The plaintiff requested that the defendant bank negotiate documents on its behalf from Oppenheimer covering a shipment of "cobalt ore analysis not less than 5 per cent pertoxide." The plaintiff specified that the bill of lading must be accompanied by a policy of insurance and a certificate of analysis from Dr. Helms, a Sydney chemist. Oppenheimer submitted for analysis phony samples of ore to the chemist, who, on the basis of this small sample, issued his certificate indicating the quality to be as described in the bill of lading. In fact, the ore contained in the actual shipment was worthless. The plaintiff brought this

action in order to recover amounts paid by the bank against the documents.

JUSTICE BIGHAM
It was no part of their duty to verify the genuineness of the documents; the duty was not cast upon them of making inquiries at the office of the ship's agent as to whether the goods had, in truth, been received on board; nor were they to examine the contents of the packages to see whether they were right; nor were they to communicate with Dr. Helms in order to ascertain whether he had properly made the analysis mentioned in the certificate. The plaintiffs' mandate amounted in

(*continued*)

*(continued)*

business to a representation to the defendants that upon all such matters they might rely on Oppenheimer, and the legal effect of such a representation is now to preclude the plaintiffs from questioning the validity of any apparently regular documents which Oppenheimer might tender. If this is so, then the only question left on this part of the case is whether the documents were apparently regular. It is admitted by the plaintiffs that the bill of lading and the policy of insurance were apparently regular, but an objection is made on this score to Helms's certificate. It is said that it professes to show merely the test of the contents of a sample packet with a mark upon it, and does not purport to show a test of the bill of lading of 100 tons of ore. This, I think, is a fanciful objection. Large quantities of produce are necessarily tested by means of samples. Such samples are drawn either by the servants of the owner of the goods or (as it seems) by the servants of the analyst, and if the samples are carefully and skillfully drawn they generally fairly represent the bulk. But in this case it would be no part of the bank's duty to see to the sampling or to ascertain that it was fairly done. The bank was entitled to assume that it was so just as they were entitled to assume that the analyst had acted skillfully in making the analysis. The certificate is, in my opinion, regular on its face, and comes within the meaning of the mandate under which the bank was acting, and the bank in taking it acted carefully and properly.

Judgment for defendants.

**Decision.** The court ruled that since the certificate on its face was regular, the bank had acted properly in paying the seller. The bank had no duty to inspect the ore itself.

## Measuring Damages for Breach of the Documentary Sale

The last chapter discussed the remedies available to a buyer and seller for breach of contract. Here, the text turns to the unique problem presented by the documentary sale. If the buyer sues the seller for nondelivery or other breach of contract, the buyer's damages may be measured by the difference between the contract price for the goods and their fair market value. How is market value determined in a documentary sale? Is it the market value at the time that the goods are shipped, the time of delivery of the goods, or the time of payment? Under the English view, damages would be based on the date that the buyer would have paid for the goods had the seller not breached. In *Sharpe & Co., Limited v. Nosawa & Co.*, 2 K.B. 814 (1917), a Japanese seller entered into a contract to ship peas to an English buyer under a documentary sale, CIF London. Neither the goods nor the documents were ever sent and the buyer sued for damages. The question was whether the buyer's damages should have been calculated on the basis of the difference between the contract price (£10.15 sterling per ton) and the market price of peas at the time of the anticipated August delivery (£17.10 sterling per ton) or the market price of peas at the time the documents would have been tendered in London July 21 (£12.00 sterling per ton). The court held that the seller's responsibility in this contract would have not been completed until he delivered the shipping documents to the buyer in London, at which time he would have been paid, and that the damages should therefore be measured by the price of peas on that date, July 21. Obviously, in a market with highly fluctuating prices, this question becomes especially important.

As the *Seaver* case illustrates, U.S. courts have taken a different view. The case involves a documentary sale calling for shipment from Chicago to London. The question is whether the buyer's damages for nondelivery are based on the difference between the contract price and the market price in London (the port of delivery) or the market price in Chicago (the port of shipment). Contrary to the English rule, the New York court states that since the seller's primary responsibility was to properly put the goods in the hands of the ocean carrier, the measure of damages should be calculated on the basis of the market price at the port of shipment.

## Seaver v. Lindsay Light Co.
*233 N.Y. 273, 135 N.E. 329 (1922)*
*New York Court of Appeals*

**BACKGROUND AND FACTS**
Seller and buyer entered into a CIF contract for the sale of thorium in six monthly shipments at the price of $4.00 per pound, with shipment from Chicago to London. After three shipments were made and paid for, the seller refused to ship the balance. The buyer brought this action to recover damages for breach of contract based on the difference between the contract price and the market price of thorium in London at the time of the breach.

**JUDGE McLAUGHLIN**
At the trial the sole issue was the proper measure of damages; the plaintiff contending it was the difference between the contract and market price at London dock at the time of the breach, and defendant contending it was the difference between the contract and market price at Chicago at that time.

If the former contention were correct, then plaintiff was entitled to recover $8,316, besides interest: if the latter contention were correct, then he was entitled to recover only $868.50 besides interest, the different amounts being the difference between the market price at London dock and Chicago at the time of the breach.

The trial court held that defendant's contention was correct, and thereupon gave judgment for the plaintiff in accordance therewith. Plaintiff appealed to the Appellate Division which reversed the judgment and ordered a new trial, holding that the measure of damage was as contended by plaintiff. Defendant now appeals to this court.

The meaning of the letters "CIF" in an executory contract is, and at the time the contract in question was made were, well understood in the commercial world. They mean the cost of the merchandise, insurance thereon, and freight charges to point of destination. Unless there is something in a CIF contract to indicate to the contrary, the seller completes his contract when he delivers the merchandise called for to the shipper, pays the freight thereon to point of destination, and forwards to the buyer bill of lading, invoice, insurance policy, and receipt showing payment of freight.

Where was the delivery of the thorium in the present case to be made? Was it at Chicago or at London dock? If delivery were to be made at the former place, then the measure of damage was as found by the trial court. If at London dock, then it was as found by the Appellate Division.

I am of the opinion that the trial court was right. When the correspondence and cablegrams are all construed together, as they must be, then it seems to me they clearly indicate an intention on the part of both parties that the delivery was to be made at Chicago, and when defendant delivered to a carrier at that point, paid the freight to point of destination, and forwarded the other necessary documents, he had fully completed his part of the contract. Failure to make delivery at that place obligated it to respond in damages in an amount corresponding to the difference there between the contract and market price of thorium at the time of the breach plus the cost of insurance and freight. There certainly is nothing in this contract to indicate that a delivery was to be made only at point of destination. Concededly, if the merchandise had been lost intermediate the delivery to the carrier and point of destination, the loss would have fallen upon the buyer and not upon the seller. That Chicago was to be the place of delivery seems to me not only to follow from the contract itself, but especially from that provision of it which required each shipment to be paid for in advance at Chicago. The trial court found as a fact that was the meaning and intention of the agreement. This finding is sustained by the evidence, and a finding to the contrary would be against the evidence.

Judgment reversed.

**Decision.** In a CIF contract, the damages for breach should be measured by the market price of the goods at the port of shipment on that date.

## Types of Ocean Bills of Lading

Bills of lading can take a variety of forms. The legal significance of each is important to all parties to the document.

**Clean Bills of Lading.** In addition to being a document of title, the bill of lading is also a receipt for the goods. A *clean bill* is one that contains no notations by the carrier that indicate any visible damage to the goods, packages, drums, or other containers being loaded. A bill of lading that is not clean is *foul.* Normally, this description applies only to the external appearance of the goods. For instance, leaking containers, rust on metal products, and external evidence of infestation by insects must be noted on the bill of lading. As a generally accepted practice, the bill of lading must state the condition of the goods themselves, even if they are not externally observable, if the carrier nonetheless *knows or should have known* that the goods are damaged. This type of inspection serves to protect the carrier from responsibility for *preshipment* damage. Buyers should insist that all contracts call for the seller to provide a clean bill.

A buyer who receives a clean bill still has no assurance that the goods will arrive in good condition. A clean bill of lading means only that the carrier noted no obvious or visible damage to the goods when they were loaded aboard ship. Of course, a clean bill of lading is also no guarantee as to the quality of the goods or whether the goods conform to the description in the sales contract. And it is no guarantee that the goods will not be damaged during the voyage.

**Onboard Bills of Lading.**   An *onboard bill of lading,* signed by the ship's master or other agent of the carrier, states that the goods have actually been loaded aboard a certain vessel. In most documentary sales, the buyer would want to specify that payment is conditional upon receipt of a negotiable, clean, onboard bill of lading. This document gives some assurance that the goods described in the bill of lading have actually been loaded on board and are underway to the buyer. It also insulates the exporter from loss of the goods before loading. An importer who buys an onboard bill also has an approximate idea of when the goods will arrive.

**Received-for-Shipment Bills of Lading.**   A *received-for-shipment bill of lading,* on the other hand, is issued by a carrier only upon having received goods for transport. It has limited use in cases of a time delay between the delivery of the goods to the carrier and their being loaded onboard ship. Imagine a buyer who is asked to pay for a received-for-shipment bill of lading for bananas being shipped from Honduras to the United States. The buyer has no guarantee that they won't

be sitting on the sun-parched dock for weeks waiting to be loaded. Most documentary sales contracts will require that sellers tender onboard (and clean) bills of lading. A received-for-shipment bill of lading can be converted into an onboard bill of lading by the carrier's noting the vessel name and date of loading on the face of the bill.

**Straight Bills of Lading.**   The bill of lading used in a documentary sale is negotiable. In nondocumentary sales, a nonnegotiable or *straight bill of lading* will suffice. They are used by ocean carriers only if the seller intends that the goods be delivered directly to a *consignee,* a specific person, named in the bill. The consignee may be the foreign buyer, as in the case of a sale on open account terms. It also may be the buyer's bank or customs agent. The consignee is not required to product the actual bill in order to receive delivery.

Straight bills of lading are also used when the exporter is shipping to its own agent (or subsidiary company) in the foreign country, with the expectation that the agent will make direct arrangements with the buyer for payment before the goods are turned over. As in the case of negotiable documents, the carrier may deliver only to the party named in the bill. If the carrier delivers the goods to anyone else, it will be liable for misdelivery. Straight bills do not represent transferable title to the goods and cannot, alone, be used as collateral for a loan. Thus, typically straight bills of lading are used when there is no financing involved.

## Other Types of Transport Documents

Many specialized types of transport documents are in use today. The ocean bills of lading just described are only a few of the most common. Transport documents have specific uses, depending on the type of carrier and the function the document is to perform. Many new types of transport documents have been developed because of modern shipping techniques. The following summary describes the different types of transport documents.

*http://www.silkweb.bc.ca/portview/k_6.htm*
See for a sample import/export manifest.

*http://www.silkweb.bc.ca/portview/k_8.htm*
Go here for a sample vessel container transaction.

**Air Waybills.** Most airfreight is handled through nonnegotiable *air waybills* issued by air cargo carriers (see Exhibit 6.4). The carrier will make delivery only to the consignee named in the bill. The importance of negotiability in airfreight is not as important as in ocean freight because the goods are not out of the control of the parties for long periods. The air waybill contains a mechanism by which the seller can guarantee payment, even though the sale is not a documentary sale. The air waybill can name a foreign bank as consignee and specify that the goods be held at the point of destination until payment is guaranteed by the bank or until the bank approves release to the buyer. COD services are also available.

International law applicable to air waybills is found in the *Warsaw Convention* of 1929 and in subsequent amendments. The convention is applicable to all international transportation by air of persons, baggage, or goods by commercial aircraft. The convention places limits on the liability of air carriers for injuries to air travelers and damage to cargo, and a two-year statute of limitations on the filing of claims. Because not all nations have ratified the amendments, a great deal of inconsistency among nations is apparent in the laws regarding air transportation.

**Forwarder's Bill of Lading.** Bills of lading, either straight or order, can be issued by freight forwarders. They allow claims only against the forwarder itself, not the carrier. The carrier is liable only to the forwarder who holds the carrier's bill of lading. These bills must be distinguished from forwarder's receipts that are mere acknowledgements that the forwarder has received goods for shipment. Such receipts are nonnegotiable and usually will not be accepted for payment under a draft unless specifically allowed.

**Multimodal Transport Documents.** When goods are transported by only one mode of transportation, the transport is referred to as *unimodal*. If the transport is executed by using more than one mode of transportation, the transport is *multimodal*. Multimodal transport or *combined transport operators* represent shippers whose cargo will be sent via several different carriers in one journey—truck, rail, barge, and/or ship. Multimodal transport has been made possible by new methods of containerizing freight that re-

placed "break bulk" cargo for all but the smallest shipments. The *combined transport document* is a single contract between the shipper and the operator, who, in turn, contracts with each of the carriers involved. The operators become responsible for the shipment of goods throughout the time of their transport.

## Electronic Data Interchange

There is a growing trend to replace written documents with a computer-to-computer messaging system. This practice has been referred to as *electronic data interchange* or EDI. Under this practice, trade documents such as bills of lading, letters of credit, and certificates of origin may be filed electronically at a central database.

The electronic transfer of documents has several advantages over paper-based transfers. First, it allows buyers and sellers to track goods that are in transit and enables the parties to make necessary adjustments when the goods are delayed. Second, the faster transmission of bills of lading and other documents enables the seller to obtain faster payment for goods, which in turn translates into an improved cash flow for the seller. Third, the elimination of the need to manually prepare multiple copies of documents reduces the redundancy of paperwork and improves efficiency and accuracy.

EDI however, also raises several issues. A principal concern is security. Traditionally, the buyer has been required to present an original signed bill of lading in order to receive the goods. Although the written signature requirement may be replaced by a "digital signature," such documents may not be protected against unauthorized access. Not all geographic regions have reliable telecommunication networks. Another issue is liability. Who bears responsibility for electronic transfers that are sent but not received? Who bears responsibility for unauthorized access to the documents? The answers to these questions depend on how such electronic transfers are characterized. A third obstacle to the global paperless system of trade is the lack of standardization. A particular trade document such as a bill of lading may have several different formats depending on the country and practices used. In order for a global system to work, the format of trade documents must be standardized.

**EXHIBIT 6.4   International Air Waybill**

| AIRPORT OF DEPARTURE | | | INTERNATIONAL AIR WAYBILL | | | |
|---|---|---|---|---|---|---|
| **037–**  0226 0123 | | | | **037–**  0226 0123 | | |

| SHIPPER'S NAME AND ADDRESS | SHIPPER'S ACCOUNT NUMBER | NOT NEGOTIABLE | USAIR |
|---|---|---|---|
| ABC Company 123 Elm St. Anytown, NC 12345 | | **AIR WAYBILL** (AIR CONSIGNMENT NOTE) | USAir, Inc. NATIONAL AIRPORT, WASHINGTON, D.C. 20001 |

Copies 1, 2 and 3 of this Air Waybill are originals and have the same validity.

| CONSIGNEE'S NAME AND ADDRESS | CONSIGNEE'S ACCOUNT NUMBER |
|---|---|
| XYZ Corporation 456 Wind St. Anycity, France | |

It is agreed that the goods described herein are accepted in apparent good order and condition (except as noted) for carriage SUBJECT TO THE CONDITIONS OF CONTRACT ON THE REVERSE HEREOF. THE SHIPPER'S ATTENTION IS DRAWN TO THE NOTICE CONCERNING CARRIERS' LIMITATION OF LIABILITY. Shipper may increase such limitation of liability by declaring a higher value for carriage and paying a supplemental charge if required.

TO EXPEDITE MOVEMENT, SHIPMENT MAY BE DIVERTED TO MOTOR OR OTHER CARRIER AS PER TARIFF RULE UNLESS SHIPPER GIVES OTHER INSTRUCTIONS HEREON.

| ISSUING CARRIER'S AGENT NAME AND CITY | ALSO NOTIFY NAME AND ADDRESS (OPTIONAL ACCOUNTING INFORMATION) |
|---|---|
| | Foreign Custom Broker 1001 Maple St. Anycity, France |

| AGENT'S IATA CODE | ACCOUNT NUMBER | ACCOUNTING INFORMATION | (SHIPPER CHECK ONE) |
|---|---|---|---|
| 1-5678 | | XX  AIR FREIGHT | AIR EXPRESS     COMAT |

| AIRPORT OF DEPARTURE (ADDR OF FIRST CARRIER) AND REQUESTED ROUTING |
|---|
| Charlotte |

| ROUTING AND DESTINATION | | | | | | CURRENCY | CHGS CODE | WT/VAL PPD COLL | OTHER PPD COLL | DECLARED VALUE FOR CARRIAGE | DECLARED VALUE FOR CUSTOMS |
|---|---|---|---|---|---|---|---|---|---|---|---|
| TO CDG | BY FIRST CARRIER US | | TO | BY | TO | BY | USD | | X | X | NVD | 5000 |

| AIRPORT OF DESTINATION | FOR CARRIER USE ONLY FLIGHT/DATE  FLIGHT/DATE US 815/01 | AMOUNT OF INSURANCE NIL | INSURANCE– If shipper requests insurance in accordance with conditions on reverse hereof, indicate amount to be insured in figures in box marked amount of insurance. | TC |
|---|---|---|---|---|

HANDLING INFORMATION  These commodities licensed by US for ultimate destination. Diversion contrary to US law is prohibited.

MKD:   AS Addr.   PO# 0001

| | NOTIFICATION (PERSON NOTIFIED) | BY |
|---|---|---|
| | DATE/TIME | DISPOSITION |

| NO. OF PIECES RCP | GROSS WEIGHT | Kg lb | RATE CLASS COMMODITY ITEM NO. | CHARGEABLE WEIGHT | RATE / CHARGE | TOTAL | NATURE AND QUANTITY OF GOODS (INCL. DIMENSIONS OR VOLUME) |
|---|---|---|---|---|---|---|---|
| 10 | 109 | K | | 109 | 2.10 | 228.90 | Leather aprons |

| PREPAID | WEIGHT CHARGE | COLLECT | P-UP ZONE | PICK-UP CHARGES | ORIGIN ADVANCE CHARGES | DESCRIPTION OF ORIGIN ADVANCE | ITEMS PREPAID |
|---|---|---|---|---|---|---|---|
| A. | 228.90 | | B. | 25.00 | K. | | |
| VALUATION CHARGE D. | | | DEL. ZONE C. | | DEST. ADVANCE CHARGES L. | DESCRIPTION OF DESTINATION ADVANCE | ITEMS COLLECT |
| TAX I. | | | SHIPPER'S R.F.C. (AMOUNT TO BE ENTERED BY SHIPPER) J. | | OTHER CHARGES AND DESCRIPTION F. | | |

| TOTAL OTHER CHARGES DUE AGENT |
|---|
| 58.00 |

SHIPPER CERTIFIES THAT THE PARTICULARS ON THE FACE HEREOF ARE CORRECT AND THAT INSOFAR AS ANY PART OF THE CONSIGNMENT CONTAINS RESTRICTED ARTICLES, SUCH PART IS PROPERLY DESCRIBED BY NAME AND IS IN PROPER CONDITION FOR CARRIAGE BY AIR ACCORDING TO APPLICABLE NATIONAL GOVERNMENT REGULATIONS, AND FOR INTERNATIONAL SHIPMENTS THE CURRENT INTERNATIONAL AIR TRANSPORT ASSOCIATION'S RESTRICTED ARTICLES REGULATIONS.

| TOTAL OTHER CHARGES DUE CARRIER |
|---|
| 10.00 |

SIGNATURE OF SHIPPER OR HIS AGENT

| I. COD | CURRENCY | EXECUTED ON |
|---|---|---|

| TOTAL PREPAID | TOTAL COLLECT |
|---|---|
| | 296.00 |

(Date)   (Time)   at   (Place)   SIGNATURE OF ISSUING CARRIER OR ITS AGENT

| CURRENCY CONVERSION RATES | TOTAL COLLECT IN DEST. CURRENCY |
|---|---|

CARRIER CERTIFIES GOODS DESCRIBED ABOVE WERE RECEIVED FOR CARRIAGE SUBJECT TO THE CONDITIONS ON THE REVERSE HEREOF, THE GOODS THEN BEING IN APPARENT GOOD ORDER AND CONDITION EXCEPT AS NOTED HEREON.

| FOR CARRIERS USE ONLY AT DESTINATION | CHARGES AT DESTINATION | TOTAL COLLECT CHARGES | **037–**  0226 0123 |
|---|---|---|---|

(ALL COLLECT CHARGES IN DESTINATION CURRENCY)

In 1996 a group of business leaders formed the Bolero project in order to develop a cross industry platform for the world-wide electronic transfer of commercial trade information. The following article discusses how the Bolero system will be used to facilitate international trade at different levels.

*Foreign Accents*

# The Bolero Project

### What Is the Bolero Project?

The Bolero Project is a cross-industry system for the electronic transfer of commercial trade information worldwide. Bolero will provide a platform for users to store and exchange electronic trade documents in a secure manner. The service will be governed by a multilateral contract called the Rule Book which specifies the rights and responsibilities of Bolero and its users. Today, commercial trade information—the documents necessary for business to be conducted—is largely paper based. This adds considerable costs to the trade cycle and has prevented the introduction of re-engineered processes and new services. By moving from paper to electronics, through Bolero, all participants in the trade cycle stand to reap significant benefits.

The system is not intended to change existing business relationships, nor to endorse the integrity of any specific trading parties or groups of trading parties. Establishing and maintaining business relationships will remain at the discretion of those involved. Similarly, the system is not intended to mandate a specific way of doing business, but to enable a variety of options. The system will not own the data it holds. Ownership of data is determined by the Rule Book. Documents will retain their integrity as no manipulation of data will be carried out by the system.

### Who Will Use the System and How Will They Benefit?
#### Users and Global Benefits
Bolero will offer a secure, single window of communication to the whole trade community: importers and exporters, as well as carriers, customs authorities, banks and freight forwarders.

Customers of 'Bolero capable' logistics and financial services suppliers will see fewer document-caused delays in the shipment of goods and associated payments. Integrating the full trade information flow will yield inventory reduction and bring administrative efficiencies. These improvements may be felt in all parts of a corporation: purchasing, inventory, accounting, sales, manufacturing and treasury.

### Importers and Exporters
EDI is already possible. Bolero adds the ability to move documents of title along with other trade documents, whether they be EDI or image or other. This will bring significant improvements particularly in cases where decisions require clusters of documents, like customs clearance and cargo release. Even just for documents of title such as the bill of lading, the incremental efficiencies are enormous. The main benefits of Bolero to importers and exporters will appear in the following areas:

- Improved supply chain management—Bolero will inhibit fraud and reduce delays caused by discrepancies in paper processing. With greater certainty of delivery, corporations will be better able to achieve 'just in time' processing. Bolero also will provide reductions in order processing time.
- Reduced occurrence of fraud—By using Bolero for the exchange of new 'virtual' documents of title, the potential for fraud arising from paper based counterfeit documents is reduced.
- Better cash management—Faster payment of sellers will be possible as the time taken to relay and manage paper documents is reduced.
- Greater control over goods traded in transit—Bolero will enable goods to be bought and sold during transit through the provision of a secure virtual registry where ownership of documents of title can be exchanged.

*(continued)*

*(continued)*

### Carriers and Freight Forwarders

- Operational benefits—With significant over-capacity and shrinking margins, cost control in the transport industry is paramount. Typical paper-based logistics administration involves expensive document relay costs, reduced opportunities for automation and scope for the fraudulent presentation of false documents. Bolero with its secure, single window interface to all users, will provide a universal solution to assist with these problems.
- Improved value added services—Logistics companies that have already automated their systems will get more from their investments by extending their current connectivity and functionality. These systems are expensive to develop and maintain, and large carriers and freight forwarders will use Bolero as a backbone on which to add value through differentiated services and customised 'front end' applications.
- Improved tracking of goods—Bolero's global cross market connectivity will enrich existing tracking systems owned by the carrier shipment sector and enable them to provide new information services to shippers addressing the status of virtual documents.
- Improved tracking of documents—Bolero will uniquely assist freight forwarders by offering a global electronic standard for the exchange of shipment data. This will facilitate the automated capture and manipulation of consignment data throughout the transport chain.

### Customs and Government Agencies

The challenges facing customs authorities today are the handling of growing volumes of trade internationally, and the pressure from governments on budgets to fund customs departments. Many countries are looking to electronic means for submitting customs documentation to reduce fraud, accelerate processing and reduce costs.

Bolero will provide single window connectivity reaching all parties in the trade chain on both a national and international basis. This, combined with a shared security standard, will assist the global customs community in the acquisition and exchange of electronic customs information. The Bolero system will also provide users with the ability to send documents to customs authorities to receive an authorisation or endorsement. Along with electronic document authorisation, Bolero will provide functionality allowing the addition of physical stamps to paper documents and their return as authorised images.

### Port Authorities and Terminal Operators

Bolero offers a global standard for document exchange which will be acceptable across markets on a global basis. With universal acceptance it will support the evolution and enhancement of existing and future port and terminal schemes around the world.

Using state of the art security, Bolero will reduce fraudulent presentations of counterfeit documentation at the dockside. It will also reduce the incidence of goods being held by ports owing to document discrepancy or delayed delivery.

The Bolero international standard for secure document exchange will provide a neutral sales channel through which existing proprietary port systems may promote their applications to regional distribution hubs and feeder links.

Edited and reprinted with permission of Bolero Association Limited, 1 Gainsford Street, LondonSE1 2NE, U.K.

## Shipping Terms and the Risk of Loss

The *shipping terms* in a sales contract are those provisions that define the seller's and buyer's responsibilities for making the shipping arrangements, paying transportation charges, procuring insurance on the goods, paying port charges, and bearing the risk that the goods may be lost or damaged in transit. In contract negotiations, the parties often consider these terms as important as the quality of the merchandise or its price. Indeed, the shipping terms are integral to the price term itself. Because of the risks of international trade and the high cost of air and ocean freight, a contract price without shipping terms is nearly meaningless. If the parties cannot reach agreement on the shipping terms, the entire deal may fail.

## Allocating the Risk of Loss

The parties to a contract must know when they are responsible for damage or loss to goods and when they are not. Clearly, the seller is responsible if the goods are destroyed by fire during production at the seller's plant. Likewise, if the goods are destroyed after they have been moved into the buyer's warehouse, then the buyer is responsible. But when does the risk pass from one party to the other? In some countries, including the United Kingdom, the party who bears the risk of loss is the party who has "title" to the goods—the party who owns them at that moment. However, since the document of title does not move physically with the goods, a determination of who owned the goods at the exact time of their destruction is often difficult. This "title" method was employed in the United States until the adoption of the Uniform Commercial Code.

Ideally, the seller wants to be free of the risk of loss as soon as the goods leave the back door. The buyer would like to delay it for as long as possible. The ability to negotiate, of course, stems from the relative bargaining position of the parties. If the seller's products contain superior technology, or if they are commodities in short supply, or patented products that the buyer needs, then the seller may be in a stronger position to shift the risk to the buyer. Similarly, if the buyer is in a dominant economic position, such as by being able to order in large quantities, the buyer may be able to dictate the terms of the contract. For example, the owner of a rare 1927 Rolls Royce in London may say to a U.S. buyer, "You may purchase my Rolls in London and drive it away, but if you want it shipped to you, you must bear all the risks of the journey from the moment it leaves my door."

Buyer and seller are always free to decide in their contract when the risk of loss will pass from one to the other. But if the parties fail to do so, and a dispute arises, the courts will be forced to decide on the basis of whether the contract is of the shipment type or of the destination type.

**Destination Contracts.** The question of whether a contract is a shipment or a destination contract will be determined by how the responsibilities of the parties are defined: Who has responsibility for shipping or transporting the goods? Who is paying the freight charges? By what means will the buyer remit payment? If the contract calls for the seller to deliver the goods to a particular destination, such as the buyer's city or place of business, the contract is a *destination contract.* Under the UCC §2-509 (see appendix), the risk of loss in a destination contract passes to the buyer when the goods are tendered to the buyer at the point of destination.

**Shipment Contracts.** If the contract calls for the seller to ship the goods by carrier, but does not require the seller to deliver the goods to a named place, then it is a *shipment contract.* In a shipment contract the risk of loss or damage to the goods passes to the buyer when the goods are given to the first carrier—be it truck, airline, or ocean carrier. Shipment contracts are more common in international trade. Where parties fail to specify who will bear the risk of loss, courts look to the language of the contract and to the totality of responsibilities of the parties to determine whether they have entered into a shipment or a destination contract.

## The Risk of Loss in International Sales under the CISG

The *Convention on Contracts for the International Sale of Goods* (CISG) contains provisions that allocate the risk of loss in Articles 66–70, reproduced in the appendix. Like the UCC, CISG provisions apply only if the parties do not specify by agreement when the risk shifts from seller to buyer. Article 67 applies to sales in which the goods will be transported by carrier. If the contract calls for the goods to be *handed over to a carrier at a particular place,* then the risk passes to the buyer at that place. However, if the seller is simply expected to ship, but not bound to hand over the goods *at a particular place,* the risk passes to the buyer when the goods are *handed over to the first carrier* for shipment to the buyer. For instance, assume that a company located in Boone, North Carolina, confirms an order for the export of its product to a foreign customer. The contract reads simply that "Seller will handle all transportation charges and arrangements." The seller arranges for a trucking company to pick up the goods and deliver them to the air carrier's terminal at the Charlotte airport, 100 miles away. The risk of loss will pass from seller to buyer when the goods are first handed over to the trucking company at the seller's factory or warehouse in Boone. If the goods are damaged from that point forth, on land or in the air (or sea, in the case of ocean shipment), the loss falls on the buyer. Of course, the seller is responsible for properly packaging and preparing the merchandise for shipment. The buyer would be relieved from any obligation to pay for the goods if the loss was due to an act or omission of the seller (see Article 66).

> **http://www.cisg.law.pace.edu/cisg/text/ cisg-toc.html**
> *The site of the contents page of the CISG. Choose Articles 66–70 for the text on risk of loss.*

**Allocating the Risk of Loss by Contract.** In most cases, the parties to a business contract will want to decide between themselves when the risk of loss passes, and will not want to risk the uncertainty of litigation. While they can do this by spelling out their intentions exactly—"This is a shipment contract"—businesspeople generally rely on the use of abbreviated symbols, or trade terms, in the contract to allocate the risk of loss. A *trade term* is a shorthand method of expressing their agreement on the risk of loss and other shipping terms as well. The UCC defines several commonly used trade terms, but the CISG does not. Here are a few examples:

- *UCC Trade Terms for Shipment Contracts. FOB (place of shipment).* Seller is located in Boone, North Carolina. A contract term *FOB Boone, North Carolina,* requires the seller to put the goods in the possession of a carrier in Boone, and to make a contract for their transportation to the buyer. The buyer will become responsible for the goods once they are picked up by the carrier in Boone [UCC 2-319(1); 2-504].

- *CIF (place of destination).* Seller is located in the United States and is shipping by ocean. A contract term *CIF Port of Liverpool* requires the seller to bear the expense and risk of putting the goods into the possession of a car-

rier at the port for shipment and obtaining a negotiable bill of lading covering the transportation to a named destination. The buyer becomes responsible for the goods once they are delivered to the carrier at the U.S. port of shipment. The designation of the place of destination in this trade term does not render it a destination contract, however (UCC 2-320).

- *UCC Trade Terms for Destination Contracts. FOB (place of destination).* A contract term *FOB Foreign Port* (to be named by buyer) requires the seller to bear the expense of transporting the goods to the named port and tendering delivery of the goods to the buyer there. The seller is not relieved of the risk of loss until that time (UCC 2-320). The seller's *tender of delivery* is complete when the seller holds conforming goods at the buyer's disposition and gives the buyer notification reasonably necessary to enable the buyer to take delivery [UCC 2-503(1)].

The meaning or definition of a trade term does not have to be left to statute. The parties—and in the event of a dispute, the courts—can look to a number of other sources for defining trade terms in an international sales contract.

> **http://www.rolandfreight.com/index.htm**
> *The site of an international freight services company. From the contents, select information on countries served, ocean and airfreight, import customs clearance, and many other detailed topics.*

## Freight and Transportation Charges

A buyer and seller must do more than merely agree on a price for the goods; they must also agree on who is going to pay the transportation charges. For the price quoted, will the seller deliver the goods to the buyer, or will the seller also put them aboard a ship, or just make them available to a common carrier at the factory door? For instance, a seller might say, "This is the price if you come to my factory and pick up the goods. If you want me to pay to get them to the seaport in my country, or even across the ocean to your country, I will; but this is what the price of the goods will be then." Moreover, the seller also has an opportunity to negotiate the passing of the risk of loss. Seller may say, "I'll be glad to ship these to you in the United States, and I'll arrange their carriage on the SS *Anna Star,* freight prepaid, but you must bear the risk of loss from the moment the goods are loaded on board."

A seller will frequently present a proposal to a buyer offering a choice of shipping terms. For instance, one proposal may show a price with ocean freight, another without. These choices provide the buyer with a breakdown of the costs and responsibility for those costs within the transaction. Buyers who have an itemized breakdown of the various transportation, handling, and insurance charges from the seller can compare those with the costs of making the shipping arrangements themselves. The document prepared by the seller and sent to the buyer that shows the description of the goods and a breakdown of the charges is called a pro forma invoice (see Chapter Five). Furthermore, transportation costs are needed if the buyer is comparing price quotations on similar goods from two different foreign suppliers. A buyer who requests all suppliers to quote prices on the same terms is able to compare "apples to apples."

A party to a contract doesn't negotiate shipping terms only on the basis of cost or the passing of the risk of loss. Sales decisions are more likely to be based on how these terms fit into a buyer's overall business needs. A buyer who imports regularly may have buying agents in the seller's country who can handle the details of moving the goods. Similarly, some buyers may take full responsibilities for chartering their own ships, as in the case of a country making a large purchase of grain for its own population. They may want the grain made available to them alongside their ship, and they will pay all expenses and bear all risks from that point. In many cases, a seller that maintains a warehouse in the buyer's country will price the goods for pickup there.

Unless a seller is in such a dominant position in the market that it can dictate terms, it may want to offer more flexible shipping terms in order to land a contract. Even if one seller offers a lower price, a competitor with better shipping terms may get the order. The buyer may be inexperienced at moving cargo, or may just not want to be bothered dealing with cargo in the seller's country. For instance, imagine a Japanese buyer who attends a trade fair in New York and concludes a contract with a company from Boone, North Carolina. The buyer may not want to bother with getting the goods from "the Boonedocks" to a U.S. seaport and then on to Japan. The buyer may just want the best price for the goods delivered and unloaded from a ship at a Japanese seaport nearest the buyer's factory.

## Trade Terms

Shipping terms, as with other terms of sale, are often drafted into contracts in detail by experienced attorneys. However, many sales contracts use trade terms as a shorthand method of expressing shipping terms as well as allocating the risk of loss. Trade terms are usually expressed in the form of abbreviated symbols, such as FOB or CIF. They permit the parties to express their agreement quickly, with little confusion, and with few language problems. If the parties use a trade term in their contract, they must define it. If it is not defined in the contract, a court would have to look to the applicable law, such as the UCC, for its interpretation. The most common method of defining trade terms, however, is to incorporate them into the contract by reference to some independent source or publication. One source for trade terms, used by a declining number of American exporters, is the *Revised American Foreign Trade Definitions of 1941;* however, these are generally not accepted in other parts of the world.

## International Rules for the Interpretation of Trade Terms

The most important set of trade term definitions are the *International Rules for the Interpretation of Trade Terms,* or *Incoterms* (1990), published by the Paris-based *International Chamber of Commerce.*[2] These definitions have the support of important business groups, including manufacturing, shipping, and banking industries worldwide. First published in 1936, the newest revision was released in 1990. The new terms accommodate the changes in airfreight, modern multimodal shipping, containerized cargo, and electronic data interchange.

*Incoterms* include approximately thirteen trade terms (more with the variations). They are classified into four groups—E, F, C, and D—according to the relative responsibilities of each party and to the point at which the risk of loss passes from seller to buyer. The terms are grouped and explained in Exhibit 6.5. (Consult the appendix for more complete definitions.) Exhibit 6.5 arranges the terms with the minimum responsibility of the seller and the maximum responsibility of the buyer appearing at the top; the minimum responsibility of the buyer and maximum responsibility of the seller appearing at the bottom. International sales people, export managers, and world traders benefit from a working knowledge of these terms. *Incoterms* are not automatically part of a contract for the sale of goods. To ensure that the *Incoterms* definitions will be applied to their contract, parties should include a clause such as "This contract is to be interpreted in accordance with *Incoterms*."

The following section looks at some hypothetical illustrations to see how these terms are used. Keep in mind that the terms represent years of work by their authors to reflect how companies actually do business. Selecting a term for incorporation in a contract is more than just bargaining over who will pay freight costs or bear the risk of loss. Certain terms may fit better with the needs of the parties. Some are suited for ocean carriage, some for airfreight, or cases in which the seller will use many modes of transport—truck to a railhead, rail to the port, and finally an ocean voyage—known as *multimodal transport.* Some terms are suited for a documentary form of payment; others are suited to open account payment terms. Be sure to study Exhibit 6.5 on pp. 208–209 before reading the following summary.

---

*http://www.iccwbo.org/Comm/comm.html*
*The site of the International Chamber of Commerce, with information on global business issues such as Advertising and Marketing, Arbitration, Commercial Crime, Extortion and Bribery, Intellectual Property, International Trade, and many others.*

---

**"E" Terms.**  *E Terms* represent the least amount of responsibility for the seller. In the following hypothetical situation, assume a buyer in the Netherlands is placing an order with a supplier in Albany, New York. The buyer states that its U.S.

subsidiary will pick up the goods at the Albany plant and arrange export. Therefore, the seller would probably quote its price in terms *EXW Albany factory.* Under this term, the seller need only make the goods available at its factory (or mill, farm, warehouse, or other place of business) and present the buyer with an invoice for payment. The buyer must arrange all transportation and bear all risks and expenses of the journey from that point. The buyer would also have to clear the goods for export by obtaining export licenses from the U.S. government. This term is most often used when the buyer will pick up the goods by truck or rail. Therefore, for international shipments, EXW terms are common in Europe where goods frequently move across national boundaries by ground transportation. This term is likely to become more popular in trade among Canada, the United States, and Mexico in the future. But unless this term has been requested by the buyer, use of it may show that the seller is not really interested in exporting and is unwilling to accommodate a foreign buyer.

**"F" Terms.**  The *F terms* are shipment contracts similar to those studied earlier. Under F terms the seller is required to deliver the goods to the designated point of departure "free" of expense or risk to the buyer. At that point the risk of loss passes from seller to buyer. The buyer arranges the transportation and pays all freight costs. However, if it is convenient and the parties agree, the seller may pay the freight and add that amount to the invoice price already quoted. F terms are often used when the buyer has contracted for a complete shipload of materials or commodities and thus had reason to assume the responsibility for arranging carriage. F terms may also be used because the buyer feels that it can obtain better freight rates than the seller. Some F terms are for ocean shipment only. Others can be used for all modes of transport.

Assume that the buyer in the Netherlands wants to arrange its own ocean transportation. The seller in Albany would like to deliver the goods to a carrier near it, for transportation to the Port of New York, so different forms of transportation will be required. For instance, the seller might deliver the goods to a barge hauler for a trip down the Hudson, or to a railroad or trucking company. The seller may want to hand over the goods to a multimodal terminal operator nearby and let it handle goods from there. This inland carrier will then transport the goods to the Port of New York for shipment to the foreign destination. If this inland carrier is in Albany, then the seller should quote prices *FCA Albany*. Here, for the contract price, the seller bears the costs and assumes all risks of getting the goods from its factory to the carrier or terminal in Albany. The seller then has the responsibility to obtain any government export licenses that are required. This term could also be used for airfreight. A term *FCA JFK Airport* means that the seller has agreed, for the contract price, to deliver the goods from Albany to the airline in New York for shipment.

Assume now that the Dutch buyer is purchasing a bulk cargo, such as agricultural commodities, and will be chartering a full ship for the overseas voyage—*a voyage charter*—departing from New York to Rotterdam. The buyer may find the voyage charter more convenient and cheaper to arrange than leaving the shipping up to the seller. The buyer would like the seller to place the goods on barges or on the pier alongside the ship, *Queen Anna E,* docked at the Port of New York. The appropriate contract terms would be *FAS Queen Anna E.* (If the name of the vessel is not yet known, the parties can contract on terms *FAS New York.*) The risk of loss passes from seller to buyer at the time the goods are placed alongside the ship. The buyer, having arranged the ocean transport, will pay the separate costs of loading and obtain necessary export licenses from the U.S. government. An FAS buyer should also provide the seller with notice of the ship's departure date and loading times. The seller's obligation is to place the goods alongside the vessel within the time called for in the contract.

Under FOB (free on board) contracts, the seller bears slightly more responsibility. In addition to obtaining export clearance, the seller is required to place the goods aboard the ship. Risk of loss passes to the buyer only when the goods cross the ship's rail. Therefore, if the contract were on terms *FOB New York* or *FOB Queen Anne E*, the seller would be required to secure export licenses, pay all costs of loading and deliver the goods over the ship's rail. Notice that the

seller's FOB responsibility under *Incoterms* differs from their responsibility under the UCC. Under the UCC, the FOB seller is only required to place the goods *in possession of the carrier,* while under *Incoterms*, the seller's responsibility does not end until the goods have actually passed the ship's rail. Therefore, it is critical for the parties to specify which set of definitions should govern the contract. Exporters should also be careful to use the FOB term as a shipment contract, because using it in conjunction with a destination location (e.g. *FOB Rotterdam*) would contradict the *Incoterms* definition and would shift the risk of the voyage to the exporter. Consider the *Knitwear* case on p. 210, in which the seller argues that the FOB trade term should be given a different meaning from what is provided in the UCC.

**"C" Terms.** *C terms* are also shipment contracts. The letter *C* indicates that the seller is responsible for certain costs after the goods have been delivered to the carrier. Like the FOB term, however, risk of loss passes to the buyer when the goods cross the ship's rail at the point of shipment. Assume that our Dutch buyer requests pricing information from Albany. As an experienced exporter, the seller might understand that the buyer has little interest in arranging transportation, let alone coming to pick up the goods. The buyer simply wants the goods delivered to the port of entry in its country closest to its company. If ocean shipment is required the seller will prepare a price quotation *CFR Port of Rotterdam* (formerly called *C & F*) or *CIF Port of Rotterdam.* For the price quoted the seller will deliver the goods to an ocean carrier, arrange shipment, prepay the freight charges to the agreed upon port of destination, obtain a clean, onboard bill of lading marked *freight prepaid,* and forward it along with the invoice to the buyer for payment.

The only difference between CFR and CIF terms, is that under CIF terms the seller must also procure and forward to the buyer a policy of marine insurance to cover the risk of loss once it passes to the buyer. (This amount is the minimum coverage; the buyer may want to request additional insurance be purchased for its own protection.) By providing both carriage and insurance coverage, the seller is able to earn additional profit

**EXHIBIT 6.5  Explanation of *Incoterms* INTERNATIONAL RULES FOR THE INTERPRETATION OF TRADE TERMS, 1990**

| Group and Type | Term Abbreviation/In Full | Mode of Transportation | Seller's Responsibilities* | Buyer's Responsibilities* | Passage of Risk |
|---|---|---|---|---|---|
| E Group | EXW *Ex Works* (works: mill, factory, mine, warehouse, etc.) | Up to buyer (all modes) | Have the goods ready for pickup at the location specified in the contract, usually seller's place of business. | Provide vehicle or rail car and load goods. Obtain export licenses. Enter goods thru customs. | When the goods are made available by seller at named location. |
| F Group *Shipment Contract* | FCA *Free Carrier* (named place) | Ocean, air, truck, rail, or multimodal (all) | Place the goods in the hands of a carrier (usually inland) named by the buyer at the place specified. Provide export license. | Choose carrier, arrange transport, and pay freight charges. On arrival, enter goods thru customs. | When the goods are delivered to the carrier or terminal operator at the named place of shipment. |
| | FAS *Free Alongside Ship* (named port of shipment) | Ocean only | Place the goods alongside the ship specified by the buyer (on the dock or barge) within the time called for in the contract, ready for loading. | Choose ocean carrier, arrange transport and pay freight. Obtain export license. Enter goods thru customs. | When the goods are delivered alongside the ship specified by buyer. |
| | FOB *Free on Board* (named port of shipment) | Ocean only | Load the goods on board the ship specified by the buyer within the time called for in the contract. Pay costs of loading. Obtain export license. | Choose ocean carrier and pay freight charges. Enter goods thru customs. | When the goods cross the ship's rail at port of shipment. |
| C. Group *Shipment Contract* | CFR *Cost and Freight* (named port of destination) | Ocean only | Contract for transport and pay freight charges to the named port of destination. Arrange for loading goods on board ship, usually at seller's choice, and pay costs of loading. Obtain export license. Notify buyer of shipment. Documentary sale is assumed. Tender documents to buyer. | Purchase document of title and take delivery from ocean carrier. No date of delivery at buyer's port is implied. Pay import duties. Enter goods thru customs. | When the goods cross the ship's rail at port of shipment. Buyer must procure own insurance or else use CIF term. |
| | CIF *Cost, Insurance and Freight* (named port of destination) | Ocean only | Same as CFR, with added requirement that seller purchase marine insurance in amount of invoice price plus 10%. Insurance policy is assigned to buyer. Documentary sale is assumed. | Same as CFR, except seller supplies insurance. Buyer may ask for additional insurance coverage at own expense. | When the goods cross ship's rail at port of shipment. If damage or loss, buyer files claim for insurance. |
| | CPT *Carriage Paid To* (named place of destination) | Ocean, air, truck, rail, or multimodal (all) | Similar to CFR, but for all modes of transport. Deliver goods to truck, rail or multimodal carrier, or to ship, and arrange for transport to destination. Freight charges prepaid. Obtain export license. Notify buyer of shipment. Seller need not insure goods. Documentary sale is assumed. | Similar to CFR. Purchase document of title and take delivery of goods from carrier. Enter goods thru customs. Pay import duties. | When goods are delivered by the seller to the first carrier. Buyer must procure own insurance or use CIP term. |

| Term | Mode of transport | Seller's duties | Buyer's duties | Transfer of risk |
|---|---|---|---|---|
| **CIP** *Carriage and Insurance Paid To* (named place of destination) | Ocean, air, truck, rail, or multimodal (all) | Same as CPT, with added requirement that seller purchase policy of marine insurance in amount of invoice plus 10%. Insurance policy assigned to buyer. | Same ast CPT. Purchase document of title and take delivery of goods from carrier. Enter goods thru customs. Pay import duties. | When goods are delivered by the seller to the first carrier. If damage or loss, buyer files claim for insurance. |
| **D Group** *Destination Contract* | | | | |
| **DAF** *Delivered at Frontier* (named place) | Usually for int'l. rail shipments (can be used for all modes) | Contract for transport and pay freight expenses to the "frontier" point in the country of importation. Buyer clears goods for import by customs authorities. | Pay freight charges from frontier point. Enter goods thru customs. Pay import duties. | When the goods are ready to be handed over to the buyer at the named (frontier point) in buyer's country. |
| **DES** *Delivered Ex Ship* (named port of destination) | Ocean (often used when ship is chartered by seller) | Arrange transport and pay all freight charges to port of foreign destination. Notify buyer of expected arrival date. Place goods at disposal of buyer aboard ship within time called for in contract. | Arrange and pay cost of unloading goods from ship and land transport. Enter goods thru customs. | When the goods are ready for unloading by the buyer at port of destination. |
| **DEQ (d/u)** *Delivered Ex Quay, duty unpaid* (named port of destination) | Ocean | Contract for transport and pay freight charges to put the goods on the quay (dock) beside the ship at specified port of destination. Notify buyer of arrival date. May be used for documentary sale. | Take delivery of goods at dock and enter goods thru customs. Pay import duties. Arrange land transport to buyer's place of business. | When the goods are placed on the dock or in terminal. Seller should insure goods for own protection. |
| **DEQ(d/p)** *Delivered Ex Quay, duty paid* (named port of distination) | Ocean | Same as DEQ (d/u) except seller pays import duties and enters goods thru customs. May be used for documentary sale by seller tendering transport document or warehouse receipt for payment. | Take delivery of goods after they have cleared customs. Arrange land transport to buyer's place of business. | When goods are placed on dock or in terminal. Seller should insure for own protection. |
| **DDU** *Delivery Duty Unpaid* (named place of destination) | Ocean, air, truck, rail, or multimodal (all) | Similar to DEQ, except used for all modes of transport. Seller usually contracts for carriage to inland port of entry in importing country. May be used for documentary sale. | Purchase document of title if required. Take delivery at specified location and enter goods thru customs. Pay import duties. | When goods are delivered at location specified. Seller should insure for own protection. |
| **DDP** *Delivery Duty Paid* (named place of destination) | Ocean, air, truck, rail, or multimodal (all) | Same as DDU, except that seller obtains import licenses, pays import duties, and clears goods thru customs. Place of destination specified is usually buyer's place of business. | Purchase document of title if required. Take delivery of goods at specified location. | When the goods are delivered to buyer at specified location. Seller should insure for own protection. |

*In all cases, seller is required to provide goods in conformance with contract; buyer is to pay invoice according to contract. Time for shipment or delivery is determined by contract. Trade term must be stated in contract and reference made therein to *Incoterms 1990* in order for these definitions to apply.

*A.M. Knitwear v. All
America Export-Import,*
41 N.Y.2d 14 (1976)
*Court of Appeals of New York*

## BACKGROUND AND FACTS

All America Export-Import ordered several thousand pounds of yarn from the seller, A.M. Knitwear. All America used its own purchase order form on which it stated "Pick Up from your Plant to Moore-McCormak [sic] for shipment to Santos, Brazil." In the price column, All America typed "FOB PLANT PER LB $1.35," but the place where FOB terms were to be entered was left blank. The seller loaded the goods into the container provided by the buyer and then notified it that the loading had been completed. The buyer advised its freight forwarder to pick up the container and deliver it to the Moore-McCormack pier. That evening, a driver arrived at the seller's place of business, signed a bill of lading, and drove off with the container. Shortly thereafter, the buyer's freight forwarder arrived to pick up the container, at which point it was determined that the first driver was a thief. The buyer stopped payment of the check.

COOKE, JUDGE

Although the seller contends that the FOB term on the buyer's form did not have its ordinary meaning, the Uniform Commercial Code provides that, unless otherwise agreed, the term FOB at a named place "even though used only in connection with the stated price, is a delivery term." Where the term FOB the place of shipment is used, as in this case with the term FOB plant, the code provides that the seller must ship the goods in the manner provided in section 2-504 of the Uniform Commercial Code and "bear the expense and risk of putting them into the possession of the carrier." . . .

Despite the provisions of the code which place the risk of loss on the seller in the FOB place of shipment contract until the goods are delivered to the carrier, here the seller contends that the parties "otherwise agreed" so that pursuant to its agreement, the risk of loss passed from the seller to the buyer at the time and place at which the seller completed physical delivery of the subject goods into the container supplied by the buyer for that purpose. In support of this contention, the seller alleges that the language of the purchase order "Pick Up from your Plant" is a specific delivery instruction and that the language "FOB PLANT PER LB. $1.35", which appears in the price column, is a price term and not a delivery term. Further support of the seller's contention is taken from the fact that

the space provided in the buyer's own purchase order form for an FOB delivery instruction was left blank by the buyer. Thus, the seller contends its agreement with the buyer imposed no obligation on it to make delivery of the loaded container to the carrier.

As often happens in commercial transactions, the parties to this action did not prepare an extensive written agreement, but merely made an arrangement that, under normal circumstances, would have been entirely satisfactory. The intervention of a wrongdoer who stole the goods that were the subject of the agreement forces the court to determine who should bear the loss resulting from the theft. In this respect, although the seller argues that only to the extent that the agreement is silent should the code apply, it should be noted that the underlying purpose and policy of the code is "to simplify, clarify and modernize the law governing commercial transactions." To this end, the code provides a framework for analyzing a variety of commercial transactions.

The seller's contention, that the parties intended the FOB term as a price term and not a delivery term, conflicts with the code provision that states that the FOB term is a delivery term "even though used only in connection with the stated price." That the FOB term was not inserted in the space provided for such an expression in the buyer's own purchase order form does not require a determination that the FOB term was intended as a price term, since the drafters of the code recognized that the term FOB will often be used in connection with the stated price . . .

The term "FOB PLANT" is well understood to require delivery to the carrier and does not imply any other meaning. If a contrary meaning was intended, an express statement varying the ordinary meaning is required. . . . To allow a commonly used term such as FOB to be varied in meaning without an express statement of the parties of an intent to do so would not serve [the purpose of the code].

**Decision.** The judgment for the buyer was affirmed. The court held that the meaning of a trade term will be interpreted according to the UCC unless expressly stated otherwise. Under the UCC definition of an FOB contract, risk of loss does not pass to the buyer until the goods are delivered to the carrier.

yet retain its rights in the goods until payment is made against documents. Upon presentation of the bill of lading, the Dutch buyer is required to make payment, but once it receives the bill of lading, it can resell the goods, or if the goods are lost, it is entitled to collect the insurance money. However, both *Incoterms* and maritime practice seem to indicate that, *if the seller desires,* it may forego its right to collect on the documents and negotiate the bill of lading directly to the buyer and make other arrangements for payment or credit.

If the seller intends to arrange ocean transportation, but will be delivering the goods to a road or rail carrier, inland waterway, or to a multimodal terminal operator for transit to the seaport, the seller may wish to quote *CPT, Port of Rotterdam.* Here, the risk of loss shifts to the buyer when the goods are delivered to the first carrier. CIP terms are the same as under CPT, with the added requirement that the seller procure insurance to cover the buyer's risk of loss.

**"D" Terms.** Contracts with *D terms* of sale are destination contracts. If the seller in Albany is willing to enter into a destination contract, then it must be willing to accept far greater responsibility than under any other terms. For the price stated in the contract, the seller must not only deliver the goods at the port of destination, but bear the risk of loss throughout the journey. Thus if the goods are lost in transit, the Dutch buyer would not be entitled to claim the insurance money although the buyer may have lost profits it was hoping to make on the goods.

DES and DEQ are destination terms used for ocean cargo. If the contract terms are *DES Rotterdam,* the seller must pay the ocean freight to Rotterdam, but the buyer pays the unloading charges at the Rotterdam terminal. Under *DEQ duty unpaid, Rotterdam,* the seller will pay the ocean freight and pay the unloading charges to place the goods on the *quay* (pronounced "kee," meaning the dock or wharf) in Rotterdam. Under *DEQ duty paid, Rotterdam,* the seller will pay the ocean freight and the unloading charges, obtain import licenses from the government of the Netherlands, and pay the import duties and taxes at the port of entry. DES and DEQ terms are commonly used with open account payment terms, although the seller may tender a negotiable bill of lading accompanied by all necessary documents to clear the goods through Dutch customs. Clearly, the seller will not want to take on the responsibility and risks of a DEQ shipment unless it is experienced in importing into the Netherlands and familiar with customs regulations and tariff laws there.

Today, destination contracts are actually becoming increasingly popular due to an increasingly competitive and globalized marketplace. Many manufacturers and other shippers find they must do more and more to win and keep customers. In other words, shippers often have to provide credit terms to their customers by shipping on open account and giving the customer time to pay. Shippers are also being forced to take greater responsibility for getting the goods into the customer's hands. For these reasons, more and more shippers are quoting prices on D terms than ever before. Still others are quoting prices on C terms to shift the risk of the voyage, but voluntarily foregoing the documentary collection and sending the bill of lading directly to the customer for payment on open account.

> **http://itl.irv.uit.no/trade_law/documents/
> sales/incoterms/nav/inc.html**
> *See for more on Incoterms.*

## Modification of Trade Terms

On occasion, the parties may be tempted to alter the meaning of a trade term in their contract to meet their own business requirements. The International Chamber of Commerce and many experienced lawyers usually recommend that buyer and seller do not attempt to add to, explain, or change the meaning of any trade term without legal advice. This "customizing" only causes needless confusion. The problem usually arises in CIF contract cases. The general rule is that if the additional shipping terms added by the parties to a CIF contract do not contradict the usual terms of a CIF contract, then the contract will still be considered a CIF contract.

On the other hand, if the parties insert additional terms that are contrary to the usual meaning of CIF, then it can destroy the CIF terms. For instance, assume that the parties enter into a contract labeled "CIF." They then add that "payment is not due until the goods are sold by the

## *Kumar Corporation v. Nopal Lines, Ltd.*
### 462 So.2d 1178 (1985)
### District Court of Appeals of Florida, Third District

BACKGROUND AND FACTS

Kumar sold 700 television sets to one of its largest customers, Nava, in Venezuela. The contract was on CIF terms, Maracaibo. However, they agreed that Nava would not pay Kumar until Nava actually sold the merchandise. Kumar obtained the televisions from its supplier, received them in its Miami warehouse, loaded them on a trailer, delivered the trailer to its freight forwarder, Maduro, in Florida, and obtained the shipping documents. The trailer was stolen from the Maduro lot and found abandoned and empty. Kumar had failed to obtain marine insurance on the cargo. Kumar sued Maduro and the carrier. The defendants argued that, since the risk of loss had passed from Kumar to Nava, Kumar did not have standing to sue. The trial court agreed with the defendants and dismissed Kumar's case. Kumar appealed.

DANIEL S. PEARSON, JUDGE

Kumar's argument that it is the real party in interest proceeds . . . from the premise that its agreement to postpone Nava's obligation to pay for the goods modified the ordinary consequence of the CIF contract that the risk of loss shifts to the buyer. A CIF contract is a recognized and established form of contract, the incidents of which are well known. Thus, if a buyer and seller adopt such a contract, "they will be presumed, in the absence of any express term to the contrary, to have adopted all the normal incidents of that type of contract," D. M. Day, *The Law of International Trade,* 4 (1981), one of which is that the buyer, not the seller, bears the risk of loss when the goods are delivered to the carrier and the seller's other contractual obligations are fulfilled. A CIF contract is not a contract "that goods shall arrive, but a contract to ship goods complying with the contract of sale, to obtain, unless the contract otherwise provides, the ordinary contract of carriage to the place of destination, and the ordinary contract of insurance of the goods on that voyage, and to tender these documents against payment of the contract price." C. Schmitthoff, *The Law and Practice of International Trade,* 26–27 (7th ed. 1980).

It is clear, however, that parties may vary the terms of a CIF contract to meet their own requirements. But where the agreed-upon variation is such that it removes a vital ingredient of a CIF contract, then the contract ceases to be a CIF contract. Thus, "if according to the intention of the parties the actual delivery of the goods [to the buyer] is an essential condition of performance, the contract is not a CIF contract." C. Schmitthoff, *supra.*

In the present case, Kumar and Nava agreed to payment upon Nava's sale of the goods in Venezuela . . . [thereby negating an essential ingredient of the CIF contract]. . . . [T]he use of the term CIF does not ipso facto make the contract a CIF contract if the contract has been altered in a manner that is repugnant to the very nature of a CIF contract. Therefore, because the record before us does not . . . conclusively show that the contract remained a true CIF contract despite the agreement between Kumar and Nava concerning the payment for the goods, it was improper for the trial court to conclude as a matter of law that the risk of loss passed to Nava when Kumar delivered the goods to the shipper.

But even assuming, arguendo, that we were to conclude, as did the trial court, that the risk of loss passed to Nava merely by virtue of the label CIF on the contract, Kumar must still prevail. Under the CIF contract, Kumar was obliged to procure insurance, and by not doing so, acted, intentionally or unintentionally, as the insurer of the shipment. As the insurer of the shipment, Kumar was obliged to pay Nava, the risk bearer, for the loss when the goods were stolen. Being legally obliged to pay Nava's loss, Kumar would thus be subrogated to Nava's claims against the appellees. Since a subrogee is the real party in interest and may sue in its own name, Kumar would have standing to sue under this theory.

Reversed and remanded for further proceedings.

**Decision.** The court held that where, under a CIF contract, the seller fails to obtain marine cargo insurance on behalf of the buyer, the risk of loss remains with the seller, who becomes a self-insurer of the property. As such, the seller has standing to sue the carrier for the cargo loss.

buyer." A court would then have to decide, looking at all the evidence, whether the contract was on CIF terms. This issue was one discussed by the court in the *Kumar* case. As you read, notice that the court decides the case on the basis of the seller's failure to obtain insurance on the cargo as required under CIF terms.

## Chapter Summary

In an international contract for the sale of goods, the terms of sale are as essential to the contract as the quality of the goods themselves. Moving goods around the world is expensive and risky. If a contract does not specify the terms of sale and who bears the risk of loss, the parties may be in for a tremendous surprise. Moreover, because of the risk of nonpayment and nondelivery, the parties may not wish to do business on cash or open account terms until a business relationship is established. Thus, an understanding of the documentary sale, as well as of the most common trade terms, is necessary for any international sales specialist or export manager.

Despite the continued widespread use of the documentary sale, its use has declined greatly in the past 30 years due to a number of factors. First, the greater reliability of international credit reporting makes open account transactions between foreign parties much safer than in previous years. Second, the increasing globalization of markets means that foreign manufactured goods are now no longer available only from foreign sources. Many of the same products can be easily purchased from domestic sources, such as domestic subsidiaries of foreign manufacturers, or through local distributors. Nevertheless, the documentary sale is often used when the credit risk is high or when the goods will be resold while in transit.

No reader should be left with the impression that the documentary sale eliminates the risk of foreign shipments. For example, the buyer might refuse the documents when they are presented by its bank, or the buyer might buy documents that appear to be in order, only to find defective merchandise in the containers. To minimize these risks, a seller can insist in the contract that the documents will be purchased, not by the buyer, but by the buyer's bank, as discussed in a later chapter.

---

## QUESTIONS AND CASE PROBLEMS

1. Banque de Depots, a Swiss bank, brought an action against Bozel, a Brazilian exporter, seeking a money judgment because Bozel allegedly misapplied the bank's funds. The bank obtained an order seizing 1.3 metric tons of calcium silicon located in a Louisiana port. The calcium silicon was shipped under ocean bills of lading by Bozel from Rio de Janeiro to New Orleans for transit to three purchasers, none of whom were domiciled in Louisiana. The documents were still in the hands of the collecting banks and had not yet been negotiated to the buyers. Bozel asked the court to free the goods because he was not the owner of the bills of lading. Can the court-ordered seizure of goods in transit stand in this case? What documents should have been seized by the court? Does the bank have any other recourse? *Banque de Depots v. Ferroligas,* 569 So.2d 40 (1990).

2. Colorado Fuel sold caustic soda to a buyer in Bombay under a CIF contract. The soda was fully loaded aboard ship when a labor strike made it impossible for the vessel to sail. As a result the soda arrived in Bombay six months late. The buyer sued for the late shipment. Was Colorado Fuel liable for damages? Does it matter that Colorado Fuel may have known that a strike was imminent? *Badhwar v. Colorado Fuel and Iron Corp.,* 138 F.Supp 595 (1955).

3. Buyer and seller entered into a contract for the sale of sugar from the Philippines to New York on CIF terms. They added language to the contract that delivery was to be "at a customary safe wharf or refinery at New York, Philadelphia, or Baltimore to be designated by the buyer." Before the sugar arrived, the United States placed a quota on sugar imports. The sugar was not allowed to be imported and was placed in a customs warehouse. The buyer refused the documents and the seller sued, claiming that the import restriction was no excuse for the buyer's nonpayment. The buyer argued that the language calling for delivery to a U.S. port converted a shipment contract into a destination contract. Was this a CIF contract or a destination contract? What was the effect of the additional shipping language used by the parties?

Why should the parties not attempt to modify a trade term or add other delivery language? *Warner Bros. & Co. v. A.C. Israel,* 101 F.2d 59 (1939).

4. Phillips contracted to buy naphtha from Tradax for shipment from Algeria to Puerto Rico on C&F terms. Shipment was to be made between September 20 and 28, 1981. The agreement incorporated the ICC *Incoterms.* It also contained a force majeure clause that stated, "In the event of any event delaying shipment or delivery of the goods by the seller, the unaffected party may cancel the unfulfilled balance of the contract." On September 16, Tradax shipped on the *Oxy Trader.* While enroute, the *Oxy Trader* was detained by maritime authorities at Gibraltar and deemed unsafe, and was not allowed to proceed. Tradax informed Phillips, which telexed back on October 1 that October 15 was the last acceptable delivery date. On October 7, its cargo had to be off-loaded in Portugal for shipment on another vessel. On October 13, Phillips refused payment of the documents due to the delay. In November, the cargo was sold by Tradax to a third party at a loss. Phillips brought this action in the United States. Tradax claimed that it had ceased to bear responsibility for the goods when it transferred the goods to the carrier for shipment. Phillips maintained that it was excused from performance because the ship's delay constituted force majeure. Judgment for whom and why? *Phillips Puerto Rico Core, Inc. v. Tradax Petroleum Ltd.,* 782 F.2d 314 (1985).

5. Design Inc., in Newport, Rhode Island, entered into a contract with Buenavista, S.A. in Barcelona, Spain to buy 1,000 sheets of stained glass. The contract contained a delivery clause which read, "FOB Hasta Luego." The contract also stated that it was to be interpreted in accordance with *Incoterms.* While the glass was being loaded onto the ship (*Hasta Luego*) one of the crates slipped from the loading mechanism and landed in the water before it crossed the ship's rail. Who bears the risk of loss of the glass? Would the answer change if the contract was governed by the UCC?

## MANAGERIAL IMPLICATIONS

Following on the discussion in Chapter Five, you receive a fax transmittal from the Japanese buyers that you had met in New York. They indicate that they would like to place an order for 5,000 down bed pillows. The pillows must contain no less than 85 percent cluster prime white goose down. In order to make the transportation as cost effective as possible, they would like to have pricing for a full ocean container. Before placing the order, they do have some questions about the details of the sale.

Their fax has indicated that although they would prefer to pay for the pillows on open account terms, they would consider your suggestions for payment options. They have indicated that they are unwilling to purchase against the documents unless they can first inspect the pillows on their arrival in Japan. They want this right of inspection to find out if the quality is what they had ordered and to look for possible freight damage. They feel strongly about this issue and insist on these conditions, unless you can show them that they can be adequately protected. In addition, they also would like to consider the cost of alternative shipping arrangements before they decide whether they want to handle this themselves.

1. Prepare a pro forma invoice giving your buyer several options for shipping the pillows. Consider how they will be packed and transported to the closest or best seaport. What facilities are available for handling containerized cargo or for multimodal transport in your region? Utilizing *Incoterms,* present a breakdown of the shipping alternatives and costs involved in the transaction. Contact a freight forwarder and inquire as to what services it can provide. Can it assist you in obtaining the information you need to prepare your pro forma invoice?

2. In determining your export price, what other factors must be taken into consideration in addition to freight costs? Do you consider additional communication expenses, port fees, trade show expense, forwarder fees, sales agents, and clerical expenses? Discuss your export pricing with your marketing team and decide on your pricing strategy.

3. Prepare a letter to accompany the pro forma invoice explaining why payment by "cash against documents" would be fair to both parties. What can you propose to address their concerns that the goods shipped will conform to their quality specifications? How will they be protected from marine risks?

## NOTES

1. For an excellent discussion of this topic, see James J. White and Robert S. Summers, *Uniform Commercial Code,* 3rd edition, West Publishing Company (1988).

2. For the complete text of *Incoterms,* explanation and graphical presentation, see Jan Ramberg, *Guide to Incoterms 1990,* ICC Publishing S.A., ICC Publication No. 461/90 (1991), available through ICC Publishing Corporation, New York, N.Y.

# Chapter Seven

# The Carriage of Goods and the Liability of Air and Sea Carriers

The last two chapters examined the legal relationship between the seller and buyer in a contract for the international sale of goods. Introduced were some basic concepts about the relationship between the seller and the carrier that undertakes to transport the goods to the buyer, such as the function and importance of transport documents. This chapter discusses the liability of the carrier for damage or loss to cargo while it is in transit. It includes the following subjects: (1) the liability of international air carriers, (2) the liability of ocean carriers, (3) selected issues in maritime and marine cargo insurance law, and (4) the liability of carriers for misdelivery of goods.

## Bailments and Common Carriers

An understanding of the legal arrangement between the one shipping the goods and the one carrying the goods is important. When a carrier accepts cargo for transport a bailment situation is created. A *bailment* is a legal arrangement whereby the owner of property, the *bailor,* transfers possession of the property to the *bailee.* One example of a bailment occurs when a bailor places goods in a warehouse for storage. The owner of the warehouse is the bailee. In the context of shipping goods, the bailor is the *shipper* who places goods in the hands of a *common carrier,* the bailee, for transport to a *consignee.* A common carrier is a carrier that contracts with the public for transportation services, and might include road, rail, air, ocean, and inland waterway carriers. As discussed in the last chapter, the contract between shipper and carrier is called a *contract of carriage,* and it is evidenced in the written *transport document.* In ocean carriage, this contract is the *bill of lading.* In air carriage it is the *air waybill.* (Copies of these documents appear in Chapter Six.) The rights and responsibilities of shipper and carrier to one another depends on the contractual provisions in the transport document and on the law applicable to that contract. In any case involving damage to cargo, the plaintiff is usually the person or party who has title to the goods, whether it is the original shipper, the consignee, or other party who has acquired title to the goods.

Under the traditional law of bailments, a carrier must return the property to the bailor (or deliver it to the consignee) in the same condition in which it was received. Thus, common carriers are held strictly liable for damage or loss to goods. If goods are destroyed or stolen, the carrier is liable even if it was not at fault. Common carriers, however, are not liable for damage or loss caused by (1) acts of God, such as an earthquake, (2) an act of a public enemy or terrorist, (3) an act of government intervention or court order, (4) an act of the shipper, such as improper packaging or mislabeling, or (5) an inherent characteristic of the goods such as perishability or chemical reaction, that causes its own destruction or waste. Moreover, carriers can limit their liability to a stated amount through *disclaimers.* In order to take advantage of the disclaimer, however, carriers in the United States must advise the shipper of its right to declare a higher value in return for which the carrier may charge a higher rate.

In the United States the liability of a carrier for damage or loss to cargo in domestic shipments is determined by a combination of the common law of bailments, and state and federal statutes (including the *Uniform Commercial Code* and regulations of U.S. government agencies). International shipments are treated much differently. They are governed primarily by international law.

# The Liability of International Air Carriers

At the beginning of air travel in the early part of this century the risk of an air disaster was far greater than today. The risk was so great, that investors feared entering the aviation industry in which their fortunes could be wiped out in one disaster. Insurance companies also feared insuring the new airlines. Lawmakers soon realized that firms entering the fledgling aviation industry required protection from such catastrophic loss in order for the industry to develop. In the late 1920s delegates from more than 20 countries met in Warsaw, Poland, to draft an international agreement that would provide a uniform limitation on the liability of an air carrier to both shippers and passengers. The *Convention for the Unification of Certain Rules Relating to International Transportation by Air,* still in effect today, is commonly known as the *Warsaw Convention.* It was adopted in the United States in 1934 and is the law in more than 120 nations.

## The Warsaw Convention

The Warsaw Convention sets uniform rules governing the carriage of international passengers, baggage, and cargo. It governs the form of air waybills, passenger tickets, and baggage claim receipts. The main provisions of the Warsaw Convention define the liability of airlines for injuries to passengers and damage or loss to their baggage or to cargo. According to the Convention, an air carrier is presumptively liable for all damage to cargo unless they can prove that (1) the damage did not occur as a result of their own fault or negligence, or (2) the loss was caused by the negligence of the shipper in handling, marking, or packing the goods. In addition, even if the carrier is liable, it is protected by a limitation on its liability. This limitation is valid unless the shipper declares the goods to be of higher value on the air waybill and pays an additional fee.

**http://ra.irv.uit.no/trade_law**
The "International Trade Law Monitor" site is the most comprehensive site for information and research on international trade law and other international legal topics. Includes full text of important international treaties and conventions, such as the Warsaw Convention and other international agreements cited in this chapter.

**The Limitation on Liability and the Gold Standard.** In drafting the convention, the delegates had difficulty in arriving at a universally accepted method for limiting the liability of a carrier. They knew that the carrier's liability would have to be limited to a certain amount of money per kilogram of luggage or cargo, but in what currency should it be payable? Getting the countries to agree would have been impossible, because all currencies fluctuate in value. So the delegates chose not to use paper money at all, but to use a common standard of value—one that was accepted in all countries regardless of the worth of their currency—gold, at a specified purity and weight. Thus the liability of airlines for damage or loss to cargo or to baggage was limited to an amount of gold per kilogram of cargo. Of course, they never intended that one collecting for damaged cargo would be paid in gold, but rather currency. Damages would be paid in any country's currency in an amount based on how much of that currency could be purchased with the weight of gold specified in the convention.

The use of gold as the measurement of liability worked in the United States until the early 1970s when the gold-based international monetary system began to collapse. Until that time, the United States had been on the "gold standard," meaning that the U.S. government had set by law the price of gold in dollars. (For nearly forty years the official price of gold in the United States was $35 per ounce.) Thus converting from gold to dollars was easy, and the dollar limits of liability under the Warsaw Convention were $7.50 per pound of cargo. But by the mid 1970s, gold ceased to be the official standard of value for the U.S. dollar, and the United States and other members of the International Monetary Fund eliminated gold as the accepted basis of international exchange. With the value of gold fluctuating, the U.S. government agency that had been charged with regulating the airline industry fixed the liability of carriers at $9.07 per pound of cargo—the last "official" price of gold. This method of determining the liability limit of a carrier was upheld by the U.S. Supreme Court in *Trans World Airlines, Inc. v. Franklin Mint Corporation,* 466 U.S. 243, 104 S.Ct. 1776 (1984). Because these limits of liability are so low, many court cases involve a shipper who tries to prove that the airline violated the terms of the Convention and thus should not be protected by these limits.

A carrier that does not provide the shipper with an air waybill does not gain the protection of the Convention. Also, the air waybill is required to contain the details in the following list:

- Place and date of the air waybill's execution.
- Place of departure and destination.
- Agreed stopping places en route.

- Names and addresses of the shipper, the first carrier, and the consignee.
- Nature of the goods.
- Number of packages, method of packing, and package markings (when commercially significant).
- Weight, quantity, volume, or dimensions of the articles shipped (when commercially significant).
- Statement that the shipment is governed by the Warsaw Convention.

In *Maritime Insurance Co. v. Emery Air Freight,* 983 F.2d 437 (2nd Cir. 1993), the U.S. court of appeals took a strict interpretation of the Convention and held that if these details are missing, the carrier will not be entitled to limited liability. In the following case, *Williams Dental Co. v. Air Express International,* a U.S. federal court considered the limits of liability of a carrier in a situation in which the shipper of dental gold had declared a higher value on the air waybill.

---

## Williams Dental Co., Inc. v. Air Express International

824 F. Supp. 435 (1993)
United States District Court,
(S.D.N.Y.)

### BACKGROUND AND FACTS

Williams Dental Company shipped 50 ounces of dental gold and equipment to Sweden aboard Air Express International, an air carrier. Williams' employees double-checked the gold, packaged and sealed it in a pail, and boxed the pail for shipment. When the shipment was delivered to the buyer in Sweden, the safety seals on the pail were broken and the gold was missing. Williams submitted a claim for the value of the gold in an amount of $23,474, but the claim was denied by the carrier. Williams sued to recover the $23,474. The defendant, Air Express, claims that its liability is limited to $1,262 under the Warsaw Convention.

### MUKASEY, DISTRICT JUDGE

. . . This case is governed by the *Warsaw Convention,* which applies to "all international transportation of . . . goods performed by aircraft for hire." Contracting parties may adopt the terms of the *Warsaw Convention,* and the air waybill at issue here incorporates the *Warsaw Convention* by reference.

*Warsaw Convention* Article 22, Clause (2) provides that "[i]n the transportation of . . . goods, the liability of the carrier shall be limited to a sum of [$9.07 per pound] of goods, unless the consignor has made . . . a special declaration of the value at delivery and has paid a supplementary sum if the case so requires. In that case the carrier will be liable to pay a sum not exceeding the declared sum". . . . see, *Trans World Airlines, Inc. v. Franklin Mint Corp.,* 466 U.S. 243, 104 S.Ct. 1776, 80 L.Ed.2d 273 (1984). Therefore, if plaintiff had not declared a special value for the shipment, defendant's liability would have been limited to $9.07 per pound.

However, plaintiff chose not to be bound by this limit. Instead, plaintiff declared a special value for the entire shipment of $23,474.50. Plaintiff claims that it declared separately a value for customs of $21,680.00 for the [gold]. . . .

*(continued)*

*(continued)*

The cases support plaintiff's expectation that in the event of loss it would receive the declared value of the lost shipment, not the *Warsaw Convention* value. For example, although the plaintiff in *Orlove v. Philippine Air Lines* had not declared the value of his shipment, the Court noted that "[i]t is clear that had the plaintiff declared the value of his shipment to the shipper, the shipper would be liable to the plaintiff for the full value of his loss." 257 F.2d at 387. In that case, the Court found that the plaintiff could recover the full value of a lost jewelry shipment, because by the time the package was delivered, the plaintiff "had already declared its value and had impliedly agreed to an increased freight charge." 257 F.2d at 388. Moreover, although *Trans World Airlines, Inc. v. Franklin Mint Corp.* did not involve a special declaration, the Supreme Court noted in that case that "[h]ad such a declaration been made, and an additional fee paid, the shipper would have been able to recover in an amount not exceeding the declared value." . . .

Holding defendant liable for the declared value of the shipment also is consistent with the goal of the *Warsaw Convention* to regulate uniformly the liability of international air carriers. The Second Circuit already has held that one who ships goods at a declared value substantially below their actual net worth in order to receive a reduced freight rate "is gambling that the goods will not be lost [and if] such loss occurs, the shipper . . . should not be entitled to recover the full value of the goods." *Perera Co. v. Varig Brazilian Airlines, Inc.,* 775 F.2d 21 (2d Cir. 1985).

This case presents the converse of *Perera*—plaintiff shipped goods at a declared value substantially above the *Warsaw Convention*'s liability limit and paid an increased freight rate. If a shipper who specifically declares a value less than full value and pays the corresponding lower rate may recover only the declared value, then a shipper, such as plaintiff, who declares a greater value (up to the actual value of the goods) and pays the corresponding greater rate also should recover the declared value. Such a rule applies uniformly to those shippers who declare a special value and pay the corresponding freight rate—all would recover the declared value. . . .

In sum, there is no genuine issue of fact that plaintiff told defendant the shipment contained one pail and two boxes of dental supplies worth almost $25,000. . . . Defendant accepted an additional rate to ship the package, based on its additional declared value. Thus, plaintiff provided information sufficient to notify defendant that the shipment contained gold. It was then up to defendant, a commercially sophisticated carrier, either (to refuse the shipment) or to assume the additional risk associated with the increased shipping rate. . . .

Under Section 22(2) of the *Warsaw Convention,* a shipper may not declare a value for a shipment greater than its market value and then recover that amount if the shipment is lost. Therefore, the maximum plaintiff may recover for the lost gold is its market value. The amount listed on plaintiff's invoice—$21,680—is consistent with the market price of gold on August 21, 1990. The additional declared amount—$1,794—relates to the other dental equipment, which was not lost and for which plaintiff may not recover.

**Decision.**   Judgment for the plaintiff for the declared value of the cargo. Although the *Warsaw Convention* sets a ceiling on the liability of an international air carrier for damage to cargo, a shipper that declares a higher value for that cargo on the air waybill may collect the declared value, provided that it does not exceed the actual market value of the cargo.

# Liability for the Carriage of Goods by Sea

Ocean-going cargo is constantly at risk. Damage can result from any number of causes, including external forces, the inherent nature of the goods, the passage of time, or any combination of factors. Typical examples of cargo damage include infestation from insects or molds, contamination from chemicals previously held in the ship's hold, rust and other moisture damage from condensation inside the hold, damage from broken refrigeration units and other equipment, storm damage from rain and seawater, losses from fire or the sinking of the ship, damage done to cargo while rescuing the ship from peril, damage resulting from cargo being improperly stowed above deck, losses from theft and piracy on the seas, damage from acts of war, and so on.

One of the greatest dangers to cargo has traditionally been pilferage and theft. This problem was particularly troublesome during the time when goods were moved by break-bulk freight. With the advent of containerization, particularly in the last 25 years, pilferage has been greatly reduced. The impact of containerization was described by the court in *Matsushita Electric Corporation v. S.S. Aegis Spirit:* 414 F.Supp 894 (1976):

The emergent use of these cargo-carrying containers marks a significant technological stride within the maritime industry, and their use seems certain to expand in years to come because of the substantial advantages they provide over conventional modes of ocean carriage for shippers and carriers alike. Their increasing popularity finds its source in the enhanced economy and efficiency they offer in the handling, loading, stowing, and discharge of most types of seagoing cargo. Their value to shippers lies in the greater protection they afford cargo from pilferage, rough handling, and the elements. Use of containers will frequently permit the shipper to substitute lighter, more economical packaging materials without increased risk to the cargo. Furthermore, the shipper can, in most container operations, personally ensure a tight stow and the careful handling of his goods, because he has the responsibility to stuff the containers under the carriage contract. The carrier, for its part, enjoys tremendous savings in labor by eliminating slow, manual handling and stowing of individual packages, and in claim payments by reason of reduced cargo loss and damage. Although shippers and freight forwarders sometimes acquire their own fleet of containers, carriers are the predominant owners of containers used in maritime commerce.

Despite the impact of containerization on international trade, damage and loss to cargo must be anticipated by any international shipper. In the event of a loss, inevitably the owner of the goods or the insurer will look to the carrier for recovery. But carriers enjoy considerable protection under the law.

---

**http://www.mglobal.com/**
*The "Maritime Gobal Net" contains information and communication resources for the international maritime community, links to ocean carriers, carrier shipping schedules, and ocean ports worldwide.*

## History of Carrier's Liability

The law regarding an ocean carrier's liability for damage or loss to cargo is rooted in the history of transportation and trade. As goods moved across the high seas on sailing ships, they were under the exclusive control of the ship's captain for months at a time. Shippers had no way of proving that goods were lost or destroyed as a result of a natural disaster, the negligence of the carrier, or from the crew's pilferage or theft. As a result, the maritime laws of both England and the United States held carriers to be absolutely liable for all loss or damage to cargo in their possession. Although a few exceptions to this liability were recognized, carriers were virtual insurers of their cargo. With the growth of trade and the advent of steamships, carriers became more economically powerful. They began to include provisions in their bills of lading (which is a contract between the shipper and carrier) that would limit their liability. These limitation-of-liability clauses attempted to free the carrier from all responsibility, including liability for its own negligence or even for providing an unfit vessel. The small shippers were at the mercy of the steamship companies. The result was a period of great uncertainty over the liability of ocean carriers.

**The Harter Act.** In 1892, the U.S. Congress first addressed the problem in the *Harter Act,* a federal law still in effect today. This act set out the liability of a carrier for the care of its cargo, and imposed restrictions on the use of exculpatory clauses in bills of lading. Subsequent developments in the law have resulted in the Harter Act's limited application. Today, the Harter Act remains applicable to contracts for the carriage of goods only from one U.S. port to another U.S. port. For international shipments, the Harter Act has been superseded by a new statute. The Harter Act also applies to the liability of the carrier for caring for the goods before they are loaded and after they are unloaded from the ship (e.g., during warehousing).

**The Hague Rules.** At the end of the first World War, other nations attempted to develop similar rules. The result was the near universal acceptance of a 1924 international convention on bills of lading known as the *Hague Rules.* These rules represent an international effort to achieve uniformity of bills of lading, and were intended to reduce the uncertainties concerning the responsibilities and liabilities of ocean carriers. The Hague Rules define the liability of ocean carriers for damage or loss to goods on the seas. Virtually every trading nation of the world today has incorporated them into its national law.

**The Carriage of Goods by Sea Act.** The Hague Rules were codified in the United States in 1936 in the *Carriage of Goods by Sea Act* or COGSA. COGSA is applicable to every bill of lading for the carriage of goods by sea, to or from ports of the United States in foreign trade. Since virtually all bills of lading issued in the United States provide that they are controlled by COGSA, the discussion here concentrates on that statute.

## Limitations of Liability under COGSA

COGSA invalidates all clauses in the bill of lading that try to exonerate a carrier from liability for damage or loss to cargo, or that attempt to lessen a carrier's liability beneath that set by the statute itself. For instance, a carrier is liable under COGSA if refrigeration units are inadequate to prevent spoilage of perishable fruit during a journey. A carrier cannot put a "fine print" provision in a bill of lading that says they are not liable for inadequate refrigeration; such an attempted provision is void.

Prior to the decision in the following 1995 case, U.S. shippers were able to rely on this provision of COGSA to invalidate clauses in the bill of lading requirements that damage claims be submitted to arbitration in a foreign country. Most U.S. federal courts sided with the shippers, and maintained that clauses in the bill of lading requiring arbitration in a foreign country would make it too costly and too difficult for them to pursue damage claims against a carrier. The argument was that a foreign arbitration clause would effectively lessen the carrier's liability, contrary to COGSA. The following case threw U.S. shippers into a panic and, as Justice Stevens' dissenting opinion clearly describes, is likely to have far reaching effects on the maritime industry.

## Nautical Liability of the Carrier

The liability of a carrier for damage or loss to ocean-going cargo is strictly defined and limited by COGSA. COGSA provides considerable protection to the carrier for damage to cargo resulting from negligence in navigating or managing the ship, or from fire or storms. The carrier, however, is liable for its failure to use due diligence in providing a seaworthy ship at the beginning of the voyage.

**Carrier's Due Diligence.** The statute of limitations for the filing of claims under the *Carriage of Goods by Sea Act* is one year. Proving liability under COGSA leads to complex litigation and has

---

BACKGROUND AND FACTS
Bacchus, a New York company, purchased fruit from Galaxie, a Moroccan supplier. The fruit was shipped on the M/V *Sky Reefer*, a cargo ship owned by Maritima, a Panamanian company, and leased for charter to Nichiro, a Japanese shipping company. Stevedores hired by Galaxie loaded the cargo. Nichiro issued a bill of lading to Galaxie for receipt of the goods. Once the ship set sail from Morocco, Galaxie sold the bill of lading to Bacchus. The bill of lading stated that it shall be governed by Japanese law, and that any disputes shall be referred to arbitration in

*Vimar Segurosy Reaseguros, S.A. v. M/V Sky Reefer, et al.*
115 S.Ct. 2322, 1995 WL 360200 (U.S.), 63 USLW 4617 (1995)
United States Supreme Court

Tokyo, and that the award of the arbitrators shall be binding on both parties. When the fruit arrived it was discovered that thousands of boxes of oranges had shifted and been crushed, resulting in over a million dollars in damage. Bacchus was paid by its insurance company, Vimar, who brought suit in the U.S. against Maritima and the *Sky Reefer* for damages. Maritima maintains that the matter must be arbitrated in Japan. Vimar contends that enforcement of the foreign arbitration provision would violate COGSA.

*(continued)*

*(continued)*

### JUSTICE KENNEDY, DELIVERED THE OPINION OF THE COURT

This case requires us to interpret the *Carriage of Goods by Sea Act* (COGSA) as it relates to a contract containing a clause requiring arbitration in a foreign country. The question is whether a foreign arbitration clause in a bill of lading is invalid under COGSA because it lessens liability in the sense that COGSA prohibits.

The leading case for invalidation of a foreign forum selection clause is the opinion of the Court of Appeals for the Second Circuit in *Indussa Corp. v. S.S. Ranborg,* 377 F.2d 200 (1967) (en banc). The court there found that COGSA invalidated a clause designating a foreign judicial forum because it "puts 'a high hurdle' in the way of enforcing liability, and thus is an effective means for carriers to secure settlements lower than if cargo [owners] could sue in a convenient forum." The court observed "there could be no assurance that [the foreign court] would apply [COGSA] in the same way as would an American tribunal subject to the uniform control of the Supreme Court." The logic of that extension would be quite defensible, but we cannot endorse the reasoning or the conclusion of the *Indussa* rule itself.

The determinative provision in COGSA, examined with care, does not support the arguments advanced first in *Indussa* and now by the petitioner, as follows:

> "Any clause, covenant, or agreement in a contract of carriage relieving the carrier or the ship from liability for loss or damage to or in connection with the goods, arising from negligence, fault, or failure in the duties or obligations provided in this section, or lessening such liability otherwise than as provided in this chapter, shall be null and void and of no effect."

The liability that may not be lessened is "liability for loss or damage . . . arising from negligence, fault, or failure in the duties or obligations provided in this section." The statute thus addresses the lessening of the specific liability imposed by the Act, without addressing the separate question of the means and costs of enforcing that liability. The difference is that between explicit statutory guarantees and the procedure for enforcing them, between applicable liability principles and the forum in which they are to be vindicated.

The liability imposed on carriers under COGSA is defined by explicit standards of conduct, and it is designed to correct specific abuses by carriers. In the 19th century it was a prevalent practice for common carriers to insert clauses in bills of lading exempting themselves from liability for damage or loss, limiting the period in which plaintiffs had to present their notice of claim or bring suit, and capping any damages awards per package. . . . Nothing in this section, however, suggests that the statute prevents the parties from agreeing to enforce these obligations in a particular forum. By its terms, it establishes certain duties and obligations, separate and apart from the mechanisms for their enforcement.

Sixty-six countries, including the United States and Japan, are now parties to the Hague Rules and it appears that none has interpreted the Hague Rules to prohibit foreign forum selection clauses. The English courts long ago rejected the reasoning later adopted by the *Indussa* court. And other countries that do not recognize foreign forum selection clauses rely on specific provisions to that effect in their domestic versions of the Hague Rules, e.g., Australia and South Africa. In light of the fact that COGSA is the culmination of a multilateral effort to establish uniform ocean bills of lading to govern the rights and liabilities of carriers and shippers inter se in international trade, we decline to interpret our version of the Hague Rules in a manner contrary to every other nation to have addressed this issue. . . .

### JUSTICE STEVENS, DISSENTING

Judge Friendly [in *Indussa*] first remarked on the harsh consequence of "requiring an American consignee claiming damages in the modest sum of $2600 to journey some 4200 miles to a court having a different legal system and employing another language." The decision, however, rested not only on the impact of the provision on a relatively small claim, but also on a fair reading of the broad language in COGSA.

The foreign arbitration clause imposes potentially prohibitive costs on the shipper, who must travel—and bring his lawyers, witnesses and exhibits—to a distant country in order to seek redress. The shipper will therefore be inclined either to settle the claim at a discount or to forgo bringing the claim at all. . . . Accordingly, courts have

*(continued)*

*(continued)*

always held that such clauses "lessen" or "relieve" the carrier's liability. Yet this Court today holds that carriers may insert foreign-arbitration clauses into bills of lading, and it leaves in doubt the validity of choice-of-law clauses.

In my opinion, this view is flatly inconsistent with the purpose of COGSA [which] responds to the inequality of bargaining power inherent in bills of lading. . . . A bill of lading is a form document prepared by the carrier, who presents it to the shipper on a take-it-or-leave-it basis. Characteristically, there is no arms-length negotiation over the bill's terms; the shipper must agree to the carrier's standard-form language, or else refrain from using the carrier's services. Accordingly, if courts were to enforce bills of lading as written, a carrier could slip in a clause relieving itself of all liability for fault, or limiting that liability to a fraction of the shipper's damages, and the shipper would have no recourse. COGSA represents Congress' most recent attempt to respond to this problem. By its terms, it invalidates any clause in a bill of lading "relieving" or "lessening" the "liability" of the carrier for negligence, fault, or dereliction of duty.

I respectfully dissent.

**Decision.**   COGSA does not invalidate a foreign arbitration clause in a maritime bill of lading.

---

resulted in untold numbers of cases in the law reports. In the event of a dispute over damaged cargo, the shipper, owner of the cargo, or holder of the bill of lading is likely to be the plaintiff. The plaintiff must show that the goods were loaded in good condition and unloaded in a damaged condition, or lost. A clean bill of lading establishes a rebuttable presumption that the goods were delivered to the carrier in good condition. The carrier must then explain the loss. Thus, the burden shifts to the carrier to show either that the damage was not caused by its failure to use *due diligence* in providing a *seaworthy ship* at the beginning of the voyage, or that the loss occurred from one of the specific exemptions in Exhibit 7.1.

In one interesting case, *Bubble Up International Ltd. v. Transpacific Carriers Corp.*, 458 F. Supp. 1100 (S.D.N.Y. 1978), the court ruled that the carrier had failed to use due diligence in inspecting the ship's engine room. Despite an exhaustive three-part inspection before leaving port, the crew failed to find one missing cotter pin on a bearing bolt inside the engine. The engine failed at sea as a result. The court ruled that the crew had failed to use due diligence in inspecting for the presence or absence of cotter pins on the ship's engine. When the carrier pointed out that COGSA relieves them from liability for failing to find a latent or hidden defect, the court disagreed and felt that they should have found it.

**Seaworthiness of the Ship.**   The carrier is liable for damage to cargo resulting from its failure to use due diligence to make the ship seaworthy at the time of its departure on the voyage. This assurance has been called the "warranty of seaworthiness." A vessel is *seaworthy* if it is reasonably fit to carry the cargo it has undertaken to carry on the intended journey. In other words, the carrier must not only use due diligence to inspect the vessel for repair, but it must be sure the vessel is the proper type for carrying this specific type of cargo on this particular voyage. The standard of seaworthiness includes a number of factors, including the type of ship and the condition and suitability of its equipment, the competence of its crew, the type of cargo being carried and the manner in which it is stowed, the weather (e.g., was the ship prepared for the type of weather expected?), and the nature of the voyage. Some courts will recognize a presumption of *unseaworthiness* at the time of departure if the ship breaks down shortly after departure in clear weather and calm seas.

The carrier is responsible for properly manning, equipping, and supplying the ship, and making the refrigerating and cooling chambers, and all other parts of the ship in which goods are carried, fit and safe for receiving, carrying, and preserving the goods. The carrier must also properly load, store, and carry the goods. For instance, the cargo holds must not be in such a condition that they cause moisture damage to the goods through condensation. Cargo should not be stowed in a manner that causes it to shift and be crushed. Cargo should not be exposed to

**EXHIBIT 7.1   "Carriage of Goods by Sea Act" Specific Exceptions to Liability**

Carriers are not liable for losses resulting from a number of specific causes listed in the statute. These exceptions include the following:

1. Errors in the navigation or in the management of the ship
2. Fire, unless caused by the actual fault of the carrier (the corporate owner of the ship)
3. Perils, dangers, and accidents of the sea
4. An act of God (a natural disaster)
5. An act of war
6. An act of public enemies
7. Legal seizures of the ship
8. Quarantine restrictions
9. An act or omission of the shipper or owner of the goods
10. Labor strikes or lockouts
11. Riots and civil commotions
12. Saving life or property at sea
13. An inherent defect, quality, or vice of the goods that causes wastage in bulk or weight or other damage or loss
14. Insufficiency of packing
15. Inadequate marking of goods or containers
16. Latent defects in ship or equipment (which might render the ship unseaworthy) were not discoverable by due diligence

rain and seas. Refrigeration units must be in working order, and so forth. The carrier must also properly unload the cargo and hand it over to the party entitled to it.

**Errors in Navigation or Mismanagement of the Ship.**   Exhibit 7.1 shows those situations in which a carrier is not liable for damage to cargo. One of the most important is that the carrier—the corporate ship's owner—is not liable for errors in navigation or mismanagement of the ship caused by the master, mariner, pilot, or a crew member (except for the crew's negligence in the care and custody of the cargo, such as during loading and unloading, for which the carrier is liable).

Understand that an error in the "navigation and management of the ship" by the crew is a very different thing than when the ship's corporate owner fails to use due diligence in providing a seaworthy ship at the beginning of the voyage. While carriers are not liable for the former, they are liable for the latter—for failing to provide a seaworthy ship. Thus, some courts have held car-

riers liable for their crew's negligence by reasoning that a crew that errs in navigating or managing a ship is not competent, and a ship is not seaworthy without a competent crew. As a result, carriers are often held liable despite the protection they receive from this defense.

**Damage from Fire Aboard Ship.**   Fire aboard ship has the potential to cause catastrophic losses at sea. Ocean carriers are not liable unless the actual negligence of the carrier—the corporate owner of the ship—caused the fire or prevented it from being extinguished. Although the U.S. federal courts disagree as to how to handle fire cases, they tend to rule that carriers will be liable for fire damage only if the corporate owner of the ship was actually at fault. The negligence of the crew is not enough to make the carrier liable. For instance, the carrier is liable if it allows the ship to leave port with inadequate firefighting equipment or with a crew untrained to fight fires.

In this instance, the carrier (i.e., the company that owned the ship) would have had control over installation of the equipment or training of the crew in firefighting. Thus, the law holds them responsible. However, once at sea, the corporate owner loses control of the ship—it becomes at the mercy of the elements and the ocean. Here, the corporate owner is not liable for losses due to fire. Once the carrier proves in court that fire damaged the cargo, the burden shifts to the plaintiff (the shipper or cargo owner) to prove that actual negligence of the ship's owner caused the fire or prevented it from being extinguished. In one of the leading fire cases, *Asbestos Corp. Ltd. v. Compagnie de Navigation,* 480 F.2d 669 (2nd Cir. 1973), a fire broke out in an engine room where large quantities of hot oil are expected to be present. The firefighting equipment was located in the engine room, and thus could not be used to extinguish the fire there. The court ruled that the ship's owner was negligent in installing the equipment, and liable for the loss to cargo as a result.

**Perils of the Sea.**   COGSA exempts carriers from liability for damage resulting from "perils, dangers, and accidents of the sea." A *peril of the sea* is a fortuitous action of the sea or weather of sufficient force to overcome the strength of a seawor-

# Sneaking Up On Security

## Innovative High-tech and Some Surprising Low-tech Strategies Help Beat Cargo Thieves

The cargo thieves were laughing. From outside a topless bar along the edge of Los Angeles Harbor, they watched each day as construction crews rolled into major container terminals across the street, expanding one of LA's big container terminals.

As it neared completion, work crews began moving fences out to the expanded perimeter. The port's trans-Pacific volume was growing so fast, the contractor ran out of heavy-security fencing in mid-job. So the crews temporarily closed the gap with lightweight fencing.

That night, while police at the LAPD station across the street were at roll call, the thieves drove a truck tractor up the construction access road, cut through the temporary fence and rolled the tractor out of sight behind a line of containers. After breaking a few container seals, they found a van full of sports shoes that sell for $140 a pair in retail stores.

While one man watched for guards, the other backed the truck up to the van and hooked it up. Moments later, they drove out the way they came in, becoming just another of the thousands of anonymous container trucks rolling around the Los Angeles-Long Beach port complex.

But the police had the last laugh. A week later, they found the container abandoned, with its cargo intact. The US-based shoe importer routinely ships all its left shoes in one container and all its right shoes in another. The thieves had stolen the container with left shoes.

This story illustrates one of the many security strategies used by shippers to ensure that thieves, smugglers or terrorists don't put kinks in their logistics pipelines.

Many shippers direct their freight forwarders or logistics providers to arrange shipments in ways that make stolen cargo hard to use and easy to identify. In the last few years, some have started using high-tech strategies that can lead police to stolen cargo.

Tiny computers hidden in the containers, the truck trailers or the cargo can calculate its position to within 10 feet, anywhere on earth, using global positioning satellites, similar to the electronic map units now used in some rental cars. They radio their position to shipping line computers, police or a regional group such as the Cargo Criminal Apprehension Teams, also known as Cargo CATs.

Capt. Michael Goodward, a Port of Los Angeles officer assigned to a Cargo CAT in Southern California, says newer containers with global positioning technology make poor targets for theft. "Probably the biggest single advance in cargo security is technological the use of global positioning to monitor containers," he notes. "Cargo thieves don't get far when the police know exactly where a stolen container is."

Another technology-based development in logistics security is the use of containers instead of railroad rackcars for shipping automobiles. Less expensive rackcars are still widely used, but auto manufacturers find that expensive cars are vulnerable to damage by transients. They break into the automobiles and live in them until the train nears its destination. The Greenbrier Cos. have led a push to popularize the use of folding rack systems that allow cars to be put on a rack and slid inside a container. Once the cars are removed, the racks fold up, leaving all but one container free to carry cargo on the return trip.

Indeed, steamship lines used the earliest containers to enhance security, not to cut labor costs. During World War II, the Army experimented with using sealed cargo vans for rapid, secure movement of equipment to the front lines. After the war ended, Matson Navigation Co. and other commercial lines began using oversized lockboxes to move liquor and other high-value cargo. By the time Malcolm McLean introduced truck-size cargo containers in 1956, their value as a security device had been established.

As the years passed, however, containers became a vehicle for crime. Not only could a sophisticated

*(continued)*

*(continued)*

thief make off with a whole truckload of cargo, but they also gave smugglers new places to hide drugs, guns or illegal immigrants. In third-world countries, containers might be stolen for use as houses. Security forces responded with drug-sniffing dogs, new types of x-ray scanners and computerized profiles of the kinds of containers smugglers might use. Marine terminals were redesigned with better lighting, fencing, security guards and container-tracking computers. Today, some sophisticated cargo scanners at seaports and airports use artificial intelligence technology to scan for drugs and explosives.

That doesn't prevent thieves from buying a tankerload of oil with a bad check, or lifting art masterpieces from temporary storage because a dealer forgot to line up a customshouse broker before importing them. At large airports, thieves frequently target expensive computer parts, gemstones and negotiable documents.

Air cargo theft has grown dramatically with the increased use of air freight and express delivery. Computer-literate bandits can go after a single object worth hundreds of thousands of dollars, amassing an entire database about how it will move before carrying out a raid with military precision.

Capt. Goodward says that's why operations such as Cargo CATs are taking on a new importance. "All the [law enforcement] agencies have got to work together if we're going to have a chance," he says.

***John Davies***
*International Business Magazine,* **November 1997.**
Reprinted by permission.

---

thy ship or the diligence and skill of a good crew. The defense often depends on the severity of the storm and the manner in which the cargo was damaged. The courts will consider the force of the wind, the height of the waves, the foreseeability of the storm when the ship set sail, the ability of the ship to avoid the storm, whether other ships in the same storm suffered damage, the type of damage to the cargo, and other factors. The negligence or lack of competence on behalf of the crew will void the *perils of the sea* defense. But if the ship was seaworthy when it left port, and was operated in a competent manner, the carrier is not liable for cargo damage from a storm so strong that it represents a peril of the sea. In the case that follows, *J. Gerber & Co. v. S.S. Sabine Howaldt,* the court

---

### J. Gerber & Company v. S.S. Sabine Howaldt
**437 F.2d 580 (1971)**
**United States Court of Appeals (2d Cir.)**

BACKGROUND AND FACTS
The SS *Sabine Howaldt,* a small cargo vessel, was chartered for a voyage from Antwerp, Belgium, to Wilmington, Delaware. The ship was carrying a quantity of steel products consigned to the plaintiff. The cargo was in good condition when loaded at Antwerp. On arrival at the port of destination in the United States, however, the steel showed extensive salt water damage from rust and pitting. In the course of her voyage across the North Atlantic, the *Sabine Howaldt* encountered extremely heavy weather. Water penetrated the ventilators and damaged the cargo. The carrier argued that the damage was caused solely by a peril of the sea, and that the ship was not unseaworthy. The district court found that the ship was unseaworthy due to the negligence of the defendant and that the winds and seas that the vessel encountered did not constitute a peril of the sea.

ANDERSON, CIRCUIT JUDGE
The ship's log records that . . . the ship was badly strained in her seams and sea water was breaking over forecastle deck, hatches, and upper works. It

*(continued)*

*(continued)*

was necessary for the vessel to heave to and she so remained for 12 hours. The hull of the *Sabine Howaldt* was twisted and strained in the turbulent cross seas; she rolled from 25 degrees–30 degrees; waves constantly broke over her; and she shuddered and vibrated as she was pounded and wrenched by the heavy seas. . . . Subsequently it was discovered that during this period of hurricane . . . a porthole in the galley was smashed; the catwalk or gangway from the amidships housing aft over the hatches and the well-deck to the poop was destroyed when it was torn loose and landed against a ventilator, which it dented.

The district court not only found that the character and nature of the winds and seas were not sufficiently severe to constitute a peril of the sea in fact, but it also found that the *Sabine Howaldt* was unseaworthy due to the neglect of the defendant carrier. It concluded that the defendant was negligent in permitting the ship to proceed on the voyage with defective hatch covers without tarpaulins over them and also because its ventilators were insufficiently protected. . . .

On arrival at Wilmington, Delaware, on January 3, 1966, the chief officer examined the hatches and found no damage to the hatches, the hatch covers, or their rubber gaskets—all were in good condition. . . . There was no evidence that there was a customary or usual standard in the exercise of good seamanship that called for the use of canvas tarpaulins over MacGregor hatchcovers. It was quite apparent that the customary practice of most steamship lines was not to use tarpaulins over such hatchcovers. . . . As there was no evidence in the case that the MacGregor hatchcovers on the *Sabine Howaldt* were not properly maintained and as there was substantial, uncontradicted evidence that they were, it was plain error to hold there was negligence in regard to a failure to cover the hatchcovers with tarpaulins.

The standard of seaworthiness must remain uncertain because of the imponderables of the forces exerted upon a ship by the winds and seas. Ship design and construction over many centuries of experience have evolved to meet the dangers inherent in violent winds and tempestuous seas. But for the purpose of deciding whether or not they constitute perils of the sea for a particular vessel for the purpose of the statutory exception there is the question of how violent and how tempestuous. These are matters of degree and not amenable to precise definition. . . . Other indicia are, assuming a seaworthy ship, the nature and extent of the damage to the ship itself, whether or not the ship was buffeted by cross-seas which wrenched and wracked the hull and set up unusual stresses in it and like factors. While the seaworthiness of a ship presupposes that she is designed, built, and equipped to stand up under reasonable expectable conditions, this means no more than the usual bad weather which is normal for a particular sea area at a particular time. It does not, however, include an unusual combination of the destructive forces of wind and sea which a skilled and experienced ship's master would not expect and which the ship encountered as a stroke of bad luck. Hurricane-force winds and turbulent cross-seas generating unpredictable strains and pressures on a ship's hull are an example.

We are satisfied that the *Sabine Howaldt* was a seaworthy vessel when she left Antwerp on December 15, 1965. . . . Throughout the voyage she was operated in a good and seamanlike manner. There was no negligence on the part of the carrier. The damage to the cargo was caused by violence of the wind and sea and particularly by the resulting cross-seas which, through wrenching and twisting the vessel, set up torsions within the hull which forced up the hatchcovers and admitted sea water to the holds.

**Decision.**    The judgment was reversed for the defendant carrier. The defendant met its burden of proof that the vessel was seaworthy when it left port, was operated in a seamanlike manner, and the damage to the cargo resulted solely from a peril of the sea.

ruled that the carrier had used due diligence to maintain a seaworthy ship and that the damage had resulted from a peril of the sea. Ships encounter tremendous forces of water and weather on the high seas. As the court notes, just because a ship is seaworthy does not mean that it can withstand every form of violent weather and turbulent sea that ocean-going ships might encounter.

**The Q-Clause Defense.** Even if a carrier cannot prove one of the sixteen exceptions shown in Exhibit 7.1, it still may be exonerated from liability under a seventeenth defense, the *Q-clause defense.* This provision states that a carrier is not liable for "any other cause arising without the actual fault and privity of the carrier . . . but the burden of proof shall be on the [carrier] to show that neither the actual fault . . . nor the fault or neglect of the agents or servants of the carrier contributed to the loss or damage." The carrier must therefore prove that it was free from any fault whatsoever contributing to the loss, damage, or disappearance of the goods entrusted to it, and it must also prove what the actual cause of the loss was. This burden is difficult for the carrier to bear, and relatively few cases in the literature describe carriers that have been successful using this defense.

> **http://www.fmc.gov**
> *The official site of the Federal Maritime Commission, the U.S. agency responsible for regulating shipping in the foreign trades of the U.S.*

## Carrier's Liability for Cargo Shortages

Ocean containers are generally loaded and sealed at the shipper's place of business and not opened until they are in the hands of the consignee. Even so, cargo shortages are a regular occurrence in the maritime trade. The legal problems here are somewhat different from the problems of damaged cargo. As the first step in any litigation, the owner of the cargo or the insurer establishes that a shortage actually occurred. Then, under the catch-all Q-clause defense that limits the carrier's liability (as discussed in the previous section), the carrier may attempt to prove that the shortage resulted despite its having exercised due care to safeguard the cargo.

A consignee can prove a shortage by showing that the quantity or weight of the cargo at the destination is less than that listed on the bill of lading. This issue can also be problematic, however. Under COGSA, a bill of lading usually lists the number of packages, the quantity, or weight of the cargo that the carrier receives for shipment; but the quantity or weight is usually supplied by the shipper. Because shipping containers are sealed at the shipper's place of business, the carrier doesn't really have the opportunity to physically count the number of packages inside. The carrier will customarily insert a disclaimer in the bill of lading stating that the cargo inside the container is the "shipper's weight, load, and count." Thus, carriers claim that they should not be liable for "missing cargo"—for delivering less cargo than described in the bill of lading. Recent cases have not recognized these disclaimers and, as in the *Westway Coffee* case, are holding carriers liable for shortages in

---

### West Way Coffee Corporation v. M.V. Netuno

528 F. Supp. 113 (1981),
aff'd 675 F.2d 30 (2d Cir. 1982)
United States District
Court, (S.D.N.Y.)

BACKGROUND AND FACTS
Westway, the consignee, purchased 1,710 cartons of coffee from Dominium, S.A., of Sao Paulo, Brazil. The cartons were loaded into six cargo containers under the supervision of a government officer who inspected and counted the cartons going into the containers. Dominium sealed and padlocked the containers. The containers were then driven from Sao Paulo to the port of Santos, where they were stored in a customs bonded warehouse prior to loading onto the MV *Netuno,* a vessel owned by Netumar. Netumar issued an onboard bill of lading listing the serial numbers of the containers, along with the gross weight of the containers filled with coffee and the number of cartons within them. Netumar did not count the cartons. The bill of lading contained disclaimers stating that the containers were "said to contain" a quantity of cargo described by the shipper, that the cargo was the "shipper's load, and count," and that the "contents of packages are shipper's declaration." After the *Netuno*'s arrival in New York, the padlocked containers were opened, revealing a shortage of 419 cartons or approximately twenty tons of coffee. Westway purchased the bill of lading and then brought this action against the carrier under the *Carriage of Goods by Sea Act.*

*(continued)*

*(continued)*

SAND, DISTRICT JUDGE

Plaintiff contends that the weights stated in the bill of lading constitute prima facie evidence of the receipt by the carrier of the goods as therein described; that it was entitled to rely on the weights stated in the bill of lading which was duly negotiated to it; and that Netumar is estopped from claiming that the missing cartons of coffee were not in the containers when Netumar took possession of them.

Defendant contends that plaintiff has failed to prove delivery of the full quantity to the carrier, and thereby has failed to establish a prima facie case; and alternatively, that defendant has established that it exercised proper care, and that plaintiff's estoppel theory does not apply to cases involving sealed containers. These contentions are based largely on the disclaimers contained in the bill of lading, and on the fact that the goods were "hidden" within the containers.

COGSA provides the answer to defendant's contention. Section 1303(3) provides:

> After receiving the goods into his charge the carrier . . . shall, on demand of the shipper, issue to the shipper a bill of lading showing among other things,
>
> (b) Either the number of packages or pieces, or the quantity or weight, as the case may be, as furnished in writing by the shipper.
>
> (c) The apparent order and condition of the goods: Provided, that no carrier, master, or agent of the carrier, shall be bound to state or show in the bill of lading any . . . quantity, or weight which he has reasonable ground for suspecting not accurately to represent the goods actually received, or which he has had no reasonable means of checking.

As our Court of Appeals has said of this section: "The Act specifically provides a method for avoiding carrier liability for false information given by the shipper, by not stating it in the bill. . . . The carrier must utilize that method, rather than the quite general reservation attempted here." *Spanish American Skin Co. v. The Ferngulf,* 242 F.2d 551, 553 (2d Cir. 1957). Thus, if defendant has reason to doubt the shipper's weights, it was required to use the method for limiting liability expressly provided by COGSA and cannot now advance the general statement in the bills, "said to weigh," against the consignee. Since plaintiff relied on the weights specified in the bills in purchasing the consignment, defendant is estopped from denying the accuracy of the description contained therein.

We thus find that despite the disclaimers stamped on the bill of lading, the weights recited in the bill established prima facie receipt by the carrier of the entire shipment of coffee.

Plaintiff having satisfied its initial burden, the burden thus shifts to defendant to establish the applicability of a COGSA exception. Defendant contends that it has satisfied this burden by demonstrating that it exercised "proper care," relying on the catchall exception contained in COGSA. Defendant must therefore prove that it was free from negligence. We find the testimony produced by defendant with respect to the loading of the containers on the *Netuno,* their stowage on the ship, and the operation of Pier 36 insufficient to satisfy that burden. We find as a matter of fact that there were significant periods of time when the container could have been pilfered . . . most notably during loading and the voyage (which included stops in three other ports), and during discharge. Moreover, we find the testimony with respect to the general security measures taken on Pier 36 insufficient to establish defendant's freedom from negligence, especially in view of the testimony that coffee was an item in high demand on Pier 36 and easily saleable to salvors during this period of time. Finally, the fact that the unnumbered seals and locks were intact when the loss was discovered is not conclusive. First, the seals, which consist of wire and a seal stamped IBC but have no identifying number or unique characteristic, could be easily duplicated. Second, as the testimony indicated and as other courts have recognized, the locks used on these containers could have been picked.

If defendant had succeeded in showing that the extent of surveillance, fending, internal security measures, and other security measures were such that pilferage could not readily have been accomplished on the pier or during the voyage, we would conclude that, although the precise technique utilized by the thief is still unknown, the defendant had absolved itself of any negligence. But defendant's showing falls far short of this, and the extent of pilferage, especially of coffee, is a matter of record. Since defendant is estopped from denying that the coffee was within the container when it came into its custody, and has not shown that it adopted security measures which would have effectively precluded the inference that the cargo was stolen, plaintiff's prima facie case has not been adequately

*(continued)*

*(continued)*

rebutted, and plaintiff is therefore entitled to recover its damages.

So ordered.

**Decision.**    The District Court ruled that the consignee was entitled to recover for the missing coffee. The carrier was not permitted to relieve itself of liability for the shortage by claiming that the weight or quantity of cargo stated on the bill of lading was the weight or count of the shipper. Further, the court held that the carrier had failed to meet its burden of proof under COGSA that it had used due care in protecting the cargo during shipment.

**Comment.**    This case illustrates the carrier's predicament. If it refuses to put the shipper's quan-

tity or weight on the bill of lading, it runs the risk that a consignee might refuse to purchase it. After all, the buyer wants assurance that the goods are actually in the container. Opening every container to check the shipper's count would be impracticable, costly, and contrary to maritime practice. Thus, the only practical alternative for the carrier might now be to omit all reference on the bill of lading to the shipper's quantity and to simply weigh the container on receipt and on discharge. On appeal, the Second Circuit confirmed that the carrier would have had a defense against a claim for shortage of weight if it had weighed the container at loading, listed that weight on the bill of lading, and then weighed it again at unloading and found the same weight.

sealed containers even where the quantity stated on the bill of lading was the shipper's count. The liability of the carrier in this case stems from the carrier's option of weighing the container when it is received in order to confirm the existence of cargo inside, and then weighing it again at its destination in order to prove delivery.

## The Per Package Limitation

In the United States, COGSA also provides that carriers are not liable in amounts in excess of

$500 "per package" where the shipper has had a "fair opportunity" to indicate the nature and value of the shipment on the bill of lading. Typically, the bill provides blank spaces on the front in which to declare a value for the goods, and a notice to the shipper on the reverse side of its right to do so. Shippers will be charged a higher rate for cargo of greater value.

Where the shipper has not declared the value of the cargo, any loss or damage to the goods is likely to lead to litigation over what constitutes a "package." Where the goods are not shipped in

---

BACKGROUND AND FACTS

The plaintiff, Z.K. Marine, is an importer of yachts for sale in the United States. In 1987, five yachts were shipped from Taiwan to the United States aboard the MV *Archigetis.* Each yacht was shipped under a clean negotiable bill of lading. Each of the five bills of lading provided on its face that one unit only was being shipped, that the yacht was being shipped on deck at the shipper's risk, and that the value of the goods could be declared with prior notice. On the back of each bill of lading, the liability for danger or loss was limited to $500 per package or customary freight unit. All five yachts were secured by cradles and shipped on deck. During tran-

### Z.K. Marine, Inc. v. M/V Archigetis
*776 F.Supp. 1549 (1991)*
**United States District Court, (S.D. Fl.)**

sit, one yacht was lost and the other four were damaged. The bills of lading were purchased by the plaintiffs while the yachts were in transit. The defendant claims that it is liable only in the amount of $500 per yacht.

HOEVELER, DISTRICT JUDGE

Defendants argue that pursuant to the *Carriage of Goods by Sea Act,* and the explicit provisions of the bills of lading, damages are limited to $500 per package. Because the bills of lading are clearly stamped "one unit," defendants contend that their liability is limited to $500 per yacht. Alternatively,

*(continued)*

*(continued)*

defendants argue that if the yachts are not one package, they are each a customary freight unit—since the freight charges were based upon a customary freight unit and yacht was used as the basis of a single freight charge—and consequently subject of the $500 limitation.

Plaintiffs argue that the terms of the bills of lading should be given no effect because the consignees had no opportunity to declare a higher value for the yachts, they now argue that the carrier cannot now limit its liability. Plaintiffs urge the Court to disregard the explicit limitation because they had no chance to bargain over this clause. Alternatively, plaintiffs argue that the limitation is for $500 per package, not per yacht, and thus the limitation does not apply to this situation. . . .

First, [plaintiffs] argue that there is no opportunity to declare a higher value because the bills of lading themselves provide no space to do so. A cursory inspection of the bills of lading reveals that this is not the case, however. On the face of the bills, in capital letters, it states that the "VALUE OF GOODS MAY BE DECLARED PROVIDED MERCHANT GIVES PRIOR NOTICE AND AGREES TO PAY GREATER FREIGHT AD VALOREM BASES SEE CL 18 ON BACK HEREOF." Clause 18 limits the value to $500 per package unless a higher value is declared and higher freight paid. Although there is no specific slot for the shipper to write in its higher value, there appears plenty of space on the face of the bills for it to do so, if desired. The bills plainly afford space and, by their terms, opportunity for the shipper to declare a higher value.

Plaintiffs argue in the alternative that even if the bills of lading offer the shipper opportunity to declare a higher value, the plaintiffs, as purchasers of the negotiable bills, had no such opportunity. Therefore, they argue that the limitation provisions should not be enforced. Purchasers of a negotiable bill of lading, however, purchase only those rights which the shipper had. The right to de-clare a higher value and pay higher freight ended when the goods were delivered on board the ship. Therefore, the purchasers of the bills cannot now complain if a higher value was not declared.

Plaintiffs' next contention is that each yacht is not a package so that the limitation to $500 per package does not apply. Plaintiffs contend that the cradles attached to the yachts for ease in transporting them do not suffice as packaging because the cradles do not enclose the yachts. Plaintiffs are mistaken in this regard. A package is some class of cargo, irrespective of size or weight, which has been prepared for transportation by the addition of some packaging that facilitates handling, but which does not necessarily enclose the goods. . . . In the instant case, the yachts were all transported on cradles, analogous, for purposes of the package analysis, to skids. Accordingly, this court finds that each yacht constituted a package within the purview of COGSA's liability limitation provisions. Therefore the limitation of $500 per package on the bills of lading applies to limit liability of the carrier to $500 per yacht. . . .

**Decision.** The court held that each yacht had constituted one package unit, that the shipper had been given a fair opportunity to declare a higher value, and that the carrier had validly limited its liability to $500 per package. The purchasers of the bills of lading are bound by the terms of the bills of lading, including the limitation provisions.

**Comment.** COGSA's limitation of liability generally does not apply to goods carried above deck, however, in this case, a provision in the bill of lading stated that it would be governed by COGSA. This type of statement is known as a *clause paramount.* Thus, the court held that the COGSA package limitation applied to these yachts.

packages, the $500 limit applies to a *customary freight unit* for goods of that type. For instance, when a large corrugated container is strapped to a wooden skid, the courts usually hold that the $500 limitation applies to each of the smaller boxes inside. In one case, the shipper entered a claim for losses to 4,400 men's suits being transported by container. Each suit was on a hanger in its own plastic wrapper. The court looked to the bill of lading, which stated that 4,400 suits were being shipped, and set the limitation of liability at a maximum of $2.2 million.

A number of carriers have tried to claim that an ocean container, in which large quantities of goods can be transported, constitutes a "package." The courts have not agreed. In *Mitsui & Co.*

*v. American Export Lines,* 636 F.2d 807 (2nd Cir. 1980), the court considered whether an ocean container is a "package" for purposes of the $500 COGSA limitation. Steel ocean containers resemble truck trailers without the wheels. They are usually 8′ × 8′ × 20′ long, or 8′ × 8′ × 40′ long. In this case, Armstrong had shipped 1,705 rolls of floor covering to Japan. Each roll was six feet long, contained 60 square yards of material wrapped around a hollow cardboard roll, and weighed about 300 lbs. Each was wrapped in brown paper. The rolls were packed and sealed in 13 containers at Armstrong's factory. The bill of lading described the shipment as "13 containers, said to contain 1,705 rolls of floor covering." It also gave the weight and measurement of the rolls, but stated no value. The containers were lost at sea during a storm. Armstrong claimed damages in excess of $350,000 for the CIF value of the merchandise. The carrier claimed it was liable for only $6,500 ($500 × 13 containers). In awarding Armstrong full value for its loss, the court stated that, "Certainly, if the individual crates or cartons prepared by the shipper and containing his goods can rightly be considered 'packages' standing by themselves, they do not suddenly lose that character upon being stowed in a carrier's container. I would liken these containers to detachable stowage compartments of the ship. They simply serve to divide the ship's overall cargo stowage space into smaller, more serviceable loci. . . . A container is not a COGSA package if its contents and the number of packages or units are disclosed (on the bill of lading)."

These cases give due warning to the export sales manager. The shipper should always be certain that the goods are correctly described, weighed, and counted, and that their value is correctly stated on the bill of lading. Moreover, a shipper must never knowingly or fraudulently misstate the identity of cargo or its value on the bill of lading, or the carrier cannot be held liable for any damage to the goods.

## Liability for a Material Deviation

In the nineteenth century, steamships commonly interrupted a voyage and detoured from their customary or shortest route if presented with the opportunity to profit by loading or discharging cargo or passengers. Today, COGSA largely prevents this practice by prohibiting a carrier from deviating from the journey unless necessary to save lives or property at sea.

Any material deviation from the terms of the bill of lading can cause the carrier to lose any immunity or protection it may have under the act. For instance, in one case an Israeli-owned vessel was transporting clock movements through the Gulf of Mexico from Israel to Louisville, Mississippi. It was ordered to unload at Mobile and return to Israel in order to join in the war effort. The clocks were left to be damaged on an unsheltered dock. The court held that this action was a material deviation for which the carrier is liable. If the material deviation is unreasonable, the carrier becomes a virtual insurer of the cargo. When a material deviation occurs, most U.S. courts have held that the carrier cannot claim protection of the $500 per package limitation.

Most courts have also held that stowage of cargo *above deck* under a clean bill of lading without the consent of the shipper is deemed to be an unreasonable material deviation from the terms of the bill of lading. Accordingly, goods can generally not be stowed above deck, where they are exposed to the weather and seas, unless the bill of lading specifically allows it, or unless the shipper knew that it was the common practice of the carrier to stow the particular type of goods in question above deck.

Several court cases have distinguished between carrying exposed cargo above deck and stowing it in a sealed ocean container. The courts noted that transporting cargo in a sealed ocean container on the deck of a modern container ship is not an unreasonable deviation, because containers stowed on deck are not necessarily subject to greater risks than containers stowed below deck (although as a practical matter, ocean containers are not entirely watertight). The court also considered the fact that many ships and loading terminals are designed exclusively for handling containerized cargo.

**Himalaya Clauses.** If a carrier is relieved from liability under COGSA, such as for an error in navigation, can a plaintiff recover against the captain and crew? Would stevedores be responsible to the owner of cargo for damage caused by the negligent operation of a crane? In many countries, the Hague Rules, from which COGSA was derived, do not apply to parties other than the carrier. These countries exclude stevedores, who are generally independent contractors of the carrier. To protect these other parties, carriers include provisions in their bills of lading extending the protection of the Hague Rules to their agents, employees, and independent contractors. These *Himalaya clauses,* named after a famous case, are recognized in some countries, including the United States, and are invalid in others (e.g., the United Kingdom and Canada).

## The Hamburg Rules

In 1978 the United Nations completed drafting a new Convention on the Carriage of Goods by Sea, known as the *Hamburg Rules*. These rules are different from the *Hague Rules* and COGSA. They do not relieve the carrier for errors in navigation or in the management of the ship, and they make ocean carriers liable for losses resulting from negligence. They also make it easier for cargo owners to win their cases against carriers. These rules were drafted by the United Nations to serve the interests of cargo owners and shippers in developing countries that do not have large carrier fleets. The rules are also supported by shippers in other countries who believe they will reduce insurance costs. As of 1994, 22 countries (mostly developing countries) had sanctioned the new rules, making them legally binding in those countries only. However, higher insurance rates for shipowners who sail to or from these countries are already being charged by international marine insurance pools. The rules are strongly opposed by carriers and insurance companies worldwide, and adoption of the Hamburg Rules in the United States and other ocean-going nations seem unlikely at present.

## The Visby Amendments

The United States may be closer to simply passing amendments to its current law than it is to adopting the Hamburg Rules. The *Visby Amendments* are amendments to the original 1924 Hague Rules. They are already in effect in some countries, in-

cluding the United Kingdom, Canada, most of Western Europe, Japan, Hong Kong, and Singapore. The Visby Amendments raise the per package limitation of carriers to an amount based on special drawing rights of the International Monetary Fund, or approximately $1,000, and make them liable for all losses resulting from the carrier's "recklessness" in the operation and navigation of the ship. The carrier is reckless if it knew or should have known that its conduct would be likely to cause damage.

> **http://www.tradeport.org**
> A comprehensive site covering all aspects of international trade. Log on to "Tradeport," go to the section on "Moving the Goods." Online shipping tutorial, export documentation, links to shipping companies and freight forwarders, seaports, and ocean shipping schedules.

# Marine Cargo Insurance

As evident from the foregoing discussions, the insuring of cargo is an essential element of international trade. The potential for damage and loss to goods, particularly during ocean shipments that are more lengthy and more hazardous than air shipments, is tremendous. The last chapter demonstrated how the risk of loss can be allocated between buyer and seller, often through the use of trade terms. If loss does occur, the party bearing the risk (perhaps the holder of the bill of lading) will surely seek to shift its financial burden to an insurer. Sellers, buyers, and even banks that finance international sales will want to be certain that their interest in the goods is fully insured. If not, the property risks will prove unacceptably high.

## Marine Insurance Policies and Certificates

While policies of insurance are issued to cover individual shipments, many shippers who do large volumes of business overseas maintain *open cargo policies*. An open policy offers the convenience and protection of covering all shipments by the shipper of certain types of goods to certain destinations and over specified routes. With an open policy in effect, the exporter is authorized by the insurance company to issue a certificate of insurance on a form provided by the company. Open cargo policies are often used by exporters shipping on CIF terms. These certificates are negotiable and are thus transferred along with the bill of lading to the party who purchases and takes title to the goods. The type or form of the certificate is determined by the contract between the parties or by the requirements of the bank that is providing financing for the sale. The insurance company must be notified as soon as possible after shipment under an open policy.

---

*Foreign Accents*

---

# Outlaws of the Ocean
## Piracy: The Jolly Roger Flies Again

The coasts of West Africa have suffered from lawlessness for centuries, and it was not the Africans who created that condition in the first place. It was the slavers of Europe and America who brought pillage, kidnapping, rape, and murder to these shores. Pirates, bent on reaping an even quicker profit, would rip off the slavers. Corruption induced among local chieftains by slave traders became enigmatic to Africa's West Coast. The heavy hand of history rests on that coast now. Nigeria's oil wealth, Sierra Leone's diamond wealth, and the Ivory Coast's agricultural success have created a purchasing power far exceeding previous experiences. Ships are arriving in great numbers from ports all over the world, bringing the bounty of industrialized economies. The ports, however, were not equipped for the import-export demands of these rapidly developing countries. Neither the physical facilities nor the staff capacity were available to handle the sudden enormous trade. Long delays would occur. Delays of ships in port mean loss of income to the line. To cut down on delays, bribes had to be offered for preferential docking rights. That fouled up matters even more. Docking facilities being as limited as they are, many ships were bound to be delayed. And these delays were now being exploited by the new breed of harbor pirates!

As one report put it:

> One ship was recently attacked 12 times in a five-day period. The port, one of the busiest in Africa, never has fewer than 50 ships at anchor at one time, and it is estimated that every freighter that has called here regularly in the last few years has been attacked at least once.

As the frequency and ferocity of incidents have increased, so have the official protests and demands for protection, yet piracy

> has reached such an outrageous level that shipping agents representing lines from the United States, Europe, and the Far East are concerned that their maritime unions might boycott the port.

The government of Nigeria acted incompetently in the deteriorating situation. Neither a curb on nighttime movement of fishing vessels, nor the establishment of a committee to study port security, nor the stationing of some sixty soldiers at the entrance to the piers did much to curb the piracy of the ships anchored in the roadstead.

> When a committee of the shipping trade groups of the Nigerian Chamber of Commerce and Industry asked the police to begin an antipirate patrol, it was told by the inspector general of police that the police did not have the means to do it.

Help was not forthcoming from the Nigerian government. The shipping lines, contractually bound to convey cargo to Lagos, had to resort to self-help. Some took the risky measure of arming the officers of their vessels. Others, relying on insurance, advised their captains to yield when necessary to protect the lives of officers and crew. The most ingenious response was that of the Norwegian Karlander Line, which hired men from Nigeria's Hausa tribe, known for their ferocity, to stand guard at anchorage in Lagos and to shoot with bows and arrows at attackers. But soon the pirates found out

*(continued)*

*(continued)*

which of the Norwegian ships had bowmen aboard and promptly attacked those that didn't. One tanker crew was so frightened after the first attack and ransacking of their ship that to a man they asked to sign off in the next harbor.

Masters of vessels and ships' agents soon suspected collusion between the pirates and port and customs officials, since pirates appeared to have accurate information on all "the ships and the flags they are flying and what kind of cargo they have." As the captain of the West German freighter *Hartford Express* reported to his country's embassy in Lagos, "The aimed proceeding of the pirates implied that they had been in possession of the stowage plan, which must have been given to them by someone on shore."

The pirates of Nigeria, and their accessories ashore, are acting out an age-old scenario. "It's our time to get rich and even. This is our opportunity!" The early American pirates used galleons, schooners, and brigantines. Today's Nigerian pirates are using dugouts with Mercury outboards. There is excitement for the loyal youths in this kind of adventure, as they swoop down from their hideouts, storm ships, and loot their cargoes. And there is large and fast profit: "Within hours the booty finds it ways into the Lagos shops and streets, where it is hawked by women and children at black market prices."

But pilferage of the cargo or of the crew's possessions is not the pirates' only goal and bounty. Entire ships simply disappear. On January 21, 1978, the *New York Times* reported that the Panamanian-registry freighter *Chief S. B. Bakare*, with $4.2 million worth of Japanese cargo aboard, had vanished off the coast of Nigeria. A ship of 12,000 tons and her entire crew!

## EPILOGUE
### Modern Piracy: A Resurgent Threat to Commerce

Piracy, the act of boarding a merchant vessel on the high seas for purposes of committing theft, robbery, or other crimes, was thought to have disappeared from the oceans—and for nearly two centuries it did. But in the mid 1970s, piracy reappeared in the Caribbean as well as off the coast of West Africa and in the Malacca Straits (between Malaysia and Singapore to the north, and Sumatra and Indonesia to the South), mostly in the form of coastal piracy. In the 1980s, incidents of piracy occurred at the rate of nearly one per day and included the taking of valuables of crew; theft of cargo; and sometimes the taking of entire vessels, often with the loss of life.

With the decline in the number of ships waiting for off-loading at Lagos, Nigeria, opportunities for piracy decreased dramatically in that part of the world, and increased security (communications, electronics, naval patrols) caused a sharp decrease of piracy in the Malacca Straits.

By the mid 1990s, piracy had moved to the ports of Cameroon and Angola, and particularly to Santos and Rio de Janeiro, Brazil, where pirates (local, organized maritime robbers) now attack mostly ships at anchor. Brazil has created a federal task force to deal with the problem, since it greatly endangers Brazilian maritime commerce, yet the problem persists.

**Mueller and Adler**
*Outlaws of the Ocean*, New York, Hearst Marine Books (1985). Copyright by Gerhard O. W. Mueller and Freda Adler.

Reprinted by permission.

When a sales contract calls for the seller to obtain a marine insurance policy or certificate on behalf of the buyer, the certificate is universally understood to be acceptable. When the parties state only that a contract is CIF, however, and make no reference to insurance, some confusion can arise as to whether a certificate will be accepted.

The English view is that a certificate of insurance will not substitute for an insurance policy. In a 1924 case, *Kunglig Jarnvagsstyrelsen v. Dexter & Carpenter, Inc.*, 299 Fed.991 (S.D.N.Y. 1924), a U.S. court rejected the English view. The court based its argument on the fact that insurance certificates are so widely recognized in commerce that they should be recognized in the law. This rule has been adopted by the UCC.

## General Average and FPA Losses

Marine insurance policies cover several different types of loss: (1) total losses of all or part of a shipment, (2) general average losses, and (3) partial or particular average losses.

The term *average* in marine insurance law means loss. A *general average* is a loss that results when extraordinary expenses or losses are incurred in saving the vessel or its cargo from danger at sea. This ancient principle of maritime law, which was developed long before insurance was available, spreads the risk of a disaster at sea by making all parties to the voyage contribute to any loss incurred. Under this rule, if A's cargo is damaged or "sacrificed" in the process of saving the ship, and B's cargo is saved as a result, B or its insurer must contribute to A for the loss. A's claim is a general average. In other words, the owner of the cargo that was sacrificed would have a general average claim for contribution against the owner of the cargo that was saved. For example, when fire threatens an entire ship, and certain cargo is damaged by water in putting the fire out, the owners of all of the cargo must contribute to the loss of the cargo that was damaged by the water. The owners of cargo that is thrown overboard to save a sinking ship may have a claim against those whose cargo was thereby saved. General average claims are typically covered by marine insurance.

In order to prove a general average claim, the claimant must show that (1) the ship, cargo, and crew were threatened by a common danger; (2) the danger was real and substantial (the older cases required that the danger also be "imminent"); and (3) the cargo or ship was voluntarily sacrificed for the benefit of both, or extraordinary expenses were incurred to avert a common peril.

**The York-Antwerp Rules.** The *York–Antwerp Rules* are a set of standardized rules on general average. An effort to develop commonly accepted principles of general average began in England as early as 1860, with work on the rules being completed in 1890. Following World War II, an international effort to achieve universally accepted general average rules resulted in the revised *York-Antwerp Rules* of 1950. The rules have achieved widespread acceptance by the maritime industry; the latest version was agreed to in 1994. The rules are not the subject of treaty or convention, and have not been enacted into national laws. They traditionally have become a part of the contract of carriage because their provisions are generally incorporated into all modern bills of lading.

**General Average Claims by the Carrier.** Surprisingly enough, ocean carriers can bring general average claims against the owners of cargo. As the following case illustrates, the principles of general average also apply when a carrier incurs extraordinary expenses in rescuing, saving, or repairing an endangered ship. In your reading, notice how carefully the court circumscribes the loss that is general average and the loss that is not.

The results of general average law must have been quite surprising to the plaintiff in *Amerada*

---

BACKGROUND AND FACTS

In 1967, the *Beauregard* was operated by Sea Land, sailing from New York with cargo in containers bound for Rio Haina, Dominican Republic. While proceeding into the harbor of Rio Haina, the *Beauregard* encountered adverse weather and seas. Strong currents beached the ship on rocks. The pilot signaled distress, and a tug was at the scene within minutes. After ten minutes of pulling, as the vessel was beginning to move but

### Sea-Land Service, Inc. v. Aetna Insurance Company
545 F.2d 1313 (1976)
United States Court of Appeals (2d Cir.)

before she was free, the towline broke. The vessel was pushed sideways by the wind and waves, causing additional damage to the ship's bottom. The *Beauregard* was eventually refloated and put on her way, arriving in Rio Haina the next morning with her cargo and crew safe and sound. The district court awarded Sea Land general average contribution for the costs of towing and removing

*(continued)*

*(continued)*

the vessel from the rocks, but denied general average for the damage to the bottom of the ship. Sea Land appealed.

## MULLIGAN, CIRCUIT JUDGE

The concept of general average contribution in maritime law is ancient, dating back to the Romans, surviving we are told the fall of the Roman Empire and recognized from the Middle Ages until the present time by all the principal maritime nations. G. Gilmore and C. Black, *The Law of Admiralty* 244–45 (2d ed. 1975). The principle is simply stated when one who partakes in a maritime venture incurs loss for the common benefit, it should be shared ratably by all who participate in the venture. Modern law and practice relating to the adjustment of general average is determined generally by the *York-Antwerp Rules,* 1950. The complaint in this action alleges in Par. 8 that the bills of lading issued for the cargo carried on board the *Beauregard* provide that "General Average shall be adjusted, stated, and settled according to the *York-Antwerp Rules,* 1950. . . ." Rule A of these Rules defines a general average act as "any extraordinary sacrifice or expenditure [which] is intentionally and reasonably made or incurred for the common safety for the purpose of preserving from peril the property involved in a common maritime adventure." There is no dispute here that the effort of the Master of the *Beauregard* to free the vessel from the strand by the use of the tow was an act of general average. The costs of the tow have already been determined and stipulated on that basis. The vessel, the crew, and the cargo were in imminent peril, and the Captain acted promptly and reasonably for the common good. No negligence on the part of either the Master or the Pilot caused the stranding.

However, it does not follow that the damage to the bottom of the *Beauregard* is recoverable as general average. Rule C of the *York-Antwerp Rules,* 1950, provides: "Only such losses, damages, or expenses which are the direct consequence of the general average act shall be allowed as general average." Moreover, Rule E provides: "The onus of proof is upon the party claiming in general average to show that the loss or expense claimed is properly allowable as general average." There was, however, no finding of fact that the damage . . .

was caused by the act of sacrifice, the towing. . . . In fact . . . the court found: "The master's action in attempting the tow in no way increased the danger to the ship." We conclude that the plaintiffs did not shoulder the burden of proof of establishing that the towing so moved the vessel that she became more vulnerable to natural forces, thereby rendering the bottom damage general average. . . .

We further agree that if the breaking of the towline permitted a sideward movement that would not otherwise have occurred, the damage would be general average . . . and cases such as *Australian Coastal Shipping Commission v. Green,* (1971) 1 Ll.Rep. 16 (C.A.1970) and *Anglo-Grecian Steam Trading Co. v. T. Beynon & Co.,* (1926) 25 Ll.L.Rep. 122 (K.B.1926) would be in point. In both cases the act of towing caused the damage. In *Green,* which involved two incidents of towing by tugs where the snapping of the towlines caused them to become ensnared in the propellers of the tugs, the resulting damage to the tugs was properly found to be the direct consequence of the sacrifice. The subsequent accident, the parting of the towline, did not break the chain of causation. In *Beynon,* the vessel was in peril and was taken into tow. The intention was to beach the vessel in the center of a bay. On the way she grounded, the towlines parted and the ship was damaged on the rocks. Again, it was held to be general average damage directly caused by the act of sacrifice. However, the applicability of these cases here depends upon Sea Land's ability to establish that the tow had permitted the vessel to be pulled free enough to permit a sideward motion which otherwise would not have occurred. In sum, Sea Land cannot escape the issue of fact which, as we have already indicated, it has failed to do.

**Decision.** The decision of the district court was affirmed. The court determined that the expenses incurred in freeing the vessel from the rocks was an act of general average, but that the damage to the bottom of the vessel resulting from natural forces occurring after the tow line parted was not.

**Comment.** The seaworthiness of the vessel in this case was not disputed. Principles of maritime law will not allow a general average if the vessel is shown to be unseaworthy (as under COGSA).

*Hess Corporation v. S/T Mobil Apex,* 602 F.2d 1095 (2nd Cir. 1979). Plaintiff shipped gasoline and naphtha. When the cargo was destroyed by an explosion and fire that had been started by sparks from machinery in the engine room, the plaintiff sued the carrier for damages. The carrier counterclaims for general average losses. The court denied recovery to the cargo owner under COGSA, holding that the carrier was not liable for the fuel, because the ship was not unseaworthy. The court then held, much to the chagrin of the plaintiff, that it was actually liable to the carrier for towing and salvage expenses incurred in arresting the fire and saving the ship.

**Real and Substantial Danger.**   Historically, the courts have allowed a general average claim only where the loss occurred as a result of the ship being in imminent peril. Today that concept has been broadened to include instances of *real and substantial danger.* In *Eagle Terminal Tankers, Inc. v. Insurance Company of USSR,* 637 F.2d 890 (2nd Cir. 1981), the ship had traveled for more than a day with a damaged propeller. It dry-docked, unloaded the cargo, had the damage repaired at a cost of $127,000 (which included the crew's expenses during that time), reloaded, and completed its voyage to Leningrad. The court awarded the carrier the general average claim. It noted that "a ship's master should not be discouraged from taking timely action to avert a disaster," and need not be in actual peril to claim general average.

## Particular Average Losses

While total and general average losses are ordinarily covered up to the policy amount, special problems result from partial or particular average losses. A *particular average loss* is a partial loss to the insured's cargo. Many insurance policies limit the insurer's liability for particular average losses. Because many losses only partially damage the cargo, a shipper must understand the particular average terms of the policy. A policy designed *free of particular average (FPA)* will not cover any partial losses. A policy FPA, followed by certain specified losses, will not pay for any partial or particular average losses of that nature. As such, an "FPA fire" policy will not pay for partial losses to the cargo due to fire.

## Types of Coverage

Marine cargo insurance is available for virtually any type of risk, for any cargo, destined for almost any port (see Exhibit 7.2). The only limitations are the willingness of the insurer to undertake the risk and the price. The types of risk covered in a policy are described in the perils clause.

**The Perils Clause.**   The *perils clause* covers the basic risks of an ocean voyage. It generally covers extraordinary and unusual perils that are not expected during a voyage. Examples of perils that are included are bad weather sufficient to overcome a seaworthy vessel, shipwreck, stranding, collision, and hitting rocks or floating objects. (An example of a perils clause follows in the next case.) But not every event that can damage goods is covered by this clause. Damage due to the unseaworthiness of the vessel is not included in a perils clause; neither is loss from explosion or pilferage, and the clause only covers losses while at sea. Moreover, only *fortuitous losses* are covered. Fortuitous is a concept that runs throughout insurance law. It means that the loss occurred by chance or accident and could not have reasonably have been predicted. For example, damage due to predictable winds or waves are generally *not* held to be fortuitous. Thus, if a ship sinks in calm seas and good weather, it is presumed that the loss was caused by the ship's own unseaworthiness. Only if it is proven that the ship was seaworthy can it then be shown that the loss was due to a fortuitous event. Courts have held that damage from seawater due to improper stowage of goods is not fortuitous.

A shipper who desires additional coverage can purchase it from the insurer at an added charge. This is called a *specially to cover clause.* For instance, while damage resulting from explosion is not generally covered in a standard perils clause, insurance to cover it can be obtained in the form of an explosion clause. Similarly, additional coverage can be purchased to protect against the risks of fresh water damage, moisture damage, and rust or contamination of the cargo from chemicals, oil, or fuel. Many insurers have recently offered specially designed import–export insurance packages for shippers of perishable foodstuffs, tobacco, steel, and other products and commodities.

**EXHIBIT 7.2**    Marine Cargo Insurance Policy

# CHUBB GROUP
## of Insurance Companies
**CHUBB**   100 William Street, New York, N.Y. 10038

# CARGO POLICY OF INSURANCE

$       Number

Issued by the stock insurance company shown below

Open Policy No.

**FEDERAL INSURANCE COMPANY**
Incorporated under the Laws of New Jersey

In consideration of a premium as agreed, the Company
**Does insure (lost or not lost)**
to the amount of               Dollars,
on

valued at       to be shipped on board of the       B/L Date
at and from
to
and it is hereby understood and agreed, that in case of loss, such loss is payable to the order of
on surrender of this Policy.

*(continued)*

Touching the Adventures and Perils which said Assurers are contented to bear, and take upon themselves, in this Voyage, they are of the Seas, Fires, Assailing Thieves, Jettisons, Barratry of the Master and Mariners, and all other like Perils, Losses and Misfortunes that have or shall come to the Hurt, Detriment or Damage of the said Goods and Merchandise, or any part thereof except as may be otherwise provided for herein or endorsed hereon. AND in case of any Loss or Misfortune, it shall be lawful and necessary to and for the Assured, his or their Factors, Servants and Assigns, to sue, labor and travel for, in and about the Defense, Safeguard and Recovery of the said Goods and Merchandise, or any part thereof, without Prejudice to this insurance; nor shall the acts of the Assured or Assurers, in recovering, saving and preserving the property insured, in case of disaster, be considered a waiver or an acceptance of an abandonment; to the charges whereof, the said Assurers will contribute according to the rate and quantity of the sum hereby insured.

In case of loss, such loss to be paid in thirty days after proof of loss and proof of interest in the property hereby insured.

In case the interest hereby insured is covered by other insurance (except as hereinafter provided) the loss shall be collected from the several policies in the order of the date of their attachment, insurance attaching on the same date to be deemed simultaneous and to contribute pro rata; provided, however, that where any fire insurance, or any insurance (including fire) taken out by any carrier or bailee is available to the beneficiary of this policy, or would be so available if this insurance did not exist, then this insurance shall be void to the extent that such other insurance is or would have been available. It is agreed, nevertheless, that where these Assurers are thus relieved of liability because of the existence of other insurance, these Assurers shall receive and retain the premium payable under this policy and, in consideration thereof, shall guarantee the solvency of the companies and/or underwriters this clause, but not exceeding, in any case, the amount which would have been collectible under this policy if such other insurance did not exist.

In all cases of damage caused by perils insured against, the loss shall, as far as practicable, be ascertained by a separation and a sale or appraisement of a damaged portion only of the contents if the packages so damaged and not otherwise.

Losses arising from breakage and/or leakage and/or loss of weight and/or loss of contents are excluded from this insurance unless caused by stranding or collision with another vessel, or unless this insurance has been expressly extended to include such losses.

Warranted free from Particular Average unless the vessel or craft be stranded, sunk or burnt, but notwithstanding this warranty these Assurers are to pay any loss of or damage to the interest insured which may reasonably be attributed to fire, collision or contact of the vessel and/or conveyance with any external substance (ice included) other than water, or to discharge of cargo at port of distress. The foregoing warranty, however, shall not apply where broader terms of average are provided for herein or by endorsement hereon.

If the voyage aforesaid shall have been terminated before the date of this policy, then there shall be no return of premium on account of such termination of the voyage.

Wherever the words "ship", "vessel", "seaworthiness", "ship or vessel owner" appear in this Policy, they are deemed to include also the words "aircraft", "airworthiness", "aircraft owner".

**THIS INSURANCE IS SUBJECT TO THE AMERICAN INSTITUTE CARGO CLAUSES (FEB. 1949) (INCLUDING THE WAREHOUSE TO WAREHOUSE CLAUSE), SOUTH AMERICAN 60 DAY CLAUSE WHEN APPLICABLE. ALSO SUBJECT TO THE AMENDED F. C. & S. AND S. R. & C. C. WARRANTIES (OCT. 1959) (*SEE REVERSE*)**

*(continued)*

**EXHIBIT 7.2    Marine Cargo Insurance Policy—(continued)**

**Original and Duplicative issued, one of which being accomplished the other to stand null and void**

| SPECIAL CONDITIONS | Marks and Numbers |
|---|---|
| ON DECK—Merchandise and/or goods shipped on deck to an On Deck Bill of Lading *which must be so specified in this policy* are insured.—Free of particular average unless caused by the vessel being stranded, sunk, burnt, on fire, or in collision, but including jettison and/or washing overboard, irrespective of percentage. | |

**Where the words "including M. E. C."** are typed in the space below at the time the policy is issued, this insurance is subject to the American Institute Marine Extension Clauses.

**Where the words "including Strike Risks"** are typed in the space below at the time the policy is issued, this insurance is subject to the Current American Institute S. R. & C. C. Clauses.

**Where the words "including War Risk"** are typed in the space below at the time the policy is issued, this insurance is subject to the Current War Risk Clauses.

In Witness Whereof, the Company issuing this policy has caused this policy to be signed by its authorized officers, but this policy shall not be valid unless signed by a duly authorized representative of the Company.

**.FEDERAL INSURANCE COMPANY**

Date:

*Henry G Gubel*
Secretary

*Henry L. Harlon*
President _____

Authorized Representative

The following Warranties shall be paramount and shall not be modified or superseded by any other provision included herein or stamped or endorsed hereon unless such other provision refers specifically to the risks excluded by these warranties and expressly assumes the said risks.

(A) "Notwithstanding anything herein contained to the contrary, this insurance is warranted free from capture, seizure, arrest, restraint, detainment, confiscation, preemption, requisition or nationalization, and the consequences thereof or any attempt thereat, whether in time of peace or war and whether lawful or otherwise; also warranted free, whether in time of peace or war, from all loss, damage or expense caused by any weapon of war employing atomic or nuclear fission and/or fusion or other reaction or radioactive force or matter or by any mine or torpedo, also warranted free from all consequences of hostilities or warlike operations (whether there be a declaration of war or not), but this warranty shall not exclude collision or contact with aircraft, rockets or similar missiles or with any fixed or floating object (other than a mine or torpedo), stranding heavy weather, fire or explosion unless caused directly (and independently of the nature of the voyage or service which the vessel concerned or, in the case of a collision, any other vessel involved therein, is performing) by a hostile act by or against a belligerent power; and for the purposes of this warranty 'power' includes any authority maintaining naval, military or air forces in association with a power.

Further warranted free from the consequences of civil war, revolution, rebellion, insurrection, or civil strife arising therefrom, or piracy."

(B) Warranted free of loss or damage caused by or resulting from strikes, lockouts, labor disturbances, riots, civil commotions or the acts of any person or persons taking part in any such occurrence or disorder.

**NOTE: It is necessary for the assured to give prompt notice to these Assurers when they become aware of an event for which they are "held covered" under this policy and the right to such cover is dependent on compliance with this obligation.**

SOURCE:    Sample policy provided courtesy of Chubb Group of Insurance Companies.

The *Shaver* case discusses a standard perils clause and several additional types of coverage purchased by the insured. Unfortunately, none of them covered the loss that the plaintiffs had incurred.

**All Risks Coverage.** An *all risks policy* covers all risks except those specifically excluded in the policy. These policies usually exclude damage from acts of war through a "free of capture and seizure" clause, damage or loss from delay

## Shaver Transportation Company v. The Travelers Indemnity Company
481 F.Supp. 892 (1979)
United States District Court,
(D. Or.)

**BACKGROUND AND FACTS**
Shaver, a barge company, contracted with Weyerhauser, the shipper, to transport caustic soda to a buyer. Shaver arranged for marine cargo insurance with Travelers. Several different types of coverage were discussed. Shaver decided on "free from particular average" and "standard perils" provisions, supplemented with "specially to cover" clauses. Shaver loaded the first shipment of caustic soda on one of its barges and transported it to the buyer. The buyer refused delivery because it had been contaminated with tallow. The contamination occurred as Shaver was loading the caustic soda aboard the barge. The barge had previously carried a load of tallow, and Shaver had not thoroughly cleaned the barge input lines. The barge was returned to Shaver's dock. Shaver and Weyerhauser filed a claim with Travelers. Travelers argued that the contamination did not represent a recoverable loss under the policy. Shaver and Weyerhauser brought this action against Travelers.

SKOPIL, CIRCUIT JUDGE, SITTING BY DESIGNATION
Although the plaintiffs request recovery under several theories, there is only one major issue in the case: Are the losses incurred by the plaintiffs the consequences of an insured event under the marine cargo insurance policy? If the losses are not insured against, no recovery is possible.

**Recovery under the Perils Clause and Free from Particular Average Clause**
The perils clause, almost identical to ancient perils provisions dating back several hundred years, defines the risks protected by the policy. In addition to a long list of "perils of the sea," the clause concludes with "and all other perils, losses, and misfortunes, that have or shall, come to the hurt, detriment, or damage to the said goods and mer-

chandise." Plaintiff argues that the "forced" disposition of the caustic soda was like jettison (an enumerated peril) and is covered by the concluding language of the clause. That language has been interpreted to include only perils that are similar to the enumerated perils.

Whether or not I conclude the forced disposition was a type of jettison, plaintiffs are unable to show an insurable loss due to jettison. The loss contamination of the cargo occurred at the time of loading. . . . Plaintiffs cannot recover under the perils clause of the policy. The term "jettison" also appears in the Free from Particular Average clause. If jettison did occur, this clause affords coverage regardless of the amount of cargo damage. However, I find that a jettison did not occur in this instance. Jettison is the act of throwing overboard from a vessel a part of the cargo, in case of extreme danger, to lighten the ship. The orderly unloading and sale of the cargo to a chemical salvage company is not "jettison." Plaintiff cannot recover under the Free from Particular Average clause.

**Recovery under the . . . Shore Coverage Clause**
The shore coverage clause provides coverage for enumerated risks occurring on shore. Plaintiffs argue that contamination while loading is a shore accident. However, since the contamination occurred within the barge's intake lines, the incident arose "on board." Therefore shore coverage does not apply. Even if it were to apply, contamination of cargo is not within the enumerated risks covered by the shore coverage clause. . . .

**Recovery under the Inchmaree Clause**
The purpose of the Inchmaree clause is to expand the coverage of the policy beyond the perils provision. Federal law allows a vessel owner to become exempt from liability for fault or error in navigation or management of the ship. In contrast, the

*(continued)*

(continued)

shipowner must retain liability for negligence in the care and custody of the cargo. The Inchmaree clause is intended to provide coverage to a cargo owner when a loss is due to error in navigation or management of the vessel since the carrier is exempt from liability. Plaintiffs argue the contamination was the result of an error in management and therefore covered under the Inchmaree clause. Defendant naturally urges the court to find the loss caused by fault in the care and custody of the cargo.

The United States Supreme Court has addressed the distinction between error in management and error in care of cargo but has not articulated a clear test. The Ninth Circuit, noting that no precise definitions exist, advocates a case-by-case determination using the following test: "If the act in question has the primary purpose of affecting the ship, it is "in navigation or in management;" but if the primary purpose is to affect the cargo, it is not "in navigation or in management." *Grace Line, Inc. v. Todd Shipyards Corporation,* 500 F.2d 361, 374 (9th Cir. 1974).

Using this test, I find that the contamination of the cargo in this case was caused by fault in the care, custody, and control of the cargo. The Inchmaree clause will not provide coverage for plaintiffs' losses under the facts of this case.

### Recovery under Negligence Clause

The Negligence clause provides coverage against losses due to enumerated perils caused by the unseaworthiness of the vessel. . . . This unseaworthiness must then cause a loss through one of the enumerated perils: "sinking, stranding, fire, explosion, contact with seawater, or by any other cause of the nature of any of the risks assumed in the policy." . . .

Since contamination is not an enumerated peril, plaintiff urges coverage . . . by suggesting the barge was in imminent danger of sinking. Although there is evidence that the caustic soda would have eventually corroded through the barge and caused it to sink, the process would have taken three to five years. This possibility is too far removed to find coverage under a provision providing for loss due to sinking. No recovery is possible under the Negligence clause of this policy. . . .

Plaintiffs suggest a number of theories of recovery under the marine cargo insurance policy. None is suited to this case. I am aided in my construction of this policy by one additional fact. Shaver rejected insurance coverage costing more but did not believe contamination was covered under the policy. Plaintiffs' present attempt to include this type of loss within the coverage of the policy is an afterthought.

Judgment shall be entered for the defendant.

**Decision.** The plaintiffs' loss due to contamination was not covered under any of the clauses of the insurance policy.

**Comment.** The following clauses were at issue in this case.

### The Perils Clause

"Touching the adventures and perils which the said Assurers are contended to bear, and take upon themselves, they are of the seas and inland waters, man of war, fires, enemies, pirates, rovers, assailing thieves, jettisons, letters of mart and countermart, reprisals, taking at sea, arrests, restraints and detainments of all kings, princes of people of what nation, condition or quality soever, barratry of the master and mariners, and all other perils, losses, and misfortunes, that have or shall come to the hurt, detriment, or damage to the said goods and merchandise, or any part thereof."

### The Shore Clause

"Including while on docks, wharves, or elsewhere on shore and/or during land transportation, risks of collision, derailment, fire, lightning, sprinkler leakage, cyclones, hurricanes, earthquakes, floods, the rising of navigable waters, or any accident to the conveyance and/or collapse and/or subsidence of docks and/or structures, and to pay loss or damage caused thereby, even though the insurance be otherwise FPA."

### The Inchmaree Clause (named after a famous British case)

"This insurance is also specially to cover any loss of or damage to the interest insured hereunder, through the bursting of boilers, breakage of shafts, or through any latent defect in the machinery, hull, or appurtenances, or from faults or errors in the navigation and/or management of the vessel by the Master, Mariners, Mates, Engineers, or Pilots; provided, however, that this clause shall not be construed as covering loss arising out of delay, deterioration, or loss of market, unless otherwise provided elsewhere herein."

### The Negligence Clause

". . . [T]he Assurers agree that in the event unseaworthiness or a wrongful act or misconduct of shipowner, character, their agents or servants, shall, directly or indirectly, cause loss or damage to the cargo insured by sinking, stranding, fire, explosion, contact with seawater, or by any other cause of the nature of any of the risks assumed in the policy, the Assurers will [subject to the terms of average and other conditions of the policy] pay to an innocent Assured the resulting loss."

in reaching the destination, or damage resulting from strikes and civil commotion. Coverage for strikes is available, but only at additional cost.

**War Risk.** Typically, marine insurance policies do not cover the risks of war. *War risk insurance* is available for ocean shipments. If war risk insurance is desired, the shipper will have to purchase it separately from the insurer. Under CIF terms, the seller is not expected to provide war risk insurance. If the buyer wants war risk coverage, it will have to agree on the price separately from the marine insurance provisions. The rates for war risk insurance are relatively stable in peacetime, but fluctuate almost daily in times of war.

## Carrier's Liability for Misdelivery

As mentioned in the last chapter, the carrier is liable for misdelivery of goods. When goods are moving under a negotiable order bill of lading, they must be delivered only to the party that presents the bill to the carrier. Under a straight bill of lading or air waybill the carrier may release the goods only to the consignee. The law is filled with cases resulting from carrier misdelivery. In many reported cases, goods moving under a straight bill of lading have been improperly delivered to the *notify party* instead of to the consignee. The notify party, usually an agent of the importer—such as a customs broker, warehousing firm, or banker—is entitled to receive notice of when the goods will arrive, but not to take custody. In the following case involving a negotiable order bill of lading, the Brazilian importer was able to obtain the goods without presenting the bill. This problem is commonly faced by exporters shipping to South America.

---

**BACKGROUND AND FACTS**
Allied Chemical, a U.S. exporter, received an order from Banylsa, a Brazilian importer, for a shipment of caprolactam, terms C&F Salvador, Brazil. Allied delivered the bags to Lloyd, the carrier, at the Port of Norfolk and received clean, order bills of lading showing that the goods were consigned to the order of Banylsa. Banylsa was also listed as the notify party. Allied sent the bill of lading, draft, and invoice to a Brazilian bank for collection, together with a letter of instruction to deliver the documents only on payment of the sight drafts. In the meantime, the goods had been put into a warehouse under the supervision of the port authority. However, in order to obtain the goods from a state warehouse, one may produce either the bill of lading or a *carta declaratoria,* a letter from the carrier stating that Brazilian import fees had been paid. Banylsa obtained a *carta declaratoria* from Lloyd and used it to obtain possession of the goods from the warehouse. Banylsa never purchased the bill of lading and never paid for the goods. Banylsa then became insolvent and filed for receivership in Brazilian civil court. Allied sued Lloyd for misdelivery in New York.

*Allied Chemical International Corporation v. Companhia De Navegacao Lloyd Brasileiro*
775 F.2d 476 (1985)
United States Court of Appeals (2nd Cir.)

**MESKILL, CIRCUIT JUDGE**
The liability question in this case inextricably involves the critical importance of the documentary transaction in overseas trade. . . . "Delivery to the consignee named in the bill of lading does not suffice to discharge the [carrier] where the consignee does not hold the bill of lading." 2 T.G. Carver, *Carriage by Sea* P. 1953 (R. Colinvaux 13th ed. 1982). If the carrier delivers the goods to one other than the authorized holder of the bill of lading, the carrier is liable for misdelivery. The ocean carrier's liability arises from rights of property and "[d]elivery to a person not entitled to the goods without production of the bill of lading is prima facie a conversion of the goods and a breach of contract." . . .

While it is clear . . . that Lloyd retained some responsibilities after discharge, the bill of lading did not specify what they might be. Therefore, "the law steps in to fill the lacuna" and provides that when Lloyd discharged the cargo, it assumed the status of a bailee. The transfer of the cargo to the port authority, without more, did not alter this status; thus Lloyd remained

*(continued)*

*(continued)*
presumptively responsible for the proper delivery of the goods. We have previously articulated the applicable standard of responsibility under admiralty law: "a bailee is absolutely liable for misdelivering cargo, unless his mistake as to the person entitled to receive the goods was induced by the bailor" or the contract of carriage otherwise reduced or eliminated his liability. There is no suggestion in the record that Allied induced the misdelivery. Allied was not even aware until well after the event that Banylsa had acquired possession of the goods. . . .

Pursuant to the Pomerene Act (Federal Bills of Lading Act), a carrier operating under an order bill of lading is justified in delivering the goods to one lawfully entitled to them or to one in possession of an order bill "by the terms of which the goods are deliverable to his order; or which has been indorsed to him, or in blank by the consignee." When Lloyd caused the goods to be released to Banylsa, by means of the *carta declaratoria,* the bill of lading was still in the custody of the Brazilian bank because payment had not been made on the sight draft. Not having paid on the draft, Banylsa was neither lawfully entitled to the goods nor in possession of the bill. Delivery to Banylsa, therefore, was not justified. . . .

The fact that the government-controlled port authority, rather than Lloyd itself, physically delivered the goods to Banylsa does not in any way relieve Lloyd from liability. As previously noted, it is undisputed that unless Banylsa presented to the port authority either the original bill of lading or a carta declaratoria issued by the carrier, the port authority would not have permitted Banylsa to take the cargo. Because Banylsa did not pay the sight draft and take possession of the bill of lading, Lloyd retained control over the goods. Thus, Lloyd acted at its peril when it authorized the release of the goods to Banylsa without demanding production of the bill. . . .

The judgment of the district court is affirmed. Appellant is liable for costs.

**Decision.** The court held that the carrier was liable for misdelivery of the goods for two reasons. First, a bill of lading is a contract of carriage that must be strictly construed against the party that drafted it, the carrier. Secondly, the court determined that the carrier was liable as a bailee of property belonging to another (the bailor). Thus, if the carrier delivers the goods to one other than the authorized holder of the bill of lading, the carrier is liable for misdelivery, resulting in the tort of conversion of the goods and a breach of contract.

**Comment.** While the court allowed the shipper to recover from the carrier, this case should still serve as a word of caution to U.S. export managers. Beware of maritime customs and shipping practices in countries in which one is inexperienced in doing business.

# Chapter Summary

The greatest portion of trade in the world today still moves on the ocean. The contract of carriage between the shipper and the ocean carrier is set forth in the bill of lading. The transport document used in the air cargo business is known as the air waybill.

The liability of an air carrier is determined by the *Warsaw Convention.* While air carriers are presumed liable for damage to cargo enroute, the amount of recovery is limited. To avoid this limitation, shippers should declare the actual value of the goods on the air waybill.

The liability of the carrier for damage or loss to ocean-going goods, in most nations of the world, is governed by the *Hague Rules,* adopted in the United States as the Carriage of Goods by Sea Act. COGSA provides many limitations on the liability of shipowners. The carrier's primary obligation is to provide a seaworthy ship. Its liability for damage to cargo resulting from errors in navigation, perils of the sea, and fire is limited. A tremendous amount of litigation in the United States concerns cargo that has been lost or damaged during ocean transport. The losses usually fall on the insurers of the cargo and vessel, who often become embroiled in the litigation.

Maritime and marine insurance law is a complicated and specialized area of the law, with concepts dating back to the days of the ancient mariners. Under the law of general average, a carrier can assert a general average claim against the owners of cargo demanding that they (or their insurers) contribute to expenses incurred in saving a vessel from a common peril on the seas. Marine insurance policies are complex contracts. Shippers must exercise caution in insuring their goods for ocean transport, seeking professional advice when deemed prudent.

---

## QUESTIONS AND CASE PROBLEMS

1. What are the policy reasons underlying the protection that the Carriage of Goods by Sea Act (COGSA) offers to ocean carriers? Explain.

2. Tradex Petroleum Services negotiated for the carriage of oil well equipment with West India. West India's agent confirmed by letter that freight rates would be based on the greater of weight or volume. The bill of lading indicated that the freight would be based on tonnage and would amount to $44,800. After reaching its destination, the cargo was unloaded and the rate recalculated on the basis of volume, a sum equal to $108,000. West India, the carrier, claims that it is due the larger amount. What was the result? *West India Industries v. Tradex Petroleum Services,* 664 F.2d 946 (5th Cir. 1981).

3. Sony Corp. packed a shipment of video cassette tapes into a forty-foot ocean container for transport to England. Sony put the tapes into 1,320 cardboard cartons, then strapped the cartons onto 52 wooden pallets. The pallets were put into one shipment container. The bill of lading stated: "1 × 40 container: 1,320 ctns. magnetic tape." The value of the tapes shown on the export certificate was $400,000. On loading, the ship's deck crane dropped the container sixty feet to a concrete deck. Sony claims it can recover the value of the tapes. The ship maintains that under COGSA its liability is limited to 52 pallets. Does COGSA apply in this situation? Why would the carrier want to make this type of argument? What would be the limits of liability for 1,320 cartons versus 52 pallets under COGSA? How many "packages" were involved here and what do you think should be the outcome? *Sony Magnetic Products Inc. of America v. Merivienti O/Y,* 863 F. 2d 1537 (11th Cir. 1989).

4. A shipper of fruits and vegetables delivered a refrigerated van of produce to the S.S. *Bayomon* at the port of Elizabeth, New Jersey, on September 22 for shipment to San Juan, Puerto Rico. The ship was supposed to sail that day, but was unable to do so because of repairs needed to correct a boiler problem. The ship sailed on September 25 and arrived in Puerto Rico on September 27. A clause paramount incorporated COGSA into the bill of lading. Upon arrival in Puerto Rico, part of the produce was found to be rotten. The shipper claims that the carrier is liable because the ship was not "seaworthy." COGSA states that the carrier shall not be liable unless it shows a failure to make the ship seaworthy before and at the beginning of the voyage. Does COGSA apply here considering that the port is domestic rather than foreign? Is the carrier liable for an unseaworthy vessel? What is the outcome? *Squillante & Zimmerman Sales, Inc. v. Puerto Rico Marine Management, Inc.,* 516 F. Supp. 1049 (D. Puerto Rico, 1981).

5. ICC, a Korean corporation, sold down garments to Down in the Village (D/V) of New York. In order to assure payment, however, the garments were consigned to Kologel, an American subsidiary of ICC, with D/V being specified on the air waybill as "notify party" only. Upon their arrival in New York, however, Northwest Airlines delivered the garments to a delivery service representing D/V. Kologel, being unable to recover either the goods or payment from D/V, is attempting to recover from the airline for misdelivery. What is the result? *Kologel v. Down in the Village,* 539 F.Supp. 727 (1982).

6. New York Merchandising Company (NYMCO) imported goods produced by C-ART in Hong Kong. The goods were shipped on the Hong Kong Island Lines (carrier). The parties' prior course of dealings had been for the carrier to release the goods to NYMCO on its presentation of a "bank guarantee." These bank guarantees released the carrier from liability for any misdelivery. On this occasion, however, the carrier released the goods upon NYMCO's corporate guarantee of payment. Soon thereafter, NYMCO filed for Chapter 11 bankruptcy. C-ART sued the carrier to recover the money owed for the goods. The carrier argued that

it was not liable for misdelivery because NYMCO had good title to the goods from the time they were shipped in Hong Kong. Do you agree with this argument? The carrier also claims that the bills of lading are not valid because the importer NYMCO was insolvent. What is wrong with this argument? *C-ART, Ltd. v. Hong Kong Islands Line America, S.A.,* 940 F.2d 530 (1991).

## MANAGERIAL IMPLICATIONS

You are CEO of a firm that regularly imports raw materials from Thailand, Malaysia, Indonesia, and the Philippines. They are shipped to you by ocean carrier through the South China Sea. Your finished goods are sold in the United States and exported to ports in Europe and the Middle East. What kind of information do you need in assessing the risk potential to your cargo passing through these dangerous waters? What will the source of your information be? What sources are available in your library? Which are commercially available? If part of your job is to keep abreast of developments on a daily basis, where will you obtain that information? What types of information might be available from freight forwarders, steamship companies, local port authorities, and insurers?

# Chapter Eight

# Bank Collections, Trade Finance, and Letters of Credit

Chapter Five discussed the law governing contracts for the sale of goods. Chapter Six described how the parties can define and allocate the risks of shipping and transporting the goods sold under a sales contract. Part of that discussion covered how a negotiable document of title can be used to transfer ownership of the goods sold from one party to another. This chapter examines how the international banking system is used to move money from one party in a transaction to another—how sellers collect for their shipments and how buyers remit payments for their purchases. It also explains how banks guarantee that sellers will be paid for their goods through the use of bank letters of credit and how they provide commercial financing for the international sale. Keep in mind that most of the concepts covered here apply not just to collecting money for the sale of goods, but are equally applicable to many different types of international transactions involving the movement of money internationally and the use of banks to provide an assurance of contractual commitments.

> **http://itl.irv.uit.no/trade_law/nav/ electronic.commerce.html**
> *International Trade Law Monitor site for information on electronic commerce.*

## The Bill of Exchange

The *bill of exchange* is a specialized type of *negotiable instrument* commonly used to expedite foreign money payments in many types of international transactions. A bill of exchange is often called a *draft,* or *international draft.* A *documentary draft* is used to expedite payment in a documentary sale. The word *draft* is more frequently used in U.S. law and banking practice, while the term *bill of exchange* is more frequently used outside the United States, particularly in England. Generally, the term *draft* is used in this text except when referring specifically to an English bill of exchange. These negotiable instruments can serve two purposes: (1) they act as a substitute for money; and (2) they act as a financing or credit device.

Although it is beyond the scope of this text to offer a thorough treatment of the law of negotiable instruments, an understanding of the importance of the draft is essential to anyone engaged in international trade.

## The Origin of Bills of Exchange

The origin of the bill of exchange lies in the history of the merchants and traders of fourteenth- and fifteenth-century Europe. As merchants visited the markets of distant cities to buy and sell their wares, they sought a safer means of transferring their gold or money than by carrying it in their caravans. It might have worked like this: Assume Merchant A delivered goods to Merchant B in a distant city, who became indebted to A for the amount of the purchase. Later Merchant A desires to purchase goods from Merchant C. Merchant A could pay Merchant C for the goods with a written piece of paper—an order—addressed by A to B to pay that money to C. Of course, Merchant B was probably wealthy and respected in the trade—one whose credit was highly regarded. Merchant C could present the written order to B for payment immediately, or if he wished, he could simply ask B to sign (or "accept") the order for future payment. The written order to pay thus became an *acceptance*. With the acceptance in hand, Merchant C could purchase new wares from yet another merchant, and use the acceptance in payment. Eventually, merchants turned to wealthy families, Italian banking societies, or medieval bankers spread throughout Europe, to transfer money over great distances by issuing payment orders to their correspondents living in distant cities. As merchants recognized that these orders could be bought and sold, the concept of negotiability evolved and negotiable instruments were born. At first English law did not recognize the validity of negotiable instruments. But merchants accepted them as substitutes for money, and they were enforceable in the merchant's private courts under the Law Merchant. As their importance and use evolved, so did their validity and treatment under the law. They became formally recognized by statute in England in 1822 in the *English Bills of Exchange Act* and in the United States in 1866 in the *Uniform Negotiable Instruments Law.*

Bills of exchange or drafts are today governed in the United States by the Uniform Commercial Code, in England by the Bills of Exchange Act, and in more than 20 other countries by the 1930 *Convention on Bills of Exchange and Promissory Notes.* Despite their common history, these laws differ in their treatment of the creation and transfer of negotiable instruments, as well as the rights of the parties should an instrument be dishonored or refused.

## Brief Requirements of a Bill of Exchange

The English Bills of Exchange Act requires that the bill of exchange be (1) an unconditional order in writing, (2) addressed by one person to another, (3) signed by the person giving it, (4) a requirement that the person to whom it is addressed pay on demand or at a fixed or determinable future time, (5) a sum certain in money, (6) to or *to the order of* a specified person, or to bearer. These characteristics are similar to the requirements for a draft set out in the U.S. Uniform Commercial Code (UCC). (The Convention on Bills of Exchange requires that the words "bill of exchange" appear on the instrument, but English and U.S. laws do not.)

Basically, a bill of exchange or international draft is similar to a check, in that it is an unconditional order to pay a sum of money. (Drafts can be made payable in any currency.) In the case of a check, the *drawer* orders its bank, the *drawee,* to pay the amount of the check to the *payee.* However, instead of being drawn against funds held on deposit in a bank (as with a check), an international draft is an order from the seller to the buyer or buyer's bank to pay the seller upon the delivery of goods or the presentation of shipping documents (e.g., an ocean bill of lading or air waybill). Thus the seller is both the drawer (the one giving the order to pay) and the payee (the one entitled to payment under the instrument). The drawee is either the buyer or its bank, depending on the arrangements made for payment.

**Negotiation and Transfer of Negotiable Instruments.** The commercial use of a draft or other negotiable instrument is derived from its negotiability, the quality that allows it to act as a substitute for money. *Negotiation* is the transfer of an instrument from one party to another so that the transferee (called a *holder*) takes legal rights in the instrument. The correct manner of negotiation depends on whether the instrument is a *bearer* or *order* instrument. Most drafts used in international trade are order instruments, because they are payable to a named payee. In order to negotiate an order instrument, *indorsement* (by signature) *and delivery* of the instrument to the holder must take place. References to the negotiation of international drafts appear throughout this chapter.

## The Documentary Draft and the Bank Collection Process

Drafts come in several different types. A draft that is to be paid upon presentation or demand is known as a *sight draft* because it is payable "on sight." The sight draft is prepared by the seller and is sent to the buyer along with the shipping documents (e.g., the bill of lading) through banking channels, moving from the seller's bank in the country of export to a foreign correspondent bank in the buyer's country and city. The draft is being sent "for collection," known as a *documentary collection.* The banks act as the agent of the seller for collection purposes. The draft and documents are accompanied by a *collection letter* that provides instructions from the seller on such matters as who is responsible for bank collection charges, what to do in the event the buyer dishonors the draft, and instructions for remittance of the proceeds back to the seller. Thus, the collection letter may specify that in the event of the buyer's dishonor of the draft, the seller's agent in the buyer's country is to be notified, and that the goods are to be properly warehoused and insured pending resolution of the problem or sale of the goods to another party.

Essentially, documentary collections function like a cash-on-delivery (C.O.D.) transaction. When the sight draft is presented to the buyer at its bank or place of business, it is paid, and the payment remitted back to the seller. Only then does the bank turn over the shipping documents with which the buyer can claim its cargo from the carrier. The transaction is somewhat risky however, because when presented with documents, there is no guarantee that the buyer will actually pay. Assuming the buyer does pay, the average cycle for completing a documentary collection is approximately three weeks (although most banks offer accelerated schedules). If a sales contract between buyer and seller calls for payment upon presentation of a sight draft, the contract terms commonly call for *cash against documents* (recall Chapters Five and Six).

**The SWIFT System.** International banking transactions are handled through a worldwide telecommunications system known as the SWIFT system, or *Society for Worldwide Interbank Financial Telecommunication.* This system has greatly expedited the remission of payments in a documentary collection. SWIFT is a private, high-speed communications network between banks, set up to transfer funds worldwide. It originated through the cooperative efforts of major banks in Europe, the United States, and Canada in the mid-1970s and is now in use in more than 50 nations. Due to its speed and cost effectiveness, it has largely replaced the use of the telex and mail-in fund transfers. Currently SWIFT is involved in the Bolero Project which is designed to eventually replace the paper-based transfer of trade documents with electronic transmissions on a global scale.

> **http://cnn.com/travel/currency**
> *CNN site performs exchange rate calculations among 164 countries.*

# Trade Finance

Banks and other financial institutions involved in commercial lending provide a wide range of financing packages for international trade, commonly called *trade finance.* Trade finance not only assists the buyer in financing its purchase, but also provides immediate cash to the seller for the sale, and is profitable for the lending institution.

The documentary draft can serve as an important financing or credit device, providing the seller and buyer with a mechanism for financing the international sale. In a competitive marketplace, an exporter must be able to offer its customers credit or other financing for their purchase. Many firms consider their ability to arrange credit a crucial component of their marketing strategy. If an exporter can prearrange financing for the buyer, it has an advantage over a competitor who cannot.

## The Use of Time Drafts and Acceptances

The use of the draft in trade finance works like this: Seller agrees to issue a draft that is due, say, 60 days after shipment of the goods. The draft states that it is due in 60 days, or on a future date specified on the instrument. A draft due at a future date or after a specified period of time is known as a *time draft,* as shown in Exhibit 8.1. The time draft is sent to the buyer for its *acceptance.* Typically, the acceptance is done by stamping the date and the word "accepted" across the face of the draft, together with the name and signature of the drawee—no party is obligated on a draft unless its signature appears on it. Under the Uniform Commercial Code, the

**EXHIBIT 8.1   Time Draft Drawn Under Letter of Credit with Banker's Acceptance**

AT SIGHT _____ DATE_____ CITY_____

(INDICATE ABOVE WHETHER PAYABLE ON DEMAND OR OTHER TIME LIMIT)

PAY TO THE ORDER OF_____ U.S.$ _____

(NAME OF PAYEE)

_____ U.S. DOLLARS

FOR VALUE RECEIVED AND CHARGED TO THE ACCOUNT OF NATIONAL BANK LETTER OF CREDIT NO. _____

THE TRANSACTION WHICH GIVES RISE TO
THIS INSTRUMENT IS THE:
☐ IMPORT  ☐ DOMESTIC SHIPMENT
☐ WAREHOUSING
OF_____
FROM _____ TO _____

ACCEPTED   Date   National Bank, N.A.   Per Authorized Signature

TO: NATIONAL BANK, N.A.
    ANYTOWN, U.S.A.
      (DRAWEE)

DRAWER'S SIGNATURE (EXPORTER)

---

acceptance "may consist of the drawee's signature alone." The buyer has thus created a *trade acceptance*. The buyer's acceptance indicates the buyer's unconditional obligation to pay the draft on the date due. A draft payable at "60 days after date" is payable by the drawee 60 days after the original date of the instrument. A draft payable at "60 days sight" means that it is due to be paid 60 days after the date of the acceptance.

As with a sight draft, a seller usually sends the time draft together with the shipping documents to the buyer through banking channels with instructions to the banks that the shipping documents should be handed over to the buyer only upon acceptance of the draft. The sales contract would have indicated the parties' agreement to this arrangement by calling for "documents against acceptance," or other clear language of similar meaning. After acceptance, the draft is then returned through banking channels to the seller. The seller can then hold the draft to maturity, or sell it at a discount to a local bank or commercial lending institution for immediate cash. The commercial lender takes the acceptance by negotiation. The greater the creditworthiness of the buyer, the greater the marketability of the

trade acceptance. Where the foreign buyer is unquestionably creditworthy, such as a major multinational corporation, the trade acceptance carries little risk and is easily saleable.

## Banker's Acceptances and Acceptance Financing

A *banker's acceptance* is a negotiable instrument and short-term financing device widely used to finance international (as well as domestic) sales. The purpose of an acceptance is to substitute a bank's credit for that of the buyer in order to finance the sale. A banker's acceptance is a time draft drawn on and accepted by a commercial bank. The bank stamps its name, date, and signature on the face of the draft to create the acceptance, and thereby becomes obligated to pay the amount stated to the holder of the instrument on the date specified. The holder of the acceptance can convert it to cash immediately at a discounted rate or hold it until it matures.

Banker's acceptances are flexible instruments, with many creative uses. Acceptance financing can be done by either the buyer's or seller's bank.

Importing buyers can use a banker's acceptance for short-term borrowing until they can resell and liquidate the goods being purchased. Sellers to export markets can use a banker's acceptance for short-term, preexport, financing of raw materials and production costs until the goods are sold to the foreign customer and payment received. Exporters can also use acceptances to grant credit terms to foreign customers. For instance, in a sale on open account, an exporter might draw a time draft on its own bank for the amount of its overseas sale. The draft is accepted by the exporter's bank, the discounted amount is paid to the exporter, and the acceptance negotiated and discounted in the credit markets. When the importer pays the invoice amount to the exporter, the proceeds are used to satisfy the acceptance at maturity. In another arrangement, the exporter's draft may be accepted by the importer's bank then discounted in the credit markets. In any case, the acceptance is satisfied at maturity through the proceeds of the sale.

In essence, the acceptance financing is self-liquidating, because repayment is made from the underlying sales transaction, using credit market monies to finance business. The bank charges the borrower a commission and the discount rate for acceptance financing, which is usually deducted from the face amount of the acceptance when paid to the borrower. Depending on market conditions, acceptance financing is often cheaper for companies than regular credit borrowing.

Banker's acceptances are generally short-term instruments, since they must be for a period of six months or less. An *eligible* banker's acceptance is one that qualifies for discount at the U.S. Federal Reserve Bank, which will buy it if it is not sold privately. Acceptances thus serve to finance international trade with outside capital. Because they are created by commercial banks, the use of banker's acceptances is subject to banking laws and Federal Reserve regulations in the United States.

## Credit Risk in Trade Finance Programs

Institutions regularly involved in trade lending commonly prearrange these financing terms by agreeing in advance to purchase the trade acceptances of the foreign buyer. They must first per-

form an analysis and evaluation of the buyer's financial position. Thorough credit checks are done on the buyer, utilizing trade and banking information, the reports of U.S. or foreign credit reporting agencies, and even site visits to the foreign firm. (While obtaining and verifying credit information is relatively easy in the United States, Canada, Japan, and Western Europe, it is somewhat more difficult, and the information is less reliable, in other regions of the world.) To reduce the credit risk and lower the cost of trade finance, several government agencies, in the United States and other countries, provide credit guarantees to back trade finance lending by commercial institutions. In the United States, these agencies include Eximbank, the Commodity Credit Corporation, and the Agency for International Development (discussed later in this chapter).

## Credit Risk in Acceptance Financing: Rights of the Holder in Due Course

One of the primary reasons for the popularity of the acceptance as a financing device is the protection provided to the financial institution or other party who purchases it, provided that party is a *holder in due course.* The detailed requirements to become a holder in due course are spelled out in the Uniform Commercial Code. A holder in due course is a holder in possession of a negotiable instrument (such as a draft or acceptance) that has been taken: (1) for value, (2) in good faith, (3) without notice that it is overdue or has been dishonored, and (4) without notice that the instrument contains an unauthorized signature or has been altered (UCC 3-302). If all of the requirements for transferring a negotiable instrument are met, and the transferee qualifies as a holder in due course, the transferee can take greater rights in the instrument than the transferor had.

According to the *holder in due course rule,* the purchaser of an acceptance, or any negotiable instrument, takes it free from most disputes that might arise between the drawer and drawee—the original parties to the underlying transaction. The most common type of dispute that might arise is breach of contract. For example, assume that DownPillow sells pillows to a

Japanese buyer and forwards documents and a draft for acceptance. DownPillow discounts the trade acceptance to a U.S. bank, who discounts the instrument in the credit markets. If the pillows turn out to be molded and worthless, the Japanese buyer must still honor and pay the acceptance upon presentation in Japan. It may then assert its separate claim for breach of contract against the seller. This rule ensures the free transferability of commercial paper in international commerce. A financial institution can discount an international draft without fear that it will be caught up in the middle of a breach of contract action between buyer and seller. If a draft did not come with this protection, banks might not be so willing to finance international sales.

## Credit Risks in Factoring Accounts Receivable: The Rights of the Assignee

As firms become more globalized, and as credit information becomes more widely available, many firms are offering open account terms to their better, long-term foreign customers. These sellers are giving their customers an open credit period of usually 30 days to several months to pay for goods received. But companies engaged in exporting products are not in business to loan money. Thus, banks are providing open account trade finance services, including the factoring of foreign accounts receivable.

An account receivable is no more than a representation of a *contract right* belonging to the seller—the right to collect money owed by the buyer under the contract for goods shipped. Contract rights can be *assigned* to another party. In a typical financing arrangement, the seller (*assignor*) assigns its right to collect the account to the financial institution (*assignee*). This is also called *factoring,* and the *assignee* is sometimes called the *factor.* Under basic contract law, the assignee "steps into the shoes" of the assignor and acquires only those rights under the contract that the assignor had against the other party to the contract (e.g., the buyer of the goods). Take the following example: Assume that DownPillow ships an ocean container of pillows to Japan and factors the account receivable with a U.S. bank

(the assignee). DownPillow now has its money and the bank is awaiting payment directly from Japan (of course, it is important for the Japanese buyer to be notified of the assignment and instructed to pay only the assignee bank). If a dispute later breaks out over the quality of the pillows, the Japanese buyer may legally assert any claims and defenses against collection by the bank that it otherwise would have had against DownPillow. Thus, for example, the buyer can successfully argue that it does not have to pay the bank because of the breach of warranty by DownPillow. DownPillow will have to repay the bank for money received, and resolve the breach of contract suit with the buyer. For this reason, banker's acceptance financing offers some advantages over accounts receivable financing. Unlike a factor, a holder in due course of a banker's acceptance is protected by the holder in due course rule. Thus, the fact that the products are defective does not provide a defense against payment to one liable on the negotiable instrument. Some insurance companies today offer commercial *credit insurance* to protect against accounts receivable that become bad debts and cannot be collected.

# The Documentary Letter of Credit

As discussed in preceding chapters, a seller to foreign markets assumes less credit risk in the documentary sale than in a sale on open account terms. Nevertheless, a seller still faces the possibility that the buyer might breach its contract and not honor the documentary draft when it is presented for payment. Any number of reasons might cause a buyer to breach a contract, including the buyer's inability to pay or to obtain financing. The buyer also might have found the merchandise at a cheaper price from another supplier. This situation could easily happen in a depressed market in which the price of the goods or commodities has dropped sharply since the time the buyer signed the contract.

Another problem is that an act of the buyer's country might prevent the buyer from making payment on the documents. Although not likely in the case of exports to Japan, Canada, or Western Europe, currency controls imposed on importers by their governments might make it impossible for their companies to obtain the foreign currency needed to purchase foreign goods from their central banks. If such an event occurs, the seller may have to wait extended periods to receive payment. Thus, a seller could quite possibly have its goods arrive at a foreign port only to find that the buyer, for one reason or another, is unable or unwilling to pay for them.

Ideally, the seller would prefer not to relinquish title to the goods until it is certain that it will be paid. The buyer, on the other hand, ideally would want to postpone payment until it is assured that the goods are what was contracted for and are no longer subject to the seller's control or disposition. In order to reconcile these conflicting objectives and reduce the risks involved in an international sale of goods transaction, the parties may arrange for payment under a letter of credit.

> **http://ananse.irv.uit.no/trade_law/nav/finance.html**
> A site containing links to information on letters of credit.

## The Letter of Credit Defined

Letters of credit are flexible commercial instruments adaptable to a broad range of commercial uses. They are the most common form of payment for the international sale of goods. This chapter covers two types of letters of credit: (1) *documentary* letters of credit (also called *documentary credits* or *commercial credits*), and (2) *standby* letters of credit. In business, letters of credit are generally referred to as L/Cs. Documentary credits are used in sale of goods transactions, and so the discussion begins with this type.

The *letter of credit* is defined as a conditional undertaking by a bank, issued in accordance with the instructions of the account party, addressed to or in favor of the beneficiary. The bank promises to pay, accept, or negotiate the beneficiary's draft up to a certain sum of money, in the stated currency, within the prescribed time limit, upon the presentation of stipulated documents.

In a sales transaction, the *account party* is the buyer, the *beneficiary* is the seller, and the *issuing bank* (or *issuer*) is the buyer's bank (see Exhibit 8.2). In a letter of credit transaction, the promise of an internationally recognized bank is substituted for that of the buyer. As long as the seller complies with all conditions in the letter of credit, such as tendering the documents called for in the letter of credit within the time allowed, the seller has more assurance of being paid than in any other form of sale except by receiving cash in advance. Letters of credit specify whether the issuing bank will pay sight drafts or accept time drafts presented by the beneficiary. Typically, bank letters of credit call for the seller's draft to be accompanied by shipping documents together with a number of other collateral documents. The shipping documents could be a negotiable ocean bill of lading, a nonnegotiable or straight ocean bill of lading, an air waybill, or a multimodal transport document. Collateral documents that might be required in the letter of credit include a commercial invoice describing the goods, a marine insurance policy, a consular invoice, a country of origin certificate, a certificate of analysis or inspection, various customs declarations, packing slips, and almost any other documentation demanded by the buyer.

The use of the letter of credit in international trade is well described by the court in *Voest-Alpine International Corp. v. Chase Manhattan Bank*. 707 F.2d 680 (2d Cir. 1983).

Originally devised to function in international trade, a letter of credit reduced the risk of nonpayment in cases where credit was extended to strangers in distant places. Interposing a known and solvent institution's (usually a bank's) credit for that of a foreign buyer in a sale of goods transaction accomplished this objective. A typical letter of credit transaction, as the case before us illustrates, involves three separate and independent relationships—an underlying sale of goods contract between buyer and seller, an agreement between a bank and its customer [buyer] in which the bank undertakes to issue a letter of credit, and the bank's resulting engagement to pay the beneficiary [seller] provided that certain documents presented to the bank conform with the terms and conditions of the credit issued on its customer's

**EXHIBIT 8.2    The Documentary Sale with a Letter of Credit**

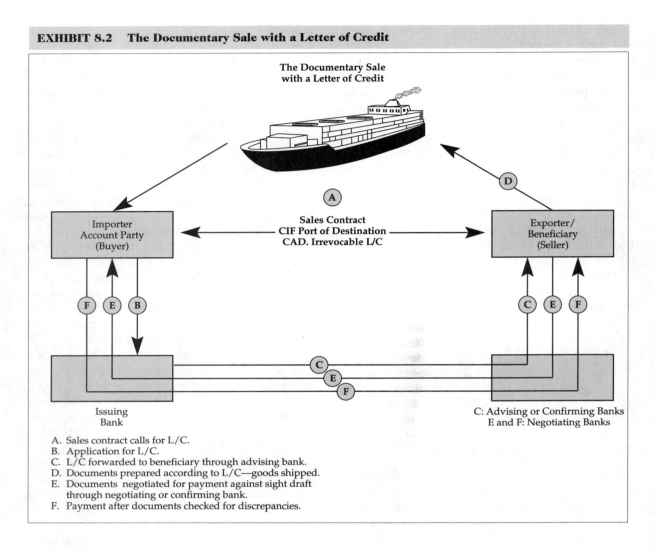

The Documentary Sale
with a Letter of Credit

Sales Contract
CIF Port of Destination
CAD. Irrevocable L/C

Importer
Account Party
(Buyer)

Exporter/
Beneficiary
(Seller)

Issuing
Bank

C: Advising or Confirming Banks
E and F: Negotiating Banks

A. Sales contract calls for L/C.
B. Application for L/C.
C. L/C forwarded to beneficiary through advising bank.
D. Documents prepared according to L/C—goods shipped.
E. Documents negotiated for payment against sight draft
   through negotiating or confirming bank.
F. Payment after documents checked for discrepancies.

behalf. Significantly, the bank's payment obligation to the beneficiary is primary, direct, and completely independent of any claims which may arise in the underlying sale of goods transaction. . . .

Letters of credit evolved as a mercantile specialty entirely separate from common-law contract concepts and they must still be viewed as entities unto themselves. Completely absorbed into the English common law by the 1700s along with the Law Merchant—of which it had become an integral part by the year 1200—letter of credit law found its way into American jurisprudence where it flourishes today. Its origins may be traced even more deeply into history. There is evidence letters of credit were used by bankers in Renaissance Europe, Imperial Rome, ancient Greece, Phoenicia, and even early Egypt.

These simple instruments survived despite their nearly 3,000-year-old lineage because of their inherent reliability, convenience, economy, and flexibility.

## Law Applicable to Letters of Credit

Letters of credit are recognized in all legal systems of the world. In the United States, the law governing letters of credit has been codified in Article 5 of the Uniform Commercial Code. In addition, in some states, notably New York, letters of credit make up a great body of case law. Perhaps the most important rules affecting letters of credit are not laws at all, but a privately developed set of guidelines based on the customs and commonly accepted practices of merchants and bankers, known as the *Uniform Customs and Practice for Documentary Credits.*

**The Uniform Customs and Practice for Documentary Credits.** The *Uniform Customs and Practice for Documentary Credits* (UCP) is a document that international bankers know well. It is a set of standardized rules for issuing and handling letters of credit, drafted and published by the *International Chamber of Commerce* (which also publishes *Incoterms*) with the assistance of the international banking community. The UCP establishes the legal format of letters of credit, sets out rules by which banks process letter of credit transactions, and defines the rights and responsibilities of all parties to the credit. Because the UCP has been drafted primarily by banks, its provisions primarily protect them in any transaction. The UCP was first introduced in the early 1930s, with the latest revision (UCP No. 500) published in 1993. The UCP is in use in virtually every nation of the world (including, for example, the People's Republic of China).

**Legal Effect of the UCP.** The International Chamber of Commerce is not a government or lawmaking body, and the UCP is not law. The UCP "governs" letters of credit only if its provisions are incorporated into the letters of credit by reference. The great majority of international letters of credit issued today state that they are to be interpreted according to the UCP. The UCP is widely recognized by judges in deciding letter of credit cases; reference to it appears in virtually every reported decision on international letters of credit. Statutes in New York and several other states specifically state that the Uniform Commercial Code is *not* applicable to any letter of credit that is subject to the UCP. As a result, the UCP has a far greater impact on the law of international letters of credit than does the Uniform Commercial Code.

> *http://itl.irv.uit.no/trade_law/documents/
> payment/ucp500/nav/ucp_a.html*
> and
> *http://www.unicc.org/unece/trade/kyoto/
> ky-01-e0.htm*
> See for information on the UCP.

## Relationship of the Letter of Credit to the Underlying Transaction

As the previous quote from the *Voest-Alpine* case states, the letter of credit is a separate contract between the account party and the issuing bank. Under this principle of independence, the letter of credit is separate from the underlying contract between buyer and seller on which it is based. The following case, *Maurice O'Meara Co. v. National Park Bank of New York,* is generally considered by writers in the United States to be the classic statement of the legal nature of letters of credit.

---

### Maurice O'Meara Co. v. National Park Bank of New York
*239 N.Y. 386, 146 N.E. 636 (1925)*
*Court of Appeals of New York*

BACKGROUND AND FACTS
National Park Bank issued a letter of credit addressed to Ronconi & Millar, beneficiary, at the request of its account party, Sun Herald, "covering the shipment of 1,322 tons of newsprint paper in 72½ inch and 36½ inch rolls to test 11–12, 32 lbs. at 8½ cents per pound net weight—delivery to be made in December 1920, and January 1921." The letter of credit did not require that a testing certificate from an independent laboratory accompany the documents. When Ronconi & Millar's invoice and draft were presented to the bank, the documents described the paper as was required in the letter of credit. But the bank refused payment because it had no opportunity to test the tensile strength of the paper. (Interestingly, the market price of newsprint paper had fallen sharply in the time period between the contract of sale and the presentation of documents, amounting to over $20,000 in this case.) Ronconi & Millar transferred their rights to collect payment to Maurice O'Meara, a financial institution, who brought this action to collect the full

*(continued)*

*(continued)*

amount of the drafts. Maurice O'Meara claims that the issuing bank had no right to test or inspect the paper.

McLAUGHLIN, JUDGE

[The letter of credit] . . . was in no way involved in or connected with, other than the presentation of the documents, the contract for the purchase and sale of the paper mentioned. That was a contract between buyer and seller, which in no way concerned the bank. The bank's obligation was to pay sight drafts when presented if accompanied by genuine documents specified in the letter of credit. If the paper when delivered did not correspond to what had been purchased, either in weight, kind or quality, then the purchaser had his remedy against the seller for damages. Whether the paper was what the purchaser contracted to purchase did not concern the bank and in no way affected its liability. It was under no obligation to ascertain, either by a personal examination or otherwise, whether the paper conformed to the contract between the buyer and seller. The bank was concerned only in the drafts and the documents accompanying them. This was the extent of its interest. If the drafts, when presented, were accompanied by the proper documents, then it was absolutely bound to make the payment under the letter of credit, irrespective of whether it knew, or had reason to believe, that the paper was not of the tensile strength contracted for. This view, I think, is the one generally entertained with reference to a bank's liability under an irrevocable letter of credit of the character of the one here under consideration.

The defendant had no right to insist that a test of the tensile strength of the paper be made before paying the drafts; nor did it even have a right to inspect the paper before payment, to determine whether it in fact corresponded to the description contained in the documents. The letter of credit did not so provide. All that the letter of credit provided was that documents be presented which described the paper shipped as of a certain size, weight, and tensile strength. To hold otherwise is to read into the letter of credit something which is not there, and this the court ought not to do, since it would impose upon a bank a duty which in many cases would defeat the primary purpose of such letters of credit. This primary purpose is an assurance to the seller of merchandise of prompt payment against documents.

It has never been held, so far as I am able to discover, that a bank has the right or is under an obligation to see that the description of the merchandise contained in the documents presented is correct. A provision giving it such right, or imposing such obligation, might, of course, be provided for in the letter of credit. The letter under consideration contains no such provision. If the bank had the right to determine whether the paper was of the tensile strength stated, then it might be pertinent to inquire how much of the paper must it subject to the test. If it had to make a test as to tensile strength, then it was equally obligated to measure and weigh the paper. No such thing was intended by the parties and there was no such obligation upon the bank. The documents presented were sufficient. The only reason stated by defendant in its letter of December 18, 1920, for refusing to pay the draft, was that— "There has arisen a reasonable doubt regarding the quality of the newsprint paper. . . . Until such time as we can have a test made by an impartial and unprejudiced expert we shall be obliged to defer payment."

This being the sole objection, the only inference to be drawn therefrom is that otherwise the documents presented conformed to the requirements of the letter of credit. All other objections were thereby waived.

Judgment should be directed in favor of the plaintiff.

**Decision.**   National Park Bank's obligation to pay the beneficiary's drafts submitted under its letter of credit is separate and distinct from the contract of sale between the buyer and seller. Banks deal in documents only. Therefore the defendant, National Park Bank, cannot withhold payment of the drafts even if it believes that the paper is not of the weight, kind, or quality ordered by Sun Herald. Defendant also has no right to demand testing of the paper or to inspect it prior to payment.

The rule of *Maurice O'Meara* is recognized in UCP 500, Article 3.

Credits, by their nature, are separate transactions from the sales or other contracts on which they may be based and banks are in no way concerned with or bound by such contracts. . . .

Consequently, the undertaking of a bank to pay, accept and pay drafts or negotiate and/or fulfill any other obligation under the credit, is not subject to claims or defenses by the applicant [account party] resulting from his relationships with the issuing bank or the beneficiary.

A beneficiary can in no case avail himself of the contractual relationships existing between the banks or between the applicant (account party) and the issuing bank.

## Rights of the Account Party in Cases of Fraud

Under the UCC, a partial exception has been created to the preceding rule if the letter of credit is fraudulent, forged, or *fraud in the transaction* exists in the underlying sales contract. This exception is governed by the UCC because the UCP is silent on the question of fraudulent documents. Under this exception, if a seller presents documents for a nonexistent shipment of goods, fraud in the transaction occurs. In such cases, a bank *can still honor* a demand for payment. If, however, the bank does choose to honor a demand for payment despite being notified of fraud, the buyer may petition a court for an injunction which would prevent the bank from paying on the credit. If the demand for payment is made by a holder in due course, however, then the bank *must* honor the demand for payment.

Compare the last case, *Maurice O'Meara*, with the following case, *Sztejn v. J. Henry Schroder Banking Corporation*. It presents a clear distinction between a mere breach of warranty and fraud. *O'Meara* involved a breach of warranty—the seller shipped newsprint paper of inferior quality. *Sztejn* involves fraud in the transaction—

---

### Sztejn v. J. Henry Schroder Banking Corp.
### 31 N.Y.S.2d 631 (1941)
### Supreme Court, Special Term, New York County

BACKGROUND AND FACTS

The plaintiff contracted to purchase hog bristles from Transea Traders in India. The defendant bank issued an irrevocable letter of credit to Transea covering a shipment of hog bristles and payable upon presentation of the proper documents. Transea filled 50 cases with cow hair and other worthless rubbish in order to obtain an ocean bill of lading from the steamship company showing the shipment of 50 cases of hog bristles. The documents and draft were presented to the defendant bank by The Chartered Bank of India, acting as agent for Transea. The plaintiff brought this action against the issuing bank to restrain it from paying on the letter of credit.

SHIENTAG, JUSTICE

One of the chief purposes of the letter of credit is to furnish the seller with a ready means of obtaining prompt payment for his merchandise. It would be a most unfortunate interference with business transactions if a bank before honoring drafts drawn upon it was obliged or even allowed to go behind the documents, at the request of the buyer and enter into controversies between the buyer and the seller regarding the quality of the merchandise shipped. . . . Of course, the application of this doctrine presupposes that the documents accompanying the draft are genuine and conform in terms to the requirements of the letter of credit. However, I believe that a different situation is presented in the instant action. This is not a controversy between the buyer and seller concerning a mere breach of warranty regarding the quality of the merchandise; on the present motion, it must be assumed that the seller has intentionally failed to ship any goods ordered by the buyer. In such a situation, where the seller's fraud has been called to the bank's attention before the drafts and documents have been presented for payment, the principle of the independence of the bank's obligation under the letter of credit should not be extended to protect the unscrupulous seller. It is true that even though the documents are forged or fraudulent, if the issuing bank has already paid the draft before

*(continued)*

*(continued)*

receiving notice of the seller's fraud, it will be protected if it exercised reasonable diligence before making such payment. However, in the instant action Schroder has received notice of Transea's active fraud before it accepted or paid the draft. . . .

Although our courts have used broad language to the effect that a letter of credit is independent of the primary contract between the buyer and seller, that language was used in cases concerning alleged breaches of warranty; no case has been brought to my attention on this point involving an intentional fraud on the part of the seller which was brought to the bank's notice with the request that it withhold payment of the draft on this account. The distinction between a breach of warranty and active fraud on the part of the seller is supported by authority and reason. As one court has stated: "Obviously, when the issuer of a letter of credit knows that a document, although correct in form, is, in point of fact, false or illegal, he cannot be called upon to recognize such a document as complying with the terms of a letter of credit." . . .

While the primary factor in the issuance of the letter of credit is the credit standing of the buyer, the security afforded by the merchandise is also taken into account. In fact, the letter of credit requires a bill of lading made out to the order of the bank and not the buyer. Although the bank is not interested in the exact detailed performance of the sales contract, it is vitally interested in assuring itself that there are some goods represented by the documents.

Accordingly, the defendant's motion to dismiss the supplemental complaint is denied.

**Decision.**    The court held in favor of the plaintiff and enjoined the bank's payment. A court can enjoin an issuing bank from honoring a draft if the bank learns that its customer is about to become the victim of a fraud.

**Comment.**    Under the Uniform Commercial Code (Section 5-114) a bank "may honor the draft . . . despite notification from the customer (the buyer) of fraud . . . but a court . . . may enjoin such honor." As an interesting note, the California legislature chose to omit the words "but a court . . . may enjoin such honor." Therefore, in California, courts have held that no injunction can be issued against a letter of credit for fraud in the transaction.

the presentation of documents covering goods, and the shipment of bales of worthless rubbish. The *Sztejn* case is one of the most widely cited cases in U.S. letter of credit law.

Compare the rule holding in *Sztejn* regarding fraud in the transaction with the circumstances which arise in the English case *United City Merchants (Investments) Ltd. v. Royal Bank of Canada.* Notice how the English court distinguishes American precedent and narrows the application of the fraud exception.

## A Letter of Credit Transaction

The following discussion examines how a letter of credit is used in a sale of goods transaction. For

*United City Merchants*
*(Investments) Ltd. v.*
*Royal Bank of Canada*
*2 Weekly Law Reports 1039*
*House of Lords, 1982*

BACKGROUND AND FACTS
The buyer, a Peruvian company, entered into a contract to purchase glass fibers at a price of $662,082 from an English seller. Payment was to be made under an irrevocable letter of credit confirmed by Royal Bank of Canada. The letter of credit called for a bill of lading dated no later than December 15, 1976. The goods were in fact loaded onto the vessel (*The American Accord*) on December 16, but the loading brokers issued a bill of lading which was dated December 15, 1976. Unaware of the false statement, the sellers submitted documents to Royal Bank who refused to pay on the credit because it suspected fraud in the documents.

*(continued)*

*(continued)*

LORD DIPLOCK

If on their face, the documents presented to the confirming bank by the seller conform with the requirements of the credit as notified to him by the conforming bank, that bank is under a contractual obligation to the seller to honour the credit, notwithstanding that the bank has knowledge that the seller at the time of presentation of the conforming documents is alleged by the buyer to have, and in fact has already, committed a breach of his contract with the buyer for the sale of the goods to which the documents appear on their fact to relate, that would have entitled the buyer to treat the contract of sale as rescinded and to reject the goods and refuse to pay the seller the purchase price. The whole commercial purpose for which the system of confirmed irrevocable documentary credits has been developed in international trade is to give to the seller an assured right to be paid before he parts with control of the goods that does not permit of any dispute with the buyer as to the performance of the contract of sale being used as a ground for non-payment or reduction or deferment of payment.

To this general statement of principle as to the contractual obligations of the confirming bank to the seller, there is one established exception: that is where the seller, for the purpose of drawing on the credit, fraudulently presents to the confirming bank documents that contain, expressly or by implication, material representations of fact that to his knowledge are untrue. . . . [*Sztejn v. J. Henry Schroder Banking Corporation* (1941) 31 N.Y.S.2d 631]. This judgment of the New York of Appeals was referred to with approval by the English Court of Appeal in *Edward Owen Engineering Ltd. v. Barclays Bank International Ltd.* [1978] Q.B. 159. . . . The courts will not allow their process to be used by a dishonest person to carry out a fraud.

The instant case, however, does not fall within the fraud exception. [The trial judge] found the sellers to have been unaware of the inaccuracy of Mr. Baker's notation of the date at which the goods were actually on board *American Accord.* They believed that it was true and that the goods had actually been loaded on or before December 15, 1976, as required by the documentary credit.

\*\*\*

It has so far as I know, never been disputed that as between confirming bank and issuing bank and the buyer, the contractual duty of each bank under a confirmed irrevocable credit is to examine with reasonable care all documents presented in order to ascertain that they appear *on their face* to be in accordance with the terms and conditions of the credit, and, if they do so appear, to pay to the seller/beneficiary by whom the documents have been presented the sum stipulated by the credit. . . . It is equally clear, and is so provided by Article 9 of the Uniform Customs, that confirming banks and issuing banks assume no liability or responsibility to one another or to the buyer "for the form, sufficiency, accuracy, genuineness, falsification or legal effect of any documents."

**Decision.**   Confirming banks are not permitted to refuse a demand payment when the documents, on their face, comply with the letter of credit. Fraud perpetuated by a third party does not constitute fraud in the transaction so as to permit the confirming bank to deny payment.

ease in understanding, the parties are referred to as "buyer" and "seller" instead of their banking terms, *account party* and *beneficiary.*

Once the sales contract calls for payment under a letter of credit (L/C), the buyer becomes responsible for applying to its bank for the L/C. The application is prepared on the bank's form. The application requests that the issuing bank honor the seller's drafts by paying or accepting them (as the case may be) up to a specified amount (usually the contract price), but *only if the drafts are accompanied by specified documents.* The buyer will specify in the application which documents must be presented in order for the bank to rightfully honor the draft. It will also specify exactly what those documents must say. For instance, the buyer might call for the L/C to require that the bill of lading be negotiable, or marked "freight prepaid," or that the packing slip or certificate of analysis contain certifications as to quality, weight, or markings. It probably would require the bank to honor the L/C only if the documents are accompanied by a marine insurance policy (such as in a CIF contract), or a country-of-origin certificate. The application may also specify any other requirements for honoring the draft desired by the buyer. To illustrate, suppose the buyer does not want the seller to make partial shipments because of the increased risk of damage or loss to the goods. It knows that unless the L/C states otherwise, the issuing bank is permitted to honor drafts on partial shipments. Therefore, it must indicate on the application that drafts drawn under the letter of credit are not to be honored in the event that the documents show a partial shipment.

Thus, the application for the letter of credit forms a *contract between the buyer and its bank* (not between buyer and seller), with the buyer agreeing to reimburse the bank for any sums properly paid out according to the terms of the L/C. If the bank does not act according to its contract with its customer, it may not be entitled to reimbursement.

**Irrevocability of Letters of Credit.**   According to UCP 500, credits may be either revocable or irrevocable, but "in the absence of such indication the credit shall be deemed to be *irrevocable.*" Revocable letters of credit are seldom used in international commerce (except perhaps between some corporate subsidiaries) because they do not provide sufficient protection to the beneficiary. An example of an irrevocable documentary letter of credit is shown in Exhibit 8.3.

**Advising the Letter of Credit.**   The letter of credit will be issued and sent to the seller via a foreign correspondent bank located in the seller's country. This bank, known as the *advising bank,* merely informs or "advises" the seller that an L/C has been issued in its favor and that the L/C is available for the seller. Under UCP 500, the L/C is advised "without engagement" by the advising bank, which is not liable on the L/C and makes no promise to pay the seller. It provides only a banking service by transmitting the L/C to the seller. The bank is responsible, however, for using reasonable care to authenticate the letter of credit, which is often done by comparing the signature on the credit with the authorized signature kept on file in the bank's signature books. UCP 500 states that L/Cs can be transmitted from issuing bank to advising bank electronically, and that no mail confirmation need be sent.

**Seller's Compliance with the Credit.**   Until the seller receives the L/C it may not want to pack-

age the goods, arrange transportation, or prepare the documentation. This reluctance is because the seller must first read the L/C and follow its instructions carefully in order to be paid by the bank.

First, the seller will want to compare carefully the terms of the L/C with the terms of the underlying contract of sale. If the documents show significant differences, the seller would want to contact the buyer to inquire why and resolve the difference. For instance, assume that a sales contract called for shipment of "4,000 lbs. washed white goose down in machine-compressed bales," and the L/C reads "3,000 lbs. washed white goose down in machine-compressed bales." The seller must stop and inquire why a difference appears in the quantities expressed. Did the buyer change its mind and decide to purchase only 3,000 lbs. instead of the 4,000 lbs. agreed to? If so, why wasn't the seller contacted to reconfirm the new order? Perhaps the bank erred in transmitting the L/C. Whatever the reason, the seller should do nothing until the problem is resolved or until an *amended* L/C is received. If the seller ships 4,000 lbs., its drafts may be refused and it may only get paid for 3,000 lbs.; if it ships 3,000 lbs., it may be losing a sale for the 1,000 lbs. difference.

The seller would want to examine many other provisions of the L/C before shipping; the L/C might prompt other questions for which the seller would want answers. In the above example, can the seller ship the goods within the time called for in the L/C? Can the down be washed, sorted, baled, delivered to the carrier, and an onboard bill of lading received within the time limits set in the L/C? If an export license is needed in order to export goose down from the seller's country, can it be processed and received on time? (Although obtaining a license is not so much a problem for exporters of products such as down, corn, or pencils, it can be a real headache for exporters of high-tech products!) An L/C that calls for shipment aboard a certain vessel sailing on a certain date may not be possible, and the seller may want to request an extension in an amended L/C. Is the total amount of the L/C sufficient to cover the drafts? Is it in the currency called for in the sales contract? Do the provisions for insurance and the payment of freight charges meet the terms of the contract of sale, or are they

**EXHIBIT 8.3    Irrevocable Documentary Letter of Credit**

IMPORTER'S BANK
CONFIRMATION OF BRIEF CABLE

# Irrevocable
# Documentary Letter of Credit

| Importer's Bank | Date of Issue | |
|---|---|---|
| Charlotte, NC | February 1, 1990 | |
| | Issuing Bank Letter of Credit No. | Advising Bank Letter of Credit No. |
| | 78346 | |

| Advising Bank | Applicant |
|---|---|
| German Bank F.R.G. | Downpillow, Inc. North Carolina |

| Beneficiary | Expiratory Date (For Negotiation) | | |
|---|---|---|---|
| Federhaus, GMBH F.R.G. | Day | Month | Year |
| | 30 | April | 90 |

| Currency | Amount | |
|---|---|---|
| U.S.A. | 35,000.00 | Thirty-Five Thousand Dollars |

Gentlemen:

We hereby issue this documentary Letter of Credit in your favor which is available against your draft at sight drawn on Importer's Bank, Charlotte, North Carolina for 100% of the invoice value bearing the clause "Drawn under documentary letter of Credit Number 78346" Accompanied by the following documents:

1. Commercial invoice in triplicate
2. U.S. special customs form #1111 in triplicate
3. Insurance policy/certificate in duplicate covering all risks
4. Certificate of origin "form A" in duplicate
5. Full set 3/3 clean on-board bills of lading issued
   to the order of Importer's bank, marked "Freight prepaid,"
   notify applicant.

Purporting to cover:   3000 lbs washed white goose down in machine
                       compressed bales,  CIF Norfolk, Va.

| Shipment from | Partial Shipments | Transshipments |
|---|---|---|
| F.R.G. To Norfolk, Va. | Prohibited | Prohibited |

Special conditions

Documents must be presented to negotiating bank within 10 days of issuance of shipping documents but within the validity of the credit.
Latest ship date March 15, 1990.

Negotiating bank is authorized to forward all documents to us via airmail.   All banking charges outside the United States are for account of the beneficiary.

| We hereby engage with the bona fide holders of all drafts under and in compliance with the terms of this letter of credit that such drafts will be duly honored upon presentation to us.  The amount of each drawing must be indorsed on the reverse side of this letter of credit by the negotiating bank. | Indications of the Advising Bank |
|---|---|
| *B. G. DeWoolfson* Authorized Signature | Place, Date, Name, and Signature of the Advising Bank |

Except so far as otherwise expressly stated this documentary letter of credit is subject to the Uniform Customs and Practices for Documentary Credits (1984 Revision) the International Chamber of Commerce Document No. 400.

agreeable to the seller? Does the L/C allow partial shipments? Has the buyer made any last-minute changes to the order that should be included in a new L/C? Finally, can the documents and the draft be presented to the issuing bank before the date of expiration of the L/C?

If the seller is unable to comply with the letter of credit for any reason, the buyer must be contacted immediately so that an amended credit can be issued. In one case, for instance, a U.S. furniture manufacturer received a letter of credit from Kuwait calling for the shipment of furniture in "one 40' ocean container." Only after packaging and loading did the manufacturer realize that a few pieces would not fit into the container. If the manufacturer's documents had shown less furniture than was called for in the L/C, its draft might not have been paid. An amended credit had to be issued covering the new quantity before it was safe for the furniture manufacturer to ship. Due to the added cost of small shipments, the potential for damage, and the difficulty of handling break-bulk cargo in modern Middle Eastern ports, the buyer simply reduced its order rather than have the pieces shipped separately.

**Collecting on the Credit.**   Once the seller knows that it is able to meet the terms of the L/C, it is ready to prepare the draft and shipping documents and present them to a *negotiating bank* in its city to be forwarded to the issuing bank. The UCP permits the issuing bank to "nominate" a negotiating bank. If not, the documents may be negotiated through the advising bank or another bank of the seller's choice. The beneficiary must present the documents within a specified number of days after shipment, or prior to the expiration of the L/C (known as the *expiry date*), whichever is earlier. If no time period is specified, the UCP requires submission of shipping documents to banks within 21 days of shipment. Both the expiration and presentment dates must be met or the documents will be rejected (unless the defect is waived by the buyer). This requirement is an assurance to the buyer that the goods have been shipped on time.

The negotiating bank then transmits the documents to the issuing bank, which then inspects them for accuracy, irregularities, and discrepancies against the letter of credit. Documents that are not in order may be rejected. If the issuing bank decides to reject, it must notify the negotiating bank within seven banking days. If the issuing bank pays out on documents that do not conform to the L/C, then the bank will be liable to its customer, the buyer, for doing so. If the documents are in order, the bank will normally pay the draft at sight or at maturity, or accept the time draft, and then negotiate the shipping documents to the buyer. Thus, with bill of lading in hand, properly indorsed by the bank, the buyer may claim its goods from the carrier.

## Examination of the Documents under the UCP

From this overview of a letter of credit transaction, the next section performs a more careful analysis of how the seller's documents must conform to the requirements of the L/C. According to the independence principle, the obligation of the issuing bank to honor the beneficiary's draft under a letter of credit is not dependent on the contract of sale between the buyer and seller. Rather, the obligation of the bank to honor drafts is conditional solely upon the beneficiary's doing exactly what is requested in the L/C. This notion is clear throughout the UCP. Article 4 states that "in credit operations all parties concerned deal with documents, and not with goods, services and/or other performances to which the documents may relate." Indeed, banks deal mainly in the appearance of documents. Article 14 requires that the issuing bank "determine on the basis of the documents alone whether or not they appear on their face to be in compliance with the terms and conditions of the credit." As long as the documents are in apparent good order, appear valid on their face, and correspond to the terms of the L/C, the bank must honor the beneficiary's draft, and will be able to seek reimbursement from its customer, the buyer, regardless of the quality or condition, or even the existence, of the goods. That the goods might have gone to the bottom of the ocean during their voyage is irrelevant to the bank's obligation. That the goods inside the container are not even close to what the buyer ordered is irrelevant. The bank has no obligation to check the quality or condition of the goods, nor to investigate rumors about them. The UCP does not require the bank to examine any documents not called for in the L/C.

**The Rule of Strict Compliance.** The prevailing rule established by the courts for examining documents is the *strict compliance rule.* According to this view, the terms of the documents presented to the issuing bank must strictly conform to the requirements of the letter of credit. When a document contains language or terms different from the L/C, or some other apparent irregularity, it is said to contain a *discrepancy.* Documents that do not conform are *discrepant.* The documents and letter of credit are literally put side by side by a document checker at the issuing bank and the terms are matched. This does not mean

that every "i" must be dotted and every "t" crossed. (As one court stated, it's not a discrepancy if Smith is spelled "Smithh.") Some typographical errors are excusable, of course. But the thrust of the rule is that every provision of the bill of lading, commercial invoice, insurance policy, and other required shipping documents must match the letter of credit. Even a small discrepancy can cause the bank to reject the documents. If the issuing bank pays against documents that contain a discrepancy, then the bank cannot seek reimbursement from the account party, its customer. A summary of common discrepancies appears in Exhibit 8.4. In the following case, *Courtaulds North America, Inc. v. North Carolina National Bank,* the court considered a discrepancy between the description of the goods on the letter of credit and on the invoice.

---

**EXHIBIT 8.4    Common Discrepancies Found in Documentation**

**Bill of Lading/Air Waybill**

- An incomplete set of bills (originals missing)
- Onboard notations not dated and signed or initialed
- Time for shipment has expired
- Unclean bill of lading shows damage
- Indorsement missing
- Evidence of forgery or alteration
- Does not show freight prepared if required under the L/C
- Description of goods differs substantially from L/C
- Name of vessel differs
- Shows partial shipment or transshipment where prohibited by the L/C

**Commercial Invoice**

- Description of goods does not conform to description in L/C
- Does not show terms of shipment
- Amount differs from that shown on draft
- Amount exceeds limits of L/C
- Weights, measurements, or quantities differ

**Draft**

- Draft and invoice amounts do not agree
- Draft does not bear reference to L/C
- Evidence of forgery or alteration
- Draft not signed
- Maturity dates differ from L/C
- Currency differs from L/C

**Insurance Policy**

- Description of goods differs from invoice
- Risks not covered as required by the L/C
- Policy dated after date of bill of lading
- Amount of policy insufficient
- Certificate or policy not indorsed
- Certificate presented instead of policy, if required in L/C

**General Discrepancies**

- L/C expired
- L/C overdrawn
- Draft and documents presented after time called for in L/C
- Incomplete documentation
- Changes in documents not initialed
- Merchandise description and marks not consistent between documents

## BACKGROUND AND FACTS

### Courtaulds North America, Inc. v. North Carolina National Bank
### 528 F.2d 802 (1975)
### United States Court of Appeals (4th Cir.)

The defendant bank issued an irrevocable letter of credit on behalf of its customer, Adastra Knitting Mills. It promised to honor 60-day time drafts of Courtaulds for up to $135,000 covering shipments of "100% Acrylic Yarn." Courtaulds presented its draft together with a commercial invoice describing the merchandise as "Imported Acrylic Yarns." The packing lists that were stapled to the invoice contained the following description: "Cartons marked: 100% Acrylic." The bank refused to accept the draft because of the discrepancy between the letter of credit and the commercial invoice. (The buyer had gone into bankruptcy, and the court appointed trustee would not waive the discrepancy.) The documents were returned and the plaintiff brought this action. The lower court held that the bank was liable to the plaintiff for the amount of the draft because the packing lists attached to each carton stated that the cartons contained "100% Acrylic," and the bank appealed.

### BRYAN, SENIOR CIRCUIT JUDGE

The defendant denied liability chiefly on the assertion that the draft did not agree with the letter's conditions, viz., that the draft be accompanied by a "Commercial invoice in triplicate stating (inter alia) that it covers . . . 100% acrylic yarn"; instead, the accompanying invoices stated that the goods were "Imported Acrylic Yarn."

. . . [T]he District Court held defendant Bank liable to Courtaulds for the amount of the draft, interest, and costs. It concluded that the draft complied with the letter of credit when each invoice is read together with the packing lists stapled to it, for the lists stated on their faces: "Cartons marked: 100% Acrylic." After considering the insistent rigidity of the law and usage of bank credits and acceptances, we must differ with the District Judge and uphold Bank's position.

In utilizing the rules of construction embodied in the letter of credit—the Uniform Customs and State statute—one must constantly recall that the drawee bank is not to be embroiled in disputes between the buyer and the seller, the beneficiary of the credit. The drawee is involved only with documents, not with merchandise. Its involvement is altogether separate and apart from the transaction between the buyer and seller; its duties and liability are governed exclusively by the terms of the letter, not the terms of the parties' contract with each other. Moreover, as the predominant authorities unequivocally declare, the beneficiary must meet the terms of the credit—and precisely—if it is to exact performance of the issuer. Failing such compliance there can be no recovery from the drawee. That is the specific failure of Courtaulds here.

. . . .[T]he letter of credit dictated that each invoice express on its face that it covered 100% acrylic yarn. Nothing less is shown to be tolerated in the trade. No substitution and no equivalent, through interpretation or logic, will serve. Harfield, *Bank Credits and Acceptances* (5th ed. 1974), commends and quotes aptly from and English case: "There is no room for documents which are almost the same, or which will do just as well." Although no pertinent North Carolina decision has been laid before us, in many cases elsewhere, especially in New York, we find the tenent of Harfield to be unshaken.

At trial Courtaulds prevailed on the contention that the invoices in actuality met the specifications of the letter of credit in that the packing lists attached to the invoices disclosed on their faces that the packages contained "cartons marked: 100% acrylic." . . . But this argument cannot be accepted.

The district judge's pat statement adeptly puts an end to this contention of Courtaulds: "In dealing with letters of credit, it is a custom and practice of the banking trade for a bank to only treat a document as an invoice which clearly is marked on its face as 'invoice.' " This is not a pharisaical or doctrinaire persistence in the principle, but is altogether realistic in the environs of this case; it is plainly the fair and equitable measure. (The defect in description was not superficial but occurred in the statement of the quality of the yarn, not a frivolous concern.) Bank was not expected to scrutinize the collateral papers, such as the packing lists. Nor was it permitted to read into the instrument the contemplation or intention of the seller and buyer. . . .

Had Bank deviated from the stipulation of the letter and honored the draft, then at once it might have been confronted with the not improbable risk

*(continued)*

*(continued)* of the bankruptcy trustee's charge of liability for unwarrantably paying the draft monies to the seller, Courtaulds, and refusal to reimburse Bank for the outlay. Contrarily, it might face a Courtaulds claim that since it had depended upon Bank's assurance of credit in shipping yarn to Adastra, Bank was responsible for the loss. In this situation Bank cannot be condemned for sticking to the letter of the letter.

Nor is this conclusion affected by the amended or substituted invoices which Courtaulds sent to Bank after the refusal of the draft. No precedent is cited to justify retroactive amendment of the invoices or extension of the credit beyond the August 15 expiry of the letter.

For these reasons, we must vacate the decision of the trial court, despite the evident close reasoning and research of the district judge. . . .

Reversed and remanded for final judgment.

**Decision.** The judgment is reversed for the defendant bank. The description of the goods in the invoice did not match the description of the goods in the credit, and the defect was not cured by a correct description in the packing list.

Apply the strict compliance rule of the *Courtaulds* case to the following situation: Suppose that a seller receives a letter of credit from a foreign buyer covering "1,000 standard-size bed pillows." Seller's export manager completes an invoice for "1,000 bed pillows, size 20 x 26 in." A discrepancy would exist. Bankers are not expected to know that a "standard" bed pillow is $20 \times 26$ inches, and even if the banker did know, he or she would still have to refuse the document because of the discrepancy (although in practice the bank would call its customer to get a waiver of the discrepancy). Assume now that the invoice matches the L/C, but that the bill of lading shows shipment of "1,000 pillows." On this point, the UCP is very clear:

The description of the goods in the commercial invoice must correspond with the description in the credit. In all other documents, the goods may be described in general terms not inconsistent with the description of the goods in the credit. (Article 37c)

Here the documents show no discrepancy. The language used in the bill of lading, "1,000 pillows," is a more general statement "not inconsistent with" the full language used to describe the pillows in the L/C.

The rule of strict compliance seems to make commercial sense. Bankers are involved every day with letters of credit from all industries, comprising all sorts of goods and services. They cannot be expected to be experts in all areas—textiles, steel, agriculture commodities, electronics, or as in our examples, the bedding business.

**Avoiding and Handling Discrepancies.** Actually, estimates are that *more than half* of the letter of credit transactions in the United States involve discrepant documents. Many discrepancies occur because of clerical errors. Thus, the seller's export clerks should follow the letter of credit when preparing their invoice and shipping documents—more than one export manager has suggested that "any words found misspelled in the L/C, should be misspelled in the documents." Other discrepancies might occur as a result of documents prepared by an insurance agent, by the seller's freight forwarder, or by the carrier. For instance, if the L/C requires an onboard bill of lading, and the representative of the carrier that issued the bill of lading forgot to sign, initial, or date it to indicate that the goods have been loaded, the bank will rightfully reject the documents. This type of error should be caught and corrected early.

The best advice is that all parties use extreme care in preparing documents. Sellers should request that as few documents as possible be required in the L/C, to lessen the chance of mistake. The seller should be certain that the freight forwarder is experienced in documentation. In addition, the seller should be sure that all deadlines are met—that the goods are shipped on time and the documents promptly presented. Finally, the seller's international banker should review the documents and give an opinion as to whether they are in compliance with the L/C. The seller should not ship until all mistakes in the documents are corrected.

**An Ethical Issue in Handling Letters of Credit.** In most cases, where a minor discrepancy occurs, the issuing bank will obtain a written waiver from the buyer, and the transaction will proceed as anticipated, but the world of international business is a perilous place. The lore of international trade is filled with stories of the unwary being taken in by the unscrupulous. Sellers and bankers beware: If a buyer is looking for a reason to reject the documents (for instance, if the market price of the goods falls, or if the buyer's country has entered a period of civil war, or if it learns that the ship has gone to the bottom of the sea during the voyage), a seller who errs in preparing the documents is giving the savvy (or unscrupulous) buyer a way out. Although banks must preserve and protect their international reputations for honoring their credits, if they realize that the buyer is going to back out of the deal, their first reaction will be to try to find a justifiable reason for rejecting the documents—the best reason is, of course, to uncover a discrepancy! (An old adage states that any banker who cannot find a discrepancy isn't worth his or her salt.) Then, when the buyer's bank refuses to honor the draft, the buyer graciously offers to waive the discrepancy—but only for a huge discount off the contract price! Of course, almost all discrepancies are honest accidents or commercial mistakes and are easily resolved.

## Relationship between Negotiating and Issuing Banks

International banks generally have cooperative relationships with one another. The UCP was drafted with the idea of fostering this cooperation. For instance, in the event that an issuing bank dishonors a draft and rejects discrepant documents, the UCP requires that it give immediate notice by telecommunication to the negotiating bank describing the discrepancies. The issuing bank then holds the documents until it receives instructions from the negotiating bank, or it returns the documents.

## Confirmed Letters of Credit

For the most part, a letter of credit will serve to adequately assure payment of the seller's drafts. In certain instances, however, the credit of the issuing bank may be insufficient to assure payment. This lack of assurance may occur when shipments are exported to countries that have shortages of foreign currencies, large foreign debts, and a poor balance of payments record. In such a situation, government currency restrictions imposed between the time the contract is agreed to and the time the drafts are tendered for payment could prevent the issuing bank from honoring its letter of credit in dollars. A U.S. seller may want to include as part of the sales contract that the buyer will furnish a letter of credit *confirmed* by a bank in the United States.

Sellers have other reasons for insisting on a confirmed letter of credit. In some instances, the seller may be unsure of the soundness of the buyer's bank and wants the backing of some reputable U.S. bank on the letter of credit. Additionally, should legal action ever be necessary to collect on a letter of credit, a seller can much more easily sue a U.S. confirming bank in the United States than a foreign bank in foreign courts. Of course, a confirmed credit is far more expensive than one that is unconfirmed because two banks are exposed to the risk of the transaction. These costs must be weighed by the parties in determining the level of acceptable risk in the transaction.

Banks in the United States that confirm foreign letters of credit try to be aware of the economic and political conditions in those foreign countries. If a buyer is unable to have an L/C from its country confirmed, then the U.S. bank is signaling that it deemed the political and credit risks too high. Certainly this type of high risk is not one an exporter wants to assume if its bank would not. In these cases, U.S. sellers often request that its foreign customer have the L/C issued from a bank in a country with less risk, such as Switzerland, Great Britain, or Japan.

**Liability of Confirming Bank.** Unlike an advising bank, a confirming bank *does* become liable on the letter of credit. Under the UCP, payment is made immediately to the seller upon its presentation of the documents. A confirming bank that negotiates documents from the seller is entitled to reimbursement from the issuing bank if the documents presented to it are in order. The confirming bank also bears the risk that the issuing bank or the buyer will become unable to reimburse it. If the confirming bank pays for documents that are not in order, it generally cannot seek reimbursement from the beneficiary. A confirming bank that cannot obtain reimbursement may be left holding title to the goods purchased. (And if the shipment contains toaster ovens or clock radios, they can give them away to people who open new accounts at their branch offices!)

While the liability of a confirming bank is based on the letter of credit, one might wonder whether a confirming bank can be held negligent under tort law for wrongfully paying out on a letter of credit. The following case, *Instituto Nacional de Comercializacion Agricola* (Indeca), involves a confirming bank in Chicago that failed to exercise good judgment in paying out on fraudulent documents. The phony documents were part of an illegal conspiracy devised by a

---

## *Instituto Nacional De Comercializacion Agricola (Indeca) v. Continental Illinois National Bank*
### 858 F.2d 1264 (1988)
### United States Court of Appeals (7th Cir.)

**BACKGROUND AND FACTS**

Indeca, the plaintiff, purchased $5 million of black beans from Rumex for import into Guatemala. Banco de Guatemala issued a letter of credit in favor of Rumex, Bell (a Chicago commodities broker), and Bell's attorney. Continental Bank in Chicago confirmed the credit. Under its terms, Continental would pay Rumex for the beans upon receipt of documents that showed that the beans had been loaded onboard ship in Hong Kong and were on their way to Guatamala. The beneficiaries presented documentation to Continental on September 5, 1980. A Continental employee examined the documents and concluded that they did not comply with the requirements of the letter of credit: The certificate of origin was not legalized, a draft was missing, the insurance certificate was not satisfactory, and the bill of lading misidentified the shipper. The items were returned to Bell, who resubmitted a new certificate of origin that was dated September 2 and typed on a different machine, and that contained a signature different from that on the original certificate. Continental contacted the steamship company listed as the carrier. This proved unsuccessful. Nevertheless, Continental paid Bell and sent the documents to Banco de Guatemala. As it turned out, the documents were forged, and Indeca never received the black beans. Bell and her accomplices were convicted of wire fraud and of submitting false statements to a bank. Indeca filed this action alleging breach of contract, fraud, and negligence against Continental. The district court concluded that Continental had no actual knowledge of the falsity, and did not act in a reckless or negligent fashion in inspecting the documents. The plaintiff appealed.

**HARLINGTON WOOD, JR., CIRCUIT JUDGE**

The correct and prudent approach . . . is to consider generally whether the letter of credit situation is even amenable to the tort of negligent misrepresentation, irrespective of that tort's requirements.

As the Illinois Code and the comments to the UCC recognize, Article 5 may not explicitly cover every conceivable letter of credit situation. . . . The comment that Article 5's principles may be extended to other situations not listed recognizes that not every situation could be provided for in the Code, and even if it could, the rules might be overly complex, restrictive, and confusing if such an attempt was made. The flexibility accorded by the Code, however, should not be mistaken for approval to range far and wide over the legal landscape in search of legal theories to invoke against the parties to a letter of credit transaction. The flexibility accorded is limited by the underlying policies of letter of credit law and Article 5. As the comments to the Illinois Code state, paragraph 5-102(3) is intended to "encourage the development of the law by usage of trade." . . . In large part then adapting letter of credit principles to varying situations in a way that encourages the use of letters of credit is the approved task under Article 5; adapting tort principles not expressly adopted and that tend to discourage the use of such devices is not.

All letters of credit are bottomed on the principle "that the parties are not required to look beyond the face of the documents presented." *Auto Servicio San Ignancio, S.R.L. v. Compania Anonima Venezolana De Navegacion*, 765 F.2d 1306,

*(continued)*

*(continued)*

1310 (5th Cir.1985). . . . As Judge Higginbotham wrote in *Auto Servicio,* "in letter of credit transactions, facial compliance is, and indeed must be, the watchword. We can require no more of [the advising, confirming, and paying bank] if we are to remain faithful to the statutory scheme as well as the customs and practices behind letters of credit." Imposing a greater duty on a confirming bank by, for example, holding it liable for negligent misrepresentation, is inconsistent with the underlying premise of letter of credit law. "The exchange function of the letter of credit rests upon objective predictable standards with defined expectations and risks. Injecting the uncertainty of the tort principles . . . is not supported by the Code, which implicitly rejects them." Moreover, *Auto Servicio* holds that to the extent a confirming bank owes any duty, or duty-like obligation, it owes that duty to its customer, the issuing bank, and not the ultimate customer, which in this case is Indeca.

Therefore, the decision of the district court is affirmed.

**Decision.**   Indeca, the buyer, has no cause of action against Continental, the confirming bank, for negligence in inspecting documents. A confirming bank owes no duty under tort law to the buyer. A confirming bank's liability to use due care in inspecting the documents is derived exclusively from the Uniform Commercial Code or the UCP. Moreover, this duty is owed solely to the issuing bank, Banco de Guatemala, and not to the buyer.

Chicago commodities broker, her attorney, a Miami freight forwarder, and a Miami commodities broker with contacts in the Far East. The case became known as the "Guatemalan Black Bean Caper." As you read, consider that maritime and documentary frauds are not unknown in the business world. Instances of altered invoices, fake bills of lading, forged certificates of origin, and even phony letters of credit have all been reported in the press. Not all frauds are perpetrated on the small, inexperienced businessperson, however; as happened in this case, and in a large number of other cases during the 1970s and 1980s, the developing countries fell victim to sophisticated con artists. Even experienced international banks are not immune.

## Standby Letters of Credit

The standby letter of credit can be used to guarantee that a party will fulfill obligations under a service contract, construction contract, or sales contract. Standby letters of credit can also be used to insure the repayment of a loan. Suppose, for example, that a subsidiary of a U.S. company operating in Latin America borrows money from a local bank. The bank can require a standby letter of credit from a U.S. bank that would allow it to draw against the credit should the subsidiary default on its obligation.

**Standby Credit as Performance Guaranty.** Most standby credits are used, however, not in sale-of-goods transactions, but as guaranties of performance under consulting and performance contracts. Although a performance bond would accomplish the same objective, U.S. banks are prevented from issuing performance bonds by the *Glass Steagall Act* which prohibits banks from entering into areas of insurance. Thus, banks instead issue standby credits which serve as guarantees of performance under consulting and performance contracts. Unlike a regular letter of credit in which the beneficiary of the credit is the seller, a standby credit is issued in favor of the buyer to guarantee the seller's performance.

For example, if an engineering firm enters into a contract with a foreign government to perform engineering services related to a major public works project, the engineering firm could apply for a standby credit to be issued that would guarantee its performance to the foreign government. A standby credit however, does not usually require the same type of documentation such as a bill of lading that would be required by a traditional letter of credit. Instead the bank is required to honor a demand for payment under a standby credit upon receiving a signed statement by the beneficiary (buyer) that the seller has not performed the contract. In this case, the government would simply have to submit a signed statement which states that the engineering firm failed to perform its services. Since all that is required for the beneficiary to receive payment is a statement that a default has occurred, a standby letter of credit is sometimes referred to as a *suicide* credit for the buyer.

Not surprisingly, standby letters of credit, which are so common in international business transactions, have led to a great deal of litigation in the courts. To protect an account party under a standby credit from an "unfair" demand by the beneficiary, many international business lawyers will require that the beneficiary's request for payment be accompanied by an independent confirmation of the account party's default by a third party.

**Middle East Politics and Standby Letters of Credit: The Iranian Claims.** The politics of the Middle East have caused a great deal of litigation

in this area. Prior to 1979, U.S. companies enjoyed lucrative business contracts with the Imperial Government of Iran, under the rule of the Shah of Iran. Many of these contracts involved the supply of the latest armaments, consumer goods, and construction projects to this Islamic nation. These contracts had often been obtained through the use of illegal payments to the Shah and his family. At the time of the revolution, and the seizing of hostages at the U.S. embassy in Tehran, many U.S. firms had outstanding commitments to the government of Iran that were guaranteed with standby letters of credit. For example, in 1978, five banks alone had $12.6 billion in outstanding standby letters of credit. The following *American Bell* case clearly illustrates that the political risks of international business can even affect letter-of-credit transactions.

## American Bell International Inc. v. Islamic Republic of Iran
474 F.Supp. 420 (1979)
United States District Court (S.D.N.Y.)

BACKGROUND AND FACTS
In 1978, American Bell International, a subsidiary of AT&T, entered into a contract with the Imperial Government of Iran to provide consulting services and telecommunications equipment. The contract provided that all disputes would be resolved according to the laws of Iran and in Iranian courts. The contract provided for payment to Bell of $280 million, including a down payment of $38 million. Iran had the right to demand return of the down payment at any time and for any reason, with the amount returned to be reduced by 20 percent of the amounts that Bell had invoiced for work done. At the time of this action, about $30 million remained callable. In order to secure the return of the down payment on demand, Bell had been required to arrange for Manufacturers Bank to issue a standby letter of credit to the Bank of Iranshahr, payable on the demand of the Iranian Government. However, in 1979, a revolution resulted in the overthrow of the imperial government. The Shah of Iran fled the country, and a revolutionary council was established to govern the country. The nation was in a state of chaos and westerners fled the country. Having been left with unpaid invoices, Bell ceased its operations. Fearing that any monies paid to Iran would never be recouped, Bell brought this action asking the court to enjoin Manufacturers Bank from honoring Iran's demands for payment under the letter of credit.

MACMAHON, JUDGE
Plaintiff has failed to show that irreparable injury may possibly ensue if a preliminary injunction is denied. Bell does not even claim, much less show, that it lacks an adequate remedy at law if Manufacturers makes a payment to Bank Iranshahr in violation of the Letter of Credit. It is too clear for argument that a suit for money damages could be based on any such violation, and surely Manufacturers would be able to pay any money judgment against it. . . .

To be sure, Bell faces substantial hardships upon denial of its motion. Should Manufacturers pay the demand, Bell will immediately become liable to Manufacturers for $30.2 million, with no assurance of recouping those funds from Iran for the services performed. While counsel represented in graphic detail the other losses Bell faces at the hands of the current Iranian government, these would flow regardless of whether we ordered the relief sought. The hardship imposed from a denial of relief is limited to the admittedly substantial sum of $30.2 million.

*(continued)*

*(continued)*

But Manufacturers would face at least as great a loss, and perhaps a greater one, were we to grant relief. Upon Manufacturers' failure to pay, Bank Iranshahr could initiate a suit on the Letter of Credit and attach $30.2 million of Manufacturers' assets in Iran. In addition, it could seek to hold Manufacturers liable for consequential damages beyond that sum resulting from the failure to make timely payment. Finally, there is no guarantee that Bank Iranshahr or the government, in retaliation for Manufacturers' recalcitrance, will not nationalize additional Manufacturers' assets in Iran in amounts which counsel, at oral argument, represented to be far in excess of the amount in controversy here.

Apart from a greater monetary exposure flowing from an adverse decision, Manufacturers faces a loss of credibility in the international banking community that could result from its failure to make good on a letter of credit.

Bell, a sophisticated multinational enterprise well advised by competent counsel, entered into these arrangements with its corporate eyes open. It knowingly and voluntarily signed a contract allowing the Iranian government to recoup its down payment on demand, without regard to cause. It caused Manufacturers to enter into an arrangement whereby Manufacturers became obligated to pay Bank Iranshahr the unamortized down payment balance upon receipt of conforming documents, again without regard to cause.

Both of these arrangements redounded tangibly to the benefit of Bell. The contract with Iran, with its prospect of designing and installing from scratch a nationwide and international communications system, was certain to bring to Bell both monetary profit and prestige and goodwill in the global communications industry. The agreement to indemnify Manufacturers on its Letter of Credit provided the means by which these benefits could be achieved. One who reaps the rewards of commercial arrangements must also accept their burdens. One such burden in this case, voluntarily accepted by Bell, was the risk that demand might be made without cause on the funds constituting the down payment. To be sure, the sequence of events that led up to that demand may well have been unforeseeable when the contracts were signed. To this extent, both Bell and Manufacturers have been made the unwitting and innocent victims of tumultuous events beyond their control. But, as between two innocents, the party who undertakes by contract the risk of political uncertainty and governmental caprice must bear the consequences when the risk comes home to roost.

So ordered.

**Decision.** The court refused to issue the injunction. The letter of credit was not enjoined because there was no clear showing of irreparable injury and because the plaintiff had an adequate legal remedy against Iran for the return of the monies that would be paid. Such a rule protects the sanctity of a bank's reputation for honoring its letters of credit. The plaintiff was aware of the risks involved and must bear the consequences.

In *KMW International v. Chase Manhattan Bank*, 606 F.2d 10 (2d Cir. 1979), the court held that the unsettled situation in Iran was insufficient reason for releasing the bank from its obligation under a letter of credit. The court in *KMW* gave perhaps the real reason for the decision in the Iranian cases when it stated, "Both in the international business community and in Iran itself, Chase's commercial honor is essentially at stake. Failure to perform on its irrevocable letter of credit would constitute a breach of trust and substantially injure its reputation and perhaps even American credibility in foreign communities. Moreover, it could subject Chase to litigation in connection with not only this matter, but also other banking affairs in Iran."

The following article provides an interesting comparison of claims involving standby credits that followed the Iranian revolution in 1978 and the effect that Iraq's invasion of Kuwait in 1990 had on outstanding standby letters of credit.

## Other Specialized Uses for Letters of Credit

Many specialized types of letters of credit provide a mechanism for financing a sale or other business transaction. Some of these types are discussed here.

**Transferable Credits.** *Transferable credits* are usually used by international traders. Traders buy and sell goods in international trade—quickly and with no view to actually using the goods themselves. They bear considerable risk every day.

# Guarantees and Political Risks: Understanding the Basic Lesson of the Gulf and Iranian Crises

## Exposure and Unfounded Calls When Political Crisis Erupts

The contrast between what occurred regarding standby letters of credit in the months following the success of the Islamic Revolution in Iran on February 11, 1979, and what happened, or, rather, did not happen, following Iraq's invasion of Kuwait on August 2, 1990, is indeed striking.

### After the Iranian Revolution

Shortly after Ayatollah Khomeini took over in Tehran, contracting parties began what seemed to be a wholesale call on letters of credit opened by their American counterparts, usually as guarantees either of performance or for the return of advance payments. Courts in the commercial centers of the United States were besieged by American contractors seeking to enjoin payment of such letters of credit.

Almost universally, such suits were in vain. Generally the most that could be achieved was a so-called "notice injunction" requiring the confirming bank to notify the account party of its intention to honor a demand on such a letter 72 hours in advance of acting, so that the account party might at least have the opportunity to persuade a court to bar payment on the ground that the call was indeed fraudulent or abusive. By and large, payments, when demanded, were not prevented. The principle of purity in matters of letters of credit prevailed over the legitimate fears of contractors.

This situation was ameliorated only when the U.S. government, on November 14, 1979, ten days after the seizure of 52 hostages of the American Embassy in Tehran, froze all Iranian assets subject to its jurisdiction. As an integral part of that measure, the Iranian Assets Control Regulations subsequently provided that a contractor subjected to an Iranian call on its standby letter of credit might, to the extent it was otherwise required to comply, simply es-

tablish a "blocked account" on its books in favor of the Iranian beneficiary, thereby avoiding any immediate economic detriment.

When the United States and Iran concluded the Algiers Accords on January 19, 1981, releasing the 52 American hostages, establishing the Iran–United States Claims Tribunal, and returning to Iran its frozen assets, the U.S. government interpreted the Accords as not requiring the funding and transfer of these previously "blocked accounts" to Iran. Thus, American contractors continued to be protected from the potential consequences of Iranian calls on their letters of credit. . . .

### After the Iraqi Invasion

No wave of activity such as followed the Iranian Revolution resulted from the Iraqi invasion of Kuwait eleven years later, on August 2, 1990. Why not? It could hardly have been that there were so few demand guarantees outstanding. Obviously, too, Saddam Hussein is not fundamentally more correct in such matters than was Ayatollah Khomeini. Wherein, then, lies the cause of the difference?

Principally, I believe, it was because, unlike in the case of the Iranian events of 1979, there was no prolonged period afforded for legal jousting. The very fact that Iraq initiated international hostilities doubtless circumscribed its ability to benefit in foreign legal proceedings. Also, because the Iraqi *Anschluss* of Kuwait, unlike the Iranian postrevolutionary upheaval, was cross-border, and hence a truly international event, and because far more than the safety of 52 individuals and the "face" of a superpower was at stake, the international community reacted, and it reacted immediately.

How did it react? On the very day of the invasion itself, it reacted with a United Nations Security

*(continued)*

*(continued)*

Council resolution of condemnation; immediate withdrawal was demanded. . . . Just four days later . . . the Security Council adopted Resolution 661 imposing sanctions. . . . Whereas the United States in 1979 had waited, for various reasons, from February 11 until November 14 before acting, in the Kuwait crisis the United Nations almost immediately preempted any possibility of normal legal processes taking place. Thus virtually from the beginning, the legal landscape was radically adjusted by sovereign acts.

How have those sovereign acts protected parties otherwise potentially "on the hook" for guarantees? First, of course, the United Nations sanctions, by their basic terms, preclude any transfers that Iraqi demands on guarantees, if made and if successful, might effectuate. Second, however, and more enduringly, relevant resolutions of the Security Council have addressed the merits of potential disputes in a way that may well preclude unjustified demands on guarantees even after sanctions are lifted. . . .

In short, Iraq may not "claim" for breach of a contract insofar as its performance was affected by the United Nations sanctions. This would appear to offer a basis for contesting any future Iraqi demand on preinvasion standby letter of credit or demand guarantee on the ground that the claimed breach cannot serve legitimately as a basis for the demand.

This disposition is, or must become, the law of all member states of the United Nations, which are required by Article 25 of the United Nations Charter to treat such Security Council decisions as legally binding. The initial (and still extant) sanctions have been broadly implemented and continue to protect contractors. Thus in the United Kingdom, legislation under the United Nations Act of 1946 prohibits any person from paying a bond either to or to the order of any person in Iraq without the permission of H.M. Treasury.

In the United States, Treasury Department regulations promulgated under the International Emergency Economic Powers Act broadly prohibit any U.S. bank from making any "transfer" of Iraqi property or property interest, unless licensed to do so by the Treasury. . . . France already has adopted implementing legislation. . . . Also, in December 1992, the EC (European Community) Council adopted a regulation that prohibits honoring any such Iraqi claim. As an EC Council regulation, it should have direct and uniform effect throughout the Community.

The EC regulation demonstrates how far sovereign authority may be exercised to preclude the operation of laws otherwise normally applicable. Under it, the government of Iraq or any Iraqi person could, of course, still claim on a guarantee where the basis for the call is entirely preinvasion and unaffected by the United Nations embargo. As the required predicate for such recovery, however, the EC regulation requires that Iraq first "prove to a court in a Member State that the claim was accepted by the parties prior to the adoption of the measures decided on pursuant to . . . [the various Security Council resolutions] and that those measures have had no effect on the existence or content of the claim." This requirement thus places a heavy burden on Iraq to prove its claim.

## Therein Lies the Lesson

. . . [T]he EC's provisions mean there will be no recovery without dispositive judicial action.

And therein lies the basic lesson of the Iranian Revolution and the Gulf Crisis: The enduring negotiating balance that seems to impel purchasers and employers to exact "clean" guarantees from contractors, and equally to reconcile contractors to providing them, even against their better judgment, is a fact of life, and of necessity it leaves contractors exposed to the consequences of unjustified individual demands. When, however, a political crisis erupts, actually or potentially entailing programmatic unfounded calls on such guarantees, a remedy, and the only remedy, lies in sovereign political action to vary, directly or indirectly, the applicable rules of law.

*Charles N. Brower, Esq.*
**Copyright 1993 Middle East Executive Reports, Ltd. Middle East Executive Reports, September, 1993.**
LETTERS OF CREDIT; Volume 16, No. 9; Pg. 9

Traders operate on little capital, buying merchandise or commodities in one country, taking title through the documents, and then, through their business contacts built up over years of experience, selling at a profit. Some traders specialize in trade with the developing world, often trading commodities for raw materials or merchandise when dollars or hard currency is not available there. For instance, a Swiss bank issues a letter of credit for the account of an African country in favor of the trader, with a part of the credit transferred to the trader's supplier in the Philippines for the cost of the goods it is supplying to the African country. This letter of credit can be split up among many suppliers around the world, each presenting documents for payment, with the trader taking its profit out of the balance of the credit. Shipments of crude oil are often bought and sold in this fashion.

**Red Clauses in Credits.** The *red clause* is a financing tool for smaller sellers who need capital to produce the products to be shipped under a letter of credit. A red clause in a letter of credit is a promise (usually written or underlined in red ink) by the issuing bank to reimburse the seller's bank for loans made to the seller. The loan, then, is really an advance on the credit. Loans can be used only for purchasing raw materials or for covering the costs of manufacturing or shipping of the goods described in the credit. Ultimately, the liability will fall on the buyer if the seller defaults on shipment or repayment of the amounts taken under the credit. This form of financing is very risky for the buyer and its bank.

**Revolving Credits.** When a buyer is planning on purchasing on a regular basis from a foreign seller, a *revolving letter of credit* may be used. Instead of having to use several different credits, one may be used with a maximum amount available during a certain period of time. As the draws against the credit are paid, the full amount becomes available again and continues until the expiration of the credit.

**Back-to-Back Letter of Credit Financing.** A *back-to-back letter of credit* is a special type of financing device. In certain circumstances, an exporter is selling goods to a buyer in one transaction and is buying supplies in another. Under a

back-to-back credit, the exporter can use its credit with the buyer to finance the purchase of goods from the supplier. Thus, a back-to-back credit is really two credits, one representing the security for the second. The bank that issues the second credit requires that it be assigned the proceeds of the original credit. Many banks will issue the second credit only if they had opened the first (known as a countercredit). Back-to-back letters of credit are usually used by traders who are not manufacturers, or by other intermediaries with minimal capital resources who buy and sell goods for delivery to others.

## Letters of Credit in Trade Finance Programs

Letter of credit financing plays an important role in export financing by government and intergovernmental agencies. U.S. exports are financed by such agencies as the *Agency for International Development* (AID), the *World Bank* (which provides financial and technical assistance to developing countries to stimulate economic growth), the *Commodity Credit Corporation* (covering surplus agricultural products), and the *Export-Import Bank of the United States (Eximbank)*. These agencies often insure payments made to U.S. sellers under letters of credit that are confirmed by U.S. banks through the use of a letter of commitment from the agency to the issuing bank.

**AID Financing.** A typical AID financing situation might include a letter of credit. A country wishing to import U.S. products, usually to be used in developmental projects such as building roads, power-generating facilities, and the like, applies to AID for financing. AID then issues its commitment to a U.S. bank that issues its letter of credit for the benefit of the U.S. supplier of eligible goods used in the project. The issuing bank receives reimbursement for payments under its letter of credit from AID.

**Eximbank Financing.** Eximbank is the largest U.S. export financing agency. It can provide guarantees on loans made by commercial banks, and insurance on credit extended by U.S. exporters to their foreign customers. It also makes loans directly from Eximbank funds. Under an

*Foreign Accents*

# Using Credit to Beat the Competition
## New Forms of Flexible Financing Can Be the Key to Winning a Foreign Contract

An exporter in the Midwest needed to prepare a bid on a $40 million contract to supply materials to a utility company in South America. But several suppliers around the world were asking almost the same price for similar quality product. The tie-breaker, the buyer made clear, would be flexible credit terms.

This left the U.S. firm faced with the challenge of offering attractive financing without exposing itself to foreign credit risk, a challenge that an increasing number of exporters are not only meeting, but are even welcoming as a way to beat the competition. Best of all, this can come at no cost to the seller, since the exporter can build financing costs into the price he or she sets—with all interest paid by the importer.

### Solutions
In the case of the $40 million sale to South America, the exporter's solution was to get the Export-Import Bank of the United States to guarantee a loan equal to 85% of the contract price. A commercial bank was then willing to fund the loan with the Eximbank guarantee, which basically represents the "full faith and credit" of the U.S. government. The strength of this guarantee also allowed the bank to charge a low interest rate, around 50 basis points over the London interbank offered rate (LIBOR).

For the remaining 15% of the contract, the exporter offered financing through the "forfait" market, which is comprised mainly of subsidiaries of large European banks. This market frequently provides medium-term (three-to-five years) financing for creditworthy companies and banks in emerging markets. Forfait market rates are higher than Eximbank rates, but since forfait was used for only 15% of the contract, the blended rate was very acceptable.

The bottom line was that by combining the forfait funds with an Eximbank guarantee, the exporter was able to offer 100% financing, at a low fixed rate for five-to-seven years. Further, no down payment was required and the importer was also able to avoid the cost and inconvenience of opening a commercial letter of credit. As in many such cases, the low interest rate and other terms proved to be the margin needed to win a close bid.

What's even more advantageous in an Eximbank guaranteed deal is that potential competitors from industrial nations, including Germany, Switzerland and Belgium, cannot match this financing. Their governments do not allow financing of 15% of the contract price when a government export assistance program (the German equivalent of Eximbank, for example) is used for the other 85% of the contract. As a result, the U.S. company may be one of the few bidders able to offer 100% financing.

### Benefits
There are a number of other reasons to set up this sort of flexible financing approach:

- The exporter usually receives cash proceeds from the sale within 60 days of shipment, with no recourse from any lender financing the importer's purchase (in the above example, Eximbank and the forfait lender). Upon receiving his or her funds, the exporter is completely removed from the financing arrangement.

Since financial intermediaries are basically purchasing the foreign trade receivables without recourse, the risk to the exporter is usually minimal. By prearranging to "sell off" these receivables upon shipment, the exporter is protected from exposure to foreign credit risk.

- The importer can bypass the impediments in local credit markets, which is often the only way he or she can afford to buy a product. Due to lack of liquidity among banks, undeveloped domestic financial systems, government intervention through reserve requirements for loans, and local stamp

*(continued)*

*(continued)*

taxes mean that, especially in emerging market countries, medium-term credit is often very scarce and/or expensive.

- The exporter often makes sales sooner, since a preestablished credit term can be an important element in the buying decision. Assuring credit terms in advance also helps avoid tension over sales terms.

- The importer can tap into projected cash flows, and not have to rely on money already in hand. Especially with capital goods, a new product purchased on credit can be expected to generate a steady flow of cash over several years.

Perhaps most important for the exporter to remember, foreign buyers are becoming increasingly aware of the existence of these new flexible financial alternatives. As a consequence, the importers are increasingly requiring their suppliers to work with them to find or provide acceptable financing. Of course, a credible prospect will not expect exporters to accept foreign exposure or carry long-term receivables. Such a request, in fact, is usually an indication of a weak prospect.

## Selling a Bill of Exchange to a Third Party

Recently a U.S. exporter received a long-awaited inquiry from a major Brazilian steel company. The international sales manager quickly assembled the product specifications and, following company policy, asked for a sight letter of credit confirmed by a U.S. bank.

The Brazilian company responded by accepting the product specifications and price, but asked for different payment terms: a documentary collection using a bill of exchange (draft) with payment deferred for six months. When the sales manager took this offer to his company's CFO, the response was sympathetic, but unyielding. The exporter's cash flow simply could not accommodate the importer's request.

In this case, the immediate solution was to find a trade finance company or international bank that would purchase, at a discount, a bill of exchange that obligates the Brazilian company to pay the amount of the invoice in 180 days (six months) from sight.

An "accepted" bill of exchange is a common instrument and may be discounted assuming the credit of the importer is acceptable.

By discounting the bill of exchange, the exporter was able to receive cash at shipment, without recourse. For the exporter, the sale became a cash transaction. For the importer, it became a credit transaction. The needs of both parties were met by a financial intermediary.

## Medium-Term Financing Through the Sale of an LC

In another case, a U.S. manufacturer of farm equipment wanted to expand sales to South America. Since most locally made equipment was of inferior quality, the company expected to tap into generally strong demand for American-made farm equipment. But the company decided to accept for payment only a "sight" letter of credit, which requires that the buyer pay cash. For most mid-range farmers, this is usually something they cannot do until they first plant, harvest and sell their crop.

The solution in this case was to find a financial intermediary to discount the letter of credit, and convert it to cash. This met the need of the exporter, who needed the cash to pay production costs. And since the deal calls for the letter of credit to come due two years from sight, it also meets the needs of the farmer, who will have ample time to plant, harvest and sell his crop and collect from his customers.

In this case, the intermediary basically accepted the risk of default by the foreign bank for two years. In the event the foreign bank had defaulted, the intermediary of course would have lost its investment. But all the risk had already been factored into the discount rate.

This method prevented any erosion of the exporter's margin, because after discounting, the exporter received the normal cash price. All parties achieved their objective, and the exporter closed a sale that was about to be abandoned.

*Roger Zlotoff*
*Export Today Magazine,* Washington, D.C. (February 1995): 32–34. Copyright 1995. *Export Today Magazine.*

Reprinted with permission. *Export Today* P.O. Box 28189, Washington D.C. 20038.

Eximbank loan program, a U.S. bank, designated by the foreign buyer, opens a letter of credit on behalf of the buyer for the benefit of a U.S. supplier. Eximbank guarantees the issuing bank repayment of sums that it pays out under the credit. Eximbank then receives its payments under the loan agreement worked out in advance between it and the foreign buyer. Despite the importance of the U.S. Eximbank, only a small percentage of U.S. exports are financed by Eximbank (about three percent). Eximbank has been subject to much criticism for failing to assist with the special needs of small business exporters. Recently, Eximbank has increased its lending guarantees for U.S. goods going to developing countries. The largest foreign market for U.S. goods financed by Eximbank guarantees is China, with over $1 billion in guarantees there in 1994. Other countries have export–import banks of their own to assist in financing their exports.

**Commodity Credit Corporation.** The Commodity Credit Corporation provides payment assurances to U.S. sellers of surplus agricultural products to approved foreign buyers. Standby letters of credit are often used, whereby the seller can draw under the credit for invoices that remain unpaid by the overseas buyer.

**Foreign Credit Insurance Association.** The Foreign Credit Insurance Association (FCIA) is an association of private insurance companies that insure U.S. exporters from political and commercial risk. It works in partnership with Eximbank. Commercial risk includes losses due to the default of the buyer and the inability of the buyer to pay because of natural disasters. Political risk (covered by Eximbank) covers the confiscation of goods by the government, nonconvertibility of the buyer's currency, war expropriation, and the inability of the buyer to obtain an import license. Typically, the FCIA provides coverage for up to 100 percent of the political risk and 90 percent of the commercial risk. The cost of this insurance is based on an analysis of the country and the foreign importer.

Another benefit to small and medium-sized exporters is that their foreign accounts receivable are more valuable to commercial banks due to the insurance protection. As such, exports sold on open account to foreign buyers can more readily be sold or assigned to a financial institu-

tion. FCIA policies are also available to cover losses under confirmed letters of credit issued in favor of U.S. exporters by U.S. commercial banks.

# Countertrade

The focus of this chapter has been on payment by documentary collection and letter of credit. Many other methods of effectuating payment between buyer and seller have developed in recent years. Firms trading with the independent states of the former Soviet Union, China, the countries of Eastern Europe, and the developing countries often have to find a substitute for hard cash if they want to sell their products there. Many nations in all regions of the world, from Mexico to Poland, have a shortage of foreign currency, a high debt burden to foreign banks that must be paid in dollars, and little currency left over to purchase the products needed for consumption by their people. As a result, they may have instituted exchange controls that make normal trade difficult or impossible. The foreign currency that is available will be allocated by central planning authorities or central banks to the purchase of only the most essential goods. As a result, many countries will attempt to find other means of paying for the products they need. They may require, for instance, that a seller take goods in return, or that every import be "offset" by the seller with an export sale of similar value. These alternatives are generally known as countertrade.

> **http://132.174.112.1/infosrc/aca/**
> *American Countertrade Association site includes reference library and overview of countertrade techniques.*

## What Is Countertrade?

*Countertrade* is the term for several different types of transactions, arising from agreement between buyer and seller, and involving an exchange of goods rather than an exchange of currency. While a large portion of the world's countertrade occurs between private firms and governments or state trading organizations, much of it takes place between private parties.

Countertrade deals span all sectors of the world economy and all regions of the globe. Given that approximately 70 percent of the world's population lives in countries with non-convertible currencies, it is no surprise that countertrade accounts for nearly 30 percent of world trade. Such deals can be large or small transactions, running into the hundreds of millions of dollars, or larger. General Electric, for example, succeeded in obtaining a $150 million power-generating project in Romania against firms from Germany and Japan, not because its technology or price was any better, but because it agreed to take $150 million in Romanian products in exchange. In the largest trade deal ever signed between the former Soviet Union and an American corporation, Pepsi-Cola agreed to trade its concentrate syrup for Stolichnaya Russian Vodka until the year 2000, a deal worth $3 billion in total retail sales. (See the following article.) Other industries active in countertrade include aerospace, weapons systems, and construction.

## Counterpurchase

The most common type of countertrade is the *counterpurchase agreement.* Counterpurchase involves the sale of goods to a buyer, often a foreign government, who requires as a condition of the sale that the seller buy other goods produced in that country. For example, the People's Republic of China may agree to purchase a firm's machine tools, but will require in return that the firm either purchase a quantity of Chinese made products—or find someone who will. These deals are usually two separate contracts where each party is paid in currency when its products are delivered to the other party. Often, the private firm is given a period of several years in which to fulfill its purchase obligation. Usually, the seller will be given a selection of items for export so that if the particular Chinese products do not fit into the seller's channels of distribution, the seller can choose other products instead. The goal of a counterpurchase arrangement, however, is for export transactions to offset the "cost" of import transactions.

## Barter

Another form of countertrade is barter. Barter is the direct exchange of goods for goods (or services). Unlike counterpurchase transactions which in-volve payment in currency, barter transaction are not pegged to market prices and therefore it is difficult to compensate for changes in the value of the goods exchanged. Barter transactions can involve a wide range of items, from pharmaceuticals and aircraft to agricultural commodities, oil, and natural resources. Some firms which specialize in barter transactions have developed creative schemes for minimizing risks for exporters. Consider the following article. Countries that are members of the Organization of Petroleum Exporting Countries (OPEC) are famous for bartering oil for many of the products they need to import.

## Buy-Back

A *buy-back agreement* is often associated with the sale of machinery or industrial equipment, or the construction of plants and factories. Here the provider of the equipment or technology will receive, as its payment, a portion of the goods manufactured by the equipment or in the factory. For example, under the Israel Cooperation Program, any foreign company which sells products to the Israeli government is required to purchase 35 percent of the value of the contract from Israeli companies in return. Consequently, when El Al (the Israeli government-owned airline) agreed to buy approximately $90 million worth of engines for its Boeing 757 jets from Rolls Royce, Rolls Royce agreed to buy Israeli technological products and engine components worth 35 percent of El Al's purchases. One of the problems for firms that enter into buy-back agreements is that they cannot effectively control the quality of the goods taken back. Another problem arises when the firm that provides the equipment also manufactures the same products as those for which the equipment will be used. The goods produced may possibly compete with those that the firm manufactures itself.

Countertrading is generally left to the more experienced multinationals, exporters, or traders, as it is considered one of the more risky ventures of international trade. Many stories tell of smaller firms that suffered great losses in countertrading, particularly when they did not have the foresight to arrange for a buyer for their countertraded products in advance. Because of the rapidly expanding market, countertrade specialists, who purchase traded goods at a discount and resell them for a profit, have emerged.

# Financing Strategies—Barter's Rebirth

NEW YORK, DECEMBER 12—Ever since the famed Stolichnaya-for-Pepsi deal, the old concepts of bilateral barter and countertrade, with which the former is sometimes confused, had been gradually falling out of favor as a way to clear international payments, particularly in currency-strapped Russia, the NIS, and to a lesser extent, Central and Eastern Europe. However, a number of multilateral trading facilitators are using computer technology and advanced global marketing techniques to improve the barter process.

As the old ways yield to a kindler, gentler, and immensely more useful multilateral clearing system, these firms have broadened barter's appeal by improving returns for their clients. "In our business, the exporter doesn't bear the risk," said William Levitz of Atwood Richards Inc., a firm that facilitates such transactions. "We assume the risk. We will buy the product from the company, pay for it with vouchers, and sometimes, a combination of cash and credits for needed services."

In what Levitz calls a "typical multilateral barter transaction," goods are paid for in a combination of cash and vouchers, exchangable for products and services from the barter firm's clients. The holders of these vouchers or "credits" can swap them for a range of raw materials, capital equipment, supplies, and worldwide services for travel, accommodations and advertising.

In the past, multinational financial and marketing managers have viewed barter as a court of last resort in which distressed exporters accept "in-kind" settlements from strapped importers, and afterwards shop the goods wherever they can, at deep discounts. This concept is "out the window" at such firms as Atwood Richards, Inc. (ARI), Icon International, Inc. (III), Tradewell Industries (TI), and others. These deals are not intended for emerging exporters or marginal MNCs [multi-national corporations]. The value of the average deal is $1 million or better and ARI, at least, hardly ever does business with a company having revenues less than $60 to $70 million. The reason for the size requirement, ARI Vice President, William Levitz, told *East/West Commersant*, is that "smaller companies would not be able to use their vouchers within an economical period of time."

## Far-Flung Markets Absorb Inventory

. . . Levitz gave this example: A baked-goods or frozen-food producer finds itself with an unwanted inventory of a certain product. It could be that there was a change in labeling, a change in regulations in the primary market, or perhaps the product was for a since-canceled promotion. Or, it could be that the product is just 'off spec' for its primary market. It is not difficult to construct parallel cases for a number of different industries.

In that case, ARI would likely make the producer an offer for the inventory. The price might be 20 percent in cash and the balance in ARI vouchers. The seller would have to store the product, maintain it, insure it, and ship it according to ARI's instructions, all at the seller's expense. ARI and similar firms scrupulously avoid re-marketing products in competition with the seller, often including a clause to this effect in documentation for the deal. Instead, the products are sold offshore, in a region in which the seller's products are little known. As a result, new markets for the seller's products are often created.

## A Case in Point

A typical ARI deal, involving the French clothing producer, Eminence, and about $10 million annually in sportswear and accessories, illustrates the way the company facilitates market penetration for its clients. Eminence found itself with excess inventory and a desire to open new markets. Competition is tough, admitted an Eminence executive, likening the company's traditional Western European markets to a chessboard. The company wanted to expand, but was not finding any free niches.

Being one of France's major clothing manufacturers, Eminence wanted to enter the fresh and tantalizingly large markets of Eastern Europe for years. But for all the opportunities, Eminence saw dozens of possible pitfalls: Where to find reliable distributors? How to deal with the transitory nature, or total

*(continued)*

*(continued)*

absence, of commercial law? And most important, how to repatriate profits from countries with scant hard-currency reserves? The company eventually contacted ARI, which marketed the sportswear products through its distributor network in the region. The results were dynamic; continuous, strong demand for the Eminence line caused the original contract for a $6 million inventory "bulge" to grow to $10 million annually over five years.

Eminence is taking its payments out in a combination of cash, media services, and raw materials. At the end of the period, the company will be free to distribute in the region without re-negotiating its contract with Atwood Richards International. The Eminence executive added that, as a result of the arrangements with ARI, "We will be the first brand in Central Europe, and we will be there for a very long time.". . .

**Keys to Success**

[ARI Vice President Levitz states]: "One of our keys to success in Central and Eastern Europe and Russia is to maintain our own offices, staffed entirely by nationals, and we constantly travel to these offices. For example, our CEO Moreton Binn, has been spending a lot of time in Uzbekistan, because we're opening a big operation there. Sure, it's a complicated market, but Uzbekistan has 24 million people, there's a tremendous demand for Western goods, and we want to be the first firm doing this kind of thing."

*George Cassidy*

Copyright 1995 *WorldTrade Executive, Inc.* 2250 Main St., Suite 100, P.O. Box 761, Concord, MA 01742, *http://www.wtexec.com, East/West Commersant* December, 1995, No. 22, Vol. 3.

# Chapter Summary

This chapter describes some of the legal issues involved in moving money from one party to another in an international transaction. The reader should understand why bills of exchange, or drafts, are the primary instrument for effectuating payment in an international transaction, and how they are used. Drafts are commonly classified as sight drafts or time drafts. When a draft is accepted by a merchant in the trade it becomes a trade acceptance. When it is accepted by a bank, it becomes a banker's acceptance. These negotiable instruments are used as substitutes for money, as well as in acceptance financing. By discounting an acceptance in the credit markets, outside capital is used by buyer and seller to finance their trade sale. A holder in due course of an acceptance is protected from disputes that might arise between buyer and seller in the underlying transaction. The ability of a seller to provide trade finance to a buyer is important in a competitive market.

While most of the discussion focused on transactions involving the sale of goods, the same negotiable instruments and legal concepts discussed apply to moving money in many different types of transactions, including licensing and investment contracts, the sale of services and construction contracts.

Drafts can be used to collect payment under a bank letter of credit. Letters of credit are not bank guarantees, but they are assurances to the seller of payment, if the seller complies with all the terms and conditions stated in the credit. Courts in most jurisdictions rely on the *Uniform Customs and Practice for Documentary Credits* (UCP) to interpret the rights of the parties to a letter of credit. Under the independence principle, a letter of credit is separate from the underlying sales transaction. Banks are required to honor a demand for payment upon presentation of documents that conform to the requirements of the letter of credit. Standby letters of credit are guarantees of the seller's performance to the buyer. Like traditional letters of credit, the beneficiary of a standby credit is entitled to payment upon presentation of the required documents to the bank.

Countertrade is a business practice involving the exchange of goods, as a substitute for money. It is used by experienced traders in all regions of the world, but especially in Russia, Eastern Europe, China, and other developing countries that are subject to a scarcity of hard currency. Countertrade accounts for a large share of world trade.

## QUESTIONS AND CASE PROBLEMS

1.  Habib Bank issued a letter of credit on the instructions of its account party calling for the payment of drafts upon the presentation of documents showing shipment by a certain date. The bank examined the documents and paid the beneficiary's draft. The account party refused to take the documents and reimburse the bank because the shipping date was incorrectly stated in the documents. The bank sued the beneficiary for a return of its money for presenting nonconforming documents. The bank brought its action under the Uniform Commercial Code, Article 5-111, which states that a presenting beneficiary warrants that "the necessary conditions of the credit have been complied with." The beneficiary claims that under the UCP the bank was precluded from complaining about the discrepancies because the bank had failed to object to the documents in a timely fashion. UCP 500, Article 14, states that an issuing or nominated bank must notify the beneficiary (or another bank from which it is receiving the documents) of the rejection *without delay but no later than the close of the seventh banking day following the day of receipt of the documents.* Judgment for whom and why? Which rule will apply, the UCC rule or the UCP rule? *Habib Bank Limited v. Convermat Corporation,* 145 Misc. 2d 980, 554 N.Y.S.2d 757 (1990).

2.  Hambro Bank, Ltd., an English bank, received a cable from a Danish company, A.O., requesting that an irrevocable letter of credit be opened in favor of J. H. Rayner and Company. A.O. instructed Hambro Bank that the letter of credit be for " . . . about \P16,975 [pounds] against invoice full straight clean bills of lading . . . covering about 1,400 tons Coromandel groundnuts." The bill of lading presented to Hambro by J. H. Rayner stated " . . . bags machineshelled groundnut kernels," with the abbreviation C.R.S. in the margin. Hambro refused to pay on the letter of credit. J. H. Rayner sued Hambro. The custom of trade holds that C.R.S. is short for Coromandel groundnuts. Why did the bank not want to pay on this letter of credit? Was the bank correct in denying payment on this letter of credit? *J. H. Rayner and Company, Ltd. v. Hambro's Bank, Ltd.,* 1 K.B. 36 (1943).

3.  Marino, a manufacturer of construction materials, agreed with a German company to ship materials to a job site in Saudi Arabia. A letter of credit was issued to Marino at the request of the German company and confirmed by Chase Manhattan Bank in the United States. To obtain payment, one of the requirements was that a certificate of receipt be presented showing that freight charges were prepaid. The certificate presented had a box at the top stating: "ACCOUNT: CASH" with the word "CASH" crossed out, but did not state that the freight had been prepaid. The freight forwarder representing Marino stated that crossing out the word "CASH" means that freight charges are prepaid. Chase refused to pay. Marino filed legal action. Was Chase correct to refuse to pay on this letter of credit? Did Chase have any obligation to check other documents Marino had presented earlier—bill of lading or invoice—to see if the freight charges were prepaid? Would Chase be obligated to know of any trade custom where crossing out "CASH" indicates freight prepaid? *Marino Industries Corp. v. Chase Manhattan Bank,* 686 F.2d 112 (2nd Cir. 1982).

4.  The seller of goods has a right to proceed judicially against an issuing bank that dishonors its obligation under an irrevocable letter of credit, just as the seller has the right to proceed directly against the buyer. Should the issuing bank also be liable for consequential damages that are reasonably foreseeable? See *Hadley v. Baxendale,* 9 Ex. 341 (1854).

5.  Lotsa Music, has signed a contract to buy "2,000 new CD players, with manufacturer's warranties" from Phoney, Inc., in Korea. Phoney is shipping the CD players CIF, and requires an irrevocable letter of credit. First Faithful Bank has issued a letter of credit on Lotsa Music's behalf promising to honor a draft accompanied by a clean onboard bill of lading and an invoice showing "2,000 new CD players, with manufacturer's warranties." Hamsung, a competitor, informs you that even though Phoney obtained a bill of lading for "2,000 new CD players, with manufacturer's warranties," the CD players are all used and partly inoperable. What can your company do? Would it make any difference if Phoney's bank had confirmed the letter of credit and already paid the amount of the draft before you learned about this problem? See *United Bank Limited v. Cambridge Sporting Goods Corp.,* 392 N.Y.S.2d 265, 41 N.Y.2d 254, 360 N.E.2d 943 (1976).

6.  A South African firm applied for a revolving letter of credit at Barclays Bank, Johannesburg, in favor of a German exporter. The L/C was issued covering shipments of pharmaceuticals, and was confirmed by Deutsche Bank, Germany. After a number of shipments, the amount of the L/C was increased. To the best knowledge of Barclays, their account party had always taken possession of the goods and sold them quickly for a profit. In the last shipment, Deutsche Bank honored the seller's sight draft for the full amount of the L/C, and presented the documents to Barclays. While Barclays was inspecting the docu-

ments, it learned that the South African buyer had ceased business. In the meantime, Deutsche Bank discovers that the seller has ceased business also. On inspection by Barclays, the cargo containers contained only worthless junk. Reports placed both buyer and seller in Brazil. What happened? What are the rights and liabilities of the advising and confirming bank? How do banks handle problems like this?

7. Pursuant to the instructions of the buyer, a Chicago bank issued its credit in favor of a bicycle exporter in Hong Kong covering "HPO 360 bicycles." The operative credit was by cable, with no mail confirmation to follow. The Hong Kong bank confirmed. On receipt of the documents, the confirming bank paid the seller and forwarded the documents to the Chicago bank. On receipt, the Chicago bank rejected the documents, claiming that the invoices showed the merchandise as "NOOHPO 360 bicycles." The confirming bank claims that the documents complied with the credit because the cable containing the credit called for "NOOHPO 360 bicycles." Later, the banks realized that although the Chicago bank had sent the cable correctly (describing HPO 360 bicycles), the Hong Kong bank had received the credit with the description "NOOHPO 360 bicycles." Investigation revealed that the error was caused by sunspots affecting satellite transmission. Under the transmission agreement, the satellite company is liable only for $250. The confirming bank in Hong Kong seeks reimbursement. What is the confirming bank's argument? What claim does the confirming bank have against the beneficiary? What is the argument of the issuing bank in Chicago? What legal and/or ethical responsibilities do the buyer and seller have to each other and to the two banks?

8. The beneficiary of a letter of credit alleges that it was unable to meet the shipping date set out in the L/C because the advising bank, Continental, delayed in advising of the L/C. The beneficiary brought an action in tort law for Continental's negligence in advising of the L/C, claiming that Continental owed a duty to the beneficiary under the common law of torts. Does an advising bank owe the beneficiary a tort duty of timely transmission? Is Continental liable for a breach of contract with the beneficiary? Was Continental a party to the L/C arrangement?

Does the beneficiary have any claim against the account party based on the underlying contract? Consider the impact of UCP 500, Article 7: "A credit may be advised to a beneficiary through another bank [the advising bank] without engagement on the part of the advising bank. . . . If the bank elects not to advise the credit, it must so inform the issuing bank without delay." *Sound of Market Street, Inc. v. Continental Bank International,* 819 F.2d 384 (3rd Cir. 1987).

## MANAGERIAL IMPLICATIONS

1. Your firm regularly sells to customers in Germany, Poland, Japan, Canada, and Venezuela. How would you evaluate the creditworthiness of firms in each of these countries? How would the credit risk differ in each of these countries? What sources of information would you use? Under what circumstances would you consider selling to firms in these countries without a letter of credit? In which of these countries would you want the buyer's letter of credit to be confirmed by an American bank? Why? What additional protection does the confirmed credit provide?

2. An advising bank presents documents to you for payment. How would you respond to each of the following discrepancies? Explain your answer.
   a. The L/C calls for an ocean bill of lading. The seller presents a trucker's bill of lading showing shipment to an ocean port.
   b. The sales contract and the L/C call for shipment of "Soda Ash Light." The invoice shows shipment of "Soda Ash Light," but the bill of lading describes the shipment as "Soda Ash."
   c. The L/C calls for shipment of 1,000 kilograms. The invoice shows shipment of an equal amount in pounds.
   d. The CIF contract with the L/C calls for onboard bill of lading to be dated by December 20. The bill of lading is dated December 20, but the insurance policy is dated December 21.

3. Your firm has contracted to purchase silk from overseas suppliers on letter of credit terms. After contracting, but before presentment of the seller's documents, China expands its production and floods the market with raw silk. The price of silk plummets on world markets. Comment on whether you should try to find a minor discrepancy in the documents to justify rejecting the documents. Is it ethical for a buyer to reject documents presented under a letter of credit that contains only a minor discrepancy between the documents and the credit? Do the reasons matter? Does it matter that the buyer may know that the shipment actually conforms to the requirements of the contract and of the letter of credit?

# *Part Three*

# International and U.S. Trade Law

art Three turns from the study of the private law of international business transactions to a study of the public law of international trade. These are actually two very different areas of the law. As we saw in the preceding chapters, the law of international business transactions is a type of private law which determines the rights and responsibilities of two or more parties in their business relationship. The law of international contracts for the sale of goods was one example. *International trade law,* on the other hand, is a body of public law used to determine the responsibilities that nations have to one another in their trade relations. An agreement between two nations to charge a certain rate of duty on imported goods would be governed by international trade law.

Before one can understand how nations agree upon and implement international trade law, one must first understand the national lawmaking process. Chapter Nine explains how the various branches of the U.S. government share the responsibility for regulating foreign commerce and trade. Once the role of the executive and legislative branches of government in regulating trade activity is explained, the discussion of public law can be extended to international trade relations.

Chapters Ten, Eleven, and Twelve cover the basics of international trade law: Chapter Ten examines the *General Agreement on Tariffs and Trade 1994,* GATT, and the *World Trade Organization.* Since its inception in 1947, GATT has provided the framework for regulating most world trade in goods. We will examine in detail the major GATT principles as newly enacted in 1994 as a result of the Uruguay Round trade negotiations. Many current events issues will be covered in this chapter, giving the reader an inside look at the trade negotiations behind some of the headline news stories of the 1990s. In Chapter Eleven we move on to special GATT problems involving the issues of free trade versus protectionism, and the regulation of import competition. Many of these topics, such as dumping and subsidies, may be familiar to the reader from courses in economics. Here we look at the very interesting legal aspects and political ramifications of these issues. Chapter Twelve examines laws that help assure access to foreign markets. The focus of the chapter is on how the U.S. government has used its economic leverage to force other countries to remove nontariff barriers to the import of U.S. goods and services. Here we will have the chance to examine many "sectoral issues," including trade in services, agriculture, textiles, and other areas.

Chapter Thirteen examines customs and tariff laws which govern the importing of goods into the United States and the relationship between a U.S. importer and the U.S. government. We will take a hands-on look at how

to enter goods through U.S. Customs and how to determine the dutiable status of goods. The chapter focuses on importing as an integral part of the global strategy of the firm, in the context of global sourcing and the location of factories and assembly plants in different regions of the world.

Chapter Fourteen covers the *North American Free Trade Agreement* (NAFTA) and trade issues affecting the Western Hemisphere. This subject is covered near the end of this part because it builds upon the principles of global trade covered in the earlier chapters. Finally, Chapter Fifteen discusses export law.

# Chapter Nine

# National Lawmaking Powers and the Regulation of U.S. Trade

The U.S. Constitution provides for a separation of powers between the executive and legislative branches of government. In the field of international economic affairs, however, the role of Congress and the president is not always clearly defined. We know that Congress has the authority to impose tariffs, to regulate commerce with foreign nations, and to declare war. But what of the president? We know that the president appoints ambassadors, negotiates with foreign nations, and is the commander-in-chief of the armed services. Of course, we should not forget that the president makes treaties, albeit only with the advice and consent of the Senate. Thus, it would seem that most of the authority to regulate U.S. trade rests with Congress, and not with the president. This is true. As we will see in this chapter, however, much of the president's role in regulating U.S. trade is delegated to him by Congress itself. This puts tremendous responsibility in the hands of the president and his cabinet, most importantly the U.S. Trade Representative, the Secretary of Treasury, and the Secretary of Commerce. In this chapter we will examine the role of the legislative and executive branches in regulating U.S. trade and how their respective functions are affected by their separation of powers. Most importantly, the reader should consider the impact of their decisions on American firms doing business around the world. An understanding of this chapter will assist the reader later, in understanding America's role in solving global trade problems.

## U.S. Trade Law and American Foreign Policy

United States trade law is that body of public law that governs America's trade relations with foreign countries, including the import and export of goods and services. Trade law is used to implement American trade policies. These policies are determined by Congress and the president, often after protracted public debate of the issues. The debates usually focus on the economic and political objectives for the nation. One possible economic objective of U.S. trade policy might be to affect the balance of trade, perhaps by promoting exports or by reducing consumption of imports. Other objectives might be to affect the strength of the U.S. dollar, to aid in promoting the economic and social development of poorer developing countries, to force foreign countries to permit U.S. goods to enter their markets freely, or to foster growth in an American industry, such as automobiles, semiconductors, or steel.

Trade law is used to implement not only economic policy but also foreign policy. Trade law can be used to encourage trade with a political ally or to discourage trade with a potential foe. It can determine those countries with which Americans will trade and do business and those with which they will not. It is trade policy that determines where on the globe U.S. firms will source raw materials, where their contract labor will be done, where their complex finished goods will be assembled, and to whom these goods will be shipped. For example, the U.S. Congress might want to restrict trade by imposing higher tariffs on the goods from countries that are non-democratic or that violate human rights. Congress might be willing to grant favorable tariff treatment to goods coming from countries that promise to protect the global environment. The president also might ban trade altogether with countries that sponsor international terrorism or an illegal drug trade. Examples of the use of trade controls for political purposes have occurred throughout U.S. history. President Kennedy embargoed trade and travel to Cuba when communist leader Fidel Castro came to power. President Nixon imposed import surcharges on U.S. imports to address an international monetary crisis. President Carter banned trade and travel to Iran after its takeover of the U.S. embassy there. President Reagan imposed trade sanctions on Panama in response to its government's sponsorship of international drug trafficking, and on Libya for sponsoring international terrorism. President Bush granted favorable trading status to Hungary and other formerly communist coun-

tries when they eased their emigration policies. President Bush and President Clinton both have imposed United Nations backed sanctions on Iraq for invading Kuwait and for developing weapons of mass destruction. In the following case, *Freedom to Travel Campaign (FTC) v. Newcomb* (1995), the company asked the federal courts to overturn restrictions on U.S. citizens traveling to Cuba. The court declines to evaluate the foreign policy underlying a U.S. law in determining its validity, holding that foreign affairs is entrusted to the "political branches of government." Also notice that the court refuses to rule that the travel ban violates one's constitutional rights.

---

### Freedom to Travel Campaign (FTC) v. Newcomb

82 F. 3d 1431
United States
Court of Appeals
(9th Cir. 1995)

**BACKGROUND AND FACTS**
In 1962 President Kennedy announced the *Cuban Asset Control Regulations* that prohibited U.S. citizens from engaging in almost any economic activity with communist Cuba without a license. The embargo has lasted through eight U.S. presidents. The regulations also restrict travel to Cuba. Certain persons, such as journalists and government officials, can qualify for a general license. Permission to travel for all other persons, including tourists, will only be considered upon the showing of "compelling need" and for such specified reasons as "clearly defined educational activities." Traveling to Cuba without a license is a criminal offense subject to imprisonment, fine, and property forfeiture. The Freedom to Travel Campaign (FTC) is an organization that organizes educational and other trips to Cuba. It brought this action challenging the regulations. The FTC claimed that (1) the regulations violate the Constitution on the theory that the government lacks sufficient foreign policy reasons to prohibit a person from traveling to another country and (2) the failure to define "educational activities" for which a travel permit may be granted renders the regulations excessively vague and therefore void.

**CYNTHIA HOLCOMB HALL, CIRCUIT JUDGE**
The FTC argues . . . that the regulations' travel ban is unconstitutional because the government lacks a

sufficient foreign policy rationale to inhibit FTC's liberty interest in travel. In substance, this appears to be a substantive due process claim and we will treat it as such. A substantive due process claim involves the balancing of a person's liberty interest against the relevant government interests. The FTC claims that its freedom to travel is trampled by the regulations' travel ban. Although the freedom to travel internationally is a liberty interest recognized by the Fifth Amendment . . . it is clearly not accorded the same stature as the freedom to travel among the states. *Haig v. Agee,* 453 U.S. 280, 101 S.Ct. 2766 (1981) ("The Court has made it plain that the freedom to travel outside the United States must be distinguished from the right to travel within the United States."). Restrictions on international travel are usually granted much greater deference. Given the lesser importance of this freedom to travel abroad, the government need only advance a rational, or at most an important, reason for imposing the ban. This the government can do. The purpose of the travel ban is the same now as it has been since the ban was imposed almost 35 years ago—to restrict the flow of hard currency into Cuba. That goal has been found "important," "substantial," and even "vital." See *Walsh v. Brady,* 927 F.2d 1229, 1235 (D.C.Cir.1991). Thus, the government seems to have satisfied its obligation.

*(continued)*

*(continued)*

The FTC, however, would have us evaluate the foreign policy underlying the embargo. It contends that the President's current reason for the embargo—to pressure the Cuban government into making democratic reforms—is not as compelling a policy for an embargo as were previous justifications that relied on national security concerns. FTC thus invites us to invalidate the ban. This is an invitation we must decline. It is well-settled that "[m]atters relating to the conduct of foreign relations . . . are so exclusively entrusted to the political branches of government as to be largely immune from judicial inquiry or interference." *Regan,* 468 U.S. at 242, 104 S.Ct. at 3038. This immunity manifests itself in a history of judicial deference.

Even were we to second guess the President, this is not a case where the government has set forth no justifications at all. It has detailed numerous reasons for the embargo. We will look no further. *The Cuban Asset Control Regulations'* travel ban is constitutional.

The FTC claims that the regulations' provisions on travel for "educational activities" are void for vagueness and therefore infringe upon its freedom to travel. . . . FTC correctly states that due process will not tolerate a law restricting the freedom of movement if its enforcement is left to the whim of government officials. . . . The Treasury Department's recent amendment to the regulations further cures any vagueness defects. Newly created Regulation 419 now defines "clearly defined educational activities" as (1) those conducted at an international meeting or conference; and (2) those related to undergraduate or graduate studies [and not solely for personal enrichment]. Thus, this aspect of [the regulations] is constitutional.

The FTC . . . argues that the regulations' vague language gives Asset Control officials the ability to arbitrarily interfere with its right to gather first-hand information about Cuba, which its members would use to participate in the public debate about the wisdom of the Cuban-American embargo. When a person's right to travel internationally is conditioned on the surrender of his First Amendment expressive or associational rights, the First Amendment is clearly implicated. . . . However, where a person seeks only to gather information, no First Amendment rights are implicated.

**Decision.** The ban on travel to Cuba is valid. The U.S. government need only have a rational basis for prohibiting travel to foreign countries, such as in this case, where the ban is intended to deprive the communist government of hard currency.

---

Many critics claim that trade policy often "falls victim" to foreign policy. They argue that trade will suffer if it is used as a tool for implementing foreign policy in an unstable political world. They claim that trade should not be used as a political carrot and stick, because in a global economy trade restrictions are seldom effective. They argue that if U.S. companies cannot sell to a country because it is governed by a cruel dictator, then that foreign country will simply purchase the needed products elsewhere. Unless all countries are willing to participate in an embargo of a rogue nation's products, the embargo is unlikely to be effective. Cuba is a good example: communism has lasted for almost forty years there, despite Cuba's near total isolation from the United States. Critics also point out that trade sanctions seldom work against "third world dictators," because the population that suffers the most, for instance the people of Iraq, is not in a position to rise up and oust the government anyway. An excellent example of how trade sanctions can backfire on the United States occurred during the late 1970s. President Carter ordered a halt of all shipment of U.S. grain to the Soviet Union when that country invaded Afghanistan. The trade ban did send a message to the Soviet Union—that the United States objected to the invasion. But the Soviets simply purchased their grain from other global suppliers—to the chagrin of the American farmers, who lost a good-paying customer. Of course, these moves also involve important moral decisions that are actually supported by many members of Congress and the American public, and the sacrifice for the sake of morality is considered by many to be worth the price.

This quandary leads us to an important point. Quite often U.S. firms are caught in the middle of international disputes. Any action by the United States involving trade sanctions against another country is liable to hurt some American interest. Therefore, it is essential that companies be able to manage the risk of doing business in a political world. In the following case, *B-West Imports, Inc. v. the United States* (1996), ten U.S. firms that had been doing business in China learned that they no longer could do so. These companies had been importing arms and munitions from China for sporting use, when they learned that their import licenses had been revoked. The revocation was based on foreign policy grounds. The court rejected their argument that they had an established right to continue importing.

---

## B-West Imports, Inc. v. The United States

75 F.3d 633
United States
Court of Appeals
(Fed. Cir. 1996)

BACKGROUND AND FACTS
The U.S. *Arms Export Control Act* (AECA) prohibits the import of arms and munitions from countries on the "proscribed list" without a license. Although China had been on the proscribed list, prior to 1994 exemptions had been made for China and import licenses issued. On May 26, 1994, however, President Clinton announced a ban on the import of arms and munitions from China, and other trading sanctions because of "continuing human rights abuses" and other foreign policy reasons. The law was enforced by the U.S. Customs Service and the Bureau of Alcohol, Tobacco and Firearms (BATF). The agencies detained all shipments of arms from China and revoked all import permits. Subsequently, Congress enacted legislation providing that the embargo would not apply to shipments that, as of May 26, 1994, were in a bonded warehouse or foreign trade zone, in port, or in transit to the United States. B-West Imports (the appellants), together with nine other importers, challenged the government's actions in the Court of International Trade. They argued that the AECA does not authorize the president or his delegates to impose an arms embargo and that the revocation of the permits violated the Due Process and Takings Clauses of the Fifth Amendment to the Constitution.

BRYSON, CIRCUIT JUDGE
In this court, the appellants renew their argument that the AECA does not authorize an arms embargo. Although the Act, 22 U.S.C. § 2778, grants the president the authority to "control" arms imports, the appellants argue that the term "control" limits the president to creating and operating a licensing system for arms importation, and does not allow the president to ban the importation of arms for which import permits have been granted.

The appellant's statutory argument is unconvincing. They concede that the term "control" is broad enough to allow the president to ban imports by denying licenses or permits for future imports. Their contention is thus limited to the assertion that "control" does not include the right to revoke licenses and permits after they are granted. . . . As the court noted in *South Puerto Rico Sugar Co. v. U.S.,* 167 Ct.Cl. 236, 334 F.2d 622 (1964), presidents acting under broad statutory grants of authority have imposed and lifted embargoes, prohibited and allowed exports, suspended and resumed commercial intercourse with foreign countries. Thus, the broad statutory delegation in the AECA incorporates the historical authority of the president in the fields of foreign commerce and of importation into the country. We therefore agree with the Court of International Trade that the AECA authorizes the president not only to regulate arms importation through a licensing system, but also to prohibit particular importations altogether when the circumstances warrant. . . .

Finally, the appellants challenge the government's actions as violative of the Takings and Due Process Clauses of the Fifth Amendment. In the *Legal Tender Cases,* 79 U.S. (12 Wall.) 457 (1870), the Supreme Court rejected just such an argument, noting that an embargo would not give rise to a compensable taking or a valid due process claim:

A new tariff, an embargo, a draft, or a war inevitably bring upon individuals great losses; may, indeed, render valuable property almost valueless. They may destroy the worth of contracts. But whoever supposed that, because of this, a tariff could not be changed, or a non-intercourse act, or an embargo be enacted, or a war be declared. . . . [W]as it ever imagined this was taking private property without compensation or without due process of law? Id. 79 U.S. (12 Wall.) at 551.

*(continued)*

*(continued)*

While it is true that takings law has changed significantly since 1870, the principles that the Supreme Court articulated in the *Legal Tender Cases* have remained valid, particularly as they apply to governmental actions in the sphere of foreign relations. . . .

The same principle is directly applicable here. While an individual who obtains a permit to import arms may make commitments in the arms market on the assumption that the permit will not be revoked before the importation is completed, that assumption does not constitute a "reasonable investment backed expectation" of the type necessary to support a takings claim. That is particularly true with respect to importations of arms from a country with which the United States has an arms embargo that is subject to an exemption that could be terminated at any time.

The appellants' due process claim fares no better. They assert that the implementation of the Chinese arms embargo deprived them of property without due process of law by denying them the opportunity to sell in the United States the munitions for which they had obtained permits prior to the announcement of the embargo. As we have discussed, however, the appellants' right to import and sell Chinese arms in the United States was subject at all times to the hazard that their permits would be revoked, pursuant to statute and regulation, on foreign policy grounds or for other reasons. The Due Process Clause does not require the government to stand as a surety against the adverse consequences sometimes suffered by persons who knowingly undertake that kind of commercial risk.

**Decision.** Judgment affirmed for the United States. Under the Arms Export Control Act, the president has wide latitude to enforce this law by prohibiting the import of controlled items. A statute that deprives one of the opportunity to import goods does not violate or "take" one's property under the Fifth Amendment without compensation, nor does it deprive the importer of due process of law.

---

For another very real example of how a U.S. firm can be affected by foreign policy, give some thought to the "managerial implications" problem at the end of this chapter. This problem involves America's relations with the poorest country in the Western Hemisphere, the island nation of Haiti, and the impact of U.S. policies on companies doing business there. Consider both the effectiveness of the trade sanction in achieving foreign policy and the firm's reaction to the ensuing crisis.

> **http://www.hg.org/hg.html**
> *The home page for Hieros Gamos, with links and information on foreign governments, including 50 "Doing Business" guides.*

## The Separation of Powers

At the time the Constitution was drafted, people were greatly concerned with how foreign commerce would be regulated. During this period of U.S. history, each state was interested primarily in its own economic well-being. States imposed regulations on commerce designed to protect their own local industries, their ports, and their agricultural interests. To ensure that states would not erect barriers to commerce among them, and to guarantee a source of revenue to the federal government in the form of import duties, the drafters of the Constitution placed the power to regulate international commerce in the hands of the federal government. The drafters believed, for example, that economic disintegration could result if states were free to tax exports, or if states located along the seacoast could tax imports passing through to states located inland. Moreover, the concern was that the United States be able to deal with foreign nations from a position of political strength and unity. The framers of the Constitution understood that trade relationships with foreign nations could not be handled successfully by each state on its own, but only by a strong federal government that could speak for the economic and political interests of the nation as a whole.

## The Executive–Legislative Debate

Today the fact that the power over both foreign affairs and foreign trade rests with the federal government arouses little controversy. Considerable debate arises, however, over how the Constitution divides that power between Congress and the president. Indeed, in recent years, both branches of government have sought greater control over international affairs.

One argument in favor of a strong executive branch is that the nation must "speak with one voice" in international affairs. If each senator or representative, perhaps motivated by the local interests of his or her own constituents, attempted to negotiate agreements with foreign nations on matters such as tariff reductions, trade in agriculture, or, say, trade in computer chips, provisions for military assistance, or even nuclear disarmament, the process would be encumbered by local interests and would be ineffective and potentially disastrous.

On the other hand, in recent years, Congress has exercised greater oversight and control over the president's conduct of foreign affairs. For a number of historical reasons, Congress has come to view the executive branch with an element of suspicion and mistrust. During the 1960s and 1970s, Congress passed several statutes attempting to limit the president's powers over foreign affairs. These laws were enacted partially as a result of the president's unpopular use of U.S. troops in the Vietnam War, and partially as a result of the illegal and unethical conduct of the president and his closest advisers during the Watergate scandal. More recently, Congress has kept strict watch over the president's actions in the Middle East and Central America to ensure that the president complies with all provisions of U.S. law in the handling of U.S. foreign policy.

The executive and legislative branches of government and their roles in setting and carrying out foreign economic and trade policies of the United States should be examined briefly now.

## The Congress

Article I of the Constitution confers "all legislative powers" upon Congress, including the power "to regulate commerce with foreign nations, and among the several states" (Section 8, clause 3). In addition, Congress has broad power to pass domestic laws, declare war, appropriate monies, lay and collect taxes, and give advice and consent to the president in making treaties with foreign nations. Considering these powers as a whole, the U.S. Supreme Court has consistently held that Congress has wide-ranging constitutional power to establish overall economic policy for the United States and to put it into effect through legislation. Congress has recognized, however, that the day-to-day conduct of trade relations with foreign nations is often best conducted through a strong executive branch. As a result, Congress has delegated the authority to the president to carry out trade policies set by statute.

## The President

Article II of the Constitution confers executive power on the president. The executive power is not clearly specified, and many court decisions interpret what the Constitution meant to confer. However, the courts and writers have said that the president has greater and wider-reaching power over foreign affairs than over domestic matters at home. One of the most famous statements about the power of the president is found in *United States v. Curtiss-Wright Export Co.,* 299 U.S. 304, 57 S.Ct. 216 (1936).

Not only, as we have shown, is the federal power over external affairs in origin and essential character different from that over internal affairs, but participation in the exercise of the power is significantly limited. In this vast external realm, with its important, complicated, delicate and manifold problems, the President alone has the power to speak or listen as a representative of the nation. He makes treaties with the advice and consent of the Senate; but he alone negotiates. Into the field of negotiation the Senate cannot intrude; and Congress itself is powerless to invade it. As Marshall said in his great argument of March 7, 1800, in the House of Representatives, "The President is the sole organ of the nation in its external relations, and its sole representative with foreign nations." . . .

It is quite apparent that if, in the maintenance of our international relations, embarrassment—perhaps serious embarrassment—is to be avoided and success for our aims achieved, congressional legislation which is to be made effective through negotiation and inquiry within the international field must often accord to the President a degree of discretion and freedom from statutory restriction which would not be admissible were domestic affairs alone involved. Moreover, he, not Congress, has the better opportunity of knowing the conditions which prevail in foreign countries, and especially is this true in time of war. He has his confidential sources of information. He has his agents in the form of diplomatic, consular and other officials. Secrecy in respect of information gathered by them may be highly necessary, and the premature disclosure of it productive of harmful results.

The president's powers over foreign affairs are derived from (1) the treaty power; (2) inherent executive power, including the power to appoint ambassadors and to act as commander-in-chief of the armed forces; and (3) powers delegated by Congress. Each of these is addressed here in turn, to provide a better understanding of the interplay between the president and Congress in setting trade policies and carrying out trade relations with foreign countries.

## The Treaty Power

Sovereign governments have been entering into military and trade alliances with one another for thousands of years. As modern nations see the growing need to come to terms with one another on important global issues, these agreements take on an even greater significance. The interdependence of all peoples of the world is expanding. Scientific and technological advances are proceeding more rapidly than ever before. Air and water pollution know no national boundaries. Toxic waste from one nation is dumped in another. Endangered wildlife slaughtered in one country is sold in another. Illegal drug trafficking, terrorism, and other forms of criminal behavior have taken on multinational dimensions. Products designed and produced in one country cause injuries to consumers in others. All of these problems have one thing in common: Resolving each of them requires the cooperation, understanding, and joint efforts of all nations of the world. In a global economy, in which the economic and financial well being of all nations is interrelated, economic cooperation thus becomes absolutely necessary.

The primary instrument for implementing foreign political and economic affairs is the *inter-*

*national agreement.* International agreements include (1) treaties and (2) executive agreements. International agreements are either *bilateral* (between two nations) or *multilateral* (among many nations).

A *treaty* is an agreement, contract, or *compact* between two or more nations, which is recognized and given effect under international or domestic law. Treaties can cover almost any subject of mutual concern to nations—from ending war and conflict to the elimination of nuclear weapons testing to enhancing the free movement of trade and investment across national borders. In the United States, the treaty power is found in Article II of the Constitution. Treaties are negotiated by the president with the "advice and consent" of the Senate, requiring passage by a two-thirds senatorial vote. A *convention* is a treaty on matters of common concern, usually negotiated on a regional or global basis and open to adoption by many nations. Many conventions discussed in this book, such as the Convention on Contracts for the International Sale of Goods or the Warsaw Convention, function to make otherwise diverse national laws uniform. A *protocol* is a common term for a draft treaty prior to ratification or an agreement used to supplement or amend an existing treaty. *Executive agreements,* made by the president without the formal treaty process in the Senate, are discussed in the next section.

## Treaty Powers and the Constitution

The *treaty power* of the United States is derived from the Constitution. Under the Constitution, a treaty is considered the "Law of the Land." It is binding on both the federal and state governments with the same force as an act of Congress. Treaties are said to be either *self-executing* or *non-self-executing* (also known as *executory* treaties). The United States is party to both types. In the United States and other countries with written constitutions, a self-executing treaty has a "domestic law effect." Thus, once the treaty has been ratified, no further presidential or legislative action is required for it to become binding law. Self-executing treaties therefore provide to individuals specific rights, which the courts will enforce.

An executory or non-self-executing treaty requires an act of Congress or of the president to give it legal effect. In many other nations, including Great Britain, all treaties must be put into force through legislation. Whether a treaty is self-executing or not depends on how a U.S. court interprets the language of the treaty and the history surrounding its negotiation and approval.

One self-executing treaty well known to all travelers is the *Warsaw Convention*. This international agreement determines the rights and remedies available to those who are injured or whose property is damaged during travel on commercial aircraft. Similarly, the Convention determines the liability and limitations on liability of the airline. On the other hand, treaties that merely express a nation's desire to cooperate with other nations in achieving broad social, economic, cultural, humanitarian, or political objectives may not be self-executing. The Charter of the United Nations, for example, is a non-self-executing international "pledge" to abide by common values for the betterment of humankind, and is generally considered by U.S. courts *not* to grant enforceable rights to private parties.

## Treaties of Friendship, Commerce, and Navigation

Treaties of Friendship, Commerce, and Navigation (FCN treaties) are self-executing bilateral agreements that provide a broad range of protection to foreign nationals doing business in a host country. Although each treaty is different, they all typically state that each country will allow the establishment of foreign branches or subsidiary corporations; the free flow of capital and technology; the equitable and nondiscriminatory treatment of foreign firms, individuals, and products; the right of travel and residence; the payment of just compensation for property taken by the state; the privilege of acquiring and owning real estate; and most-favored-nation trading status for goods.

The self-executing nature of FCN treaties is illustrated in *MacNamara v. Korean Air Lines*. This case involved a conflict between a federal statute that protects workers against discrimination in employment and the FCN treaty between the United States and Korea that allows foreign firms to give preference in hiring their own foreign nationals for executive, managerial, and technical positions.

---

### MacNamara v. Korean Air Lines
**863 F.2d 1135 (1988)**
**United States Court of Appeals (3rd Cir.)**

BACKGROUND AND FACTS
MacNamara brought this action against his former employer, Korean Air Lines (KAL), for discrimination under Title VIII of the Civil Rights Act of 1964 and the U.S. Age Discrimination in Employment Act. KAL is a Korean company. MacNamara, an American citizen, was a district sales manager in Philadelphia who had worked for the defendant airline since 1974. In 1982, at age 57, he was dismissed from employment. KAL claimed that his dismissal was part of KAL's reorganization plan, which included merging the Philadelphia and Atlanta offices into one office located in Washington, D.C. KAL had also dismissed six American managers and replaced them with four Korean citizens. The Korean citizen who replaced MacNamara was 42 years old. After exhausting his administrative remedies, MacNamara filed suit claiming that KAL had discriminated against him on the basis of race, national origin, and age. KAL moved to dismiss on the ground that its conduct was protected by the Treaty of Friendship, Commerce, and Navigation between the United States and Korea. The motion to dismiss was granted and the plaintiff appealed.

CIRCUIT JUDGE STAPLETON
The Korean FCN treaty is one of a series of friendship, commerce and navigation treaties the United States signed with various countries after World War II. Although initially negotiated primarily
*(continued)*

*(continued)*

for the purpose of encouraging American investment abroad, the treaties secured reciprocal rights and thus granted protection to foreign businesses operating in the United States. The specific provision of the Korean FCN treaty relied upon by KAL in this case provides as follows:

> Nationals and companies of either party shall be permitted to engage, within the territories of the other party, accountants and other technical experts, executive personnel, attorneys, agents, and other specialists of their choice.

We agree with the Courts of Appeals for the Fifth and Sixth Circuits that Article VIII(1) goes beyond securing the right to be treated the same as domestic companies and that its purpose, in part, is to assure foreign corporations that they may have their business in the host country managed by their own nationals if they so desire. We also agree with the conclusion of the Sixth Circuit Court of Appeals that Article VIII(1) was not intended to provide foreign businesses with shelter from any law applicable to personnel decisions other than those that would logically or pragmatically conflict with the right to select one's own nationals as managers because of their citizenship. Insofar as Title VII and the ADEA proscribe intentional discrimination on the basis of race, national origin, and age, we perceive no theoretical or practical conflict between them and the right conferred by Article VIII(1). Thus, for example, we believe that a foreign business may not deliberately undertake to reduce the age of its workforce by replacing older Americans with younger foreign nationals. On the other hand, to the extent Title VII and the ADEA proscribe personnel decisions based on citizenship solely because of their disparate impact on older managers, a particular racial group, or persons whose ancestors are not from the foreign country involved, we perceive a potential conflict and conclude that it must be resolved in favor of Article VIII(1).

Having concluded that KAL cannot purposefully discriminate on the basis of age, race, or national origin, we now turn to the most difficult aspect of this case. To this point we have confined our analysis to liability for intentional discrimination. The reach of Title VII and the ADEA, however, extends beyond intentionally discriminatory employment policies to those practices fair in form, but discriminatory in operation. *Griggs v. Duke*

*Power Co.,* 401 U.S. 424, 91 S.Ct. 849, 28 L.Ed.2d 158 (1971). Accordingly, Title VII and ADEA liability can be found where facially neutral employment practices have a discriminatory effect of "disparate impact" on protected groups, without proof that the employer adopted these practices with a discriminatory motive.

The fact that empirical evidence can satisfy the substantive standard of liability would pose a substantial problem in disparate impact litigation for corporations hailing from countries, including perhaps Korea, whose populations are largely homogeneous. Because a company's requirement that its employees be citizens of the homogeneous country from which it hails means that almost all of its employees will be of the same national origin and race, the statistical disparity between otherwise qualified noncitizens of a particular race and national origin, and citizens of the foreign country's race and national origin is likely to be substantial. As a result, a foreign business from a country with a homogeneous population, by merely exercising its protected treaty right to prefer its own citizens for management positions, could be held in violation of Title VII. Thus, unlike a disparate treatment case where liability cannot be imposed without an affirmative finding that the employer was not simply exercising its Article VIII(1) right, a disparate impact case can result in liability where the employer did nothing more than exercise that right. For this reason we conclude that disparate impact liability under Title VII and the ADEA for a foreign employer based on its practice of engaging its own nationals as managers cannot be reconciled with Article VIII(1). Accordingly, we hold that such liability may not be imposed.

**Decision.** The Court of Appeals reversed and remanded for a trial on the question of whether KAL's discriminatory treatment was intentional. The court ruled that the FCN treaty that authorized foreign employers to engage executives and technical specialists "of their choice" permits discrimination on the basis of citizenship. Although the treaty does not grant foreign employers a blanket exception to the civil rights laws, and employers are liable for *intentional* discrimination (disparate treatment) on the basis of race, national origin, or age, the treaty *does permit* foreign employers to retain their own nationals in executive and techni-

*(continued)*

*(continued)*

cal positions even where the *effect* of such personnel decisions is discriminatory and would otherwise subject the employer to disparate impact liability under the law.

**Comment.** In a U.S. Supreme Court decision, relied upon by the *MacNamara* court, *Sumitomo v. Avagliano,* 457 U.S. 176, 102 S.Ct. 2374 (1982), it was held that the FCN treaty between the United States and Japan did not provide immunity to a Japanese trading company for liability under Title VII of the Civil Rights Act of 1964. In *Sumitomo* the Court ruled that since the employer was a wholly owned U.S. subsidiary of a Japanese company, incorporated under the laws of the United States, it was not a Japanese company but a U.S. one. Thus, it was not entitled to protection under the treaty.

Other self-executing treaties (in the United States) discussed elsewhere in this text include the *Hague Convention,* the *Convention on Contracts for the International Sale of Goods,* and the *U.N. Convention on Recognition and Enforcement of Foreign Arbitral Awards.* Tax treaties are also considered self-executing in that the provisions of these treaties, like those of the others mentioned, need no further legislation to make them a binding source of law in U.S. courts.

## The Equal Dignity Rule

Self-executing treaties have the same legal effect statutes passed by both houses of Congress. How, then, do we resolve conflicts between treaties or statutes, the terms of which are inconsistent with one another? In these cases, the rule is that the *last in time prevails.* A treaty will override an inconsistent prior act of Congress. Similarly, an act of Congress can override an inconsistent prior treaty, provided that Congress had expressed its intention to do so. The rule is easy to understand and based on the idea that statutes and treaties are of equal legal importance or of *equal dignity.*

## Executive Agreements

*Executive agreements* are international agreements between the president and a foreign country, entered into without resort to the treaty process. They are binding obligations of the United States government and have the effect of law in the United States. Executive agreements are not provided for in the Constitution, as are treaties. Yet throughout U.S. history, presidents have utilized executive agreements to conduct foreign affairs. For many practical and political reasons, presidents often favor the executive agreement over the treaty. Since World War II, most international agreements of the United States have not been treaties; they have been executive agreements.

Of the two types of executive agreements, a *sole executive agreement* is one that the president can negotiate and put into legal effect without congressional approval. The *congressional-executive agreement* is based on authority granted by Congress to the president in a joint resolution or statute, or by treaty.

## Sole Executive Agreements and the President's Inherent Power

The president's authority to enter a sole executive agreement is based on powers inherent in the executive office. *Inherent powers* are either stated expressly in the Constitution or found to be there by judicial interpretation. The president may only rely on this inherent power when Congress has not passed a law directing otherwise. If Congress has passed a statute on a subject, the president's inherent power does not grant "license" to violate that law. Sole executive agreements are usually reserved for agreements with foreign countries that do not affect the broad interests of the nation as a whole. Most sole executive agreements, such as the one in *Dole v. Carter,* are between two countries on specific matters.

### Dole v. Carter
*444 F.Supp. 1065 (1977)*
*United States District*
*Court (D.Kansas)*

### BACKGROUND AND FACTS

This action was brought by a U.S. senator against the president to enjoin him from returning the Hungarian coronation regalia to the People's Republic of Hungary. The Holy Crown of St. Stephen had been held by the Hungarian people as a treasured symbol of their statehood and nationality for nearly 1,000 years. At the close of World War II, it was entrusted to the United States for safekeeping by Hungarian soldiers. In 1977, the governments of the United States and Hungary entered into an agreement returning the crown to Hungary. Many Hungarians living in the United States were opposed to the return of the crown. The plaintiff filed this action seeking an injunction against delivery of the crown to Hungary on the ground that such action was tantamount to a treaty undertaken by the president without the prior advice and consent of the Senate.

### DISTRICT JUDGE O'CONNOR

We turn now to the plaintiff's argument that the agreement to return the coronation regalia to Hungary in and of itself constitutes a treaty which must be ratified by the Senate. It is well established, and even plaintiff admits, that the United States frequently enters into international agreements other than treaties. Indeed, as of January 1, 1972, the United States was a party to 5,306 international agreements, only 947 of which were treaties and 4,359 of which were international agreements other than treaties. These "other agreements" appear to fall into three categories: (1) so-called congressional-executive agreements, executed by the president upon specific authorizing legislation from the Congress; (2) executive agreements pursuant to treaty, executed by the president in accord with specific instructions found in a prior, formal treaty; and (3) executive agreements executed pursuant to the president's own constitutional authority (hereinafter referred to as "executive agreements"). Defendant contends that his agreement to return the coronation regalia to Hungary falls into the latter category, and the court agrees.

Since the *Curtiss-Wright* decision, the Supreme Court has twice upheld the validity of an executive agreement made by President Franklin Roosevelt with the Soviet Union. In the Litvinov Agreement, the president recognized and established diplomatic relations with that nation. In addition, for the purpose of bringing about a final settlement of claims and counterclaims between the Soviet Union and the United States, it was agreed that the Soviet Union would take no steps to enforce claims against American nationals, but all such claims were assigned to the United States with the understanding that the Soviet Union would be notified of all amounts realized by the United States. In speaking for the Court in *United States v. Belmont,* 301 U.S. 324, 57 S.Ct. 758, 81 L.Ed. 1134 (1937), Justice Sutherland, who also authored the majority opinion in *Curtiss-Wright* . . . stated:

> (A)n international compact, as this was, is not always a treaty which requires the participation of the Senate. There are many such compacts, of which a protocol, a *modus vivendi,* a postal convention, and agreements like that now under consideration are illustrations.

The United States enters into approximately 200 executive agreements each year, and it has been observed that the constitutional system "could not last a month" if the president sought Senate or congressional consent for every one of them. *L. Henkin, Foreign Affairs and the Constitution* . . . Congress itself recognized this fact in passing P.L. 92-403, 1 U.S.C. s 112b, requiring the secretary of state to transmit for merely informational purposes the text of all international agreements other than treaties to which the United States becomes a party. The House Committee on Foreign Affairs stated in recommending passage of that statute that while it wished to be apprised of "all agreements of any significance," "[c]learly the Congress does not want to be inundated with trivia." 1972 *U.S. Code Cong. and Admin. News,* p. 3069. While the president's understanding to return the Hungarian coronation regalia is hardly a "trivial" matter to either the United States or the people of Hungary, the court is yet convinced that the president's agreement in this regard lacks the magnitude of agreements customarily concluded in treaty form. The president's agreement here involves no substantial ongoing commitment on the

*(continued)*

*(continued)*

part of the United States, exposes the United States to no appreciable discernible risks, and contemplates American action of an extremely limited duration in time. The plaintiff presented no evidence that agreements of the kind in question here are traditionally concluded only by treaty, either as a matter of American custom or as a matter of international law. Indeed, while the court has not exhaustively examined all possibly pertinent treaties, the court can hardly imagine that any such examination would lend support to the plaintiff's position. Finally, the agreement here encompasses no substantial reciprocal commitments by the Hungarian government. As a matter of law, the court is therefore persuaded that the president's agreement to return the Hungarian coronation regalia is not a commitment requiring the advice and consent of the Senate under Article II, Section 2, of the Constitution.

**Decision.** The plaintiff's motion for a preliminary injunction is denied. The agreement to return the coronation regalia was not a treaty requiring ratification by the Senate, but a valid executive agreement based on the president's inherent power.

## Congressional-Executive Agreements

In performing its duties, Congress has broad legislative power to establish policy for the nation. It passes laws and enters treaties to implement that policy. Then Congress delegates to the president and the executive branch the responsibility to carry out or enforce those laws, which is known as the president's *delegated power.* If the president enters into an executive agreement pursuant to this delegated authority, the agreement is valid and has the effect of binding law. This action is known as a *congressional-executive agreement.*

Congressional-executive agreements serve much the same purpose as treaties. Their legal nature, however, is different. Unlike treaties, congressional-executive agreements are not described in the Constitution. Their use grew out of the constitutional history of the United States during the present century. For the most part, they were born of the Roosevelt era of the 1930s and 1940s, when the president was seeking new and more flexible ways of dealing with the nation's economic problems during the Great Depression and World War II. By the close of World War II, the House and Senate had informally agreed with the president to provide a substitute process for approving international agreements— one that would not require a two-thirds vote of approval of the Senate, as do treaties. Instead, they agreed on a substitute process permitting international agreements to be approved either by statute or by joint resolution of both houses of Congress. Statutes and joint resolution can pass on a *simple majority vote* of both houses. Presidents usually prefer the congressional-executive agreement process to the treaty process because it is often easier for them to obtain congressional approval by majority vote of both houses than by a two-thirds vote of one house. (Thus the legislature and president become partners in forming international agreements—a real "balance of power.") Today, congressional-executive agreements, based on the majority vote of both houses of Congress, are recognized as having the same binding legal effect as treaties.

## Trade Agreements

Like treaties, executive agreements cover a wide range of subjects. For instance, bilateral agreements might attempt to open investment opportunities in one nation for citizens of the other. *Trade agreements,* discussed here, are executive agreements among countries on matters involving international trade and related issues. They are used to implement the trade policies of a nation. If, for instance, a nation takes a liberal, open-market view of trade, then it might seek to enter agreements with foreign nations to further that goal (e.g., reducing tariffs and nontariff barriers to trade). If it seeks to protect key domestic industries from foreign competition, it can try to negotiate trade agreements for that purpose (e.g., imposing quotas or increased tariffs). Trade agreements can be either bilateral or multilateral. The United States' first trade agreement was with France, in 1778. Today, the United States participates in many trade agreements, affecting virtually every major industry and sector of the American economy. For instance, the United States is a party to nearly 50 bilateral trade agreements affecting trade in textiles alone. Other industries regulated by trade agreements include semiconductors, steel, and automobiles. Companies that import and export these products are directly affected by the trade and tariff regulations outlined in these agreements. The most important trade agreements are of the congressional-executive type. Some of the most important trade agreements of the United States since World War II include:

- General Agreement on Tariffs and Trade, 1947 (and subsequent GATT agreements)
- U.S.–Israel Free Trade Agreement
- U.S.–Canada Free Trade Agreement
- North American Free Trade Agreement
- General Agreement on Tariffs and Trade, 1994 (GATT Uruguay Round Agreement), including the Agreement Establishing the World Trade Organization

Some of the most important U.S. trade and tariff statutes follow. Most of them provide authority to the president to negotiate and conclude congressional-executive trade agreements.

- Smoot-Hawley Tariff Act of 1930
- Reciprocal Trade Agreements Act of 1934
- Trade Expansion Act of 1962
- Trade Reform Act of 1974
- Trade Agreements Act of 1979
- Trade and Tariff Act of 1984

- Omnibus Trade and Competitiveness Act of 1988
- The Uruguay Round Agreements Act of 1995

## The Smoot-Hawley Tariff Act of 1930

The United States has had trade and tariff laws since its founding. In the 1800s, these laws gave virtually no authority to the president other than to collect taxes; Congress established tariff rates. Shortly after World War I, as a result of isolationist sentiments at home, the United States began to increase tariffs on imported goods. In 1930, the U.S. Congress imposed the highest tariff levels in the nation's history when it enacted the *Smoot-Hawley Tariff Act*. The bill was signed by President Herbert Hoover. Under Smoot-Hawley, tariffs on more than 1,000 items were increased to levels so high that other nations raised their tariffs in retaliation. Some tariff rates reached nearly 100 percent of the cost of the goods. Economic activity declined precipitously. It is generally accepted today that these high tariffs worldwide contributed to the Great Depression of the 1930s. The newly elected president, Franklin Roosevelt, recognized the immediate need to reduce tariffs and "liberalize" trade. At that time, however, the president simply did not have the legal authority to take any significant action without congressional approval, and the treaty process was too cumbersome. Roosevelt thus worked with Congress to pass the *Reciprocal Trade Agreements Act of 1934,* which provided the president with the authority needed to lower tariffs.

*Foreign Accents*

# Shades of Smoot-Hawley
## The Politics of Protectionism: A Look Back at History

As the bill moved through Congress, formal protests from foreign countries flooded into Washington, eventually adding up to 200 pages. Both houses voted aye nonetheless. While the legislation sat on the president's desk, 1,028 American economists called for a veto. Herbert Hoover made it the law of the land anyway, swallowing his own reservations and, on June 17, signing the Tariff Act of 1930.

Known as Smoot-Hawley after its legislative

*(continued)*

*(continued)*

sponsors, the bill promptly fulfilled the worst fears of critics. A new panic seized the already battered stock market; the slide continued for two years. In raising import duties on scores of items, in some cases to 50 percent, the measure provoked angry retaliation by twenty-five of the nation's trading partners. U.S. exports fell by nearly two-thirds in just two years.

How did Hoover, a president well versed in international commerce, fall into such a trap? In part, he was bound by the 1928 Republican platform, which promised tariffs to help the ailing farm economy. A crisis atmosphere took hold a year later with the stock market crash and the onset of the Great Depression. For decades the Republicans had been sympathetic to protectionism; now they saw trade barriers as a means of placating demands that the government do something concrete to fight unemployment.

Willis Hawley of Oregon chaired the House Ways and Means Committee, and Reed Smoot of Utah headed the Senate Finance Committee. Both were fiscal experts with more than twenty years of service on Capitol Hill. But, responding to pressure from organized labor and some sectors of industry, they transformed what was to be an agricultural measure into a comprehensive increase in tariffs.

Hoover was hemmed in by tradition and the G.O.P. platform. Henry Ford spent an evening at the White House pleading for a veto of what he called "an economic stupidity." Other automobile executives backed Ford. But no president had ever vetoed a tariff measure, and Hoover was not about to be the first.

"With returning normal conditions, our foreign trade will continue to expand," he said hopefully.

In 1932, with international trade in collapse, Franklin Roosevelt denounced Smoot-Hawley as ruinous. Hoover responded that Roosevelt would have Americans compete with "peasant and sweated labor" abroad. Then, as now, protectionism had a strong if superficial political appeal: by election eve, F.D.R. had backed down, assuring voters that he understood the need for tariffs. Protectionist politicking, however, could not save the Republicans in 1932. Smoot and Hawley joined Hoover in defeat. The Democrats dismantled the G.O.P.'s legislative handiwork with caution, using reciprocal trade agreements rather than across-the-board tariff reductions. The Smoot-Hawley approach was discredited. Sam Rayburn, House Democratic Speaker from 1940 until 1961, insisted that any party member who wanted to serve on the Ways and Means Committee had to support reciprocity, not protectionism.

Though some legislators today might be reluctant to make such a promise, no one in Congress is seriously proposing anything as drastic as Smoot-Hawley. Still, the pro-tariff mania that swept Washington fifty-five years ago remains a danger. "What we are afraid of," says S. Bruce Smart, undersecretary of commerce of international trade, "is that people are so emotional that they will do something that they know is foolish, just to do something."

## The Reciprocal Trade Agreements Act of 1934

Prior to 1934, the president had little or no discretion in setting tariff rates. The reciprocal Trade Agreements Act provided the president with a mechanism not only for lowering U.S. tariffs, but also for encouraging other countries to lower their rates as well. This act granted the president far more flexible powers to adjust tariffs than under any prior legislation. The president was granted the authority to negotiate tariff reductions on a product-by-product basis with other countries on the basis of *reciprocity.* The United States would reduce a tariff on a foreign product if the foreign country would reciprocate by lowering its tariffs. An agreement to reduce a tariff to a specified level is known as a *tariff concession.* If the United States was to lower an existing tariff on an imported product from, say, France, then France would have to make similar concessions on the same or other products coming from the United States.

The 1934 law also introduced what is known as *unconditional most-favored-nation* (MFN) *trade.* It provided that a lower tariff rate negotiated with one nation would automatically be granted to like products imported from all other nations that had signed an MFN agreement with the United States, without any concession being requested from those nations in return. Moreover, if two other nations reached agreement to lower tariffs on a given product, then that new rate would apply to U.S. products imported into those nations as well. This system served to quicken and expand the process of lowering duties worldwide.

In the following case, *Star-Kist Foods, Inc. v. United States,* the constitutionality of the tariff-setting process of the Reciprocal Trade Agreements Act was upheld against a charge that it was an unconstitutional delegation of power by Congress to the president.

## More Recent U.S. Trade Legislation

The *Reciprocal Trade Agreements Act of 1934* provided the basic system for trade negotiations

---

### Star-Kist Foods, Inc. v. United States
275 F.2d 472 (1959)
United States Court of Customs and Patent Appeals

**BACKGROUND AND FACTS**
Star-Kist Foods, a U.S. producer of canned tuna, instituted a lawsuit to protest the assessment of duties made by the collector of customs on imported canned tuna fish. The canned tuna was assessed at the rate of 12.5 percent pursuant to a trade agreement with Iceland. Prior to the agreement, the tariff rate had been set by Congress in the Tariff Act of 1930 at 25 percent *ad valorem.* The trade agreement with Iceland, which resulted in lowering the rate of duty, was executed pursuant to the Reciprocal Trade Agreement Act of 1934. That act authorized the president to enter into foreign trade agreements for the purpose of expanding foreign markets for the products of the United States by affording corresponding market opportunities for foreign products in the United States. To implement an agreement, the president was then authorized to raise or lower any duty previously set by Congress, but not by more than 50 percent. Star-Kist brought this action contending that the delegation of authority under the 1934 act and the agreement with Iceland were unconstitutional.

**JUDGE MARTIN**
A constitutional delegation of powers requires that Congress enunciate a policy or objective or give reasons for seeking the aid of the president. In addition the act must specify when the powers conferred may be utilized by establishing a standard or "intelligible principle" which is sufficient to make it clear when action is proper. And because Congress cannot abdicate its legislative function and confer carte blanche authority on the president, it must circumscribe that power in some manner. This means that Congress must tell the president what he can do by prescribing a standard which confines his discretion and which will guarantee that any authorized action he takes will tend to promote rather than flout the legislative purpose. It is not necessary that the guides be precise or mathematical formulae to be satisfactory in a constitutional sense.

In the act before us the congressional policy is pronounced very clearly. The stated objectives are to expand foreign markets for the products of the United States "by regulating the admission of foreign goods into the United States in accordance with the characteristics and needs of various branches of American production so that foreign markets will be made available to those branches of American production which require and are capable of developing such outlets by affording corresponding market opportunities for foreign products in the United States. . . . "

Pursuant to the 1934 act the presidential power can be invoked "whenever he [the president] finds as a fact that any existing duties or other import restrictions of the United States or any foreign country are unduly burdening or restricting the foreign trade of the United States and that the [purpose of the act] will be promoted." . . .

Under the provisions of the 1934 act the president by proclamation can modify existing duties and other import restrictions but not by more than 50 percent of the specified duties nor can he place articles upon or take them off the free list. Furthermore, he must accomplish the purposes of the act through the medium of foreign trade agreements with other countries. However, he can suspend the operation of such agreements if he discovers discriminatory treatment of American commerce,

*(continued)*

*(continued)*

and he can terminate, in whole or in part, any proclamation at any time. . . .

In view of the Supreme Court's recognition of the necessity of flexibility in the laws affecting foreign relations . . . we are of the opinion that the 1934 act does not grant an unconstitutional delegation of authority to the president.

Affirmed.

**Decision.** The court held in favor of the United States. The congressional delegation of authority under the 1934 statute was constitutional because Congress had provided the president with a sufficiently discernible standard to guide any decisions in carrying out the purposes of the act.

---

until 1962. In that year Congress passed the *Trade Expansion Act of 1962* that authorized the president to negotiate *across-the-board* tariff reductions instead of using the tedious product-by-product system set up in 1934. This law also created the *Office of Special Trade Representative* (today the *U.S. Trade Representative*), empowered to conduct all trade negotiations on behalf of the United States. The *Trade Reform Act of 1974* replaced most provisions of the 1962 law, and delegated even more authority to the president. The president was given wide latitude in reducing or eliminating duties (with authority to reduce duties by up to 60 percent and simply end any import duties of less than 5 percent), and in negotiating a reduction of nontariff barriers during the *Tokyo Round*. The *Trade Agreements Act of 1979* continued congressional support for expanding free trade by approving the president's trade agreements to reduce nontariff barriers. The *Trade and Tariff Act of 1984* authorized the president to negotiate agreements related to high-technology products, trade in services, and barriers to foreign investment. It also authorized the free trade area between the United States and Israel. In 1988 President Reagan signed a bill into law ratifying the *U.S.–Canada Free Trade Agreement*, creating a duty-free trade area between the two countries. In 1988 Congress passed the *Omnibus Trade and Competitiveness Act* that extended the president's authority to negotiate trade agreements, including an expansion of the U.S.–Canadian free trade area to include Mexico in the *North American Free Trade Agreement* (NAFTA). It also gave even broader powers to the president to "pry open" foreign markets that have unfair barriers to the entry of U.S. goods and services (through both negotiations and sanctions). As can be seen, many of the basic principles and programs established in the 1930s and 1940s are, in a modern form, still in existence today. To this day, every U.S. president has returned to Congress to ask for needed authority to negotiate congressional-executive agreements on trade and investment issues with foreign nations.

### The General Agreement on Tariffs and Trade

The *General Agreement on Tariffs and Trade,* or GATT, became effective in 1947 for the purpose of promoting and expanding trade through multilateral trade negotiations among member nations. As the most important trade agreement of the twentieth century, it has provided a global framework for reducing tariffs and nontariff barriers to trade. Today, more than 100 nations are signatories of GATT. The most recent GATT, the *General Agreement on Tariffs and Trade 1994* (commonly called the *Uruguay Round Agreement*), led to the creation of the new *World Trade Organization* (WTO), the subject of the next chapter.

**GATT's Legal Status in the United States.**   The original General Agreement on Tariffs and Trade of 1947 was not a treaty, nor was it a typical congressional-executive agreement. Rather, it was an international agreement adopted only by a proclamation of the president. Despite no explicit congressional approval, GATT has been accepted as a binding agreement of the United States, and its legal status today is completely accepted (although legal scholars still debate GATT's constitutional basis under U.S. law).

**Presidential Authority for GATT Multilateral Trade Negotiations.**   GATT succeeded in liberalizing trade in this century because it provided a forum for bringing nations together in *multi-lateral trade negotiations*. GATT negotiations are called "rounds." The most notable GATT rounds were the *Dillon Rounds* (1950s), the *Kennedy Rounds* (1960s), the *Tokyo Rounds* (1970s), and the *Uruguay Rounds* (1980s and 1990s). Each set of rounds resulted in improvements in the world trading environment. The president has sought congressional approval for trade agreements negotiated under GATT, granted under the statutes listed in the preceding sections.

## Fast-Track Negotiating Authority

Congressional-executive trade agreements require congressional approval in order to be binding. If a foreign nation thought that an agreement with the president of the United States might later be rejected by Congress, it might be less willing to bargain. To assure legislative approval of an agreement, the Trade Reform Act of 1974 instituted a *fast-track* procedure. Under fast-track procedures, (1) the president must notify Congress of the intention to enter an agreement prior to it being concluded with the foreign nation; (2) Congress authorizes the president in advance to conduct bilateral or multilateral negotiations for the purpose of furthering stated policy objectives; (3) the agreement must be completed and submitted to Congress for approval within a specified period of time or by a certain date; and (4) Congress must vote within a specified time period (usually 60 or 90 days) to either accept or reject the agreement in its entirety, without amendment. The most important U.S. trade agreements of the past 20 years have been negotiated pursuant to fast track authority.

**Expanded Powers.**   Today the president is not just authorized to reduce duties on products, but to take a wide range of executive actions to deal with the complexities of the modern business world. This authority is in keeping with the modern notion that the president needs increased flexibility in handling matters related to international trade and foreign affairs. For example, under the Trade Act of 1974 and the Omnibus Act, the president has been given authority to negotiate special trade relations with developing coun-

tries; to negotiate rules for dealing with agricultural trade problems; to coordinate international monetary policies; to negotiate better mechanisms for protecting copyrights, patents, and trademarks in foreign countries; to negotiate a reduction of barriers to trade in high technology; and to ensure equal access to foreign high technology by U.S. firms.

In addition, the president has been given broader powers to deal with a range of complex economic problems. For example, the president may take certain authorized measures (tariffs, quotas, and the like) designed to protect U.S. industry from foreign competition under certain well-defined situations, such as when U.S. industry is being injured by increased imports of particular foreign products. The president is also authorized to invoke emergency regulations to deal with severe international economic problems, such as U.S. balance of payments shortages. These problems are discussed in later chapters.

> **http://www.ita.doc.gov**
> *See for country-by-country expertise from the U.S. Department of Commerce (DOC).*

## Presidential Acts in Contravention of Congress

In order for an executive agreement to be valid, either the president must have the inherent power to enter into it (e.g., the *Dole v. Carter* case) or the power must be delegated from Congress (e.g., the *Star-Kist Foods, Inc. v. United States* case). Even when Congress delegates the power to the president to deal with a trade problem, however, the president may still seek a separate solution. In the following case, *U.S. v. Guy W. Capps, Inc.*, Congress had addressed the problems of agricultural imports in the Agricultural Act of 1948, but the president tried to circumvent the statute and impose his own solution for reducing potato imports from Canada. His actions were invalidated by the court.

## The President's Emergency Powers

The president can also justify executive actions by invoking far-reaching *emergency powers*. Dating

BACKGROUND AND FACTS

During the 1940s, the U.S. government instituted a price support system for domestic potatoes. In order to protect the potato market from imported Canadian potatoes, the U.S. secretary of state entered into an executive agreement with the Canadian ambassador in which they agreed, in return for certain U.S. concessions, that Canada would permit the export of potatoes into the United States only if they were to be used for seed and not for food. The agreement was not submitted to or approved by Congress. Guy W. Capps, Inc., the importer, assured the Canadian exporter that the potatoes were destined for planting, but while they were in transit, they were sold to A&P grocery stores for resale. The United States brought suit against the defendant for damages. The court entered judgment for the defendant and the government appealed.

CHIEF JUDGE PARKER

The power to regulate foreign commerce is vested in Congress, not in the executive or the courts; and the executive may not exercise the power by entering into executive agreements and suing in the courts for damages resulting from breaches of contracts made on the basis of such agreements.

In the Agricultural Act of 1948, Congress had legislated specifically with respect to the limitations which might be imposed on imports if it was thought that they would render ineffective or materially interfere with any program or operation undertaken pursuant to that act. Section 3 of the act, provided

> (a) Whenever the president has reason to believe that any article or articles are being or are practically certain to be imported into the United States under such conditions and in such quantities as to render or tend to render ineffective, or materially interfere with, any program or operation undertaken under this title . . . he shall cause an immediate investiga-

### United States v. Guy W. Capps, Inc.
*204 F.2d 655 (1953)*
*United States Court of Appeals (4th Cir.)*

tion to be made by the United States Tariff Commission. Such investigation shall be made after due notice and opportunity for hearing to interested parties.

(b) If, on the basis of such investigation and report to him of findings and recommendations made in connection therewith, the president finds the existence of such facts, he shall by proclamation impose such . . . quantitative limitations on any article or articles which may be entered . . . for consumption as he finds and declares shown by such investigation to be necessary.

There was no pretense of complying with the requirements of this statute. The president did not cause an investigation to be made by the Tariff Commission, the commission did not conduct an investigation or make findings or recommendations, and the president made no findings of fact and issued no proclamation imposing quantitative limitations and determined no representative period for the application of the 50 percent limitation contained in the proviso. All that occurred in the making of this executive agreement, the effect of which was to exclude entirely a food product of a foreign country from importation into the United States, was an exchange of correspondence between the acting secretary of state and the Canadian ambassador. Since the purpose of the agreement as well as its effect was to bar imports which would interfere with the agricultural adjustment program, it was necessary that the provisions of this statute be complied with and an executive agreement excluding such imports which failed to comply with it was void. . . .

The judgment for defendant will accordingly be affirmed.

**Decision.** The court ruled that the executive agreement was invalid because it was entered into without congressional authorization and in express contradiction to the provisions of a prior statute.

back to the time of the Civil War, Congress has granted extraordinary powers to the president to deal with a variety of "national emergencies." Although originally conceived to allow the president to deal with the economic problems arising during wartime, the concept of a *national emergency* has gradually been expanded to include a broad range of situations affecting international trade.

## Trading with the Enemy Act

The *Trading with the Enemy Act* (TWEA) was passed in 1917 for the purposes of "punishing trading with the enemy." Section 5(b) originally empowered the president to regulate international financial transactions during times of war. In 1933, however, President Roosevelt used this statute during a domestic economic crisis to declare a national banking emergency, close the nation's banks, and prevent the hoarding of gold. Within three days, Congress ratified the president's actions and amended Section 5(b). The amendments expanded the president's emergency powers to include peacetime crises, which included a wide range of situations, each determined by the president to be a "national emergency."

## International Monetary Crisis

In *United States v. Yoshida International, Inc.,* 526 F.2d 560 (1975) the U.S. Court of Customs and Patent Appeals approved a far-reaching use of emergency economic powers by the president under the TWEA. The case exemplifies how the definition of "national emergency" could be expanded to give a president broad powers in times of domestic economic crisis. During the 1960s, a crisis in the foreign exchange and gold markets upset the international monetary system and caused a lack of confidence in the U.S. economy, as well as speculative trading in currencies across national borders. The U.S. balance of payments was in disequilibrium, the nation's trade deficit was increasing, and U.S. reserves of gold had fallen sharply. In a large-scale sale of dollars, capital flowed out of the United States to Europe where interest rates were higher.

To rectify the situation, President Nixon took a number of steps, including halting conversions of foreign-held dollars into gold, reducing taxes and foreign aid, and imposing a 90-day wage-price freeze. Under Proclamation 4074, the president also imposed a 10 percent across-the-board surcharge on all imported goods. The proclamation stated that a "national emergency" had existed and that the president's actions were being taken pursuant to the trade acts, the Trading with the Enemy Act, and inherent presidential power under the Constitution. When the 10 percent surcharge was placed on Yoshida's imported zippers, the company challenged the president's authority to do so. The Court of Customs and Patent Appeals upheld the surcharge and ruled that Congress had intended that the president should have far-reaching powers during the national emergency. As a result of the president's actions, the United States was able to pressure other nations into agreeing on a system for stabilizing international exchange rates. Known as the *Smithsonian Agreement,* this effort resulted in a complete revision of the international monetary system.

In the 1970s, Congress generally came to believe that the TWEA provided the president with far more sweeping powers to regulate nonwartime emergencies than had ever been intended by the law. After all, this was the time of Vietnam, a war undeclared by Congress. The excesses of presidential power were becoming evident as the Watergate disclosures and abuses of public office were made public. Executive actions of the president were considered suspect. In this climate, Congress sought to increase its role in making U.S. foreign policy and to impose new controls on the president's actions during national emergencies. By 1977, Congress had passed new emergency powers statutes that repealed the TWEA with the exception of the provisions restricting trade with Cuba, North Korea, Vietnam, and Cambodia, or with any country during time of a declared war.

## National Emergencies Act

In 1976, Congress passed the *National Emergencies Act* (NEA), which ended four existing states of emergency and established new procedures for declaring new ones. (Ironically, the banking emergency declared by President Roosevelt during the Great Depression had remained in effect until 1976.) Under the NEA, the president can still declare a state of emergency, although the authority to act under it lasts for only one year. At the end of that period, the president must ask Congress to renew authority over that situation. The president must consult with Congress prior to declaring an emergency and report to Congress every six months while the emergency continues. Congress votes every six months on whether to continue the emergency and may terminate a national emergency declared by the president through a joint resolution of both houses of Congress.

While the procedures for congressional oversight are set out in the National Emergencies Act, the powers and the scope of remedies available to the president are set out in the 1977 *International Emergency Economic Powers Act* (IEEPA).

# International Emergency Economic Powers Act

This statute provides the current grant of authority to the president to regulate economic and financial transactions, and to place restrictions on importing or exporting, during a peacetime (or wartime) national emergency. The statute states that the president may declare a national emergency in the event of "any unusual and extraordinary threat, which has its source in whole or substantial part outside the United States, to the national security, foreign policy, or economy of the United States." IEEPA allows the president wide discretion in controlling international financial transactions, including the transfer of monies, goods, and securities to and from the United States. It allows the president to seize foreign assets held in U.S. banks or foreign branches of U.S. banks. The statute also allows the president to impose a trade embargo with a foreign country and to take a wide range of other economic sanctions. The president's policy decisions under IEEPA are often implemented by the U.S. Treasury, whose regulations are published in the *Federal Register.*

**Economic Sanctions under IEEPA.**   Since its enactment, IEEPA has been used to impose economic sanctions against Nicaragua, South Africa, Panama, Libya, Haiti, and Iraq in response to the political situations in those and other countries. These sanctions, tailored to the special problems presented by each individual country, have included a ban on the import and export of goods (computers, arms, and nuclear equipment to South Africa), prohibitions on financial transactions (a ban on the import of South African gold krugerrands and a prohibition on U.S. loans to South Africa), a ban on air flights between United States and Nicaragua, and a ban on

Nicaraguan and Panamanian ships entering U.S. ports. The embargo against Libya, in the wake of Libyan-sponsored terrorism, included a ban on travel to that country by U.S. citizens and a freeze on all Libyan property in the United States.

**IEEPA and U.N. Sanctions Against Iraq.**   In 1990, shortly after the Iraqi invasion of Kuwait, President Bush used his authority under IEEPA to impose economic sanctions on Iraq. Because Congress had not voted on a war resolution at that time, the president could not rely on the Trading with the Enemy Act. In an effort to block Iraq from seizing Kuwait assets, the Treasury Department used IEEPA to freeze all assets of both countries held in U.S.-owned or -controlled banks, or by U.S. firms. The sanctions were administered by the Treasury's *Office of Foreign Assets Control.* All sales between Iraq and U.S. companies were halted.

The Iraqi case presented a unique situation under IEEPA. The legal authority for U.S. action against Iraq was broadened by international cooperation and by the force of international law. The United States was not acting unilaterally against Iraq; it was, rather, responding to calls from the United Nations for sanctions against Iraq. This case was also unique in that IEEPA sanctions were used to aid in the protection of foreign assets (those belonging to the government and people of Kuwait), not just to punish an offending country. The sanctions resulted in lost business, disruption of the international oil markets, blocked letter-of-credit transactions, and a regulatory nightmare for U.S. companies doing business in the Middle East. The Gulf War began when the U.S. administration determined that the sanctions would not be effective.

**Court Challenges to IEEPA.**   When Libya was implicated in supporting international terrorism in the late 1980s, the president prohibited U.S. citizens from performing any contract in support of commercial, industrial, or governmental projects there. In *Herman Chang v. United States,* 859 F.2d 893 (1988), a group of petroleum engineers brought suit against the United States alleging that the termination of their employment with a Libyan oil company by an executive order under IEEPA violated their constitutional protection against the taking of private property without the payment of just compensation. In upholding the president's order, the court dismissed the argument that the U.S. government may not act in an emergency situation in a way that causes economic harm to individuals or companies. The court stated, "A new tariff, an embargo, a [military] draft, or a war may inevitably bring upon individuals great losses; may, indeed, render valuable property almost valueless. They may destroy the worth of a contract. But whoever supposed that, because of this, a tariff could not be changed . . . or an embargo be enacted, or a war be declared?"

The political turmoil that struck Iran during the 1979 Islamic Revolution, and the taking of hostages in the U.S. embassy in Tehran, led to perhaps the greatest legal challenge to IEEPA. In *Chas. T. Main v. Khuzestan,* the court discusses two important questions: first, whether the president has the authority to interfere with a court-ordered attachment against foreign assets held in U.S. hands; second, whether the president may negotiate the settlement of claims that Americans might have against foreign governments.

---

### BACKGROUND AND FACTS

This suit was brought by a U.S. contractor contesting an executive agreement between the United States and Iran. In 1979, the Shah of Iran was overthrown in a violent revolution leading to the establishment of the Islamic Republic of Iran. During the revolution, Iranian militants seized the U.S. Embassy in Tehran, taking U.S. diplomatic personnel hostage. Having received information that Iran was about to withdraw its deposits from U.S. banks, President Carter declared a national emergency and froze all Iranian property ($12 billion) held by U.S. banks or by U.S. corporations here and abroad. All trade was halted and travel restricted between the two countries. In order to free the hostages President Carter negotiated an executive agreement (the *Algiers Agreement*) with Iran. Under the terms of this agreement, the United States agreed to transfer Iranian monies (then frozen) either back to Iran or into trust accounts set up in British banks. One billion dollars of these trust funds was held in a security account to cover future claims that U.S. individuals or firms might have against Iran for damages (such as damages for the breach of a business contract). In addition, the president issued an executive order suspending all claims in U.S. courts by U.S. nationals against Iran for damages. The Iran–U.S. Claims Tribunal was then established, sitting at The Hague, to arbitrate any claims or disputes between U.S. nationals and Iran. Chas. T. Main International, Inc., a U.S.

### Chas. T. Main International, Inc. v. Khuzestan Water and Power Authority
*651 F.2d 800 (1981)*
*United States Court of Appeals (1st Cir.)*

engineering firm, had been doing consulting work in Iran related to the building of a hydroelectric power plant. It brought this action in the United States to recover monies owed to it under its contract with Iran and to have the Algiers Agreement declared unconstitutional as exceeding the president's authority.

---

LEVIN H. CAMPBELL, CIRCUIT JUDGE

The International Emergency Economic Powers Act (IEEPA) enables the president, in times of declared national emergency, to: (A) investigate, regulate, or prohibit

(i) any transactions in foreign exchange,

(ii) transfers of credit or payments between, by, through, or to any banking institution, to the extent that such transfers or payments involve any interest of any foreign country or a national thereof. . . .

The president relied on his IEEPA powers in November 1979, when he "blocked" all Iranian assets in this country, and again in January 1981, when he "nullified" interests acquired in blocked property, and ordered that property's transfer.

Main argues that IEEPA does not supply the president with power to override judicial remedies, such as attachments and injunctions, or to extinguish "interests" in foreign assets held by United States citizens. But we can find no such limitation in

*(continued)*

*(continued)*

IEEPA's terms. The language of IEEPA is sweeping and unqualified. It provides broadly that the president may void or nullify the "exercising (by any person of) any right, power, or privilege with respect to . . . any property in which any foreign country has any interest . . . " 50 U S C s 1702(a)(1)(B).

We therefore hold that the president had authority to order the transfer of blocked Iranian assets without regard to attachments or other judicial orders against the assets obtained subsequent to the November 14, 1979, blocking order.

The president's order suspending claims stands on a different footing. While it is not impossible to read IEEPA itself as providing authority for the president to suspend or terminate claims against a foreign sovereign, the statutory meaning in this regard is scarcely clear, and there is no precedent for such a reading. Though we read IEEPA as giving some support to the president's order, we cannot say that it provides sufficient authority. We therefore approach the president's order in terms of whether he had inherent power under the Constitution to take such action. We hold that he did. . . .

International agreements settling claims by nationals of one state against the government of another "are established international practice reflecting traditional international theory." L. Henkin, *Foreign Affairs and the Constitution* 262 (1972). In numerous instances, dating back to the earliest days of this country's history, the president, often acting without the advice or consent of the Senate, has agreed to extinguish claims of United States nationals against foreign governments, in return for lump sum payments or the establishment of arbitration procedures.

To be sure, such settlements were often encouraged by the U.S. claimants themselves; a claimant's only hope of obtaining any payment at all might lie in having his government negotiate a diplomatic settlement with the foreign power. However, the president has "sometimes disposed of the claims of [U.S.] citizens without their consent, or even without consultation with them, usually without exclusive regard for their interests, as distinguished from those of the nation as a whole." . . .

This case well illustrates the imperative need to preserve a presidential flexibility sufficient to diffuse an international crisis, in order to prevent the crisis from escalating or even leading to war. As the Supreme Court has consistently recognized, it is the president who is charged with responsibility as the United States' representative and negotiator in the international arena. . . .

To be sure, arbitration before the Tribunal poses, from Main's perspective, certain obvious disadvantages. Main might fear that a panel composed partly of Iranians will approach Main's claims with less sympathy than might a United States district court. The Tribunal could become stalled in procedural wrangles. On the other hand, there may, in fact, be some advantages to the arbitration process. Iran will be unable to present sovereign immunity or act of state defenses, and thus, at the least, potentially troublesome pre-trial skirmishes will be avoided. Main will also derive some protection from a $1 billion security account, although it maintains this security represents only a fraction of all claims and thus may be inadequate. The Declarations also provide that Tribunal awards will be enforceable in any country in accordance with its laws. Thus, even should the security account prove insufficient, the Tribunal award may nevertheless be more valuable, in terms of enforcement abroad, than an equivalent unsecured United States court judgment. And, of course, the amount the Tribunal will award Main on its claim is at present uncertain.

For the reasons stated above, we affirm the dismissal of the complaint in *Main v. United States.*

**Decision.** The court upheld the president's authority to transfer the blocked Iranian assets over Main's claim. Under IEEPA, the president has the authority to dissolve a court-ordered attachment against foreign assets held in the United States and to negotiate the settlement of claims that U.S. nationals might have against foreign governments.

**Comment.** Main eventually won an award against Iran in the Iran–U.S. Claims Tribunal. The president's authority to order the transfer of blocked Iranian assets pursuant to the hostage release agreement was later upheld by the United States Supreme Court in *Dames & Moore v. Regan, Secretary of Treasury,* 453 U.S. 654, 101 S.Ct. 2972 (1981).

# Federal–State Relations

Thus far our discussion has focused on the relationship between the executive and legislative branches of the federal government. But the notion of "federalism" also implies that the United States has two levels of government—state and federal. The Constitution has several provisions that touch upon the relationship between the state and federal governments and that determine a state's authority to regulate international (as well as interstate) trade. These include the *Supremacy Clause,* the *Import–Export Clause,* and the *Commerce Clause.*

## The Supremacy Clause

When a law or regulation of the federal government directly conflicts with those of the state (or local) government, the federal law sill generally prevail when Congress either expresses the intention that the federal law shall prevail or when it is implied in the legislation or from the circumstances. For example, when Congress enacts a comprehensive scheme of legislation, such as regulations governing commercial aviation, it includes an implication, known as *federal preemption,* that the federal rule will prevail over an inconsistent state rule. The inconsistent state law will be void to the extent of the conflict.

Because international trade is so heavily regulated by the federal government, many such conflicts have arisen. In the following case, a federal law was designed to provide a tax-free "home" for goods imported temporarily into the United States and intended for reexport. A local Texas law imposed a property tax on those same goods. The United States Supreme Court struck down the Texas law on the basis of federal preemption.

---

### Xerox Corporation v. County of Harris, Texas
459 U.S. 145, 103 S.Ct. 523 (1982)
United States Supreme Court

BACKGROUND AND FACTS

Xerox manufactured parts for copy machines in the United States that were shipped to Mexico for assembly. The copiers were designed for sale exclusively in Latin America. All printing on the machines was in Spanish or Portuguese. The copiers operated on a 50-cycle electric current unavailable in the United States. The copiers had been transported by a customs bonded trucking company to a customs bonded warehouse in Houston, Texas, where they were stored pending their sale to Xerox affiliates in Latin America. (Prior to this case, the copiers had been stored in Panama, but anti-U.S. sentiment there forced Xerox to remove them temporarily to the United States.) Under federal law, goods stored in a customs bonded warehouse are under the supervision off the U.S. Customs Service. Goods may be brought into a warehouse without the payment of import duties and stored for up to five years. At any time they may be reexported duty-free or withdrawn for domestic sale upon the payment of the duty. Harris County and the city of Houston assessed a nondiscriminatory *ad valorem* personal property tax on the copiers.

Xerox brought this action in Texas courts to have the tax declared unconstitutional. The Texas court upheld the tax and Xerox appealed.

CHIEF JUSTICE BURGER

Pursuant to its powers under the Commerce Clause, Congress established a comprehensive customs system which includes provisions for government-supervised bonded warehouses where imports may be stored duty free for prescribed periods. At any time during that period the goods may be withdrawn and reexported without payment of duty. Only if the goods are withdrawn for domestic sale or stored beyond the prescribed period does any duty become due. While the goods are in bonded warehouses they are in the joint custody of the United States Customs Service and the warehouse proprietor and under the continuous control and supervision of the local customs officers. Detailed regulations control every aspect of the manner in which the warehouses are to be operated.

Government-regulated, bonded warehouses have been a link in the chain of foreign commerce since "a very early period in our history." *Fabbri v. Murphy,*

*(continued)*

*(continued)*

95 U.S. 191, 197 (1877). A forerunner of the present statute was the Warehousing Act of 1846. A major objective of the warehousing system was to allow importers to defer payment of duty until the goods entered the domestic market or were exported. The legislative history explains that Congress sought to reinstate the sound though long-neglected maxim of Adam Smith, "That every tax ought to be levied at the time and in the manner most convenient for the contributor to pay it; [by providing] that the tax shall only be paid when the imports are entered for consumption."

The Act stimulated foreign commerce by allowing goods in transit in foreign commerce to remain in secure storage, duty free, until they resumed their journey in export. The geographic location of the country made it a convenient place for transshipment of goods within the Western Hemisphere and across both the Atlantic and the Pacific. A consequence of making the United States a center of world commerce was that

> our carrying trade would be vastly increased; that shipbuilding would be stimulated; that many foreign markets would be supplied, wholly or in part, by us with merchandise now furnished from the warehouses of Europe; that the industry of our seaports would be put in greater activity; [and] that the commercial transactions of the country would be facilitated. . . . Cong. Globe, 29th Cong., 1st Sess., App. 792 (1846) (remarks of Sen. Dix).

To these ends, Congress was willing to waive all duty on goods that were reexported from the warehouse, and to defer, for a prescribed period, the duty on goods destined for American consumption. This was no small sacrifice at a time when customs duties made up the greater part of federal revenues, but its objective was to stimulate business for American industry and work for Americans.

In short, Congress created secure and duty-free enclaves under federal control in order to encourage merchants here and abroad to make use of American ports. The question is whether it would be compatible with the comprehensive scheme Congress enacted to effect these goals if the states were free to tax such goods while they were lodged temporarily in government-regulated bonded storage in this country.

In *McGoldrick v. Gulf Oil Corp.,* 309 U.S. 414 (1940), the City of New York sought to impose a sales tax on imported petroleum that was refined into fuel oil in New York and sold as ships' stores to vessels bound abroad. The crude oil was imported under bond and refined in a customs bonded manufacturing warehouse and was free from all duties. We struck down the state tax, finding it preempted by the congressional scheme.

The analysis in *McGoldrick* applies with full force here. First, Congress sought, in the statutory scheme reviewed in *McGoldrick,* to benefit American industry by remitting duties otherwise due. The import tax on crude oil was remitted to benefit oil refiners employing labor at refineries within the United States, whose products would not be sold in domestic commerce. Here, the remission of duties benefited those shippers using American ports as transshipment centers. Second, the system of customs regulation is as pervasive for the stored goods in the present case as it was in *McGoldrick* for the refined petroleum. In both cases, the imported goods were segregated in warehouses under continual federal custody and supervision. Finally, the state tax was large enough in each case to offset substantially the very benefits Congress intended to confer by remitting the duty. In short, freedom from state taxation is as necessary to the congressional scheme here as it was in *McGoldrick.* . . .

Accordingly, we hold that state property taxes on goods stored under bond in a customs warehouse are preempted by Congress's comprehensive regulation of customs duties.

**Decision.** Judgment reversed for Xerox. The Court ruled that the imposition of *ad valorem* property taxes on imported goods stored in a customs bonded warehouse and destined for foreign markets was preempted by Congress's comprehensive regulation of international trade.

**Comment.** In *R. J. Reynolds Tobacco Co. v. Durham County,* 107 S.Ct. 499 (1986), the Court ruled that imported goods stored in a customs bonded warehouse may be subjected to an *ad valorem* property tax *where the goods are intended not for reexport but for domestic use.*

## The Import–Export Clause

The *Import–Export Clause* (1) prohibits the federal government from taxing *exports* and (2) prohibits the states from taxing either *imports* or *exports*. Historically, three reasons prompted such a provision. First, the federal government must be able to "speak with one voice" on matters related to foreign affairs. Second, import duties provided an important source of revenue for the federal government. And third, seaboard states were prevented from imposing burdensome regulations and taxes on "in transit" goods that were destined for inland states.

In *Michelin Tire Corporation v. Wages,* 423 U.S. 276, 96 S.Ct. 535 (1976), the U.S. Supreme Court addressed the issue of the state's power to tax imports. Michelin Tire Corporation imported tires manufactured in France and Nova Scotia, Canada, by Michelin Tires, Ltd. The company maintained a distribution warehouse in Georgia. The state assessed an *ad valorem* property tax against the tires being held in inventory. The tax was nondiscriminatory in nature in that the same tax was imposed upon all property similarly being held for resale in Georgia. The petitioner filed suit to have the collection of the tax enjoined as being unconstitutional under the Import–Export Clause. The Supreme Court ruled that the tax was permitted under the Import–Export Clause because the tax was imposed on all products for the purpose of supporting the cost of public services, the tax was nondiscriminatory, and did not interfere with the federal government's regulation of international commerce.

In 1978, the Supreme Court considered the constitutionality of a Washington state tax on stevedoring (the process of loading and unloading cargo on ships). Relying on the *Michelin* decision, the Court in *Department of Revenue of the State of Washington v. Association of Washington Stevedoring Companies,* 435 U.S. 734, 98 S.Ct. 1388 (1978) held that "the tax does not restrain the ability of the federal government to conduct foreign policy. As a general business tax that applies to virtually all businesses in the state, it has not created any special tariff. The assessments in this case are only upon that business conducted entirely within Washington. No foreign business or vessel is taxed. . . . The tax merely compensates the state for services and protection extended by Washington to the stevedoring business." In discussing interstate rivalries, the Court concluded that if it were to strike down the tax, then the state of Washington would be forced to subsidize the commerce of inland consumers. The tax was upheld under the Import–Export Clause.

## The Commerce Clause

As we discussed earlier in the chapter, the broadest power of the federal government to regulate business activity is derived from Article I, Section 8, of the Constitution. The *Commerce Clause* vests the federal government with exclusive control over foreign commerce. Conversely, in what is known as the *negative implication doctrine,* state governments may not enact laws that impose a substantial burden on foreign commerce. Where there is an existing federal law governing some aspect of foreign commerce, a conflicting state statute may be invalid (preempted) under the Supremacy Clause.

**The Commerce Clause and Multiple Taxation.** A state's authority to tax a business engaged in foreign commerce is also determined by whether or not the tax imposed results in *multiple taxation.* Multiple taxation occurs when the same service or property is subjected to the same or a similar tax by the governmental authorities of more than one nation.

The following case, *Japan Line, Ltd. v. County of Los Angeles,* discusses the problems of multiple taxation.

The purpose of restricting multiple taxation is to strengthen the government's ability to foster domestic participation in the international marketplace. By not prejudicing foreign companies operating in the United States, this country does not risk retaliation by foreign governments against U.S. firms operating abroad.

**State Income Taxation of Multinational Corporations.** The issue of multiple taxation was recently considered in *Barclays Bank PLC v. Franchise Tax Board of California,* 114 S.Ct. 2268 (1994). This important case upheld the constitutionality of California's "unitary" method of assessing income

## Japan Line, Ltd. v. County of Los Angeles
441 U.S. 434, 99 S.Ct. 1813 (1979)
United States Supreme Court

### BACKGROUND AND FACTS

The state of California imposed an *ad valorem* property tax upon cargo containers owned by Japanese companies and temporarily located in California ports. The containers were used exclusively for transporting goods in international commerce. They were based, registered, and subjected to property taxes in Japan. The containers spent, on average, only three weeks a year in California. Japan Lines contended that the tax was invalid because it subjected the containers to multiple taxation in Japan and the United States.

The California Supreme Court upheld the statute and the ship owners appealed.

### JUSTICE BLACKMUN

This case presents the question whether a state, consistently with the Commerce Clause of the Constitution, may impose a nondiscriminatory *ad valorem* property tax on foreign-owned instrumentalities (cargo containers) of international commerce. . . .

In order to prevent multiple taxation of commerce, this Court has required that taxes be apportioned among taxing jurisdictions, so that no instrumentality of commerce is subjected to more than one tax on its full value. The corollary of the apportionment principle, of course, is that no jurisdiction may tax the instrumentality in full. "The rule which permits taxation by two or more states on an apportionment basis precludes taxation of all of the property by the state of the domicile. . . . Otherwise there would be multiple taxation of interstate operations." The basis for this Court's approval of apportioned property taxation, in other words, has been its ability to enforce full apportionment by all potential taxing bodies.

Yet neither this Court nor this Nation can ensure full apportionment when one of the taxing entities is a foreign sovereign. If an instrumentality of commerce is domiciled abroad, the country of domicile may have the right, consistently with the custom of nations, to impose a tax on its full value. If a state should seek to tax the same instrumentality on an apportioned basis, multiple taxation inevitably results. Hence, whereas the fact of apportionment in interstate commerce means that "multiple burdens" logically cannot occur, the same conclusion, as to foreign commerce, logically cannot be drawn. Due to the absence of an authoritative tribunal capable of ensuring that the aggregation of taxes is computed on no more than one full value, a state tax, even though "fairly apportioned" to reflect an instrumentality's presence within the state, may subject foreign commerce "to the risk of a double tax burden to which [domestic] commerce is not exposed, and which the commerce clause forbids."

Second, a state tax on the instrumentalities of foreign commerce may impair federal uniformity in an area where federal uniformity is essential. Foreign commerce is preeminently a matter of national concern. "In international relations and with respect to foreign intercourse and trade the people of the United States act through a single government with unified and adequate national power." *Board of Trustees v. United States.* . . .

A state tax on instrumentalities of foreign commerce may frustrate the achievement of federal uniformity in several ways. If the State imposes an apportioned tax, international disputes over reconciling apportionment formulae may arise. If a novel state tax creates an asymmetry in the international tax structure, foreign nations disadvantaged by the levy may retaliate against American-owned instrumentalities present in their jurisdictions. Such retaliation of necessity would be directed at American transportation equipment in general, not just that of the taxing state, so that the Nation as a whole would suffer. . . .

It is stipulated that American-owned containers are not taxed in Japan. California's tax thus creates an asymmetry in international maritime taxation operating to Japan's disadvantage. The risk of retaliation by Japan, under these circumstances, is acute, and such retaliation of necessity would be felt by the Nation as a whole. . . .

We hold the tax, as applied, unconstitutional under the Commerce Clause.

**Decision.** The Supreme Court reversed, holding that the tax was unconstitutional. The Court ruled that an *ad valorem* property tax applied to cargo containers used exclusively in foreign commerce violates the Commerce Clause because it results in multiple taxation of instrumentalities of foreign commerce.

tax on companies in California that are subsidiaries of foreign multinational corporations.

Barclays Bank of California (Barcal), a California banking institution, was a subsidiary of the Barclays Group, a multinational banking enterprise based in the United Kingdom. The Barclays Group included more than 220 corporations doing business in 60 nations. In 1977 Barcal reported taxable income only from its own operations within California. California claimed that Barcal was a member of a multinational "unitary" business, and that the *entire worldwide income* of the unitary business—the income of all of the subsidiaries within the Barclays Group operating anywhere in the world—was taxable in California. Under the unitary method, taxes were assessed on the percentage of worldwide income equal to the average of the proportions of worldwide payroll, property, and sales located in California. Thus if a multinational corporation had 8 percent of its payroll, 3 percent of its inventory and other property, and 4 percent of its sales in California, the state imposed its tax on 5 percent of the multinational's total income. (The weight given to each category can vary under different formulas.) California used the unitary method because it believed that under traditional methods of tax accounting, conglomerates had the ability to manipulate transactions between affiliated companies so as to shift income to low-tax jurisdictions (although to guard against such manipulation, transactions between affiliated corporations are generally scrutinized to ensure that they are reported on an "arm's length" basis). Barclays claimed that California's tax resulted in multiple taxation, in violation of the Commerce Clause.

Citing its previous decisions, the U.S. Supreme Court upheld the California tax because seven requirements were met: (1) the tax applied to an activity with a substantial connection to California; (2) the tax was "fairly apportioned"; (3) the tax did not discriminate against interstate commerce; (4) the tax was fairly related to the services provided by the state; (5) the tax did not result in multiple taxation; (6) the tax did not impair the federal governments ability to "speak with one voice when regulating commercial relations with foreign governments"; and (7) compliance with the formula was not so impossible as to deprive the corporation of its due process of law.

Even before this case went to court, foreign corporations doing business in California had objected strongly to the unitary tax. Foreign governments also objected, claiming it violated international law. In response to this outcry, the state of California in 1986 dropped its unitary tax requirement and substituted a *water's edge election* allowing corporations the option of being taxed only on their California income—up to the "water's edge." Nevertheless, the case is important because it stands for the principle that unitary taxation is constitutional. It is still used in a few states.

**State Restrictions on Exports.** The Commerce Clause prohibits state governments from restricting, taxing, or otherwise imposing undue burdens on exports. In *South-Central Timber Development, Inc. v. Wunnicke,* 467 U.S. 82, 104 S.Ct. 2237 (1984), the Supreme Court considered an Alaska regulation that required that all timber taken from state lands be processed within the state prior to being exported. South-Central was an Alaskan company engaged in purchasing timber and shipping logs overseas. It filed suit claiming that the regulation violated the negative implications of the Commerce Clause. Alaska argued that the Commerce Clause did not apply because the state was acting as a "market-participant" (a vendor of lumber), not as a regulator. The Court agreed with South-Central. The Court concluded,

The limit of the market-participant doctrine must be that it allows a State to impose burdens on commerce within the market in which it is a participant, but allows it to go no further. The State may not impose conditions, whether by statute, regulation, or contract, that have a substantial regulatory effect outside of that particular market. . . . [A]lthough the state may be a participant in the timber market, it is using its leverage in that market to exert a regulatory effect in the processing market, in which it is not a participant.

In addressing the Commerce Clause question directly, the Court also noted, "In light of the substantial attention given by Congress to the subject of export restrictions on unprocessed timber, it would be peculiarly inappropriate to permit state regulation of the subject."

**State Restrictions on Imports.** State government restrictions on imports are severely limited. User fees for the use of port facilities are generally permitted. Also, states may impose restrictions directly related to the protection of the public health and safety. For example, Florida could limit, restrict, or ban the import of fruits or vegetables suspected of carrying a disease that could contaminate the local crop. In one case, however, a labeling and licensing statute was invalidated by the courts even though its alleged purpose was the protection of the public health and safety. Tennessee had enacted a statute calling for the licensing of all persons who deal in foreign meat products in the state and the labeling of all foreign meats sold in the state as being of foreign origin. The court concluded that "The regulation here involved cannot fairly be construed as a consumer protection measure, and if it should be, it would be interdicted by the Commerce Clause because it unreasonably discriminates against foreign products in favor of products of domestic origin."

# Federal Agencies Affecting Trade

Thus far, this chapter has discussed the constitutional role of government in regulating international trade. The remainder of the chapter briefly discusses the various agencies and executive branch departments of government that carry out the functions of government on a daily basis. U.S. government agencies that provide technical and financial assistance for exporters, such as the Small Business Administration, the Export-Import Bank, the Overseas Private Investment Corporation, the Commodity Credit Corportion, the Agency for International Development, the Trade and Development Program, the U.S. Department of Agriculture, and others are discussed elsewhere in the text. The following agencies are primarily concerned with the establishment of trade policy and the handling of trade disputes.

## U.S. Department of Commerce

The *Department of Commerce* (DOC) has the broadest authority over international trade of all department-level agencies in the federal government. The department's functions include approving export license applications for U.S. companies and fostering trade and promoting exports of U.S.-made products. The *International Trade Administration,* housed within the department, investigates certain unfair U.S. import cases, including those discussed in the next chapter. The *U.S. & Foreign Commercial Service* has a network of commercial officers assigned to 63 foreign posts serving in U.S. embassies worldwide. Their function is to promote U.S. trade with the countries in which they are assigned and to gather data and commercial intelligence about their areas.

## Department of Treasury

The *Treasury Department* administers the *U.S. Customs Service.* U.S. Customs plays a primary role in regulating the import of goods into the United States, including the classification and valuation of imports for customs purposes and the assessment and collection of duties. Customs also supervises U.S. Foreign Trade Zones and enforces the export control laws of the United States. The Treasury Department also plays an important role, along with the Federal Reserve, in setting the international financial policy of the United States. Other functions of the department include negotiation of tax treaties, enforcement of the tax laws applicable to foreign business operation, and control of foreign-held monies and assets during presidential-imposed embargoes.

## United States Trade Representative

The *United States Trade Representative* (USTR) is a cabinet-level post reporting directly to the president. The USTR carries on all bilateral and multilateral trade negotiations on behalf of the United States, serves as the principal adviser on trade matters to the president, represents the United States at all GATT meetings, coordinates the trade agreements program, and coordinates all U.S. trade policies, including those related to agricultural, textile, and commodity trade and unfair trade practices. Much of the responsibility for trade matters once held by the Department of State has been transferred to the USTR.

## International Trade Commission

The *International Trade Commission* (ITC), formerly called the U.S. Tariff Commission, is an independent agency of government created by Congress in 1916. The ITC maintains a highly trained cadre of professional economists and researchers who conduct investigations and prepare extensive reports on matters related to international economics and trade for Congress and the president. The role of the ITC (along with that of the International Trade Administration) in investigating unfair trade practices will be thoroughly discussed in future chapters. Because of the highly political nature of many of the investigations related to the impact of imported goods on U.S. domestic industry, the ITC is a bipartisan agency. The members of the commission must be appointed by the president from both political parties and are subject to Senate confirmation.

**www.embpage.org**
*Go to this address for embassies, consulates, and other links.*

## The U.S. Court of International Trade

The *Court of International Trade* (CIT) consists of nine judges who hear cases arising from the trade or tariff laws of the United States. Appeals from the U.S. Customs Service regarding duties assessed on imported goods and appeals from decisions of the International Trade Commission in unfair import cases are heard by the CIT. Appeals from the CIT go to the Court of Appeals for the Federal Circuit and, where appropriate, to the United States Supreme Court.

The court has exclusive jurisdiction over all civil actions commenced against the United States involving (1) revenue from imports or ton-nage; (2) tariffs, duties, fees, or other taxes on importation of merchandise for reasons other than the raising of revenue; (3) embargoes or other quantitative restriction of the importation of merchandise for reasons other than the protection of the public health or safety; and (4) administration or enforcement of the customs laws.

# Chapter Summary

Although the roles of the legislative and executive branches of government are set forth in the Constitution, considerable debate in recent years has surrounded the power of the president in regulating foreign commerce and foreign affairs. The president's power in these areas is derived from the treaty power, the inherent power under Article II, and the power delegated by Congress.

Trade policies are implemented through treaties or executive agreements. Treaties are negotiated and made by the president with the advice and consent of the Senate. Many treaties, such as FCN treaties, are self-executing. They require no act of the legislature to become effective, binding law.

Sole executive agreements relating to international affairs are valid if undertaken pursuant to the president's inherent power. Congressional-executive agreements are binding upon approval of both houses. Most major trade agreements today, such as those creating free trade areas, are negotiated under fast-track authority. Congress has set trade policies for the United States in the Tariff Act of 1930 and in subsequent acts that authorize the president to enter into trade agreements with foreign countries to reduce tariffs on imports. These agreements have helped achieve today's level of global prosperity.

The role of the states in regulating trade is limited. They may not tax imports or otherwise obstruct international commerce. States may levy reasonable fees to cover the cost of inspecting imports in the interest of the public health and safety.

---

QUESTIONS AND CASE PROBLEMS

1. North Carolina, South Carolina, and Georgia produce a large amount of cotton each year. In an effort to protect their farmers from overseas competition, the governors of these three states met and agreed on a uniform "inspection fee" to be imposed on all foreign cotton coming into their states

through their ports. They vowed to do their best to get their state legislatures to adopt this fee as law. Would any problem arise with such a fee?

2. From what four sources does the president draw the power to regulate foreign commerce or international trade? Explain each source.

3. The U.S. State Department negotiated directly with European and Japanese steel producers to limit their exports to the United States. This was done as a result of threats by the president to set import quotas. No foreign government was party to the agreement. Although the president had been granted express authority to limit imports by an act of Congress, this act required that he either hold public hearings through the Tariff Commission about setting import quotas or deal directly with foreign governments about limiting imports. The Consumers Union of U.S., Inc., felt that when Congress gave the president this express power, it preempted any other action by the president. They brought an action against the secretary of state to have the president's agreement with private steel producers in Europe and Japan declared illegal. What should be the result of such an action? *Consumers Union of U.S., Inc. v. Kissinger,* 506 F.2d 136 (D.C. Cir. 1974).

4. The Trade Expansion Act of 1962 as amended by the Trade Act of 1974 stated that if the secretary of the treasury finds that an "article is being imported into the United States in such quantities or under such circumstances as to threaten to impair the national security," the president is authorized to "take such action . . . as he deems necessary to adjust the imports of the article . . . so that [it] will not threaten to impair the national security." Does this grant of power to the president by Congress allow the president to establish quotas? If importation of foreign oil were determined to be "a threat to national security," could the president implement a $3–4 per barrel license fee? See *Federal Energy Administration v. Algonquin SNG, Inc.,* 426 U.S. 548 (1976).

5. What is a treaty? Where does the treaty power of the United States come from? What is the difference between a self-executing treaty and a non-self-executing treaty? How does the treaty approval process differ from the approval process for congressional-executive agreements?

6. The president has been holding discussions with several countries concerning lowering the tariff rates on certain U.S. goods shipped to those countries. Each of the countries in question wants the United States to lower tariff rates for items it imports into the United States. Does the

president have the power to negotiate such tariff changes? If so, from what does the president derive such a power and what would such an agreement be called?

7. If the president feels that human rights matters in a foreign country are not being handled correctly or that change is not occurring at a rapid enough pace, from a trade standpoint is there anything the president can do? Does the president have the power to do this? From what source is this power derived?

8. The state of Tennessee passed legislation requiring that any person selling or offering for sale in the state of Tennessee any meats that are the products of any foreign country shall so identify such product by labeling it "This meat is of foreign origin." The state law did not require a higher standard of purity and sanitation than that required by the U.S. Department of Agriculture. A New York corporation selling imported meats to customers in Tennessee challenged this state statute in U.S. District Court. The corporation's sales of imported meat to customers in Tennessee was one-half its volume prior to enactment of the statute. What do you think the legal basis was for this challenge to the Tennessee law? What do you think Tennessee's legal argument was for passing the law? What do you think the court decided? See *Tupman Thurlow Co. v. Moss,* 252 F.Supp. 641 (M.D. Tenn. 1966).

9. Name the federal agencies that deal with the day-to-day functions of U.S. trade.

10. Both the North American Free Trade Agreement (NAFTA) and the 1994 Uruguay Round GATT Agreement were negotiated according to fast-track authority from Congress. They were passed by slim margins, and only after much heated debate. Research the history of fast-track authority stemming from the Trade Reform Act of 1974 through today. Then examine the political and economic issues that were the focus of this debate.

## MANAGERIAL IMPLICATIONS

Your firm, Day-O Shoes, Inc., manufactures deck shoes in the Caribbean island country of Haiti. Haiti is the poorest nation in the Western Hemisphere. Your plant there employs more than 400 workers, and has always considered itself a good citizen of both Haiti and the United States. Most of the shoes are imported for sale into the United States, where you maintain a 30 percent share of a competitive market. In 1991, the freely elected president of Haiti is removed from office by military officers who install a dictator of their choice. In response, the president of the United States exercises authority under the International Economic Emergency Powers Act and issues an executive order imposing a complete embargo on trade with Haiti. The Treasury Department's Office of Foreign Assets Control is charged with enforcing the embargo. Facing the impending embargo, your firm shuts down its production operations there, one week prior to the date set for the embargo. Feeling some obligation to the unemployed workers, your company's chief executive ships over ten tons of food and clothing to the people who have lost their jobs.

Believing that the United States is serious about the embargo, and that it would remain in effect until the rightful president was returned to Haiti, your firm ships its U.S.-made raw materials, such as rubber soles and leather uppers, from Haiti to your other factory in Costa Rica. But you soon discover, much to your surprise, that your competitors are continuing to produce and stockpile their shoes in Haiti in the belief that the embargo would soon be lifted. Three months after you had ceased operations, the U.S. government decides to lift the embargo because it has resulted in the loss of 50,000 Haitian jobs. With no inventory of finished shoes, and your raw materials enroute to Costa Rica, your firm is unable to fill existing orders. Your competitors are ready, however, to ship their shoes from Haiti immediately.

1. Evaluate the course of action taken by Day-O Shoes. How did Day-O Shoes balance its responsibility under U.S. law to comply with the embargo with its need to remain competitive in the industry? What could it have done differently? Evaluate the ethics of Day-O's actions.
2. Was Day-O Shoes required to stop producing in Haiti? Were its competitors violating U.S. law by continuing to produce and stockpile their inventories? Were they violating any moral code, or even the "spirit of the law" by continuing to produce there? Evaluate the risks taken by the competitors in continuing their operations in Haiti during the embargo.
3. The embargo was intended to put economic pressure on Haiti so as to encourage political reform. Is the U.S. government saying that the embargo worked too well? Do you think that the embargo was lifted because of its impact on the Haitian workers or on U.S. firms doing business there? Critics argue that the U.S. government's attempts to use trade policy as a means of conducting foreign policy lead to confusion and uncertainty, and are counterproductive. Evaluate this argument.

## Chapter Ten

# GATT Law and the World Trade Organization: Basic Principles

The last chapter discussed how the responsibility for formulating and implementing the trade policies of the United States is shared between the legislative and executive branches of government, but the United States is only one nation in the world community. Every nation establishes its own trade policies and has its own best national interests at heart when dealing with other nations. Nowhere is this clearer than in the post-World War I policies of isolationism and protectionism. The Great Depression of the 1930s showed what can happen when nations try to isolate themselves economically and politically from the world solely for their own economic interests.

Yet from the economic and industrial ruin of the Great Depression and World War II came a renewed belief in free trade and a new international approach to dealing with common economic problems. Nations learned that their mutual interests could be best served if they could find a way to encourage free trade in goods, unfettered by high tariffs and other barriers, by enacting "liberalized" trade rules. However, they first needed to reach an agreement on trade issues of common concern, and then to find a way to resolve their disputes when they occurred.

The global framework for liberalizing trade rules and reducing barriers to the free movement of goods was established shortly after World War II by the *General Agreement on Tariffs and Trade* (GATT)—and the modern global trading system was born. GATT today provides the framework for most multilateral (many nations) trade negotiations aimed at reducing trade barriers. For nearly 50 years GATT has functioned to set the rules of international trade and provide a forum for settling international disputes. In 1994 a new world trade agreement was reached, called the *General Agreement on Tariffs and Trade 1994* that enhanced the role of international law in regulating trade and created the *World Trade Organization* (WTO), an international organization charged with administering the GATT world trade system.

> **http://itl.irv.uit.no/trade_law/documents/ freetrade/wta-94/nav/toc.html**
> *Contains links to the Articles of GATT 1994.*

## Import Barriers to Trade

A *trade barrier* is any impediment to trade in goods or services. An *import* trade barrier is any impediment, direct or indirect, to the entrance or sale of imported goods or services existing in the country of importation. A *trade barrier* usually refers to *laws or government regulations* that make selling foreign-made goods more difficult or costly than competing domestic-made goods. The term may also include *many other nonlegal* factors that discourage the sale or purchase of imported products.

All countries have trade barriers. While the United States is generally considered to be a "free trade" nation, with relatively few barriers to imports as compared to some other countries, it too has many trade barriers. The United States has accused Japan of having many unfair barriers to the import of U.S.-made products; however, Japan has responded with similar accusations against the United States. The United States has also accused many developing countries of erecting barriers to U.S. goods and services. Even countries such as Canada and the United States, which are similar in many respects, have come to blows over trade—including such products as beer, lumber, and automobiles. When nations are unable to resolve these disputes through negotiated agreements, *trade wars* can erupt.

## Anatomy of a Trade War: Auto Parts to Japan

To understand how a trade war can develop, let us use automotive trade as an example. Remember that the automobile industry is one of the most, if not the most, economically important manufacturing industries in the world—and also one of the most competitive. So a trade war here can cause tremendous economic hardship. Our example involves a long standing dispute between the United States and Japan in which the U.S. government and U.S. car manufacturers claimed that Japan unfairly restricts the import and sale of U.S. cars and car parts there.

At the end of World War II the Japanese government wanted to rebuild its ruined economy. In order to foster the growth of its own automobile industry, the Japanese government restricted the import and sale of foreign automobiles. The problem never made much notice outside of U.S. automobile circles until the late 1960s when more and more Japanese cars started to be sold in the U.S. Ever since then, the United States has tried to persuade the Japanese government to make it easier for U.S. cars and car parts to be sold in Japan. But by 1994, U.S. cars had made up less than 3 percent of all cars sold in Japan. Also in that year the U.S. government reported that of the total $62 billion trade deficit that the U.S. had with Japan, $36 billion was attributable to automobile trade. The United States claimed that this was largely due to actions of the Japanese government and its failure to permit U.S. companies to have free and fair access to its market. In 1995 the U.S. Trade Representative called for Japan to agree to opening its car market—or else.

**The U.S. Position.** The U.S. pointed out that U.S.-made cars were selling in Japan at prices nearly 40 percent higher than similar cars in the U.S. and far higher than similar Japanese models. The U.S. blamed the Japanese distribution system which favors Japanese products and the ex-

cessive costs required to make U.S.-made cars comply with Japanese requirements. The U.S. felt that the Japanese government as well as Japanese car manufacturers had pressured car dealers in Japan to not carry U.S. brands. For example, all Japanese car dealers were bound by a "prior consultation clause" in their franchise contracts that required them to "consult" with Japanese car manufacturers before selling U.S. brands.

The U.S. wanted Japanese car manufacturers to purchase more "original equipment" parts from U.S. companies for use in their auto assembly plants both in Japan and in North America. (Japanese auto plants in North America are commonly referred to as "transplants.") Also, the United States argued that Japanese regulations restricted the sale of U.S.-made "after market" parts (replacement parts for car repairs and accessories such as mufflers, towing hitches, mud flaps, and roof racks). The United States argued that Japanese requirements affecting the sale of after-market car parts were unreasonable, discriminatory, excessive, and anticompetitive. The United States cited Japanese regulations that required most repairs (e.g., brake, suspension, and engine repairs) to be done in a government-licensed garage. Any repair or alteration to the car that changed its height or external dimensions, no matter how slight, had to be inspected and approved at a licensed garage according to strict standards. Virtually all of the licensed garages in Japan are either owned or controlled by the Japanese automobile and automobile parts manufacturers, limiting the opportunities for U.S.-made parts to break into the market.

The problem is part of a larger dilemma in Japan's highly integrated vertical distribution system resulting in part from Japan's *keiretsu* system of business relationships. A *keiretsu* is the Japanese practice of having interlocking directorships, joint ownership, and other linkages between Japanese companies. *Keiretsu* companies share corporate directors and develop long-term contractual relationships that favor *keiretsu* members, thus keeping foreign firms from many business opportunities. The United States maintained that many *keiretsu* relationships are actually illegal collusion, which would violate antitrust laws if they occurred in the United States. Japanese new car manufacturers have vertically integrated *keiretsu* relationships with Japanese parts manufacturers, and thus bought, and still buy, only from them. The large parts manufacturers also control the distribution of after-market parts to the wholesalers and to the licensed garages that make repairs, inspections, sell, and install the parts for retail customers. Moreover, many of the garages are owned by Japanese parts manufacturers and carry only Japanese parts. Regulations increase the difficulty for new auto repair shops to become licensed. Inspections are rigorous and expensive (the installation and inspection of even minor parts, such as trailer hitches or shock absorbers, can run many hundreds or thousands of dollars). The system effectively prohibited U.S. firms from the parts market in Japan. The United States had for years called on Japan to deregulate its inspection and licensing system.

**The Japanese Position.** The Japanese tell a different story. Reports of the *Japan Fair Trade Commission* and the Japanese *Ministry of International Trade and Industry,* claimed that U.S.-made cars did not sell in Japan simply because of the preferences of Japanese consumers. For instance, they argued that U.S. manufacturers did not make enough right-hand drive models (for driving on the left-hand side of the road). With regard to the U.S. demands, Japan argued that the U.S. insistence that Japanese car manufacturers commit to purchase specified quantities of U.S. parts was a "results based" strategy that put the United States in the position of "managing trade" in violation of free market principles. They refused to submit to purchasing quotas imposed by the United States. They also argued that any agreement with the United States would discriminate against European, Mexican, and other parts suppliers in violation of international law. Moreover, the Japanese government claimed that *keiretsu* relationships were based on Japanese tradition, on cultural and social norms, and on business decisions—not on conspiracy and collusion. They argued that car parts were purchased from long-standing Japanese suppliers in order to ensure consistent quality control. The Japanese also pointed out that their requirements are based on safety considerations, with which the United States should not interfere.

**A Breakdown in Negotiations.** In 1995 trade talks between the U.S. and Japan took place in Canada. The U.S. refused to accept the few concessions made by the Japanese (e.g., the Japanese government offered to write a letter to sellers of car parts in Japan telling them that they may offer U.S. parts for sale). The issue reached the boiling point when the U.S. Trade Representative threatened to impose $6 billion in trade sanctions against Japan by increasing tariffs on Japanese luxury cars entering the United States to 100 percent of their value. U.S. car dealers worried that prices of Japanese cars could nearly double as a result, and that hundreds or thousands of dealerships could close and that tens of thousands of U.S. jobs would be lost. Japanese government officials threatened counter sanctions against a list of U.S. products, including aircraft and farm products, and fears of an all out economic war with Japan loomed.

Japan immediately filed a petition with the *World Trade Organization* in Geneva, Switzerland, to have the matter resolved before an international tribunal.

**An "Eleventh Hour" Settlement.** Trade negotiations were moved to Geneva, Switzerland, to the headquarters of the World Trade Organization, where in June of 1995 they continued virtually 24 hours a day. For weeks, U.S. negotiators continued to threaten to impose the punitive tariffs of 100 percent on Japanese luxury cars if a deal was not reached. Japanese negotiators, bolstered by Japanese public opinion, steadfastly maintained their markets were open, and refused to give in to "unreasonable" U.S. pressure. But, with only a few hours left before U.S. tariffs became effective, an agreement was reached.

The settlement called for Japanese auto manufacturers to purchase more U.S.-made auto parts, increase the number of Japanese-model cars made in the U.S., and to increase the number of Japanese dealerships carrying U.S. models. The agreement called for reform to the distribution system in Japan. For example, the Japanese government agreed to tell all car dealers that they were free to carry U.S. brands. The agreement also required the elimination of "prior consultation clauses" that had been used by Japanese manufacturers to pressure their dealers to not carry imported cars. The government agreed to aid in the marketing and promotion of U.S. cars through trade shows and exhibitions, and to provide financial incentives. Japan also agreed to speed up the delivery of imported cars to dealerships by sending inspectors (e.g., to inspect for compliance with safety and emission standards) directly to the dealerships. With regard to the repair parts market, the agreement called for Japan to permit more small, independently owned garages to do repair work and to sell and install U.S.-made parts. For example, Japan decreased the square footage requirement for garages to service large cars, thus allowing more garages to service bigger U.S. cars. The agreement also called for Japan to eliminate restrictions on the use of accessories, such as roof racks. With regard to Japanese transplant companies in the United States, the Japanese government agreed to get them to do more than just assemble cars in the U.S. by encouraging them to build research and development facilities here as well. Japan also pledged itself to expand its investigations and prosecutions of violations of the *Japanese Antimonopoly Act*, which prohibits restrictive and anticompetitive business practices.

The U.S. had to abandon its insistence on enforceable, mandatory requirements for Japanese imports and instead agree to voluntary goals that would be monitored in the future. The agreement did little to affect the Japanese *keiretsu* system. At the same time, U.S. automakers announced that they were going to be more aggressive marketing in Japan. For instance, Chrysler announced a major capital investment in Japan and the opening of new dealerships. All the U.S. auto companies announced that they would build more cars with right-hand drive for export to Japan. In the end, U.S. public opinion saw the Clinton Administration as being "tough on Japan." Also, many observers noted that Japanese negotiators are famous for stalling, and then reaching a last minute compromise. On the other hand, the opinion of many commentators and of the world trade community was that the Japanese commitment was an empty promise. The U.S. was criticized for resorting to threats and intimidation. They argued that if the U.S. had actually imposed sanctions against Japan—a "trading partner"—without the full approval of the world

community, it would have destroyed the spirit of cooperation and negotiation on which the world trading system is built. They also argued that it set a dangerous precedent for brinkmanship in future trade relations.

The U.S.–Japanese auto dispute was important because of the volume of trade that would have been affected, but the problems and principles are the same regardless of the product, industry, or money involved. With this dispute as our introduction, this chapter will examine the basic international legal principles affecting trade and the legal mechanisms for resolving trade disputes and preventing trade wars before they occur.

## Reasons for Regulating Imports

Nations impose import trade barriers for many economic and political reasons. Several broad policy reasons prompt the regulation of import or export of goods and services. These include the following:

1. *Collection of revenue* (taxing imports).
2. *Regulation of import competition* (the protection of domestic industry, agriculture, or jobs).
3. *Retaliation against foreign government trade barriers.*
4. *Implementation of foreign policy* (prohibition on allowing the import of goods from a country that violates international norms or is a military adversary).
5. *Implementation of national economic policies* (preservation of foreign exchange; implementation of industrial policy).
6. *Protection of the national defense* (erection of barriers to foreign firms selling defense-related equipment or essential products such as machine tools; protection of strategic national industries such as aerospace or telecommunications).
7. *Protection of natural resources or of the environment* (ban on export of scarce minerals; a requirement that imported cars be equipped with anti-pollution devices; or ban on import of tuna caught in fishing nets that trap dolphins).
8. *Protection of public health, safety and morals, and plant and animal life* (ban on the import of disease-carrying fruit, explosives, or obscene materials; use of safety requirements for construction equipment or consumer goods).

9. *Protection of local cultural, religious, or ethnic values* (limitations on foreign television programming; prohibition of the import of religiously offensive materials in fundamentalist Middle Eastern countries; ban on export of artifacts or antiques).

Import trade barriers can take many different forms and are usually classified as either tariff barriers or nontariff barriers. (For an interesting view of tariffs and nontariff barriers in China, see the following article, *China, 1997 National Trade Estimate Report.*)

> **http://www.ustr.gov**
> *The home page for the United States Trade Representative.*

---

*Foreign Accents*

---

# China
## 1997 National Trade Estimate Report on Foreign Trade Barriers

In 1996, the U.S. trade deficit with China was over $39.5 billion, an increase of more than $5.7 billion from the U.S. trade deficit of $33.8 billion in 1995. U.S. merchandise exports to China were nearly $12.0 billion, an increase of $230 million (2.0 percent) from the level of U.S. exports to China in 1995. China was the United States' fifteenth largest export market in 1996. U.S. imports from China were nearly $51.5 billion in 1996, an increase of over $5.9 billion (13.0 percent) from the level of imports in 1995. The U.S. Department of Commerce has estimated that for services trade in 1995, the U.S. exported $2.5 billion to China and imported $1.6 billion in services, resulting in a positive service trade balance with China of $937 million. A 1996 services trade balance is not yet available. The stock of U.S. foreign direct investment (FDI) in China in 1995 was $2.0 billion. . . . U.S. FDI in China is concentrated largely in the manufacturing and petroleum sectors.

**Import Policies**

China restricts imports through a variety of means, including high tariffs and other taxes, non-tariff measures, limitations on which enterprises can import, and other barriers. . . .

*Tariffs and Taxes*

China's tariffs have traditionally been so high as to be prohibitive to foreign exporters. In fact, in 1996, most-favored-nation (MFN) tariffs facing goods entering China ranged as high as 120 percent. In 1996, China lowered its average import tariff from 35.9 percent to 23 percent. Despite recent tariff reductions, however, U.S. industry continues to express concern that tariff rates for sectors in which China is seeking to build its international competitiveness, such as chemicals, remain extremely high. In addition to high tariff rates, unpredictable application creates difficulties for companies trying to export to, or import into, the Chinese market. Tariffs may vary for the same product, depending on whether the prodict is eligible for an exemption from the published MFN tariff. High-technology items whose purchase is incorporated into state or sector plans, for instance, have been imported at tariff rates significantly lower than the published MFN rate. In addition, import tariffs have sometimes been reduced or even not applied, either through temporary tariff rates published by China's General Administration of Customs (Customs) or through informal means.

China has taken steps to reduce tariffs pursuant to its bilateral commitments and in an effort to support its WTO accession bid. While many of the tariff reductions are still under negotiation in the context of WTO discussions, in November 1996, China's President Jiang Zemin announced that China would reduce the simple average tariff rate from the current 23 percent to 15 percent by the year 2000, as well as make further reductions in the medium- and long-term.

\*\*\*

*(continued)*

*(continued)*

Different ports of entry may charge significantly different duty rates on the same products. Because there is flexibility at the local level in deciding whether to charge the official rate, actual customs duties, like many taxes, are often the result of negotiation between businesspeople and Chinese customs officers. Allegations of corruption often result.

\*\*\*

### Non-Tariff Measures

Non-tariff barriers are administered at national and subnational levels by the *State Economic and Trade Commission* (SETC), the *State Planning Commission* (SPC), and the *Ministry of Foreign Trade and Economic Cooperation* (MOFTEC). These non-tariff barriers include import licenses, import quotas, and other import controls. The levels of specific non-tariff barriers are the result of complex negotiations between the Central Government and Chinese ministries, state corporations, and trading companies. Central Government agencies determine the levels of import quotas through data collection and negotiating sessions, usually late each year. These agencies—including the SETC, SPC, and MOFTEC—determine the projected demand for each product subject to import restrictions. Such restrictions generally include quantitative restrictions. Officials at central and local levels evaluate the need for particular products for individual projects or quantitative restrictions for the products. Once demand is determined, Central Government agencies allocate quotas that are eventually distributed nationwide to end-users and administered by local branches of the Central Government agencies concerned. China provides little transparency regarding the quantity or value of products to be imported under a quota, notwithstanding bilateral obligations and WTO requirements to provide such information.

### Transparency *[Government rules and regulations are open to view by the public]*

. . . While the MOFTEC *Gazette* was established to carry official texts of all trade-related laws and regulations at the national level—and has been a significant step toward transparency—its coverage of trade-related regulations is still incomplete and not always timely. In addition, important steps toward making the import approval process transparent, especially for industrial goods such as machinery and electronics products, are offset by the opaque nature of customs and other government procedures. Central Government agencies have published many—though not all—of their import administration laws and regulations, making China's trade regime more transparent.

\*\*\*\*

### Trading Rights and Other Restrictions

China restricts the types and numbers of entities within China which have the legal right to engage in international trade. Only those firms with important trading rights may bring goods into China. In addition, some goods that are of great commercial value to both China and its trading partners, such as grains, cotton, vegetable oils, petroleum, and certain related-products are imported principally through state trading enterprises.

In some cases, specific bureaus or ministries impose informal market access barriers for imports that fall under their jurisdictions. For example, the State Pharmaceutical Administration is responsible for issuing quality certificates for pharmaceutical products. Some Chinese organizations require end-users to acquire purchase certificates before they can receive permission to import.

As a result, China's real demand for these types of imported products greatly exceeds the supply made available through the official system. For example, the U.S. spirits industry estimates that only five percent or less of imported distilled spirits enter the Chinese market through official channels. Thus, a large illegal market for spirits has grown up around the official system. Sales of such products have resulted in revenue losses for China, because of rampant smuggling and the associated corruption. Another side effect of the smuggling that suppressing demand engenders is counterfeiting and passing off of poor quality or even dangerous products as the much sought after but difficult to obtain legitimate imports.

\*\*\*\*

*(continued)*

*(continued)*

**Lack of Intellectual Property Protection**

U.S. efforts to protect intellectual property rights (IPR) in China took a major step forward in 1996. In an effort to ensure effective enforcement by the Chinese of the 1995 U.S.-China IPR Agreement, in May 1996 the Clinton Administration threatened to impose increased tariffs on $2 billion of China's exports to the United States. In June 1996, China and the United States signed an IPR Accord which set out the steps [toward compliance] that China had taken in recent months and further steps that it would take in the future. At that time China reported on its recent efforts to crack down on piracy which included shutting 15 illegal CD factories and over 500 laser disc cinemas nationwide. Imports of CD presses were also stopped unless central government authorities granted express approval for the import. Since June 1996, the Chinese have made significant progress in combating IPR violations. Specifically, Chinese officials have closed 9 factories and 28 illegal production facilities and confiscated millions of illegal and unauthorized LDs, CDs, VCDs and other publications. In addition, Chinese authorities launched 37,300 checks across the country on IPR related cases and collected US $491 million in revenue from IPR related fines, up to 33 percent over 1995. To date, more than 3,000 judges have been specifically trained to hear IPR cases, and significant rewards have been paid for information leading to the arrest of pirates. Significantly, China's customs authorities have notably increased IPR enforcement efforts at the border. Imports of CD presses through the ports of Shantou and Foshan have been stopped. In Guangdong province, over 6,000 smuggling cases involving goods worth approximately US $1.2 million were uncovered (up 18 percent over 1995). Cooperative efforts between Guangdong province and Hong Kong customs officials have paid off, resulting in 15 joint crackdown operations in 1996. Enforcement of IPR protection has become part of China's nationwide anti-crime campaign, thus ensuring Chinese police involvement in arresting IPR piracy. The Administration commends China for taking these promising steps on effectively enforcing IPRs.

\*\*\*\*

**Services Barriers**

\*\*\*\*

U.S. financial institutions, law firms, and accounting firms, among others, must largely limit their activities to serving foreign firms or joint ventures. U.S. companies still are not permitted to offer after-sales services, except in collaboration with a Chinese partner. Although some U.S. companies, such as those involved in joint-ventures, are allowed to hire and fire based on demand and performance and pay wages according to market rates, the representative offices of U.S. service suppliers are still required to hire, recruit, or register all local staff through state labor services companies which collect large monthly fees for each employee hired. Access to distribution outlets remains severely restricted, and foreign firms are even barred from transferring products among various subsidiary production facilities.

**Office of the United States Trade Representative**

## Tariffs

The most common device for regulating imports is the *tariff* or *import duty*. (Note: these terms are used interchangeably in this text.) A tariff is a tax levied on goods by the country of importation. It is usually computed either as a percentage of value (*ad valorem* tariffs) or on the basis of physical units (also called specific or flat tariffs). Goods that are fungible (e.g., crude oil, wheat, or standard-sized graded lumber) are usually subject to a specific or flat-rate tariff, while goods which vary in value (e.g., chairs, machinery, or specialized steel) are usually subject to an *ad valorem* tariff. Tariffs are generally considered to be one of the least restrictive types of trade barriers.

## Nontariff Barriers to Trade

*Nontariff barriers to trade* are any impediment to trade other than tariffs. This rather broad definition, can be broken down into *direct* and *indirect* nontariff barriers. *Direct nontariff barriers* include those barriers that specifically limit the import of goods or services, such as embargoes and quotas. *Indirect nontariff barriers,* discussed in the next section, are those which on their face seem perfectly neutral and nondiscriminatory against foreign-made products, but which in their actual use and application make it difficult or costly to import foreign-made goods.

**Embargoes.**   The most restrictive of the direct nontariffs barriers is the embargo. An *embargo* can be either a complete ban on trade with a certain foreign nation (e.g., the United States embargo on trade with Iraq or North Korea) or a ban on the sale or transfer of specific products (e.g., ivory) or technology (e.g., nuclear). The embargo can be both on imports from, or exports to, that nation. While a quota is used for economic purposes, the embargo is usually reserved for political purposes. The use of this extraordinary remedy is usually designed to implement foreign policy objectives, such as to "punish" another country for some offensive conduct in world affairs. In recent years the United States has imposed embargoes on Cuba, Iran, Iraq, North Korea, Libya, and a few other countries.

**Quotas.**   Perhaps the *direct nontariff barrier* that most people think of first is the *quota.* A quota is a quantitative restriction on imports. It can be based either on the value of goods or on quantity (weight, number of pieces, etc.). A quota can also be expressed as a percentage share of the domestic market for that product. Quotas can be placed on all goods of a particular kind coming from all countries, a group of countries, or only one country. Thus, a quota to protect U.S. garment manufacturers could limit imports of men's trousers either to a specified number of trousers or to a given percentage of the U.S. market for men's trousers. *Global quotas* are imposed by an importing nation on a particular product regardless of its country of origin. They are filled on a first-come, first-serve basis. *Bilateral quotas* are placed on a particular product on the basis of its country of origin. A *zero-quota* is a complete ban on the import of a product by permitting *zero* quantities to be imported.

Quotas are used either to protect domestic industry from foreign competition or as a tool for implementing a nation's economic policy of reducing imports. Governments sometime prefer the use of quotas to tariffs because quotas work more quickly in restricting imports. Quotas can work quickly to protect a domestic industry threatened with increased imports of competing goods. A country which experiences a domestic economic crisis caused by excessive imports (such as during a *balance-of-payments crisis,* when an excessive amount of foreign exchange leaves the country to purchase imported products) can use quotas immediately to restore economic equilibrium.

Because of the ease in administering and applying a quota, it is a more flexible tool for regulating imports than a tariff. It can, therefore, be used to reduce imports on a specific product or commodity to correct short-term market conditions. Also, government policy makers can more easily assess the potential impact of a quota than of a tariff, because no one can predict with absolute certainty what the economic effect of a tariff will be. Another advantage is that quotas can either be applied across the board to all imports from a particular nation or be applied to the products of several nations. These *allocated quotas* can thus serve important foreign policy objectives because the ability to allocate additional quota rights to certain countries can become a powerful economic incentive in world politics. Quotas have been widely used in regulating trade in textiles and agricultural products.

Quotas of course also have several disadvantages. First, a costly governmental *licensing scheme* is necessary to enforce them. Imports may need to be tracked on the basis of their country of origin, requiring complex recordkeeping. Second, most quotas provide no revenue to the importing nation. Third, they are often politically unpopular because they deprive importers and consumers of the ability to make a choice of products in the marketplace. Fourth, the imposition of quotas often can lead to retaliation by foreign governments whose products have been restricted. Fifth, the complex licensing schemes used to enforce quotas are difficult for many foreign exporters to understand, who therefore may not know what barriers they will face when their goods reach the foreign country. Sixth, and most importantly, quotas interfere with the *price mechanism* in the marketplace, affecting prices by reducing supply. Firms able to import the product under the quota receive a monopoly profit, which contributes to considerable price increases to consumers. Indeed, the reduced supply and increased prices attributable to quotas and other restraints on imported products restrict competition and allow the price of competing domestic products to increase correspondingly.

U.S. presidents have not favored the use of quotas to protect U.S. industry for fear that the foreign nations affected would retaliate, giving rise to trade wars. Import quotas are more likely to be used when increased foreign imports threaten national security. For instance, in the 1980s, quotas were placed on imported machine tools for this reason. This quota prompted foreign manufacturers to invest in factories in the United States to avoid these restrictions.

**Auctioned Quotas.** A quota which is sold to the highest bidder is known as an *auctioned quota.* One advantage of auctioned quotas is that they allocate import rights by price, rather than by government restrictions on supply. Moreover, auctioned quotas minimize the cost of relief to the economy by transferring the profits gained from owning quota rights from the foreign producer or importer to the country imposing the quota.

**Tariff-Rate Quotas.** A *tariff-rate quota* is not really a quota at all, but a tariff that increases according to the quantity of goods imported. It is a limitation or ceiling on the quantity of goods that may be imported into a country at a given tariff rate. Let's use bedspreads as an example. A country that wants to protect its domestic textile industry might impose a tariff rate of, say, 7 percent on the first 500,000 bedspreads to be imported into the country in a given year; 14 percent on the next 500,000 bedspreads; and an even higher rate, perhaps, 25 percent, on all bedspreads imported above 1,000,000 pieces. The use of tariff-rate quotas is quite common worldwide.

## Indirect Nontariff Barriers

*Indirect nontariff barriers* include laws, administrative regulations, industrial or commercial practices, or even social and cultural forces, that have the *effect of limiting or discouraging the sale or purchase of foreign goods or services in a domestic market,* regardless of whether the

barrier is intended as a measure to control imports. All countries have indirect nontariff barriers of some sort. Many indirect barriers are intended to protect domestic industries from foreign competition. Consider some examples.

To restrict imports, countries may impose *monetary and exchange controls* on currencies that limit the amount of foreign currency available to purchase foreign goods. Foreign *government procurement* policies may encourage government agencies to buy goods and services primarily from domestic suppliers. Foreign administrative regulations can impose *technical barriers to trade,* including performance standards for products, product specifications, or product safety or environmental engineering standards. Examples might include national standards for electrical appliances, health standards for food or cosmetics, safety standards for industrial and consumer goods, and even automotive emission requirements. Unless foreign suppliers of goods can meet these standards in the same fashion as domestic suppliers, they will be frozen out of the foreign market. The refusal to allow the import of beef containing growth hormones would effectively shut down imports of beef from countries in which virtually all beef produced contains such chemicals. Governmental restrictions on the use of food preservatives, such as those that have been imposed by Japan, are another excellent example of a trade barrier in disguise—as foods without preservatives cannot be transported long distances. Other common examples might include requirements that instruction manuals for consumer goods be written in the language of the importing nation, that only metric sizes appear on the product or packaging, or that imported goods be subject to stringent inspections or fees that are not applicable to domestic products. In the accompanying article, "Mail-Order Firms Also Face Myriad Trade Rules in Japan," U.S. firms such as L.L. Bean and Lands' End have made successful inroads into the Japanese catalog business despite Japanese postal regulations.

**The Japanese Large-Scale Retail Stores Law.** Another good example of an indirect nontariff barrier in Japan that impedes the ability of foreign firms to sell there is the *Japanese*

*Foreign Accents*

# Mail-Order Firms Also Face Myriad Trade Rules in Japan

## Direct Marketing in Japan Requires Business Savvy

Tokyo—To fully appreciate the beauty of selling mail-order products in Japan, you only need to look at the endless trade negotiations covering autos, flat glass or paper.

"They're struggling to compete," said Marc Fuoti, chairman of the direct marketing committee of the American Chamber of Commerce in Japan. "There's no fundamental restrictions to U.S. catalogs. And there are millions of consumers dying to buy."

That said, the industry is not completely free of regulations. Some leather products, including luggage, jackets and shoes, face tariffs that can undercut their price advantage.

### Mail Regulations

There are also mail regulations to cope with. American mail-order companies with an office in Japan aren't allowed to send catalogs from their U.S. headquarters. In Japan, which has some of the highest postage rates in the world, domestic rates often exceed rates for delivery from outside the country.

In addition, sales promotions are severely limited in Japan under rules overseen by Japan's Fair Trade Commission. Giveaways are limited to 10% of the product cost or a maximum of about $500, whichever is less, making most sweepstakes impossible.

Thus Reader's Digest Book's popular $1 million sweepstakes in the United States wouldn't be allowed since $1 million is worth far more than the book's value.

Japan's Fair Trade Commission has taken the stance that this is fooling consumers and that the product's merits must stand on its own.

"It's an archaic way the FTC responds to this," Mr. Fuoti said.

"We say, we're not talking about consumers in the war-torn 1940s. [Japanese consumers] are very sophisticated."

### Customs Minor Concern

Another minor concern is customs. Right now, products worth up to $100 can be imported by mail without duty. The U.S. Chamber of Commerce is trying to get that boosted to about $400.

Mr. Fuoti pegs Japan's total mail-order business at about $40 billion, compared with more than $300 billion in the United States. He estimates the foreign mail-order share at more than $1 billion.

Japan's direct-market business—which includes orders taken by mail and phone—grew by 3% in 1993, which is quite strong given that most other retail sectors shrunk.

In 1993, 55% of Japan's adult female population and 18% of the adult male population bought something through direct marketing.

In the Japanese market, meanwhile, catalog sales continue to grow. But the market has slowed relative to double-digit growth rates seen in the late 1980s and early 1990s. This is due to a weaker Japanese economy and more industry competition.

### Shakeout Beginning

"This is the beginning of a shakeout," Mr. Fuoti said, "with very general catalog companies—which still make up 45% of the market—starting to have more trouble." Still, the concept of well-targeted niche marketing has not yet caught on among Japanese companies.

Because many U.S. companies are able to penetrate the Japanese market without translating or spending extra money, some find themselves making $500,000 to $700,000 more a year without doing anything. "For a $40 million company, that's 4% of sales," Mr. Fuoti said. "That's making marketing managers sit up and notice."

The first U.S. company to enter the Japanese market in a big way was L. L. Bean. It has been very

*(continued)*

*Large-Scale Retail Stores Law.* This law protects the small "mom and pop" retail stores by limiting the location and operations of large retail stores and supermarkets in Japan. Since large retail chains are high-volume purchasers, and since large U.S. exporters are set up to sell to high-volume buyers, this law has the effect of limiting U.S. imports. Moreover, it perpetuates the vertically integrated distribution system in Japan and allows large Japanese manufacturers to control the distribution of their products through many small retail stores to the consumer. The effect is to strengthen their market position to the exclusion of foreign firms. The problem is exacerbated because of high land prices in Japan that make it costly for foreign companies to obtain suitable real estate for large-scale retail operations. This law is an excellent example of a nontariff barrier that on its face is completely neutral. It does not discriminate against products because they are of foreign origin, yet it has the effect of limiting Japanese imports of foreign goods.

The *Japanese Large-Scale Retail Law* began as the Department Store Law in 1937. The law, which came about as a compromise among the department stores, small and medium size retailers, and superstores, was enacted in 1973. By 1978, it protected retailers with stores as small as 500 square meters by giving them a voice in determining whether any large stores could come into their locale. By 1979, the Japanese Ministry of International Trade and Industry refused to accept a retailer's notification that it planned to open a new store unless there was also a document indicating the terms under which local merchants agreed to the large store's opening. Negotiations between new store owners and local merchants frequently took seven or eight years to reach an accord.

Both domestic and international pressure led to changes in the law and in its application in the 1990s. The Japanese Parliament changed the law by enlarging the size of the small stores entitled to participate in the approval for a new store, shortening the notification period that required a new store to meet before it could open and replacing the local approval board with a larger and less protectionistic regional board. By 1994, there had been an increasing number of new large volume stores, a growth in direct importing by retailers, and implementation of new marketing strategies bringing business suits, British whiskey, and U.S. cosmetics to a variety of large retail outlets.

The first half of the 1990s also saw a rapid growth in discounting. While critics still continued to call for total repeal of the law, the dramatic amendments and policy changes to it moved this law away from center stage in international trade negotiations. Consumers in Japan were the clear beneficiaries.[1]

**Import Licensing Schemes and Customs Procedures as Trade Barriers.** Some of the most insidious indirect barriers to trade are import licensing schemes and customs procedures. Some governments require importers to apply for permission to import products, subject to meeting many complex and often discriminatory requirements. The licensing is often expensive and time consuming. For instance, an importer may have to make a deposit of foreign exchange in order to get the license, or the license may be based on a discriminatory quota system.

A host of governmental red tape, administered by entrenched bureaucracies, can also cause delays of days or weeks in bringing goods into a country. Import documentation and inspection requirements, for instance, can be so unreasonable that firms cannot comply without incurring delays and unanticipated expense. Bribery and corruption in a foreign government office can stall an importer's paperwork endlessly. Administrative regulations might be impossible to comply with. For instance, imagine a country that requires all foreign-made jewelry be marked with the country of origin, but provides no exemption for jewelry too small for engraving. Inspection procedures have also been used to stall shipments. To illustrate, in 1995 the United States accused Korea of using delaying tactics, in the form of inspections, to hold shipments of U.S.-grown fresh produce on the docks until it rotted.

## Transparency

When a foreign government's import regulations are not made readily available to the public, or are hidden or disguised in bureaucratic rules or practices, the regulations are not *transparent*. For instance, government procurement policies *lack transparency* when the requirements for bidding on a project are made available only to select domestic firms. A licensing scheme used to enforce a quota is not transparent when the "rules of the game" are not made known to foreign exporters. When a nation's import regulations or procedures lack transparency, foreign firms cannot easily gain entrance to its markets. Many trade laws today incorporate transparency by requiring nations to publish all regulations directly or indirectly affecting imports.

## Impact of Trade Barriers on Managerial Decisions

In making import–export decisions, the international manager needs to assess the impact of trade barriers on a business strategy. For example, the decision to ship goods into a foreign market, or to license or produce there, might be made on the basis of government policies that either restrict or promote trade. To the exporter of manufactured goods, regulations of the importing country may mean the difference as to whether the firm's products can be successfully imported and marketed at all. To the importer, regulations may dictate those countries from which the firm may "source" raw materials, purchase machine parts, or locate finished goods. To the service provider, governmental regulations may determine when and on what terms it can successfully enter the banking, insurance, architectural, or engineering market. And to the investor who is considering building a plant, entering into a joint venture, or forming a subsidiary abroad, governmental regulations and trade barriers may indicate how suitable the economic and political climate is for the enterprise.

## Trade Liberalization Through Cooperation

Most nations have come to realize that trade barriers are damaging to the international economy—and ultimately to their own. Moreover, they have realized that if they restrict the products of their trading partners in order to protect one segment or sector of their economy, then another sector will suffer. For instance, restrictions on the import of steel benefit domestic steel producers, but injure the automakers that use the finished product (as well as increase automobile prices to consumers). Similarly, import restrictions that protect one sector sometimes result in foreign retaliation against another sector. For instance, Korea might put strict quotas on U.S. beef imports, but the U.S. might respond by placing retaliatory tariffs on Samsung appliances or Hyundai cars. So, in order to limit the snowball effect of protectionism, nations have established certain rules.

## The Bretton Woods System and GATT's Founding

Even while World War II was being fought, the United States and its allies were charting a course to rebuild and revitalize the world's economy and to ensure that the economic mistakes of the 1930s would not be repeated. In 1944 the allied nations met at the *Bretton Woods Conference* in New Hampshire and established several important international economic institutions, including the

*International Monetary Fund* and the *International Bank for Reconstruction and Development,* or *World Bank.* At that time, a third specialized agency was planned to promote and stabilize world trade by reducing tariffs. In international meetings held in the United States and in Geneva, Switzerland, in 1947 a *General Agreement* was reached that reduced tariffs and set rules to hold countries to their tariff commitments.

After World War II national leaders and policy makers stressed a more international view of the world's economy. At the same time, the United Nations and other new international organizations were born. Led by the United States, other nations embraced free trade and open market policies; they wanted to continue to reduce tariff and nontariff barriers to trade. But most importantly, they wanted to ensure that the world would never again fall victim to the forces of protectionism that existed in the 1930s. Their efforts to establish new rules for conducting their trade relations resulted in the creation of an international legal system to handle trade matters, complete with international law, dispute settlement mechanisms, and agreed-upon codes for regulating trade. This system is based on the *General Agreement on Tariffs and Trade.*

## The General Agreement on Tariffs and Trade

The General Agreement on Tariffs and Trade (GATT) has been the most important multilateral agreement for liberalizing trade by reducing tariffs, opening markets, and setting rules for promoting freer and fairer trade. The original GATT agreement, completed in 1947, governed most of the world's trade in goods for almost 50 years.

Twenty-three nations, including the United States, were the original signatories to GATT in 1947. The agreement became effective through the signing of the *Protocol of Provisional Application.* Although GATT 1947 was never ratified by the U.S. Congress as a treaty, it has consistently been accepted as a binding legal obligation of the United States under international law. Until January 1, 1995, the GATT agreement was administered by *The GATT,* a multilateral trading organization based in Geneva, Switzerland, composed of countries that were signatories to the GATT agreement.

In 1994, after nearly a decade of negotiations, the world community adopted a new General Agreement on Tariffs and Trade that made many changes to the original 1947 agreement. GATT 1994 was signed by 125 nations on April 15, 1994, as a result of the *Uruguay Round* of multilateral negotiations that had begun in 1986. The United States negotiated and adopted GATT 1994 under "fast-track" negotiating authority as a congressional-executive agreement. The agreement was negotiated by three U.S. presidents, and was submitted to Congress by President Clinton. Congress approved the agreement at the close of 1994 to become effective on January 1, 1995.

GATT 1994 establishes rules for regulating trade in goods and services that are broader in scope than those of GATT 1947. It also resulted in the creation of the *World Trade Organization* (WTO), which replaced the original GATT organization that had operated for nearly 50 years. Countries that were signatories to GATT 1947 were called *contracting parties* to reflect that GATT is a contract between nations. Under GATT 1994, signatory nations are called *members.* Selected provisions of GATT 1994, which includes GATT 1947, are reproduced in the appendix.

## GATT and a World Trading System

GATT provides an organized global structure to improve the economic, political, and legal climate for trade, investment, and development. Its primary goal is to achieve distortion-free trade through the removal of artificial barriers and restrictions imposed by self-serving national governments. The GATT system includes an international legal system with rules, a mechanism for interpreting those rules, and a procedure for resolving disputes under them.

GATT rules are created by international agreement and become guiding principles of international trade law, upon which a WTO member nation's own trade regulations are to be based. In theory, the GATT legal system exists side by side with the domestic legal systems of sovereign nations. GATT anticipates that national legislatures and government agencies will comply with GATT's principles in setting tariffs and regulating imports. For instance, when a nation imposes a tariff or quota on imported products, it is to use guidelines established by GATT. If it does not follow the GATT principles, the offending nation may suffer economic or political sanctions imposed by other GATT members. Although absolute enforcement of international law is not possible except through war between nations, international trade law is to some extent enforceable because it is in the best economic and political interests of nations to comply with it. In essence, then, international trade law serves as a check upon the actions of governments that might otherwise severely and unnecessarily restrict the free flow of trade and commerce between nations. At the close of the Uruguay Round, the United States implemented the GATT 1994 agreement in the *Uruguay Round Agreements Act,* effective January 1, 1995.

## GATT and U.S. Law

GATT is not like most national laws. It does not provide individual rights and remedies to private parties. It cannot be used by private litigants to assert rights or claims for compensation in lawsuits against the U.S. government, nor to challenge the legality of a federal statute. For instance, in a recent federal court decision, a U.S. Court of Appeals ruled that "GATT does not trump domestic legislation." The *Uruguay Round Agreements Act* states that "No state law . . . may be declared invalid . . . on the ground that the provision or application is inconsistent with any of the Uruguay Round Agreements, except in an action brought by the United States for the purpose of declaring such law or application invalid."

The 1995 *Uruguay Round Agreements Act* states that "No provision of the Uruguay Round Agreements . . . that is inconsistent with any law of the United States shall have effect. Nothing in this Act shall be construed to amend or modify any law of the United States relating to the protection of human . . . life, the protection of the environment, or worker safety." If a private firm or industry in the United States believes that its rights under GATT are being violated by a foreign company or foreign government, then it may seek redress either with the appropriate federal administrative agency or before the courts *on the basis of a U.S. statute,* but not under GATT. Of course, it can also communicate its grievance to the U.S. government, which can at its discretion negotiate with the foreign government under GATT rules in an attempt to resolve the trade dispute—nation to nation.

## Scope and Coverage of GATT 1947

Before examining GATT's major principles, a reader needs to understand generally the scope and coverage of the GATT agreements. The rules of GATT 1947 applied only to trade in goods. Because most of the major trading nations of the world have been members, GATT has controlled more than 80 percent of the world's trade in goods. GATT 1947 was successful in reducing tariffs and nontariff barriers to trade worldwide. However, nations encountered many trade issues over which GATT had no responsibility. Trade in services, such as banking or insurance, was specifically excluded from GATT 1947. It also failed to regulate agricultural trade, an area of constant dispute between nations. Trade in textiles and apparel was also not covered because of the politically sensitive nature of these industries. (Trade in textiles and apparel has been regulated by other international agreements between textile producing and textile importing nations.) Because GATT 1947 only dealt with trade in goods, it did little or nothing to protect intellectual property rights, such as copyrights and trademarks. GATT 1947 also did not regulate the use of restrictions on foreign investment that interfered with the free movement of goods. GATT 1947 failed to provide adequate standardized rules for nations to deal with "unfair trade" problems. Finally, the dispute settlement process set up under GATT 1947, used to resolve trade conflicts between countries, was filled with loopholes and was often ineffective. Many of these deficiencies were remedied in GATT 1994.

## Scope and Coverage of GATT 1994

GATT 1994 is much broader in scope and coverage than the original 1947 agreement, and addresses many of the latter's limitations. The two most important agreements included in GATT

1994 are the *Final Act Embodying the Uruguay Round of Multilateral Trade Negotiations* and the *Agreement Establishing the World Trade Organization* (see Appendix). In addition to the original provisions of GATT 1947, GATT 1994 includes the following multilateral trade agreements on specific issues:

- General Agreement on Tariffs and Trade 1994
- Agreement on Agriculture
- Agreement on the Application of Sanitary and Phytosanitary Measures
- Agreement on Textiles and Clothing
- Agreement on Technical Barriers to Trade
- Agreement on Trade-Related Investment Measures
- Agreement on Implementation of Article VI (Dumping)
- Agreement on Implementation of Article VII (Customs Valuation)
- Agreement on Preshipment Inspection
- Agreement on Rules of Origin
- Agreement on Import Licensing Procedures
- Agreement on Subsidies and Countervailing Measures
- Agreement on Safeguards (Import Relief)
- General Agreement on Trade in Services
- Agreement on Trade-Related Aspects of Intellectual Property Rights
- Understanding on Rules and Procedures Governing the Settlement of Disputes
- Trade Policy Review Mechanism
- Understanding on Commitments in Financial Services
- Agreement on Government Procurement, and miscellaneous sectoral trade agreements

This chapter examines the basic principles of GATT trade and tariff law and the role of the World Trade Organization. Most of these principles are applicable to all of the agreements shown above. Later chapters deal with more specific GATT issues, such as those related to agricultural trade, trade in textiles, and trade in services.

## The World Trade Organization

As of January 1, 1995, the World Trade Organization (WTO) replaced the original GATT organization. It provides an umbrella organization that sets the rules by which nations regulate trade in manufactured goods, services (including banking, insurance, tourism, and telecommunications), intellectual property, textiles and clothing, and agricultural products. The role of the WTO is to facilitate international cooperation to open markets, provide a forum for future trade negotiations between members, and provide a forum for the settlement of trade disputes. The WTO will have a stature equal to that of the IMF or World Bank, and will cooperate with those agencies on economic matters. The WTO's membership includes those countries that previously belonged to GATT, and will eventually be open to other countries, if accepted by a two-thirds majority vote of the members. Possible new members in the future include China, Taiwan, and Russia.

*http://itl.irv.uit.no/trade_law/documents/ freetrade/wta-94/status/wto-status.html* Lists the members of the WTO.

## Organization of the WTO

The organization of the WTO is shown in Exhibit 10.1. The WTO is overseen by the *Ministerial Conference,* made up of high-ranking representatives from all WTO member countries. They plan to meet at least once every two years to direct the policies, activities, and future direction of the WTO. The Ministerial Conference appoints the WTO *Director-General* and specifies his or her duties. The work of the Director-General is supported by the WTO *Secretariat* staff. Beneath the Ministerial Conference is the *General Council,* made up of representatives of each nation and responsible for overall supervision of the WTO's activities. The General Council also oversees the work of the lower councils, which carry out the work of the WTO in specialized areas. When the WTO took over the GATT's headquarters in Geneva, Switzerland, the former GATT organization had 350 employees and a $70 million budget.

The *Trade Policy Review Body* periodically reviews the trade policies and practices of member countries for transparency and to assure that member nations adhere to the rules and commitments of GATT. The body is a policy body only and has no enforcement powers. The *Council for Trade in Goods* oversees the functioning and

**EXHIBIT 10.1** **Structure of the World Trade Organization**

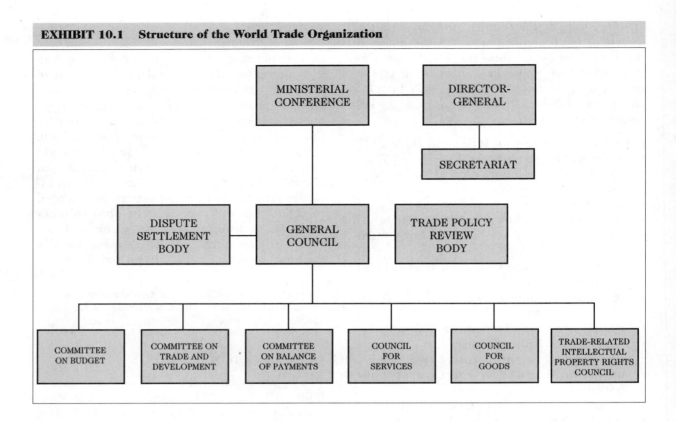

implementation of the multilateral trade agreements. The *Committee on Trade and Development* reviews the treatment received by least-developed countries under GATT, considers their special trade problems, and makes recommendations to the General Council for appropriate action.

Decision making by the WTO is by consensus. If the countries cannot agree by consensus, voting is by majority vote, with each member having one vote (each European Union country also has one vote). The Ministerial Conference and the General Council have the authority to adopt interpretations of the GATT agreements. For countries that experience extraordinary circumstances, the Conference may grant a temporary waiver of an obligation imposed under GATT by three-fourths vote of the members.

*http://www.wto.org*
*Takes you to the home page of the WTO.*

## GATT/WTO Dispute Settlement Procedures

GATT 1994 envisions that one nation will not take unilateral retaliatory action against another nation in a trade dispute, but that the parties will rely on GATT *dispute settlement procedures* to avert a trade war. GATT's dispute settlement procedures are a quasi-judicial process for resolving trade disputes when attempts by the countries involved to reach a settlement become deadlocked. This process is intended to resolve conflicts before "trade wars" erupt. For instance, if nation **A** imposes a "GATT illegal" quota on nation **B**'s products, then nation **B** may file a complaint with GATT. In the meantime, nation **B** is not supposed to unilaterally retaliate with quotas or tariffs on **A**'s products and, in fact, needs GATT approval to do so. Only a government can bring a GATT complaint against another government. Complaints are not filed by or against firms or individuals (although as a practical matter GATT cases are often brought by nations upon the instigation of private industry).

## WTO Dispute Settlement Procedures

Under GATT 1947, panel decisions were released only to the countries involved to give them another chance to resolve the issue. Panel decisions did not have the force of international or domestic law. Decisions did not acquire legal effect until they were adopted by the GATT Council of Ministers. Under the rules, valid through 1994, panel decisions were effective only if both sides in the dispute agreed to be bound. Either party could "block" or veto a panel's decision before it was sent to the Council. (Many nations chose not to block GATT panel decisions because they did not want to undermine a process for resolving disputes that they might want to use in the future. Furthermore, GATT/WTO panel decisions do carry the voice of world opinion and serve as an international conscience for determining which trade practices are acceptable and which are not.)

Under GATT 1994 the dispute settlement process has been strengthened and the deficiencies remedied. The WTO is given far more authority in handling trade disputes than the former GATT organization had, and individual countries can no longer block panel decisions from going into force. Among the most important changes are new procedures and timetables to assure prompt handling of disputes. The following provisions are expressed in the WTO *Understanding on Rules and Procedures Governing the Settlement of Disputes* known as the *Dispute Settlement Understanding* (DSU).

- Responsibility for dispute settlement now rests with the WTO's General Council, which oversees the work of the *Dispute Settlement Body.* The Dispute Settlement Body appoints panels, adopts panel decisions, and authorizes the withdrawal or suspension of concessions.
- A complaining party can request *consultations* to seek a solution. If no solution is found within 60 days, the complaining party may request that a panel hear the case. In urgent

cases, such as in cases involving perishable goods, members must enter into consultations within 10 days, and if they fail to reach agreement within 20 days thereafter, they may request that a panel be convened. The panel will consist of three to five individuals nominated by the Secretariat, but subject to rejection by a party for compelling reasons.

- Other member nations with a "substantial interest" in the case may make written submissions and an oral argument before the panel. More than one member nation may join in bringing a related complaint to a single panel established by the Dispute Settlement Body.
- A panel must make an *objective assessment* of the facts of the case and determine whether the terms of a GATT agreement have been violated. It may call on experts for advice on scientific and technical matters. All panel deliberations are confidential. The panel must submit a written report to the parties and to other members within six months (three months in urgent cases). Unless the parties file for an appeal to the *Appellate Body,* the panel's report will be adopted by the Dispute Settlement Body. However, the Dispute Settlement Body may vote by consensus not to accept the report. Thus, the offending nation in a dispute settlement case can no longer "block" the decision of the panel without a unanimous vote of all members.
- An *Appellate Body* of three people will hear appeals from a panel case. They may uphold, modify, or reverse a panel decision. People serving on the Appellate Body will be chosen by the Dispute Settlement Body on the basis of their expertise in law and international trade to serve for four-year terms. Other member nations with a substantial interest in the case may file written submissions and appear before the Appellate Body. Appeals are limited to issues of law covered in the panel report and legal interpretations considered by the panel. The appellate report is final unless the Dispute Settlement Body rejects it by consensus vote within 30 days.
- If the panel report finds that the offending party has violated a GATT agreement, the Dispute Settlement Body can recommend ways for the offending party to come into compliance. The offending party has 30 days in which

to state how it plans to comply with the panel's ruling. Compliance must be within a reasonable time. If no immediate solution is available, the offending party can voluntarily make compensatory adjustments to the complaining party as a temporary measure.

- If no settlement is reached, or if the trade violation is not removed, the panel may authorize the complaining party to impose a retaliatory trade sanction against the offending party by withdrawing or suspending a concession. The sanction should be imposed on the same type of goods imported from the offending nation, or on goods from the same type of industry or economic sector. Sanctions should be in an amount equal to the impact that the GATT violation had on the complaining party. Sanctions are to be temporary and in force only until the offending party's violation is removed.

The following WTO Appellate Body Report, *European Communities—Regime for the Importation, Sale and Distribution of Bananas,* involves a long-running trade dispute between the European Community, Latin America, and the United States. It addresses the issue of who may request a WTO panel in a trade dispute.

---

## BACKGROUND AND FACTS

### European Communities— Regime for the Importation, Sale and Distribution of Bananas

WT/DS27/AB/R
September 9, 1997
Report of the Appellate Body
World Trade Organization

In recent years the European Community (EC) has been the world's largest importer of bananas, accounting for 38 percent of world trade in bananas. In 1991, the EC imported over 3.65 million tons, two-thirds of which was grown in Latin America. Almost 19 percent came from developing countries that were once colonies of Britain, Spain, and France, located in Africa, the Caribbean, and the Pacific (known as ACP Countries). Growers in the ACP Countries could not compete with the highly efficient non-ACP producers, most of which are in Latin America. In order to encourage the import of ACP-grown bananas, and to aid in the development of ACP economies, the EC devised a host of tariff and non-tariff barriers aimed at non-ACP bananas. For example, a complex quota scheme was used permitting only a limited quantity of non-ACP bananas to be imported each year. While licenses to import ACP bananas were granted routinely, only importers who met strict requirements could receive licenses to import Latin American and other non-ACP bananas. While most ACP bananas entered duty free, other bananas had a very substantial tariff rate. Several Latin American countries requested consultations, claiming that the EC regulations violated GATT by discriminating against bananas grown in their countries. The United States joined with the Latin Amerian coun-

tries arguing that it too had a substantial interest in the issue. While the U.S. was not an exporter of bananas, the U.S. government felt that U.S. companies, such as Chiquita Brands and others, conducted a wholesale trade in bananas amounting to hundreds of millions of dollars a year and would lose market share because of the EC's actions. The EC maintained that the U.S. had no grounds for complaining about the EC regulations because it was not a producer and grower. A WTO panel was convened, and its decision was appealed to the WTO Appellate Body.

## REPORT OF THE APPELLATE BODY

The EC argues that the Panel infringed Article 3.2 of the Dispute Settlement Understanding (DSU) by finding that the United States has a right to advance claims under the GATT 1994. The EC asserts that, as a general principle, in any system of law, including international law, a claimant must normally have a legal right or interest in the claim it is pursuing. . . . The EC asserts that the United States has no actual or potential trade interest justifying its claim, since its banana production is minimal, it has never exported bananas, and this situation is unlikely to change due to the climatic and economic conditions in the United States. In

*(continued)*

*(continued)*

the view of the EC, the panel fails to explain how the United States has a potential trade interest in bananas, and production alone does not suffice for a potential trade interest. The EC also contends that the United States has no right protected by WTO law to shield its own internal market from the indirect effects of the EC banana regime. . . .

We agree with the Panel that no provision of the DSU contains any explicit requirement that a member must have a "legal interest" as a prerequisite for requesting a panel. We do not accept that the need for a "legal interest" is implied in the DSU or in any other provision of the WTO Agreement. . . . [We believe] that a member nation has broad discretion in deciding whether to bring a case against another member nation under the DSU. . . .

The participants in this appeal have referred to certain judgments of the International Court of Justice and the Permanent Court of International Justice relating to whether there is a requirement, in international law, of a legal interest to bring a case. We do not read any of these judgments as establishing a general rule that in all international litigation, a complaining party must have a "legal interest" in order to bring a case. Nor do these judgments deny the need to consider the question of standing under the dispute settlement provisions of any multilateral treaty, by referring to the terms of that treaty.

We are satisfied that the United States was justified in bringing its claims under the GATT 1994 in this case. The United States is a producer of bananas, and a potential export interest by the United States cannot be excluded. The internal market of the United States of bananas could be affected by the EC banana regime, in particular, by the effects of that regime on world supplies and world prices of bananas. We also agree with the Panel's statement that: " . . . with the increased interdependence of the global economy, . . . member nations have a greater stake in enforcing WTO rules than in the past since any deviation from the negotiated balance of rights and obligations is more likely than ever to affect them, directly or indirectly."

Accordingly, we believe that a member nation has broad discretion in deciding whether to bring a case against another member under the DSU. The language of Article XXIII:1 of the GATT 1994 and of the DSU suggests, furthermore, that a member is expected to be largely self-regulating in deciding whether any such action would be "fruitful."

**Decision.** The Appellate Body held that the United States could call for the convening of a WTO panel to question EC import barriers even though its exports were not directly affected.

## WTO Reports as Legal Precedent

The issue arises as to whether WTO reports carry precedential value for future panels as do the decisions of American common law courts. According to the language of GATT and recent WTO reports, the answer seems to be no. The Appellate Body, in *Japan—Taxes on Alcoholic Beverages* (1996) addressed the status of a report that is adopted by the Dispute Settlement Body, as follows: "We do not believe that the contracting parties [WTO member nations] in deciding to adopt a panel report, intended that their decision would constitute a definitive interpretation of the provisions of GATT 1947. Nor do we believe that this is contemplated under GATT 1994. . . . Adopted panel reports can play an important part of the GATT *acquis.* They are often considered by subsequent panels. They create legitimate expectations among WTO members, and, therefore should be taken into account

where they are relevant to any dispute. *However, they are not binding. . . .* " This statement is reaffirmed in the actual language of GATT 1994, which states that interpretations of the agreement may only be made by the Ministerial Conference and the General Council.

Certainly, all trade disputes are intertwined with politics. The following article, *WTO's Kodak Ruling Heightens Trade Tensions,* illustrates the political nature of trade disputes. In this 1997 case, a WTO panel determined that Japan had not unfairly deprived Kodak of access to its photographic products market. This case was one of the few disputes up to this time in which a WTO panel found against the U.S. Prior to this case, the U.S. had been successful in more than a dozen WTO disputes. As you read, compare the WTO process to the unilateral action taken by the United States against Japan in the automobile trade war, discussed at the beginning of this chapter.

# WTO's Kodak Ruling Heightens Trade Tensions

The World Trade Organization's resounding rejection of U.S. claims of Japanese protectionism in photographic film promises to heighten trade tensions and increase competitive pressures on Eastman Kodak Co. . . .

While the U.S. does have the right to challenge the decision, it could be awkward. The U.S. doesn't want to be seen as contradicting an organization it worked hard to create. Also, it doesn't want to turn up the heat too high on Japan while Tokyo is trying to deal with its economic problems. But the U.S. believes Japan can only deal with economic stagnation if it opens up its economy—exactly what it was calling for in its complaint.

The decision was also a setback for Kodak Chief Executive George Fisher, who has billed the case as critical not just for Kodak but for all U.S. industries seeking to break down alleged "internal barriers" to trade in Japan—such as the locked-up film-distribution system that Kodak portrayed in the WTO case.

Mr. Fisher called the decision "totally unacceptable" and called for the administration to develop a "concrete plan to open the Japanese market." . . .

Thomas H. Shay, a spokesman for Fuji's American subsidiary, praised the ruling as "a complete win before a worldwide, neutral umpire." . . .

Many trade experts, including some U.S. officials, had viewed the case as weak, partly because it relied on old evidence and attacked vertical distribution alliances common in many countries.

A three-member WTO panel agreed with them. The U.S., Kodak and Fuji—which have viewed the otherwise unreleased decision—said the panel rejected all 21 claims of Japanese government measures that allegedly violated multilateral trade agreements. Partly because of these measures, Kodak says none of the four main film distributors who control Japanese retail channels will buy large amounts of Kodak film.

The 21 claims were made in support of three main Kodak legal claims, the central one of which was that Japanese regulations and business practices had deprived Kodak of fair access to the market and therefore negated trade benefits granted to the U.S. in reduced tariffs over many years. But the WTO panel ruled that the Japanese regulations predated any lowered tariffs and therefore couldn't have negated them.

The decision is a preliminary one, but a reversal is seen as highly unlikely before the final decision in January. . . .

The somewhat technical nature of the film ruling allowed the WTO to sidestep the thorny issue of internal barriers and avoid what might have become and endless stream of disputes had it ruled in Kodak's favor. Prior to film, the U.S. had won outright victories or concessions in all 14 of the other cases it brought at the WTO. . . .

***Robert S. Greenberger, Laura Johannes, Ross Kerber, and Bhushan Bahree***
[Reporting for] *The Wall Street Journal*, December 8, 1997. Copyright © 1997 The Wall Street Journal.

Reprinted with permission.

## GATT 1994: Major Principles of Trade Law

In addition to member nations' commitments to consult with each other over trade differences and to resort to dispute settlement, GATT 1994 continues four basic principles of international trade law.

1. *Multilateral trade negotiations:* nations will meet periodically to reduce tariffs and nontariff barriers to trade.
2. *Nondiscrimination and unconditional most-favored-nation trade:* members will not give any import advantage or favor to products coming from one member over the goods of another member.

3. *National treatment:* members will not discriminate in favor of domestically produced goods and against imported goods, nor treat the two differently under their internal tax laws, regulations, and other national laws.
4. *Elimination of quotas and other nontariff barriers:* nations first "convert" their nontariff barriers to tariffs (through a process called *tariffication*), and then engage in negotiations to reduce the tariff rates.

In addition, GATT contains provisions to promote trade with developing nations and special rules allowing the establishment of free-trade areas and customs unions. Other special rules allow restrictions on imports when necessary to protect the public health and safety or to protect domestic firms from unfair trade practices or increased levels of imports that cause serious economic injury to domestic industries.

## Multilateral Trade Negotiations

Since 1947 the GATT organization has served to bring member nations together to negotiate tariff reductions and the opening of markets. Under the auspices of the GATT, the contracting parties have completed eight major *rounds*, or *multilateral negotiating sessions.*

1. Geneva, Switzerland, in 1947
2. Annecy, France, in 1948
3. Torquay, England, in 1950
4. Geneva, Switzerland, in 1956
5. *Dillon* Round, 1960–1961
6. *Kennedy* Round, 1964–1967
7. *Tokyo* Round, 1973–1979
8. *Uruguay* Round, 1986–1994

## Tariff Concessions, Bound Rates, and Tariff Schedules

Article II of GATT calls for member nations to cooperate in lowering tariffs through negotiations. In a *tariff concession,* one country promises not to levy a tariff on a given product at a level higher than agreed upon. In essence, each country makes a concession to the products of the other country and receives reciprocal treatment. This process does not set the same tariff rate on a particular product for every nation, but determines a tariff rate that is said to be *bound*. The rates are arrived at through compromise, and these concessions are recorded in *tariff schedules,* which are detailed product-by-product listings of all tariff obligations for a particular nation. (Tariff schedules for the United States are found in the *Harmonized Tariff Schedule of the United States.*) GATT calls for its members to negotiate reciprocal reductions in tariffs, either on a product-by-product basis or across the board.

The following case, *European Economic Community—Import Regime for Bananas,* Part II, illustrates the importance of countries honoring their tariff rates granted by concession to foreign countries. As the case shows, government and business planners alike rely on access to foreign markets. If an importing nation unexpectedly raises its tariff rate, contrary to its concession, this would cause market disruption and injury to foreign exporters. The GATT Panel ruled that the change in EC tariff schedules had "nullified and impaired" the rights of foreign banana exporters who should have been able to rely on the existing tariff structure.

---

BACKGROUND AND FACTS
This case was decided in 1995 by a GATT Dispute Settlement Panel prior to GATT 1994 and the creation of the WTO. It resulted from the same "Banana Trade Wars" as a case appearing earlier in this chapter. Since 1963 the EEC had negotiated tariff rates with the

*European Economic Community (EEC)— Import Regime for Bananas (Part II)*
*34 I.L.M177 (1995)*
*Report of the GATT Dispute Settlement Panel (not adopted by the Council)*

developing countries that export bananas, and these concessions were bound in the tariff schedules at 20 percent *ad valorem*. In 1993 the EEC took over banana import regulation from the individual countries. The EEC set up uniform rules on quality,

*(continued)*

*(continued)*

marketing standards, and tariffs. Under the EEC regime the tariff rates on bananas from the Latin American countries were increased between 20 and 180 percent. A complex licensing scheme was also set up to limit foreign banana traders (e.g. Chiquita, Dole, and DelMonte) access to sell in the EEC. The Latin American countries claimed that the regulations impaired their Article II tariff concessions, violated Article I MFN principles and other GATT provisions.

REPORT OF THE PANEL

*Article II—Schedules of Concessions:* [Central and South American] banana producers had assessed their competitive position on the basis of the bound tariff level. They had made strategic decisions and investments on that basis; they had cultivated substantially more land specifically for this export trade; and they had pursued marketing ties with European importers. The new tariff quota undermined the legitimate expectations upon which these actions were based and severely disrupted the trade conditions upon which the these producers had relied, regardless of the actual protective effect of the new regime.

The Panel noted that Article II required that each contracting party "accord to the commerce of the other contracting parties treatment no less favourable than that provided for in the . . . *Schedule of Concessions.*" The Panel then considered whether the introduction of a specific tariff for bananas in place of the *ad valorem* tariff provided for in its *Schedule* constituted "treatment no less favourable" in terms of Article II. . . . The Panel

consequently found that the new specific tariffs led to the levying of a duty on imports of bananas whose *ad valorem* equivalent was, either actually or potentially, higher than 20 percent *ad valorem*. . . .

The Contracting Parties had consistently found that a change from a bound specific to an *ad valorem* rate was a modification of the concession. A working party examining a proposal by Turkey to modify its tariff structure from specific to *ad valorem* had stated: "The obligations of contracting parties are established by the rates of duty appearing in the schedules and any change in the rate such as a change from a specific to an *ad valorem* duty could in some circumstances adversely affect the value of the concessions to other contracting parties. Consequently, any conversion of specific into *ad valorem* rates of duty can be made only under some procedure for the modification of concessions." . . .

The Panel found therefore that the specific tariffs applied by the EEC on imports of bananas since 1 July 1993 accord treatment to imports of bananas less favourable than that provided for in the EEC's *Schedule of Concessions* and were, therefore, inconsistent with the EEC's obligations under Article II:1. . . .

**Decision.** The panel held that the EEC had deprived (also called "nullified and impaired") the complaining Latin American countries of the benefits to which they were entitled under the bound tariff schedules. However, the EEC "blocked" the decision from going to the GATT council, as it could do under the GATT 1947, and the "banana wars" continued.

## Tariffication

*Tariffication* refers to the process by which quotas, licensing schemes, and other nontariff barriers to trade are "converted" to tariffs. Tariff rates can then be reduced through negotiation and the global economic environment for trade improved. For example, under GATT 1994 quotas on agricultural products will be converted to tariffs and gradually reduced. Tariffication has been a GATT policy since 1947.

**The Kennedy Round.** In the early rounds, countries negotiated on a product-by-product basis by simply presenting lists of tariff reductions

that they desired from other countries, who submitted requests for concessions that they wanted in return. These rounds resulted in lowering *ad valorem* tariffs from roughly 40 percent in 1945 to approximately 20 percent in 1961. The *Kennedy Round,* which took place from 1964 to 1967, resulted in even larger across-the-board tariff cuts, particularly in manufactured goods, averaging nearly 40 percent reductions and covering $40 billion in trade. More than 60 nations participated in the Kennedy Round. During this period, many developing countries joined GATT.

**The Tokyo Round.** By the 1970s, GATT's efforts had proven so successful that tariffs ceased to be the world's greatest barrier to trade in goods. Indeed, without GATT, decades of bilateral negotiations may have been necessary to achieve the reductions that multilateral negotiations reached within a few years. In the *Tokyo Round* more than 100 participating nations agreed to tariff cuts averaging 34 percent and covering $300 billion in trade, which effectively lowered the average level of tariffs to about five percent. In addition, the parties established a number of GATT *codes* that attempted to remove nontariff barriers. These codes have addressed issues such as subsidies, technical barriers to trade, government procurement rules, customs valuation, and dumping (discussed in Chapter Eleven).

### The Uruguay Round: Market Access Provisions

The *Uruguay Round* negotiations lasted from 1986 to 1994 and resulted in GATT 1994. Its *market access provisions* are expected to add trillions of dollars to the world's economy in the years to come. The Clinton Administration estimated that it will add at least $100 billion to $200 billion to the U.S. gross domestic product annually. It is expected to increase total U.S. employment, at a minimum, by hundreds of thousands of jobs and increase U.S. labor productivity and wages (United States Trade Representative, Office of Chief Economist, January 31, 1994). The market access negotiations resulted in worldwide tariff cuts averaging 35 to 40 percent on merchandise, farm products, and industrial goods.

Some products have much greater tariff reductions, including 50 to 100 percent on electronic items such as semiconductors and computers. In addition to tariff cuts, tariffs have been *bound,* or capped, at their rate effective at the time of the agreement. A country that raises a bound tariff will have violated GATT and would have to withdraw the increase or reach agreement with the affected countries to lower tariffs on some other product.

**Zero-for-Zero Tariff Elimination.** During the Uruguay Round, the United States adopted a *zero-for-zero* tariff reduction policy. U.S. negotiators sought reciprocal tariff elimination in key industry sectors. The agreement eliminates tariffs in ten product areas over time (averaging five

years): agricultural equipment, medical equipment, construction equipment, beer, distilled spirits, chemicals, furniture, paper, and printed matter; tariffs on pharmaceuticals and toys were eliminated on January 1, 1995. Each nation's tariff schedules deposited with the WTO reflect the new rates. Current U.S. legislation grants the president the authority to negotiate additional market access agreements in future WTO negotiations on a zero-for-zero basis.

## Nondiscrimination, Most-Favored-Nation Trade, and National Treatment

The principle of *nondiscrimination* has long been a guiding concept of international economic relations and of trade liberalization. Defined most broadly, nondiscrimination means that in every aspect of economic life, all nations should be treated equally and without discrimination. For example, if a nation taxes wire transfers of money sent to a recipient in a foreign country, then it should tax similar transfers equally, regardless of what country will receive the money. In terms of international trade, nondiscrimination means that the products of all nations should be treated equally and without discrimination by importing and exporting nations. Simply put, nations should not "play favorites" with each others' products. Although this ideal has rarely, if ever, been achieved, the concept of nondiscrimination runs throughout GATT law. It is most evident in the following areas: (1) the concept of *most-favored-nation trade*, that favorable tariff treatment on goods imported from one country shall be extended to similar goods from all other countries; (2) the concept of *national treatment,* that an importing country shall treat imported goods the same as its own domestic goods for purposes of all internal (domestic) laws, regulations, and taxes; and (3) that while GATT calls for countries to not regulate trade with quotas or other quantitative restrictions on imports, if a country does use them, they must be employed without discrimination and without regard to the country of origin of the goods.

### Most-Favored-Nation Trade

Nondiscrimination is the principle behind *unconditional most-favored-nation* (MFN) trade.

MFN principles require that any trade advantage or privilege granted by one GATT member to the goods of another member should be granted to all. Any tariff, tax, or other restriction on imports should be applied equally to products, without regard to origination. Because the products of all MFN countries are treated equally, products shipped from both economically powerful countries and small countries will be treated the same in the foreign market. While MFN trade has been in use for at least 300 years, it is now a basic principle of GATT law, found in Article I:

With respect to customs duties and charges of any kind imposed on or in connection with importation or exportation . . . and with respect to the method of levying such duties and charges, and with respect to all rules and formalities in connection with importation and exportation . . . Any advantage, favour, privilege, or immunity granted by any other member to any product originating in or destined for any other country shall be accorded immediately and unconditionally to the like product originating in or destined for the territories of all other members.

*At http://itl.irv.uit.no/trade_law/nav/ conventions.html#1940's*
Select GATT and scroll down to Article I regarding MFN status.

**Unconditional MFN Trade.** *Unconditional* MFN trade requires that when a nation extends some privilege or right to one of its trading partners, such as a reduced tariff rate, that privilege *automatically* becomes applicable to all other trading partners. So, if nation **A** negotiates a reduced tariff rate on a particular product imported from nation **B,** that new rate becomes applicable to like products imported from MFN nation **C** and from *all* nations that have MFN status with the importing country. Unconditional treatment is granted merely because nation **C**'s product is "entitled" to be treated equally and without discrimination, and does not require further concessions to be in effect.

*Unconditional* MFN trade is different from conditional MFN trade. *Conditional* treatment requires that a trading partner give something in return for a tariff concession. Conditional MFN trade was used by the United States in its first trade pact made in 1778 with France and through the end of World War I. Then the United States found out that conditional MFN trade allowed other countries to discriminate against U.S. exports, and the practice was phased out. MFN trade today is unconditional.

MFN treatment for imported goods greatly influences trade flows among nations. If a country's products do not qualify for MFN tariff rates in an importing nation, then it may not be economically practical to import those products at all. For example, assume that a company desires to import products into nation **A** that originated in nation **B.** If nation **B**'s goods do not qualify for MFN tariff treatment in nation **A,** then the transaction may not be profitable because of the high tariff rates. For instance, an MFN rate on a particular product might typically be 5 percent of the value of the import. Without MFN treatment, however, the rate on the same goods might be 90 percent on the value of the import. The importer may actually have to find substitute products in some other country that is an MFN trading partner of nation **A.**

Most people understand MFN trade as special treatment given to products imported from a nation's best trading partners. Actually, it is the norm. Europe, Japan, and most developed countries of the world are MFN trading partners with the United States. However, products of some countries can receive *less favorable than* MFN treatment and others can receive *more favorable than* MFN treatment. Some developing countries' products can be imported into a developed country at tariff rates *even lower* than the MFN rate—such as when the United States or European Union is trying to encourage imports from poorer developing countries. Similarly, some countries' products come into the U.S. at a rate higher than the MFN rate—such as when the United States is restricting trade with another country for political reasons.

Each nation's law determines the qualifications for granting MFN status to a trading partner, as long as those laws comply with GATT's general provisions. However, membership in GATT does not automatically guarantee MFN treatment. For example, the United States denied MFN treatment to imports of Polish goods in the period from

1982 to 1987—because of the Polish communist government's tough stand against economic and political reform—even though Poland was a GATT member. Also, a trading partner that is not a GATT member may still be granted MFN status. China and Russia are MFN trading partners of the United States, although they have not yet been admitted to GATT at the time of this writing.

## MFN and Human Rights

The use of unconditional MFN tariff treatment is subject to several exceptions. U.S. laws authorize the president to deny MFN status to any nation on the basis of national security, foreign policy, or a foreign government's denial of fundamental human rights to its citizens. The *Jackson-Vanik Amendment* to the *Trade Act of 1974* (Title IV) is a statute that grew out of the Cold War. It prohibits the granting of MFN status to any nation whose government unreasonably restricts the right of its citizens to emigrate. The statute was primarily aimed at the former Soviet Union and other communist countries. It requires the president to review the human rights records of foreign countries and to make reports to Congress annually. The president may grant *temporary* MFN status only if the country improves its human rights record. Since 1989, as communism collapsed and political reform occurred, the president has granted temporary MFN status to more countries. The United States has granted MFN status to Russia and most of the other newly independent states. Permanent MFN status can be granted by Congress (exempting them from annual review by the president).

## MFN and China

In recent years, an important political debate in the United States has surrounded the issue of the MFN status of the People's Republic of China. Although China has been ruled by a communist government for almost 50 years, temporary MFN status was granted to China by the United States in 1980. More than one-third of China's exports are to the United States. (In 1996 the United States had an annual trade deficit with China of $39.5 billion.) As an MFN trading partner, China's products enter the United States with an average 3 percent import tariff. Because China's status is temporary, it must be renewed by the president every year. Congress can vote to override the president's decision with a two-thirds vote, although it has not done so. If MFN status were to be revoked, the average import duty on Chinese goods would rise to over 70 percent.

This favorable trading status was called into question in 1989 when the Chinese government used military force to stop public demonstrations against the government at Tiananmen Square (during which many students were arrested as political prisoners or killed). People who are opposed to continuing MFN status for China make the following political arguments: China's human rights record has deteriorated; China does not allow the free emigration of its citizens; China does not treat prisoners humanely; China has allowed violations of U.S.-owned patents, copyrights, and trademarks; China has shipped textile and apparel products to the United States in violation of U.S. quotas by fraudulently labeling them as having been made in a different country; China has exported products to the United States that have been made in brutal slave labor camps; and considerable evidence indicates China has been responsible for exporting nuclear technology and Scud missiles to the Middle East.

Arguments for extending permanent MFN status to China are becoming more popular in the United States. First, China has made many economic and political reforms in recent years. It has strengthened its intellectual property laws, reformed its tax laws, opened its borders to foreign direct investment, reformed its currency laws, released political prisoners, and more. Other arguments are that trade is ineffective as a political weapon. Depriving China—or any nondemocratic country—of MFN status will not effectively change its domestic policies. Another argument is that by closing the doors to trade with China, the United States loses its ability to influence Chinese domestic political policies. Moreover, it would stifle economic development in China and make it harder for China to move from a socialist economy to a free market economy. If the United States denies MFN status to China, or to any other single country on the basis of its human rights record, that country will still be able to trade with other countries in

Europe or Asia. The argument, then, is that MFN tariff treatment by the United States should be used only as a trade policy and not as a diplomatic tool to gain political leverage over the Chinese government.

Despite the controversy, and despite considerable debate in the U.S. Congress, the United States has continued temporary MFN status for China. In 1994 President Clinton announced that renewal of MFN status for China would be "virtually automatic," a pragmatic recognition that trade with China—with 1.2 billion people and the largest potential market in the world—would not be tied to political events. Obviously, MFN status is a hot political issue. Therefore, the cautious importer will always be aware of the latest political developments that might threaten MFN treatment of foreign goods.

China was an original party to GATT 1947, but it withdrew in 1950 as a result of the communist takeover of mainland China. China reapplied for GATT membership in the 1980s and 1990s, but has been denied. As of 1997, China had not been admitted to the WTO. In addition to the arguments already discussed, critics argue that despite its reforms, China is still a socialist country and its economic policies are not compatible with GATT's free market principles. Critics point out that China must reduce state controls over its economy, including eliminating price controls, licensing schemes, and subsidies to industries, to name a few. Nevertheless, admission to the WTO seems likely in the not-to-distant future.

**Other MFN Exceptions.** The GATT Agreement provides for trade relationships that may be even more favorable than MFN treatment. These include free-trade areas (e.g., the North American Free Trade Agreement) and common markets (e.g., the European Union). GATT also provides for special trade "preferences" for developing countries under which their products qualify for better-than-MFN treatment.

## National Treatment

The *national treatment* provisions of GATT are intended to ensure that imported products will not be subjected to discriminatory treatment under the laws of the importing nation. Under Article III, imported products must not be regulated, taxed, or otherwise treated differently from domestic goods once they enter a nation's stream of commerce. GATT Article III:2 provides that imports shall not be subject to internal taxes or charges in excess of those applied to like domestic products.

### Article III

1. The contracting parties recognize that internal taxes and other internal charges, and laws, regulations and requirements affecting the internal sale, offering for sale, purchase, transportation, distribution or use of products, and internal quantitative regulations requiring the mixture, processing or use of products in specified amounts or proportions, should not be applied to imported or domestic products so as to afford protection to domestic production.

2. The products of the territory of any contracting party imported into the territory of any other contracting party shall not be subject, directly or indirectly, to internal taxes or other internal charges of any kind in excess of those applied, directly or indirectly, to *like domestic products.* Moreover, no contracting party shall otherwise apply internal taxes or other internal charges to imported or domestic products in a manner contrary to the principles set forth in paragraph 1.

### *Ad* Article III (Annex) to Paragraph 2

A tax conforming to the requirements of the first sentence of paragraph 2 would be considered to be inconsistent with the provisions of the second sentence only in cases where competition was involved between, on the one hand, the taxed product and, on the other hand, a *directly competitive or substitutable product* which was not similarly taxed.

The even broader provisions of Article III:4 state that imported products shall be given "treatment no less favourable than that accorded to like products of national origin in respect of all laws, regulations, and requirements affecting their internal sale." This provision has been interpreted as prohibiting discrimination against imports resulting from a wide range of nontariff barriers to trade, including discriminatory customs procedures, government procurement policies, and product standards. In the following case, *Japan—Taxes on Alcoholic Beverages,* the

WTO Appellate Body undertook a thorough analysis of Japan's Liquor Tax Law and found that the Japanese tax violated GATT Article III. As you read, look not only for its interpretation of national treatment, but also look at the Appellate Body's reflections on GATT as international law.

### Japan—Taxes on Alcoholic Beverages
WT/DS11/AB/R
Report of the Appellate Body
World Trade Organization
October 4, 1996

### BACKGROUND AND FACTS

The Japanese Liquor Tax Law, or *Shuzeiho,* taxes liquors sold in Japan based on the type of beverage. There are ten categories of beverage (the categories are *sake, sake* compound, *shochu, mirin,* beer, wine, whiskey/brandy, spirits, liqueurs, and miscellaneous. *Shochu* is distilled from potatoes, buckwheat or other grains. *Shochu* and vodka share many characteristics. However, vodka and other imported liquors fall in categories with a tax rate that is seven or eight times higher than the category for *shochu.* Foreign spirits account for only 8 percent of the Japanese market, whereas they account for almost 50 percent of the market in other industrialized countries. The U.S., the European Union and Canada called for consultations before the WTO. The panel held that the Japanese tax law violated GATT, and Japan appealed to the Appellate Body.

### REPORT OF THE APPELLATE BODY

The WTO Agreement is a treaty—the international equivalent of a contract. It is self-evident that in an exercise of their sovereignty, and in pursuit of their own respective national interests, the Members of the WTO have made a bargain. In exchange for the benefits they expect to derive as Members of the WTO, they have agreed to exercise their sovereignty according to the commitments they have made in the WTO Agreement. One of those commitments is Article III of the GATT 1994, which is entitled *National Treatment on Internal Taxation and Regulation.*

The broad and fundamental purpose of Article III is to avoid protectionism in the application of internal tax and regulatory measures. More specifically, the purpose of Article III is to ensure that internal measures not be applied to imported or domestic products so as to afford protection to domestic production. Toward this end, Article III obliges Members of the WTO to provide equality of competitive conditions for imported products in relation to domestic products. "[T]he intention of the drafters of the Agreement was clearly to treat the imported products in the same way as the like domestic products once they had been cleared through customs. Otherwise indirect protection could be given. Moreover, it is irrelevant that "the trade effects" of the tax differential between imported and domestic products, as reflected in the volumes of imports, are insignificant or even non-existent; Article III protects expectations not of any particular trade volume but rather of the equal competitive relationship between imported and domestic products. Members of the WTO are free to pursue their own domestic goals through internal taxation or regulation so long as they do not do so in a way that violates Article III or any of the other commitments they have made in the WTO Agreement. . . .

[I]f imported products are taxed in excess of like domestic products, then that tax measure is inconsistent with Article III. . . . [We must determine first] whether the taxed imported and domestic products are "like" and, second, whether the taxes applied to the imported products are "in excess of" those applied to the like domestic products. If the imported and domestic products are "like products," and if the taxes applied to the imported products are "in excess of" those applied to the like domestic products, then the measure is inconsistent with Article III:2.

We agree with the Panel also that the definition of "like products" in Article III:2 should be construed narrowly. How narrowly is a matter that should be determined separately for each tax measure in each case. [A 1970 GATT Report] set out the basic approach for interpreting "like or similar products":

> . . . [T]he interpretation of the term should be examined on a case-by-case basis. This would allow a fair assessment in each case of the different elements that constitute a "similar" product. Some criteria were suggested for determining, on a case-by-case basis, whether a product is "similar": the product's end-users in a given market; consumers' tastes and habits, which change from country to country; the product's properties, nature and quality.

*(continued)*

*(continued)*

The concept of "likeness" is a relative one that evokes the image of an accordion. The accordion of "likeness" stretches and squeezes in different places as different provisions of the WTO Agreement are applied. [The definition of "likeness" must be narrowly interpreted]. The Panel determined in this case that *shochu* and vodka are "like products."

A uniform tariff classification of products can be relevant in determining what are "like products." Tariff classification has been used as a criterion for determining "like products" in several previous adopted panel reports. . . . There are risks in using tariff bindings that are too broad as a measure of product "likeness." . . . It is true that there are numerous tariff bindings which are in fact extremely precise with regard to product description and which, therefore, can provide significant guidance as to the identification of "like products." Clearly enough, these determinations need to be made on a case-by-case basis. However, tariff bindings that include a wide range of products are not a reliable criterion for determining or confirming product "likeness" under Article III:2.

The only remaining issue under the first sentence of Article III:2 is whether the taxes on imported products are "in excess of" those on like domestic products. If so, then the Member that has imposed the tax is not in compliance with Article III. Even the smallest amount of "excess" is too much. The prohibition of discriminatory taxes in Article III is not conditional on a "trade effects test" nor is it qualified by a *de minimis* standard.

If imported and domestic products are not "like products" . . . those same products may well be among the broader category of "directly competitive or substitutable products" that fall within the domain of the second sentence of Article III:2. How much broader that category of "directly competitive or substitutable products" may be in any given case

is a matter for the panel to determine based on all the relevant facts in that case. In this case, the Panel emphasized the need to look not only at such matters as physical characteristics, common end-uses, and tariff classifications, but also at the "market place." This seems appropriate. The GATT 1994 is a commercial agreement, and the WTO is concerned, after all, with markets. It does not seem inappropriate to look at competition in the relevant markets as one among a number of means of identifying the broader category of products that might be described as "directly competitive or substitutable." Nor does it seem inappropriate to examine elasticity of substitution as one means of examining those relevant markets. In the Panel's view, the decisive criterion in order to determine whether two products are directly competitive or substitutable is whether they have common end-uses, *inter alia,* as shown by elasticity of substitution. We agree.

Our interpretation of Article III is faithful to the "customary rules of interpretation of public international law." WTO rules are reliable, comprehensible and enforceable. WTO rules are not so rigid or so inflexible as not to leave room for reasoned judgements in confronting the endless and ever changing ebb and flow of real facts in real cases in the real world. They will serve the multilateral trading system best if they are interpreted with that in mind. In that way, we will achieve the "security and predictability" sought for the multilateral trading system by the Members of the WTO through the establishment of the dispute settlement system.

**Decision.**  The Japanese Liquor Tax Law violated the national treatment provisions of GATT Article III. *Shochu* is a "like product" and is "directly competitive and substitutable" with other imported spirits. The imported spirits were taxed higher than the *Shochu.* The decision of the panel was upheld and Japan was request to bring its tax law into compliance with GATT.

**Customs User Fees and Nondiscrimination.** Although discriminatory charges on imported goods are prohibited, charges imposed upon the *movement* of goods are generally permitted. GATT Article VIII permits fees to be imposed on imports approximately equal to the cost of services rendered to the importer. For example, user fees imposed on the use of port and harbor facilities or fees for inspecting imported products are permitted if they are reasonable and based on ac-

tual costs. In 1986, the United States instituted a user fee of 0.17 percent on imports of merchandise. A GATT panel investigation determined that it was in excess of the actual costs of operation and declared it illegal. The U.S. Congress responded with a proposal to place a per shipment dollar limit on the fee, thereby excluding from coverage the costs of processing air passengers, export controls, and the indirect costs of conducting international affairs.

# GATT and the Elimination of Quotas

The GATT Agreement permits the use of tariffs as the acceptable method of regulating imports, but not quotas or other quantitative restrictions. Since 1947 the agreement has called for countries to give up using quotas. Of course, many countries still utilize them—because they are a sure and certain way of keeping out foreign-made goods. The GATT prohibition of quotas is found in Article XI:

No prohibitions or restrictions other than duties, taxes, or other charges, whether made effective through quotas, import or export licenses, or other measures, shall be instituted . . . on the importation of any product . . . or on the exportation or sale for export of any product.

The use of quotas, even where they are permitted by GATT, is subject to the principle of nondiscrimination. GATT Article XIII states that an importing nation may not impose any quantitative restriction on a product unless it imposes the same restriction on all like or similar products coming from all other WTO member nations.

Despite the prohibition on the use of quotas, countries still do use them for many economic and political reasons. Quotas have been used to protect essential industries from foreign competition and to implement national economic policies. They are used by virtually all countries, including (although to a lesser extent) the United States. GATT permits the use of quotas to relieve food shortages and to restrict the import of agricultural and fishery products subject to governmental price support mechanisms. Quotas are also widely used to regulate world trade in textiles and apparel (see Exhibit 10.2). Also, quotas are used by importing countries facing severe balance-of-payments deficits in order to temporarily preserve needed foreign exchange.

---

**EXHIBIT 10.2   Trade in Textiles Strictly Enforced Through Rigid Quota and Licensing Scheme**

**QUOTA WATCH**

*Current Textile and Apparel Quotas:*
Average recent utilization rate indicates full quota utilization within four weeks from May 30, 1995.

| Country | Category | Description | Percent Fill |
|---|---|---|---|
| China . . . . . | 336 | Cotton Dresses | 97.98 |
| China . . . . . | 352 | Cotton Underwear | 93.06 |
| Egypt . . . . . | 448 | Wool Trousers, Breeches & Shorts, Women's and Girls' Shorts | 82.24 |
| U.A.E. . . . . . | 336/636 | Cotton and Man-Made Fiber Dresses | 96.10 |

**Note:** The above list was compiled using U.S. Customs Service data. Potential adjustments to quotas or charges have not been factored into the analysis.

*Fully Utilized Quotas*
*As of May 30, 1995*

| Country | Category | Description |
|---|---|---|
| China . . . . . | 362 | Cotton Bedspreads & Quilts |
| Kuwait . . . . | 361 | Cotton Sheets |
| U.A.E. . . . . . | 315 | Cotton Fabric, Printcloth |
| U.A.E. . . . . . | 361 | Cotton Sheets |
| U.A.E. . . . . . | 369 O | Cotton Other than Shop Towels |
| U.A.E. . . . . . | 369 S | Cotton Shop Towels |

**Note:** The above list was compiled using U.S. Customs Service data. Potential adjustments to quotas or charges may allow for reopening of quotas.
© *The Journal of Commerce.* Reprinted by permission (May 31, 1995).

SOURCE:   International Development Systems Inc., Washington.

## Balance-of-Payments Exception to GATT

A nation requires a ready reserve of foreign currency so that it (and its firms) may fulfill its international contracts and meet other legal obligations. When its payments of foreign exchange exceed receipts, a balance-of-payments deficit can arise. For a nation like the United States, whose currency is widely accepted, this situation is not usually a problem. For many other countries, particularly developing countries, it can be a major crisis. A nation might deal with the crisis by restricting imports through the use of quotas or surcharges. The resulting corrective action can have a dramatic impact on firms. Because of the impact on business, businesspeople need to understand the legal framework by which nations are permitted to take corrective action.

Despite GATT's prohibition of quotas, a nation may impose quotas on imported goods under Article XII in order to "safeguard its external financial position and its balance of payments . . . necessary to forestall the imminent threat of, or to stop, a serious decline in its monetary reserves." As the following GATT panel report, *Republic of Korea—Restrictions on Imports of Beef*, shows, the restrictions are supposed to be temporary and gradually eliminated as economic conditions improve.

---

### Republic of Korea— Restrictions on Imports of Beef
I.E.L. I-B-49 (1989)
*Report of the GATT Dispute Settlement Panel*

BACKGROUND AND FACTS

Since 1967 Korea maintained quotas and other restriction on imports of beef and 358 other products. In 1979 the tariff on beef was lowered. As beef imports rose, prices fell on the Korean domestic market. To force prices higher, Korean beef farmers pressured the government to reduce imports. Korea instituted strict controls over beef imports, including quotas and licensing requirements supervised by a state monopoly board. From 1985 to 1988 no imports of beef took place, although Korea partially reopened its market in 1988. At a meeting of the GATT Balance-of-Payments Committee, Korea maintained that it was instituting the quotas to prevent an outflow of foreign exchange, due to a balance-of-payments emergency pursuant to GATT Article XI. The committee disagreed and found that Korea had a continuing favorable economic situation, with 12 percent growth. Korea's current account for 1988 showed a reserve U.S. currency of $12 billion. After negotiations to reach a settlement broke down, the United States requested the GATT Council to establish a panel.

REPORT OF THE PANEL SUBMITTED TO THE PARTIES ON 25 APRIL 1989 AND ADOPTED 7 NOVEMBER 1989

The United States argued that the quotas, import bans, state-trading monopoly and other restrictions maintained by the Government of Korea were inconsistent with Articles II, X, XI and XIII, and nullified or impaired benefits accruing to the United States within the meaning of Article XXIII of GATT. . . .

The United States contended that the import restrictions on beef imposed for balance-of-payments reasons were not justified because Korea no longer had balance-of-payments problems. The Panel noted that Korea had maintained import restrictions on beef on balance-of-payments grounds since 1967. The Panel noted the condition in paragraph 9 of Article XVIII that "import restrictions instituted, maintained or intensified shall not exceed those necessary: (a) to forestall the threat of, or to stop, a serious decline in its monetary reserves, or (b) in the case of a contracting party with inadequate monetary reserves, to achieve a reasonable rate of increase in its reserves." The Panel noted further that paragraph 11 required the progressive relaxation of such restrictions "as conditions improve" and their elimination "when conditions no longer justify such maintenance."

The Panel noted that all available information, including figures published by the Korean authorities and advice provided to it in February 1989 by the International Monetary Fund, had shown that the reserve holdings of Korea had increased in 1988, that Korea's balance-of-payments situation had continued to improve at a good pace

*(continued)*

*(continued)*

since the November 1987 consultations, and that the current economic indicators of Korea were very favourable. According to information provided to the Panel by the International Monetary Fund, the Korean gross official reserves had increased by 9 billion dollars to 12 billion dollars (equivalent to three months of imports) by end 1988. The Panel concluded that in the light of the continued improvement of the Korean balance-of-payments situation, and having regard to the provisions of Article XVIII:11, there was a need for the prompt establishment of a timetable for the phasing-out of Korea's balance-of-payments restrictions on beef, as called for by the Contracting Parties in adopting the 1987 Balance-of-Payments Committee report.

In the light of the findings above, the Panel suggests that the Contracting Parties recommended that: (a) Korea eliminate or otherwise bring into conformity with the provisions of the GATT agreement the import measures on beef introduced in 1984/85 and amended in 1988; and, (b) Korea hold consultations with the United States and other interested contracting parties to work out a timetable for the removal of import restrictions on beef justified since 1967 by Korea for balance-of-payments reasons and report on the result of such consultations within a period of three months following the adoption of the Panel report by the Council.

**Decision.** The balance-of-payments exception to GATT, permitting the use of quotas on a temporary basis in emergency economic circumstances, could no longer be justified. The Panel recommended that Korea remove the restrictions and comply with its GATT obligations.

Reproduced with permission from *International Economic Law Documents.* © The American Society of International Law.

In response to the problems illustrated in the Korean beef case, GATT 1994 has instituted new requirements for using the balance-of-payments exception. A member must use the least restrictive mechanism possible for correcting the problem, preferably a price-based measures, such as a surcharge or tariff increase, rather than pure quantitative limitations. Justification for the measures must be given to the *Balance-of-Payments Committee* of the World Trade Organization, and the action is subject to WTO surveillance and periodic review. The action may not exceed what is necessary to correct the problem. The restrictions must be transparent and the member must publicly announce its time schedules for removing them. The new regulations will have the greatest impact on companies exporting to India, Egypt, Pakistan, and Korea.

## Chapter Summary

The General Agreement on Tariffs and Trade has provided a framework for the international trading system since the close of World War II by establishing the principles of international trade law upon which national trade laws are based.

GATT prevented reactionary forces from drawing the world back into the isolationism and protectionism of the 1930s. GATT's multilateral trade negotiations have resulted in tariff concessions and a worldwide lowering of duties. Today, GATT has succeeded in reducing tariffs to levels that no longer act as a barrier threatening world trade. GATT's trade liberalization rules have also opened markets for foreign goods by reducing nontariff barriers to trade.

The Uruguay Round, completed in 1994, resulted in worldwide tariff reductions of almost 40 percent and will gradually eliminate many duties entirely under the zero-for-zero tariff concessions. The most-favored-nation and national treatment principles are based on the concept of nondiscrimination. These important principles ensure that importing nations will treat the goods of all GATT members equally in terms of taxes, charges, and administrative regulations. GATT provides for the eventual elimination of all quotas, although the balance-of-payment exception allows countries to impose temporary quantitative measures in a financial emergency. GATT 1994 consists of the original 1947 agreement, numerous multilateral agreements negotiated since 1947, and the Uruguay Round Agreements.

GATT 1994 created the new World Trade Organization. This institution took over the responsibilities of the former GATT organization (1947–1994) effective January 1, 1995. At the end of 1997 there were 132 members of the WTO. As of early 1998, Russia and China were not members of GATT, but they continue to seek membership. If their economic reforms continue they are likely to gain entrance to the WTO. Even though these countries are not GATT members, they enjoy MFN status with the United States.

GATT also provides a dispute settlement mechanism by which nations can settle their differences before a trade war begins. From 1995 through 1997 there were 115 trade disputes brought to the WTO for consultation. Dispute settlement under the WTO has made many improvements over GATT 1947 methods. The WTO has greater power to enforce the decisions of the panel because no single country can veto their adoption.

This chapter focused on the basic principles of GATT international trade law and dispute settlement. However, the Uruguay Round also addressed many other specialized areas of trade relations. GATT 1994 contains agreements related to trade in agriculture, services, and textiles; these are trade-related investment measures and aspects of intellectual property rights; government procurement; technical barriers to trade; and more. The next chapter addresses some of these other issues.

## QUESTIONS AND CASE PROBLEMS

1. Every year the United States Trade Representative issues a report of foreign government trade barriers to U.S. goods and services. Locate these reports and describe the nature of these trade barriers. Which countries are the greatest "offenders"? What industries are most affected?

2. Look at the WTO website (http://www.wto.org) and access the Dispute Settlement section. How many consultations have occurred among WTO members? How many disputes have been decided by the panels? How many have been submitted to and reviewed by the Appellate Body? Do you agree with William Davey, Director of the WTO's Legal Division, that the increased WTO caseload (almost twice as many cases submitted to the WTO as were submitted during a period comparable to that of the GATT) indicates that both developed and developing countries are using the WTO dispute settlement procedures? Why do you think the caseload has increased?

3. Do you think that Russia and the People's Republic of China should be admitted to membership in the WTO? Describe the key economic and political issues in this decision. What is the position of the United States and other members? Why would this issue be important to those countries?

4. Describe MFN trade status. What is unconditional MFN trade? Should MFN trade be used as a tool of foreign affairs to influence the conduct of other countries? What were the issues and concerns in granting MFN status to Russia and China?

5. One of the central obligations of WTO membership is a limit on tariffs on particular goods according to a nation's tariff commitments. If a member does not abide by its agreement, can another WTO member unilaterally raise its agreed-upon tariff? Describe the dispute settlement mechanism in the WTO. Reports of the dispute settlement panels are available in the *International Legal Materials,* published by the American Society of International Law. Locate a WTO panel decision and summarize the main issues and arguments of the parties and the panel's recommendation.

6. The U.S. auto industry has had its problems in the past from foreign competition. If the auto industry lobbied the president and Congress for implementation of a quota on the total number of imported automobiles and trucks, would such a quota be in violation of GATT 1994? Under what circumstances may a country impose a quota?

7. The WTO comprises many nations from all regions of the world. As such, the GATT/WTO system takes a global view of trade liberalization based on nondiscrimination, unconditional MFN, national treatment, tarrification, and multilateral trade negotiations. The GATT agreement recognizes that nations may form free trade areas and customs unions. Yet a free trade area only has free trade among the countries that belong to it. How does the concept of a free trade area, such as the North American Free Trade Agreement (NAFTA) fit into

the GATT/WTO global framework? Do free trade areas violate the principle of nondiscrimination and MFN trade? Evaluate these arguments.

8. Farr Man & Co., Inc., imports sugar from Argentina into the United States. In 1978 the U.S. president imposed fees on the importation of sugar under the authority of the U.S. Agricultural Adjustment Act. The Act had been passed by Congress for the purposes of stabilizing farm prices and protecting domestic price supports on sugar and agricultural products. The Act granted to the president the discretionary authority to impose restrictions on agricultural imports if they were deemed to be interfering with the domestic price support program. In exercising this authority, the president's proclamation imposed import fees on all sugar except that of Malawian origin. Plaintiff contends that either the proclamation is invalid or that Argentinean sugar is entitled to a similar exemption because of the most-favored-nation provisions of a 1941 bilateral treaty between the United States and Argentina as well as the MFN provisions of GATT. Does the act preempt the MFN provisions of an earlier treaty or international agreement? *Farr Man & Co., Inc. v. United States,* 544 F.Supp. 908 (C.I.T. 1982).

## MANAGERIAL IMPLICATIONS

Your firm manufactures children's toys in the People's Republic of China for export to the United States. About 35 percent of your total worldwide production comes from China. While you market many styles of toys in other countries, the toys made in China are intended for the U.S. market. You have invested heavily in China in the last five years and have come to depend greatly on inexpensive Chinese labor. You are concerned because of increasing tension between China and the United States over trade issues. Moreover, some members of the U.S. Congress are calling for sanctions against China for its imprisonment of pro-democracy student demonstrators. Recent news stories on cable television vividly show the abuse of prison labor in Chinese camps. The president recognizes the importance of trade with China and thus far has not shown any interest in breaking off trade relations.

1. Describe the impact that a trade war would have on your firm.
2. Describe the impact on your firm if China were to lose its MFN trading status.
3. What strategic actions might you take now in order to reduce your firm's exposure to the risks of these political events?
4. How has GATT 1994 affected the import of your products into the United States?

## NOTES

1. *See* Frank K. Upham, "Privatized Regulation: Japanese Regulatory Style in Comparative and International Perspective," *Fordham International Law Journal,* 20 (December 1996), 396.

## Chapter Eleven

# Regulating Import Competition and Unfair Trade

The last chapter examined the basic principles of GATT law found in the General Agreement on Tariffs and Trade 1994. The key principles dealt with nondiscrimination, most-favored-nation trade, national treatment, and the elimination of quotas and nontariff barriers. A knowledge of this material is essential here, because these concepts are carried throughout this chapter as well as the remainder of the book. Chapter Ten also described how the new World Trade Organization has become the primary international body for liberalizing trade, and how the WTO's dispute settlement procedures work. This chapter discusses many of the specific agreements under GATT 1994 with a far-reaching impact on the global economy and competitive environment.

This chapter covers two areas: The first is the regulation of import competition through laws that "safeguard" domestic industries. These laws protect industries that say, "We're trying as best we can to compete, but foreign competitors seem more efficient and more productive. They're shipping ever-greater quantities of products here, and we need time to adjust—to retool our plants and retrain our workers to become more competitive again. Just give us some time!"

The second area covers the regulation of "unfair trade," more specifically, the two most common unfair trade practices of dumping and government subsidies. Here domestic industries might say, "Foreign firms compete unfairly. They dump their goods in our market at ridiculously low prices. They absorb the losses until they drive us all out of business so they'll have the whole U.S. market to themselves!" Or, "How can we expect to sell our products here at home when

we can't match the price of imports. Our overseas competitors are subsidized; they're paid by their own government, with their taxpayer's money, to build products and ship them here. We've got to stop this!"

## The Double-Edged Sword of Import Regulation

Trade wars are often depicted in nationalistic terms as an us-against-them problem. Pictures of unemployed factory workers fill the television screens. Politicians call for greater protectionist measures. Of course, these familiar stories have two sides: U.S. auto workers and manufacturers scream for the president to put high tariffs on imported cars and trucks. Yet the Japanese government claims that the Japanese manufacturers are only producing cars that Americans want. The few remaining U.S. manufacturers of display screens for portable computers call for protection against an onslaught of imports. Yet U.S. computer manufacturers who use the screens threaten to close shop in the United States and move overseas if more duties are placed on the imported screens. U.S. steel makers want higher tariffs on imported steel, while high-tech companies fear that they will pay the price in higher tariffs placed on their products in return. Examples such as these come from every agricultural, industrial, and service sector of the world's economy. Amid the clamoring for protection against imports, calls for free trade come from the heads of those firms whose exports might suffer from foreign retaliation, or by leaders of consumer groups concerned about the rising price of imported consumer products. The discussion in this chapter attempts to break through this protectionism-versus-free-trade morass by focusing on how international rules serve as a check on these competing national political interests.

## Impact on Management Decision Making

Governments impose countless regulatory methods to control imports into their markets. These controls cause a ripple effect on national economies as well as on business and business decision making. Controls on import competition affect all players in the international marketplace—exporter, importer, licensor, joint venture partner, or foreign subsidiary.

Even purely domestic firms that do not import or export must have an understanding of how governments regulate import competition. Virtually all domestic products compete with products made abroad, and U.S. managers require a knowledge of how U.S. trade policies and trade laws affect their firms' competitive positions. Managers may need to determine whether legal action could forestall a flood of competing imports, and on what grounds such a lawsuit could be based. Would an action for relief be brought in the courts or before an administrative agency? Do any government programs exist to provide benefits to workers whose jobs are lost due to import competition? In the United States many industries have sought protection against foreign competition. Some notable examples include apparel, shoes, gloves, motorcycles, steel, chemicals, foodstuffs, microwave ovens, typewriters, minivans, glass, and automobiles.

U.S. exporters must also be prepared to confront possible trade barriers in a foreign market. If their marketing and local political efforts fail, can they call on the U.S. government for negotiating assistance or retaliatory measures against foreign countries that treat their products unfairly? Are WTO international dispute mechanisms available to ensure that U.S. products are treated "fairly" and without discrimination abroad? Does U.S. law provide for any unilateral actions against offending countries—either with or without WTO approval? Some industries that have succeeded in obtaining government negotiating assistance in breaking down foreign trade

barriers include computers and semiconductors, automobiles, agriculture (notably rice and beef), and telecommunications. The service industries, such as insurance, banking, and transportation have also been successful in working through the government.

> **http://www.wto.org**
> *Provides links to international trade issues.*

# Safeguards Against Injury

Economic and political realities often force nations to take temporary corrective action to protect a domestic industry from severe market disruptions and dislocations of the workforce resulting from increased imports. A country takes legal action to protect a domestic industry by granting *import relief* or *adjusting imports,* commonly known as a *safeguard against injury.* Safeguards are generally used to protect a domestic industry from increasing volumes of imported goods (regardless of any wrongdoing or unfair trade practice by a foreign firm or foreign government). These safeguards include temporarily increasing tariffs, imposing quotas, or by some other (lawful) method to restrict or discourage imports. The legal authority for a GATT member nation to safeguard its firms from injury comes from the GATT escape clause.

## The GATT Escape Clause

If a nation reduces its tariffs, the result is frequently increased imports and possibly serious market disruption to a domestic industry. Article XIX of GATT 1947, known as the *GATT escape clause,* authorizes a country to take temporary corrective action to adjust import levels of a certain product and thus safeguard domestic industry. The escape clause is so named because it temporarily permits a country to "escape" from previous promises (tariff concessions) it may have made to lower tariffs on that product. Article XIX was included in the GATT agreement at the insistence of the United States, which had previously used similar provisions in bilateral treaties. Today, the GATT 1994 *Agreement on*

*Safeguards* establishes rules for safeguarding domestic industry and providing import relief.

## The GATT 1994 Agreement on Safeguards

The Agreement on Safeguards provides that a member may apply a safeguard measure (e.g., increase tariffs) to a product only if that product "is being imported in such increased quantities and under such conditions as to cause or threaten to cause serious injury to the domestic industry that produces like or directly competitive products." The term *serious injury* is defined as a "significant overall impairment in the position of a domestic industry." The term *domestic industry* means "producers as a whole," as opposed to just one firm within the industry.

In order to apply a safeguard, a country must first undertake an administrative investigation, which includes a public hearing at which importers, exporters, and other interested parties can present evidence and their views of whether the safeguard would be in the public interest. The investigating body is required to evaluate all relevant economic factors bearing on the industry's position, and it must find that the increased imports are the actual cause of the domestic industry's decline. If other factors are shown to be causing injury simultaneously, then the increased imports are not considered to be the cause. Emergency action can be taken without the investigation if clear evidence justifies the safeguards, but any additional tariffs imposed must be lifted within 200 days.

**Limits on the Use of Safeguards.**   GATT places limits on safeguards, because they are a temporary remedy to be used only until the problem is resolved. They may not exceed four years (with an extension to eight years). The restrictions on imports must be gradually lifted as conditions warrant. Imposing safeguards on a product can only be done without discrimination, regardless of the product's country of origin, and only as is necessary to prevent or remedy serious injury. Tariffs are the preferred safeguard. A quota, if used, may not reduce the quantity of imports below the average level of imports of the prior three years. Quotas should be allocated among supply-ing nations based upon their proportion of the total quantity of imports during the preceding years. Nations must follow certain limits when imposing safeguards on products from developing countries. All safeguards in existence when the GATT 1994 agreement became effective must be lifted by the end of 1999.

**Trade Compensation.**   GATT 1994 encourages a country imposing a safeguard to compensate a supplying nation for the burden the safeguard measure has imposed on it. For instance, if the United States imposes safeguard tariffs on imported bicycles, and Taiwan supplies large numbers of bicycles to the United States, then the United States should make *trade compensation* to Taiwan by reducing tariffs on other Taiwanese imports in an equivalent amount. The countries are expected to negotiate trade compensation; if they fail to reach agreement, then the supplying nation may "suspend . . . substantially equivalent concessions"—or raise tariffs in retaliation.

**The WTO Committee on Safeguards.**   Countries must notify the *Committee on Safeguards* when taking safeguard actions. The Committee reports to the WTO *Council for Trade in Goods*. It monitors compliance with GATT safeguard provisions and assists countries in negotiating trade compensation.

## Safeguards Against Injury under U.S. Law

The U.S. escape clause is found in Section 201 of the *Trade Act of 1974* as amended by the *Omnibus Trade and Competitiveness Act of 1988* and the *Uruguay Round Agreements Act* (URAA). U.S. law now follows the guidelines of GATT Article XIX and the Agreement on Safeguards. However U.S. law does not refer to the term *safeguards,* but rather to the "positive adjustment to import competition" or import relief.

**Standard for Import Relief.**   Under U.S. law, import relief can be granted when "an article is being imported into the United States in such increased quantities as to be a substantial cause of serious injury or threat thereof to the domestic industry producing an article like or directly competitive with the imported article." The president may make an adjustment to imports (e.g., impose tariffs or quotas) only after an investigation by the U.S. International Trade Commission (ITC), and if, in the president's discretion, it will "facilitate efforts by the domestic industry to make a positive adjustment to import competition and provide greater economic and social benefits than costs." Because of this discretionary power, a president who adopts free trade or free market concepts, such as President Reagan did during the 1980s, might be reluctant to exercise the escape clause remedy at all. Although largely political in nature, a president's decision is usually based on the national interest.

**ITC Investigations.** A petition for relief may be filed with the ITC by any firm, trade association, union, or group of workers, or by Congress or the president, or it may be initiated by the commission itself. The ITC gives public notice in the *Federal Register* of its investigation and hearings. If it finds that the requirements of the law are met, it may advise the president as to what action to take. The commission conducts public hearings at which interested parties may present evidence and make suggestions as to the form of import relief. The ITC prepares a detailed economic analysis of the affected market and then makes its determination. The factors that the commission considers in determining whether increased imports are a substantial cause of serious injury include:

1. A significant idling of productive facilities in the industry.
2. The inability of firms to operate at a reasonable profit.
3. Unemployment or underemployment in the industry.
4. Growing inventories.
5. A decline in sales, market share, production, wages, or employment.
6. A firm's inability to generate capital for plant and equipment modernization or for research and development.
7. An actual increase in imports or in market share held by imports.
8. Other factors that may account for the serious injury to the domestic industry (e.g., incompetent management or lack of technological innovation).

The law defines *substantial cause* as "a cause which is important and not less than any other cause." The ITC may not consider overall economic trends, such as the impact of a recession on the industry, but must look at the impact of the increased imports. In the following ITC report on the U.S. motorcycle industry, Commissioner Eckes found that increased imports of heavyweight motorcycles threatened serious injury to the petitioner, Harley-Davidson, despite the severe impact of a long recession on total sales in the industry.

BACKGROUND AND FACTS

In 1982, the ITC instituted an investigation to determine if motorcycles having engines with displacement more than 700 cubic centimeters are being imported into the United States in such increased quantities as to be a substantial cause of serious injury, or threat thereof, to domestic industry producing like or directly competitive articles. The investigation was in response to a petition for relief filed by Harley-Davidson Motor Co., a U.S. firm. The investigation showed that from 1977 to 1981, U.S. shipments of motorcycles grew by 17 percent,

*Heavyweight Motorcycles, and Engines and Power-Train Subassemblies*

Report to the President on Investigation No. TA-201-47 United States International Trade Commission 1983

with domestic productive capacity increasing by nearly 82 percent (largely as a result of American Honda's increased production in the United States). During that same period the number of U.S. jobs increased by 30 percent. In 1982, however, consumption fell, domestic shipments declined, and employment dropped. In the first nine months of 1982, domestic shipments fell by 13 percent and inventories rose, leaving large numbers of unsold motorcycles. Production during that period showed a decline of 36 percent,

*(continued)*

*(continued)*

profits were down by 20 percent, and employment was down by 12 percent. Inventories of imported motorcycles doubled in that period, representing a tremendous threat to Harley-Davidson. The country as a whole was in the midst of a recession, and demand for heavyweight motorcycles was depressed.

## VIEWS OF CHAIRMAN ALFRED ECKES

The primary factor underlying the threat of injury to this industry consists of importers' and dealers' inventories. Importers' inventories have tripled since 1979, and most recently doubled in the first nine months of 1982 over the same period in 1981. Total inventories of imported motorcycles held by dealers and importers on September 30, 1982, exceed actual domestic consumption for the period January–September 1982. From another analytical perspective, it is clear that these inventories represent 158 percent of total importers' shipments during that period. In short, domestic producers, importers, and dealers have enough motorcycles on hand to meet total consumption of imported and domestic motorcycles for approximately one year.

It is evident that inventories of imported motorcycles have increased significantly during the most recent period. These increases exceed growth in consumption and surpass historical shipment trends for importers. The mere presence of such a huge inventory has had and will continue to have a depressing effect on the domestic industry. Also, given the natural desire of consumers for current design and up-to-date performance capabilities, motorcycles cannot be withheld from the market indefinitely. They must be sold. And given the realities of the market place, there is a strong incentive to liquidate these inventories as quickly as possible. The impact of such a massive inventory build-up on the domestic industry is imminent, not remote and conjectural.

I have seen no persuasive evidence that would suggest imports of Japanese heavyweight motorcycles will decline in the near future. Instead, the Japanese motorcycle industry is export oriented—exporting in 1982 some 91 percent of the heavyweight motorcycles produced in Japan. Because motorcycles of more than 750cc, which include the merchandise under investigation here, cannot be sold in Japan under current law, Japa-

nese producers cannot consider domestic sales as a replacement for exports. The other option, which they apparently pursued in 1982, is to push export sales in the face of declining demand in the U.S. market. This tactic helps to maintain output and employment in the producing country but it shifts some of the burden of adjustment to competitors in the importing country. Evidence that the Japanese producers will seek to maintain a high level of export sales to the U.S. is found in an estimate of the Japanese Automobile Manufacturer's Association. This organization estimated that exports of 700cc or over motorcycles to the United States for 1982 and 1983 would average 450,000 units or less for both years combined. That figure results in import levels higher than recent levels.

Finally, imports of finished heavyweight motorcycles pose a "substantial cause" of threat of serious injury. Under section 201(b)(4), a "substantial cause" is a "cause which is important and not less than any other cause." In my view, there is no cause more important than imports threatening injury to the domestic motorcycle industry.

In reaching this conclusion I have considered the significance of the present recession in my analysis. Without a doubt the unusual length and severity of the present recession has created unique problems for the domestic motorcycle industry. Without a doubt the rise in joblessness, particularly among blue-collar workers, who constitute the prime market for heavyweight motorcycles, has had a severe impact on the domestic industry. Nonetheless, if the Commission were to analyze the causation question in this way, it would be impossible in many cases for a cyclical industry experiencing serious injury to obtain relief under section 201 during a recession. In my opinion Congress could not have intended for the Commission to interpret the law this way.

There are other reasons for doubting the domestic recession is a substantial cause of injury or threat to the U.S. industry. During the current recession, imports from Japan have increased their market share from domestic producers, gaining nearly six percentage points. Imports have taken market share from the domestic facilities of Honda and Kawasaki as well as Harley-Davidson.

Moreover, while the current recession has undoubtedly depressed demand for heavyweight motorcycles, economic conditions are beginning

*(continued)*

*(continued)*

to improve in this country.... As demand responds to this improvement, the domestic industry will be pre-empted from participating in any growth because of the presence of a one-year supply of motorcycles poised and ready to capture market share. Consequently, not the recession, but the inventory of motorcycles coupled with anticipated future imports constitute the greatest threat of injury in the months ahead.

**Decision.** The commission recommended that incremental duties be imposed for five years at the declining rate of 45, 35, 20, 15, and 10 percent, in addition to the existing rate of 4.4 percent *ad valorem*.

**Comment.** The president followed the commission's recommendations, but added tariff-rate quotas of 5,000 units in order to keep the U.S. market open to European firms that exported to the United States in smaller quantities. The remedy has been considered one of the successful uses of the escape clause. Under protection, Harley-Davidson recapitalized, introduced a statistical quality control process and just-in-time inventory control, and regained its competitiveness.

**Available Remedies under U.S. Law.** Any relief granted by the president must be temporary (limited to four years, with an extension to eight years if the firms in the industry are making needed changes), and designed to allow those firms sufficient time to regain their competitive position in the market. Relief should only provide time to retool, modernize, streamline, recapitalize, improve quality, or take other actions to better meet new competitive conditions in the market. The president's options for adjusting imports include (1) tariff increases subject to a maximum increase of 50 percent, (2) tariff-rate quotas, which allow a certain number of articles to be imported at one tariff rate, while all excess amounts enter at a higher rate, (3) absolute quotas, (4) quotas administered through the auctioning of import licenses, and (5) negotiated agreements with foreign countries, which limit their exports to the United States.

## The Steel Industry Example

The U.S. steel industry is a classic example of how a combination of import relief actions and international agreements have been used to protect a U.S. industry. After World War II, the United States dominated the world steel industry. With German and Japanese steel operations in ruin, those countries had the opportunity to rebuild with the most modern plants and techniques. The large U.S. steel companies did not modernize their plants, however, and by the late

1960s found themselves operating inefficiently and at a competitive disadvantage to the new foreign mills. As foreign plants increased capacity, not only in Germany and Japan, but in developing countries as well, foreign steel users no longer turned to U.S. suppliers. U.S. steel companies also faced higher wage rates than did foreign companies, and a loss of market share to plastics, aluminum, and other newer technologies.

Government protection of the U.S. steel industry began in the late 1960s when low-priced foreign steel started making inroads into the U.S. market. When steel imports reached over 15 percent of U.S. demand, President Nixon obtained the promises of foreign steel producers to voluntarily restrict their exports of steel to the United States. The legality of the president's action was called into question in *Consumer's Union v. Kissinger,* 506 F.2d 136 (D.C. Cir. 1974). The Court of Appeals, however, upheld the president's authority to negotiate voluntary restraint agreements (VRAs) with foreign producers—to the displeasure of consumer groups who maintained that the restraints were too costly to U.S. consumers. VRAs on steel imports lasted through the 1970s and early 1980s. The 1994 GATT Agreement on Safeguards states that VRAs and other orderly marketing agreements are not to be used and any in existence must be phased out.

In 1984, foreign steel accounted for nearly 20 percent of the U.S. market. U.S. steel producers and steelworkers petitioned the International Trade Commission for import relief. After an exhaustive analysis, the ITC recommended that tariffs and tariff-rate quotas be imposed for five years to allow U.S. steel makers to regain their competitive position. President Reagan rejected the call for quotas and instead negotiated new VRAs with nineteen countries and the European Community. The import restrictions were flexible but limited each foreign country's share of the U.S. market. The VRAs restricted the penetration of foreign steel in the United States, but at the same time allowed import quantities to rise according to demand. A system of export licenses granted by the foreign country provided enforcement of the VRAs. Without the license, the steel could not enter the United States. Through the use of the VRAs, the president was able to address the demands of U.S. steelmakers while still maintaining the position that quotas were protectionist and contrary to the interests of U.S. consumers. The VRAs expired in 1992.

Critics claim that VRAs have been too costly and ineffective. As foreign imports were restricted, domestic steel companies took advantage of the lack of competition to raise prices. These price increases were reflected in the price of automobiles, appliances, and construction. U.S. companies then became reliant on protection, returning every few years to have the restrictions extended. On the other hand, by the early 1990s, steel imports dropped considerably and U.S. exports climbed. Some economists attributed this to a more favorable exchange rate for U.S. exports, as well as the increased competitiveness of smaller mills that produce specialty steel in more efficient plants. Still, older U.S. plants continued to close. Since 1990, 30 steel-producing nations have worked on an agreement to eliminate the VRAs, quotas, and tariffs that have been in place more than 20 years. A number of cases brought by U.S. steel companies have alleged dumping or the subsidized sale of a variety of steel products in the U.S. from at least a dozen other countries. The decisions of the courts have been mixed.

## Trade Adjustment Assistance

If the ITC finds that increased imports caused serious injury to a U.S. industry, then workers who are unemployed as a result may be entitled to federal *trade adjustment assistance* (TAA). Assistance to workers, in the form of direct cash payments, is intended to cover the expenses of job retraining and relocation. (More than 1,000 petitions covering over 115,000 workers were certified in 1996.) For workers to be eligible to apply for TAA, the Secretary of Labor must determine that workers in a firm have become, or are threatened to become, partially or totally separated; that the firm's sales or production have decreasd absolutely; and that increases in like or directly competitive imported products contributed importantly to the separation and the decline in the firm's sale or production.

Proving that imports contributed to unemployment is not easy. In one case, the Court of International Trade ruled that U.S. oil geologists who lost their jobs in cutbacks caused by a worldwide glut of crude oil and a resulting decline in world oil prices were not entitled to adjustment assistance. Sales of crude oil and natural gas had increased in quantity during 1986, but revenues had declined by 30 percent due to a drop in prices. Noting that revenues and prices were not to be considered under the law, the court ruled that the increased imports did not contribute importantly to the loss of jobs. The court reasoned that Congress had not intended to provide assistance to all workers who lost their jobs due in some measure to imports.

Another common difficulty is proving that the import is "like" the article made by the firm or group of workers petitioning for relief. One U.S. court decided that workers who manufactured parts of shoes were not eligible for benefits when they lost their jobs as a result of increased imports of finished shoes. In another case, a court denied adjustment assistance to workers who manufactured component parts of televisions, and whose jobs were displaced because of increased imports of finished television sets.

Workers have been certified in many TAA programs. The six industries with the largest concentration of certified workers during the last two decades were working in: automotive equipment, apparel and other finished products made from fabrics and similar materials, primary metal industries, oil and gas production and services, leather and leather products, and electrical and electronic machinery equipment and supplies.

# Unfair Import Laws: Dumping and Antidumping Duties

In importing, *dumping* is the unfair trade practice of selling products in a foreign country for less than the price charged for the same or comparable goods in the producer's home market. It is a form of price discrimination causing injury to domestic competitors through artificially low prices against which domestic producers cannot compete at a profitable level. GATT has prohibited dumping since 1947, and in the United States it has been illegal since 1916.

Virtually all developed nations have statutes, patterned after GATT, that permit the importing country to impose antidumping duties on dumped products to offset the unfair low price and to prevent injury to a domestic producer. The United States, the European Union, Canada, and Australia all have antidumping laws. In the European Union the anti-dumping laws are imposed only on trade between a member country and a non-member country. The Japanese have similar laws, although they are not widely enforced. Developing countries such as Mexico, Brazil, Argentina, and Korea are currently enacting antidumping codes. Antidumping laws are used more frequently than any other trade law in the United States and Europe. For instance, from 1990 through 1996, 320 antidumping petitions were filed in the United States. Japan has been the most important single target for both EU and U.S. antidumping laws. Fifteen percent of all EU and U.S. actions against market economies in the 1980s were brought against Japan.

## The Economics of Dumping

The theories that explain the economic motivation for dumping fill entire volumes and are certainly beyond the scope of this book. At first glance, one might wonder what is wrong with consumers of one country being able to buy the products of another nation cheaply. As long as the products remain available at a reasonable market price, nothing is wrong. But the lower prices charged in an importing country are often not related to superior efficiencies in production. Rather, dumping is often intended to drive competitors out of business so that the dumping firms

will ultimately be free to raise their prices to monopoly levels.

Dumping has become a fairly persistent problem in international trade, often practiced by those firms wishing to sell their excess production capacity at bargain prices to cover fixed costs and to avoid cyclical worker layoffs. As long as dumped products are not sold in the producer's own country, causing price suppression in the producer's home market, then the dumping firm has everything to gain and little to lose. Some economists point out that dumping is not always predatory, but may be related to market conditions. An exporting firm may not be able to command the same prices from foreign buyers as in its domestic market, where it has brand-name recognition and greater market power.

Critics of antidumping laws claim that they injure consumers by "fixing prices" at high levels. Once the prices rise for imported products, domestic manufacturers follow suit by raising their prices as well. In one case, reported in *The Journal of Commerce,* U.S. manufacturers of portable computers moved their assembly operations out of the United States, causing a loss of U.S. jobs, in order to avoid the punishing antidumping duties on imported flat panel computer screens used in their computers. Critics cite the fact that antidumping laws are designed to *correct* an unfair trade practice and not to *protect* domestic companies. They also maintain that antidumping laws do not require the United States to assess the impact of additional duties on the public interest (i.e., the cost to consumers), and do not provide an exception for goods that are in short supply in the United States.

## The GATT 1994 Antidumping Agreement

The GATT provisions on dumping are found in GATT 1994 Article VI and in the *1994 Antidumping Agreement* (see Appendix). Earlier GATT codes on dumping merely condemned dumping as injurious to competition; however, the 1994 rules are more explicit. The 1994 agreement provides complex rules for determining when dumping has occurred and for resolving dumping disputes.

In the United States, the Uruguay Round Agreements Act amended U.S. antidumping laws to reflect the new GATT provisions. The agreement provides that an importing country may impose an antidumping duty when foreign goods are imported for sale at a price less than that charged for comparable goods in the exporting or producing country, and only when the dumping threatens or causes material injury to a domestic industry producing like products (the material injury requirement is discussed later in this chapter). GATT requires that an importing country resort to antidumping duties only after conducting a formal investigation to determine both the amount of the dumping and the extent of material injury. In these generally administrative agency proceedings, the offsetting duties are imposed on imported merchandise when the United States International Trade Administration (ITA) of the U.S. Department of Commerce determines that the merchandise is being dumped and the International Trade Commission (ITC) determines that there is material injury or the threat of material injury "by reason of" the imports.

**Calculating the Dumping Margin.**   GATT 1994 states that dumping is the sale of a product in a foreign country at *"less than normal value."* The U.S. statute refers to a sale below normal value as a sale "for less than fair value." Contrary to popular belief, dumping does not require that the product be sold in the importing country for less than the cost to produce it, although a sale at below cost is certainly below normal value. A sale at *less than normal value* occurs where the *export price* is less than the *normal value* of the product in the exporting or producing country. This price differential is known as the *dumping margin.* When dumping causes or threatens material injury to domestic producers of like products, the importing nation may equalize the price differential by imposing an additional tariff, above the normal tariff charged for that product. These *antidumping duties* are assessed in an amount equal to the dumping margin. Thus, if a Korean company sells a widget in Korea at $100, and sells the same widget in the United States at $80, then the dumping margin is $20 and an antidumping duty of $20 can be imposed on the imported widget.

**Calculating the Export Price.**   The *export price* is the price (usually the *ex factory* price without shipping charges) at which a product is sold to an unaffiliated or unrelated buyer in the importing country. When a price charged for a product does not reflect an "arms length," or freely negotiated transaction, a *constructed export price* must be used. A constructed export price is used when the exporter and importer are related companies or the product price is "hidden" in some other type of compensatory arrangement (such as barter). In these cases the constructed price is deemed to be the price at which the imported product is first resold in its original condition to an independent buyer.

**Calculating the Normal Value of Like Products in the Exporting or Producing Country.**   Normal value is the price at which *like products* are sold in the exporting or producing country for consumption, in the ordinary course of business, and at the same level of trade—in other words, comparing wholesale sale to wholesale sale, or retail to retail—as the dumped product. If insufficient quantities of like products are sold in the exporting country with which to make a fair comparison, then normal value is calculated on the basis of sales to third countries, or on the basis of a constructed value. Constructed value is calculated on the basis of what it might actually cost to produce the product in the exporting country, plus a reasonable profit.

The dumping margin can be calculated either by comparing average prices (average normal value) for comparable goods sold in the exporting or producing country with average export prices, or by comparing prices in individual transactions. When *spot dumping* to particular customers occurs, or dumping is limited to a particular geographical region or on an occasional basis, a comparison may be made between *individual* export prices in the importing country to *average* market prices in the exporting country. Currency conversions use the rate on the date of sale. For purposes of calculating the dumping margin, price and cost information can be used from records kept by the producers or exporters under investigation, provided that their records follow generally accepted accounting principles.

**Making a Fair Comparison.** Calculating the dumping margin requires a *fair comparison* of the export price of the dumped product in the foreign export market with the price of a like product sold in the ordinary course of trade in the exporting or producing country (i.e., the normal value). A fair comparison often requires adjustments to either the export price or to normal value to compensate for differences in the sale—comparing "apples to apples." For example, if the German manufacturer of ball bearings must pay a sales commission to sales representatives for ball bearings sold in Germany, but does not pay commissions on sales to the United States, then the difference must be accounted for in the calculation. Adjustments can be made for differences in the terms and conditions of sale, for the cost of ocean containers and packaging, for freight and warehouse expenses, customs brokerage fees, insurance on the goods in transit, and other expenses. Adjustments should also be made for differences in taxes, advertising and sales commission expenses, quantity discounts, and other factors that might legitimately cause the export price to be lower than normal value. The rules for making adjustments in U.S. dumping cases are spelled out in U.S. law.

The following case, *Smith-Corona Group v. United States,* illustrates the complexity of determining if a product is sold at less than normal value. In this case, adjustments to the normal value and export price were necessary in order to make an accurate comparison. Because the case was decided under an older statute, it uses the term *foreign market value* instead of *normal value,* and it refers to *United States price* instead of *export price.*

---

### Smith-Corona Group v. United States
713 F.2d 1568 (1983)
United States Court of Appeals
(Fed. Cir.)

BACKGROUND AND FACTS
The plaintiff was the last remaining manufacturer of portable electric typewriters in the United States. This action was brought to challenge the method used by the International Trade Administration to determine whether the Japanese typewriter companies, Brother and Silver Seiko, had engaged in dumping in the United States. The typewriters in question were sold in Japan (the home market) under different circumstances of sale than in the United States. In Japan, Silver Seiko provided volume rebates to its customers based on total sales of all merchandise sold. Brother incurred advertising expenses in Japan, as well as expenditures for accessories that accompany typewriters sold in Japan but not in the United States. The ITA subtracted these amounts from foreign market value in calculating the dumping margin. The Court of International Trade upheld the ITA's position and the plaintiff appealed.

CIRCUIT JUDGE SMITH
The Antidumping Act provides that if foreign merchandise is sold or is likely to be sold in the United States at less than its fair value to the material injury of a United States industry, then an additional antidumping duty shall be imposed. The amount of the duty shall equal the amount by which the foreign market value [now normal value] exceeds the United States price [now export price] for the merchandise.

Foreign market value and United States price represent prices in different markets affected by a variety of differences in the chain of commerce by which the merchandise reached the export or domestic market. Both values are subject to adjustment in an attempt to reconstruct the price at a specific, "common" point in the chain of commerce, so that value can be fairly compared on an equivalent basis. . . .

Silver granted volume rebates to Japanese customers for purchases of targeted quantities of certain Silver typewriters. Commerce computed the adjustments on the basis of expense to Silver. Silver granted rebates on sales of portable electric typewriters and other merchandise, necessitating apportionment of the rebate expense. Commerce initially computed the ratio of the total sales amount of portable electric typewriters to the total sales amount of all merchandise subject to the rebate program. This ratio, multiplied by the total amount of rebate paid, yields the total amount of

*(continued)*

*(continued)*

rebate paid for portable electric typewriters sales. . . .

Smith-Corona challenges these specific rebates as not directly related to the sales under consideration because they were based on total sales. Allegedly, the rebates are not identified with specific sales and are not properly quantifiable and, therefore, not properly subject to adjustment.

The statute requires that the adjustment be for differences in circumstances of sales. Brother and Silver both offer the rebate in Japan and not in America. Thus, the rebates constitute differences that may be adjustable. The rebates based on total sales were apportioned, as described above, in an attempt to correlate the rebates with the appropriate sales of portable electric typewriters within the pool of merchandise upon which the rebates were based. . . .

The rebates were actually paid on the sales under consideration. The effective cost to the manufacturer of the specific transactions subject to the rebates was increased by the amount of the rebates. More importantly, the apportionment of rebate cost was made on the basis of actual cost and sales figures. Despite the necessity of apportionment calculations to unravel the rebate transactions, the cost of the rebates can be directly correlated with specific merchandise using verified cost and sales information. While it would be simpler to make adjustments for a more direct rebate scheme, the necessity to undertake a straightforward mathematical analysis on the basis of verified, actual cost and sales data does not deprive these rebates of their direct relationship to the sales under consideration.

We conclude therefore that, in allowing these adjustments, the ITA acted within the framework of the statute and regulations and that the adjustments were based on substantial evidence. . . .

Commerce also made certain adjustments to foreign market value for certain "direct" advertising expenses incurred by Brother in the home market. The ITA allowed adjustments for twelve advertisements financed by Brother and aimed at the ultimate consumer. Some of these ads were for multiple products or involved a commemorative announcement. Commerce considered the adjustments to be for direct advertising expenses that were attributable to a later sale by a purchaser. . . .

The ITA also made adjustments to foreign market value for differences in the physical characteristics of the goods. Certain allowances were based on accessories and printed materials furnished with the merchandise by Brother. Portable electric typewriters sold in Japan were accompanied by spare typewriter ribbons and a pamphlet including a text on how to type. The merchandise sold for export to America consisted of the typewriter, without accessories, and with a pamphlet that did not include a typing instruction text.

Smith-Corona argues that the definition of the subject "merchandise" should be limited to portable electric typewriters. Consequently, differences in accessories or the pamphlet would not constitute differences in the physical characteristics of the merchandise.

The ITA has defined the term differently, however, and our inquiry is at an end if that interpretation is reasonable. The statute attaches significance to differences in value. Accessories included in sales to one market could enhance the value of the merchandise in that market relative to the value in the market not provided with those accessories. There is no evidence of record tending to show that value was not enhanced. It is, therefore, reasonable for the ITA to make adjustments on the basis of those features as physical characteristics of the merchandise. We hold that the ITA acted within the framework of the statute and regulations and that the allowances for differences in the physical characteristics of the merchandise on the basis of accessories provided with the principal goods were supported by substantial evidence.

**Decision.** The judgment is affirmed for the government. The ITA had correctly determined the dumping margin by making the proper adjustments to the price of the typewriters sold in Japan.

**Market Viability Test and Constructed Value.** A price comparison between the export price in the foreign market and the normal value of the product in the exporting country only works if the exporting country has a *viable market*. If the exporting country has insufficient sales of a like product, then the *normal value* is difficult to determine. When sales in the exporting country are less than 5 percent of the sales of the dumped product in the foreign market, the dumping margin is calculated by comparing the dumped product to the price of a like product when it is exported to a third country—provided that this price is representative. If sales to a third country are also insufficient, then a constructed value for the product is substituted for normal value. In this case, the price of the dumped product is compared to the cost of producing the product in the exporting country plus a reasonable amount for administrative, selling, and other costs, and for profits. The amount of profit to be added into constructed value is based on (1) actual profits in the transaction, (2) average profits on sales of the same product made by other producers, *or* (3) profits made on different products sold by the same producer.

**Sales below Cost.**    If a product is sold in the exporting country or in a third country at a *price below per unit cost of production* (including fixed and variable costs plus administrative and selling costs), the below-cost sales may be disregarded in determining a dumped product's normal value. The below-cost sales may be also disregarded if they make up a substantial portion—normally 20 percent or more—of the sales in question. Normal value would then be calculated using the constructed value method.

**The Level-of-Trade Problem.**    A producing firm that sells to its local market at a different level in the chain of distribution than in foreign markets presents a common problem in the evaluation of dumping cases. For example, a higher normal value frequently occurs when the producer sells directly to retailers or to end-users in the home country, whereas in the export market the producer may be selling to distributors or to wholesalers. The dumping margin would be attributed to the different costs of sale and different markups required. In a *level-of-trade problem* such as this, the ITA adjusts the price differential so that figures for normal value and export price are comparable. In *American Permac v. United States,* 703 F.Supp. 97 (1988), the Court of International Trade considered the level-of-trade problem of a German manufacturer of dry cleaning equipment and stated, "The additional costs of selling the merchandise to the end-users in Germany were amply provided by plaintiffs in

this case. Unless the ITA has specific evidence that these additional costs are not reflected in the prices of the merchandise in Germany, the ITA may not reject this data as too 'speculative.'"

## Imposition and Collection of Antidumping Duties

If the dumping margin is below 2 percent of the value of the products, the dumping is considered *de minimis* and no duties are imposed. Any antidumping duties that are imposed may not exceed the calculated dumping margin, and they must be imposed on all imports of the dumped products that cause injury, from all sources without discrimination. Assessments of antidumping duties and refunds of antidumping duties paid by importers in excess of the dumping margin must be made promptly. Antidumping duty orders should remain in force only as long as necessary to remedy the dumping that is causing the injury.

A *provisional measure* is an antidumping duty, cash deposit, or bond collected by the importing country upon entry of the product that is currently under a dumping investigation. This practice assures payment of the additional duties once a final assessment is made. However, final assessments may not be made in an amount higher than the provisional duty already paid.

Many dumping disputes are settled before antidumping duties are imposed. A *price undertaking* is a voluntary action of the foreign exporter or producer to raise prices so as to eliminate the dumping margin. If the price undertaking is satisfactory, the dumping proceeding may be terminated, and no antidumping duties need be imposed.

While dumping laws of different countries or regions generally must conform to the GATT 1994 provisions, there are some important distinctions in each area. Exhibit 11.1 depicts several comparisons between the dumping laws of the United States and those of the European Union.

## Dumping Investigations

GATT requires countries to conduct formal antidumping investigations, usually through an administrative process conducted by a

**EXHIBIT 11.1  Comparison of Antidumping Laws in U.S. and in the EU**

| Topic | U.S. | EU |
|---|---|---|
| 1. When Are Duties Imposed? | Retrospectively after goods are imported | Prospectively for future imports |
| 2. Duration | No time limit | 5 years maximum |
| 3. Determination of Amount | Equals dumping margin | Varies based on injury |
| 4. Measures to Stop Actions That Seek to Avoid Duties | Looks to see if alternative is a "like" product | Uses rules of origin for goods |
| 5. Discretion | Application of duties based on transparent and publicly available data | Has greater discretion; EU Commission doesn't reveal all calculations |

SOURCE:  This chart is based on an article, *Antidumping and Tariff Jumping: Japanese Firms' DFI in the European Union and the United States,* Rene A. Belderbos, *Weltwirtschaftliches Archiv* 133(3) (1997), 419.

governmental agency. The purpose of the investigation is to determine whether dumping has occurred, the amount of the dumping margin, whether it has caused or threatened material injury to a domestic industry, and the amount of antidumping duties to be imposed. In the European Union, the European Commission receives the complaint, decides whether to investigate it, carries out the investigation to determine if both dumping and injury is occurring, and has the power to establish provisional duties. The European Council of Ministers makes comments during the investigation and imposes final duties. In the United States, a dumping investigation is initiated by the filing of a complaint jointly with the U.S. International Trade Administration (ITA) and the U.S. International Trade Commission (ITC), who have shared responsibilities under the law. The ITA determines whether, and to what extent, dumping has occurred, and the ITC determines whether the dumping has materially injured or threatened material injury to a competing U.S. industry. Petitions may be filed by "an interested party . . . on behalf of domestic industry" that produces a like product. *Interested parties* include manufacturers, producers, wholesalers, labor unions, or groups of workers in the United States.

The following case, *Brother Industries (USA), Inc. v. United States,* addresses the question of who is a "manufacturer in the United States." While reading the case, consider the function of the antidumping duty laws and their impact on both the national and global economies.

---

BACKGROUND AND FACTS
This case is part of a continuing saga in the battle over the protection of the U.S. typewriter industry. In the 1970s, Smith-Corona was the last remaining typewriter manufacturer in the United States when Brother Industries moved into the U.S. market. Brother is a billion-dollar Japanese electronics company many times larger than Smith-Corona. Brother's products

**Brother Industries (USA), Inc. v. United States**

*801 F.Supp. 751 (1992)*
*United States Court of International Trade*

were of high quality and priced well below Smith Corona's. In 1980 Smith-Corona petitioned the U.S. government to impose antidumping duties on Brother's Japanese-made typewriters (as mentioned earlier in the chapter). But the new duties prompted Brother to open a typewriter plant in Bartlett, Tennessee, in 1986. The plant is owned by

*(continued)*

(continued)

BIUSA, a subsidiary of Brother. Brother invested $13 million and employed 450 workers at its plant. Smith-Corona was then purchased by a British company, which opened plants in Singapore, and later Mexico, to lower labor costs and become more competitive. The company closed its New York plant, eliminating hundreds of jobs, while adding even more jobs at its foreign factories. British-owned Smith-Corona then began exporting low-priced Singapore-made typewriters to the United States. In a petition that led to this case, Brother filed for antidumping duties against Smith-Corona. Brother claimed that it is a "United States manufacturer" and as such is entitled to have antidumping duties placed on unfairly low-priced typewriters made in Singapore—by Smith-Corona. Smith-Corona countered that Brother is only a foreign-owned "assembler" of typewriters, not a "manufacturer in the United States." The International Trade Administration (ITA) agreed because the research and development of the typewriters were not done in the United States, despite Brother's Tennessee plant. Brother appealed to the Court of International Trade.

JUDGE RESTANI

The plant has three product assembly lines and one circuit board assembly line. The operations at Bartlett [Tennessee] consist of welding of the chassis or metal frame from fabricated metal parts. The circuit boards are then assembled, using parts from outside vendors. The electronic components are inserted either automatically or manually onto the boards. Electrical connections are made with a soldering machine. . . . BIUSA has commenced production of its own liquid crystal display circuits. . . . All plastic housing, ribbons, correction tapes, cartons, and packing materials are sourced in the United States, and BIUSA estimates that outside vendors employ an additional 2,000 people. . . .

ITA found that the absolute levels of investment and employment were not instructive given the high output from the plant. It discounted both elements, finding that neither argues strongly for or against BIUSA's status as a domestic producer. After describing BIUSA's operations at Bartlett, ITA characterized the level of technical expertise as "what could be expected in any large assembly operation." . . .

ITA then turned to the final factor—other costs and activities leading to production of the like product. This factor proved dispositive. ITA found:

> Brother's products have been developed, designed, and engineered outside the United States over several years. . . . Though some market research is done by Brother in the United States, this is to be expected in the course of selling any product, domestic or imported. It is however, much less critical to the manufacture of a product than is the research, development, design and engineering activity. This factor, when considered in combination with the nature of Brother's operation, the low number of domestic parts, and its domestic value-added, is one of the most compelling factors affecting our analysis. . . .

ITA concluded that BIUSA was not an interested party under the statute and lacked standing to maintain the action. . . .

ITA's analysis, however, imposes burdens on a petitioner for which there is no support in the statute. . . . ITA elevates the situs of research, development, design and engineering to a primary position. As BIUSA notes . . . without U.S. research and development, a "company is cast outside the pale of qualified antidumping petitioners." Thus, any company that is manufacturing a product that has been researched and developed outside the United States likely would be disqualified under ITA's analysis. . . . It does not, as ITA suggests, depend on a showing that its product is "domestic" in the sense that it was conceived and developed in the United States. A company may be a U.S. manufacturer for purposes of the standing requirements even though its product is designed abroad.

Smith-Corona claims that the record establishes the importance of the design and engineering factors to the determination. Yet, Smith-Corona does not provide citations to the record nor elaborate on its argument. . . . Moreover . . . the situs of research and development is not dispositive, and its relative importance declines as an industry matures. As BIUSA has noted, the industry at issue here is a mature industry. This is not to say that the standing requirements are without teeth or that a company that merely completes a product in the United States would have standing. In this case, however, ITA has erected an onerous and unwarranted barrier to BIUSA's petition.

(continued)

*(continued)*

In emphasizing the situs of design and engineering, ITA has given inadequate consideration to several other factors such as capital investment and employment levels, even though it characterized these factors as "substantial" and "not insignificant." It also fails to note that BIUSA's U.S. value-added figures [adding value to raw materials] . . . compare favorably to at least one other case where International Trade Commission found the firm was part of the domestic industry. No adequate explanation for distinguishing this case has been provided. . . . Finally, the fact that BIUSA imports critical component parts from Japan does not preclude a finding that BIUSA is an interested party.

. . . Here, ITA's focus on the situs of design and engineering leads to an unwarranted concern with the intrinsic nature of the product rather than the nature of production in the United States. Because ITA's determination that BIUSA is not a manufacturer is not supported by substantial evidence and is not in accordance in law, it cannot stand. Moreover . . . the facts of record demonstrates that BIUSA is a United States "manufacturer" with a clear stake in the outcome of the antidumping investigation. The investment and employment levels at BIUSA, even as characterized by ITA, are not insignificant. The value-added is also significant, and at least as great as in another case where a firm has been found to be part of the domestic industry.

Based on the record before the court . . . BIUSA's operations at Bartlett can only be described as "manufacturing." Accordingly, ITA's determination is reversed, and the case is remanded for ITA to consider whether BIUSA has filed the petition "on behalf of" the domestic industry, and if so, to proceed with an investigation under the antidumping laws.

**Decision.**    BIUSA is a "manufacturer in the United States" and may therefore bring an action under U.S. antidumping laws, despite the fact that it is Japanese-owned. The ITA must consider all relevant factors when investigating charges of dumping, including the correct determination of whether the petitioner is a manufacturer in the United States.

**Comment.**    Consider the irony: In essence, the United States ended up placing antidumping duties on products made by a British-owned company in Singapore at the request of a Japanese-owned company. Critics of the antidumping laws point out that the real losers in these industry battles are U.S. consumers, who are likely to question whether antidumping legislation is in the best national interest. After all, cross-border investments in a global economy (such as Brother's operation in Tennessee) confuse the determination of who the laws are supposed to protect. On the other hand, if price discrimination is an evil to be addressed, does the nationality of the perpetrator and victim matter? In 1994, Brother and Smith-Corona agreed to petition the U.S. government to lift the antidumping duties on each other's typewriters; the order became effective in May 1995. In the end, U.S. consumers had paid the cost of antidumping duties on typewriters for 14 years.

Dumping investigations may not be initiated if the volume of dumped imports is negligible or if imports from any one country constitute less than 3 percent of total imports of that product, or countries that individually have less than 3 percent of the imports collectively account for more than 7 percent of the dumped imports. In addition, GATT 1994 requires that administrative rules concerning dumping investigations be transparent, that all notices and hearings be made public, that affected companies be given the chance to present their arguments, that all published decisions of administrative agencies state the reason for their findings, and that independent administrative appeals or judicial review be available to affected parties. Investigations must be concluded within 18 months.

An investigating agency may carry out investigations in the country in which the dumped products were produced or exported, provided it has the consent of the dumping firms and notifies their government accordingly. If the agency is not given freedom to pursue an investigation in the exporting country, it may make its decision on the basis of facts available to it. Companies asked for information by government agencies should respond fully and quickly (this applies to dumping actions in any country) to avoid possible negative consequences of a decision that is made on what information is available. Companies that do not respond might discover that their products are charged even higher duties than products from companies that do respond.

## GATT Dispute Settlement in Dumping Cases

Prior to the WTO agreement in 1994, GATT was sometimes criticized for its inability to control dumping or resolve dumping disputes. The 1994 agreement creates the *WTO Committee on Antidumping Practices,* which is responsible for assisting countries in implementing the agreement.

Dumping disputes may be taken to the WTO *Dispute Settlement Body* for negotiation or resolution. (The procedures for WTO dispute settlement were discussed in Chapter Ten.) The parties to dispute settlement, of course, are the nations involved and not the sellers and buyers of the dumped products—although individual companies often have considerable influence in initiating dumping investigations.

The WTO panel may review a final antidumping order of an administrative agency in the importing country to determine if it is consistent with the GATT Antidumping Agreement. The panel can look to see if the agency misinterpreted the provisions of the agreement, or whether it properly followed all administrative procedures in an "unbiased and objective" manner as called for in the GATT agreement. If the panel finds that an antidumping order violates GATT, the panel can recommend measures to be taken against the importing country. However, the scope of review of an agency's investigation and antidumping order is limited.

A dispute panel cannot reconsider issues of fact determined during a dumping investigation or overturn an interpretation of the agreement made by the investigating agency. Thus in reviewing U.S. dumping cases, a panel must accept the facts as found by the ITA and ITC in their investigations and look only to see whether the agencies correctly applied GATT law. This standard of review is similar to the process found in the United States in which courts of law review decisions of administrative agencies.

The following GATT dispute panel report was issued in 1985. The case is noted in the history of GATT law because the panel recommended that a government repay an antidumping duty already collected. Normally, GATT remedies are intended to end violations of the GATT agreement and to bring countries' future regulations and administrative practices into compliance. In this case, the panel attempted to correct a wrong that had already occurred by recommending compensation to a private party—that the government reimburse the importer for duties paid.

---

### Report on New Zealand Imports of Electrical Transformers from Finland

*Document I-B-18 (1985)*
*Report of the GATT Dispute Settlement Panel*

**BACKGROUND AND FACTS**

A Finnish exporter obtained a contract with a New Zealand importer for the sale of two large custom-built power transformers valued at approximately $NZ 150,000. The contract was obtained through competitive bidding. Following the award of the contract, New Zealand's largest manufacturer of transformers, which had also bid on the contract, requested that the New Zealand Customs Department initiate dumping proceedings against the Finnish exporter. The complaining company produced 92 percent of total domestic production in 1983. The transformers arrived in New Zealand and were delivered to the importer. During its dumping investigation, New Zealand Customs determined that the transformers had been sold at below their normal value and that the New Zealand domestic industry had suffered material injury, and, based on this determination, imposed an antidumping duty equal to the full dumping margin. Calculations of normal value were based on a constructed value method using data on the costs of production. The antidumping duty of $NZ 49,543 was paid. Total sales by value of domestic producers amounted to $NZ 5,920,000 in 1982–83. Finland maintained that the antidumping duties nullified

*(continued)*

*(continued)*

and impaired its rights under GATT, and requested that a panel be convened to resolve the dispute.

## REPORT OF THE PANEL ADOPTED ON 18 JULY 1985

The Panel based its consideration of the case before it on Article VI of GATT. . . . The first question which the Panel addressed was whether the Finnish exporter, in its sale of the two transformers in question to New Zealand, had engaged in dumping in terms of Article VI. The Panel noted that—in the absence of a domestic price in Finland for custom-built transformers of this kind—the New Zealand authorities had based their determination of normal value on the cost-of-production method. . . . The Panel also noted that Finland, while not objecting to the use of this method as such, had contested the individual elements of the calculation as being too high, resulting in a constructed price much higher than the actual price of the Finnish exporter. In the Finnish view, the New Zealand authorities should have instead used the cost elements provided by the exporter. The Panel, having heard the arguments put forward by both sides and having perused the documents submitted, concluded that the Finnish exporter, whether through its own fault or not, had not provided all of the necessary cost elements which would have enabled the New Zealand authorities to carry out a meaningful cost-of-production calculation on the basis of the information supplied by the exporter alone. . . . In the view of the Panel, the New Zealand authorities were therefore justified in making a cost calculation, where necessary, on the basis of price elements obtained from other sources.

In its examination, the Panel then turned to the question whether the New Zealand transformer industry [which is actually the complaining company] had suffered material injury as a result of the imports of the two transformers from Finland. The Panel did not question that this industry had been in a poor economic situation, due to lack of new orders, diminishing orders on hand in certain product categories, declining profitability, a large increase in imports and considerable uncertainty as to new orders. The Panel noted, on the other hand, that the Finnish imports in question . . . represented only 2.4 percent of total sales of the New Zealand transformer industry in 1983. . . . The Panel also considered it significant that imports increased from 1981/82 to 1982/83 by 250 percent . . . and that the imports from Finland represented only 3.4 percent of this increase. In view of these facts, the Panel concluded that while the New Zealand transformer industry might have suffered injury from increased imports, the cause of this injury could not be attributed to the imports in question from Finland, which constituted an almost insignificant part in the overall sales of transformers in the period concerned. In this connection, the Panel rejected the contention advanced by the New Zealand delegation that, at least as far as material injury in terms of Article VI was concerned, "any given amount of profit lost" by the complaining firm was in some sense an "injury" to a domestic industry. . . . The Panel noted in addition that at the time the ministerial decision was taken, the Finnish exporter had not attempted to make any further sales to the New Zealand market. The Panel could therefore not agree that the imposition of antidumping duties could have been based on threat of material injury in terms of Article VI.

In view of the reasons contained in the preceding paragraphs, the Panel came to the conclusion that New Zealand had not been able to demonstrate that any injury suffered by its transformer industry had been material injury caused by the imports from Finland. The Panel therefore found that the imposition of antidumping duties on these imports was not consistent with the provision of Article VI:6(a) of GATT.

In accordance with established GATT practice, the Panel held that where a measure had been taken which was judged to be inconsistent with the provisions of GATT, this measure would prima facie constitute a case of nullification or impairment of benefits which other [GATT member countries] were entitled to expect under GATT.

The Panel proposes to the Council that it addresses to New Zealand a recommendation to revoke the antidumping determination and to reimburse the antidumping duty paid.

**Decision.** The panel determined that the sale of the two transformers was not the cause of material injury to the New Zealand industry. The panel recommended that the antidumping order be lifted and that the antidumping duty be reimbursed to the importer.

## Dumping and Nonmarket Economy Countries

The United States has special rules for calculating the dumping margin of products imported from nonmarket economy countries such as China, because the governments of these countries can control the allocation of resources, production, and labor as well as pricing. The ITA generally determines normal value on the basis of costs of production—hours of labor, raw materials, energy, capital investment, etc.—plus an amount for general expenses and profit. If these data are not available due to governmental controls, then the normal value is considered to be the price at which comparable merchandise is produced in a market economy country at the same level of economic development as the nonmarket economy country. The case *Certain Headwear from the People's Republic of China* illustrates the difficulty in calculating the value of imports from a communist country.

---

### Certain Headwear from The People's Republic of China
54 Fed. Reg. 11983 (1989)
U.S. International Trade Administration

FINAL DETERMINATION OF SALES AT LESS THAN FAIR VALUE

Imports covered by this investigation are caps, hats, and visors made from knitted or woven cloth of vegetable fibers including cotton, flax, and ramie, of man-made fibers, and/or of blends thereof, and which are cut and sewn. . . .

To determine whether sales of the subject merchandise in the United States were made at less than fair value, we compared the United States price with the foreign market value. . . . We have examined information submitted by parties concerning this issue and have determined that, although the degree of state control has lessened, particularly with respect to the production and exportation of headwear, the PRC is appropriately treated as a state-controlled economy for purposes of this investigation.

As a result of our determination to treat the PRC as a state-controlled economy, section 773(c) of the Act requires us to base foreign market value on either the prices of, or the constructed value of, such or similar merchandise in a "non-state-controlled-economy" country. . . .

As noted in the preliminary determination, we sent a questionnaire to, and received a response from, a headwear producer in the Philippines. Since the preliminary determination, we have received a supplemental response from this manufacturer. . . . We did not use information on domestic sales provided by this "surrogate" producer as the foreign market value for PRC sales of polyester headwear since . . . the surrogate merchandise was not sufficiently similar to serve as a basis of comparison. For these sales, we constructed foreign market value by valuing the factors of production employed by the PRC manufacturers using factor cost information provided by the surrogate. This methodology was also utilized for sales of cotton hats with the exception of the cotton input. For the value of the cotton input, we based the factor information on the customs value of U.S. imports from Egypt. For . . . sales (of converted, nonmanufactured items), we constructed foreign market value by valuing the factors of production employed by the PRC manufacturers in performing the conversion using factor cost information provided by the surrogate. Foreign market value based on valuing factors of production includes the statutory minimum for SG&A and profit.

**Decision.** The International Trade Administration ruled that the baseball caps had been dumped at low prices in the United States. The foreign market value of the caps in China was determined on the basis of estimates of the cost of producing like merchandise in the Philippines (using raw material costs from Egypt).

**Comment.** The ITA discussed the reasons that China should be treated as a state-controlled economy in this investigation. The ITA took into consideration: (1) the degree of government ownership—of the twenty-six factories producing headwear, four were state-owned, sixteen cooperatives were collectively owned, and six were foreign-owned. Of the eight trading companies, all

*(continued)*

*(continued)*

were state-owned; (2) the degree of centralized government control over the allocation of resources or inputs—control over cotton and other raw materials and their allocation to different factories; (3) the degree of centralized control over production of goods or outputs; (4) the degree of centralized government control over the country's currency and trade—the *renminbi* is not convertible, which requires that most foreign trade be conducted through state agencies. Since 1988, the national trading compa-

nies have operated autonomously, with responsibility for their own profit and loss. Profits go into employee welfare, expansion, and retained earnings at levels set by the state. Each agency makes its own product export decisions within limits set by the central government. Based on these factors, the ITA concluded that although the economy of the People's Republic of China is in transition, it is still significantly state-controlled for purposes of the investigation.

## Dumping and the World Market in Computer Chips

In the 1980s the United States had a 10 percent share of the $20 billion Japanese semiconductor (computer chip) market. At the same time, Japanese firms had an 85 percent share of the world market. Many reasons explain Japan's success in the semiconductor industry: Government funding spurred research and development by cutting the risk of private expenditures, which, in turn, allowed Japanese firms to quickly reach the technological level of U.S. companies. Protection of the Japanese market for computer chips through trade barriers insulated domestic companies from competition. Moreover, agreements among Japanese firms to buy semiconductors only from domestic suppliers effectively closed the market to outside firms. Finally, aggressive marketing and pricing strategies for export gave Japanese producers an edge in world markets.

To build their market share, Japanese firms had been dumping semiconductors in foreign markets since the early 1980s. Although the United States instituted antidumping proceedings, industry experts realized that antidumping duties would not prevent the chips from entering the United States in the form of finished products. In addition, the Japanese would do nothing to open their domestic market to U.S. semiconductor firms. By the time all dumping investigations would have been carried out and the duties imposed, U.S. firms could not have regained the lead lost in high-technology products. As a result, in the mid-1980s President Reagan imposed $300 million in punitive tariffs on a wide range of Japanese products. Thus, under duress, Japan agreed to enter into a

*Semiconductor Agreement,* by which Japanese semiconductor firms would monitor the export prices of chips sold in third-country markets to prevent excessively low-priced chips from being dumped on the U.S. market.

The European Union, however, was not pleased with this agreement. The same low prices that injured U.S. semiconductor manufacturers were welcomed by European computer manufacturers. In 1987, the European Union instituted a complaint with GATT, which declared the agreement in violation of the GATT Antidumping Code. Under the Antidumping Code then in effect, a country could not take corrective action against dumping in a third country. Japan announced that it would modify its price monitoring program in third countries to comply with the panel's recommendation. (Under GATT 1994 countries may now petition for investigations of dumping in third countries.)

By 1991, the original semiconductor agreement had expired, and the U.S. share of the Japanese semiconductor market had reached over 13 percent. In that year, the United States and Japan entered into a new agreement. This agreement put more responsibility on private firms in the United States and Japan to do business together, and less responsibility on the governments. A stated goal of the agreement called for U.S. semiconductors to reach a 20 percent share of the Japanese market.

The Japanese promised both to encourage Japanese firms to purchase foreign semiconductors and to provide to U.S. firms information for locating customers and marketing their semiconductors in Japan. Perhaps most importantly, the new agreement called for Japanese and U.S. companies to develop long-term business relationships. This aspect of the agreement was essential because many semiconductors must be designed into a finished product, such as a watch or automobile component, and the design stages may take several years. As U.S. competitiveness improved, by 1994 U.S. firms reached 24 percent of the Japanese semiconductor market.

In 1995 the Clinton administration saw the success of the semiconductor agreements as a sign that the United States could "manage" its trade relations with Japan. (*Managed trade* is a principle under which a government sets trade goals for an industry and then uses a system of government incentives and controls to guide trade in the direction of the goals set. Most "free traders" object to the use of managed trade.) Many in Washington also believed that the semiconductor example shows that the Japanese government is likely to enter trade agreements only when they are under the threat of retaliatory tariffs. As a result, the Clinton administration has used the semiconductor negotiations as a guide in conducting trade relations with Japan in other industries, most notably the automotive sector.

In March, 1997, 39 countries concluded negotiations that led to the *Information Technology Agreement* under the sponsorship of the World Trade Organization. The agreement provides for the elimination of tariffs on information technology products by the year 2000. The participants have also agreed to review non-tariff barriers that impede market access for information technology products.

The countries that have signed the agreement represent over 92 perent of the world's trade in information technology products. In addition to the U.S. and the EU countries, Asian nations like Hong Kong, India, Japan, Korea, Malaysia, Singapore, and Thailand have agreed to abide by the agreement's terms. The United States is the largest single exporter of information technology products, accounting for approximately 25 percent of global trade. The agreement is open for signing by all current and applicant WTO members. The products covered by the agreement include semiconductors, computers, telecommunications equipment, and software.

The World Trade Organization recently agreed to hear allegations brought by the United States that the European Union, as well as its members of the United Kingdom and Ireland, have improperly classified local area network equipment and personal computers with multimedia capabilities for customs purposes. The three cases are being heard together after the Dispute Settlement Body of the World Trade Organization established a panel in early 1997.

> **http://www.ita.doc.gov/import_admin/
> records**
> *See for additional material on antidumping and other issues.*

## Unfair Import Laws: Subsidies and Countervailing Duties

A second type of unfair trade practice is subsidies. *Subsidies* are financial contributions or benefits conferred by a government to a domestic firm or industry to achieve some economic or social objective. Subsidies might be granted to assist the start-up of new companies, to retire old factories, to help firms meet new environmental regulations, or to protect industries such as steel, aircraft, or agriculture that are essential to national security. They may take many forms, including low interest loans, direct cash payments, export financing and credit assistance, favorable tax treatment, and so on. Subsidies are granted by all industrialized nations to virtually all segments of their economies, and not just to manufacturing firms. The European Union, the United States, and Japan each spend tens of billions of dollars annually on agricultural subsidies alone, including direct payments to farmers.

Subsidies have long been recognized as damaging to the international economy. Subsidized industries are able to sell their products in foreign markets at prices lower than would otherwise be possible, which distorts trade patterns based on comparative advantage, and gives an unfair competitive advantage to subsidized industries. Subsidies also encourage private industries to embark on commercial ventures that, once the subsidy ends, may prove unprofitable or commercially disastrous. These drawbacks of subsidies can be illustrated in the case of the *Concorde* supersonic aircraft, which flies from Europe to the United States in less than half the time of a regular jet. The aircraft's development by a consortium of European companies was spurred not by demand, but by a host of European Union subsidies. In commercial use, the plane turned out to be highly unprofitable. Without the subsidy, the plane would have proved too costly to merit production.

## GATT 1994 Agreement on Subsidies and Countervailing Measures

Subsidies have been regulated by GATT since 1947. The current law is found in the GATT 1994 *Agreement on Subsidies and Countervailing Measures,* negotiated during the Uruguay Round. The basic terms of the new GATT agreement have been incorporated into federal law in the Uruguay Round Agreements Act.

Under the GATT agreement, subsides may be dealt with in several ways. First, a WTO member country may appeal to the WTO for dispute resolution. The WTO may recommend that the subsidy be discontinued, that its harmful effects be eliminated, or that some countermeasure be taken by the importing country. Secondly, an importing country may initiate its own administrative proceedings, similar to antidumping proceedings, to impose a countervailing duty on the subsidized goods in order to eliminate their unfair price advantage. A *countervailing duty* (CVD) is a special tariff, in addition to the normal import tariff, imposed on imports of subsidized goods in an amount equal to the amount of the countervailable subsidy. A CVD action may be brought at the same time as the WTO dispute settlement action. However, only one form of relief—either the CVD or a countermeasure approved by the WTO—is available.

## Definition of a Subsidy

A subsidy exists if a government *confers a benefit* on a domestic firm or industry *and* provides any form of income or price support *or* provides a financial contribution by

1. Providing a grant or making loans at less than prevailing commercial interest rates, or loan guarantees that allow the company to receive loans at rates more favorable than nonguaranteed commercial loan rates;

2. Not collecting revenue or taxes otherwise due;
3. Providing investment capital if the investment decision is inconsistent with the usual practices of private investors;
4. Furnishing goods or services other than general infrastructure, such as building a road or bridge;
5. Purchasing goods from firms at a higher price than would be paid in the marketplace.

GATT 1994 provides for three types of subsidies: prohibited subsidies, domestic or adverse effects subsidies, and nonactionable or socially beneficial subsidies. All three types must meet the preceding definition.

## Prohibited Subsidies

*Prohibited subsidies* include export subsidies or import substitution subsidies. An *export subsidy* is made available to domestic firms upon the export of their product, or is contingent upon export performance. An *import substitution subsidy* is a governmental subsidy whose payment is contingent on its recipient using or purchasing domestically made goods over imported goods. Both of these are completely prohibited under GATT. An importing country that is a WTO member can request dispute settlement before a WTO panel regardless of whether the subsidy causes injury to any of its firms or industries. WTO dispute resolution should take less than a year to complete. Countervailing duties may be imposed on export subsidies through administrative or legal proceedings in the importing country. In CVD proceedings, export subsidies must be shown to have caused or threatened material injury to a domestic industry producing a like product.

Examples of an export subsidy include money paid on the basis of the number of exported goods, free or subsidized transportation provided for export shipments, rebates of taxes paid on the export of products, export credit guarantees at below market rates, and special tax treatment of income earned through export sales. In an interesting example of an export subsidy, Germany assisted the development, manufacture, and export of the European Airbus (a jumbo jet that competes with U.S. planes) by providing no-interest loans and currency stabilization guarantees to the manufacturers. These subsidies allowed the manufacturers to enter contracts to sell planes to U.S. airlines without assuming any currency fluctuation risk. In 1992, a GATT panel ruled that the German currency stabilization guarantees violated GATT.

## Domestic Subsidies

Many subsidies take the form of government programs designed to achieve some greater social or national economic objective, ranging from health care to national defense, and indirectly give firms an advantage in world markets. After all, when a government makes large purchases of overpriced military jets, it subsidizes (and lowers the cost of) passenger aircraft. These purchases generally fall in the category of *domestic subsidies,* and must be distinguished from export subsidies. Examples include the provision of capital or low-cost loans for modernizing factories or for buying land on which to build new factories; providing industry with low-cost oil, chemicals, or other raw materials at discount prices from government-owned stockpiles; government defense spending on military aircraft or ships; grants for research and development of medicines; cash payments for apprentice programs or tax deductions to employers that pay college tuition for employees; government-supplied utilities; tax deductions or tax credits to encourage investment in capital equipment. Domestic subsidies such as these are generally permissible as a part of the legitimate responsibility of government to direct its industrial growth and fund social programs.

**Remedies for Adverse Effects of Domestic Subsidies.** Some domestic subsidies, however, give unfair competitive advantage to domestic firms and are known in GATT as *adverse effects subsidies.* They are actionable at the WTO only if they (1) cause injury to a domestic industry of another WTO member country, (2) cause nullification and impairment of rights accruing to a member country under GATT, or (3) cause serious prejudice to another member. *Serious prejudice* is *presumed to exist* if the subsidy of a product exceeds 5 percent of its value, if the subsidy covers a firm's operating losses, or if the government forgives a debt owed to it. Serious

prejudice *may exist* if (1) the subsidy impedes world trade in similar products produced in member countries; (2) the subsidy causes lost sales or price undercutting by the subsidized product; or (3) in the case of a subsidy of a primary product or commodity, it causes an increase in the subsidizing country's world market share of that product. In these cases, the WTO may recommend that the subsidizing country remove the prohibited subsidy or that the complaining country take some countermeasures against it. In a CVD proceeding conducted by an administrative agency in the importing country, the requirement is different; a complaining party need only show that the domestic subsidy caused or threatens to cause *material injury* to domestic producers of like products.

**What Makes a Subsidy Specific?** The second requirement, for both WTO actions and CVD actions, is that the domestic subsidy be *specific. All* prohibited (export and import substitution) subsidies are presumed to be specific. All other subsidies are specific if they are limited to an enterprise or industry. A government's objective criteria for eligibility for a domestic subsidy is *not* specific if eligibility is automatic and does not favor one enterprise or industry over another. For instance, suppose that tax authorities allow all taxpayers to deduct $35,000 of the cost of new machinery as an ordinary operating expense in the year of purchase instead of $17,500 that had been allowed. Because the tax reduction does not favor one industry over another, it is not specific. However, if the companies receiving the subsidy are limited in number, if one firm or industry is the predominant user of the subsidy, or if the subsidy is limited to firms within a certain geographical region, then the subsidy is probably specific. In the next case, *Cabot Corporation v. United States,* a U.S. court adopted the "specificity test." The test was enacted into law by Congress in 1988 and subsequently brought to the Uruguay Round Agreement by the United States.

**Upstream Subsidies.** An *upstream subsidy* is one that is granted by a government to a firm or industry that produces raw materials or component parts (input products) that are used in an

## Cabot Corporation v. United States
620 F.Supp. 722 (1985)
United States Court of International Trade

### BACKGROUND AND FACTS

Plaintiff, Cabot Corporation, is contesting the International Trade Administration's finding that the Mexican government's provision of carbon black feedstock and natural gas to Mexican producers at below-market prices did not constitute a countervailable subsidy. Carbon black feedstock and natural gas are used in the production of paints, inks, plastics, and carbon paper. The feedstock is a by-product of crude oil and sold in Mexico through PEMEX, the government-owned oil company. Pursuant to a comprehensive economic development plan, PEMEX supplied the feedstock and natural gas at below-market prices to two Mexican producers of carbon black. The plaintiff, U.S. producer of carbon black, contends that under U.S. law the actions of the Mexican government amount to a countervailable domestic subsidy.

### JUDGE CARMAN

The chief issue presented to the Court is whether benefits that are available on a nonpreferential basis—that is, benefits obtainable by any enterprise or industry—can be [a prohibited subsidy] and therefore countervailable. Since any industrial user in Mexico could purchase carbon black feedstock and natural gas at the same price, the ITA viewed PEMEX's provision of these inputs at well below world market prices as not constituting a countervailable practice. The ITA view was based on the "generally available benefits rule," which has evolved within the administrative agency and was adopted by the court in *Carlisle Tire & Rubber Co. v. United States,* 5 C.I.T. 229, 564 F.Supp. 834 (1983).

The generally available benefits rule as articulated by the defendant is essentially that benefits available to all companies and industries within an economy are not countervailable subsidies. Defendant's conclusions are primarily drawn from [the federal statute] which refers to countervailable domestic subsidies as being those provided to "a specific enterprise or industry, or group of enterprises or industries." Thus, argues defendant, benefits "generally available" to all enterprises or industries are not subsidies under [federal law]. . . .

The court in *Carlisle* recognized the absurdity of a rule that would require the imposition of CVDs where producers or importers have benefited from general subsidies, as "almost every product which enters international commerce" would be subject to CVDs. Alternatively, the court [in another case] recognized the absurdity of a law that would transform an obvious subsidy into a noncountervailable benefit merely by extending the availability of the subsidy to the entire economy. Thus, although a bounty or grant is preferential in nature, bestowed upon an individual class, the generally available benefits rule as developed and applied by the ITA is not an acceptable legal standard for determining the countervailability of benefits. . . .

In the case before the Court, the availability of carbon black feedstock and natural gas at controlled prices does not determine whether the benefits actually received by these two carbon black producers are countervailable subsidies. The programs appear to effect specific quantifiable provisions of carbon black feedstock and natural gas to specific identifiable enterprises. That additional enterprises or industries can participate in the programs, whether theoretically or actually, does not destroy the programs as subsidies. The programs are apparently available to all Mexican enterprises, but in their actual implementation may result in special bestowals upon specific enterprises. . . .

The rule of not countervailing generally available benefits as developed by the ITA does not render a correct result in this case. The availability of carbon black feedstock at government-set rates is not the determinative factor regarding countervailability. Rather, the inquiry for the ITA is whether the rates in fact afford the carbon black producers a benefit or competitive advantage. The case must therefore be remanded for further investigation and redetermination consistent with the requirements set forth in this opinion to determine if CVDs should be assessed.

**Decision.** The court reversed the ITA's determination and remanded the case to the ITA for further investigation. The Court rejected the ITA's "general availability" test for the existence of a domestic subsidy. The Court held that a domestic subsidy exists if a benefit is in fact bestowed upon a specific enterprise or industry.

exported product. For instance, a subsidy on coal might also be considered a subsidy on steel made in furnaces that burn that coal. A subsidy on European wheat might be considered a subsidy upon Italian pasta made from that wheat. Similarly, a subsidy on live swine might be considered an upstream subsidy of unprocessed pork exports. A subsidy of semiconductors would amount to a subsidy of computers in which they are installed. Upstream subsidies are subject to countervailing duties if the input product is made available at a below-market price and has a significant effect on the cost of manufacturing the final product. Under the U.S. Uruguay Round Agreements Act, upstream subsidies include only domestic subsidies, and not export subsidies. Upstream subsidies may be countervailed only when they bestow a competitive benefit on the goods in question.

## Nonactionable or Socially Beneficial Subsidies

*Socially beneficial subsidies* are not actionable under the WTO and not countervailable if they meet the requirements of the GATT agreement. They include (1) certain subsidies granted to industry or universities for expanding knowledge through research and development, provided it does not directly create an unfair competitive advantage to exported products; (2) certain subsidies to poor, depressed, or underemployed geographic regions—U.S. law requires that per capital GDP or income does not exceed 85 percent of the national average or that unemployment be at least 110 percent of the rate in the subsidizing country; and (3) certain subsidies granted on a one-time basis to help companies meet costly environmental or antipollution regulations, provided it is limited to 20 percent of the cost and made available to all companies that require the new pollution control equipment or technology. Member countries should notify the WTO Committee on Subsidies and Countervailing Measures in advance of granting a socially beneficial subsidy. A socially beneficial subsidy is not countervailable if the country that granted it notified the WTO Committee on Subsidies and Countervailing Measures in advance. An importing country's

only recourse in this case is at the WTO which uses binding arbitration in these cases.

## Subsidies and Countries That Are Moving to Market Economies

Applying the principles of countervailing duty law to goods exported from nonmarket economy countries presents several problems. Nonmarket economy countries, such as China or former communist countries, have such great control over economic planning that, in effect, *all* goods are subsidized. Historically, the governments in nonmarket countries allocated raw materials, determined wages and production schedules, set prices, and fixed currency exchange rates— functions normally determined by market forces. Moreover, foreign trade decisions were made by the state trading organization charged with the responsibility for that particular sector of the economy. In *Georgetown Steel Corporation v. United States,* 801 F.2d 1308 (Fed. Cir. 1986), the court ruled that the U.S. countervailing duty statute could not be applied to imports from nonmarket countries. The court believed Congress had designed the statute to remedy subsidies that distort the free market process by altering the market decisions of manufacturers and exporters. In nonmarket economy countries, the subsidy is, in a sense, made only to the government itself, with no resulting effect on market decision making.

Since the late 1980s, the political systems and economies of these countries have undergone great change. Significant private investment from North America, Europe, and Japan, the transfer of ownership to private hands, and the introduction of market principles are taking place. Suppose a company was at one time state-owned, but has been sold to private investors. It might be located in a formerly communist country, a developing country such as Brazil, or in an industrialized country such as Great Britain or France.

While the company was state owned, it had received subsidies from the government to assist in the costs of operation. Now the newly privatized company exports goods to the U.S. Are these goods countervailable on import into the United States even though the subsidies have ceased? In

1994 the U.S. Court of International Trade ruled that if the company was sold to private investors for fair market value and in an arms-length transaction, then the goods currently being imported into the U.S. were not countervailable. The court believed that the economic advantages of the subsidies received while the firm was government-owned did not pass through to the new private owners.

> **http://www.doc.gov**
> Search here for information on subsidies, as well as other information and links.

## Countervailing Duty Investigations

Countries are expected to try and settle their disputes at the WTO before initiating CVD complaints. As with antidumping proceedings, U.S. CVD proceedings take place before federal administrative agencies. Investigations are initiated by domestic industry through petitions filed with the ITA, which determines if a subsidy exists, and with the ITC, which determines if a material injury has occurred. CVD investigations must be dismissed where the volume of subsidized imports is negligible, less than 3 percent. CVDs must be removed when the subsidy has ended. In recent years, the number of CVD complaints filed in the United States has dwindled considerably. From 1994 through 1996, only nine complaints were filed and in only four of those cases were orders imposed.

## Material Injury in Unfair Import Cases

In unfair trade actions between WTO members, the administrative agency must find that a domestic industry has been materially injured, threatened with material injury, or that the establishment of an industry has been materially retarded. This requirement applies to both antidumping actions and CVD actions. The term *domestic industry* means "domestic producers as a whole of like products" or those firms whose collective output constitutes most of the total domestic production of a given product. In the case of a smaller number of domestic firms that sell their products only in isolated regional markets within a country, material injury can be found by examining the impact on those firms selling within that market.

The U.S. CVD law distinguishes between subsidized products imported from WTO member countries and those imported from nonmember countries. Products subsidized by countries that are *not* members of the WTO do not have the full protection of the GATT agreement; their products can be countervailed regardless of whether they cause injury. Of course, subsidies from member countries can only be countervailed if they cause or threaten material injury to a U.S. industry.

The material injury requirement under the unfair import statutes prescribes a finding of less harm than does the serious injury requirement in the escape clause. Material injury has generally been defined as injury that is not inconsequential or unimportant. In determining material injury under the unfair trade laws, the ITC must consider all relevant economic factors. Factors used to determine material injury include (1) the volume of the dumped or subsidized imports (Have dumped imports increased significantly?); (2) the effect of the imports on prices in the domestic market for like products (Have prices been undercut significantly? Have prices been depressed? Are domestic firms unable to raise prices to cover increased costs?); and (3) the impact of the imports on the domestic industry, including all relevant economic data reflecting industry sales, profits, market share, productivity, return on investment, utilization of capacity, cash flow, wages, unemployment, growing inventories, and so on. A finding of material injury must be reviewed every five years after an antidumping order is issued. As the following case, *American Spring Wire Corporation v. United States*, illustrates, profitability of the industry alone is an insufficient indicator of material injury.

## Judicial Review in International Trade Cases

Decisions of the ITA or ITC in both countervailing duty cases and antidumping duty cases are reviewable in the U.S. Court of International Trade if they are final decisions or if they are negative

## BACKGROUND AND FACTS

Plaintiffs are U.S. manufacturers of prestressed concrete steel wire (strand). They brought this action to challenge the International Trade Commission's negative injury determination with regard to imports of strand from Spain, France, the United Kingdom, and Brazil. The investigations were conducted pursuant to antidumping proceedings against imports from the United Kingdom and countervailing duty proceedings against imports from the remaining countries. The commission found that domestic production capacity, plant utilization, and shipments of strand had increased significantly from 1979 through 1981. Employment showed no discernible changes. Hourly wages had increased in the industry. Although sales also increased, net profits had declined and losses occurred during the first nine months of 1982. Based on this evidence, the plaintiffs brought this action contending that the commission's determination was not based on substantial evidence.

## American Spring Wire Corporation v. United States
*590 F.Supp. 1273 (1984)*
*United States Court of International Trade*

## SENIOR JUDGE MALETZ

"Material injury" has been defined by Congress as "harm which is not inconsequential, immaterial, or unimportant." Congress has directed the ITC to consider "all relevant economic factors which have a bearing on the state of the industry," including, but not limited to:

I. actual and potential decline in output, sales, market share, profits, productivity, return on investments, and utilization of capacity,
II. factors affecting domestic prices, and
III. actual and potential negative effects on cash flow, inventories, employment, wages, growth, ability to raise capital, and investment.

The list is illustrative, but not exclusive. The flexibility afforded to the ITC is evidenced by the legislative history. ("The significance of the various factors affecting an industry will depend upon the facts of each particular case. Neither the presence nor the absence of any factor listed in the bill can necessarily give decisive guidance with respect to an injury determination.") . . .

Examination of the record of the four investigations demonstrates that there is substantial evidence to support the finding that the domestic PC strand industry was not suffering material injury. For the record shows the following:

Market demand for PC strand remained relatively constant during the periods of the investigations. It was not seriously affected by the recession or other forces that had an adverse impact on other segments of the steel industry. Indeed, the domestic industry expanded vigorously throughout the periods covered by the investigations—an expansion that appears to have resulted in part from a 1978 antidumping order issued against PC strand from Japan. Three producers entered the market in 1980, and domestic productive capacity was substantially greater for the first nine months of 1982 than it was for the whole of 1979.

Moreover, domestic strand production and shipments increased markedly in the period from 1979 to 1981, although they declined slightly in 1982. Capacity utilization too rose steadily after the 1978 antidumping order against Japan, even in the face of the major increases in productive capacity. That is, domestic producers' shipments grew even faster than their productive capacity. In addition, employment in the domestic industry was steady and actually increased through 1981, though it fell slightly in 1982.

Net sales figures likewise increased throughout the period under investigation, although they showed some decline during 1982. Domestic producers were not required to warehouse excessive production, with inventory levels remaining virtually constant throughout the period of the investigations, increasing slightly only during 1982.

The domestic industry had no trouble raising capital, as demonstrated by its capital expenditures for new plants and equipment and by its interest expenses for working capital and new capital investments. What is more, the domestic producers have grown rapidly and gained an ever-increasing share of the domestic market.

*(continued)*

*(continued)*

In fact, the record reveals only one negative factor—lack of profitability during 1982. Looking at the industry as a whole, however, it had a net profit in every year except 1982, and the loss it experienced in the first nine months of 1982 was not significant in proportion to net sales. Moreover, if operating profit is considered, the domestic industry was profitable in every year. The loss in 1982, therefore, was accounted for by nonoperating expenses, which appear related to the domestic industry's large increase in capacity during 1982. Given this capacity increase—with its attendant capital costs and diseconomies of scale while the capacity came on stream—the performance of the domestic industry appeared extremely strong.

Plaintiffs, however, contend that the losses suffered by the domestic industry during the last nine months of 1982 preclude any finding that the industry is healthy and mandate a finding of material injury. But profitability is only one of the factors to be considered by the ITC. This does not denigrate its importance to the Commission's analysis of material injury, but it does underscore the legislative intent that absence of profits shall not act as a proxy for injury. Whatever the importance of a particular factor, the ITC is obligated "to consider and weigh a number of other pertinent economic and financial criteria, and consider all the facts and circumstances, including the health of the domestic industry." *SCM Corp. v. United States,* 4 C.I.T. 7, 13, 544 F.Supp. 194, 199 (1982).

Under the circumstances, substantial evidence supported the Commission's conclusion that the industry was not suffering material injury, notwithstanding the loss it suffered in 1982—a loss that was not unusual considering the industry's rapid expansion in that period. It was thus reasonable for the ITC to find that the loss was insufficient to outweigh other significant economic factors, including increased productive capacity, increased shipments, and all the other indications of a healthy industry.

For the foregoing reasons, plaintiffs' motion for judgment on the agency record is denied and the negative injury determinations of the ITC are affirmed.

**Decision.** The decision of the ITC is affirmed. The court found that the negative injury determination was based on substantial evidence. Profitability data, standing alone, are not sufficient to support a finding of material injury or threat of material injury under the antidumping and countervailing duty laws. The court ruled that the level of profitability of an industry is only one factor to be considered by the ITC and that it would not outweigh other indicia of a healthy industry. The ITC must weigh all relevant economic and financial criteria in making its determination.

determinations. A *negative determination* is a decision by the agency either to not initiate an investigation or that a material injury does not exist. If an antidumping determination involves Canadian or Mexican goods, appeals may be made to a binational arbitration panel established under NAFTA. The number of both antidumping and countervailing orders issued has declined in the last several years. In 1996 less than a dozen orders of either kind were imposed.

In escape clause cases, the courts have far less control over the president's decisions. The following escape clause case, *Maple Leaf Fish Co. v. United States,* illustrates the limitations on judicial review in international trade cases in which Congress has granted wide discretion to the president.

## Maple Leaf Fish Co. v. United States
### 762 F.2d 86 (1985)
### United States Court of Appeals (Fed. Cir.)

BACKGROUND AND FACTS
In 1980, the American Mushroom Institute, a trade association representing U.S. canners and growers of mushrooms, filed a petition with the International Trade Commission for import relief under Section 201 of the Trade Act of 1974. The ITC initiated an investigation to determine if articles classified under TSUS 144.2, "mushrooms . . .

*(continued)*

*(continued)*

otherwise prepared or preserved were being imported in such substantial quantities as to cause or threaten serious injury to a like or competing domestic industry. The investigation determined that U.S. producers of fresh and canned mushrooms had suffered serious injury, although no mention was made in the report of frozen mushrooms. The president then proclaimed increased duties on all mushrooms covered by TSUS 144.2. Maple Leaf Fish, an importer of frozen and breaded mushrooms, filed this action to protest the assessment of these higher duties. Maple Leaf contended that no evidence showed injury to the frozen mushroom industry and that the president had no authority to levy duties on that product.

CIRCUIT JUDGE DAVIS

Appellant makes the argument as if the ITC had gone wildly beyond its own investigation to include frozen mushrooms, without the slightest basis in the record before it. The fact is, however, that a part of the report entitled "Information Obtained in the Investigation" contains a section headed "Dried, frozen and fresh mushrooms," giving in detail the statistics on imports of those particular varieties, including imports from Canada. We, therefore, have before us an ITC report which followed an investigation that actually included frozen mushrooms, and a report which covered frozen mushrooms in its final determinations.

The question then is to what extent the courts can review the challenged actions of the Commission and the president in such a case. The critical element is that the area of the "escape clause" legislation undoubtedly involves the president and his close relationship to foreign affairs, our nation's connections with other countries, and the external ramifications of international trade. More than that, Congress has vested the president with very broad discretion and choice as to what he decides to do affirmatively, or even whether he should do anything. Similarly, the ITC has great leeway to consider various factors—including all economic factors it deems relevant—bearing on its final determination "whether an article is being imported into the United States in such increased quantities as to be a substantial cause of serious injury, or the threat thereof, to the domestic industry producing an article like or directly competitive with the imported article" 19 U.S.C. at 2251(b)(1)-(6).

In international trade controversies of this highly discretionary kind—involving the president and foreign affairs—this court and its predecessors have often reiterated the very limited role of reviewing courts. For a court to interpose, there has to be a clear misconstruction of the governing statute, a significant procedural violation, or action outside delegated authority. On the other hand, "[t]he President's findings of fact and the motivations for his action are not subject to review." The same is true, we think, of ITC "escape clause" action which is preparatory to, and designed to aid, presidential action. The same factors which have led, in this kind of discretionary case, to strict confinement of the court's intervention vis-à-vis the president are equally applicable to the ITC in its "escape clause" functioning.

**Decision.** On appeal, the court affirmed the judgment for the government. The determinations of fact (i.e., whether or not there was injury) and the decision of the president to impose duties are not subject to judicial review in the courts, unless they exceed the authority granted by the statute. In international trade controversies, the ordinary standard for judicial review of administrative decisions is not applicable. The court here will not look to see if there is "substantial evidence" to support the decisions of either the commission or the president.

# Unfair Trade: The Use of Convict and Forced Labor

When we think of convicts and forced laborers in prison camps in totalitarian countries we naturally think of them in humanitarian terms. But there is also an economic aspect to their plight. In non-democratic societies the government can use convict labor to produce goods to compete unfairly in world markets against goods made by paid workers in democratic countries. As you read the following case, consider both the economic and moral basis of U.S. policy.

## China Diesel Imports, Inc. v. The United States

870 F.Supp. 347 (1994)
United States Court of International Trade

### BACKGROUND AND FACTS

Diesel engines made by the JINMA Diesel Engine Factory in the People's Republic of China were prohibited from entering the United States by the U.S. Customs Service because it was believed that they were produced by convict labor. U.S. law provides that "All goods, wares, articles, and merchandise mined, produced, or manufactured wholly or in part in any foreign country by convict labor or/and forced labor or/and indentured labor under penal sanctions shall not be entitled to entry at any of the ports of the United States, and the importation thereof is hereby prohibited. . . . " The importer, China Diesel Imports, Inc., brought this action to have the engines entered for sale in the United States.

### JUDGE RESTANI

Both documentary evidence published for internal Chinese consumption and official U.S. government publications are consistent in their description of the basic Chinese penal institutions. Specifically, China has traditional style prison facilities, but it also maintains "Reform Through Labor" facilities, which may be either camps or factories. Persons convicted of crimes are assigned to both types of institutions. In addition, China has "Education Through Labor" facilities, to which persons are assigned following local administrative action. All three facilities are forced labor institutions. The first two, however, are clearly penal, and the inmate workers therein are convicts.

The model 1100 diesel engines at issue were produced by the JINMA Diesel Engine Factory in Kunming, China. The JINMA factory is described as a "Reform Through Labor" facility in at least two Chinese publications. This information is corroborated by unplanned interviews conducted by a U.S. State Department employee with persons living in the vicinity of the JINMA factory. The conclusion is also corroborated by the prevarication of the JINMA factory manager and what the court concludes were staged tours of the facility.

Next, the factory manager defended the plant against "local talk" that it was a prison by explaining that the facility was originally established to provide work for families of prison employees. Thus, the factory was owned by the Ministry of Justice. This does not comport with Chinese publications that place the factory under the Ministry of Justice because it is a "Reform Through Labor" facility. Further, many of the factory buildings were not open to view, even when a request was made. Other evidence falls in place as well, such as a prison truck observed leaving from the direction of the JINMA gate, a worker hiding her face from the video camera used by plaintiff during one visit, hesitancy about showing the U.S. State Department observers the location of the Yunnan No. 1 Prison wall, a blank space on a city map for both the admitted prison and the factory grounds, and the repeated failure to tender any documentation on production and personnel.

**Decision.** The court held that the diesel engines are convict-made and are to be excluded from entry into the customs territory of the United States.

# Chapter Summary

A nation's choice either to protect its domestic industries from foreign competition or to adopt free trade policies is an economic and political decision. A country that joins the World Trade Organization pledges to protect domestic industries from foreign competition only within the guidelines and international legal standards set out in the General Agreement on Tariffs and Trade. This chapter discussed how GATT permits countries to "safeguard" domestic industries from increasing imports and offset the price advantage of "unfairly" imported goods. The Uruguay Round agreements significantly changed international trade rules. The United States has implemented the GATT 1994 rules in the Uruguay Round Agreements Act, effective January 1, 1995.

A country may safeguard a domestic industry from serious injury caused by increasing imports, by providing import relief or adjusting import competition. The president may provide import relief in the form of temporary tariff increases or quotas only upon investigation by the International Trade Commission and its finding that increasing imports are the substantial cause of serious injury to a domestic industry producing like products. The purpose of the relief is to give the domestic industry time to adjust to market conditions. The willingness of the president to protect an industry depends on national interests as well as the president's own economic and trade philosophies.

Unfair trade includes dumping and subsidies. Both practices allow foreign products to be imported at unfairly low prices. The GATT Agreement on Dumping allows a nation to impose an antidumping duty on imports sold for less than normal value. The GATT Subsidies Agreement permits countervailing duties on subsidized imports to offset the foreign government subsidy. In both cases, the unfair action must have materially injured a domestic industry. WTO dispute resolution is available for resolving unfair import disputes between nations.

---

## QUESTIONS AND CASE PROBLEMS

1. What makes an import practice "unfair"? What remedies are available under U.S. law to protect domestic industries from unfair imports?

2. Describe the role of the International Trade Administration and the International Trade Commission in regulating import competition.

3. One form of relief provided to industries adversely affected by foreign imports is federal adjustment assistance, or cash payments, to displaced workers. To be eligible after the ITC affirmatively invokes an escape clause action, the secretary of labor must determine that (1) a significant number of workers lost their jobs; (2) production of the firm has decreased; and (3) increased imports of articles, like or directly competitive with those made by the workers, contributed importantly to loss of their jobs. Great Western Sugar Co. produced refined sugar directly from sugar beets. In 1985, it closed its doors and filed for bankruptcy. Its workers sought adjustment assistance. The secretary of labor determined that the first two requirements were met but that the third—increased imports of like or directly competitive articles contributing to the loss of jobs—was not met. Records show that raw sugar imports increased during three of the four years prior to Great Western ceasing business. However, refined sugar imports did not increase. The secretary of labor denied assistance, stating that raw sugar importation was not a "like or directly competitive article . . . contributing importantly" to the loss of jobs. The workers appealed. Their argument was that raw sugar was "directly competitive" with their refined sugar after it was processed. Give your opinion of their argument and what you think was the result of their appeal? *West-*

*ern Conference of Teamsters v. Brock,* 709 F.Supp. 1159 (C.I.T. 1989).

4. Samsung Electronics America, Inc., which manufactures color televisions in Korea for export to the United States, has been accused of dumping. What information will the ITA use to determine if Samsung is selling televisions in the United States for less than normal value? What if Samsung were to contend that bad debt expenses in Korea should be a factor in determining normal value? Are warranty expenses and volume rebates in Korea also used in determining the normal value in the home market? See *Daewoo Electronics Co., Ltd. v. United States,* 712 F.Supp. 931 (C.I.T. 1989).

5. The U.S. Department of Commerce's International Trade Administration (ITA) determined that several Taiwanese companies sold color televisions (CTVs) in the United States at less than fair value. The International Trade Commission (ITC) found that the Taiwanese imports posed a threat of material injury to the domestic industry. The U.S. Customs Service then imposed antidumping duties on CTVs and determined that the actual duties would be set through six periodic reviews.

During one of those reviews, the ITA determined that the exporter AOC sold its CTVs in its home market at below the cost of production. AOC claimed that it had higher labor costs for CTVs as opposed to other products coming from the same production center, and that its sole local distributor had agreed to pay some of its research expenses which AOC therefore alleges should be deducted from its total expenses. In its review, the Court of International Trade denied both of AOC's claims because the records to show the research work done by AOC for its distributor were not adequate and the differential in production costs could not be related to any specific cost centers. AOC appealed to the Court of Appeals. Should it affirm the decision of the Court of International Trade?

6. Grupo Industries Camesa (Camesa) a Mexican producer of steel wire rope was charged with selling in the United States steel wire rope that was priced at less than fair value. The Court of International Trade affirmed a final decision from the International Trade Commission that an industry in the U.S. was materially injured by reason of those imports. Camesa argues that the imported steel wire rope did not compete with the domestic steel wire rope and that the Commission did not consider the industry's business cycle.

   It alleges that, while domestic and imported steel wire ropes are physically fungible, the market share for each shows that they are not commercially fungible inasmuch as the domestic product has 60 percent of the market even though it charges 30 percent higher prices. It also noted that some domestic firms imported rope from Mexico and sold it at higher prices than those charged for the rope from Camesa. Testimony indicated that the products had similar uses and were often sold by the same distributors.

   Camesa also alleges that the industry was in a downturn in the period under review and that the downturn, not the imports, caused the domestic industry to suffer. It notes that the ITC made no specific finding regarding the influence of the business cycle on the domestic industry. Would these factors cause the court to reverse the ITC decision against Camesa?

7. The American Grape Growers alleged that imports of wine from France and Italy were being subsidized and sold in the U.S. at less than fair value. The ITC's preliminary review found no reasonable indication that a U.S. industry was threatened with material injury by reason of those imports. The American growers said the ITC decision did not cumulate the imports from France and Italy as they should have been. It instead had considered the two products different, since the French wines were primarily white wines, and the Italian wines were primarily red and effervescent. The growers also said the ITC was wrong to base its decision on whether an injury had been proved, as opposed to whether there was a possibility of injury. Do you agree with the grape growers that the ITC preliminary decision was wrong?

8. Your company manufactures golf clubs and has expanded its market to Europe. The wholesale price of the clubs in the United States is $500 per set. In an effort to get a greater share of the European market, your company is selling the same clubs for $395 per set in Europe. What are the possible legal and ethical implications of this pricing scheme?

9. Are there any places where antidumping, countervailing duties, and other trade disputes can be resolved other than through the U.S. Department of Commerce and the International Trade Commission? Will the U.S. courts make all ultimate determinations on all such disputes?

## MANAGERIAL IMPLICATIONS

Your firm manufactures optic transistors (OTs) used as a component part of personal computers. U.S. firms control 60 percent of the U.S. market for OTs. The market has done well overall, but recently, Japanese manufacturers of computers have increased their market share. Over the past two years the Japanese have been exporting OTs to the United States in larger quantities. You have noticed that in the past two years your share of the U.S. market for OTs has dropped from more than 25 percent to less than 20 percent. In addition, your total sales have declined, your inventories are at their largest levels, and you have had to postpone hiring new employees. You have been informed by one of your better customers that it can purchase imported OTs for $0.95 each, ex factory, or $1.00, CIF American port. Your U.S. price has been $1.20, FOB your factory, with your costs at $0.90. The same OTs are sold to Japanese computer firms at $1.15. Furthermore, you have learned that the Japanese government assists OT manufacturers by rebating the value-added tax normally assessed on all products manufactured in Japan.

To complicate your problems, you have experienced difficulty cracking export markets. You noticed that countries in which personal computers are now being assembled, such as Brazil, Korea, and Taiwan, have restricted your imports through a maze of complex regulations. These regulations require that you disclose important manufacturing and design techniques before import licenses will be granted. You are also concerned that your design patents will not be protected there, because Korean patent protection laws are not enforced. Korea has imposed quotas on OTs that make it virtually impossible to export to that market.

What remedies are available to your firm under U.S. law? What factors (economic, political or other) will affect the outcome of the case? Discuss.

# Chapter Twelve

# Laws Governing Access to Foreign Markets

The process of opening a country's markets to competition by foreign firms is often a slow and painful one, burdened by local political concerns. Many trade disputes over foreign market access have lasted for years. But as more and more industries become dependent on export sales, they become more vulnerable to foreign trade barriers. Open access to foreign markets thus becomes critical to business survival.

This chapter examines a few separate GATT 1994 agreements that are intended to open markets for goods and services in WTO member nations. These agreements cover the following areas: (1) technical barriers to trade, including product standards; (2) import licensing procedures; (3) government procurement of goods and services; (4) trade in services, including consulting, engineering, banking and financial services, insurance, telecommunications, and the professions; (5) trade in agricultural products; (6) trade in textiles and apparel; (7) trade-related investment measures; and (8) trade-related aspects of intellectual property rights. The United States has implemented these new GATT agreements in the *Uruguay Round Agreements Act.* The chapter concludes with a look at the U.S. response to foreign trade barriers that deny access to U.S. products and services or that treat U.S. firms unfairly. The United States hasn't always been willing to rely on GATT dispute settlement procedures, but has instead resorted to threats of retaliation against other countries to assure open access to their markets and fair treatment of U.S. products there.

**http://www.mac.doc.gov/tcc/treaty.htm**
*or*
**http://www.mac.doc.gov/**
Go to this site for the Trade Compliance Center of the U.S. Department of Commerce. One of the most complete on-line sources for all trade and related agreements entered into by the United States. Research trade agreements by indexing on the agreement, country, or issue. Also market access reports by country or region.

## Technical Barriers to Trade

A *technical regulation* is a law or regulation affecting a product's characteristics—such as performance, design, construction, chemical composition, materials, packaging, labeling, etc.—that must be met before a product can be sold in a country. A *product standard,* or *standard,* is a voluntary guideline for product characteristics established by a recognized private or administrative body. Technical regulations are mandatory and imposed by government regulations, whereas standards are usually voluntary and issued by either private industry groups or government agencies. Although a standard may be "voluntary," it may very well be that a product will not be accepted by consumers in the marketplace unless it complies with the standard. Technical regulations and standards that apply to imported foreign products, even if they also apply equally to domestic products, are called *technical barriers to trade.*

## The Protection of Public Health, Safety, or Welfare

Almost all products are subject to technical regulations or standards set by either government regulators or private standard-setting groups. They are generally imposed for the protection of public health, safety, or welfare. Examples might include standards for the safe design and manufacture of consumer or industrial goods, applied to an endless list of products, from machine lathes or automobiles to infant car seats or toothpaste. Imagine multinational companies such as Ford, General Electric, or Procter & Gamble and the incredibly diverse product standards they must meet in each country in which their products are sold. Other standards might protect consumers from fraud or deception; environmental standards on appliances and other products, such as the widely used restrictions on ozone-damaging refrigerants; fuel economy or exhaust emission standards for automobiles; packaging requirements on products such as plastic bottles to aid in recycling; technical specifications to standardize electrical power or telecommunications; building and construction standards such as common sizes for lumber and building materials; and many others.

**Restrictions on Sale and Distribution: Testing and Inspections.** Regulations can require the inspection of the factory or plant where a product is made. Some products must be tested prior to sale and certified by a government agency or independent laboratory. For instance, in the United States, the *Flammable Fabrics Act* places technical restrictions on the sale of all bed mattresses. The law is administered through regulations of the Consumer Products Safety Commission. Six prototypes are subjected to a controlled cigarette burn test under laboratory conditions to determine whether they meet federal safety requirements. If the length of the char is longer than allowed or if the mattress ignites, then it does not pass. The manufacturer usually arranges to have the test performed by an independent laboratory. They are required to keep photographs and records of the results at their place of business, and to make them available to retailers, customers, or agency regulators when

requested. Importers are also subject to the regulations; any of their products entering into the United States must meet these standards. If they cannot produce the certification, the goods will be denied entry. Thus, foreign manufacturers and importers alike must be familiar with the regulations of the countries to which their products will be shipped.

Because they often cause delays in getting goods to market, inspection and testing requirements can prove to be a tremendous barrier to trade. This is especially true if the product has a short shelf life, as with produce or other food products, or a short technological life (semiconductors or computer parts). In 1989, the European Community complained that the United States was delaying the inspection of perishable products by making them wait in turn behind nonperishable goods such as steel products, causing the perishables to spoil in the process. Entire shipments of citrus fruit from Spain had to be dumped, and the importer received no compensation.

In the United States, technical regulations and product standards are set by many federal agencies, including the Department of Agriculture, the Consumer Product Safety Commission, the Food and Drug Administration, the Federal Communications Commission, the Department of Energy, and the Department of Transportation. To illustrate, the U.S. Department of Agriculture is required by law to review meat inspection standards in foreign countries to ensure that imported meat products comply with USDA standards. The Federal Communications Commission promulgates uniform standards for telecommunications equipment that apply to foreign products. The Consumer Product Safety Commission's rules apply to all consumer products, regardless of where they are made. In 1994 the Commission learned that children's crayons imported from China contained hazardous amounts of lead in violation of U.S. regulations. The crayons were removed from stores.

## Why Technical Regulations and Standards Are Barriers to Trade

Of course, a regulation or standard that applies only to foreign goods and not to domestic goods discriminates against the foreign goods. However, many technical barriers do not discriminate on their face, but only in their application. As a result, discrimination may occur even when imported and domestic products are treated the same. A manufacturer whose product meets local regulations may find that building another product specially to meet foreign regulations is cost prohibitive. For instance, if U.S. wallboard manufacturers produce wallboard that is 3/8" thick, and Europe requires wallboard to be 1.5 cm. thick, then the firm will have to produce specially made wallboard for export to Europe. Certainly the European nations have the right to determine safety standards for construction, but the regulation does not allow the U.S. firm to take advantage of economies of scale and is thus an indirect technical barrier to trade. Another problem is that many technical barriers are not disclosed to foreign firms. Either they are not published or are made known only to domestic firms. Moreover, foreign companies are generally not a part of the standard-setting process. Domestic firms are typically invited to participate in developing and writing regulations or standards; foreign firms are not. Thus, they often experience delays in adapting their products for sale in the foreign market, causing them to lose competitive advantage to local firms. The U.S. Department of Commerce maintains a collection of international standards so that U.S. exporters have access to foreign technical regulations and standards applicable to their industries.

**Technical Barriers in the European Union.** The problem of technical barriers is critical to firms operating in the European Union where national standards vary tremendously. Consider the impact of such barriers on a firm such as Phillips, a Dutch electronics company, which has had to manufacture 29 different types of electrical outlets. Thus, the standards policy of the European Union is designed to balance the health and safety interests of member countries with the need for the free flow of goods. Despite decades of work by the EU Commission to reduce technical barriers to trade, thousands of new national standards have arisen. Even after years of debating detailed standards for thousands of products, companies wishing to sell their products in Europe still face a maze of complex regulations, applicable to a wide range of products from beer to hair dryers, automobiles to plywood. However, EU countries understand that uniform standards are essential to achieving a unified market.

The EU's effort to reduce technical barriers is reflected in many opinions of the European Court of Justice. As noted in Chapter Three, the *Cassis de Dijon* case, arising over the sale of liquor made in France and sold in Germany, illustrates that an EU member country cannot prohibit the sale of a product produced in another EU member country when that product had already met the technical specifications of the producing country. In decisions handed down in the 1980s, the Court rejected attempts by two EU countries to protect centuries-old industries. Disregarding consumer protection arguments, the Court of Justice struck down Germany's beer purity law that had kept out foreign beers containing preservatives and required that beer only be made from wheat, barley, hops, and yeast (beer made in other European countries often contains rice and other grains), and Italy's pasta content regulations. In one long-standing dispute with the United States, the European Union prohibited the import of beef with hormones, and because the hormones are widely used in the United States, U.S. beef was kept out of European markets.

Most standard setting in the European Union takes place through the *European Committee for Standardization,* which sets standards for non-electrical products, the *European Committee for Electrotechnical Standardization,* and the *European Telecommunications Standards Institute.* These intergovernmental agencies work with manufacturers, including some European subsidiaries of U.S. firms, and scientists to develop workable product standards. These standards then become binding on manufacturers in all EU countries. For U.S. and other non-EU firms, compliance with European standards is still difficult. Many products must be tested for compliance by European laboratories; certifications from U.S. laboratories are not accepted. For this reason, many non-EU companies want to participate in the European standard-setting process (although U.S. firms have not been very successful in doing this).

The European Union has attempted to increase its standardization through the use of the "CE Mark," meaning *Conformité Européene*. Like the ISO 9000 mark, the CE Mark is an internationally recognized symbol for quality and product safety for many different types of products, such as medical and electrical equipment. European manufacturers are inspected and audited by an EU authorized body. Once the mark is received, a European manufacturer may sell its products throughout the EU without undergoing inspections in each individual country. Manufacturers outside the EU may submit their products to an independent laboratory for testing before attaching the CE Mark.

**Technical Barriers in Japan.** Japan and the United States have had a long history of disputes over Japanese technical barriers to trade.[1] U.S. and other non-Japanese firms have lodged many complaints against Japan's technical barriers, most of which involve unreasonable and burdensome inspection procedures or import licensing requirements, and the arbitrary enforcement of overly strict standards. Japan has maintained complex technical regulations on thousands of important products, including electrical appliances, telecommunications and medical equipment, lumber, electronic components, pharmaceuticals, and food. The prolific use of technical requirements in Japan is rooted in Japan's protective attitude toward consumers, the historical role of the Japanese government in economic life, and the Japanese people's acceptance of governmental regulation of business. Products standards in Japan have been generally based on *design* characteristics—how a product should be designed and manufactured. U.S. standards, by contrast, are usually based on *performance*. Thus, products designed according to foreign regulations can pass U.S. regulations if they perform according to standards. Products capable of inflicting injury on consumers or that affect public health are more highly regulated than other products. For example, for many years Japan banned the import of cosmetics containing colorants and preservatives for health reasons, despite the fact that they are approved for use in the United States.

Japanese agencies that enforce technical regulations include the *Japanese Ministry of International Trade and Industry,* which has the widest authority, and the ministries that oversee the health, agriculture, and transportation sectors. Many products require testing and *prior approval* before they can be sold. For instance, prior to the mid-1980s foreign products could not be inspected for pre-clearance at the foreign factory, but could only be inspected, shipment by shipment, as they arrived in Japan. Items had to be individually inspected and tested for compliance with the technical regulations or standards. Legal changes have now made it possible for a foreign firm to register with the appropriate regulatory ministry and to obtain advance product approval without going through a Japanese importer or intermediary. Another problem occurs when Japanese technical regulations and standards lack transparency. Their agencies still generally do not permit foreign input into the drafting of the regulations, although on occasion U.S. industry groups, under pressure, have succeeded in being heard by Japanese standard-setting groups. During the 1980s new Japanese regulations provided that advance announcements of product standards be made by the *Japan External Trade Organization.*

The symbol of an approved product in Japan is the government-authorized *Japan Industrial Standards Mark,* or JIS Mark. Its appearance on a product, although voluntary, indicates that the manufacturer has submitted to on-site inspections by the appropriate Japanese ministry and has met accepted standards for quality control, production techniques, and research methods. Because this mark has become widely recognized, foreign products without it are often not competitive in the Japanese market.

**http://www.jetro.go.jp**
*The official site of JETRO, the Japanese External Trade Organization. Contains essential information for investment and exporting to Japan. Information on trade opportunities and access to the government procurement market in Japan. Take the "Business Japanese Test" and "Business Japanese Lessons."*

## The GATT 1994 Agreement on Technical Barriers to Trade

The GATT 1994 *Agreement on Technical Barriers to Trade* is one of the Uruguay Round agreements. It governs the use of technical regulations, product standards, testing, and certifications among WTO member countries. It improves on the older standards code that had been in effect since the Tokyo Round in 1979. Unlike the 1979 code that was signed by about only 30 countries, the new agreement is binding on all WTO member countries. Remember that this agreement does not contain standards of its own. It makes no attempt to say how a product should perform or be designed, or when a product is safe or unsafe. These are matters for nations and local governments to decide. But the GATT Agreement on Technical Barriers does prohibit countries from using their regulations or standards to discriminate against the import of foreign goods.

The 1994 Agreement on Technical Barriers to Trade builds on the 1979 agreement. It applies to all products, including agricultural, industrial, and consumer goods. The agreement's main provisions can be outlined as follows:

1. All technical regulations shall be applied on a nondiscriminatory basis, without regard to the national origin of the products.
2. Regulations must not be made or applied to create an *unnecessary obstacle* to trade, and they must not be more trade-restrictive than necessary to fulfill a legitimate objective such as national security, preventing fraud or deception of consumers, protecting public health or safety, or protecting the environment.
3. The agreement requires that countries take into account available scientific and technical information in writing their standards. This provision is intended to assure that standards are not made just to keep out foreign goods, but that they have some scientific foundation.
4. Wherever possible, product requirements should be based on performance abilities of the product rather than on design or descriptive characteristics.
5. The agreement recommends that countries develop and use internationally accepted standards where they exist. International standards will be presumed to be in compliance with GATT.
6. Proposed standards must be published and made available to foreign countries, and an opportunity be given to those countries to make written comments prior to adoption.
7. Final regulations must be published, with a reasonable time given before they become effective so that foreign producers have time to adapt their products.
8. Testing and inspection procedures should restrict trade as little as possible and should not discriminate. The agreement encourages on-site factory inspections instead of port-of-entry inspections for foreign goods.
9. Nations should try to see that states and local governments, as well as private standard-setting groups, comply with the agreement.
10. Disputes between countries may be referred to the WTO for negotiation and settlement.

> **http://itl.irv.uit.no/trade_law/documents/ freetrade/wta-94/art/iia1a6.html**
> See for the complete text of the Agreement on Technical Barriers to Trade.

## The Principle of Least-Restrictive Trade

The principle of *least-restrictive trade* is found both in the Agreement on Technical Barriers to Trade and other GATT agreements. It means that a country, in setting otherwise valid restrictions on trade (such as those to protect public health), shall make them no more restrictive than necessary to achieve the goals for which they were imposed. The following GATT panel decision, *Thailand Restriction on Importation of Cigarettes*, was issued in 1990, before the Uruguay Round agreements. It discusses least-restrictive trade in the context of Thailand's effort to reduce cigarette smoking.

## International Organization for Standardization

The most internationally accepted standards are those promulgated by the *International Organization for Standardization*, based in Geneva. The standards have become widely recognized

## Report on Thailand Restrictions on Importation of Cigarettes

*I.E.L. Document I-B-56 (1990)*
*Report of the Dispute Settlement Panel*

### BACKGROUND AND FACTS

The Royal Thai Government maintains restrictions on imports of cigarettes. The Tobacco Act of 1966 prohibited the import of all forms of tobacco except by license of the Director-General of the Excise Department. Licenses have only been granted to the government-owned Thai Tobacco Monopoly, which has imported cigarettes only three times since 1966. None have been imported in the ten years prior to this case. The United States requested the Panel to find that the licensing of imported cigarettes by Thailand was inconsistent with GATT Article XI and could not be justified under Article XX(b) since, as applied by Thailand, the licensing requirements were more restrictive than necessary to protect human health. Thailand argued that cigarette imports were prohibited to control smoking and because chemical and other additives contained in U.S. cigarettes might make them more harmful than Thai cigarettes.

### REPORT OF THE PANEL ADOPTED ON 7 NOVEMBER 1990

The Panel, noting that Thailand had not granted licences for the importation of cigarettes during the past 10 years, found that Thailand had acted inconsistently with Article XI:1, the relevant part of which reads: "No prohibitions or restrictions . . . made effective through . . . import licenses . . . shall be instituted or maintained by any [country] on the importation of any product of the territory of any other [country]." . . .

The Panel proceeded to examine whether Thai import measures affecting cigarettes, while contrary to Article XI:1, were justified by Article XX(b), which states in part:

> [N]othing in this Agreement shall be construed to prevent the adoption or enforcement by any [country] of measures: . . .
> (b) necessary to protect human, animal or plant life or health.

The Panel then defined the issues which arose under this provision. . . . [The] Panel accepted that smoking constituted a serious risk to human health and that consequently measures designed to reduce the consumption of cigarettes fell within the scope of Article XX(b). The Panel noted that this provision clearly allowed [countries] to give priority to human health over trade liberalization; however, for a measure to be covered by Article XX(b) it had to be "necessary." . . .

The Panel concluded from the above that the import restrictions imposed by Thailand could be considered to be "necessary" in terms of Article XX(b) only if there were no alternative measure consistent with the GATT Agreement, or less inconsistent with it, which Thailand could reasonably be expected to employ to achieve its health policy objectives. The Panel noted that [countries] may, in accordance with Article III:4 of the GATT Agreement, impose laws, regulations and requirements affecting the internal sale, offering for sale, purchase, transportation, distribution or use of imported products provided they do not thereby accord treatment to imported products less favourable than that accorded to "like" products of national origin. The United States argued that Thailand could achieve its public health objectives through internal measures consistent with Article III:4 and that the inconsistency with Article XI:1 could therefore not be considered to be "necessary" within the meaning of Article XX(b). The Panel proceeded to examine this issue in detail. . . .

The Panel then examined whether the Thai concerns about the quality of cigarettes consumed in Thailand could be met with measures consistent, or less inconsistent, with the GATT Agreement. It noted that other countries had introduced strict, non-discriminatory labeling and ingredient disclosure regulations which allowed governments to control, and the public to be informed of, the content of cigarettes. A non-discriminatory regulation implemented on a national treatment basis in accordance with Article III:4 requiring complete disclosure of ingredients, coupled with a ban on unhealthy substances, would be an alternative consistent with the GATT Agreement. The Panel considered that Thailand could reasonably be expected to take such measures to address the quality-related policy objectives it now pursues through an import ban on all cigarettes whatever their ingredients.

*(continued)*

(continued)

The Panel then considered whether Thai concerns about the quantity of cigarettes consumed in Thailand could be met by measures reasonably available to it and consistent, or less inconsistent, with the GATT Agreement. The Panel first examined how Thailand might reduce the demand for cigarettes in a manner consistent with the GATT Agreement. The Panel noted the view expressed by the World Health Organization (WHO) that the demand for cigarettes, in particular the initial demand for cigarettes by the young, was influenced by cigarette advertisements and that bans on advertisement could therefore curb such demand. At the Forty-third World Health Assembly a resolution was approved stating that the WHO is: "Encouraged by . . . recent information demonstrating the effectiveness of tobacco control strategies, and in particular . . . comprehensive legislative bans and other restrictive measures to effectively control the direct and the indirect advertising, promotion and sponsorship of tobacco."

A ban on the advertisement of cigarettes of both domestic and foreign origin would normally meet the requirements of Article III:4. . . . The Panel noted that Thailand had already implemented some nondiscriminatory controls on demand, including information programmes, bans on direct and indirect advertising, warnings on cigarette packs, and bans on smoking in certain public places.

The Panel then examined how Thailand might restrict the supply of cigarettes in a manner consistent with the GATT Agreement. The Panel noted that [countries] may maintain governmental monopolies, such as the Thai Tobacco Monopoly, on the importation and domestic sale of products. The Thai Government may use this monopoly to regulate the overall supply of cigarettes, their prices and their retail availability provided it thereby does not accord imported cigarettes less favourable treatment than domestic cigarettes or act inconsistently with any commitments assumed under its Schedule of Concessions. . . .

For these reasons the Panel could not accept the argument of Thailand that competition between imported and domestic cigarettes would necessarily lead to an increase in the total sales of cigarettes and that Thailand therefore had no option but to prohibit cigarette imports.

In sum, the Panel considered that there were various measures consistent with the GATT Agreement which were reasonably available to Thailand to control the quality and quantity of cigarettes smoked and which, taken together, could achieve the health policy goals that the Thai government pursues by restricting the importation of cigarettes inconsistently with Article XI:1. The Panel found therefore that Thailand's practice of permitting the sale of domestic cigarettes while not permitting the importation of foreign cigarettes was an inconsistency with the GATT not "necessary" within the meaning of Article XX(b).

**Decision.** The licensing system for cigarettes was contrary to Article XI:1 and is not justified by Article XX(b). The Panel recommended that Thailand to bring its laws into conformity with its obligations under the GATT.

**Comment.** As an additional note to this case, GATT Article XVII permits a country to create state agencies and "marketing boards" that have the authority to import and export goods. The Thai Tobacco Monopoly is an example. State trading enterprises are often used in developing countries and usually have the exclusive rights to import or export certain classifications of goods. Products traded by state enterprises might include foodstuffs, medicines, liquor, or in this case, tobacco. Article XVII requires that state enterprises not discriminate against the purchase of foreign goods, or treat them differently than domestic goods.

throughout the world and have become required in many industries. The most commonly known standard is ISO 9000. Since 1987, ISO 9000 is the standard used for assuring product quality through product design and manufacturing process. Companies become certified through a costly and rigorous inspection of their facilities and documentation of their quality control systems. They are audited on a regular basis for compliance. In order to sell in Europe, many U.S. firms have obtained ISO certification. By meeting ISO requirements, the firms no longer have to certify each product individually in every European country. ISO certification is required under EU law for certain regulated products, such as medical devices and construction equipment. Market demands make compliance for other products equally essential. In the United States, a number of firms offer assistance to U.S. companies seeking ISO certification. New ISO 14000 standards, now being released, will provide the guidelines in environmental management and labeling (e.g., advertising claims that a product is "environmentally safe," etc.).

**http://www.iso.ch/welcome.html**
The site of the ISO.

## Import Licensing Procedures

The case of Thailand's cigarette restrictions is an example of how an import licensing scheme can work to block foreign imports. Of course, Article XI does permit a country to use licensing in a nondiscriminatory, MFN, and transparent fashion in order to regulate imports in certain cases. For instance, a country may use licensing to enforce its technical regulations or standards laws. Thus, in such a case a health department would appropriately permit importation of say, pillows and mattresses *only* upon a license indicating that the products were made from sterilized materials. Customs officials might request to see this license at the border. Revenues from license fees could go to support the costs of inspection and administering the law. Import licenses are also used to track the quantities of imported goods subject to a quota. For instance, textile products from certain countries enter the United States under a quota. The textile importer must hand over the license for the given quantity to U.S. Customs. The license appears in the precise form (including typeface and color) as agreed between the U.S. and foreign governments so it can be authenticated. The license information is then sent to Washington, where the Customs Service tracks the quantity of each type of textile product entered from each foreign country so far in that year.

### The GATT 1994 Agreement on Import Licensing Procedures

The GATT 1994 *Agreement on Import Licensing Procedures* sets guidelines for countries issuing import licenses. It calls for the procedures to be fair, reasonable, and nondiscriminatory, and that application procedures to obtain a license should be as simple as possible. Applications should not be refused because of minor errors in paperwork. In other words, governments should see that clerical workers and bureaucracies do not use the licensing procedures to stand in the way of trade. Where licenses are used to administer quotas, the amount of the quota already used must be published for all importers to see. The WTO *Import Licensing Committee* must be notified if any new products will become subject to licensing requirements.

## Government Procurement

Governments are among the largest business customers in the world. GATT Article III permits an exception from its national treatment provision for government procurement, allowing governments to favor domestic suppliers. Article III, which normally prohibits laws that discriminate against foreign goods, states that,

[T]his article shall not apply to laws, regulations or requirements governing the procurement by governmental agencies of products purchased for governmental purposes and not with a view to commercial resale or with a view to use in the production of goods for commercial sale.

Most nations of the world have laws that require their own government agencies to give some preference to domestically made products. The laws often apply to goods purchased by defense-related agencies or by the military. Other laws might require that the purchased product contain a certain proportion of domestically made component parts or raw materials. In the United States, the *Federal Buy American Act* as well as state and local Buy American laws allow preferences for the purchase of domestic goods. The federal government is required to buy domestic products unless such purchases are not in the public interest or the costs are unreasonable. The U.S. Department of Defense must purchase domestic products unless those products are more than 50 percent more expensive than competing foreign goods. Japan has come under criticism for its discriminatory procurement rules. For the company that is considering bidding on a foreign government procurement contract, knowledge of the specific rules applicable to that bid is essential.

## The GATT 1994 Agreement on Government Procurement

The Uruguay Round *Agreement on Government Procurement* (AGP) is causing many changes in procurement practices in the United States and other countries. The AGP requires fair, open, and nondiscriminatory procurement practices and sets up uniform procurement procedures to protect suppliers from different countries. It applies to the purchase of goods or services worth more than $182,000 (approximately) or to construction contracts (building, dams, power plants, etc.) worth more than $7 million. Unlike the other GATT agreements, the AGP applies only to those countries that have signed it. (As of mid-1995 they included the United States, the European Union, Austria, Canada, Finland, Israel, Japan, Norway, Sweden, Switzerland, Korea, and Hong Kong. Other countries are expected to join.) The countries negotiated with each other as to how the AGP will be applied among them, and so the rules can differ depending on the countries involved in a purchase. For instance, the AGP says that Japan will not receive the benefit of the agreement if it wants to sell goods or services to NASA because Japan has not treated U.S. companies equally in procuring satellite technology. The purpose of the agreement is to bring competition to world procurement markets. The International Trade Commission estimates that the agreement will open up export markets for U.S. companies worth hundreds of billions of dollars.

**Agencies Excluded from the Procurement Rules.** The agreement applies to almost 90 U.S. federal agencies, large and small—from the Department of Labor to the Peace Corps to the American Battle Monuments Commission—and includes the executive branch departments. Several exclusions from the procurement rules include purchases to be sent to foreign countries as foreign aid; purchases by the Department of Agriculture for food distribution or for farm support

programs; and some purchases made by the Federal Aviation Administration, the Department of Energy, and the Department of Defense that are related to national security or to the military. In the United States, 37 states have also agreed to comply, and more will do so in the future. Many states—based on political reasonings—opted to exclude certain items: New York excluded subway cars and buses, and South Dakota excluded purchases of beef. Thus, state agencies in these states may give preferences to local producers when awarding procurement bids for these products.

**Procurement Rules.** The new AGP reverses the general GATT rules that allow government agencies to favor domestic products. It brings the principles of most-favored-nation trade, nondiscrimination, and transparency to government procurement. A procuring agency must treat the products, services, and suppliers from all other countries that have signed the agreement equally *and no less favorably than* if they were from its own country. Moreover, a government agency may not discriminate against local suppliers just because they are foreign-owned. The agreement prohibits *offsets,* which occur when a firm is awarded a contract only when it gives something to the government in return. Contracts cannot be awarded to a firm because it had agreed to utilize domestic materials, parts, or labor. Offsets also can be complex. For instance, assume that Aeroflop, a U.S. firm, wants to sell several million dollars worth of airplanes to a government-owned airline in a European country famous for cheese. In order to get the contract it agrees to pay a 5 percent kickback to another U.S. company, Cheezy, if Cheezy agrees to buy all of its cheese from a seller in that European country. If the cheese-producing country requires Aeroflop to make the offset, it violates the AGP.

Other rules state how the country-of-origin of products sold to a government agency is to be determined. For instance, a supplier that sells a product that is fraudulently labeled with the incorrect country-of-origin may be subjected to severe penalties under the law of the country involved.

**Transparency in Procurement Procedures.** To assure that the new rules are applied fairly, the

AGP sets up procedures for governments to follow. When a government agency intends to make a purchase by inviting suppliers to "bid on the job," the agency must give adequate notice to potential bidders when the contract is announced and disclose all the information necessary for them to submit their bid. The agreement requires fairness in qualifying foreign companies to bid (e.g., countries can disqualify companies that are not technically or financially capable of delivering). In the event of a disagreement between a supplier and a procuring agency, countries must allow the supplier to challenge the contract either before an independent administrative review board or the courts.

### Administering Government Procurement Rules in the United States

Congress has placed responsibility for implementing the AGP with the president. Basically, the president may waive the requirements of the Buy American Act for suppliers from any country that is party to the AGP *and* that complies with its terms in its own procurement practices. Suppliers from a least-developed country also receive the waiver. This waiver entitles those foreign suppliers to nondiscrimination and equal treatment with U.S. domestic suppliers.

The president must compile an annual report of those countries that have adopted the AGP but that do not abide by it. The USTR negotiates with violating countries to get them to end their unfair practices and give equal access to U.S. firms. If no agreement is reached, then the USTR must present the case to the WTO for dispute settlement. If an agreement or resolution is still not reached within 18 months of initiating dispute settlement, then the president must revoke the waiver of the Buy American Act, and preferences for domestic suppliers will be allowed.

In certain cases the president must completely prohibit U.S. government agencies from procuring products from suppliers in a foreign country, such as where the country "maintains a significant and persistent pattern or practice of discrimination against U.S. products or services which results in identifiable harm to U.S. business." The prohibition also applies to a country that has not joined the AGP—but from whom the U.S. government buys significant amounts of goods or services—that fails to provide U.S. firms with equal access to its procurement markets, or that permits its agencies to engage in bribery, extortion, or corruption in procuring goods or services. This severe sanction can only be used if the president has first consulted interested U.S. companies and if it will not harm the public interest of the United States and does not unreasonably restrict competition.

**Other Procurement Agreements.** The United States has negotiated several other procurement agreements with foreign nations. On behalf of the U.S. telecommunications industry, it entered into an agreement with Japan to help open opportunities for U.S. firms bidding on contracts there. A 1993 agreement between the United States and the European Union opened up the $15 to $20 billion heavy electrical equipment (power plant) market in Europe. The *North American Free Trade Agreement* (NAFTA) also contains its own provisions to guarantee U.S., Canadian, and Mexican firms "equal access" and "equal opportunity" to government contracts over $25,000.

## Trade in Services

Service industries such as travel and tourism, transportation, professional services, finance and insurance, and telecommunications account for the majority of the gross domestic product in the United States and most developed countries. Indeed, in 1994, service industries accounted for 76.6 percent of U.S. GDP, according to the U.S. Department of Commerce. While much attention is given to the U.S. merchandise trade deficits, the United States consistently runs a trade surplus in services. In 1995, U.S. exports of services amounted to $196 billion, or 21 percent of total U.S. trade volume, generating a trade surplus in services of $68.4 billion. According to the World Trade Organization, total cross-border services accounted for almost 12 percent of world trade. Although the GATT agreement regulated trade in goods for more than 45 years, it did not regulate trade in services until the Uruguay Round agreements. (Also, the *North American Free Trade*

*Agreement* permits a free flow of services among the U.S., Canada, and Mexico.)

## The GATT 1994 General Agreement on Trade in Services

As a result of the Uruguay Round, the *General Agreement on Trade in Services,* or GATS, is the first multilateral, legally enforceable agreement to establish rules for international trade in services. It is a part of the World Trade Organization system, and is overseen by the *Council for Trade in Services.* The agreement is largely patterned after the concepts that GATT applies to trade in goods. The agreement covers trade in most services, including health services, architecture, engineering and construction, travel and tourism, legal and other professional services, rental and leasing, education, management and environmental consulting, market research and advertising consulting, computer services, repair and maintenance, sanitation and disposal, franchising, entertainment, and others. GATS applies to the federal government as well as to state and local governments. Two areas, telecommunications and air transportation, are not included in the agreement. They are the subject of separate GATS agreements that as of mid-1995 remained uncompleted. An *agreement on financial services* was entered into in 1995 between the EU, Japan, and about 30 other countries. This agreement applies free trade principles to the commercial banking, securities, and insurance industries. However, the United States did not actually join the agreement, and the advantages to U.S. firms may yet be several years away. Thus our discussion focuses on GATS.

GATS principles are similar to the GATT principles studied in previous chapters. Rules affecting service providers must be transparent and made readily available. Signatory countries to

the agreement can place no limit on the number of service providers or on the number of people they may employ. The agreement also prohibits a requirement that local investors own any percentage of the service company (although they may if the parties choose). Like GATT, the GATS agreement also contains most-favored-nation trade and national treatment (nondiscrimination) provisions. Countries may not treat foreign service providers less favorably than they treat domestic providers. Also, they may not unreasonably restrict the international transfer of money by service industries.

GATS contains a set of schedules, or commitments, wherein each country lists its specific commitments for each type of service, which amounts to an exception to the nondiscrimination provision for certain types of services. For example, the United States excluded transportation services from GATS. Japan excluded repair services for certain automobiles and motorcycles, as well as courier services with respect to letters. In Canada, GATS applies to legal services only for law firms or attorneys advising on foreign or international law. Many countries excluded printing and publishing services. Thus, a country may not treat foreign services or service providers any less favorably than promised in the schedules. As a result, no new or additional restrictions may be imposed in the future. Countries also are bound to negotiate an eventual elimination of the exceptions made in the schedules.

**Licensing and Professional Qualifications.** GATS also has special provisions governing the qualifications of service providers set by national or local governments. Most governments license certain service providers at some level; in the United States, licensing generally occurs at the state level. Of course, areas such as law, nursing, architecture, and accounting will continue to have more strict professional licensing requirements than, say, management consulting. Countries can continue to license professionals and other service providers as necessary to insure the quality of the service provided that it is not made overly burdensome just to restrict trade. Licensing must be based on objective criteria, such as education or ability. It must not discriminate on the basis of the person's citizenship. Countries may recognize the licenses of other countries, but only if they choose to do so.

To illustrate the impact of GATS licensing provisions, it was reported by the *Bureau of National Affairs* in the United States that in 1999 the Japanese Ministry of Finance will hold national accreditation examinations for foreign certified public accountants for the first time since 1975. From 1950 through 1975 only 74 foreign CPAs had been certified to practice in Japan. Typically, foreign CPAs in Japan only provide auxiliary services to clients in Japan through Japanese CPA offices because of the requirements to register as a member of the Japan Institute of CPAs and laws that allow only Japanese nationals to own and run CPA offices. Japan announced that it plans to follow international standards and eventually sign mutual recognition agreements with other countries.

## Trade in Agriculture

Agricultural exports are an important part of world trade. The United States exports almost 20 percent of its agricultural production, worth over $40 billion in 1994. However, agricultural products are among the most heavily protected products traded in the world. No nation wants to be dependent on other nations for its food supply. Also, agriculture represents a politically powerful and important constituency in most countries. To protect farmers, governments strictly control the domestic pricing structure in order to provide market stability. These agricultural price supports set prices at higher-than-world-market prices and contribute to the buildup of food surpluses. To avoid disrupting their price support systems, most countries impose strict import restrictions on both raw and processed food products. The United States, Japan, and the European Union provide farming subsidies, controls on prices, and restrictions on imports. GATT Article XI, which prohibits quantitative restrictions, contains a loophole allowing quotas on agricultural imports when necessary to protect government price support programs. Thus agricultural products have really escaped control by GATT. In the following GATT panel decision, *Report on Thailand Restriction on Importation of Cigarettes* (continued from a case appearing earlier in the chapter), the Thai government tried to argue that the restrictions on cigarettes as an agricultural product were permitted under Article XI.

---

BACKGROUND AND FACTS

This report given here is a continuation of the case that appeared earlier in the chapter. In the earlier quoted portion of the case, the panel ruled that Thailand's restrictions on the import of cigarettes were not justified on public health grounds. Here, the court discusses whether the cigarette restrictions are permissible under Article XI in order to prevent disruption to a domestic agricultural market.

*Report on Thailand Restrictions on Importation of Cigarettes (continued)*
*I.E.L. Document I-B-56 (1990)*
*Report of the Dispute Settlement Panel*

REPORT OF THE PANEL ADOPTED ON 7 NOVEMBER 1990

The Panel then examined Thailand's claim that its restrictions on the importation of cigarettes were necessary to enforce domestic marketing or production restrictions for leaf tobacco and cigarettes and that they were therefore justified by Article XI:2(c)(I), the relevant part of which reads:

*(continued)*

*(continued)*

[T]his Article shall not extend to . . . Import restrictions on any agricultural or fisheries product, imported in any form, necessary to the enforcement of governmental measures which operate . . . to restrict the quantities of the like domestic product permitted to be marketed or produced.

The Panel noted that this provision refers to "agricultural products" and agricultural products "imported in any form," and defines the latter [in a note] as covering "the same products when in an early stage of processing and still perishable, which compete directly with the fresh product and if freely imported would tend to make the restriction on the fresh product ineffective."

In the view of the Panel, the reference to "the fresh product" . . . makes clear that the agricultural products subject to marketing or production restrictions must be fresh products. It noted that a previous panel had reached the same conclusion, stating that "the focus of this provision was limited to a fresh product" and that "the domestic product subject to restrictions had to be the product produced by farmers." . . .

The Panel found for these reasons that the only domestic marketing and production restrictions that would be relevant under Article XI:2(c)(I) were those that Thailand claimed to have imposed on the production of leaf tobacco—not those on cigarettes—and that consequently this provision would cover import restrictions only on (a) products that were "like" domestic leaf tobacco and (b) products processed from such "like" products that met the conditions of the Note at Article XI:2(c). The Panel, noting that cigarettes were not "like" leaf tobacco, but processed from leaf tobacco, examined whether cigarettes fell within the range of products covered by this Note. It recognized that a central requirement of the Note was that the product processed from the fresh product was still "in an early stage of processing." It noted that a previous panel had found that agricultural products not normally intended for further processing such as ketchup could not be regarded as eligible for import restrictions under Article XI:2(c)(I). Since cigarettes could not be described as "leaf tobacco in an early stage of processing" because they had already undergone extensive processing and, moreover, were not intended for further processing, the Panel found that they were not among the products eligible for import restrictions under Article XI:2(c)(I).

**Decision.** The panel rejected Thailand's argument and held that the import restrictions (licensing only through the government-owned Thai Tobacco Monopoly) could not be justified as being necessary for the protection of domestic agriculture under GATT Article XI.

Reproduced with permission from *International Economic Law Documents*. © The American Society of International Law.

---

Agricultural price supports in the EU are handled through a *Common Agricultural Policy,* which uses a variable levy to bring the world price of an agricultural import up to the domestic price level. Expenditures for agricultural subsidies and price supports cost billions of dollars each year, constituting nearly three-quarters of the annual total budget of the European Union. In the United States, the Farm Bill provides billions of dollars to subsidize farm exports.

No other single trade issue has created so much international disagreement and controversy as trade in agriculture. The United States has generally demanded that EU farm subsidies, including direct payments to European farmers, be reduced. France, Europe's largest grain exporter, has been unwilling to reduce farm subsidies because French farmers are politically powerful. (Pictures of rioting French farmers setting trucks afire in the early 1990s, to contest their government's negotiations with the United States over agricultural subsidies, filled the TV screens around the world.)

The largest purchaser of U.S. agricultural products is Japan, but farmers in Japan are still highly protected. The *Japanese Staple Food Control Law* puts strict limitations on the import of foreign agricultural products. The most protected item is rice. In 1991, U.S. rice exhibitors at a Japanese trade fair were threatened with arrest for merely exhibiting U.S. rice products there. The U.S. rice had to be removed from the show. Clearly, with such displays of protection-ism, liberalization of trade in agriculture will continue to take many years of negotiations.

http://itl.irv.uit.no/trade_law/documents/
freetrade/wta-94/art/iia1a3.html
*See for information on trade in agriculture.*

## The GATT 1994 Agreement on Agriculture

The Uruguay Round resulted in a new GATT *Agreement on Agriculture.* It is expected to increase export opportunities for agricultural products and to reduce government subsidies. Nontariff barriers will gradually be converted to tariffs. Japan and Korea agreed to open their markets to farm products and to end their ban on rice imports, although progress is sure to be slow. As quotas end, these countries will likely purchase more citrus, poultry, beef, and pork. The United States also agreed to allow more imports of foreign cotton, beef, sugar, and cheese. Domestic subsidies will be reduced worldwide by 20 percent and export subsidies by 35 percent.

**Measures to Protect Human, Animal, and Plant Life from Pests, Disease, and Toxins.**  Trade in agricultural goods has been impeded because some countries use food safety as an excuse for blocking agriculture imports. No one doubts the right of a government to take extraordinary measures to protect the people from contagious disease or to protect food or agricultural products from infestation. If a blight, fungus, or insect were found in orange groves in Mexico, no one argues against the right of the United States to keep out Mexican oranges to protect the U.S. crop. The GATT *Agreement on the Application of Sanitary and Phytosanitary Measures* is specifically designed to allow governments to protect human, animal, and plant life from infestation, contaminants, pesticides, toxins, food additives (including hormones), or disease-carrying organisms. However, the restrictions may not be used as an excuse to keep out foreign goods. (The Agreement on Technical Barriers to Trade does not apply to sanitary and phytosanitary regulations.)

The agreement opens markets for agricultural exports by requiring that: (1) the measures must be not more trade-restrictive than required and may be applied only to the extent necessary for the protection of human, animal, or plant life; (2) measures may not be a disguised restriction on trade; (3) measures must be based on a risk assessment made according to scientific principles and scientific evidence; (4) the measures may not unjustifiably discriminate among countries where similar threatening conditions prevail; and (5) countries must insure that inspections or controls are fair and reasonable, and that they are instituted without delay. Consider an example: If an Asian country sets a short shelf-life for a food product, say hot dogs, then hot dogs shipped from the U.S. will be discriminated against because their shelf-life has been "used up" in the time it takes to ship across the Pacific. Under the Sanitary and Phytosanitary Agreement, however, the shelf-life restrictions cannot stand unless they are based on scientific evidence. Another novel case might be the strict Japanese laws prohibiting thoroughbred race horses from entering Japan—this prohibition would violate the agreement if the laws are unnecessary, discriminatory toward the United States, or not backed by scientific evidence. Citing the GATT agreement, the U.S. Department of Agriculture in 1995 partially repealed an 81 year-old prohibition against the import of Mexican avocados.

In the following 1997 WTO panel decision, *EC Measures Concerning Meat and Meat Products (Hormones),* the panel held that the European ban on the sale of beef containing residues of growth hormones violated the *Sanitary and Phytosanitary Agreement.*

## Trade in Textiles and Clothing

The textile and apparel industries are among the most "import sensitive" sectors of the world economy. They are labor intensive, allowing developing countries quickly to become major competitors in world markets. In 1994 the United States had a trade deficit in textiles of almost $35 billion, to the chagrin of U.S. textile workers and politicians in textile producing states. Until 1995, the textile trade remained outside of the GATT system, thus allowing strict regulation of textile imports into the United States.

## BACKGROUND AND FACTS

Throughout the 1970s European consumers became more concerned over the use of hormones to speed the growth of livestock. Their fears were in part based on the fact that some people had been injured by the illegal use of certain banned hormones. Some consumer organizations boycotted meats. By 1986 the EC had banned the sale of beef from cattle given growth hormones. The EC maintained that such measures were necessary to protect public health (primarily from hormone related illnesses and cancer), and necessary to restore confidence in the meat industry. The United States began contesting the hormone ban in 1987 at GATT. In January 1989, the United States introduced retaliatory measures in the form of 100 per cent ad valorem duties on a list of products imported from the European Communities. The United States, together with Canada, Australia, and New Zealand, maintained that the ban was unlawful under the 1994 *Agreement on the Application of Sanitary and Phytosanitary Measures* ("SPS Agreement"). The U.S. argued that the ban was not based on an assessment of risk, not based on scientific principles, more trade-restrictive than necessary, and a disguised restriction on trade. In June 1996, the European Communities requested the establishment of a panel to examine this matter, and the United States terminated its retaliatory action entirely. Prior to the ban U.S. firms exported hundreds of millions of dollars annually to Europe. After the ban exports plummeted to nearly zero. The European Communities argued that its measures offered equal opportunities of access to the EC market for all third-country animals and meat from animals to which no hormones had been administered for growth promotion purposes. Of the 31 countries which were authorized to export meat to the European Communities, only six apparently allowed the use of some or all of these hormones for growth promotion purposes.

## REPORT OF THE PANEL

Article 3.1 requires Members to base their sanitary measures on international standards, guidelines or recommendations [where they exist]. We note,

**Report of the Panel on EC Measures Concerning Meat and Meat Products (Hormones)**

*Complaint by the United States*
*World Trade Organization*
*WT/DS26/R/USA (18 August 1997)*

therefore, that even if international standards may not, in their own right, be binding on Members, Article 3.1 requires Members to base their sanitary measures on these standards. . . . We shall therefore, as a first step, examine whether there are international standards, guidelines or recommendations with respect to the EC measures in dispute and, if so, whether the EC measures are *based on* these standards, guidelines or recommendations in accordance with Article 3.1. . . .

Article 3.1 of the SPS Agreement reads as follows:

> To harmonize sanitary and phytosanitary measures on as wide a basis as possible, Members shall base their sanitary and phytosanitary measures on international standards, guidelines or recommendations, where they exist, except as otherwise provided for in this Agreement. . . .

. . . For food safety . . . the SPS Agreement defines "international standards, guidelines or recommendations" as "the standards, guidelines and recommendations established by the Codex Alimentarius Commission relating to food additives, *veterinary drug* and pesticide *residues,* contaminants, methods of analysis and sampling, and codes and guidelines of hygienic practice" (emphasis added). . . . [The Codex Alimentarius Commission is an advisory body to the World Health Organization. The purpose of this programme is to protect the health of consumers and to ensure fair practices in food trade by establishing food standards. These standards, together with notifications received from governments with respect to their acceptance or otherwise of the standards, constitute the *Codex Alimentarius* . . . a collection of internationally adopted food standards presented in a uniform manner]. . . . We note that [there are] five Codex standards . . . relating to veterinary drug residues . . . with respect to five of the six hormones in dispute when these hormones are used for growth promotion purposes. . . . We find, therefore, that international standards exist with respect to the EC measures in dispute. . . .

*(continued)*

*(continued)*

The amount of residues of these hormones administered for growth promotion purposes allowed by these Codex standards is . . . higher than zero (a maximum level of such residues has not even been prescribed). The EC measures in dispute, on the other hand, do not allow the presence of any residues of these three hormones administered for growth promotion purposes. The level of protection reflected in the EC measures is, therefore, significantly *different* from the level of protection reflected in the Codex standards. The EC measures in dispute are . . . therefore, *not based on* existing international standards as specified in Article 3.1. . . .

[For those sanitary measures for which no international standards exist] . . . a Member needs to ensure that its sanitary measures are based on an assessment of risks. The obligation to base a sanitary measure on a risk assessment may be viewed as a specific application of the basic obligations contained in Article 2.2 of the SPS Agreement which provides that "Members shall ensure that any sanitary . . . measure is *applied only to the extent necessary to protect* human, animal or plant life or health, is *based on scientific principles* and is *not maintained without sufficient scientific evidence* . . . " (emphasis added). Articles 5.1 to 5.3 sum up factors a Member needs to take into account in making this assessment of risks. . . . [A]n assessment of risks is, at least for risks to human life or health, a *scientific* examination of data and factual studies; it is not a policy exercise involving social value judgments made by political bodies. . . .

We recall that under the SPS Agreement a risk assessment should, for the purposes of this dispute, identify the adverse effects on human health arising from the presence of the specific hormones at issue when used as growth promoters in meat or meat products and, if any such adverse effects exist, evaluate the potential or probability of occurrence of these effects. We further recall that a risk assessment should be a scientific examination of data and studies and that the SPS Agreement sets out factors which need to be taken into account in a risk assessment.

[The panel conducted a review of the scientific studies]. All of the scientific studies outlined above came to the conclusion that the use of the hormones at issue for growth promotion purposes is safe; most of these studies adding that this conclusion assumes that good practice is followed. We note that this conclusion has also been confirmed by the scientific experts advising the Panel. Accordingly, the European Communities has not established the existence of any identifiable risk against which the EC measures at issue . . . can protect human life or health.

**Decision.** The EC's ban on the sale of beef containing residues of growth hormones violates the *Agreement on the Application of Sanitary and Phytosanitary Measures*. Where an existing internationally accepted standard permits beef to contain a residue of a certain growth hormone, an EC regulation permitting zero residue is in violation of the agreement. Where no internationally accepted standard exists on the residue of a certain hormone, the EC ban on that hormone is not permitted because it is not based on a risk assessment made using scientifically accepted principles.

**Comment.** The panel's decision was upheld by the WTO Appellate Body in January 1998.

---

The process of "managing" trade in textiles and apparel began in the early 1960s when the developed countries were flooded with textile imports from low-wage developing countries, such as China, India, the Philippines, Egypt, Pakistan, Hong Kong, Indonesia, Korea, Taiwan, and Mexico. Indeed, textiles account for nearly one-half of the total Chinese exports to the United States, so the regulation of trade in textiles has a considerable impact on U.S. relations with that country. Now countries in Eastern Europe, such as the Czech Republic and Bulgaria, have joined in the export of textile products.

Trade in textile products made from cotton, wool, and other natural and synthetic fibers was governed by the 1974 *Multifiber Arrangement* (MFA), an international agreement between textile importing countries and more than 40 textile-producing nations. The purpose of the MFA was to promote exports from developing countries, while avoiding market disruption in developed importing countries. The MFA was a system of bilateral agreements among importing and producing countries setting quota limits on a country-by-country basis for each product category (e.g., silk blouses from India, cotton sweaters from Pakistan, down-filled comforters from China). A complex licensing system was established to track shipments and monitor quota limits. In the United States, textile negotiations were, and still are, conducted by the *Committee for the Implementation of Textile Agreements* (CITA). CITA is a U.S. agency made up of members from five departments of government. The agency also administers the textile quota system. (Under the North American Free Trade Agreement, Mexican-made textiles entering the United States or Canada are not subject to quotas.)

## The GATT 1994 Agreement on Textiles and Clothing

The Uruguay Round resulted in the GATT *Agreement on Textiles and Clothing*. This agreement puts an end to the MFA quota system, improves access to foreign markets, and liberalizes world trade in textiles. During the Uruguay Round negotiations, the agreement was supported by U.S. textile importers and retailers but was opposed by U.S. textile manufacturers and textile workers. The agreement brings textiles within the scope of normal GATT rules, under the auspices of the WTO. GATT calls for textile quotas to be phased out, and tariffs reduced, over a ten-year period. Relatively high U.S. tariffs will remain after that period, however. By 2004 all textiles and clothing will be covered by the basic GATT principles of most-favored-nation trade, non-discrimination, and the elimination of quotas. Until then, a country may temporarily reinstate quotas as a safeguard if increased textile imports cause serious injury to a domestic industry. Tariffs on textiles will also be reduced over the ten-year period. Many U.S. retailers and textile importers believe that the economic impact of the textile agreement will not occur until after the full ten-year period is up. The agreement creates the WTO *Textile Monitoring Body* to oversee trade in textiles and assist countries in complying. Any disputes not resolved by this body, can be settled before the WTO Dispute Settlement Body.

**Preventing Illegal Textile Transshipments.**   For many years the United States has had a significant problem in enforcing its textile quotas. Some exporters and importers have been trying to avoid U.S. quotas by illegally rerouting or *transshipping* textile products to a third country whose quota is not yet used up, relabelling the products with bogus country-of-origin labels, and shipping them to the United States. Such merchandise has ended up on store shelves of major retailers throughout the United States. The U.S. Customs Service estimates that $4 billion in illegal textiles reach the United States every year, most of it from China. In 1995 the U.S. government took action against China for failing to stop transshipments, and reduced the quota allotment for many categories of textiles coming to the United States. Importers and retailers in the U.S. who had expected shipments from China were forced to find alternative sources of supply. For instance, shipments of quilts and comforters from China can generally be brought into the United States through most of the year. In 1995 the category filled and the quota closed on March 6th, sending unprepared U.S. importers into a panic for lack of merchandise to sell. In the new textile agreement, the countries pledge to end illegal transshipments, false shipping documents, and false fiber-content labels. They have agreed to share information, make investigations, and to cooperate in policing the law. While the United States may still use quotas or even deny entry to goods from countries that do not cooperate in stopping illegal transshipments, most U.S. firms hope that the problem can be controlled and stability returned to the textile and clothing markets.

# Other WTO Trade Agreements

Two other agreements that will have an effect on world trade are the 1994 *Agreement on Trade-Related Investment Measures* and the 1994 *Agreement on Trade-Related Aspects of Intellectual Property Rights*. These issues are mentioned only briefly here, because they are discussed more fully in Part Four of this book.

## Trade-Related Investment Measures

Multinational firms are well aware of the many restrictions on their investments in foreign countries. *Trade-related investment measures* (commonly called TRIMS) are those restrictions a nation places on foreign investment that adversely affect trade in goods or services. WTO members entered into the Agreement on Trade-Related Investment Measures as a part of the Uruguay Round agreements.

The agreement does *not* set broad rules for investors in a WTO country. It simply prohibits laws or regulations that condition a company's right to import foreign goods on the volume of goods exported. For instance, Argentina may not say to a U.S. multinational corporation: "We will finance the construction of a new automobile factory for you, but only if you guarantee us that 25 percent of the component parts used in assembling cars are made in this country," or "You may only import foreign raw materials on condition that you export an equal volume of finished goods from our country." These requirements would violate the prohibition of quantitative restrictions of GATT Article XI. Also prohibited are laws that condition the receipt of foreign exchange on the company's foreign exchange revenues. Thus, Argentina may not demand: "Our central bank will only permit you to transfer U.S. dollars out of the country if you have brought into the country an equivalent amount this year in dollars, yen, or other hard currency."

## Trade-Related Aspects of Intellectual Property Rights

*Intellectual property rights* (IPRs) include copyrights, trademarks, and patents. The economic value of an IPR lies in the right of its owner to the sole use of the IPR or to license its use to someone else, but it only has worth if the owner can prevent its unauthorized use. Because IPRs are not "goods," they did not fall within the bounds of the 1947 GATT agreement. However, IPRs are often attached to, and used to sell, goods. Thus, if IPRs are not protected from unauthorized use, then trade in goods and services suffer as a result. For this reason, the Uruguay Round negotiations focused on IPRs and resulted in the *Agreement on Trade-Related Aspects of Intellectual Property Rights,* or TRIPS.

TRIPS sets new, comprehensive standards for the protection of IPRs in all member countries of the World Trade Organization. It requires every WTO country to abide by the most important international intellectual property conventions and then calls on countries to grant even greater protection to inventors, authors, and trademark owners. The agreement requires that all domestic and foreign IPR owners, regardless of their citizenship, be treated the same under a country's IPR laws. It prohibits countries from imposing requirements on foreign firms in exchange for being granted a trademark, patent, or copyright. For instance, a WTO country will not be able to condition the award of a patent on the basis of the inventor's promise to manufacture the item in that country. Countries must publish all laws, regulations, and administrative rulings that pertain to the availability, application, protection, or enforcement of IPRs. Enforcement efforts will be strengthened worldwide to reduce the billions of dollars worth of losses every year due to counterfeit and pirated goods (e.g., fake Rolex watches or Microsoft software). WTO member countries will bring their IPR laws into compliance with TRIPS, as the United States has already done. For example, in 1995 the United States increased the patent period from 17 years to 20 years to comply with TRIPS longer period. The TRIPS Council of the World Trade Organization will monitor compliance with TRIPS, and after the year 2000 disputes may be settled before the WTO Dispute Settlement Body (see Exhibit 12.1 for an example of a WTO dispute resolution).

## Information Technology Agreement

In 1996, 42 nations entered into the *International Technology Agreement.* The agreement includes the United States, Canada, the European Union, Japan, Hong Kong, Singapore, and other countries accounting for over 90 percent of world trade in information technology products. The agreement calls for the elimination of tariffs on computers, semiconductors, telecommunications equipment, software, scientific instruments, and other information technology products by the year 2000.

---

**EXHIBIT 12.1    Trade Compliance Center**
**Japan Resolution of WTO Dispute on Sound Recordings**

United States Trade Representative-designate Charlene Barshefsky today announced that the United States and Japan have resolved the dispute over Japan's protection of U.S. sound recordings. Japan recently adopted amendments to the Japanese Copyright Law to provide protection to U.S. recordings produced between 1946 and 1971. These amendments are scheduled to come into effect before the end of March 1997 and are intended to bring Japan's copyright law into compliance with the WTO *Agreement on Trade-Related Aspects of Intellectual Property Rights,* or "TRIPS Agreement."

"We launched this case on a clear principle to protect intellectual property rights," said Barshefsky. "We sought—and will now obtain—protection for U.S. sound recordings from one of the most vibrant and popular periods in the history of American music—from the swing music of Duke Ellington, the bebop jazz of John Coltrane, the rock and roll of Elvis Presley, Chuck Berry, Little Richard, Johnny Cash, Patsy Cline and the Sixties sounds of Bob Dylan, the Beach Boys and Otis Redding. The remarkable range and stature of the music produced in that quarter-century makes it an important part of our heritage."

Barshefsky also said, "Japan's action provides a clear indication of the enormous value of the TRIPS Agreement and WTO dispute settlement procedures for U.S. industry and workers. I am especially pleased that we were able to resolve this issue through WTO dispute settlement consultations."

It is estimated that approximately 6 million unauthorized recordings, from the pre-1971 period are manufactured and sold in Japan annually. Industry estimates are that U.S. rights holders in these sound recordings lost half a billion dollars annually because of the absence of such protection in Japan.

The U.S. recording industry, along with other entertainment industries, is a key U.S. industry. Recorded music is a $40 billion dollar industry. In 1995, industry sales in the United States reached over $26 billion. Over 60% of that topped $14 billion, and sales in the rest of the world. $26 billion in industry foreign sales was of products made by Americans. The recording industry employs tens of thousands of workers in our country and in every state in the nation. Along with the musicians and sound engineer who record the music, there are countless others, including the workers who press and make the CDs, truckers who transport them, and retail clerks who sell them.

**Background on the Dispute**

Prior to the adoption of these amendments, Japan's copyright law only granted protection to foreign sound recordings that were produced on or after January 1, 1971, the date on which Japan first provided specialized protection for sound recordings under its copyright law.

The absence of protection for works produced between 1946 and 1971 put Japan squarely in conflict with Article 14.6 of the TRIPS Agreement, which applies the provisions of Article 18 of the Berne Convention to the protection of sound recordings. These provisions generally require that a country—in this case, Japan—provide a 50-year term of protection to pre-existing works originating in another WTO member-country—in this case, the United States—if those works have not already enjoyed a full term of protection in both countries. Since Japan, along with other developed countries, was required to fulfill its TRIPS Agreement obligations by January 1, 1996, all sound recordings produced in other WTO member-countries after January 1, 1946, were required to be eligible for protection.

On February 14, 1996, the United States initiated WTO dispute settlement proceedings against Japan and several rounds of formal and informal consultations took place over the course of 1996. Based on the Government of Japan's promulgation on December 26, 1996, of amendments providing U.S. sound recordings retroactive protection, the United States and Japan notified the WTO that a mutually satisfactory solution had been reached, thus terminating the dispute settlement proceeding.

SOURCE:    Office of the United States Trade Representative.

# Trade Sanctions and U.S. Section 301: The Threat of Retaliation

One of the most important weapons in the U.S. arsenal against foreign trade barriers and unfair trade practices is commonly known to businesspeople and lawyers alike as Section 301. *Section 301* refers to the provisions found in that section of the Trade Act of 1974, although it has been amended by Congress three times since then. The latest version of Section 301 is based on the *Omnibus Trade and Competitiveness Act of 1988.* The law permits the United States to retaliate unilaterally against other countries—not against foreign *companies*—that violate GATT, that are unfair in restricting the import of U.S. goods or services, or that maintain unreasonable or discriminatory policies or practices. Congress believed that other countries would only comply with GATT if the United States could threaten retaliation for violations. After all, if other countries were threatened with being denied access to the vast U.S. market, they would be less likely to discriminate against U.S. goods or services. While most experts think that the law has been successful in achieving its goals, many others do not (see article, "Past Market Access . . . "). The law really contains four different provisions: (1) Basic Section 301, (2) Special 301, (3) Telecommunications 301, and (4) Super 301.[2]

## Basic Section 301

In Basic Section 301, Congress instructs the United States Trade Representative (USTR) when retaliatory action against a foreign country in a trade dispute is *discretionary,* and when it is *mandatory.* Retaliatory action may be taken at the discretion of the USTR against any foreign country whose policies or actions are *unreasonable* or *discriminatory* and which *burdens* or *restricts* U.S. trade or foreign investment. A foreign country acts unreasonably if its policies toward U.S. firms are unfair or inequitable, even though not in violation of any international agreement, including unfair restriction of foreign investment, denial of equal access to their markets, failure to protect U.S. intellectual property rights, or subsidization of a domestic industry. Section 301 gives the president sufficient flexibility to attack a wide variety of foreign unfair trade practices. Retaliation by the USTR in these instances is discretionary. The USTR also has the discretion to take retaliatory action when a foreign government (1) fails to allow workers the right to organize and bargain collectively; (2) permits forced labor; (3) does not provide a minimum age for the employment of children; or (4) fails to provide standards for minimum wage, hours of work, and the health and safety of workers.

Retaliation is *mandatory* if the USTR determines that (1) a foreign country has denied the U.S. its rights under any of the GATT agreements; or (2) a foreign country's actions or policies are unjustifiable, violate the legal rights of the United States, *and* burden or restrict U.S. commerce. Unjustifiable acts or polices include illegal tariffs or quotas, denial of most-favored-nation treatment, illegal import procedures, overly burdensome restrictions on U.S. foreign investment, and intellectual property rights violations. In a case of a violation of GATT, the "burden" to U.S. commerce is presumed. Mandatory action need not be taken if a WTO panel has upheld the foreign government action, if the foreign country has agreed to eliminate the illegal policy, if the USTR believes that a negotiated solution is imminent, or if in extraordinary cases the USTR believes that retaliation would have a greater adverse impact to the U.S. economy than benefit.

**Section 301 Procedures.** A Section 301 action begins with the filing of a petition by an interested party, such as a U.S. company, or on the initiative of the USTR. The petition asks the USTR to conduct an investigation of the foreign unfair trade practice. The USTR has 45 days in which to decide whether to conduct the investigation. Petitions for investigation are usually granted only when an entire U.S. industry is affected. An opportunity must be provided for interested parties to submit their views in writing, and a hearing must be provided if requested. All decisions of the USTR are published in the *Federal Register.* Once an investigation is begun, the USTR must also begin negotiations with the foreign government involved. If the petition claims that the foreign government has violated GATT, and the dispute is not resolved within 150 days or within the time required in the agreement, then the USTR must invoke the formal WTO dispute settlement procedures. The USTR must complete its investigation and determine whether to impose sanctions within 18 months of having initiated the investigation, or within 30 days after conclusion of WTO dispute procedures, whichever occurs first. When sanctions are authorized by the WTO, Section 301 is used to carry them out under U.S. law.

**Sanctions and Retaliatory Measures.** Investigations are conducted not on behalf of the petitioning firm, but on behalf of the U.S. government itself. The purpose of Section 301 is to end the illegal foreign practice, not to compensate the petitioning U.S. firm. No benefits accrue directly to the petitioning firm other than those that affect all U.S. companies or industries in a similar position. The USTR has a wide range of retaliatory measures, or *trade sanctions,* that can be used. Generally, the most common form of retaliation is to assess additional import duties on products from the offending nation in an amount that is equivalent in value to the burden imposed by that country on U.S. firms. The sanctions may be imposed against any type of goods or against any industry. A country might put quotas on U.S. food products, and the United States can retaliate against their electronic parts. For instance, when the United States threatened trade sanctions against Japan for unfairly keeping out U.S. auto parts, the USTR proposed 100 percent import duties on imports of Japanese luxury automobiles. When China refused to protect U.S. copyrights, the U.S. threatened to impose over $1 billion a year in trade sanctions on Chinese imports. In the 1980s, President Reagan retaliated against Japanese restrictions on computer chips by imposing punitive tariffs of 100 percent on Japanese power tools, color television sets, and personal computers.

> **http://miti.go.jp/**
> The official website of Japan's Ministry of International Trade and Industry. Contains MITI's report on foreign trade barriers facing Japanese products, Japanese trade statistics, and statements of Japanese trade policy.

> **http://ustr.gov/**
> The homepage of the United States Trade Representative. Contains valuable links to all trade agreements negotiated by the United States, press releases, and USTR reports, including the National Trade Estimate Report on Foreign Trade Barriers and the report on the Identification of Trade Expansion Priorities.

## Special 301

*Special 301,* enacted in 1988, is used by the United States against countries that fail to protect U.S. intellectual property rights. By April 30th of each year the USTR must identify foreign countries that deny adequate and effective protection. The worst offenders will be designated as *priority foreign countries* and placed on either the *watch list* or the *priority watch list.* The USTR has six months to decide whether to invoke sanctions according to basic Section 301.

## Telecommunications 301

*Telecommunications 301* is another special statute which calls for an annual review, by March 31st of each year, of foreign barriers to U.S. telecommunications firms. It requires *mandatory* retaliation against countries that block access to their markets by U.S. telecommunications companies.

---

NOTICE OF DETERMINATION OF VIOLATION OF TRADE AGREEMENT SUMMARY
Section 1377 of the Omnibus Trade and Competitiveness Act of 1988 requires the U.S. Trade Representative (USTR) to review annually the operation and effectiveness of each telecommunications trade agreement in force between the United States and another country or countries, and to determine whether any act, policy, or practice of the foreign country that entered into the agreement (1) is not in compliance with the terms of the agreement, or (2) otherwise de-

*Access to Japanese Markets for U.S. Cellular Phone Companies*
59 FR 9503 (February 28, 1994)
Office of the United States Trade Representative

nies, within the context of the agreement, mutually advantageous market opportunities to U.S. telecommunications products and services.

Pursuant to section 1377, USTR has determined that certain practices of Japan with respect to cellular telephone products and services are not in compliance with Japan's commitments under a June 28, 1989, agreement on third-party radio and cellular telecommunications equipment. Section 1377

*(continued)*

*(continued)*

requires this affirmative determination to be treated as an affirmative determination under section 304(a)(1)(A) of the Trade Act of 1974. Accordingly, USTR will request the section 301 Committee to recommend what action, if any, should be taken under section 301. USTR will publish notice of any proposed action and will provide an opportunity for interested persons to present views.

SUPPLEMENTARY INFORMATION

This determination is the second affirmative determination under section 1377 on this issue. In the first determination, made on April 28, 1989, USTR found that, for the reasons cited below, Japan was not in compliance with agreements on third-party radio and cellular telecommunications equipment encompassed in a series of letters and joint communications between the United States and Japan pursuant to the "MOSS" (*Market-Oriented Sector-Selective*) discussions that took place between 1985 and 1987.

Specifically, USTR found that the Japanese Ministry of Posts and Telecommunications (MPT) had declined to license the operation in the Tokyo and Nagoya area of a cellular telephone system based on U.S. technology. This system was licensed in the rest of Japan, but subscribers to the system could not use their cellular telephones in the Tokyo-Nagoya area, i.e., they could not "roam" into Tokyo-Nagoya. Users of competing Japanese-technology cellular systems could "roam" throughout the country. USTR determined that the failure to approve operation of a U.S. technology-based system in the Tokyo-Nagoya area was inconsistent with the MOSS agreements, in which the Government of Japan committed to take measures with respect to roaming in Tokyo-Nagoya by users of the U.S. technology-based system.

Following that determination, consultations led to the June 28, 1989, third-party radio and cellular agreement that is the subject of this determination. In the 1989 agreement, the Government of Japan committed to measures to enable users of

the U.S. technology-based system to roam in the Tokyo-Nagoya region. In the agreement, Japan reaffirmed its commitment to the principle of "comparable market access."

In its review of the 1989 agreement, USTR found the following. To install the U.S. technology-based system in the Tokyo-Nagoya region, MPT selected, notwithstanding concerns expressed by USTR and U.S. industry, a company that operates a competing system in the Tokyo-Nagoya area using Japanese technology. This company has substantially delayed installing the U.S. technology-based system in Tokyo. Nearly five years after the 1989 agreement, and nine years after the MOSS discussions began, the new system covers only 40 percent of the Tokyo-Nagoya area. As a result, because users of the U.S. technology-based system still are unable to roam throughout Tokyo-Nagoya, the U.S. technology-based system does not have comparable market access with the Japanese systems, which offer full geographic coverage.

USTR has consulted with other executive agencies and the private sector during this review, and has had discussions with the Japanese Government regarding this agreement on more than seven occasions between July 1993 and February 15, 1994.

As a result of this review, USTR has determined that MPT's failure to ensure full coverage for the U.S. technology-based system in the Tokyo-Nagoya area nearly five years after the 1989 third-party radio and cellular agreement is inconsistent with the terms of that agreement, and denies, within the context of the terms of that agreement, mutually advantageous market opportunities in Japan for telecommunications products and services of the United States.

**Comment.** Only a few weeks later the United States and Japan reached an agreement intended to give U.S. telecommunications firms equal access to the Tokyo cellular phone market. The United States announced that it would not impose trade sanctions.

Reprinted from the *Federal Register*.

## Super 301

The so-called *Super 301* law is the most controversial piece of trade legislation that the United States ever enacted. It was passed in 1988 by a Congress vowing to "get tough" on trade issues. The law has been extended in the 1990s by executive orders of President Clinton. It requires the USTR to identify and report to Congress those *priority trade practices* that pose the greatest barriers to U.S. trade in foreign countries. The USTR also has to identify those *priority countries* that exhibit a pervasive pattern of discrimination against U.S. firms. Within 21 days of the report, the USTR must initiate investigations of the countries named. If a priority country does not remove a trade barrier, then retaliation by the USTR is required. The act provides a real threat to other countries—if they block U.S. firms from their markets they will lose access to the U.S. market (see *Report on Trade Expansion Priorities,* USTR, 1997, in Exhibit 12.2). This report is based on the USTR's *National Trade Estimate Report on Foreign Trade Barriers,* prepared annually for Congress and the president. The *Trade Estimate* is a "laundry list" of U.S. complaints about trade barriers in foreign countries. The 1998 *Trade Estimate* focused on Japan, South Korea, Europe, and China.

**Assessing the Impact of Unilateral Action.** Many experts believe that Section 301, Special 301, and Super 301 have been successful in getting other countries to open their markets to U.S. goods and services. A look at the reports of the USTR, and its announcements in the *Federal Register* (see Exhibit 12.2) reveal many cases in which Section 301 has resulted in increased market access. In the early 1990s, Section 301 was helpful in getting Japan to reduce its restrictions on the import of citrus products, supercomputers, and satellites. Korea, China, Brazil, Poland, Saudi Arabia, Thailand, and countries in every region of the globe, agreed to provide greater protection to IPRs; Taiwan reduced import barriers on foreign tobacco, beer, and wine; Brazil improved market access for the U.S. software industry; Canada agreed to change its marketing restrictions on the sale of U.S. beer. Market access has been improved in dozens of countries around the world. Yet, the use of trade sanctions in these cases is actually rare. In virtually all cases, trade disputes have been resolved through negotiation or panel decisions. The very existence of the law has provided the USTR with the "negotiating leverage" needed to resolve a dispute and avoid a trade war. The threat of action has prompted other nations to open markets for U.S. products and to protect U.S. intellectual property rights. Many problem areas remain, however. The USTR cites Japanese restrictions inherent in their distribution system that discriminate against foreign suppliers, Japanese standards that discriminate against U.S.-designed products, and Japanese government procurement practices. In terms of product areas, Japan is still criticized by the USTR for unfair treatment of U.S. auto parts, wood products, fish, glass, and steel. Europe is criticized for quotas on U.S. television programming, and intellectual property violations continue worldwide. Long-running disputes over Korean restrictions on imports of U.S. products continue (see Exhibit 12.2). Almost all observers believe that Section 301 will continue to be used in the future, and that it will aid in the enforcement of WTO dispute panel decisions.

Most countries, especially Japan and those in Europe, have criticized Section 301 and Super 301 as a one-sided "strong-arm" tactic that violates U.S. commitments to settle trade wars through WTO dispute resolution. They will surely continue to press the United States not to use Section 301 without authorization by the WTO.

---

**http://dylee.keel.econ.ship.edu/intntl/ ecn321/lecture/uspolicy.htm**
*See for information on the "Super 301" clause.*

*CFR Code of Fed. Regulation*

**EXHIBIT 12.2 Report on Trade Expansion Priorities ("Super 301"),
Office of the United States Trade Representative,
62 FR 52604 (October 8, 1997),
October 1, 1997**

Under the Executive Order the United States Trade Representative (USTR) is required, by September 30, 1997, to "review United States trade expansion priorities and identify priority foreign country practices, the elimination of which is likely to have the most significant potential to increase United States exports, either directly or through the establishment of a beneficial precedent."
\*\*\*

### Priority Foreign Country Practice

*Korea—Barriers to Auto Imports*
Specific Korean practices of concern include an array of cumulative tariff and tax disincentives that disproportionately affect imports; onerous and costly auto standards and certification procedures; auto financing restrictions; and a climate of bias against imported vehicles that Korean officials have not effectively addressed. . . . Meanwhile, Korean auto manufacturers are expanding domestic capacity, which is forecast to rise from 2.8 to over 5 million units by the year 2000. Although some progress was made during recent bilateral negotiations to improve market access in Korea for foreign automobiles, Korea was not prepared to undertake the reforms which are necessary for real opening of its autos market. In light of the foregoing, the USTR has decided to identify Korea's barriers to imported automobiles as a priority foreign country practice under the Executive Order and will initiate a section 301 investigation of Korea's practices. The United States continues to hope that it can reach an agreement with Korea that will effectively address U.S. concerns.

### New Cases to Be Launched

As a result of this year's review of its trade expansion priorities, and its monitoring of compliance with U.S. trade agreements, the Administration will take the following actions to enforce U.S. rights under those agreements, with heavy emphasis on challenging foreign government actions that appear to circumvent the WTO rules on export subsidies.

*Japan—Market Access Barriers to Fruit*
USTR will initiate a section 301 investigation and in that context, request the establishment of a WTO panel to challenge the Japanese government requirement of separate efficacy testing of certain quarantine treatments for each variety of imported fruit, even where the same treatment has been accepted by Japan as effective for another variety. Although the fruit of immediate export concern is apples, Japan's requirement operates as a significant import barrier to nectarines, cherries, and other fruits that are of export interest to the United States. The United States and Japan have already completed consultations on this matter pursuant to WTO dispute settlement procedures, so the United States will proceed directly to request a panel.

*Canada—Export Subsidies and Import Quotas on Dairy Products*
USTR will invoke WTO dispute settlement procedures in the context of a section 301 investigation to challenge practices that subsidize exports of dairy products from Canada, and Canadian implementation of its import quotas on milk. The U.S. dairy industry has petitioned USTR to initiate this investigation on the grounds that both of these practices are inconsistent with Canada's WTO obligations and adversely affect U.S. exports.

*EU—Circumvention of Export Subsidy Commitments on Dairy Products*
USTR also will invoke WTO dispute settlement procedures in the context of a section 301 investigation to challenge practices by the European Union (EU) that circumvent the EU's commitments under the WTO to limit subsidized exports of processed cheese and adversely affect U.S. exports to third markets. The EU is counting these exports against its limits on powdered milk and butterfat to avoid the limits on subsidies of cheese. USTR will also closely monitor EU compliance with its WTO agricultural subsidy commitments on all other agricultural products.

*Australia—Export Subsidies on Automotive Leather*
Following bilateral and multilateral consultations, Australia agreed to eliminate export subsidies for leather used in automobiles. However, Australia's subsequent package of assistance for its industry (comprised of a sizable loan and grant), has raised similar concerns regarding consistency with WTO subsidies rules. While some progress has been made in recent months, these concerns have not yet been adequately addressed. Thus USTR will invoke WTO dispute settlement procedures, but remains hopeful that a solution satisfactory to both countries can be reached.

*(continued)*

**EXHIBIT 12.2    (continued)**

**Recent Enforcement Actions**

During the past year, USTR has invoked WTO dispute settlement procedures to challenge a wide variety of foreign government practices, covered by the broad range of agreements administered by the WTO, seeking to enforce the rules on tariffs, agriculture, services, intellectual property rights, antidumping measures, and sanitary and phytosanitary measures. Those complaints include challenges of:

- Argentina's import duties on footwear, textiles, and apparel that exceed the maximum to which Argentina is committed under WTO tariff rules;
- licensing requirements in Belgium that discriminate against U.S. suppliers of commercial telephone directory services;
- Brazilian government measures that give certain benefits to manufacturers of motor vehicles and parts, conditioned on compliance with average domestic content requirements, trade-balancing and local content requirements with regard to inputs;
- the failure of Denmark to provide adequate measures to enforce intellectual property rights;
- reclassification by the European Union, the United Kingdom, and Ireland of certain computers and computer-related equipment to different tariff categories with higher tariff rates;
- import restrictions on more than 2700 agricultural, textile and industrial products imposed by India for which India can no longer claim a justification for balance-of-payments reasons;
- Indonesia's programs granting preferential tax and tariff benefits to producers of automobiles based on the percentage of local (Indonesian) content of the finished automobile;
- Ireland's failure to expeditiously bring its copyright laws into compliance with the WTO agreement on intellectual property rights;
- Japan's barriers to market access for photographic film and paper, and barriers to distribution and retail services in Japan;
- Korea's taxes on Western-style distilled spirits that are higher than those assessed on the traditional Korean-style spirit soju;
- an antidumping action by Mexico of high-fructose corn syrup imports from the United States that does not conform to WTO procedures;
- a licensing system in the Philippines that discriminates against U.S. exports of pork and poultry; and
- the failure of Sweden to provide adequate measures to enforce intellectual property rights.

*Japan—Port Practices*
Restrictive practices in Japanese ports have caused serious difficulties for U.S. shipping companies for many years. After initial consultations with Japan failed to resolve these problems, on September 4, 1997, the Federal Maritime Commission imposed sanctions of $100,000 per voyage on container vessels owned or operated by Japanese companies entering the United States. Consultations to remove the restrictive practices which impede open and efficient business operations of our carriers continue.

*Argentina—Patent Protection*
On January 15, 1997, the Administration decided to withdraw 50 percent of Argentina's tariff benefits under the Generalized System of Preferences as a result of its continued delay in providing adequate patent legislation, particularly for pharmaceutical products.
***

*Mexico—Telecommunications*
USTR cited Mexico for not fulfilling its NAFTA obligation to accept other parties' laboratory or test facility test data relating to product safety in certifying telecommunications equipment for safe use. An agreement reached in April 1997 established procedures to resolve this issue, which will further facilitate the export of U.S. telecommunications products to Mexico.

*Honduras—Piracy*
In response to the failure of Honduras to address effectively the unauthorized broadcasting of pirated U.S. videos and the rebroadcasting of U.S. satellite-carried programming, the Administration is taking steps to withdraw some of the tariff benefits accorded Honduras under the Generalized System of Preference and Caribbean Basin Initiative programs.
***

*(continued)*

**EXHIBIT 12.2 (continued)**

*China—IPR Enforcement*
We have seen progress through closure of 58 pirate compact disc production lines and the establishment of an infrastructure for enforcement of IPRs. Continuing problems exist regarding computer software piracy and trademark counterfeiting, however, since Chinese authorities often fail to impose penalties sufficient to deter illegal activities. U.S. negotiators are continuing to work with Chinese authorities to improve compliance with our IPR agreements.
\*\*\*

*China—Insurance Providers*
Foreign insurers' access to the Chinese market is severely restricted. U.S. insurers must first establish a representative office for two years before applying for a license. If China grants the company a license, numerous non-prudential restrictions apply on doing business, including restrictions on the form of investment, scope of business lines, and geographic location. We are seeking elimination of these non-prudential restrictions.

*Korea—Impediments to Entry and Distribution of Cosmetics*
The Korean government uses measures that restrict the entry and distribution of cosmetics including: restrictions on sales promotions (premiums), including changes to the valuation methodology; delegation of authority to a Korean industry association to screen advertising and information brochures prior to use; mandatory provision of proprietary information on imports to Korean competitors; redundant testing; unreasonable prior-approval requirements on cosmetic tester labels; and burdensome import authorization and tracking requirements. After bilateral talks with U.S. officials, Korea stated its intention to change some of these measures, but the Korean government still has not fully addressed U.S. concerns. . . .

*Korea—Import Clearance Procedures*
After WTO dispute settlement consultations with Korea on its long, burdensome, and non-science-based import clearance procedures, the Korean government made changes, including expediting clearance for fresh fruits and vegetables; instituting a new sampling, testing, and inspection regime; eliminating some phytosanitary requirements; and starting the process of updating Korean Food Additives Code standards. However, Korean port inspectors have failed to implement changes to which the Korean government has committed, including the elimination of requirements for proprietary information (on manufacturing process and ingredient listing by percentage) and for sorting of produce.
\*\*\*

As a result of intense efforts in the past year, the Administration has resolved technical issues bilaterally to permit exports of tomatoes to Japan; table grapes to China; lemons, table grapes, kiwis, oranges and grapefruit to Chile; sweet cherries to Mexico; rough rice to Honduras; live swine to Argentina and Peru; and live cattle to Peru. The Administration will continue to press our trading partners to remove unjustified SPS barriers facing U.S. agricultural exports, including:

*EU—Specified Risk Material (SRM) Ban and Cosmetics Directive*
Two recent directives approved by the European Commission prohibiting the sale in the EU of cosmetic products containing tallow and its derivatives, and governing the production of certain materials, due to concerns regarding the transmission of Bovine Spongiform Encephalopathy (BSE), raise concerns with respect to the EU's WTO obligations. The directives fail to recognize that BSE is not known to occur in the United States and that the United States maintains an aggressive surveillance program for BSE that exceeds international standards. The EU has failed to provide a scientific basis for these requirements, and both directives are expected to have severe negative effects on U.S. exports of pharmaceutical, cosmetic and tallow products; and the potential impact on the international availability of essential pharmaceutical products also raises serious public health concerns.

*France—Pet Food Imports*
In September 1996, France adopted new requirements for pet food production, restricting the use of certain animal products or proteins and prohibiting the use of certain material. The regulation requires that manufacturers exclude materials from the rendering process that are commonly considered safe by renderers and

*(continued)*

**EXHIBIT 12.2** **(continued)**

this has effectively stopped all U.S. pet food exports to France. France has not demonstrated the scientific principle underlying the restriction of non-mammalian material as a protective measure against any risk factor. This issue was raised by the United States at the July 1997 meeting of the WTO SPS Committee.

### EU—Design Restrictive Standards
U.S. firms continue to encounter difficulty in obtaining market access for certain products in Europe due to design-restrictive standards that may have no bearing on the safety and performance of the product.

### EU—Ecolabeling Directive
The EU Ecolabeling Directive sets forth a scheme whereby EU Member States will grant voluntary environmental labels based on criteria approved by the European Commission for products in specific sectors. The United States affirms its support for the concept of ecolabeling and has previously expressed appreciation for the EU's attempts to address problems raised by the United States regarding its ecolabeling program. However, while improvements in the transparency of procedures and opportunity for foreign participation in the EU's ecolabeling program have been reported, concern remains that the EU ecolabeling program favors European industry, thus leading to trade concerns.

### EU—Units of Measurement Directive
The EU plans to implement a directive requiring that after December 31, 1999, the only indications of measurement that can be used on product labels will be metric units. Currently, labels may include other units (e.g., inches, pounds) in addition to metric units. Such a step is unnecessary and burdensome, and will affect many U.S. companies, particularly in those industries where packaging and labeling are key aspects of placing a product on the market (e.g., food products, consumer goods and cosmetics).

## Early Victories

The United States has won the first five cases that it has taken through the WTO dispute settlement panel process.

### Japan—Liquor Taxes
The United States—joined by the EU and Canada—successfully challenged a discriminatory Japanese tax scheme that placed high taxes on whisky, vodka, and other Western-style spirits, while applying low taxes to a traditional Japanese spirit (shochu).

### Canada—Restrictions on Magazines
The United States successfully challenged a recently enacted Canadian law that placed a high tax on American magazines containing advertisements directed at a Canadian audience. This tax, which was the latest in a series of Canadian government measures designed to protect the Canadian magazine industry from U.S. competition, was specifically calculated to put the Canadian edition of Sports Illustrated, published by the Canadian subsidiary of Time Warner, Inc., out of business. By ruling in favor of the United States, this case makes clear that WTO rules prevent governments from using "culture" as a pretense for discriminating against imports.

### EU—Banana Imports
The United States joined Ecuador, Guatemala, Honduras, and Mexico in challenging an EU import program that gave French and British companies a big share of the banana distribution services business in Europe that U.S. companies had built up over the years. Ruling against the EU, the WTO panel and Appellate Body found that the EU banana import rules violated both the General Agreement on Trade in Services and the General Agreement on Trade in Goods by depriving U.S. banana distribution services companies and Latin American banana producers of a fair share of the EU market.

### EU—Hormone Ban
Both the United States and Canada challenged Europe's ban on the use of six hormones to promote the growth of cattle, and a WTO panel agreed that the EU has no scientific basis for blocking the sale of American beef in Europe. . . . The panel affirmed the need for food safety measures to be based on science, as they are in the United States.

(continued)

---

**EXHIBIT 12.2 (continued)**

*India—Patent Law*
The United States recently obtained a panel ruling against India for failing to provide procedures for filing patent applications for pharmaceuticals and agricultural chemicals, as required by the WTO agreement on intellectual property protection.

*Korea—Shelf-Life Requirements*
Consultations under WTO procedures resulted in a commitment by Korea to phase out its shelf-life restrictions on food products—which removed a major barrier to US exports of beef, pork, poultry and frozen products.

*EU—Grains Imports*
By demonstrating our resolve to refer the matter to a panel, we succeeded in pushing the EU to implement a settlement agreement on grains that benefits U.S. exports of rice and malting barley.

*Japan—Sound Recordings*
In only a matter of months after we held WTO consultations, the Government of Japan amended its law to provide U.S. sound recordings with retroactive protection, as required by the WTO agreement on intellectual property rights.

*Portugal—Patent Law*
After the United States requested WTO consultations, Portugal agreed to revise its patent law to provide a 20-year term to old, as well as new, patents, as required by the WTO agreement on intellectual property rights.
***

*Turkey—Film Tax*
The United States has used the WTO dispute settlement process to convince the Government of Turkey to eliminate discriminatory tax treatment currently given to box office receipts from exhibition of foreign films. Turkey has agreed to change its practice.

SOURCE: Office of the United States Trade Representative.

## Chapter Summary

As industries become more dependent on export sales, they become more vulnerable to foreign trade barriers that deny them access to export markets. The Uruguay Round trade negotiations resulted in many important GATT 1994 agreements designed to remove trade barriers and improve access to foreign markets, including agreements on technical barriers, import licensing, government procurement, services, agriculture, textiles, intellectual property, and foreign investments. For the first time, GATT now governs trade in services, textiles, agriculture, and intellectual property. Most economists predict that the impact will be felt by U.S. firms, and by firms around the world, stimulating economic growth for years to come.

The Agreement on Technical Barriers to Trade will guide WTO nations in their use of technical regulations and product standards. It does not set standards of its own for product performance, design, safety, or efficiency, but it guides nations in the application of their own regulations and standards through legal principles of nondiscrimination, transparency, and MFN trade. The agreement applies broadly to regulations imposed to protect the public health, safety, and welfare, including consumer and environmental protection. Health and safety regulations may not be used unless they are "trade neutral" and restrict trade no more than necessary, according to the principle of least-restrictive-trade.

Government procurement is a key sector of the world's economy. *The Agreement on Government Procurement* provides an exception to the rule that governments may treat goods and services from domestic suppliers more favorably than those from foreign suppliers. Countries must "free up" their procurement policies and practices by giving foreign firms equal access in bidding on government contracts, and providing transparent and easily obtained rules for submitting bids.

About 20 percent of world trade is in services. The General Agreement on Trade in Services applies basic GATT principles to service industries for the first time since 1947. This agreement will open access to foreign markets in construction, engineering, health care, law, and other services. Eventually the industries that may benefit the most are in banking, insurance, securities, and transportation.

Trade in agriculture has been distorted by billions of dollars worth of government subsidies granted to farming interests worldwide, and restrictions on food imports. Attempts to limit government support of agriculture has been met by attacks from politically powerful farm groups, particularly in France and other European countries. The Agreement on Agriculture is expected to reduce government subsidies on farm products by 20 to 35 percent and to open access to markets. Exports of farm products have suffered because of discriminatory trade barriers imposed under the guise of health standards. Under the *Sanitary and Phytosanitary Agreement,* countries cannot impose restrictions to protect animal and plant life from pests or contagious diseases unless those restrictions are applied fairly and equally to goods from all countries that present a risk of infection. Restrictions must be supported by scientific evidence and be the least restrictive to trade as possible.

Textiles are one of the most import sensitive industries of all. Many jobs in developed countries have been lost to low-wage jobs in the textile-producing developing countries. Quotas are used to control and monitor textile and apparel shipments for each product category. The quota is administered through a licensing system. Textiles imported from most countries cannot enter without a license. The *Agreement on Textiles* is intended to eliminate quotas over a ten-year period. When quotas close on Chinese textiles, some shippers illegally transship or reroute Chinese textiles through other countries whose quota allotment is still open. They are subject to severe criminal penalties in the United States.

GATT 1994 also sets new rules on *Trade-Related Investment Measures* that limit the use of trade-restrictive conditions on investment. The rules on *Trade-Related Aspects of Intellectual Property Rights* change the copyright, patent, and trademark laws of many nations, including the United States. It makes them more uniform and provides greater protection to the holders of intellectual property rights. (These topics will be discussed in greater detail in Part Four.)

No one knows whether the promise of the World Trade Organization will be fulfilled in the future. Whether it will be able to assure that all companies will have greater access to foreign markets or be as successful in promoting trade in services, agriculture, and textiles as it has been for 45 years in promoting trade in goods remains to be seen. The ability of the WTO to resolve countries' disputes before trade wars erupt will be critical to its overall success.

One of the new issues likely to appear is the link between trade and the environment—trade in tropical products, trade in endangered species, the destruction of the world's forests, pollution, and degradation of the air and water. These environmental issues may reach the WTO's agenda in the not-too-distant future. Another difficult issue is that of labor and workers' rights. The WTO, as a trade organization that functions by consensus, may be rigorously tested as it addresses such a political issue as this. The WTO will most likely be involved in the controversial treatment of children or women in the workforce, or the use of prison labor in the developing countries of Asia. If you wonder whether this is a "trade" problem appropriately addressed by the WTO, consider that products made by children or abused workers in poor countries are bought by consumers in the rich countries. One questions whether countries will give the WTO sufficient authority and clout to deal with these problems, or whether solutions lie in other realms.

---

## QUESTIONS AND CASE PROBLEMS

1. Immediately after India was targeted under Super 301 for restricting market access by U.S. firms, it began a public relations campaign against the United States. Its representatives stated that India would not negotiate "at the point of a gun." Evaluate this statement. Do you agree that unilateral

retaliation by the United States has been the best way to improve access to foreign markets and to protect U.S. intellectual property rights?

2. What are the real economic impacts and long-term effects of trade sanctions? Assume that the United States imposes punishingly high tariffs of 100 percent on, say, Japanese cars. Immediate costs might be borne by the Japanese manufacturers, U.S. dealerships, or consumers; but what does such a measure do to the long-term health and competitiveness of the U.S. car industry? Could you see any impact on the U.S. lead in innovation, design, and quality? Discuss.

3. What is *managed trade?* Do you agree or disagree that trade can be "managed"? Give examples from the text, and from your reading, of how governments manage trade. Can you cite successful or unsuccessful cases? What is the position of recent U.S. administrations in regard to "managing" trade?

4. Do you think that the United States is guilty of "Japan Bashing"? What have been the key issues affecting trade between the United States and Japan? How has their relationship been affected by political considerations?

5. At the request of the Canadian owner of a country music channel, Canada removed from the air a Nashville-based country music channel. This effort is only one in a series made by Canada to restrict U.S. programming. Canadians argue that their country is dominated by U.S. culture on television and want it restricted. The U.S. firm petitions the USTR for trade sanctions unless the Canadian policy is changed. After an investigation, the USTR threatens the Canadian government with $500 million in punitive tariffs. Discuss whether the USTR should have threatened sanctions before the case is heard by the WTO. See *Initiation of Section 302 Investigation Concerning Certain Discriminatory Communications Practices,* 60 FR 8101 (February 10, 1995).

6. The marketing and sale of beer and alcoholic beverages in Canada are governed by Canadian provincial marketing agencies or "liquor boards." In most of the ten Canadian provinces, these liquor boards not only regulate the marketing of domestic beer in the province, but serve as import monopolies. They also warehouse, distribute, and retail imported beer. Canada imposed restrictions on the number of locations at which imported beer could be sold; authorization from the liquor board was needed to sell a brand of beer in the province; and higher markups were required on the price of foreign beer than on domestic beer sold by the liquor boards. Do the regulations violate the nondiscrimination provisions of GATT? May Canada use state trading mo-

nopolies to regulate imports of this kind? Are Canada's provisions valid public health regulations or illegal discrimination? If trade statistics showed that foreign beer sales have actually increased, could an exporting country's rights under GATT still be subject to "nullification and impairment"? Would Section 301 apply to this case? See, 56 FR 60128 (1991). See *GATT Dispute Settlement Panel Report: Canada Import, Distribution and Sale of Alcoholic Drinks By Canadian Provincial Marketing Agencies,* Document I-B-38, International Economic Law Documents (1988).

7. Thailand has been slow to protect copyrights. Although the Thai government has conducted raids and taken other steps that have reduced pirated goods on the market, prosecution of pirates of U.S. works in the Thai courts has not been successful. Of the cases filed, many have been pending for nearly two years with little result. Evidentiary requirements, limits on raids and other problems make enforcement difficult. Under the Thai copyright law, computer software is not protected. Unauthorized public performances of copyrighted recordings are also not controlled. Although Thailand passed a patent law in 1992, it allows the government extremely broad authority in using foreign patents without compensation. The law also establishes a Pharmaceutical Patent Board with extraordinary authority requiring owners of pharmaceutical patents to provide sensitive cost and pricing information; it also imposes draconian fines for failure to provide such information. What recourse would U.S. intellectual property owners have under Special 301? Is this case actionable at the WTO? See *Identification of Priority Foreign Countries* 58 FR 26991 (May 6, 1993); *Thailand: Revocation of Priority Foreign Country Designation* (September 21, 1993). For additional information, see Chapter Twenty.

8. What is the status of multilateral negotiations for trade in financial services, and how will they affect the banking, insurance, and securities industries?

## MANAGERIAL IMPLICATIONS

1. Your company is a U.S. multinational corporation with a 40 percent share of the world market for its product. Over the past decade management has invested more than $500 million dollars trying to get its products into Japanese stores. After all of its efforts the company has less than a 10 percent share of the Japanese market, and only 15 percent of Japanese stores carry its products. Company in-

vestigations show that its major Japanese competitor has a virtual monopoly there and has violated Japanese antitrust laws by fixing prices and refusing to sell to any store that carries your firm's products. Most distributors and retailers are linked to your competitor through *keiretsu* relationships. Management believes that by "having the Japanese market all to themselves," the competitor is able to maintain prices sufficiently high in Japan to permit them to undersell your company in the United States. Apparently, the Japanese government simply "looks the other way." Moreover, your firm has been effectively restrained by the bureaucracy that administers government procurement contracts in Japan. As a result, management estimates that it has lost several billion dollars in exports since the company first entered the Japanese market. Your competitor responds that they are not the only producer in Japan, that the market there is very competitive, and besides, they also outsell your firm's products in several other Asian countries.

1. If you petition for a Section 301 action, do you think the USTR will begin an investigation? What political factors in the United States might affect the USTR's decision to investigate? What is the attitude of the current U.S. administration toward the use of Section 301?
2. Management thinks that the Japanese government should require distributors to agree to import a given quantity of U.S.-made products in a year's period. How would the Japanese government mandate this? Do you think the Japanese distribution system or its *keiretsu* practices can be reformed? What other remedies or sanctions might be appropriate in this case? What is the likelihood that the threat of sanctions by the United States will affect the Japanese position? Given the history of U.S.—Japanese trade relations, and authority of the new World Trade Organization, what do you think is the likely outcome of this case? Based on your study of the last three chapters, what provisions of the GATT agreement, if any, might apply to this case?
3. Are the market share statistics relevant to your case? What other data or information will be important?

II. The Asian country of Tamoa imports large quantities of down pillows each year. DownPillow, a U.S. company, would like to do more business there, but it has a problem. Tamoa has a number of regulations affecting the importation and sale of down bedding. Consider the following 5 regulations:
1. Pillows made from down harvested from Tamoan flocks may be labeled as "goose down" even though they contain up to 25 percent duck down. (Down is taken from both geese and ducks, but duck down is considered inferior.) If the pillow is made from foreign down, then a pillow labeled "goose down" may contain no more than 5 percent duck down. U.S. regulations recognize that geese and ducks often get plucked together, and therefore permit goose down to contain up to 10 percent duck down. DownPillow believes the 10 percent "tolerance" is reasonable, but given farming methods in most countries it is not possible to sort out the geese and the ducks any better than that. Tamoa believes that the stricter standard for imported pillows is justified to protect Tamoan consumers from fraud, and since Tamoan farmers do not raise any ducks, the 25 percent domestic standard is irrelevant anyway.
2. Tamoa also requires that the cotton coverings of all pillows be certified to meet certain ecology and human health standards for textiles—that they not contain any harmful chemicals such as formaldehyde or chlorine and that they have been tested according to minimum standards set by the International Organization for Standardization. Certifications are accepted from qualified testing laboratories in any country. U.S. regulations do not require certification.
3. All pillow imports must be inspected on arrival in Tamoa. No inspections are permitted at the foreign factory. Tamoa has only one full-time inspector, who must remove down from at least three pillows from every shipment and subject it to laboratory analysis. Given the current backlog, inspections and analysis are taking up to four weeks, during which time the pillows are often damaged by Tamoa's high humidity.
4. Tamoan regulations also require that Down Pillow's plant be inspected and that the sterilization process be approved by Tamoan officials. In the United States the down is washed, sanitized, and subjected to hot air heat several hundred degrees in temperature, all under health department supervision. The Tamoan ministry of agriculture refuses to accept the sterilization permits, inspections, and approvals from state health departments in the United States. Tamoa does not pay the overseas travel expenses of its inspectors.
5. Tamoan regulations prohibit pillows and comforters from being compressed or vacuum packed for shipment to assure the down will not be damaged in shipment. DownPillow ships smaller orders by airfreight and larger orders by ocean container.

DownPillow and other U.S. firms are not pleased with these requirements. Evaluate the legality of the regulations and their impact on DownPillow. What course of action should DownPillow take?

## NOTES

1. For an article based on original research that details the history of Japanese technical barriers to trade, see Peter B. Edelman, *Japanese Product Standards as Non-Tariff Barriers: When Regulatory Policy Becomes a Trade Issue,* 24 Stan.J. Int'l. L. 389 (1988).

2. For an article comparing U.S. Section 301 with its counterpart in European Union law, see Wolfgang W. Leirer, *Retaliatory Action in United States and European Union Trade Law: Comparison of Section 301 of the Trade Act of 1974 and Council Regulation 2641/84,* 20 N.C. J. Int'l. & Com. Reg. 41 (1994).

# Chapter Thirteen

# Imports, Customs, and Tariff Law

Importing is the process of entering goods into the customs territory of a country. The study of importing should not be approached from the perspective of an isolated transaction. Rather, importing should be viewed as an integral part of a global company's operations. For instance, a chemical company might find that raw materials can be sourced from foreign suppliers at a net cost far less than if purchased at home. A leading apparel designer might ship garments to the United States that had been assembled in Honduras, from parts of clothing that were cut and sewn at plants in Hong Kong, from fabric that had been woven in China. An automobile company might ship cars to the United States from assembly plants in Mexico that used component parts sourced from Japan or Europe. A Japanese-owned electronics company might assemble televisions in the Caribbean using both Japanese and U.S. parts, with the finished products shipped back to U.S. markets. A large retailer might import foreign-made consumer goods, such as toys or appliances, because they are cheaper from overseas sources. U.S. distributors of Swiss watches, Danish cheese, or French wine, also might import these foreign brands because customers perceive them to be of superior quality. Each of these companies views the operation of their firm in a global context, and they are aware that their global strategy will be affected by the customs and tariff laws applicable to their products as these goods cross national borders.

Whereas the preceding chapters discussed the process by which nations regulate international trade, this chapter focuses on the specific problems of importing goods into the United States. It examines U.S. regulations governing the admis-sion of goods into the country, the calculation of import duties, tariff preferences for developing countries, the marking requirements for goods, and the use of many duty-saving devices, such as foreign trade zones. The chapter begins with an explanation of how imports into the United States are supervised by the U.S. Customs Service and how the customs and tariff laws are administered.

---

**http://www.ita.doc.gov/import_admin/ records**
See for links to many of the topics in this chapter.

---

## The Administration of Customs and Tariff Laws

The customs and tariff laws of the United States are enacted by the U.S. Congress and implemented and enforced by the *U.S. Customs Service,* referred to as Customs. Customs is an agency within the Department of Treasury, and is headed by the Commissioner of Customs. The agency's functions are to assess and collect the tariff revenue of the United States, enforce the customs laws, which includes regulating the entry of products under quota, enforcing the labeling statutes, supervising exports, administering of duty-free zones, and other functions. As a law enforcement agency, U.S. Customs combats smuggling and investigates tariff fraud cases. The agency is responsible for the administration of customs laws throughout the customs territory of the United States, which includes the U.S. Virgin Islands and Puerto Rico. U.S. Customs officers are assigned to U.S. embassies in many foreign countries to assist in the administration of U.S. customs laws.

The Customs Service is divided into seven geographic regions, each headed by a regional commissioner. The regions are further divided into customs districts, headed by a district director. Customs offices are located at the *ports of entry,* including major seaports, airports, inland ports, and border crossings. Within each district are *field import specialists,* who make initial determinations as to the entry of goods. They can seek advice from the *national import specialists.* Some officers are specialists in particular types of products, such as textiles. The district director supervises all imports within the district and makes sure that imported goods are entered in accordance with the rules of the agency and decisions of the courts.

> **http://www.customs.ustreas.gov**
> See for the official site of the U.S. Customs Service.

## The Entry Process

The *entry process* refers to the administrative process required to import goods into the stream of commerce of a country. The process begins upon the arrival of the merchandise at a U.S. port of entry. Entry must be made within five days of the arrival of the goods. The goods may be entered by the owner, purchaser, consignee (the party to whom the goods are shipped or to be delivered), or customs broker. A *customs broker* is an agent, licensed by federal law, to act for and on behalf of importers in making entry of goods. Over 90 percent of all entries are made by customs brokers. A customs broker must possess a written power of attorney from the party making entry. Nonresident individuals and foreign corporations may make entry, but they are bound by much stricter rules.

**Required Documentation.** When goods are entered, the entry documents must be filed within five days. The documents necessary to enter goods generally include the following items:

1. An entry manifest or merchandise release form (see the *Entry/Immediate Delivery Form* in Exhibit 13.1).

2. U.S. Customs *Entry Summary* Form (Exhibit 13.2).
3. Proof of the right to make entry (a bill of lading, air waybill, or carrier's receipt).
4. The commercial invoice (or a pro forma invoice when the commercial invoice is temporarily delayed by the seller).
5. Packing slips to identify the contents of cartons.
6. Other documents required by special regulations (e.g., certificate of origin, quota visa, textile declaration, etc.).

**The Commercial Invoice.** A seller must provide a separate invoice for each commercial shipment entering the United States. The *commercial invoice* is required for all shipments greater than $500 and intended for sale or commercial use in the United States. The invoice must provide all pertinent information about the shipment, in English, and be signed by the seller. One invoice can be used for installment shipments to the same consignee if the shipments arrive within ten days of each other. The invoice must include the following information:

- Name of the port of shipment and the destined port of entry.
- Name of buyer and seller or consignee.
- Common or trade name for the goods and their detailed description.
- Country-of-origin.
- Currency of payment.
- Quantity and weight of the goods shipped.
- Value of the goods accurately and correctly stated, including a breakdown of all itemized charges such as freight, insurance, packing costs, the costs of containers, and any rebates and commissions paid or payable.
- A packing list stating in detail what merchandise is in each individual package.
- Special information for certain classes of merchandise (e.g., bedspreads must indicate whether they contain any embroidery, lace, braid, or other trimming).

Customs regulations in the United States and in most other countries are strict about the content and proper form for invoices. For example, in the United States, customs regulations require that importers write on an invoice only in black

**EXHIBIT 13.1    Entry/Immediate Delivery Form**

DEPARTMENT OF THE TREASURY
UNITED STATES CUSTOMS SERVICE

FORM APPROVED
OMB NO. 1515-0069

# ENTRY/IMMEDIATE DELIVERY

19CFR 142.3, 142.16, 142.22, 142.24

| 1. ARRIVAL DATE | 2. ELECTED ENTRY DATE | 3. ENTRY TYPE CODE/NAME | 4. ENTRY NUMBER |
|---|---|---|---|
| 060999 | | 01   ABI/S | 669-2242260-6 |

ABI CERTIFIED

| 5. PORT | 6. SINGLE TRANS. BOND | 7. BROKER/IMPORTER FILE NUMBER | |
|---|---|---|---|
| 1512 | X   891 | 617795E | |
| | 8. CONSIGNEE NUMBER | | 9. IMPORTER NUMBER |
| | | | 12-34567 |

SAME

**10. ULTIMATE CONSIGNEE NAME**

Importer's Company
Anytown, NC 20000

| 12. CARRIER CODE | 13. VOYAGE/FLIGHT/TRIP | 14. LOCATION OF GOODS–CODE(S)/NAME(S) |
|---|---|---|
| 111 | 444 | L362 |

**15. VESSEL CODE/NAME**

LUFTHANSA

| 16. U.S. PORT OF UNLOADING | 17. MANIFEST NUMBER | 18. G.O. NUMBER | 19. TOTAL VALUE |
|---|---|---|---|
| 1704 | | | $3331 |

**20. DESCRIPTION OF MERCHANDISE**

Bedding

| 21. IT/BL/AWB CODE | 22. IT/BL/AWB NO. | 23. MANIFEST QUANTITY | 24. H.S. NUMBER | 25. COUNTRY OF ORIGIN | 26. MANUFACTURER ID. |
|---|---|---|---|---|---|
| I | 22069456995 | | 6304.99.60107 | DE | DEBILRHE4044KRA |
| M | 22069456995 | | | | |
| H | 4850228 7 | 5 | | | |
| | | | | | |
| | | | | | |
| | | | | | |

| 27. CERTIFICATION | 28. CUSTOMS USE ONLY |
|---|---|

**27. CERTIFICATION**

I hereby make application for entry/immediate delivery. I certify that the above information is accurate, the bond is sufficient, valid, and current, and that all requirements of 19 CFR Part 142 have been met.

SIGNATURE OF APPLICANT

X    Importer's Customs Broker

| PHONE NO. | DATE |
|---|---|
| | 6/11/99 |

**29. BROKER OR OTHER GOVT. AGENCY USE**

**28. CUSTOMS USE ONLY**

☐ OTHER AGENCY ACTION REQUIRED, NAMELY:

☐ CUSTOMS EXAMINATION REQUIRED.

☐ ENTRY REJECTED, BECAUSE:

JUN 12  8 23 AM '99

| DELIVERY AUTHORIZED: | SIGNATURE WRL | DATE 6-12-99 |
|---|---|---|

Customs Form 3461 (010189)

**EXHIBIT 13.2   Entry Summary Form**

DEPARTMENT OF THE TREASURY
UNITED STATES CUSTOMS SERVICE

Importer's Broker
P.O. Box 123
Charlotte, N.C. 28219

| 1. Entry No. 2242260-6 | 1. Entry No. 01 ABI/S | 3. Entry Summary Date 6/26/99   414 |
|---|---|---|
| 4. Entry Date | 5. Port Code 1512 | ABI APPROVED |
| 6. Bond No. 891 | 7. Bond Type Code SEB -9 | 8. BROKER/IMPORTER FILE NO. 123456ab-6 |

| 9. Ultimate Consignee Name and Address | 10. Consignee No. | 11. Importer of Record Name and Address Same | 12. Importer No. 12-34567 |
|---|---|---|---|

Importer's Company
Anytown, NC 20000

| 13. Exporting Country DE GERMANY | 14. Export Date 06/06/99 |
|---|---|
| 15. Country of Origin DE | 6. Missing Documents |
| 17. I.T. No. 22069456995 | 18. I.T. Date 6/06/99 |

| 19. BL or AWB No. 22069456995 | 20. Mode of Transportation 40 | 21. Manufacturer I.D. DEBILRHE4044KRO | 22. Reference No. |
|---|---|---|---|
| 23. Importing Carrier LUFTHANSA | 24. Foreign Port of Lading Frankfurt | 25. Location of Goods/G.O. No. L362 | |
| 26. U.S. Port of Unlading 1704 ATLANTA | 27. Import Date 06/06/99 | | |

| 28. Line No. | 30. (A) T.S.U.S.A. No. (B) ADSA CVD Case No. | 31. (A) Gross Weight (B) Manifest Qty. | 32. Net Quantity in T.S.U.S.A. Units | 33. (A) Entered Value (B) CHGS (C) Relationship | 34. (A) T.S.U.S.A. Rate (B) ADA/CVD Rate (C) I.R.C. Rate (D) Visa No. | 35. Duty and I.R. Tax Dollars | Cents |
|---|---|---|---|---|---|---|---|
| | 48502287 | | | | | | |
| | INV. NO.  9999/99/89591 | | | | | | |
| 001 | FURN ARTICLES:N/KNIT:WOOL/HAIR | | | | | | |
| | 6304.99.60107 | 193 | 193KG | 3331 709 | 6.4% | 213 | .18 |
| | MERCHANDISE PROCESSING FEE | | | | .17% | 5 | .66 |
| | INV VAL      4039.98 | | | | | | |
| | LESS NDC      709.00 | | | | | | |
| | 3330.98 | | US DOLLAR  AT 1.00000000 | | | | |
| | ENT. VAL   3330.98 AS | | 3331    TOTAL | | | | |
| | | | | 3331 | | 234 | .18 |
| | 5 PCS TOTAL | | | | | | |
| | BLOCK 39 SUMMARY: | | | | | | |
| MPF | 499 | 21.00 | | | | | |
| TOTAL: | | 21.00 | TEV: | 3331 | | | |

| 36. Declaration of Importer of Record (Owner or Purchaser) or Authorized Agent | ↓ U.S. CUSTOMS USE ↓ | TOTALS |
|---|---|---|

I declare that I am the
[ ] importer of record and that the actual owner, purchaser, or consignee for customs purposes is as shown above.   OR  [X] owner or purchaser or agent thereof.

I further declare that the merchandise
[X] was obtained pursuant to a purchase or agreement to purchase and that the prices set forth in the invoice are true.   OR  [ ] was not obtained pursuant to a purchase or agreement to purchase and the statements in the invoice as to value or price are true to the best of my knowledge and belief.

I also declare that the statements in the documents herein filed fully disclose to the best of my knowledge and belief the true prices, values, quantities, rebates, drawbacks, fees, commissions, and royalties and are true and correct, and that all goods or services provided to the seller of the merchandise either free or at reduced cost are fully disclosed. I will immediately furnish to the appropriate customs officer any information showing a different state of facts.

Notice require by Paperwork Reduction Act of 1980. This information is needed to ensure that importers/exporters are complying with U.S. Customs laws, to allow us to compute and collect the right amount of money, to enforce other agency requirements, and to collect accurate statistical information on imports. Your response is mandatory.

| A. Liq. Code | B. Ascertained Duty | 37. Duty 213.18 |
|---|---|---|
| | C. Ascertained Tax | 38. Tax .00 |
| | D. Ascertained Other | 39. Other 21.00 |
| | E. Ascertained Total | 40. Total 234.18 |

-17:09

| 41. Signature of Declarant, Total and Date Importer's Broker | 6/11/99 |
|---|---|

STATISTICAL

Customs Form 7501 (030984)

or blue ink. Shippers should be experienced in invoicing foreign shipments. Invoices are often sent via airmail to the importer or broker to arrive in time to make entry when the goods arrive. Penalties are assessed for failing to provide the U.S. Customs Service with an invoice.

**The Entry Summary.** Within ten days the importer must file the *Entry Summary Form* with the Customs Service at the port of entry (see Exhibit 13.2). The information on the form is used to determine the amount of duties owed, to gather import statistics, and to determine if the goods conform to other U.S. regulations. Because this critical information is provided by the importer, the cooperation and full disclosure of the importer are essential in making the U.S. Customs system work.

**Payment of Duties.** If import duties are assessed on the goods by U.S. Customs, the importer must deposit estimated duties with Customs at the time of filing the entry documents or the entry summary form. The duties must be in an amount determined by U.S. Customs, pending a final calculation of the amount actually owed. Payment to a customs broker does not relieve the importer of liability to pay the duties. The liability for duties constitutes a personal debt of the importer, and a lien attaches to the merchandise. At the time the entry summary is filed, a bond is also usually required. A customs bond can be purchased for a single shipment or for all shipments over the course of a year and up to the amount stated in the bond. The purpose of the bond is to assure the payment of duties on final calculation. In some cases, goods can be released for transportation or storage *in-bond,* with the payments of duties suspended until the goods are released for sale or use in the United States. There is no liability for duties on unordered or unclaimed merchandise.

**Postal Entries.** Some smaller commercial shipments valued at $2,000 or less may be cleared through the U.S. Postal Service. The letter carrier acts as the agent for the U.S. Customs Service for the purpose of collecting import duties. This practice has several advantages. Postal rates can be far less for smaller packages than commercial airfreight. The entry process is quicker and less expensive, with no customs broker needed. The documentation and marking requirements are still strict, however, and the importer should check with the postal service before attempting a postal entry. A commercial invoice must accompany the shipment. In addition, many products have a $250 limit on postal entries; these include furniture, flowers, textiles, and leather goods. Wool products and wearing apparel from the Pacific Rim countries requires a formal customs entry regardless of value. If a mail article is found to contain merchandise subject to an import duty, and the article is not accompanied by a customs declaration and invoice, it is subject to seizure and forfeiture.

## Trends in Customs Administration

The administration of customs is undergoing many changes. In 1993 Congress passed the *Customs Modernization and Informed Compliance Act* (Mod Act) to make customs procedures more uniform nationally, improve compliance, reduce operating costs, and speed entries. The Mod Act calls for electronic entry processing and other improvements.

**Electronic Entry Processing.** The Mod Act calls for the Customs Service to adopt a paperless entry process, known as the *Automated Commercial System.* It is designed to reduce costs to business and government and to speed the entry process. The system allows entry documents to be filed electronically through an automated hook-up between importers, customs brokers and the Customs Service via the *Automated Broker Interface.* Many companies, primarily the largest and most sophisticated importers, are already filing electronically. By the end of the 1990s, the majority of entries will be done electronically.

**Remote Location Filing.** Until recently entry processing had to take place at the same port that the goods were located. Thus importers had to rely on the services of a broker at the port of entry, even if the goods were being entered in a distant location. Large importers who move goods through different ports asked Congress to permit entry processing from remote locations. The Mod Act charged U.S. Customs with developing the Remote Location Filing system that would allow brokers in all parts of the country to make remote entries at distant ports. The system became effective in 1998.

## Enforcement and Penalties

The Customs Service has broad authority to enforce the customs and tariff laws. The Mod Act increased customs enforcement powers and stiffened penalties for violations. The law imposes both civil and criminal penalties against violators. Penalties and fines vary according to whether the violator was *negligent, grossly negligent,* or committed *fraud.* Negligence occurs if an importer fails to use reasonable care and skill to ensure that all customs documents are materially correct. This is known as the rule of *informed compliance.* Importers are expected to have enough information and knowledge in order to comply with the law. Inexperienced importers can protect themselves from penalties for negligence by relying on licensed customs brokers or customs attorneys. Any importer unsure of the U.S. Customs regulations should seek advice or a ruling directly from customs authorities or their attorneys. In 1997 U.S. Customs adopted a "checklist" to provide guidance regarding an importer's obligation to use reasonable care. Customs noted that a "black and white" definition of reasonable care is impossible, because the concept of acting with reasonable care depends upon individual circumstances. This checklist is not a law or customs regulation, and it merely serves to provide guidance and information to importers to assist them in meeting reasonable care obligations. Rather, the checklist serves as a flexible tool to help importers find and/or understand statutory and regulatory obligations involved in the importation process. It is important to remember that not every incident of non-compliance involves a failure to exercise reasonable care. The circumstances surrounding an incident of non-compliance determine whether or not the incident involves culpable conduct. (See Exhibit 13.3.)

An importer is grossly negligent if the act is done with actual knowledge or wanton disregard

for the relevant facts, and with a disregard for the importer's obligations under the law. Penalties for negligence or gross negligence are usually based on the value of the goods, the seriousness of the offense, and the amount of revenue lost to the government. Fraud is committed by knowingly making a materially false statement to customs. An importer that knowingly makes a false statement to customs to get a reduced tariff rate, such as misdescribing the goods or stating a false country-of-origin, can be fined up to $100,000. Special rules apply to the conduct of licensed customs brokers.

Criminal penalties of fines and imprisonment apply to anyone who knowingly provides false information to any customs official, intentionally conceals or destroys information, or conceals any country-of-origin mark on the goods. In addition, the merchandise imported can be confiscated and forfeited.

**Recordkeeping and Penalties.** The Mod Act requires importers to keep records for five years from the date of entry and to give Customs access to those documents on demand. The records include U.S. Customs documents and all other documents "normally kept in the ordinary course of business," including sales contracts, purchase orders, government certificates, letters of credit, internal corporate memoranda, bills of lading, etc. Establishing a customs compliance and recordkeeping program is highly recommended for any corporate importer. The willful failure to keep records about the entry is punishable by (the lesser of) a $100,000 fine or 75 percent of the value of the goods. Even negligent recordkeeping is punishable by fines up to $10,000 or 40 percent of the value of the goods, unless caused by an "act of God." Concealment of records carries an additional $5,000 fine or up to two years' imprisonment, or both. In certain cases an importer may be barred from importing goods into the United States in the future, since the courts have held, "There is no constitutional right to import." U.S. Customs conducts audits to verify business records. The Mod Act sets new standards for conducting audits. Inspections can take place on reasonable notice to the importer, and documents can be seized under court order.

1.  If you have not retained an expert to assist you in complying with U.S. Customs requirements, do you have access to the *Customs Regulations* (Title 19 of the *Code of Federal Regulations*), the *Harmonized Tariff Schedule of the United States,* and the GPO publication *Customs Bulletin and Decisions*? Do you have access to the *Customs Internet Website, Customs Electronic Bulletin Board* or other research service to permit you to establish reliable procedures, and facilitate compliance with customs laws and regulations?

2.  Have you consulted with a customs "expert" (e.g., lawyer, broker, accountant, or customs consultant) to assist in preparation of documents and the entry of the merchandise? If the expert is not a licensed broker or attorney, have you checked his or her qualifications and experience?

3.  If you use an expert to assist you in complying with U.S. Customs requirements, have you discussed your importations in advance with that person and have you provided that person with full, complete, and accurate information about the import transactions?

4.  Has a responsible and knowledgeable individual within your organization reviewed the customs documentation prepared by you or your expert to ensure that it is full, complete, and accurate?

5.  Are identical transactions or merchandise handled differently at different ports or customs offices within the same port? If so, have you brought this to the attention of the appropriate customs officials?

6.  Have you established reliable procedures within your organization to ensure that you provide complete and accurate documentation to U.S. Customs?

7.  Have you obtained a customs ruling regarding the importation of the merchandise?

8.  Do you know the merchandise that you are importing and have you provided a detailed and accurate product description and tariff classification of your merchandise to U.S. Customs? Is a laboratory analysis or special procedure necessary for the classification?

9.  Have you consulted the tariff schedules, U.S. Customs' informed compliance publications, court cases, and/or U.S. Customs rulings to assist you in describing and classifying the merchandise? Have you consulted a customs expert on the product's tariff classification?

10. If you are claiming a free or special tariff treatment for your merchandise (e.g., GSP, HTS Item 9802, NAFTA, etc.), have you established a reliable program to ensure that you reported the required value information and obtained any required or necessary documentation to support the claim?

11. Do you know the customs value of the imported products? Do you know the "price actually paid or payable" for your merchandise? Have you obtained advice from an "expert" regarding the customs value of the merchandise?

12. Do you know the terms of sale; whether there will be rebates, tie-ins, indirect costs, additional payments; whether "assists" were provided, commissions or royalties paid? Have all costs or payments been reported to U.S. Customs? Are amounts actual or estimated? Are you and the supplier "related parties" and have you disclosed this to U.S. Customs?

13. Have you taken reliable measures to ascertain the correct country-of-origin for the imported merchandise? Have you consulted with a customs expert regarding the country-of-origin of the merchandise?

14. Have you accurately communicated the proper country-of-origin marking requirements to your foreign supplier prior to importation and verified that the merchandise is properly marked upon entry with the correct country-of-origin?

15. If you are importing textiles or apparel, have you developed reliable procedures to ensure that you have ascertained the correct country-of-origin and assured yourself that no illegal transshipment (rerouting through a third country for illegal purposes) or false or fraudulent documents or practices were involved? Have you checked the U.S. Treasury's published list of manufacturers, sellers, and other foreign persons who have been found to have illegally imported textiles and apparel products? If you have obtained your textiles from one of these parties have you adequately verified the country-of-origin of the shipment through independent means?

16. Is your merchandise subject to quota/visa requirements and, if so, have you provided or developed a reliable procedure to provide a correct visa for the goods upon entry?

17. Have you determined or established a reliable procedure to permit you to determine whether your merchandise or its packaging bear or use any trademarks or copyrighted matter or are patented and, if so, that you have a legal right to import those items into, and/or use those items in, the United States?

18. If you are importing goods or packaging which contain registered copyrighted material, have you checked to ensure that it is authorized and genuine? If you are importing sound recordings of live performances, were the recordings authorized?

19. Have you checked to see that your merchandise complies with other government agency requirements (e.g., FDA, EPA/DOT, CPSC, FTC, Department of Agriculture, etc.) prior to or upon entry and procured any necessary licenses or permits?

20. Have you checked to see if your goods are subject to a Commerce Department dumping or countervailing duty determination and reported that to U.S. Customs?

SOURCE:    Excerpted and adapted by the authors from TD 97-96 (1997), United States Customs Service.

## Binding Rulings

Informal information received from a customs officer about an import is not binding. However, an importer may make a written request for a *binding ruling* from the Customs Service in advance of an entry. Rulings are important to all importers, especially to those dealing in new or unusual merchandise that they have not imported before. It relieves them of the uncertainty of how their product will be treated by customs upon entry and what the rate of duty will be. It also shows that the importer used reasonable care in making the entry.

A request for a ruling should be submitted by written letter to the appropriate customs office and should contain a statement of all relevant facts, a description of the goods, their price or value, and their country-of-origin. Some rulings may be addressed to the district office. Photographs and samples are often submitted for inspection. The ruling is issued on the basis of the facts submitted by the importer. A ruling letter is addressed to the importer and assures that the products described will be entered according to the terms set out in the ruling. The ruling contains an analysis of prior law on the subject and a holding. It can take from one to nine months to receive a ruling. Rulings are valid for all ports of entry unless revoked by notification to the party to whom the ruling had been issued. The ruling letter is presented to Customs officials at the port when entering the goods. All rulings issued by Customs are made available for inspection by any person requesting to see them. Many are now available at the U.S. Customs website. Importers often follow an existing published ruling, even though it was not addressed to them, where they believe it covers the circumstances of their import transaction. However, they do so at their peril because the rulings are only binding for the importer to whom they were addressed.

## Liquidation and Protest

*Liquidation* is the final computation and assessment of the applicable duty on an import by the Customs Service. When the entry summary and documents are accepted by the Customs Service as entered, liquidation occurs immediately. However, when the Customs Service at the port of entry determines that additional duties are owed, a *notice of adjustment* is sent to the importer. The importer must respond to the notice, or the duty will be assessed as corrected by the government. If a question or dispute arises concerning the dutiable status of the goods, as in the case of technical or unusual products or in complex cases, either the importer or customs officials may seek an *internal advice* from the Customs Service headquarters. The advice represents the official position of the U.S. Customs Service, but is not binding in future cases. The official liquidation becomes effective when it is posted on a bulletin board or otherwise made available to the public at the customshouse at the port of entry. The Customs Service also sends a *courtesy notice* to importers advising them of the amount of the liquidation, although this notice is not legally effective. If the actual duties owed exceed the estimated duties paid at the time of entry, the importer must pay them within 15 days of the posting of the notice of liquidation.

**Time Limits on Liquidation.** Liquidation must occur within one year of entry. This period can be extended by the Customs Service for good cause. An entry not liquidated within one year from the date of entry—such as cases in which customs officers are awaiting the results of an internal advice—are "deemed liquidated" by operation of law. According to the case law, under a *deemed liquidation,* the goods are dutied at the rate at which the Customs Service allowed entry as accepted on the entry summary form. A liquidation can be reopened by the Customs Service within two years if it has probable cause to suspect that the importer committed fraud in the entry.

**Time for Protest.** In the event of a dispute over a liquidation, an importer may seek administrative review by filing a timely *protest of entry* with the port director within 90 days. A protest cannot be filed before liquidation. The Customs Service has 30 days to respond in cases in which the protest is filed in response to goods having been excluded from entry; otherwise they have two years to act. Upon a request for further review, the protest will be considered by the commissioner of customs. If the protest is successful, the goods will be released or a refund will be made of duties paid. If the protest is denied—as most are—the importer may seek judicial review by the Court of International Trade.

## Judicial Review

Denial of a protest is necessary before the importer can request judicial review. However, an importer may seek judicial review under limited conditions prior to the filing of a protest. The *National Juice Products* case illustrates a situation in which the importer was granted judicial review by the Court of International Trade, because not to have done so might have subjected the importer to irreparable harm.

---

### National Juice Products Association v. United States
628 F.Supp. 978 (1986)
Court of International Trade

BACKGROUND AND FACTS
The National Juice Association and other plaintiffs brought this action challenging the Customs Service ruling that country-of-origin marking requirements apply to frozen concentrated orange juice and reconstituted orange juice made from imported concentrate. In September 1985, the U.S. Customs Service issued ruling C.S.D. 85-47, requiring that the juice be marked with the foreign country-of-origin. The directive was to take effect on January 1, 1986, but was postponed until March 1, 1986. The plaintiffs brought this action in the Court of International Trade seeking a preimportation judicial review of the ruling. The government contended that the court lacked jurisdiction to hear the matter prior to the actual importation.

JUDGE RESTANI
The Court of Appeals for the Federal Circuit has defined the requirements for invoking this court's declaratory judgment jurisdiction:

1. judicial review must be sought prior to importation of goods;
2. review must be sought of a ruling, a refusal to issue a ruling, or a refusal to change such ruling;
3. the ruling must relate to certain subject matter; and
4. it must be shown that irreparable harm will occur unless judicial review is obtained prior to importation.

The second requirement under dispute is whether plaintiffs will be irreparably harmed if they are unable to secure preimportation review. The essence of "irreparable injury" is that it is harm that "cannot receive reasonable redress in a court of law." *Manufacture de Machines du Haut Rhin v. von Raab,* F.Supp. 877 (Court of International Trade, 1983). In making this determination, what is critical is not the magnitude of the injury, but rather its immediacy and the inadequacy of future corrective relief.

Plaintiffs offer the following reasons to support their claim that they will suffer irreparable harm if they are unable to secure preimportation review.

First, plaintiffs maintain that their packaging suppliers will be unable to provide the necessary labels and cans by the current effective date of March 1, 1986, and that the unavailability of such packaging will result in the inability to fill orders placed by retail customers. In support of this proposition, plaintiffs offer affidavits of three packaging company representatives. These affiants estimate that the transition to packaging complying with the new ruling would take a year to two-and-one-half years.

As plaintiffs have noted, under the country-of-origin marking statute, Customs is required to withhold delivery of imported merchandise until it is properly marked or until proper certifications are filed. Therefore, to the extent that plaintiffs cannot comply with Customs' ruling by March 1, 1986, they will be unable to use foreign manufacturing concentrate and will not be able to satisfy all of their customers' orders for retail orange juice products. This court has recognized that severe disruption of business operations can constitute irreparable injury under certain circumstances. . . .

Plaintiffs have provided undisputed documentation of the possibility of significant disruption of their business operations that will result if they are required to comply with the ruling.

*(continued)*

*(continued)*

Plaintiffs' second argument is that they will be forced to discard millions of dollars worth of non-complying labels that are currently in inventory. Plaintiffs have provided documentation that demonstrates that if they are unable to secure preimportation review they will be required to either warehouse this inventory or destroy the labels. Either way, plaintiffs will be required to expend funds that will not be recoverable should they ultimately prevail on the merits. This factor also applies to plaintiffs' third argument that they will be forced to spend millions of dollars to redesign packaging to comply with Customs' ruling. Plaintiffs support this argument with affidavits from a sampling of processors, whose estimates of their costs for new labels and packaging, even under normal conditions, proved to be substantial. These costs, also, could not be recouped if the court were to rule in plaintiffs' favor.

The final consideration is whether there exists a viable temporary measure for providing the country-of-origin information without forcing plaintiffs to incur these nonrecoupable costs. The availability of such alternatives can reduce the impact of the change in the labeling and substantially mitigate the damage.

In the present case, none of the temporary measures suggested by defendant is a feasible alternative. The first alternative, the use of adhesive stickers, is not a feasible alternative. In the summer of 1985, Citrus World attempted to apply foreign language stickers to frozen concentrated orange juice cans. These attempts were unsuccessful because the cans are sprayed with water to wash off excess juice and the stickers will not stick to a wet surface. . . .

The final suggestion offered by defendant is that the U.S. orange juice processing industry could rely exclusively on the supply of domestic manufacturing concentrate to avoid the requirements of the marking ruling. The evidence indicates that this, too, is not a realistic alternative. In four out of the last five seasons, severe freezes have substantially diminished the availability of U.S. oranges and their by-products, including manufacturing concentrate. Defendants offer no evidence to refute this conclusion.

In sum, plaintiffs have demonstrated by clear and convincing evidence that they will suffer irreparable injury if they cannot procure preimportation review. The cumulative impact of the facts stated by plaintiff, specifically, the business disruption likely to occur because of the inability of the industry packagers to satisfy the simultaneous demand for new labels, the cost of discarding or storing noncomplying labels, and the cost of redesigning packaging, would be substantial and none of these expenses could be recouped should plaintiffs ultimately prevail on the merits. The impact of these injuries would not be alleviated by any of the alternatives suggested by defendants. This showing of irreparable harm allows the court to exercise jurisdiction under section 1581(h) and to provide, if appropriate, declaratory relief.

**Decision.** The court held that it had jurisdiction to hear the plaintiffs' petition for review. Under its "residual jurisdiction," the Court of International Trade may review rulings of the U.S. Customs Service prior to importation, protest, and denial when extraordinary circumstances exist that could cause the importer to suffer irreparable harm unless judicial review is granted.

# Dutiable Status of Goods

Tariffs are applied to goods according to the item's *dutiable status.* The dutiable status of goods is determined by (1) the classification of the merchandise (What is it?), (2) the value of the merchandise, and (3) the country-of-origin of the merchandise (What country does it come from for purposes of determining the tariff rate or applicability of a quota?). An accurate estimate of the duties owed on imports provides essential information for business planning, for the development of cost estimates, and for pricing and marketing decisions.

Determining the dutiable status of merchandise can require importers to negotiate a maze of regulatory barriers. For importers who enter a wide variety of products or materials, or who enter them from many different countries, the potential for problems increases significantly. For U.S. exporters trying to enter goods into foreign countries, the regulatory headaches can become nightmarish. Lessons learned from importing into one country are not necessarily transferable when importing into another.

In recent years, worldwide efforts have attempted to make customs procedures and import regulations more uniform, more understandable, and easier to follow, so that even foreign firms can comply more easily. These efforts have resulted in the development of uniform rules for classifying and valuing imports and for determining their country-of-origin. These include a standardized system for classifying products (the *Harmonized Commodity Description and Coding System,* or *Harmonized System*), the GATT 1994 *Rules on Customs Valuation,* and the GATT 1994 *Agreement on Rules of Origin.*

Despite the increasingly widespread applicability of these uniform rules, each nation's customs rules still differ dramatically. Thus, no international manager can be expected to know every rule for importing into every country in which he or she is doing business. For this reason, competent advice and assistance are necessary. Most firms rely on the services of a customs broker to assist in importing into the United States, or of a foreign agent when importing into a foreign country. Foreign counsel is also often used when planning business strategies both in the United States and overseas. For instance, if a firm is importing chocolate, they may encounter distinct cost differences between importing chocolate in solid bars or as a liquid in tank cars. Among the many factors to be considered by management are the differences in purchase price, insurance, transportation costs, warehousing and storage fees, and import duties. The documentation required by the foreign customs authority (including language requirements) will certainly be different from country to country. The advice of a customs broker or an attorney specializing in importing will be invaluable in comparing these costs and in evaluating alternate business strategies. Many specialized reference materials can also be found in libraries designed for use by U.S. exporters. In addition, the U.S. Department of Commerce maintains a trained staff in Washington ready to advise U.S. firms on how to comply with foreign import regulations and about the problems of getting particular goods into foreign countries.

## The Harmonized Tariff Schedule

All goods entering the United States are dutiable unless specifically exempted. Because all goods carry their own tariff rate, the first step in determining the dutiable status of goods or materials is to properly classify the items being imported. From 1963 to 1989, the United States had used a system for classifying goods that was found in the *Tariff Schedules of the United States* (the TSUS). All duties and quotas were imposed on the basis of the classification of imports under this statute. But on January 1, 1989, the United States undertook the most significant effort ever made to internationally coordinate its customs classification system by adopting the *Harmonized Commodity Description and Coding System* and incorporating it into federal law in the *Harmonized Tariff Schedule of the United States (HTSUS).* (Canada enacted its version of the Harmonized Code in 1988.) The Harmonized Code was part of a worldwide effort, spanning nearly two decades, to standardize tariff nomenclature. It provides the mechanism for defining all commodities, materials, and articles sold in international trade, but does not set the tariff rate. Tariff rates are set by each nation in its own statutes. The code was developed by the World Customs Organization, an international organization located in Brussels.

**http://dataweb.usitc.gov**
*See for tariff information.*

**Using the Harmonized Tariff Schedule.** The Harmonized Tariff Schedule of the United States divides products into approximately 5,000 tariff classifications, ranging from basic commodities and agricultural products to manufactured goods. It is organized into 22 sections, covering products from different industries. Sections are broken down into 99 chapters, each covering the commodities, materials, and products of a distinct industry. The chapters are arranged in a progression from livestock and agricultural products or component materials to finished products such as vehicles and aircraft. The following list provides a few examples:

| Chapter 1 | Live animals |
| Chapter 9 | Coffee, tea, spices |
| Chapter 22 | Beverages, spirits, vinegar |
| Chapter 30 | Pharmaceuticals |
| Chapter 44 | Wood and articles of wood |
| Chapter 51 | Wool, fine or coarse animal hair |
| Chapter 62 | Articles of apparel, accessories not knitted |
| Chapter 63 | Other textile articles, sets, worn clothing |
| Chapter 76 | Aluminum and articles thereof |
| Chapter 84 | Nuclear reactors, boilers, parts |
| Chapter 85 | Electrical machinery, sound recorders, television image |
| Chapter 88 | Aircraft, spacecraft, parts |
| Chapter 94 | Furniture, bedding, lamps |
| Chapter 97 | Works of art, collectors' pieces |
| Chapter 98/99 | Reserved for special tariff classifications (e.g., imports that enter the United States only temporarily or for service and repair, etc.) |

Chapters are broken down into headings, subheadings, and tariff items. Tariff items are denoted by eight-digit codes. In the United States, the schedules break out to ten digits to allow for compiling of statistical data on imports.

*Chapter:* first two digits

*Heading:* four digits

*Subheading:* six digits

*Tariff items:* eight digits

*Statistical break:* ten digits

Consider the example in Exhibit 13.4. Tents made of synthetic fibers—such as (nylon)—used fo24r backpacking are classified as item 6306.22.10. They are found within subheading 6306.22, for tents of synthetic fibers, and heading 6306 for "Tarpaulins, awnings and sunblinds, tents, sails for boats . . ." and within chapter 63

for "Other textile articles." Countries that use this international coding system have "harmonized" their classifications to six digits—at the subheading level. After the first six digits, each country assigns its own numbers.

After locating the article in the schedule, the importer can determine the tariff rate. The schedule is divided into two columns (see Exhibit 13.4). Column 1 contains a *general rate* applicable to imports from MFN nations, and a *special rate* applicable to one or more special tariff programs. The special rate applies to goods coming from developing countries under the Generalized System of Preferences, to goods coming from Canada or Mexico under the *North American Free Trade Agreement,* or to goods imported from the Caribbean Basin or Israel. Column 2 rates are the original *Smoot-Hawley* rates applicable to non-MFN countries under the Tariff Act of 1930, although few countries fall in this category today. (See the General Notes to the HTS, appearing in Exhibit 13.4).

Tariffs are imposed on imports either on the basis of ad valorem, specific, or compound rates. The most common type of tariff is the ad valorem rate, based on a percentage of the value of the materials or articles imported. A specific rate is a specified amount per unit of weight or measure. A compound rate is a combined ad valorem and specific rate.

Over the years, a large body of customs law has developed interpreting the tariff schedules. The *Camel Manufacturing Co. v. United States* case, decided before the Harmonized Tariff Schedule went into effect, illustrates the problems of classifying merchandise. While reading the case, consider the impact of the decision on the importer involved and the implications in planning future import decisions.

## The Classification of Goods

Tariff rates are based on an article's HTS classification. However, a product does not always fit clearly into a category. Many products can easily fall into more than one category. Naturally, importers will want to classify their products in that category with the lowest tariff rate. U.S. Customs, whose job it is to collect the tariff revenue of the United States, will want to classify the products at the highest rate. (Initially, the classification is

**EXHIBIT 13.4   Harmonized Tariff Schedule of the United States (1995), Annotated for Statistical Reporting Purposes**

| Heading/ Subheading | Stat. Suffix | Article Description | Units of Quantity | Rates of Duty | | Column 2 |
|---|---|---|---|---|---|---|
| | | | | **Column 1** | | |
| | | | | **General** | **Special** | |
| 6306 | | Tarpaulins, awnings and sunblinds; tents; sails for boats, sailboards or landcraft; camping goods; . . . | | | | |
| 6306.11.00 | 00 | Tarpaulins, awnings and sunblinds: Of cotton . . . . . . . . .(369) | kg . . . . . . | 15.2% | Free (IL) 4.8% (CA) 10.7% (MX) | 90% |
| 6306.12.00 | 00 | Of synthetic fibers. . . (669) | kg . . . . . . | 9.9% | Free (IL) 3% (CA) 7.2 (MX) | 90% |
| 6306.19.00 | | Of other textile materials | | 5.7% | Free (E*, IL) 1.7% (CA) 4.3% (MX) | 40% |
| | 10 | Of artificial fibers. .(669) | kg | | | |
| | 20 | Other . . . . . . . . . .(899) | kg | | | |
| | | Tents: | | | | |
| 6306.21.00 | 00 | Of cotton . . . . . . . . . . . . | kg . . . . . . | 15.2% | Free (IL) 4.0% (CA) 10.7% (MX) | 90% |
| 6306.22 | | Of synthetic fibers: | | | | |
| 6306.22.10 | 00 | Backpacking tents . . . . . | No. . . . .v kg | 4.2% | Free (A,E,IL,J,MX) 1.3% (CA) | 90% |
| 6306.22.90 | | Other . . . . . . . . . . . . . | . . . . . . . | 9.9% | Free (IL) 3% (CA) 7.2% (MX) | 90% |
| | 10 | Screen houses . . . . . . | kg | | | |
| | 30 | Other . . . . . . .(659) | kg | | | |
| 6306.29.00 | 00 | Of other textile materials. . | kg . . . . . | 5.5% | Free (E*,IL,J*) 1.7% (CA) 4.3% (MX) | 40% |
| | | Sails: | | | | |
| 6306.31.00 | 00 | Of synthetic fibers . . . . . . . | kg . . . . . . | 3.8% | Free (A,E,IL,J,MX) 1.2% (CA) | 30% |
| 6306.39.00 | 00 | Of other textile materials . . | kg . . . . . . | 3.8% | Free (A,E,IL,J,MX) 1.2% (CA) | 30% |
| | | Pneumatic mattresses: | | | | |
| 6306.41.00 | 00 | Of cotton . . . . . . . . . . . . | kg . . . . . . | 4.2% | Free (IL) 1.2% (CA) 3.2% (MX) | 25% |
| 6306.49.00 | 00 | Of other textile materials . . | kg . . . . . . | 4.2% | Free (A,E,IL,J,MX) 1.2% (CA) | 25% |
| | | Other: | | | | |
| 6306.91.00 | 00 | Of cotton . . . . . . . . . . . . | kg . . . . . . | 6.6% | Free (IL) 2.1% (CA) 5.2% (MX) | 40% |
| 6306.99.00 | 00 | Of other textile materials . . | kg . . . . . . | 8.6% | Free (E*,IL,J*) 2.7% (CA) 6.5% (MX) | 78.5% |

*(continued)*

**EXHIBIT 13.4   (continued)**

**General Notes**

3. *Rates of Duty.* The rates of duty in the "Rates of Duty" columns designated 1 ("General" and "Special") and 2 of the tariff schedule apply to goods imported into the customs territory of the United States as hereinafter provided in this note:

(a) <u>Rate of Duty Column 1.</u>

(i) The rates of duty in column 1 are rates which are applicable to all products other than those of countries enumerated in paragraph (b) of this note. Column 1 is divided into two subcolumns, "General" and "Special", which are applicable as provided below.

(ii) The "<u>General</u>" subcolumn sets forth the general most-favored-nation (MFN) rates which are applicable to products of those countries described in subparagraph (i) above which are not entitled to special tariff treatment as set forth below.

(iii) The "<u>Special</u>" subcolumn reflects rates of duty under one or more special tariff treatment programs described in paragraph (c) of this note and identified in parentheses immediately following the duty rate specified in each subcolumn. These rates apply to those products which are properly classified under a provision for which a special rate is indicated and for which all of the legal requirements for eligibility for such program or programs have been met. Where a product is eligible for special treatment under more than one program, the lowest rate of duty provided for any applicable program shall be imposed. Where no special rate of duty is provided for a provision, or where the country from which a product otherwise eligible for special treatment was imported is not designated as a beneficiary country under a program appearing with the appropriate provision, the rates of duty in the "General" subcolumn of Column 1 shall apply.

(iv) Products of Insular Possessions (omitted)

(v) Products of the West Bank or Gaza Strip (omitted)

(b) <u>Rate of Duty Column 2.</u> Notwithstanding any of the foregoing provisions of this note, the rates of duty shown in Column 2 shall apply to products, whether imported directed or indirectly, of the following countries and areas:

    Afghanistan   Cuba   Laos   North Korea   Vietnam*

(c) <u>Products Eligible for Special Tariff Treatment.</u>

(i) Programs under which special tariff treatment may be provided, and the corresponding symbols for such programs as they are indicated in the "Special" subcolumn, are as follows:

Generalized System of Preferences . . . . . . . . . . . . . . . . . . . . . . . . . . . . . . . . . . . . . . . . .A
Automotive Products Trade Act . . . . . . . . . . . . . . . . . . . . . . . . . . . . . . . . . . . . . . . . . . . . .B
Agreement on Trade in Civil Aircraft . . . . . . . . . . . . . . . . . . . . . . . . . . . . . . . . . . . . . . . .C
North American Free Trade Agreement:
   Goods of Canada, under the terms of
     general note 12 to this schedule . . . . . . . . . . . . . . . . . . . . . . . . . . . . . . . . . . . . . . .CA
   Goods of Mexico, under the terms of
     general note 12 to this schedule . . . . . . . . . . . . . . . . . . . . . . . . . . . . . . . . . . . . . . .MX
Caribbean Basin Economic Recovery Act . . . . . . . . . . . . . . . . . . . . . . . . . . . . . . . . . . . .E
United States-Israel Free Trade Act . . . . . . . . . . . . . . . . . . . . . . . . . . . . . . . . . . . . . . . . .IL
Andean Trade Preference Act . . . . . . . . . . . . . . . . . . . . . . . . . . . . . . . . . . . . . . . . . . . . . .J
Agreement on Trade in Pharmaceutical Products . . . . . . . . . . . . . . . . . . . . . . . . . . . . .K
Uruguay Round Concessions on Intermediate
   Chemicals for Dyes . . . . . . . . . . . . . . . . . . . . . . . . . . . . . . . . . . . . . . . . . . . . . . . . . . .L

*NOTE:   Status as of May 1998. Vietnam will likely be removed from Column 2 in the future.

## BACKGROUND AND FACTS

The plaintiff imported nylon tents into the United States. The tents were designed to hold up to nine people and weighed over thirty pounds, including carrying bag, stakes, and frames. The floor sizes ranged from eight feet by ten feet to ten feet by fourteen feet, and when folded for carrying were approximately fifty inches long. It was undisputed that the tents were used as shelter by people who wish to camp outdoors, either purely for that purpose or for the purpose of engaging in other outdoor activities such as fishing, hunting, and canoeing. The importer entered the tents as "sports equipment" under Item 735.20 of the TSUS, thus carrying a 10 percent ad valorem import duty. The U.S. Customs Service ruled that the tents were properly classifiable under TSUS Item 389.60 as "Textile articles not specially provided for" and imposed a duty of 25 cents per pound plus 15 percent ad valorem. Upon liquidation, the importer appealed.

### *Camel Manufacturing Co. v. United States*
*686 F.Supp. 912 (1988)*
*Court of International Trade*

## JUDGE WATSON

The basic question before the court is whether or not the activity in which the tents are used, which we shall call by the name of "camping out" is a sport, which would then lead to the conclusion that these tents are sporting equipment.

In a previous opinion, *The Newman Importing Co., Inc. v. United States,* 415 F.Supp. 375 (1976), this court decided that certain light tents used in backpacking were sports equipment because the activity of backpacking was found to be a sport. In this action, the court was given a generous range of opinions regarding what it is that makes an activity a sport. Seven witnesses testified on behalf of the plaintiff and two witnesses testified on behalf of the defendant. The witnesses had a wide range of familiarity with the use and manufacture of tents. Although these opinions were extremely interesting, the fact remains that in the end the question of defining the term "sporting equipment" is really one of legal interpretation for the court.

The rationale used in the *Newman Importing* case will not suffice here because these tents are not suitable for backpacking. The court finds that these tents are too heavy for that particular activity and, in fact, are generally used by persons who are camping in the outdoors and are not subject to strict limitations of weight in the tenting equipment which they can take with them. In the absence of persuasive proof regarding any special attributes of these tents which may contribute to their use in backpacking, the court finds it quite reasonable for the Customs Service to have excluded them from the category of backpacking tents on the basis of their weight and carrying size.

The basic question before the court is whether the general activity of camping out, i.e., taking up temporary residence in the outdoors, is a sport within the meaning of the Tariff Schedules.

The court is unable to expand its view of the term "sports" to include the activity of camping out. To do so would require a definition of the term so loose that it would cover almost any purposeful activity engaged in by humans in a natural setting. If it were simply a question of whether an activity had a certain degree of challenge and skill then the activity of gardening, which has in it a good measure of challenge, skill, and struggle and offers in innumerable ways the "joy of victory and agony of defeat," would also have to be considered a sport. This tells us that as a matter of simple logic and meaning, it does not appear that the term "sport" can be carried past the point which was expressed in the *Newman* case.

It follows that these tents are not "sports equipment" within the meaning of the tariff law.

For the reasons given above, it is the opinion of the court that plaintiff's claim for classification must be denied and judgment must issue dismissing that claim.

**Decision.**   The importer's classification was rejected and the decision of the government upheld. The tents were not properly classifiable as "sporting goods" because the tents were designed for camping out, which was held not to be a sport.

made by the importer in the entry form filed with Customs, which can then accept or reject the classification.) In order to decide whether an article falls within a certain tariff classification, the Customs Service (or the courts if the case is appealed) must first determine the meaning of the language used to describe the items within that class. Customs must ask, "What are the items listed here?" The second step is to determine whether the articles being imported come within the description of the terms as interpreted. Customs will base its decision on what articles they think Congress intended to be included in the classification at the time it was established, and must rely on its prior administrative rulings and on judicial decisions. If a classification is protested and appealed to the courts, the agency's classification of the goods will be presumed to be correct. On review, the courts will consider whether the agency properly interpreted the meaning of the items listed in the tariff schedules. The agency's determination of whether a given article falls within that classification, however, is a question of fact that will not be overturned by the courts unless the agency made a clear error.

**Interpreting the Tariff Descriptions: The Common Meaning Rule.** Articles are described in the tariff schedules in several ways: by common name (known as an *eo nomine* description), by a description of the article's physical characteristics, by a description of their component parts, or by a description of the article's use.

To understand the meaning of terms used in the tariff schedules, the courts look to the common meaning of the articles described. According to the cases, the *common or popular meaning* of terms used in the tariff schedules applies unless Congress clearly intended a *commercial meaning* to prevail. Courts will often examine the legislative history of the tariff act and will consult lexicographic sources such as dictionaries and encyclopedias to determine the common or commercial meaning of the terms used (e.g., is an *anchovy* commonly understood to be the same thing as a *sardine?*). The courts also rely on scientific authorities and expert witnesses during the trial.

Determining the common meaning is not always so simple. In *Texas Instruments v. United States,* 518 F.Supp. 1341 (1981), aff'd. 673 F.2d 1375 (1982), the court was faced with determining the common meaning of a watch movement under the TSUS. The plaintiff, Texas Instruments, Inc., had entered solid-state electronic watch modules and electronic watches. The articles consisted of an integrated circuit chip, a capacitor, a quartz crystal, a liquid crystal display for digital readouts, and plastic cases within which the modules were encased. Since digital watches had not yet been invented at the time the TSUS was enacted by Congress, the court upheld the Customs Service's determination that the common meaning of watch movement in the horological industry did not include these electronic modules. The court believed that Congress could not have intended the term "movement" to include the mere vibration of a quartz crystal in a digital watch. In addressing the impact of technological development on Customs law, the Court of International Trade stated that

The courts cannot be asked to restructure the tariff schedules by judicial fiat in order to accommodate scientific and engineering innovations which far transcend the vision and intent of the Congress at the time of the enactment of the tariff schedules. It is true . . . that it is an established principle of customs law that tariff schedules are written for the future as well as for present application and may embrace merchandise unknown at the time of their enactment. It must be borne in mind, however, that . . . in applying a tariff provision to an article, unknown at the time of the enactment thereof, such an article must possess an essential resemblance to the characteristics so described by the applicable tariff provision.

Accordingly, the court ruled that the solid-state electronic module was not a "watch movement" within the meaning of the TSUS.

In a similar case, *C. J. Van Houten & Zoon v. United States,* 664 F.Supp. 514 (1987), the court ruled that tariff schedule items for "bars or blocks" of chocolate weighing ten pounds or more did not apply to imports of molten, liquid chocolate imported into the United States in tank cars. Rather, the molten chocolate was to be classified as "sweetened chocolate in any other form." After consulting several dictionaries for the common meaning of the terms "bars and blocks," the court concluded that this meant only solid materials. The court noted that "[A]ltering of the state of an article temporarily to facilitate transportation without changing the essential nature of the goods may not control classification," *unless* it causes the product to fall under another category better describing the product.

Similarly, the tariff schedules do not call for the use of scientific terminology or scientific meanings in describing products. When the scientific meaning of a term used in the tariff schedule differs from the term's common or commercial meaning, the latter applies (unless a contrary intent is expressed by Congress).

## General Rules of Interpretation

Because many products could conceivably fit into more than one tariff category, the importer must consult the *General Rules of Interpretation* (GRI), found at the beginning of the *Harmonized Tariff Schedules* when two or more classifications conflict. In brief, they state:

GRI 1.    Classification shall be determined according to the terms of the headings and any relative section or chapter notes and, provided such headings or notes do not otherwise require, according to the following provisions:

GRI 2. (a)    An article described in the schedules includes the completed, finished article as well as one that is incomplete or unassembled, provided that the incomplete or unassembled article has the essential character of the complete or finished article.

GRI 3.    When goods are classifiable under two or more headings, the article shall be classified as follows:

(a)    According to the rule of specificity: The heading which provides the most specific description shall be preferred to headings providing a more general description.

(b)    Mixtures, composite goods consisting of different materials or made up of different components, and goods put up in sets for retail sale, which cannot be classified by reference to 3(a), shall be classified as if they consisted of the material or component which gives them their essential character, insofar as this criterion is applicable.

(c)    When goods cannot be classified by reference to 3(a) or 3(b), they shall be classified under the heading which occurs last in numerical order among those which equally merit consideration.

GRI 4.    Goods which cannot be classified in accordance with the above rules shall be classified under the heading appropriate to the goods to which they are most akin.

GRI 5.    In addition to the foregoing provisions, the following rules shall apply in respect of the goods referred to therein:

(a)    Camera cases, musical instrument cases, gun cases, drawing instrument cases, necklace cases and similar containers, specially shaped or fitted to contain a specific article or set of articles, suitable for long-term use and entered with the articles for which they are intended, shall be classified with such articles when of a kind normally sold therewith. This rule does not, however, apply to containers which give the whole its essential character;

(b)    Subject to the provisions of rule 5(a) above, packing materials and packing containers entered with the goods therein shall be classified with the goods if they are of a kind normally used for packing such goods. However, this provision is not binding when such packing materials or packing containers are clearly suitable for repetitive use.

**The Rule of Relative Specificity.**    When an item could be properly classifiable in more than one tariff classification, it must be classified under the provision *that most specifically describes the item.* This is known as the rule of *relative specificity.* A description of an item by use is considered more specific than a description by name *(eo nomine).* An *eo nomine* description is considered more specific than a description of an item by its physical characteristics.

A good example of the rule of relative specificity is found in *Humphrey's v. U.S.* 272 F.Supp. 951 (1967). Packard-Bell had imported wooden cabinets used for housing stereo systems. Electrical components were then installed in the cabinet, including speakers, a tuner, an amplifier, and a turntable. The unit was to be sold through furniture stores, appliance and television stores and department stores. Customs classified the items as "radiotelegraphic transmission and reception apparatus" dutiable at 15 percent ad valorem. The plaintiff contended that the articles were classified as "furniture, and parts thereof, not specially provided for: of wood" and dutiable at 10.5 percent. In holding for the government, the court stated that:

Even though the cabinets are furniture, they are more specifically provided for within the superior heading encompassing radio-phonographic combinations. To be classifiable as "not specially provided for, furniture of wood," an article of wood need only be a movable article of utility used to equip dwellings or other establishments. To meet the requirements for a part of a radio-phonographic combination, the cabinets also had to be dedicated to a sole and specific use

and to serve a useful function in connection with the radio-phonographic combination.

**Classification by Essential Character.** If the conflicting classifications describe only certain parts or components of the article, the article is to be classified under the heading describing those materials or components of the item that give it its essential character. The term *essential character* refers to that attribute or quality that is indispensable to the structure, condition, or use of the article. In *Better Home Plastics Corp. v. United States,* 916 F.Supp. 12265 (1996), the court had to determine whether a shower curtain set was classified under the heading for "Curtains" or under the heading for "Tableware, kitchenware, other household articles and toilet articles, of plastics: Other: Curtains and drapes, including panels and valances." The court found that it was the inner liner that gave the sets their essential character, and thus they were classified in the latter category.

---

## Better Home Plastics Corp. v. United States
### 916 F.Supp. 1265 (1996)
### United States Court of International Trade

BACKGROUND AND FACTS

Plaintiff, Better Home Plastics Corp., imported shower curtain sets. The shower curtain sets consisted of an outer textile curtain, inner plastic magnetic liner, and plastic hooks. The plastic liner prevents water from escaping the shower while the shower is in use. The liner—which is opaque—also protects the textile curtain from mildew. The liner is color coordinated to match the outer curtain, and adds to the set's decorative appearance. The textile curtain is intended to be decorative, and does not block the water from getting out on the floor. The curtain is also semi-transparent, permitting the color of the plastic liner to show when the curtain and the liner are drawn. The imported articles are at the "low end" of the shower curtain market. Better Home Plastics sells the sets to budget stores at prices ranging from $5.00–$6.00, and retailers resell them at prices from $9.00–$12.00. Customs classified the merchandise under the provision for the set's outer curtain at a duty of 12.8% ad valorem according to Chapter 63, Subheading 6303.92.0000 of the Harmonized Tariff Schedule

(HTSUS). Better Home Plastics asserts classification of the set is properly determined by the set's inner plastic liner under Chapter 39, Subheading 3924.90.1010, HTSUS, at a duty of 3.36% ad valorem.

DiCARLO, CHIEF JUDGE

The *General Rules of Interpretation* (GRI) govern the classification of the imported shower curtain sets under the HTSUS. GRI 1 establishes the general presumption for classification under the rules. GRI 1 provides that the headings and relative section or chapter notes determine the classification of the imported merchandise, so long as those headings or notes do not require otherwise.

GRI 3 governs where the merchandise at issue consists of more than one material or substance, such as a textile curtain and an inner plastic liner, as here. GRI 3 mandates that, when "goods are, prima facie, classifiable under two or more headings," the court must classify the merchandise in question pursuant to the heading providing the

*(continued)*

*(continued)*

most specific description. This is known as the *rule of relative specificity.* An exception to this rule exists. When, however, two or more headings each refer . . . to part only of the items in a set put up for retail sale, those headings are to be regarded as equally specific . . . even if one heading provides a more complete or precise description of the goods. Accordingly, the rule of relative specificity does not apply when two of the headings each refer only to part of the items within the set.

Goods put up in sets for retail sale, which cannot be classified according to the most specific heading, are classified by the "component which gives them their essential character" (the *essential character test*). Better Home Plastics contends the court must apply the essential character test, in classifying the applicable merchandise. Application of the test, Better Home Plastics asserts, would mandate classification of the set on the basis of its inner plastic liner pursuant to Subheading 3924.90.1010, HTSUS. . . .

Defendant contends the essential character of the curtains are embodied in the textile curtain. Defendant raises numerous arguments to support its position, particularly that (1) the plastic liner is replaceable at 1/3 to 1/4 the price of the set; (2) the consumer purchases the set because of the decorative function of the outer curtain, and not for the protection afford by the liner; and (3) the liner is only employed for the limited period that someone is utilizing the shower, whereas the decorative outer curtain is employed, at a minimum, when the bathroom is in use, and as much as 24 hours a day. Defendant also contends Better Home Plastics' invoice description supports Customs' classification. Pursuant to the invoice description, the set is sold as "Fabric Shower Curtain and Liner." Therefore, defendant argues, this description serves as an admission that the curtain provides the essential character of the set.

Although the court agrees that the curtain in the imported set imparts a desirable decorative characteristic, nonetheless, it is the plastic liner that provides the indispensable property of preventing water from escaping the shower enclosure. The liner (1) prevents water from escaping when the shower is in use; (2) protects the fabric curtain from mildew and soap scum; and (3) conceals the shower and provides privacy when the shower is in use. Further, the plastic liner can serve its intended function without the outer curtain and contributes to the overall appearance of the set. The outer curtain, in contrast, merely furthers the sets decorative aspect. The court therefore concludes the essential character of the set is derived from the plastic liner.

Defendant's other contentions are also unpersuasive. The manner in which the set is invoiced does not definitively determine which component provides the essential character of the set. See 2 Sturm, *Customs Law and Administration* S 57.6 (1993). The invoice description is intended to characterize the shipped item; it is not a declaration of the relative importance of its component parts. Finally, while the court takes into consideration the relative cost of the component parts, this point alone is not dispositive, nor very persuasive against the competing arguments.

It is the essential character of the set—derived in part from the plastic's ability to repel water— that denotes the set's utility, purpose, and accordingly, character. Inclusion of the textile curtain within the classification for the plastic liner does little to change the qualities or the basic nature of the set in meeting this purpose.

The court finds Better Home Plastics has overcome the presumption of correctness accorded to Customs, and the shower curtain sets were improperly classified under subheading 6303.92.0000, HTSUS. In addition, the court agrees with Better Home Plastics' proposed classification of the sets under subheading 3924.90.1010, HTSUS.

This decision is limited to its facts, i.e., that the set at issue is at the low end of the shower curtain market. The court does not offer an opinion on the proper classification of sets targeted to a different market segment.

**Decision.** When articles are made up of component parts, or are in sets, and their parts are refereed to in two equally specific headings, then the rule of relative specificity does not apply, and their classification must be determined by which part gives the article its essential character. In this case, the shower liner imparts the essential character to the set.

**Comment.** Judge DiCarlo's opinion was affirmed by the U.S. Court of Appeals in *Better Home Plastics Corp. v. United States,* 119 F.3d 969 (Fed. Cir. 1997).

In a similar case, *Mita Copystar America, Inc. v. United States,* 96 F.Supp. 1245 (CIT 1997), the court had to decide whether toner cartridges for photocopy machines are classified as "chemical preparations for photographic uses" or as "parts and accessories of electrostatic photocopying apparatus." Classifying the toner as a chemical, the court stated:

The factor which determines essential character will vary as between different kinds of goods. It may, for example, be determined by the nature of the material or component, its bulk, quantity, weight or value, or by the role of a constituent material in relation to the use of the goods. . . . The basic function of a toner cartridge is to supply toner to the photocopier as efficiently and effectively as possible. In this context, the toner is the principle product. Although packaging the toner in cartridges enhances the efficiency of toner delivery and prevents spills during installation, the cartridge only plays an auxiliary role in the process.

**Classification by Actual or Principal Use.** The tariff schedules also describe articles by use. To classify a product according to its *actual use,* the product must be used for the purposes or functions listed in the schedule. In order to classify an article by actual use, the intent to use it must be stated to U.S. Customs at the time of entry, and the imported article must actually be used in that manner. When the article is placed into actual use, the actual use is subject to verification by the Customs Service for three years. When an article is described in the tariff schedule by both its use and by name, the *use* provision is generally deemed to be more specific, and thus controls. When an article might have several uses, the *principal use* controls. Principal use is the use that is greater than any other single use of the article.

**The Doctrine of Entireties: Classification of Component Parts.** Another problem under the customs laws concerns the classification of parts or components that combine to produce a finished product. The tariff classification for parts is usually found within the same subheading as the complete article (e.g., "furniture and parts thereof"). To be entered and dutied as a part,

Customs requires that the imported items have no commercial use of their own unless combined with other items. When parts are entered separately, they must be dutied as individual parts. But when they are imported in the same shipment and under a single entry, it is possible that they could be dutiable as the finished product. As an example, consider the entry of an unassembled roll-top desk reproduction. The individual pieces, cut and carved to fit together, are clearly a piece of furniture and not pieces of wood. Under the *doctrine of the entireties,* if an entry consists of unjoined parts that when assembled form an article that is commercially different from any of the parts, then the proper classification is the one for the completed article and not for the parts separately. As such, the desk becomes a "complete commercial entity" and is thus dutied as an entirety.

In *Standard Brands Paint Co., Inc. v. United States,* 511 F.2d 564 (1975), the plaintiff imported packages invoiced as "wooden picture frames." They consisted of moldings of different styles and lengths. Each package contained two pieces of molding with mitered ends, drilled for nails, and two nails. The purchaser could buy the size and style desired to make custom picture frames. The Customs Service classified the articles as "wood moldings . . . whether or not drilled" and assessed the duty at 10 percent to 17 percent. The plaintiff claimed that the articles were properly classifiable as unassembled picture frames dutiable at the rate of 7 percent to 12 percent. Noting that the importer "has merely given the consumer . . . the opportunity to choose the size of the picture frame he desires to assemble," the court held in favor of the importer.

To take another example, consider the components of a stereo system. Are they properly classified and dutied individually or as one stereo sound system? In *Sears, Roebuck & Co. v. United States,* 723 F.Supp. 805 (1989), the Court of International Trade upheld the classification of a shipment of amplifiers, tuners, turntables, cassette decks, and wooden racks as individual components rather than as one stereo rack system. The evidence showed that each component could be used with other components made by other manufacturers, that the components did not lose their individual identities just because they were sold together, and that advertisements for the stereo "system" described each component separately. The court rejected the use of the doctrine of the entireties because each component had retained its essential characteristics as a component.

**Chief Weight System for Textiles.** An additional rule is applicable to textile imports. Under the HTSUS, they will be classified according to those fibers that constitute the *chief weight* of the article. Under this method, the importer must determine the weight of each component fiber or yarn, and the fiber that has the greatest weight determines the classification of the merchandise. Under the new chief weight system, an imported bedspread that contains 30 percent linen, 40 percent synthetic polyester, 10 percent natural ramie, and 20 percent cotton would be classified under the rate for bedspreads of synthetic fiber.

**http://www.customs.ustreas.gov/ imp-exp/rulings/harmoniz** See for the HTSUS.

## Customs Valuation

The customs value, often called *dutiable value,* of all goods entered into the United States must be established. That value is defined by U.S. law as the *transaction value* of the goods. The transaction value of the merchandise is *the price actually paid or payable* for the merchandise when sold for exportation to the United States, plus the following amounts if not included in the purchase price: (1) packing costs (including containers, covers, and labor for packing) incurred by the buyer, (2) any selling commission incurred by the buyer, (3) the value of any assist, (4) any royalty or license fee that the buyer is required to pay as a condition of sale, and (5) the proceeds of any subsequent resale of the merchandise that accrues to the seller. Transaction value does not include international freight charges, insurance or customs brokerage fees, inland freight after importation, charges for assembling or maintaining the goods after importation, or import duties. Charges for transporting the goods in the country of exportation (e.g., from the seller's factory to the port) are also excludable when these charges

are identified separately on the seller's invoice. Transaction value is not affected by whether the sales contract called for CIF or FOB payment terms. If the price is expressed as CIF, the freight and insurance will be deducted; if FOB, the freight and insurance were not included anyway.

When a seller provides financing on goods exported to the United States, the interest payments are not includable in the transaction value of the goods when the interest is identified separately (rather than as a part of the purchase price), the financing contract or note is in writing, and the interest rate is not unusual.

Importers are often required to pay royalties or license fees to the holders of copyrights, trademarks, or patents for the privilege of importing merchandise subject to those rights. Sometimes these payments are made through the seller or exporter of the merchandise. When such payments are made "as a condition of sale of the imported merchandise for exportation to the United States," they are includable in transaction value. For instance, if a firm imports blue jeans manufactured in Hong Kong, and as a condition of sale makes royalty payments to the designer of the jeans in Paris, the royalty would be includable in the transaction value of the merchandise.

The GATT 1994 *Agreement on Customs Valuation* attempts to unify the various nations' methods of calculating dutiable value on the basis of transaction value. It also attempts to toughen rules for dealing with importer fraud in stating value. Its greatest effect will be in assuring U.S. exporters that their goods will be fairly valued in foreign countries according to international principles.

**Agency Commissions.** The importance of transacting business through a foreign agent is stressed many times in this text. Agents are used both by sellers attempting to export to foreign markets and by buyers attempting to source materials or goods from foreign suppliers. The terms of the relationship between the importer and the agent can have a distinct impact on the calculation of transaction value. As the *Rosenthal-Netter* case illustrates, while commissions paid to a buying agent (an agent of the buyer/importer) are generally not included in transaction value, payments made to, or for the benefit of, the seller or

## BACKGROUND AND FACTS

Rosenthal-Netter, the plaintiff, began importing rattan furniture from the People's Republic of China (PRC) in 1974. Mr. Rosenthal sought the assistance of Mr. Wong of the Hongson Arts Company of Hong Kong in furthering his business in China. In 1975, Mr. Rosenthal attended the Commodities Fair with Mr. Wong in Canton, China, under an oral agreement not to buy goods directly from the PRC but to purchase them only through Mr. Wong. In 1976, the agreement was put into writing. Under the agreement, Mr. Wong traveled to the PRC for the plaintiff nearly every week. He obtained samples, placed orders, and spoke with the PRC trading companies. He also received, unpacked, and warehoused the furniture in Hong Kong. The furniture was inspected for damage and proper markings, and consolidated for shipment to Rosenthal-Netter. Wong negotiated all freight contracts with the steamship companies. For these services he received a "5% Commission" and a "10% Handling Charge." The plaintiff contended that these amounts paid to Mr. Wong were properly excludable from dutiable value of the merchandise as bona fide "buying commissions." The U.S. Customs Service included these amounts in the dutiable value of the goods on the basis that Mr. Wong was not a buying agent of the plaintiff. The plaintiff brought this action contesting this determination of dutiable value.

## JUDGE TSOUCALAS

It is well settled that bona fide buying commissions are not a proper element of dutiable value. Plaintiff has the burden of proving the existence of a bona fide agency relationship and that the charges paid were, in fact, bona fide buying commissions. If plaintiff does not clearly establish that such a relationship existed, then the relationship is not that of agency.

It is not disputed that Hongson did engage in activities indicative of an agency relationship. Mr. Wong accompanied Mr. Rosenthal to the Canton Fair. He helped plaintiff obtain samples, place orders, compare trading companies, translate, take measurements, and acquire quotes on prices. These services are typical of those rendered by buying agents.

### Rosenthal-Netter, Inc. v. United States
679 F.Supp. 21, Aff'd.,
861 F.2d 261
(Fed. Cir. 1988) Court of
International Trade

Mr. Rosenthal, by attending the fair, meeting suppliers, and participating in negotiations engaged in activities which undoubtedly support an agency relationship. Likewise, being able to purchase directly without the assistance of Mr. Wong also evidences an agency relationship.

However, the court must examine all relevant factors in deciding whether a bona fide agency relationship exists. Although no single factor is determinative, the primary consideration is the "right of the principal to control the agent's conduct with respect to the matters entrusted to him."

There are several aspects of Mr. Wong's conduct plaintiff failed to control. First, plaintiff did not control from which factory Hongson selected the subject merchandise. Hongson's quote sheet on its own invoice paper to plaintiff omits the name of any manufacturer. Therefore, plaintiff could not have known from which factory Hongson purchased the goods. A factor which negates the existence of any agency relationship is the lack of control over the choice of factories. Failure to substantiate the names of manufacturers is evidence that no agency relationship existed.

Second, Hongson purchased quantities up to ten times greater than the amount ordered by plaintiff. The larger shipments make it apparent that the manufacturers could not have known that one-tenth of the order was purchased on behalf of Rosenthal-Netter, a factor which militates against an agency relationship.

Third, plaintiff did not control the amount of discretion exercised by Hongson in the purchasing process. Specifically, no instructions were given with respect to how the goods were to be handled or shipped. Similarly, Hongson retained all discretion to negotiate price and to negotiate the means of transport with the freight companies. Additionally, Hongson bought in bulk, making it unlikely that plaintiff exerted control over the purchasing process.

Fourth, plaintiff allowed Hongson to absorb the cost of shipping and handling.

The fact that the intermediary absorbs the cost of shipping and handling out of its commission is evidence that the agency relationship did not exist.

*(continued)*

*(continued)*

Fifth, plaintiff did not control the manner of payment. The letters of credit opened by plaintiff to pay for the subject merchandise were made payable to Hongson Arts Co. Hongson used the letters of credit as master receipts to open new letters of credit to pay the suppliers. From the master letters of credit, Hongson also deducted its commission, handling charges, freight charges, and the costs of opening all letters of credit. An importer's failure to control the manner of payment is a factor evidencing the nonexistence of an agency relationship.

The transaction documents reveal that Hongson operated an independent business, primarily for its own benefit. The government introduced as evidence: a sales confirmation from the PRC to Hongson, and a sales confirmation from Hongson Arts to Rosenthal-Netter, Inc., which lists Rosenthal-Netter as the "buyer" and states "confirmation of order given by the undermentioned (plaintiff) and accepted by Hongson Arts Company." These documents reflect two separate transactions: Hongson buying from the PRC and Rosenthal-Netter buying from Hongson. Plaintiff failed to refute defendant's evidence establishing a relationship between itself as the buyer and Hongson as the seller of merchandise.

The pricing structure employed by Hongson also demonstrates that Hongson traded on its own account, for its own benefit. Mr. Garretto, who reviewed plaintiff's protest, testified that the Customs Service rejected plaintiff's claim primar-ily because Hongson Arts was selling to Rosenthal-Netter at a higher price than he was buying from China. In one instance, a PRC manufacturer charged Hongson 88 cents for an item, but plaintiff paid Hongson $1.01 for the same merchandise. Thus, the pricing structure reflects Hongson's lack of financial detachment from the suppliers, indicating Hongson traded on its own account primarily for its own benefit.

It is uncharacteristic of an agency relationship to allow the intermediary to bear the risk for damaged, lost, or defective merchandise. Losses which were greater than the "10% Handling Charge" were left to Hongson's "own devices as far as recoupment from the supplier of the defective merchandise is concerned.". . . .

On balance, taking into consideration the amount of control exerted over Hongson, the pricing structure, the risk of loss allocation, the transaction documents, the discretion allowed Hongson and the credible testimony, the court holds that plaintiff failed to meets its burden of proof and overcome the presumption of correctness afforded the government. Therefore, the action is dismissed and the appraisement by the Customs Service is sustained.

**Decision.** The plaintiff's action was dismissed and the determination of the Customs Service sustained. Although bona fide buying commissions paid to the buyer's agent are not included in dutiable (transaction) value, the facts of this case prove that no such agency relationship existed.

seller's agent are included. Notice how carefully the Customs Service scrutinizes these business relationships.

In *Monarch Luggage Co. v. United States*, 715 F.Supp. 1115 (1989), the importer successfully structured a business transaction so that the buying commissions were excludable from transaction value. Although representatives of Monarch traveled to the Far East several times a year to meet with their suppliers, inspect their facilities, and place orders for luggage, they nevertheless maintained a local agent there. Under a written agreement, the agent was to locate the best sources for luggage and visit the suppliers to determine the quality of the luggage, but could place orders only at Monarch's direction. The agent coordinated payment for the luggage and arranged transportation according to Monarch's explicit instructions. The supplier and not the agent absorbed the loss of defective merchandise. The agent bore no risk of loss to the goods and never took title to them. The agreement further stated that "the agent shall never act as a seller in any transaction involving the principal." Most importantly, Monarch made the payments to its agent directly and separately and not as a part of the invoice price paid to the supplier of the luggage.

## Texas Apparel Co. v. United States
### 698 F.Supp. 932 (1988)
### Court of International Trade

BACKGROUND AND FACTS

In 1981 and 1982, Texas Apparel Company made 266 entries of wearing apparel from Mexico. The company had provided sewing machines to the Mexican manufacturer, and paid the cost of repairs to the machines. The sewing machines were essential to the production of the garments. The U.S. Customs Service included the value of the machines, spare parts, and repair costs in the calculation of dutiable value of the garments as an assist. The importer brought this action to contest the government's appraised value of the imported garments.

CHIEF JUDGE RE

Plaintiff contests the inclusion in the appraised value of the cost or value of the sewing machines as dutiable assists, and contends that 19 U.S.C. §1401a(h)(1)(A)(ii) does not include general purpose machinery as assists. It maintains that "the only production equipment included as assists are the `tools, dies, molds, and similar items . . .' which are special purpose equipment having the dedicated and exclusive function of producing the discrete article in question." Specifically, plaintiff claims that the sewing machines are "general purpose equipment," and are not "tools, dies, molds, and similar items used in the production of the imported merchandise." Hence, plaintiff contends that the appraisement of the imported merchandise should not have included an addition for the cost or value of the sewing machines, and seeks a refund of the excessive duties paid, with interest.

Computed value is defined in 19 U.S.C. §1401a(e) as follows:

(1) The computed value of imported merchandise is the sum of
   (A) the cost or value of the materials and the fabrication and other processing of any kind employed in the production of the imported merchandise;
   (B) an amount for profit and general expenses equal to that usually reflected in sales of merchandise of the same class or kind as the imported merchandise that are made by the producers in the country of exportation for export to the United States;
   (C) any assist, if its value is not included under subparagraph (A) or (B); . . .

On judicial review, the fundamental question presented is whether, based upon the statutory language and the legislative intent which underlies the pertinent statutory provision, the interpretation of the statute by the Customs Service was reasonable.

An examination of the legislative history of the Trade Agreements Act reveals that Congress did not intend as narrow or restrictive a view of computed value, or of the term "assist," as suggested by plaintiff. The legislative history of the Trade Agreements Act of 1979 indicates that the act "revise(s) section 402 of the Tariff Act of 1930, which specifies the methods for determining the value of an import for purposes of applying ad valorem duties, to make it consistent with the Customs Valuation Agreement negotiated in the (Multilateral Trade Negotiations)." The amended version of section 402 contains five methods of customs valuation including computed value which is "based on production costs, profit and overhead."

The new code simplifies valuation since it "confines the computed value standard to the cost of producing the imported merchandise. . . ." Accordingly, the Custom Service's interpretation of 19 U.S.C. § 1401a (h)(1)(A)(ii) as including items directly related to the production of merchandise, such as a sewing machine to the sewing of wearing apparel, cannot be said to be contrary to the goals and intent of the new valuation code. Including the value of the sewing machine, which is essential to the fabrication of the apparel, fairly and accurately reflects "the cost of producing the imported merchandise."

Defendant stresses that the Customs Service, in interpreting the statute, has differentiated between those general purpose machines which are used in the actual production of the specific imported article, and those that are not used in the actual production of the merchandise. Indeed, the Customs Service has specifically interpreted the statute to include "general purpose equipment, such as sewing machines, ovens, drill presses, etc., . . . used abroad in the production of merchandise imported into the United States, (as) dutiable under section 401(h)(1)(A)(ii)." On the other hand the Customs Service has held that "air conditioning equipment, a power transformer, telephone switching equipment, and emergency generators do not fall within the definition of

*(continued)*

*(continued)*

assist, as they are not used in the production of the merchandise." Customs' interpretation clearly distinguishes between machinery which works directly on the merchandise or contributes directly to its manufacture, e.g., sewing machines, drill presses, and ovens, and machinery which although used by the industry is not used directly in the production of the merchandise itself, e.g., air conditioners and emergency generators.

It is well settled that the court will defer to the agency's interpretation of the statute if the interpretation is reasonable, and is consistent with the legislative intent and guiding purpose of the statute. See *Chevron U.S.A. Inc.,* 104 S.Ct. at 2781–82. Machinery such as air-conditioning and power generators, which may be used by manufacturers and may be invaluable, is not used directly to produce the merchandise. The sewing machines in issue, however, are used directly "in the production of the imported merchandise." Hence, the court concludes that Customs' interpretation of the statute is reasonable and consistent with congressional intent. . . .

In the present case, the function performed by the sewing machines, which is to construct the apparel by sewing together the fabric, is essentially or principally the same as that of a tool, die,

or mold. Although a tool may be defined as plaintiff suggests, as a manual instrument, a tool may also be defined more broadly as "an implement or object used in performing an operation or carrying on work of any kind . . . " See *Websters Third New International Dictionary* 2408 (1981). It is clear, therefore, that in this industry a sewing machine is a device similar to a "tool, die, (or) mold . . . used in the production of the imported merchandise."

In view of the foregoing, the court holds that the cost or value of the sewing machines, repair parts, and the cost of repairs were properly included by the Customs Service in the computed value of the imported merchandise as an "assist" under 19 U.S.C. § 1401a(h)(1)(A)(ii). Accordingly, plaintiff's motion for summary judgment is denied, and defendant's cross-motion for summary judgment is granted.

**Decision.** Summary judgment was entered for the U.S. government. General purpose machines supplied by the importer free of charge or at a reduced cost to a foreign manufacturer are properly included in computed value of the imported merchandise as an assist when they are used directly in the production of articles imported into the United States.

**Assists.** Importers will often provide some form of assistance to a foreign manufacturer from whom they are purchasing goods. If this *assist* is provided free of charge or at a reduced cost, for use in the production of or sale of merchandise for export to the United States, the value of the assist is includable in transaction value. Assists generally include (1) raw materials and component parts used in the production of the imported merchandise; (2) tools, dies, or molds; and (3) engineering, development, artwork, and design, or plans and sketches performed by a foreign firm or person not domiciled within the United States.

**Other Methods of Calculating Dutiable Value.** When the transaction value of imported merchandise cannot be determined, the Customs Service will look to the value of identical merchandise. If identical merchandise cannot be found, then the value of similar merchandise will

be used. The identical or similar merchandise used in the comparison must have been recently sold for export to the United States at the same level of trade (manufacturer to distributor, distributor to retailer, for example) and in quantities similar to the entry being valued.

If dutiable value cannot be determined by any of these methods, the Customs Service will utilize the deductive value or computed value methods. *Deductive value* is the resale price of the goods (including packaging costs) in the United States after importation, less international and inland freight, insurance, customs duties, brokerage fees, commissions, and expenses of refining, assembling, or further manufacturing incurred in the United States. The final method for calculating the value of imports gives the computed value. *Computed value* is calculated by adding the costs of raw materials, processing or fabricating, overhead, labor costs, packing costs, the value of any assist, and an amount for profit.

## Country-of-Origin

Imagine that a trading company has firm commitments from buyers in the United States to take all of the ostrich chicks that it can provide during the next year. After considerable searching and time spent traveling the world, the trading company finds an ostrich hatchery in England. It enters into a sales contract with the hatchery, with payment to be made under a confirmed letter of credit. The bank pays the seller cash on the documents and the chicks arrive peeping and squawking at a U.S. port of entry. The chicks are entered with their country-of-origin listed as Great Britain. An astute customs inspector realizes that the chicks could not possibly have "originated" in that country and corrects the country-of-origin to South Africa, where the eggs actually originated. The trading company agrees that the fertilized eggs originated in South Africa, but argues that their incubation and hatching in Great Britain amounts to a "substantial transformation" and that Great Britain therefore became the country-of-origin. The U.S. Customs Service rules that the processing of the eggs in Great Britain was a natural biological consequence of the initial fertilization of the eggs in South Africa, that the chicks continued to be a product of South Africa, and that they are prohibited from entering the United States under a U.S. law banning the import of products from South Africa (which, of course, is no longer the case since the end of *apartheid* and the election of Nelson Mandela as president). This not-so-hypothetical case illustrates, once again, the importance of planning import decisions well in advance.

**Rules of Origin.**   Goods cannot be imported into any country without knowing and properly reporting their country-of-origin. The *country-of-origin* determines the tariff rate on imported goods as well as the applicability of quotas and other trade restrictions. *Rules of origin* refer to those laws that determine an article's country-of-origin. All countries have rules of origin. According to these rules, the country-of-origin is *that country where an article was grown, mined, produced, or manufactured.* Thus, bananas grown in Honduras and shipped directly to supermarkets in the United States are a product of Honduras. However, determining the country-of-origin is not always easy. As the importer in the ostrich case soon discovered, country-of-origin can be difficult to determine when an article originates in one country and is then shipped to some intermediary country where it is subjected to a manufacturing process that transforms it in a significant way before it is reshipped to another country of ultimate destination. Because more and more products are subjected to refining, manufacturing, and assembly operations on a global scale, country-of-origin determinations become even more complicated. A good example is agricultural products that are grown in China, refined and processed into food in the Philippines, and sold in the European Community. Steel rods might be forged in Spain, shipped to Canada for processing into wire, and then sold in the United States. Automobiles offered for sale in the United States also may have been assembled in Mexico from parts that had been manufactured in perhaps a dozen countries. As a general rule, the country-of-origin is *that country where the goods last underwent a substantial transformation.*

**Applying the Rules of Origin.**   The first consideration is exactly how the rules of origin affect an import transaction. First, the country-of-origin determines the proper tariff rate under the Harmonized Tariff Schedule. The tariff rate can be substantially lower for goods originating in MFN nations than for goods originating in those nations that are not MFN trading partners. It can be even lower for goods that originate in a developing country that is entitled to a trade preference under U.S. law. Suppose that Country A's goods are subjected to a relatively high tariff on entry into the United States, but that Country B's goods are entitled to a relatively low tariff. If a U.S. importer ships materials from Country A to Country B for manufacturing, processing, refining, or assembly, the rules of origin determine if the articles imported into the United States are still a product of Country A or whether they have been transformed into a product of Country B for tariff purposes.

Second, an importer needs to know the country-of-origin in order to determine whether imported goods are affected by country-specific import restrictions. These restrictions might include country-specific quotas, countervailing duties, government procurement regulations, or even an embargo or quarantine affecting imports from a specific country. Importers have often attempted to use the rules of origin in order to circumvent quotas and countervailing duties.

Third, the rules of origin determine how products of foreign origin are to be labeled. U.S. tariff law strictly requires that every article imported into the United States (e.g., a Japanese-made television sold to a U.S. consumer), be marked or labeled so as to indicate to the *ultimate purchaser* the country-of-origin of the article. On the other hand, if an article originates in Country A and is subjected to a substantial transformation in Country B, it must be labeled as a product of Country B when it is imported into the United States. Moreover, if raw materials are imported into the United States and put through a manufacturing or refining process that substantially transforms them, they need not be marked as a foreign product when sold to a U.S. consumer or other "ultimate purchaser." In other words, the raw materials have been transformed into products of the United States. For instance, if U.S.-made ice cream contains imported guar gum, a minor ingredient, the quart container of ice cream need not disclose that the guar gum is of foreign origin.

Finally, the *North American Free Trade Agreement* (NAFTA) between the United States, Canada, and Mexico grants duty-free status to many products originating in one country and being imported into the other. Thus, U.S., Canadian, and Mexican customs agencies need to know when an import originated in one of the other countries. The purpose of the free trade agreements would be frustrated if consistent rules of origin did not guide when a product was entitled to favorable tariff treatment under the agreement.

**The Substantial Transformation Test.** The oldest and most important rule of origin is based on the *substantial transformation test*. Under this legal theory, the country-of-origin of imported goods of any kind is deemed to be the country in which it last underwent a substantial transformation. The substantial transformation test is one of the most important aspects of customs law and has held the interest of U.S. courts for nearly the entire century. In a line of cases dating back to 1908, the courts have consistently held that a substantial transformation occurs *when the original article or product loses its identity as such and is transformed into a new and different article of commerce having "a new name, character, or use" different from that of the original item.* In that year, the U.S. Supreme Court ruled that imported cork had not been substantially transformed when it was dried, treated, and cut into smaller sections for use in bottling beer, because the cork did not take on a new "name, character, or use."

The landmark case, *Gibson-Thomsen Co. v. United States,* 27 CCPA 267 (1940), involved the application of the *name, character, or use test* under the marking and labeling laws of the United States. The court ruled that when wooden handles and blocks were imported into the United States from Japan, drilled with holes into which American bristles were inserted, with the final product being sold in the United States as toothbrushes and hair brushes, that the imported wooden components had "lost their identity in a tariff sense" and had been transformed into products of the United States. The court took account of the fact that the bristles, which had been of U.S. origin, were a key component of the new product. Because the transformation took place in the United States, the wooden handles did not have to be marked as having originated in Japan. *Gibson-Thomsen* is often cited by courts today.

Since 1940, the courts have interpreted and refined the "name, character, or use" concept. Some courts have looked to see if a "new article of commerce" emerges from the transformation. For instance, in a 1970 case, a court ruled that unfinished furniture chair parts were substantially transformed by the importer into chairs that were new and different articles of commerce. Similarly, wooden sticks imported into the United States and then set into liquid ice cream and frozen have been held to be substantially transformed into a new product having a new name, character, and use. In a 1960 case, a court ruled that the winding of typewriter ribbon onto imported spools resulted in a substantial transformation of the spools because the imported spool became an integral part of the whole product with which it was combined. In 1984, the Customs Service used the same rationale for deciding not to impose country-of-origin marking requirements on the plastic spools and shells in which audio cassette tape is wound. While many cases look to see if the name commonly given the transformed article has changed, a product's name is generally considered to be only one of several factors to take into account. Greater emphasis is usually placed on whether the *character*—sometimes said to be the "essential nature" of the product—or its *use* have changed.

Many of the modern cases also look to see whether the substantial transformation has resulted in an increase in value, called the *value-added test*. In *National Juice Products Association v. United States,* 628 F.Supp. 978 (C.I.T. 1986), a U.S. company had imported evaporated orange concentrate and blended it with water, orange oils, and fresh juice to make frozen orange concentrate. The blending and processing in the United States had added only a seven-percent value to the orange juice. The court held that the orange juice sold to consumers had to be labeled with the foreign country-of-origin.

In *Uniroyal, Inc. v. United States,* 542 F.Supp. 1026 (1982), *aff'd. per curiam* 702 F.2d 1022 (Fed. Cir. 1983), the court ruled that a substantial transformation had not occurred when the leather upper portion of a shoe was imported and then attached to the preformed rubber sole in the United States and sold as a "Sperry Topsider."

The court relied heavily on evidence that the time and cost of producing the leather upper in Indonesia were much greater than the time and cost of attaching it to the rubber sole (called a "minor assembly operation"). The court also considered that the fashioning of the leather uppers in Indonesia required far greater skill than was required to attach the sole in the United States. The court stated that "[I]t would be misleading to allow the public to believe that a shoe is made in the United States when the entire upper—which is the very essence of the completed shoe—is made in Indonesia and the only step in the manufacturing process performed in the United States is the attachment of an outsole." The court noted that unlike the earlier case involving typewriter spools, the upper leather portion of the shoe was not just a vehicle for selling something else, but was the major reason that consumers selected this shoe.

The *Ferrostaal Metals* case, involving the applicability of voluntary restraint agreements to imported steel, illustrates the difficulty in determining whether a substantial transformation has occurred. As this case shows, the precise definition of substantial transformation is unclear because so many factors can be considered. Faced with complex cases, courts have developed rules on a case-by-case basis. The unpredictable nature of these court rulings increase importers' difficulties in interpreting and applying the rules of origin, as evidenced by the large number of customs cases appealed to the courts.

---

### Ferrostaal Metals Corporation v. United States
**664 F.Supp. 535 (1987)**
*Court of International Trade*

**BACKGROUND AND FACTS**
Plaintiff attempted to enter steel products at the Port of Seattle. They consisted of unpainted steel sheets that had originated in Japan but had been hot-dip galvanized in New Zealand. Plaintiff's entry documents identified New Zealand as the country-of-origin. The Customs Service ruled that the country-of-origin was Japan and that the steel was therefore subject to a voluntary restraint agreement between the United States and Japan. Customs contended that hot-dip galvanizing of Japanese steel sheets in New Zealand was merely a "finishing process" carried out to improve certain performance characteristics of the steel sheets and not a process that results in a substantial transformation so as to change the country-of-origin. The plaintiff disagreed and brought this action for review.

**JUDGE DiCARLO**
Substantial transformation is a concept of major importance in administering the customs and

*(continued)*

*(continued)*

trade laws. In addition to its role in identifying the country-of-origin of imported merchandise for purposes of determining dutiable status, or, as in this case, the applicability of a bilateral trade agreement, substantial transformation is the focus of many cases involving country-of-origin markings. . . .

The essence of these cases is that a product cannot be said to originate in the country of exportation if it is not manufactured there. The question, therefore, is whether operations performed on products in the country of exportation are of such a substantial nature to justify the conclusion that the resulting product is a manufacture of that country. "Manufacture implies a change, but every change is not manufacture. . . . There must be transformation; a new and different article must emerge, `having a distinctive name, character, or use.' " *Anheuser-Busch Brewing Ass'n v. United States,* 207 U.S. 556, 562, 28 S.Ct. 204, 206 (1908). The criteria of name, character, and use continue to determine when substantial transformation has occurred, and the prior cases of this court and our predecessor and appellate courts provide guidance in the application of this test.

The argument that the court should apply a more stringent test depending on the context in which the substantial transformation issue arises is . . . misplaced. Defendant [Customs] says that "decisions of the courts hold that the various criteria applied in substantial transformation cases must be considered in light of the objectives of the statute in question. . . . Thus, in this case, where the purpose of the VRA and its statutory foundations is to limit imports of Japanese steel products and to foster the growth of the American steel industry, the nature of the overall changes which occur to the product in New Zealand must be more substantial than when a statute fostering operations in a foreign country [is] being construed." However, none of the cases cited even remotely suggests that the court departed from policy-neutral rules governing substantial transformation in order to achieve wider import restrictions in particular cases.

In this case, the bilateral agreement between the United States and Japan is designed to limit steel imports from Japan, not to limit imports of steel generally. Under these circumstances the standard rule for substantial transformation should be applied to determine whether steel is covered by the Agreement. No legitimate purpose is served by employing some other test in order to bring within the terms of the Agreement steel which the United States had not attempted to restrict. As a practical matter, multiple standards in these cases would confuse importers and provide grounds for distinguishing useful precedents. Thus, the court applies the substantial transformation test using the name, character, and use criteria in accordance with longstanding precedents and rules. . . .

Whether galvanizing and annealing change the character of the merchandise depends on the nature of these operations and their effect on the properties of the materials. . . . To produce one of the types of imported sheet . . . the sheet must be heated to 1,350 degrees F, at which point recrystallization of the grains of steel occurs. The sheet is then brought down to 880 degrees F, before galvanizing begins. At 880 degrees F, the sheet enters a pot of molten zinc and is dipped. The molten zinc reacts immediately with the solid steel, and begins a process known as "alloying." Alloying constitutes a chemical change in the product, characterized by the formation of iron-zinc alloys at the interface between the steel and the zinc. The galvanized steel sheet emerging from the bath has a mixed zinc-steel surface with an identifiable atomic pattern. The formation of a galvanized surface is an irreversible process which provides electrochemical protection to the sheet. As a result of the galvanic protection, the steel will last up to twenty years, or ten times as long as ungalvanized steel. . . .

The alloy-bonded zinc coating affects the character of the sheet by changing its chemical composition and by providing corrosion resistance. The court also finds that the hot-dip galvanizing process is substantial in terms of the value it adds to full hard cold-rolled steel sheet. The evidence showed that the Japanese product is sold for approximately $350 per ton, while the hot-dipped galvanized product is sold for an average price of $550 to $630.

Taken as a whole, the continuous hot-dip galvanizing process transforms a strong, brittle product which cannot be formed into a durable, corrosion-resistant product which is less hard, but formable for a range of commercial applications. Defendant's witness stated that the imported sheet has a "different character from the standpoint of durability." The court finds that the annealing and galvanizing processes result in a change in character by significantly altering the mechanical properties and chemical composition of the steel sheet.

*(continued)*

*(continued)*

The court also finds substantial changes in the use of the steel sheet as a result of the continuous hot-dip galvanizing process. Testimony at trial overwhelmingly demonstrated that cold-rolled steel is not interchangeable with steel of the type imported, nor are there any significant uses of cold-rolled sheet in place of annealed sheet.

The name criterion is generally considered the least compelling of the factors which will support a finding of substantial transformation. Nonetheless, the satisfaction of the name criterion in this case lends support to plaintiffs' claim. The witnesses for both parties testified that the processing of full hard cold-rolled steel sheet results in a product which has a different name, continuous hot-dip galvanized steel sheet.

The court also considers relevant whether the operations underlying the asserted transformation have effected a change in the classification of the merchandise under the Tariff Schedules of the United States. Change in tariff classification may be considered as a factor in the substantial transformation analysis. Here this factor supports a substantial transformation. Full hard cold-rolled steel sheet is classified under item 607.83, TSUS, while continuous hot-dip galvanized steel sheet is classifiable under item 608.13, TSUS.

Based on the totality of the evidence, showing that the continuous hot-dip galvanizing process effects changes in the name, character, and use of the processed steel sheet, the court holds that the changes constitute a substantial transformation and that hot-dipped galvanized steel sheet is a new and different article of commerce from full hard cold-rolled steel sheet.

**Decision.** Japanese steel that had been galvanized in New Zealand prior to its importation into the United States was substantially transformed so that it had become a product of New Zealand and thus was not subject to voluntary restraint agreements between the United States and Japan.

## GATT 1994 Agreement on Rules of Origin

GATT 1994 calls on countries to harmonize and clarify their rules of origin. According to the *Agreement on Rules of Origin*, the country-of-origin will be defined as either where the article and all of its constituent materials have been wholly obtained, or if the article is produced in more than one country, it is that country where the article last underwent a change in tariff classification. This provision is known as the *tariff-shift rule*. These rules will apply to all trade between countries that are members of the World Trade Organization. The United States is moving toward the use of the tariff-shift rule. Rules of origin based on the tariff-shift rule state precisely—for every given category of product in the HTS—what tariff classification changes will result in a substantial transformation. This rule is already in effect under the *North American Free Trade Agreement* for trade between Canada, Mexico, and the United States. (See Chapter Fourteen for a detailed discussion of North American rules of origin).

As of 1998 the WTO had agreed on over 1,000 rules covering non-agricultural products. The goal is to complete a single set of rules of origin covering over 5,500 products in both the agricultural and non-agricultural sectors that would be applied by all WTO member countries.

## Special Rules of Origin for Textiles and Apparel

The world's textile and apparel industry operates on a global scale. Textile firms shift the site of spinning, weaving, cutting, sewing, and other operations from country to country, and region to region, to take advantage of low-cost labor and materials, and to benefit from customs and tariff laws in the country in which the goods will be sold. For instance, cotton might be grown and spun into yarn in China, where it is woven into cloth. The cloth might be sent to Hong Kong where it is cut to form pieces of garments (e.g., sleeves, collars, etc.), and then sent to Honduras for assembly. Textile firms require regular legal advice on using the rules of origin and often obtain advance rulings from U.S. Customs in determining dutiable status of their goods.

In the past, the country-of-origin of apparel was where the cutting took place—where they were cut to shape—regardless of where the garments were assembled. This rule was used because Customs felt that this step changed the product from fabric, which could be used for any purpose, to a garment part (e.g., a sleeve) that had only one specific use. In 1995 the Customs Service adopted new textile rules of origin. The new rules eliminate the cut-to-shape rule. Under the new rules, the country-of-origin for textile and apparel is determined as follows: If all constituent materials are obtained, processed, and assembled in *only one country,* then the article originates in the country where the product is *wholly obtained or produced.*

If the constituent materials in an article (e.g., yarn, cloth, embroidery, lining material, etc.) are obtained, processed, or assembled in *more than one country,* then the following rules apply: For some articles, the country-of-origin will be that country in which *all* the constituent materials last underwent a change in tariff classification—the tariff-shift rule. If the article is "knit-to-shape" (e.g. pantyhose or socks) then the country-of-origin is that single country in which the good was knit. If the tariff-shift rules do not apply, and if the good was *not* "knit-to-shape" (e.g. woven cloth cut and sewn to make a garment), then the country-of-origin is where the product was *wholly assembled.* If it was not wholly assembled in one country, then the country-of-origin is the country in which the *most important assembly or manufacturing process* took place.

Yarn or thread originates in the country *where the fibers are spun.* Fabric originates in the country *where the fibers or yarns are woven or knitted* by a fabric-making process. If the process starts with fabric and transforms it into a different kind of fabric, the country-of-origin does not change.

Special rules apply to certain types of goods (handkerchiefs, quilts, comforters, blankets, bed sheets, curtains, tents and sails, and filled pillows and comforters). For these articles, U.S. Customs has adopted the *fabric-forward rule.* The country-of-origin is where the product's fabric was woven, regardless of where the product was cut, sewn, or assembled. Consider the result to business: Assume that China is the largest producer of fabric for curtains. Not all curtains are cut and sewn

in China, however; many are finished in other countries, such as Honduras or the Philippines, from Chinese fabric shipped there. Now assume that U.S. quotas limit imports of "curtains from China." Under the old rules the curtains made in the Philippines could enter under Philippine quota limits, not China's. Under the new rules, quotas on "curtains from China" include all curtains made anywhere in the world if they are made from Chinese fabric. As a result of the quotas, U.S. importers and retailers will not be able to get all the curtains they need for U.S. consumers at the lowest available world price.

**Opportunities for Business Planning.** The rules of origin can provide a resourceful importer with significant opportunities for good business planning. With proper legal advice, a firm can structure its global operations so as to minimize tariffs and to take advantage of the favorable trade and tariff treatment granted to goods coming from particular foreign countries. After all, trade and tariff laws are designed in part to either encourage or discourage trade with particular nations. Many firms, particularly multinational corporations, are therefore capable of shifting global resources and production facilities to those countries whose goods receive the most favorable trade and tariff treatment in the United States or other major importing nation. But to do this, the corporation must follow the importing nation's rules of origin meticulously. The tariff savings can be so great that some unscrupulous U.S. importers have been tempted to transship articles through developing countries, repackage or relabel them, and then enter them into the United States at the lower tariff rate. The penalties for furnishing false information to U.S. Customs authorities are quite severe.

## Marking and Labeling of Imports

The United States has two primary laws that require imports to be labeled with the country-of-origin: the marking rules of U.S. Customs and the Federal Trade Commission rules.

**Customs Marking Rules.** We have already learned that the marking rules require that every article of foreign origin imported into the United

States must be indelibly and permanently marked in English in a conspicuous place and in such a manner as to indicate to the *ultimate purchaser* in the United States the name of the country-of-origin of the article. The ultimate purchaser may be defined as the last person in the United States who will receive the article in the form in which it was imported. Thus, if an importer resells an imported article in its original state to a consumer, then the article must be labeled with the country of origin for the consumer to see. However, it's not always easy to know who is going to be considered the ultimate purchaser. For instance, patrons of a racetrack who were given umbrellas upon admission—not the racetrack owner who had purchased boxes of them from the importer—were held to be the ultimate purchasers of the umbrellas. Each umbrella had to be individually marked. But in another case, the ultimate purchaser of frozen airline meals was the airline and not the passenger. Thus in this case only the packages containing the meals, which were seen only by the airline, had to be marked with the country-of-origin. Because product labeling changes can be costly and disruptive to business, it is often wise to obtain a preimportation ruling from U.S. Customs.

If the imported article is converted, processed or combined with other articles or ingredients in the United States, so that it undergoes a substantial transformation resulting in a new article with a new name, character and use, as defined by the *Gibson-Thomsen* case, then it is exempted from the marking requirements—it has been transformed into a product of the United States. In *CPC International, Inc. v. United States,* 933 F.Supp. 1093 (Ct. Int'l Trade 1996), the court examined Custom's marking requirements for Canadian made goods entering the United States under the *North American Free Trade Agreement* (NAFTA). The plaintiff, CPC, a major multinational food producer, proposed to import Canadian-origin "peanut slurry" (a gritty paste made from shelled peanuts that have been roasted, blanched, split, and ground) to be processed, together with other ingredients, in the manufacture of CPC's "Skippy" brand peanut butter. In a preimportation ruling the Customs Service applied NAFTA's tariff-shift rules and stated that the finished peanut butter must be marked as a product of Canada because both peanut slurry and finished peanut butter are in the same tariff classification. The Court of International Trade concluded that U.S. Customs had failed to additionally address whether the peanut butter might be excused from the marking requirements under *Gibson-Thomsen's* substantial transformation test. In the court's words, "Congress intended that the interpretation of the ultimate purchaser provision in *Gibson-Thomsen* should remain in full force and effect as a case-specific test in addition to and independent of the application of the NAFTA Marking Rules and NAFTA exemptions from marking based on those rules." Labeling and marking can be quite costly, and changes in these aspects are disruptive to business operations. As a result, many court cases involve disputes over Custom's labeling regulations.

**Items Not Requiring Marks.** Customs regulations specify many articles by name that are exempt from marking requirements. These are generally objects that are incapable of being marked because of their size or special characteristics. Examples include works of art, unstrung beads, rags, nuts and bolts, screws, cigarettes, eggs, feathers, flowers, cellophane sheets, livestock, bamboo poles, maple sugar, vegetables, newsprint, and many others. In addition, the following general exemptions exist for certain categories of products: (1) products incapable of being marked; (2) products that cannot be marked without injury; (3) crude substances; (4) articles produced more than twenty years prior to importation; (5) products of possessions of the United States; (6) articles imported solely for the use of the importer and not intended for resale (e.g., personal articles purchased abroad by a tourist); (7) products of American fisheries that are entered duty free; and (8) certain products of the United States that are exported and returned. In addition, articles used by an importer as samples in soliciting orders and that are not for sale are exempted from the marking requirements. When an item is exempted from markings, the container in which it is sold to the consumer must be marked. To illustrate, while imported carpentry nails need not be marked, the box in which they are sold to the consumer must be.

**FTC Rules.** Under Federal Trade Commission regulations in effect in the United States, selling a product without disclosing a foreign country-of-origin is an unfair trade practice. The purpose of the regulations is to enable consumers to be informed as to where an item was grown or made. According to the FTC, a product sold in the United States does not have to be marked with a foreign country-of-origin if its domestic content is 51 percent or more. A product *assembled* in the United States of foreign components may be labeled as "Assembled in the U.S.A." However, a product may not be labeled as "Made in the U.S.A." unless the product is virtually completely made in the United States of U.S.-made component parts. Imported products need not be labeled if (1) the products are generally not native to the United States, such as diamonds or pearls; or (2) no clear public preference has been shown for U.S.-made goods of that kind, such as scotch or vodka. As of 1995 the FTC was considering changing its labeling rules to conform to the rules used by U.S. Customs.

> **http://www.ita.doc.gov/**
> *See for the home page of the U.S. I.T.A.; select "Regions and Countries" for country-specific information.*

> **http://www.mof.go.jp/~customs/ conte-e.htm**
> *See for the official website of Japanese Customs.*

# U.S. Trade Preferences for Developing Countries

The United States has recognized that trade with developing countries, and particularly with the poorer nations of the Western Hemisphere, is essential to the economic development and political stability of these countries. U.S. law provides trade and investment incentives in the form of *trade preferences* for goods imported from these countries. These preferences generally take the form of reduced tariffs or duty-free status for goods. These laws include the Generalized System of Preferences and the Caribbean Basin Economic Recovery Act.

## The Generalized System of Preferences

Under the *Generalized System of Preferences* (GSP) the United States aids in the economic development of certain developing countries by allowing their products to enter the United States at reduced rates of duty, or duty-free, until such time as these countries establish their own competitive industries. Such a trade preference is allowed under the terms of GATT and is similar to programs that other industrialized nations offer developing countries (notably the preferences granted by European nations to the products of many African nations). The program was begun in the United States in 1976 and has been renewed regularly by Congress. Mexico no longer qualified for the GSP when it joined the North America Free Trade Agreement in 1994. In 1998 approximately 140 countries received GSP status.

**Eligibility for GSP Status.** In order for a country to be eligible for GSP status, it must be designated a *beneficiary developing country.* Countries are not eligible for GSP status if they (1) have participated in an organized embargo of oil against the United States, (2) do not cooperate with the United States in the enforcement of narcotics laws (e.g., Panama), (3) aid and abet international terrorism, (4) have unlawfully expropriated the property of U.S. citizens, (5) do not recognize or enforce the arbitral awards of U.S. citizens, or (6) are controlled by communist governments (several of the formerly communist countries of Eastern Europe are now eligible for GSP tariff treatment). In addition, the president has wide authority under the GSP statute to deny duty-free treatment on political and economic grounds. For instance, the president can deny GSP status to any country that does not protect the patents, trademarks, and copyrights of U.S. citizens; maintains unreasonable restrictions on U.S. investment; does not grant internationally recognized worker rights to its workers; or whose exports to the United States injure a U.S. industry.

The product must also be eligible for duty-free treatment; approximately 3,000 classifications of products are eligible. Many of the eligible products are agricultural. Other typical products admitted under the GSP include sugar, jewelry, leather shoe uppers, wooden furniture, Christmas tree lighting, and telephones. Certain import-sensitive products such as textiles, footwear, steel, watches, and some electronic items are not eligible. A country may lose GSP benefits for specific products under competitive need limits. *Competitive need* is determined by an annual review process conducted on a product-by-product basis. Usually the duty-free status of a country's product will be terminated when more than half of the total U.S. imports of that product are imported from one GSP country or when imports of that product from the GSP country exceed $80 million (for 1997). U.S. firms, labor unions, and even foreign governments may petition that products be added to, or removed from, the GSP list.

Once a developing country reaches a per capita gross national product of $8,500, it becomes ineligible for GSP treatment, and is considered *graduated*. By the close of the 1980s, the four "Asian tigers" of Hong Kong, Singapore, South Korea, and Taiwan were graduated from the GSP.

**GSP Rules of Origin.**   In order for an article to qualify for duty-free treatment, it must meet the following requirements: (1) it must be imported into the United States directly from the beneficiary developing country; (2) it must be the "growth, product, or manufacture" of the beneficiary developing country (or substantially transformed there into a product with a new name, character and use); and (3) at least 35 percent of the value of materials and the direct cost of processing operations must have been added to the article in a single beneficiary developing country (or in any two or more GSP countries that are members of the same free trade association, such as ASEAN or Andean Group). A special rule applies when raw materials are brought to the GSP country from another country and then made into a finished article and shipped to the United States. In this case, the law requires a *dual transformation*. The raw materials brought from another country into the GSP country must first undergo a substantial transformation in the GSP country resulting in a new and different article of commerce. Then that article must undergo a second transformation into another new and different article of commerce, which is then shipped to

the United States. Consider this example: In a 1989 case, Azteca Milling was denied duty-free status for breakfast cereal that had been made in Mexico from corn originally grown in the United States. The production in Mexico required a two-step process: the converting of corn to dry corn flour and the subsequent production of breakfast cereal. Although the production of cereal from the flour was a substantial transformation that had created a new and different article of commerce (food), the converting of corn into dry corn flour was not. This decision was based on a ruling that dry corn flour was not a new and different article of commerce from corn.

To better illustrate, consider the following example of a dual transformation adapted from the *Code of Federal Regulations:*

A raw, perishable skin of an animal grown in a nonbeneficiary country is sent to a beneficiary country where it is tanned to create nonperishable leather. The tanned leather is then cut, sewn, and assembled with a metal buckle imported from a nonbeneficiary country to create a finished belt that is imported directly into the United States. Because the operations performed in the beneficiary country involved both the substantial transformation of the raw skin into a new or different article (tanned leather) and the use of that intermediate article in the production or manufacture of a new or different article imported into the United States, the cost or value of the tanned leather used to make the imported article *may be counted* toward the 35 percent value requirement. The cost or value of the metal buckle imported into the beneficiary country *may not be counted* toward the 35 percent value requirement because the buckle was not substantially transformed in the beneficiary country into a new or different article prior to its incorporation in the finished belt.

**The Lome Convention.**   Under the 1989 *Lome IV Convention,* the European Community nations granted trade preferences and development aid to 68 countries of Africa, the Caribbean, and the Pacific. It is broader in scope than the American GSP, applies to trade in services, and has provisions that deal with other issues ranging from the transport of radioactive waste to the preservation of cultural and historical values in the developing country.

## Caribbean Basin Economic Recovery Act

According to the U.S. Department of Commerce, U.S. exports to the Caribbean in 1995 were $15 billion. U.S. imports from the Caribbean for 1995 were $12.5 billion. Under the *Caribbean Basin Economic Recovery Act* (CBERA), enacted in 1983, the president has the authority to grant tariff reductions and duty-free status to imports from 24 eligible countries in order to increase imports from the region. (See Exhibit 13.5.) This law was part of a larger program to stimulate investment in the Caribbean known as the *Caribbean Basin Initiative.* These nations include Central America and the island nations of the Caribbean, although communist Cuba is excluded from eligibility. A few of the leading participants in the CBERA program are the Dominican Republic, Costa Rica, and Guatemala. A few of the most important products benefiting from CBERA are cane sugar, beef, medical appliances, orange juice, bananas and tropical fruits, ethyl alcohol, baseballs, and rum. Products excluded from CBERA treatment include footwear, certain leather goods such as handbags and gloves, luggage, oil, canned tuna, watches, and certain textile products.

Many countries that qualify for favorable CBERA treatment also receive GSP treatment. Also, many products qualify under both laws. However, the criteria are not the same for eligibility. Unlike the GSP, CBERA has no provisions for

**EXHIBIT 13.5    Caribbean Basin Initiative Participant Countries**

| | |
|---|---|
| Antigua | Haiti |
| Aruba | Honduras |
| Bahamas | Jamaica |
| Barbados | Montserrat |
| Belize | Netherlands Antilles |
| British Virgin Islands | Nicaragua |
| Costa Rica | Panama |
| Dominica | St. Kitts & Nevis |
| Dominican Republic | St. Lucia |
| El Salvador | St. Vincent |
| Grenada | & Grenadines |
| Guatemala | Trinidad & Tobago |
| Guyana | |

graduating Caribbean countries on the basis of any economic criteria. The CBERA applies to a greater variety of products than the GSP, and the competitive need requirements of the GSP are not applicable. As of 1990, CBERA became a permanent program with no date set for expiration of the law. In 1995, bills were pending in the U.S. Congress to grant the Caribbean countries the same trade preferences as are granted to Mexico under the North American Free Trade Agreement. NAFTA membership would further improve the trade and investment environment there.

**http://americas.fiu.edu/customs97/**
*See for a Customs Guide to the Americas.*

**CBERA Rules of Origin.**    CBERA rules of origin are similar to those of the GSP. In order for an article to be eligible for duty-free treatment or duty reduction (1) it must be imported directly from the CBERA country; (2) it must be the "growth, product, or manufacture" of that country (or substantially transformed in that country into a product with a new name, character and use); and (3) at least 35 percent of the value of materials and the direct cost of processing operations must have been added to the article in that country (although of that 35 percent, 15 percent may be U.S.-made components or materials). Suppose raw materials are brought into the Caribbean country from a non-CBERA country for use in making a finished product for sale in the United States. As with the GSP, the cost or value of materials imported into the Caribbean country may be included in calculating the 35 percent value-added requirement for an eligible article only if a *dual transformation* takes place—the materials must first be substantially transformed into a new and different article of commerce and then used as constituent materials in the production of the finished article exported to the United States.

CBERA grants duty-free entry into the United States for articles that have been "assembled or processed" in CBERA countries from U.S.-made "components, materials, or ingredients." In other words, U.S.-made parts that have been subjected to minor assembly, finishing, and processing operations in the CBERA country, and then shipped back to the United States qualify for duty-free entry. For these products, the substantial transformation requirement has been eliminated.

# Other Customs Laws Affecting U.S. Imports

This section examines three other laws affecting U.S. imports: drawback provisions allowing a refund of duties paid, the duty-free return of U.S. exports, and foreign trade zones.

## Drawbacks

A *drawback* is a refund of duties already paid. The most common type is the *manufacturing drawback,* designed to encourage U.S. manufacturers to export. A manufacturing drawback is a 99 percent refund of duties and taxes paid on merchandise that is imported, subjected to manufacture or production, and then exported within five years. U.S. firms are becoming increasingly sophisticated in using manufacturing drawbacks. For instance, duties paid on imported yarn will be refunded to the importer who exports a finished fabric made from that yarn. Similarly, a poultry farm that imports chicken feed can receive a drawback on duties paid on the imported feed when the chickens are slaughtered and exported. Drawbacks such as these allow the exporter to purchase materials from low-cost foreign suppliers, including non-MFN countries, without having to pay prohibitively high duties. The use of drawbacks in U.S.–Canadian trade was eliminated in 1996. In U.S.–Mexican trade, drawbacks will be eliminated by 2001.

*Same condition drawbacks* are utilized when the imported goods are not processed or manufactured, but are reexported in the "same condition" as they were imported. These products are not significantly altered while in the United States (although they may be repackaged, cleaned, tested, or displayed). For example, nuts and bolts can be entered in bulk, and sorted and repackaged in packages with foreign-language labeling. On export, the drawback applies. Many trading companies utilize same condition drawbacks.

In certain cases, an importer may export U.S.-made goods in the substitution of imported goods that are of the "same kind and quality" (i.e., interchangeable) and receive the drawback on the imported items. This practice is known as a *substitution drawback.* Substitution drawbacks are applicable to both manufacturing and same condition drawback situations. For instance, assume that a U.S. manufacturer imports semiconductors for use in making computers. The manufacturer may receive a drawback on duties paid if it exports, within three years, products containing U.S.-made semiconductors of the same kind and quality. If the company exports only 40 percent of its production, it can claim a drawback for 40 percent of the duties paid (a manufacturing/ substitution situation). To take another example, the importer of soda ash can decide to resell the foreign soda ash in this country and export the same quantity of U.S.-made soda ash to a foreign buyer, and then receive a drawback on duties paid on the imported soda ash (a same condition/ substitution situation). In most instances, these substitution drawbacks deal with fungible goods or commodities such as agricultural products.

A drawback of 99 percent is also allowed for imported merchandise that does not conform to specifications or to samples (e.g., zippers that do not zip; receipt of cotton sweaters instead of wool), provided that the error was the fault of the foreign shipper (not of the importer) and the merchandise is returned to U.S. Customs within 90 days for inspection and return to the seller under Customs' supervision. A similar drawback is allowed for merchandise shipped to a U.S. firm without its consent. If a U.S. firm imports foreign goods and finds that they are useless and cannot be returned, the importer can receive a drawback on the duties paid on the merchandise, which is subsequently destroyed.

A drawback is essentially a contract with the U.S. Customs Service. Firms wishing to arrange a drawback need competent advice in doing so. The procedures, time limits, documentation, and accounting requirements for obtaining all drawbacks are complex and exact, and many U.S. companies use the services of specialist firms for advice on structuring drawback transactions. Some firms utilize specially developed software to help track and document a drawback transaction. Civil penalties are imposed for violating the provisions of the law. Many firms do not file for drawbacks for fear of being assessed a penalty for clerical errors. The criminal penalties for fraudulently claiming a drawback are severe.

## Returns of U.S. Exports

If U.S. exports are returned to the United States they are dutiable just as though they were foreign products. This rule has three general exceptions: (1) U.S.-made products that were exported and returned to the United States and that were not substantially transformed or advanced in value while outside the United States (e.g., samples sent to a prospective buyer and returned; articles such as equipment leased to a foreign firm and returned at the end of the lease term; articles subjected to minor processing); (2) articles exported for repair or alteration, which are dutiable on the value of the repair or alteration provided that they were not substantially transformed while outside the United States; and (3) component parts made in the United States and assembled in a foreign country under special provisions of the tariff laws designed to promote economic development in certain developing countries. (This provision is discussed in the next chapter.)

**http://imex.com/naftz.html**
*The home page of the National Association of Foreign Trade Zones.*

## Foreign Trade Zones

*Foreign trade zones* (FTZs) are legally defined areas outside the customs territory of the country in which they are located. They are monitored by, and under the control of, the customs authorities of that country. Foreign trade zones exist under the laws of most nations, including the United States and European countries. In the United States, imported goods may be brought into an FTZ without being subjected to tariffs until such time as the goods are released into the stream of commerce in the United States.

Foreign trade zones are operated by state or local governments or specially chartered corporations who charge private firms for their use. Originally, FTZs were intended to encourage U.S. firms to participate in international trade by providing a "free port" into which foreign-made goods could be transported, stored, packaged, and then reexported without the payment of import duties. Today, FTZs are used for many different purposes, ranging from warehousing to actual manufacturing. The length of time that these goods can be held in a zone is not limited.

The flexibility offered to an importer through the use of FTZs provides many opportunities for creative importing strategies. For example, firms can ship goods to their zone duty-free and hold them for later entry and sale in the United States pending buyer's orders or more favorable market conditions. Foreign goods can also be held for exhibition and display in the zone for unlimited periods without the payment of duties. Foreign goods that arrive damaged or defective may be destroyed without the payment of duties. Goods in an FTZ are not subject to quotas, and may remain in the FTZ until the quota opens and their entry is permitted. Title to goods held in an FTZ may be transferred to another party without the payment of duties (although not to a retail customer for consumption outside of the FTZ). Opportunities for creative business planning are almost endless. As another example, if a commodity is dutied by weight, it may be brought into an FTZ for drying and may be entered without the excess weight caused by the moisture. But perhaps the most unusual use of an FTZ is the Cape Canaveral Zone in Florida. There, foreign payloads can be imported into the United States, processed and made ready for a space launch, and "exported" to space without the payment of U.S. import duties! Nearly 150 general purpose foreign trade zones and more than 125 subzones exist in the United States.

In addition to general purpose zones, firms are able to establish their own special purpose *subzones*. The following case arose out of Nissan's importation of equipment into an automotive manufacturing subzone in Tennessee.

## Nissan Motor Mfg. Corp., U.S.A. v. United States
### 884 F.2d 1375 (1989)
### United States Court of Appeals (Fed. Cir.)

BACKGROUND AND FACTS

Nissan operates a foreign trade zone subzone at its automotive manufacturing and assembly plant located in Smyrna, Tennessee. Nissan imported production machinery for use in the subzone consisting of industrial robots, automated conveyor systems, and a computerized interface. The machinery was to be assembled and tested in the zone, and if it proved unsatisfactory it was to be replaced, redesigned, or scrapped. Customs ruled that production equipment was not "merchandise" as defined under the FTZ act and was therefore dutiable. Duties were liquidated at $3 million and Nissan filed a protest. On denial, the Court of International Trade ruled that the equipment was dutiable and this appeal was filed.

CIRCUIT JUDGE ARCHER

The activities performed by Nissan in the foreign trade zone subzone with the imported equipment are not among those permitted by a plain reading of the statute. Section 81c provides that merchandise brought into a foreign trade zone may be "stored, sold, exhibited, broken up, repacked, assembled, distributed, sorted, graded, cleaned, mixed with foreign or domestic merchandise, or otherwise manipulated, or be manufactured. . . ."

The act does not say that imported equipment may be "installed," "used," "operated" or "consumed" in the zone, which are the kinds of operations Nissan performs in the zone with the subject equipment. Alternative operations of a different character should not be implied when Congress has made so exhaustive a list.

Nissan relies upon the case of *Hawaiian Indep. Refinery v. United States*, 460 F.Supp. 1249 (Cust.Ct. 1978), in support of its position. The merchandise there involved was crude oil which was entered into a foreign trade zone for manufacture into fuel oil products. This, of course, is an activity delineated by the act and entry into the zone was exempted from Customs duties. Thereafter, a portion of the crude oil was consumed in the manufacturing process and Customs assessed duty on the theory that there had been a "constructive" entry into the Customs territory of the United States. In holding that the assessment was improper, the Court of International Trade did not have to deal with the question at issue here of whether the initial entry into the zone was exempt. Clearly, in that case the crude oil was exempt at the time of entry. Thus, the Court of International Trade properly concluded that the *Hawaiian Indep. Refinery* case was not dispositive of this case.

We are convinced that the Court of International Trade correctly determined that the importation by Nissan of the machinery and capital equipment at issue into the foreign trade zone subzone was not for the purpose of being manipulated in one of the ways prescribed by the statute. Instead it was to be used (consumed) in the subzone for the production of motor vehicles. Under the plain language of the 1950 amendment to the act and the legislative history of that amendment, and Customs' published decision interpreting the act as amended, such a use does not entitle the equipment to exemption from Customs duties. Accordingly, the judgment of the Court of International Trade is affirmed.

**Decision.** The decision of the lower court is affirmed. Machinery entered into a foreign trade zone for use in the manufacture and assembly of automobiles is not "merchandise" under the act and may not be entered duty-free.

# Chapter Summary

The entry process is used to determine the dutiable status of goods. Information needed by the Customs Service to enter goods is obtained from the commercial invoice and other required documents. The penalties for filing false statements on the entry forms can be severe. Importers have 90 days from the date of liquidation of an entry to file a protest. In most cases, a denial of a protest by Customs is required before judicial review becomes available.

Dutiable status is determined by classification, valuation, and country-of-origin. In many countries, including the United States, goods are classified according to the Harmonized Customs Code. Ad valorem duties are based on the transaction value of the import, including commissions paid to a selling agent and the value of any assists.

All imported articles must be marked to show the country-of-origin. Where articles are transshipped through intermediary countries, they must be substantially transformed there in order for the intermediary country to be considered the country-of-origin.

The customs laws provide many duty-reducing mechanisms, including the planned use of drawbacks, trade preferences for developing countries, and the use of foreign trade zones.

Most importantly, the importer, international trader, and multinational firm must prepare their import strategies carefully. In order to remain competitive in international markets, they must make the best use of every opportunity available under the customs and tariff laws not only of the United States, but of all countries in which they are doing business. Whether a firm is exporting, sourcing globally, or manufacturing on a worldwide basis, careful evaluation of the impact of customs regulations and tariffs is essential to the success of its business plan.

## QUESTIONS AND CASE PROBLEMS

1. Inner Secrets entered 2,000 dozen boxer-style shorts from Hong Kong. The boxer shorts are made of cotton flannel in a plaid pattern, with a waistband that is not enclosed or turned over, a side length of 17 inches, and two small nonfunctional buttons on the waistband above the fly. Two seams have been sewn horizontally across the fly, dividing the fly opening into thirds. The boxers do not have belt loops, inner or outer pockets or pouches, or button or zipper fly closures. They are marketed under the label "No Excuses." Customs classified the garments as outerwear shorts under HTSUS 6204.62.4055: "Women's or girls' suits, ensembles, suit-type jackets and blazers, dresses, skirts, divided skirts, trousers, bib and brace overalls, breeches and shorts. . . . Trousers, bib and brace overalls, breeches and shorts . . . of cotton . . . 17.7%. The Customs Service based its decision on its determination that the boxers will be worn by women as outer clothing. Inner Secrets maintains that the items are not outerwear, as Customs claims, but are actually *underwear* properly classified under HTSUS 6208.91.3010: "Women's or girls' singlets and other undershirts, slips, petticoats, briefs, panties, nightdresses, pajamas, negligees, bathrobes, dressing gowns and similar articles . . . of cotton . . . 11.9%." Inner Secrets filed a protest with the agency, which was denied. Inner Secrets brought this action with the Court of International Trade. What is the proper classification of the boxers? How would a camisole worn under a sport jacket or a slip worn as a dress be classified? *Inner Secrets v. United States*, 1995 WL 227372 (C.I.T. 1995).

2. SDI, Inc. (Soundesign) is a consumer electronics manufacturer of CD players, "boom boxes," VCRs, and audio rack systems. The audio rack system assembly included an electronic chassis consisting of an unhoused printed circuit board assembly and face plate which were combined with speakers and other components and installed in a wood-laminate cabinet. The chassis was imported from China to SDI's manufacturing operation in Juarez, Mexico (which then qualified for GSP status) for assembly. On entry of the final product, the U.S. Customs denied GSP tariff preferences claiming that the goods were not a product of Mexico. SDI asserts that before it completed the assembly process, the chassis functioned only as an audio recording and reproduction device, yet after the addition of two speakers, the chassis was transformed, gaining the ability to produce sound, and thus became capable of "audio entertainment." The majority of the operations in SDI's plant in Juarez, Mexico only required a skill level of a first to sixth grade education. Is the chassis a product of Mexico? What is the proper test to tell if the imports qualify for GSP treatment? *SDI Technologies, Inc. v. U.S.* (C.I.T. 1997).

3. Sport graphics imported soft-sided "Chill" coolers from Taiwan. The coolers consist of an outer shell of a vinyl-coated nylon material; an insulating core of approximately 1/2 inch thick polymer-based closed cell foam; a top secured by a zippered interlocking flap; an inner liner of vinyl; a handle or shoulder strap of nylon webbing and plastic fixtures as a means of carrying the merchandise; and exterior pockets secured by VELCRO or zippered closures. Customs classified the merchandise under the luggage provision, which included "Trunks . . . satchels, suitcases, overnight bags, traveling bags, knapsacks, and like articles designed to contain . . . personal effects during travel . . . and brief cases, golf bags, and like containers and cases designed to be carried with the person. . . . Luggage and handbags, whether or not fitted with bottle, dining,

drinking . . . or similar sets . . . and flat goods . . . of laminated plastics . . ." at a 20 percent rate of duty. Sports Graphics contended that the imported soft-sided coolers were properly classifiable as "Articles chiefly used for preparing, serving, or storing food or beverages" at a rate of 4 or 3.4% ad valorem. What is the proper classification? Does the use of this product have a bearing on its classification? *Sports Graphics, Inc. v. U.S.,* 24 F.3d 1390 (Fed. Cir. 1994).

4. Fathom imported scuba diving wetsuits, wetsuit shoes, headgear, gloves, and weight belts. The items are made from neoprene rubber and textile laminate in St. Lucia, West Indies. The suit works by allowing water to enter the suit, and allowing it to reach an equilibrium temperature with the body. Plaintiff entered the items as "other water-sport equipment," under Chapter 95: "Articles and equipment for gymnastic, athletics, other sports . . . swimming pools, wading pools . . . water skis, surf boards, sailboards and other water sport equipment" dutied at 4.64 percent. U.S. Customs claimed that Chapter 95 applied only to "apparatus and appliances," and classified the items under HTS chapter 61–65 "Garments, made up of . . . man-made fibers" dutiable at 16.1 percent. Do you agree? Is there a difference between the wetsuits and the weight belts? *H.I.M. Fathom, Inc. v. U.S.* 981 F.Supp. 610 (C.I.T. 1997).

5. Mita imported toner cartridges for photocopy machines. U.S. Customs classified the items as "chemical preparations for photographic uses" under HTSUS subheading 3707.00.30 dutied at 8.5 percent ad valorem. Mita believed that the toner cartridges should be classified as "parts and accessories of electrostatic photocopying apparatus" under HTSUS 9009.90.30, duty free. Which classification is correct? What is the proper test to determine the classification of the items, relative specificity or essential character?

6. Superior Wire, a Michigan corporation, imports steel wire from its parent company, Superior Products Company, of Canada. The wire is processed in Canada from wire rod produced in Spain. The Customs Service excluded the wire on the basis that the country-of-origin was Spain rather than Canada. A voluntary restraint agreement existed between Spain and the United States over importation of wire rod. The wire rod was made into steel wire in Canada by a cold drawn process, meaning the wire rod is fed through a machine, unheated, and stretched and formed into wire. Superior Wire claimed this was a substantial transformation and that because of this substantial transformation, the

country-of-origin was Canada, not Spain. What is substantial transformation, and what does it have to do with country-of-origin? Do you think this was a substantial transformation? *Superior Wire v. United States,* 669 F.Supp. 472 (C.I.T. 1987).

7. "Sperry Topsider" is a brand of shoe denoting a boat-type nonslip sole or "deck shoe." Do you agree with the case discussed in the chapter, *Uniroyal, Inc. v United States*? Are leather uppers the major reason for buying "deck shoes"? What do you think the country-of-origin should have been?

8. The different components of pantyhose—sewing yarn, labels, the two tubes (legs), gusset, and the plastic bag and stickers—manufactured in the United States by L'Eggs Products, Inc., were exported to Colombia for assembly. The assembled pantyhose were then imported back into the United States by L'Eggs Products, Inc., with a duty of 23.6 percent. L'Eggs received a duty allowance for the sewing yarn, labels, gusset, and plastic bag, but not the two tubes. The Customs Service determined that sewing the two tubes closed to make the legs was a further fabrication and not an assembly process. To receive favorable treatment—a duty allowance—under the U.S. import (Section 9802) law, required that articles assembled abroad of exported, fabricated U.S. components must "not have been advanced in value or improved in condition except by being assembled." The Customs Service contends that the definition of assembly requires the joining of two or more solids, parts, or pieces, and that the sewing together of the tubes is not "assembly." L'Eggs argues that the thread and fabric of the tubes constitutes two components being joined and, therefore, the duty allowance should be given. How do you feel about the government policy of allowing a duty allowance for items assembled abroad of U.S.-exported components? From an ethical standpoint, how do you think the workers in Colombia should be treated—i.e., medical care, pension plans, worker safety, and so on—when these worker benefits are not required by that country's laws? Do you think this instance was an "assembly" qualifying for the Section 9802 allowance? *L'Eggs Products, Inc. v. United States,* 704 F.Supp. 1127 (C.I.T. 1989).

## MANAGERIAL IMPLICATIONS

Your firm is one of the last remaining manufacturers of bicycles in the United States. Z-Mart is a U.S. retail chain with nearly 1,000 stores in 15 countries. Z-Mart has asked you to prepare a proposal for a large number of bicycles to be sold at discount prices under the Z-Mart brand name. They must have a U.S. retail price of no more than $100. Z-Mart would also like to sell these bikes through its stores in France and Italy in order to compete with the European bikes made in that market. You begin to analyze your costs of materials and production. The first step of production is the sourcing of a tubular frame, a major component. You can purchase the bare frames in the United States, Canada, or Taiwan. You must clean and paint the frames before assembly. The high-performance wheels, another major component, are made from an aluminum alloy. The aluminum is made in Japan and shipped in the form of strips and rods to the Philippines, where it is cut into lengths, molded into wheel parts, and assembled. They will arrive at your plant covered in a film of oil to protect them during shipping. The tires are available from companies in Japan or Brazil. Most of the component parts, such as brakes, gears, and chains, are available directly from firms in the United States and Canada.

At a meeting of management, you are asked to prepare a plan for the production of the bicycles that will price them for Z-Mart's discount stores. In doing so, you must give consideration to the following questions. (You may make certain assumptions as to the relative costs of materials and labor if necessary.)

1. Explain how U.S. trade and tariff laws would affect your plans for bicycle production. What influence would U.S. tariff preference laws have on the sourcing of component parts? Explain how the rules-of-origin might affect the importation of the tubular frame. Would the North American Free Trade Agreement have any impact on how you structure your operations?

2. What factors would be taken into consideration in determining where to assemble the finished bicycles? In the United States? In Taiwan? In the Philippines? You have heard that U.S. automakers are assembling cars in Mexico using workers that are paid about $10 a day. What factors would influence your decision to assemble in Mexico? What processes could you do or not do in Mexico in order to obtain the most favorable tariff treatment? What are the advantages and disadvantages of assembling there?

3. Evaluate the potential for using a foreign trade zone. What advantages or disadvantages would your firm experience in this case?

4. Determine the applicability of U.S. marking and labeling requirements with regard to the finished bicycles sold in the United States.

# Chapter Fourteen

# North American Free Trade Law

Up to this point, this text has discussed international trade law, including the basic principles of GATT law and the World Trade Organization, laws regulating import competition and unfair trade, and laws governing access to foreign markets. It has examined how the growth of free trade principles, or trade liberalization, has led to increased trade in goods and services, and an improved quality of life for people around the world. The preceding few chapters have focused on trade liberalization at the global level, through GATT and the WTO. Yet GATT clearly encourages countries to cooperate on trade liberalization at the regional level as well. In Chapter Three, the discussion of the European Union introduced basic concepts of regional economic integration. Recall how the European countries, over a period spanning 40 years, reduced barriers to trade, investment, and the free movement of people, money, information, and technology. What began in the 1950s as the "European Common Market," later became the European Economic Community, and today the European Union. As the name changes signify, each step along the way increased the economic and social ties between European countries.

GATT recognizes the formation of regional free trade blocs despite an apparent conflict between regionalism and multilateralism. GATT Article 24 states that "[T]he provisions of the Agreement shall not prevent . . . the formation of a customs union or of a free trade area." These trading blocs allow members to grant each other even more favorable trade terms than those granted to either WTO members or to other most-favored-nation (MFN) countries. Of course, GATT cautions that "the purpose of a customs union or of a free trade area should be to facilitate trade between the constituent territories and not to raise barriers to the trade of other [WTO member countries]." The WTO stands ready to deal with conflicts and complaints that regional groups have become too protectionist.

This chapter examines how Canada, Mexico, and the United States have formed a regional trading bloc in North America. These countries share trade privileges with each other beyond what is required by GATT or the WTO. For instance, while Canada might impose a 15 percent import duty on a certain product coming from another WTO country, it may admit similar products from the United States or Mexico at a lower tariff rate, or for no tariff at all. Thus the world of doing business is greatly affected not only by global trading rules, but by regional rules as well. The trading bloc between Canada, Mexico, and the United States is known as the *North American Free Trade Area*. The purpose of the North American Free Trade Area is to spur trade and investment in North America, and to improve the standard of living throughout the continent.

## The North American Free Trade Area

Canada, Mexico, and the United States each have separate economic and political systems as well as different cultures, geographies, and climates. Together, they encompass a market of 370 million people, with $6.5 trillion in production. (References to dollars in this chapter refer to U.S. dollars, or their equivalent.) They have long had close trading relationships. Canada and the United States are far more similar to each other than to their southern neighbor. They are in advanced stages of economic development, with comparable levels of productivity and per capita gross domestic products of about $23,000. Mexico is a developing country with a 1994 per capita gross domestic product of about $4,300.

For many decades, Mexico had a tightly controlled and protected economy. Its policies restricted imports and discouraged foreign investment. Many key industries were (and some remain) in the hands of government-owned monopolies. Companies that wanted to do business there had to break through a mass of government bureaucracy red tape, trade barriers, corruption, and an outdated infrastructure. Hampered by inefficient industries, Mexico during the 1970s and early 1980s suffered low productivity, staggering rates of inflation (of several hundred percent per year), and overwhelming foreign debt. Its foreign income was almost totally dependent on exports of oil. New liberal policies in the late 1980s and 1990s opened the Mexican economy to trade and investment. Mexico's gross domestic product has grown rapidly. Benefiting from an influx of foreign capital, technology and management skills, Mexican companies have become far more efficient than before. Mexican exports are competitive on world markets, including Europe and Asia. As a result, Mexico has become less dependent on oil exports and now has a broader-based economy.

Canada and the United States are each other's largest trading partner. Many people are surprised to learn that the United States actually exports more goods to Canada ($114 billion) than to all the countries of the European Union combined, and more than twice as much as to Japan. The United States purchases slightly more merchandise from Canada ($129 billion) than it does from any other country, with Japan a close second. Based on figures contained in a 1997 report to Congress on NAFTA, Mexico is expected to become the number-two trading partner of the United States, supplanting Japan. (See the following information and statistics in Exhibits 14.1 and 14.2.)

Despite Mexico's continued economic growth over the last 10 years, it has suffered several setbacks. Mexico underwent a severe financial crisis in 1994 that rocked international financial markets. Economists believe the crisis was precipitated by Mexico's devaluation of its peso. The

United States arranged international financial guarantees worth $58 billion to support the Mexican peso, and the crisis was resolved. (In 1995 the leaders of the world's seven largest economies, known as G-7 nations, met in Canada in an effort to bolster the international monetary system in order to avert similar crises from occurring in other developing nations.) Trade and investment may suffer in Mexico in the next few years as a result of the crisis.

The United States has considerable cross-border investment in both Canada and Mexico. The largest U.S. investors in those countries are GM, Ford, and Chrysler, followed by a host of companies in the oil industry, computers, supermarkets, fast-food franchising, telecommunications, pharmaceuticals, retailing, and beverages. The President of the United States was required to report to Congress on NAFTA. President Clinton submitted the report in July 1997. (See excerpt in Exhibit 14.3 on page 457.)

## What Is NAFTA?

The North American Free Trade Area was created on January 1, 1994, by the *North American Free Trade Agreement,* both of which are called *NAFTA.* A *free trade area* is a group of two or more sovereign countries in which import duties and other trade barriers are reduced or eliminated. NAFTA is not a customs union or common market, as is the European Union. A *customs union* is a free trade area with a common external tariff; the European Union goes beyond a free trade area with its common economic and agricultural policies. On trade issues, the European Union deals with other countries as outsiders, and represents its members in trade negotiations at the World Trade Organization. NAFTA does not. NAFTA fosters trade and investment among Canada, Mexico, and the United States by reducing tariffs and nontariff barriers. It also facilitates transportation of goods, provision of services, and financial transactions among the three countries. Each country will generally continue to maintain its own tariff rates and quotas on imports from outside the area. (Actually, NAFTA countries have agreed to adopt a common external tariff on certain computer parts after the year 2004, but NAFTA is still not considered a customs

**EXHIBIT 14.1   Business Fact Sheet: Mexico (1996)**

**Profile/Economy**

**Population:**   91.6 million

**Capital:**   Mexico City

**Nationality:**   mestizo 60%, Amerindian 30%, white 9%, other 1%

**Language:**   Spanish, various Mayan dialects

**Religion:**   Roman Catholic 89%, Protestant 6%, Other 5%

**Currency:**   New peso

| **Unemployment Rate (%, official Mexican statistics)** (In billions of U.S. dollars unless otherwise stated) | **1992** | **1993** | **1994** | **1995** | |
|---|---|---|---|---|---|
| | 2.8 | 3.7 | 3.2 | 6.3 | |

| **U.S.-Mexico Trade** (In billions of U.S. dollars unless otherwise stated) | **1992** | **1993** | **1994** | **1995** | |
|---|---|---|---|---|---|
| Trade Balance | 5.4 | 1.7 | 1.3 | −15.4 | |
| U.S. Merchandise Exports to Mexico (FAS value) | 40.6 | 41.6 | 50.8 | 46.3 | |
| U.S. Merchandise Imports from Mexico (Customs value) | 35.2 | 40.0 | 49.5 | 61.7 | |

| **World Trade** (In billions of U.S. dollars unless otherwise stated) | **1991** | **1992** | **1993** | **1994** | **1995** |
|---|---|---|---|---|---|
| Total Exports (FOB, Mexican official statistics) | 42.7 | 46.2 | 51.9 | 60.9 | 79.5 |
| Total Imports (FOB, Mexican official statistics) | 49.9 | 62.1 | 65.0 | 79.3 | 72.5 |
| Trade Balance | −11.1 | −15.9 | 13.4 | −18.4 | 7.4 |

*Foreign Supplier Percentage Share of Mexican Imports (Mexican official statistics, 1995):*
1. United States (74.3%); 2. Japan (5.0%); 3. Germany (3.7%); 4. Canada (1.9%); 5. France (1.4%)

*Import Policy:*
Most Favored Nation tariffs range from 0 to 35 percent. Additional Taxes: 0.8% Customs Handling Fee; 15.0% Value Added Tax Licensing. Under NAFTA, Mexico retains the right until January 1, 2003 to require import permits for certain used goods (including computers and construction equipment). With the implementation of the North American Free Trade Agreement on January 1, 1994, 50% of all tariffs on U.S. industrial goods by value were eliminated. The remaining dutiable industrial goods will be subject to either a 5- or 10-year tariff phase-out period, while U.S. agricultural goods will be subject to five-, ten-, and fifteen-year tariff phase-out periods.

*Best 10 U.S. Export Prospects:*
Automotive Parts & Service Equipment, Franchising Services, Pollution Control Equipment, Chemical Production Machinery, Telecommunications Equipment, Building Materials, Management Consulting Services, Apparel, Aircraft and Parts, and Electronic Components.

| **Authorized Foreign Direct Investment** (In billions of U.S. dollars unless otherwise stated) | **1992** | **1993** | **1994** | **1995** |
|---|---|---|---|---|
| Cumulative Direct Foreign Investment in Mexico | 37.5 | 42.4 | 49.5 | 56.1 |
| U.S. Direct Investment in Mexico | 13.7 | 15.2 | 16.4 | NA |

*Other Principal Foreign Investors (percent of total through Dec. 1995):*
United Kingdom (7.2%), Holland (5.1%), Japan (5.0%), Germany (4.1%), Switzerland (3.5%), France (3.4%), Canada (2.0%).

**Commercial Information**

*Top U.S. Investors:*
General Motors of Mexico, Ford Motor Company, Chrysler of Mexico, IBM, Celanese Mexicana, Kimberly Clark, American Express, Anderson-Clayton, Xerox, Dupont, Hewlett-Packard, Vitronatic

SOURCES:   U.S. Department of Commerce; U.S. Embassy, Mexico City; Bank of Mexico; Government of Mexico.

**EXHIBIT 14.2    Business Fact Sheet:  Canada (1996)**

**Profile/Economy**

**Population:**   29,529,800 (December 1995)

**Capital:**   Ottawa

**Religion:**   Roman Catholic 42%, Protestant 40%

**Language:**   English and French

**Currency:**   Canadian dollar

**Nationality:**   British Isles origin 40%, French origin 27%, Other European 20%, Native American 1.5%, Other 11.5%

**Average Unemployment Rate (%)**

| (In billions of U.S. dollars unless otherwise stated) | 1991 | 1992 | 1993 | 1994 | 1995 |
|---|---|---|---|---|---|
| | 10.3 | 11.3 | 11.2 | 10.4 | 9.5 |

**Trade**

| (In billions of U.S. dollars unless otherwise stated) | 1991 | 1992 | 1993 | 1994 | 1995 |
|---|---|---|---|---|---|
| Canadian Total Merchandise Exports | 122.4 | 128.9 | 140.6 | 159.5 | 184.6 |
| Canadian Total Merchandise Imports | 119.2 | 123.4 | 133.2 | 148.5 | 164.1 |
| Trade Balance | 6.5 | 5.5 | 7.4 | 11.0 | 20.5 |
| U.S. Merchandise Exports to Canada | 85.1 | 90.6 | 100.2 | 114.8 | 126.9 |
| U.S. Merchandise Imports from Canada | 91.1 | 98.5 | 111.2 | 128.4 | 145.1 |

*Principal U.S. Exports to Canada (U.S. $billions, 1995):*
Machinery ($1.9), Cars/Other Motor Vehicles ($2.3), Electrical Products ($1.3), Plastic Products ($0.4), Optical and Medical Instruments ($0.3).

*Principal U.S. Imports from Canada (U.S. $billions, 1995):*
Cars/Other Motor Vehicles ($3.1), Mineral Fuel/Petroleum ($1.2), Machinery ($1.0), Paper Products ($0.6), Electrical Products ($0.5).

*Canadian Merchandise Trade Balance with Three Leading Trade Partners in Canadian $ (1995):*
United States (+33), Japan (+3), United Kingdom (−1).

*Import Policy:*
Most Favored Nation tariffs range from 0 to 25 percent.

*Additional Taxes:* 7% Goods and Services Tax; certain provinces assess sales taxes.

*Licensing:* Import permits are required for certain agricultural products, clothing and textile items, and steel products. Under the U.S.–Canada Free Trade Agreement (CFTA) and, subsequently, NAFTA, all tariffs on qualifying goods are traded between the U.S. and Canada were eliminated in stages. All dutiable products are assigned to the following staging categories: duty-free immediately (on January 1, 1989, with the implementation of the CFTA); elimination in five equal annual cuts, which became duty free on January 1, 1993; and elimination in ten equal annual cuts which became duty free on January 1, 1998.

*Best U.S. Export Prospects:*
Computer Software, Computers and Peripherals, Telecommunications Equipment, Pollution Control Equipment, Automotive Aftermarket Parts, Furniture, Medical Equipment, Electronic Components, Sporting Goods, Machine Tools and Metalworking Equipment, Materials Handling Machinery, Plastic Materials and Resins, Automotive Parts and Service Equipment, Apparel, Textile Fabrics, Building Products, Aircraft and Parts, Household Consumer Goods.

*(continued)*

**EXHIBIT 14.2** (continued)

| Foreign Direct Investment (In billions of U.S. dollars unless otherwise stated) | 1991 | 1992 | 1993 | 1994 | 1995 |
|---|---|---|---|---|---|
| Cumulative Direct Foreign Investment in Canada | 118.7 | 115.0 | 113.1 | 108.8 | 122.4 |
| U.S. Direct Investment in Canada | 75.5 | 73.2 | 73.3 | 74.6 | 82.3 |
| U.S. Percentage of Direct Foreign Investment | 63.6 | 63.7 | 64.8 | 64.9 | 65.0 |
| Canadian Direct Investment in the U.S. | 51.0 | 50.9 | 50.5 | 49.8 | 55.0 |

*Other Principal Foreign Investor (percent of total, 1994):*
United Kingdom 12.6%

**Commercial Information**

*Top U.S. Investors:*
General Motors of Canada, Ford Motor Company of Canada, Chrysler Canada, Imperial Oil (Exxon), IBM Canada, Canada Safeway, Amoco Canada Petroleum Company, Sears Canada, Maple Leaf Foods, Total Petroleum, Great Atlantic and Pacific Tea, Mitsui & Company, Honda Canada, BC Telecom, Cargill Limited, Consumers Gas, Canadian Ultramar, Price Costco Canada, Medis Health and Pharmaceutical, Pepsi Cola, DuPont Canada, McDonald's Restaurants, General Electric, Pratt and Whitney Canada.

SOURCES: U.S. Department of Commerce, U.S. Embassy-Ottawa Office of Canada, Statistics Canada, Bank of Canada.

union.) Each country will continue to establish its own economic policies and each country will represent itself in the WTO system.

**Survey of NAFTA's Coverage.** Historically, trade agreements focused on the lowering of tariffs, but NAFTA is a trade agreement that does more than just lower import duties among Canada, Mexico, and the United States. It liberalizes trade in goods, trade in services, cross-border investments, and more (see Exhibit 14.4 on page 460). It also addresses many regional issues that are of concern to the three countries. For instance, it contains specific provisions for protecting intellectual property rights. It makes cross-border investment easier, and serves to protect the interests of foreign investors from arbitrary government action. It allows easier access for business travel among the countries. NAFTA encourages cooperation among governments on setting antitrust policy (called *competition law* in many countries) to deal with monopolies and unfair methods of competition. NAFTA also has provisions concerning worker safety, child labor, and environmental protection. Thus, NAFTA is far broader in scope than most typical trade or investment agreements. Only the European Union treaties and perhaps GATT are as broad in scope as NAFTA.

## How NAFTA Came into Being

NAFTA was built upon the *U.S.–Canada Free Trade Agreement* (CFTA), which had been in effect since January 1, 1989. CFTA called for the gradual reduction of tariffs over a ten-year period and loosened restrictions on investment, government procurement, travel, and many other areas. CFTA also created a U.S.–Canadian Trade Commission and dispute settlement panels to settle trade disputes. Almost immediately after CFTA was established, the United States and Mexico began negotiating a trade agreement between themselves. Not wanting to be left out, Canada entered the negotiations. After four years of negotiations and political debate, and with CFTA as its prototype, NAFTA was born. NAFTA not only includes Mexico, but expands the terms of CFTA generally. It also addresses new issues, such as the protection of intellectual property, easing restrictions on financial services and trucking companies operating in North America, environmental protection, labor issues, and others. As of 1995 these three countries had opened negotiations to expand the agreement to include Chile and possibly other Latin American and Caribbean countries.

**The Political Debate: Pro NAFTA.** Although NAFTA had to be approved by legislatures in all

**EXHIBIT 14.3    Executive Summary:    Operation and Effect of the NAFTA**

TO THE CONGRESS OF THE UNITED STATES:

I am pleased to transmit the Study on the Operation and Effect of the North American Free Trade Agreement (NAFTA), as required by section 512 of the NAFTA Implementation Act (Public Law 103-182; 107 Stat. 2155; 19 U.S.C. 3462). The Congress and the Administration are right to be proud of this historic agreement. This report provides solid evidence that NAFTA has already proved its worth to the United States during the 3 years it has been in effect. We can look forward to realizing NAFTA's full benefits in the years ahead. . . .

**Trade in North America**

U.S. trade with Canada and Mexico is much larger relative to the size of these economies than with any other trading partners, in large part reflecting shared land borders and geographical proximity.

- In 1996, nearly one-third of U.S. two-way trade in goods with the world was with Canada and Mexico ($421 billion). Two-way trade with our NAFTA partners has grown 44 percent since the NAFTA was signed, compared with 33 percent for the rest of the world. Mexico and Canada accounted for 53 percent of the growth in total U.S. exports in the first four months of 1997.
- Canada was in 1993—and remains today—our largest trading partner, accounting for $290 billion in two-way trade in 1996. Between 1993 and 1996, U.S. goods exports to Canada were up by 33.6 percent to $134.2 billion.
- U.S. exports to Mexico grew by 36.5 percent (or $15.2 billion) from 1993 to a record high in 1996, despite a 3.3 percent contraction in Mexican domestic demand over the same period.
- Exports to Canada and Mexico supported an estimated 2.3 million jobs in 1996; this represents an increase of 311,000 jobs since 1993, 189,000 supported by exports to Canada and 122,000 by exports to Mexico.
- Exports to Mexico were up by 54.5 percent in the first four months of 1997 relative to the same period in 1993. In the first four months of 1997, U.S. exports to Mexico virtually equalled U.S. exports to Japan, our second largest market—even though Mexico's economy is one twelfth the size of Japan's.

**NAFTA's Effect on Trade Barriers**

Under NAFTA, Mexico has reduced its trade barriers on U.S. exports significantly and dismantled a variety of protectionist rules and regulations, while the United States—which started with much lower tariffs—has made only slight reductions.

- Before NAFTA was signed, Mexican applied tariffs on U.S. goods averaged 10 percent. U.S. tariffs on Mexican imports averaged 2.07 percent, and over half of Mexican imports entered the United States duty-free. (Figure 1.)
- Since NAFTA was signed, Mexico has reduced its average applied tariffs on U.S. imports by 7.1 percentage points, compared with a reduction of 1.4 percentage points in the United States. The United States would have made some of these tariff reductions under the Uruguay Round even in the absence of NAFTA.

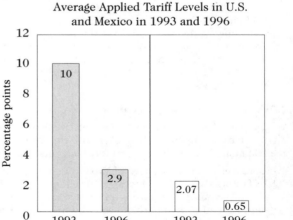

Average Applied Tariff Levels in U.S. and Mexico in 1993 and 1996

**Figure 1**

*(continued)*

**EXHIBIT 14.3** (continued)

### NAFTA's Effects on the U.S. Economy

Several studies conclude that NAFTA contributed to America's economic expansion. NAFTA had a modest positive effect on U.S. net exports, income, investment and jobs supported by exports.

- It is challenging to isolate NAFTA's effects on the U.S. economy, since NAFTA has only been in effect for three years, and events such as the severe recession in Mexico, the depreciation of the Mexican peso, and U.S. tariff reductions under the Uruguay Round have taken place during the same period.
- Nonetheless, several outside studies conclude that NAFTA has resulted in a modest increase in U.S. net exports, controlling for other factors. A new study by DRI estimates that NAFTA boosted real exports to Mexico by $12 billion in 1996, compared to a smaller real increase in imports of $5 billion, controlling for Mexico's financial crisis. An earlier study by the Dallas Federal Reserve finds that NAFTA raised exports by roughly $7 billion and imports by roughly $4 billion. The relatively greater effect on exports partly reflects the fact that under NAFTA Mexico reduced its tariffs roughly 5 times more than the United States.
- DRI estimates that NAFTA contributed $13 billion to U.S. real income and $5 billion to business investment in 1996, controlling for Mexico's financial crisis.
- These estimates suggest that NAFTA has boosted jobs associated with exports to Mexico between roughly 90,000 and 160,000. The Department of Commerce estimates that the jobs supported by exports generally pay 13 to 16 percent more than the national average for nonsupervisory production positions.

### NAFTA's Effects on the Mexican Economy

In 1995, Mexico experienced its most severe economic recession since the 1930s. Comparing Mexico's recovery in 1996 with Mexico's recovery from its last financial crisis in 1982, when NAFTA was not in effect, reveals that both the Mexican economy and American exports recovered more rapidly following the 1995 crisis than the 1982 crisis, in part because of the economic reforms locked in by NAFTA. Mexico's strong economic adjustment program and bilateral and multilateral financial support were also important.

- Following Mexico's 1982 financial crisis, Mexican output drifted down for nearly two years before rising again and did not recover to pre-crisis levels for five years. Although Mexican economic output dropped more quickly in 1995, it also rebounded more quickly, reaching pre-crisis peaks by the end of 1996. Similarly, following the 1982 crisis, it took Mexico 7 years to return to international capital markets, while in 1995, it took 7 months.
- Following Mexico's 1982 financial crisis, Mexico raised tariffs by 100 percent, and American exports to Mexico fell by half and did not recover for seven years. In 1995, Mexico continued to implement its NAFTA obligations even as it raised tariffs on imports from other countries. As a result, American exports recovered in 18 months and were up nearly 37 percent by the end of 1996 relative to pre-NAFTA levels, even though Mexican consumption was down 3.3 percent.

### NAFTA's Effects in Key Sectors

U.S. suppliers hold dominant shares of Mexico's import markets and in many sectors have expanded their shares significantly under NAFTA, at the expense of suppliers from other countries. In almost all sectors, Mexico has made large reductions in tariff barriers under NAFTA, compared with only slight U.S. reductions.

- Increases in the U.S. share of Mexico's import market are indicative of NAFTA's effects, since they control for factors that affect all foreign suppliers similarly, such as Mexico's recession. Since NAFTA went into effect, U.S. suppliers have seen their share of Mexico's import market grow from 69.3 percent to 75.5 percent, reflecting a 10 percentage point average tariff advantage over foreign suppliers. Mexico's share of American imports has risen from 6.9 percent to 9.3 percent.
- Reductions in Mexican barriers in key sectors have led to U.S. share gains in Mexican import markets. Since NAFTA was signed, the U.S. share of Mexican imports is up 17.2 percentage points to 86.4 percent in the textiles sector, where Mexico has cut tariffs by 10.7 percentage points under NAFTA. The U.S. share is up 19.2 percentage points to 83.1 percent in the transport equipment sector, where Mexico has cut tariffs 10.2 percentage points under NAFTA. And the U.S. share is up 5.7 percentage points to 74.3 percent in the electronic goods and appliances sector, where Mexico has cut tariffs by 9.0 percentage points under NAFTA.

*(continued)*

**EXHIBIT 14.3 (continued)**

- Under NAFTA, Mexican tariff reductions of 9.0 percentage points on electronic goods and appliances are more than 4 times greater than U.S. reductions; Mexican tariff reductions on transport equipment of 10.2 percentage points are more than 9 times greater than U.S. reductions; and Mexican tariff reductions of 6.2 percentage points in the chemicals industry are more than 10 times greater than U.S. reductions.
- Since NAFTA was signed, U.S. exports to Mexico have made significant gains in several sectors, despite the severe Mexican recession. However, analysis by the International Trade Commission (ITC) shows that data inadequacies at the sectoral level make it difficult to isolate the effects of NAFTA on absolute trade flows.
- In industries such as autos, chemicals, textiles and electronics, NAFTA is permitting American companies to achieve synergies across the North American market, improving their strategic positions abroad and contributing to strong growth in employment, production, and investment at home.
- In several industries that have experienced strong import growth from Mexico, Mexican imports have largely displaced imports from other regions, which have lower U.S. domestic content. In the apparel industry, the share of U.S. imports supplied by Mexico rose from 4.4 percent in 1993 to 9.6 percent in 1996, while the share of U.S. imports from China, Hong Kong, Taiwan and Korea fell from 39 percent in 1993 to 30 percent in 1996. (Figure 2.) Close to 2/3 of the value of Mexican apparel imports in 1996 was comprised of U.S. content. . . .

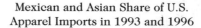

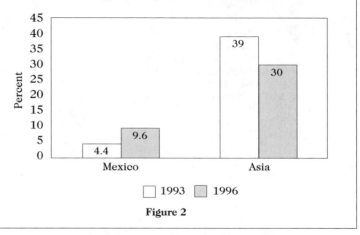

**Figure 2**

three countries, the greatest debate took place in the United States. NAFTA was a classic case of pitting free traders against protectionists, with the battle raging in the halls of Congress and on TV talk shows. It culminated with a televised debate, on the eve of the U.S congressional vote, between Vice President Albert Gore and the self-proclaimed leader of the anti-NAFTA forces, Ross Perot. The dispute was intensified because of the differences between the economy of Mexico and that of its wealthy and industrialized neighbors to the north. NAFTA supporters claimed that the agreement would permit U.S. firms to ship more high-value products to Mexico, adding good-paying jobs to the U.S economy. This argument was backed by U.S. exporters who railed against high Mexican tariffs and nontariff barriers. Exporters pointed out that U.S. shipments to Mexico faced tariffs two-and-a-half times the average U.S. rates. Moreover, under the *General-*

*ized System of Preferences,* more than half of Mexico's goods were already entitled to enter the U.S. duty free. They claimed that Mexico's import licensing scheme made shipping U.S. agricultural products there nearly impossible. Supporters also claimed that if U.S. firms did invest in manufacturing and assembly plants in Mexico, those manufacturers would serve as a springboard to markets throughout Latin America, such as Chile and Argentina. Next, they argued that closer ties to the United States would insure that Mexico's economic and political reforms of the 1980s would continue, and that its continued economic growth would ultimately benefit the United States. As a by-product of this economic growth, many hoped that illegal immigration from Mexico into the United States would be reduced.

**The Political Debate: Anti NAFTA.** NAFTA detractors in both the United States and Canada,

**EXHIBIT 14.4    Best Prospect for U.S. Product Exports, in North America, by Rank (1995)**

| Potential Exports to Canada | Potential Exports to Mexico |
|---|---|
| Computers and parts | Auto parts |
| Software | Electrical power systems |
| Auto after-market parts | Machine tools |
| Telecommunications equipment | Franchising services |
| Medical equipment | Pollution control equipment |
| Pollution control equipment | Chemical production machinery |
| Building products | Computers and parts |
| New auto parts | Telecommunications equipment |
| Plastic and resins | Wood products |
| Sporting goods | Paper |
| Electronic components | Management consulting services |
| Household consumer goods | Mining equipment |
| Apparel | Apparel |
| Materials handling equipment | Building products |
| Furniture | Aircraft and parts |
| Textile and fabrics | Agricultural machinery |
| Aircraft parts | Electronic components |
| Electrical power systems | Medical equipment |
| Machine tools | Textile and fabrics |
| Scientific equipment | Scientific equipment |
| Packaging equipment | Cosmetics |
| Industrial process controls | Hotel and restaurant equipment |
| Airport equipment | Toys and games |
| Dental equipment | Software |
| Veterinary equipment | Jewelry |

SOURCE:   U.S. Department of Commerce, 1995.

supported by labor unions and automobile and textile workers, claimed that NAFTA would cause U.S. firms to move jobs to Mexico to take advantage of low-cost labor (which can run as low as 10 to 20 percent of U.S. hourly wages for comparable manufacturing jobs). Labor groups were supported by environmental groups that feared U.S. firms would locate plants in Mexico to take advantage of weaker environmental laws, thus worsening the already serious pollution problem in Mexico and along the U.S.–Mexican border. Of course, Mexican firms feared that they would be unable to compete against the larger, better capitalized, and better managed U.S. and Canadian companies. Interestingly, people in both Canada and Mexico feared that U.S. products and advertising would eventually destroy their distinctive cultures and traditions.

**Regional versus Global Trade Liberalization.** A major criticism raised against NAFTA, and

equally applicable to any free trade area, is that it divides the world into regional trading blocs. Some people and nations fear that regional protectionism will threaten GATT's global trade liberalization achievements. Despite GATT's qualification that free trade areas not be used as a barrier to trade, goods not produced in the area will be discriminated against. An illustration can be found in the Caribbean countries who depend on the North American market for their exports. Although many Caribbean products enter the U.S. and Canada duty free, some products are excluded, such as watches, shoes, and clothing. Caribbean countries fear that these industries will move their operations to Mexico to take advantage of NAFTA. Many Caribbean governments are pushing for admission to NAFTA as a result. Interestingly enough, Japanese firms are apparently concerned about the same issue. Press reports in *The Journal of Commerce* and elsewhere indicate that a number of Japanese firms have already built facilities in Mexico, rather than in other Asian countries such as Thailand, in order to take advantage of NAFTA tariff rates, Mexico's low wage rates, and its close proximity to the U.S. and Canadian markets. (See the following article.)

---

*Foreign Accents*

---

# Asian Investment Floods into Mexican Border Region
## Access to U.S. Market Draws Makers of Televisions, Toys—and Shabu-Shabu

MEXICALI, MEXICO—Here along the dusty border where North meets South, there's a remarkable trade story unfolding. Call it, East meets West.

Along a 700-mile strip stretching from Tijuana to Ciudad Juarez, dozens of Asian manufacturers have swooped in to take advantage of cheap, abundant labor and Mexico's special trade relationship with the U.S.

Asian consumer-electronics giants such as **Matsushita Electric Industrial** Co., **Mitsubishi Electric** Corp., **Daewoo** Corp. and **Sony** Corp. have erected massive assembly plants up and down Mexico's border with the U.S., transforming the region into a virtual Detroit of television manufacturing. This year, more than 10 million sets will be produced in Northern Mexico.

But televisions aren't the only fruit of Asian investment. **Sinomex** SA, a toy company based in Hong Kong and Los Angeles, recently began manufacturing computer toys in Hermosillo, in the border state of Sonora. **Devanshi de Mexico** SA, an Indian company, makes blue jeans in San Luis Rio Colorado, just across the border from Yuma, Ariz. In the same small town, **Sana Internacional** SA, a joint Japanese-Mexican venture, processes and exports thinly sliced *shabu-shabu* beef to Tokyo and to Japanese restaurants in the U.S.

All together, Asians have invested some $2 billion in "brick-and-mortar" projects such as plants and equipment since the beginning of 1994, according to the Mexican government, much of it along the border, against some $10 billion from the U.S. But the official statistics understate the Asian contribution: Billions of dollars in additional funds have come from the U.S. subsidiaries of giant South Korean and Japanese exporters, sometimes recorded as U.S. investments in Mexico.

Of course, Mexico's international appeal has dimmed some in recent weeks, since a new leftist guerilla movement began staging assaults in southern Mexican states. And violence has touched Asian companies directly: Mamoru Konno, president of **Sanyo Electric** Co.'s Video Component USA unit in San Diego, was kidnapped by unknown assailants during a visit to the company's Tijuana facilities last month, and released after the company paid a ransom. Even so, there's no sign that the problems are discouraging investment, and several Asian companies have vowed to step up their efforts along the border.

Most of the new money is being poured into assembly plants known as *maquiladoras* which allow non-Mexican companies to import machinery and raw materials duty-free, then export finished products paying duty only on the value added by local labor.

For Asian companies seeking access to the U.S. market these days, there is often little alternative. With local wages rising in places such as South Korea and Taiwan, Mexican workers are a bargain, especially in the wake of a 1994 devaluation that cut the value of the Mexican peso nearly in half. Equally important is the impact of the North American Free Trade Agreement, which since 1994 has been lowering duties on goods traded among the U.S., Mexico and Canada. Thus, for goods they produce in Mexico and then export to the U.S., Asian companies generally pay duties only on the value of materials brought in from outside the three-country region.

For a typical consumer-electronics appliance, the economics are compelling. Alan Foster, vice president of Sanyo's Video Component USA, says the company can shave its costs by $10 to $20 per set by manufacturing televisions in Tijuana, thanks to savings on freight, labor and tariffs—a significant

*(continued)*

*(continued)*

amount for a product that retails for about $250. "It's basically a commodity, so any way you can save helps," he says.

Geography is another big reason for the Asian influx. The northwest corner of Mexico is handy to the U.S. interstate highway system, and just a few hours from Long Beach, Calif., the busiest Pacific port in the U.S.

It's also close to big Asian population centers in Southern California, another source of capital. Chinese and Taiwanese trading companies established in California to import goods from Asia are starting to encourage manufacturing operations across the border.

"Importers see the problems China has with Most Favored Nation status [with the U.S.] and they get nervous," says Tom Chang, San Diego branch manager for General Bank of Los Angeles, which was founded by Taiwanese immigrants in 1980 and caters to Asian businesses seeking a toe-hold in Mexico. "Essentially they want a second door."

**Delta Products,** a Taiwanese company with sales offices in Fremont, Calif., is typical of this breed. Delta invested $4 million for a factory in Nogales to make battery packs for computers. The company already manufactures offshore in Thailand and mainland China, but sourcing in Asia puts distance between the product and the end-user.

"We are looking to give better service to our customers, to have quick response and flexibility," says Parkson Hwang, manager of Delta's Nogales maquiladora. "You build in the Far East, you're too far away. You can't do last-moment modification while the product is on the ocean."

Another benefit of moving to Mexico, says Delta's President Elson Chang, was finding a multilingual Asian population close by in California. Delta's managers communicate with customers in English, suppliers in Chinese and laborers in Spanish. All senior staffers have to be able to speak either Spanish or English in addition to Chinese, says Mr. Chang. "Most of our managers are recruited in Southern California."

One of the fastest-growing sources of investment these days comes from smaller South Korean companies that have begun pouring in to service giant South Korean *chaebol,* or conglomerates, that have operations here. Over the past two years, companies like LG Electronics, Daewoo and **Samsung Electronics** Co. have been forcing suppliers to accompany them across the Pacific or risk losing their business.

"Korea's market is so small, everyone relies on exports," explains J. W. Cho, president of **GumSung Plastics** USA in Mexicali. GumSung uses robots and plastic-molding presses to churn out 25-inch and 27-inch frames for televisions and computer monitors. It can produce 1,500 frames a day, and sell all of them along the border.

GumSung, a small, family-owned plastics company with just 150 employees, spent $8 million in start-up costs, but felt it had little choice. Back in South Korea, Mr. Cho explains, it is getting harder and harder to find people willing to work for $45 a day, the prevailing South Korean wage, which is three times the rate in Mexicali.

What's more, he adds, small companies are being squeezed, forced to import laborers from other Asian countries. After GumSung factors in the cost of importing workers from Malaysia and Indonesia— some 20% of its work force in South Korea—the Mexican advantage looks even better.

At another plant, Suk Hee Jang explains that his company, **J. Cox Mexico** SA, also had to come here. J. Cox makes plastic-foam packaging for television sets. His company can produce a pair of plastic-foam pads here for 85 cents each, about the same cost as in South Korea. But he adds his clients "won't pay freight costs to ship it over."

*Joel Millman*

**Extension of NAFTA.**  President Clinton sought Fast Track authority (see Chapter 9) to negotiate an extension of NAFTA to include Chile and possibly other countries. During the 1996 presidential campaign, however, Congress was not interested in cooperating with him. Both Republicans and Democrats support and oppose the measure. Clinton promised between 1 and 4 billion dollars in worker aid over a period of 5 years to garner additional support for the measure. He has not succeeded at time of this writing. (See the following article).

**http://www.iep.doc.gov/nafta/nafta2.htm**
The site of the NAFTA home page, with links to NAFTA text, documents, facts, and other relevant sites.

*Foreign Accents*

# U.S. to Report to Congress
## NAFTA Benefits Are Modest

WASHINGTON, JULY 10—Four years after a bitterly divisive debate over how a free-trade pact with Mexico and Canada would affect American workers, the Clinton Administration will report to Congress on Friday that the North American Free Trade Agreement has so far generated modest benefits for the United States.

The report provides ammunition to both supporters and critics of the trade pact, and is unlikely to defuse the coming debate over the Administration's plan to extend free trade throughout the hemisphere.

"The facts point to only one conclusion; NAFTA hasn't measured up," said Representative Richard A. Gephardt of Missouri, the Democratic leader in the House and one of the most insistent critics of the agreement. "Before we proceed with further trade negotiations we need to insure that trade results in real progress for the broadest cross section of people."

The Administration report, the White House's first formal assessment of the trade agreement since it went into effect in January 1994, said exporters in many industries like textiles, transportation equipment and electronics had benefited from the reduction in Mexican tariffs and that the direct benefits to the American economy would mount over time.

The report said that the pact stimulated greater exports to Mexico, despite the deep financial crisis that engulfed Mexico in 1995 and turned a small American trade surplus with the country into a deficit that reached $17.5 billion last year.

The pact also increased United States exports to Canada during the last three years, the report said, although the trade deficit with Canada doubled from 1993 to 1996, to $21.7 billion, because of a surge of imports from that country.

But the Administration, which fought hard for approval of the pact despite strong opposition from labor unions, environmentalists and other Democratic constituencies, found only sketchy evidence that the agreement had helped American workers.

The Administration said studies it commissioned suggested that 90,000 to 160,000 American jobs relied on increased exports to Mexico that have come as a result of the pact.

The report did not provide—or even try to provide—a precise accounting of how many American jobs might have been lost as companies moved manufacturing to Mexico to take advantage of lower wages there. Official said there were largely unsolvable problems in generating an accurate estimate of job losses. But the report said the number of people whose jobs were lost to Canada or Mexico was probably somewhere between 32,000, the number of those who applied for unemployment and retraining benefits under Government programs for workers displaced by changing trade patterns with those countries and nearly 100,000, those who were certified by the Government as eligible for those programs, which often cover workers not directly affected by NAFTA.

While the Administration reiterated its long-held position that export-oriented jobs paid better than the national average for production workers, the report did not directly address whether the new jobs were better paying than those lost as companies shifted employment to take advantage of the new trade rules.

The trade agreement "has made a modest positive contribution to the U.S. economy in terms of net exports, G.D.P., employment and investment," said the report, which the Administration is required to submit to Congress.

*(continued)*

*(continued)*

While upbeat about the long-term outlook for the trade pact, the Administration report largely avoided the kinds of sweeping claims made on its behalf in 1993 when President Clinton rallied support over the intense opposition of critics who contended that free trade with Mexico would send jobs streaming south of the border. Supporters argued at the time that the agreement would create hundreds of thousands of jobs even after accounting for jobs lost; critics said the effect would be precisely the reverse.

The Administration's conclusions are largely in line with those of the last major study of NAFTA, issued last year by researchers at the University of California at Los Angeles. The U.C.L.A. study found that the trade pact's effect on employment in the United States was probably a "moderately positive number."

But critics of NAFTA, including unions, industries subject to greater competition and environmental watchdogs, continue to argue that the pact has been harmful to American interests and that it is a flawed model for the Administration's plans to extend free-trade agreements throughout the hemisphere.

"Wages and living standards have seen downward pressure in all three countries, and workers' rights and bargaining power have been weakened," said a report issued recently by a coalition including labor-backed groups, environmentalists and other opponents of the pact.

"For the average citizen of any of the three signatory countries, NAFTA has been a failure," said the opponents' study, which was compiled in anticipation of the Administration's report by groups including the labor-backed Economic Policy Institute, the International Labor Rights Fund, Public Citizen's Global Trade Watch and the Sierra Club.

The Administration said a study commissioned from DRI/McGraw Hill, the economic consulting firm, found that exports to Mexico from the United States last year were $12 billion higher than they would have been without NAFTA, after factoring out the effects of the Mexican economic crisis of 1995. The corresponding increase in imports from Mexico because of the trade pact was $5 billion, the study found.

The Administration also cited a study by the Federal Reserve Bank of Dallas that found a $7 billion increase in American exports attributable to NAFTA, and a $4 billion increase in imports.

The report said that based on figures from the first four months of the year, Mexico would likely pass Japan to become the nation's No. 2 trading partner, behind Canada.

The report said tariff reductions and other market-opening steps would be phased in over the next 12 years, so it might be too early to assess the accord's full impact.

It said that the short-run effect was to increase United States gross domestic product by $13 billion last year, a small amount in an $8 trillion economy. Gains could increase to $40 billion a year in the long run, it said.

*Richard W. Stevenson*

# Survey of Trade and Tariff Provisions

NAFTA will gradually eliminate tariffs and non-tariff barriers to trade on North American-made products sold in North America. Tariff levels will fall below the MFN rate or the rate applicable to other WTO member countries. NAFTA does not raise tariffs on non-North American products; all provisions of NAFTA are in compliance with GATT/WTO requirements. In many cases NAFTA's rules are more liberal than GATT and specifically address the issues of regional importance in North America.

## National Treatment

NAFTA's *national treatment* principle is similar to that found in GATT. It states that once goods arrive from another NAFTA country, they must be treated without discrimination and no differently than domestically made goods. So, if the United States imports taco shells from Mexico, it cannot require that only Mexican-made taco shells contain 90 percent cornmeal without setting the same standard for U.S.-made taco shells. Of course, the rule has wide application to all U.S. laws, regulations, and taxes. This provision also applies to regulations of individual U.S. states and Canadian provinces.

## Tariff Elimination

In 1989, the U.S.–Canadian Free Trade Agreement set out a ten-year timetable for the elimination of import tariffs on North American goods between the United States and Canada. For example, tariffs on computers, subway cars, furniture, unprocessed fish, leather, and most machinery have already been eliminated. Tariffs on most agricultural products, steel, textiles and apparel, softwood, plywood, tires, and other products will be eliminated by 1999. The NAFTA agreement continues that same schedule as set between the United States and Canada, and also sets timetables for eliminating tariffs in trade with Mexico.

When NAFTA became effective in 1993, it eliminated many tariffs on North American goods immediately. After five years, 65 percent of tariffs will be eliminated. The remainder are scheduled to be phased out over a period ranging from ten to fifteen years, depending on the product. The fifteen-year phase-out period will apply to certain sensitive industries, such as watches, ceramic tile, shoes, tuna, orange juice, sugar, and some fruits and vegetables. The phase-out can be speeded up by agreement, however, and many industries are asking their governments to do so. The elimination of tariffs applies only to products that are really products of Canada, Mexico, or the United States. A foreign product cannot simply be channeled through one North American country for sale in another North American country to avoid the payment of duties. For example, European or Asian products cannot be brought into Canada and then imported duty-free into the United States as a product of Canada. In order to know which products qualify for NAFTA's duty free treatment, one will have to consult the applicable rule of origin. Rules of origin are discussed in the next section.

**Elimination of Nontariff Barriers.** Most quotas, import licenses, and other quantitative restrictions will be eliminated within five years under NAFTA. Special rules allow each country to impose import restrictions to protect human, animal, or plant life, or the environment. Other special rules affect key economic sectors, including automobiles, agriculture, energy and textiles.

NAFTA prohibits new *export taxes* on goods, unless the taxes are also applied to similar goods sold for domestic consumption (although Mexico can stop the export of food in cases of critical shortages). *Customs user fees*—fees imposed on importers to help fund the cost of customs enforcement and ports services—will be eliminated by 1999. NAFTA also addresses issues related to customs administration, the public disclosure of customs regulations, fairness-in-labeling requirements for products, and other barriers to trade.

> **http://www.sice.oas.org/trade/nafta/ naftatce.stm**
> *Provides an index for the text of NAFTA. Select Articles from Section B on Tariffs.*

## Rules of Origin

Rules of origin were introduced in the last chapter and are a critical issue to importers and exporters. Businesspeople need to understand and be able to apply the rules of origin on products. This is the only way to determine the rate of duty or even quotas that might apply to the product being bought or sold. Thus, rules of origin partly determine the *true cost* of an imported product. Companies seeking a source for goods or materials will look to suppliers in countries that can provide the products needed at the lowest cost (considered together with a host of other factors such as quality, delivery, and service). Ultimately, the cost differences in sourcing goods from different countries will influence investment decisions, such as where companies locate their own factories and plants. Rules of origin, for example, have spurred Japanese automobile companies to build plants in the United States.

Because of the importance of knowing the country of origin in advance, businesspeople often seek binding rules from U.S. Customs Service on the origin of products to reduce the risk in a transaction. NAFTA's tariff provisions apply only to goods originating in North America. Companies cannot simply ship goods from, say, Europe to Canada and then re-export them to the United States as products of Canada, even if the product undergoes some minor changes in Canada or is relabeled or repackaged. A product labeled "Made in U.S.A." does not assure a purchaser that it will receive NAFTA tariff rates. Only goods that qualify under NAFTA's rules of origin can obtain NAFTA tariff rates. NAFTA sets out several rules of origin to determine whether a good produced in Canada, Mexico, or the United States qualifies for NAFTA tariff treatment. The most important general rules are (1) the goods are *wholly produced or obtained* in Canada, Mexico, or the United States; and (2) the goods contain nonoriginating inputs (components or raw materials), but meet the *Annex 401 rule of origin*.

## Goods Wholly Produced or Obtained in North America

NAFTA applies to goods wholly produced or obtained in North America. These goods may not contain any non-North American parts or materials. NAFTA Article 415 states that the qualifications apply only to minerals mined in North America, vegetables grown in North America, live animals born and raised in North America, fish and fish products, waste, and scrap derived from production in North America. "Produced or obtained" does not mean "purchased." The definition also includes goods produced in North America *exclusively* from the raw materials just mentioned. Thus, NAFTA applies to coal mined in Tennessee, lead mined in Canada, cotton grown in Mississippi, and cattle born in Mexico and raised in Mexico or Texas. It also includes silver jewelry made in Arizona from silver mined in Mexico or taco shells made in Mexico entirely from corn grown in Iowa. The producer, however, must be able to trace *all inputs* to raw materials mined, grown, or born in North America.

## Annex 401 Rule of Origin

Chapter Thirteen discussed the *substantial transformation test* that courts use to determine the country of origin of goods. This test is difficult to apply, and different courts often come up with different results. The variation in court decisions leads to great uncertainty in applying the test to any given case and complicates importers' sourcing decisions. NAFTA avoids this problem by setting out a simpler rule for when a foreign or non-North American product is "transformed" into a product of North America. NAFTA substitutes a tariff classification change for the vague substantial transformation test. When non-North American goods or materials are brought into a NAFTA country, they can be transformed into a product of North America as long as each non-North American input undergoes a tariff classification change as specified in NAFTA Annex 401. The Annex 401 rules of origin may be based on either a *change in tariff classification,* a *regional value-content requirement,* or both, depending on the requirements for that particular product.

**Changes in Tariff Classification.** To know if a product has undergone a change in tariff classification, importers and exporters must refer to the particular rule for their product in Annex 401. This judgment requires a good understanding of the *Harmonized Tariff Schedules* (HTS), as discussed in the preceding chapter. The HTS system is used by Canada, Mexico, and the United States. First, importers and exporters must know the HTS classification of the parts, materials, or goods brought into one of the NAFTA countries. Then they must determine the HTS classification of the goods after processing in that NAFTA country. If the finished goods are then shipped to another NAFTA country they will only qualify for NAFTA tariff treatment if the processing resulted in a change in tariff classification (sometimes called a *tariff-shift*) as specified in Annex 401. The following example demonstrates how a product's tariff classification can change.

Recall that the harmonized system breaks down product classifications into 10 digits, as follows:

*Chapter:*  first 2 digits

*Heading:*  4 digits

*Subheading:*  6 digits

*Tariff item:*  8 digits

*Statistical break:*  10 digits

Countries that have adopted the HTS system have "harmonized" their classification of products internationally at the subheading level. After the first six digits, each country assigns its own numbers. For example, a down-filled comforter (HTS 9404.90.9005) is classified in chapter 94 (which covers a conglomerate of unrelated manufactured articles, including furniture), heading 9404 (covering bedding and similar furnishings, stuffed), subheading 9404.90 (comforters and similar textile articles), and tariff item 9404.90.9005 (down filled comforters).

NAFTA rules of origin require knowing the tariff classification at least to the subheading level. For instance, consider pastries that are made in Canada for shipment to the United States. Pastries, breads, cakes, and biscuits fall under subheading 1905.90. Assume their only non-North American input is flour, imported from Europe. The Annex 401 rule of origin for subheading 1905.90 states that the item will be treated as a North American product if it undergoes "A change to heading 1902 through 1905 from any other chapter." The pastries would qualify for NAFTA tariff treatment because the European-made flour was classified outside of HTS chapter 19. However, the baker must be careful. If the pastries had been made from a prepared mix (containing flour, shortening, sugar, baking powder, etc.), they would not qualify as a North American product because mixes are classified under chapter 19, the same chapter as the pastries themselves.

**Regional Value Content Requirement.** For most products undergoing a transformation in North America, the rule of origin will be based on its tariff classification. In limited cases, NAFTA requires a specified amount of *regional value content* (a similar rule is used for trade in automobiles and parts). For example, a rule might require that at least 50 percent of the value of a

finished product be North American. Regional value may be calculated either by *transaction value* or *net cost* methods. Transaction value is the price actually paid for a good. The net cost method removes sales and marketing costs, shipping costs, and certain other expenses from the calculation. The value of non-North American materials is then subtracted from the total cost of the product. Usually the regional value content must be at least 60 percent for transaction value method and at least 50 percent for the net cost method. The value of packaging materials and containers in which a product is packaged for retail sale must be taken into account as either North American or non-North American materials, as the case may be.

**Transaction Value Formula**

$$RVC = \frac{TV - VNM}{TV} \times 100$$

**Net Cost Formula**

$$RVC = \frac{NC - VNM}{NC} \times 100$$

$RVC$ = Percent regional value content

$TV$ = Transaction value of good, FOB basis

$VNM$ = Value of nonoriginating material

$NC$ = Net cost of good

The importer may generally choose which method it wants to use. (For an example of the calculations, see Exhibit 14.5.) For automobiles and parts, shoes, and word processing machines, however, only the net cost method may be used.

**Goods With Minimal Amounts of Non-North American Materials.** If the amount of non-North American materials in a finished product is minimal (defined as less than seven percent of the total cost of the product), the product will still be eligible for NAFTA tariff rates. Thus if Japanese thread is used to sew together the sleeves on (an otherwise 100 percent) Mexican-made jacket, and the thread is less than seven percent of the total cost of the jacket, the finished jacket can be exported to Canada or the United States under NAFTA tariff rates.

**EXHIBIT 14.5   Rules of Origin Example**

**Product:**   Wooden Furniture (HS # 9403.50)

**Non-North American Inputs:**   Parts of furniture classified in 9403.90

**Rule of Origin:**

"A change to subheading 9403.10 through 9403.80 from any other chapter; or

A change to subheading 9403.10 through 9403.80 from subheading 9403.90, provided there is a regional value-content of not less than:

a) 60 percent where the transaction value is used, or

b) 50 percent where the net-cost method is used."

**Explanation:** Wooden furniture can qualify for NAFTA tariff preference under two scenarios—a tariff shift, or a combination of a tariff shift and regional value content requirement.

The first option—the tariff-shift rule—requires that all non-originating inputs be classified outside of HS chapter 94 (furniture and bedding). Since the non-originating inputs (furniture parts) are classified in chapter 94, (subheading 9403.90), then the product cannot qualify based on tariff shift. However, it may still qualify based on the second part of the rule.

The second option has two components—a tariff shift requirement, and a regional value content requirement. The tariff shift requirement is satisfied since the non-originating input (furniture parts) is classified in subheading 9403.90 as specified by the rule. The product must meet its regional value content requirement using the transaction value or the net cost methodology.

Given the following values, furniture qualifies for NAFTA tariff preference using the net cost methodology. The calculation is found below, with the following example.

| | |
|---|---|
| Producer's Net Cost | $182.00 each (not including shipping, packing royalties, etc.) |
| Transaction Value | $200.00 each piece |
| Value of Non-Originating Parts | $90.00 |

---

**Transaction Value Method**

$$\frac{(200 - 90)}{200} \times 100 = 55$$

Good does not qualify under transaction value method, because it does not have at least 60 percent regional value content.

**Net Cost Method**

$$\frac{(182 - 90)}{182} \times 100 = 50.5$$

Good qualifies under net cost regional value requirement because it has at least a 50 percent regional value content.

SOURCE:   U.S. Department of Commerce, 1995.

## Understanding the Mexican Tariff Schedules

Mexico, like Canada and the United States, has adopted the harmonized tariff system, which means that the classification of products, up to the six-digit subheading level, will be the same in all three countries. Of course, the tariff rates will be different, until such time as they are completely eliminated under NAFTA over the 10- to 15-year phase-out period. U.S. exporters can ob-tain information on exporting to Mexico from several U.S. government sources, particularly the U.S. Department of Commerce. But the Mexican customs broker representing the importer should be able to provide more information on product classification, tariff rates, required customs documentation, and shipping and warehousing arrangements. Also, as in the United States and Canada, the Mexican customs authorities (the *Administración Especial Juridica de Ingresos*) issue legally binding rulings on the classification of products. With this in mind, the following example should aid in understanding the Mexican tariff schedules. Assume that the company, DownPillow, Inc. wants to export down comforters or pillows—with 100 percent North American content—to Mexico. The proper HTS classification subheading is 9404.90. Exhibit 14.6 is an excerpt from the Mexican tariff schedule for heading 9404. The product heading and subheadings are on the left, with the description in Spanish. The *Tasa Base* is the base rate for imports. Mexican base tariffs are generally either 5, 10, 15, or 20 percent. It is followed by two columns representing the phase-out tariffs for those products originating in the United States or Canada. The phase-out period is indicated by the codes A, B, B6, or C.

Once the exporter knows that the base rate is 20 percent and the phase-out code is B6 (for U.S. comforters), it can consult the phase-out schedule. DownPillow learns that the 1994 tariff rate is 16 percent, and that the rate declines in equal amounts until it reaches zero in 1999 (similar charts are used for all codes and base rates; see Exhibit 14.7.)

In Mexico, all imports must be handled by a licensed Mexican customs broker. All tariffs and other custom fees are paid by the broker to a Mexican bank, and not by the importer. (In addition to the duty, Mexico currently imposes a 0.8 percent customs processing fee and a 10 percent value-added tax.) Mexican customs will not release the goods to the importer unless the broker can produce the receipt showing that the duties are paid. When the bank remits payment to the government, the importer reimburses the broker.

## The NAFTA Certificate of Origin

As discussed in the preceding chapter, a U.S. importer is responsible for making entry of goods and paying the import duties owed. Under NAFTA, the exporter in Canada, Mexico, or the United States must determine whether its shipment qualifies for NAFTA's preferential tariff treatment. This information must be documented in the NAFTA *Certificate of Origin* (see Exhibit 14.8). The exporter must then provide the importer with the certificate of origin so that

---

**EXHIBIT 14.6   NAFTA Tariff Phase-out Schedule for Mexico**

| Fracción Arancelaria | Descripción | Tasa Base | *Productos de* EE.UU. (I) | Canadá (II) |
|---|---|---|---|---|
| 94.04 | SOMIERES; ARTICULOS DE CAMA Y ARTICULOS SIMILA RES (POR EJEMPLO: COLCHONES, CUBREPIES. EDRE DONES, COJINES, PUFES, ALMOHADAS), CON MUELLES O BIEN RELLENOS O GUARNECIDOS INTERIORMENTE CON CUALQUIER MATERIA, INCLUIDOS LOS DE CAUCHO O DE PLASTICO CELULARES, RECUBIERTOS O NO. | | | |
| 9404.10 | -Somieres. | | | |
| 9404.10.01 | Somieres. | 20 | A | A |
| | -Colchones: | | | |
| 9404.21 | —De caucho o plástico celulares, recubiertos o no. | | | |
| 9404.21.01 | Colchones. | 20 | C | C |
| 9404.21.02 | Colchonetas. | 20 | A | A |
| 9404.29 | —De otras materias. | | | |
| 9404.29.99 | De otras materias. | 20 | C | C |
| 9404.30 | —Sacos (bolsas) de dormir. | | | |
| 9404.30.01 | Sacos (bolsas) de dormir. | 20 | A | A |
| 9404.90 | -Los demás. | | | |
| 9404.90.01 | Almohadas, almohadones, cojines. | 20 | B6 | C |
| 9404.90.99 | Los demás. | 20 | B6 | C |

**EXHIBIT 14.7** **Mexican Phase-Out for Textile Products Coded B6 (see tariff schedule to determine code)**

| Tasa Base | 1994 | 1995 | 1996 | 1997 | 1998 | 1999 |
|-----------|------|------|------|------|------|------|
| 20%       | 16%  | 12.8% | 9.6% | 6.4% | 3.2% | 0%   |

the importer can claim the tariff preference. The certificate of origin is required unless the shipment is of a "low value." Mexico defines low value as $1,000. In Canada, low value is 1,600 Canadian dollars, and in the United States it is $2,500. If the shipment is less than $1,000, the statement of North American origin may be included on the invoice, as long as the small shipment is not part of a larger series of shipments. The importer must be in possession of an original certificate of origin before claiming the NAFTA tariff preference, and it must have the exporter's original signature. Field 7 of Exhibit 14.8, titled "Preference Criterion," is the place that the importer states the rule of origin applicable to the shipment. (Note: Codes are given in the instructions on the reverse side of the certificate, but are not included in this book.) The importer must provide this information to their customs authorities on import. If the importer cannot produce the certificate of origin, then the higher MFN rate of duty will apply. The importer, however, has up to one year to file for a refund of duties paid if they later receive a certificate of origin. The certificate can be completed either in the language of the country of export or country of import, at the exporter's discretion. It may cover a single shipment or multiple shipments of identical goods; a *blanket certificate* covers multiple shipments and is good for up to twelve months. A certificate is not required for temporary imports, such as those sent for repair or servicing. In the United States, the importer is required to keep the certificate on file for no fewer than five years.

Generally, the certificate is prepared by the producer of the goods. If the exporter is not the producer but an intermediary, then the exporter should be sure of where the goods originated or be reasonable in relying on the producers representation of where the goods originated. Intermediaries will be safer if they have the certificate

filled out by the producer. An exporter that does not want to disclose to the importer who actually produced the goods may state that the name is "Available to customs on request" (see field 3, Exhibit 14.8).

## Standards and Technical Barriers to Trade

All countries can maintain product regulations to protect public health, consumer safety, the environment, and areas of public welfare. However, NAFTA encourages that standards and technical regulations not be used as a nontariff barrier. For instance, Mexico cannot set unnecessary technical regulations and long, drawn-out approval processes for the sale of telecommunications equipment only to discourage entry to the Mexican market by U.S. or Canadian firms. Technical requirements for telecommunications equipment such as telephones may only require that the equipment not harm the telephone network in order to be approved for use or sale. Standards can be set for energy efficiency in appliances, safety in automobiles, or chemical additives in food. NAFTA requires that each country notify the others when the development of a technical regulation or standard begins, give public notice of the proposed regulations, and provide a 60-day comment period for interested firms or individuals to submit their arguments and concerns.

Standards and technical regulations in Mexico are called *normas. Normas* are either mandatory—the *Normas Oficiales Mexicanas,* or "official norms"—or voluntary. They are drafted by dozens of committees operating under the aegis of the *Secretaria de Comercio y Formento Industrial,* commonly called *Secofi,* the Mexican Ministry of Commerce and Industrial Development. *Normas* are published in the *Diario Oficial,* which is similar to the *Federal Register* in the United States. Mexico

**EXHIBIT 14.8** **NAFTA Certificate of Origin**

## DEPARTMENT OF THE TREASURY
## UNITED STATES CUSTOMS SERVICE

Approved through 12/31/96
OMB No. 1515-0204
See back of form for Paper-
work Reduction Act Notice.

### NORTH AMERICAN FREE TRADE AGREEMENT
# CERTIFICATE OF ORIGIN

*Please print or type*       19 CFR 181.11, 181.22

| 1.EXPORTER NAME AND ADDRESS | 2. BLANKET PERIOD (DD/MM/YY) |
| --- | --- |
| | FROM |
| TAX IDENTIFICATION NUMBER: | TO |
| 3. PRODUCER NAME AND ADDRESS | 4. IMPORTER NAME AND ADDRESS |
| TAX IDENTIFICATION NUMBER: | TAX IDENTIFICATION NUMBER: |

| 5. DESCRIPTION OF GOOD(S) | 6. HS TARIFF CLASSIFICATION NUMBER | 7. PREFER-ENCE CRITERION | 8. PRODUCER | 9. NET COST | 10. COUNTRY OF ORIGIN |
| --- | --- | --- | --- | --- | --- |
| | | | | | |

SAMPLE

I CERTIFY THAT:
• THE INFORMATION ON THIS DOCUMENT IS TRUE AND ACCURATE AND I ASSUME THE RESPONSIBILITY FOR PROVING SUCH REPRESENTATIONS. I UNDERSTAND THAT I AM LIABLE FOR ANY FALSE STATEMENTS OR MATERIAL OMISSIONS MADE ON OR IN CONNECTION WITH THIS DOCUMENT;

• I AGREE TO MAINTAIN, AND PRESENT UPON REQUEST, DOCUMENTATION NECESSARY TO SUPPORT THIS CERTIFICATE, AND TO INFORM, IN WRITING, ALL PERSONS TO WHOM THE CERTIFICATE WAS GIVEN OF ANY CHANGES THAT COULD AFFECT THE ACCURACY OR VALIDITY OF THIS CERTIFICATE;

• THE GOODS ORIGINATED IN THE TERRITORY OF ONE OR MORE OF THE PARTIES, AND COMPLY WITH THE ORIGIN REQUIREMENTS SPECIFIED FOR THOSE GOODS IN THE NORTH AMERICAN FREE TRADE AGREEMENT, AND UNLESS SPECIFICALLY EXEMPTED IN ARTICLE 411 OR ANNEX 401, THERE HAS BEEN NO FURTHER PRODUCTION OR ANY OTHER OPERATION OUTSIDE THE TERRITORIES OF THE PARTIES; AND

• THIS CERTIFICATE CONSISTS OF _____ PAGES, INCLUDING ALL ATTACHMENTS.

| 11. | 11a. AUTHORIZED SIGNATURE | 11b. COMPANY | |
| --- | --- | --- | --- |
| | 11c. NAME (Print or Type) | 11d. TITLE | |
| | 11e. DATE (DD/MM/YY) | 11f. TELEPHONE ▷ NUMBER | *(Voice)* — *(Facsimile)* |

has hundreds, if not thousands, of *normas* that apply to both goods and services, and many U.S. exporters argue that these are really used to discourage the sale of their goods in Mexico.

In 1995 the U.S. *National Trade Estimate Report on Foreign Trade Barriers,* submitted to Congress by the U.S. Trade Representative, focused on Mexico's standards as an unfair barrier to trade. The report cited Mexico's lack of notification to U.S. parties before changing its regulations—for instance, Mexico changed its import requirements on one day and put them into force the next day, leaving no time for companies to comply. The report also cited the inconsistency in which customs agents apply the law. Moreover, the report maintained that Mexico makes U.S. exporters submit their products for testing and certification only to Mexican labs, and requires detailed inspections of goods at border check-points, tying up shipments for excessively long periods.

## Marking and Labeling Rules

Another controversial area of customs law has been Mexico's marking and labeling requirements. The *Normas Oficiales Mexicanas,* promulgated by *Secofi,* contains specific labeling requirements for certain products (e.g., appliances, electronics, textiles, and food products). All others fall into the more general requirements for general merchandise. Mexico's labeling requirements are strict and often burdensome to U.S. and Canadian exporters. The cost of compliance is often so difficult that many small exporters cannot afford to sell their products there. Mexico has dictated the content, form, size, and even the appearance, of product labels. The Spanish language labels must include the generic name of the product, the name and address of the importer and exporter, contents, and the country of origin. Instructions and warnings as to use and care of the product may be enclosed separately, but an invitation to read them must appear on the label. Product warranties must be clearly stated. The following incident illustrates the confusion of Mexican labeling laws: *Secofi* announced in the *Diario Oficial* that it would require that all labels be preprinted on the product or package itself, and not "stickers." Apparently the agency did not want Spanish language labels stuck over English

language packaging. After a year of uncertainty and haggling, the *Bureau of National Affairs* reported that *Secofi* would probably accept stickers as long as they were as large and "as pretty" as the English language print. Exporters to Mexico need to seek good advice in labeling and marking products to avoid long delays in getting their goods to markets in Mexico. (Some products are exempt from labeling, such as bulk commodities, products destined for industrial use, goods in a passenger's luggage, personal items shipped home by a person domiciled in Mexico, samples that have been destroyed or mutilated to prevent sale, live animals, books, and others.)

> **http://www.sice.oas.org/trade/nafta/naftatce.stm**
> The index for NAFTA; select Articles from Chapter 4—Rules of Origin.

# Trade in Goods:  Sectoral Issues

*Sectoral issues* are issues of concern to a particular industrial, agricultural, or service sector of the economy. Examples might be automobile manufacturing and assembly, telecommunications, agriculture, or financial services. NAFTA has specific provisions that reduce tariffs and liberalize trade and investment in these and other sectors. The most important and most controversial industry in North American trade relations is motor vehicles and parts.

## Trade in Motor Vehicles and Parts

Perhaps no other sector will be affected by NAFTA as much as the automobile industry. Mexico had long tried to manage its automobile industry through strict trade and investment restrictions. For instance, prior to NAFTA automobiles sold in Mexico had to contain a minimum of 36 percent Mexican-made parts. Tariffs on cars imported into Mexico were 20 percent, and 13.2 percent on automobile parts (as compared to a 2.5 percent tariff on the import of Mexican-made cars into the United States). The result was a Mexican auto parts industry that was largely inefficient and noncompetitive in world markets. Of course, many modern automotive parts and assembly plants in Mexico are owned and operated by U.S., European, and Japanese firms. As discussed later in this chapter, cars assembled there cannot be released for sale into Mexico without meeting Mexican customs regulations and without the payment of duties. Cars assembled there from U.S. parts can only be returned to the U.S. at lowered tariff rates if they meet the strict requirements of U.S. customs law.

Canada and the United States eliminated duties on imports of their automobiles under CFTA. NAFTA eliminates tariffs and restrictions on Mexican auto trade over a ten-year period. First, U.S. duties on imports of passenger cars from Mexico were removed immediately. Duties on light trucks were reduced from 25 percent to 10 percent and will be phased out over five years. Mexico immediately reduced its 20 percent tariff on cars and its 13.2 percent tariff on auto parts by one half, with the remaining duties eliminated over ten years. Canada will also eliminate its duties on Mexican autos over the same period. NAFTA also phases out restrictions on the cross-border trade in used cars.

**Special Rules of Origin for Automobiles.** To qualify for duty-free treatment, a motor vehicle that is made or assembled in North America must contain a specified percentage of North American content. For motor vehicles, these rules supersede the regional value content rules for other products, discussed earlier in the chapter.

Beginning in 1993, and for four years, automobiles and light trucks must contain at least 50 percent North American content. During the next four years automobiles and light trucks must contain at least 56 percent North American content. In 2001, the content requirement will rise to 62.5 percent. Automobile manufacturers building factories to produce a new model not yet made in North America will have to meet an accelerated schedule, meeting the 62.5 percent requirement by 1999. The same content requirements apply to engines and transmissions for these vehicles. Other vehicles will have to meet a 60 percent content requirement. One of the major purposes of local content rules has been to encourage investment in North America. As Japanese plants began to build vehicles in North America, their use of North American parts increased. Both U.S. and Japanese transplant auto makers are not expected to have trouble meeting the content requirements.

## Trade in Textiles and Apparel

No other trade sector is as complex or as highly regulated as trade in textiles. The NAFTA textile provisions are of major significance because of the U.S. position as a major textile importer (with a large domestic industry arguing for protection from low-cost imports), and the role of Mexican plants in assembling apparel for sale in the United States. Imports of Mexican textiles and apparel were limited by quotas in the United States and Canada. Mexico has also had 20 percent tariffs on U.S. textile products. NAFTA provisions will take precedence over these tariffs, quotas, and other laws applicable to the textile trade.

Canada, Mexico, and the United States will phase out, over a period of ten years, all tariffs on textile and apparel goods that meet the North American rules of origin. All U.S. quotas on imports of Mexican textiles were immediately eliminated, and no new quotas can be used except in "emergency" situations. (In 1995 the *Diario Oficial* announced that Mexico had raised its tariff on non-North American textiles to 35 percent. This move should further benefit U.S. textiles and apparel in Mexican markets. However, the *Bureau of National Affairs* reported in 1995 that U.S. retailers, such as Wal-Mart or Sears, were concerned that the new high tariffs would make it more difficult for them to sell a mix of products—some of which come from Asia or Europe—in their Mexican stores.

**Textile Rules of Origin.** Strict rules of origin are used to assure that no foreign textile products take advantage of NAFTA's tariff preferences unless they qualify as having originated in North America. U.S. law contains specific rules of origin for textile and apparel products. Those rules apply to U.S. imports of apparel worldwide. As with the automotive rules of origin just discussed, however, NAFTA contains specific rules of origin for determining when a textile product has originated in North America. NAFTA adopts a rule of origin known as *yarn-forward,* meaning that textile goods must be produced from yarn made in a NAFTA country. Yarn-forward requires a *triple transformation test.* The yarn must be spun, the fabric woven, and the clothing sewn and assembled in North America. This rule will encourage Mexican and Canadian garment manufacturers to purchase yarn from U.S. mills, instead of Japanese or European mills, in order to sell their products in the United States at NAFTA's preferential rates.

Certain products such as cotton and synthetic fibers will use a rule known as the *fiber-forward* rule, which means that the goods must be produced from fiber made in a NAFTA country. NAFTA does include exceptions to the rules for fibers not generally produced in North America, such as silk (spun from silk worms primarily in China) or linen (made from the flax plant). Apparel that is cut and sewn in North America from these fabrics, even though of foreign origin, will qualify for NAFTA tariff preferences.

## Trade in Agriculture

NAFTA either eliminates each country's tariffs immediately or phases them out over fifteen years. Most tariffs will be eliminated earlier, by 2004. The *more import-sensitive products* will be controlled for the longer periods through the use of *tariff-rate quotas*—no tariff is assessed if only small quantities have been imported in a given year, but the tariff rate increases as imports rise. Agricultural products are included in this category. For instance, Canada will maintain tariffs over the imports of dairy products; the United States will maintain tariffs on imported orange juice, sugar, eggs, and poultry; and Mexico will continue tariffs on corn, beans, and dairy products. Mexico also pledged an immediate elimination of burdensome import licensing requirements for U.S. agricultural products, replacing them with tariffs that will be phased out over ten years. The U.S. government estimates that the lifting of restrictions will cause a tremendous growth in agricultural trade in the future.

## Government Procurement

Like many of the topics of this chapter, the basic principles of government procurement were examined in earlier chapters. NAFTA will allow North American companies to compete for contracts for the supply of goods and services to agencies of the three governments. NAFTA's government procurement rules apply to contracts for goods and services greater than $50,000, and construction contracts greater than $6.5 million. The agreement does not cover weapons, equipment, and systems needed for national defense.

When a government agency announces its request for submission of bids, it must publish the technical specifications, qualifications of suppliers, and the time limits for submission. Bids from suppliers in all NAFTA countries must be treated without discrimination. Each country has established a bid protest system that allows firms to challenge procurement procedures and awards. Countries will exchange information on bidding procedures to encourage cross-border bidding, particularly from small and medium-sized firms.

## Safeguards Against Injury

Through 1996 NAFTA permitted a country to take *emergency safeguard actions* to temporarily protect industries from surges in imports from other NAFTA countries. Safeguards must be in the form of higher tariffs up to the pre-NAFTA level, not quotas, and the country using them must offer the exporting country *trade compensation*—reduced tariffs on imports of other products or in some other sector. Special safeguards for textiles may be applied where increased imports cause "serious damage" to the domestic industry. Safeguards are available for ten years for certain agricultural products.

**GATT's Global Safeguards.** GATT permits safeguards to be imposed on goods on a global basis (i.e., imposed on a product without regard to the country of origin), if the increased imports are the *substantial cause of serious injury.* NAFTA provides that global safeguards may be applied to goods originating in another NAFTA country as well, but only if the imports comprise a *significant share* of the total imports of that type of good and *contribute importantly* to the serious injury. According to GATT, these safeguards may take the form of either tariffs or quotas.

---

*http://www.sice.oas.org/trade/nafta/ naftatce.stm*
*See Articles in Chapters 6 and 7.*

# Trade in Services

NAFTA provisions on cross-border services are aimed at facilitating trade in services in North America. The provisions affect a wide range of service providers, including transportation and package delivery, consulting, banking and insurance, and others. The principles of national treatment and most-favored-nation trade apply. No NAFTA country may require a North American service provider to have a residence or office within its borders. Each country will be able to continue to certify and license professionals, such as doctors, lawyers, and accountants; however, the countries are working to recognize the foreign credentials of a professional, especially foreign lawyers and engineers. For instance, many professional organizations from NAFTA countries are negotiating *mutual recognition agreements*. Once ratified by state and federal governments they will permit recognition of professional licenses in all three countries. As of 1995, the countries eliminated citizenship requirements to obtain a professional license.

## Financial Services

U.S.–Canadian cross-border investment in financial services was largely opened in 1989. Thus the most important impact of NAFTA's financial services provisions is that they open Mexican financial service industries to investment by U.S. and Canadian companies. Banks, insurance companies, securities firms, and other financial service providers will be able to open branches and offices throughout North America. Mexico will phase out restrictions on foreign ownership of financial service companies within seven to ten years. Initially, foreign ownership of Mexican banks will be restricted to an 8 percent market share of the banking industry. Investors in securities firms will be limited to 10 percent of the securities brokerage industry. Restrictions in both industries will be phased out by the year 2000, permitting a full 100 percent foreign ownership of Mexican financial institutions. Similar provisions apply to insurance companies (100 percent U.S. ownership of some Mexican insurance companies was permitted as early as 1996), and other finance companies (commercial credit, real estate lending, leasing, and credit card services).

# Transportation

Almost 90 percent of goods sold across the 2,000 mile U.S.–Mexican border moves by rail or truck transportation—some two million truckloads a year. In the past, Mexican truck regulations have severely limited U.S. truck access there. Typically, U.S. carriers have had to hand over their cargo to Mexican truckers at the border. The border is known for traffic congestion and delays. Mexican truckers have been limited to a 75-mile incursion into California and to four counties in Texas. NAFTA significantly frees up cross-border transportation and opens trucking companies to foreign investment.

NAFTA does not affect regulations applied to purely domestic truck or bus transportation, and drivers will always be bound by the "rules of the road" in any foreign country in which they operate a vehicle. NAFTA did, however, provide limited cross-border truck and bus access in 1995 and will provide full access by 2000. U.S. and Canadian trucking companies will be able to make deliveries and pickups in Mexico, and Mexican trucking companies will have similar access to their customers north of the border. The three countries are developing common safety standards for vehicles—(tires, brakes, truck and cargo weight, etc.—and driver's license certifications, including testing). After 2001, U.S. and Canadian companies will be able to own a 51 percent majority interest in Mexican trucking companies, and a 100 percent ownership interest after 2004.

# Telecommunications

NAFTA eliminates all tariffs on telephones, cellular phones, and trade in telecommunications equipment by 2004. Given that the number of telephones per capita in Mexico is only a fraction of the per capita number of phones in the United States, Mexico is considered a giant untapped market for all forms of communications equipment and services. NAFTA provides that Canadian, Mexican, and U.S. telecommunications companies have nondiscriminatory access to all North American public telecommunications networks. They must be granted access to public and private (leased) lines and networks only upon conditions that are reasonable and necessary.

Access to public telecommunications networks must be at rates related to the cost of operations. Technical standards may be imposed only for safety or to prevent damage to the equipment.

Mexico's telephone system had been operated as a government-owned monopoly, *Telefonos de Mexico.* Today the company has considerable private investment and is even traded on the New York Stock Exchange. Mexico has been developing a telecommunications law that would set limits on foreign investment and otherwise regulate foreign firms entering its market. During the mid 1990s, U.S. firms such as AT&T, MCI, and Sprint, and Canada's Northern Telecom, were teaming up in partnerships with many Mexican companies to take advantage of growing opportunities in the telecommunications market.

> **http://www.sice.oas.org/trade/nafta/**
> **naftatce.stm**
> See Chapters 12, 13, and 14.

## Cross-Border Investment

As noted earlier in the chapter, Mexico has had a history of strictly regulating or even prohibiting foreign investment. For instance, until recent years, Mexico has required that foreign investors include local participants—Mexican stockholders or partners—in any new factory or investment venture. If a foreign firm wanted to purchase an interest in a local company, Mexico usually limited them to a minority, noncontrolling interest. Mexico, as with many developing countries, has required foreign manufacturing firms located there to export finished goods to other countries for foreign currency. Investors in manufacturing companies were required to use a certain portion of domestic content in the finished goods, thus discouraging imports. Limits were placed on how much money could be transferred out of the country. A common requirement was that foreign investors had to introduce their most advanced technology to the host country. In the 1980s Mexico turned away from the philosophies of government control as in the best interest of the country and of seizing property through *expropriation* and *nationalization;* it became more hospitable and adopted forward-thinking

liberal policies toward foreign investment. It still exercises some control over foreign investment, particularly in the energy and petroleum industries, but not to the extent it did in the past. (See Chapter One and Part Four of this text for additional information on foreign direct investment.)

## NAFTA's Investment Provisions

NAFTA eliminates most of the restrictions placed on investors as noted in previous text. Investors from all three countries can now establish new companies and purchase existing ones across North American borders. Foreign-owned companies are to be treated equally with locally owned firms. Parent companies can transfer profits from a subsidiary in one NAFTA country to another NAFTA country without restriction. Firms operating in any NAFTA country can convert foreign exchange at local banks. No NAFTA country may expropriate property of NAFTA investors, unless it is done pursuant to internationally accepted rules: that it only be done for a public purpose, on a nondiscriminatory basis, in accordance with principles of due process of law, and with the payment of fair compensation (according to market value of the property taken). NAFTA's investment provisions apply to investments made by citizens or nationals of another NAFTA country and to investments made by investors that have substantial business activities in another NAFTA country. For example, if a parent company in Sweden owns an incorporated subsidiary company in the United States, then the U.S. subsidiary may make investments in Canada or Mexico according to the open investment policies of NAFTA. With regard to management personnel, NAFTA prohibits the host country from requiring that local firms owned by investors from other NAFTA countries fill senior management positions with local citizens.

**Environmental Measures Applicable to Investments.** Mexico does not have the strict environmental laws that the United States has. For many U.S. firms, compliance with U.S. laws can be costly. When NAFTA was negotiated, heated debate surrounded the issue of whether U.S. companies, especially polluting ones, would flock to open plants in Mexico to avoid U.S. law. As a compromise in the negotiations, NAFTA provides that "it is inappropriate to encourage investment by relaxing domestic health, safety, or environmental measures. Accordingly, a [NAFTA country] should not waive . . . such measures as an encouragement for the establishment, acquisition, expansion or retention in its territory of an investment."

**Exceptions to the Investment Agreement.** Canada reserved the right to review acquisitions of local companies of $150 million (Canadian) or more under the *Investment Canada Act*. Mexico also retained the right to review acquisitions worth $25 million (U.S.) or more (increasing to $150 million in 2004). Mexico also may restrict ownership of land, cable television companies, air and land transportation, oil production and refining, and retail sales of gasoline and oil. The United States excluded investments in nuclear power, broadcasting, mining, customs brokerages, and air transportation, and may block the takeover of U.S. firms on the basis of national security (see Chapter One).

---

**http://www.sice.oas.org/trade/nafta/ naftatce.stm**
*See Chapter 11.*

---

# Other NAFTA Provisions

In negotiating NAFTA, the United States was able to see the broader implications of free trade and investment in North America. For instance, what if an unscrupulous company in Mexico produces counterfeit software and smuggles it across the border in violation of the copyrights of a U.S. company? Or suppose that a firm emits poisonous gas or pollutants from a smokestack at its Mexican plant, and they are carried by air currents to the United States? What if the top management of several competing companies meet in Denver or Mexico City and fix prices to consumers for a product that they each make? Although these problems undoubtedly occurred before NAFTA, and are tremendous issues that no one trade agreement is likely to change, the U.S. negotiators of the agreement used the opportunity to address them openly.

## Intellectual Property Rights

Intellectual property rights (IPR) are generally protected by national law, but as discussed in previous chapters, IPR is the subject of several international conventions (e.g., the *Berne Convention*) and agreements (e.g., GATT/TRIPS). Intellectual property is covered in greater detail in Part Four of this book. NAFTA adopts the basic tenets of these international agreements and builds upon them. NAFTA's provisions protect the IPR of North American firms. No country can make citizenship a requirement for IPR protection. Applicants for trademarks, copyrights, and patents must be treated equally and without discrimination. NAFTA guarantees that any IPR is freely transferable by the owner to another party.

**Trademarks.** Trademarks and service marks will be protected for ten years, and can be renewed indefinitely. The owner of a registered trademark has the right to prevent others from using identical or similar signs for goods or services if it would result in a likelihood of confusion (and a *likelihood of confusion* is presumed unless the offender can prove otherwise). Specific provision prohibit the use of the names of geographical regions (e.g., Tennessee Whiskey), unless the products are actually derived from that area. Actual use of a trademark cannot be a condition for filing an application for registration. NAFTA requires fair procedures for obtaining a trademark, including notice and an opportunity to be heard. Registration may be canceled if the trademark is not used for an uninterrupted period of at least two years.

**Copyrights.** Copyrights will be protected equally in all three countries. Computer programs will be protected as literary works, and motion pictures and sound recordings protected for 50 years. (Canada has made some exceptions for "cultural industries.") NAFTA prohibits the importation of copies of a sound recording made without the producers' authorization.

**Patents.** Patents must be made available for any invention "in all fields of technology" (including pharmaceuticals), whether it is a product or process. It must be new, result from an inventive step (i.e., be "nonobvious"), and be capable of industrial application (i.e., be "useful"). They are effective for a period of 20 years from the date of application, or 17 years from the date when the patent was granted.

**Enforcement and Penalties.** NAFTA requires that each country enforce its IPR laws, both internally and at the border to prevent smuggling of counterfeit items. IPR owners will be able to protect their rights through administrative action and judicial relief. Courts will have the authority to order seizure and destruction of infringing items, to issue injunctions against their sale, and to permit lawsuits for damages against infringers. The NAFTA countries must provide criminal penalties for cases in which willful trademark counterfeiting or copyright piracy occurs on a commercial scale. Penalties may include imprisonment or monetary fines, or both.

## Environmental Issues

NAFTA does not set environmental or ecological standards, as does national law, but it does call for the three countries to cooperate in protecting the environment. The countries have promised to enforce their laws more effectively. They also promise to develop environmental emergency procedures and to share information on protecting the environment. They are also working to develop common environmental standards. All countries must notify the others before banning a pesticide or chemical, and afterward, all are urged to prohibit the export of such products to other countries.

The agreement created the NAFTA *Commission for Environmental Cooperation* to oversee this portion of the agreement. The commission is headed by a council made up of three cabinet-level officers of the three governments. The commission may convene panels to resolve disputes between countries. The panel can authorize tariff increases against a party found in violation of the environmental provisions of the agreement. In one of the NAFTA's first environmental cases, *The Journal of Commerce* reported in 1995 that the commission was investigating the death of 40,000 wild birds in Mexico. The commission acted quickly to determine the cause—

apparently the birds died from the industrial dumping of either chromium or red dye—and made recommendations in order to protect other migratory birds that were due to return to the area. Mexico took quick action as a result of the commission's investigation. It was the first time in North America that authorities from other countries investigated an environmental disaster solely within another country. However, no one knows yet how willing Canada, Mexico, and the United States will be to opening these types of incidents to NAFTA investigations.

NAFTA created the CEC (Commission on Environmental Compliance) to address complaints. Reportedly, 11 complaints have been lodged at the time of this writing, resulting in only one investigation involving the construction of a cruise ship pier in Cozumel, Mexico. There was a concern about damage to delicate ocean reefs. Perhaps the clearest signal regarding the impotence of the commission is the recent statement by the Director of the CEC, quoted in *The Wall Street Journal,* noting that the objective of the CEC is "to clarify the state of the facts, not to enforce compliance."

## Labor and Worker Rights

Many people worried that NAFTA would cause U.S. companies to move to Mexico to take advantage of cheap labor and weakly enforced labor laws. With this in mind, the United States insisted on a side agreement called the *North American Agreement on Labor Cooperation,* intended to make labor policies more uniform by promoting the following basic labor principles in the region:

- Freedom of association
- Right to bargain collectively
- Right to strike
- Prohibition of forced labor
- Restrictions on child labor
- Minimum working conditions
- Elimination of employment discrimination
- Equal pay for men and women
- Prevention of accidents and occupational disease
- Protection of migrant workers

NAFTA does not set specific rules, but requires countries to enforce those rules that they already have. A *North American Labor Commission* was created to oversee the agreement and to promote cooperation in labor issues. The commission is headed by a council, consisting of the U.S. Secretary of Labor and labor ministers from the other countries. Dispute panels may be convened to investigate issues involving worker health or safety, the abuse of child labor, or the failure to enforce minimum wage laws, and may make recommendations for solutions.

There is some criticism of the efficacy of this agreement. One attorney quoted in *The Wall Street Journal* who litigated five cases before the NAO (National Administrative Office) noted:

Technically speaking in all cases we won. But in all cases workers are left with a piece of paper that says 'you were right.' Not a single worker was ever reinstated, not a single employer was sanctioned, no union was ever recognized.

At best, the agreement provides a forum to discuss disputes. Many labor groups are poised to push vigorously for new safeguards in any future agreements.

## Antitrust and Competition Policy

*Antitrust laws,* also called *competition law,* prohibit illegal monopoly control of industries, price fixing and a range of anticompetitive and unfair business practices. Both the United States and Canada have long had strong antitrust laws. Mexico adopted an antitrust law in 1993. NAFTA countries agreed to cooperate in the enforcement of these antitrust laws, including mutual legal assistance, consultations, and exchange of information. For industries in which the countries permit legal monopolies, such as Mexico's state-owned oil company, NAFTA sets rules to minimize the anticompetitive impact of the monopoly on other industries.

## Rights to Temporary Entry

Unlike the European Union, NAFTA does not create a common market in labor. Each country will still determine its own qualifications for employment and its own immigration policies. NAFTA countries, however, have agreed to give business-people easy access to their customers, clients, factories, and offices across the borders. NAFTA permits temporary entry in the following cases:

1. Business visitors engaged in international business activities related to research, manufacturing, marketing, sales, and distribution; those who are service providers; and those servicing products after-the-sale (repair or maintenance of products after the sale must be done pursuant to a warranty or other service contract on the products).
2. Traders employed by a company in a NAFTA country, and those who are buying and selling substantial amounts of goods and services.
3. Potential investors.
4. Management or executive employees transferred to subsidiary companies in another NAFTA country.
5. Qualified professionals (in 63 professions, ranging from teachers and lawyers to hotel managers) entering to do business (separate licensing qualifications must also be met if they intend to practice a profession).

Mexico requires these travelers to obtain the FMN card (*Formularia Migratorio* NAFTA), which is valid for 30 days. Special visas are available for periods of stay longer than 30 days. Normal tourist cards are still available.

*http://www.sice.oas.org/trade/nafta/
naftatce.stm*
*See Chapters 15, 16, 17, 27, and 28 for details on
Other NAFTA Provisions.*

## Administration and Dispute Settlement

NAFTA does not have the type of lawmaking institutions that the European Union has. However, an administrative body oversees implementation of the agreement, and a dispute resolution process is available to NAFTA countries. The dispute resolution process is similar to that at the World Trade Organization.

## NAFTA Fair Trade Commission

The *Fair Trade Commission* supervises the implementation of the agreement and attempts to resolve disputes that may arise regarding its interpretation or application. One cabinet-level official from each of the three governments, supported by an administrative staff and committees, form the commission.

**Arbitral Panels.** When one NAFTA country accuses another of violating NAFTA's principles, it must first attempt to negotiate a settlement. If a settlement is not reached, then the countries can seek dispute resolution. When the issue falls under both NAFTA and GATT, the countries must agree on whether it will be heard by the NAFTA Fair Trade Commission or the World Trade Organization. If they cannot agree on which forum, the case will normally be heard before the Fair Trade Commission. If a settlement is not reached, the commission may convene an *arbitral panel,* which consists of five members who are experts in trade or law. They decide whether one country has violated NAFTA and recommend a solution. If the recommendations of the arbitral panel are not followed, and no agreement is reached within 30 days, the complaining country may retaliate by raising tariffs, but no panel has the authority to tell a country to actually change its laws or policies. Take a hypothetical example: If a panel rules that a regulation of the U.S. Consumer Product Safety Commission, the National Park Service, or other agency is violating NAFTA, an individual cannot obtain a court order compelling the agency to alter its decision solely on the basis of the panel report.

**Antidumping and Countervailing Duty Cases.** The Fair Trade Commission also hears cases involving countervailing and antidumping duties. These cases are treated differently from other disputes. Recall that *countervailing duties* are imposed on imported goods that received an unfair price advantage because a part of their cost of production was subsidized by the exporting country. *Antidumping duties* are imposed on "dumped" products. Dumping, another unfair trade practice, is the selling of goods in a foreign market for less than the price charged in the country in which they were produced. Anti-dumping and countervailing duties are only imposed pursuant to an order of an administrative agency in the importing country. This practice will continue under NAFTA; however, the appellate process has been changed greatly. In the United States, an appeal of an agency decision in an international trade case normally goes to the U.S. Court of International Trade, but appeals from administrative orders in NAFTA cases now go to NAFTA *binational panels,* not to courts of law. (This practice started in 1989 in the U.S.–Canada Free Trade Agreement.) The role of the panel, and its *standard of review,* in reviewing agency decisions is limited. Binational panels apply the same standard of review as would a court of law convened in the country where the case originated. Because it is not an appellate court, a panel does not make law in the traditional sense, but applies the existing law of the country from which the case was appealed. This legal process is quite unusual and controversial, because private businesses will be bound by the decision of an intergovernmental panel with no recourse to judicial review. The following case illustrates the appellate function of a binational panel in a dumping case. (Refer to Chapter Eleven for a review of the law of dumping.)

**Extraordinary Challenge Committees.** Appeals of a binational panel decision may be taken only to a NAFTA *Extraordinary Challenge Committee,* and not to courts of law. A challenge committee examines a case only to see if a panelist was biased or guilty of misconduct, or whether the panel departed from a fundamental rule of procedure, or *exceeded its powers, authority, or jurisdiction.* A binational panel must apply the correct standard of review. Under NAFTA, a binational panel that fails to apply the correct standard of review would be considered to have exceeded its powers, authority, or jurisdiction. In the *Certain Softwood Lumber Products* case, decided under CFTA, a challenge committee reviewed the decision of a binational panel to see if it had applied the correct standard of review. It also considered whether the panelists were biased. After reading the case, consider how the problems discussed here resulted in new qualifications for panelists. Today, under NAFTA,

## BACKGROUND AND FACTS

Poli-Twine and other Canadian twine manufacturers, filed an antidumping complaint in Canada against synthetic baler twine imported from the United States. The Canadian International Trade Tribunal found that the twine was causing material injury to the production of like goods in Canada. Bridon Cordage, a U.S. exporter of twine, challenged the Tribunal's decision on the grounds that the Tribunal committed an error in applying a Canadian statute, the *Special Import Measures Act* (SIMA). A NAFTA binational panel was requested. Three aspects of the panel's decision are discussed here: (1) the standard of review; (2) whether the Tribunal properly determined that the dumping had injured Canadian industry; and (3) whether the Tribunal properly determined that the dumped goods are likely to cause injury in the future. The panel applied Canadian law because it was reviewing a decision of a Canadian government agency.

## DECISION OF THE PANEL

This Binational Panel was constituted pursuant to Chapter 19 of the North American Free Trade Agreement (NAFTA) to review a finding of the Canadian International Trade Tribunal (the Tribunal). The Tribunal found that the dumping of synthetic baler twine exported from the United States of America had caused, and was likely to cause material injury to the production of like goods in Canada.

### I. Standard of Review

Binational Panels are directed by NAFTA Article 1904(3) to apply the standard of review set out in the general legal principles that a court of the importing party [Canada] otherwise would apply to a review of a determination of the competent investigating authority. In the case of Canada . . . the standard of review is set forth in the [Canadian] *Federal Court Act.* . . . [The Act] provides that the Tribunal's decisions will be reviewed on the grounds that it: (a) acted without jurisdiction, acted beyond its jurisdiction or refused to exercise its

*Synthetic Baler Twine with a Knot Strength of 200 lbs or Less Originating in or Exported from the United States of America*
CDA-94-1904-02
*(NAFTA Binational Panel, 1995)*

jurisdiction; (b) failed to observe a principle of natural justice, procedural fairness or other procedure that is required by law to observe; (c) erred in law in making a decision or order, whether or not the error appears on the face of the record; (d) based its decision or order on an erroneous finding of fact that it made in a perverse or capricious manner or without regard for the material before it; (e) acted, or failed to act, by reason of fraud or perjured evidence; or (f) acted in any other way that was contrary to law.

Complainants contend that, because binational Panels are themselves expert in international trade, the Tribunal is not entitled to the same degree of deference that ordinarily would be accorded to it by the [Canadian] Federal Court. The Panel disagrees. Pursuant to the NAFTA binational Panel review replaces judicial review by domestic courts in certain defined circumstances. NAFTA provides: The Panel shall apply the standard of review set out in NAFTA Annex 1911 and the general legal principles that a court of the importing Party otherwise would apply to a review of a determination of the competent investigating authority. NAFTA Annex 1911 states that the standard of review for Canada means "the grounds set out in subsection 18.1(4) of the Federal Court Act." Under section 18.1(4) the Federal Court is obliged by law to give "considerable deference" to the decisions of the Tribunal. In fulfilling their mandate to "apply the standard of review . . . that a court of the importing Party otherwise would apply" binational Panels are obliged to apply the same standard that would be used by the Federal Court.

The Panel holds that the requirement that Panelists be familiar with international trade law under paragraph 1 of the NAFTA, Annex 1902.2 is not intended to modify the standard of deference that is ordinarily accorded an expert tribunal. The requirement that Panelists be familiar with international trade law assists Panelists to fulfil their mandate by making it easier for them to understand the types of issues that are dealt with by the Tribunal. . . .

*(continued)*

*(continued)*

## II. Errors of Law and Fact

Complainants contend that the Tribunal erroneously violated its legal duty under the Special Import Measures Act (SIMA) by failing to [determine all possible factors that could have caused injury to the Canadian twine industry]. This would have essentially required the Tribunal to quantify each and every factor that might be a cause of material injury, not limited to dumped goods from the United States. . . .

It is true that the effects of dumping must be segregated from other causes, and the Tribunal is required under SIMA to determine whether the dumped goods are a cause of material injury. However, neither SIMA, nor the GATT rules as incorporated in SIMA, require that the other causes be calculated or quantified beyond what is necessary to assure that injury from dumped goods is not being attributed to those other causes. . . . Of course, there may be other factors which may have contributed to the injury. As a matter of common sense, it seems to me that there almost always will be. Such matters as efficiency [of Canadian twine producers], quality, cost control, marketing ability, accuracy in forecasting, good luck and a host of others come to mind. It is the function of a specialized tribunal such as the Canadian International Trade Tribunal to weigh and balance those factors and to decide the importance to be given to each.

## III. Future Injury

The amount of evidence required in order to sustain the Tribunal's findings of fact is modest. This, however, does not mean the Tribunal's determination will be upheld in the absence of any evidence in the record to support its conclusions. Such is the situation we find here.

While . . . it may be logical to assume that injury will continue as long as conditions remain the same, we are unwilling to hold that such an assumption is the equivalent of evidence. The Tribunal here based its conclusion on the "belief" that Poli-Twine will [in the future] be faced with the same market conditions as in the recent past . . . and the view that as long as the U.S. has excess production, injury will continue. These assertions may or may not be true, and if so would appear to support a conclusion of future injury, but there are not—on the basis of anything that has been brought to our attention in the briefs or oral argument—in the record as established facts. The references in the record offered in support amount to conjecture, falling short of evidence.

**Decision.** The Panel affirmed the Canadian Tribunal's determination that the sale of U.S. twine in Canada at unfairly low prices caused past injury to Canadian twine producers. But the Panel held that there was not sufficient evidence to support the Tribunal's conclusion that injury would continue in the future. The case was remanded to the Tribunal to reconsider new evidence on the question of future injury. The Panel applied the same standard of review that a Canadian appellate court would have applied if a court had been reviewing the case.

**Comment.** When reviewing an order from a U.S. agency, a NAFTA Panel applies U.S. standards for judicial review. In *Live Swine from Canada*, USA-94-1904-01(May 30, 1995), a NAFTA panel stated that, "The Panel steps into the shoes of the Court of International Trade and the Court of Appeals for the Federal Circuit and is to apply the standards and the substantive law that those courts apply when they review a . . . determination by the Department of Commerce. This in turn means that the Panel is to hold unlawful 'any determination, finding or conclusion found . . . to be *unsupported by substantial evidence.*' . . . The Panel is not to substitute its own judgment, and the only question before it is whether the agency's action had appropriate support in fact and/or law."

panelists are chosen from a roster of impartial judges or former judges whenever possible, both for binational panels and extraordinary challenge committees, but not arbitral panels.

http://www.sice.oas.org/trade/nafta/ naftatce.stm
*Chapter 20 of NAFTA discusses dispute settlement procedures.*

### BACKGROUND AND FACTS

Canada and the United States have disputed trade in softwood lumber for more than twelve years. Canada assesses a "stump charge" to private companies cutting timber on government land. In 1991 the U.S. Department of Commerce held that the stump charges were below market price and constituted an illegal subsidy. Commerce ordered countervailing duties on the lumber. The Canadian government appealed the action to a binational panel under the (pre-NAFTA) U.S.–Canadian Free Trade Agreement. In 1992 the binational panel ruled that no subsidy existed and requested that the countervailing duties be removed. The United States requested an extraordinary challenge committee (ECC).

### JUSTICE GORDON L. S. HART

The Constitution and authority of an ECC is derived solely from the United States–Canada Free Trade Agreement. It is an international committee intended to be the ultimate vehicle in a dispute resolution system agreed to by the parties to the FTA. It was not intended to be an appellate court but rather a committee of limited jurisdiction to protect the integrity of the system. Where, within a reasonable time after the panel decision is issued, a Party alleges that: (a) a member of the panel was guilty of gross misconduct, bias, or a serious conflict of interest, (b) the panel seriously departed from a fundamental rule of procedure, or (c) the panel manifestly exceeded its powers, authority or jurisdiction set forth in this Article, and any of these three actions has materially affected the panel's decision, that party may avail itself of the extraordinary challenge procedure.

There have been only two previous ECCs. In *Live Swine from Canada*, ECC-93-1094-01 USA (1991), the unanimous decision of the committee stated:

> The ECC should be perceived as a safety valve in those extraordinary circumstances where a challenge is warranted to maintain the integrity of the binational panel process. . . . The ECC should address systemic problems and not mere legal issues that do not threaten the integrity of the FTA's dispute resolution mechanism itself. A systemic problem arises whenever the binational panel process itself is tainted by failure on the part of a panel or a panelist to follow their mandate under the FTA.

## *Certain Softwood Lumber Products from Canada*
### ECC-94-1904-01USA
### (Extraordinary Challenge Committee, 1994)

The [*Live Swine*] decision goes on to state that if a panel failed to apply the appropriate standard of review it would manifestly exceed "its powers, authority or jurisdiction" and would be guilty of one prong of the test. The committee must assess whether the panel accurately articulated the standard of review and whether it had been conscientiously applied.

[After a lengthy analysis of U.S. countervailing duty law, Justice Hart concluded]: In my opinion the panel followed an appropriate standard of review and properly interpreted United States law when it ruled that Commerce was required to assess whether or not there was any competitive advantage or market distortion created by the Canadian stumpage systems before determining whether or not a countervailable subsidy existed. Furthermore, having determined that there was no such distortion according to the evidence there was nothing to countervail. The panel was correct in directing Commerce to remove the countervailing duties which they had imposed.

The United States alleges that two members of the panel materially violated the FTA rules of conduct by failing to disclose information that revealed, at least the appearance of partiality or bias, and with regard to one of the panelists a serious conflict of interest.

Before participating in a panel each member is required to submit a disclosure statement under the panelist's *Code of Conduct* which states:

> The governing principle of this Code is that a candidate or member must disclose the existence of any interests or relationships that are likely to affect the candidate's or member's independence and impartiality or that might reasonably create the appearance of bias.

Most panelists, like these two men, work with large law firms, some with offices in different cities and it is difficult to know always what work is being conducted by their partners and associates. They each made reasonable efforts to make sure that there was no work being conducted by their firms that would in any way interfere with their impartiality in the matter before the panel. Firms like theirs, both in Canada and the United States, are regularly employed by various government agencies and unless the employment relates to the matter in dispute

*(continued)*

*(continued)*

it should not be used to bar a roster member from serving on a panel. Otherwise it would be very difficult to get competent people to serve.

It was known here that both [panelists in question] worked with law firms that represented the various governments in Canada on unrelated matters and it was also known that one of the American members of this panel was associated with a firm that billed over $3,800,000 to an American government agency during 1992–93. Neither party considered it necessary to treat these facts as an indication of bias on the part of any of the panelists and did not do so. It was only when the final decision was in that the matter was raised.

**Decision.** The request for an extraordinary challenge committee was denied. The binational panel applied the correct standard of review, and was justified in its decision that no countervailing duty was authorized by U.S. law. The circumstances did not indicate that the panel decision was based on misconduct, bias, or a conflict of interest.

## In-Bond Assembly Plants and the Mexican Maquiladora

Long before NAFTA existed, other trade preferences had a tremendous impact on the North American region. As mentioned in Chapter Thirteen, many Mexican goods shipped to the United States received special tariff preferences under the GSP, or *Generalized System of Preferences,* which were available to any developing country that qualified under the GSP law. They had either a low tariff, or no tariff at all. Canada offered similar preferences for Mexican goods. The purpose of these programs was to encourage trade with developing countries to aid in their economic growth.

Another U.S. government program that has had a tremendous impact on North American business is found in Section 9802 of the *Harmonized Tariff Schedule.* This law contains a special provision allowing U.S.-made articles or component parts to be shipped to factories in a foreign country, assembled there, and returned to the United States with duties assessed only on the value of the newly assembled product *less the value of the U.S.-made article or component parts.* The law thus permits U.S. firms, such as the "Big Three" automakers, to purchase auto parts from U.S. suppliers and assemble them in foreign plants using low-cost labor. Assembly plants can be established in all areas of the world and owned by companies from all countries. For instance, a Japanese automaker can produce cars in a Mexican assembly plant, using parts sourced from countries around the world, and then ex-port the Mexican-made car to the United States. The car will be dutied on the value of the car less the value of the U.S. component parts. In one Ford Motor Company plant, steel from Japan is stamped into body parts, assembled together with Japanese-made engines and U.S. component parts, and the finished car is exported to the United States (much to the chagrin of U.S. autoworkers). Because of the nature of the operation, the process is sometimes called *production sharing.* It is intended to create U.S. jobs by encouraging the use of U.S.-made components when assembly of a product takes place in a foreign country. The automobile industry has invested heavily in plants in Japan, Canada, Sweden, Germany, and Mexico; the electronics industry in Asia; and the textile industry in Mexico and the Caribbean. These plants are often called *offshore assembly plants, in-bond plants,* or *border plants.* The Spanish term is *maquiladora,* or *maquila.*

### Mexican Customs Rules

For the past 25 years, Mexico has used the maquiladora industry as a means of attracting foreign investment and increasing jobs, without having an influx of foreign-made goods. The Mexican government allows the temporary, duty-free import of articles or parts brought into Mexico for assembly *if they are returned to the United States or exported to a third country.* Mexico permits the import of machinery, equipment, parts, raw materials, and components for use in assembly operations. The articles enter

Mexico *in-bond* and cannot be released for sale in Mexico without going through normal Mexican customs procedures—the importer must post a bond as assurance to the government that the goods will not be sold in Mexico without payment of duties. Mexico has permitted only 50 percent of the prior year's production to be released for sale within Mexico. Some of the special income tax treatment of maquiladoras was eliminated by the Mexican government in 1995.

## Assembly Plant Tariff Treatment in the United States

Section 9802 tariff treatment is available only where (1) the imports were assembled in the foreign plant from U.S.-made fabricated components, (2) which had been exported "ready for assembly without further fabrication," (3) and which have not lost their physical identity and have not been advanced in value or improved in condition abroad except by being assembled and except "by operations incidental to the assembly process," (such as

cleaning, trimming, calibrating, or lubricating). Examples of fabricated components that would qualify as being ready for assembly without losing their physical identity include transistors, machine parts, semiconductors, precut parts of wearing apparel, lug nuts, and automobile engines or tires. Bolts of fabric sent abroad to be cut into parts of shirts do not qualify as an assembly, but the sewing of two sleeves to the body of a shirt does. It is not an assembly when lumber, leather, or plastic is sent abroad to be formed into component parts. Section 9802 applies only to assembly operations, which includes any method of joining together, such as welding, gluing, or sewing. Combining chemicals, liquids, gases, or food ingredients is not considered an assembly. In addition to automobiles and clothing, other representative products include telecommunications and electronic equipment, computers, televisions, sausage casings, miniblinds, and stuffed toys—almost any product capable of *assembly*. In the case *Samsonite Corporation v. United States*, the operations of the plant were held to be a fabrication and not a mere assembly.

---

*Samsonite Corporation v. United States*
889 F.2d 1074 (1989)
United States Court of Appeals (Fed.Cir.)

BACKGROUND AND FACTS

Samsonite Corporation assembles luggage in Mexico for import into the United States. Many component parts used in the assembly process are made in the United States. Samsonite had shipped steel strips from the United States to Mexico for use as luggage handles. When the strips left the United States, they were five inches long, straight, and bearing a coat of oil. Their value ranged from 95 cents to $1.26. In Mexico, the strips were bent by machine into a form resembling a square-sided letter *C*, cleaned, covered with a vinyl sheath, and riveted to plastic frame assemblies. The assemblies were then placed in, and fastened to, bags of vinyl to make soft luggage. On import into the United States, the Customs Service dutied the luggage, including the value of the steel strips at the rate of 20 percent ad valorem. The Court of International Trade upheld the government's contention that the steel strips had not been "exported in a condition ready for assembly" and that the process in Mexico amounted to a fabrication and more than a mere assembly. Samsonite appealed.

SENIOR CIRCUIT JUDGE FRIEDMAN

To obtain a deduction for American-fabricated articles assembled abroad, the components

a. must have been exported from the United States "in condition ready for assembly without further fabrication,"
b. not have lost their physical identity in the articles by change in form, shape, or otherwise, and
c. not have been advanced in value or improved in condition "except by being assembled" and except "by operations incidental to the assembly process such as cleaning, lubricating, and painting."

As the Court of International Trade correctly pointed out, since the "foregoing three conditions for a deduction are set forth in the conjunctive, . . . each must be satisfied before a component can qualify for duty-free treatment." We agree with

*(continued)*

*(continued)*

that court that the steel strips involved in this case did not meet those conditions.

The critical inquiry is whether the bending and shaping that the strips underwent constituted "fabrication" or mere assembly and operations incidental to the assembly process. We hold that what was done to the strips in Mexico was fabrication and not mere assembly.

When the steel strips were exported from the United States, they were just that: five-inch strips that could not serve as the frame of the luggage without undergoing a complete change in shape. Prior to assembling the luggage, the strips were bent by machine into a carefully and specially configured rectangular shape that was necessary before the original strip would serve its ultimate function as part of the frame of the luggage.

In short, what emerged after the bending operation was a different object from that which left the United States. The latter was a steel strip, the former was a metal frame for a piece of luggage. The transformation of the strip in this manner into a luggage frame was a fabrication. The strips therefore had not been exported from the United States "in condition ready for assembly without further fabrication."

Samsonite contends, however, that prior decisions of the Court of Customs and Patent Appeals require a contrary conclusion. It relies particularly on *General Instrument Corp. v. United States,* 499 F.2d 1318 (CCPA 1974). That case involved wire wound on spools that had been exported from the United States to Taiwan. There the wire was removed from the spools, formed into a horizontal coil by a winding machine, taped to prevent unraveling, dipped in cement, dried, precision shaped, removed from the spools, and wound around a core. The end product made from the wire was a component of a television set that was imported into the United States.

The Court of Customs and Patent Appeals held that: "The steps performed upon the wire after its exportation to Taiwan are not 'further fabrication' steps, but rather assembly steps within the meaning of [the statute]."

Samsonite argues that far more was done to the wire in *General Instrument* than was done to the steel strips in this case. It argues that if the processing the wire underwent in *General Instrument* was not "fabrication," a fortiori "the one simple-minded act of bending a straight frame into a *C* was neither a further fabrication nor a nonincidental operation."

The critical inquiry in determining whether fabrication rather than mere assembly took place here, is not the amount of processing that occurred in the two cases, but its nature. In General Instrument, the wire, when it left the United States and when it returned as part of a finished product, was a coil. The wire was taken directly from the supply spool on which it was wound and, after processing, was used in assembling the TV set components. The wire underwent no basic change in connection with its incorporation into the television set component.

In contrast, in the present case the steel strips had to undergo a significant change in shape before the actual assembly of luggage could begin. Until the steel strips had been made into $C$ shapes they could not be used as a part of the luggage. Unlike the "assembly" that the court in *General Instrument* held the processing of the wire involved, here "further fabrication" of the steel strips was required in order to change them into frames for luggage, before the assembly of the luggage could take place.

**Decision.** The Court of Appeals upheld the decision of the lower court. The bending and processing of the steel strips in Mexico was fabrication and not a mere assembly and therefore did not qualify for duty-free treatment under Section 9802.

**Comment.** In a case of major economic importance to the auto industry, *General Motors Corporation v. U.S.,* 976 F.2d 716 (Fed.Cir. 1992), the court ruled that automotive topcoat painting performed on sheet metal parts shipped to foreign countries for assembly into automobiles were not "operations incidental to assembly." The parts were cleaned and sprayed with zinc, submerged in an electro-primer tank, baked, sanded, and sealed. Then the topcoat paint was applied and the body oven baked. GM claimed this to be an assembly operation, pointing out that customs has held painting to be an operation incident to assembly with other items. The court disagreed, relying on the extent of capital investment in GM's painting operation in Mexico and the time factor involved in the process. Based on this court decision, U.S. Customs later ruled that the value of "stonewashing" bluejeans in a Mexican or Caribbean plant is to be included in dutiable value on their re-export to the United States, because stonewashing is not a minor operation incident to assembly.

## The Mexican Maquiladora Industry

Most Section 9802 assembly plants have been built in Mexico, due to its close proximity to the United States. U.S. firms are also able to take advantage of Mexico's lower wage rate, with the average manufacturing hourly wage between $1.25 and $2.75 per hour, depending largely on the value of the peso at any given time. (However, Mexican plants often require more supervisory personnel, higher quality control costs, and have higher worker training costs than in the United States.) Almost 500,000 people are employed in more than 2,500 Mexican maquiladoras. Many of them are concentrated along Mexico's border with the United States, which means lowered inventory requirements and transportation costs. Many firms also use their Mexican plants as a base for shipments to South America. Maquilas will most likely have far less importance under NAFTA than they did before the free trade pact went into effect. Of course the plants will continue operation, but their reliance on special customs laws will be replaced by NAFTA's general tariff preferences.

## The Social Responsibility of U.S. Firms in the Maquiladora Industry

Maquiladoras have had a tremendous economic and social impact on the people of Mexico—and on sections of California and Texas as well—and account for the second-largest source of income, next to oil, for Mexicans. The maquiladora industry presents many of the same social, political, and economic issues faced by multinational firms operating anywhere in the developing world. Mexico desires the economic opportunities created by foreign plants situated there, poised on the doorstep of the U.S. market. To attract foreign investment, it offers many economic and regulatory incentives. On the other hand, Mexico expects these companies to be good citizens and to operate within the law. Most firms do understand their responsibility to comply with Mexican regulations and to contribute to the betterment of Mexican society, but man-

agers face many perplexing problems. For instance, should a U.S. firm operating a maquila in, say, Chihuahua City provide a clinic for dealing with employee drug or alcohol problems engendered by the many workers who have left their homes and traveled to northern Mexico in search of jobs? Should they provide these facilities even though Mexican law may not require them to do so? Should a U.S. firm in Mexico operate voluntarily under the same health and safety standards that they are expected to conform to in the United States, or merely conform to the minimum standards required under Mexican law? Should the U.S. company introduce the latest technologies to the Mexican plants and fund worker training programs? With new investment opportunities made possible by NAFTA, U.S. and Canadian companies operating throughout Mexico will face these kinds of ethical issues.

No issue is more pressing in the border regions than the degradation the plants have caused to the environment. In the early 1990s, the governments of the United States and Mexico began negotiations on protecting the Rio Grande, and on building municipal sewer systems, water treatment plants, and solid-waste disposal sites. Their greatest concern is how to deal with hazardous waste. The two governments are attempting to devise ways of tracking hazardous waste and regulating disposal sites. Mexico has reportedly closed hundreds of plants for environmental violations. Complicating the problem are the thousands of trucks that cross the border daily, causing severe air pollution and damage to roads and bridges. Governments will spend hundreds of millions of dollars, at a minimum, in dealing with these social and environmental problems. Industry investors will bear an increasing share of these costs in the future.

*http://www.customs.ustreas.gov/ imp-exp/rulings/harmoniz/*
*The site of the Harmonized Tariff Schedule. The index links you to sites of the text on specific commodities.*

*Foreign Accents*

# "A DIFFERENT WORLD"

## Companies Are Often Unprepared for Just How Different Mexico Is

MEXICO CITY—The North American Free Trade Agreement may be knocking down tariffs and stimulating trade, but U.S. companies operating here know that Mexico is still Mexico.

That means lots of unfamiliar customs and invisible barriers that can create anything from a corporate nuisance to a migraine headache. None of the conveniences that Americans count on—from reliable postal service to working telephones—can be taken for granted. Intersections between major highways go unmarked; street addresses have no logic; and laws are applied so haphazardly that an American can end up in jail without ever being accused of a crime. Though Mexico is just across the border, it can seem farther away than countries across the Atlantic.

"This is a very difficult place to do business," says Carol Kolozs, an American who runs Lotto Italian Sports Design, a sportswear company here. He says he once had a desperately needed shipment of thousands of shoes held up at the border for weeks because of confusion over the country of origin in a handful of pairs.

Almost nothing in Mexico is completely straightforward. Bill collecting, for instance, ought to be simple. Just mail out a bill and wait 30 days for a check. If the customer doesn't pay promptly, pester him. If all else fails, sue.

### Postal Roulette

In Mexico, though, it doesn't work that way. The mail system is so unreliable that few companies would trust it with anything as important as a bill. So someone billing a customer needs to present the bill in person. Usually that means the salesperson has to quit selling for a while and become a bill collector.

Companies generally accept bills only for a few hours, one day a week, and if a bill doesn't arrive during that window it has to wait another seven days. Many salespeople outside the biggest cities have huge territories; if they miss the time for presenting a bill, they may not pass that way again for a month.

There are often problems with the bills, too, because of all the documentation required. It's generally not enough in Mexico just to send out a sheet of paper requesting payment. The bill has to be presented together with the original invoice. If goods have been shipped, the customer must also include a seal showing that the shipment was in order. Then the government demands additional documentation. Salespeople often create further trouble by making oral promises of a discount that they fail to relay to the person preparing the bill. The discrepancies can add another week or two to the billing process.

Companies that promise to pay their bills in, say, 30 days don't start the clock ticking until they've received a bill and decided it's acceptable. There's little that can be done to pressure people into paying.

### Capricious Judicial System

"You can almost forget about taking them to court, because that process will take years," says Laurence Noclain, senior vice president in charge of REL Consultancy Group's Mexico practice, which specializes in helping companies improve their cash flow. "There's a lot of bad debt in Mexico that's pretty much unrecoverable."

Indeed, the justice system is another of the areas that foreigners—and Mexicans—find hard to fathom. There are plenty of laws on the books, but many are just ignored, and many more are enforced in accordance with the plaintiff's political influence. There are even stories of Americans who thought they were involved in a minor civil dispute only to find themselves thrown in jail because they tangled with the wrong person.

Alex Argueta, a resort developer from Tucson, Ariz., for instance, was renegotiating a bank loan he had been slow to repay. He was grabbed from his hotel room late one night and spent 16 months in jail, even though he was never charged with a crime.

Ernesto Zedillo, elected president in August, said in an interview that, while many Mexicans and foreign investors are focusing on his efforts to revive the economy, he figures that will be the easy part. His other priority—establishing a clear, consistent judicial system—may well be much tougher, he said.

*(continued)*

*(continued)*

But even in regard to the economy, the new president faces enormous obstacles because Mexico's infrastructure is in such lousy shape. For example, in many neighborhoods here—even the ritziest—electricity can go off once a day.

## Crossed Calls

While Mexico is the 14th-largest economy in the world, it is only around 70th in density of phone lines, with fewer than nine for every 100 people. Phone lines still get crossed often enough that a common first question from a caller is "Whom have I reached?" Getting a phone line installed typically takes months, and costs $1,100 for a business. Rates on calls to the U.S. from Mexico are about twice as high as for calls made in the other direction.

The ports are badly managed. "And, of course, the railroads are a disaster," says Jesus Olivas, director of finance at International de Ceramica SA, a maker of floor and wall tile. Even though a rail spur runs right next to Interceramic's plants in Chihuahua, the rail lines to other regions are so inadequate and in such disrepair that Interceramic sends products to only one city by rail. The rest of its shipments go by truck.

The roads aren't so great, either. Though the current administration has been on a road-building binge, only about a third of the roads in Mexico are paved. So little preparation is done for laying roads, too, that many have potholes or bumps in them the day they open. It doesn't help that countless trucks roll over the roads, or that these trucks may be carrying twice the weight the U.S. allows.

Some of the new toll roads are beautifully constructed, but financing in Mexico is so expensive that many companies decide the lofty tolls aren't worth the price. The six-hour round trip between Mexico City and Acapulco, for instance, costs about $150 in tolls for a passenger car, and much more for a truck or bus.

To top it all off, just getting goods into the country in the first place is difficult—especially now, in the early stages of NAFTA. Many U.S. companies have complained that the Mexicans have been overly cautious about certificates of origin, as they try to make sure that the required percentage of a shipment into Mexico actually originated in North America. The companies also complain that the Mexicans are understaffed, undertrained, and undersupplied with the sort of technology that would speed the customs process.

U.S. companies are finding that in Mexico customs brokers aren't optional, as they are in the U.S. And they seem to complicate the process, even though they are there to make sure the paperwork is properly filed. One day a broker will say he needs an additional document faxed to him. The next day, he'll say he needs the original of the document. This continues as the broker, paid by the day, runs up his fees.

"Customs brokers are like New York plumbers," says Ray Shaw, a senior manager in the international-trade and customs-services group of Arthur Andersen & Co., the accounting firm. "They pretty much work on their own time." He says he knows of one big U.S. company that was desperate to get a shipment into Mexico, but its broker was off playing golf; he couldn't be bothered to come back to sort out the problem.

An executive from Grupo Casa Autrey SA, a big distributor in Mexico, says even highly organized Wal-Mart Stores Inc. has found out how hard it is to fathom distribution in Mexico. When Wal-Mart set up its huge store in Mexico City, it turned down a proposal from Autrey to supply the M&M candies sold there. Wal-Mart knew it could use its purchasing power to get a much better price in the U.S. and could then ship the product to Mexico itself. But, the executive says, after a few months Wal-Mart ran into so many shipping and customs problems that it decided the cost of providing M&Ms to its Mexico City store was almost identical to the price Autrey wanted to charge. So it gave Autrey the contract—and let Autrey deal with the headaches.

As if all these problems weren't enough, kidnapping has surfaced this year as a major worry. Security experts say Mexico has become the third-biggest trouble spot in Latin America for kidnappings, after Rio de Janeiro and Colombia. So far, kidnappers have grabbed only Mexican executives—including billionaire banker Alfredo Harp Helu and billionaire retailer Angel Losada Moreno—inspiring sensationalistic headlines this spring. Security experts are optimistic that foreigners won't become targets, because they aren't as well known as the wealthy Mexicans and don't have so much money readily available in the country. Nonetheless, many foreign executives are stepping up security.

*Mr. Paul B. Carroll*
is *The Wall Street Journal's* Mexico City Bureau Chief.

# Chapter Summary

The North American Free Trade Agreement encompasses the largest free trade area in the world—Canada, Mexico, and the United States. The agreement became effective on January 1, 1994, and will have far reaching effects well into the next century. NAFTA was based on the earlier U.S.–Canadian Free Trade Agreement of 1989. NAFTA was agreed to by the legislatures of the three countries only after heated debate. Proponents of the agreement saw it as a means of expanding trade opportunities for North American products, spurring cross-border investment, increasing the number of high-paying U.S. jobs in export industries, and bringing greater economic and social stability to Mexico. Opponents argued that it would result in large-scale loss of U.S. and Canadian jobs to low-wage workers in Mexico. Since the agreement went into effect, some U.S. factories have moved to Mexico, but many Asian manufacturers have also moved operations to Mexico to give them a jumping-off platform to the Americas. In the short time that NAFTA has been in effect, trade and cross-border investment in North America has grown. Although Mexico suffered a severe financial crisis in 1994, most businesspeople, investors, and traders are optimistic about the future of business there.

NAFTA is more than just a trade agreement. It contains broad provisions affecting a wide range of topics—trade in goods and services, cross-border investment, the protection of intellectual property, the protection of the environment, the health and safety of workers, and more. It calls on each of the three countries to harmonize their laws in these areas. Special rules apply to key industries, such as automobiles and telecommunications.

North American trade and investment laws are complex. Anyone buying or selling goods must be keenly aware of the complicated customs procedures that must be followed in moving goods across borders. For instance, a product is qualified for NAFTA trade preferences or advantages only if it originated in North America. To know its country-of-origin, the exporter and importer must have a working knowledge of the rules of origin applicable to that product. NAFTA also sets out special rules for cross-border trade in services that affect banking, insurance, and transportation. Although NAFTA generally makes investment in Mexican firms easier, when starting new companies or purchasing existing ones, potential investors must have good legal advice covering investment rules as well as good advice on how they might be affected by future economic or political changes.

Finally, keep in mind that NAFTA is a part of a wider free trade movement encompassing the entire Western Hemisphere. No sooner was NAFTA effective than did the Caribbean countries ask to join. They feared being left behind as free trade leads to economic growth in the hemisphere. They were concerned that investors from the United States and other countries would relocate their factories to Mexico to qualify for NAFTA treatment. Admission to NAFTA would mean access to North American markets for their products and increased investment from sources worldwide.

In 1994, 34 nations met in Miami for the *Summit of the Americas,* at which their heads of state announced their intention to negotiate a *Free Trade Agreement of the Americas* by the year 2005. Trade ministers from these countries met in 1995 to continue negotiations in that direction. In that year, negotiations opened to permit Chile to join NAFTA. However, the U.S. Presidential race of 1996 slowed the momentum. Some observers predict that Chile, and possibly other Latin American countries, will join NAFTA in the not-too-distant future. While the movement to free trade and investment policies can be derailed by any number of events, such as political change and economic crisis, the end of the twentieth century seems a time of trade liberalization in the Americas.

## QUESTIONS AND CASE PROBLEMS

1. Based on discussions in this chapter and Chapter Three, explain how a free trade area differs from a common market. Give examples of each.

2. Consider a study of doing business in Mexico. How does the economic, cultural, social, and political climate affect a business there? Describe Mexico's form of government. How are business relations conducted there? Are they more or less formal than in other Western countries? Describe how Mexico's policies toward trade and investment have changed over the years. Do you believe that Mexico provides a stable climate for trade and investment? What products or industries would seem to do well in the Mexican market?

3. Given the evidence about the ineffectiveness of the labor and environmental side agreements to NAFTA, do you think they should be included in any expansion of NAFTA? In a different form? Explain.

4. Your company produces "Big Duster" tires. Your most popular styles are the ones with the raised white lettering on the outside of the tire. You would like to export tires to Mexico, but cannot pass the Mexican labeling and marking requirements. Among the many other requirements, to remold the tires in Spanish would be costly. You do not think the regulations are fair. Do the requirements violate NAFTA? What course of action should you take?

5. Your company distills Kentucky bourbon. A Canadian competitor is also selling Kentucky bourbon in Ontario, but their bourbon is made in Canada. Canada's liquor control agency has looked the other way and ignored your requests to enjoin the sale. Does the sale violate NAFTA? GATT? Would this action be heard before the NAFTA Free Trade Commission or the World Trade Organization? What steps can be taken to force Canada to enjoin the sale? What remedies are available? If the Canadian products are exported to the United States, can they be stopped at the border?

6. Compare and contrast other trade preference programs such as the Generalized System of Preferences and the Caribbean Basin Initiative, with NAFTA. If the Caribbean countries already receive trade preferences under the CBI, why would many of them want admission to NAFTA?

7. How does the function of a NAFTA arbitral panel differ from that of a binational panel? What is the standard of review in binational panel decisions? Describe the role of an extraordinary challenge committee. Why does NAFTA recommend that panelists on binational panels and extraordinary challenge committees be judges or former judges whenever possible, but arbitral panelists may be specialists in international business or trade?

8. What is a rule of origin? Why is it important to the operation of a free trade area?

9. Discuss the social responsibility of a Canadian or U.S. manager working in Mexico. If a certain course of action were illegal in the manager's own country, but lawful and accepted in Mexico, which standard should the manager follow? Describe the social responsibility of firms operating in Mexico in regard to environmental protection, worker health and safety, and corrupt practices.

10. As you read this, what progress has been made toward wider Western Hemisphere free trade? In the Caribbean? In Central and South America?

## MANAGERIAL IMPLICATIONS

Consider the following NAFTA management problem in a global business context.

DownPillow, Inc., a small U.S. manufacturer of down comforters and pillows, sells nationally through high-quality retailers. The company is known for its quality of materials and production. Its raw materials include cotton fabric, unfilled cotton shells and down fills. These materials are not produced in the United States in sufficient quantities to meet the needs of the U.S. market. The Harmonized Tariff Schedule classification for unfilled comforter shells is 6307.90. The classification for finished down comforters is HTS 9404.90.

For many years, DownPillow purchased materials from Europe and paid in foreign currency. Gradually, costs rose because European suppliers faced higher labor and overhead costs. A declining U.S. dollar made goods more costly, but as costs rose, the company couldn't pass them on in price increases. When the U.S. market became more competitive in the early 1990s, DownPillow looked to China for cheaper materials. China is the world's leading producer of cotton textiles and down fill. Chinese textiles enter the United States under strict quota limits, enforced by U.S. Customs. Quota category 362 includes unfilled shells, comforters, quilts, bedspreads, and other top-of-the-bed products. DownPillow negotiated with a Chinese manufacturer for low-cost materials, priced in dollars. The new products were introduced to U.S. customers in 1993 at competitive prices. The new lower-priced goods quickly became an important part of the company's line.

In the following year the political situation changed. The United States accused China of illegally transshipping textiles through third countries to "get around" the U.S. quota. In response, the United States reduced the quota on category 362. In 1994, the annual quota closed in early fall. Goods anticipated for shipment during the Christmas season sat in a customs-bonded warehouse at the port until released by U.S. Customs on January 2, 1995. By 1995 the largest U.S. importers of comforters and bedspreads had bought their merchandise early, and the quota closed on March 6. DownPillow was barely able to obtain sufficient unfilled shells for its production needs. When it tried to switch its customers back to the higher-priced merchandise made from European materials, they balked. Many threatened to take their business elsewhere.

1. Management is desperate for a solution. It has learned that Canada will permit the entry of Chinese textiles. They also know that Canadian trade negotiators put a little-known rule of origin in NAFTA providing that a product that undergoes a change from category 6307.90 to category 9404.90 will become a product of North America. (Tariff shifting is not generally available for textile articles, but widely available for many other manufactured and processed goods.) They would like your opinion on answers to the following questions:
   a. May they bring the Chinese cotton shells into Canada, and ship them to the United States despite the quota? What processes would have to take place in Canada to do this. If they did, what would the tariff rate be? Would they see any net tariff savings?
   b. Production in Canada would give ready access to the Canadian home-fashions market. Should the company explore the possibility of investment in a plant in Canada? What are the pros and cons of such a move? How would they be affected by NAFTA investment provisions?
   c. Canada is a good supplier of goose down. Would it make a difference if they used down from Canadian geese, as opposed to down plucked from geese in, say, Poland?
   d. Every state requires that comforters may only be sold if they are manufactured or imported by licensed bedding manufacturers. Does NAFTA prohibit the application of these rules to Canadian and Mexican companies? What is the purpose of these rules?
   e. The company also has had some interest from buyers in Mexico. Would any import duties apply on shipments of either its U.S.- or Canadian-made products to Mexico? What would the tariff rate be? What special textile labeling rules are applicable, and how would they affect the company's ability to market there?
   f. Management is concerned about meeting foreign health standards applicable to a natural product like down and feathers. Where would they go for information on foreign regulations?
2. Management is concerned that this rule of origin will soon be eliminated and that the basic rules of origin for textiles will apply—the fiber-forward rule would cause the items to remain a product of China. Discuss what other courses of action might be open to them. What would they have to do in order to produce a comforter that originates in North America?
3. Discuss the wisdom of DownPillow's decision to switch sources of supply to China. Describe the impact of customs and tariff law on a North American firm's strategy. Describe how this small company was affected by international political events out of its control. Do you think the company underestimated its customers and its market?

# Chapter Fifteen
# The Regulation of Exports

Building on previous discussions of laws and regulations relating to the import of goods, this chapter examines the U.S. regulation of exports. In Western European and North American countries, the inflow of technology is relatively free. The principal issues in those countries arise from the varying interpretations of national antitrust limitations, which are discussed in Chapter Twenty-three. For the U.S. investor, the principal concerns arise in U.S. laws regulating the outflow of technology.

Historically, the United States has been concerned about its technology and weaponry falling into the hands of its enemies. The "enemy" has been defined differently from decade to decade as allegiances shifted, but the conviction that one should provide neither a military nor an economic advantage to the current enemy has remained constant. Therefore, the United States, in conjunction with its allies, has chosen to regulate the export and re-export of arms, technology, commodities with military applications, and other strategic commodities including technical data, component parts, and chemicals. *Technical data* is a specialized term that refers to technical information about a product or process that is not available to the general public.

Initially, the focus was on controlling technology moving from "West to East" to communist countries. The emphasis has shifted because of the collapse of the USSR and the end of the cold war to "North-South" concerns or movement of technology to belligerent or unstable Third World countries. Nonetheless, controls still exist to the former communist countries as well.

The government agencies that handle the control of exports are the Department of Commerce Bureau of Export Administration, Department of State Office of Defense Trade Controls, Department of the Treasury Office of Foreign Assets Control, Department of Defense, Department of Energy (nuclear area), and the intelligence community. The Department of Commerce plays the greatest role in the control of "dual use" commodities—those that have both a business use as well as a potential military application. The controls cover equipment, software, and technology. The breadth of the technology covered by the export control regulations is expansive, ranging from formulas to make toxic chemicals to computers (including data and its application).

Controlling exports is not as simple as, say, a basketball game where the object is to keep the ball from the other side and to score points for one's team. The United States and its allies, including Japan, are theoretically on the same team, yet each has concerns about sharing technology among teammates or allies. For example, pitched battles were waged over agreements to cooperate with Japan in developing specialized missile systems, because some people feared the agreements would give some economic advantage to the already powerful Japan. Lurking behind the economic argument lay concern about delivering a military advantage to a current ally but a former formidable enemy. Friendly nations also compete to develop particular kinds of technology, e.g., high-definition television, so that one country may enjoy the economic rewards of being first.

Many items are routinely allowed to be exported without an individual export license because of the decontrol of technology, however, knowing which ones are still controlled requires attention. Thus, for the first-timer, as well as the seasoned exporter, a review of how the law and regulations will affect their product is essential.

This chapter examines the history of U.S. export controls, the current export laws, the concurrence of other nations with U.S. law, and the enforcement of these laws. It concludes with an assessment of the effectiveness and necessity of such controls, and their impact on business.

## History of Export Controls

The rationale for controlling exports is not a complicated one. An example with hypothetical countries illustrates the problem: If the country, Igo, is an "enemy" of Mabu, then it is reasonable that Igo does not want Mabu to have any advantage supplied directly or indirectly by Igoan business people that will adversely affect Igo militarily or economically. Yet if Mabu can buy the same technology from Rowa, doesn't that only hurt Igoan business?

Therein lies the dilemma of export controls: If one refuses to supply the desired goods to the "enemies," then someone else will. As a consequence, not only will the hostile country have the technology, but U.S. businesses will have lost a sale. Yet no one wants to assist in fulfilling Lenin's alleged prophecy that "The capitalists will sell us the rope we need to hang them." As the definition of "enemy" changes and becomes less clear-cut (and is by no means uniformly agreed upon), the task is made more difficult. Even within the United States, significant disagreements arise within the business community and the defense establishment on these issues. For example, the United States encouraged trade with Iraq until Iraq's invasion of Kuwait in August 1990.

### The Development of the Legal Framework

During the American Revolution, Congress outlawed exports to Britain. The United States utilized export controls during the early 1900s in response to either war or emergency conditions. They were reintroduced during World War II and were intended to last only until the war ended. When hostilities ceased, the justification of preventing critical shortages of necessary goods was no longer relevant, but the cold war tensions developed in which old allies of World War II, the So-

viet Union and United States, who had fought the common enemy of Germany, themselves became enemies. The archetypal battle between democracy and communism had begun in earnest, and export controls were a way to ensure that the West proffered no economic or military help to the Eastern Bloc. The *Export Control Act of 1949* reflected this philosophy. This Act controlled the exporting of commodities with military application to communist countries and gave the president power to restrict exports based upon three criteria: national security, foreign policy, or the preservation of materials in short supply. Thereafter, Congress renewed the powers of the president under this Act and in subsequent acts. Congress has the power under the U.S. Constitution "to regulate commerce with foreign nations." Article I, section 8. Under the law, Congress delegated power to the president, who in turn delegated it to the secretary of commerce.

The United States was not alone in its efforts to control exports. Concurrently, in 1949, the United States and six European countries formed the *Coordinating Committee for Multilateral Export Controls* (COCOM).

In the United States, many revisions and acts followed the original Export Control Act. In 1951, the *Battle Act* (Mutual Defense Assistance Act), which controlled arms exports, made official the U.S. role in COCOM and tied foreign aid to compliance with the goals of export controls. This Act was followed by the *Mutual Security Act of 1954*. In 1962, because of escalating U.S.-Soviet tensions relating to Cuba, the Export Control Act was strengthened to authorize the denial of export licenses to ship goods "detrimental to the national security and welfare of the United States." Subsequent enactments of the *Export Administration Acts* of 1969, 1974, and 1977 stated that the purpose was "to restrict the export of goods and technology which would make a significant contribution to the military potential of any other nation or nations which would prove detrimental to the national security of the United States."

At the same time export controls were being strengthened, the law reflected a growing recognition that the United States and allied countries must be able to export in order to be competitive. In 1979, Congress enacted the *Export Administration Act* (EAA), which acknowledged the necessity of balancing the need for trade and exports with national security interests. Subsequent changes were made by the *Export Administration Act Amendments of 1985* and the *Export Enhancement Act of 1988* (part of the *Omnibus Act*). The 1988 law substantially liberalized U.S. export controls, easing license restrictions and decontrolling some items while increasing penalties and reinforcing the enforcement process. These controls expired in 1990.

Subsequently, Congress enacted extensions of the EAA. In April 1993, Congress extended the Act through June 30, 1994. When the extension expired—Congress was stymied on a more controversial overhaul of the entire export system proposed by the Clinton administration—President Clinton was forced to use powers granted under IEEPA (International Emergency Economic Powers Act) and extend the provisions of the EAA. Because of the concern over the Fall 1994 elections and the GATT vote, the Senate did not vote on the reauthorization. As of this writing, the EAA is extended by Executive Order 12924 (reprinted in Exhibit 15.1) and extended annually by notice in the Federal Register.

Export controls have been dramatically reshaped by a number of factors. The end of the cold war and the struggle to identify who is the "enemy" as well as the Gulf War and the apparent ease with which Suddam Hussein was able to acquire so much military equipment created a significant impact. These events shifted the focus of the debate to controlling the end use or user of the technology.

New regulations were adopted in 1996 (15 C.F.R. 730) but did not go into effect until March 1997. The regulations are supposed to be more "user friendly" and shift the presumption to no export license required unless specifically stated. The regulations are still cumbersome and lengthy, however.

## Multilateral Export Control

The Coordinating Committee for Multilateral Export Controls (COCOM) was formed in 1949 to coordinate the exports of technology to communist countries. Seventeen countries were members including Australia, Belgium, Canada, Denmark, Germany, Greece, Italy, the United Kingdom, France, Japan, Luxembourg, the Netherlands, Norway, Portugal, Spain, Turkey, and the United States. Several countries, Ireland, Sweden, Switzerland, Finland, Austria, Singapore, and New Zealand, had agreements to enforce export controls and thus share some of the benefits of more liberal intramember exporting. Under COCOM, members reviewed certain licenses.

The end of the cold war also signalled a major reassessment of export controls by the members. COCOM ceased to exist on March 30, 1994. The Wassenaar Arrangement formed in 1996 (named after a suburb of the Netherlands near the Hague) does not have the single-country veto, as COCOM did. The 33 current member countries include the United States, countries of Europe, Russia, Japan, Turkey, and many Eastern European countries. Thus the United States cannot veto another country's decision to issue an export license. This loose arrangement reflects the lack of consensus about the level of control necessary in today's world. There is a serious question about the utility of any export controls imposed by only one country (see the article on the next page). It is interesting to note that in such an important matter, there is no treaty; essentially there is a notice requirement wherein member countries will give another country the opportunity to object to the issuance of an export license.

## The Purpose of the Current Law

The purpose of the current law remains much the same as in the earlier laws:

It is the policy of the United States that export trade by United States citizens be given a high priority and not be controlled except when such controls (A) are necessary to further fundamental national security, foreign policy, or short supply objectives. . . .

It could be estimated that approximately 80 percent of the controls are concerned with national security and foreign policy. Adherence to the goals of nuclear nonproliferation and noncooperation with boycotts are also goals of the legislation.

Controls apply to four types of transactions:

1. Export of commodities and technical data from the United States.
2. Re-exports of U.S.-origin commodities and technical data among foreign countries.

**EXHIBIT 15.1    Executive Extension of EAA**

### Executive Order 12924

*Continuation of Export Control Regulations*

By the authority vested in me as President by the Constitution and the laws of the United States of America, including but not limited to section 203 of the International Emergency Economic Powers Act, I, William J. Clinton, President of the United States of America, find that the unrestricted access of foreign parties to U.S. goods, technology, and technical data and the existence of certain boycott practices of foreign nations, in light of the expiration of the Export Administration Act of 1979, as amended, constitute an unusual and extraordinary threat to the national security, foreign policy, and economy of the United States and hereto declare a national emergency with respect to that threat.

Accordingly, in order (a) to exercise the necessary vigilance over exports and activities affecting the national security of the United States; (b) to further significantly the foreign policy of the United States, including its policy with respect to cooperation by U.S. persons with certain foreign boycott activities, and to fulfill its international responsibilities; and (c) to protect the domestic economy from the excessive drain of scarce materials and reduce the serious economic impact of foreign demand, it is hereby ordered as follows:

*Section 1.* To the extent permitted by law, the provisions of the Export Administration Act of 1979, as amended, and the provisions for administration of the Export Administration Act of 1979, as amended, shall be carried out under this order so as to continue in full force and effect and amend, as necessary, the 1979, as amended. . . .

*Section 2.* All rules and regulations issued or continued in effect by the Secretary of Commerce under the authority of the Export Administration Act of 1979, as amended, including those published in Title 15, Subtitle B, Chapter VII, Subchapter C, of the Code of Federal Regulations, Parts 768 through 799, and all orders, regulations, licenses, and other forms of administrative action issued, taken, or continued in effect pursuant thereto, shall, until amended or revoked by the Secretary of Commerce, remain in full force and effect as if issued or taken pursuant to this order, except that the provisions of sections 203(b)(2) and 206 of the Act shall control over any inconsistent provisions in the regulations. Nothing in this section shall affect the continued applicability of administrative sanctions provided for by the regulations described above.

*Section 3.* Provisions for administration of section 38(e) of the Arms Export Control Act may be made and shall continue in full force and effect until amended or revoked under the authority of section 203 of the Act. To the extent permitted by law, this order also shall constitute authority for the issuance and continuation in full force and effect of all rules and regulations by the President or his delegate, and all orders, licenses, and other forms of administrative actions issued, taken, or continued in effect pursuant thereto, related to the administration of section 38(e).

*Section 4.* Executive Order No. 12923 of June 30, 1994, is revoked, and that declaration of emergency is rescinded. The revocation of Executive Order No. 12923 shall not affect any violation of any rules, regulations, orders, licenses, and other forms of administrative action under that order that occurred during the period the order was in effect.

*Section 5.* This order shall be effective as of midnight between August 20, 1994, and August 21, 1994, and shall remain in effect until terminated.

William J. Clinton

The White House, August 19, 1994.

---

*Foreign Accents*

# The Limited Utility of Export Controls

## Should Export Controls Be Used for Political Purposes?

As United Nations inspectors scour Iraq in a desperate hunt for contraband and nuclear materials, Washington is abuzz with schemes to insure that future Saddam Husseins don't turn up on the world stage. The coming debate over the lapsed Export Administration Act will enable members of Congress and the Administration to offer their plans, and high on the list will be proposals for the United States to impose even tighter export controls.

*(continued)*

*(continued)*

Yet as we approach the first anniversary of the Gulf War, one lesson that every policy maker should have absorbed is this: Export controls are no panacea. Such controls, especially unilateral ones, have proved inadequate against the determined efforts of governments to develop a capacity for the mass destruction of their neighbors.

During the 1980's, Saddam Hussein managed to obtain—from many suppliers—sensitive technologies and more than $40 billion in military equipment. During the Cold War, despite history's most prolonged and ambitious system of export controls, the Soviet Union designed and produced tens of thousands of nuclear warheads and created a formidable conventional capability.

If export controls are to be effective, they must be focused narrowly and have multilateral support. American controls against the Soviet Union, for instance, were most successful when coordinated with other countries and targeted at technologies with clear military significance. Compare this with Washington's first moves after the Gulf War. To control the spread of biological and chemical warfare capabilities, it tried to ban anything—even trucks and typewriters—that seemed destined for use at such facilities. And, according to current plans, export licenses are required for anything an exporter "knows" will contribute to development of lethal weapons. The House's version of the legislation contains some control proposals that are similarly comprehensive—and equally unlikely to win multilateral support.

Measures like these play well in Peoria. The Government gives the appearance of leaving no stone unturned as it tries to bottle up gruesome technologies and punish companies that trade with the enemy. And the Administration knows that nobody wants to be accused of promoting the spread of chemical and biological weapons—least of all an American exporter who might one day need the support of regulators.

Yet such measures actually do great mischief. They undermine the chances of establishing a system of deterrents that may really count. And, with enterprises and technology moving easily across borders, they invite American producers to move their facilities elsewhere. They also weaken the United States economy and saddle exporters with the stigma of being unreliable.

For 40 years, the United States has led the world in the zealous use of export restrictions, with efforts that, at times, have seemed ludicrous. These efforts have included attempts in the 50's to control the export of machetes and mosquito netting to suppress agrarian rebels in Latin America, and efforts in the 70's and 80's to restrain the export of personal computers and oilfield equipment in the Soviet Union. At times, other nations have been greedy and irresponsible in resisting sensible American appeals for their cooperation. Just as often, their resistance has been based on the conviction that the American proposals were futile, misguided and counterproductive. Export controls should be used more as a scalpel than as a wrecking ball. They cannot produce results when sources of supply are numerous and the products are common commodities.

The key ingredient for maintaining peace in the modern world is nurturing and strengthening a consensus worth maintaining. Such a consensus was an indispensable element in NATO's success in containing the Soviet Union and in the success of Desert Storm in containing Iraq. Any policy that weakens the chances of building and maintaining such a consensus—such as the indiscriminate use of export restrictions—must be curbed.

*Michael Mastanduno and Raymond Vernon*
*The New York Times Company,* 1991.

3. Exports and re-exports from a foreign country of products with U.S.-origin parts.
4. Exports and re-exports from a foreign country of products based on U.S. technical data (products designed from U.S.-origin research and technical data; re-exports include goods shipped from the United States to Singapore, for example, and from Singapore to India).

Thus, shipments out of the United States as well as from foreign countries are affected by this law.

## Reasons for Control

The possible reasons for control of exports include:

AT    Antiterrorism
CB    Chemical and biological weapons
CC    Crime control
MT    Missile technology
NS    National security
NP    Nuclear nonproliferation
RS    Regional stability
SS    Short supply
XP    Computers

## Problems with Control

The Soviet pipeline dispute exemplifies some of the frustration companies may have in dealing with the ever-changing regulations. Dresser Industries, Inc., a U.S. corporation, had a French subsidiary, Dresser France, which made compressors and pumps to be used in oil and gas development. Dresser France signed a contract with V/O Machino-Import (a Soviet entity) and Creuset Loire (a French entity) to deliver twenty-one gas compressors to be used in the construction of a pipeline between the Soviet Union and Europe. Dresser, Inc., had licensed its technology to Dresser France.

In 1981, because of Soviet interference in Poland, the U.S. Commerce Department issued a series of export regulations that specifically restricted export of gas technology. The U.S. company ordered its French subsidiary to cease shipment under the contract, but the French government instructed the company to honor its contract. Dresser France began to ship the compressors.

The Department of Commerce placed Dresser France on the Table of Denial Orders (TDO), thereby denying the company export licenses and preventing other U.S. companies from doing business with Dresser France.

Dresser France complied with the order, but appealed it in the United States, seeking to enjoin the issuance of the TDO. Its motion was denied. On November 16, 1982, however, the Department of Commerce moved to vacate the TDO because the controls established on oil and gas technology in 1981 and 1982 were rescinded by the U.S. government, thus voiding any enforcement action brought under them.

Export controls are also necessary to prevent "excessive drain of scarce materials and to reduce serious inflationary impact of foreign demand." The law provides a mechanism whereby any entity may petition to the secretary of commerce, claiming the need for controls. These controls have been utilized for metallic materials, crude oil, refined petroleum products, certain agricultural products, and unprocessed red cedar.

An interesting example of how the export laws may be used to suit other purposes is the inclusion of a prohibition on the shipment of horses by sea without special permission. This case was a victory for animal rights activists who were intent on slowing down the export of wild horses for processing overseas into horsemeat, a staple item in some cultures.

Another interesting example involved copper. During the Korean War, copper was selling for a higher price in Europe than in the United States. The United States began to have difficulty supplying the military needs for copper. The president had to restrict the export of copper to ensure the supply for the war effort. At a later date, in the 1970s, when the United States was experiencing a grain shortage, export controls were placed on grain and soybeans. Foreign buyers immediately had to turn to other sources, which made it difficult for the grain farmers to regain their foreign markets when controls were eased.

## Antiboycott Provisions

Antiboycott law provisions are also included in the act. The section on foreign boycotts makes it illegal to "comply . . . [with or] support any boycott fostered or imposed by a foreign country against a country which is friendly to the United States." This provision was primarily aimed at Middle Eastern countries that tried to orchestrate a boycott of Israel. The following case addresses a challenge to the constitutionality of both the Export Administration Act and the Antiboycott Regulations published in the Code of Federal Regulations.

## BACKGROUND AND FACTS

In December 1954, the League of Arab States called for an economic boycott of Israel. Under the "General Principles" worked out by the Arab states, a firm could be blacklisted if it traded with Israel.

The plaintiff manufactures internal combustion engines. Its products are often used as component parts. Briggs has been blacklisted because of dealing with Israel.

In May of 1977, Briggs received a letter from its Syrian distributor telling it that it had been blacklisted and refused an import license. He also received a questionnaire, which was translated as follows:

1. Has the company now or in the past main or branch factories in Israel?
2. Has the company now or in the past general offices in Israel for its regional or international works?
3. Has it granted now or in the past the right of utilizing its name or trademarks or patents to persons or establishments or Israel works inside or outside Israel?
4. Does it share in or own now or in the past shares in Israel works or establishments inside or outside Israel?
5. Does it now or did it offer in the past any technical assistance to any Israeli work or establishment?
6. Does it represent now or did it represent in the past any Israel establishment or work inside or outside Israel?
7. What are the companies which it shares in or with, their nationality and the size or rate of this share.

Briggs answered the questions "no," but did not have it authenticated because of the new antiboycott regulations. The blacklisting continued, but subsequently the company was removed from the blacklist. Briggs was unquestionably injured economically by the blacklisting. Briggs brought an action against the officials charged with enforcing the act and regulations, claiming that they violated the First, Fifth, and Ninth Amendments to the U.S. Constitution.

## Briggs and Stratton Corp. v. Baldridge

539 F.Supp. 1307 (E.D. Wis. 1982) aff'd., 728 F.2d 915 (1984)
United States Court of Appeals (7th Cir.)

## DISTRICT JUDGE GORDON

... The Commerce Department regulations are consistent with this express policy to require persons to refuse to furnish information which would have the effect of furthering a boycott against a nation friendly to the United States. Thus the regulations are not inconsistent with the policies of the act.

I also reject Briggs' argument that the regulations permit a firm to supply information in the absence of a questionnaire that it cannot supply if it gets one. Example (ix) following the intent regulation reads:

"U.S. company A is on boycotting country Y's blacklist. In an attempt to secure its removal from the blacklist, A wishes to supply to Y information which demonstrates that A does at least as much business in Y and other countries engaged in a boycott of X as it does in X. A intends to continue its business in X undiminished and in fact is exploring and intends to continue exploring an expansion of its activities in X without regard to Y's boycott.

"A may furnish the information, because in doing so it has no intent to comply with, further, or support Y's boycott." 15 C.F.R. 369.1(e), Examples of Intent.

Briggs' interpretation of this example goes too far. The example merely permits a company on its own initiative to demonstrate non-discriminatory conduct. . . .

Briggs argues that because the regulations cause Briggs to be blacklisted, and thus affect its worldwide sales, the government has totally destroyed Briggs' rights to its foreign trade. Briggs likens the effect to a restriction on private property which "forc[es] some people alone to bear public burdens which, in all fairness and justice, should be borne by the public as a whole."

In *Andrus v. Allard*, the Supreme Court held that the denial of one traditional property right, where the others were not disturbed, did not always amount to a taking. In *Andrus*, there was no physical invasion or restraint on the property in question; the regulation only prohibited the sale

*(continued)*

*(continued)*

of the property. The Court did not find dispositive the fact that the regulations prevented the most profitable use of the property.

> When we review regulation, a reduction in the value of property is not necessarily equated with a taking. . . . [L]oss of future profits—unaccompanied by any physical property restriction—provides a slender reed upon which to rest a takings claim.

The reed is equally slender here. The regulations apply to all Americans equally. It is possible that they have a somewhat greater impact on Briggs than they do on others, but that does not constitute a taking. Briggs has lost some profits because it has lost some sales, but its property has not been seized or restrained by the government. There is no restriction by the challenged regulation on Briggs' efforts to export its products. In prohibiting Briggs from answering certain questions, the government has not taken Briggs' property in violation of the Fifth Amendment.

Therefore, IT IS ORDERED that the motion of the plaintiffs for summary judgment be and hereby is denied.

IT IS ALSO ORDERED that the defendant's motion for summary judgment be and hereby is granted.

IT IS FURTHER ORDERED that this action be and hereby is dismissed upon its merits.

**Decision.** Thus, the antiboycott regulations were upheld by the court despite the difficulty business may have in complying with them.

---

Other countries' companies do cooperate with the boycott. Companies have honestly replied that their internal sales policy forbids transactions with Israel. In the following case, an Israeli corporation unsuccessfully tried to use U.S. law to coerce a U.S. subsidiary of a Japanese bank to lend it money.

---

*Israel Aircraft Industries Ltd. v. Sanwa Business Credit Corporation and the Sanwa Bank, Ltd.*
16 F.3d 198 (1994)
United States Court of Appeals
(7th Cir.)

BACKGROUND AND FACTS

Sanwa Business Credit Corporation, the principal lender to Fairchild Aircraft Corporation, is the American subsidiary of a Japanese bank. After Fairchild entered bankruptcy, Israel Aircraft Industries, Ltd. (an Israeli corporation) and Quadrant Management, Inc., formed a joint venture to acquire Fairchild. They were unwilling to pay off Fairchild's debts at face value and asked Sanwa to accept the joint venture in lieu of Fairchild as the borrower under a revised credit arrangement. According to the complaint Sanwa said no, on instructions of its parent, for the sole reason that Sanwa Bank will not deal with any Israeli corporation so long as the League of Arab States maintains its boycott of Israel. The district court dismissed the complaint, holding that § 8 of the Export Administration Act does not create a private right of action in favor of victims of foreign boycotts.

EASTERBROOK, CIRCUIT JUDGE

. . . A look beneath the surface of this legislation reinforces the inferences from its text and structure. When Congress enacted the statute in 1977, it recognized that there would be no private enforcement.

The Senate Committee wrote of "[t]he danger of unwarranted allegations in this highly sensitive area." What makes the subject especially "sensitive" is that it concerns the foreign relations of the United States. Nations use boycotts and other forms of commercial pressure to achieve diplomatic and military ends. The United States uses the device frequently (at the moment, commerce with Cuba, Haiti, Iran, Iraq, Vietnam, and Yugoslavia is severely limited) and has no objection to the principle of international boycotts. Whether

*(continued)*

*(continued)*

to recognize or instead to resist a boycott announced by some other nation—and what form any resistance will take—depends on the degree of friendliness between the United States and its target, and on the other options available to the United States. This nation recognizes not only that foreign nationals may be under pressure by their home governments to comply with boycotts we seek to break, but also that diplomatic overtures may be more successful than awards of damages in undermining unwelcome boycotts. Our case, a suit by an Israeli corporation against a Japanese bank to obtain damages on account of the bank's decision to respect a boycott by the Arab League, exposes some of the complications. Would the State Department find it as easy to enlist Japanese aid in bringing about harmony between the Palestinians and Israel—a subject on which mighty strides have been made while this case was in progress—if American courts were compelling Japanese firms and their subsidiaries to pay large sums? Whatever bargaining space the State Department enjoys could be curtailed by the presence of actors (judges and private litigants) beyond the influence of U.S. negotiators. No surprise, then, that Congress left implementation of § 8 to the President, who establishes the foreign policy of the United States. It would be imprudent for a court to create rights of action that might interfere with the conduct of foreign policy. . . .

Israel Aircraft makes a claim under state law in addition to § 8. It contends that by refusing to advance credit to the joint venture, Sanwa tortiously interfered with its business opportunities—whether with Israel Aircraft's opportunity to deal with Quadrant, or the joint venture's ability to acquire Fairchild's assets, the complaint is not quite clear. . . .

Sanwa did not induce any third party to cease dealing with Israel Aircraft. It simply refused to lend any money to the joint venture. Israel Aircraft and Quadrant could have borrowed from any of a hundred other lenders and purchased Fairchild's assets in bankruptcy. Because the joint venture was unwilling to pay off Fairchild's loans in full (and apparently feared that it would not be the highest bidder at an auction in bankruptcy), it sought concessions from Sanwa, Fairchild's principal creditor. Sanwa balked. Israel Aircraft has not cited, and we could not find, any case holding a financial institution liable in tort for failing to make a concession that would have facilitated an extension of credit. By refusing to lend money, a bank does not "tortiously interfere" with the use the borrower would make of the funds. Other ways of characterizing Sanwa's conduct are possible but do not change the result under state law.

Affirmed.

---

To provide a sense of the volume of antiboycott prosecutions, consider the fact that in 1993 the Commerce Department imposed fines of $6.8 million on 37 companies and individuals. Recently, in September of 1994, two companies agreed to pay civil penalties of $410,000 (Kessler Inc., Rockville, Maryland) and $18,000 (Kenclaire Electrical, Westbury, New York). The companies had agreed to boycott Israel in selling railroad equipment and electrical equipment to the United Arab Emirates and Kuwait. Neither company admitted nor denied violating U.S. law. These companies chose to accept the penalty rather than fight the case in court. Even if a company believes it did nothing wrong, it may, as a business decision, accept the penalty without a trial because the penalty will be less costly.

An example of the first company to plead guilty to criminal violations of the antiboycott law is the hospital supply company, Baxter International (see the following article).

After the Gulf War, the Arab League announced that Coca-Cola was removed from the list of companies it has asked countries to avoid doing business with. Kuwait announced that it would resume doing business with companies that have ties to Israel and would urge other countries to do the same, however, the boycott did not end.

As a result of the Middle East peace process, however, in October of 1994 Saudi Arabia and the five members of the Gulf Cooperation Council (Kuwait, Oman, Bahrain, Qatar, and the United Arab Emirates) announced a partial lifting of the boycott by ending the blacklisting of companies that do business with Israel. They also expect to allow travelers to their counties to have passports that reflect travel to Israel, flights crossing airspace en route to Israel, postal

*Foreign Accents*

# A Company's Dilemma

Baxter International was faced with a dilemma and for its choice paid a price. Baxter International, a hospital supply company, through its general counsel Mr. Abbey, made contact with a Syrian national, Mr. Raslan living in Paris. They began to pay Mr. Raslan $30,000 a month to assist them in getting Baxter off the blacklist. Mr. Raslan told them they could be delisted if they invested as much in the Arab world as they had in Israel. They paid Mr. Raslan more than $700,000.

Baxter was also being pressured by a Swiss partner, Nestle SA, who stated that they would not proceed with a deal if Baxter was still blacklisted. Simultaneously, Teva, an Israel company made an offer to buy Baxter's Israeli plant. This proposition seemingly offered a helpful way out of Baxter's blacklist dilemma.

In the meantime, a disgruntled employee at Baxter, Dr. Fuisz, who was fired, used his contacts in the Arab world to amass the evidence against Baxter. He also contacted the Commerce Dept. The man in charge at the Commerce Dept. refused to pursue a criminal complaint, so the lower-level Commerce Dept. employee went over his boss' head and notified the Commerce Dept.'s inspector general. The case was ultimately turned over to federal prosecutors.

Some of the evidence used by federal prosecutors in the case included a letter by Counsel Abbey to Syrian officials stating, "there is no present intention to make new investments in Israel or to sell technology to Israeli companies." Mr. Abbey allegedly said that this statement should not be construed as a promise. Another piece of evidence was Mr. Abbey's annual report in which he allegedly listed his 1989 achievements as the delisting of Baxter. He noted that he had achieved this at "great personal and professional risk." Another Baxter employee negotiated to sell $3 million of supplies to a Syrian company for $1 million with the rest to be used as "fees"—another "helpful" factor in the delisting. The government also had as evidence a letter prepared by the Swiss unit manager of Baxter to a Syrian general in which he offered to give details of Baxter's sale of its plant in Israel.

Baxter plea bargained and agreed to pay a $3,382,000 civil fine, to accept a prospective denial of export privileges to Syria and Saudi Arabia for two years, and to pay the maximum criminal fine of $500,000. IMT, a Baxter subsidiary (of which Abbey was president), paid a civil fine of $2,527,500; Baxter AG, a Swiss subsidiary, paid $50,000 civil penalty. Mr. Abbey, the general counsel, paid a fine of $101,000, but did not resign. The company and officials only admitted to attempting to get off the blacklist and supplying information and money to achieve that objective. The case contained no finding about the sales of the plant in Israel.

Prior to this case, the largest fine had been $1 million without any admission of wrongdoing by Safeway. In 1992, 30 cases were settled under the boycott law for $2.1 million.

Baxter noted that it allocated $7.5 million to pay the fines, which would not affect the bottom line of $436 million earned on $8.47 billion of sales in 1992. The bad publicity and whether it will affect doing business with Jewish hospitals in the future is the unanswered question and hidden cost.

*The New York Times,* March 26, 1993, p. D1; *The Wall Street Journal,* March 29, 1993 p. B1; and *The Wall Street Journal,* March 26, 1993, p. A1.

deliveries, and transshipment and ships permitted to stop in a GCC country as well as stop at an Israeli port. On the other hand, the Arab League countries are on record as saying that the boycott will not end until Israel returns land taken in the 1967 war and progress is made with Israel, Syria, and Lebanon. Egypt had officially ended the boycott when it signed the peace agreement with Israel, but businesses continue to report problems.

## Power Politics in Export Controls

Historically, the U.S. export control laws have reflected objectives that often conflict. The United

States wants to encourage the development of U.S. companies' export business, but not at the expense of national security interests and foreign policy objectives.

This dilemma is exacerbated by the ever-dynamic relationship between the United States and different countries. For example, when Secretary Khrushchev concluded his visit to the United States by pounding his shoe on the desk and exclaiming, "We will bury you," the balance shifted more in the direction of national security. Later, when the politics of "detente" led to a thawing of international relations, loosening controls came under discussion. The 1988 trade bill reflected this philosophical shift. Nevertheless, a military change may send the seesaw teetering back in the other direction toward stricter controls, as occurred earlier when the Soviets invaded Afghanistan. Although they insisted they were invited, the invasion precipitated an increase in U.S. rhetoric. Ronald Reagan, then a candidate for president, dubbed the Soviet Union the "evil empire." President Jimmy Carter took the step of imposing a grain embargo that prohibited the shipment of U.S. grain to the Soviets. He also took the unusual step of withdrawing U.S. athletes from participation in the Moscow Olympics.

The collapse of the Soviet Union and Soviet bloc countries has encouraged optimism, particularly among the European allies who are eager to begin or expand a harmonious, productive, and unfettered trading relationship with their geographically close neighbor. The United States is facing increased pressure from the world community to decontrol many items. One must realize that the source of the authority is now the president's executive order under IEEPA, which could change when Congress agrees on new authorization legislation.

The major changes in Poland, Hungary, and the Czech Republic have logarithmically raised expectations of future trade partnerships. U.S. allies, as well as the countries that are former members of the Warsaw Pact, will increase their demands for an easing of restrictions on trade (export controls), as well as on licensing and investment. If countries feel that the former Soviets are no longer a threat waiting to pounce at the borders (as they did in the past in Prague and Afghanistan), then their concern will be transformed into a desire to sell and profit from the transfer of technology to these technologically hungry markets. President Clinton continued in the footsteps of President Bush in decontrolling many items. Computers and high-tech equipment were significantly decontrolled in 1993. In March of 1994 the old cold war bans on selling telecommunications and computer equipment to the former Soviet Union and China were ended. In 1997 to prevent a former Soviet Republic from selling off military equipment to Third World countries, the United States purchased them instead. This subsidization may have to substitute for a weaker multilateral export control regime.

> **http://www.bxa.doc.gov/**
> The home page of the Bureau of Export Administration (BXA), which enforces the EAA.

## Mechanics of the Law

This section examines in greater detail the mechanics of how the law and accompanying regulations contained in the Code of Federal Regulations are applied to companies engaged in export trade.

The new regulations break down export controls into 29 steps. Basic questions begin the process:

What is the item?

Where is it going?

Who will use it?

What will it be used for?

The first 6 steps are:

1. Which items are under jurisdiction of another agency?
2. Are they publicly available?
3. Are they re-exports of U.S.-origin items?
4. Are they foreign items made with *de minimis* U.S. parts?
5. Are they foreign made items with more than *de minimis* U.S. parts?
6. Are they foreign made item with U.S.-origin technology?

Step 7 requires a classification of the item on the Commerce Control List (CCL). Step 8 looks at the country destination, while Step 9 cross checks by chart whether a license is required.

There are ten general prohibitions:

1. Export and re-export of controlled items to listed countries.
2. Re-export and export from abroad of foreign-made items with more than a *de minimis* amount of controlled U.S. content.
3. Re-export and export from abroad of the foreign-produced direct product of U.S. technology.
4. Action prohibited by denial order.
5. Export or re-export to prohibited end-use or end-user.
6. Export to embargoed destination.
7. Export supporting proliferation activity or encryption.
8. Shipment through Albania, Armenia, Azerbaijan, Belarus, Bulgaria, Cambodia, Cuba, Estonia, Georgia, Kazakhstan, Kyrgystan, Laos, Latvia, Lithuania, Mongolia, North Korea, and Russia.
9. Violation of license or of regulation.
10. Proceeding with transaction with knowledge of a violation.

Source:   15 CFR §736.2

The regulations continue to monitor, in theory, the re-export of goods. Thus, if a controlled product moves from the U.S. to Thailand to India, the U.S. law purports to cover this transaction, even after a lapse of time. This extraterritorial application of U.S. law offends many countries. Its effectiveness may also be questioned in light of the Wassenaar arrangement supplanting COCOM.

## License

If an item is controlled, then the exporter must apply for a license. The exporter must use the ECCN, along with the Commerce Control List and Country Chart. There may be special exceptions based on item, country, license, or special conditions.

If no license is required, then *NLR* (no license required) is reported on the Shipper's Export Declaration (SED).

A new license, called the *Special Comprehensive License* (SCL) replaces earlier distribution and service supply licenses.

An exporter who does not know the ECCN, can request a classification. It is also possible to ask for an advisory opinion from the BXA. (See Exhibit 15.2 for a summary of the ECCN system.)

**Extraterritorial Application.**  A little-known fact is that the export control law covers the movement of U.S.-origin commodities and technical data or products containing U.S.-origin parts from one foreign country to another. This extraterritorial application of the law has caused some political problems for the United States. Its allies, including the United Kingdom, were not pleased that the United States (prior to 1989) did not have sufficient faith in each allied country's export control system.

The extraterritorial application of the law means that to move U.S.-origin goods controlled by export laws from India to Taiwan, one needs a U.S. export license. The law also covers the movements or the export and re-export of foreign products from a foreign country when the product is based on U.S.-origin technical data. Under these provisions, the United States has been pursuing high-level discussions with Israel for allegedly violating the Export Control Law by sharing what the United States believes was U.S.-origin technical data with South Africa for use in constructing a bomb.

## Licensing Review Process

One of the difficulties exporters face is that of trying to comply with the law in a way that allows them to do business in a timely manner and meet the demands of their clients. The Bureau of Export Administration (BXA) must review and rule on licenses within 90 days or send the matter to the president. This problem is compounded by the overlapping jurisdictions of the various U.S. agencies that administer the U.S. export laws, a situation that results in confusion over which agency has jurisdiction over a particular question.

Once the application for a type of validated license is received, the Office of Export Licensing reviews the application. (See Exhibit 15.3 for a sample of a multipurpose license application form.) If it is complete, the specialist will either make a determination about the license or refer the application to the relevant agency:

**EXHIBIT 15.2   Summary of Commerce Control List Numbering System Making Up the ECCN (Export Control Classification Number)**

(1) The CCL is divided into ten general categories, indicated by the first character, numbered from 0 to 1, as follows:
   0—Nuclear Materials, Facilities and Equipment, and Miscellaneous
   1—Materials
   2—Materials Processing
   3—Electronics
   4—Computers
   5—Telecommunications and Information Security
   6—Sensors and Lasers
   7—Avionics and Navigation
   8—Marine Technology
   9—Propulsion Systems and Transportation Equipment
(2) Five groups of products fall within each category; the second character is identified by the letters A through E as follows:
   A—Equipment, Assemblies, and Components
   B—Production and Test Equipment
   C—Materials
   D—Software
   E—Technology
(3) Reasons for control:
   0—National Security (including dual use)
   1—Missile Technology
   3—Nuclear Nonproliferation
   3—Chemical and Biological Weapons
   9—Antiterrorism, Crime Control, Short Supply, United Nations Sanctions

The ECCN is made up of these letters and numbers.

SOURCE:   15 C.F.R. §736

---

Department of Defense (national security)

Department of Energy (nuclear nonproliferation)

Department of State (reviews both the equipment and end-user for foreign policy concerns) (OTC—Office of Defense Trade Control)

Intelligence Community (end-user checks dealing with weapons of mass destruction)

Department of the Treasury (can also become involved in dealing with embargoed countries as well as tobacco and firearms)

OFAC (Office of Foreign Assets Control)

If the departments cannot reach consensus, the application goes through several layers of interagency committees including the Operating Committee, Advisory Committee on Export Policy (ACEP), Export Administration Review Board (EARB), culminating in a final decision by the president. Time limits prescribe when a matter must move to the next level, but no limits are placed on the total time the government can take to consider the application. At any time, an agency may send the matter out to the National Security Council for review.

For an example of a company's problem with the licensing process, see the article on page 507.

## Computerized Processing

A business deal that cannot be consummated because $10 million worth of computers are waiting for licenses so they can be shipped can cause the calmest executive to have a "Maalox moment." The Department of Commerce regulations have addressed a number of businesses' concerns about timeliness by installing an *Electronic License Application Information Network* (ELAIN) and an Electronic Request for Item

**EXHIBIT 15.3    Form BXA-748P: Multipurpose Application**

**B**

FORM BXA-748P
FORM APPROVED: OMB NO. 0694-0088, 0694-0089

**U.S. DEPARTMENT OF COMMERCE**
Bureau of Export Administration

**MULTIPURPOSE APPLICATION**

Information furnished herewith is subject to the provisions of Section 12(c) of the Export Administration Act of 1979, as amended, 50 U.S.C. app. 2411(c), and its unauthorized disclosure is prohibited by law.

**DATE RECEIVED**
(Leave Blank)    **X**

1. CONTACT PERSON

2. TELEPHONE

3. FACSIMILE

APPLICATION CONTROL NUMBER
**This is NOT an export license number.**

**Z 132248**

4. DATE OF APPLICATION

| 5. TYPE OF APPLICATION | 6. DOCUMENTS SUBMITTED WITH APPLICATION | 7. DOCUMENTS ON FILE WITH APPLICANT | 8. SPECIAL COMPREHENSIVE LICENSE |
|---|---|---|---|
| ☐ EXPORT | ☐ BXA-748P-A   ☐ LETTER OF EXPLANATION | ☐ BXA-711 | ☐ BXA-752 OR BXA-752-A |
| ☐ REEXPORT | ☐ BXA-748P-B   ☐ FOREIGN AVAILABILITY | ☐ LETTER OF ASSURANCE | ☐ INTERNAL CONTROL PROGRAM |
| ☐ CLASSIFICATION REQUEST | ☐ BXA-711   ☐ OTHER | ☐ IMPORT/END-USER CERTIFICATE | ☐ COMPREHENSIVE NARRATIVE |
| ☐ SPECIAL COMPREHENSIVE LICENSE | ☐ IMPORT/END-USER CERTIFICATE | ☐ NUCLEAR CERTIFICATION | ☐ CERTIFICATIONS |
| ☐ OTHER | ☐ TECH. SPECS. | ☐ OTHER | ☐ OTHER |

9. SPECIAL PURPOSE

10. RESUBMISSION APPLICATION CONTROL NUMBER

11. REPLACEMENT LICENSE NUMBER

12. FOR ITEM(S) PREVIOUSLY EXPORTED, PROVIDE LICENSE EXCEPTION SYMBOL OR LICENSE NUMBER

13. IMPORT/END-USER CERTIFICATE COUNTRY:          NUMBER:

| 14. APPLICANT | | 15. OTHER PARTY AUTHORIZED TO RECEIVE LICENSE | |
|---|---|---|---|
| ADDRESS LINE 1 | | ADDRESS LINE 1 | |
| ADDRESS LINE 2 | | ADDRESS LINE 2 | |
| CITY | POSTAL CODE | CITY | POSTAL CODE |
| STATE/COUNTRY | EMPLOYER IDENTIFICATION NUMBER | STATE/COUNTRY | TELEPHONE OR FAX |
| 16. PURCHASER | | 17. INTERMEDIATE CONSIGNEE | |
| ADDRESS LINE 1 | | ADDRESS LINE 1 | |
| ADDRESS LINE 2 | | ADDRESS LINE 2 | |
| CITY | POSTAL CODE | CITY | POSTAL CODE |
| COUNTRY | TELEPHONE OR FAX | COUNTRY | TELEPHONE OR FAX |
| 18. ULTIMATE CONSIGNEE | | 19. END-USER | |
| ADDRESS LINE 1 | | ADDRESS LINE 1 | |
| ADDRESS LINE 2 | | ADDRESS LINE 2 | |
| CITY | POSTAL CODE | CITY | POSTAL CODE |
| COUNTRY | TELEPHONE OR FAX | COUNTRY | TELEPHONE OR FAX |
| 20. ORIGINAL ULTIMATE CONSIGNEE | | 21. SPECIFIC END-USE | |
| ADDRESS LINE 1 | | | |
| ADDRESS LINE 2 | | | |
| CITY | POSTAL CODE | | |
| COUNTRY | TELEPHONE OR FAX | | |

| 22. (a) ECCN | (b) CTP | (c) MODEL NUMBER | | (d) CCATS NUMBER | 23. TOTAL APPLICATION DOLLAR VALUE |
|---|---|---|---|---|---|
| (e) QUANTITY | (f) UNITS | (g) UNIT PRICE | (h) TOTAL PRICE | (i) MANUFACTURER | $ |
| (j) TECHNICAL DESCRIPTION | | | | | |

24. ADDITIONAL INFORMATION

**For all applications:** I certify that to the best of my knowledge, all the information on this form is true and correct, and that it conforms to the instructions accompanying this form and the Export Administration Regulations. **For license applications:** I certify or agree, as appropriate that (a) to the best of my knowledge all statements in this application, including the description of the commodities, software or technology and their end-uses, and any documents submitted in support of this application are correct and complete and that they fully and accurately disclose all the terms of the order and other facts of the transaction; (b) I will retain records pertaining to this transaction and make them available as required by the Export Administration Regulations; (c) I will report promptly to the Bureau of Export Administration any material changes in the terms of the order or other facts or intentions of the transaction as reflected in this application and supporting documents, whether the application is still under consideration or a license has been granted; and (d) if the license is granted, I will be strictly accountable for its use in accordance with the Export Administration Regulations and all the terms and conditions of the license. A number of the parts of this form include certifications based on a person's knowledge. As defined in Part 772 of the Export Administration Regulations, "Knowledge" of a circumstance includes not only positive knowledge that the circumstance exists or is substantially certain to occur, but also an awareness of a high probability of its existence or future occurrence. Such awareness is inferred from evidence of the conscious disregard of facts known to a person and is also inferred from a person's willful avoidance of facts.

25. SIGNATURE (of person authorized to execute this application)    NAME OF SIGNER    TITLE OF SIGNER

This license application and any license issued pursuant thereto are expressly subject to all rules and regulations of the Bureau of Export Administration. Making any false statement or concealing any material fact in connection with this application or altering in any way the license issued is punishable by imprisonment or fine, or both, and by denial of export privileges under the Export Administration Act of 1979, as amended, and any other applicable Federal statutes. No license will be issued unless this form is completed and submitted in accordance with Export Administration Regulation.

**X**          **X**          **B**

USCOMM-DC 96-24024

# US-China Catch-22 Thwarts Elatec
## Private Firm Finds Conflicting Policies on Exports Are Difficult to Overcome

WILMINGTON—If exports to China are as important to the nation's trading future as the US government claims, William L. Kovacs wants to know:

• Why did the Commerce Department issue him a license to sell a $500,000 industrial machine to China—only to cancel that license after the machine was built but before it was shipped?

• Why did the US Export-Import Bank, which guaranteed the loan Kovacs took to build the machine, balk at paying out on an insurance policy it had issued to cover possible losses?

• And why, when sands seem to be shifting in US–China relations, does the government continue to promote China as an export opportunity to small businesses that can ill afford the political risks that his case demonstrates?

To be sure, this was no ordinary machine, nor was the buyer an ordinary customer.

The device built by Kovac's company, Elatec Technology Corp., is a vacuum-induction casting furnace, a specialized high-temperature unit used to melt metals ranging from titanium used in golf club heads to uranium for nuclear applications.

The privately held company, with 35 employees and $3.5 million in sales last year, has an impressive customer list, including the US Navy, the Pratt & Whitney aircraft engine division of United Technologies Corp., and Nuclear Metals Corp. of Concord.

But the customer for this particular furnace was China's government import-export agency, which would turn it over to the Shaan Xi Hongguang Machinery Factory in Xian, China, acknowledged to be an arm of the Chinese aerospace ministry.

Nevertheless, government and business observers agree the questions Kovacs asks after sustaining a costly reversal are legitimate, reflecting a tension between business and the Commerce Department over conflicting policies that, on the one hand, promote China exports, and, on the other, obstruct them.

And the squeeze on business, especially small business, appears to be getting tighter, especially where prospective exports might be classified as "dual use," meaning they could be put to either civilian or military applications.

Swirling allegations of big donations by China lobbyists to US politicians are part of the reason for Commerce's behavior, government sources say. But the department's stance also seems guided by a perennial and growing debate over whether the United States should renew China's most-favored-nation trading status—a topic due to go before Congress again this year.

Small businesses, ranging from software manufacturers to tool shops and lacking the well-oiled lobbying machinery that Fortune 500 companies can afford, say the bind on them is acute. Last month two congressional subcommittees heard from Midwestern machine-tool makers who want to know why they can't ship semirobotic lathes and other equipment that China could just as easily buy from manufacturers in other countries.

The Commerce Department's concern, said Philip Eskeland, an aide to US Representative Donald A. Manzullo (R-Ill.), is that these tools could be put to "dual use." The tool makers' view, he said, is that "Commerce is erring on the side of caution."

Elaborating, an aide to US Senator John F. Kerry (D-Mass.), who interceded on Kovacs's behalf to get the Ex-Im Bank to pay out Elatec's insurance claim, says that while the Cold War may be history, concern over China's military capabilities is not.

"It is really the intelligence community and the State Department that is calling the shots in cases like these," he said. "The mood seems to correlate with whatever the temperature of the bilateral relationship may be at any given time."

The Commerce Department's Bureau of Export Administration, through a spokesman, refused to discuss the Elatec case on grounds of confidentiality. Neither the bureau nor the Export-Import Bank returned phone calls seeking other information.

*(continued)*

(continued)

Says Kovacs, who simmers when he thinks of all the seminars and workshops on exports to China to which he's been invited:

"Everybody thinks there is a gold mine in China. Maybe for some people there is. But there are a hell of a lot of risks, too. The first is that you are subject to the politics of the moment."

What goes on at the Hongguang Machinery Factory is no secret. Business cards passed out by officials there display a color photo of a rocket blasting off into space.

And even while Kovacs's sales manager, John C. Welch Jr., was in Xian negotiating the deal, US intelligence agents were asking questions. Kovacs won't talk about it. Welch, who left Elatec last month but still does work for Kovacs, says it was the Central Intelligence Agency that came knocking.

Nevertheless, six months later, in November 1995, the Commerce Department OK'd an export license that identified the buyer and made note of its potential strategic uses by including a condition banning its use for "by nuclear end users or for nuclear end uses."

Documents that Elatec submitted to the Commerce Department say that the Hongguang Machinery Factory wanted the furnace "to manufacture automobile turbocharger turbine blades." Kovacs said he questioned that use from the outset. The unit, with a smelting capacity of 220 pounds of metal, is too small for manufacturing, he says. "It's a toy," he said, more suited for research or perhaps prototype production.

The furnace, standing two stories tall when assembled and weighing several tons, today stands collecting dust in the back of Elatec's plant in an industrial park in North Wilmington.

It now belongs to the Export-Import Bank, Kovacs says, as a result of the $418,000 insurance payment to the Family Bank of Haverhill, which wrote the working-capital loan. It's for sale—although, Kovacs says he's been told, not to China or Hong Kong.

Independent business consultants who specialize in China trade shake their heads when they hear about Elatec's decision to accept the order in the first place. But Bryan Batson of the Boston-based China Business Group says small businesses often find the Commerce Department's shifting priorities hard to fathom. Paul Marcus of Boston Business Consultants, who advises Fortune 500 corporations on China investments, adds that companies proposing long-term investments get more respect both in Washington and Beijing than small exporters. "People trying to go in there and sell widgets don't do very well," he said.

Kovacs says he was aware that he was walking on egg shells. But he thought the issuance of an export license on Nov. 14, 1995—six months after those intelligence inquiries—meant what it said. The license openly identified the buyer and made note of the furnace's strategic uses by including the ban on nuclear-related uses. Looking back, Kovacs and Welch think the subsequent lifting of their license—after the machine was built and two weeks before it was to be shipped—might have been triggered by their own desire to cover higher costs and boost profit.

After getting the export license and while awaiting a letter of credit from Beijing, Kovacs and Welch decided to renegotiate the contract's terms. The sale price was boosted, from $442,000 to $518,000, and a Hong Kong trader who initiated the deal was cut out in return for a commission. The change would mean $10,000 more profit, Welch said.

In July 1996 Welch, on behalf of Elatec, applied to the Commerce Department for an export license modification to reflect these changes. That, he and Kovacs believe, set off an entirely new review—under new rules, which took effect in August, that gave veto powers to the Department of Defense, the Department of Energy, and several intelligence agencies.

And veto they did. Kovacs and Welch say they weren't told exactly who was responsible for the blackball. One hint came, though, in a December 1996 letter warning the license was being voided. It was from the Bureau of Export Administration's office of nuclear and missile technology controls.

The final order, dated last Feb. 4, declared: "The Department of Commerce has concluded that this export would be detrimental to US foreign policy interest."

Kovacs says that if the Ex-Im Bank can't recover its insurance payout by selling the furnace, Elatec's losses could grow. Even if that sale breaks even, he says, Elatec has lost between $50,000 and $75,000 in interest and associated carrying charges—"a year's worth of profit."

Kovacs says his insurance policy cost about $3,000 and that he took it out because he knows Sino-American relations are always edgy. He considered a break in diplomatic relations a possibility, as well as nonpayment. "What I didn't foresee," he said, "was that the government would pull my permit."

**Jerry Ackerman**
*The Boston Globe*, May 18, 1997, p. F4.

Copyright © 1997 by *The Boston Globe*. Reprinted with permission.

Classification (ERIC). Once an exporter receives a *personal identification number* (PIN), similar to a bank card teller number, it can hook up the office computer to ELAIN or ERIC with a modem and obtain information on the application process. Through the *System for Tracking Export License Applications* (STELA), an automated voice response system in the Commerce Department, the exporter can learn the status of the application by punching in the case number on a pushbutton phone.

Automation has shortened the processing time considerably. For example, Commerce reported that the time required for processing licenses to free-world destinations has dropped from 46 days to less than five days.

The Department of Commerce basically has 90 days to issue or deny any export license. The Department of Defense and other agencies, including the intelligence community, may also become involved.

## Foreign Availability

Finally, authorities in the United States are beginning to recognize that if a product is available from another source besides the United States, export controls make little sense. The Office of Foreign Availability within the Department of Commerce allows U.S. companies to petition for a review of the foreign availability of products and technology. If the office determines that a non-U.S. item of comparable quality is available for the proscribed country buyer, making the controls ineffective, the Department of Commerce may recommend decontrol of the item. Decontrol does not happen immediately, however, because the president may override the office's finding for national security reasons.

A recent example of this process was an OFA-initiated investigation (June 1993) into controlled oil well perforators. U.S. companies export $450 million in oil well perforators annually, representing 75 percent of their business. In March of 1994, based on a finding by the OFA, the Bureau of Export Administration removed national security validated license requirements for items exported to country groups Q, W, Y, and Z and the PRC. Although this process took less than one year, many sales were lost during this period.

## Export Management System

One of the problems companies face is how to comply with the ever-changing export regulations. The need for management controls that are not exorbitantly expensive nor stifling to business development is clear. (See Exhibit 15.4 for an example.)

Management must create a system that maintains the required records for at least two years including invoices, shippers export declarations, bills of lading, and air waybills. (Keeping the records longer may be advisable since the statute of limitations is five years for criminal actions.) A company should have a policy in place, with trained personnel to implement the policy, as well as a system of internal audits and notification of the BXA in case of irregularity. A significant part of the process is an effective screening operation that searches orders for prospective problems (see Exhibit 15.5). Every export decision should be screened for the following:

- Parties on the table of denial orders.
- Classification and need for validated license.
- Possible diversion from original use stated in application.
- Nuclear end-use and end-user.
- Missile end-use and end-user.
- Chemical and biological end-use and end-user.
- Violation of new denial orders in recent federal registers.

These requirements place a burden on the seller to ensure that the buyer does not violate the EAA. Weekly readings of the *Federal Register* to update the companies barred from doing business is essential.

A firm's voluntary disclosure of export violations to the BXA discovered as the result of an internal audit may lessen the ultimate penalties imposed. For example, Sigma Designs, a California computer component company, concluded, based upon an independent audit, that they had violated the law 237 times between 1988 and 1990, with computer parts shipments worth more than $9 million. In January 1994, Sigma signed a consent agreement that levied a civil fine of $750,000. The company, however, paid only $237,000; the remaining $513,000 was suspended for two years and will be waived if Sigma

---

**EXHIBIT 15.4    An Export Management System Outline**

**Administrative Elements:**

- A clear statement of corporate policy emphasizing the importance of compliance with U.S. export laws and regulations.
- A clear identification of individuals and positions that have export control compliance authority and responsibilities.
- A program for clear and concise record keeping.
- A continuing education program to ensure export control personnel are informed on changes to the export regulations.
- A system of internal review to ensure compliance with export regulations.
- A system for notifying BXA when noncompliance is discovered.

**Screening Elements:**

- **A screening procedure to ensure compliance.** This procedure could include:

  **A Classification/Licensing Determination Screen.** *Does my item require a license? If so, under whose licensing authority does it fall? Which federal agency has jurisdiction? Does my item require a license because of the country of destination? Can I ship under a general license or do I need an individual validated license or special license? Is my item controlled for national security concerns under the new Commerce Control List? Is it controlled for foreign policy reasons such as the EPCI regulations; is it controlled for sensitive nuclear end-uses under the Nuclear Non-Proliferation Act; or is the export of my commodity restricted under the short supply provisions of the Export Administration Act?*

  **A Table of Denial Orders Screen.** *Have any of the parties to this transaction been denied export privileges?*

  **A High Risk for Diversion Screen.** A system for identifying transactions and end uses that are high risks for diversion. For example:

  > *The customer is small and little known. The customer does not wish to utilize commonly available installation or maintenance services. It is reluctant to provide end-use/end-user information. It requests atypical payment terms or currencies. The order amounts, packaging, or delivery routine do not correspond to industry practice. The export is incompatible with the customer's line of business or stated end-use. The customer uses a post office box address or his facilities are inappropriate. The customer is known to have, or is suspected of having, unauthorized dealings with parties in country groups Q, S, W, Y, and Z, China, Afghanistan, Syria, Iraq, and/or Iran.*

  **A Nuclear End-Use/End-User Screen.** *Is there any information that my shipment may be destined for a sensitive nuclear end-use or is my product on the Nuclear Referral List?*

  **A Missile End-Use/End-User Screen.** *Is there any information that my shipment may be used in the design, development, or production of a missile?*

  **A Chemical and Biological Weapons End-Use/End-User Screen.** *Is there any information that this export may be used in the development, stockpiling, or production of chemical or biological weapons?*

- **An order-processing system that documents management oversight of export control actions and decisions.**

---

does not violate the law during that period. An export management system may have avoided the errors and the resulting fine. Nonetheless, the prompt action taken allowed Sigma to reduce the damage of its violation.

**http://www.ita.doc.gov/how_to_export/license.html**
*Provides information and links relevant to export licenses and controls.*

**http://www.ita.doc.gov/how_to_export/country.html**
*See this address on country-specific export counseling.*

## Diversion

*Diversion* refers to the illegal placement of goods or commodities in the hands of an individual(s) for whom an export license would not be granted

**EXHIBIT 15.5    General Guidelines to Avoid Export Violations**

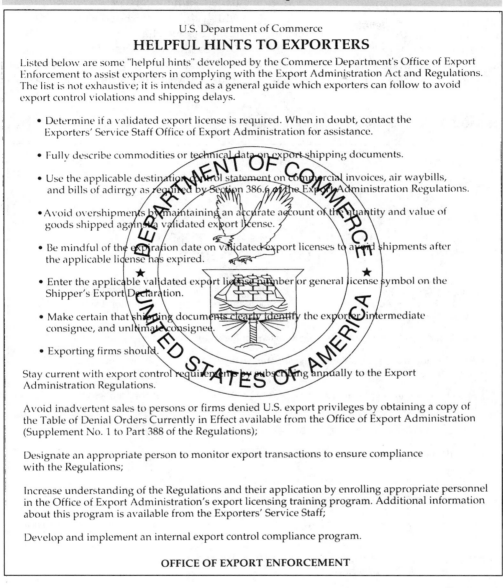

U.S. Department of Commerce
# HELPFUL HINTS TO EXPORTERS

Listed below are some "helpful hints" developed by the Commerce Department's Office of Export Enforcement to assist exporters in complying with the Export Administration Act and Regulations. The list is not exhaustive; it is intended as a general guide which exporters can follow to avoid export control violations and shipping delays.

- Determine if a validated export license is required. When in doubt, contact the Exporters' Service Staff Office of Export Administration for assistance.

- Fully describe commodities or technical data on export shipping documents.

- Use the applicable destination control statement on commercial invoices, air waybills, and bills of adirrgy as required by Section 386.6 of the Export Administration Regulations.

- Avoid overshipments by maintaining an accurate account of the quantity and value of goods shipped against a validated export license.

- Be mindful of the expiration date on validated export licenses to avoid shipments after the applicable license has expired.

- Enter the applicable validated export license number or general license symbol on the Shipper's Export Declaration.

- Make certain that shipping documents clearly identify the exporter, intermediate consignee, and ultimate consignee.

- Exporting firms should:

Stay current with export control requirements by subscribing annually to the Export Administration Regulations.

Avoid inadvertent sales to persons or firms denied U.S. export privileges by obtaining a copy of the Table of Denial Orders Currently in Effect available from the Office of Export Administration (Supplement No. 1 to Part 388 of the Regulations);

Designate an appropriate person to monitor export transactions to ensure compliance with the Regulations;

Increase understanding of the Regulations and their application by enrolling appropriate personnel in the Office of Export Administration's export licensing training program. Additional information about this program is available from the Exporters' Service Staff;

Develop and implement an internal export control compliance program.

**OFFICE OF EXPORT ENFORCEMENT**

either because of country group, end-use of the product, or the product itself. Although diversion stories might seemingly belong in a Grade B movie, with North Korean agents in trench coats, walking around with briefcases full of cash, such stories are not so far from the truth. Both the newspapers and enforcement agencies are replete with accounts of schemes to divert sensitive technology to a prohibited destination. One recent case involved a "sting" operation in which agents substituted 200 pounds of kitty litter for avionic-equipment sent from the United States to England and then to Iran.

Another example of diversion is the reported scheme to ship U.S.-origin helicopters to North Korea through a West German firm, Delta-Avia Fluggerate, GmbH. Although a number of them were shipped, finally the U.S. was able to intercede and prevent the final fifteen from reaching their destination. The company was denied export privileges by the Department of Commerce while an investigation of the incident proceeded.

Many companies face the problem of how to determine when a buyer may be planning to divert the goods to an ultimate buyer who would not have been able to purchase the same item directly. The Department of Commerce has published *Indications of Potential Illegal Exports*, which should assist exporters in identifying when a buyer may have a diversion scheme in mind (see Exhibits 15.6 and 15.7).

An exporter who had reason to know that an end-user was going to direct the products to an em-

**EXHIBIT 15.6    Possible Export Violations**

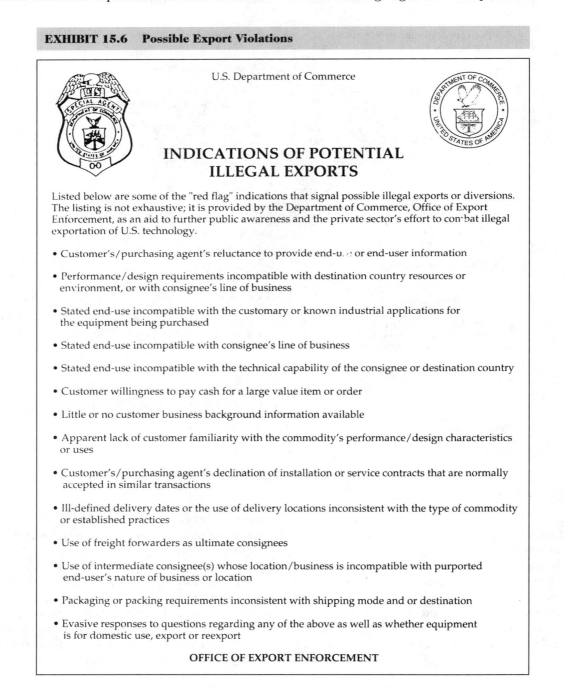

U.S. Department of Commerce

## INDICATIONS OF POTENTIAL ILLEGAL EXPORTS

Listed below are some of the "red flag" indications that signal possible illegal exports or diversions. The listing is not exhaustive; it is provided by the Department of Commerce, Office of Export Enforcement, as an aid to further public awareness and the private sector's effort to combat illegal exportation of U.S. technology.

- Customer's/purchasing agent's reluctance to provide end-use or end-user information

- Performance/design requirements incompatible with destination country resources or environment, or with consignee's line of business

- Stated end-use incompatible with the customary or known industrial applications for the equipment being purchased

- Stated end-use incompatible with consignee's line of business

- Stated end-use incompatible with the technical capability of the consignee or destination country

- Customer willingness to pay cash for a large value item or order

- Little or no customer business background information available

- Apparent lack of customer familiarity with the commodity's performance/design characteristics or uses

- Customer's/purchasing agent's declination of installation or service contracts that are normally accepted in similar transactions

- Ill-defined delivery dates or the use of delivery locations inconsistent with the type of commodity or established practices

- Use of freight forwarders as ultimate consignees

- Use of intermediate consignee(s) whose location/business is incompatible with purported end-user's nature of business or location

- Packaging or packing requirements inconsistent with shipping mode and or destination

- Evasive responses to questions regarding any of the above as well as whether equipment is for domestic use, export or reexport

**OFFICE OF EXPORT ENFORCEMENT**

| EXHIBIT 15.7 | Table of Denial Orders | | | |
| --- | --- | --- | --- | --- |

| Name and Address | Effective Date | Expiration Date | Export Privileges Affected | Federal Register Citation |
| --- | --- | --- | --- | --- |
| Brownhill, David<br>13 Robin Road<br>Northcliff Ext. 12<br>Johannesburg,<br>    South Africa | 9/11/95 | 10/6/03 | General<br>and validated<br>licenses, all<br>commodities,<br>any destination,<br>also exports<br>to Canada. | 60 F.R. 48961<br>9/21/95 |
| Carlson, Paul C.<br>P.O. Box 3125<br>Brockton,<br>    Massachusetts<br>and<br>87 Springhill Avenue<br>    Bridgewater,<br>    Massachusetts | 3/5/85 | 3/5/00 | General<br>and validated<br>licenses, all<br>commodities,<br>any destination,<br>also exports<br>to Canada.<br>See: Contel<br>        Equipment | 50 F.R. 9699<br>3/11/85<br>50 F.R. 18281<br>4/30/85 |
| CCC Inc.<br>Frankfurt, Germany<br>    c/o Pars<br>    Hafezeh<br>    Tehran, Iran | 9/25/93 | 9/25/13 | See: Amiri, Reza | 57 F.R. 57155<br>12/3/92 and<br>58 F.R. 31361<br>6/2/93 and<br>58 F.R. 51610<br>10/4/93 and<br>60 F.R. 8221<br>2/13/95 |
| Chan, Anthony<br>a/k/a<br>Chan Sum-Tai Anthony<br>c/o Shuttle Long Co., Ltd.<br>Ka Wah Bank<br>    Center Building<br>19th Floor<br>232 Des Voeux Road<br>Hong Kong Central | 12/6/84 | Indefinite | General<br>and validated<br>licenses, all<br>commodities,<br>any destination,<br>also exports<br>to Canada.<br>    See: Wysh Data<br>    Systems, Ltd. | 49 F.R. 48591<br>12/13/84 |

bargoed destination is liable. This liability places a burden and duty on the exporter to inquire about the projected buyer and the anticipated uses for the product. Thus, the pressure to make a fast sale must be tempered by judicious inquiry.

The following case on page 514 details a complicated diversion scheme in which the perpetrators were caught.

## Enforcement

The penalties for violations of the EAA before it lapsed were severe. The law states that whoever "knowingly violates or conspires or attempts to violate any provision of this Act or any regulation, order, or license issued thereunder shall be fined not more than five times the value of the exports involved or $50,000, whichever is greater or imprisoned not more than 5 years, or both." The penalty for "willful violations" of the provisions regarding countries embargoed for either national security or foreign policy reasons is a fine of $250,000 for individuals and/or five years in prison, and for other than individuals (business entities) the penalty is five times the value of the exports or $1,000,000, whichever is greater.

The Act also makes room for civil penalties and administrative sanctions. An entity may be

*U.S. v. Elkins*
885 F.2d 775 (1989)
United States Court of Appeals
(11th Cir.) Cert. Den.
110 S.Ct. 1300 (1990)

BACKGROUND AND FACTS

The defendant, an owner of a California company, Armaflex, was convicted in Federal District Court of conspiracy to defraud the government and of engaging in or aiding and abetting illegal export activity in violation of the Export Administration Act and Arms Export Control Act. Elkins and six others purchased planes, KC-130, through a West German company (owned and operated by Libyans), routed the planes through Bordeaux, France, and Benin, Africa, and then to Libya. A license had been issued by the Department of Commerce. When Commerce raised questions about the Libyan-owned West German firm, Elkins explained that the company was hostile to Libya and the planes were destined for Benin. One of the planes was later seen in Egypt with indications it was with the Libyan Arab Air Force.

CIRCUIT JUDGE JOHNSON

. . . Defendant also challenges the fine imposed on count two. There may be circumstances where an excessive fine constitutes cruel and unusual punishment in violation of the Eighth Amendment. *Monroe,* We need not identify those circumstances in this case. Defendant made a gross profit of $13,049,474, a net profit of $7,336,233, and an after-tax profit of $3,368,917 from the sale of these aircraft. Defendant's fine of $6.6 million was less than his gross profit and less than his net profit from the sale of these planes. Although a large amount, we hold that a fine representing an amount less than the net profit of an illegal transaction does not violate the Eighth Amendment absent a showing of severe, particularized hardship suffered by defendant.

Defendant also argues that this fine exceeds the maximum prescribed by law. We disagree. Violation of the export control laws generally results in fines up to $250,000; however, the district court could have imposed a fine up to five times the value of the exports.

. . . Defendant could have been fined twice the gross gain from the sale of the planes, unless imposition of such a large fine would have unduly complicated or prolonged the sentencing process. This fine was less than the amount defendant earned as a gross profit on the sale, and is well within the limits of section 3623. Consequently, we conclude that this fine does not exceed the maximum fine allowed for this offense.

Defendant argues that the district court did not consider the impact of this fine on his family. This argument has no merit. That information was before the district court, and the transcript indicates that the court considered these factors.

**Decision.** Affirmed the lower court conviction and penalty of a five-year sentence on count 1 and ten-year consecutive sentence on count 2 and a $6,600,000 fine. A $50 per count special assessment was also upheld.

**Comment.** This case illustrates the extremes a company utilizes to circumvent the law. Diversion represents a serious threat to security. Well-intentioned companies may find themselves victimized, however. Individuals such as Elkins were clearly aware of the circumstances of the sale. Companies need to establish a review process for both foreign and domestic sales to screen for possible diversion. A control system will help them in any prosecution for export violations because it will show that they exercised good faith and due diligence in trying to comply with the law. Thus, at a minimum, they may avoid a finding of willful violation, which carries more serious penalties.

denied exporting privileges via a temporary denial order. This list is published in the *Federal Register* (see Exhibit 15.7). The Department of Commerce may also impose a $10,000 penalty. The law also provides that persons convicted under the statute may forfeit their property. Both the Office of Export Enforcement within the Department of Commerce and the U.S. Customs office are charged with enforcement. The penalties provided for under IEEPA are less than provided for by the EAA. The IEEPA assesses only $50,000 per transgression, which is further evidence of the need for either a new law or reauthorization of the old.

In the *Dart* case, prosecutors alleged that an exporter knew or should have known that a validated license was needed to export upgraded wafer (computers) polishers to Czechoslovakia. The case raises the issue of the Secretary of Commerce's power and the recourse available to an exporter.

## BACKGROUND AND FACTS

William Dart and two corporations in which he was a principal and several others planned to sell and ship to Czechoslovakia two wafer polishers used in the manufacture of integrated circuits, without export licenses. These polishers had been "upgraded" so that they were in the category of goods that needed a license for that destination. One of the executives from the company doing the upgrading agreed to travel to Washington to determine if a license was needed and if it would be granted. Dart gave the executive the name of an individual at the Commerce Department with whom to discuss this issue. The executive returned and said that no license was necessary, and the goods were prepared for shipment. Customs seized the machines at Los Angeles International Airport. In November 1984, the Commerce Department secured a temporary denial order, blocking Dart's export privileges. In April 1985, a "charging letter" was issued by Commerce including allegations that Dart had attempted to violate the law by shipping without a license. An administrative law judge (ALJ) ruled that the Department of Commerce failed to prove that Dart "knew or reasonably should have known" of the need for an export license. Charges were dismissed against Dart. The secretary of commerce reversed the ALJ decision, fined Dart $150,000, and prohibited him from exporting for fifteen years. The district court upheld Commerce's decision and Dart appealed.

## CIRCUIT JUDGE MIKVA

. . . Here, a citizen charged with violating an export law was absolved of liability by an independent administrative law judge who presided over five days of evidentiary hearings. Yet, that judgment was summarily reversed by a higher official who did not witness the presentation of evidence, who gave no reasons for his action, and who was a member of the prosecuting agency. This reversal was contrary to law, and the result was far from inconsequential: appellant was fined $150,000 and essentially prohibited from pursuing his present livelihood for fifteen years.

### Dart v. United States
### 848 F.2d 775 (1988)
### United States Court of Appeals
### (D.C. Cir.)

In vacating this result, therefore, we are motivated by much more than a belief in administrative punctilio. We find that the agency official had no authority to reverse the administrative law judge's decision. The enforcement action against appellant thus disregarded an important procedural safeguard—one that Congress expressly enacted to protect citizens accused of violating the export law at issue here. We also find that, notwithstanding a statutory provision that precludes judicial review of most enforcement decisions under this export law, Congress did not withdraw from the courts the power or obligation to enforce the procedural safeguard that was flouted here. Accordingly, we vacate the agency decision and remand the case for further consideration. . . .

In drafting the EAA's enforcement provisions, Congress steered a path between two competing concerns: the need to protect national security by controlling exports of advanced technology and the need to treat individuals fairly in the administrative process. We find that Congress struck the balance in favor of a greater degree of fairness than either the department or the trial court recognized.

The EAA no longer gives the secretary power to reverse an ALJ's decision as to sanctions. Therefore, the secretary's order against Dart—imposing $150,000 in fines and barring all export privileges for fifteen years—cannot stand. Though issued in the guise of a modification, the order clearly reversed the ALJ's key findings and thus exceeded the secretary's authority. The result was a denial of the procedural protections that Congress expressly extended to accused EAA violators—namely, a determination regarding civil sanctions that is firmly grounded in a required hearing and that is justified in terms of the evidence adduced therein. Without examining the merits of the secretary's determination, we conclude that the order "on its face" violated the EAA. We also find that Congress has permitted judicial review of such "facial" violations.

**Decision.**  The court vacated the agency decision and remanded the case for further consideration.

In another case in which the *Dart* holding was discussed, Justice Ruth Ginsburg, in one of her last D.C. Circuit opinions before assuming her Supreme Court duties, underscored the interpretation that civil penalties can be imposed on a strict liability basis without proving "scienter" or criminal intent.

---

### Iran Air v. Kugelman
**996 F.2d 1253 (D.C. Cir. 1993)**
*United States Court of Appeals (D.C. Cir.)*

**BACKGROUND AND FACTS**

In August 1985, Iran Air placed an order for three top-of-the-line signal generators with a German-based company, Fluke Germany, for export to Iran. The purchase order stated: "Please ship to Iran Air Frankfurt Airport for reforwarding to Tehran Iran." Fluke Germany did not have the generators in stock, and therefore referred the order to its affiliate, Fluke Holland. Fluke Holland, which was also out of the signal generators, obtained them from the United States manufacturer, Fluke USA. The invoices associated with the transactions between Fluke USA and Fluke Holland and between Fluke Holland and Fluke Germany bore the destination control statement: "These commodities were licensed for ultimate destination Fed.Rep. Germany. Diversion contrary to United States law is prohibited."

On October 17, 1985, Fluke Germany delivered the Fluke USA generators to Iran Air in Frankfurt, Germany. In contrast to the previous invoices, the invoice for this transaction contained no destination control statement. A few days later, Iran Air shipped the generators to Iran. . . .

Five years later, in October 1990, the Commerce Department's Office of Export Enforcement (OEE) instituted administrative proceedings against Iran Air—though apparently not against any of the Fluke companies—for the imposition of civil sanctions. OEE charged Iran Air, with causing the reexport of U.S.-origin Fluke signal generators . . . from . . . Germany to Iran without obtaining . . . the reexport authorization.

In 1985, Iran Air unwittingly violated the Export Administration Act of 1979 in connection with the shipment of three U.S.-made "signal generators" from Germany to Iran. In 1990, the Commerce Department's Office of Export Enforcement sought to impose civil sanctions against Iran Air, but the Administrative Law Judge (ALJ) assigned to hear the case ruled that the Export Act authorized sanctions only for knowing violations. Because the Office of Export Enforcement had neither alleged nor proved that Iran Air knowingly violated the law, the ALJ dismissed the charge. On final agency review, [Kugelman] the Acting Under Secretary of Commerce for Export Administration emphasized that the ALJ's interpretation of the Act clashed with the Department's firm position that "knowledge" is not a requirement in a civil penalty case. The Under Secretary imposed a $100,000 civil penalty (the statutory maximum) and a suspension of export privileges for twenty-four months, twenty-one of them to be waived if Iran Air paid the penalty in full within thirty days of the Under Secretary's order.

On petition for review to this court, Iran Air asserts that, as the ALJ ruled, only knowing violations of export administration regulations are sanctionable. In any event, Iran Air insists, this court's decision in *Dart v. United States,* precludes a ruling by the Under Secretary overturning that of the ALJ.

We adhere to the holding in *Dart* that the agency head may not, under section 2412(c)(1), overturn an ALJ's findings of fact and, on that basis, entirely reverse the initial decision, imposing a "diametrically oppos[ite]" result. We decline, however, to extend our *Dart* precedent beyond fact findings to questions of agency law or policy. For in that domain, which was not traversed in *Dart,* it would be senseless to give to the ALJ not simply the first, but also the last word.

Section 2412(c)(1), in short, does not limit the agency head's authority to check an ALJ's interpretation of the Export Act.

We hold that both sides have misperceived our ruling in *Dart.* That decision does not permit the agency head to reject the ALJ's fact findings, but neither does it allow the ALJ to supplant the head of the agency in construing the applicable law and regulations. Accordingly, we affirm the Under Secretary's construction of the governing statute and regulation: we remand, however, for a reasoned determination of the appropriate penalty.

**Decision.** The court upheld the right of the Department of Commerce to impose a civil penalty and remanded the case for a determination of the appropriate penalty.

## Toshiba-Kongsberg Sanctions

The U.S. Navy discovered in 1986 that Soviet submarines were able to move without noise, a first for the subs, which made them a greater threat to U.S. security. The USSR had acquired advanced milling machinery from Toshiba Machine Co., Ltd., a subsidiary owned by Toshiba Corporation (it owned 50 percent). Both the United States and COCOM had prohibited the sale of these machines, which could affect the propellers of submarines. Toshiba had changed the description of the package and thus secured the appropriate permissions to ship the machinery to the Soviets. Concurrently, Kongsberg, a Norwegian company, shipped control devices to Toshiba to be used with the milling machines. Soviet agents tested the machines in Japan, and they were ultimately shipped to the Soviet Union where they were fitted by both Toshiba affiliate and Kongsberg employees.

The news coverage of these events disturbed the U.S. public as well as elected officials and members of the defense establishment. The shipment highlighted the lax enforcement by fellow COCOM members and the ridiculous ease with which the Soviets were able to acquire the technology. In 1987, the House of Representatives voted that the State Department should seek damages from Japan and Norway for this infraction. The Defense Department canceled a $100 million contract with Toshiba for laptop computers.

Japan itself imposed sanctions on Toshiba barring it for one year from honoring contracts worth $18 million and imposing a one-year ban on exports to communist countries. The Japanese later reversed this decision, allowing the corporation to go ahead on seven of the contracts. Despite complaints that this was not sufficient punishment, the Japanese court aroused further controversy when it gave suspended sentences to the Toshiba Machine executives and imposed a $16,000 fine on the subsidiary.

After much discussion, the U.S. Congress decided that Toshiba Machine imports should be banned for three years and that the parent company, Toshiba Corporation, should be banned for three years from doing business with the U.S. government, although certain loopholes would allow some purchases from the Toshiba Corporation. Some have argued that, because of all the loopholes, the sanctions were not effective. Nevertheless, the example illustrates that the United States may punish foreign companies for violating foreign export control laws and COCOM policy.

Another case, *U.S. v. Pervez,* illustrates the undercover enforcement operations to stem illegal exports.

---

### U.S. v. Pervez
*871 F.2d 310 (3d Cir. 1993)*
*United States Court of Appeals*

CIRCUIT JUDGE SCIRICA

Defendant Arshad Pervez appeals his conviction on charges of conspiring to defraud the government, attempting to export beryllium, and submitting false statements to the Department of Commerce. The principal issue raised by this appeal is whether defendant is entitled to a new trial in light of the Supreme Court ruling on entrapment.

BACKGROUND AND FACTS

Arshad Pervez, a native of Pakistan, moved to Canada in 1967. In 1986, Pervez incorporated his own import–export business, A. P. Enterprises, in Toronto. Pervez contracted with companies in Saudi Arabia and Pakistan to export pillows, food, mini-TVs, satellite antennas, computers, and lumber.

In October 1986, Pervez contacted a business acquaintance in an effort to locate a source of "maraging steel." He was referred to and eventually spoke with Mr. Del Guidice and Mr. Tomley at Carpenter Technology Corporation, a Pennsylvania company that manufactures specialty steel for use in high-technology products and in the oil industry. In particular, Carpenter manufactures "maraging 350 steel," a steel with a high tensile strength, a limited market, and a very high cost.

*(continued)*

*(continued)*

Maraging 350 steel is used in the nuclear industry in gas centrifuge enrichment plants. Because maraging steel has nuclear application, its export is governed by the Export Administration Act and its regulations, which require a U.S. Department of Commerce export license for intended use in an unsafeguarded nuclear facility. (Pakistan has not signed the nuclear nonproliferation treaty.) Because of restrictions placed on the export of maraging steel, Tomley notified the Nuclear Regulatory Commission and met with United States Customs Service personnel, informing them that A. P. Enterprises was interested in purchasing maraging steel for export to Pakistan and that Pervez had alleged that the steel was to be "remelted." At the direction of the United States Customs Service, Tomley forwarded a price quotation to Pervez. Pervez then arranged to meet with Carpenter representatives to discuss the sale. In November 1986, Tomley and U.S. Special Customs Agent John New, acting undercover as an international marketing analyst for Carpenter, met with Pervez in Toronto. At this meeting, Pervez identified his client as Mr. Inam Ul-Haq of Multinational Corporation of Lahore, Pakistan. Tomley told Pervez that Carpenter previously had been directed by the United States Department of Commerce not to manufacture maraging steel for use in Pakistan because it was believed that the material was destined for Pakistan's unsafe nuclear facility. Tomley also told Pervez that Carpenter would not manufacture the steel unless Pervez obtained the proper license from the U.S. Department of Commerce.

In a telephone conversation in December 1986, Pervez and New discussed the Export Administration's licensing requirements. New told Pervez that the Department of Commerce would not issue a license unless Pervez obtained a letter from Multinational stating the intended end use of the maraging steel. New informed Pervez that it might be necessary to make a cash payment to the Department of Commerce licensing officer to ensure the issuance of the license. Pervez said that he would be willing to pay $5,000 to obtain the export license, but later asked if he could reduce the "kickback" to $3,000. Pervez gave $1,000 to undercover Commerce license officer Rovello, to "secure the license."

About one month later, Pervez mailed Tomley two end-use statements, which declared that the maraging steel would be used to manufacture high-speed turbines and compressors. One end-use statement purported to be from Noeem Pasha, general manager of Multinational, and the other from the Pakistan Council of Scientific and Industrial Research.

For the purpose of its investigation, on March 31, 1987, the Department of Commerce issued a false "license" to Pervez to export the steel. Shortly thereafter, New met with Pervez in Toronto to review export documents and finalize the terms of the sale. At the meeting, Pervez told New for the first time that his buyer also wanted beryllium, a highly controlled specialty metal that also requires a validated export license from the Department of Commerce. When told that export of beryllium was also restricted, Pervez suggested that Rovello be contacted again. New and Pervez then discussed alternative methods to export the beryllium from the United States, including diverting it through other countries, identifying the shipment as something other than beryllium, or shipping it directly. When New expressed concern that shipping beryllium was illegal, Pervez remarked that "the United States won't mind a small piece." Pervez also stated that his customers in Pakistan were looking for other hard metals.

New again told Pervez that beryllium was a restricted material requiring an export license, and that it had a nuclear application. When Pervez inquired whether it could be shipped under another label, New stated, "You tell me what you want me to put on the box." Pervez then said that he wanted New to commingle the beryllium with the maraging steel for shipment to Pakistan. During the same conversation, Pervez also inquired whether New could procure a "gamma scanning unit" for use in an "oil refinery." New recommended that Pervez inquire elsewhere for such a unit. Finally, in July 1987, Pervez drove to Philadelphia to facilitate the first shipment of maraging steel and to make another payment to Rovello. At that time, he was arrested.

On July 28, 1987, a federal grand jury returned an eight count indictment against Pervez and his co-defendant in Pakistan, Inam Ul-Haq. Pervez was charged with conspiracy to defraud the government, bribery, interstate travel in aid of racketeering, submitting false statements to the Department of Commerce, and violating the Export Administration Act through the payment of a bribe for the export of maraging 350 steel and

*(continued)*

*(continued)*

through the attempt to export beryllium. Pervez was convicted of conspiring to defraud the United States (Count One), and of submitting statements to the Department of Commerce that misrepresented the end-use for the maraging steel. He admitted the elements of the charges in Count Five (attempting to export beryllium), claiming entrapment, and was found guilty of the offense. He also admitted the elements of the bribery counts, claiming entrapment, and was found not guilty (Counts Two and Four—bribery of a United States Customs agent, and Count Three—interstate travel to bribe a federal employee). Pervez was sentenced to five years imprisonment on Count One, the conspiracy. On Counts Five, Six, Seven, and Eight, the imposition of sentence was suspended and he was placed on probation for a period of five years on each count to run concurrently. The appeal followed.

**Decision.** The Pervez conviction was vacated and remanded for a new trial on Counts One and Five (conspiracy and export of beryllium), and he had a new hearing to present evidence of entrapment because of the intervening Supreme Court case, *Matthews* (stating that a defendant need not admit all the elements of a crime before he can argue entrapment). Subsequently, Mr. Pervez pleaded *nolo contendere* to export violations. He then filed a civil lawsuit seeking compensatory and punitive damages, claiming among other issues false imprisonment, interference with economic advantage, and intentional infliction of emotional distress. The civil case was dismissed in April 1991.

While the preceding cases have dealt with equipment that has obvious strategic importance, problems can also arise with less obvious but nevertheless controlled items. For example, in August of 1994, the Department of Commerce announced that Asia Motors of South Korea was fined $70,000 for violating the EAA. The company did not admit or deny the charges but agreed to pay the fine. Asia Motors seven times re-exported U.S.-origin trucks in disassembled kits from Korea to Thailand, Saudi Arabia, and Libya without applying for a re-export license at the Department of Commerce. Thus the long arm of the U.S. law reaches overseas. Obviously the company wanted to continue to trade with the United States, so it cooperated in the investigation.

## Current Issues

The major issues in export control remain: Who is the enemy? Will there be effective multilateral controls? What will be controlled? If there are no multilateral controls, what about unilateral controls? Can the Department of Commerce both promote and control exports?

The reelection of President Clinton has not seemed to eliminate the previous election year legislative gridlock. Thus we may not see quick resolution of these issues.

The debate over the level of control over encryption software is a good example of the dilemas (see the following article).

*http://www.bxa.doc.gov/bxaissue.htm*
*The BXA site on current issues.*

---

*Foreign Accents*

# Between a Hacker and a Hard Place
## Data-Security Export Law Puts Businesses in a Bind

Matt Blaze, a researcher for the AT&T Corporation, had never thought of himself as an arms exporter. But just before he was to fly to Europe recently on business, Federal Customs agents at Kennedy International Airport in New York detained him for more than an hour while they puzzled over the "munitions" device in his carry-on bag.

*(continued)*

*(continued)*

When the head Customs official was summoned to the back room where he was being questioned, Mr. Blaze realized the Orwellian scope of the Federal export laws governing technology that safeguard international business communications.

"Are you the guy who wants to export the fancy gun?" the Customs man asked, peering at Mr. Blaze's documents.

"It's not a gun, it's a telephone," Mr. Blaze said. The small box connected to a handset was in fact a scrambling device to thwart hackers, corporate spies and even foreign governments from eavesdropping on his calls back to the United States. But because the device can also thwart American law enforcement, military and national security agents from eavesdropping on terrorists, drug dealers or foreign agents, the Federal Government defines it as "munitions"—right up there with rockets, nuclear warheads and fancy guns.

While Mr. Blaze produced the required license at the airport, the Customs official was clearly unfamiliar with this particular twist in United States export law. "Why do you need a license to export a telephone?" he asked.

"Good question," Mr. Blaze recalls thinking.

Good question, indeed, in the view of a growing number of American businesses that want the equivalent of seat belts and air bags as they set out on the global information highway in search of new markets and international partnerships.

Alarmed by accounts of hackers making off with credit card numbers and computer passwords and of saboteurs intercepting trade secrets, American businesses are being advised—often by the Government itself—to encode their sensitive electronic information with data encryption hardware or software. Such equipment scrambles phone calls and electronic mail into gibberish that remains unintelligible to anyone not holding the key to the code.

But at the same time, the Government prohibits businesses from providing their overseas customers or partners with the most advanced American-made cryptographic tools needed to safeguard their communications. It fears that the American technology could be used to break American laws, though few examples of such cases involving encryption have been made public.

There's just one problem: The export policy is honored mainly in the breach. Each day, copies of highly sophisticated cryptographic programs are transmitted out of the United States over computer networks, carried out unseen in laptop computers or secure telephones, or simply sold to foreign citizens in America's software and computer stores. The same technology is already in wide use overseas, available to anyone conected to the Internet global web of computers. . . .

Some Federal officials say the Government may relax the export-control policies in coming weeks, in part to make it easier for traveling executives like Mr. Blaze to take security devices on business trips. But for now, critics say the export restrictions have businesses caught between hackers and a hard place.

"They impede American businesses from having secure global communications," said Bill Moroney, president of the Electronic Messaging Association, a trade group in Washington. "Faced with this dilemma, companies can do it and violate U.S. laws somehow, or not do it and suffer."

The Federal Government says it has ample reason to worry about the consequences of letting American encryption technology into the hands of criminals or hostile governments, but can't discuss its concerns. . . .

"I empathize tremendously with the Government's fear of not being able to crack codes, but what it really comes down to is that export controls don't stop crooks from exporting encryption," Mr. Moroney said. "They only stop United States software companies from having a global market." . . .

The Government is now said to be leaning toward endorsing a commercially developed cryptography system in which a trusted third party—not the Government—would hold a spare copy of the code keys. These keys could be made available to law-enforcement officials bearing a warrant. Such a system would still be unpalatable to many privacy advocates, who argue that they have a right to private communications beyond the ear of Uncle Sam.

American companies that want to build their own forms of strong encryption into their products include **I.B.M., Digital Equipment, Microsoft, Sun Microsystems, Apple Computer, Lotus Development,**

*(continued)*

*(continued)*

**Novell** and nearly every other company making hardware or software for the so-called information highway. They say that the Government's export restrictions cost them hundreds of millions of dollars in lost sales and drain millions more in extra development and administrative fees. They also say the United States risks losing its historic leadership role in data security technologies. . . .

The Commerce Department is currently surveying American software and computer companies to determine what economic harm, if any, has been sustained by companies as a result of the export restrictions.

To obtain a Federal license to use the most advanced American encryption technology, businesses must often struggle through endless red tape—and even then run the risk of rejection. That puts them in a quandary, according to the director of network security for a multi-billion-dollar corporation based in the Middle West. Like most executives interviewed for this article, he spoke on the condition that neither he nor his company be identified.

"We end up importing foreign encryption tools so that we can communicate with our partners overseas," he said, "Or, we get around the policy with a wink and a nod." . . .

At an informal hearing at a recent computer conference near San Francisco, six members of a Government task force listened as a procession of petitioners—including several corporate security managers, representatives of high-tech companies and privacy advocates—appealed for quick relief from what they described as impractical, ineffective and harmful restrictions.

The result of the Government policy "is that computers on networks are less secure than they should be," said John Gilmore, an executive with Cygnus Support, a software support company in Mountain View, Calif. "Unless the policy is changed, we will continue to see plenty of large- and small-scale intrusions like Keven Mitnick's."

Mr. Mitnick, who was arrested in January after a two-year Federal manhunt, is accused of breaking into many private computers and making off with information that would have been useless to him had it been encrypted.

Mr. Mitnick was unusual, law-enforcement agents and security experts acknowledged, because he apparently did not seek to profit from his collected data. In an era when financial data and intellectual property are often more valuable than physical property, computer networks are an attractive target.

"I know for a fact that hackers are paid to get information," said James Bidzos, president of **RSA Data Security** of Redwood City, Calif., whose company's technologies are at the core of many popular encryption systems. "People have made offers to us to break into other people's systems, or they want to retain us to decrypt information they got from someone else's computers."

Mr. Ozzie of Iris Associates said he agreed that current policies do not work. "But that doesn't mean they have no basis in logic," he said. "The fact is, law enforcement and national security interests rely on access to unencrypted data. What are they going to do?"

*Peter H. Lewis*

# Chapter Summary

Within the United States, regardless of the agency structure, the pursuit of both export promotion and control will always be a deliberate balance between trade growth and national security and foreign policy interests. Internationally, forging a consensus and enforceable regulations becomes more difficult as countries' perceptions and definitions of the "threat" evolve. The efficacy of the Wassenaar Arrangement will be tested in the future.

## QUESTIONS AND CASE PROBLEMS

1. "Unilateral export controls are expensive, serve no purpose, and only injure our own business. It's like borrowing a gun to shoot yourself in the foot, or more like in the heart." Agree or disagree with this statement. Give support for this answer. Who is most likely to have said something like this? Who is most likely to disagree?

2. Explain the difference between unilateral and multilateral export controls. How has the end of the Cold War affected the multilateral export control system?

3. Mega Computer Corporation of California was convicted of EAA violations for shipping computers to Singapore without an export license. The company's export licenses were revoked for ten years. Does this penalty violate the Constitution? What are the ramifications for the business?

4. How would you determine whether you could legally export military aircraft tires for F14 planes to Iran? See *U.S. v. Geissler,* 731 F.Supp. 93 (E.D.N.Y. 1990).

5. Is an indictment for criminal prosecution sufficient when it charges violations of the Export Administration Act, 50 U.S.C.S. Appendix Sec. 2401, but fails to define "export" and does not specify how and from what points exports were to be made? See *U.S. v. Moller-Butcher,* 560 F.Supp. 550 (D.C. Mass. 1983).

6. IBZ, a computer company, sells a "supercomputer" to a London-based company, Argo. IBZ applies for and receives a validated license for this export. After the sale, an IBZ saleswoman in London overhears a conversation at a bar from which she infers that Argo is a corporation set up to channel unauthorized technology to Libya. What legal obligation does she have, if any? How is your answer affected if the sale has not been completed?

8. Is it ethical to hold a businessperson legally responsible if he or she sells controlled technology to a second party that is then diverted to a third prohibited end-user? What factors will influence your answer?

9. The defendant was convicted of violations of the EAA for trying to export a controlled microwave amplifier. The defendant was trying to purchase it for a German man whom he had befriended. The German had said that one could purchase things more cheaply in the United States. The seller, a California company, because they had only sold one other such amplifier, contacted the Department of Commerce when the defendant called them. The defendant told the seller that the amplifier would not be exported. The defendant purchased the amplifier for $6,500 and sold it to Mr. Mann for $7,500. There was no evidence that Mr. Mann had any plans to sell the technology to an embargoed or forbidden end-user. The defendant was sentenced to 41 months in prison. He appeals on the basis that if the equipment costs less than $5,000 he did not need a validated license and that the government did not prove its net value was over $5,000. He also argued that the jury was not properly instructed on the issue of the requirement of "knowingly violates or conspires to or attempts to violate," arguing that the government has to prove a willful violation. Was he successful in his appeal? *United States v. Shetterly,* 971 F. 2d 67 (7th Cir. 1992).

10. In May 1994, the Atlanta branch of an Italian bank, BNL, agreed to pay a civil penalty of $475,000 for 104 alleged violations of EAA and regulations based on the antiboycott provisions. BNL, in seeking reimbursement on letters of credit, provided information to Iraqi banks on the company's business dealings with Israel. These events occurred between 1987 and 1990. The Georgia state courts had ordered the bank to pay $17 million owed to a German manufacturer on a letter of credit after presented with the appropriate documents, despite language on the documents that stated, "We declare that the goods are neither of Israeli origin nor do they contain Israeli materials nor are they being exported from Israel." The Bank filed a petition for certiorari with the U.S. Supreme Court on June 16, 1994. What ruling do you think the Court made? Why? Is this a "Catch-22" for the bank? What could they do to avoid this problem?

## MANAGERIAL IMPLICATIONS

1. Your company, AJAX Pharmaceutical, based in New Jersey, is approached by an agent for a company in Egypt and Jordan about participating in several joint ventures in the Middle East and Asia. The agent inquires about the status of your investment in Israel. You currently have an offer from a newly formed Israeli investment group to purchase your 30 percent share of Drugisco, an Israel-based company. How do you respond? What is your legal obligation? What other information do you need to answer the question?

You are also asked about your ability to ship certain chemicals that are controlled. Do you have any obligation to report this inquiry? You initially ship the requested items to Japan. You discover through a late-night meeting in a Karaoke bar that those items were being sold through a middleman and are now headed to Afghanistan. What is this called and do you have any legal responsibility? Ethical? What managerial controls can you implement to reduce the likelihood of this happening in the future?

2. Your company, Enzyme, Inc., manufactures both biological and chemical agents that have potential military uses. You understand that Congress is considering the contentious issue of how to revamp the entire export control regimen. Prepare a letter to your state's senators, articulating your company's position about decontrol. Do you think your company should take an active position in lobbying for a new law? What are the risks associated with such a position? Will you discuss these issues with your board of directors?

# Part Four

# Regulation of the International Marketplace

The issues addressed in Parts Two and Three of this text are applicable to any U.S. enterprise that wishes to transport its goods to another country, even if that enterprise is physically located inside the United States. Part Two considered international commercial law, which creates a reliable framework assuring exporters and importers in different parts of the world that they will receive money for goods and services. International trade law, discussed in Part Three, involves the framework of barriers and openings to trade among nations. In Part Four, the focus turns to the legal complications that arise when one actually moves a portion of one's enterprise outside the United States.

Numerous business factors may prompt a business to take this step. First, most businesses, from Madagascar to Minnesota, find that one sells more goods if one employs a local sales representative. A business that wishes to promote sales abroad will be greatly advantaged if it retains the services of an individual abroad to promote sales. If such a retention proves successful, the business may then wish to establish an office in that country. Indeed, the business might eventually experience greater profitability from making its product abroad and selling it there— or even exporting it back into the United States.

When the U.S. business first creates a presence abroad, it becomes subject to regulation by the foreign country being "penetrated" and to a series of U.S. laws that apply to such "penetrators." As the presence in the host country progresses from the local office phase through the manufacturing plant phase, the level of "host country" regulation becomes more intense. For instance, a U.S. company that establishes a factory in a foreign nation may become subject to national and provincial labor laws, environmental laws, tax laws, laws governing the transfer of technology, laws governing the appropriate level of foreign ownership of businesses, laws regarding how profits from the operation are repatriated to the United States, possible nationalization by the foreign country, the U.S. Foreign Corrupt Practices Act, and a plethora of U.S. and foreign country antitrust laws.

Part Four treats that immense body of law in a thematic and general way. Such a treatment is necessary because in contrast to international commercial law, in which great consistency has developed, and trade law, in which substantial harmonization has emerged through the General Agreement on Tariffs and Trade (GATT) and the World Trade Organization (WTO), local laws governing foreign investment vary widely among the more than 200 nations on the planet. Furthermore, these laws are constantly evolving. Many countries, including the United States, have fluctuated from the extreme of being aggressively hostile to foreign investment back to a more friendly attitude.

The position of any given country at any given time on this spectrum depends upon mercurial international and domestic political conditions. For instance, from the 1950s through the mid-1970s, many developing countries grew progressively more antagonistic toward foreign investment, reflecting emerging national self-esteem and wariness of their former colonial masters. But when anti-foreign investment laws resulted in those economies running out of capital resources in the late 1970s and early 1980s, many of the governments began to pass more receptive laws.

In short, no one can possibly predict precisely what foreign investment laws will be tomorrow. People can, however, identify different approaches that nations have taken in regulating foreign business penetration. A working knowledge of these approaches provides an analytical framework that a business can employ to assess different aspects of the legal environment in the country in which it is considering an investment.

The analysis in this part begins at the least intrusive and, hence, the least regulated, foreign presence and moves through increasingly substantial and regulated forms of establishment. Chapter Sixteen reviews issues that arise once the enterprise retains an agent or a representative abroad. Such retention triggers the host country's requirements for agency relationships, as well as its laws relating to advertising and marketing. It also unleashes one of the principal concerns of U.S. business abroad, the U.S. Foreign Corrupt Practices Act. Chapter Seventeen reviews licensing and other arrangements through which a U.S. enterprise is paid for permitting a foreign entity to use its technology. These arrangements are closely regulated by some host countries that are often desirous of capturing the technology

for their own nationals. Chapter Eighteen turns to the legal peculiarities of operating in another country—subjecting oneself to the full array of the host country's corporate and tax laws. Chapter Nineteen considers the political risk associated with committing capital resources in a foreign country: nationalization or expropriation of one's investment by the foreign sovereign. Chapter Twenty explores the flip side of nationalization, the emerging process of privatization, and reviews the different ways in which formerly public assets are transferred to private hands. Ironically, most assets nationalized in the 20th century are now being privatized. Chapter Twenty-one discusses labor laws, which mirror the broadly varying concepts of the proper relationship between employees and their places of work. Chapter Twenty-two provides an in-depth treatment of international environmental law, one of the most dynamic legal disciplines in recent years. Finally, Chapter Twenty-three addresses the pinnacle of foreign penetration, situations in which U.S. investors have come to so dominate the relevant market that they become subject to the antitrust or competition laws of various countries—including the United States—against monopolization of markets.

As the foregoing summary suggests, confronting foreign law is a bit like taking on Hydra, the many-headed monster of Greek mythology. In these succeeding chapters, the student may find that every time he or she cuts off one of the law monster's heads, like Hydra, the monster will replace it with two new heads.

# Chapter Sixteen

# International Marketing Law: Sales Representatives, Advertising, and Ethical Issues

A s noted in Chapter Five, an American business can sell its goods abroad by simply delivering them FOB a U.S. port onto an ocean-bound vessel. If the business sells its products abroad in that fashion and does not otherwise have any contacts with the country to which its goods are bound, it will generally escape regulation by the foreign country. Why then, would a U.S. business place a representative abroad and begin to enmesh itself in foreign regulation?

First, a business should promote its product where it wishes to sell it. If a business advertises popcorn poppers only in Topeka, Kansas, it will sell popcorn poppers only to Zimbabwean buyers who happen by Topeka. If, on the other hand, it markets in Zimbabwe, the enterprise will encounter more prospective Zimbabwean buyers. Thus, the enterprise that believes Zimbabwe is a "hot" prospective market for poppers will retain the services of a sales representative located in Zimbabwe.

Second, a local presence permits the Topeka enterprise to maintain the popcorn poppers sold abroad. Zimbabweans are more likely to buy a Topeka popper if they know they can get it repaired in Harare rather than have to send it back to Topeka for maintenance. Thus, if the initial sales efforts bear some fruit, the Topeka enterprise may wish to establish a sales and service facility in Harare.

Before embarking on these initiatives, however, the Topeka enterprise should review the Zimbabwe law affecting representatives of foreign enterprises.

**http://www.ita.doc.gov/ita_home/ itamac.html**
*Provides information and links on market access and compliance.*

## Regulation of Relationships with Representatives

Relationships with representatives take two basic forms: the agency and the independent contract. An *agency* is a business arrangement in which one party, the agent, performs a variety of functions on behalf and at the direction of another party, the principal. More simply put, the agent performs specific acts at the specific direction of the principal. Most employees of a corporation, for example, are agents of that corporation for one purpose or another.

*Independent contractors,* who are often known as *independent agents* outside the United States, perform general tasks for the business, but retain substantial discretion and independence in carrying them out. Consultants to a corporation are often viewed as independent contractors. Under U.S. law, the main importance of the distinction between agents and independent contractors is that third parties can generally sue the principal for acts of an agent, but not for those of an independent contractor. This distinction is important to principals because they wish to avoid paying for their representatives' injuries to third parties. The distinction does not, however, change the deal between the agent and principal; the substantive terms of the agreement are those developed between the principal and the agent.

The United States places few restrictions on the substantive terms of the representative–principal relationship. Two sophisticated parties can agree on virtually any compensation they wish, from a few dollars to an ownership interest in the principal's enterprise. They can decide on the extent to which one will indemnify the other. They can expand or restrict the representative's scope of discretion as they mutually deem appropriate. Accordingly, a U.S. enterprise is accustomed to shaping representative–principal relationships without worrying about governmental intervention. The enterprise assumes it will make its own deal with the agent; the government will not alter that arrangement.

## Supersession of Agreement with Representative

In many countries, the assumption that an enterprise can make its own deal would be in error. Often nations have laws calculated to protect local representatives irrespective of the deal that the representative has negotiated. In effect, local law may state that, notwithstanding the written agreement between the principal and the representative, the representative has certain rights. Stated another way, even if the representative agrees to a commission of one percent with the U.S. principal, the principal might find that it is obligated to pay the representative no less than two percent. Little surprises like this commission requirement can greatly affect the profitability of a foreign venture.

The supersession problem is particularly acute when the U.S. business terminates the agency arrangement. Irrespective of what the contract provides, the U.S. investor may need to make a large payment to the representative in order to terminate, or the U.S. principal may not have a right to terminate the agent at all. For example, the *Voyageur, Representant et Placier* (VRP)—a type of representative—is entitled to special protection under the French labor code; every representative is assumed to be a VRP unless the written agreement specifies otherwise. Similarly, under Council Directive 86/653 of the European Union, parties may agree to a fixed-term contract. But if the parties continue their relationship after the stated term, it becomes an *evergreen contract*—one that may be terminated only by a three-month written notice for any relationship that has lasted for three years or more. The complications associated with representative terminations are apparent in the following German case.

---

### Judgment of 30 January 1986

IZR 185/83 Neue Juristische Wochenschrift (NJW) 1931 (1986)

Bundesgerichtshof of the Federal Republic of Germany

BACKGROUND AND FACTS In 1954, plaintiff was appointed an independent agent (*Handelsvertreter*) for the distribution of textile products manufactured by the principal. In 1968, the parties amended the agency agreement to permit the principal to terminate the agency by notice to be given "not earlier than July 1, 1970, to take effect on December 31, 1970," in case of a restructuring of the principal's business. The principal continued the agency beyond that date. After the principal suffered significant losses in 1979, it notified its distribution agents in early February 1980 that it would cease all distribution by the end of that month. The principal then limited its activities to the production of a modified collection of textiles. These products were distributed by an affiliate to whom the principal had transferred its list of customers without any further compensation.

The *Handelsvertreter* brought suit against the principal, seeking damages for breach of contract, asserting that the principal terminated the agency prematurely. In addition, this independent agent sought compensation for the continuing benefits that the principal allegedly derived from the agent's former services.

The principal argued that it was justified in terminating the agency "for cause" because it had suffered severe losses that necessitated not only a cessation of its distribution but also a significant alteration of its production. Furthermore, the principal argued it did not receive any compensation for the distribution of its products by its affiliate nor was it credited for any sales to its former customers.

German law requires that if an agency for an indefinite duration has lasted for more than three

*(continued)*

*(continued)*

years, it can be terminated only upon a three-month notice and the termination can only take effect at the end of a calendar quarter. The parties may agree to a longer notice period; should the length of the notice period differ for each party, the code prescribes that the longer period will govern. Under certain extraordinary circumstances, each party may terminate the agency "for cause" without need to observe a notice period. The parties may not modify or limit these rights contractually. A party that terminates an agency prematurely without justification breaches the contract.

The courts below had awarded the agent compensation for the continuing effects of its previous activities for the principal but denied the claim for damages. The German *Bundesgerichtshof* (Supreme Court) reversed the lower courts.

### THE COURT

In terminating the agency effective February 28, 1980 by notice dated February 5, 1980, defendant breached the obligation under the agency contract to take into account the interests of the plaintiff in making its decisions.

The court below was correct when it held that a principal may invoke the right to terminate the agency for cause if it would be inequitable to require, in light of all circumstances of the case and considering the interests of both parties, that the principal continue the agency until the end of any required ordinary notice period. . . . But the facts established by the court below do not support the conclusion that defendant was entitled to terminate the agency for cause.

The fact that defendant ceased to distribute its products and transferred distribution activity to an affiliated company is not sufficient cause for a termination of the agency arrangement without observing the ordinary notice period. The court below found that neither the change in defendant's operations nor the transfer [of the distribution operations] occurred suddenly or unexpectedly. The fact that the parties agreed in 1968 that notice of termination should be given from "July 1, 1970, to take effect on December 31, 1970," in case of a restructuring of defendant's business showed that defendant had been considering such a measure for a long time. When defendant thereafter continued the contract with plaintiff for many years, it could not terminate the contract [in 1980] upon two weeks' notice without the occurrence of additional circumstances; rather, it would have been fair for it to wait until the ordinary notice period had lapsed. This is true irrespective of whether the arrangement of 1968 regarding a notice period from "July 1, 1970, to take effect on December 31, 1970," was still in effect at the time [defendant terminated the agency in 1980]. Defendant knew that plaintiff was particularly interested in receiving early notice of any planned restructuring or termination of the agency. This meant that under the given circumstances defendant had to honor the ordinary notice period. It would not have been unduly burdensome for defendant to await the expiration of the ordinary notice period because it continued its production business, albeit with certain modification, and could have continued its distribution activity for a transition period during which it could have used plaintiff's services.

The termination upon two weeks' notice is thus invalid; defendant is liable for any damage suffered by plaintiff as a result of the fact (asserted by plaintiff) that it was not able to find any substitute for the agency until the end of 1980.

**Decision.** The *Bundesgerichtshof* reversed the lower courts' finding that the termination was valid and remanded the case back to the trial court for determination of damages. The trial court was instructed to ascertain the extent to which defendant benefited from plaintiff's services so as to determine the amount of compensation due to plaintiff.

The *Judgment of 30 January 1986,* illustrates that legal requirements may be applicable to the termination of the representative, irrespective of what the agreement with the representative says. In short, a deal between two parties is not a deal. The U.S. entrepreneur should, therefore, seek local advice on what requirements will be appended to its deal by operation of law. Within the European Union (EU), there should be somewhat less discrepancy in the future; Council Directive 86/653 on agency requires each EU member state to pass national laws consistent with its terms. Nevertheless, the Directive includes a few mandatory provisions that may seem odd to Americans. For instance, it provides for an *economic conditions alarm:* The principal must notify the agent if it expects that the agent's volume of business—and thus the agent's commission—will be "significantly lower" than what the agent "normally" expects. The Directive also requires payment of a commission not only when a transaction is concluded because of the agent's efforts, but also whenever a transaction is made between the principal and a party the agent previously acquired as a customer. Further, a *commission override* is included: Whenever a principal makes a sale in a territory or a market sector reserved for the agent, the agent must be paid a commission, whether or not the agent participated in the sale. Under the Directive, these commissions accrue when the customer "should have [executed its part of the transaction] if the principal has executed its part of the transaction." Thus, commissions must be paid even if the deal is not done.

## Tax and Labor Regulation and Principal Liability: The Dependent–Independent Distinction

The retention of a representative often leads to principal liability and triggers tax and labor law requirements. The burden of these regulations frequently increases upon a finding by the host country that the representative is a *dependent agent* rather than an *independent agent.*

For tax purposes, the principal is often viewed as having opened an office once that principal hires a dependent agent within the host country. Upon such an office opening, the principal's transactions become subject to the host country's corporate tax laws.

Similarly, a dependent agent is viewed as an employee for purposes of the host country's labor law. As in the United States, having an *employee* subjects a company to pension law, tax withholding law, labor negotiations law, and other legal consequences. But, in many countries, such a determination can also affect the control of the U.S. investor's foreign enterprise. For example, as Chapter Twenty-One explains, in many countries employees may have statutory rights to representation on the company's board of directors.

Finally, if an agent is *dependent,* its principal will be vicariously liable to third parties for the

agent's misdeeds. In the context of *product liability*—responsibility to consumers for defects in one's product—the agent–principal relationship is not a critical consideration. As long as the U.S. manufacturer's product enters the foreign market, the manufacturer is likely to be in the "chain of distribution" and subject to suit whether it does business through a dependent or independent agent. But it makes a difference if the U.S. manufacturer has no hand in the agent's liability-creating act. If the entrepreneur's Nairobi dependent agent runs over a medical student in the agent's delivery truck, the entrepreneur may be liable in Kenya for a lifetime of lost income. If the agent is independent, the entrepreneur probably has no such liability.

In hiring a representative, therefore, a firm must determine whether the arrangement is characterized as creating a dependent agent or an independent agent. Unfortunately, this distinction is not based on any single definitive test. Instead, courts review a variety of factors and determine which type of agency, after considering all facts, has been created.

As noted previously, the more flexibility and discretion the agent has, the more likely the agent is to be considered independent. Agents who personally organize, pursue, and set the schedule for the marketing program—that is, those who have great discretion in organizing their time and work—are more likely to be considered independent. If, on the other hand, the U.S. principal creates the marketing program in detail and the agents simply carry it out, the agents are likely to be dependent. Similarly, agents who have an obligation to follow the specific instructions of the principal are likely to be dependent. In contrast, agents who are given a task to perform, but no obligation to follow the principal's instructions in carrying out that task, are more likely to be viewed as independent. The EU Agency Directive, for example, simply defines independent agents as those with "continuing authority to negotiate the sale or purchase of goods" on behalf of the principal. A compensation package that is based solely on commissions, rather than on periodic payments or a fixed salary with reimbursement of overhead expenses, is also indicative of independence. In this regard, independent agents typically rent their own office space and hire subagents to carry out the tasks. Finally, agents who serve more than one principal are more likely to be considered independent. Exhibit 16.1 lays out these considerations in graphic form.

Of course, the U.S. investor may not wish to give an agent the level of discretion required to be an independent agent. The U.S. company may wish to have a greater level of quality control and a greater share of the entrepreneurial profits in the venture. These benefits often outweigh the costs of greater regulation. But in weighing the business benefits of retaining a dependent agent, the U.S. investor should thoroughly understand the local legal costs it will incur.

## Regulation of Advertising Abroad

If the Topeka enterprise wishes to sell its popcorn poppers to the Zimbabwean public, merely hiring an agent in Zimbabwe may not be enough. The enterprise will need to determine how best to advertise its poppers to the Zimbabwean consumer. This task will require consideration of a number of marketing strategies calculated to be attractive to the local culture. In other words, the soccer-loving Zimbabweans will be singularly unimpressed by endorsements from U.S. football players. One cannot do justice to this fascinating area of marketing in a book principally concerned with the effect of law on business; however, marketing abroad requires a sensitivity to

the limits that foreign law can place on marketing efforts.

In most countries, the marketer may not place just anything on television or in the newspapers. These local legal limits do not always correspond with local interests. For instance, a commercial that features an explicit sexual message might well spur sales both in Denmark and in Saudi Arabia; after all, a percentage of individuals in all cultures have an interest in things prurient. In Denmark, the authorities would take no interest in such a commercial, but in Saudi Arabia, the "religious police" might mete out corporal punishment to one's local representative. An ineffective advertising campaign may simply prove unprofitable, but an *illegal* advertising campaign may lead to an unexpected stay at a local prison facility.

### Truth in Advertising

One of the founding concepts of libertarian capitalism is that of *caveat emptor* (let the buyer beware). According to this precept, government should not intervene in commercial relations. Buyers should investigate the seller's claims or obtain contractual representations and warranties. If they fail to do so and the claims turn out to be false, they have only themselves to blame. Under classic capitalist theory, the *invisible hand* of the market will, in time, ferret out consistently dishonest sellers and consistently careless buyers.

---

**EXHIBIT 16.1  The Distinction between Independent and Dependent Agents**

| | Scheduling | Work Organization | Instructions | Compensation | Expenses | Number of Principals |
|---|---|---|---|---|---|---|
| Independent | Details created by agent within principal's general requirements | Principal identifies strategic objectives; agent determines tactics and has continuing authority for achieving objectives | Principal does not instruct; change in direction causes change in compensation | Commissions; fixed amount of money | Included in compensation amount | Works for many clients |
| Dependent | Details provided by principal | Principal is involved in working out details | Agent is always subject to change in instructions | Hourly pay or salary | Specific expense reimbursement | Works for one client |

Ultimately, the philosophy of the Ninth Commandment decisively triumphed over *caveat emptor;* virtually every nation, at least formally, now prohibits false advertising. The European Union, for example, specifically excludes fraudulent advertising from its general protection of commercial speech. Even during the late nineteenth century—the high water mark of libertarian capitalist thought—courts found ways to protect the unwary. In a country with no consumer protection laws, English courts protected consumers by stretching old common law principles of contract law to apply to newspaper advertising. If one promises that one's product can specifically do something, they reasoned, one is liable if the product fails to live up to the promise.

The universal distaste for deceptive advertising illustrated in the *Carbolic Smoke Ball* case is shared to varying degrees throughout the world. But some cultures are less tolerant of "puffing"—vagueness and exaggeration—in advertising than other cultures. The Teutonic penchant for accuracy, for example, prevented a German snack food marketer from making an unspecific claim that its potato chips contained "40 percent less fat." When a competitor brought action, a German court felt obliged to determine whether the chips contained 40 percent less fat when compared with every existing brand. Finding that they did not, the court enjoined the advertising program.

**http://adage.com/international/index.html**
*See this address for news and information on international advertising and marketing.*

## Carlill v. Carbolic Smoke Ball Co.
### 1 Q.B. 256 (1893)
### Queen's Bench

**BACKGROUND AND FACTS**
The defendants, proprietors and vendors of a medical preparation called the "Carbolic Smoke Ball," inserted the following advertisement in the *Pall Mall Gazette* of 13 November 1891:

100 £ reward will be paid by the Carbolic Smoke Ball Company to any person who contracts the increasing epidemic influenza, colds, or any disease caused by taking cold, after having used the ball three times daily for two weeks according to the printed directions supplied with each ball. 1000 £ is deposited with the Alliance Bank, Regent Street, showing our sincerity in the matter. During the last epidemic of influenza many thousand carbolic smoke balls were sold as preventives against this disease, and in no ascertained case was the disease contracted by those using the carbolic smoke ball.

The plaintiff was a lady who, relying on this advertisement, bought one of the balls at a chemist's shop, and used it as directed, three times a day, from 20 November 1891, to 17 January 1892, when she was attacked by influenza.

**LORD JUSTICE LINDLEY**
The first observation I will make is that we are not dealing with any inference of fact. We are dealing with an express promise to pay 100 £ in certain events. Read the advertisement how you will, and twist it about as you will, here is a distinct promise expressed in language which is perfectly unmistakable—"100 £ reward will be paid by the Carbolic Smoke Ball Company to any person who contracts the influenza after having used the ball three times daily for two weeks according to the printed directions supplied with each ball."

We must first consider whether this was intended to be a promise at all, or whether it was a mere puff which meant nothing. Was it a mere puff? My answer to that question is No, and I base my answer upon this passage: "1000 £ is deposited with the Alliance Bank, showing our sincerity in the matter." Now, for what was that money deposited or that statement made except to negative the suggestion that this was a mere puff and meant nothing at all. . . .

Then it is contended that it is not binding. In the first place, it is said that it is not made with anybody in particular. Now that point is common to the words of this advertisement and to the words of all other advertisements offering rewards. They are offers to anybody who performs the conditions named in the advertisement, and anybody who does perform the condition accepts the offer. . . .

*(continued)*

*(continued)*

[I]t is said that this advertisement is so vague that you cannot really construe it as a promise—that the vagueness of the language shows that a legal promise was not intended or contemplated. The language is vague and uncertain in some respects, and particularly in this, that the 100 £ is to be paid to any person who contracts the increasing epidemic after having used the balls three times daily for two weeks. It is said, When are they to be used? According to the language of the advertisement no time is fixed, and, construing the offer most strongly against the person who has made it, one might infer that any time was meant. . . . I do not think that business people or reasonable people would understand the words as meaning that if you took a smoke ball and used it three times daily for two weeks you were to be guaranteed against influenza for the rest of your life, and I think it would be pushing the language of the advertisement too far to construe it as meaning that. . . . [I]t strikes me that there are two, and possibly three, reasonable constructions to be put on this advertisement, any one of which will answer the purpose of the plaintiff. Possibly it may be limited to persons catching the "increasing epidemic" or any colds or diseases caused by taking cold, during the prevalence of the increasing epidemic. That is one suggestion; but it does not commend itself to me. Another suggested meaning is that you are warranted free from catching this epidemic, or colds or other diseases caused by taking cold, whilst you are using this remedy after using it for two weeks. If that is the meaning, the plaintiff is right, for she used the remedy for two weeks and went on using it till she got the epidemic. Another meaning, and the one which I rather prefer, is that the reward is offered to any person who contracts the epidemic or other disease within a reasonable time after having used the smoke ball. . . . What is a reasonable time? It has been suggested that there is no standard of reasonableness; that it depends upon the reasonable time for a germ to develop! I do not feel pressed by that. It strikes me that a reasonable time may be ascertained in a business sense and in a sense satisfactory to a lawyer. . . . It strikes me, I confess, that the true construction of this advertisement is that 100 £ will be paid to anybody who uses this smoke ball three times daily for two weeks according to the printed directions, and who gets the influenza or cold or other diseases caused by taking cold within a reasonable time after so using it; and if that is the true construction, it is enough for the plaintiff.

**Decision.**   The Queen's Bench found that the advertisement was, in the parlance of contract law, a definite and operative offer that the plaintiff had accepted through her performance. It entered judgment of 100 £ on her behalf.

The exacting standards of the Japanese are similarly intolerant of exaggeration. In Japan, PepsiCo, Inc., cannot advertise its cola drink as the choice of "generation neXt" as it does in the United States. After all, members of the Japanese Fair Trade Committee argue, it is currently second to Coca-Cola in the Japanese market.

By contrast, other nations are far more flexible. In some countries—among them, the People's Republic of China—hucksters have been victimizing others for centuries. While investors can, they may wish to take advantage of such greater latitude abroad. But the trend is clear: Even in China, the authorities are catching up to the philosophical descendants of the *Carbolic Smoke Ball* medical science entrepreneurs (see the following article).

The sanctions for false advertising also vary from place to place. Of particular interest is the South Korean sentence, which requires a public apology. Although to a Westerner such a sanction would be little more than a slap on the wrist, the ignominy of a public apology caused an advertiser to appeal the public apology sentence to the High Court of Seoul. The Seoul Court found that the advertiser was guilty of deception, but it also found extenuating circumstances in the case. Therefore, it reversed the sentence of a public apology, finding it too harsh a penalty.

## Content-Specific Regulations

Advertising can also be outlawed even if its content is perfectly true. Advertising aimed at children, for example, is closely and diversely

*Foreign Accents*

# China Fights Wild Ad Claims
## The Universality of Truth in Advertising

China has issued tough new regulations aimed at protecting consumers and raising the standard of advertising produced here.

The State Council, China's highest administrative body, said ads must be "true, wholesome, clear, and understandable," reported Xinhua, the official China news agency.

The new regulations, effective this month, are an effort to crack down on domestic advertisers that misrepresent products and to improve advertising's overall quality.

Under the new rules, ads containing obscene, superstitious, and absurd content are outlawed.

Many Chinese products—particularly medicines—carry labels proclaiming the contents can cure ailments ranging from stomach pains and headaches to cancer and impotence. . . .

[R]egulations on alcohol and tobacco may hit Western marketers especially hard as the imported goods try to break into the market, [an observer] said.

The regulations also stipulate that Chinese journalists no longer are allowed to solicit advertising, and the media must stop carrying advertisements in the form of news reports.

China's national anthem, emblem, and flag also are banned from advertisements as are ads that belittle other products.

Xinhua reported advertisers will be taxed and will be subject to supervision and examination by auditing, commercial, and financial authorities.

Violators will be subject to criticism or fines and serious offenders will have their licenses revoked or their businesses shut down.

*Advertising Age,* **December 21, 1987.**

regulated. More than 40 countries prohibit or greatly limit such advertising, reasoning that children cannot intelligently assess the content of commercials. Many of these bans are rather curious. In Italy, for example, appeals to children are generally permitted—but children cannot be shown eating. Other nations prohibit children's commercials that use public or fictional figures. Many countries require prior government clearance of advertising to children. The province of Quebec completely prohibits all advertising directed at children.

In some nations, *language laws* can complicate cross-border advertising. In Indonesia, the municipal government of Jakarta bans languages other than Indonesian from billboards, and violators may be jailed for up to three months for breaking the law. The marketing difficulties created by this law become apparent when one realizes that, for most of the 180 million people on the Indonesian islands, Indonesian is a second language.

In France, every word used in advertising must be French, even if the French population more commonly uses the English word. For example, although virtually all French businesspeople prefer to use the English term *cash flow,* the language law recently required them to reflect the concept in writing and public speeches in its lengthy, seldom-used French incarnation of *marge brute d'auto-financement.* If similar laws prevailed in the United States, advertisers would have to refer to *paté* by its less appetizing English equivalent, *ground goose liver.* The advertising laws in some of the relatively new Eastern European democracies indicate a remaining socialist distrust of advertising in a capitalist economy. The Czech Republic bans "hidden seduction" and insists that advertising be based on the "specific features of the goods." Hungary demands that the advertiser have sufficient inventories of advertised goods on hand before beginning an advertising campaign.

Other advertising regulations are aimed at specific types of products. For instance, almost all countries limit the advertising of "sin" products—tobacco and alcohol. As in all advertising, however, regulations reflect the idiosyncrasies of the countries that enact them.

Starting in 1993, France banned all tobacco advertising and most liquor advertising—direct or indirect, including sponsorship of sports events. The only exception, of course, is French wine. With a ferocity mindful of its recent totalitarian heritage, Bulgaria has banned all tobacco advertising outside of tobacco shops and threatened violators with $50,000 in fines per violation. The anti-authoritarian British, on the other hand, do not forbid tobacco advertising, but insist on self-imposed and highly subjective industry guidelines. This approach led to the banning of an ad campaign featuring two overweight, balding, middle-aged men whom the industry watch group deemed "too appealing" to young people. Belgium permits cigarette advertising, but only those that focus on the package or on part of its design. Even more curiously, Belgium generally permits advertising of alcoholic beverages, but not for absinthe drinks. The Belgian enmity to the green liqueur may not be intuitively obvious to Americans. Even the definition of "sinful liquor" can be counterintuitive. In 1995, Iran's spiritual leader ruled that foreign soft drinks such as Coca-Cola and Pepsi-Cola are forbidden because they somehow advance Zionism.

As the following excerpt from Kenya demonstrates, all of these "anti-sin" laws in developed nations have caused a migration of "sin" products to people in the Third World. But their reaction may not be what marketers would want.

---

*Foreign Accents*

## Tobacco Firms Looking South

While the smoking habit is dying out in the developed world, it is on the increase in Third World countries where it is killing an estimated one million people every year. Faced with shrinking markets and a hostile population in the West, tobacco companies are now turning their full advertising efforts towards winning consumers in the Third World.

According to London-based Panos Institute, multinational tobacco companies are frantically looking for new markets in the Third World and Eastern Europe. In their home countries, more and more people are quitting smoking and few are starting because of greater awareness of the health dangers associated with smoking. . . .

Smoking is on the rise in the Third World mainly because of ignorance about its dangers. Children and women are taking up the habit. Two decades ago, few women and teenagers in Kenya smoked. Today, more and more women are smoking and many children are starting the habit very early. Figures . . . indicate that smoking has fallen by half in the past 40 years in the developed world. By contrast in the Third World, smoking has risen to a level where one in every two men is a smoker and eight percent of our women smoke. . . .

The [World Health Organization] projects a very grim forecast for smoking trends in developing countries where per capita consumption of tobacco has risen by 70 percent during the last 25 years. In the next two to three decades, seven million deaths a year will result from smoke related diseases in Eastern Europe, Asia, Latin America, and Africa.

It is surprising that so little is being done in Kenya to fight the rising rates of tobacco use. The very opposite is happening instead. Promotion of smoking is being done in our radio, in our print media, on buildings like Tawfiq Shopping Centre in Eastleigh, on our highways, on ubiquitous giant billboards and signboards, and on gigantic mounted metal cigarette packets in the city.

In Kenya, *Embassy* [cigarette brand] is still the smooth way to go places. *Sweet Menthol (SM)* will win you friends. The time has come to tell our youngsters that smoking *Embassy* is the smooth way to go to the grave and that smoking *SM* will only win you friends to die with. . . .

In Kenya, tobacco companies still sponsor radio programs and sporting events. This should be prohibited. Sponsorship of public events is a way these

*(continued)*

*(continued)*

companies use to create a favorable attitude to their killer tobacco products.

In Kenya, we have done so little to fight smoking. But it is not due to lack of good examples from other (even African) countries. In Burkina Faso, for instance, the government prohibits all cigarette advertising on billboards and screens. Cigarette packs must indicate tar and nicotine content of cigarettes in addition to carrying a health warning. In Nigeria, advertising of tobacco and sponsorship of sports events by tobacco companies is restricted. Cigarette packaging must carry two warnings: "The federal ministry of health warns that tobacco smoking is dangerous to health," and "smokers are liable to die young." In China—the world's largest tobacco producing country—tobacco advertising on TV, radio and print media was banned in January 1992.

But the most ambitious campaign against smoking is taking place in Singapore, which targets to become the world's first smoke-free city in two decades. In Singapore, dropping a cigarette butt on the street will earn you a fine of $300. . . . Since 1989, four different messages are carried on cigarette packs: "Smoking causes heart disease," "Smoking causes cancer," "Smoking damages your lungs" and "Smoking harms those around us," in Singapore.

In Kenya and other Third World countries, efforts to fight tobacco use may face frustrations because of interference from the multinational tobacco companies. These have billions and are prepared to use them to buy influence in poor Third World and stop laws harsh to them being enacted.

The argument by tobacco companies that they pay taxes is also easily proven fallacious. Wangai said that for every shilling paid by tobacco companies [Kenya] Shs 20 are spent dealing with health problems caused by tobacco use. In any event, no paying of any amount of tax on a product or employment creation can be justified if that product will kill prematurely a half of all those who use it—which in the Third World means a quarter of all adult males who now smoke.

Tobacco farming also causes environmental degradation through deforestation. A half of all tobacco produced in the Third World is dried (cured) using firewood. To cure a kilo of tobacco requires 7.8 kg of wood. This means that for every hectare of tobacco grown, an hectare of forest is cleared. No tree planting effort can replace trees felled this fast, considering that even fast-growing trees take five years to mature.

Perhaps the greatest challenge to the global smoke-out lobby is what to do with the many workers employed in tobacco production when business shrinks as a result of the ongoing campaign. But we should never hesitate to dismantle a dangerous army to safeguard the jobs of soldiers. The giant tobacco companies should use their accumulated billions to give workers pensions. But where possible, small companies could be helped to voluntarily wind up from a global smoke-out fund.

**Dr. Kangethe Mungai**
*The East African Standard*, December 20, 1994.

The central point in advertising abroad is that the U.S. enterprise must seek legal advice from local practitioners and fashion local advertising appropriately. Indeed, in many countries the guiding norms are not in laws at all but in industry codes observed by the local marketing organizations. The rules in this area are as diverse and arbitrary as human culture itself and as transitory as political opinion. Perhaps the primary general principle is that no useful general principles apply to all cultures.

**http://www.stetson.edu/~ldenecke/
mktplan.html**
*The PepsiKona Marketing Plan for Columbia S.A.*

## Marketing Considerations: The Nestlé Instant Formula Case

An enterprise that seeks to market a product in a new nation must be alert to unanticipated risk associated with the product in the new environment. If such risk exists, even if a marketing campaign is technically lawful, the law, public scorn, or both will in time catch up with the entrepreneur. The Nestlé infant formula case is an excellent illustration of this problem.

Infant formula manufacturers have long provided hospitals with free or low-cost formula as a marketing technique. The concept is that the mother develops a brand loyalty from the child's birth that is unlikely to change over time. In addition, formula manufacturers promoted their products, like all other merchants, through mass media. Some have argued that these marketing techniques have the effect of discouraging mothers from breast-feeding, which is widely regarded to be superior to infant formulas. This discouragement is said to be particularly influential in the Third World, where mothers are less educated and more impressionable.

Critics argue that in such developing countries, forsaking breast-feeding can have especially grim consequences. Outside hospitals, the water supply may not be sanitary and mothers may not understand usage instructions. Improper use can lead to malnutrition, diarrhea, and gastroenteritis.

Nestlé, S.A., a Swiss concern with over 40 percent of the $3 billion baby formula market, became a lightning rod for criticism. Critics charged that Nestlé was discouraging uneducated Third World mothers from breast-feeding by luring them through its marketing activities. These critics organized a series of boycotts against all Nestlé products throughout developed countries.

---

### Foreign Accents

# Murphy Brown Goes to Canada or *Parlez-Vous* Long Distance

### Candice Bergen's Television Ad Campaign for Sprint Canada Is Running into Some Crossed Signals in Quebec

Response to the commercials for discount long-distance service, which features a 1-800 number to order, is lagging that in English-speaking Canada, according to executives at Sprint Canada and Grey Advertising in Toronto, who are in the process of figuring out why.

"We're having a closer look at the Quebec market," says Malcolm MacKenzie, an account executive at Grey.

The U.S.'s Sprint Corp., which is based in Kansas City, Missouri, owns 25 percent of Sprint Canada's parent, Call-Net Enterprises, Inc.

Last July, Ms. Bergen, who speaks French, filmed two sets of ads for Sprint's "The Most Worldwide" service, called *Le Maxiphone* in French.

*Alors, quel est le probleme?*

Although many Quebec residents can get the U.S. networks, they tend to watch made-in-Quebec shows and, therefore, weren't as exposed to Sprint's U.S. campaign, says Sprint Canada vice president David Hagan.

Also, Ms. Bergen's popular show "Murphy Brown" isn't a hit in Quebec—where it's dubbed into French. The voice Quebec viewers associate with Candice Bergen isn't that of Candice Bergen. When they hear the actress's natural voice, it seems unreal.

"For us, it was an Englishwoman speaking French. She's not a star at all in Quebec," says Luc Merineau, a senior copywriter at Le Groupe BCP, a Montreal ad agency. Grey Advertising is based in Toronto but says its Montreal office wrote the copy for the French commercials.

Although the copy and Ms. Bergen's command of the French won praise in one Quebec newspaper, the expressions used by the actress, such as *"Tigidou, mon minou,"* ("OK, my pussycat") are "not the type of expressions young people use every day," according to Mr. Merineau.

Overall, Sprint Canada says it has reached its goal of 200,000 new customers this year. But for next year, according to Mr. Hagan, the company is preparing "new creative execution" in English and French.

**Solange de Santis**
*The Wall Street Journal*, November 25, 1994.

Reprinted by permission. Copyright © Dow Jones & Co., Inc., 1994.

In response, Nestlé changed its promotional practices and in 1976 phased out mass media advertising. Still Nestlé did not escape criticism, because it continued to provide free and low-cost formula. The World Health Organization promulgated an "International Code of Breast Milk Substitutes," which some ten countries have implemented as law. Nestlé voluntarily agreed to follow the code in 1982, agreeing to supply formula only upon request by hospital administrators. Third World administrators, however, continued to order formula and give it to virtually all mothers. Accordingly, in 1989, several groups in Britain, Ireland, and Sweden reactivated the boycott because of what they viewed as continued promotion. Finally, in January 1991, Nestlé committed to stop supplying free and low-cost formula completely.

In short, although Nestlé acted in conformance with the law, it still found itself in a vortex of controversy that adversely affected its profitability throughout the world. Marketing often involves understanding that corporations may be held to a higher standard than that mandated by law.

# The Foreign Corrupt Practices Act

In most nations, the government is far more immersed in the day-to-day functioning of commerce than is the government of the United States in its economy. Favorable government action or inaction is frequently a prerequisite to concluding a transaction in many nations. Naturally, such governmental action or inaction results from the exercise of discretion by government officials, giving such officials greater influence in commercial transactions than their counterparts in the United States. Many of these foreign government officials are not above informing their discretion with a bribe. Indeed, in many countries, bribery of public officials is virtually a way of life.

This is the case even though almost every nation in the world formally outlaws bribery of its own officials. For example, the Russian Federation, which in recent years has obtained a dubious reputation for official corruption, has a complex legal framework to deter corruption. Since April 1992, Presidential Decree 351 has, as a prophylactic measure, barred civil servants from participating in entrepreneurial activities, managing commercial activities, or accepting foreign business trips paid by commercial entities. The Russian Federal Anti-Monopoly Law restricts government officials from owning enterprises or serving in a voting capacity in a commercial enterprise. Penalties for violation include fines, dismissal from office, and imprisonment. South Korea, which in early 1998 experienced a near-collapse of its financial system due to the business consequences flowing from official corruption, also has an impressive and strict anti-bribery legal framework. Article 129 of the Korean Criminal Code prohibits not only receipt or solicitation of a bribe but also "manifestation of a will to deliver" a bribe. There certainly is increasing enforcement. In August 1996, two former South Korean Presidents were convicted of criminal bribery—having accepted hundreds of millions of dollars from business enterprises. One was sentenced to death, while the other was sentenced to 22 years and six months in prison.

A foreign investor who makes a payoff to a foreign official risks criminal prosecution by the official's country. But in many countries, this risk is not great. For instance, prior to very recent events, South Korean prosecutors had enforced bribery laws only against lower level officials and had exercised their prosecutorial discretion to avoid actions against politically powerful high-level officials. The much greater risk is often that of official persecution if the payment is not made.

One country in the world also outlaws bribes by its citizens to public officials in other countries. Because that country is the United States, every American who retains an agent abroad should be familiar with the *Foreign Corrupt Practices Act* (FCPA).

> **http://www.utc.com/corrupt/corrmain.htm**
> or
> **http://www.mac.doc.gov/bisnis/fcp1.htm**
> Information on the FCPA.

## Origins of the FCPA

In the mid-1970s, the press in the United States uncovered a number of instances of U.S.-based corporations making payments to foreign leaders for official favors. An aircraft manufacturer was widely alleged to have made payments to the Japanese prime minister and a Dutch prince in exchange for assistance in obtaining government contracts. At the same time, alleged payments to a number of members of the Italian government caused its president to resign.

Concerned by these embarrassing incidents, the U.S. Securities and Exchange Commission instituted a voluntary disclosure program to assess the frequency of the phenomenon. Firms were invited to tell of their payoffs abroad under a loose understanding of nonprosecution.

The volume of the response was remarkable. More than 400 U.S. companies revealed that they had bribed foreign public officials. The amounts paid aggregated into the hundreds of millions of dollars. Although corporations based in other countries allegedly engaged in the same practices, no nation had ever publicly confessed to such a massive pattern of corrupting behavior.

The U.S. public was in no mood to condone such frank admissions of immorality. Scarcely a year before, the president of the United States had resigned because of the so-called Watergate coverup. Nor had any nation ever faced the embarrassment of admitting such an extensive pattern of corrupt activity. U.S. public opinion and the world's disdain demanded prompt and decisive action.

They got it. By December 1977, Congress had passed and the president had signed the world's first law outlawing its citizens' bribes to officials of another nation. In the decades since, the United States has amended its own statute to a limited degree, but no nation has followed the U.S. lead. To the contrary, as noted in the following section, some nations now permit tax deductions for such payments. Some multilateral organizations, however, such as the World Bank and the International Monetary Fund, have finally begun to follow the United States' lead, seeking to deny international funding from nations which continue to permit public corruption. The United States has long been a lonely voice in the wilderness, but it may finally be evoking a positive response.

## Structure of the Act

The Foreign Corrupt Practices Act seeks to punish bribery of foreign officials and to establish internal accounting mechanisms that will prevent such bribery. Criminal punishment is accomplished through the so-called *antibribery* provisions. The prevention function is accomplished through provisions that seek to detect illegal payments through the *accounting and record-keeping systems* of the enterprise.

**The Antibribery Provisions.** In essence, the antibribery provisions prohibit U.S. firms from "corruptly" paying or offering to pay a "foreign official" for assistance in obtaining or retaining business. Most significantly, it also prohibits payments to a person—such as a foreign agent—when the payer knows that a portion of the payment will go to a public official.

Violation of the antibribery provisions is a serious offense. Any individual convicted can be jailed for up to five years and fined up to $100,000. Any corporation convicted can be fined $2 million per violation. Unfortunately, the law does not clearly define what one has to do to commit this serious criminal act. It contains three principal points of ambiguity: the "routine governmental action" exception, the "corruptly" requirement, and the "knowing" requirement.

Congress recognized that in many countries petty graft is so common that to forbid U.S. companies from engaging in it would be tantamount to forbidding them from doing business there. Accordingly, Congress excluded from the coverage of the FCPA any payment that is a "facilitating or expediting payment . . . the purpose of which is to expedite or secure the performance of a routine governmental action." Such "routine actions" can include the granting of qualification to do business, processing of visas, providing police and mail service, or providing basic utilities or transportation services.

The routine governmental action exception is limited—few government actions do not involve some discretion, particularly in countries outside the United States. As discussed in other chapters, foreign statutes tend to lay out broad general outlines and allow bureaucrats to fill in the interstices. In short, U.S. executives must guess whether the role of any given government official will ultimately be determined by some court to be "routine." If they guess wrong, they can go to jail. Under such circumstances, taking chances is probably not advisable.

Where gratuity payments to customs officials are routine, the U.S. investor must make a careful assessment of its potential FCPA liability vis-à-vis its ability to operate effectively without making facilitating payments. Many U.S. companies have simply determined that the profits of operating in such countries are not worth the overwhelming risk.

Although the word "corrupt" is used in a number of criminal statues, the legal concept is not well defined. Someone who is simply negligent in making a payment, however, is not generally considered corrupt. Thus, a businessperson who, through lack of sophistication, fails to realize that part of a payment to a local foreign agent is in fact going to a government official may not have the corrupt state of mind required for a violation of the antibribery provision. (Such a businessperson might, however, be in violation of the accounting provisions, which have no such corruptness requirement.) Corruptness requires that the businessperson display a reckless or conscious disregard for the consequences of personal actions. In other words, even if payers do not have actual knowledge that a payment is being made, they are corrupt if they act as if they do not care whether it is going to a government official.

The corruptness requirement does not excuse the U.S. victim of extortion. Even where a foreign official is extorting a payment from a U.S. investor, the firm is corrupt if it makes the payment. When faced with an extortion request in a country in which a U.S. firm already has substantial assets, therefore, the firm must refuse to make the payment and suffer the consequent losses. The situation, of course, again suggests that the investor should carefully review the business climate in the foreign country before entering it.

The ambiguities that accompany the corruptness concept are similar to those that surround the knowing requirement. Although Congress has now made clear that "mere foolishness" is insufficient for liability, the standard is intended to cover "any instance where 'any reasonable person would have realized' the existence of the circumstances or result and the [person] has 'consciously chosen not to ask about what he had reason to believe he would discover.'" The danger is that foreign agent might be asking for a commission that will ultimately end up in the hands of a foreign official. If a firm discovers that its agent made a payment to a government, the U.S. prosecutorial authorities would be able to review the circumstances surrounding the payment to the agent to determine whether the firm "knew" of the agent's bribe. Suffice it to say that whenever an agent asks for a big fee or commission, a U.S. investor has reason to be nervous. Extracts on the following page from an SEC consent decree illustrate a number of the techniques that crooked agents employ to effect transfers to foreign officials.

**The Accounting and Recordkeeping Requirements.** The FCPA also requires a U.S. investor to "make and keep books, records, and accounts which, in reasonable detail, accurately and fairly reflect the transactions and dispositions of its assets." It further requires an investor to "devise and maintain a system of internal accounting controls sufficient to provide reasonable assurances" that all transactions are authorized and that access to assets is tracked. These are commonly referred to as the *accounting and recordkeeping provisions.*

The principal objection to the accounting provisions is that they fail to incorporate any concept of *materiality.* U.S. businesses are not normally expected to unearth every fact in their financial statements; aside from its impracticality, the reader of the financial statements would drown in a sea of detail. Thus, accounting systems are generally geared to tracking "material" facts—facts that a prudent investor in the company should know. A $5,000 problem in a $5 billion company, for instance, would not normally be perceived as material.

By not including a concept of materiality, the accounting provisions of the FCPA require the U.S. company's accounting system to be able to pick up bribery irrespective of how small it may be. Although $5,000 might be a great deal of money to an individual, tracking every such problem represents a formidable task for a multi-billion-dollar company. Nevertheless, as a technical matter, ignoring such a task is a possible violation of the FCPA.

## The DOJ Review Process

Before entering a transaction raising a possible FCPA issue, an investor can seek an

## Securities and Exchange Commission v. Tesoro Petroleum Corp.

2 FCPA Repors 63F(1980)
United States Securities &
Exchange Commission

## BACKGROUND AND FACTS ALLEGED IN COMPLAINT

Defendant Tesoro is an integrated natural resources company which has since 1946 engaged in or endeavored to engage in the exploration, development, production, purchase, and sale of oil and gas [throughout the world]. Defendant Tesoro and others have engaged in a course of business in connection with acquiring material foreign assets . . . whereby they made or caused to be made substantial payments to "finders" and "consultants," where such payments, with respect to multimillion dollar contracts, were disproportionate to the business obtained or the service rendered, were not usual or customary. . . . In certain instances involving payments made in connection with foreign business activities, the circumstances of the payments indicate that the funds, in whole or in part, may have been directly or indirectly transferred to foreign government officials or political leaders.

As part of said conduct, since at least 1974 Defendant Tesoro through the participation of the chairman of its board, Robert V. West (West), has caused payments and loans totaling approximately $460,500 to be made to or on behalf of entities associated with James L. Morgan (Morgan), "finder/consultant" who assisted Tesoro in obtaining certain foreign oil and gas concessions from a foreign government. Of the $460,500 paid by Tesoro in connection with its successful signing of a production-sharing contract with a foreign government in 1974, $200,000 in cash was paid to Morgan when West delivered to Morgan, and immediately thereafter assisted Morgan in cashing, a Tesoro check payable to a foreign entity in which Morgan was a partner. After the check was cashed, the $200,000 in cash was delivered by Morgan to Morgan's home where an official of the national oil company of the country involved was waiting. West accompanied Morgan to Morgan's home and met with the official of the national oil company. . . . In 1974, in connection with the successful signing of this production-sharing contract, Tesoro, in addition to the $200,000 direct payment to Morgan, arranged and guaranteed a $200,000 bank loan to a United States entity controlled by Morgan as additional payment for Morgan's "consulting services." The note became past due in December 1977 and subsequently Tesoro,

under its guarantee, paid the note plus $60,500 in interest when Morgan defaulted on the note.

As further part of said conduct between December 1973 and September 1974, Tesoro paid $120,000 to a consultant in connection with an application to do business in another foreign country, and in connection with subsequent applications by Tesoro to do business in that country and a refinery joint venture. These payments, made pursuant to an agreement between the consultant and Tesoro which provided that the consultant would be paid $10,000 monthly for one year, were disproportionate to the business obtained or the services rendered, were not usual or customary, and were made under circumstances indicating that the funds, in whole or in part, may have been passed on to government officials. . . .

On December 6, 1973, during the period when Tesoro's application to do business was pending, Tesoro conveyed $30,000 to a bank account of the consultant at a United States bank as payment for the first three months of the agreement. . . . In January 1974, just prior to the time that the consultant informed West that Tesoro would soon be notified that it had qualified to bid on exploration areas, the consultant paid a director of the national oil company $20,000 via two $10,000 checks drawn on the same U.S. bank account to which Tesoro deposited the consultant's fees. In late March, while Tesoro's application to do business was still pending, the consultant paid an additional $30,000 to the director of the national oil company. The check was again drawn on the same U.S. bank account in which Tesoro had deposited the fees. As of March 1974, the consultant had transferred to a director of the national oil company an amount equivalent to all the money paid the consultant by Tesoro at that time.

Tesoro has in connection with the acquisition of material foreign assets, made substantial payments over three years to a foreign consultant—payments represented the substantial majority of Tesoro's entire cost of acquiring the assets. The consultant primarily provided service in connection with the successful negotiation of an agreement with a foreign government with whose official he had direct access. The agreement subsequently enabled Tesoro to obtain an interest in

*(continued)*

*(continued)*

certain material foreign assets. The payments to the consultant were made without benefit of a written contract, and in a manner designated to conceal the transaction thorough multiple bank transfers terminating in a deposit in a Swiss bank account of a Liechtenstein corporation.

**Decision.** Tesoro, without admitting or denying any of the allegations in the complaint . . . consented to the entry of the Final Judgment of Permanent Injunction in the form annexed hereto, enjoining it from violating . . . the Securities Exchange Act of 1934.

interpretation of these somewhat ambiguous provisions from the U.S. Department of Justice (DOJ). But the investor may not like the process.

The firm first submits all relevant details of the proposed transaction to the DOJ, including appropriate documentation—the DOJ will not respond to hypothetical situations. The firm must be willing to risk the confidentiality of the deal—all documents in the DOJ's possession are subject to the Freedom of Information Act, which permits any American to request disclosure of documents in the government's possession. Even when the specifics of the deal are afforded confidential treatment, the DOJ will always issue a release that describes the general nature of the transaction and the identity of the parties involved. Thus, the procedure has the initial disadvantage of subjecting the transaction to the scrutiny of the public at large, including the U.S. firm's competitors. These competitors may be attracted to the opportunity and lure the U.S. firm's proposed business partners away with a more attractive deal. Furthermore, disclosure of the deal has other adverse side effects. The public officials involved may resent having their integrity publicly questioned. Indeed, such public disclosure might well have adverse effects on the officials' standing in their own home country.

The DOJ will respond in thirty days unless it requires the submission of additional information. If it does require such additional information, the Department will have an additional thirty days from the time of receipt of that information. At the end of this two-month period, the DOJ will either express an interest to pursue or not to pursue a prosecution under the FCPA—or simply decline to state any position. This delay is not very satisfactory in most business transactions. While the parties await a response, mar-

ket conditions may change so as to make the deal less attractive or entirely unattractive for one of the parties.

Perhaps because of these problems, the DOJ review procedure is used infrequently. Although millions of foreign transactions have occurred since the procedure was instituted in 1980, only a few dozen requests have been made under the DOJ procedure. In the overwhelming majority of cases, U.S. firms are choosing not to avail themselves of the procedure. It seems unlikely that they are failing to do so because FCPA issues are not surfacing. Nevertheless, the examination of the FCPA review process in Exhibit 16.2 may provide a sense of its general outlines.

The saving grace of this ambiguous criminal statute is that it is seldom enforced. Although the FCPA is now over 20 years old, the *Tesoro* case is one of the few occasions that U.S. authorities actually initiated formal enforcement actions in connection with alleged payments to foreign officials. A recent FCPA investigation, relating to alleged payments by Northrop Corporation to South Korean officials to persuade them to purchase F-20 fighter planes, was dropped with no action in 1993. Apparently, U.S. authorities are using their prosecutorial discretion not to go after businesses in borderline cases. While FCPA is almost certainly to remain on the books, as time goes on without significant enforcement, it becomes less menacing. It seems somewhat clear, after all these years, that the Department of Justice will exercise its prosecutorial discretion to enforce the spirit of the law vigorously, rather than in an unrealistically broad interpretation in order to go after legitimate U.S. businessmen.

The United States' complex legislation to prevent bribery of foreign officials is in stark contrast to attitudes in other nations. Not only has no

---

**EXHIBIT 16.2    FCPA Review Procedure Release 85-1**

**2 FCPA Reports 722 (1985) United States Department of Justice**

The Department of Justice has received a review request from the Atlantic Richfield Company (ARCO) pursuant to the Foreign Corrupt Practices Act Review Procedure, 28 C.F.R. 50.18. ARCO, doing business through its wholly owned subsidiary, ARCO Chemical Europe, Inc. (ACEI), has announced plans for the construction of a chemical plant to be located in Fos-sur-mer, Bouches du Rhone, France. The proposed plant will produce large quantities of propylene oxide and gasoline-grade tertiary butyl alcohol.

ARCO intends to invite officials of the French government ministry responsible for that nation's industrial financial and development programs and for the issuance of permits and licenses necessary for the Fos-sur-mer project. The French government will designate an official or officials to meet with ARCO Chemical Company management personnel in Philadelphia and to inspect an ARCO chemical plant at Bayport, Texas, similar to the plant proposed for Fos-sur-mer. The meetings and plant inspections are to address environmental and management concerns raised by French authorities in connection with the operation of a large scale chemical plant.

ARCO has furnished an opinion that the proposed conduct does not violate French law. The travel will occur during a period of not more than one week and ARCO will pay the necessary and reasonable expenses of the French delegation, which will include those for air travel, lodging, and meals.

Based on all the facts and circumstances, as represented by the requestor, the department does not presently intend to take an enforcement action with respect to any of the prospective conduct described in this request.

The FCPA review letter and this release have no application to any party not joining in the request, and may be relied upon by the requesting party only to the extent that the disclosure of facts and circumstances in the request is accurate and complete and continues to accurately and completely reflect the actual facts and circumstances.

---

country followed the United States' example, but some regard the entire FCPA as yet another instance of U.S. naiveté. Indeed, as reflected in the next article, some European governments permit the deduction of illicit payments to government officials as just another cost of doing business.

The problem of official corruption has certainly not gone away. In 1993, the president of Brazil was impeached for accepting illegal payments. In Ecuador, the government somehow purchased nine French railroad locomotives that were far too heavy for any of the railroad track in the entire country. As noted above, in 1996, two former South Korean presidents were convicted of criminal bribery.

While FCPA has clearly not solved the problem, it has greatly diminished participation by Americans in the problem. Frightened by the possibility of prison sentences and adverse publicity, major U.S. firms expend substantial resources assuring that they are not associated with questionable foreign representatives.

Because U.S. firms are therefore at a competitive disadvantage vis-à-vis the rest of the world,

they are working hard to prevent such practices by foreign firms. Major U.S. firms have helped fund Transparency International, a nongovernmental organization that assists developing countries in devising anticorruption schemes. They have also urged European parliaments to pass legislation akin to the FCPA. By late 1996, the heads of the International Monetary Fund (IMF) and the World Bank had both weighed in against corruption. The IMF said that Fund officials would henceforth regard it as their duty to press for anti-corruption reforms in countries seeking to borrow money. The World Bank noted that in projects financed by the Bank, if evidence of corruption were found, it would cancel the project. The FCPA's slow and modest beginning has not ruled out its potential for success in cleansing international business ethics of official corruption.

## Prudent Behavior for the U.S. Businessperson

Achieving greater profits for one's company is certainly not worth a five-year prison sentence,

# Bribing Foreigners Can Be Deducted in Much of Europe

Responding to a parliamentary question earlier this month, Denmark's tax minister advised Danish companies to use the term "consultant fees" rather than "bribes" in filling out tax returns. But he made it clear that greasing palms to secure deals in Eastern Europe or Africa can be written off as legitimate business expenses.

"Bribe expenses are tax deductible provided companies can document that they were necessary to secure a sale of goods or a business contract," said the minister, Ole Stavad.

Denmark is not alone.

Many other countries in Europe also allow bribes to be tax deductible under certain conditions, and a special report on the practice from a panel set up by the Organization for Economic Cooperation and Development is expected by year end.

According to a publication from the Paris-based agency, "All OECD countries have some sort of legislation against bribery of their own national officials. But with the exception of the United States, national legislation does not address actions committed abroad by its citizens."

Mark Pieth, a criminal law professor at the University of Basel who is chairman of the OECD panel, fears that a lax attitude toward kickbacks creates a "climate of corruption" that favors organized crime. The panel within the OECD's Commission on International Investment and Multinational Enterprises was set up on the urging of the United States.

But experts say there is a disagreement within the OECD over how strong any recommendation to do away with such tax deductibility might be, because some countries contend it would be nearly impossible to win certain contracts—especially in Africa—without bribing local officials.

In Britain, the Inland Revenue Department proposed tax-law changes on Friday that would forbid companies from claiming deductions for illegal bribes or money paid to terrorists for protection. But a spokesman for the department says some bribes paid to foreign officials might still be deductible under the changes.

The spokesman says, "If it's an accepted business practice in that particular country, a company may be able to get a deduction." The British regulations generally allow deductions for expenses "wholly and exclusively" for the benefit of the company.

In Switzerland, kickbacks are tax deductible if a company bribes a foreign official to land a contract in a country where corruption is considered rife.

Says federal tax official Roland Montangero: "If a company can prove a bribe was necessary to get a contract, naturally it's tax deductible. It's an extra expense." He says Swiss tax authorities don't expect the company to produce a receipt, but "some sort of proof is required."

If, however, a company tried to deduct a bribe taken by a Swiss official, "There would be a real stink," says Mr. Montangero, and tax authorities would inform prosecutors. Tax is paid on the federal and cantonal level in Switzerland. A majority of cantons seem to accept bribes as a tax deduction subject to varying conditions, but the canton of Geneva allows no such deductions.

*Charles Goldsmith*
*The Wall Street Journal Europe*, June 15, 1993.

improbable as prosecution may be. Furthermore, any detection of any corruption will increasingly lead to a termination of financing from multilateral institutions leading to disastrous consequences for the investor. Therefore, the best course of action for the U.S. entrepreneur abroad is vigilance against foreign corruption. First, direct payments to government officials, other than those associated with the most ministerial tasks of clearing customs, should be completely avoided. They should be avoided even if the foreign official is wrongfully extorting money by threatening to terminate existing business with the U.S. firm. These considerations suggest that the businessperson may wish to avoid nations in which such extortion is known to be likely to occur. Such situations put the U.S. firm between a rock and a hard place: If they accept the extortion demand, they risk U.S. criminal conviction; if they refuse the demand, they face a substantial business loss in the country of the corrupt official.

Second, foreign agents should be carefully selected and even more carefully paid. Preferably, the U.S. businessperson should build an ample file of the references upon which the foreign agent was retained and of investigations into the person's character. Commissions and other payments should conform to customary rates in that nation. "Premium" transactions should be avoided in nations with suspect reputations. An appropriate inquiry should be made with respect to the government officials whose discretion is involved in any given transaction.

> **http://adage.com/international/index.html**
> See this address for news and information on international advertising and marketing.

## Chapter Summary

If a U.S. enterprise chooses to expand into a foreign nation by hiring an independent agent, it may avoid much of the foreign regulation inherent in establishing a full corporate presence or in cross-border licensing. It will, however, need to take care that the independent agent is indeed recognized as independent. Furthermore, the enterprise will benefit from a familiarity with the statutory framework of rights that protect the agent, irrespective of any agreement between them.

Once armed with a local agent, the U.S. enterprise must be mindful of advertising and promotional efforts abroad and their regulatory requirements that reflect the sensitivities of the local culture. It must be particularly careful that such "promotion" does not include a quaint local custom of official bribery.

### QUESTIONS AND CASE PROBLEMS

1. Suppose that Roger Sobodka, a U.S. executive stationed in Paris, wishes to build a support office for his firm's technicians in the suburb of Asnieres. He enters into an agreement with Francois Demblans, a homebuilder, to do the work for $100,000. M. Demblans may, however, seek reimbursement of costs created by unforeseen circumstances. The agreement further specifies that the office building will be completed in nine months and that M. Demblans will modify his work upon Mr. Sobodka's reasonable instructions. Assuming that French agency law is consistent with that discussed in this chapter, is M. Demblans a dependent or an independent agent for Mr. Sobodka?

2. After conducting a market survey, Penton Intergalactic, Ltd., a manufacturer of plows, believed that there is pent-up demand for its product in the expanding agricultural economy of Paraguay. Penton retains Saul Ortiz, a Paraguayan with a substantial business selling agricultural implements. Penton's New York City advertising agency develops the ad campaign and strategy for introduction of the product, including a rather precise time schedule. Señor Ortiz is to follow Penton's instruction as the project develops. Señor Ortiz will use the same employees that he uses in his business operations, except that a few Penton employees will be on site to assist him. He will be paid a commission on each plow sold, plus reimbursement of marketing expenses identifiable as related to the Penton program. Assuming that Paraguayan agency law is consistent with that discussed in this chapter, is Señor Ortiz a dependent or an independent agent?

3. Jordan Motors, Inc., opens a dealership in Frankfurt, West Germany, selling American cars. In its advertising campaign, Jordan claims that for the next two weeks only, it will beat the price on any comparable German car by 1,000 Deutsche marks. Faced with this threat to its market share, Hartman Autos, A. G., slashes its prices to cost. Andrea Giebbels comes to Jordan's showroom with a written quote of Hartman's price for its bottom-of-the-line German car and demands that Jordan sell her twenty of its bottom-of-the-line cars for a substantial loss. Jordan

refuses. If Giebbels brings action, will she be able to enforce Jordan's offer? If Hartman sues, can it have Jordan's advertising campaign enjoined?

4. Borges Meat Marketing, Inc., a Nebraska corporation, wishes to establish a network of gourmet butcher shops in India. It has a well-developed introductory advertising campaign that it has employed in establishing similar butcher shops in the United States and does not wish to go to the expense of developing a new one. What should it do?

5. Joseph Supersonic Company, a U.S. jet fighter manufacturer, is eager to sell its aircraft to the state-owned airline of the Republic of Platano and wishes to retain a local representative to assist it. Maria de la Concepcion Casañas y Diaz is reputed to have the best government contracts in Platano; her clients have been successful in garnering contracts a high percentage of the time. Accordingly, she is more in demand than other local representatives, and her fee is the highest in the country. What are the implications of hiring Casañas y Diaz?

6. Assume the facts in Question 5 and assume further that a reference check has uncovered rumors that Casañas y Diaz has had intimate relations with Platano's assistant secretary for government procurement, although there are no plans for more permanent relationship. What are the FCPA implications now?

7. Assume that Casañas was retained, but Joseph failed to obtain the contract. To Joseph's chagrin, however, it subsequently learns that Casañas y Diaz used part of her fee to make a $10,000 payment to a government official. If Joseph has total assets of $5 billion, should the episode be reported on its financial statement?

## MANAGERIAL IMPLICATIONS

Your firm, Flyboy, Inc., is a successful U.S. manufacturer of aircraft. Flyboy would like to expand its market to Pamonia, a small, oil-rich kingdom that was once an Italian colony. The principal purchaser of aircraft in Pamonia is the government, although some private families have the resources to purchase the product. The same private families are, not coincidentally, also the nobility of the Pamonian kingdom. For a new entrant like Flyboy, breaking into the market without a local representative is not possible. You are also aware that local custom includes "grease payments" and lavish gifts to customers in Pamonia.

1. Prepare a paper considering the pluses and minuses of entering the Pamonian market, focusing on the legal risks posed by the proposed investment and how Flyboy might avoid them.

2. Describe the arrangements into which you would enter with your Pamonian agent.

3. Evaluate the possibility of using an Italian firm as your distributor in the country. What would be the FCPA implications if Flyboy simply delivered the aircraft FOB Pamonia and had no involvement in marketing? What implications would this have for Flyboy's profit margin?

# Chapter Seventeen

# Licensing Agreements and the Protection of Intellectual Property Rights

## Reasons for Intellectual Property Transfer Arrangements

The most rapidly growing method of doing business abroad is to transfer *intellectual property rights* (IPRs)—technological know-how or artistic work—to a foreign business in exchange for a fee or other form of remuneration. Like the simple engagement of a representative discussed in the preceding chapter, IPR transfers need not involve any capital investment. They usually involve, however, manufacturing or merchandising one's product or service in the foreign country. By engaging a foreign party to do this manufacturing or merchandising, the U.S. investor avoids the substantial risks and legal entanglements of capital investments abroad, discussed at length in chapters to follow.

An owner of IPRs would be inclined to transfer the technology for a broad variety of reasons. The U.S. firm might, for a fee sometimes called a *royalty,* grant a license to a foreign company that would permit it to use the U.S. firm's trademarks, copyrights, or know-how in making products for sale in the vicinity of the foreign company's country. Alternatively, the U.S. company might provide the IPR and components to a foreign manufacturing plant that will fabricate the product for re-export back to the U.S. concern. In many cases, the foreign product is itself a component of the U.S. company's product. Upon receipt, the U.S. company will integrate it into the ultimate product in the United States. In addition, a U.S. firm can use a transfer of technology as its contribution to a joint venture abroad in exchange for a share of the joint venture. The joint venture would use the technology to manufacture and, perhaps, market the product or component.

A U.S. company typically enters into one of these arrangements because it provides market or other opportunities that the firm otherwise could not exploit efficiently by itself. The firm may already be producing at the full extent of its domestic manufacturing capacity and may not have the resources to expand significantly. Licensing or teaming with a foreign company with adequate capital and perhaps other attractive assets—for instance, a ready marketing network in desired export markets—is a way to expand the company's market without raising substantial additional capital.

Another North American firm may have ample funds and a good product, but an inadequate *research and development* (R&D) capability. Confronting the need to improve its technology quickly before it is nudged out of market share by competing technologies, such a company may wish to team with a foreign company that has a strong R&D staff in order to expand to new geographic markets in the short term, while developing enhanced products for the future.

Yet another company may possess technology that has a broad range of potential applications, but lacks the breadth of management capabilities, developmental resources, and marketing skill to exploit all of these attractive alternatives simultaneously. After such a company reserves for itself the technology applications that seem most consistent with its skills and orientation, the company might license the basic technology to several other firms, each of which is authorized to develop a specified product and/or geographic market.

The appeal of substantially cheaper labor costs in a host country might also tempt a U.S. company to shift its production offshore. The U.S. company may not, however, know its way around the foreign country or may fear the risk of nationalization. In such a situation, the U.S. firm might prefer contracting with a local firm for its production requirements, rather than setting up its own factory abroad.

While there are many positive reasons for an IPR owner to transfer its technology, the principal risk associated with such transfers generally remains the same—the risk of losing control of one's proprietary technology and helping establish a competitor. For example, a small U.S. chemical manufacturer may provide its basic patent to a large French manufacturer through a joint venture in the hope of exploiting the European market and obtaining added R&D capacity. In doing so, however, it may simply be giving the powerful foreign firm an opportunity to research around the patent to develop non-infringing alternatives—or infringing products that cannot be proved to infringe. With such products, the French firm may come to dominate Europe, as well as pose a threat in the U.S. firm's own home market.

> **http://itl.irv.uit.no/trade_law/nav/i_p.html**
> *See this site for links on protection of intellectual property.*

> **http://www.wto.org**
> *See for information and links on topics in this chapter.*

# Intellectual Property Rights: Transfer Agreements

The heart of any IPR transfer is a grant of license that permits the other party to use the relevant rights. The conditions of and compensation for that use form the balance of the agreement.

## Right to Use and Conditions of Use

The licensor often agrees to provide various services to facilitate the anticipated activities, such as assistance in setting up an assembly line or other training and technical support. The licen-

sor generally seeks to restrict the licensee's use of the transferred IPR in a number of ways. Common restrictions include *geographic limitations* on the licensee's manufacturing and/or marketing activities, and *field of use limitations,* which restrict the applications for which the licensee may employ the IPR. For example, the licensor of a laser technology might permit one licensee to use the technology only in connection with medical applications, while retaining for itself the right to use the technology for communications applications, manufacturing applications, or other uses. Similarly, a licensor of a "name brand" doll may limit the licensee's sale of that doll within a specific nation. Other potential restrictions on the licensee might be *output* or *customer restrictions,* especially if the licensor plans to use the licensee as a source of products for the licensor's own distribution requirements.

When the licensor's economic return depends on the licensee's marketing success, the licensor may seek to impose various obligations on the exploitation of the licensed IPR. The licensee will usually be expected to pledge to use its "best efforts" to develop a market for the products manufactured with the IPR. Many licensors go farther, demanding that the licensee comply with specific marketing quotas under pain of losing its license.

## Competitive Circumstances

When exploitation of the licensed IPR will require significant financial or other resources by the licensee, it will often demand *exclusive rights* in the IPR within some geographic area in order to enhance its chances of earning an adequate return on its investment. The licensor, on the other hand, may not want to "put all of its eggs in one basket" in a potentially large market. A licensee could fail for many reasons, such as lack of commitment, inability to secure financing on the necessary schedule, or marketing inadequacies. Meanwhile, competing technologies may come into the market, the licensor's patents may expire, or other events may intrude to reduce the long-term prospects for the venture. Licensors who have reasons to be concerned about such risks sometimes grant rights to two or more licensees who are willing to compete to develop the target market. Licensees faced with this situation will probably attempt to negotiate some offsetting advantage, such as a reduced royalty obligation.

Setting the royalty level for a particular IPR can be a difficult proposition, especially when the degree of market demand for the IPR may not yet be clear. Setting the royalty level too high may boost the total price for the end products to a level that is not competitive with substitute products available in the market. Demand may be high in Dijon for a hamburger sold in McDonalds' trademarked materials and quality control practices, justifying a higher price; but at some point, consumers will be happier with a Brand X hamburger produced by someone who does not pay royalties. At that point, sales—and royalties— will decline, hurting licensor and licensee alike. The trick is to identify a royalty level that allows both licensor and licensee to optimize the return on their respective investments in developing and employing the licensed IPR.

## Confidentiality and Improvements

When the IPR being licensed is technology that is protected primarily by trade secret procedures rather than patent law, another key license provision will be the clause setting forth the licensee's obligation to keep the licensed technology confidential so that third parties cannot exploit the technology or compromise its protected status. The licensee often will try to limit the length of the period during which it must maintain confidentiality, while the licensor's interest is to preserve confidentiality as long as the anticipated useful life of the trade secret. The parties may also bargain over the specific means by which the licensee will be expected to safeguard the confidential technology. For instance, the licensor may demand that the licensee's employees enter into confidentiality and non-exploitation agreements that the licensor could enforce in the event of a breach or threatened breach. The licensor might also demand that only employees who "need to know" the technology be informed of it.

The parties will also usually negotiate over ownership and use rights in the event that the licensee develops improvements in the licensed technology or creates new inventions based on that technol-ogy. Reasoning that the licensee would not have had the opportunity to develop these useful technologies without the know-how supplied by the licensor, the licensor may seek a *grant back* to itself of ownership in or, at a minimum, the right to use—often without compensation—such new technology. In addition, the parties often bargain over whether the licensor shall be obligated to disclose to the licensee, and allow the use of, improvements made by the licensor.

Licensors and licensees also haggle about termination issues. These principally include the period of time during which the licensee may exploit the licensed IPR, what events may cause the license to be terminated short of the normal license period, and the rights of the licensee in the IPR, if any, after the agreement has expired or terminated. Thus, in the contract permitting use of the IPR, the licensor will try to be sure that the licensee agrees not to use the IPR in competition with the licensor or to disclose it to a potential competitor. The licensee, on the other hand, will try to keep royalties low and minimize or abbreviate the noncompetition/nondisclosure provisions.

Enforcing confidentiality provisions or commitments to obtain appropriate IPC protection abroad can be difficult. Courts in different nations will enforce them to varying degrees and, even when the provisions are enforceable, will apply widely different sanctions for misuse.

Many of the conflicts discussed here are often at issue during negotiations of IPR transfer agreements, whether domestic or international. One principal difference in the international scenario is that in many instances the host government creates circumstances that favor the local licensee.

## Policies Underlying International IPR Transfer Law

Host countries can promote or undermine potential transfers of IPR through a variety of direct and indirect means. Without laws protecting patents, copyrights, trade secrets, and trademarks, foreign owners of IPR will be most unwilling to share their valuable intangible assets with citizens in the host country because of the possibility that the IPR will be stolen.

# International Protection for Patents, Trademarks, and Other Intellectual Property

For approximately the last century, nations have been struggling to establish a consistent international legal system of intellectual property. As the computer revolution dramatically increased the value of that property, nations finally began to develop a coherent system in the mid-1990s. Despite the existence of a number of international treaties and conventions on the protection of intellectual property, most real protection is still found in national laws and practices. When the U.S. entrepreneur wishes to protect its IPR in a number of countries, it must file and pursue a separate application in each of the countries.

The seminal patent protection treaty is the *International Convention for the Protection of Industrial Property,* better known as the *Paris Convention.* The Paris Convention guarantees that foreign trademark and patent applications from signatory countries receive the same treatment and priority as domestic applicants: "Nationals of each of the [signatory] countries . . . shall, as regards the protection of industrial property, enjoy in all the other countries . . . the advantages that their respective laws now grant, or may hereafter grant, to nationals. . . . " In other words, no signatory country can give intellectual property protection to its own citizens unless it provides the same protection to the citizens of the other signatories. The Paris Convention also gives a trademark holder in any signatory country a 12-month period of priority within which to make similar applications in other signatory countries.

*The Patent Cooperation Treaty* (PCT) supplemented the Paris Convention by streamlining the patent application process. The PCT gives a patent applicant in a signatory country a *priority claim* once it files an international application in the format designated in the PCT. The applicant then has at least eight months to prosecute the application in the countries in which it wishes to obtain protection.

There were two main problems with the Paris Convention scheme. First, the Convention did not require any minimum substantive standard of patent protection within any signatory country. Thus, if a nation has no pharmaceutical research and development capability, it can decide that it is "immoral" to permit pharmaceutical patents and deny patent protection to pharmaceuticals. Such a law would be in compliance with the Paris Convention, as long as it applied to the nation's citizens as well as foreigners. Under such a scheme, Brazilian entrepreneurs were able to sell copies of U.S. drugs for years without paying the drug owners any royalties at all or violating any international law.

Another significant drawback of the Convention is the lack of an enforcement mechanism. Disputes under the treaty are to be resolved by the International Court of Justice, but most signatory countries either do not recognize that Court's jurisdiction or ignore rulings with which it does not agree. There was no real procedure for enforcing verdicts other than voluntary compliance.

Another prominent international intellectual property treaty is the *Berne Convention for the Protection of Literary and Artistic Works,* better known as the *Berne Convention.* The Berne Convention, which deals with the granting of copyrights among member nations, is also based on a *national treatment* scheme: Each signatory nation must afford foreigners the same treatment as its own citizens. Unlike the Paris Convention, the Berne Convention requires all signatory nations to enact certain minimum substantive laws. These *minima* include prohibitions against copying literary and artistic works and granting authors exclusive rights to adaptations and broadcasts of works. In contrast to the fragmented patent and trademark system, all an author needs to do is affix the symbol © and the year of authorship to provide copyright protection throughout the world. The coming of the computer revolution and the Internet rocked the staid world of international copyright law. First, there was a significant dispute as to whether computer programs were copyrightable subject matter. This was resolved in late December 1996, when the World Intellectual Property Organization (WIPO) approved the Draft Treaty on Certain Questions Concerning the Protection of Literary and Artistic Works, providing that: "Computer programs are protected as literary works within the meaning of Article 2 of the Berne Convention. Such protection applies to the expression of a computer program in any form."

This treaty, also known as the *WIPO Copyright Treaty* or the *Protocol* to the Berne Convention, expands the scope of broadcasts that an author must permit to include "any communication to the public of their works, by wire or wireless means, including the making available to the public of their works in such a way that members of the public may access these works from a place and a time individually chosen by them." Naturally, this is carefully crafted to include access through the Internet. Together with the *Performances and Phonograms Treaty,* passed at the same time, the Protocol sought to tighten international law by requiring signatory nations to provide: adequate legal protection against the circumvention of technological security measures; effective remedies against the knowing removal of electronic rights-management information and the related acts of distribution; measures necessary to permit effective action against any act of infringement of rights covered by the Treaties.

The United States wanted to go even further, seeking to cover even temporary reproduction of copyrighted material unless the nation enacted certain minimum standards of protection. Because the Internet works by sending packets of data into a computer's temporary memory, this would have created significant issues as to Internet "browsing." The dispute was temporarily resolved through an Agreed Interpretation of a Treaty provision, but it is unclear whether or how that interpretation will be implemented.

All these provisions had dubious significance in the context of the Berne Convention. Like the Paris Convention, it has been very difficult to enforce the Berne Convention effectively.

The only place with a single multinational patent application is the European Union. Since 1978, one has been able to obtain protection in all countries of the Union by filing a single application under the *Community Patent Convention.* This system was enhanced in December 1989 when the member states signed the *Agreement Relating to Community Patents,* which creates a unitary system for the application and grant of European patents and a uniform system for the resolution of litigation concerning patent infringement. Under this system, all persons seeking a European patent fill the same PCT application form. European patents would be granted or revoked by a *Revocation Division* and a *Patent Administration Division* of the *European Patent Office,* and infringement actions would be brought in *Community Patent Courts of First Instance* and *Second Instance,* with all appeals to a single *Common Patent Appeal Court* for the entire Union.

The European Union has also pioneered a single multinational trademark registration system. Since 1996, the Community Trademark Regulation, administered by the Office for Harmonization in the Internal Market (OHIM), has allowed a single trademark registration which is enforceable in all members of the Union. The Trademark Regulation also provides a unified enforcement authority; infringement in any member state can be prosecuted within OHIM. Perhaps the principal obstacle to the international unification of patent and trademark laws has been that the U.S. system has traditionally based priority on which entrepreneur was the *first to invent* priority, while most other countries—including the foregoing international treaty arrangements—give priority to the *first to file* the application, irrespective of who invented the item first.

Advocates of the first-to-file system point to its ease of application; it allows little room for litigation as to which person filed first, while determining who invented an innovation first can be the source of interminable dispute. Apologists for the first-to-invent system, on the other hand, note the great potential for abuse in the first-to-file system. In many first-to-file nations, companies with little capacity for exploiting a trademark will race to obtain rights to a trademark being exploited by its inventor elsewhere. When the inventor tries to exploit its trademark in the filer's nation, the first filer can prevent it from doing so. Even in most first-to-file nations, courts will provide relief to one who can prove that the first filer never used the mark and that it has used the mark elsewhere. While the litigation proceeds, however, the foreign owner cannot use its mark, losing potential sales. The only way to avoid that loss of money quickly is to pay the first filer a blackmail payment. Similarly, people in first-to-file nations sometimes illegally copy U.S. technology such as computer software and then file patents to win full rights to the copied invention in the first-to-file country.

The United States, whose entrepreneurs have been most frequently victimized by IPR infringement, spearheaded an effort to create a viable international intellectual property protection system during the Uruguay Round of General Agreement on Tariffs and Trade. These efforts bore fruit in the GATT *Agreement on Trade-Related Aspects of Intellectual Property Rights* (TRIPS), which strives to create the first truly effective international system for protection of IPRs. TRIPS requires every member of the World Trade Organization (WTO) to abide by the Paris and Berne Conventions—including the recent protocols to those treaties—applying those treaties' national treatment requirements so that all foreign IPR owners receive the same protection as local nationals. It establishes fifty year copyright protection pursuant to the Berne Convention. All WTO members must recognize patent holders' right to assign or license their patents and the term of patent protection must be at least 20 years. Further, patent protection is now to be available for "any new inventions, whether products or processes, in all fields of technology, provided that they are new, involve an inventive step (*nonobvious*) and are capable of industrial application (*useful*)."

TRIPS also seeks to remedy some of the acknowledged problems of the Paris and Berne Conventions. First, unlike the Paris Convention, TRIPS sets minimum standards of intellectual property protection. A nation can no longer comply with international intellectual property law by having its law provide no protection. Second, TRIPS tries to solve the enforcement problem that has plagued prior regimes. It requires signatory countries to "ensure that enforcement procedures as specified in this Part are available under their laws so as to permit effective action against any act of infringement of intellectual property rights covered by this Agreement, including expeditious remedies to prevent infringements and remedies which constitute a deterrent to further infringements." Furthermore, if one nation believes that another is out of compliance, it can initiate a dispute proceeding before a WTO panel.

TRIPS has significant drawbacks. The United States was compelled to accept an "escape clause" to the minimum substantive standards. Signatory nations may:

exclude from patentability inventions, the prevention within their territory of the commercial exploitation of which is necessary to protect *ordre public* or morality, including to protect human, animal or plant life or health or to avoid serious prejudice to the environment, provided that such exclusion is not made merely because the exploitation is prohibited by domestic law.

Arguably, therefore, Brazil may again decide that pharmaceutical patents are immoral and not face international repercussions. The issue is likely to be litigated in the WTO's dispute process.

Another drawback is the length of the transition period allowed to certain nations. While most Western nations were subject to the treaty as of January 1996, TRIPS gives certain developing nations a transition period until 2000 during which they are to bring their laws and enforcement into specified norms. Another group of "less developed" nations have until 2006, with a possibility for further extensions. Until all countries are brought under the same IPR scheme, violations of that scheme are not remediable in GATT forums.

Notwithstanding the hope created by TRIPS, the owners of IPRs must rely on national systems for protection from violations of those rights. After all, only nation-states may bring claims under TRIPS and then only to point to deficiencies in national systems, not to supplant them. National laws can vary significantly from one another. The following case underscores just how narrowly national the focus is and how difficult proving infringement can be.

The worldwide liquor name wars shown in this case have resulted in an armistice of sorts between the United States and the European Union. In a bilateral agreement concluded in 1994, the United States agreed to prevent its companies from labeling U.S.-made liquor as *Scotch whisky, Irish whiskey, cognac, Armagnac, Calvados,* or *brandy de Jerez.* In exchange, Europeans may not label European-made products as *bourbon* or *Tennessee whiskey.*

As the *Champagne* case makes clear, intellectual property protection is an intensely national phenomenon: The level of protection that an investor receives in any given nation will depend largely on the attitudes, history, and/or law in that nation. Accordingly, investors need a sense

## Comite Inter-Professionel du Vin de Champagne v. Wineworths Group, Ltd.
*(1991) 2 N.Z.L.R. 432*
*High Court of Wellington*

## BACKGROUND AND FACTS

An Australian company sought to sell in New Zealand sparkling wine made in Australia from grapes grown in Australia but bottled with the word "champagne" on the label. The *Comité Interprofessionel du Vin de Champagne* (the CIVC), a group of champagne producers from the French department of Champagne, sought an injunction to prevent the Australians from "passing off" as wine produced in the region of Champagne wine not so produced.

## JUDGE JEFFRIES

These proceedings are brought by the plaintiffs to protect their claimed property right in the word "Champagne." As an editorial policy in this judgment I am using the word champagne with a capital when it refers to the district and the wine from the district. The plaintiffs seek in effect to prevent the defendant from importing into New Zealand sparkling wine from Australia labelled champagne. . . . The plaintiffs say according to the law of New Zealand they cannot do that for it constitutes deceptive conduct because the wine labelled champagne was made in Australia from grapes grown there.

Champagne as we know it is relatively new, having its origin in time at the end of the seventeenth century but its final development was a nineteenth century phenomenon. Dom Perignon of the Benedictine Abbey of Hautvillers near Epernay in the Champagne district is credited with its beginning. There are four generally acknowledged ingredients of Champagne being its wine type, the grapes used, most importantly the location of a sparkling wine, usually but not always, white in colour. The two features of Champagne of prime importance for its uniqueness are the soil and climate in which the grapes are grown, and the method of manufacture by skilled personnel. . . . For the production of grapes for Champagne there are strict geographical limitations imposed by law. On 22 July 1927 a law strictly delimited the boundaries of the vine growing Champagne area. Within those boundaries, and in each village, the soil suitable for planting vines has been meticulously indexed. By law the wine allowed to carry the appellation Champagne must be produced exclusively within precise zones. . . .

Champagne is a wine that must be made and elaborated into the final style with care and attention to detail. The essence of the methode champenoise is that the process of second fermentation takes place in the bottle in which it is sold. That requires an operation for shifting the yeast by gradual manipulation down the neck of the inverted bottle for its removal and then final corking. . . .

This proceeding is about New Zealand law and the understanding of its people so it is appropriate to say something of the wine industry and wine drinking by New Zealanders. Viticulture commenced with the first settlers 150 years ago and never abated, but New Zealanders did not early develop a widespread interest in and use of wines either locally made or imported. This was in contrast to Australia where indigenous wine manufacture and drinking became a more integral part of the lifestyle of that country and that partly accounts for the differences with New Zealand to be detailed later. New Zealanders' attitude toward wine underwent a marked change commencing from about thirty years ago. . . . The population became markedly more knowledgeable on wines and the demand for information was met principally by newspaper columns and books on wine.

Champagne has been exported to New Zealand from about the middle of the last century in small quantities until 1979, and increasingly in the 1980s. It is certain there were quite small volume exports of Australian champagne from 1977 onwards. . . . New Zealand has, apart from the foregoing, no history of material consumption, or manufacture, of sparkling wine prior to 1980. . . . In about 1981 Montana Wines, Ltd., which is New Zealand's largest maker, launched a sparkling wine produced by methode champenoise and labelled it "Lindauer New Zealand Champagne." Proceedings were issued in 1982 against Montana and after four years were settled by a consent order of the Court issuing an injunction generally restraining the use of the word champagne on that defendant's products. Over about the last four years all New Zealand makers have observed that order and all leading wine importers have declined to import Australian sparkling wine labelled champagne. Absenting the events now to be described New Zealand, judged by the attitude of

*(continued)*

*(continued)*

markers and importers, conceded to the plaintiffs their legal proprietary right in the appellation champagne.

Indigenous wine making and consumption were much more a part of Australian life than they were in New Zealand until about thirty years ago. Australia has a record of well over a century of making acceptable wines of great variety and styles which have been consumed by its people. Sparkling wine calling itself champagne made from grapes grown in Australia by the methode champenoise, and by other methods, has been entirely accepted and without direct challenge from the CIVC. The plaintiffs recognize, and although reluctantly accept, for Australia, like Canada and the United States of America, there is no legal protection available to them over the use of the appellation champagne.

The sparkling wine market in New Zealand changed dramatically with the introduction here from Australia in 1986 of Yalumba Angas Brut Champagne. The wine was of good quality and reasonably priced. It was a stunning success and other wine importers began a serious search in Australia for competitors.

In August 1987 [Australia's wine maker, Penfolds Wine Pty., Ltd.] reached agreement with the defendant Wineworths Group, Ltd., to export into New Zealand a sparkling wine made by its wholly owned subsidiary Seaview Winery Pty., Ltd., bearing the label "Australian Champagne." Before this arrangement Penfolds through another agent in 1986 had sold a Seaview wine labelled "Brut Champagne."

It is appropriate here to emphasize the plaintiffs' view of what makes the product and therefore the name of Champagne so special. The product is a quality one and by virtue of the cost of manufacture it is necessarily expensive, which is part of its exclusivity. From the quality product the reputation has developed, which reflects the specialness of the wine itself arising from factors outlined above. Whilst it has developed a reputation as a quality sparkling wine the consumption of it has also become widely associated with certain types of human activity which are mobilized around celebration and joy. Champagne is appropriate as a wine with which to celebrate (a characteristic is that it palpably agitates in the glass) and that is reinforced by exotic origin (for all but the French) and its cost. The plaintiffs say the excellent wine, whose quality is secured by the law of France, is rolled up with its deserved reputation and the name is a valuable right to them as owners. . . .

Through the early '80s Penfolds quite vigorously expanded its market for champagne by taking the celebratory theme for which it is renowned and expanding that so as to encourage greater volume drinking. . . .

The particular attraction of Seaview was that its champagne was made by methode champenoise. The leading high-volume champagne for Penfolds is Minchinbury which is made by the transfer method recognized as inferior to methode champenoise. Also market research revealed the general public was manifesting a preference for methode champenoise over transfer.

The Court thinks a deliberate choice was made by Penfolds to test the New Zealand law with a middle- to upper-bracket sparkling wine made by methode champenoise rather than a wine made by the transfer method, and specifically labelled it "Australian Champagne." That action labelling by Penfolds set up these proceedings.

It is appropriate here to deal with a phenomenon which is occurring in Australia . . . whereby [s]parkling wines at the lower end of the price range not made from the classic Champagne grape varieties and using the transfer method are continued to be called champagne but those at the upper end of the price range made by methode champenoise are tending not to be called champagne, but given a brand name with the label showing it was produced by methode champenoise. That trend clearly suggests that the word champagne has been so devalued in the market in Australia that the public now needs a word, or words, that will convey the excitement and quality surrounding the word champagne say in New Zealand or the United Kingdom.

What the defendant [says] is that the word *champagne* has in New Zealand lost its distinctive significance so as to be properly defined now as a generic term having generic use within the wine market. It is in the same category as many other words whose origins are almost identical such as sherry, port, burgundy, graves, and chablis.

No case was cited to the Court how it should go about making a decision on a fact of that nature. To decide whether a word has become (for there is no doubt it once was not) a generic word is not a how, when, where fact. The task of the Court is to decide how the adult population of New Zealand as a group perceives the word. One has only to frame the task in that way to demonstrate its immense difficulty.

*(continued)*

*(continued)*

The Court holds [market research] studies supported the contention that there is significant evidence that champagne is not a generic word by usage in New Zealand. . . . From the evidence of the wine experts emerged two other observations worth making. If Australian wine interests were able to export sparkling wines to New Zealand it would have overall a deleterious effect by setting back the desirable goal of attainment of the maximum accuracy and fair labelling on wine bottles. . . . The countries who are members of the Common Market strictly adhere to France's proprietary right in the world Champagne. . . . There was a conscious attempt to supply [restaurant wine] lists encompassing a wide range of restaurants from the select and expensive ones downwards. . . . the great majority make the distinction between sparkling wines and Champagne. Notwithstanding some interesting and persuasive evidence to the contrary, the Court's decision is that the word champagne in New Zealand is not generically used to describe any white sparkling wine.

The word *champagne* does in my view, have a special impact or impression on ordinary, average New Zealanders for whom wine drinking generally plays no significant part in their lives. This non-expert, phlegmatic, even uninterested representative New Zealander does have a definite response to the word *champagne* over and above noting it to be a white sparkling wine, or one with bubbles in it. That response if pushed to articula-

tion might be, a wine for celebration, expensive, of French origin, special method of manufacture, name of district in France, consumed by a certain social class, a wine ships are launched with or crowds are sprayed with after a major sporting event is won. . . .

The question for the Court is whether importation into New Zealand as aforesaid by the defendant advertising and selling Seaview Champagne, is deceptive in the way complained of by the plaintiffs. The Court's decision is that it is deceptive. To begin with the finding of the Court is that the word *champagne* is distinctive and that in New Zealand it has not passed into generic territory. Having found it is not generic then to use it in the market previously described is deceptive. The public in purchasing wine labelled champagne will think that it is being supplied wine having all the attributes of Champagne, even if they understand it is manufactured in Australia from Australian grapes. By using the word *champagne* on the label the defendant is deceptively encroaching on the reputation and goodwill of the plaintiffs.

In short the Court says the word *champagne* is distinctive in New Zealand for the French product and it would be deceptive for other traders, foreign or domestic, to seek to attach themselves to that reputation by using the word *champagne* to describe sparkling wine made out of Champagne, France.

**Decision.**   Judgment for plaintiffs.

---

of the host nation's relevant attitudes and history before investing there.

In addition to their laws on the fundamental underpinnings of technology transfer, host countries may insert themselves into particular proposed transfers by a number of techniques. These techniques often vary, depending on the stage of internal development the country has reached.

> **http://itl.irv.uit.no/trade_law/documents/**
> **freetrade/wta-94/art/iia1c.html**
> *See for the TRIPS agreement.*

> **http://lcweb.loc.gov/copyright/forms**
> *See for GATT intellectual property copyright applications.*

## Government Policies in Emerging Nations

Industries in emerging nations are typically in great need of technological know-how. The significant research and development that leads to technological innovation is generally the product of substantial capital investment, long lead times, and a strong educational infrastructure. Less developed countries have a great shortage of these commodities. To industrialize, such nations—whether modern Brazil or post-war Japan—must rely on important technology.

Nevertheless, emerging countries have historically not tolerated unrestricted technology transfer. First, poorer nations typically husband hard currency reserves with great care. They permit the outflow of hard-currency royalties only for particularly attractive technologies. Such nations are understandably reluctant to squander foreign exchange so that their citizens may have a higher-quality soft drink. And such nations often severely restrict or prohibit trademark royalties that are not accompanied by a right to use concomitant technology. Indeed, the central banks of these countries will sometimes unilaterally restrict remittances of hard currency royalty payments. Peru, for instance, froze all such hard-currency royalty remittances without warning during the late 1980s and early 1990s. Whenever possible, the intellectual property owner should make firm arrangements with the relevant government authorities in advance about royalty arrangements.

One way for the foreign owner to avoid this repugnance to hard currency royalties is to raise the price of production equipment, input materials, or other goods that the licensee is contractually obligated to purchase from the owner to produce the end product. In more comprehensive arrangements, the licensee can accept a lower commission for distributing the end product in the host country, or perform assembly or other manufacturing functions for other goods at a reduced rate. In these ways, the owner obtains the same financial yield without having any part of the money placed in the royalty category. When these solutions do not lead to the same return, the owner can consider deferring royalties during the initial years of the agreement until the licensee can earn substantial hard currency through exports and use those earnings to pay the owner.

Second, the host country may be concerned about the anti-competitive effects of a licensing agreement. If the foreign entity is not forced to license the technology to local competitors, it might enjoy a local monopoly on the product. If so, one would expect that its pricing policies would reflect its monopolisitc market position to the detriment of the local economy. Largely based on the strength of this anti-competitive rationale, the *Andean Common Market* issued its Decision 220, which, *inter alia,* forbade provisions in technology transfer agreements that (1) attempted to fix the price of goods manufactured with the licensed technology, (2) prohibited the licensee from using competing technologies, (3) required the use of goods sold

by the technology owner, which in turn blocked one of the methods for avoiding restrictions on royalties, or (4) limited the volume of end products manufactured with the technology.

Third, the local government might simply wish to obtain the long-term benefits of the technology for its own nationals by wresting control of it from foreign hands. This objective is often justified with the argument that royalties are redundant, because the cost of technology should be included in the cost of the products sold. In the context of trademarks, this argument has been extended to say that, because trademarks do not produce value in and of themselves, trademark royalties are inherently exploitative. These arguments, of course, disregard the benefits of encouraging technological innovation or of creating a reputation for quality in a trademark.

If local entrepreneurs are given an opportunity to employ foreign technology, in time they might become dominant not only in the local economy but might even give the original licensor some competition throughout the world. The Japanese success in the period after World War II is largely attributable to an ability to cause the transfer of technology. The Japanese philosophy was essentially that a transfer-of-technology contract is a "sale" rather than a temporary lease of the technology. At the end of the term of the license, the licensee should be free to use the technology.

This former Japanese philosophy has been faithfully followed by Brazil's technology transfer watchdog, the National Institute of Industrial Policy (INPI). Regardless of what a technology agreement stated, INPI regarded a technology transfer agreement as a sale of the technology rather than a license. In other words, at the end of the term the licensee could, in INPI's eyes, freely use the technology to make end products for the local Brazilian market or for *export into the technology owner's home market.*

Unfortunately for Brazil, technology owners had also learned a lot from the Japanese appropriation of technology in the postwar era. Accordingly, the Brazilian policy did little more than catch a few uninitiated owners unaware. Most technology owners did not repeat the error of their postwar counterparts and merely steered clear of Brazil, inhibiting that nation's industrial development. In time, INPI changed its approach.

Many nations use these philosophical foundations to restrict license terms and cap royalty payments, all to the benefit of local licensees. In India, for example, licenses once could not last longer than eight years—and in many types of technologies, less than that. In Colombia, all agreements have to be approved by the Royalties Committee, which permits agreements to last only three to five years. In both nations, royalties were limited to an inflexible percentage cap. Another outgrowth of this philosophy is that local subsidiaries are often forbidden to send royalty payments home. This policy assures that the foreign technology owner must part with its technology to a locally controlled entity in order to pull any royalties out of the nation.

Over time, these practices have damaged local developing economies more than the potential licensors, who now simply avoid such economies as too dangerous for licensing. Many emerging nations have come to this realization and turned their backs on these restrictive systems.

A prominent case in point has been the resistance of many emerging nations to IPR protection for biological life forms that are increasingly important in biotechnology. This resistance has been justified in philosophical terms: Anything occurring in nature should not be patented or that the "Northern" companies are trying to steal "Southern" plants and crop varieties. If one reviews the dispute more carefully, however, one can readily see that less metaphysical motivations are at work. The equatorial countries that provide the raw material for many of these life forms receive almost none of the economic benefit of biotechnological developments of companies in developed nations. Instead, these countries purchase the new crop hybrids or pharmaceuticals developed by the "Northern" companies. In short, the emerging countries want a cut of the action.

Eventually, however, most emerging nations—by economic compulsion—appear to have slowly come around to the view that life is patentable. The "Northern" inventors simply did not make their discoveries available in nations that were inhospitable to their IPR. Those nations that lacked the advantages of the newly devised hybrids realized that they were less productive; eventually, they began to change their position. Chile passed a law permitting the patenting of microorganisms and genes. Mexico now allows companies to patent life forms up to the level of a plant. The process continues.

---

*Foreign Accents*

# IPR and Biological Life Forms: An Indian View
## Biodiversity and Germ Plasm Issues

The Convention on Biological Diversity (CBD) which was negotiated under the auspices of the U.N. Environment Programme was adopted in May 1992 at the Earth Summit in Rio-de-Janeiro. As of July 1, 1996, 152 countries had become parties to the convention and the current membership is placed at 170, practically all the members of the United Nations. The U.S. which initially did not ratify the treaty under the Bush administration, presumably on the grounds that the terms will seriously affect its own biotech industry, finally endorsed the document. . . . The administration further emphasised the need to resist any action taken by any party to the CBD that led to inadequate levels of protection of intellectual property rights. As of now, the U.S. is fully behind the concept of providing just rewards to countries which possess unique genetic resources. . . .

[T]he resources of developing countries such as India in the area of natural products, represented by their rich biodiversity, have hardly been exploited to gain economic strengths. The potential to produce valuable chemical compounds, genes or germ plasms by industries in such sectors as pharmaceuticals and biotechnology, agrochemicals, food prod-

*(continued)*

*(continued)*

ucts, industrial enzymes, phytomedicines and the like has not been recognised.

The developing countries, with their rich pool of genetic resources should, therefore, achieve their comparative advantage through the exploitation and use of their unique natural resources. . . .

Very few countries have laws on access to natural products and therefore, pending such legislation, a voluntary code needs to be established to encourage equitable sharing of benefits arising from R & D on natural products. Some of the terms of such a code are:

Wherever possible, efforts should be made to give value added natural products rather than the crude raw materials, so that the additional benefits accruing from value addition reside with the indigenous supplier.

Fair compensation to source countries for natural products or value-added products should include (1) monetary payments or non-monetary compensation such as technology, training or equivalent for source country scientists and owners of natural resources; (2) royalties for marketed products derived from the natural products; and (3) earmarking by the source country, a certain percentage of revenues for conservation and development of natural products in the source country. . . .

A bioprospecting model in search of medicinal plants for new life-saving drugs, without destroying natural resources, has been drawn up by the Conservation International, a Surinamese pharmaceutical firm and the National Herbarium of Surinam, which have agreed to participate in a long-term effort to expand drug research. The agreement provides for financial returns to Surinam and its people and fully endorses the rights of the local people to their natural forest resources. . . .

Merck of the U.S., the world's largest pharmaceutical company and Costa Rica's National Biodiversity Institute (IN Bio) have agreed that Merck will evaluate a limited number of plant, fungal and environmental samples from Costa Rica's protected national resources. The samples are collected and processed by IN Bio for which Merck pays $1 million to IN Bio and the processed samples are screened by Merck for a variety of biological activities. Royalties are payable for any product which Merck develops from IN Bio samples and data. It is not clear how Costa Rica shares the revenues collected by IN Bio with land-owners and communities. . . .

Article 15 of CBD recognises the "sovereign rights" of governments over their genetic resources which can be used as tradable commodities with economic value. Based on the models delineated earlier, parties from the source countries and sourcing agencies could negotiate and sign material transfer agreements prior to granting permission to use genetic resources for R & D or for commercial exploitation.

## TRIPS and CBD

In many areas, the provisions under TRIPS, the section dealing with Intellectual Property Rights under GATT and provisions under the convention of biodiversity are not consistent. The patent laws do not permit patenting of natural products under the doctrine of nature principle. Hence, to protect the biodiversity resources uniquely available to sovereign states, fresh legislations are required. Very few countries have so far legislated appropriate statutes to protect biodiversity and therein lies the immediate problem of establishing legal rights to indigenous natural resources. . . .

The new cell line for a new and "improved" (as claimed) variety of Basmati rice was derived from the original germ plasm or cell line of an indigenous variety from the Indian sub-continent. The development of the new variety by Rice-Tec, the patentee, would not have been possible if the original cell line was not available to it. Consequently, on the basis of the case for equitable returns for the use of an indigenous germ plasm, Rice-Tec in all fairness owes to the source country a share of the benefits that has accrued or will accrue from the commercial exploitation of the new variety. Even in the absence of the needed legal statute, India and Pakistan should negotiate with Rice-Tec and arrive at a mutually agreeable formula, consistent with the provisions under CBD. . . .

It is unfair to believe that all natural resources (biodiversity) can be profitably converted into commercial products and that every one of the accessed material will lead to a valuable product, be it a pharmaceutical, agrochemical or any other product. It is, therefore, difficult to assess the real value of such

*(continued)*

*(continued)*

a resource at the time of signing an agreement, particularly since an enormous amount of financial, infrastructural and scientific inputs extending over long periods of time need to be deployed before success is achieved.

The most equitable way, therefore, would be to pay a relatively low up-front compensation followed by a reasonable royalty payment as percentage of commercial revenue for a specified period. That way, the benefit to the source country will be commensurate with the success achieved. . . .

Without prejudice to Indian efforts to get the Rice-Tec patent revoked and sort out trade mark and geographical indication issues, India should take a long-term perspective on the whole matter of exploitation of Indian biodiversity and germ plasm resources by third parties. To deny access to our national resources would be counterproductive and a physical ban on material transfer would not only be impractical, but would also be negating the virtues of new and better R & D for the discovery and development of new products for health care, agriculture and ecological improvements from natural products.

India neither has the capability nor the resources to exploit the full potential of its natural resources and consequently it will be beneficial to enter into formalised collaborative agreements with international companies and agencies on clearly defined terms and conditions. The CBD fully provides for such an alternative, and it will be in the country's interest to expeditiously bring in appropriate legislation to ensure legitimacy for its approaches.

*Dr. M. D. Nair*
*The Hindu*, May 6, 1998.

M. D. Nair, A-11 Sagarika, 3rd Seaward Rd., Valmikinagar, Chennai, 600041, India. Published in *The Hindu*, May 6, 1998.

## Policies Influenced by Marxist Ideology

Marxist theory on the individual's role in creative activity has historically complicated intellectual property policy in communist countries. Marxist philosophy regards intellectual innovation as a product of society that is manifested through individuals. Because the society is the true author of the creation, the individual should have no independent right to the profits from the creation—all such benefits should be owned by the state. Communist intellectual property regulation has greatly restricted the monetary benefits individuals receive from their inventions and has discouraged the recognition of compensable IPRs.

These policies had negative effects on innovation in communist nations. To be blunt, individuals are far more likely to be innovative if they will grow rich as a result of their innovation; fewer individuals are motivated to be innovative for the greater good of the homeland. The disastrous economic consequences of Marxist disincentives have, over time, caused communist governments to develop regulatory schemes that reward individual initiative while bowing to Marxist tradition. For instance, the Chinese have afforded certain inventions eligibility for *certificates of authorship*. While the ownership right in the invention remains in theory in the state, the inventors are entitled to a monetary award by virtue of their certificate of authorship. Over time, the Chinese have grown more comfortable with permitting collective bodies, such as corporations—as distinct from individuals—to obtain trademark and other intellectual property protection.

The vestiges of these Marxist attitudes have retarded the protection of IPR in former communist nations. In Poland, Hungary, and the former Czechoslovakia, piracy boomed. The new IPR laws protected authors, but not performers or producers. In addition, even these limited laws were not enforced. In a place where all property had belonged to the state, the victimless crime of copyright or trademark infringement had not triggered prosecutions during the past 40 years. In fact, the Czech Ministry of Culture blithely granted licenses for the importation of pirated video and audio cassettes. Simply put, the local citizens, who had not been trained to understand the existence of private IPR, could not really understand what the fuss was all about. In due course, private entrepreneurs from the West, together with their governments, applied pressure to change these attitudes.

As on other subjects, different views on the protection of intellectual property are prevalent among the remaining Marxist countries. Nevertheless, the few nations that remain in the Marxist camp are devising methods that, while making obeisance to tradition, protect the benefits to the individual inventors that are so necessary to technological innovation. The U.S. business should review the laws of the communist state in which it is interested in investing prior to making the investment.

## Attitudes in Developed Nations

National chauvinism does not end once a country becomes developed. The tendencies of licensing laws to favor local licensees persist in developed countries. In many high-technology electronic fields, for instance, European nations have been well behind U.S. firms. Not coincidentally, significant disputes have arisen between the *European Telecommunication Standards Institute* (ETSI)—which must certify all electronic products in the European market for safety and compatibility purposes—and U.S. computer hardware manufacturers. Purportedly to assist its technical research efforts, ETSI sought to require all firms seeking to sell equipment in Europe to sign an "undertaking" agreeing to grant licenses to any other merchant for patented technology necessary to implement ETSI standards. U.S. manufacturers immediately complained, noting that this gave them a Hobson's choice of agreeing to forego potential licensing income or being excluded from the European market. The U.S. government soon intervened on behalf of its manufacturers, and the dispute turned into an old-fashioned, nation-against-nation fight. As local licensees become more capable of defending their own interests, however, the cloak of protectionism does not wear as well. More importantly, as local enterprises become more sophisticated, they require greater amounts of IPR. The same local enterprises that once may have relied on government intervention to procure more favorable terms become impatient at the delays and obstacles inherent in their obtaining much-needed technology.

Perhaps the clearest example of this evolution is the transformation of Japan's policy toward technology licensing over the past several decades. Through the 1960s, each and every technology transfer agreement required governmental approval. As discussed previously, the Japanese government ministries used this process to negotiate a better deal for the Japanese licensees than the licensees had been able to do in their own negotiations. The Japanese government could do this because under its system it could simply prevent a technology transfer agreement by taking no action on a request for approval.

As Japan became an economic powerhouse, however, this system increasingly became an impediment to Japanese industrialists. Even today, Japan is a net importer of technology; in light of the vastly increased number of such agreements and the need for greater speed in international transactions, the approval process grew to be a hindrance. Moreover, in light of the great economic strength of Japanese corporations, the pro-Japan function of government approval had become archaic. And by the 1970s, Japan certainly had no difficulty in conserving foreign exchange reserves. To accommodate these new realities, the Japanese system was transformed in the late 1970s to *notification* only. The government had a number of days within which to object to an approval for a technology transfer agreement; if it took no action, the agreement was approved. This trend is also being reflected in other newly developed countries such as South Korea. In cases in which the need for protection of fledgling domestic enterprises has waned and the need for additional technology has waxed, the more restrictive policies relating to technology transfer tend to be eased.

A similar phenomenon may now be seen in some developing countries on the verge of a breakthrough. Mexico, for instance, abruptly shifted in January 1990 from being one of the most restrictive nations on technology transfer agreements to being one of the most open. The principal requirement became merely that technology transfer agreements be registered. The power of government bureaucrats to modify agreements was dramatically curtailed. Limits on royalty payments and on agreement terms were lifted. Moreover, the agreements could now require confidential treatment for the technology after expiration of the contract term, reflecting the technology owner's right to the continued value of its intellectual property. As a result, Mexico experienced an economic boom even while its principal international trading partners labored through a recession.

Capitalism, therefore, seems to be slowly conquering chauvinism. Chauvinism is not completely dead, though; the Japanese government has changed its regulatory focus from the import of technology to the export of technology. Some officials seem concerned that other nations will use the Japanese model of technological development against Japan.

## Non-enforcement of IPR Laws

As has been demonstrated in this chapter, the varying attitudes of nations are generally reflected in their laws. Often, however, attitudes in the IPR context—particularly in the areas of software, recordings, and chemical/pharmaceutical products—are reflected more accurately in the enforcement of those laws.

It is one thing to enact laws and quite another to enforce them. A number of countries—particularly in Asia, Latin America, Africa, and the Middle East—have a panoply of laws designed to protect domestic and foreign IPR, but fail to enforce the laws or do not have adequate procedures to enable foreign parties to take advantage of the laws. After NAFTA, for example, Mexico adopted most internationally accepted standards with respect to IPR. To this day, however, Mexico City streets are littered with pirated music and videos because Mexico has not devoted many of its scarce resources to enforcing those laws.

Still others enforce their laws in a discriminatory fashion so that foreign parties do not have confidence that their rights will be vindicated against clear infringement. Indeed, some nations tacitly encourage piracy of such IPR by their citizens. In South Korea, the government once published details of pharmaceutical and pesticide formulations to facilitate their copying by locals. In China, after a great deal of prodding from developed nations, the Chinese government enacted modern copyright infringement legislation

and even created special IPR tribunals. But in the meantime, China allowed construction of 26 compact disk plants with the capacity to manufacture over 50 million compact disks a year, despite the fact that China has a relatively small number of consumers who can purchase CDs and that virtually no Western companies have licensed the reproduction of their products in China. A particularly flagrant violation occurred in 1994 when a relative of the Chinese premier opened a huge laser disk and compact disk factory with the capacity to manufacture 5.5 million CDs and 1.5 million laser disks a year. Despite open violations of the ostensible IPR protection laws, Chinese authorities refused to permit even an inspection of the facility by Westerners.

This piracy is very big business. The Motion Picture Association of America estimates that the American movie industry alone loses $150 million a year due to piracy. Accordingly, in recent years, the U.S. government and leaders of its domestic "high-tech" and entertainment industries have focused a great deal of attention on the interrelationship between the quality of foreign intellectual property protection and the vitality of U.S. trade in foreign countries and, indeed, the U.S. domestic market. Many international firms from developed nations joined to form the *International Counterfeiting Coalition* to pressure governments into enforcement of IPR laws.

At the urging of these industry groups, the U.S. government has become active in promoting the adoption and effective enforcement of intellectual property laws by its various trading partners. As noted above, the TRIPS agreement requires WTO countries to insure that IPR laws are enforced and to call for seizure of goods infringing upon IPR rights; failure to enforce such laws now gives rise to a WTO trade proceeding. Taiwan, once an internationally notorious haven of piracy, largely eliminated piracy after the United States was on the verge of enacting retaliatory tariffs on Taiwanese products. When the United States threatened to block hundreds of millions of Brazilian products from entering the United States, the government of Brazil agreed to a strict timetable for implementing patent and copyright reforms. U.S. movie industry officials, in partnership with the U.S. government, have used the threat of Super 301 trade proceedings against

Italian products to prod Italian officials into more diligent enforcement of its copyright laws. And the United States was instrumental in preventing China from being admitted into the World Trade Organization as long as it continued to be an IPR outlaw. The following case illustrates that this relentless pressure has resulted in some enforcement, even in the People's Republic of China.

## Walt Disney Company v. Beijing Publishing Press, et al.

*Zhongjing zhichu No. 141 (1994)*
*Beijing First Intermediate Court*

### BACKGROUND AND FACTS

Beijing Publishing Press, Beijing Children's Publishing Press, and the Beijing Distribution Office of New World Bookstore Distribution Center published and distributed a series of books called *Collection of Disney Moral Tales.* The collection included reproductions of Mickey Mouse, Cinderella, Peter Pan, Snow White, and other cartoon characters, although the Chinese had not received authorization from the copyright holder. The Walt Disney Company, which created and holds copyright registrations in the United States for the cartoon characters, brought action in Chinese court against the Chinese entities for infringement of copyright. Specifically, the Disney Company asked that the Court order the defendants to cease immediately their publication, issuance, and sale of the collection, to guarantee in writing that they will not again infringe Disney's copyright interest, to make an open apology in a newspaper published both within and outside China, and to compensate for economic losses alleged by the Disney Company to be more than RMB 1,770,000 yuan.

Beijing Publishing Press and its corporate affiliate, Children's Press, countered that use rights for the cartoon likenesses had been obtained through a Contract for Assignment of Publishing Rights to Disney's Reading Materials for Children in Simplified Chinese Characters Versions (the Contract for Assignment of Simplified Versions) executed with Maxwell Communications Corporation plc. Maxwell had since gone bankrupt and was not joined as a defendant.

Beijing Publishing Press and Children's Press further relied on an agreement with Maxworld (China) Publishing Corp., Ltd., a joint venture between Children's Press and Maxwell, under certification that the foreign party had confirmed publishing rights to the collection. Beijing Publishing Press and Children's Press took the view that, in light of this latter agreement, they had no obligation to contact the foreign party regarding copyright matters. They brought in Maxwell as a third party defendant.

Beijing Distribution Office asserted that it was merely a distributor, not a publisher, and was under no obligation to investigate the legality of copyright of books and periodicals.

### CHIEF JUDGE SU CHI

[P]rocedures for registration of copyright for the Mickey Mouse likeness were completed . . . in the United States, and the copyright belonged to the Disney Company. The Beijing Publishing Press, in each of August 1991, November 1992 and November 1993, printed and published "Bambi," "Dumbo," "101 Dalmatians," "Alice in Wonderland," "Lady and the Tramp," "Sleeping Beauty," "Cinderella," "Snow White," and "Peter Pan" in which the cartoon likeness were exactly the same as those appearing in the original versions provided by the plaintiffs. . . .

The Disney Company and the Maxwell Company signed an agreement on 19 August 1987 which provided: "Disney Company licenses to Maxwell Company exclusive rights to publish and sell within China Chinese-language publications based on Disney World characters. The license granted under this License Agreement may not be assigned by the Licenses to any third party in any manner or by means of any legal procedure." . . . [T]he Maxwell Company signed the "Contract for Assignment of Simplified Versions" with the Children's Press on 21 March 1991, which contract provided: "Under authorization from the Disney Company, the Maxwell Company possesses an exclusive right to publish Chinese language versions of Disney children's reading materials and to represent the Disney Company in regard to copyright trading of such publications. Maxwell Company assigns the authorization from the Disney Company to the Children's Press." On the same day, the Children's Press and the Maxworld

*(continued)*

*(continued)*

Company, in order to implement the "Contract for Assignment of Simplified Versions," signed an agreement whereby the Children's Press entrusted the Maxworld Company to finalize, arrange composition of, and make printing plates for and of the text of Disney children's reading materials. . . . Maxworld also undertook to provide to the Children's Press confirmation by the foreign party of the copyright contract relating to the Disney Collection, which would serve as the legal basis for possession within China of the copyright by the Children's Press. Following this, the Maxworld Company obtained film costs for the Collection in the amount of RMB 69,750 yuan, which, after deducting costs of RMB 59,312.40 yuan, resulted in a profit of RMB 10,437.60 yuan.

On 11 March 1992, the Children's Press delivered the "Contract for Assignment of Simplified Versions" to the Beijing Municipal Copyright Authority for examination and approval. Because no authorization had been issued by the Disney Company, this Authority could not complete registration procedures. No supplemental registration procedures were ever completed by the Children's Press.

[T]he Beijing Publishing Press and the Beijing Distribution Office signed a working agreement on 1 February 1991 which provided . . . "Where it publishes foreign products and books, the publishing press shall enter into a publishing contract with the copyright owner and shall register the contract with the Copyright Registration Authority. After obtaining a registration number, the book shall be passed to the Beijing Distribution Office for preselling and publication. Failing this, the publishing press shall be responsible for any disputes that may arise regarding publication, distribution and selling of foreign copyrighted materials. . . . "

After entry into force of the 17 March 1992 Sino-U.S. Memorandum of Understanding, the Beijing Publishing Press published 118,200 volumes of the Collection, of which it published 41,779 volumes on its own, stored 33,341 volumes, and entrusted the Beijing Distribution Office to distribute 43,080 volumes . . . gross profits were RMB 5,999.04 yuan. . . .

This Court, based on the provisions of the Sino-U.S. Memorandum of Understanding, concludes that, effective 17 March 1992, products of United States nationals have received the protection of Chinese law. Disney Company, in regard to the cartoon likeness germane to this matter—Mickey Mouse, Cinderella, Snow White, Peter Pan, Bambi,

Dumbo, 101 Dalmations, Alice, Lady, etc.—enjoys copyright protection. Absent authorization by the Disney Company, commercial use of these cartoon likenesses constitutes infringement.

Although the Disney Company had previously authorized the Maxwell Company to publish and print an album of cartoon likenesses in China, it never authorized the Maxwell Company to assign such publishing and printing rights to third parties. Accordingly, assignment by the Maxwell Company of its publishing and printing rights in respect of these products . . . to the Children's Press constitutes, on the one hand, an infringement of Disney's rights and, on the other hand, is a fraud on the Children's Press. The Contract by which this assignment was made is void as a matter of law.

From a legal perspective, the Maxwell Company's use of fraudulent means to sign the "Contract for Assignment of Simplified Versions" was the main cause of this infringement of rights. . . . [C]onsidering that the Maxwell Company became bankrupt in July 1993, this Court will not offer any opinion regarding the liability of the Maxwell Company in this matter.

That the Children's Press, without having first investigated whether the Maxwell Company had any right to assign publication rights to the Disney Company products, nonetheless concluded a publishing agreement with it, was extremely reckless. [In a publication of] the State Copyright Administration, . . . there is a provision as follows: "Effective 1 March 1988, any unit or individual entering into publishing trading contract with Taiwan, Hong Kong or Macao, and regardless of whether it provides for licensing out of copyrights or for authorizing use or for taking assignment of authorizations, shall be submitted to the Copyright Administration Authority for review and registration. Where a contract has not been reviewed and registered, it shall, prior to 1 March 1990, be submitted to the review and registration authority in accordance with procedures. Contracts not reviewed and registered shall be void."

The Children's Press, after being refused permission by the relevant department of the State Copyright Administration to register this contract on the ground that it could show no legal proof of copyright, did not conduct any inquiry, and did not implement registration procedures in accordance with relevant national legislation, and proceeded

*(continued)*

*(continued)*

to publish picture albums containing likenesses of Disney cartoon characters. That it was aware it was at fault in so doing is clear. Since the Children's Press is not an independent legal person, its liability shall be borne by the Beijing Press. . . . Since the first occasion on which the Beijing Publishing Press published the products occurred prior to entry into force of the Sino-U.S. Memorandum of Understanding, this Court will not address this issue. Both of the second and the third occasions on which the Beijing Publishing Press published the products occur following entry into force of the Sino-U.S. Memorandum of Understanding, and constituted infringement for which the Beijing Publishing Press should assume responsibility.

The Beijing Distribution Office participated in marketing the second and third publications by the Beijing Publishing Press of the Collection. In accordance with . . . "Implementing Regulations of the People's Republic of China on the Law of Authorship Rights," marketing, regardless of whether it takes the form of "consignment sales" or "distribution" is a form of publishing. . . . A publisher has a legal responsibility to know whether or not the publications it handles are legally defective. The cooperative agreement signed by the Beijing Distribution Office and the Beijing Publishing Press provides that, where foreign products or books are published, the Beijing Publishing Press and the owner of the copyright shall sign a publishing agreement and register it with the Copyright Administration Authority. . . . In fact, whether or not the Beijing Distribution Office ever obtained a registration number from the Copyright Administration Authority was not investigated. This demonstrates clearly that the Beijing Distribution Office, at the time it signed the agreement, took notice of the regulations of relevant State departments but did not implement them. We hold that the Beijing Distribution Office was aware of its fault in this regard and that it should accept responsibility for infringement in publishing the infringed books. The Beijing Publishing Press is jointly liable with the Beijing Distribution Office in respect of the latter's illegal marketing activities. Inasmuch as the "cooperative agreement" provides that all disputes relating to foreign copyright will be handled by the Beijing Publishing Press . . . the liability of the Beijing Distribution Office to compensate for infringement shall be borne by the Beijing Publishing Press. However, it cannot avoid its obligation to cease infringement, and it must give over all gains obtained illegally. . . .

Maxworld Company, according to the agreement signed with the Children's Press, was responsible for providing to the Beijing Publishing Press confirmation by the foreign party of the publishing contract relating to the Disney Collection, which confirmation was to be the legal basis by which the Children's Press enjoyed copyrights in China. By the "confirmation by the foreign party," this court accepts the explanation of the Maxworld Company, which is to say, confirmation by the Maxwell Company. However, confirmation by the Maxwell Company cannot serve as the legal basis upon which the Children's Press enjoyed copyrights in China. Accordingly, Maxworld Company could not implement its promised guarantee obligations to the Children's Press. Since the agreement provided for guarantee obligations by the Maxworld Company, the Maxworld Company should have carefully investigated whether the "confirmation by the foreign party, i.e., by the Maxwell Company" was or was not legally valid. . . . The Maxworld Company claims that it only introduced the parties, but no one could believe its contention that it did not assume guarantee responsibilities. . . . Accordingly, the Maxworld Company shall assume responsibility for part of the obligations of the Beijing Publishing Press to pay compensation for economic losses arising out of the infringement and, in addition, its illegal gains shall be forfeited. . . .

During its investigation, the conclusion of the Beijing Tianzbeng Accounting Office's audit of the financial results of the infringement by the Beijing Publishing Press was that the Beijing Publishing Press lost money. This Court is of the view that the profits or losses of actual business operations are not always the same as the illegal benefits it can obtain. Profits, as a legal matter, should be determined based on the total amount made by the Beijing Publishing Press from publication of infringed works minus reasonable costs (of printing and for payment of taxes). At the same time, the amount payable to the plaintiff as compensation should be this amount plus reasonable bank interest and reasonable fees of the plaintiff incurred in the course of prosecuting this lawsuit.

With regard to the request by the plaintiff, the Disney Company, for an order "that the defendants guarantee in writing that they will never again infringe the copyrights of the plaintiff," this is not a usually available civil remedy, and cannot, therefore, be supported by this Court.

*(continued)*

---

*(continued)*

**Decision.** The Beijing First Intermediate Court entered an order providing, among other things, that (1) Beijing Publishing Press and the Beijing Distribution Office should cease all publication and distribution of the *Collection of Disney Moral Tales* and that all volumes in their possession should be confiscated, along with the colored films thereof; (2) Beijing Publishing Press should make a public apology to the Walt Disney Company in a Chinese newspaper published and printed throughout China; (3) Beijing Publishing Press should make a one-time compensation payment to the Disney Company of RMB 227,094.14 yuan and pay a fine of RMB 50,000 yuan; (4) Maxworld should pay RMB 90,837.66 yuan to the Beijing Publishing Press and RMB 10,437 in its illegal income should be confiscated; (5) RMB 5,000.04 yuan in illegal income earned by the Beijing Distribution Office should be confiscated; and (6) the defendants should bear RMB 40,000 yuan of Disney's attorneys' fees.

---

# The Mechanics of IPR Transfer Regulations

Roughly three basic types of regulatory schemes provide the format for IPR transfer agreements. They range from preapproval to notification/registration to no regulation. The third scheme is obviously the most beneficial to the U.S. entrepreneur. Because the absence of law is somewhat uninteresting to one studying legal issues, however, the text focuses on the preapproval and registration/notification systems in selected countries.

## Prior Approval Schemes

The requirement of substantive prior approval from a government agency is the more intrusive government regulatory scheme and is indicative of a relatively protectionist government policy. The degree to which it intrudes on private enterprise depends largely on the attitude and mandate of the relevant regulatory agencies.

In India, for example, licensing agreements must be approved by the Indian Foreign Investment Board. Before the board can give that approval, however, it is required to seek the opinion of each governmental ministry that may be concerned with the product involved. Depending on the product, this process can include quite a number of agencies. Moreover, the guidelines for approval laid down by the central Indian government are quite demanding. The Indian licensee should be free to sublicense the technical know-how to local Indian companies, sometimes eviscerating the licensor's nondisclosure provisions.

Further, the Indian government forbids payment of a minimum guaranteed royalty to a foreign licensor. To make matters worse, the Indian party to the agreement should be able to export the products it makes with the license—the greatest fear of the licensor.

Most prior approval schemes are not so detailed in their delegation of authority. Instead, the laws are written in general terms with broad interpretive and administrative powers vested in the bureaucracy. Some nations call for the exercise of this discretion by giving government officials a broad range of reasons for disapproving a transfer of technology. For instance, in Colombia the government could refuse to register a technology transfer agreement for any one of many reasons. Prominent among these are the requirements that no license continue confidentiality obligations after its term, and that no term extend for more than three to five years.

Other countries have taken the approach that depends even more on discretion: All transfer-of-technology agreements are prohibited unless a specific reason can be found for them to be permitted. The Japanese *gensoku kinshi* (prohibited in principle) system was a good example. In this system, the principal variable was not any doctrine of law, but bureaucratic practice over time that decided what transactions should be exempted from the presumption of prohibition. The key "legal" insight to the foreign investor would come from those familiar with the personalities administering the process.

In fact, a company is not necessarily free of government discretion even after prior approval is obtained. Its license agreement must still be upheld in a local court system, and many countries provide for the non-enforcement of contracts on public policy grounds. In some foreign courts, these public policy grounds are used more frequently than in the United States, where they are employed only rarely.

These discretionary systems are well adapted to reject requests for technology transfers by mere delay. In its heyday, the Japanese approval mechanism once held up a request for a technology transfer by Texas Instruments, Inc., to a proposed Texas Instruments subsidiary in Japan for more than four years. While Texas Instruments was stalemated, Japanese competitors were able to develop technologies that would help them combat the Americans once they arrived, and many companies that were not as dogged as Texas Instruments were driven away by delay.

Delay is also used as a weapon in technology transfers that require a patent. For instance, in some Latin American countries, the patent process commonly took eight years from start to finish. During that entire period, all fees payable to the owner of the patent were held up.

The flexibility inherent in granting government officials great discretion can also have positive effects on business. In many countries, such as Mexico, official discretion has increasingly been exercised in favor of approving promising projects on terms that are advantageous to the foreign investor. In such countries, businesses should obtain local advice from legal and other consultants familiar with the local patterns in the exercise of discretion.

## Notification/Registration Schemes

A notification or registration system is more open to technological transfer. The Japanese *gensoku kinshi* (prohibited in principle) system was transformed over time to *gensoku jiyu* (free in principle) system. Similar instances may be found in South Korea, Venezuela, and Mexico, where prior approval schemes have been displaced by a simple registration procedure. Countries with a general system of notification often make exceptions for areas of heightened concern. One of these areas commonly involves technology agreements between foreign companies and their controlled subsidiaries. Because of

the patent inequality in bargaining position in such situations, countries that generally have a notification/registration system will require specific approval of technology transfer agreements between such companies.

A danger in notification/registration countries is that some provisions of a registered contract might not be enforceable under those countries' laws. Thus, license royalties in a given contract might be ruled excessive and re-characterized as taxable income to the foreign company. Indeed, in some Chinese special economic zones, the foreign investor must compensate the local licensee for losses incurred in sales of products manufactured by the transferred technology.

A significant danger in any approval or notification system is that leaks in the government bureaucracy can cause a disclosure of the U.S. investor's intellectual property. Some commentators have suggested that, notwithstanding its advanced new laws, Mexico is not acquiring the most modern industrial technology because foreign investors do not wish to risk piracy of their intellectual property rights. In Japan, foreign investors cast a wary eye on the Japanese government's continuing requirements for specificity in describing transferred technology even under the notification system. Although Japanese authorities respond that such information is necessary for statistical purposes, and that any disclosure by a government official could lead to criminal sanctions, foreign investors remain concerned about possible leaks from government ministries to Japanese firms.

One final provision of U.S. trade law is Section 337 of the Tariff Act, which prohibits, among other things, the importation of articles that infringe a U.S. patent, trademark, or copyright. For example, if someone tries to import "fake" Rolex watches into the United States from a country that does not enforce its IPR laws, the Rolex trademark holder may seek to exclude the fakes through Section 337. The International Trade Commission (ITC) carries out investigations under this provision upon the filing of a complaint by the trademark holder or by the ITC on its own initiative. If the ITC determines that an article is being imported in violation of Section 337, the U.S. Customs Service may stop the article from entering the United States or, upon subsequent violation, the property may be seized and forfeited to the U.S. government. Proof of injury is not required in order to block the imported items.

In 1988, a GATT panel ruled that Section 337 violated GATT's nondiscrimination provisions, but the United States initially refused to comply with its decision. The United States would consider a modification of Section 337 only in the context of the development of an international intellectual property rights system in the Uruguay Round of GATT negotiations. In short, the United States, which is perhaps the greatest source of technological innovation, simply refused to comply with the GATT judgment until a world system was developed that would treat its intellectual property owners more equitably. Finally, after the TRIPS was accepted by other nations effective in 1995, Congress amended Section 337 in the *Uruguay Round Agreement Act* to respond to the panel's concerns.

## The Gray Market

As noted earlier, an important fear of the prospective U.S. licensor is that the IPR that it licenses abroad will come back into the home market in the form of products that will compete with its goods. This situation can occur when, after the expiration of a license and its anti-competition restrictions, the licensee makes the product for itself and invades the U.S. market. Even before that occurs, however, a licensor must contemplate the danger that a completely unrelated party—with whom the licensor has no anti-competition agreement—will purchase the licensed product and import it back into the United States. This importation of merchandise produced and sold abroad and then imported back into the United States for sale in competition with the U.S. trademark owner is referred to as the *gray market* or *parallel trade*. The products imported back are *"gray market goods"* or *"parallel imports."*

> **http://www.arentfox.com/features/
> counterfeit/counterfeit5c.htm**
> See this site for gray market issues.

### The Nature of the Problem

The gray market principally threatens the U.S. licensor if the product is sold at a lower price abroad than in the United States, which can happen for a variety of reasons. The U.S. licensor might have established such a reputation of quality in the U.S. market that it can command a substantial premium for its product there. Before its product builds a similar reputation abroad, however, the licensor will not be able to charge a similar premium. In the meantime, the gray marketeer could simply purchase the goods abroad more cheaply, transport them back to the United States, and place them in direct competition with the U.S. licensor.

The gray market is also stimulated by international currency fluctuations. Relative currency values vary minute by minute during each business day. Retailers and wholesalers of goods are much slower to react, however. Thus, upon a negative movement by, say, the Mexican peso, a nimble arbitrageur can purchase the U.S. product in Mexico at a price that is a bargain in U.S. dollars.

Holders of U.S. trademarks are incensed by the gray marketeers. They note that some products sold abroad under their trademarks are actually different from the domestic products. For instance, soft drinks sold in the Far East are sweetened more than their U.S. counterparts. U.S. licensors argue that sale of the foreign product in the United States could have a detrimental impact on the reputation of their domestic product.

U.S. licensors also argue that gray marketeers receive a "free ride" on their development efforts. They point out that a substantial investment in time, effort, and capital is required to develop the sort of reputation that commands a premium in the United States. Consequently, they argue, the gray marketeer who comes in without making any payment to the U.S. trademark holder is stealing some of the return on the holder's investment.

U.S. consumers, on the other hand, are generally delighted by the gray market. It often enables them to obtain goods of the same or comparable quality as well-known brands at a lower price. Thus, consumer advocates and merchandise retailers argue that the gray market gives the consuming public the benefits of price competition in otherwise noncompetitive markets.

### Resolution of the Dispute

In this hotly debated area, courts have gone in a variety of directions. Moreover, national legislatures, including the U.S. Congress, are often called upon to provide assistance to one side or the other in the struggle. As with all political struggles, its outcome is impossible to predict.

Under one view, the trademark holder has no right to control goods after it sells them in commerce. After such a sale, the trademark holder has *exhausted* its control, and once its control has been exhausted, the trademark holder cannot complain of competition by others. Thus, exhaustion doctrine would create a wide-open gray market.

Courts seem to have accepted the proposition, however, that if a gray market product is so different as to call into question the quality of the domestic product, the licensor should be granted relief, especially if the seller of the domestic product has independently developed goodwill in its home country. Justice Oliver Wendell Holmes, in the following case, wrote one of the opinions that formed the foundation for analysis in this area.

In situations with relatively little possibility of confusion, in which the quality of the gray

---

### A. Bourjois & Co. v. Katzel
*360 U.S. 689, 43 S. Ct. 244 (1923)*
*United States Supreme Court*

**BACKGROUND AND FACTS**
**JUSTICE HOLMES**
In 1913 A. Bourjois & Cie., E. Wertheimer & Cie., Successeurs, doing business in France and also in the United States, sold the plaintiff for a large sum their business in the United States, with their good will and their trade marks registered in the Patent Office. The latter related particularly to face powder, and included the above words. The plaintiff since its purchase has registered them again and goes on with the business that it bought, using substantially the same form of box and label as its predecessors and importing its face powder from France. It uses care in selecting colors suitable for the American market, in packing and in keeping up the standard, and has spent much money in advertising, & c., so that the business has grown very great and the labels have come to be understood by the public here as meaning goods coming from the plaintiff. The boxes have upon their backs: "Trade Marks Reg. U.S. Pat. Off. Made in France—Packed in the U.S.A. by A. Bourjois & Co., Inc., of New York, Succ'rs. in the U.S. of A. Bourjois & Cie., and E. Wertheimer & Cie."

The defendant, finding that the rate of exchange enabled her to do so at a profit, bought a large quantity of the same powder in France and is selling it here in the French boxes which closely resemble those used by the plaintiff except that they have not the last quoted statement on the backs, and that the label reads, "Poudre de Riz de Java," whereas the plaintiff has found it advisable to strike out the suggestion of rice powder and has "Poudre Java" instead. There is no question that the defendant infringes the plain-

tiff's rights unless the fact that her boxes and powder are the genuine product of the French concern gives her a right to sell them in the present form.

After the sale the French manufacturers could not have come to the United States and have used their old marks in competition with the plaintiff. . . . If for the purpose of evading the effect of the transfer, it has arranged with the defendant that she should sell with the old label, we suppose that no one would doubt that the contrivance must fail. There is no such conspiracy here, but, apart from the opening of a door to one, the vendors could not convey their goods free from the restriction to which the vendors were subject. . . . It deals with a delicate matter that may be of great value but that easily is destroyed, and therefore should be protected with corresponding care. It is said that the trade mark here is that of the French house and truly indicates the origin of the goods. But that is not accurate. It is the trade mark of the plaintiff only in the United States and indicates in law, and, it is found, by public understanding, that the goods come from the plaintiff although not made by it. It was sold and could only be sold with the good will of the business that the plaintiff bought. It takes the reputation of the plaintiff upon the character of the goods.

**Decision.** The plaintiff has sought a preliminary injunction restraining the defendant from infringing its copyrights. The U.S. Supreme Court reversed the decision of the U.S. Court of Appeals not to grant such a preliminary injunction.

market product is indistinguishable from the domestic product, courts have not been solicitous of the rights of licensors. In such cases, courts prize the benefits of price competition over concerns about a free ride for the gray marketeer, particularly within the European Union. Courts there have enforced common market competition laws with great aggressiveness. The *Deutsche Grammophon* decision excerpted in the following case is an illustrative precedent from Europe.

In the United States, pro-gray market forces also seem to be on the rise. This international

---

## Deutsche Grammophon
## v.
## Metro-SB-Grossmarkte
### Common Market Reports
### (CCH)8106 (1971)
### Court of Justice of the
### European Communities

### BACKGROUND AND FACTS

Deutsche Grammophon Gesellschaft (D.G.) was a German company whose main product was phonograph records. It distributed them either directly or through its subsidiaries established in several European nations. Among these was Polydor S.A., a French Company in which D.G. had a 99.55 percent interest.

In Germany, D.G. sold the phonograph records directly through retailers and two wholesale booksellers for Deutche Mark 12.33 and required a final price to the consumer of DM 19.00. In the other European Union countries, D.G. distributed its records through licensing contracts with its subsidiaries or other corporate affiliates. Each of these licensing contracts granted to the licensee the exclusive right to make commercial use of its recording in the contract territory.

Metro-Grossmarkte GmbH & Co. KG (Metro) had purchased D.G. records from Polydor and, because it was not bound under a price agreement, had offered these records to its customers in Germany for DM 14.85 in May 1969, and for DM 13.50 in August 1969. D.G. believed that the sale of its records by Metro violated the German copyright law and thus constituted an infringement of its exclusive right to distribute the records in Germany. It obtained an injunction from the Landgericht (District Court) at Hamburg, prohibiting metro from selling or otherwise distributing D.G. records bearing the Polydor label. Metro appealed to the Hanseatisches Oberlandesgericht (Hanseatic Superior Court), which deferred judgment and, pursuant to the EEC Treaty, submitted to the Court of Justice the issue whether continuation of the injunction would violate the Treaty.

### PER CURIAM

It follows from the facts given by the Hanseatisches Oberlandesgericht at Hamburg that the question submitted is essentially whether the exclusive right to sell the protected goods, which the manufacturer of sound records has under a national law, can, without jeopardizing the Union rule, prevent the sale on the domestic territory of products normally sold in the territory of another Member State by that manufacturer or with its consent. . . .

Under Article 85, paragraph 1, of the [EU] Treaty, "all agreements between enterprises, all decisions of associations of enterprises, and all concerted practices that are likely to affect trade between Member States and whose object of effect is to prevent, restrict, or distort competition within the Common Market are prohibited." The exercise of the exclusive right referred to in the question could fall within the prohibition set forth in that provision wherever it appears to be the object, the means, or the result of an agreement which, by prohibiting imports from other Member States of products lawfully sold in those States, would have the effect of partitioning the market. However, where such exercise would escape the elements of contract or concert contemplated in that provision, the answer to the question submitted would make it necessary to determine whether the exercise of the right to protection is compatible with other provisions of the Treaty, particularly those relating to the free movement of goods.

The principles that must be considered in this case are those which, for the realization of a single market between the Member States, are stated in the second part of the Treaty, which is devoted to the foundation of the Union, under the title of free movement of goods, and in Article 3(f) of the Treaty, which provides for the establishment of a system that ensures that competition in the Common Market is not distorted. Where, moreover, the Treaty, in Article 36, permits certain prohibi-

*(continued)*

*(continued)*

tions or restrictions on trade between Member States, it refers to them specifically, stipulating that such exceptions shall not be used "as a means of arbitrary discrimination nor as a disguised restriction on trade between Member States." It is therefore in the light of these rules, particularly of Articles 36, 85, and 86, that the extent to the exercise of a national right to protection, akin to a copyright, might prevent the sale of products coming from another Member State must be determined. . . .

Assuming that a right akin to a copyright can be covered by these provisions, it nevertheless follows from that article that while the Treaty does not affect the existence of the rights recognized by the laws of a Member State in the matter of industrial and commercial property, the exercise of such rights can, however, be subject to the prohibitions, set forth in the Treaty. While Article 36 permits prohibitions or restrictions on the free movement of goods that are justified for reason of industrial and commercial property protection, it permits exception from this freedom only to the extent that they are justified in order to safeguard rights that are the specific object of such property.

"Where a right akin to a copyright is invoked to prohibit the sale in a Member State of products that are distributed by its holder, or with the holder's consent, in the territory of another Member State, for the sole reason that the distribution does not take place on the domestic territory, such prohibition, since it serves to isolate national markets, conflicts with the essential goal of the Treaty, which is to merge the national markets into a single market. This goal could not be achieved if, because of the various legal systems of the Member States, nationals of such States were able to partition the market and bring about arbitrary discrimination or disguised restrictions on trade between the Member States. That is why the exercise, by a producer of sound recordings, of the exclusive right under the laws of a Member State to distribute the protected products, in order to prohibit the sale in that State of products that were distributed in another Member State by the producer or with its consent, solely for the reason that such distribution did not take place in the territory of the first Member State, is contrary to the rules providing for the free movement of goods within the Common Market."

**Decision.** The Court of Justice of the European Communities held that prohibition of Metro's sales of records would violate the EEC Treaty and so advised the Hanseatic Supreme Court.

Reproduced from the Common Market Reporter by permission of CCH Editions Limited. 8106 (1971).

---

trend has been confirmed in the United Sates by the Supreme Court in *K Mart Corp. v. Cartier, Inc.*, in which the Court allowed the entry of gray market imports if the foreign manufacturer and the domestic trademark owner are subject to common control.

---

## K Mart Corp. v. Cartier, Inc.
### 486 U.S. 281, 108 s. Ct. 1811 (1988)
### United States Supreme Court

BACKGROUND AND FACTS
The Court noted that the gray market arises in three contexts, only two of which are relevant for the purposes of these cases. In case 1, despite a domestic firm's having purchased from an independent foreign firm the rights to register and use the latter's trademark as a U.S. trademark and to sell its foreign-manufactured products here, the foreign firm imports the trademarked goods and distributes them here, or sells them abroad to a third party who imports them here. In case 2, after the U.S. trademark for goods manufactured abroad is registered by a domestic firm that is a subsidiary of (case 2a), the parent (case 2b), or the same as (case 2c), the foreign manufacturer, goods bearing a trademark that is identical to the U.S. trademark are imported. Section 526 of the Tariff Act of 1930 prohibits the importation of certain gray market goods. The Customs Service's implementing regulation permits the entry of goods manufactured abroad by the "same

*(continued)*

*(continued)*

person" who holds the U.S. trademark or by a person who is "subject to common control" with the U.S. trademark holder, and permits importation where the foreign manufacturer has received the U.S. trademark owner's authorization to use its trademark. The *Coalition to Preserve the Integrity of American Trademarks* and two of its members filed suit against the government seeking injunctive and declaratory relief, asserting that the regulation was inconsistent with §526 and therefore invalid. Some U.S. retailers, including K Mart Corporation, intervened on the side of the government.

The Court split along three camps, making clear interpretation of its views on a number of technical issues difficult. A majority agreed, albeit for different reasons, that the "common control" exception was consistent with Section 526. Justice Brennan, concurring in part.

A comparison of [the U.S. face powder company in Bourjois] to the parties seeking § 526's protection in this ligation aptly illustrates the profound difference between the equities presented by the prototypical gray-market victim and those implicated in case 2. First, the U.S. trademark holder that, like Bourjois, has purchased trademark rights at arm's length from an independent manufacturer stands to lose the full benefit of its bargain because of gray-market interference. In contrast, a U.S. trademark holder that acquires identical right from an affiliate (case 2a) or creates identical rights itself and permits them to be used abroad by an affiliate (cases 2b and 2c) does not have the same sorts of investment at stake.

Second, without §526, the independent trademark purchaser has no direct control over the importation of competing goods, much less over the manufacturer's sale to third parties abroad. In contrast, if the gray market harms a U.S. trademark holder in case 2a, 2b, or 2c, that firm and its foreign affiliate (whether a parent, subsidiary, or division) can respond with a panoply of options that are unavailable to the independent purchaser of a foreign trademark. They could, for example, jointly decide in their mutual best interest that the manufacturer (1) should not import directly to any domestic purchaser other than its affiliate; (2) should, if legal, impose a restriction against resale (or against resale in the United States) as a condition on its sales abroad to potential parallel importers; or (3) should curtail sales abroad entirely.

These differences furnish perfectly rational reasons that Congress might have intended to distinguish between a domestic firm that purchases trademark rights from an independent foreign firm and one that either acquires identical rights from an affiliate foreign firm or develops identical rights and permits a manufacturing subsidiary or division to use them abroad.

**Decision.** In the relevant part of the ruling, the U.S. Supreme Court reversed the Court of Appeals' grant of declaratory judgment to the plaintiffs.

# Franchising: Licensing Outside the Technological Context

*Franchising,* the fastest-growing form of licensing, seldom involves technological complexity. In this text, the term refers to the arrangement in which the licensor permits the licensee to sell certain goods under the licensor's trademark or service mark under a franchising agreement. To prevent devaluation of its trademark, the licensor will typically condition its use on the licensee's observance of certain quality standards. Thus, a Muscovite who wishes to open a McDonald's restaurant will contract with McDonald's Corporation for a franchise; a condition of the franchise will likely be that the franchisee follow specified processes in cooking hamburgers.

Several observations may be made about franchises. First, although franchising seldom involves significant patent law or other technological issues, many of the considerations noted in other licensing contexts apply with equal force. The franchisor will often wish to condition retention of the franchise on the franchise meeting defined marketing quotas. The franchisee will attempt to obtain exclusive rights within some geographic area, while the franchisor will resist granting such rights or will try to narrow the geographic area. Franchisors must make the same balancing considerations as other licensors in arriving at an appropriate royalty level. And the duration of the franchise will be hotly disputed.

Second, while patent law protection is generally not a significant issue in franchising, trademark protection is. Quite often, the most valuable asset that the franchisee purchases is the right to use the franchisor's good name and trademarks on what are otherwise local products. If trademark protection is lax in the local jurisdiction, the value of the franchise accordingly declines. Thus, the extent of legal protection and actual enforcement of trademark rights is a key consideration in franchising decisions.

Third, as discussed in the succeeding chapter on antitrust and competition laws, *competition* laws have greatly affected a number of these issues. For instance, the European Commission has invalidated franchisors' *quality assurance* provisions when they were deemed unduly restrictive of the franchisee's ability to compete. Franchisors must also be concerned about the application of competition laws to *tied purchase* clauses that require the franchisee to buy certain goods from the franchisor. Such provisions are sometimes difficult to justify on quality control grounds. And geographic exclusivity will not be permitted if it unduly restricts competition within the host country.

Fourth, because franchisees typically sell to the local domestic market and generate few exports, franchisors face special difficulties repatriating profits from soft currency countries. This problem is solved by creating sections within franchise stores within which the identical products are sold for hard currency at relatively favorable exchange rates. Even if this is a small part of the total sales, as long as it is equal to the franchisee's payments due to the franchisor, it can largely relieve the problem. Another approach has been *countertrade:* payment to the franchisor with goods instead of hard currency. Thus, PepsiCo, Inc., is partially paid for its cola products by its Russian co-venturers with mushrooms for the pizzas of PepsiCo's Pizza Hut subsidiary. But the potential for countertrade is limited in most soft currency countries. Aside from commodities, goods from such nations are often not competitive with those from hard currency countries.

Fifth, in a few nations, a number of laws are specifically directed at the franchising phenomenon. The franchisor must be alert for *franchise tax* laws, which can impose taxes based on the franchisor's worldwide operations—even if the local operations fizzle. Such taxes may sometimes be avoided by structuring the franchise agreement in accordance with local preferences. If such structuring is not possible, the local profit opportunity must be sufficiently large and fast to justify an instant drain on revenues.

Sixth, *system* franchisors—those with a prepackaged program of instruction and initiation for prospective franchisees—should take care to avoid the entanglements of *language politics.* A few countries contain regions in which business must be conducted in a certain language. A prominent example is in the province of Quebec in Canada; the law there requires that business is done in French. A U.S. franchisor that brings its standard English-language package into such an area may be subject to significant civil penalties.

Finally, some nations impose stringent disclosure requirements on who may be a franchisor and what must be disclosed to prospective franchisees. These restrictions include registration requirements for highly detailed disclosure about the franchisor's business that the franchisor may not wish to make. The Australian case of *Hamilton v. Casnot,* although perhaps no longer good law, illustrates the web of legal snares that can ensnare the unwary franchisor.

---

### http://www.franchise.org
*See for information from the International Franchise Association.*

## Hamilton v. Casnot Pty. Ltd.
### 5 A.C.L.R. 279
### Supreme Court of Western Australia

### BACKGROUND AND FACTS

Casnot Pty., Ltd., a franchisor of carpet and cleaning businesses, placed an advertisement in *The West Australian,* a newspaper in Perth, Australia, which read as follows:

> Cleaning business, full price $7,500, including equipment. Metro cleaning business using new system which opens untapped market; work from home, etc. All contracts arranged. Company guaranteed income; finance on $2,500 deposit. Apply for appointment, 325 2455, Accent Services. 159 Adelaide Terrace, Perth.

Individuals who responded to the advertisement were advised that the business involved cleaning carpets and curtains and that substantial profits could be made by contracting with Casnot.

The prospective franchisee would pay to Casnot, a deposit of $3,450, purchase plant and equipment for $3,670, and pay to Casnot 20 percent of all gross income received from customers, together with $5 per customer. Casnot would spend money on advertising and employ staff to locate customers. Each "agent" would solely operate an allotted area within the metropolitan area of Perth.

Government authorities brought proceedings against the franchisor for violation of the provision of the Australian Companies Act that requires registration with the government of public offers to invest. The trial court, the Court of Petty Sessions, had dismissed the complaints, reasoning that Casnot's activity did not fall within the scope of the Companies Act.

### JUDGE WALLACE

The question is as to whether such an agreement comes within the definition of interest as appearing in section 76 of the Companies Act and in particular as to whether it "means any right to participate or interest whether enforceable or not and whether actual perspective or contingent;

(a) in any profits, assets, or realization of any financial or business undertaking or scheme whether in the State or elsewhere;

(b) in any common enterprise whether in the State or elsewhere in which the holder of the right or interest is led to expect profits, rent, or interest from the efforts of the promotor of the enterprise or a third party."

Authority to date has placed a wide construction upon the above-mentioned definition. It must be understood that the legislation does not prohibit the creation of an interest. It merely precludes such an interest being offered to the public where necessary compliance with statutory protective conditions is absent. . . .

His Worship [the Court of Petty Sessions] found that the "investors" involved in approaching the respondent Casnot were buying either a franchise or a small business. This gave them the right to clean curtains and carpets for householders within a specified area for which they paid money to the respondent. By this means his Worship reached the conclusion that there was no evidence to show that the company was engaged in a promotional scheme whereby capital was required to be raised. With respect this is not the criterion. The test is as laid down in the statutory definition. It is clear that both "investor" and Casnot became engaged in a common enterprise pursuant to which the investor held the right to expect profits from the efforts of Casnot and thus came clearly within the definition of para (b) or §76(1) of the Companies Act.

For these reasons I ordered that the matters should be referred back to the learned magistrate with a direction to convict the respondents and deal with them further in accordance with law.

**Decision.** The Supreme Court of Western Australia reversed the decision of the Court of Petty Sessions and remanded with directions that convictions be recorded against the defendants and that the lower court "attend to the appropriate punishment involved."

# Chapter Summary

In general, licensing provides to a firm with intellectual property a means for increasing the returns yielded by that property by permitting someone else to exploit it. In the international context, this capability is particularly useful: A U.S. concern with little or no experience in Nepal can contract with someone with such experience to exploit the Nepalese market. In the normal course, licensor and licensee will negotiate over matters such as conditions and extent of use, compensation, and confidentiality. The negotiations between licensor and licensee are complicated in the international context. Many countries seek to assist local licensees in their efforts to acquire advanced technology. Local legislation may supersede contractual provisions in order to permit host-country nationals to possess the intellectual property more rapidly. Lax enforcement of local legislation may provide a further source of mischief. Under some approval systems, nothing is likely to happen without cooperation of a local licensee. Unfortunately, efforts by the U.S. government to rectify the situation have often come to grief.

If all these complications were not bad enough, the U.S. firm that sends goods abroad may find them exported back to its local market. The trend among developed countries has been to permit such increased competition.

Notwithstanding all of these hazards, the efficiency and technical advances underlying licensing makes it a rapidly expanding and highly profitable form of doing business abroad. It is, however, an endeavor that must be pursued cautiously.

---

## QUESTIONS AND CASE PROBLEMS

1. Hirt Systems Company is a U.S. company with a strong market in the United States for its "securing" of computer terminals (that is, enveloping such terminals with lead so as to prevent the emission of microwaves that can be picked up by "spy receivers"). The key to Hirt's success is its know-how in design. Because the application is labor intensive, models produced abroad are significantly cheaper. Hirt has been affected by these lower-priced models, though it has held its own because of the superiority of its design. As part of its expansion program, Hirt is considering construction of a new assembly plant. Discuss the relative benefits and risks of building it as a Hirt-owned concern in a Third World country under the direction of Hirt's U.S. management as opposed to building it in the United States.

2. Assuming the same facts as in Question 1, what would be the advantages and disadvantages of a joint venture with a major foreign company abroad compared to the alternatives discussed in Question 1?

3. Scott Hill, a U.S. inventor, has developed and patented a revolutionary new running shoe that increases one's speed significantly. His invention has achieved considerable success in his native American Midwest. Two European companies have offered him joint venture packages to take his invention to the track-happy Europeans. Barthelemy Plus Grande, S.A., is a French sportswear giant with a marketing and distribution system that includes every major city in Western Europe and massive capital resources. Pék Társaság, a recently privatized Hungarian firm, offers substantially lower labor costs. Which should Mr. Hill choose as a joint venture partner? Why?

4. Mr. Hill's marketing experts advise him that the Japanese market is hungry for his shoes. Focusing on technology transfer issues, discuss whether he should seek a Japanese joint venture partner or enter through a wholly owned subsidiary.

5. Analyze the same questions raised in Problem 4, but assume Mr. Hill is considering entry into a "prior approval" country.

6. Laffitte Enterprises, Inc., a U.S. firm, has purchased the right to use the trademark of Wellington Imperial, Ltd., in the United States for a high-quality line of Napoleonic War reproductions. Wellington has a cheap line of Napoleonic trinkets that it sells in France. Dégas Magazines, S.A., a French firm, begins to import the low-priced Wellington line into the United States. If Laffitte brings action against Dégas, how would a U.S. court address the policy considerations presented?

7. Geyer Schokolade, A.G., makes the bonbon of choice for the German yuppie; its product's cachet permits Geyer to charge a hefty premium at home. Geyer expands into the U.S. market—where no one has heard of its bonbons—and charges a more reasonable price to garner market share. Henry Joseph, a U.S. entrepreneur, re-imports the bonbons into Germany and offers them at a substantial saving below Geyer's price. What will be the result of Geyer's attempt to stop Mr. Joseph at the EEC Court of Justice?

## MANAGERIAL IMPLICATIONS

I. You work for Wilbur Intergalactic, Ltd., a leading North Carolina processor and purveyor of North Carolina-style pork barbecue. Certain areas of North Carolina centered around Wilson, NC, are known for producing superior pork barbecue because of the peculiar nature of the soil in which the pigs wallow and because of the method for preparing barbecue developed in that area. Soon, Limited Wilbur and other purveyors begin to refer to their barbecue as "Wilson-Style Barbecue" as a promotional name for their product. In 1999, the North Carolina Legislature designates Wilson County as a special barbecue area and prohibits anyone from using the designation "Wilson-Style Barbecue" for barbecue not made from Wilson-bred hogs, in Wilson, pursuant to the Wilson method. Soon thereafter, the Professional Committee of Wilson Barbecue secures the U.S. trademark "Wilson-Style Barbecue" for Limited Wilbur and its other members.

In 2001, Limited Wilbur's management learns that, at France's Euro Wally World, a French firm has been selling pork barbecue with the words "Method Wilson" on the label. The barbecue is made from local French hogs, but pursuant to the Wilson method of barbecuing. The committee has not secured trademark protection in France.

1. Explain how a French court would analyze the issue of whether the French barbecuers are infringing upon Limited Wilbur's property rights. In this analysis, discuss whether "Wilson-Style Barbecue" is too generic to receive protection and what Limited Wilbur's rights are under the various intellectual property treaties.

2. Develop a plan for expanding Limited Wilbur's product marketing to France, giving consideration to steps that it should take to preserve its "Wilson-Style Barbecue" trade name.

II. Undertake a study of the trade war between China and the United States over intellectual property rights. After years of trying to get China to protect American IPRs, an agreement was reached between the two countries in 1992. Reports of copyright and trademark violations continued, and in June 1994 an investigation was initiated under Special 301. China was identified as a priority country in July 1994 (59 FR 35558). A determination was made to take action against China on February 7, 1995 (60 FR 7230). The nation's press covered the story daily, describing how it would cost U.S. consumers billions of dollars a year. China embarked on its own public relations campaign, with U.S. television showing bulldozers crushing thousands of bootlegged and counterfeit CDs on a street in China. A month later, on March 7, 1995 the USTR announced that China had agreed to take the needed action to protect IPRs of U.S. film, recording, and software companies.

1. What is the annual cost of Chinese IPR violations to U.S. companies? How have IPR violations affected the decision of American companies to do business there? What has been the response of private firms to these violations and how have they tried to control it?

2. What positive actions has China taken to correct the problem? What new laws have been passed for the protection of IPRs and how are they enforced?

3. Consider specifically the problems of U.S. software companies in China. Can you find any information about Microsoft's position on doing business in China. What has been their strategy to tap into the potentially huge Chinese market, while assuring that their copyrights on software remain protected? If the Chinese government views IPR violations as a legitimate way to make a profit, would bringing the government in as a joint venture partner be one way to get the Chinese to see the need for IPR protection?

# Chapter Eighteen

# Host-Country Regulation: Corporate Law, Taxation, and Currency Risk

Business that operates in a foreign country must comply with the laws of that country. This "rule" of international business has significant implications for U.S. business managers. A projected high profit margin may be irrelevant if local law prevents repatriation of the profits to the United States. Low per-hour labor costs may seem less attractive if local law dictates that employees control 50 percent of the local board of directors. The anticipated capital cost of building a factory may be grossly in error if the manager fails to consider that he or she is in an Islamic country in which it is more difficult to arrange short-term financing. These legal differences are not all bad for U.S. companies; many foreign nations attract investment precisely because of less-demanding laws.

For better or worse, foreign law is almost always different from U.S. law. First, as noted in earlier chapters, the U.S. common law system, founded on Anglo-Saxon antecedents, is fundamentally different from the legal system in all non-English-speaking nations. Second, these fundamental technical differences are compounded by the cultural and political differences that are reflected in law. For instance, the United States strongly favors the free flow of capital, and its laws impose relatively few barriers to that flow. Countries that are concerned about their foreign reserves or that favor central governmental control place many more restrictions on the flow of capital.

Business managers trained in the business environment of the United States must become familiar with the legal schemes created by foreign cultures before subjecting their companies to them. This chapter reviews the limits on foreign investment imposed by host-country corporate securities laws and tax laws.

> **http://www.imex.com/uscib**
> *See for links through the OECD home page.*

## Host-Country Corporate Law Affecting Foreign Investment

Nationalization—which is discussed in this chapter—once seemed a quick route to dominance over enterprises operating in a host country, but it has adverse long-term effects. Once a nation nationalizes its industries, potential foreign investors stay away and capital resources dry up. Furthermore, because the government that takes over the enterprises—like all governments—lacks the entrepreneurial skills necessary to have the business prosper, the economy soon stalls.

Accordingly, most countries now focus on preventing a resurgence of foreign economic domination rather than impeding the trend of foreign investment. Host nations regulate the form and substance of foreign investment through a wide assortment of domestic corporate laws. These laws largely reflect the nation's preoccupation with foreign economic domination that previously led to nationalization. This concern is particularly in evidence with respect to strategic industrial sectors.

Those nations that tend to be more concerned about foreign domination tend to have more restrictive laws against foreign penetration of their economies. For example, the massive U.S. economy has relatively little fear of being dominated by outsiders and has few obstacles to foreign investors. By contrast, developing economies that can easily be overwhelmed by more sophisticated capitalists place many preconditions to such investment. Within those more restrictive countries, regulation tends to be more stringent as the level of an enterprise's foreign ownership or foreign operational control grows. Nations in transition to entrepreneurial systems—where privatization is proceeding—find vestiges of suspicion of foreign penetration even as they try to enact free enterprise legal systems.

The chapter first discusses foreign investments that leave majority ownership in the hands of home nationals, and then turns to those that do not. In its examination of the former, the text addresses corporate requirements associated with all investments, irrespective of control considerations. In the discussion of the latter, the chapter addresses the additional considerations that arise once foreign ownership exceeds 50 percent of an enterprise.

## Minority Ownership Investments

Among minority investments, it is useful to distinguish between passive and active investments. For our purposes, a *passive investment* is one in which the investor limits its involvement to providing equity or debt capital in an enterprise managed by another in the hope of a profitable return. The classic passive investment is the acquisition of a non-controlling amount of stock in or a loan to a company with no participation in management of the enterprise. With an *active* investment, the investor participates in the management of the enterprise. The prototype of an active minority investment is the joint venture.

Because passive minority investments create the least risk of foreign control, they are the least regulated of foreign investments. Active minority ownership investments, on the other hand, begin to raise the specter of foreign influence and thus are the subject of greater governmental regulation.

### Passive Debt Investments

Perhaps the least intrusive of all investments is the extension of credit. In a loan, the foreign investor analyzes the proposed foreign activity and evaluates its commercial prospects and "political risk." If the activity seems profitable and likely to be able to repay the loan, the foreign lender will make its advance in exchange for repayment at an agreed-upon interest rate before any equity owners in the enterprise are repaid. Because lenders are *senior* to other investors, they are willing to accept a fixed, lower return than others and to participate very little in management. Indeed, any significant participation in management can, in some countries, lead to "lender liability," a partial or total forfeiture of the lenders' special status.

Because it is relatively unintrusive, the international lender faces relatively few governmental regulations. For the international lender, the principal form of risk apart from enterprise risk is currency risk, discussed at greater length later. Legal and administrative restrictions on the conversion of local currency into hard currency and on the transfer of hard currency out of the country can endanger loan repayment. Currency fluctuation can also create difficulties; if the local currency is sinking for reasons beyond the local enterprise's control, it will suddenly need a higher margin to be able to meet its loan obligations and that may not be possible.

In the Islamic world, however, religious law adds additional complications to the passive foreign lender. The Koran prohibits money to be made out of money. Because bank financing is necessary for effective business, however, lenders have devised an interesting array of financing techniques that do not violate scripture. The following article explains this fascinating phenomenon.

### Passive Equity Investments

The capital markets of North America, Western Europe, and Japan are becoming increasingly unified. Investors from each area feel confident in their investments in securities issued in the other areas. Consequently, "foreign" money has become an important segment of each of these markets. In fact, one can monitor the price quotations of an internationally traded stock on the different stock exchanges in order to seek the best price. As long as the foreign investors do not

# Unlocking Islamic Finance

There's no two ways about it: The Koran says money should not be created out of money. This scriptural injunction is the touchstone for the vast world of Islamic financial institutions that don't collect or pay any interest (*riba*). Instead, they share in the risks and rewards facing their customers and pay their depositors and investors on the same basis. Recently, this ancient formula has been winning a growing following in the modern world of project finance.

The mushrooming capital requirements for infrastructure projects in the Muslim countries of the Middle East and Asia have increased the need for project sponsors to tap private-sector funds. And in such countries as Kuwait, Pakistan and Malaysia, Islamic banks are proving themselves to be a viable new source of this capital.

Islamic banks, for their part, have welcomed project finance transactions as a religiously acceptable long-term investment alternative. "The nature of profit- and loss-sharing and nonrecourse finance fits well within the Islamic perspective," says Richard Thomas, head of the Islamic Investment Banking Unit of the United Bank of Kuwait in London. "Even from an ethical perspective, deploying your funds to increase economic capacity is deemed better by Islam than keeping funds idle in a local bank account."

Those who consume interest shall not rise again, except as one arises whom Satan has prostrated by the touch; that is because they have said: "Bargaining is the same as interest." God has permitted bargaining but has forbidden interest. Sura 2: 275–276, The Koran.

While statistics about Islamic financial institutions are scarce, according to Harvard University's Islamic Finance Information Program, there are now 133 Islamic financial institutions in 24 countries worldwide, with total assets of $101 billion and capital of $4.9 billion. Most of these are located in Pakistan, Indonesia and Sudan. However, the largest in terms of assets are concentrated in the Middle East countries of Bahrain, Kuwait, Saudi Arabia and Iran.

In addition to the Islamic financial institutions, a growing number of conventional banks also handle certain funds in accordance with Islamic law and offer Islamic banking services.

### The Oil Boom

The first Islamic bank was incorporated in Egypt in the mid-1960s. But it wasn't until a decade later and following the oil boom that the concept took on a more visible role. Devout Muslims in the Persian Gulf region and other oil-rich Arab states realized that instead of putting their new wealth in conventional banks, they could build a business catering to depositors like themselves who shunned interest, yet sought profits.

However, Islamic banks soon realized that many depositors had little taste for risk-taking and long-term investments. As a result, many of these banks began focusing on products that provide predetermined rates of return in the short term, such as commodities and trade financing. In these transactions the banks would arrange for a trader to buy goods on the banks' behalf and resell them to clients at a markup.

In searching for new investment products, Islamic banks and their *shari'a* boards (which assess the religious acceptability of the bank's transactions) have found a natural fit with project finance. "Philosophically, there are a lot of similarities between the two," says Isam Salah, attorney. "In project finance, you are basing the success of your loan on the success of the project [because the lender cannot sue the borrower but must rely on the project for repayment], as opposed to a conventional loan, where you are not necessarily tied in to the success of the venture. That is what Islamic finance principles call for—that you share the risks as well as the rewards."

For example, *ijara*, the Islamic leasing structure, fits well with nonrecourse finance. Using an *ijara* contract, Islamic project financiers purchase the assets of a power plant and lease them back to the project sponsor at a markup and on a deferred-payment basis during the life of the lease. This is not only compatible with Islamic law, it is often a favored approach of conventional banks financing independent power projects.

*(continued)*

*(continued)*

Another alternative is the *istisna* structure, which resembles a supplier's credit or a preproduction facility for advanced funding of a large project. In this case, the Islamic bank funds the project's major suppliers, acquires title to the equipment, and passes the title on to the project company on the basis of an agreed-upon deferred-payment structure.

The applicability of Islamic finance to large infrastructure projects was first demonstrated in 1993 with the 1,292-megawatt (MW) Hub River power project in Pakistan. The project set a precedent by obtaining religious approval for an Islamic bridge financing, arranged by ANZ Grindlays, to be used alongside conventional project financing.

Richard Duncan, director of global Islamic finance at ANZ Investment Bank in London, explains that efforts to raise medium-term funds were bogged down in lengthy negotiations, leaving the project stalled. At that point, Saudi Arabia's Al Rajhi Banking & Investment Corp. stepped in and provided a $92 million *istisna* preproduction bridge financing.

Al Rajhi bought the rights to equipment (turbines) that had not yet been manufactured, and sold these rights to the project company on a markup basis. Although the cost was comparable to the cost of a standard short-term trade finance facility, a conventional financing alternative was not available at the time. The *istisna* facility was extended twice before it was finally repaid when financing closed on the project in 1994.

### Islamic Instruments

Structuring a limited-recourse or nonrecourse project finance transaction with Islamic capital requires the use of several Islamic financing instruments. "It is important to identify the short-, medium-and long-term needs of a project and then to apply appropriate Islamic financing instruments to raise funds," says IICG's Fakih.

The short-term needs and working-capital requirements of a project are best addressed by *murabaha* financing contracts (cost-plus financing), in which the Islamic bank buys equipment, fuel or raw materials and sells them to the project company at a markup and on a deferred-payment basis. The *murabaha* is then taken out by an *istisna* financing (preproduction facility), which in turn is taken out

by an *ijara* financing—which resembles conventional lease financing. Once the *ijara* contract has expired, the project company takes title to the assets.

All of these Islamic financing mechanisms get around the prohibition on interest payments by having the financiers take ownership of assets and lease or resell them to the project company. To mitigate the risks associated with asset ownership, Islamic banks often opt for finance leases, as opposed to operating leases. "You can have a full pay-out lease, which pays itself over the life of the lease," says Citibank's Rehman. "And you have a residual risk, which is covered by a buy-back agreement from the project itself or a third party."

While Islamic finance meshes well with project finance, industry watchers don't expect projects costing more than $200 million to be financed by Islamic funds alone. Given the capital requirements of many deals, especially those in the Middle East's oil and gas sectors, most will need to combine Islamic tranches with conventional financing.

Marrying these two seemingly incompatible approaches in a single financing isn't easy. "There are major issues and conflicting desires," says ANZ's Duncan, "but the key to successfully bringing the two together is in resolving the intercreditor issues." For example, the Islamic financiers want to own assets while the conventional lenders typically want to have all the assets held by the project company. In addition to this basic difference, "the intercreditor agreements need to satisfy the *shari'a* boards that the conventional debt facilities are in no way tainting the Islamic facility," explains Neil Miller, managing partner in the Bahrain office of Norton Rose, the London-based law firm.

Conventional banks, meanwhile, have their own concerns about what the Islamic institutions are entitled to. For example, Rose explains, the conventional banks will require the intercreditor agreements to clearly describe and identify different income streams and work out the entitlements under each of them.

### Rouch

In the case of the $507 million financing for the 412-MW Rouch power project in Pakistan's Punjab province, the project company agreed to sell certain project assets to three syndicates of Pakistani fi-

*(continued)*

*(continued)*

nanciers who agreed to put up funds under Islamic principles. The three Islamic tranches consisted of a rupee-denominated working-capital facility of approximately $7 million for purchases under the fuel supply agreement; an $18 million letter-of-credit facility, which allowed the project company to post the required letters of credit under the power purchase agreement; and a rupee-denominated $40 million standby term facility arranged by Pakistan's National Development Finance Corp. to meet cost overruns.

The working-capital and standby facilities, arranged by ANZ Grindlays, which was also financial adviser to the project, were both structured as *murabaha* contracts. Under each contract, the marked-up price covered the price at which the project company sold the assets to the financiers, and included an additional amount for profit as well as compensation in case of payment delays.

According to Duncan, the Western conventional lenders were initially concerned about how the priority payments would be calculated. Because the Islamic facilities are non-interest bearing and do not specify the return on capital on the same basis as the conventional Libor-based facilities, it was necessary to come up with a mechanism that would identify which amounts payable under the Islamic facilities are applicable to principal and which to interest. This would avoid the possibility of the Islamic financiers' receiving repayment of principal prior to the Western lenders.

In these mixed financings, says Citibank's Rehman, "You not only have to do the Islamic financing documentation, but you have to marry that with the conventional financing documentation, and then top it off with the intercreditor arrangements. It is quite time consuming."

## Impediments

In terms of participating in project finance deals, perhaps the most perplexing challenge facing the Islamic banks is recourse to liquidity. "Project finance tends to be long-term, and Islamic investors tend to have their money invested short-term," notes United Bank of Kuwait's Thomas. As a result, many Islamic banks end up either running large gapping risks or simply staying away from longer-term commitments.

The gapping risk is magnified because Islamic banks do not have an inter-bank market where they can swap out short-and medium-term deposits against longer-term investments. Nor do they have mechanisms similar to interest-rate-swap instruments. As a result, Thomas says, "the biggest problem is matching funding to the term and matching the pricing mechanism, fixed or floating."

For now, some Islamic banks, such as the Islamic Investment Co. of the Gulf, circumvent these problems by raising project-specific funds or special pools of funds which are deployed for project financings. "That way investors understand the projects and take a view in terms of tenor, associated risks and rewards and the banks avert the risk of maturity mismatches," says Fakih. Other institutions, including Kuwait Finance House, are planning to set up unit trust or mutual fund types of investment vehicles aimed at longer-term investors.

The *shari'a* court, explains Citibank's Rehman, is about 1,500 years old and is not clear on many issues. "A lot," he says, "is subject to interpretation." There is growing enthusiam among Islamic scholars for industry-wide standards, but that may take years to develop.

## A Guide to Islamic Banking

| | |
|---|---|
| *Halal:* | Practices permitted under Islamic law |
| *Harram:* | Practices forbidden under Islamic law |
| *Ijara:* | A leasing structure based on risk sharing. The financier acquires title to the asset and leases it at a predetermined fee. Title is passed on to the client once the lease expires. |
| *Istisna:* | A supplier's credit or preproduction facility. The financier acquires equipment and passes the title on to the client on a predetermined deferred-payment basis. |
| *Modaraba:* | A partnership agreement where one party contributes financing and the other contributes assets (i.e.: property, equipment or expertise). Profit sharing is predetermined. Losses are borne by the financier. |

*(continued)*

*(continued)*

**Murabaha:** A short-term commercial finance agreement. The financier acquires goods on behalf of the client, who purchases and takes title to the goods at an agreed-upon date and at a price that includes a predetermined markup.

**Musharaka:** A joint-venture agreement where both financier and client contribute capital and share the profits and losses in proportion to their investment.

**Riba:** Interest charged by a lending institution

**Shari'a:** Doctrines regulating Islam

**Sara Khalili**

© *Infrastructure Finance,* 1997, Vol. 6, No. 3, Euromoney Publications. Reprinted by permission.

try to accumulate a block sufficient in size to exert control, thus ceasing to be passive, their money is welcome.

Through the device of *American Depository Receipts*—certificates held by U.S. trust institutions representing interests in stock held by a bank in a foreign country—many fledgling non-U.S. companies have become available to U.S. investors. Americans also can do more than invest abroad: They can now offer their securities to investors abroad through the Euroequity market. Indeed, the phenomenon of transnational takeovers is beginning to occur as European investors take over U.S. concerns and U.S. investors take over European concerns. In Europe, many national firms are merging across borders to form multinational concerns better suited to survival in the continent-wide competitive environment of the European Union.

In this world market, a U.S. investor needs to investigate nuances of overseas equity markets. One of the major differences abroad is in the regulation of trading in securities by people with access to nonpublic information, or *insider trading.* In the United States, insider trading is a criminal violation. In the late 1980s, their participation in insider trading resulted in the downfall of Ivan Boesky, Michael Milken, and other Wall Street moguls. By contrast, many foreign nations view insider trading as "a mere violation of the rules of ethics," rather than a violation of law. Other nations, such as Japan, have anti-insider trading laws on the books, but are generally perceived not to enforce them. Thus, U.S. investors must approach a purchase of securities abroad carefully; the sellers may have adverse nonpublic information about what they are selling.

Because regulated, honest markets tend to attract more investors, however, the international trend is now decisively toward U.S. forms of securities regulation. In Europe, this enlightened self-interest has now led France, Germany, England, Denmark, and Switzerland to outlaw insider trading. Even infant markets such as those in China are seeking to implement regulatory schemes that ensure broad dissemination of information about companies whose shares are publicly traded.

Other peculiarities of foreign equity markets are more subtle. In certain Swiss industries, for instance, a company's capital stock is divided into bearer shares (*inhaberaktien*) and registered shares (*namensaktien*). Although both kinds of shares are publicly traded, only Swiss citizens may purchase registered shares. Moreover, because registered shares most often hold the majority of the Swiss company's voting power, Swiss control is generally assured.

In some countries, legal structures do not create formal impediments to foreign equity investments; however, the country's tradition can frustrate attempts to convert a passive investment into a more active holding. In Japan, efforts by large, minority U.S. stockholders to gain greater influence have been unsuccessful. In the absence of a mutually acceptable joint venture arrangement, minority investment there is often viewed as permanently passive.

## Active Investments

For the U.S. investor that wishes to exercise a measure of control over its minority investment—the active investor—joint ventures are often the vehicle of choice. A foreign investor may enter into a joint venture by combining with a national of the host country to create a new entity, or by acquiring a portion of an existing local entity. The four basic forms of a joint venture are (1) a foreign corporation, (2) a foreign partnership, (3) a U.S. corporation with a foreign branch, or (4) a U.S. partnership with a foreign branch.

The precise shape of the joint venture depends largely on the participants' relative treatment under the tax laws of the host country and the United States, and whether the countries have entered into a tax treaty that might affect the application of those laws. In many cases, for instance, remittances from branches may be taxed at higher rates than dividends from a foreign subsidiary. Generally, taxes are deferred until dividends are declared.

In some strategic sectors of the economy, however, many nations strictly limit foreign investment. In the United States, for instance, foreign nationals may not hold more than a 25 percent voting interest in an airline or a company that owns an earth station or microwave license, or controls a defense contractor producing certain technologies. In countries even more fearful of foreign domination, foreigners are excluded from a larger number of sectors. Prior to its conversion to privatization, Argentina required prior approval of any investments in defense or national security, electricity, gas, telecommunications, public utilities, radio and television stations, insurance companies, or financial entities. In many of these cases, the government's inability to run these sectors effectively without private initiative and foreign capital and expertise have caused restrictive governments to open up these sectors through privatization.

Even if a foreign entity cannot own a majority of a joint venture, it may be able legally to obtain operational control through other means: One may surround the joint venture with contractual obligations to the foreign venturer. For example, if the joint venture is to assemble components manufactured in the United States, the U.S. investor retains significant control over the joint venture regardless of how many shares the investor owns or how many directors it can name to the board because it controls the supply of components. Similarly, a U.S. investor can exercise control through supply contracts, marketing agreements, management contracts, and veto power in the joint venture agreements.

Perhaps these operational means of control have led some nations to initiate full substantive pre-approval procedures for active foreign invest-

ment. India once was one of the nations most wary of foreign influence and had a particularly elaborate example of this pre-approval procedure. Foreign investment proposals in India were evaluated by the Project Approval Board, whose members were representatives of relevant government agencies. The Project Approval Board submitted the proposal to a variety of committees that acted as arms of the board in determining whether the proposed joint venture complied with five different Indian laws governing foreign investment. Needless to say, the administrative difficulties involved in such a process are discouraging.

India also provides an example of how such pre-approval procedures have been reformed to encourage investment. In 1993, India changed the clearance procedure for all foreign investments of less than $120 million. As long as the foreign investor limits its equity stake to 51 percent or less in 34 selected industries, the only approval necessary would be from the Reserve Bank of India. This simplification and centralization of the approval process has created a boom in foreign investment in India in the 1990s. Indeed, this unified approval entity has now become accepted throughout the Third World, from Egypt's semi-autonomous Investment Authority to Kenya's Foreign Investment Agency.

Conversely, many countries give preferences and incentives to certain types of foreign investments, especially high-technology companies and export-oriented industries. For instance, in India, export-oriented businesses are granted special relief from duties normally imposed on foreign components and are given assistance in obtaining import licenses. The People's Republic of China tries to make up for its poor infrastructure by giving high-technology firms priority access to its public utilities.

As the foregoing discussion suggests, foreign investment laws can take many forms. Most are dozens and even hundreds of pages long. One of the decrees issued by a former Soviet republic, as shown in Exhibit 18.1, provides an indication of how such laws appear in a country that has not yet decided how capitalist it really wishes to be.

## Local Assistance

The infinite variety and complexity of laws and regulations affecting foreign investment make it

**EXHIBIT 18.1    Law on Foreign Investments in the Republic Kyrgyzstan**

Vedomosti Kyrgyzstan no. 13, item 449
(1991) Adopted by the Kyrgyzstan Supreme Soviet, 28 June 1991

The present Law is directed towards ensuring the effective participation of the Republic Kyrgyzstan in international economic links and attracting additional material and financial resources and progressive foreign technology in the form of foreign investments. . . .

### Article 1.  Foreign Investments in Republic Kyrgyzstan

Foreign investments in Republic Kyrgyzstan are monetary and material contributions in the sphere of economic and other activity, and also the transfer of rights to intellectual property, by foreign States, juridical persons, and citizens. . . .

### Article 4.  Forms of Foreign Investments Authorized in Republic Kyrgyzstan

The following forms of foreign investments shall be authorized in the Republic Kyrgyzstan: participatory share in joint enterprise; foreign enterprises; acquisition of stocks and other securities; special-purpose monetary contributions; scientific-technical product; intellectual valuables; other forms of economic and other activity not prohibited by laws of the Republic Kyrgyzstan.

### Article 5.  Legislation of Republic Kyrgyzstan on Foreign Investment Activity

Relations connected with the effectuation of foreign investment activity shall be regulated by the present Law, other legislation of the Republic Kyrgyzstan, and also the provisions of international treaties of which the Republic Kyrgyzstan is a participant.

If other rules have been established by international treaties than those which are contained in legislation of the Republic Kyrgyzstan, the provisions of the international treaty shall apply.

### Article 6.  Contractual Regulation of Foreign Investment Activity

The principal document regulating the legal status of foreign investors and participants of investment activity shall be the contract (or agreement).

The choice of partners, the concluding of contracts, and the determination of obligations and other conditions of economic relations which are not contrary to the legislation of Republic Kyrgyzstan shall be the exclusive competence of the foreign investors and participants of investment activity.

The conditions of contracts concluded between foreign investors and participants of investment activity shall retain their force for the entire period of operation of the contracts and in instances when after the concluding thereof conditions worsening the position of the parties are established by legislation of the Republic Kyrgyzstan.

### Article 7.  Guarantees for Foreign Investors in Republic Kyrgyzstan

The Republic Kyrgyzstan shall guarantee the stability of rights of foreign investors and other forms of legal protection thereof.

The legal regime of foreign investments may not be less favourable than the legal regime for investments effectuated by juridical persons and citizens of the Republic Kyrgyzstan and other republics.

Losses (including profit not received) caused to foreign investors in connection with the adoption of laws and other legal acts limiting their rights shall be compensated by State agencies which adopted these acts. If the assets of State agencies are insufficient, the damage shall be compensated from the State budget of the Republic Kyrgyzstan. . . .

### Article 8.  Economic Autonomy of Foreign Investors

Foreign investors shall have the right autonomously to determine the amounts, orientations, and effectiveness of investments and to involve juridical persons and citizens, including foreign, on a contractual basis who are needed for the realization of the investments.

Foreign investors directly or through intermediaries shall have the right to acquire the property needed without limitation as regards volume or nomenclature from juridical persons and citizens at prices and on conditions which are not contrary to laws of the Republic Kyrgyzstan.

A foreign investor may transfer the right to possession, use, and disposition of investments to other juridical persons and citizens in the procedure established by a law of the Republic Kyrgyzstan. The mutual relations of the parties in the said transfer of rights shall be regulated by a contract. . . .

*(continued)*

**EXHIBIT 18.1 (continued)**

### Article 10. Freedom of Use by Foreign Investors of Results of Investments

Foreign investors shall have the right to possess, use, and dispose of the results of their investments, including reinvestment and trade operations in the territory of the Republic Kyrgyzstan.

Foreign investors may export profit or part thereof in the form of products of own production or purchased on the market of goods and services.

The export of goods and services purchased on the market shall be in the procedure established by legislation of the Republic Kyrgyzstan concerning export-import operations.

The export by foreign investors of Soviet and foreign currency shall be effectuated in the procedure provided for by legislation of the Republic Kyrgyzstan on currency regulation.

### Article 11. Compliance by Foreign Investors with Financial, Ecological, Urban Construction, and Other Requirements

Foreign investors shall be obliged to comply with the ecological, financial, urban construction, and other requirements established by legislation of the Republic Kyrgyzstan.

### Article 12. Prohibition of Unfair Competition

Foreign investors must not permit unfair competition and shall be obliged to fulfill the requirements of anti-monopoly legislation of the Republic Kyrgyzstan. . . .

### Article 13. Licensing of Foreign Investments in Republic Kyrgyzstan and Registration Thereof

A license (or authorization) for a foreign investment in the Republic Kyrgyzstan shall be issued by the Cabinet of Ministers of the Republic Kyrgyzstan not later than 30 days after the application of the foreign investor is received.

The form of the application and list of documents substantiating it shall be confirmed by the Cabinet of Ministers of the Republic Kyrgyzstan.

Foreign investors shall be registered by the Ministry of Finances of the Republic Kyrgyzstan.

Payment for the license for foreign investment activity shall be established in the amounts and in the procedure provided for by the law on taxes in the Republic Kyrgyzstan. . . .

### Article 15. Joint Enterprises in Republic Kyrgyzstan

Joint enterprises shall be enterprises in which the participatory share of the charter fund belongs to a foreign investor(s). The amount of this participatory share shall be determined on a contractual basis.

The contract on the founding of a joint enterprise shall be concluded between a juridical person(s) or citizen(s) and a foreign investor(s). . . .

### Article 16. Foreign Enterprises in Republic Kyrgyzstan

Enterprises, the charter fund of which belongs entirely to a foreign investors(s), shall be foreign enterprises in the Republic Kyrgyzstan. . . .

### Article 17. Acquisition by Foreign Investors of Stocks and Other Securities in Republic Kyrgyzstan

Foreign investors in the Republic Kyrgyzstan shall have the right to acquire stocks and other securities in the procedure established by legislation of the Republic Kyrgyzstan. . . .

### Article 20. Additional Tax Privileges for Foreign Investors in Republic Kyrgyzstan

Additional privileges relating to tax on declared profit shall be granted to foreign investors if:

- the foreign investor has contributed to the capital of a juridical person a participatory share in convertible currency in the amount of 20% or more or in an amount exceeding 0.3 million US dollars or the equivalent in another convertible currency, then for ten years it shall be exempt from tax on 25% of the profit;
- the contribution of a foreign investor to the capital of a juridical person made in convertible currency exceeds 30% or 0.8 million US dollars, then during the first five years shall be exempt from tax on 30% of the profit, and during the next five years, on 50% of the profit;
- the foreign investor has contributed its participatory share in the capital of a juridical person engaging in the activity specified in the Annex to the present Law, then during the first five years shall be exempt from tax on 100% of the profit, and during the next five years, on 60%. . . .

*(continued)*

**EXHIBIT 18.1   (continued)**

#### Article 22.  Taxation of Profit Exported by Foreign Investors from Republic Kyrgyzstan

Profit received by foreign investors who have paid taxes on the profit shall not be levied with taxes for exporting it abroad.

Foreign investors shall pay tax in the amount of 5% of the profit exported which is exempt from the payment of profit tax. . . .

#### Article 25.  Procedure for Settlement of Disputes Connected with Foreign Activity in Republic Kyrgyzstan

Disputes connected with foreign investment activity in the Republic Kyrgyzstan shall be considered in accordance with legislation prevailing in the Republic Kyrgyzstan in courts, State Arbitrazh, or, by arrangement of the parties, in an arbitration court.

#### Article 26.  Insurance of Foreign Investments in Republic Kyrgyzstan

Foreign investments in the Republic Kyrgyzstan may, and in the instance provided for by legislation of the Republic Kyrgyzstan must, be insured.

#### ANNEX

*LIST of Investment Activity, Participation in Which by a Foreign Investor Gives Him the Right to Privileges When Paying Taxes*

1. Electronics:

   - production of components;
   - production of computers and computer peripherals;
   - production of electronic equipment and rendering of services connected therewith provided by the manufacturer, including the production of electronic consumer goods

2. Production of means of auto transport, spare parts and parts
3. Production of machine tools
4. Manufacture of machines and equipment for agriculture and production of food products

---

particularly important for the U.S. investor to retain the assistance of host-country nationals familiar with local law and customs. For example, acquisition of a Brazilian export license has been estimated to require 1,470 separate legal acts. Few U.S. investors would be able to work their way through such extensive bureaucracy without someone who is thoroughly familiar with the process and the people who administer it. Paperwork for truck shipments into Mexico is notoriously complex; a Mexican customs broker is a must. Similarly, in Germany, businesses must be members of a *Handelskammer,* a society of merchants. Because many registered *Handelskammer* members have been working together for decades, for practical purposes, an investor cannot conduct business without someone who has an established relationship within that circle.

In short, the foreign investor may have to navigate around substantial corporate and cultural barriers. Typically, the only way it can do this is by enlisting the assistance of local individuals.

# Majority Ownership Interests

## Establishing a Foreign Branch or Subsidiary

An enterprise typically has a number of important business reasons why it would prefer to establish an entity it controls through majority ownership, rather than an entity in which it owns a minority interest and does not control. For instance, the firm that greatly fears disclosure of its soft drink formula would be reluctant to enter into any venture that it did not fully control, whether the potential co-venturer was a Mongolian or a Virginian. The international context places an additional layer of complexity over the businessperson's decision-making process. For example, certain nations simply do not permit 100 percent foreign ownership of soft drink manufacturers, or they impose taxes that make such ownership extremely unattractive.

An enterprise that wishes to establish an entity abroad under its control may create a subsidiary or a branch. This step is not to be taken lightly, however. Whether the company establishes a subsidiary or a branch, it may waive rights of protection under the bilateral investment protection agreements of the United States. Furthermore, the company subjects itself completely to the foreign nation's corporate tax laws.

Certain differences separate the subsidiary approach from the branch approach. If a company chooses to establish a branch abroad, it faces greater potential vicarious liability. In essence, the company is directly answerable for any liabilities of a branch, which is not the case for a separate corporation that is a subsidiary. Thus, if the foreign activity involves potential product or environmental liability, a subsidiary corporation is indicated. On the other hand, the establishment of a branch as opposed to a subsidiary may have significant consequences under local tax law and U.S. tax law. Because tax laws often distinguish among different forms of an enterprise, such laws could dictate, or at least influence, establishment of a U.S. branch, a U.S. partnership, a foreign corporation, or a foreign partnership.

## Tax Issues Associated with Foreign Branches and Subsidiaries

Tax issues are as varied as local tax laws and the circumstances of the individual ventures. Despite the tax treaties among nations, methods of calculating income, deductions, and depreciation differ significantly. Further complications occur when these different systems are applied to multinational transactions.

One textbook could not possibly address the tax systems of all nations in the world. Indeed, the U.S. Internal Revenue Service by itself is the subject of numerous different courses in American law schools. The U.S. investor should, however, be aware of the more important provisions of the U.S. tax law that affect international transactions.

**Foreign Tax Credits.** Under U.S. tax law, corporations are taxed on all income, including income from foreign sources, regardless of where it is earned. The United States, however, does not tax foreign subsidiaries of U.S. companies on the income that they earn abroad; U.S. law taxes income that is repatriated or paid as a dividend to the U.S. parent. Thus, if the tax systems of different countries were not coordinated to some degree, companies would face double taxation on the same business profits: once by the host country when it is earned by the subsidiary and once by the United States when it is earned as a return on investment by the parent.

Because such double taxation discourages international transactions, different nations have developed their own systems for avoiding it. France and the Netherlands, for example, simply exempt the foreign source income of their firms. The United States uses a tax credit method, allowing a 100 percent credit for foreign income taxes paid. If the foreign tax is lower than the U.S. tax, the U.S. company must pay the difference. If the foreign tax is greater, the U.S. company does not get a refund, but need not pay any U.S. tax on the foreign source income.

The strength of international pressure to compel cooperation on these tax issues can be decisive. In recent years, the state of California defied international convention by taxing the foreign income of foreign affiliates of companies with a California presence. Because this "worldwide reporting method" did not correspond with the usual taxation of income "where earned," it created a double taxation problem for all foreign firms doing business in California. Accordingly, these firms sent their U.S. lawyers to challenge the constitutionality of the worldwide reporting method. California successfully defended its system against this attack for years, finally winning in the United States Supreme Court in the 1994 case of *Barclays Bank v. Franchise Tax Board of California*. But the British Exchequer and the Organization for Economic Cooperation and Development condemned the California tax system and threatened retaliatory action against California firms. With this threat to California's business community—and why would a firm stay in California rather than Utah if it would be substantially disadvantaged—California backed down. Its legislature enacted "water's edge" legislation, which limited taxation to the activities of a firm within the United States.

One recurring tax issue revolves around the U.S. investor's ability to credit taxes it has paid to a foreign country against taxes it would have to pay on its U.S. tax return. In essence, a U.S. enterprise receives a credit for appropriate foreign taxes against its U.S. taxes with respect to income from foreign sources. Thus, an investor needs to consider (1) the tax rates applicable to a particular form of organization and (2) whether the foreign impositions are creditable taxes for U.S. purposes.

Because the issue of whether foreign impositions are creditable taxes for U.S. purposes is so central to the investment decision, it may be instructive to review how the courts resolved one such controversy.

---

## Bank of America National Trust & Savings Assn. v. United States
### 459 F.2d 513 (1972)
### United States Court of Claims

### BACKGROUND AND FACTS

Plaintiff Bank of America conducted a general banking business in the Kingdom of Thailand, the Republic of the Philippines, and the Republic of Argentina. With respect to this business, Bank of America paid the three jurisdictions various types of taxes. Bank of America demanded a credit for most of these assessments either on its federal income tax returns or by refund claim.

The Internal Revenue Service disallowed a number of the credits claimed and Bank of America appealed to a trial commissioner. The trial commissioner held for the Bank of America with respect to the Thailand Business Tax, Type 1 and Type 2; the Philippine Tax of Banks; and the City of Buenos Aires Tax on Profit-Making Activities. The matter was appealed to the Court of Claims.

### JUDGE DAVIS

For a domestic corporation, § 901(a) and (b)(1) of the Internal Revenue Code . . . allows a credit against federal income taxes of "the amount of any income, profits, and excess profits taxes paid or accrued during the taxable year to any foreign country or to any possession of the United States." It is now settled that the question of whether a foreign tax is an "income tax" within § 901(b)(1) must be decided under criteria established by our revenue laws and court decisions, and that the foreign tax must be the substantial equivalent of an income tax as the term is understood in the United States. . . .

[T]he Thailand Business Tax . . . states that . . . persons engaged in business have the duty to pay business tax on the "gross takings" for each tax month at [rates ranging from 2.5 percent to 10.5 percent]. "[G]ross takings" from the business of banking [are] (a) interest, discounts, fees, or service charges, and (b) profit, before the deduction of any expense, from the exchange, purchase, or sale of currency, issuance, purchase, or sale of notes or foreign remittances.

The City of Buenos Aires Tax on Profit-Making Activities . . . imposes a tax on the gross receipts of banks, insurance, savings and loan, and security and investment companies, and . . . provides that, in the case of banks and other lending institutions, "the taxable amount shall be composed of interest, discounts, profits from nonexempt taxable securities, and other revenue, resulting from profits and remuneration for service received in the course of the last business year."

The Philippines Tax on Banks provides . . . that there shall be collected a tax of 5 percent on the gross receipts derived by all banks doing business in the Philippines from interest, discounts, dividends, commission, profits from exchange, royalties, rentals of property, real and personal, and all other items treated as gross. . . . For none of the three taxes was the taxpayer permitted to deduct from gross income the costs or expenses of its banking business or of producing its net income.

The problem, then, is whether such imposts on gross banking income . . . are "income taxes" under the foreign tax credit—"income taxes" as we use that term in the federal system under our own revenue laws.

There is consensus on certain basic principles, in addition to the rule that the United States notion of income taxes furnishes the controlling guide. All are agreed that an income tax is a direct tax on gain or profits, and that gain is a necessary ingredient of income. . . . Income, including gross income, must be distinguished from gross receipts which can cover returns of capital. . . . Only an "income tax," not a tax which is truly on gross receipts, is creditable.

*(continued)*

*(continued)*

[W]e cannot accept the position that all foreign gross income taxes, no matter whether or not they tax or seek to tax profit or net gain, are covered by that provision. [F]rom 1913 on, Congress has always directed the domestic levy at some net gain or profit, and for almost sixty years the concept that the income tax seeks out net gain has been inherent in our system of taxation. That is the "well-understood meaning to be derived from an examination of the [United States] statutes which provide for the laying and collection of income taxes"—the basic test . . . for determining whether a foreign tax is an "income tax" under the foreign tax credit. . . . Where the gross income levy may not, and is not intended to, reach profit (net gain), allowance of the credit would serve only haphazardly to avoid double taxation of net income, since only the United States tax—under the concept followed since 1913—would necessarily fall upon such net gain. There would not then be any significant measure of commensurability between the two imposts (except by chance).

We do not, however, consider it all-decisive whether the foreign income tax is labeled a gross income or a net income tax, or whether it specifically allows the deduction or exclusion of the costs or expenses of realizing the profit. The important thing is whether the other country is attempting to reach some net gain, not the form in which it shapes the income tax or the name it gives. In certain situations a levy can in reality be directed at net gain even though it is imposed squarely on gross income.

For instance, it is almost universally true that a wage or salary employee does not spend more on expenses incident to his job than he earns in pay. A foreign tax upon the gross income of an employee from his work should therefore be creditable by the employee under 901(b)(1) despite the refusal of the other jurisdiction to permit deduction of job-related expenses. The reason is, of course, that in those circumstances the employee would always (or almost always) have some net gain and, accordingly, the tax, though on gross income, would be designed to pinch net gain in the end—and would in fact have that effect. In those circumstances, a loss (excess of expenses over profit) is so improbable, and some net gain is so sure, that the tax can be placed on gross income without any real fear or expectation that there will be no net gain or profit to tax.

Our review of the [law] persuades us that the term "income tax" in 901(b)(1) covers all foreign income taxes designed to fall on some net gain or profit, and includes a gross income tax if, but only if, that impost is almost sure, or very likely, to reach some net gain because costs or expenses will not be so high as to offset the net profit. . . .

Do the three foreign taxes we are now discussing . . . meet this test?

Each of the taxes is levied on gross income from the banking business and allows no deductions for the costs or expenses of producing the income. Any taxpayer could be liable whether or not it operated at a profit during the year. The only question is whether it is very unlikely or highly improbable that taxpayers subject to the impost would make no profit or would suffer a loss. Obviously, plaintiff and the other institutions subject to the taxes had substantial costs in their banking business, salaries and rent being the major items. The covered banks must also have had bad debts and defaults, and these would have to be taken into account in calculating annual net gain. . . .

Nor can one say on this record that the three governments felt that net gain would always (or nearly so) be reached by these special banking levies, or that they designed these particular taxes to nip such net profit. Each of the three jurisdictions had a general net income tax (comparable to ours, and admittedly creditable) which the Bank of America and other banks had to pay. That was the impost intended to reach net gain.

We cannot say, therefore, that there was only a minimal risk that the combination of a bank's expenses plus its debt experience (and other losses) would outbalance its net gain or profits in any particular year—or that the foreign countries so considered. . . .

**Decision.**   The United States Court of Claims dismissed Bank of America's petitions for a tax credit.

**Transfer Pricing.**   A second major recurring tax issue is generically referred to as transfer taxes or the *transfer pricing* provisions. The transfer pricing provisions are an attempt by the Internal Revenue Service to prevent evasion of U.S. tax laws. When a U.S. corporation enters into a contract with a foreign subsidiary that it controls, it may obviously structure the transaction so that only the subsidiary profits from the deal. If international firms had free rein to do this, they would price their transactions so that all profit would be realized by subsidiaries in low-tax or no-tax jurisdictions, depriving Uncle Sam of his cut of the action.

To prevent this type of tax avoidance, transfer pricing provisions require that pricing in such inter-company transactions be conducted at "arm's-length" prices—the prices that would have resulted from negotiation among unrelated parties. Failure to achieve such pricing allows the Internal Revenue Service to reconstruct retroactively what the arm's-length price should have been and to impose penalties based upon that revised computation. Virtually all developed nations have also adopted similar transfer pricing provisions, with the same objective of preventing tax evasion through manipulation of intercompany transactions.

In the *Sundstrand* case, the U.S. Tax Court illustrated the limits of the discretion of the IRS in this area and the complex and somewhat artificial methodology of arm's-length determinations.

---

### Sundstrand Corp. and Subsidiaries v. Commissioner
96 TC (CCH) Dec. No. 47, 172 (1991)
United States Tax Court

#### BACKGROUND AND FACTS

Sundstrand Corporation, the petitioner, manufactured constant speed drives (CSD), avionic devices that drive an airplane's generator at a constant speed irrespective of the speed of the engine. Sundstrand entered into a license agreement with SunPac, a wholly owned foreign subsidiary of Sundstrand located in the Republic of Singapore, under which SunPac was authorized to manufacture CSD spare parts in Singapore and to sell them throughout the world. From 1976 through 1978, pursuant to a distribution agreement, Sundstrand bought all of SunPac's production at Sundstrand's catalog price less a discount of 15 percent.

The Commissioner of the Internal Revenue Service (IRS) determined that under this arrangement SunPac was in substance a subcontractor of Sundstrand. Accordingly, the IRS contended that fair remuneration should have been based on a less lucrative cost-plus system.

#### JUDGE HAMBLEN

Section 482 gives respondent [the IRS] broad authority to allocate income, deductions, credits, or allowances between commonly controlled organizations, trades, or businesses if [the IRS] determines that the allocation is necessary to prevent the evasion of taxes or clearly to reflect the income of the controlled entities. The purpose of section 482 is to prevent the artificial shifting of the net incomes of controlled taxpayers by placing controlled taxpayers on a parity with uncontrolled, unrelated taxpayers.

Thus, the regulations attempt to identify the "true taxable income" of each entity based on the taxable income which would have resulted had the entities been uncontrolled parties dealing at arm's length.

Up through the trial, respondent argued that SunPac should be viewed as a machine shop which provided a manufacturing service to petitioner. . . .

[The IRS contended] that SunPac was merely a contract manufacturer for whom the sale of its total production was assured and who, thus, was not entitled to the return normally associated with an enterprise which bears the risk as to the volume of the product it can sell and the price it can charge.

Here, SunPac had no guarantee that petitioner would purchase all of SunPac's production. The Distributor Agreement places no obligation on petitioner to purchase any or all of SunPac's output. The record establishes that petitioner planned to purchase all of SunPac's initial production, but only until SunPac itself developed the capability to distribute SunPac parts directly to its customers. Thus, petitioner and SunPac initially intended to operate under the Distributor Agreement only until SunPac's direct distribution system could be implemented. The airlines' unanticipated reluctance to purchase directly from SunPac forced both SunPac and petitioner to develop alternative plans for the distribution of the SunPac parts which included continuing the Distributor Agreement through the years in issue. This unexpected change in plans did not convert SunPac to petitioner's subcontractor, however.

*(continued)*

*(continued)*

The record shows that petitioner consistently paid SunPac petitioner's catalog prices less a 15 percent discount for the SunPac parts. The Distributor Agreement's prices for SunPac parts, set forth in Attachment A to the agreement, however, could be and were revised by amendment from time to time to reflect changes in the prices. Although SunPac may have anticipated the transfer price less a 15 percent discount, the Distributor Agreement made no such guarantee. . . .

Petitioner, therefore, has carried its burden of proof as to this matter.

The regulations specify three methods, in the order of priority, which respondent must use to determine an arm's-length price for the sale of tangible property: the comparable-uncontrolled price method, the resale-price method, and the cost-plus method. Where none of these three methods can reasonably be applied under the facts and circumstances of a particular case, the regulations authorize use of any other appropriate method, or variations of such methods, for determining an arm's-length price. . . .

Under the comparable-uncontrolled price method, the arm's-length price of a controlled sale is equal to the price paid in comparable uncontrolled sales. Uncontrolled sales for purposes of the comparable-uncontrolled price method include: (1) sales made by the taxpayer to an unrelated party, (2) purchases made by the taxpayer from unrelated parties, and (3) sales made between two unrelated parties. Controlled and uncontrolled sales are deemed comparable if the physical property and circumstances involved in the uncontrolled sales are identical to the physical property and circumstances involved in the controlled sales; or if such properties and circumstances are so nearly identical that any differences either have no effect on price, or can be measured and eliminated by making a reasonable number of adjustments to the price of the uncontrolled sales. Some of the differences which may affect the price of property are differences in quality of the product, terms of sale, intangible property associated with the sale, time of the sale, the level of the market, and the geographic market in which the sale takes place.

We find that the physical property and circumstances involved in the sales to petitioner are not identical in all respects to the physical property and circumstances relating to the parts sold to SABENA [the customer alleged by the taxpayer to be comparable]. SABENA agreed to handle for petitioner and SunPac those parts most relevant to airline customers operating in Europe, the Middle East and Africa, and which turned over in inventory within four months. Furthermore, only FAA PMA parts could be sold to SABENA. Petitioner, on the other hand, was willing to accept any and all of the parts SunPac manufactured, regardless of how quickly the parts turned over in inventory or whether SunPac had its FAA PMA certifications. Thus, SunPac did not sell SABENA all of the types of parts it produced while it did sell all types to petitioner. Moreover, SunPac sold some unfinished parts and defective parts to petitioner for which petitioner incurred the costs of finishing, reworking, or scrapping. No semi-finished parts were included in the SABENA consignment inventory. SunPac, moreover, bore the costs for reworking or replacing any defective parts assigned to SABENA.

Based on the available record, we conclude that the comparable-uncontrolled price method . . . is not applicable to the transactions involved in this case.

Neither party argues the applicability of the resale-price method in this case nor does the record contain sufficient information upon which we could make a determination under that method. . . .

Under the cost-plus method, an arm's-length price is determined by adding to the seller's cost of producing the property involved in the controlled sale the gross profit percentage (expressed as a percentage of cost) earned on the uncontrolled sale or sales of property most similar to the controlled sales in question.

Since the comparable companies all acted as subcontractors to other prime contractors, we cannot conclude that the aerospace product sales of these companies are sufficiently similar to SunPac's sales to petitioner to derive the appropriate gross profit percentage. Moreover, the record does not contain sufficient information for us to determine what differences in the uncontrolled and controlled sales warrant adjustments to the arm's-length price or whether the costs of producing the property involved in the uncontrolled sales or the costs which entered into the computation of the gross profit percentage calculated by respondent were computed in a consistent manner as the costs of producing the SunPac parts. . . . Therefore, we conclude that the cost-plus method is not applicable here.

*(continued)*

*(continued)*

We hold that for 1977 and 1978 the arm's-length consideration for SunPac parts is the applicable catalog price, less a discount of 20 percent. In arriving at this discount rate we have relied heavily on certain sales and/or distribution agreements petitioner had with unrelated third parties and on certain representations petitioner made to the U.S. Customs Service.

We believe that under the circumstances here, as revealed in this record, petitioner's catalog prices for spare parts are the appropriate starting point for establishing an arm's-length consideration for the SunPac parts. The record shows that generally petitioner sold its CSD parts to all unrelated purchasers . . . at the catalog price, without any discount. However, petitioner did have some history of granting discounts for some of its aerospace products.

For example, on several occasions, petitioner entered into distribution agreements with various firms relating to the distribution by these firms of certain aerospace products manufactured by petitioner. Petitioner paid these firms commissions, or gave them discounts, ranging from five percent . . . to 20 percent. . . .

Furthermore, since petitioner had to resell the SunPac parts at the catalog price to its own customers, the Spare Parts Lists prices establish the outermost boundary for the prices petitioner would be willing to pay an unrelated third party. We believe that petitioner would demand a discount rate from the catalog price from an unrelated third party which would allow petitioner to recover its costs and give it a reasonable profit.

In early 1976, petitioner represented to the U.S. Customs Service that petitioner estimated its costs to act as a distributor of the SunPac parts would range between 9.5 percent and 13.5 percent of the catalog prices. This determination does not take into account internal use of the SunPac parts,

the costs of defective or unfinished parts, or the cost of inspecting the parts until SunPac received its FAA PMA certification.

Petitioner's management employees who testified at the trial regarding the transfer price issue impressed us as astute businessmen. Around the time that these men arrived at the 15 percent discount rate for SunPac parts, they estimated petitioner's costs to distribute the parts to between 9.5 percent and 13.5 percent. In February 1977, petitioner examined its costs to distribute parts as spare parts only. Petitioner concluded then that there was no need to change its pricing system for SunPac parts. Therefore, we believe that, had SunPac been an unrelated manufacturer, petitioner would not have accepted a discount rate of less than 15 percent for the finished parts it would sell.

At the time, however, petitioner anticipated it would use approximately 50 percent of the SunPac parts internally. It also knew that some of the parts would be unfinished. Other distributors of aerospace parts commonly received a discount off catalog of at least 20 percent. Those aerospace products presumably were finished parts only. In 1976, when petitioner and SunPac entered into the Distributor Agreement, SunPac did not have its own FAA PMA certification. Therefore, it had no prospects of selling the SunPac parts directly to airline customers or overhaul centers in the near future. Consequently, considering these circumstances, we believe that, had SunPac been unrelated to petitioner, petitioner would have demanded, and SunPac would have agreed to give, a discount at least equal to the 20 percent discount petitioner gave to Standard Aircraft and Avio-Diepen for finished Pesco spare parts. Consequently, we find that a discount rate of 20 percent is appropriate here.

**Decision.** The United States Court of Claims dismissed Bank of America's petitions for a tax credit.

---

In the 1992 presidential elections, abuse of transfer pricing by foreign corporations became a significant campaign issue. It seems that foreign firms collectively reported a return on assets that was only one-third of comparable domestic competitors—suggesting widespread underreporting. As a result of the notoriety that the problem received, the Internal Revenue Service

enacted new regulations to increase reporting in the area in order to permit detection of evasion. The basic structure of transfer pricing, however, remained in place. Despite much discussion of "minimum taxes" against foreign corporations doing business in the United States, the threat of foreign retaliation against U.S. firms cooled legislators' ardor.

**Foreign Sales Corporations.**    Virtually all nations provide incentives to companies that export. In the United States, tax incentives are provided in part through the *Foreign Sales Corporation Act.* Under this law, U.S. firms may create a foreign subsidiary, called a *foreign sales corporation* (FSC), to handle their export taxation. The U.S. parent may sell goods directly to the FSC who will resell them in export markets, or the parent may export directly overseas and pay a commission to the FSC for assisting in making the sale. The earnings of the FSC are called *foreign trade income.* Of the foreign trade income earned, just over one-third is taxable to the FSC at regular corporate rates. The earnings can be repatriated to the U.S. parent without incurring further tax liability.

A foreign sales corporation must meet certain requirements in order to obtain FSC tax status. The FSC must: (1) have no more than 25 shareholders (a "shared FSC"); (2) have at least one nonresident director; (3) have qualified "export activity," including the sale of goods and certain service activities (excluding intellectual property, oil, and gas); (4) have management outside the U.S. in one of the countries approved by the Treasury Department; (5) hold all director and shareholder meetings outside the U.S.; (6) make all disbursements of cash from non-U.S. banks; and (7) participate in soliciting, negotiating, or contracting with a foreign party (advertising is insufficient to qualify). Companies involved in a shared FSC can sometimes obtain export trading company immunity from U.S. antitrust laws so that they may divide export territories, use common export marketing plans, share export pricing information, and engage in other joint marketing activities. They do not normally share profits or bear the risks of the sale of each other's products.

## Laws Prohibiting Foreign Control

Virtually every country prohibits entities controlled by foreigners in particularly sensitive sectors. As noted previously, the United States outlaws foreign control in fields such as telecommunications, air transportation, and government procurement. Governments that feel more insecure about foreigners tend to exclude foreign-controlled investments from more sectors of their economies. Until the recent privatization trend, Mexico generally prohibited 100 percent foreign investment, permitting it only in 34 designated industrial activities. The Mexican government permitted its bureaucracy to add to or subtract from that list, depending on changing conditions. More recently, the laws have been changed to give government officials discretion to permit 100 percent foreign ownership in many industries and majority shares in even more.

Other countries are even more restrictive, permitting foreign control only in sectors in which they have the greatest interest in development. India and China, for example, have until recent years generally permitted full foreign ownership only in firms that manufacture exclusively for export. Such firms were tolerated because they earned needed foreign exchange for the host country. India and China also permitted high levels of foreign majority ownership in high-technology firms. In that instance, the overwhelming desire for modernization outweighed distrust of foreign control.

Finally, a few nations such as North Korea are so xenophobic that they do not permit foreign majority ownership at all. The collapse of the Communist system and the extreme unavailability of capital to isolationist nations in the 1990s, however, has pushed nearly all countries to accept foreign majority ownership. Even formally communist nations such as Cuba and Vietnam now permit foreigners to own and control investments within their borders.

An example of the evolution in anti-majority ownership laws was seen in the Commonwealth of Independent States. The joint venture law passed in the Soviet Union in January 1987 limited foreign ownership in a joint venture to 49 percent or less. Although the law sought to promote foreign investment and was widely publicized and discussed in the West, restrictions on ownership and other barriers to foreign investment continued to limit the number of entrepreneurs willing to risk investing in the Soviet Union. In December 1988, responding to criticisms of its 1987 law, the Soviet Union passed another law that, among other things, eliminated the 49 percent ownership requirement. The foreign investment laws of the Russian Federation and most of the Commonwealth of Independent States (CIS) republics also have become even more accepting of foreign participation in all sectors of the economy.

## Effects of Prohibition of Control

Investors prize control of foreign ventures highly. Firms that have valuable technology or know-how fear that it could be transferred into unfriendly hands. Investors that are more interested in the long-term equity growth of the joint venture are vitally interested in guiding the venture's progress through its startup period and in holding the reins as the venture matures.

Accordingly, investor reaction to legal measures prohibiting control has always been negative. India's enactment of a general 40 percent limitation on foreign ownership, for example, led to a 55 percent drop in foreign investment between 1975 and 1987. Similarly, Mexico's enactment of a 49 percent foreign investment limit—since modified in most industries outside of the petroleum sector—led to an abrupt reduction of foreign investment from over 10 percent of all private investment to about 3 percent. Just as the flight of foreign capital has made nationalization an endangered species, the need for foreign capital has reversed the trend toward broad prohibition of foreign control. Thus, the U.S. investor might hope to see a more open environment for commercial activities in future years, involving a greater tolerance for foreign-controlled private entities as well as a larger number of sectors of the economy in which foreigners can invest. Indeed, through the process of privatization, U.S. investors increasingly are buying into sectors of the economy that recently had been owned by the state.

> **http://www.wto.org**
> The WTO home page.

> **http://www.wto.org/wto/links/**
> **wtolinks.htm**
> Go to this site for links on related topics through the WTO.

## Controlling Currency Risk

One of the most distinctive aspects of doing business outside of the United States is currency risk. *Currency risk* simply does not exist in domestic transactions. An entrepreneur who makes an investment in a domestic business is principally concerned with its operational profitability. If the investment is in an enterprise that will be earning foreign currency, however, the entrepreneur must also consider fluctuation risk, inconvertibility risk, and non-transfer risk.

*Fluctuation risk* is simply the likelihood that the currency of the country in which the U.S. investor has put its money will devalue against the U.S. dollar. For example, from late 1994 through early 1995, a series of disclosures as to Mexico's trade balances caused the Mexican peso suddenly to devalue 30 percent against the U.S. dollar. When a foreign currency devalues against the dollar, the value of the investment's profit—and the rate of return on the entrepreneur's dollar investment—declines. Furthermore, if the U.S. investor borrowed the U.S. dollars that it invested abroad, a dollar devaluation may prevent the investment from generating enough U.S. dollars to repay the debt.

*Inconvertibility risk* is the risk that the government of a country with soft currency, in which the U.S. investor has put its money, will hinder the entrepreneur from trading the foreign currency back into U.S. dollars. A *soft currency* is one that is not freely exchangeable on public markets for currencies of other nations. To obtain hard currencies such as the U.S. dollar in soft-currency countries, one must generally go through the country's government, which will exchange the local currency for dollars at an "official rate," usually a rate favorable to the government.

In a soft-currency nation, hard currency is in short supply. At the time of the initial investment, the U.S. investor must often hand over its dollars to the local central bank, which will incorporate them into the government's hard currency reserves and exchange them for the local currency. To get dollars back for *cruzeiros,* for example, the U.S. investor must fill out an application and await a response. The government then decides who gets to exchange the local soft currency for its supply of hard currency.

Through a wide variety of diverse and imaginative ceilings, prohibitions, and controls, such governments often limit access to hard currency to foreigners seeking to take profits out of the local economy. The local country may, for instance, require central bank approval of all remittances, permitting the bank to place moratorium on remittances during periods that the government's hard currency needs exceed its resources. The nation may impose a huge surtax on out-of-country royalty fee remittances. It may prohibit remittances on returns on capital for a period of years after the initial investment. Remittances of fees from local subsidiaries to U.S. parent corporations may be limited or proscribed altogether. The most common and effective technique is for the government simply to sit on the investor's application indefinitely.

Because inconvertibility controls can effectively destroy profit, investors need to understand how to limit this risk. The U.S. entrepreneur's principal concern is how to limit the risk posed by the fact that the investment will be earning some other currency from an investment made in U.S. dollars. A broad assortment of financial instruments may be purchased to hedge against fluctuation risk, but such purely financial devices are beyond the scope of a legal textbook. A number of legal approaches can, however, minimize this risk even before hedging.

## Arrangements with the Soft-Currency Country

The most direct way of assuring access to hard currency is to obtain that access from the government of the soft-currency country. The essential problem in soft-currency countries is the great demand for a limited amount of hard currency. Accordingly, the queue for hard currency is long and when the investor finally gets to the front of the queue, it receives only its ration of foreign currency.

If the investor proposes bringing a desired industry to the soft-currency nation—a high-technology plant or a hard-currency earner—it can negotiate with the government in advance for preferential access to hard currency. The resulting *currency exchange rights* can solve the inconvertibility problem for the foreign investor.

If preferential currency exchange rights prove unattainable, the U.S. investor may seek *import substitution rights* from the government. These rights are available when the new venture will manufacture a product in the soft-currency country that the nation had previously imported. In import substitution rights, the government permits the U.S. investor to repatriate profit up to the amount of money the country would have otherwise spent importing what the new venture is providing. Again, however, an investor must conclude this agreement before actually committing capital to the soft-currency nation.

## Payment and Price Adjustment Approaches

In most situations, the government will not be willing or legally able to provide the foreign investor either currency exchange or import substitution rights. The investor must therefore create legal structures for its investment that will maximize the U.S. dollar resources of the foreign venture. One way to protect against currency risk is through the structure of payments back to the U.S. investor.

First, whenever possible, the investor should negotiate for lump sum, hard-currency payments as early as possible rather than a series of future installments, even in situations in which one would normally extend installment financing in the domestic context. Thus, even in a royalty deal for intellectual property, the investor may opt for a single payment for the present value of the anticipated income stream.

This up-front payment avoids the uncertainty of whether the foreign customer will receive hard-currency allocations in future years—a function not only of the nation's foreign exchange success but also of the investor's political prowess. Hard currency today is the best antidote to fluctuation and inconvertibility risk.

The obvious drawback with this approach is that foreign customers and foreign investments often cannot yield immediate cash. First, foreign ventures are startup operations, relying on future earnings to pay a return. Second, the approach does not work at all for a U.S. firm that plans to generate revenue by selling its products abroad for foreign currency.

A second approach is to build currency adjustment mechanisms into contractual payment terms through *profit margin preservation* provisions or *unitary index adjustment* factors. Under the profit margin preservation approach, the price or payment to the U.S. investor will be adjusted periodically to maintain the same profit margin by contractually identifying a cost structure in the relevant currency and agreeing to modify the price as the cost of the cost structure's elements change over time. Profit margin preservation, however, discloses the U.S. company's cost structure, which is often valuable information to its competitors and therefore highly confidential.

This serious problem does not exist if the parties provide for formulaic adjustment of payment terms based on an accepted unitary index. This index can be a commonly accepted measure of relative currency value or national inflation. The drawback of indexes is that they are frequently independent of the facts of the transaction. In addition, many public indices relating to soft-currency values are notoriously unreliable.

Finally, neither the profit margin preservation nor the unitary index adjustment approach addresses the issue of repatriation. In other words, if one's cost structure is stated in zlotys or adjusted to an acceptable index, one is protected against 300 percent devaluation against the dollar, but one has no way of exchanging one's many zlotys for dollars.

## Structuring of Hard-Currency Obligations and Revenues

Another series of methodologies for dealing with currency risk involves structuring transactions so as to conserve U.S. dollar resources. An investor can achieve this type of risk reduction by avoiding dollar-denominated obligations and by conserving hard currency earned by the venture.

Few investments are funded entirely through contributions of equity from the entrepreneur. In most cases, the entrepreneur borrows a significant portion of the capital necessary to launch the venture. An important rule in currency risk avoidance in a venture that will be generating local currency revenues is to borrow that money, to the greatest extent possible, in local currency.

In that way, the local outpost will be able to use its revenues directly to service its obligations without being concerned about the vagaries of the international currency markets or the whims of local authorities who control access to hard currencies.

The Mexican peso devaluation also illustrates this point. Emboldened by the passage of NAFTA in 1994, many North American entrepreneurs came to regard the peso's exchange rate to the dollar as relatively stable. Because Mexican loan interest rates were significantly higher than U.S. rates—because international financiers considered the peso more volatile—many U.S. investors borrowed money for their Mexican projects in dollars in the United States. But when the peso crashed in late 1994 and early 1995, the pesos the Mexican ventures earned suddenly were worth 30 percent less in dollars; the ventures could no longer make their debt payments and went into bankruptcy. On the other hand, those investors who had borrowed in pesos fared much better. The peso had dropped in value relative to the dollar, but within Mexico it still was the unit of exchange; the ventures could simply continue to use their pesos within Mexico to pay their debts. In fact, because the devaluation was accompanied by some inflation, those with fixed interest rate debt actually had to devote less of their cash flow to debt service. Of course, the value of their profits in dollars did fall, but many took the excess pesos to purchase, at bargain rates, ventures being abandoned by those who had shown less foresight in their borrowing structure.

The same rule applies with respect to contracts between the venture and *trade creditors,* the entities that sell supplies or services to the venture. To the greatest extent possible, the venture should buy locally so that it can pay for the goods and services in local currency. This again conserves the enterprise's hard currency resources so that as much of these resources as possible can be available for transfer back to the U.S. investor.

If the investor anticipates that the foreign venture will experience significant hard-currency earnings, it should take steps to prevent the hard currency from re-entering the soft-currency country. Instead of transferring payment for the foreign venture's products directly to the venture, hard-currency customers would be instructed to pay the U.S. investor directly. The investor takes what the foreign venture owes it in debt payments, fees, or dividends and transfers the balance to the foreign venture.

Through a related approach, the U.S. investor "calls" a percentage of the foreign venture's production. In other words, the investor actually finds hard-currency customers, sells the product to them, obtains the payment, takes its agreed upon share, and transfers the remaining share to the venture. This practice is particularly common in situations in which the foreign venture is the manufacturing or assembling arm of the U.S. investor.

## Countertrade

*Countertrade* is a particularly popular way of dealing with currency inconvertibility. In countertrade, local currency earnings are used to purchase local products, which are then exported to a hard-currency country for sale. The proceeds of the hard-currency sale are then converted into dollars and returned to the U.S. investor.

A particularly innovative example of countertrade was pioneered by PepsiCo, Inc. Pepsi was faced with the prospect of holding a large amount of volatile rubles for the sale of its soft drink products in the Russian Federation, which it wished to exchange promptly for dollars. To resolve its dilemma, Pepsi structured a complex multiparty transaction whereby rubles were used to purchase Russian mushrooms for Pepsi's Pizza Hut affiliate. Pizza Hut then paid Pepsi for the mushrooms the dollar amounts that it would have otherwise had to spend.

The principal difficulty with countertrade is that the U.S. investor must find a supply of quality local goods that are in demand in hard-currency countries. After all, if the country had many such goods, it probably would not be a soft-currency country.

---

*Foreign Accents*

# The Cultural Environment
## Negotiating the Investment Contract

The need to be wary of cultural differences in international business was illustrated in a recent corporate acquisition. After substantial negotiation, a U.S. company was on the verge of signing an agreement to acquire a significant portion of a Swiss company for a stated amount of Swiss francs. Under the terms of the agreement, the deal would be closed and money would change hands one month after the agreement was signed. In the interim, the Swiss company would seek shareholder approval and comply with other corporate requirements.

This U.S. company, although quite large, had virtually no experience in international transactions, because it had grown in the vast U.S. market. On the eve of signing, the U.S. negotiators realized that, under the agreement, they would assume 100 percent of the currency fluctuation risk for the one-month waiting period. During that time, the Swiss franc could rise against the U.S. dollar, making the deal significantly more expensive. If, on the other hand, they bought dollars a month in advance, they took the risk that the shareholders would not approve the transaction and the U.S. dollar would rise against the Swiss franc. Startled, they demanded that the purchase price be renegotiated in dollars.

Because a Swiss company must sell outside of the tiny Swiss market to become large, its typical deal is international. Thus, to the Swiss, it was simply unbelievable that a vast U.S. concern would be so ignorant of the currency futures market. Indeed, the somewhat smaller Swiss firm had an entire department devoted to acquiring currency risk protection every day. They initially interpreted the U.S. demand as a ploy and considered walking away from the table.

Fortunately, the high level of trust and good feeling that had been built during the negotiations pulled the parties through. After determining that the U.S. negotiators were sincerely confused, the Swiss familiarized them with some currency protection options, and the deal was done.

## Informal Consortia or Parallel Exchanges

In some soft-currency countries, foreign investors form consortia to trade local soft currency. At various times, some members of a consortium would have more of the local currency that they can get rid of, while others may need more than they can earn to develop profitable business. By broadening the base of foreign investors, a private *parallel exchange* is thereby formed in countries without a formal currency exchanges.

One of the most notable of these consortia was the American Trade Consortium formed in the Russian Federation in the spring of 1988, which permitted U.S. firms to freely exchange currencies among themselves. This consortium permitted U.S. firms to exchange currency at market, rather than artificial official rates, and provided immediate availability in the midst of fiscal chaos.

The parallel exchange has long existed among hard-currency investors in Latin American countries. The key to participating in these informal exchanges is to be sure that the U.S. investor does not inadvertently violate local currency exchange laws.

## Inconvertibility Insurance

A final alternative for the U.S. investor is an *inconvertibility/non-transfer insurance* policy. Such policies can be purchased for *"hard blockages"*—when the government actually passes a law that prevents conversion or transfer. For a somewhat higher fee, a businessperson may purchase a policy that also protects against *"soft blockages,"* excessive delays in processing a request to convert or transfer by the local government authorities. Protected items can include repatriation of profits, dividends, loan repayments, management and royalty fees, technical assistance fees, and any other form of income considered to be earnings or return on capital. Inconvertibility insurance is a type of political risk insurance and is provided to companies in the same manner as other forms of political risk insurance (described in Chapter Nineteen).

## Chapter Summary

Companies operating in other countries must abide by that nation's laws. The level of foreign investment regulation in a given country depends on a number of factors, including the amount of foreign currency reserves, whether the government favors central control, and their fear of foreign control. In minority ownership investments (owning less that 50 percent of the enterprise), an investor can have either an active investment and participate in managing the enterprise, or a passive investment that provides only equity capital managed by others. Many countries create a legal structure that limits foreign majority control of businesses. For the more active investor, a joint venture is often the best form of foreign investment. Local traditions, regulations, and tax laws all influence what form of joint venture is most attractive.

Currency risk in foreign business transactions comes in two forms. Fluctuation risk for a U.S. investor in the likelihood that the value of a given foreign currency will decrease against the value of the U.S. dollar. Inconvertibility risk occurs in soft-currency countries. Governments that do not allow their currency to be exchanged in public international markets often lack a supply of hard currency they can use in conducting business with other countries. Because of their low reserves of easily exchangeable currency, these countries often limit repatriation of foreign profits through a wide range of regulations, such as central bank approvals for money transfers, surtaxes, and legal prohibitions.

These risks can be minimized by hedging with a variety of financial instruments, or through legal approaches such as prior arrangements with the soft-currency government, payment and price adjustments, countertrade, consortia or parallel exchanges, and inconvertibility insurance.

## QUESTIONS AND CASE PROBLEMS

1. Keefe Energy, Inc., a U.S. firm, enters into a joint venture with Energia Guerra, S.A., a Mexican firm, to build and operate a coal-fired electric-power-generating plant with an estimated useful life of 35 years. The building and land will be owned by G/K, S.A., a company 80-percent owned by Guerra and 20-percent owned by Keefe. G/K will enter into an agreement with Keefe under which Keefe is to build and operate the plant and receive 95 percent of the projected profit from the plant for the first 20 years of its operation. Is Keefe making a minority investment? What sort of scrutiny is the joint venture likely to receive from government officials?

2. Assume the same facts as in Question 1, except that the joint venture is to build and operate a computer microcircuit manufacturing plant. What different considerations come into play in government review? What is the likely outcome?

3. Aloysius Beardsky, famed American corporate raider, initiates a hostile takeover of Bundesbank Freidumia (BF), the largest commercial bank in Freidumia. In purchasing 70 percent of BF's shares, Beardsky pays a substantial premium for control. After he concludes the transaction, Freidumia outlaws any foreigner or person under foreign control from voting shares in a commercial bank corporation, thereby wresting control from Mr. Beardsky. Has a nationalization taken place? An expropriation?

4. What financing alternatives would be available to a U.S. firm that was interested in investing in a proposed manufacturing plant in a small country that recently left the communist bloc and did not wish to invest much of its own resources?

5. If a U.S. company establishes a 100 percent subsidiary in another country, what three general aspects of U.S. income tax law should the company be sure it has addressed?

6. What are the implications for an American who purchases shares in a German company on the basis of inside information?

## MANAGERIAL IMPLICATIONS

You work for Luree Intergalactic, Inc., a Montana Alpine ski manufacturer. Because of attractive relative labor costs found in Latvia, Luree joins forces with Aivars, AG, a Latvian firm, to build a new factory in Riga to serve the European market. Together, Luree and Aivars establish Udris, Ltd., a Latvian joint stock company that will own the factory and sell products from it. Udris will be free to sell its skis to anyone, but expects to sell most of its initial output to Luree and Aivars. Under an agreement between Luree and Aivars, Luree will purchase skis from Udris for resale in Europe east of Ukraine, and in North and South America, New Zealand, and Japan; Aivars will market the remaining portion of Udris's production to the rest of the world.

1. Because Luree has greater financial resources than does Aivars, its capital contribution will entitle it to 90 percent of Udris. Aivars also recognizes that it has received the less attractive ski markets. It expects to derive most of its income from a special contract with Udris to test new ski models on mogul runs. Prepare a memorandum that anticipates what principal corporate law concerns will need to be addressed in this arrangement.

2. Aivars suggests that, as compensation for being Udris's first customers, Luree and Aivars receive a discount off the price that Udris charges other purchasers. Analyze the transfer pricing issues raised by this proposal.

# Chapter Nineteen

# Political Risk: Nationalization, Expropriation, and Other Takings of Investment

The preceding chapters discussed the gradual progression of commitment by a U.S. investor in a nation from appointment of representative through transfer of intellectual property rights and commitment of capital resources abroad. Up to now, the discussion has covered the increasing vulnerability to regulation under the laws of the host country. In a sense, the differences in risk that follow from doing business in the United States are only of degree and local peculiarity. After all, the United States also has similar regulations.

Political risk is an altogether different kind of risk. Perhaps the most elementary and important distinction between investment in the United States and investment abroad is that the foreign government might simply take one's investment without paying full compensation. Thus, a central element in understanding the risks attendant to foreign investment is understanding *political risk* and how it can be avoided.

## International Theories Relating to Takings of Foreign Property

Western legal scholars have debated the propriety of taking of foreign property for hundreds of years. This dialectic can be summarized in two major theories: the *traditional* theory and the *modern traditional* theory.

## Traditional Theory: The Prohibition of All Takings

The classic doctrine on the taking of the property of foreign citizens was developed in Europe from the 17th through the 19th centuries. Because the European states were capital exporters during that period, the doctrine was predictably protective of foreign investment. As early as 1646, Hugo Grotius enunciated the fundamental principle that foreign investors, unlike local merchants, should be exempt from the sovereign's condemnation rights: "The right of subjects then differs from the right of foreigners in this, that over those who are in no way subject, the power of eminent domain has no control."

In essence, the taking of foreign property was forbidden altogether. The state that took property had a duty of complete restitution to the foreign investors. Furthermore, as illustrated in the *Chorzow Factory* case, courts went to great pains to assure that the "taker" made absolutely full restitution.

---

BACKGROUND AND FACTS
During the First World War, the Chancellor of the German Empire contracted with the Bayerische Stickstoffwerke to construct a nitrate factory at Chorzow, Upper Silesia, then a part of Germany. On December 24, 1919, soon after the end of the fighting but before a final

### The Chorzow Factory
*1 World Court Reports 646 (1928)*
*Permanent Court of*
*International Justice*

peace treaty was signed, the Reich sold the factory to Oberschlesische Stickstoffwerke, A.G. for 110 million Reichsmarks. Under the acquisition documents, operation and management of the factory was to remain in the hands of the Bayerische.

*(continued)*

*(continued)*

A few months later, Germany and Poland signed the Geneva Convention, which ceded Upper Silesia to Poland as war reparation. After the signature of this Convention, but before the actual cession, the owner of Oberschlesische offered to a company from Geneva, Switzerland, an option for the purchase, at a price of 55 million Reichsmarks, of one-half of the Oberschlesische shares. This offer, however, came to nothing.

Two years later, the Polish Court of Huta Krolewska decreed that the registration of the Oberschlesische as owner of the factory was to be canceled and that the right of ownership was to be registered in the name of the Polish treasury. Relief for this alleged expropriation was sought by the Germans in the International Court of Justice.

JUDGES ANZILOTTI, HUBER, FINLAY, LODER, NYHOLM, DE BUSTAMANTE, ALTAMIRA, ODA, PESSOA, BEICHMAN, RABEL, AND EHRLICH

The action of Poland which the Court has judged to be contrary to the Geneva Convention . . . is a seizure of property, rights, and interests which could not be expropriated even against compensation. . . .

It follows that the compensation due to the German government is not necessarily limited to the value of the undertaking at the moment of dispossession, plus interest to the day of payment. This limitation would only be admissible if the Polish government had had the right to expropriate. . . . [I]n the present case, such a limitation might result in placing . . . the interests [for which] the German government is acting, in a situation more unfavorable than that in which . . . these interests would have been if Poland had respected the said Convention. Such a consequence would [be] incompatible with . . . the prohibition, in principle, of the liquidation of the property, rights, and interests of German nationals. . . .

The essential principle contained in the actual notion of an illegal act—a principle which seems to be established by international practice and in particular by the decisions of arbitral tribunals—is that reparation must, as far as possible, wipe out all the consequences of the illegal act and reestablish the situation which would, in all probability, have existed if that act had not been committed. Restitution in kind, or, if this is not possible, payment of a sum corresponding to the value which a restitution in kind would bear; the award, if need be, of damages for loss sustained which would not be covered by restitution in kind or payment in place of it—such are the principles which should serve to determine the amount of compensation due for an act contrary to international law.

The dispossession of an industrial undertaking . . . then involves the obligation to restore the undertaking and, if this be not possible, to pay its value at the time of the indemnification, which value is designed to take the place of restitution which has become impossible. To this obligation, in virtue of the general principles of international law, must be added that of compensating loss sustained as the result of the seizure.

[I]t is by no means impossible that the cost of construction of a factory may not correspond to the value which that factory will have when built. This possibility must more particularly be considered when, as in the present case, the factory was built by the state in order to meet the imperious demands of public necessity and under exceptional circumstances such as those created by the war.

Nor yet can the Court, on the other hand, be satisfied, with the price stipulated in the contract of December 24th, 1919, between the Reich, the Oberschlesische and [Oberschlesische's corporate parent], or with the offer of sales of the shares of the Oberschlesische to the Geneva Compagnie. . . . [T]he moment of the contract of sale and that of the negotiations with the Genevese Company belong to a period of serious economic and monetary crisis; the difference between the value which the undertaking then had and that which it would have had at present may therefore be very considerable. And further, it must be considered that . . . the offer to the Genevese Company is probably to be explained by the fear of measures such as those which the Polish Government in fact adopted afterwards against the Chorzow undertaking. . . .

This being the case, and in order to obtain further enlightenment in the matter, the Court . . . will arrange for the holding of an expert enquiry. . . . This expert enquiry . . . will refer to the following questions:

I. A. What was the value [at the time of the taking], expressed in Reichsmarks current at the present time, of the undertaking for the manufacture of nitrate products . . . in the state in which that undertaking (including the lands, buildings, equipment, stocks and processes at its disposal, supply and delivery contracts, goodwill, and future prospects) was, on the date indicated, in the hands of the Bayerische and Oberschlesische Stickstoffwerke?

*(continued)*

*(continued)*

B. What would have been the financial results, expressed in Reichsmarks current at the present time (profits or losses), which would probably have been given by the undertaking thus constituted from [that date] to the date of the present judgment, if it had been in the hands of the said companies?

II. What would be the value of the present judgment, expressed in Reichsmarks current at the present time, of the same undertaking (Chorzow) if that undertaking . . . had remained in the hands of the

Bayerische and Oberschlesische Stickstoffwerke, and had either remained substantially as it was in 1922 or had been developed proportionately on lines similar to those applied in the case of other undertakings of the same kind, controlled by the Bayerische, for instance, the undertaking of which the factory is situated at Piesteritz?

**Decision.** The Permanent Court of International Justice ordered an expert inquiry to proceed to arrive at a restitution award in accordance with the terms of the foregoing opinion.

## Modern Traditional Theory: "Prompt, Adequate, and Effective" Compensation for Takings

In its most extreme form, the traditional doctrine afforded a foreign investor even more protection than a local investor had. The local investor was subject to expropriation by the sovereign under the legal doctrine of *eminent domain*. For example, a government can condemn a U.S. citizen's land if it needs the land to build a highway, so long as it compensates that citizen for the fair value of the land. Under the traditional theory, however, the foreign investor was exempt from such takings. This made some sense in the context of the pre-20th-century international system in which citizens of the advanced mercantile or industrial countries were considered wholly immune from the judicial power of the less-developed host state. As the sovereign equality of nations be-

came accepted, however, the traditional doctrine developed to a point that the foreign investor now has no greater rights than the domestic investor.

Developed in the 20th century, this traditional theory is known, somewhat oxymoronically, as the *modern traditional theory*. It recognizes the sovereign's right to nationalize foreign-owned property, but places conditions on the proper exercise of that right. The exercise of the right must be (1) for a public purpose; (2) nondiscriminatory, not directed specifically against a foreign person; and (3) accompanied by *prompt, adequate, and effective compensation*. Thus, a sovereign cannot take foreign property for harassment, personal aggrandizement, or other nonpublic purposes, and cannot target the property of one nationality discriminatorily. Moreover, compensation must be paid. To modern traditional thinkers, "adequate" compensation meant fair market value as a

**BACKGROUND AND FACTS**
Agrarian expropriations began in Mexico in 1915. As of August 30, 1927, 1,621 moderate-sized properties of American citizens had been taken. Subsequent to 1927, additional properties, chiefly farms of a moderate size, with a value claimed by their owners of $10,132,388, were expropriated by the Mexican government. The claims of their owners were referred to a General Claims Commission established by agreement between the two govern-

*Diplomatic Note from the Secretary of State of the United States of America to the Minister of Foreign Affairs of Mexico*
*July 21, 1938*
*United States Department of State*

ments, but as of 1938, when Secretary Hull sent his letter, not a single claim had been adjusted and none had been paid.

SECRETARY OF STATE
CORDELL HULL
The taking of property without compensation is not expropriation. It is confiscation. It is no less confiscation because there may be an expressed intent to pay

*(continued)*

*(continued)*

at some time in the future. If it were permissible for a government to take the private property of the citizens of other countries and pay for it as and when, in the judgment of that government, its economic circumstances and its local legislation may perhaps permit, the safeguards which the constitutions of most countries and established international law have sought to provide would be illusory. Governments would be free to take property far beyond their ability or willingness to pay, and the owners thereof would be without recourse. We cannot question the right of a foreign government to treat its own nationals in this fashion if it so desires. This is a matter of domestic concern. But we cannot admit that foreign government may take the property of American nationals in disregard of the rule of compensation under international law. Nor can we admit that any government unilaterally and through its municipal legislation can, as in this instant case, nullify this universally accepted

principle of international law, based as it is on reason, equity and justice. . . .

The whole structure of friendly intercourse, of international trade and commerce, and many other vital and mutually desirable relations between nations indispensable to their progress rest upon the single and hitherto solid foundation of respect on the part of governments and of peoples for each other's rights under international justice. The right of prompt and just compensation for expropriated property is a part of this structure. It is a principle to which the government of the United States and most governments of the world have emphatically subscribed and which they have practiced and which must be maintained. It is not a principle which freezes the status quo and denies changes in property rights but a principle that permits any country to expropriate private property within its borders in furtherance of public purposes. It enables orderly change without violating the legitimately acquired interests of the citizens of other countries.

going concern, including future earnings and intangibles; "prompt" meant as soon as reasonable; and "effective" meant cash or a commodity immediately available and freely convertible to cash. This modern traditionalism was eloquently advanced by Secretary of State Cordell Hull in his response to the expropriations triggered by the Mexican Revolution.

This modern traditional theory is accepted as customary international law among the countries that have historically been capital exporters: the North American and Western European nations. A large number of arbitrations in the 1970s and 1980s arising out of the expropriation of foreign oil holdings by oil pronouncements of the Iran–United States Claims Tribunal in The Hague seem to have confirmed that modern traditional theory remains the accepted international standard.

Thus, while an overseas investment is normally subject to the host country's sovereign right to expropriate, in Western developed countries the investor should be entitled, under customary international law, to full compensation—at least if the investor can obtain arbitration of the dis-

pute. The modern traditional theory, however, has not been accepted everywhere.

## Non-Western Theories: The Preeminence of the Sovereign Rights of the State

The traditional requirement of full compensation has been questioned or rejected in many parts of the world. The foreign investor must therefore be aware of the extent of that risk in order to understand how to limit it.

**Sources of Rejection.** The first intellectual counterpoint to the traditional theory came from Latin America in the nineteenth century through the so-called *Calvo Doctrine*. As described in greater detail in the next section, Argentine Professor Carlos Calvo placed the sovereign ahead of the foreign investor within the sovereign's territory and challenged any intervention by foreign states in investment disputes as a violation of the territorial jurisdiction of the host country. Calvo proponents argue that nationalization is a legitimate exercise of the sovereign's preeminent right to restructure the economy and is not subject to the law of any other jurisdiction, including international law. The appropriate recourse of the foreign investor, argued Calvo, should be no greater than that of any domestic investor: to appeal to the courts or political branches of the sovereign nation taking the "nationalizing" action. No foreign nation or entity had any right to impose itself simply because the investor happened to be of foreign origin.

The emphasis of the Calvo Doctrine on the primacy of the state corresponded nicely with the concept of state property inaugurated by the Bolshevik Revolution. To communists, the theory that the sovereign state had a right to restructure its own economy was consistent with the unprecedented scale of expropriations that followed the events of November 1917. Other communist states followed the Soviet example.

Finally, when Europe's former Asian and African colonies became politically independent in the years following World War II, they came to view nationalization as a *sine qua non* of economic independence. In their view, as long as foreigners controlled the economy, they effectively controlled the country, irrespective of who nominally controlled the political apparatus. The newly emerging states could not begin to pay full compensation for such nationalizations. Hence, the communist-sovereign state countertheories seemed quite persuasive.

In short, for entirely different but complementary reasons, over the past hundred years much of the world rejected traditional theory and adopted theories that in one way or another asserted that the state had a right to take foreign property upon payment of less than full compensation. Whatever the intellectual basis for the takings, for the foreign investor, the results were the same. Its property was taken and the investor was paid less than the property was worth.

In recent years, the number of adherents to sovereign rights theories have been in a steep decline. When Latin American countries defaulted on their loans from North American and European banks, capital for their economies dried up. As a prerequisite of attracting new capital investment—in many cases for the re-privatization of assets these countries had nationalized—they were compelled to assure prospective foreign investors that future investment would be treated under the modern traditional theory. This was accomplished through both domestic legislation and international treaties. Similarly, when the Eastern European communist bloc collapsed in the 1989–91 period, the new democracies adopted modern traditional theory in a series of bilateral treaties so as to attract foreign investment. In the 1990s, former Asian colonies accepted the modern traditional theory as a prelude to attracting foreign capital. The sovereign rights club declined in size. Nonetheless, the theory to which they once subscribed remains alive as an intellectual force. In many of these nations, it may be no farther away than another change in the international economic climate.

**Public Purpose, Nondiscrimination, and the Expropriation/Nationalization Distinction.** Sovereign rights proponents like Professor Calvo rejected the modern traditional theory's "prerequisites" of public purpose and nondiscrimination. They argue that the right to take foreign property is an attribute of national sovereignty and, as such, cannot be conditioned on whether an international tribunal characterizes the taking as discriminatory or as furthering a private purpose. In essence, the sovereign has a right to take foreign property without having outsiders imposing preconditions.

Paradoxically, sovereign rights states have nevertheless incorporated public purpose concepts in deciding whether a taking is one that merits full compensation—an expropriation—or a nationalization, which merits less compensation. The classic *expropriation* is a taking of an isolated item of property. The foreign investor is singled out as the target of governmental action in a fashion that might be viewed as discriminatory and not part of a national public plan. By contrast, the prototype of a *nationalization* is the taking of an entire industry or a natural resource as part of a plan to restructure the nation's economic system. In this instance, the values underlying sovereign rights theories are most strongly implicated, and full compensation is not required by those theories.

One of the few nations that has recently not been precluded by treaty from espousing sovereign rights theories is the Islamic Republic of Iran. The INA Corporation arbitration demonstrates that some jurists still accept sovereign rights concepts.

## BACKGROUND AND FACTS

On May 3, 1978, a subsidiary of INA Corporation (INA), INA International Insurance Company, Ltd. (INA International), acquired 20 percent of the shares of Bimek Shargh, an Iranian insurance company. The proposed investment by INA International was approved by Central Insurance of Iran (CII), the government body responsible for the regulation of insurance activities in Iran, by a letter to Shargh of December 27, 1977. INA International paid 20 million rials for the shares of Shargh.

On June 25, 1979, the Law of Nationalization of Insurance and Credit Enterprises was enacted in Iran. Article 1 provided as follows:

> To protect the rights of the insured, to expand the insurance industry and the entire State and to place it at the service of the people, from the date of this law, all insurance enterprises in Iran are proclaimed nationalized with acceptance of the principle of legitimate conditional ownership.

By operation of this law, Shargh, along with other Iranian insurance companies, was brought under the control of a joint board of directors consisting of the president of CII, the executive director of Iran Insurance Company, and representatives from certain government ministries. INA's shares were annulled.

INA claimed U.S. $285,000 representing what it alleged to be the going value of its Shargh shares, together with interest and legal costs.

## JUDGE LAGERGREN

The essence of the dispute between the Parties lies not in the fact of nationalization having taken place, which is agreed, but in the determination of the level of compensation, if any, which should be paid to the shareholders of Shargh as a consequence. No compensation has been paid to date, INA argues for compensation that is "prompt, adequate and effective," on the basis both of general principles of international law and the Treaty of Amity, Economic Relations, and Consular Rights of 15 August 1955. INA asks the Tribunal to accept the amount of its initial investment in Shargh as the best available indicator of the value of the

### INA Corporation v. Islamic Republic of Iran
*8 Iran-U.S. Claims Tribunal Reports 373*
*Iran-United States Claims Tribunal*

company as a going concern at the time of nationalization just over one year later.

The respondent government concedes that, in principle, the working of Article I of the nationalization law does, in appropriate cases, envisage the payment of compensation to private shareholders of nationalized insurance companies, but that this must be based on the "net book value" of the company.

It has long been acknowledged that expropriations for a public purpose and subject to conditions provided for by law—notably that category which can be characterized as "nationalizations"—are not *per se* unlawful. A lawful nationalization will, however, impose on the government concerned the obligation to pay compensation.

This case presents, in addition, a classic example of a formal and systematic nationalization by decree of an entire category of commercial enterprises considered of fundamental importance to the nation's economy. During the course of the post-Revolutionary economic restructuring in Iran, the banks were nationalized on 7 June 1979. The insurance companies, including Bimek Shargh, were nationalized by decree on 27 June 1979, and then on 5 July 1979 there followed the nationalization of heavy industries. Such measures number among the risks which investors must be prepared to encounter.

In the event of such large-scale nationalizations of a lawful character, international law has undergone a gradual reappraisal, the effect of which may be to undermine the doctrinal value of any "full" or "adequate" (when used as identical to "full") compensation standard as proposed in the case.

However, the Tribunal is of the opinion that in a case such as the present, involving an investment of a rather small amount shortly before the nationalization, international law admits compensation in an amount equal to the fair market value of the investment.

**Decision.** The Iran–United States Claims Tribunal awarded INA Corporation $285,000 plus simple interest at 8.5 percent per annum from the date of nationalization.

The approach suggested by the panel in the *INA* case—less than full compensation in the event of any large-scale nationalization—remains a distinct minority view. Most international tribunals, including most panels of the Iran–United States Claims Tribunal, continue to adhere to the modern traditional theory. No less an authority than the Third Restatement of Foreign Relations Law, which ostensibly reflects the consensus view, states that less than full compensation may be acceptable in "exceptional circumstances" such as agricultural land reform. The modern traditional theory continues to be under attack.

**Level of Compensation.** Once it has been determined that a taking was a "nationalization," sovereign rights advocates uniformly reject the traditional formula of "prompt, adequate, and effective compensation." First, marshaling a variety of different arguments, they often disavow any obligation to provide fair market value compensation. With respect to the taking of lands or natural resources, for instance, they argue that the state already owns the resources and need pay only for the foreign owners' improvements to the land or resources.

If one scratches the surface of these arguments, one will uncover the practical point that the nation taking the goods cannot afford or does not wish to pay its fair market value. If, in the view of such a nation, a taking of foreign property is necessary for effective political independence, those imperatives override mere commercial considerations. Thus, a number of sovereign-rights states have favored measures of compensation that bear only an attenuated relationship to fair market value. An example is *net book value* of the nationalized business's asset, which reflects the depreciated cost of assets without regard to their appreciation over time or the "going concern value" of the business of which they are a part.

Second, sovereign rights states generally insist on the right to schedule payment of the compensation over time. This installment method has sometimes been accomplished through devices such as the issuance of national bonds payable in the local currency. In addition to being paid less than market value, the victim of nationalization must bear the risk of the devaluation of the local currency and of the local country's ability to repay. Because of these risks, such bonds might be transferable to others only at a further discount, if at all.

**Creeping Expropriation.** Short of outright expropriation, the foreign nation may impose regulations that gradually limit the exercise of ownership rights: so-called *creeping expropriation*. Creeping expropriation regulations include discriminatory taxes, legislative controls over management of the firm, price controls, forced employment of nationals, license cancellation, and, as discussed in Chapter Eighteen, restrictions on currency convertibility. Unlike straightforward expropriation, creeping expropriation requires a determination as to whether a "taking" or mere regulation has occurred before any compensation is deemed to be justified, making it even more dangerous to the foreign investor.

Investors in emerging nations need also concern themselves with the business consequences of politically unstable environments. For example, the Indonesian government's refusal to comply with International Monetary Fund mandates caused an economic crisis that sparked massive and destructive riots in Jakarta during the spring of 1998. This violence triggered coverage under each of the following insurance policies. Apart from causing widespread *physical damage* to business assets, such *"political violence"* created *business interruptions* to enterprises with operations in Indonesia. The violence and governmental countermeasures in many cases led to *forced abandonment* of projects by firm employees fleeing the country for their lives. All of these italicized words are *"casualties"* against which the prudent business manager will want to insure.

> *http://www.textor.com/cms/Political_Risk_Services.html*
> *See for publications on political risk.*

## Amelioration of Political Risk

As Latin American and Eastern European countries turn to the modern traditional theory, the sovereign rights approaches recede as threats. Indeed, former communist nations have turned so completely from the sovereign rights approach that they have created procedures for compensating Western firms for nationalizations that occurred many decades ago. The U.S. Foreign Claims Compensation Commission, which resolves claims by U.S. citizens against countries that have nationalized their assets without adequate compensation, has been aggressively pursuing U.S. claims in the new democracies.

It is too early, however, to forget the threat posed by the sovereign theorists. If economic conditions do not improve, today's modern traditionalist might be tomorrow's nationalizing government. As recently as 1995, for example, the head of privatization of the Russian Federation bemoaned the "excesses" of privatization and called for "re-nationalization" of selected privatized assets. The Communist Party, an electoral force to be reckoned with in the new Russia, to this day includes selective re-nationalization as a significant plank in its party platform. The bottom line is that the U.S. investor in countries that once espoused the sovereign rights countertheory is exposed to substantial risk of loss from political action. Its investment can be taken for a fraction of its true value. In addition, compensation can take the form of bonds in a tenuous currency that the investor cannot convert to dollars.

Having defined the problem, the investor must determine how to ameliorate it. The investor essentially has a choice of two ways of doing so: purchasing insurance against the event before it happens or bringing legal action against the wrongdoer after it happens.

## Political Risk Insurance

Entrepreneurs normally assume the risk that their business will fail because their service or product is unable to find an adequate market. Usually, however, the entrepreneurs will try to avoid the risk of failing due to extraneous events completely beyond their control, such as fire, earthquake, or employee dishonesty. To cover those risks, they normally contract with an insurance company, which assumes this risk for a fee called a *premium,* based on an actuarial assessment of the probability of loss among all of the company's insureds.

From this practice arose the general concept of insurance against political risk. Entrepreneurs who are unwilling to hazard the risk of a foreign

government taking will pay a premium to a public or private insurance concern, which will spread the cost over all of its insureds in an actuarially meaningful way.

Obviously, the cost of this insurance is a disincentive to investment abroad. In order for the U.S. investor to justify foreign investment, the anticipated increased marginal returns on the foreign venture as compared to a comparable domestic investment must be greater than the cost of the insurance. If political risk and the cost of insurance become too great, the foreign investment becomes financially unjustifiable. Indeed, the historic commitment of the United States to protecting private property from public seizure—eliminating political risk and political risk insurance—is one of the qualities that makes it one of the world's most attractive markets.

**Political Risk Insurance from Government Agencies.** A number of capital-exporting nations have established government corporations that provide political risk insurance. In the United States, Congress established the *Overseas Private Investment Corporation* (OPIC) in 1971. In essence, national agencies like OPIC hope to promote exports to foreign countries by guaranteeing investments in such countries. Thus, the underlying purpose is both good and bad for the U.S. investor; insurance is provided at rates that do not include a significant profit for the insurer, but is subject to politically motivated conditions that exclude many projects. For example, when India tested nuclear weapons in May 1998, OPIC funding for projects based in India immediately became unavailable. OPIC provides coverage to U.S. firms for expropriation (including creeping expropriation), nationalization, revolution, insurrections, and currency inconvertibility. Because it is a governmental program, however, the insurance is available only for projects that satisfy certain U.S. policy imperatives:

First, the investor must be a U.S. person. Although this is not an issue for most Americans, in the day of the multinational corporation, the answer to this question is not always clear.

Second, investments must not adversely affect the U.S. balance of payments or U.S. employment. Under this condition, the host country must not impose performance regulations that are likely to reduce "positive trade benefits likely to accrue to the United States." Obviously, many projects cannot possibly satisfy this requirement. A manufacturing joint venture that makes nothing but components for export back to the United States may not advance these objectives. Even if an investment can satisfy them, the investor must wait while OPIC goes through the administrative procedures necessary to ensure compliance.

Third, OPIC has been obliged to give preference to investments in countries with relatively low per capita annual income. This condition targets the insurance coverage to the poorest countries, which coincidentally also have the least viable infrastructure. It is precisely in those countries where the commercial risk is often so high that the foreign investor would not wish to enter, irrespective of the political risk.

Finally, OPIC can operate only in a country with which the United States has concluded a bilateral investment agreement. Because under these bilateral investment agreements the host country effectively agrees to waive its sovereign rights views on takings in disputes with the United States, some nations have not entered into them.

The OPIC scheme has had a significant effect. Its insurance volume is only a few billion dollars, a relatively small amount when one considers the hundreds of billions of dollars annually in international investments. OPIC and similar programs, however, act as catalysts for additional investment. Private insurers who would not invest in a particular nation by itself will participate in a group of political risk insurers led by OPIC. OPIC's unique ability to prevent foreign governments from misbehaving gives the greater assurance sometimes needed to obtain the necessary coverage. Nonetheless, OPIC cannot be everywhere. The U.S. investor must become familiar with other sources of political risk insurance.

A similar, but internationally based, investment insurance company is the *Multilateral Investment Guarantee Agency* (MIGA). Started in early 1988 as an independent affiliate of the World Bank, MIGA issues insurance guarantees to protect a foreign investor from expropriation,

war, revolution, or other noncommercial risks. MIGA guarantees are granted for 15-year terms. To qualify, both the investor's home country and the country into which it is investing must be parties to the MIGA convention. Most nations have joined MIGA, including the United States. Even though MIGA offers comprehensive protection to qualifying projects, the potential investor should be sensitive to its multilateral political nature.

**Private Political Risk Insurance.** Two principal markets provide private political risk insurance. Lloyds of London insurance *syndicates*—pools of money provided by investors to insure specific projects—provide such insurance on a case-by-case basis. In this market, the U.S. investor engages a broker for a specific transaction, and the broker negotiates terms with heads of syndicates specializing in political risk insurance. The syndicate heads then obtain commitments from other syndicates in order to spread the risk exposure.

Alternatively, the investor can approach a lead underwriter of a group operating under a *reinsurance treaty,* an agreement with other insurers whereby the underwriter spreads the risk. Under the terms of the reinsurance treaty, the lead underwriter can commit the resources of the entire group after negotiating the transaction with the U.S. investor.

Private insurance has many advantages. Private insurers have no political agendas and therefore have no special political prerequisites to issuing insurance. The host country need not be destitute and the foreign investor can hail from anywhere. In addition, the private insurance approval process can be faster than is the case with public agencies.

Private insurers, however, are in business for profit. Accordingly, their coverage can be quite expensive as compared to the government programs. Second, private syndicates will often not enter particularly politically volatile areas without a public agency as a partner. Third, the term of private insurance policies is generally limited to five to seven years, longer than in the past but still too short for an adequate return from larger capital-intensive construction projects.

In recent years, trends toward the modern traditional theory and international investment treaties and codes, have lowered the perceived risk of political risk insurance. The result has been an explosion in the availability of such insurance.

# 1998 RIMS Report
## Political Risk Creates Need to Choose Strategy

Political risk insurance is becoming more widely available and on better terms for the commercial buyer.

"There's a lot of capacity out there," said Alan Fine, San Ramone, Calif.-based field vp. . . . He added that such coverage is being more frequently offered in multiline insurance policies. However, Mr. Fine also noted that despite coverage becoming more readily available, capacity for political risk coverage still is limited enough that it can sometimes influence rates more than any actuarial assessment of the risk involved. . . .

Defining political risk as "unanticipated government action and/or cessation of law and order which affects the economic viability of a foreign enterprise or project, or repudiates a contractual agreement between a company and a foreign government," Mr. Fine said it is a risk that exists everywhere. As a result, it creates vulnerabilities for assets and investments overseas; for contracts and guarantees; from political violence; and from the disruption of trade.

From time to time, the specific issues of political risk that fit this definition change. Among the leading emerging issues today are government action affecting environmental impacts; human and labor rights; and intellectual property and discriminatory tax policies. . . .

He said the risk manager has to decide whether to fully hedge his company's political risks through the use of insurance, partially hedge them, actively or passively manage them, or not bother to hedge or monitor them at all. The most common approach he has seen is active management, he said.

Cedric Hughes, corporate risk manager for Hewlett-Packard Co. of Palo Alto, Calif., said the basis of his strategy in this regard is "to manage the political risk, not transfer it."

Hewlett-Packard manufactures its computers and business machines at 60 locations in 16 countries and sells to 120 countries, so it has considerable political risk exposures, he pointed out. He added that given the company's highly leveraged, highly interdependent production and distribution chain involving large numbers of subcontractors in numerous locations, the "domino effect" of business interruption at any one site could be considerable.

Mr. Hughes said Hewlett-Packard's philosophy of managing rather than transferring political risk reflects an "aggressive risk identification and mitigation" approach that he regards as proactive. Hewlett-Packard has three global crisis management teams—its corporate team in the United States and regional teams based in Europe and the Far East. The regional teams operate an early warning system, whereby any incident at a particular subsidiary or site is reported to the regional office and then to the corporate crisis management team.

Mr. Hughes said Hewlett-Packard's risk mitigation strategies include recognition of and focus on real exposures, strategic planning centered on making the risks obvious, and business continuity/ business recovery plans.

Mr. Wickham of RiskPro Consulting . . . recommended an "enterprise" risk management process for dealing with political risks. It should include:

Identifying risks—recognizing the assets invested; the company's country diversification; possible political violence; the possible disruption of trade; and the use of contractors and subcontractors.

Assessing and measuring those risks—gauging country exposures, including local investment and potential volatility; enterprise/project issues, such as business interruption; facility interdependency; currency and banking; and trade disruption.

Mitigating and planning—evaluating countries; business recovery plans; and traditional risk control, including facility protection, environmental and human rights issues; and embedded technology.

*(continued)*

*(continued)*

Funding—including retention capabilities; insurance mechanisms; government entities; and alternative risk treatments. A risk manager should also analyze the "risk appetite" of the company to determine how much risk it is prepared to carry. When buying insurance coverage, a realistic approach should include consideration of the capacity available, the terms of the coverage, its pricing, the replenishment of limits, and whether to insure through private insurers or government bodies.

Claims management—understanding before buying political risk coverage how a claim is defined in the policy; how to make a claim; who will be negotiating on the company's behalf; who communicates with corporate management and how; and details of the waiting periods.

*Edwin Unsworth*
*Business Insurance.*

As the foregoing article suggests, even in a world with highly available political risk insurance, the prudent entrepreneur does not rely on insurance alone. An investor needs to know the alternatives to such insurance in order to assess its benefits vis-à-vis its costs. This means that the foreign investors must understand the risks associated with seeking relief itself from U.S. or international forums if its prospective investment is nationalized. That subject involves a further review of time-honored international theory.

> **http://www.opic.gov**
> See for the Overseas Private Investment Corporation.

> **http://www.opic.gov/subdocs/public/publications/insguide.htm**
> See for information on political risk insurance coverage.

## Resolving Investment Disputes with Foreign Nations

The first alternative for a victim of nationalization would be to seek relief in the courts of the country where property was nationalized. In countries with well-developed traditions of an independent judiciary, this alternative is feasible. As German or Japanese investors in the United States will tell you, even there the foreigner is at a disadvantage as a stranger in the other party's "home court." Countries with significant political risk, however, tend not to have independent judiciaries. Further, if the country happens to ascribe to sovereign right principles, recourse to its judiciary would be rather fruitless for the injured U.S. investor. Nevertheless, under traditional international law principles, an injured investor may need to exhaust local remedies before invoking diplomatic or international adjudication.

A second possibility would be for the investor to sue the host state in the United States. After all, most states have assets in the United States that would be subject to attachment by U.S. courts. The Boeing 747 of a state-run airline on the tarmac of O'Hare Airport can satisfy most judgments, but there are serious obstacles to this course of action.

First, under the *Foreign Sovereign Immunities Act of 1976,* a federal court would not have jurisdiction over the foreign nation unless the court finds that the state's acts fall within a *commercial activity exemption* to immunity. Second, even if the court had jurisdiction over the foreign state, it might abstain from exercising it under principles of abstention referred to as the *Act of State Doctrine.* Finally, if the foreign investor can get a U.S. court to hear the case, the investor should be prepared to rely on a treaty or powerful international law argument, because U.S. courts generally apply the governing law of the host country.

In light of these difficulties, the foreign investor may wish to bring its case to an international arbitration. To do this, however, the host nation must have consented to such dispute resolution in advance.

**The Foreign Sovereign Immunities Act.** In 1976, Congress enacted the *Foreign Sovereign Immunities Act* (FSIA), making the United States the first country to codify the law of sovereign immunity in a statute. Under FSIA, foreign states are generally immune from the jurisdiction of U.S. courts. The FSIA then sets forth the exceptions to this general grant of immunity: (1) waiver by the foreign state; (2) if the state's action constitutes commercial activity carried on by the state; (3) if rights in property are taken in violation of international law; (4) if rights in property are acquired through inheritance or gifts in the United States; (5) noncommercial torts within the United States; (6) maritime liens based on the foreign state's commercial activity; and (7) certain types of counterclaims if the foreign state is the one that starts the lawsuit against a U.S. citizen. The U.S. Supreme Court has held that these are the only exceptions to FSIA's grant of immunity and has interpreted these exceptions narrowly. A clear statement of the Court's view may be found in *Argentine Republic v. Amerada Hess.*

> **http://www.autohuna.com/intlbusn/ statetrd/usa.htm**
> *See for the FSIA.*

---

### Argentine Republic v. Amerada Hess Shipping Corp., et al.
#### 488 U.S. 428 (1989)
#### United States Supreme Court

BACKGROUND AND FACTS
In 1982, the Argentine Republic and the United Kingdom fought a war over possession of the South Atlantic islands variously known as the Falkland Islands or the Islas Malvinas. In June 1982, Argentine warplanes bombed the *Hercules,* a Liberian crude oil tanker, while it was in international waters outside the war zone designated by the two warring nations. After the war, the owner of the *Hercules* sued Argentina in the United States, claiming that the Argentine action had violated the Geneva Convention on the High Seas and the Pan American Maritime Neutrality Convention, to which both the United States and Argentina are parties.

CHIEF JUSTICE REHNQUIST
We think that the text and structure of the FSIA demonstrate Congress' intention that the FSIA be the sole basis for obtaining jurisdiction over a foreign state in our courts. Sections 1604 and 1330(a) work in tandem: section 1604 bars federal and state courts from exercising jurisdiction when a foreign state is entitled to immunity, and section 1330(a) confers jurisdiction on district courts to hear suits brought by United States citizens and by aliens when a foreign state is not entitled to immunity.

Having determined that the FSIA provides the sole basis for obtaining jurisdiction over a foreign state in federal court, we turn to whether any of the exceptions enumerated in the Act apply here. We agree with the District Court that none of the FSIA's exceptions applies on these facts.

Respondents assert that the FSIA exception for noncommercial torts . . . is most in point. This provision denies immunity in a case "in which money damages are sought against a foreign state for personal injury or death, or damage to or loss of property, occurring in the United States and caused by the tortious act or omission of that foreign state.

[This exception] is limited by its terms, however, to those cases in which the damage to or loss of property occurs in the United States. Congress' primary purpose in enacting section 1605(a)(5) was to eliminate a foreign state's immunity for traffic accidents and other torts committed in the United States, for which liability is imposed under domestic tort law.

In this case, the injury to respondents' ship occurred on the high seas some 5,000 miles off the nearest shores of the United States. [Respondents] point out that the FSIA defines "United States" as including all "territory and waters, continental and insular, subject to the jurisdiction of the United States," section 1603(c), and that their injury occurred on the high seas, which is within the admiralty jurisdiction of the United States.

We find this logic unpersuasive. We construe the modifying phrase "continental and insular" to restrict the definition of the United States to the

*(continued)*

*(continued)*

continental United States and those islands that are part of the United States or its possessions. Likewise, the term "waters" in section 1603(c) cannot reasonably be read to cover all waters over which United States courts might exercise jurisdiction. Because respondents' injury unquestionably occurred well outside the three-mile limit then in effect for the territorial waters of the United States, the exception for noncommercial torts cannot apply. The result in this case is not altered by the fact that petition's alleged tort may have had effects in the United States. Respondents state, for example, that the *Hercules* was transporting oil intended for use in this country and that the loss of the ship disrupted contractual payments due in New York. Under the commercial activity exception to the FSIA, a foreign state may be liable for its commercial activities "outside the territory of the United States" having a "direct effect" inside the United States. But the noncommercial tort exception, upon which respondents rely, makes no mention of "territory outside the United States" or of "direct effects" in the United States. Respondents do not claim that [the commercial activity exception] covers these facts.

We also disagree with respondents' claim that certain international agreements entered into by petitioner and by the United States create an exception to the FSIA here. As noted, the FSIA was adopted "[s]ubject to international agreements to which the United States [was] a party at the time of [its] enactment." Respondents point to the Geneva Convention on the High Seas, and the Pan American Maritime Neutrality Convention. These conventions, however, only set forth substantive rules of conduct and state that compensation shall be paid for certain wrongs. They do not create private right of action for foreign corporations to recover compensation from foreign states in United States courts. Nor do we see how a foreign state can waive its immunity [the FSIA waiver of immunity exception] by signing an international agreement that contains no mention of a waiver of immunity to suit in United States courts or even the availability of a cause of action in the United States.

We hold that the FSIA provides the sole basis for obtaining jurisdiction over a foreign state in the courts of this country, and that none of the enumerated exceptions to the Act apply to the fact of this case.

**Decision.** The Supreme Court reversed the decision of the United States Court of Appeals for the Second Circuit, dismissing the lawsuit against the Argentine Republic on the grounds of sovereign immunity.

---

The most significant of the exceptions to FSIA is the "commercial activity" exception. In relevant parts, the exception provides that a

foreign state shall not be immune from the jurisdiction of the United States or the states in any case . . . in which the action is based . . . upon an act outside the territory of the United States in connection with the commercial activity of the foreign state elsewhere and it causes a direct effect on the United States.

This exception is principally aimed at situations in which the state enters into a commercial contract with an investor and is acting as a private commercial party. Thus, the exception would permit suit where the foreign investor has a direct contractual relationship with a foreign state.

One of the most comprehensive analyses by the Supreme Court on what constitutes "commercial activity" under the FSIA is found in the *Saudi Arabia v. Nelson* case. Writing for a slim majority of the Court over a spirited dissent and reversing a lower appellate court decision, Justice Souter was careful to contrast the actions charged against Saudi Arabia with Argentina's sophisticated attempts to clothe its actions with official enactments in an earlier case. This is an area rife with dispute.

When the foreign state is not as clearly a commercial contractor as Argentina was in the preceding case, the analysis of what constitutes commercial action under sovereign immunity doctrine under the *Saudi Arabia v. Nelson* analysis becomes more difficult. A nationalization of an entire industry pursuant to an official act, for example, certainly has commercial effects, but is not really a commercial act. In other words, in "nationalizing," the state is not acting as a merchant because a merchant could never nationalize assets; only a state can do so.

## Saudi Arabia v. Nelson
### 507 U.S. 349 (1993)
### Supreme Court of the United States

**BACKGROUND AND FACTS**

The Nelsons, a married couple, filed an action for damages against the Kingdom of Saudi Arabia, a Saudi hospital, and the hospital's purchasing agent in the United States. The purchasing agent had, at the direction of the Saudi Government, recruited the husband through advertising in the United States to work at a hospital in Saudi Arabia. The plaintiffs alleged that the husband suffered personal injuries as a result of the Saudi Government's unlawful detention and torture of him. They also based their suit on the defendants' negligent failure to warn him of the possibility of severe retaliatory action if he attempted to report on-the-job hazards. The Court of Appeals found subject matter jurisdiction, concluding that the husband's recruitment and hiring were "commercial activities" of Saudi Arabia and the hospital, carried on in the United States and that the Nelsons' action was "based upon" these activities within the meaning of the statute. There was, the Court of Appeals reasoned, a sufficient nexus between those commercial activities and the wrongful acts that had allegedly injured the Nelsons.

**JUSTICE SOUTER**

The Foreign Sovereign Immunities Act of 1976 entitles foreign states to immunity from the jurisdiction of courts in the United States . . . subject to certain enumerated exceptions. One is that a foreign state shall not be immune in any case "in which the action is based upon a commercial activity carried on in the United States by the foreign state. . . . " The Act defines such activity as "commercial activity carried on by such state and having substantial contact with the United States" . . . and provides that a commercial activity may be "either a regular course of commercial conduct or a particular commercial transaction or act," the "commercial character of [which] shall be determined by reference to" its "nature," rather than its "purpose". . . .

We begin our analysis by identifying the particular conduct on which the Nelsons' action is "based" for purposes of the Act. . . . Although the Act contains no definition of the phrase "based upon," and the relatively sparse legislative history offers no assistance, guidance is hardly necessary. In denoting conduct that forms the "basis," or "foundation," for a claim . . . the phrase is read most naturally to mean those elements of a claim that, if proven, would entitle a plaintiff to relief under his theory of the case. . . . Earlier, see n. 3, supra, we noted that [the commercial activity exception] contains two clauses following the one at issue here. The second allows for jurisdiction where a suit "is based . . . upon an act performed in the United States in connection with a commercial activity of the foreign state elsewhere," and the third speaks in like terms, allowing for jurisdiction where an action "is based . . . upon an act outside the territory of the United States in connection with a commercial activity of the foreign state elsewhere and that act causes a direct effect in the United States". . . . Congress manifestly understood there to be a difference between a suit "based upon" commercial activity and one "based upon" acts performed "in connection with" such activity. The only reasonable reading of the former term calls for something more than a mere connection with, or relation to, commercial activity. (We do not mean to suggest that the first clause of [the exception] necessarily requires that each and every element of a claim be commercial activity by a foreign state, and we do not address the case where a claim consists of both commercial and sovereign elements. We do conclude, however, that where a claim rests entirely upon activities sovereign in character, as here, jurisdiction will not exist under that clause regardless of any connection the sovereign acts may have with commercial activity.)

In this case, the Nelsons have alleged that petitioners recruited Scott Nelson for work at the hospital, signed an employment contract with him, and subsequently employed him. While these activities led to the conduct that eventually injured the Nelsons, they are not the basis for the Nelsons' suit. Even taking each of the Nelsons' allegations about Scott Nelson's recruitment and employment as true, those facts alone entitle the Nelsons to nothing under their theory of the case.

*(continued)*

*(continued)*

The Nelsons have not, after all, alleged breach of contract . . . but personal injuries caused by petitioners' intentional wrongs and by petitioners' negligent failure to warn Scott Nelson that they might commit those wrongs. Those torts, and not the arguably commercial activities that preceded their commission, form the basis for the Nelsons' suit. Petitioners' tortious conduct itself fails to qualify as "commercial activity" within the meaning of the Act, although the Act is too "'obtuse'" to be of much help in reaching that conclusion. . . . We have seen already that the Act defines "commercial activity" as "either a regular course of commercial conduct or a particular commercial transaction or act," and provides that "[t]he commercial character of an activity shall be determined by reference to the nature of the course of conduct or particular transaction or act, rather than by reference to its purpose.". . . If this is a definition, it is one distinguished only by its diffidence; as we observed in our most recent case on the subject, it "leaves the critical term 'commercial' largely undefined." *Republic of Argentina v. Weltover, Inc.,* 504 U.S. 607, 612, 112 S.Ct. 2160, 2165, 119 L.Ed.2d 394 (1992). . . . We do not, however, have the option to throw up our hands. The term has to be given some interpretation, and congressional diffidence necessarily results in judicial responsibility to determine what a "commercial activity" is for purposes of the Act.

We took up the task just last Term in Weltover, supra, which involved Argentina's unilateral refinancing of bonds it had issued under a plan to stabilize its currency. Bondholders sued Argentina in federal court, asserting jurisdiction under the third clause of [the exception]. In the course of holding the refinancing to be a commercial activity for purposes of the Act, we observed that the statute "largely codifies the so-called 'restrictive' theory of foreign sovereign immunity first endorsed by the State Department in 1952." We accordingly held that the meaning of "commercial" for purposes of the Act must be the meaning Congress understood the restrictive theory to require at the time it passed the statute.

Under the restrictive, as opposed to the "absolute," theory of foreign sovereign immunity, a state is immune from the jurisdiction of foreign courts as to its sovereign or public acts (jure imperii), but not as to those that are private or commercial in character (jure gestionis). . . . We explained in Weltover . . . that a state engages in commercial activity under the restrictive theory where it exercises "only those powers that can also be exercised by private citizens," as distinct from those "powers peculiar to sovereigns." Put differently, a foreign state engages in commercial activity for purposes of the restrictive theory only where it acts "in the manner of a private player within" the market. . . . We emphasized in Weltover that whether a state acts "in the manner of" a private party is a question of behavior, not motivation:

> [B]ecause the Act provides that the commercial character of an act is to be determined by reference to its 'nature' rather than its 'purpose,' the question is not whether the foreign government is acting with a profit motive or instead with the aim of fulfilling uniquely sovereign objectives. Rather, the issue is whether the particular actions that the foreign state performs (whatever the motive behind them) are the type of actions by which a private party engages in 'trade and traffic or commerce.'

We did not ignore the difficulty of distinguishing "'purpose' (i.e., the reason why the foreign state engages in the activity) from 'nature' (i.e., the outward form of the conduct that the foreign state performs or agrees to perform)," but recognized that the Act "unmistakably commands" us to observe the distinction. Because Argentina had merely dealt in the bond market in the manner of a private player, we held, its refinancing of the bonds qualified as a commercial activity for purposes of the Act despite the apparent governmental motivation.

Unlike Argentina's activities that we considered in Weltover, the intentional conduct alleged here (the Saudi Government's wrongful arrest, imprisonment, and torture of Nelson) could not qualify as commercial under the restrictive theory. The conduct boils down to abuse of the power of its police by the Saudi Government, and however monstrous such abuse undoubtedly may be, a foreign state's exercise of the power of its police has long been understood for purposes of the restrictive theory as peculiarly sovereign in nature. . . . Exercise of the powers of police and penal officers is not the sort of action by which private parties can engage in commerce. "[S]uch acts as legislation, or the expulsion of an alien, or a denial of justice, cannot be performed by an individual acting in his own name. They can be performed only by the state acting as such."

*(continued)*

*(continued)*

The Nelsons and their amici urge us to give significance to their assertion that the Saudi Government subjected Nelson to the abuse alleged as retaliation for his persistence in reporting hospital safety violations, and argue that the character of the mistreatment was consequently commercial. One amicus, indeed, goes so far as to suggest that the Saudi Government "often uses detention and torture to resolve commercial disputes." Brief for Human Rights Watch as Amicus Curiae 6. But this argument does not alter the fact that the powers allegedly abused were those of police and penal officers. In any event, the argument is off the point, for it goes to purpose, the very fact the Act renders irrelevant to the question of an activity's commercial character. Whatever may have been the Saudi Government's motivation for its allegedly abusive treatment of Nelson, it remains the case that the Nelsons' action is based upon a sovereign activity immune from the subject-matter jurisdiction of United States courts under the Act.

In addition to the intentionally tortious conduct, the Nelsons claim a separate basis for recovery in petitioners' failure to warn Scott Nelson of the hidden dangers associated with his employment. The Nelsons allege that, at the time petitioners recruited Scott Nelson and thereafter, they failed to warn him of the possibility of severe retaliatory action if he attempted to disclose any safety hazards he might discover on the job. . . . In other words, petitioners bore a duty to warn of their own propensity for tortious conduct. But this is merely a semantic ploy. For aught we can see, a plaintiff could recast virtually any claim of intentional tort committed by sovereign act as a claim of failure to warn, simply by charging the defendant with an obligation to announce its own tortious propensity before indulging it. To give jurisdictional significance to this feint of language would effectively thwart the Act's manifest purpose to codify the restrictive theory of foreign sovereign immunity.

**Decision.** The Supreme Court reversed the judgment of the Court of Appeals, dismissing the case.

**Act of State Doctrine.** If a court decides that, under the FSIA, it has jurisdiction over the sovereign state that the U.S. investor is suing, the investor must still persuade the court to exercise this jurisdictional power despite the *Act of State Doctrine*. The doctrine was historically referred to as a choice-of-law doctrine under which, for reasons of *comity* among nations (i.e., friendly relations marked by mutual recognition of laws), a U.S. court will refuse to inquire into the validity of any act of a foreign government.

In more recent cases, however, the U.S. Supreme Court has increasingly turned from the comity rationale to one of a *rule of repose* that recognizes the finality of foreign sovereign acts. In the *W. S. Kirkpatrick* case, the Supreme Court made this trend established law by holding that the doctrine applied only where the decision by a U.S. court would require a finding that a foreign sovereign act was invalid. In so doing, the Court rejected the broader position, favored by U.S. diplomats, that even when a finding as to the validity of a foreign sovereign's actions was not at issue, a U.S. court should abstain if it might cause the foreign sovereign embarrassment.

BACKGROUND AND FACTS

The government of Nigeria awarded a military contract to W. S. Kirkpatrick & Co. The losing bidder, Environmental Tectronics Corporation (ETC), investigated the circumstances under which the contract had been awarded and learned that the winner had bribed key government

*W. S. Kirkpatrick v. Environmental Tectronics Corp.*
*110 S. Ct. 701 (1990)*
*United States Supreme Court*

officials who were responsible for making the award. Ultimately, the U.S. Department of Justice conducted an investigation that confirmed ETC's findings, and high Kirkpatrick officials pled guilty to violations of the Foreign Corrupt Practices Act.

*(continued)*

*(continued)*

Thereafter, ETC brought a civil lawsuit against Kirkpatrick in the United States under the Racketeer Influenced Corrupt Organizations Act and the United States antitrust laws. Kirkpatrick moved to dismiss the lawsuit on the basis that the act of state doctrine prohibited the federal court from considering the matter. The district court granted Kirkpatrick's motion, but the Court of Appeals reversed the district court.

### JUSTICE SCALIA

This Court's description of the jurisprudential foundation for the act of state doctrine has undergone some evolution over the years. We once viewed the doctrine as an expression of international law, resting upon "the highest considerations of international comity and expediency." We have more recently described it, however, as a consequence of domestic separation of powers, reflecting "the strong sense of the Judicial Branch that its engagement in the task of passing on the validity of foreign acts of state may hinder" the conduct of foreign affairs. Some Justices have suggested possible exceptions to application of the doctrine, where one or both of the foregoing policies would seemingly not be served: an exception for example, for acts of state that consist of commercial transactions, since neither modern international comity nor the current position of our Executive Branch accorded sovereign immunity to such acts; or an exception for cases in which the Executive Branch has represented that it has no objection to denying validity to the foreign sovereign act, since then the courts would be impeding no foreign policy goals.

The parties have argued at length about the applicability of these possible exceptions. We find it unnecessary, however, to pursue those inquiries, since the factual predicate for application of the act of state doctrine does not exist. Nothing in the present suit requires the Court to declare invalid, and thus ineffective as "a rule of decision for the courts of this country," the official act of a foreign sovereign.

In every case in which we have held the act of state doctrine applicable, the relief sought or the defense interposed would have required a court in the United States to declare invalid the official act of a foreign sovereign performed within its own territory. In the present case, by contrast, neither the claim nor any asserted defense requires a determination that Nigeria's contract with Kirkpatrick International was, or was not effective.

Petitioners point out, however, that the facts necessary to establish respondent's claim will also establish that the contract was unlawful. Specifically, they note that in order to prevail respondent must prove that petitioner Kirkpatrick made, and Nigerian officials received, payments that violate Nigerian law, which would, they assert, support a finding that the contract is invalid under Nigerian law. Assuming that to be true, it still does not suffice. The act of state doctrine is not some vague doctrine of abstention but a "principle of decision binding on federal and state courts alike." "The act within its own boundaries of one sovereign State . . . becomes . . . a rule of decision for the courts of this country." Act of state issues only arise when a court must decide—that is, when the outcome of the case turns upon—the effect of official action by a foreign sovereign. When that question is not in the case, neither is the act of state doctrine. That is the situation here. Regardless of what the court's factual findings may suggest as to the legality of the Nigerian contract, its legality is simply not a question to be decided in the present suit, and there is thus no occasion to apply the rule of decision that the act of state doctrine requires.

Petitioners insist, however, that the policies underlying our act of state cases—international comity, respect for the sovereignty of foreign nations on their own territory, and the avoidance of embarrassment to the Executive Branch in its conduct of foreign relations—are implicated in the present case because, as the District Court found, a determination that Nigerian officials demanded and accepted a bribe "would impugn or question the nobility of a foreign nation's motivations," and would "result in embarrassment to the sovereign or constitute interference in the conduct of foreign policy of the United States." The United States, as amicus curiae, favors the same approach to the act of state doctrine, though disagreeing with petitioners as to the outcome it produces in the present case. We should not, the United States urges, "attach dispositive significance to the fact that this suit involves only the 'motivation' for, rather than the 'validity' of, a foreign sovereign act," and should eschew "any rigid formula for the resolution of act of state cases generally." . . .

*(continued)*

*(continued)*

But what is appropriate in order to avoid unquestioning judicial acceptance of the act of foreign sovereigns is not similarly appropriate for the quite opposite purpose of expanding judicial incapacities where such acts are not directly (or even indirectly) involved. It is one thing to suggest, as we have, that the policies underlying the act of state doctrine should be considered in deciding whether, despite the doctrine's technical availability, it should nonetheless not be invoked; it is something quite different to suggest that those underlying policies are a doctrine unto themselves, justifying expansion of the act of state doctrine (or, as the United States puts it, unspecific "related principles of abstention") into new and uncharted fields.

The short of the matter is this: Courts in the United States have the power, and ordinarily the obligation, to decide cases and controversies properly presented to them. The act of state doctrine does not establish an exception for cases and controversies that may embarrass foreign governments, but merely requires that, in the process of deciding, the acts of foreign sovereigns taken within their own jurisdictions shall be deemed valid. That doctrine has no application to the present case because the validity of no foreign sovereign act is at issue.

**Decision.** The U.S. Supreme Court affirmed the decision of the Court of Appeals, permitting ETC to proceed with its lawsuit against Kirkpatrick.

The Act of State Doctrine is also not an obstacle if the foreign state has entered into an investment treaty that is applicable to the U.S. investors. Thus, this factor is yet another reason that investors who wish to improve their odds should determine whether a treaty is in effect in the country where they propose to invest and should check the terms of such a treaty. Indeed, this principle permits U.S. agencies to rely on bilateral investment treaties to exert significant influence on foreign governments not to take adverse political action against U.S. investment. In the *American International Group* case which follows, the U.S. investor was favored by such a treaty.

---

## American International Group v. Islamic Republic of Iran

*493 F. Supp. 552 (1980)*
*United States District Court for the District of Columbia, remanded by 657 F.2d 430 (D.C. Cir. 1981)*

BACKGROUND AND FACTS
Plaintiffs were three groups of insurance companies that owned equity interests in several Iranian insurance companies. Defendant Islamic Republic of Iran was a sovereign state and a party to the bilateral Treaty of Amity, Economic Relations, and Consular Rights Between the United States of America and Iran. Article XI, paragraph 4 of the Treaty of Amity expressly provided that

No enterprise of either High Contracting Party . . . which is publicly owned or controlled shall, if it engages in commercial, industrial, shipping, or other business activities within the territories of the other High Contracting Party, claim or enjoy . . . immunity therein from . . . liability to which privately owned and controlled enterprises are subject there.

Article IV, paragraph 2 of the treaty provided:

Property of nationals and companies of either High Contracting Party, including interests in property, shall receive the most constant protection and security within the territories of the other High Contracting Party, in no case less than that required by international law. Such property shall not be taken except for a public purpose, nor shall it be taken without the prompt payment of just compensation.

On June 25, 1979, the insurance industry in Iran was nationalized. Immediately following nationalization, defendant CII (Central Insurance of Iran) assumed control of plaintiffs' business and assets in Iran. The nationalization had

*(continued)*

*(continued)*

the effect of terminating all reinsurance and other business relations between the plaintiffs and defendants and the Iranian insurance companies in which plaintiffs had invested. The plaintiffs did not receive compensation for their losses due to the nationalization, nor did the law of Iran provide a mechanism for determining or paying compensation.

### JUDGE HART

Plaintiffs can assert their rights to recover damages in this Court for violations of the Treaty and international law. First, the right of individuals and companies to enforce a private right of action in a United States court under the property protection provisions of a treaty of friendship, commerce, and navigation has consistently been upheld. . . . Second, since Article IV, paragraph 2 of the Treaty is self-executing, plaintiffs have a right of action before this court. The Treaty clearly meets the criteria considered significant in determining whether a Treaty is self-executing and, therefore, capable of enforcement in a United States court.

The Act of State Doctrine does not preclude this court from awarding summary judgment in this case. First, the theory underlying the Act of State Doctrine is inapplicable in this litigation. The Court is not asked to judge the validity of defendants' expropriation of plaintiffs' interests in Iran, but rather defendants' failure, in violation of the treaty and international law, to make adequate provision for the determination and payment of prompt, adequate, and effective compensation. Second, the Act of State Doctrine does not preclude judicial review where, as here, there is a relevant, unambiguous treaty setting forth agreed principles of international law applicable to the situation at hand. . . . Third, the Act of State Doctrine does not apply since defendants' failure to compensate plaintiffs occurred in connection with a commercial activity of defendants.

**Decision.** The U.S. District Court granted partial summary judgment for the plaintiffs with respect to defendants' liability. It further ordered that a hearing be held at a later date on the amount of damages owed.

---

If a treaty is not applicable, the best way around the Act of State doctrine is through the doctrine's own "commercial activity" exception. Strange as it may seem, the commercial activity exception to the Foreign Sovereign Immunities Act is not viewed by all courts as the same as the commercial activity exception to the Act of State doctrine. The FSIA focuses on whether the act of the defendant itself is commercial. The Act of State doctrine raises a broader question: Will the court's judgment result in a violation of the laws of a fellow sovereign? In *Callejo v. Bancomer*, the Fifth Circuit analyzed this distinction. Consider whether this Act of State analysis is consistent with the Supreme Court's highly literal analysis in *Saudi Arabia v. Nelson*.

---

### Callejo v. Bancomer
*764 F.2d 1101 (1988)*
*United States Court of Appeals for the Fifth Circuit*

### BACKGROUND AND FACTS

This suit was one of several arising from the promulgation by Mexico of exchange control regulations on August 13, 1982, and from the subsequent nationalization of privately owned Mexican banks on September 1, 1982. (Incidentally, most of these banks were re-privatized in the early 1990s.) The exchange control regulations mandated that all deposits in Mexican banks, however denominated, be repaid in Mexican pesos at specified rates of exchange. Because the dollar rate of exchange was well below the market rate, U.S. investors who had dollar deposits in Mexican banks lost money. A number of these indisposed investors, including the plaintiffs in the present suit, brought claims against Mexican banks for breach of contract.

### JUDGE GOLDBERG

In determining whether [the FSIA] applies, [the following question is] relevant: Is the Callejos' suit

*(continued)*

*(continued)*

"based upon a commercial activity" by Bancomer? In the present case, the district court held that the action was "based upon" the promulgation by Mexico of exchange control regulations—a sovereign act—not upon Bancomer's banking activities. We disagree.

In determining whether the commercial activity exception [to the FSIA] applies, the critical question is usually whether the relevant activity is commercial or sovereign in nature—whether it is a *jure gestionis* or a *jure imperii,* a private or a public act. Here, however, there is little doubt about how to characterize the activities at issue: Bancomer's actions in selling the certificate of deposit were clearly commercial in nature. . . . The question, instead, is defining with precision which of these activities is the relevant activity—that is, the activity on which the Callejos' suit is "based."

The district courts that have considered this question have given different answers. . . .

Under the FSIA, sovereign immunity depends on the nature of those acts of the defendant that form the basis of the suit. Here, the act complained of was Bancomer's breach of its contractual obligations to the Callejos, not the promulgation by Mexico of exchange control regulations. . . . These contractual obligations were commercial in nature; they were of kind that a private individual would customarily enter into for profit. Indeed, at the time that Bancomer sold the certificates of deposit, it was a private entity and did so as part of its general commercial activities. The fact that Bancomer was later nationalized is, in the current context, irrelevant. Even if Bancomer had remained a private entity, it would have been obligated under Mexican law to breach its contractual obligations to the Callejos. Its actions in doing so were not actions that only a sovereign could perform, but were instead commercial.

In Part III of *Alfred Dunhill of London, Inc. v. Republic of Cuba* . . . a plurality of the Court enunci-

ated a commercial activity exception to the act of state doctrine. This exception states that the act of state doctrine does not apply to "the repudiation of a purely commercial obligation owed by a foreign sovereign or by one of its commercial instrumentalities."

In the present case, we need not decide whether to adopt the commercial activity exception, since Mexico's actions were clearly sovereign and not commercial in nature. For the act of state (as opposed to sovereign immunity) purposes, the acts are not merely those of the named defendants, but any governmental acts whose validity would be called into question by adjudication of the breach of contract claim would necessarily call into question the Mexican regulations. Under these regulations, Bancomer has discharged its obligations to the Callejos by paying off the certificates in pesos at the established rate of exchange. Thus, we could require Bancomer to honor the terms of the certificates only by disregarding the regulations. . . .

The power to issue exchange control regulations is paradigmatically sovereign in nature, it is not a type that a private person can exercise. Unlike in Dunhill, where Cuba repudiated a single debt, here Mexico promulgated comprehensive, national decrees in response to a national monetary crisis. . . .

Were we to disregard the exchange regulations by enforcing the Callejos' certificates of deposit, we would render nugatory the attempts by Mexico to protect its foreign exchange reserves. While we are doubtful of our ability to foresee what will vex the peace of nations, we have no doubt that disregarding the Mexican regulations would be very vexing indeed. We therefore reject the Callejos' commercial activity argument.

**Decision.** The U.S. Court of Appeals for the Fifth Circuit affirmed the trial court's dismissal of the plaintiffs' lawsuit.

It bears emphasis that the "commercial activity" exception to the Act of State doctrine is not universally recognized. The last time that the United States Supreme Court passed on it, four justices supported it and four justices opposed it. Some lower courts, such as the Ninth Circuit Court of Appeals, the highest federal court on the West Coast, have expressly rejected the existence of such an exception. Other courts have recognized and applied it. Only the future will tell what happens to this exception over time.

**International Adjudication.** If the difficulties in proceeding in either the host country or in the United States are too redoubtable, the investor should look into the possibility of dispute resolution in an international tribunal—a subject that has been generally addressed in a previous chapter. As pointed out there, however, arbitration is by nature a voluntary action. If one is concerned about a hostile sovereign act, the time to seek the host state's consent to arbitration is before the investment is made, not after it has been expropriated. A carefully drawn arbitration clause in a contract with a government agency can provide reasonable assurance that an expropriation will be adjudicated according to the prevailing principles of international law requiring full compensation.

When contracting with a government agency, the entrepreneur should not blindly rely on the arbitration provision in the contract (the *clause compromissoire*), for the government official agreeing to the provision might have no power to do so. In many nations, national legislation or the national constitution supersedes contractual provision under which an arbitrator would be passing judgment on the exercise of sovereign state powers or would affect public institutions. In other cases, certain areas of law are excluded from coverage. For example, Andean Pact Decision 24, now superseded, excluded foreign investment contracts and foreign transfer of technology contracts from the jurisdiction of any foreign court or arbitrator. Similarly, Article 100 of the Argentine Constitution prohibits the state from submitting to arbitration on issues arising out of remittance of capital or profits abroad. Generally speaking, relatively straightforward matters such as the payment of damages to the entrepreneur upon the state's breach of an agreement not to take property is deemed by the legislature to be within an arbitrator's power.

The entrepreneur should also be on the alert for special procedural requirements imposed by national laws. Perhaps the most common of these in the context of arbitration is the requirement for a document (the *compromise*), signed by the parties to the clause compromissoire, which submits the specific dispute at issue to arbitration. The theory of the compromise is that the parties will begin to come together through the process of framing the dispute for the arbitrator. Obviously, a recalcitrant party can instead make this process the source of unnecessary delay.

These national procedural requirements are as diverse as nations themselves. In the following case, a foreign investor neglected to structure its contract with a government entity so as to assure that its choice of a foreign arbitral tribunal would be honored under local law. The case illustrates that even when a country has agreed to enforce foreign arbitral awards, the investor must understand clearly what is a foreign arbitral award for purposes of that country's domestic legislation.

---

### National Thermal Power Corp. v. The Singer Company
#### May 7, 1992
#### The Supreme Court of India

**BACKGROUND AND FACTS**

The National Thermal Power Corporation of India (NTPC) entered into a contract with The Singer Company, a British concern, to supply equipment and erect certain projects in India. A dispute arose between the parties and Singer sought arbitration under International Chamber of Commerce (ICC) rules in London. Singer won the arbitration and was granted an award by the ICC tribunal. Singer then sought to enforce the award in India under the Indian Foreign Awards Act, which limits the role of Indian courts to recognition and enforcement of the foreign arbitral award. The NTPC filed an application to set aside the award, arguing that notwithstanding the fact that the award was made by a London tribunal under ICC rules, because the contract was governed by Indian law, it was not a "foreign award" and could thus be relitigated in detail in Indian courts under the Indian Foreign Arbitration Act of 1940. The Delhi High Court dismissed the application and NTPC appealed to the Supreme Court of India.

**JUSTICE THOMMEN**

The General Terms and Conditions of Contract dated 14.2.81 are expressly incorporated in the agreements and they state:

> the laws applicable to this Contract shall be the laws in force in India. The Courts of Delhi shall have exclusive jurisdiction in all matters arising under this Contract. (7.2)

*(continued)*

*(continued)*

Sub-clause 7 of the agreement deals with arbitration in respect of a foreign contractor. The latter provision says:

27.7 In the event of foreign Contractor, the arbitration shall be conducted by three arbitrators. . . . [A]ll Rules of Conciliation and Arbitration of the International Chamber of Commerce shall apply to such arbitrations. The arbitration shall be conducted at such places as the arbitrators may determine.

The General Terms further provide:

the Contract shall in all respects be construed and governed according to Indian laws.

[T]he dispute which arose between the parties was referred to an Arbitral Tribunal constituted in terms of the rules of arbitration of the ICC Court. In accordance with Article 12 of those Rules, the ICC Court chose London to be the place of arbitration. . . . The award was made in London as an interim award in an arbitration between the NTPC and a foreign contractor. . . . The fundamental question is whether the arbitration agreement contained in the contract is governed by the law of India so as to save it from the ambit of the Foreign Awards Act and attract provisions of the Arbitration Act, 1940. Which is the law which governs the agreement on which the award has been made? . . .

[Counsel for Singer contends] that while the main contract is governed by Indian law, as expressly stated by the parties, arbitration being a collateral contract and procedural in nature, it is not necessarily bound by the proper law of the contract, but the law applicable to it must be determined with reference to other factors. . . . London having been chosen in accordance with the ICC Rules to be the seat of arbitration, English law is the proper law of arbitration, and all proceedings connected with it are governed by that law and exclusively within the jurisdiction of the English court. . . .

In the absence of an express statement about the governing law, the inferred intention of the parties determines that law. The true intention of the parties, in the absence of an express selection, has to be discovered by applying "sound ideas of business, convenience and sense to the language of the contract itself." . . . [S]election of courts of a particular country as having jurisdiction in matters arising under the contract is usually, but not invariably, an indication of the intention of the parties that the system of law followed by those courts is the proper law by which they intend their contract to be governed. However, the mere selection of a particular place for submission to the jurisdiction of the courts or for the conduct of arbitration will not, in the absence of any other relevant connecting factor with that place, be sufficient to draw an inference as to the intention of the parties to be governed by the system of law prevalent in that place. This is specifically so in the case of arbitration, for the selection of the place of arbitration may have little significance where it is chosen, as is often the case, without regard to any relevant or significant link with the place. This is particularly true when the place of arbitration is not chosen by the parties themselves, but by the arbitrators or by an outside body, and that too for reasons unconnected with the contract. . . .

[I]f the parties have specifically chosen the law governing the conduct and procedure of arbitration, the arbitration proceedings will be conducted in accordance with that law so long as it is not contrary to the public policy or the mandatory requirements of the law of the country in which the arbitration is held. If no such choice has been made by the parties, expressly or by necessary implication, the procedural aspect of the conduct of arbitration (as distinguished from the substantive agreement to arbitrate) will be determined by the law of the place or seat of arbitration. Where, however, the parties have, as in the instant case, stipulated that the arbitration between them will be conducted in accordance with the ICC Rules, those rules, being in many respects self-contained or self-regulating and constituting a contractual code of procedure, will govern the conduct of the arbitration, except insofar as they conflict with the mandatory requirements of the proper law of arbitration, or of the procedural law of the seat of arbitration. . . .

The proper law of the contract in the present case being expressly stipulated to be the laws in force in India and the exclusive jurisdiction of the courts in Delhi in all matters arising under the contract having been specifically accepted, and the parties not having chosen expressly or by implication a law different from the Indian law in regard to the agreement contained in the arbitration clause, the proper law governing the arbitration agreement is indeed the law in force in India, and the

*(continued)*

*(continued)*

competent courts of this country must necessarily have jurisdiction over all matters concerning arbitration. Neither the rules of procedure for the conduct of arbitration contractually chosen by the parties (the ICC Rules) nor the mandatory requirements of the procedure followed in the courts of the country in which the arbitration is held can in any manner supersede the overriding jurisdiction and control of the Indian law and the Indian courts.

This means questions such as the jurisdiction of the arbitrator to decide a particular issue or the continuance of an arbitration or the frustration of the arbitration agreement, its validity, effect and interpretation are determined exclusively by the proper law of the arbitration agreement, which, in the present case, is Indian Law. The procedural powers and duties of the arbitrators, as for example, whether they must hear oral evidence, whether the evidence of one party should be recorded necessarily in the presence of the other party, whether there is a right of cross-examination of witnesses, the special requirements of notice, the remedies available to a party in respect of security for costs or for discovery, etc., are matters regulated in accordance with the rules chosen by the parties to the extent that those rules are applicable and sufficient and are not repugnant to the requirements of the procedural law and practice of the seat of arbitration. . . .

A "foreign award," as defined under the Foreign Awards Act, 1961 means an award made . . . on differences arising between persons out of legal relationships, whether contractual or not, which are considered to be commercial under the law in force in India. To qualify as a foreign award under the Act, the award should have been made in pursuance of an agreement in writing for arbitration to be governed by the New York Convention or the Recognition and Enforcement of Foreign Arbitration Awards, 1958, and not to be governed by the law of India. Furthermore, such an award should have been made outside India in the territory of a foreign state notified by the Government of India as having made reciprocal provisions for enforcement of the Convention. An award is "foreign" not merely because it is made in the territory of a foreign State, but because it is made in such a territory on an arbitration agreement not governed by the law of India. An award made on an arbitration agreement governed by the law of India, though rendered outside India, is attracted by the saving clause . . . of the Foreign Awards Act and is, therefore, not treated in India as a "foreign award."

A "foreign award" is . . . recognized and enforceable in India as it were an award made on a matter referred to arbitration in India. . . . Such an award will be ordered to be filed by a competent court in India which will pronounce judgment according to the award.

The Foreign Awards Act contains a specific provision to exclude its operation to what may be regarded as a "domestic award" in the sense of the award having been made on an arbitration agreement governed by the law of India, although the dispute was with a foreigner and the arbitration was held and the award was made in a foreign State. . . .

Such an award necessarily falls under the Arbitration Act, 1940, and is amenable to the jurisdiction of the Indian Courts and controlled by the Indian system of law just as in the case of any other domestic award. . . .

In sum, it may be stated that the law expressly chosen by the parties in respect of all matters arising under their contract, which must necessarily include the agreement contained in the arbitration clause, being Indian law and the exclusive jurisdiction of the courts in Delhi having been expressly recognized by the parties to the contract in all matters arising under it, and the contract being most intimately associated with India, the proper law of arbitration and the competent courts are both exclusively Indian, while matters of procedure connected with the conduct of arbitration are left to be regulated by the contractually chosen rules of the ICC to the extent that such rules are not in conflict with the public policy and the mandatory requirements of the proper law and of the law of the place of arbitration. The Foreign Awards Act, 1961, has no application to the award in question which has been made on an arbitration agreement governed by the law of India.

**Decision.** The Supreme Court of India set aside the judgment of the Delhi High Court with instructions to consider the NTPC application on its merits.

Many countries have agreed to arbitration in cases of investment disputes in *foreign investment codes.* The investor should, of course, investigate the existence of such a provision before committing to the investment.

An additional source of consent to arbitration is by treaty. The United States has negotiated bilateral investment treaties with a large number of its trading partners under which the host countries consent to arbitration in case of dispute with U.S. investors.

The arbitration agreement can provide for *ad hoc* arbitration, as under the United Nations' UNCITRAL Rules, or may refer to one of the arbitral institutions listed in Chapter Nine. Perhaps the most significant case in arbitration involving a government is the *Convention on the Settlement of Investment Disputes Between States and Nationals of Other States,* to which the United States is a party. The Convention provides a forum and a set of rules for the arbitration of disputes between U.S. citizens and signatory countries. Both the citizen and the host country agree that the Convention governs and that all disputes will be resolved by the *International Centre for the Settlement of Investment Disputes* (ICSID), an affiliate of the World Bank. These forums provide the establishment and proceedings of an arbitration, and ensure that as long as the claimant follows the rules, a recalcitrant government respondent cannot thwart the arbitration by refusing to participate. Indeed, as the *Alcoa* case in Chapter Twenty illustrates, once a country has given its consent, it cannot revoke it unilaterally.

The business manager should understand, of course, that a commitment to arbitration is not a one-way street. The flip side of the commitment is that once the foreign investor consents to arbitration, it cannot bring action for a nationalization in its own country. As the *Republic of Guinea* case illustrates, the investor must decide on its dispute resolution strategy at the outset.

---

### La République Populaire De Guinée v. La Société Atlantic Triton
*(October 26, 1984)*
*Cour d'Appel de Rennes*

BACKGROUND AND FACTS
In August 1981, the People's Revolutionary Republic of Guinea (Guinea) entered into an agreement with Societe Atlantic Triton (Atlantic), a Norwegian company, for Atlantic to convert and equip three shipping vessels for a Guinean industrial fishing project. The agreement included an arbitration clause under which ICSID was granted sole jurisdiction for the resolution of disputes pursuant to the convention under which it was established.

Atlantic performed the work, but it proved unsatisfactory. Guinea claimed that the ships, built to Norwegian specifications, were inadequate for fishing in tropical Guinean waters. It further alleged a number of other technical deficiencies. Attempts to resolve the dispute failed and Atlantic cancelled the contract, demanding payment of U.S. $571,311 that it was still owed.

Meanwhile, Guinea had taken the three ships to a shipyard in Piriou, France, to remedy the perceived shortcomings of Atlantic. Lacking any response to its demand, Atlantic sought and obtained an order from the Tribunal of Commerce of Quimper to effect the seizure of the three vessels pending resolution of the dispute. Guinea appealed, asserting that, in light of the ICSID arbitration provision, the French tribunal had no jurisdiction to act.

PRESIDENT LELION
Whereas the convention for the settlement of disputes relative to investments between states and nationals of other states . . . , ratified by a large number of states including France, Norway, and Guinea instituted an International Center for the Settlement of Investments Disputes (ICSID) which comprises the "mechanisms for conciliation and arbitration." . . .

Whereas the handbook of ICSID . . . specifies . . . that in the absence of a contrary agreement by the parties, the consent given to ICSID arbitration excludes all other recourse, and that consequently the parties cannot address themselves to the local authorities or judges to obtain provisionary measures before calling on the arbitral tribunal.

*(continued)*

*(continued)*

Whereas the goal of the convention was to institute mechanisms . . . to which the contracting states can submit their disputes relating to private international investments, in preference over domestic lawsuits.

Whereas in perspective, . . . the spirit of the convention revealed by the rules of arbitration indicates that the arbitral tribunal had a general and exclusive competence to settle not only the core dispute but all other provisionary measures; . . . that to leave to the domestic jurisdictions the power to issue orders of provisionary measures, would have the effects of instigating a parcelling out of the jurisdiction and the not-negligible risk of taking decisions likely to make more difficult the task of the arbiters. . . .

Whereas in international law it is acknowledged that the parties must abstain from all measures which could have a prejudicial repercussion on the enactment of a decision. . . .

Whereas the parties to the contract are bound to resort to [the clause providing for ICSID arbitration] and cannot bypass it; particularly as to emergency protective measures in a case where, as here, there is no urgency, the vessels having been

more than six months in the Piriou shipyards at the time of the proceeding before the commercial tribunal at Quimper had been sought; that a like and similar process fails to recognize the spirit of the [arbitration] clause and of the convention and proceeds from the wish to obtain advantages in an illegitimate way at the threshold of the arbitral proceedings. . . .

Whereas in light of these observations the consular magistrate lacked jurisdiction to pass on the request for the authorization of the sequestration of the three boats. . . . *On these grounds:*

We sustain the Popular Revolutionary Government of Guinea and [the Guinean government company] in their appeal;

The summary order rendered by the president of the Tribunal of Commerce on Quimper on 6 April 1984 is annulled.

**Decision.**   The Court of Appeals of Rennes held that it lacked jurisdiction to entertain the request for authorization of sequestration presented by Atlantic Triton. Accordingly, it ordered the lifting of the seizure enacted by the minister of Rabadeux.

## Chapter Summary

U.S. citizens who invest in sovereign rights countries need to consider seriously the possibility that the foreign sovereign will take their investment. All such investors must decide whether they wish to assume the risk of litigating such a taking or whether they wish to obtain political insurance to cover it. Those investors who choose the former, will wish to place themselves in the best position possible by having appropriate international arbitration or litigation provisions that both establish the measure of compensation due and identify the arbiter that will do the measuring. Arbitration or litigation is perhaps best done in a nation where the ground rules have been set by a bilateral investment treaty between the foreign nation and the United States. If the investors decide to obtain insurance covering political risk, they will wish to avail themselves of the alternative with the best mixture of cost and flexibility. In making these decisions, investors should consider the fact that the law in this area is in a state of evolution; risk is enhanced by the element of unpredictability.

---

QUESTIONS AND CASE PROBLEMS

1. In the *Chorzow Factory* case, why would the cost of construction of the factory not be indicative of its value? What additional elements of value would be missing? To the extent that the owners were given wartime concessions by the German Reich, would award of the true cost of construction exceed the owners' cost?

2. How should future prospects and existing contracts of the Chorzow factory be analyzed? Would this analysis take into account the discounted value of the profits that would have been generated throughout the useful life of the factory? Would a projection of future profits or the useful life of the factory be precise?

3. Pursuant to Bulgaria's new joint venture program, Zasada, Inc., a U.S. firm, constructs a football helmet manufacturing facility in Sofia to produce hel-

mets for export to the United States. Four years later, a change in the Russian Parliament leads to domestic policy reversals. Russia annexes Bulgaria as a member of its federation and takes possession of all Bulgarian factories that employ more than 25 people, including Zasada's helmet facility. Was this a nationalization or an expropriation? How would the *INA Corporation* tribunal assess the appropriate compensation to Zasada? How would the *Chorzow* court measure that compensation? What do these decisions suggest about the development of compensation theory?

4. Economic development in the Republic of Costa Azuli is perceived to be hindered by the ownership of all farmland by a few families and firms—some of which are U.S.-owned. A new government is democratically elected on a platform of land redistribution; the government, however, has no currency to buy such land and lacks the credit necessary to borrow significant sums. If Costa Azul cannot afford to pay "prompt and just" compensation for foreign private property, should it refrain from initiating social change? Does it make a difference if Costa Azuli refrains from taking the land and instead increases property taxes 100 times on lots greater than 25 hectares?

5. In *Texas Trading*, Judge Kaufman asserted that when a government enters into a private contract, it loses its sovereign status. How should the FSIA apply if a government purchases private property as an embassy and violates local ordinances in its operation? What if a government-owned airline sells a tour package to a private citizen, then detains and refuses her entry into the country as an undesirable? What if the government retains a consulting firm to develop a national agricultural development plan and then refuses to pay because its agricultural policy changes?

6. Was the "confiscation" of all cigar manufacturers by the Cuban government in the early 1960s an expropriation or a nationalization? Was this confiscation a commercial activity in which a private businessperson could engage? Was the Cuban government's assertion of rights to post-intervention sums paid for cigars a commercial act? Is the analysis any different with respect to pre-intervention shipments?

7. Maria Hartman, a U.S. investor, owns a toy assembly plant in the Kingdom of Fromage Vert. At a tennis match between a leading U.S. player and a star Fromagian, Maria irritates the king by cheering for the American. The next day, the king issues an edict taking Ms. Hartman's plant for the kingdom. Ms. Hartman sues Fromage Vert in U.S. District Court for the Southern District of New York, where the kingdom's airline owns an office. Would the U.S. court have jurisdiction in the absence of a treaty? Do you think the Fromagian taking of the toy assembly plant was a commercial activity? Was it an "act of state"?

8. In the *Callejo* case, Judge Goldberg referred to the *Dunhill* case with approval. Yet, did the Supreme Court in *Dunhill* refuse to pass on Cuban government regulations regarding the nationalization of cigar companies? What distinction did Judge Goldberg make between *Callejo* and *Dunhill*? Is this distinction valid?

9. Manuel Aviation Co. enters into an agreement with the People's Republic of Tibia to sell it a number of personal jets on credit. Under the agreement, Tibia consents to the sole jurisdiction of ICSID in resolving disputes. After receiving the planes, Tibia promptly defaults on its payments, refuses to return its jets, and withdraws its consent to ICSID jurisdiction. A month later, en route to a state visit to England, one of the jets refuels in Paris. Manuel seeks an emergency seizure order from a Parisian court. Does the *Atlantic Triton* case control? If Manuel proceeds in ISCID, will Tibia's withdrawal be effective?

# Chapter Twenty

# Privatization: Regulation of the International Marketplace

**P**rivatization is the transfer of government-owned assets to the private sector. In that sense, it is simply the reverse of the nationalization/expropriation process addressed in Chapter Nineteen, and illustrates that trends in international law, like the political environment that law reflects, are cyclical.

## Historical Development of Privatization

In the Middle Ages, the national monarch owned the great bulk of property. Indeed, the monarch's grant of fiefs in that property formed the basis for the feudal system and, in time, for the nation-state. Not until the Enlightenment of the 16th century did liberal/libertarian economics and individual freedom—and the concomitant rise of the merchant and industrial middle classes—begin to significantly affect the law of property. As noted in the preceding chapter, within this environment, Grotius and others shaped the limitations on the powers of a sovereign to nationalize or expropriate the property of a foreign merchant.

Soon sovereigns began to realize that their interests were best served by transferring property to private parties who would develop the property, thereby adding significant wealth to the nation and, thus, to the sovereigns themselves. One of the first "sovereigns" to do so was the United States of America, a nation founded in the libertarian economic philosophy of the Scottish Enlightenment and possessing vast undeveloped natural resources. For example, the right of millers to dam a river was favored over the rights of downstream property owners because of the pro-development effects of mills. Similarly, entrepreneurs were given concessions to build and collect tolls from canals they built due to the pro-development implications of canals.

The process of privatization continued in the United States throughout the 19th and 20th centuries and was largely responsible for its growth into the world's largest economy. A few examples are illustrative: *Homestead Acts* that transferred government land to those who farmed it, federal land management laws that permitted private ranchers to graze on government land at low fees, government mining leases to private mining interests, and the Oklahoma Land Rush. A similar privatization trend was taking place throughout the world, particularly in Europe's colonial possessions. By the end of the 19th century, the bulk of the world's wealth was in private hands.

This trend was reversed by Marx's indictment of the excesses of liberal capitalist economics. Marx's views were fully or partially accepted in Russia and other communist countries, newly independent African and Asian nations, and newly elected labor or other leftist governments in Western Europe and Latin America. In the 20th century, these governments nationalized or expropriated all or large parts of the private sector, especially those parts of the private sector owned by foreigners, in an ostensible effort to redistribute wealth. Through the 1970s, the law of nationalization and expropriation was the hot topic in international law.

In most instances, nationalization ultimately did not redistribute wealth as much as it destroyed wealth. Without the engine of the individual profit incentive, enterprises grew inefficient and flaccid. The nationalized enterprise gradually went from producing profits for the government to requiring subsidies from the government to cover its losses.

In time, the political tide turned once more; the nationalization trend ran out of steam and privatization came roaring back. In the late 1970s and the 1980s, Great Britain's libertarian Thatcher government began a series of wide-ranging sales of government assets. Margaret Thatcher was the primary political spokesperson for the proposition that the British economy would function more effectively if all of its components were in private hands, subjected to the discipline of the free capitalist market. Accordingly, she moved aggressively to reverse the nationalization of industry effected by Labour governments decades earlier. Privatizations of British Steel and British Petroleum pioneered the sale of public assets in modern financial circumstances. Eventually, Mrs. Thatcher's ideas became fashionable in other developed nations and the privatization process took hold—countries as diverse as France, Japan, and the United States had soon effected privatizations of their own.

The privatization trend slowly gained ground in developed nations but was not triumphant everywhere. While pro-privatization governments went on an uninterrupted run in Great Britain and the United States during the 1980s, privatization stalled in France and Spain during periods that Socialist governments held power in the legislature. Eventually, however, at different paces and to different degrees, most Western European political parties came to accept the utility of privatization. An estimated $125 billion in privatizations was completed by the end of 1998. Privatization in these developed Western nations, however, did not create a particularly big stir in the international community. Even after the nationalizations effected by left-leaning governments, the greatest majority of assets in those capitalist economies had remained in private hands, so the privatization process, while important, did not amount to a fundamental restructuring of the economies. Moreover, in each of those countries a large domestic capital market existed; on the whole, the sales were from the local government to local private investors. Even though foreigners participated as passive investors, no huge influx of foreign control occurred.

Things changed when the trend expanded to less-developed and former nonmarket economies. The governments in most Latin American countries, through the nationalizations of the 1960s and 1970s, had come to own vast segments of the economy, such as natural resource exploitation, electric power, and telecommunications, reserved in most capitalist countries to the private sector. But by the early 1990s the nationalistic fervor fueling nationalization had given way to more economically rational considerations. As Mrs. Thatcher and her disciples had pointed out, state-owned businesses were inefficient and wasteful, placing a significant drain on poorer countries' finances. Indeed, according to the World Bank, large state-owned enterprises owed about 60 percent of the external debt of Latin American countries. The nationalized industries' demand for subsidies effectively bankrupted Latin American governments, causing them to default on their loans from international banks and triggering massive and contentious debt restructuring negotiations. Once burned, international debt lenders were twice shy about advancing any more credit to Latin American countries. International equity investors— including Latin America's own middle class—kept their investment funds out of the region due to fear of Latin America's laws favoring nationalization. Latin American economies stagnated because they could not attract any long-term capital investment. The nationalization experiment had failed, and there was little alternative but to turn to privatization with substantial foreign participation. A profound shift in the role of government in Latin countries ensued.

At the same time, the communist experiment also failed. For reasons too numerous even to outline here, the European nations that had formerly been nonmarket economies decisively turned toward capitalist economic models. Consistent with Marxist theory, the former communist governments had owned virtually everything. Thus, privatization there meant a massive series of transfers, unprecedented in number and total value of assets sold. For instance, in the first five years after its 1989 Velvet Revolution, the Czech government privatized more than two-thirds of its entire economy. Because the communist economies were even more bereft of investment capital than Latin America, such privatization necessarily involved a large foreign involvement.

Asia and Africa saw similar evolutions. In Africa, virtually devoid of foreign investment since the nationalizations of the 1960s, enterprises once expropriated from European nationals are slowly being sold back to European nationals. In Zambia's privatization program, for example, the multinationals that had owned assets before nationalization were even granted a right of first refusal at buying them back. Egypt and other governments with substantial debt to the World Bank—largely created by subsidies to nationalized industries— were pressed to privatize those industries in exchange for new loans. In India, Malaysia, and Singapore, turning infrastructure development to the private sector conserves state revenues. Even mainland China and Vietnam, the last major bastions of communism, developed business forms that transferred control of assets to private entrepreneurs, especially foreign investors.

Many more people know that privatization is a trend than know precisely what privatization really is. The focus of this chapter now turns to the specifics of the structure of the privatization transaction.

> **http://www.un.org/ecosocdev/geninfo/
> afrec/vol11no3/privatz.htm**
> A UN site with links to information on privatization in Ghana.

## Preparation for Privatization

In the complex world of modern finance, privatization takes many forms. Indeed, each combination of assets, sellers, and purchasers requires its own particular structure for privatization. While in many ways privatization can be like the acquisition of a division of a private company, the steps that sellers take to prepare for privatization, the patterns of those sales, and the legal concerns that they raise tend to be different from those of other asset transfers. To understand the principal considerations at issue, a description of the process of preparing government assets for privatization is presented entailing four generic models of privatization.

At the outset, the industry to be privatized is a functioning unit of the national government.

Whether it is a major steel manufacturer or an independent power plant, its purpose is to further national interests, as defined by the government's political leaders. These interests are most frequently defined in terms of volume of output or number of persons employed. Profit is only incidentally one of these interests; in fact, in many former communist countries, the concept of profit was unknown. Prestige for a manager in this context is derived from high employment levels. The fact that the expenses associated with those bloated employee numbers overwhelm the enterprise's revenues was not a source of concern. All revenues went into the State and all expenses were covered by the State. Government employees, whose purpose is public service, not private gain, staff the government enterprise. The equipment of the enterprise may have been chosen to maximize employment, rather than to minimize unit cost. If the enterprise received free supplies or natural resources from other government divisions, those supplies may have been used in a wasteful manner.

If such an enterprise were immediately put on the block, it would not fetch an attractive price. The private entrepreneur would not even have reliable financial information from which to make a risk assessment. Privatizing governments soon discovered that unless they prepared the asset for sale before privatizing, they would have no takers, certainly not at a reasonable price.

Similarly, the legal infrastructure for private investment must be created. International investors require a functioning commercial code. They require an understandable regulatory regime governing the newly privatized enterprise. They need to understand competitive requirements. Preparation of national assets for privatization has become a critical and standardized part of the process.

> **http://bgbio.aubg.bg/econ/fin_instr.shtml**
> A site with links to finance and other information on privatization from the American University in Bulgaria.

## The Creation and Organization of an Independent Government Corporation

The process typically begins with a functioning unit of the government—the national telecommunications ministry, the national steel manufacturing ministry, or some other governmental unit. The assets that are necessary or important for the continued progress of the unit are segregated and transferred to a new private entity, the stock of which is wholly owned by the government. Thus, for example, the Telecommunications Administration of the Ministry of Communication becomes Telco, Inc., a government-owned company.

Generally, the transfer is followed by a transitional period during which the new entity begins to operate as a private enterprise. It will record its expenses and its revenues separately from those of the government and develop financial statements that will permit potential purchasers to assess its performance. During this transitional period, the government funds all capital needs of the fledgling enterprise.

The government will frequently retain an independent financial adviser to organize the financial information of the company so as to allow private sector investors to assess its strengths and weaknesses. These advisors uncover the company's financial performance, which is generally hidden by a web of unfair market value exchanges with other government units and lax accounting practices. They then arrange this data into pro forma financial statements prepared in accordance with generally accepted accounting standards. Applying internationally accepted valuation methodology—such as discounted cash flow analysis and comparable earnings multiple analysis—they arrive at a range of values for the new company. This process takes much of the guesswork out of privatization acquisitions, permitting the right investor to come into the company at the right price.

## Preparation of a Legal System for Privatization

Before foreign investors acquire an interest in former government assets, they will want a solid legal infrastructure in place. This infrastructure creates clear rights of property and enforceability of contracts.

**"Clearing" of Expropriation Claims.** A significant legal mechanism that the government must work out before any transfer takes place is a property system that permits *clearing of title* to the assets being transferred. As previously noted, many assets currently owned by governments were once expropriated from private parties. The people who owned the assets before the government nationalized them—and who may have a claim against the government for a wrongful taking under the theories discussed in Chapter Nineteen—may have a restitution claim against the government. Without clearing of title, that claim might be available against the purchaser of the asset. The government frequently creates a legal network whereby the victim of expropriation must either assert its claim within a specified period or waive it. After the period passes without a claim, the government can transfer the asset with clear title. A system must also be developed for prompt rulings when restitution claims are asserted. A lengthy claim resolution process can destroy privatization before it begins.

If a quick sale is desired, the government may forego a title-clearing procedure and assume responsibility for the possible adverse claim. For example, Germany's privatization trust, the *Treuhand,* may issue an Investment Preference Decision (*Investitionsvorrangbescheid*) when it wishes to promote prompt investment in a priority sector. Upon the investor's compliance with the conditions of the decision—such as a specified level of investment—the restitution claim is blocked. In such instances of *blocked claims,* the government often limits the expropriation victim to the proceeds of the sale of the asset if the sale is deemed to have been conducted under reasonable commercial terms.

The investor must be sure that the government office with the authority to waive these restitution liabilities has approved the transaction; frequently that office is different from the office actually selling the asset.

**Property and Contract Law.** In some nations, the process of expropriation and nationalization had progressed to a point at which viability of private property as a legal concept was in question, particularly in former communist countries, where the state was the only legitimate repository of wealth.

The recognition of private property rights is a sine qua non of privatization. The whole concept of private enterprise is that ownership of an asset gives the owner an incentive to modernize the asset, make further investments in the asset, and put it to its most productive—and profitable—use. Without clear assurance to the investor of its right to own the property, the incentive is diminished. A functioning system of private property requires establishment of laws governing the acquisition and transfer of title, filing registries for real property mortgages, systems for acquiring and recording chattel mortgages, and other nonglamorous mechanics of a functioning private property system. The devil is in such details: Russia, for example, passed a law on mortgages back in 1991 but was very slow to establish the filing registries necessary to implement the law. Without the registries, mortgage financing—a bedrock of capital investment in the West—can operate only with great complexity, unnecessary expense, and substantial risk.

A free market maximizes value by permitting and enforcing voluntary exchanges among independent merchants. Contract law based on liberal economics performs this exchange function. Without a modern commercial code, the privatized entity may be no more than a collection of machinery and equipment. Before launching privatization, therefore, a government is wise to implement a modern contract law system.

## Methods of Distribution

Perhaps the final preparation for privatization is the development of a plan to distribute shares.

**Private and Public Equity Placements.** The simplest transfer of ownership is to a single investor or single united group of investors. Typically, such an investment is part of a strategic entry into the local market or acquisition of new manufacturing capacity. In direct negotiations between government and investor the deal is worked out and made firm in a shareholders' agreement between the parties.

The government may also sell to the passive investing public through the direct sale of the enterprise's stock in small lots directly to individual investors, or in large blocks to financial intermediaries, called underwriters, for resale to the public. Under either the small lot or underwriter scenario, the government may reserve a portion of the offering for sale to local nationals on local stock exchanges, and direct another portion for sale in foreign equity markets through U.S. depository receipts or other similar securities. An example of this form was seen in the 1990 sale of 40 percent of Ibusz, the Hungarian travel and tourism agency.

**Voucher Systems.** Governments also occasionally transfer public assets to their citizens for free. The concept underlying these *voucher* systems is that, in order for capitalism to take hold, stock ownership should be widespread among the national population. In populations in which the standard of living is low, most people do not have the resources to invest, so the objective of wide distribution can only be achieved through free distribution. Further the theory continues, the people have paid for their shares through years of laboring for a state-owned system.

This type of distribution typically begins with the issuance of voucher coupon booklets that contain points for bidding on shares in state firms to the entire population or to a portion of the population with a specific interest in the enterprise being privatized. For example, vouchers may be issued only to the citizens of a region greatly affected by the enterprise to be privatized or to the workers in the enterprise.

Often these private citizens entrust their vouchers to large private investment funds that pool vouchers. These funds then bid against one another to acquire specific entities being privatized. After a fund or group of funds acquires the asset, as the owners of the enterprise they then enter into transactions with foreign investors who are usually barred from the voucher program. Indeed, with the financial assistance of multilateral banks such as the European Bank for Reconstruction & Development, many of these funds actually finance and direct the process, described above, of preparing the former public entity for the subsequent transfer of interests to international investors. In this way, the investment funds effectively take the place of the government in privatizing the enterprise. This method tends to get bureaucrats out of the process, permitting faster transfer of shares directly from the funds or from stock markets.

Unfortunately, voucher systems do not always work this well in practice. In countries such as Russia, private citizens, who lacked any knowledge about capital markets and who often were in dire need of cash, promptly sold their vouchers to unscrupulous individuals at low prices. Massive numbers of vouchers were soon concentrated in the hands of people with few entrepreneurial credentials. Many of these persons took over enterprises that they had no ability to operate. The resulting dislocation only further battered the already overwhelmed Russian economy. Other similar experiences have led subsequent voucher programs, such as Poland's National Investment Fund program, to require a modest payment for the vouchers from eligible members of the public. In Hungary, the government permits payment of the modest sum over a number of years and does not transfer the vouchers until final payment is made. Other nations, like Kyrgyzstan, simply make the vouchers personal and not tradable, preventing transfers during the transitional period.

**Debt-for-Equity Swaps.** A popular mechanism in selling state assets is the *debt-for-equity swap*. Of the two types, the first type of debt swap involves the exchange of external sovereign debt for internal equity. In essence, the government permits foreign investors to pay for the government's equity in the entity to be privatized with debt instruments of that government.

The debt of many governments, of course, is in default and may be purchased at a substantial discount from current holders. If the investor can purchase a government's debt for twenty cents on the dollar, it can buy $1 million in the government's debt for only $200,000, thereby conserving its hard currency. By pursuing such a strategy in its many privatizations, the Argentine government drastically slashed the amount of the country's debt; in fact, it actually erased more debt than it received cash.

In the second type of swap, external debt is exchanged for internal debt. Host-country investors obtain debt instruments of the government being traded abroad at a discount with their hard currency assets, convert it into local-currency-denominated debt, and resell it in the host country as internal debt. This latter approach has the positive side effect of reversing capital flight from the host country. By allowing residents to use assets abroad to purchase external debt and convert it to domestic debt, privatization of a company actually improves the nation's balance of payments. In Chile, this process has substantially reduced the country's sovereign debt difficulties.

## Models of Privatization

There are as many different types of privatizations as there are types of private transactions. But the peculiar characteristics of privatizations make it possible to organize them into different categories in order to facilitate one's understanding of those characteristics. Privatizations can be organized into four groups or "models." Keep in mind, however, that these are only somewhat artificial illustrative models. Few real world transactions will be "pure" examples of the models, but rather, will include elements of more than one model.

> **http://www.enr.com/new/c826.htm**
> The site of an Engineering News Record *article* on international privatization.

### Sale of a Noncontrolling Interest

The least radical type of privatization involves the sale of a substantial but *noncontrolling interest* in the enterprise to private investors. The predominant feature of this model is that control will remain in the hands of the government employees who formerly managed the asset for the government, and the government retains a substantial equity interest in the new enterprise (see Exhibit 20.1).

Once the new government enterprise has a sufficient track record and has otherwise been prepared for privatization as discussed in the preceding text, the government begins its disengagement by seeking equity capital from the private sector in any of the for-profit distribution techniques previously discussed. If the sale does not involve a strategic investor, however, the privatization of a minority holding will not bring in new expertise. The passive investor, after all, is

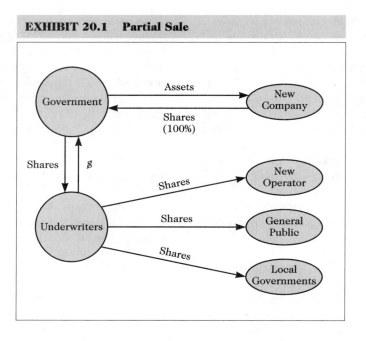

**EXHIBIT 20.1　Partial Sale**

interested in picking a manager for its investment and then looking for other investments. Such a sale does not, therefore, achieve the objective of injecting entrepreneurship into the entity, but instead results in lower private investor interest and a smaller capital investment. In short, a strategic investor is a critical element in this model.

A noncontrolling interest is often sold to a single strategic investor. In such cases, the purchaser can try to ameliorate the downside of continued government control through the shareholder agreement between the government—in its capacity as a shareholder—and the private shareholder. Such shareholder agreements lay out terms, under which the shareholder takes the stock, that give it specified rights and protections over and above those normally accorded to minority shareholders by the applicable corporate law.

Some governments have devised a way of trying to retain control even after selling a controlling interest in the enterprise. The *golden share* gives the government a continuing voice in the new company's board of directors that can protect a company from foreign takeover. A golden share may limit the private investors' voting rights over a certain set threshold, place government appointees on the company board, and/or give the government the power to veto decisions of the board in certain specified areas. At times this veto power is stated in general "wherever-necessary-to-further-national-interest" terms. The government does not wish to turn a significant source of national employment and manufacturing over to people outside its control; in short, it does not wish to give up power.

This retention of control, of course, has a negative effect on potential investors. They typically do not wish to invest money in an enterprise in which critical decisions affecting profit will be made by an entity that does not react to the profit motive. A proposed merger between A. B. Volvo and Renault S. A., for example, crumbled when Swedish shareholders could not accept the French government's retention of a golden share of the reorganized company. Notwithstanding assurances by the French that the share would be exercised sparingly, if ever, the Swedes could not accept the specter of potential governmental direction of their private investment.

Another way for the government to retain control while theoretically transferring a controlling interest is to reserve a substantial portion of the shares for local or provincial governments or labor unions. Unless the private entrepreneur is well-connected with the local polity, the local government can be expected to vote in a manner consistent with the national government, particularly on issues of short-term employment reductions. Public employee labor unions, of course, tend to protect their members' work rule prerogatives and to oppose privatization-related efficiency measures.

Obvious drawbacks also characterize the noncontrolling interest model of privatization. First, one of the reasons some governments' units are consistently ineffective is that in a government bureaucracy, managers are often selected for reasons unrelated to their business acumen. If the government remains in operational control, the likelihood that this defect will be remedied remains small. Indeed, some would say that privatization is a misnomer if the government remains in control.

Second, a government has many interests that are inconsistent with those of a private shareholder and may not use its control consistently with the harsh discipline of capitalism. For governments, production volume and full employment are the typical motivating forces rather than brisk sales, efficient cost structures, and competitive pricing. In short, by retaining old managers and old owners, this model preserves much of the inefficient system that privatization was developed to displace. As long as such inefficiencies exist, the services provided to the nation will be substandard, and/or the public treasury will be called upon to continue to subsidize the firm. Also, any privatization will attract less capital.

Third, this model discourages foreign entrepreneurs from introducing successful management and industrial techniques into antiquated enterprises. Unless the investor can control its investment, that is bring in its own experienced management team, it is unlikely to expend effort and resources to force-feed relatively inexperienced local managers. Further, in the absence of extensive protection in shareholder agreements, foreigners will not bring new technologies into enterprises that they do not control.

Notwithstanding these disadvantages, some governments pursue this model, particularly in sectors in which a perceived nonfinancial public interest needs to be protected. On a positive note, some government-controlled companies actually have a positive track record.

> **http://www.public-policy.org/~ncpa/ pd/pdint173.html**
> *The site for material on privatization attempts in China.*

## The Trade Sale

At the opposite end of the privatization spectrum is the *trade sale model,* the transfer of control of the unit's assets to a single, private investor or group of investors. The distinguishing feature of this model is that when the smoke clears, the purchaser controls the use of the assets. It decides which of the former employees are kept and what capital plant improvements are to be made. The government may pursue the trade sale either as a stock sale or as a sale of assets.

**Stock Trade Sale.**   In the case of a *stock sale,* the government will proceed, as previously discussed, to create a new private entity, transfer assets to it, and develop a financial track record. Once a salable—even if as yet unprofitable— entity is created, the government will seek an experienced and financially strong concern to purchase the new enterprise and take over its management. At times the transfer can be initially made to private investment funds, controlled by local natives, which will seek to prepare the enterprise for privatization before transferring control to international entrepreneurs (see Exhibit 20.2).

**Asset Trade Sale.**   A second alternative under this model is the *direct sale of assets* to a private entity. The government under this scenario looks for a quick, relatively inexpensive exit from a sector of the economy; it pulls together those assets thought necessary to make the enterprise succeed and negotiates with an investor to take over operations. The balance of assets, which are deemed to be unnecessary, are "junked," causing this type of trade sale to be sometimes referred to as a *liquidation.* This approach may surrender a great deal of value to the

**EXHIBIT 20.2  Trade Sale**

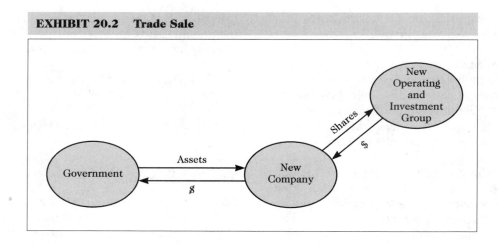

potential purchaser. Without any record of performance, any potential purchaser would need to discount its purchase price by a host of imponderables. After all, even if a new firm's performance is poor, detailed financial statements would at least identify to the purchaser the areas that require improvement or elimination and permit it to develop a projection of future cash flow from which it can base a reasonable purchase price. Without any track record, the analytical process becomes too much of a guessing exercise. Not surprisingly, in its pure form, an asset trade transaction has principally been found in the sale of mineral extraction firms, whose principal worth consists of the value of their access to identifiable natural resources.

For cases in which the former government unit principally provided services, the government may achieve privatization through management contracts with private parties for services as diverse as maintenance of port facilities and trash pickup. In this scenario, the government contracts with a private firm to perform services formerly provided by the government. *Contracting out* in this fashion may mean that some state-owned assets can be sold off because they are no longer needed now that the contractor is handling the enterprise's function. Some of these assets may be sold to the very company that has entered into the management contract to perform the work.

A variation of this asset trade sale concept occurs when a private firm is sold the right, or *con-*

*cession,* to provide a service and/or infrastructure that the state has never previously offered but over which it can exercise substantial control. The concession is discussed in greater depth in the following section.

**Advantages and Disadvantages of the Trade Sale.**  A trade sale has many advantages. First, of course, it is the liberal economic ideal of privatization. It brings assets into the hands of private entrepreneurs with a strong financial incentive in transforming the former state entity into one that can function in a competitive market. Second, it is the speediest way in which to effect privatization, reducing the need for unhelpful government interference during any transitional period. Third, it is especially useful in selling small companies for which demand is low in equity markets. In countries such as the Czech Republic, small shops were simply transferred to the individuals or families who had previously operated them for the state.

In general, however, the trade sale also presents significant disadvantages. First, the complete takeover by a foreign entity of a national company can lead to chauvinistic backlash from the local population. When Spanish-owned Iberia Airlines acquired Aerolineas Argentinas, many Argentines condemned a "new Spanish colonialization." Such publicity can be decidedly unhelpful to a firm such as Aerolineas Argentinas that relies on the patronage of Argentines.

Thus, in a trade sale the new entrepreneur group can often benefit by including significant local participation.

Second, a trade sale also places a great deal of responsibility on private entrepreneurs who may not have the capital resources necessary to pull off a successful privatization. In fact, some would-be privatizers have collapsed into bankruptcy soon after the sale. Thus, the government has a stake in carefully exploring the financial depth of the buyer in a trade sale.

Third, some governments view the national interest as harmed if the future of a significant national firm is a small piece of a multinational company's worldwide strategies. Accordingly, many national governments attach a series of *conditions subsequent* to trade sales. These can include commitments to invest in new capital equipment for the new firm, maintain specified minimum employment levels, transfer technology to the new firm and train local employees in its use, and remedy environmental problems that may exist at the company sites. The price at which the company is sold often takes a subordinate priority to the foregoing considerations.

## The Sale to Employees

Privatization can also be structured as a transfer to the enterprise's former employees, without retention of control by the government. Under this model, existing management and employees become the new owners, most often in conjunction with a group of outside private investors (see Exhibit 20.3 on page 634).

Within the private sector in developed economies, acquisitions of companies by their management and supporting investment groups, known as *leveraged buyouts* (LBOs), were common in the 1980s. In essence, when management perceived that the public equity markets undervalued the stock of their companies, it sometimes sought to purchase the company from its shareholders at a premium over its market price. Management would enlist private investors with the resources to purchase the company as majority partners; the investors would give the members of management a substantial equity stake be-

cause of the value they were perceived to add to the bare assets of the company. Further, an equity stake presumably gave management a large financial incentive to make the enterprise succeed. This trend slowed abruptly in the early 1990s as companies which had been overburdened with LBO debt began to fail.

In the context of public enterprises, giving the current senior government employees an equity stake in the new enterprise serves the same objectives and some others peculiar to privatizations. First, privatizations are necessarily political transactions that require broad support within the government. Obviously, senior government officials with a financial stake in privatization as future shareholders will favor it more readily than if they have none.

Second, lower-level employees will generally be asked to make significant wage, pension, and work rule concessions to the new private entity. In order to compensate the employees for these sacrifices, the new owners appropriately give them a "piece of the action" in the new venture. In the absence of such equity rights, labor unions might use their political clout to forestall privatization.

Third, not all traces of socialist ideology have been erased from the Eastern European consciousness; the concept of excluding workers from ownership remains a politically unattractive concept. Indeed, Russian lawmakers have entertained legislation that called for leasing of state property to the workers' collectives with a subsequent option to purchase. Similarly, the Czech and Slovak privatizations issue a percentage of shares to workers for free. In a recent privatization of a Polish chocolate waffle manufacturer by a Swiss concern, 20 percent of the new company's privatization order specifically provides for sale of equity to workers at half price.

This LBO model has occurred in a relatively pure form in some developed nations, such as in the privatization of British Telecomm. But in less-developed nations, it occurs principally as a facilitating element. Most government units are being privatized largely because they are poorly managed; existing upper government officials are not viewed as adding any value to the underlying assets. One of the first things that the foreign

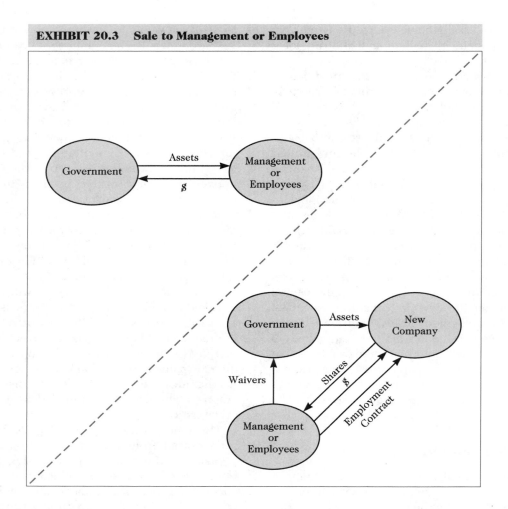

**EXHIBIT 20.3   Sale to Management or Employees**

entrepreneur will want to do is to radically modify management techniques.

As for the rank and file, privatization is often a prelude to "streamlining" of enterprises—the dismissal of large segments of the bureaucracy that cannot be justified under a regime in which expenses are principally incurred to generate revenues. In that context, placing substantial numbers of shares in the hands of ex-employees could prove to be bad policy.

Indeed, resistance from government employees is one of the greatest remaining barriers to privatization. For those who have long had a secure position at the public trough, the rigors of efficient, bottom-line oriented capitalism is not a welcome prospect. In many Latin American countries, for example, union representatives of these employees have used their considerable political influence to prevent or retard privatization. In such circumstances, notwithstanding the disadvantages already noted, a significant employee ownership element in the privatization structure may be necessary as a way of moderating opposition from employee groups.

Foreign investors can expect to issue a small number of shares to employees of the old government unit in privatizations as a necessary part of concluding the acquisition of government assets. But most transactions are not likely to be principally structured in what could be described as the LBO model.

Argentina has developed an innovative ESOP model that illustrates a likely direction in this area. The government sets aside 10 percent of each company in trust for the employees. The workers do not immediately pay for their shares, but the purchase price is paid with the shares' dividends over time. The workers elect representatives to administer the trust, and the trust is allowed one board seat.

---

*Foreign Accents*

# Selling the State, Piece by Piece: Privatization Boom Goes Global

Last year, officials in Fuyang, China, got fed up with the conditions of that city's public toilets. So they did something a little unusual. They hired a private firm to maintain those facilities. Now the city says its privies are much cleaner than when government workers kept them up.

For the last 20 years, governments around the world have been moving services and assets to the private sector. The trend has even penetrated socialist strongholds such as the People's Republic of China. And experts say that the movement shows no sign of stopping. Recent victories by leftist parties in Western Europe may slow the tide there. And in the U.S., the federal government has been slow to join the parade. But analysts say that these are mere speed bumps, not roadblocks, on the road to privatization. The trend to shifting services to the private sphere will continue. Based on prior experience, this means better service for customers. It means lower taxes for taxpayers. And it means greater wealth for the owners of private firms that take over government functions.

"The trend towards privatization is well established," said Henry Gibbon, editor of the London-based newsletter, *Privatisation International.* Since 1985, countries all over the world have sold more than $600 billion worth of state-owned enterprises. Gibbon projects another $90 billion in sales this year. It's hard to find a type of asset that hasn't been privatized somewhere. "In dollar terms the single largest category has been telephone systems," said Robert W. Poole Jr., president of the Reason Foundation. "But over the last few years, there's been a fairly sizeable amount of privatization of electricity assets, so that category is catching up, " added Poole, the man who first coined the term *privatization.*

Many nations have also sold their national oil and gas firms to private owners. It isn't just commercial enterprises that are being turned over to the private sphere. Following the U.S. lead, some nations have hired private firms to run prisons. Last year, the United Kingdom contracted with private firms to build and run three separate prisons. Also in 1996, the Australian state of Victoria hired private firms to build and run three prisons. Some nations have started allowing private firms to build and operate toll roads. And others have begun selling existing toll roads to private firms. China is an example of that. Last year, there were public offerings for four different toll-road firms in that nation. Australia has two private toll roads in operation. Last year, construction started on a third, and a fourth got governmental approval.

In the United Kingdom, most of the major airports have been sold to investors. Last year, Germany, Italy, and Portugal announced plans for airport sales. But the big news in aviation in 1996 was Canada's sale of its air-traffic control system. That made Canada the 16th country in the world to commercialize its air-traffic control system.

Privatization has taken off elsewhere around the world. Many Latin American nations have hired private firms to run their sea ports for instance. Africa has been something of a laggard, but even there, South Africa and Egypt have started to privatize some assets," said Poole. In the U.S., state and local governments have been privatizing for years, but the federal government lags behind. "The U.S. is one of the few nations not to have an organized privatization program on the national level," noted Poole. "The U.S. has not had the extensive state

*(continued)*

*(continued)*

ownership of commercial assets that other nations have." Still, experts point to plenty of assets that Washington could sell to the private sector: buildings, land and electric plants, among others.

While the U.S. shows few signs of adopting a national privatization plan, the trend grows in other parts of the world. Gibbon says governments will sell about $350 billion in state-owned projects over the next five years. Even the recent victories by leftist parties in European elections shouldn't slow the trend too much. In Great Britain, Labor Prime Minister Tony Blair will likely finish the plans of his Tory predecessors to sell off state assets. He has already signed off on a proposal to sell the London Underground. In France, the fate of privatization is less clear. The socialists have announced a halt to all sell-offs. They've stopped the planned sale of electronics giant Thomson-CSF. But in the long-term they may have no choice. "There are fiscal pressures there, the need to get their deficit in line," said Gibbon. . . .

But privatization provides more than a way for government to raise revenue. Last year, the World Bank looked at the results of global privatization among 61 privatized firms in 18 countries. The bank gave a solid thumbs up to these efforts. It found that profitability grew in these firms by an average of 45% after they were sold. Efficiency jumped 11%. Investment in new plants and equipment rose 44%. Output grew 27%. And employment rose 6%. In fact, two-thirds of the firms increased employment after being sold. Studies of privatization in the U.S. show similar improvements in performance. This success bodes well for future privatization. It shows that customers and taxpayers and even workers can benefit when a state-owned firm is sold to private buyers.

*Charles Oliver*
*Investor's Business Daily*

## Concessions: BOTs and BOOs

A different sort of privatization involves the "conceding" to private parties, the right to perform a function historically reserved to the government. The most common of these is the right to build different types of national infrastructure—electric generation plants, ports, airports, highways, bridges, tunnels, mineral extraction facilities, and the like—and the accompanying right to collect revenues generated by the infrastructure project. In contrast to other privatizations, the government is not transferring an existing asset, but a right to earn revenues in order to encourage the building of a new asset.

The concession is fast becoming the most important form of privatization. After all, the existing government assets can only be sold once. Once all of the saleable assets are in private hands, there can be no more privatization of existing assets. In Argentina and Chile for example, classic sale of existing government assets has been virtually over for years. Such innovative governments, however, are increasingly turning to the efficient private sector to perform more and more of their former functions.

**BOTs and BOOs.** There are two basic types of concessions. In the more common concession, the government grants the right to collect revenues for a number of years. After the term of the concession, the right, together with the asset built by the concessionaire, reverts back to the State. Under this model, often referred to as a *Build-Operate-Transfer* (BOT) transaction and shown in Exhibit 20.4, the government obtains an infrastructure asset that promotes development of the greater economy without making any current capital expenditures.

The term of the BOT concession is generally sufficient for the investor group to repay the debt it incurred and recoup its equity outlay with a substantial profit. This time period can vary widely depending upon the project: The period in the British Channel Tunnel is 50 years; the period in the Malaysian North/South Expressway is 30 years; power generation projects often have periods of 15 to 25 years. At times, the parties will use benchmarks, such as the repayment of debt financing, rather than a fixed term of years.

In the second major type of concession, the government actually sells the concessionaire a

**EXHIBIT 20.4   BOT Transaction**

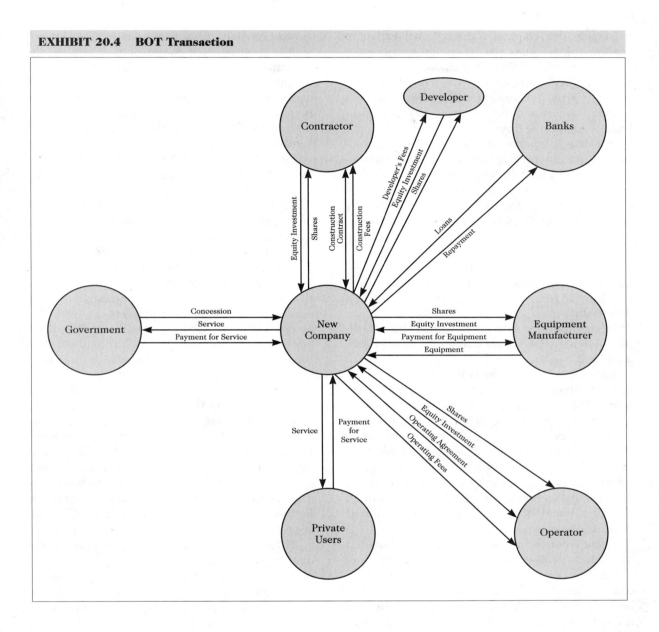

"permanent" concession. These transactions, called *Build-Operate-Own* (BOO) deals, are common in infrastructure projects that involve particularly high risk and therefore require particularly high incentive. For example, the high risk normally associated with doing business in many less developed African nations often requires that the BOO model be followed. Similarly, in countries with an emphatic history of

state intervention in the economy, governments pursue BOO projects as an added measure of assurance to the private investment community that the move to privatization is not a passing political phase.

**The Concession and Anti-Competitive Considerations.**   Because the government is granting a right to perform an activity in which it has a monopoly, the recipient of the right will expect to receive at least some part of the monopoly right for some period of time. For example, a concessionaire will not assume the risk of building a railroad line if the government is then free to use the roadbed that the concessionaire has graded to build a competing line.

Because infrastructure projects by their nature generally involve modifying the environment in a way that facilitates future competitive investment, such monopoly concessions are common. The concession to the company which built the English Channel Tunnel specifies that England and France may not take any steps to facilitate any other transportation connection until the year 2000. Even more significantly, the two governments agreed that during the 50-year term of the concession, they would not help finance through public funds or public guarantees any such connection. Without such state help, any competitor would face a difficult road.

This aspect of concessions can be politically sensitive in environments in which privatization is justified by a need to abolish state monopolies. More to the point, the government must take steps to prevent abuse of the economic power that a monopoly implies. This includes not only the obvious pricing abuses but asset maintenance and service issues as well. In the absence of a free market to assure good service through safe equipment at fair prices, the government must devise reasonable alternatives.

These concerns are properly addressed through controls on the concessionaire's pricing, either through regulation or in the concession contract itself. For example, if the project suffers cost overruns due to fault of the concessionaire, it must not be permitted to recover that overrun through price increases. When the government lacks the resources to put up infrastructure that the society needs to advance the general economic good, innovative compromises are the government's best alternative.

Of course, the best remedy to monopoly of power is to end it. Accordingly, governments have been increasingly aggressive in limiting the terms of monopoly rights to reasonable periods for the repayment of debt and return on investment.

**Advantages and Disadvantages of the Concession.** In granting a concession, of course, the government cedes control for the duration of the concession over a crucial aspect of the national economy—its infrastructure—to people who may not have the greater interests of the nation foremost in their minds. There are, however, substantial advantages that counter the drawbacks.

First, as noted earlier, the government adds an infrastructure asset to the nation without having to spend any sums from the national treasury. Better infrastructure, in turn, attracts other forms of investment to boost the economy. An international shoe manufacturer is more likely to locate in a nation with a reliable power supply to run its equipment and good roads and port facilities to bring in components and ship product. Each of these new investors will employ citizens; both employer and employees will pay taxes. Instead of an outflow from threadbare public coffers, there is a substantial positive inflow. National development is advanced while enhancing, rather than adversely affecting, the national budget.

Second, the cost of services is shifted from taxpayers to users of the services. Instead of a road which is paid for equally by those who never use it and those who routinely send 50 ton semitrailers over it, there is a toll road which charges by use. This, in turn, introduces market discipline. If the road concessionaire is to keep winning customers over from their free alternatives, he must deliver well-maintained, fast roads that are worth the price of admission.

Third, in some transactions, the government may be able to negotiate an equity share of the project company. In such cases, the government can actually earn a profit from its own concession. This is not so much important for the revenue that it brings the national treasury, but for the financing flexibility that it introduces into transactions. For example, when the Turkish State decided to create a new telecommunications network, it felt that given the potential market it should receive $500 million for its telephony license offering. When it found no takers, it put its money where its mouth was by accepting a $100 million BOT proposal to build the system. To make up for what it viewed as lost value, it retained a nonvoting participation in 52% of the project's profits. That interest is projected to bring the Turkish State more than its first "fixed price" deal.

Fourth, by offering an equity interest in the project, the government can more readily attract foreign capital. Typical "turn-key" construction projects do not present the entrepreneurial potential of a long-term BOT project. Therefore, the former typically attracts such interest only if they offer the foreign firms a high fixed profit margin. BOT projects can generate interest at lower initial rates, with the potential entrepreneurial payoff resulting from good long-term service and client development.

Fifth, at the end of the term of a BOT transaction, the government receives an infrastructure asset of substantial value. Some equipment assets, such as power plants, may have lost much of their value by the end of the term. Others, such as roads and bridges, may actually appreciate in value over time. The more businesses attracted to the neighborhood of a bridge, for example, the more valuable the bridge becomes.

Finally, concessions enhance the nation's physical and human technological infrastructure. Such projects bring in and improve the use of modern technology and train local citizens in the use of such technology. A modern power generation station, for instance, is a computer-driven technological wonder, manufactured with state-of-the-art construction techniques and equipment. The engineers that will run and maintain the plant will require a high level of training and expertise to do so successfully. Without such projects, in many nations there would otherwise be little occasion for such technology to appear. To continue the power plant example, existing generation plants with obsolete technology from the 1950s would unreliably sputter along, its workers learning nothing of significant value in the modern world.

On the negative side, the government is losing a measure of control over the nation's destiny since a large project is likely to represent a high percentage of a smaller country's infrastructure needs. To the extent that the private entrepreneur does a poor job, the government will not have the technical expertise to replace it and may be a bit at its mercy. The government must also be concerned about the reliability, safety, and cost of the now private services. These risks can be ameliorated in a number of ways.

First, the government can control the central network into which these infrastructure projects join. An independent electric power producer must generally sell all or a substantial portion of its output into the national grid, a bridge services the national road system, and so on. By controlling the concessionaire's access, and conditioning the terms of that access, the government can maintain a measure of control over the concessionaire.

Further, the concession will also often contain performance requirements. If the concessionaire fails to achieve certain project completion benchmarks or specified plant generation goals within stated periods, it pays significant penalties or forfeits the concession. The same can be done with safety and employment concerns.

Finally, the government can do what the United States has historically done with its private utility, telecommunications, transportation, and health care sectors, among others: It can regulate.

Concession transactions are becoming an increasingly accepted method for building infrastructure throughout the world. Originally viewed as a sophisticated financing technique only for institutional investors, the model has progressed to financing by the general public. In the United States and the United Kingdom, such projects are now financed by securities listed on public exchanges.

## The Models in Combination

As noted at the outset, the models of privatization discussed here seldom occur in a pure form. For instructive purposes, a review of a few "impure" variations is helpful.

**The Joint Venture Privatization.** A government may compromise its desire for control enough to grant the investor group an even share of the new enterprise, but not enough to give it minority control. The resulting joint venture privatization is really a mix of the trade sale model and the noncontrolling interest model (see Exhibit 20.5).

Because of the ensured equity deadlock in the joint venture structure, most of the important structural issues are addressed in the shareholders' agreement between the parties. In typical

**EXHIBIT 20.5    Joint Venture**

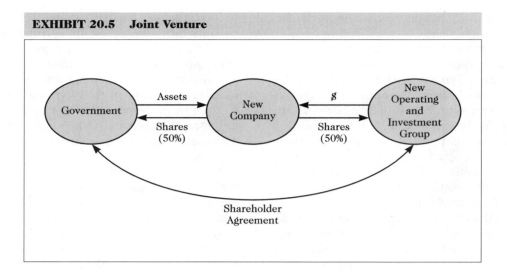

government/foreign investor joint ventures, such shareholder agreements will grant the investor control over most day-to-day operating matters. The government maintains control over certain issues in which it has a special interest, such as minimum production or employment levels. Finally, other areas will be specified over which both parties have an equal say and, thus, the ability to deadlock the firm.

**Example of Privatization Mixing Models.** Some privatization deals include a little of everything. The following model, which is outlined in Exhibit 20.6, addresses a number of issues.

The transaction begins by the government transferring public assets, including a concession, to a new company for 40 percent of the shares and a waiver of some pension and other rights from its former employees. Simultaneously, the private operator makes a significant capital contribution in the new firm in exchange for 50 percent of the new company. At the same time, the employees enter into a labor contract with the new firm on more favorable terms than their former contract with the government and waive rights against the government in exchange for 10 percent of the new company.

To obtain cash for the national treasury immediately, the government sells three-fourths of its holding (30 percent of the new company) to underwriters for distribution to the general public.

As a condition of the sale, the government may require that the underwriters resell a portion of the stock to the local national public on local stock exchanges. In addition to generating revenue for the public coffers, the offering gives a broad segment of the citizenry a stake in the venture. The government maintains a 10 percent interest in order to retain a voice in the affairs of the firm and to realize some of the long-term equity growth associated with a successful new venture.

Similarly, the operator reduces its capital exposure by reselling part of its stake (20 percent of the new company) to the public in an underwritten offering. The sale to the international public market assures the highest possible return to the operator. The operator retains a 30 percent block, which is sufficient in light of the wide holding of the balance of the stock. After the smoke clears, the passive investing public holds 50 percent of the stock, assuring the operator continuing effective control with its 30 percent block.

The transaction is essentially a trade sale but has broad elements of the employee purchase, noncontrolling interest, and concession financing models—in short, privatization soup.

*http://www.ncpa.org/~ncpa/pi/internat/*
*intdex7.html*
*Contains links to privatization information on several countries, including Peru, the Czech Republic, and Poland.*

**EXHIBIT 20.6   Mixed Example**

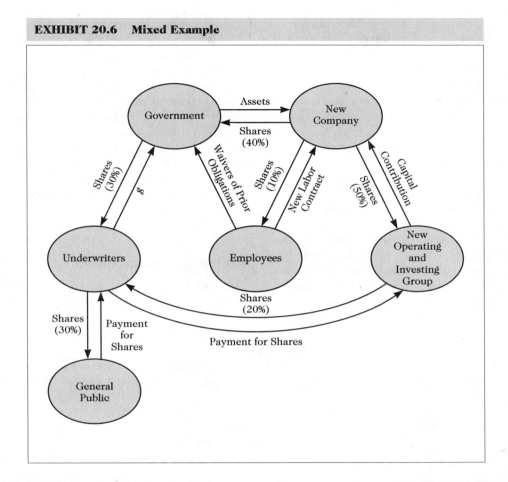

## Regulation of the Privatized Entity

Once a nongovernment entity is providing a product or service, it will typically seek to do so in a fashion that maximizes return to that entity. Accordingly, a new regulatory scheme is often necessary for the new private industry to assure some accountability to the general welfare.

The government is not free to regulate as it pleases. If a state is to privatize successfully, it must attract investment capital and it is in competition with others for investment dollars, marks, pounds, yen, pesos, and francs. Western European nations, for instance, have modified their tax laws to make equity investment in privatized entities as attractive as in the United States and the United Kingdom. Even the resolutely impassive Bundesbank has on occasion succumbed to pressures to lower short-term rates in order to attract funds into new Eastern German equity issues. In this highly competitive environment, governments must strike a balance between safeguarding the national welfare and attracting capital. In the context of privatization, regulation is as much about creating incentives to investment as disincentives to bad acts.

### Taxation

The most significant type of regulation is taxation. When the enterprise was a unit of the government, it was exempt from taxation, so the government and entrepreneur have a full range of options in structuring the taxation of the enterprise. The government may offer tax benefits to make the new company more profitable; a tax holiday on the company's initial profits, investment tax credits, accelerated depreciation, or other incentives may be advanced to the new company. The active investor and passive-investing public can be offered favorable tax treatment for long-term capital gains on privatization investments. Such benefits may facilitate a transfer by reducing one major expense during the enterprise's initial period. Moreover, they permit the government to realize a higher up-front price. Of course, these benefits should be weighed against the reduction in tax revenues to the government from the firm. Many laws around the world, for example, effect a compromise by granting a temporary tax exemption to newly privatized companies.

Tax codes, though, may always be changed. If the tax holiday is merely reflected in the law of the land, it is safe only until the next day that the legislature meets. In the 1980s, one session of the U.S. Congress, for example, repealed many provisions of the Internal Revenue Code favoring capital investment: the investment tax credit and acceler-

ated depreciation, historic renovation, and other similar provisions. Every year, new provisions are enacted and other provisions are tossed out.

Foreign investors in privatization demand and generally obtain greater certainty. They do so by securing covenants in the transfer documents contractually obligating the government to a set of commitments on tax issues. Paradoxically, these agreements on tax issues have greater binding force than legislation. As the *Alcoa Minerals* case made clear, once a government makes an agreement with respect to tax issues and agrees to have the agreement enforced by international arbitration, it must abide by it.

## Repatriation and Other Currency Issues

A regulatory issue of major concern to the new company involves the rules that determine the

---

### BACKGROUND AND FACTS

In an agreement concluded in 1968 for a term of 25 years, Alcoa agreed with Jamaica that it would construct an aluminum refining plant in Jamaica. Under the agreement, Jamaica granted Alcoa long-term concessions for the mining of bauxite in Jamaica. The agreement contained a "no further tax" clause according to which Jamaica would not impose any taxes on Alcoa's mining and refining operations other than those specifically provided in the agreement. The agreement also contained a clause referring to ICSID arbitration of any dispute arising under the agreement.

After Alcoa had constructed the alumina plant and had begun the mining of bauxite, Jamaica announced in 1974 that the taxes on the mining of bauxite were to be increased. When the subsequent negotiations with the mining companies did not result in an agreement on the amount of the increase, Jamaica enacted the Bauxite (Production Levy) Act of 1974. Under this Act, the taxes to be paid by Alcoa in respect to its mining operations rose from U.S.$2.2 million to U.S.$2.8 million.

On May 8, 1974, shortly before enacting the Bauxite Act, Jamaica notified ICSID as follows:

### Alcoa Minerals of Jamaica, Inc. v. Government of Jamaica
*IV Yearbook of Commercial Arbitration 206 (1975) International Centre for Settlement of Investment Disputes*

The Government of Jamaica hereby notifies the Centre that the following class of dispute at any time arising shall not be subject to the jurisdiction of the Centre.

**Class of Dispute.** Legal dispute arising directly out of an investment relating to minerals or the national resources. Considering Jamaica's imposition of the production levy to be a violation of the "no further tax clause," Alcoa initiated ICSID arbitration and approached Jamaica for the constitution of an arbitral tribunal. When, after three months, Jamaica had not answered, Alcoa appointed its arbitrator. Upon the continued refusal of Jamaica to appoint its arbitrator, the chairman of the Administrative Council of ICSID appointed two other arbitrators.

### MESSRS. KERR, ROUHANI, AND TROLLE

The arbitral tribunal considered next the issue of the parties' consent to arbitrate. Art. 25, para. 1, of the Convention specifies that the consent must be in writing. Para. 24 of the Director's Report . . . states that one of the examples of consent is the clause included in an investment agreement, providing for the submission to the Centre of future

*(continued)*

*(continued)*

disputes arising out of that agreement. Accordingly, the arbitral tribunal found that the arbitral clause in the 1968 agreement between Alcoa and Jamaica satisfied the requirement of written mutual consent to arbitrate.

The above-mentioned para. 24 of the Directors' Report states "Consent of the parties must exist when the Centre is seized." . . . This raised the question whether the Jamaican notification of May 8, 1974, to ICSID affected the prior agreement to arbitrate.

To assess the jurisdictional import of this notice, the arbitral tribunal quoted the last sentence in Art. 25, para. 1, "When the parties have given their consent, no party may withdraw its consent unilaterally." The arbitral tribunal applied Art. 25, para. 1, without limitation, and held the notification ineffective to abrogate Jamaica's prior consent to ICSID arbitration of disputes arising out of the investment agreement with Alcoa. The arbitral tribunal stated in particular:

> In the present case, the written consent was contained in the arbitration clause between the government and Alcoa which has already been quoted. This consent having been given could not be withdrawn. The notification under Article 25 only operates for the future by way of information to the Centre and potential future investors in undertakings concerning minerals and the natural resources of Jamaica.

The arbitral tribunal concluded that to decide otherwise "would largely, if not wholly, deprive the convention of any practical value." In addition, in denying the Jamaican notification retroactive effect, the arbitral tribunal relied again upon the Directors' Report, which states in para. 31 in part that:

> [A]rt. 25, para. 4, expressly permits contracting states to make known to the Centre in advance, if they so desire, the classes of disputes which they would or would not consider submitting to the Centre.

**Decision.** As a preliminary matter in the proceeding, the arbitral tribunal held that the dispute was within its jurisdiction and that the Jamaican notification did not affect its agreement to arbitrate.

---

amount of its profits that, as a foreign investor, the company may repatriate and the exchange rate at which they may be repatriated. Lenders in the buyer's home country generally want assurances that the new company will be able to exchange its local cash flow into hard, internationally convertible currency, so that the investor can service its debts at home. Potential foreign investors in the privatized company will put their capital at risk only if they see a reasonable prospect of being able to realize a profit in their home currencies.

These repatriation impediments can be significant. For example, at one time under the Dominican Republic's Foreign Investment Law, the foreign investor could repatriate only the value of its capital investment plus annual net profits not exceeding 25 percent of that value. If annual net profits ever exceeded 25 percent of the capital investment value, repatriation of the excess was permanently prohibited. Obviously, such regulation poses serious problems for enterprises that

are not capital intensive or those that rely on high returns in later years after losses in the initial years. Faced with a pressing need to attract foreign investment, many nations have addressed the problem of repatriation by lifting all controls. The Polish privatization law, for instance, specifically allows income received by foreign parties to be transferred abroad. Similar liberalization has been seen in connection with the privatization movement in countries as disparate as Chile, Ghana, Zaire, and Argentina.

In the absence of a general law permitting repatriation, potential privatization investors frequently seek *remittance rights on capital* from the government as part of their privatization deal. These rights permit the owner to take specified sums out of the country, irrespective of legal limitations of general applicability. These rights must usually be acquired from the national bank of the finance ministry rather than the privatizing agency. The foreign investor must, therefore, carefully coordinate the process.

# Argentina Shops Shares in Its Telephone System
## Privatization in Latin America: Placing State Owned Property into Private Hands

The Argentine Government, hoping to sustain its economic turnaround and hasten its privatization program, went on the road to persuade international investors to buy shares in the country's telephone system.... The Government sold 60 percent of Telefonica de Argentina, representing half of the nation's service, to an investment group last November, but this is the public's first chance to buy shares. Beginning in Madrid and Minneapolis last Monday and continuing throughout Europe and the United States last week, the lead underwriters, Government officials and officers of the company are presenting their roadshow to pension fund managers, mutual fund companies and other institutions.

Thirty percent of the company will be sold, with shares selling for a minimum price of 16.5 cents to raise at least $600 million. Officials hope that an auction similar to the process of selling United States Treasury securities will push the price above 20 cents a share, or more than $800 million.... Bankers say this departure from the fixed prices of most initial public offerings could discourage some investors. Moreover, they say, only last Monday did the Government release a prospectus and other documentation on the company's balance sheet. "How can I advise my clients if only today I received the documents," said Gordon Davis, broker on the Buenos Aires Stock Exchange.

Government officials say the offering must take place as soon as possible. "The probability is that they will not maximize value," said one banker close to the negotiations. "But politically it is extremely important that you do this deal before the end of the year. They need the money, and they need to show a credible deal."

The cash is vital for President Carlos Saul Menem's Government to maintain the kind of budget surplus that international lending organizations like the International Monetary Fund (IMF) are demanding for the country to prove its fiscal stability and responsibility.... IMF officials have repeatedly voiced concerns that Argentina is not running a large enough budget surplus and thus depends heavily on the cash from privatizations to meet its obligations. They note that such sales are one-time events that may cover deficits now but not in the future.

The country's Economy Minister, Domingo F. Cavallo, argues that much of the proceeds from sales are being used for one-time payments of pension fund obligations of the privatized companies.... In Argentina, four of the largest banks—Banco Roberts, Banco Galicia, Banco Rio de La Plata, and Banco Tornquist—are leading domestic sales. Small investors, buying $5,000 or less, will get a 5 percent discount.

Latin American telephone companies have been hot stocks this year. Telefonos Mexicanos, also called Telmex, issued stock to the public in May at the equivalent of $1.36 a share. The shares have risen 85 percent and have recently been trading at around $2.15. On the New York Stock Exchange, Telmex American Depository Shares, each representing 20 shares of the underlying stock, were originally sold for $27.25 and are now trading at around $43. "The telephone is an essential tool for almost everybody," said Douglas A. Campbell, president of D.A. Campbell Company, a money management firm in Santa Monica, California. "Thus, it is a very stable business, almost like food."

Mr. Campbell added that Latin American phone companies tend to be especially productive cash cows, since most have barely begun to saturate their market. California has 85 telephones for every 100 people, he said, while Latin America generally has fewer than 10. "You have almost unlimited demand, and all you have to do is keep pumping in telephones," he said. "It has got to be one of the most profitable businesses in the world."

For Argentina, the initial public offering of Telefonica comes a year after the nation sold a controlling interest in its telephone system to private

*(continued)*

*(continued)*

investors. In November 1990, Argentina split its telephone company, Entel, in two, giving each company about half of the nation's population. It sold a 60 percent interest in Telefonica to a group of investors led by Citicorp [which paid for much of its interest by canceling Argentina's debt to private banks], Spain's national telephone company, and an Argentine industrial group called Techint.

A 60 percent interest in the other company, called Telecom, was sold to a group led by J. P. Morgan [which also paid for its interest with sovereign Argentine debt], Italy's telephone company, France's telephone company, and Perez Companc,

an Argentine industrial group. The combined sales earned the government $214 million in cash and the right to retire almost $5 billion in debt. It plans to sell 30 percent of both entities to the public, and eventually 10 percent to employees. The Telecom shares are expected to be sold in March. . . .

Mr. Campbell noted that Telefonica, at 16.5 cents a share, has a price-to-earnings ratio of almost 12, equivalent to the other major international telephone stocks. "That's no bargain," he said. "It is very full price." Mr. Davis, the Buenos Aires broker, agreed. "For a good deal, you want to price it a little low so that people want to come back for the second offering next year," he said.

## Regulation of Operations

Aside from regulation of the financial aspects of the privatized entity, the government must establish a system to regulate the actual operations of the entity. In essence, once the government ceases to control the operation of the enterprise, it needs to ensure that the new private entity operates in a way that is not contrary to the public interest. New general regulations on competition, safety, and technical standards are needed. In many sectors of the economy, these requirements involve the creation of a new regulatory agency. The new company, however, must not be so controlled as to curtail the independent action and management decision making that are essential if any gains are to be realized from privatization.

One of the technical tasks often funded by the World Bank is the creation of such regulatory schemes. If the government is no longer the sole source of television programming, a regulatory commission must determine how to distribute available television channels and what material may be aired to the public. If the government is no longer providing electricity and hands over a limited power generation monopoly to private hands, it must find a way to prevent abusive rate setting. International teams of regulatory lawyers are employed to assist fledgling privatizing governments in setting up such structures. In many instances, the regulations in developing nations are somewhat more forgiving than in developed countries in order to encourage privatization investment.

In some cases, the new enterprise is given quasi-governmental powers to carry out its business. For example, a utility may be authorized to use eminent domain to acquire rights of way for transmission lines. New British public telecommunications operators can install equipment and acquire land compulsorily and are even protected from certain criminal offenses in exercising these rights.

The government may also provide for exemptions from otherwise applicable general regulations as a way of assisting the new company in achieving profitability. For example, in the United States, the Northeast Rail Service Act privatized Conrail and relieved the new company from state taxes and labor protection requirements, significantly reducing its initial operating costs. The act also gave Conrail greater flexibility in abandoning unprofitable lines than is commonly the case for other U.S. rail carriers.

**http://www.ncpa.org/pd/pdmonth.html**
and
**http://pw2.netcom.com/~interdev/risk.htm**
*Sites on privatization issues.*

## Chapter Summary

The privatization of formerly state-run enterprises is the most important development in international corporate law in recent memory. Its dramatic rise has virtually eliminated nonmarket economies and has made the private corporation or partnership the most important economic factor in the international marketplace. With its rise, nations have lost direct control over labor and environmental issues and have turned to regulation as a way to curb capitalism's less attractive tendencies.

---

## QUESTIONS AND CASE PROBLEMS

1. Is privatization a recent phenomenon? Why has it become more prominent in recent years? What triggered the move to more privatization in Latin American countries? In former communist nations?
2. Briefly describe the partial sale model of privatization. What is the predominant characteristic of the partial sale? How can a minority private investor try to protect itself from abuse by the majority government owner?
3. Briefly describe the trade sale model of privatization. What is the distinguishing feature of the trade sale? How is privatization achieved through management contracts?
4. List three reasons why giving employees an equity share in the new private entity makes sense. Give a reason that is principally applicable in Eastern Europe. What are two disadvantages associated with transferring shares to employees? What are two types of consideration that employees can be asked to give in exchange for their shares?
5. Briefly describe the concession model of privatization. How long should the term of the concession be?
6. Name four types of adjustments to regulations that are often addressed in the context of privatizations. Explain how they may be addressed.

## MANAGERIAL IMPLICATIONS

Your firm, Lloyd Aviation Company, is a leading U.S. manufacturer of helicopters. While on a trip to Moscow, you met Gennady Tupolev, the head of the former Soviet Air Force division that once manufactured military helicopters. The Russian government has no funds to finance further operations for the Tupolev Division and he needs to privatize its operations. The Russian government is reluctant to cede control over an industry that is so central to its national security; however, its conversion to commercial production will require thorough control by Lloyd. The division has a strong research and development department. Many of the division's lower-level employees, however, will need to be laid off if it is to be a commercially viable operation.

1. Prepare a memorandum to Lloyd's board of directors outlining your plan for privatizing the Tupolev Division.
2. What regulatory arrangements should Lloyd make with the Russian government?

# Chapter Twenty-One

# Labor and Employment Discrimination Law

Corporations are lifeless entities with one principal objective: maximizing profit for their stockholders. To be sure, many corporate leaders seek to run them in a way that is solicitous of the people who work for them. In many cases, the best policy is that which is most respectful of the enterprise's workers. Hard experience in the industrialized world, however, teaches that unless government intervenes, corporations will often subordinate the interests of their workers to those of their stockholders. Accordingly, virtually all societies have enacted laws that protect workers from abusive or discriminatory practices.

This regulation varies widely from place to place. For example, the protective framework that safeguards and enfranchises German workers is extremely different from the United States' emphasis on individual achievement by workers and on control by managers. This chapter examines different approaches in this important area and their effect on international business transactions.

## General Directions of Labor Law Abroad

Any active investment, whether controlled by investors from the United States or from some other country, relies on employees. As such, it is influenced by the labor laws in the host country. Because these laws are often different from those encountered in the United States, investors must review them and the attitudes they reflect. Although a more detailed study would reveal countless differences between U.S. and foreign labor laws, a review of three principal areas gives a general sense of the distinctions.

First, many nations require employee consultation or participation in management decisions that Americans view as being central to the managerial prerogative. Second, many countries place restraints on employee dismissal that are completely unfamiliar to the U.S. investor. Third, the U.S. investor should bear in mind that when it acquires a foreign business, it may also be acquiring the industry's labor arrangements.

> **http://www.ilo.org**
> *See for links to relevant topics from the ILO.*

## Employee Participation in Strategic Decisions

A current controversy in managerial theory involves the extent of freedom that owners and management should have in making strategic decisions and whether labor may participate in such decisions. The positions that nations take on these issues are strongly influenced by their respective sociopolitical traditions. One of the interesting phenomena of modern society is how these approaches are tending to merge.

**The U.S. View.** Notwithstanding recent legislative initiatives such as the *Worker Adjustment, Retraining, and Notification Act,* which at times requires sixty days' notice of the closing of a plant with more than 100 employees, U.S. companies come from an environment that allows them great flexibility. Traditionally in the United States, management, completely by itself and in secret, makes strategic decisions such as whether to close a plant or reduce manpower levels. In the United States, management decides and labor carries out those decisions at an agreed hourly rate. Indeed, the U.S. Supreme Court has squarely held that an employer need not bargain with its employees over whether to shut down part of its business. The Court viewed this prerogative as akin to the closing down of a business, where "an employer has the absolute right to terminate his entire business for any reason he pleases."

**The German Approach.** Europeans have traditionally viewed the role of workers quite differently. In many continental countries, workers are granted a right of consultation about or notice before the implementation of decisions resulting in workforce reductions.

In this regard, Germany tends to be particularly generous in granting its workers rights of participation. By law, each plant with more than five employees must have a *Betriebsrat* (works council) to represent that plant's interest. In contrast to any U.S. counterpart, these works councils are independent from trade unions. They represent the interests of plant employees as distinct from those of the employer or those of the trade unions.

Under the *German Works Constitution Act,* the employer must fully inform the works council in "due time" of any plant changes that might result in "substantial disadvantages for employees" and consult with it on such proposals. In the course of that consultation, the employer solicits the works council's approval of the employer's method of selecting persons to be terminated as a result of the plant change. If the employer and the works council cannot resolve a dispute through this methodology, they then appear before an arbitration committee. In addition, the employer notifies the regional office of the Federal Employment Institute. If this office believes the plant change would strain local resources, it can delay the change until two months after notice. As these examples illustrate, U.S. companies can be confronted with a radically different labor situation once they go abroad.

## Mandatory Employee Representation on Boards of Directors

A number of countries—particularly those with a two-tiered board structure—require substantial employee representation on the board of directors. The two-tier board consists of a large *Aufsichtsrat* (supervisory board) and a *Vorstand* (management board). The Aufsichtsrat is responsible for representing shareholder interests, while the Vorstand manages the firm from day to day.

In Germany, the Netherlands, and Luxembourg, employees have direct representation in the Aufsichtsrat. Indeed, in Germany, companies that employ more than 2,000 workers must establish Aufsichtsrate representation that is 50 percent labor and 50 percent shareholders. In companies with more than 500 workers, one-third of the Aufsichtsrat must be composed of workers.

This Germanic focus on worker participation in corporate decisions has proved attractive to former communist nations. Nearly 50 years of Marxist emphasis on the rights of workers, after all, is not discarded completely when a nation takes tentative steps toward capitalism. The Czech Republic and Poland, among others, have followed the German model of worker boards.

The implications for U.S. investors are important. All significant strategic decisions require supervisory board approval. Thus, the Vorstand must present persuasive reasons for a strategic plan that involves workforce reductions. Clearly, the flexibility of management is not as great in Germany as in the United States.

In Japan, management–labor strife is rare because of traditional and structural factors that blur distinctions between management and workers. Union leadership is a stepping stone to management; nearly 15 percent of union officials rise to serve as executives of the company. Consequently, union leaders have little incentive to take strident labor positions against those responsible for their advancement.

## Impediments to Dismissal

Law is a reflection of prevailing social norms. Nowhere is this as clear as in how different nations address the issue of employee dismissal. National attitudes toward the proper relationship between manager and employee heavily color the content of national law.

**Underlying Philosophical Foundations.**   People in the United States, perhaps the most capitalistic of nations, do not commonly believe that anyone is *entitled* to a job. Once an individual ceases to be productive, his or her future employment is in jeopardy. Severance pay is viewed as nothing more than a humane cushion to help the discharged until they can find new employment.

Europeans, on the other hand, feel that employees acquire a property interest in their jobs over time. Thus, the more senior an employee, the greater is his or her property interest. Accordingly, severance pay is viewed more as compensation for the taking of substantial property, and it increases as the employee becomes more senior. For the most senior employees, the high severance level can be so prohibitive as to strongly discourage involuntary dismissal.

The Japanese generally view a person's job as a central part of his or her place in society and believe that a job largely defines who a person is. An individual is expected to hold a job for the same company for a lifetime. In Japan, the focus is not on the conditions of dismissal but on the propriety of dismissal.

**Legal Frameworks Reflecting Philosophy.**   In the United States, employers historically have been able to terminate employees with little, if any, notice. Without a collective bargaining agreement in place, U.S. management is not limited in its employee termination options. This picture has changed somewhat as U.S. businesses have been influenced by European and Japanese practices. New federal legislation now gives employees unpaid leave to care for family members, guarantees workers their jobs back after such leave, and requires warning of plant closings. Some U.S. managers have begun to build employee loyalty by taking a page from Japanese companies and seeking ways of providing greater assurance of employment. Nonetheless, U.S. entrepreneurs remain relatively free to do what they wish with their employees. They face quite a different world beyond their shores.

In the United Kingdom, an employer must consult with the appropriate trade union before making a dismissal. If the workforce is to be reduced by ten or more employees, a consultation must take place sixty days prior to termination. In Germany, the works council must approve any dismissal. If it does not, the employer may appeal to a labor court, but is likely to lose the appeal. Indeed, the Betriebsrat can affirmatively call for the dismissal of employees even without a request from the employer.

Japan is perhaps the most interesting case. There the written law seems to permit relatively free dismissal of employees. But tradition, embodied in decisional law, protects the employee (see the *Kochi Hoso* case).

---

### *Kochi Hoso (Broadcasting Co.) Case*
*Rokeisokv No. 937 (1977)*
*Supreme Court of Japan*

BACKGROUND AND FACTS
Like all Japanese firms with more than ten employees, Kochi Hoso was required to maintain rules of employment that specified the conditions under which an employee might be discharged. Kochi Hoso, a radio broadcasting company, clearly specified that tardiness for a broadcast was cause for dismissal. No contractual provision excused such tardiness.

The plaintiff, a radio announcer, had twice failed to arrive at the studio in time for a news broadcast. After the second offense, Kochi Hoso discharged the plaintiff, pointing to the unambiguous rules.

Plaintiff sought reinstatement, arguing that although the discharge was within the rules, it was unreasonable or contrary to public policy. The Supreme Court found no reasonable cause for termination.

PER CURIAM
Even when an employee's conduct constitutes a cause for a discharge, an employer may not always discharge the employee. It should be noted that when the said discharge is found to

*(continued)*

---

*(continued)*

be significantly unreasonable under the specific situation so that it could be hardly approved as being appropriate in the light of the socially accepted view, such a discharge should be considered to be

an abusive exercise of an employer's power to discharge employees and, thus, to be invalid.

**Decision.** The Supreme Court of Japan ordered that the radio announcer be reinstated in his job.

---

A similar attitude is reflected in Japan's approach to plant closings. Japanese companies in financial stress seldom close factories. Instead, plants are taken over by friendly affiliates in good financial condition, or workers are handed over to local successful firms. In this cultural context, U.S. companies, such as Procter & Gamble and Chase Manhattan Bank, have faced court proceedings from local unions challenging plant shutdowns in Japan as "unfair labor practices." And this has occurred even when the U.S. firms offered the dismissed employees new jobs in different locations.

Some signs indicate, however, that just as U.S. employment practices are being influenced by those of Europe and Japan, the Japanese are being influenced by Westerners. During the recession of the early 1990s, giants such as Nippon Telephone & Telegraph, NKK Corporation, and Nissan Corporation all announced reductions in their workforces, threatening the tradition of lifetime employment. These companies did not actually lay off employees, but instead effected the reductions through normal attrition, intra-company transfers, and transfers to subsidiaries. But because many employees predictably rejected unattractive transfers and many of the subsidiaries went out of business, this shift proved to be significant. At the same time, surveys of Japanese executives indicated a broad consensus that the days of lifetime employment and strict seniority advancement systems were numbered. In short, the differences among nations with respect to the permanence of employment are still quite significant, but over time, they are becoming less profound.

### Assumption of Employment Arrangements

A U.S. investor must also beware of existing labor arrangements when it acquires a foreign firm. Unlike the practice in the United States, many foreign nations—particularly European countries—compel corporate acquirers to adhere to existing employment arrangements. Thus, a U.S. investor must assess this possibility before acquiring a foreign company.

> **http://www.mac.doc.gov/tcc/treaty.htm**
> See for links to specific labor/employment topics through the TCC.

## Employment Discrimination Outside the United States

The United States almost certainly has the most comprehensive set of laws against discrimination of all sorts in employment. Because other countries are dominated by homogeneous ethnic groups, they have experienced relatively little need to develop antidiscriminatory schemes. Germany, after all, is where ethnic Germans live and Japan is where ethnic Japanese live; historically, there has not been a similar perception of a need to protect against ethnic discrimination. At the opposite extreme, the Baltic countries, formerly part of the Soviet Union, have passed laws mandating discrimination against the ethnic Russian minority.

Accordingly, the principal employment discrimination issue for U.S. companies has been whether U.S. laws apply to their overseas operations. Foreign laws, however, are becoming more important as international transportation brings ethnic minorities to virtually every nation, and the issue of discrimination against women comes to the fore.

### The Extraterritorial Application of U.S. Employment Discrimination Law

Over the past several years, significant disagreement has arisen in Congress and in the legal community concerning the extent to which U.S. discrimination laws apply abroad and how they could apply if they did. For instance, how can a U.S. company operate in Islamic countries that discriminate against Christians and Jews if it has to treat everyone equally? In 1991, the U.S. Supreme Court first gave some direction in this area.

---

### Equal Employment Opportunity Commission v. Arabian American Oil Co.

*499 U.S. 244 (1991)*
*United States Supreme Court*

#### BACKGROUND AND FACTS

The respondents are two Delaware corporations, Arabian American Oil Company (Aramco) and its subsidiary, Aramco Service Company (ASC). Aramco's principal place of business is Dhahran, Saudi Arabia, and it is licensed to do business in Texas.

In 1979, Boureslan was hired by ASC as a cost engineer in Houston. A year later he was transferred, at his request, to work for Aramco in Saudi Arabia. Boureslan remained with Aramco in Saudi Arabia until he was discharged in 1984. He instituted this suit in the United States District Court for the Southern District of Texas against Aramco and ASC. He sought relief under Title VII of the Civil Rights Act on the ground that he was harassed and ultimately discharged by respondents on account of his race, religion, and national origin.

#### CHIEF JUSTICE REHNQUIST

Both parties concede, as they must, that Congress has the authority to enforce its laws beyond the territorial boundaries of the United States. Whether Congress has in fact exercised that authority in this case is a matter of statutory construction. It is our task to determine whether Congress intended the protections of Title VII to apply to United States citizens employed by American employers outside of the United States.

It is a long-standing principle of American law "that legislation of Congress, unless a contrary intent appears, is meant to apply only within the territorial jurisdiction of the United States." It serves to protect against unintended clashes between our laws and those of other nations which could result in international discord.

Title VII prohibits various discriminatory employment practices based on an individual's race, color, religion, sex, or national origin. An employer is subject to Title VII if it is "engaged in an industry affecting commerce." "Commerce," in turn, is defined as "trade, traffic, commerce, transportation, transmission, or communication among the several States; or between a State and any place outside thereof." . . .

Petitioners . . . assert that since Title VII defines "States" to include States, the District of Columbia, and specified territories, the clause "between a State and any place outside thereof" must be referring to areas beyond the territorial limit of the United States.

The language relied upon by petitioners—and it is they who must make the affirmative showing—is ambiguous, and does not speak directly to the question presented here. The intent of Congress as to the extraterritorial application of this statute must be deduced by inference from boilerplate language which can be found in any number of congressional acts, none of which have ever been held to apply overseas.

If we were to permit possible, or even plausible interpretations of language such as that involved here to override the presumption against extraterritorial application, there would be little left of the presumption.

Petitioners argue that Title VII's "alien exemption provision . . . clearly manifests an intention" by Congress to protect U.S. citizens with respect to their employment outside of the United States. The alien exemption provision says that "the statute" shall not apply to an employer with respect to the employment of aliens outside any State." Petitioners contend that from this language a negative inference should be drawn that Congress intended Title VII to cover United States citizens.

If petitioners are correct that the alien-exemption clause means that the statute applies to employers overseas, we see no way of distinguishing in its application between United States employers and foreign employers. Thus, a French employer of a United States citizen in France would be subject to Title VII—a result at which even petitioners balk. The EEOC assures us that in its view the term "employer" means only "American employer," but there is no such distinction in this statute.

It is also reasonable to conclude that had Congress intended Title VII to apply overseas, it

*(continued)*

*(continued)*

would have addressed the subject of conflicts with foreign laws and procedures. In amending the Age Discrimination in Employment Act of 1967 to apply abroad, Congress specifically addressed potential conflicts with foreign law by providing that it is not unlawful for an employer to take any action prohibited by the ADEA "where such practices involve an employee in a workplace in a foreign country, and compli-ance with the ADEA would cause such employer . . . to violate the laws of the country in which such workplace is located." Title VII, by contrast, fails to address conflicts with the laws of other nations.

**Decision.** Petitioners failed to present sufficient affirmative evidence that Congress intended Title VII to apply abroad. Accordingly, the judgment of the Court of Appeals was affirmed.

Soon after the Supreme Court had spoken, Congress sought to overrule the *Aramco* case by at least partially extending United States employment law overseas. In the *Civil Rights Act of 1991,* Congress expressly extended Title VII to firms operating outside the United States under the "control" of a U.S. entity (see Exhibit 21.1). As the *Aramco* court predicted, Congress made an exception for situations where compliance with Title VII would violate the law of the country where the firm is located.

Congress' enactment did not prove to be the last word. A few years after the enactment of the Act (Title VII) the *Equal Employment Opportunity Commission* (EEOC) sought to give some direction to U.S. employers in its Enforcement Guidance Memorandum No. 915.002. In doing so, the EEOC also enunciated its views on the extraterritorial application of the *Americans with Disabilities Act* (ADA). But U.S. courts did not readily accept EEOC guidance. They have developed three principal defenses to U.S. challenges of employment decisions abroad. These are whether (1) the decision is made by "a foreign person not controlled by an American employer," (2) United States Title VII and the ADEA conflict with a host country's laws, so that the employer faces "foreign compulsion" because to comply with U.S. law would violate the host country's laws, and (3) performance of the job requires a

---

**EXHIBIT 21.1    Extension of Title VII to Foreign Operations of U.S. Firms**

**Civil Rights Act of 1991**
**Pub. L. No. 102–166, 105 Stat. 1071, 1077–78 (1991)**
**United States Congress**
**Sec. 109. Protection of Extraterritorial Employment**

a. Definition of Employee. [The Civil Rights Act and the Americans with Disabilities Act] are each amended by adding to the end the following: "With respect to employment in a foreign country, such term includes an individual who is a citizen of the United States." . . .

b. "It shall not be unlawful under [the Civil Rights Act] for an employer (or a corporation controlled by an employer), . . . to take any action otherwise prohibited . . . with respect to an employee in a workplace in a foreign country if compliance with such section would cause such employer (or such corporation), . . . to violate the law of the foreign country in which such workplace is located.

c. 1. If an employer controls a corporation whose place of incorporation is a foreign country, any practice prohibited by section 703 or 704 engaged in such corporation shall be presumed to be engaged in by such employer.

   2. Sections 703 and 704 shall not apply with respect to the foreign operations of an employer that is a foreign person not controlled by an American employer.

   3. For purposes of this subsection, the determination of whether an employer controls a corporation shall be based on:

     A. the interrelation of operations;

     B. the common management;

     C. the centralized control of labor relations; and

     D. the common ownership or financial control of the employer and the corporation.

trait such as a specific religion or gender, allowing the employer the "bona fide occupational qualification" defense. Each of these will be reviewed in turn.

## Control by a Foreign Person

When Congress passes the ADEA amendments, there was still some hope of clearly defining the nationality of a corporation's controlling person. As international business hopelessly intertwines ownership of entities in industrialized countries beyond recognition. In the following case, after careful examination, the District Court rejected the EEOC's view of nationality and prevented a United States citizen from bringing suit against a firm with very substantial U.S. operations.

---

*Denty v. SmithKline Beecham*
*907 F. Supp. 879 (1995), affd,*
*109 F.3d 147 (1997)*
*United States District Court*
*for the Eastern District*
*of Pennsylvania*

BACKGROUND AND FACTS

The plaintiff Denty was originally hired by SmithKline French, a Pennsylvania corporation, and performed a number of responsible jobs. Denty performed these jobs at SmithKline's offices in Philadelphia. In April 1989, SmithKline merged with the Beecham Group plc, a British corporation. The resulting company was called SmithKline Beecham plc (SB plc). SB plc is organized under the laws of England, and its headquarters are located in Brentford, Middlesex, England. The American operations became SmithKline Beecham Corporation (SBC), a wholly-owned subsidiary of SB plc. According to plaintiff, in 1990, he allegedly was informed that he would not be promoted to a new position because of his age. At the time, plaintiff was 52 years old. Plaintiff claims that in 1992 he applied for four other positions at the vice-president level—and that he was denied these positions on the basis of age. The promotion decisions were made by SB plc executives in England, while Denty worked for SBC in Philadelphia. It was undisputed that all the positions Denty sought were based outside the United States.

DISTRICT JUDGE LOUIS H. POLLAK

Plaintiff Denty alleged that SBC denied him promotions due to his age, in violation of the Age Discrimination in Employment Act (ADEA). . . . SBC sought to dismiss the plaintiffs' compliant, contending that the extraterritorial application of the ADEA and the PHRA do not reach this case because the positions plaintiff sought were located outside the United States for an English company. . . .

In 1984, Congress amended the ADEA to give it a limited extraterritorial reach. . . . Together, the 1984 amendments establish that the ADEA applies abroad only when (1) the employee is an American citizen and (2) the employer is controlled by an American employer. Non-citizens working outside the United States are not protected because they are not considered "employees." And American citizens working abroad for companies not controlled by American companies are not protected because the practices of such companies are not covered by the ADEA. . . .

Defendant argues that the ADEA does not apply to the employment decisions Denty challenges because they all involved positions outside the United States for an English corporation. Denty asserts that the nature of his claim is purely domestic—involving an American citizen working for an American company in the United States. According to Denty, the site of the workplace is the key factor in determining whether a claim exceeds the extraterritorial reach of the ADEA. Denty argues that the relevant work site was SBC's Philadelphia office, where he worked at the time of the alleged discrimination. The proposition that the site of the workplace determines the application of the ADEA is indeed supported by the cases Denty cites. The courts which denied the extraterritorial application of the pre-1984 ADEA held that it was the place of the plaintiffs' employment that led to the dismissal of their claims. In those cases it did not matter that the plaintiffs worked for American corporations or that the allegedly discriminatory decisions were made in the United

*(continued)*

*(continued)*

States; the ADEA claims failed merely because the site of plaintiffs' employment was outside the United States. . . . The plaintiffs in *Cleary, Zahourek,* and *Thomas* were all denied the protection of the ADEA despite the fact that they were directly employed by American companies and not by foreign subsidiaries of the companies. . . . The proposition that the site of the workplace determines the applicability of the ADEA—a proposition in which I acquiesce—does not, however, lead to the conclusion advanced by Denty. The employment decisions at issue here involve Denty's application for positions outside the United States. The relevant work site is the location of these positions, not the location of Denty's employment at the time of the alleged discrimination. . . . The relevant work site in a case of alleged discrimination against a job applicant is the location of the position for which the plaintiff applied. . . . If the ADEA does not apply, Denty asserts, a foreign company with an office in the United States could lawfully discriminate against its American employees on the basis of age by transferring them to the company's foreign office, where, under the laws of the foreign state, the employees could be dismissed on the basis of age. This hypothetical method of evading the ADEA has already been considered by two courts, which have concluded that the problem can be addressed without redefining the definition of a workplace. In Wolf, the court stated, "An exception is made when it is necessary to prevent a transparent evasion of the Act, as where an employer transfers an employee abroad for a short period of time for the purpose of avoiding the Act's coverage." . . . Even if these courts are mistaken that such an exception can be read into the statute, the problem is one to be fixed by Congress, which limited the extraterritorial application of the ADEA. . . .

Because the positions Denty sought were outside the United States, the ADEA only applies if SB plc can be considered to be controlled by an American employer. The ADEA declares that its prohibitions apply when an "employer controls a corporation whose place of incorporation is in a foreign country." . . . Conversely, the ADEA does not apply "where the employer is a foreign person not controlled by an American employer." . . . Denty does not dispute the fact that SB plc was in-

corporated in England. Nor does Denty dispute the fact that SB plc is the 100% owner of SBC, a fact that makes it extremely difficult to believe that SB plc is controlled by SBC. Nonetheless, applying the four-factor test established by the ADEA, Denty argues that SB plc and SBC are indistinguishable and should be considered a "single employer." The "single employer" inquiry advocated by Denty is not the correct inquiry in this case. It derives from cases in which courts have considered whether the number of employees of two nominally distinct entities can be aggregated in determining whether a firm employs the minimum number of employees necessary to be covered by the National Labor Relations Act and, by extension, the ADEA. . . . In this case, the issue is not whether SB plc and SBC should be considered a single employer but whether Denty sought employment with an employer "controlled" by an American firm. Nonetheless, the four-factor test used to determine whether two firms should be considered a single employer is identical to the test specified by the ADEA for "the determination of whether an employer controls a corporation." . . . These factors are "interrelation of operations," "common management," "centralized control of labor relations," and "common ownership or financial control." . . . Operations at SB plc and SBC are highly integrated, organized by the type of work performed and not by location; thus, SmithKline Beecham Pharmaceuticals operates as a unified corporate division in England, in the United States, and elsewhere. Deposition testimony further reveals the interrelationship between the two firms in that SBC employees such as Denty report directly to SB plc employees. Moreover, the two corporations have common management—one CEO, whose offices are in England. Labor relations are similarly centralized—directed by a single Director and Vice-President, whose office is also in England. One annual report is prepared for the two entities, in which revenues are reported on a consolidated basis. . . . The annual report speaks of the corporation in singular terms, as an English corporation. While all of this suggests that SmithKline Beecham's American and English operations overlap to a great extent, it in no way suggests that SB plc is controlled by its American subsidiary. On the contrary, the evidence garnered by Denty leads to the unsurprising conclusion that the American

*(continued)*

*(continued)*

subsidiary is controlled by its English parent. While the two entities have interrelated operations and common management, the common management is focused in England, at the corporation's primary headquarters. There may be central control of the two entities' labor relations, but again control lies in the English entity. Ownership too lies entirely with the English corporation, which wholly owns its American subsidiary. Denty has produced no evidence to establish a genuine

dispute of fact as to the control of SB plc. He can only claim that he applied for positions outside the United States for an English corporation. The ADEA has no application in this situation, and summary judgment is therefore granted to defendant on Denty's failure-to-promote claim.

**Decision.** The Court dismissed the plaintiff's failure-to-promote claims because the ADEA does not cover decisions regarding employment outside the United States for a foreign-run company.

## The Foreign Compulsion Defense

Congress also clearly intended to permit United States firms flexibility when the enforcement of U.S. employment laws overseas would result in a violation of foreign law. As in all things legal, however, the interesting questions arise in difficult

cases. In the following case, the United States Court of Appeals for the District of Columbia found that where U.S. law would cause a U.S. firm to violate a foreign collective bargaining agreement—not a law strictly speaking—the foreign compulsion defense nonetheless applied. Again a court rejected the view advanced by the EEOC.

### Mahoney v. RFE/RL, Inc.
*47 F.3d 447*
*United States Court of Appeals*
*for the District of Columbia*
*Decided Feb. 28, 1995.*
*Rehearing and*
*Suggestion for Rehearing*
*In Banc Denied April 19, 1995*

BACKGROUND AND FACTS: RFE/RL, Inc. is a Delaware non-profit corporation that is funded but not controlled by the federal government and is best known for its broadcast services, Radio Free Europe and Radio Liberty. RFE/RL's principal place of business is Munich, Germany. In 1982, the company entered into a collective bargaining agreement with unions representing its employees in Munich. One of the provisions of the labor contract, modeled after a nationwide agreement in the German broadcast industry, required employees to retire at age sixty-five.

After Congress amended the Age Discrimination in Employment Act (ADEA) to cover American citizens working for American corporations overseas, RFE/RL thought its American employees in Munich would no longer have to retire at the age of sixty-five, as the collective bargaining agreement provided, and could continue to work if they chose. In order to implement this understanding, the company applied to the "Works Council" for limited exemptions from its contractual obligation. Rejecting RFE/RL's requests, the

Works Council determined that allowing only those employees who were American citizens to work past the age of sixty-five would violate not only the mandatory retirement provision, but also the collective bargaining agreement's provision forbidding discrimination on the basis of nationality. RFE/RL appealed the Works Council's decisions with respect to the plaintiffs to the Munich Labor Court and lost. The Labor Court agreed with the Works Council that RFE/RL must uniformly enforce the mandatory retirement provisions because exemptions would unfairly discriminate against German workers. The Labor Court also held that the company's retaining employees over the age of sixty-five despite the collective bargaining agreement would be illegal. The company terminated plaintiff De Lon in 1987, and plaintiff Mahoney in 1988. Both plaintiffs were working for the company in Munich, both were United States citizens, and both were discharged pursuant to the labor contract because they had reached the age of sixty-five.

*(continued)*

*(continued)*

CIRCUIT JUDGE RANDOLPH

If an American corporation operating in a foreign country would have to "violate the laws" of that country in order to comply with the Age Discrimination in Employment Act, the company need not comply with the Act. The question here is whether this "foreign laws" exception . . . applies when the overseas company, in order to comply with the Act, would have to breach a collective bargaining agreement with foreign unions. . . .

The parties agree that RFE/RL thereby violated the ADEA unless the "foreign laws" exception applied. The Act prohibits employers from discriminating against employees on the basis of age. "Employee" includes "any individual who is a citizen of the United States employed by an employer in a workplace in a foreign country"; and it is common ground that the Act covers RFE/RL.

The "foreign laws" exception to the Act states: It shall not be unlawful for an employer, employment agency, or labor organization—(1) to take any action otherwise prohibited under subsections (a), (b), (c), or (e) of this section where . . . such practices involve an employee in a workplace in a foreign country, and compliance with such subsections would cause such employer, or a corporation controlled by such employer, to violate the laws of the country in which such workplace is located. The district court held [the provision] inapplicable because the mandatory retirement provision "is part of a contract between an employer and unions—both private entities—and has not in any way been mandated by the German government. Second, the provision does not have general application, as laws normally do, but binds only the parties to the contract. . . .

If RFE/RL had not complied with the collective bargaining agreement in this case, if it had retained plaintiffs despite the mandatory retirement provision, the company would have violated the German laws standing behind such contracts, as well as the decisions of the Munich Labor Court. In the words of [the foreign compulsion defense], RFE/RL's "compliance with [the Act] would cause such employer . . . to violate the laws of the country in which such workplace is located." Domestic employers of course would never face a comparable situation; the Supremacy Clause of the Constitution would force any applicable state laws to give way, and provisions in collective bargaining agreements contrary to the Act would be superseded. Congressional legislation cannot, however, set aside the laws of foreign countries. When an overseas employer's obligations under foreign law collide with its obligations under the Age Discrimination in Employment Act, [the foreign compulsion defense] quite sensibly solves the dilemma by relieving the employer of liability under the Act. . . .

We recognize that RFE/RL's collective bargaining agreement is legally enforceable, which necessarily means that breaching the agreement in order to comply with the Act would . . . "cause" RFE/RL "to violate the laws of" Germany. Plaintiffs complain that RFE/RL could have bargained harder for a change in the labor contract. But application of [the foreign compulsion defense] does not depend on such considerations. The collective bargaining agreement here was valid and enforceable at the time of plaintiffs' terminations, and RFE/RL had a legal duty to comply with it. There is not, nor could there be, any suggestion that RFE/RL agreed to the mandatory retirement provision in order to evade the Age Discrimination in Employment Act. Such provisions are, the evidence showed, common throughout the Federal Republic of Germany, and RFE/RL entered into this particular agreement before Congress extended the Act beyond our borders.

**Decision.** The Court of Appeals reversed the District Court opinion and remanded the matter back with instructions to dismiss the matter.

## The Bona Fide Occupational Qualification Defense

The bona fide occupational qualification defense, both in the Title VII and the ADEA, provides that an employer may engage in discrimination if it is "reasonably necessary to the normal operation of the particular business or enterprise." But this is not much of a "safe harbor" for U.S. employers: What is "reasonably necessary" for one person is not to another. For example, when an American hospital refused to send Jewish anesthesiologists to Saudi Arabia, a court held that the BFOQ defense to the Jewish doctors' suit did not apply. The court found that the employer had not made appropriate efforts to determine the Saudi Arabian policy regarding the entry of Jewish doctors into the country and that the Saudi government had never directed the employer that American Jews could not participate in the program. Another court found the BFOQ defense did not justify a refusal to promote a woman to a senior position in a Latin American country. The court found inadequate the company's reasoning that she would have to deal with men in Latin America, where, they argued, businesspeople believe that women belong in the home. The BFOQ defense might be useful to the litigator trying to defend company action after the fact, but it seems too uncertain to be a useful tool for business planning.

## Antidiscrimination Laws Outside the United States

The history of the United States is peppered with the successive immigrations by various ethnic groups, each seeking civic and economic freedom. Even the framers of the Constitution, while virtually all of British ancestry, were products of four different migrations from different parts of Britain, with distinctly different religious persuasions. Not surprisingly, the United States has a highly developed legal system proscribing favoritism by the state or discrimination based on religion, ethnicity, or national origin. As we have seen in the preceding section, this body of law has in turn given rise to related legal principles prohibiting discrimination based on other socially unacceptable criteria, such as age and gender.

The multiethnic makeup of the United States has been an unusual occurrence in the world. Historically, most Europeans lived in geographic regions inhabited by their ethnic brethren. The same has been true in Asia, and, to a lesser extent, Africa. Even today, the competing desires of ethnic groups to dominate a geographically contiguous zone are a primary cause of civil strife in these continents. For example, "ethnic cleansing" in Bosnia is an effort to create geographic regions where only one ethnic group resides. While Latin America does not have the same tie to the

land as do the peoples of Europe, Asia, and Africa, the dominance of Spanish culture in Hispanic Latin America and of Portuguese culture in Brazil has prevented legal developments similar to those in the United States.

The increased mobility made possible by advances in transportation and communications is ending ethnic homogeneity in the Old World. Ethnic North Africans work in Paris, ethnic Pakistanis in London, and ethnic Turks in Frankfurt. And women are not as willing to accept discrimination in the workplace. As a result, this area of the law is slowly beginning to change in the Old World.

**Discrimination Based on National Origin.** The legal prohibitions against discrimination on the basis of national origin or ethnic background are highly developed in the United States. As F. Scott Fitzgerald elegantly noted, "France was a land, England was a people, but America having about it that quality of the idea, was harder to utter. . . . It was a willingness of the heart." When a country is synonymous with an ethnic group, that ethnic group can more easily justify preservation of ethnic identity by methodical exclusion of those outside it. Thus, Estonia has created citizenship laws the plain intent of which is to deny citizenship to ethnic Russians who arrived during the years of Soviet rule. Because Estonia confers employment and other benefits on the basis of citizenship, its citizenship law is a device for favoring ethnic Estonians over ethnic Russians in employment opportunities.

The European Union has in recent years taken significant steps in the area of ethnic discrimination. EU treaties clearly do prohibit discrimination on the grounds of nationality—ethnic identity—within the Union. Articles 7, 48, 52, and 59 of the EU Treaty forbid different types of discrimination within the Union on the basis of nationality. The driving principle behind these provisions is that nationals from each Member country should be free to pursue their economic interests anywhere within the unified European economy without fear of differential treatment. The following case demonstrates the Community's commitment to protect even the oldest of professions.

## Bezguia Adoui v. Belgian State and City of Liège; Cornuaille v. Belgian State

*E.C.R. 1665 (1982)*
*Court of Justice of the European Communities*

### BACKGROUND AND FACTS

On 3 June 1980, Miss Adoui, a French national, submitted an application to the City of Liège for a permit to reside in Belgium. The Minister of Justice denied her application and ordered her to leave the country because her personal conduct made her residence undesirable. This order was based on the Minister's finding that she worked in a bar in which waitresses displayed themselves in the window and were able to be alone with their clients for sexual encounters. Such conduct was contrary to the laws of Liège. She was not actually found to have so displayed herself, however.

Miss Adoui refused to comply with the expulsion order, asserting that she was the victim of discrimination based on national origin. In essence, Miss Adoui took the position that no similar action was taken against Belgian women merely suspected of engaging in display activities in furtherance of the business of prostitution. She sought relief from a court with jurisdiction over the Minister of Justice, the Tribunal de Prémière Instace at Liège.

Miss Cornuaille, another French national, was similarly accused of being a waitress of questionable moral character who "in scant dress displays herself to clients" for purposes of prostitution. The Committee of Aliens Office issued an opinion recommending her expulsion, without having taken account of the matters which had been the subject of the complaint to the criminal authorities. Like Ms. Adoui, Miss Cornuaille summoned the Committee to the Liège Tribunal, alleging discrimination on the basis of national origin.

The President of the Liège Tribunal stayed the proceedings in both cases and to refer to the Court of Justice under Article 177 of the Treaty of Rome, questions for a preliminary ruling to determine whether a foreign national could be expelled on the basis of conduct for which a citizen was not normally reprimanded.

J. MERTEN DE WILMARS, PRESIDENT;
G. BOSCO AND A. TOUFFAIT, PRESIDENTS OF CHAMBERS; P. PESCATORE, LORD MACKENZIE STUART, A. O'KEEFE, T. KOOPMANS, U. EVERLING, AND A. CHLOROS, JUDGES

The questions were raised in actions brought against the Belgian State by the Plaintiffs in the main proceedings, who are of French nationality, in connection with the refusal by the administrative authority to issue a permit enabling them to reside in Belgian territory, on the ground that their conduct was considered to be contrary to public policy by virtue of the fact that they were waitresses in a bar which was suspect from the point of view of morals.

The Belgian Law of 21 August 1948 terminating official regulation of prostitution prohibits soliciting, incitement to debauchery, exploitation of prostitution, the keeping of a disorderly house or brothel, and living on immoral earnings. The police regulation of the City of Liège of 25 March 1957 and subsequent orders provide that persons engaged in prostitution may not display themselves to passers-by, that the doors and windows of the premises where they pursue their activity are to be closed and covered so that it is impossible to see inside, and that those persons may not stand in the street near such premises.

[The questions referred to the Court] are essentially concerned with the question whether a Member State may, by virtue of the reservations contained in Articles 48 and 56 of the EEC Treaty, expel from its territory a national of another Member State or deny him access to that territory by reason of activities which, when attributable to the former State's own nationals, do not give rise to repressive measures.

Those questions are motivated by the fact that prostitution as such is not prohibited by Belgian legislation, although the Law does prohibit certain incidental activities, which are particularly harmful.

The reservations contained in Articles 48 and 56 of the EEC Treaty permit Member States to adopt, with respect to the nationals of other Member States measures which they cannot apply to their own nationals, inasmuch as they have no authority to expel the latter from the national territory or to deny them access thereto. Although that difference of treatment, which bears upon the nature of the measures available, must therefore be allowed, it must nevertheless be stressed that, in a Member State, the authority empowered to adopt such measures must not base the exercise

*(continued)*

*(continued)*

of its powers on assessments of certain conduct which would have the effect of applying an arbitrary distinction to the detriment of nationals of other Member States.

Although Community law does not impose upon the Member States a uniform scale of values as regards the assessment of conduct which may be considered as contrary to public policy, it should nevertheless be stated that conduct may not be considered as being of a sufficiently serious nature to justify restrictions on the admission to or residence within the territory of a Member State or a national of another Member State in a case where the former Member State does not adopt, with respect to the same conduct on the part of its own nationals, repressive measures or other genuine and effective measures intended to combat such conduct.

The answer to [the questions referred to the Court] should therefore be that a Member State may not, by virtue of the reservation relating to public policy contained in Articles 48 and 56 of the Treaty, expel a national of another Member State from its territory or refuse him access to its territory by reason of conduct which, when attributable to the former State's own nationals, does not give rise to repressive measures or other genuine and effective measures intended to combat such conduct.

**Decision.** On those grounds, The Court, in answer to the questions referred to it by the President of the Tribunal de Prémière Instance, Liège, hereby rules:

[A] Member State may not, by virtue of the reservation relating to public policy contained in Articles 48 and 56 of the Treaty, expel a national of another Member State from its territory or refuse him access to its territory by reason of conduct which, when attributable to the former State's own nationals, does not give rise to repressive measures or other genuine and effective measures intended to combat such conduct.

The notification of the grounds relied upon to justify an expulsion measure or a refusal to issue a residence permit must be sufficiently detailed and precise to enable the person concerned to defend his interests.

The person concerned must be entitled to put forward to the competent authority his arguments in defense and to be assisted or represented in such conditions as to procedure as are provided for by domestic legislation. Those conditions must not be less favorable to the person concerned than the conditions applicable to proceedings before other national authorities of the same type.

---

EU anti-discrimination law has not historically prohibited discrimination against ethnic individuals who are not Member State nationalities. This is changing. The EU's group on Treaty Amendment and Community Competence has in recent years noted that measures prohibiting racism and xenophobia should become part of the EU's discussion on EU Treaty amendments. Among the measures discussed have been the granting of legal status to resident non-EU citizens and of third country nationals EU-citizen status upon completion of a five-year lawful residency requirement in one of the Member States.

**Discrimination Based on Gender.** In recent years, there have been significant developments in the area of gender discrimination. Perhaps the efforts to eradicate it are more intense because such discrimination is so widespread. Worldwide,

working women earn between 55 and 65 percent of what men earn. In Japan, a 50 percent gap separates the earnings of men from the earnings of women, and women compose only 3.6 percent of middle management. There is only slightly more female participation in Europe, with only 5 percent reaching managerial levels and only 0.5 percent of women among those in the top 10 percent in compensation.

Lawmakers have begun to address the situation, particularly with respect to maternity leave. A European Union directive now provides for a minimum of 14 weeks of maternity leave and an allowance of at least 75 or 80 percent of net salary. It further stipulates that pregnant workers cannot be fired. In Hong Kong, a new law provides for ten weeks maternity leave at two-thirds of the woman's latest salary. India requires six weeks leave at full pay.

There has also been progress in the area of equal pay for equal work. Article 119 of the EU Treaty and Community Directives 75/117 and 76/207 require equal pay for equal work and equality in access to employment. As noted in the *Bilka-Kaufhaus* case that follows, the European Union's "effect-oriented" test in this area is quite similar to that adopted in the United States.

## Bilka-Kaufhaus Gmbh v. Karin Weber von Hartz
### E.C.R. 1607 (1986)
### Court of Justice of the European Communities

**BACKGROUND AND FACTS**

By order of 5 June 1984 the Bundesarbeitgericht (German Federal Labour Court) referred the following questions to the Court for a preliminary ruling:

May there be an infringement of Article 19 of the EEC Treaty in the form of "direct discrimination" where a department store which employs predominantly women excludes part-time employees from benefits under this occupational pension scheme although such exclusion affects disproportionately more women than men?

LORD MACKENZIE STUART, CHIEF JUDGE; KOOPMANS, EVERLING, BAHLMANN, AND JOLIET, PPC; BOSCO, DUE, GALMOT, AND KAKOURIS, JUDGES

By order of 5 June 1984, received by the Court on 2 July 1984, the Bundesarbeitsgericht (Federal Labour Court) requested a preliminary ruling pursuant to Article 177 of the EEC Treaty . . . concerning the interpretation of Article 119 of the Treaty.

The questions have arisen in the context of an action brought against Bilka Kaufhaus GmbH (Bilka) by its previous employee, Karin Weber von Hartz, concerning her entitlement to a retirement pension under the supplementary pension scheme set up by Bilka for its employees.

It appears from the file that Bilka has for several years had a supplementary pension scheme (occupational pension) for its employees. . . . According to the version in force from 26 October 1973, part-time employees qualify under the scheme only if they have been in full-time employment for fifteen years out of a total of twenty.

Mrs. Weber was employed by Bilka as a sales assistant from 1961 to 1976. After working full-time, she opted to work part-time from 1 October 1972 up to the date when her contract of employment came to an end. As she had not worked a minimum of fifteen years full-time Bilka refused her an occupational pension.

Mrs. Weber challenged the legality of Bilka's refusal in the German labour courts on the ground, inter alia, that the occupational pension scheme was in breach of the principle of equal pay for men and women, enshrined in Article 119 of the EEC Treaty. On this point Mrs. Weber argued that the requirement, for receiving an occupational pension, of a minimum period of full-time employment is to the detriment of female workers who, in order to be able to take care of their family and children, are more likely to be induced to choose part-time work than their male colleagues.

Bilka, on the other hand, maintained that it could not be accused of violating the principle of equal pay because the decision to exclude part-time employees from the occupational pension scheme was based on objectively justified economic grounds. In this connection it emphasized that the employment of full-time workers, by comparison with part-time workers, involves fewer ancillary costs and permits staff to be used for the whole period during which stores are open.

In the first question on which it seeks a preliminary ruling, the national court asked whether the staff policy of a department store company, consisting in excluding part-time employees from an occupational pension scheme, constitutes discrimination prohibited by Article 119 if the exclusion affects far more female workers than males.

For a reply to this question, reference should be made to the judgment of 31 March 1981. In that judgment the Court considered the question whether a pay practice consisting in fixing a lower hourly rate of pay for part-time work than for full-time work is compatible with Article 119. A practice of this kind is comparable to that referred to by the national court in the present case because, although Bilka makes no distinction in relation to hourly pay as between part-time or full-time employees, it grants an occupational pension only to employees in the latter category. As an occupational pension is within the definition of pay given by paragraph 2 of Article 119, as shown above, it follows that the

*(continued)*

*(continued)*

global pay given by Bilka to full-time employees is higher than that for part-time employees, assuming an equal number of hours worked.

It follows that, if it were found that a considerably smaller percentage of women than men work full-time, the exclusion of part-time workers from the occupational pension scheme would be contrary to Article 119 of the Treaty if, taking account of the difficulties encountered by women in arranging matters so as to be able to work full-time, this measure cannot be explained by factors excluding discrimination based on sex.

However, if the enterprise is able to show that its pay practice can be explained by objectively justified factors which are unrelated to discrimination based on sex, it would not be possible to find a breach of Article 119. Therefore the reply to the first question by the national court should be that Article 119 of the EEC Treaty is infringed by a department store company which excludes part-time employees from its occupational pension scheme where that exclusion affects a much greater number of women than men, unless the enterprise shows that the exclusion is based on objectively justified factors which are unrelated to any discrimination based on sex.

In the second question the national court aims in substance to establish whether the reasons put forward by Bilka to explain its pay policy can be considered "objectively justified economic reasons" within the meaning of the judgment of 31 March 1981, when reasons of commercial expediency in the department store sector do not necessitate such a policy.

It falls to the national court, which alone is competent to assess the facts, to decide whether, and if so to what extent, the grounds put forward by an employer to explain the adoption of a pay practice which applies irrespective of the employee's sex, but which in fact affects more women than men, can be considered to be objectively justified for economic reasons. If the national court finds that the means chosen by Bilka meet a genuine need of the enterprise, that they are suitable for attaining the objective pursued by the enterprise and are necessary for that purpose, the fact that the measures in question affect a much greater number of women than men is not sufficient to conclude that they involve a breach of Article 119.

Therefore the answer to question 2(a) should be that, according to Article 119, a department store company may justify the adoption of a pay policy involving the exclusion of part-time employees from its occupational pension scheme, regardless of sex, by contending that it seeks to employ as few workers of this kind as possible, if it is found that the means chosen to attain this objective meet a genuine need of the enterprise, are suitable for attaining the objective in question and are necessary for that purpose.

Finally the national court, in question 2(b), asks whether the employer is compelled, pursuant to Article 119 of the Treaty, to organize the occupational pension scheme for employees in such a way as to take account of the fact that the family commitments of female employees prevent them from fulfilling the conditions for entitlement to a pension.

It should be observed that the ambit of Article 119 is limited to the problem of discrimination in pay between men and women. On the other hand, problems connected with other conditions of work and employment are envisaged generally by other provisions of Community law, particularly Article 117 and 118 of the Treaty, with a view to harmonization of the social systems of Member States and approximation of their legislation in this field.

This imposition of an obligation of the kind described by the national court in its question goes beyond the ambit of Article 119 and has no other basis in Community law as it stands at present.

Therefore the reply to question 2(b) must be that Article 119 does not have the effect of compelling an employer to organize the occupational pension scheme for employees in such a way as to take account of the special difficulties encountered by employees with family commitments in fulfilling the conditions entitling them to such a pension.

**Decision.** The Court of Justice remanded the case to the German Federal Labor Court for proceedings consistent with the foregoing rulings.

Sex discrimination cases have even found success in Japan, a former bastion of male domination. In July 1990, a Tokyo district court ruled for the first time that female employees were denied promotions due to sex discrimination. The court awarded 18 women $640,000, although consistent with Japan's respect for the integrity of the workplace, the court declined to direct promotions because such action would interfere with personnel decisions. Progress may be slow, but it seems consistent throughout the world.

# Ethical Issues in the Employment of Persons Abroad

One of the principal reasons for locating a plant abroad is relative cost advantage. This is, of course, quite appropriate: One's dollars go farther paying salaries in an economy with weaker currencies. Many Third World countries lack burdensome work rules that add unnecessary costs. Other nations boast smooth labor–management relations that avoid expensive disputes.

In a few cases, however, the cost savings are attributable to work conditions that are not tolerated in industrialized Western nations. Any U.S. investor who is tempted to take advantage of such cost advantages should do so only after an unblinking look at the conditions from which these profits come.

U.S. companies almost never directly engage in dubious employment practices. Rather, they often place orders for a product or a component with a foreign buying agent that submits a low bid. These agents procure foreign suppliers to assemble the products or components in accordance with the U.S. company's specifications. These suppliers in turn subcontract parts of the product to smaller shops. Typically the worst abuses occur in these low-cost small shops—several steps removed from the U.S. purchaser. While some U.S. firms suspect wrongdoing, they choose to look the other way.

The problem is not one of laws that are on the books. The practices clearly violate nonbinding standards issued by the *International Labor Organization.* Further, virtually all of the practices described in this section are illegal under the laws formally in effect in the respective countries. Rather, the problem is one of enforcement.

Local governments often fear that if they enforce the laws, they will become a relatively high-cost nation, allowing manufacturers in nations that do not enforce such laws to underbid local manufacturers. Further, if that happens, the local manufacturer will simply move to the low-cost nation, leaving the higher-cost nation with unemployment. Accordingly, local government employs grossly inadequate numbers of inspectors to enforce the laws. Further, the inspectors are paid very poorly, making them susceptible to bribes.

Different people can arrive at different conclusions as to the ethics of promoting this race to the bottom. But in order to reach informed conclusions on this subject, one must examine the consequences of this race.

## Unsafe Labor Conditions

When a manufacturer has only one objective—production at low cost—and is not constrained by any government regulation, it will sometimes stop at nothing to reduce costs. Thus, such manufacturers routinely block and lock all exits to their facilities as a low-cost measure to prevent pilfering, an action that has caused thousands of workers to be trapped and burned alive when fire broke out in such buildings. Recently, a fire in a locked toy factory near Bangkok killed more than 240 workers and injured hundreds of others. In a separate incident, a fire in a locked facility killed 80 young women in Dongguan, China. The lack of ventilation in such factories also increased the incidence of tuberculosis and sinusitis among workers.

In order to maximize output per worker and thereby reduce cost per unit, some manufacturers permit assembly line workers to use the restroom only three times in a twelve-hour day. This practice not only subjects workers to great physical discomfort, it increases the incidence of urinary tract infections.

As manufacturers strive to increase rate of production and reduce expenses, they acquire and only poorly maintain antiquated equipment. Outdated equipment and insufficient maintenance, in turn, causes the rate of work injuries to balloon. Indeed, in many emerging nations, work-related injuries have doubled in the last five years.

Such injuries and illness have even more serious effects in nations where adequate health care is quite scarce. And seldom is health care provided by these employers.

## Child Labor

Because wages for children tend to be quite low, child labor is common in "low-cost" nations. For instance, although work during school hours is illegal for anyone under fourteen years of age in both Sri Lanka and Mexico, 500,000 children under fourteen work in Sri Lanka and millions in Mexico work anyway. Children form the labor foundation for Bangladesh's garment industry and India's carpet industry.

Naturally, children who are employed cannot attend school and receive formal education. Also, children are not as resistant to disease in unsanitary environments. Children in Indian carpet shops, for example, have a high incidence of tuberculosis, worm infestation, skin disease, and enlarged lymph glands.

---

*Foreign Accents*

# Working Children
## Underage Laborers Fill Mexican Factories, Stir U.S. Trade Debate

**E**ON, MEXICO—When Vicente Guerrero reported for work at the shoe factory, he had to leave his yo-yo with the guard at the door. Then Vicente, who had just turned 12 years old, was led to his post on the assembly line: a tall vertical lever attached to a press that bonds the soles of sneakers to the uppers.

The lever was set so high that Vicente had to shinny up the press and throw all his 90 pounds backward to yank the stiff steel bar downward. It reminded him of some playground contraption.

For Vicente this would have to pass for recreation from now on. A recent graduate of the sixth grade, he joined a dozen other children working full time in the factory. Once the best orator in his school and a good student, he now learned the wisdom of silence; even opening his mouth in this poorly ventilated plant meant breathing poisonous fumes.

Half of Mexico's 85 million people are below the age of 18, and this generation has been robbed of its childhood by a decade of debt crisis. It's illegal in Mexico to hire children under 14, but the Mexico City Assembly recently estimated that anywhere from five million to ten million children are employed illegally, and often in hazardous jobs. "Economic necessity is stronger than a theoretical prohibition," says Alfredo Farit Rodriguez, Mexico's Attorney General in Defense of Labor, a kind of workers' ombudsman.

Young Vicente Guerrero's life exemplifies both the poverty that forces children to seek work and the porous regulatory system that makes it all too easy for them to find jobs. In the shantytown where Vicente lives and throughout the central Mexico state of Guanajuato, it is customary for small and medium-sized factories to employ boy shoemakers known as zorritas, or little foxes.

School was the one place Vicente had no problem setting himself apart from other kids. Classmates, awed by his math skills, called him "the wizard." Nearly as adept in other subjects, Vicente finished first among 105 sixth-graders in a general knowledge exam.

Vicente's academic career reached its zenith during a speaking contest he won last June on the last day of school. The principal was so moved by the patriotic poem he recited that she called him into her office to repeat it just for her. That night, Vicente told his family the whole story. He spoke of how nervous he had been on the speaker's platform and how proud he was to sit on the principal's big stuffed chair.

After he finished, there was a strained silence. "Well," his father finally said, "it seems that you've learned everything you can in school." Mr. Guerrero then laid his plans for Vicente's next lesson in life.

*(continued)*

*(continued)*

In a few weeks, there would be an opening for Vicente at Deportes Mike, the athletic shoe factory where Mr. Guerrero himself had just been hired. Vicente would earn 100,000 pesos a week, about $34. Last August Vicente was introduced to the Deportes Mike assembly line. About a dozen of the fifty workers were underage boys, many of whom toiled alongside their fathers. One youth, his cheek bulging with sharp tacks, hammered at some baseball shoes. A tiny 10-year-old was napping in a crate that he should have been filling with shoe molds. A bigger boy was running a stamping machine he had decorated with decals of Mickey Mouse and Tinker Bell. The bandage wrapped around the stamper's hand gave Vicente an uneasy feeling.

Vicente's favorite part of his new job is running the clanking press, though that usually occupies a small fraction of his eight-hour workday. He spends most of his time on dirtier work: smearing glue onto the soles of shoes with his hands. The can of glue he dips his fingers into is marked "toxic substances . . . prolonged or repeated inhalation causes grave health damage; do not leave in the reach of minors." All the boys ignore the warning.

Impossible to ignore is the sharp, sickening odor of the glue. The only ventilation in the factory is from slits in the wall where bricks were removed and from a window near Vicente that opens only halfway. Just a matter of weeks after he started working, Vicente was home in bed with a cough, burning eyes, and nausea.

What provoked Vicente's illness, according to the doctor he saw at the public hospital, was the glue fumes. Ingredients aren't listed on the label, but the glue's manufacturer, Simon S. A. of Mexico City, says it contains toluene, a petroleum extract linked to liver, lung, and central nervous system damage. The maximum exposure to toluene permitted under Mexican environmental law is twice the level recommended by recently tightened U.S. standards. And in any event, Deportes Mike's superintendent doesn't recall a government health inspector coming around in the nine years the plant has been open.

When Vicente felt well enough to return to work a few days later, a fan was installed near his machine. "The smell still makes you choke," Vicente says, "but el patron says I'll get used to it."

"The system makes protecting the zorritas very, very difficult," says Teresa Sanchez, a federal labor official in Guanajuato state. The national labor code gives the federal government jurisdiction over only a limited number of industries that make up just 3 percent of businesses in the state. "The important industries, like shoes," she says, "are regulated by the states, and the states . . . ," she completes the sentence by rolling her eyes.

At the state labor ministry, five child labor inspectors oversee 22,000 businesses. The staff has been halved in the decade since Mexico's economic crisis erupted, says Gabriel Eugenio Gallo, a subsecretary. The five regulators make a monthly total of 100 inspections. At that rate it would take them more than two decades to visit all of the enterprises under state jurisdiction. Because child labor violations weren't even punishable by fines until very recently, state regulators say they have a hard time getting the tradition-bound employers they do visit to take them seriously. "Ultimately the schools must be responsible for these kids," Mr. Gallo concludes.

Located just four blocks from where Vicente Guerrero labors, the Emperador Cuauhtemoc school employs two social workers to reclaim dropouts. (Children are required by law to stay in school throughout the sixth grade.) One-third of the students at Cuauhtemoc never finish the Mexican equivalent of junior high. With their huge caseloads, the two social workers certainly have never heard of Vicente Guerrero. "Utimately it's the boy's own responsibility to see to it that he gets an education," says Lourdes Romo, one of the counselors.

*Bernard Wysocki*
*The Wall Street Journal*, **April 18, 1991.**

## Prison Labor

A few nations permit the staffing of manufacturing facilities with prisoners. Prison labor exists to some extent in virtually all countries. Most of the license plates in the United States have been manufactured by prisoners, and Alabama's revival of chain-gang road construction labor has been praised in some circles. But when prisoners work in traditionally commercial forms of manufacturing, grave concerns typically arise. If developed nations have difficulty competing with low-cost labor in underdeveloped countries, they have even less chance of competing with free, involuntary labor from such nations. The use of such labor is anathema to organized labor in developed countries.

With the close relationship in communist China between government and "business," the practice of prison labor became particularly prevalent in the late 1980s. This development did not go unnoticed by the United States, China's largest trading partner and a staunch opponent of prison labor. When the labor-backed Clinton campaign exerted pressure on the Bush administration in 1992, the United States stepped up the pressure on China to exclude prison labor products from exports to the United States. The result was the diplomatic Memorandum of Understanding shown in Exhibit 21.2. As is often the case in

---

**EXHIBIT 21.2    U.S. Memorandum on Prison Labor in China**

**Memorandum of Understanding Between the United States of America and the People's Republic of China on Prohibiting Import and Export Trade in Prison Labor Products**

*31 International Legal Materials 1071 (August 7, 1992)*

The Government of the United States of America and the Government of the People's Republic of China (hereinafter referred to as the Parties),

Considering that the Chinese Government has noted and respects United States laws and regulations that prohibit the import of prison labor products, has consistently paid great attention to the question of prohibition of the export of prison labor products, has explained to the United States its policy on this question, and on October 10, 1991, reiterated its regulations regarding prohibition of the export of prison labor products;

Considering that the Government of the United States has explained to the Chinese Government U.S. laws and regulations prohibiting the import of prison labor products and the policy of the United States on this issue; and

Noting that both Governments express appreciation for each other's concerns and previous efforts to resolve this issue,

Have reached the following understanding on the question of prohibiting import and export trade between the two countries that violates the relevant laws and regulations of either the United States or China concerning products produced by prison or penal labor (herein referred to as prison labor products).

The Parties agree:

1. Upon the request of one Party, and based on specific information provided by that Party, the other Party will promptly investigate companies, enterprises or units suspected of violating relevant regulations and laws, and will immediately report the results of such investigations to the other.
2. Upon the request of one Party, responsible officials or experts of relevant departments of both Parties will meet under mutually convenient circumstances to exchange information on the enforcement of relevant laws and regulations and to examine and report on compliance with relevant regulations and laws by their respective companies, enterprises, or units.
3. Upon request, each Party will furnish to the other Party available evidence and information regarding suspected violations of relevant laws and regulations in a form admissible in judicial or administrative proceedings of the other Party. Moreover, at the request of one Party, the other Party will preserve the confidentiality of the furnished evidence, except when used in judicial or administrative proceedings.
4. In order to resolve specific outstanding cases related to the subject matter of this Memorandum of Understanding, each Party will, upon request of the other Party, promptly arrange and facilitate visits by responsible officials of the other Party's diplomatic mission to its respective companies, enterprises or units.

This Memorandum of Understanding will enter into force upon signature.

DONE at Washington, in duplicate, this 7th day of August, 1992, in the English and the Chinese languages, both texts being equally authentic.

matters of international trade, however, the matter did not end with the signing of an agreement. Two-and-one-half years after the Memorandum of Understanding, the United States received renewed reports of prison labor generating exports to the United States. One such report is reprinted in the following article.

The situation described in the child labor article might ultimately raise more than a philosophical dilemma; the U.S. investor might have to see the workers on the other end of a summons in the United States. As noted earlier in Chapter Eight, in *Dow Chemical v. Domingo Castro Alfara et al.,* the Texas Supreme Court found that 80 Costa Rican banana plantation workers could sue the U.S. manufacturers of a pesticide in Texas for alleged medical injuries. This decision—rendered in a products liability

---

*Foreign Accents*

# China Still Exporting Prison Labor Products to U.S., Group Says

Materials smuggled out of a Chinese labor camp by a political dissident show China is violating its agreement not to sell prisoner-made products to the United States, investigators said Tuesday.

The dissident, an inmate in a southern China re-education camp, said in a letter that prisoners are forced to make artificial flowers for export at night after working in a stone quarry during the day. He attached labels for Ben Franklin Stores and Universal SunRay, a Springfield, Missouri, importer. Universal SunRay, which supplies Ben Franklin with flowers, said it purchased its goods through a Hong Kong company and "has had no knowledge of the labor situation in any of the Chinese flower factories."

The Laogai (Reform Through Labor) Research Foundation, a Milpitas, California, organization that opposes China's prison policies, also produced documents showing that since 1991 a Japanese company had shipped to the United States nearly 50 tons of green tea produced on a Chinese prison farm. . . .

[T]here have been persistent reports that goods from China's Laogai gulag, more than 1,000 camps with millions of prisoners throughout the country, still enter the U.S. market through Chinese and Hong Kong traders. In previous reports, the foundation has provided evidence that prison-made steel pipes, hand tools, shoes and toys are sold in this country.

"It's definitely widespread and there's no doubt" the authorities in Beijing know about it, said Jeffrey L. Fiedler, director of the foundation. The foundation said there is no evidence that American importers of the artificial flowers or tea were aware of the prison connection.

The prisoner, Chen Pokong, 30, said he understood that "once my letter is published, I might be persecuted even more harshly. I might even be killed. But I have no choice." Chen, a university teacher, served three years in prison for participating in the 1989 pro-democracy movement. He escaped to Hong Kong after completing his term, but was sent to a forced labor camp in Guangzhou province after Hong Kong rejected his asylum request and returned him to the mainland. . . .

In May [the executive director of the foundation] visited the eastern province of Zhejiang, where he found the forced labor camp producing tea and learned that it had joint venture ties with a Japanese company that exported to the United States. [The executive director] said one-third of all tea in China is produced in the "Laogai."

*Jim Abrams*
*The Associated Press,* October 4, 1994.

context—opens the door to the massive liability associated with U.S. forums like Texas.

http://www.abcnews.com/onair/nightline/
html_files/transcripts/ntl0521.html
*See for an article on prison labor.*

## Approaches to the Issue of Work Conditions

As previously noted, reliance on low-cost nations to police dubious work conditions has proved ineffective. Those who find these conditions unacceptable have turned to other approaches to end the race to the bottom line.

Multinational trade treaties are the most promising vehicles. Relatively few workers in the developed world have been historically threatened by questionable conditions in the developed world. Children and workers under trying conditions tend to lack the education and reliability to be productive in sophisticated manufacturing operations. As the number of areas in which low-cost operations can be competitive increases, such workers have voiced more concern. At the same time, more people have expressed moral misgivings about being part of a world economic system that promotes such practices.

As a result of this increased awareness, some developed nations have attempted to make non-enforcement of employment laws a violation of international trade agreements, just as dumping or subsidies discussed in Chapter Eleven. The United States has proposed amendments to the World Trade Organization trade rules that ties labor standards to international trade. These amendments were stalled and the delegates decided that labor issues should instead be discussed in the context of the ILO, where discussion has not been particularly effectual. In its effort, the United States has focused on providing a tool for enforcing ILO conventions on unsafe working conditions, minimum age for child labor, and forced labor, without addressing any issues on minimum wages. Developing nations cried foul, asserting that such standards would be misused by the developed world to bar their products from developed markets. The matter remains under intense negotiation.

The U.S. Congress has reacted to the stalled effort to tie labor standards to international trade by entertaining a unilateral expansion of its own trade laws. Under a proposed revision of Section 301 of the Trade Act of 1974, discussed in Chapter Twelve, the harsh Section 301 sanctions and retaliatory measures would be available if it could be proved that an importer is violating an established set of labor standards. Because such a measure is not addressed in the global trade rules, however, the law might itself have been deemed a violation of the international trade agreement. In October 1997, Congress did pass the Sanders Amendment, which bans the import of any product made by forced child labor. In addition, Congress established the Child Labor Command Center, to be located at U.S. Customs headquarters, which will act as a clearinghouse for information and provide 24 hour "hotline" telephone service to a wide variety of audiences in order to provide a venue for allegations about prohibited importations. Second, the Initiative increases foreign staffing by assigning three additional special agents to areas where forced child labor is the most common. Third, Customs is to engage in outreach programs with the trade, government, and nongovernment organizations to achieve successful enforcement of the Sanders Amendment.

A third, private initiative is also making significant progress. Some U.S. firms—of which Levi Strauss & Co. is particularly prominent—have instituted global "sourcing guidelines" to determine with whom they will do business. Levi Strauss requires a certification from suppliers that they are in compliance with the guidelines. If Levi Strauss has reason to believe that a supplier or its subcontractors have violated one of these guidelines, it will investigate the matter. If it finds a violation, it will terminate its contract with the supplier. As a result of this program, Levi Strauss stopped manufacturing jeans in China in 1993. Finally, as seen in the following article, by April 1998, China had made sufficient concessions to human rights to permit Levi Strauss to return. Such a guidelines approach, if adopted by more firms, would go a long way to eradicating questionable conditions.

---

*Foreign Accents*

# It's All in the Jeans as Levi Returns to China

Millions of Levi Strauss jeans—the real ones—will be rolling out of Chinese factories next year for the first time since the company pulled out of the country in 1993.

Privately-owned Levi Strauss & Co of San Francisco, the world's largest brand-name apparel manufacturer, has claimed it has perceived improvements in human rights in China and plans to resume product sourcing operations there.

The company quit manufacturing in China five years ago over human rights concerns at a time when demand for jeans there was soaring and China turned out 836 million square metres of denim a year—one third of global denim output.

But Levi is going back in, its president and chief operating officer Mr. Peter Jacobi has said. . . . "We are going to re-engage in China for a number of reasons. One, we believe that the environment has improved to the point that we can operate consistent with what we are. Part of that's because the human rights environment has improved."

He said Levi Strauss is confident it will find contracting partners in China who fitted the ethical and business standards set down in the company's sourcing guidelines. He expected Levi Strauss products to start coming off Chinese production lines again in 1999. The company produced 2.8 million items a year in China from third party contractors at the time of its dramatic high-profile withdrawal five years ago.

Levi has diversified its products in recent years, and classic blue jeans are no longer its only sought after apparel . . .

Levi Strauss has no plan to become an owner-operator of factories in China, Mr Jacobi said, but would rely on partners. "We'll go through contractors, we're not going to owner operate. There's no reason to," he said. "We believe there are contractors that can be good partners working with us with our sourcing guidelines." . . .

Levi quit China to safeguard its global image at a time when China's human rights record was widely condemned. "The major concern was that we couldn't conduct our business in a way that was consistent with our sourcing guidelines because of the (human rights) environment," Mr Jacobi said. "We felt that because of our reputation, because of our desire to run our business consistent with what we care about and what we value, that the environment was hostile to that."

"We felt it was better that we begin the process of winding down our business there and extricating ourselves." But he said the company now felt able to find partners in tune with Levi's guidelines, which cover issues ranging from ethics and employment standards to legal requirements and a ban on using child labour or prison convicts.

Levi announces no profit figures but it reported global sales last year of GBP4.2 billion, down 3.9 per cent from record 1996 sales. It also announced last November the closure of 11 North American plants in a bid to stay competitive.

*The Birmingham Post*, April 11, 1998.

Copyright © 1998 The Birmingham Post; Source: World Reporter™.

---

## Chapter Summary

The investor must weigh the benefits of establishing a presence abroad against the costs of foreign regulation. Corporate regulation will be more significant as the U.S. investor gains more active control of the foreign entity. Indeed, local law may prevent such active control altogether.

Labor law poses particular difficulties for the U.S. investor because of markedly different attitudes toward employer-employee relations in other nations. Especially surprising are laws that require employee input into strategic decisions, prescribe employee representation on boards of directors, and place impediments to dismissals.

## QUESTIONS AND CASE PROBLEMS

1. Would a U.S. court, as did the Supreme Court of Japan, overrule an employer's contractual rights because of a countervailing "socially accepted view"? What if the employment contract was between a drug lord and his "trigger man"? Do you think that the relative homogeneity of a national culture affects the breadth of issues on which society has a "socially accepted view"?
2. Susan Currie is a U.S. manufacturer of tear gas, which she sells to various governments for crowd control. To reduce transportation costs to the interested governments, Ms. Currie is considering building a new plant in Germany. The plant will employ 2,500 people. What foreign labor law and environmental law considerations should she take into account?

## MANAGERIAL IMPLICATIONS

Your firm is Crystallina, a U.S. mineral water producer and distributor. A strong market for mineral water is South Moravia, a nation dominated by a fundamentalist state religion that prohibits drinking any alcohol or carbonated beverages. Market studies indicate that if Crystallina established offices in South Moravia, it would reap rich profits. If employees of a company like Crystallina violate South Moravian religious law, however, the company is liable for severe fines.

1. The South Moravian religious law prohibits women from engaging in gainful employment. Accordingly, if Crystallina establishes an office there, it will not be able to offer any of its women executives an opportunity to work there. What U.S. legal issues are raised for Crystallina? Should Crystallina establish an office in South Moravia?
2. Now assume that the South Moravian religious law permits women to work, but strictly prohibits homosexual behavior of any kind. Accordingly, if Crystallina establishes an office there, it will not be able to offer any of its gay executives an opportunity to work there. Are there any U.S. legal issues raised for Crystallina? Should Crystallina establish an office in South Moravia?
3. Now assume that the South Moravian religious law permits women to work and has no particular concern about private homosexual behavior, but strictly prohibits Christian worship of any kind. Because Roman Catholics recognize a duty to worship on Sundays and holy days, if Crystallina establishes an office in South Moravia, it will not be able to offer any of its Catholic executives an opportunity to work there. What U.S. legal issues are raised for Crystallina? Should Crystallina establish an office in South Moravia?

# Chapter Twenty-Two

# Environmental Law

Laws protecting the environment once deserved only a brief mention in a book about law affecting foreign investments. In recent years, however, there has been extraordinary activity in international environmental law. There have been large-scale international environmental disasters such as the Chernobyl nuclear plant disaster, the Sandoz chemical spill into the Rhine River, the *Exxon Valdez* oil spill, and the Persian Gulf War oil spill. At the same time, concern over the possible thinning of the ozone layer and "global warming" has intensified. "Green" political parties have formed around environmental issues. Consequently, nations have been furiously enacting legislation and entering into treaties concerning the environment. Although this body of international law is not yet as well developed as other areas that have been the subject of argument for centuries, its impact on commercial activity has become noteworthy.

## Ethical and Practical Considerations of Varying Environmental Requirements

Virtually all human activity alters the environment in some way. The central problem in environmental law lies in determining which activities alter the environment to an unacceptable degree. Those determinations, like all human judgments, vary depending on the circumstances of the person making them. Cutting down huge forests is just as acceptable to Brazilian pioneers as it was to North American pioneers—such as Abraham Lincoln—who turned the dense forests of Illinois and Indiana into the heart of the grain belt. But in the late 20th century, most North Americans find Brazilian tree cutting unacceptable, though none have proposed a reforestation of Peoria.

All things being equal, most people favor a clean and aesthetic environment. But all things are not equal. Poorer nations tend to oppose extensive international environmental regulation because it impairs their ability to profit from less-sophisticated production procedures. Wealthy countries tend to favor environmental protection not only because they can afford to, but also because they benefit economically from it. Indeed, sometimes wealthy nations use environmental and health issues as a pretext for keeping foreign competition at bay. Understanding the reasons for differences in environmental views among nations is critical to understanding the dynamics of traditional and emerging legal remedies.

## Differences in Regulatory Schemes

Differences in nations' circumstances and views lead to differences in their respective environmental laws. First, the cost-benefit analysis with respect to any environmental alteration often varies from country to country. A country with an opportunity to profit from a sulfur-belching power plant is more likely to think that the plant's alteration of the environment is acceptable than its neighbor nation, which does not profit but suffers from the plant's acid rain. Second, countries that are happy with the economic status quo are more inclined to favor environmental measures. For example, relatively wealthy nations tend to have more laws to reduce pollution from industrial processes than countries plagued with rampant malnutrition. Third, some nations lack the technological infrastructure to produce without pollution. In a strict economic sense, enacting a regulatory scheme that mandates buying such infrastructure greatly benefits wealthier nations which manufacture and sell such equipment and hampers less-developed nations that must spend scarce resources to purchase it. Finally, some governments permit officials to profit from environmental modifications. Thus, a nation may be lax in regulating hazardous waste disposal if the families of government officials greatly profit from the activity.

Obviously, many of these factors tend to place the wealthier, more developed democracies on the side of international environmental regulation and the less-developed nations in opposition of such regulation. This dichotomy between the rich "North" and the poor "South" forms the principal division in virtually all issues relating to international environmental law.

For foreign investors, these differences have meant advantages in locating their facilities in countries with fewer environmental restrictions. A steel factory will cost millions less to build in South Korea than if it were built in the United States, where sophisticated antipollution equipment would be required. A hazardous waste dump is easier to locate in Ghana than in Germany because Germany has a more comprehensive legal framework protecting groundwater from such waste.

These incentives have not been lost on the generally well-developed countries pursuing conservation. Because nature is blissfully unaware of political boundaries, one nation's ban of chlorofluorocarbons (CFCs) only postpones depletion of the ozone layer if its neighbors continue to produce them. Canada's laws against acid rain are not fully effective if its large southern neighbor does not enact similar laws. Moreover, to make matters worse, the environmental regulations of the conservation-minded nation would make its products more expensive, placing it at a competitive disadvantage vis-à-vis countries less concerned about the environment. Accordingly, conservationists have sought legal relief through international dispute resolution, import bans, and multilateral treaties.

In other words, foreign investors must consider the risk that the host country's less restrictive environmental laws will be changed through international action. This risk can be substantial. The installation of antipollution devices after a plant is built, for example, can be vastly more expensive than including them during construction. In many circumstances, the better choice for the risk-averse investor might be not to build on the assumption that environmental laws will remain as they are. Those investors whose political views favor more aggressive environmental laws may not wish to avail themselves of more lenient environmental laws in any event.

---

*Foreign Accents*

# The Environment Strikes Back

The environment is playing an increasingly important role in deciding whether a project goes ahead or not. In the developed world, sponsors have been used to seeing projects scuppered, or at the very least delayed, by environmental pressures. Now they can expect the same wherever they go in the world.

Consider this: Phuket, Thailand, a tantalum smelter was due to be developed. Bankers were happy with the economics, good project partners were in place, even the IFC was willing to make a direct loan. One problem though—the locals did not share this enthusiasm. Worried about the smelter's impact on the local environment they burned the plant to the ground.

Or this: construction of the world's largest nickel mine, at Voisey Bay in Canada, is held back for a year because of an injunction lodged against the project by Inuit tribespeople.

*(continued)*

*(continued)*

Or this: U.S. oil firm, Occidental Petroleum, given the go-ahead by the Colombian government in March to conduct exploratory drilling in northeast Colombia is now threatened with blood on its hands. The Uwa Indians, native to the disputed area, are threatening to commit a mass suicide from a nearby cliff if drilling proceeds.

Welcome to the broadest and most varied of risks facing projects—environmental risk. More and more, sponsors, lawyers and bankers are having to pay heed to this ever-changing risk. It is found in the wastelands of Canada as Voisey Bay can attest, to the dust and heat of Australia's deserts as many a mining financier knows from bitter experience. The term environmental risk is as broad as it is vague. It is a micro-issue springing up into the broader term that catches these projects out.

### Knowing No Bounds

Environmental risk is not just the risk a project poses to the environment, immediate or at large, it is also, and more commonly, the risk projects face from environmental regulations pushed for by campaigners.

Environmental risks can be split into two main categories. Physical or green risks which are direct risks a project presents to the environment and the repercussions that these pose to a project's viability. The second category is contextual, and more tricky to mitigate against or anticipate. This involves the global relationship of one project to another and of other events which make a project harder to achieve. For example, a petrochemical spillage in one country may make a similar project harder to bank in another.

An important new factor however is the tightening of environmental regulations in emerging markets. Traditionally seen as the place to develop dirty projects using cheaper technology, emerging markets are now making a stand. "There is a noticeable evolution of environmental standards and regulations in the emerging markets," says William Chew, head of project finance ratings at Standard & Poor's in New York.

### Multilaterally Driven

Much of this has been led by multilateral institutions who are needed in many projects if private finance is to follow. The World Bank, its regional affiliates, and MIGA have environmental guidelines delineating which projects are suitable from an environmental position to receive their support. The Asian Development Bank, for example, has decided that 50% of its financings be directed towards projects with environmental and social objectives as their main purpose. It is also working with some governments to introduce programmes to integrate environmental policies into national economic plans.

Commercial banks too are developing an environmental mandate of sorts. In 1992 a group of leading international banks signed up to a Statement by Banks on Sustainable Development. These banks promise to apply the same standards to environmental risk assessment to both their domestic and overseas business.

Even export credit agencies are beginning to join in. US Ex-Im was given a mandate from Congress to fulfill environmental criteria in projects it supports as part of its reauthorization process in 1992. Early this year, the bank chose not to issue letters of intent to provide loan guarantees to Caterpillar, Rotec Industries and Voith Hydro who were bidding for contracts for the $75 billion Three Gorges hydroelectric dam in China. . . . So far, US Ex-Im stands alone as the only export credit agency which has a clear environmental mandate.

Yet, emerging markets themselves are not entirely convincing in their attitude to the environment. There is an ambivalence among some as to the relationship of environmental regulations and politics. There is also a danger that environmental concerns are abused and used as a pretext for political and economic motivations. The Dabhol power plant in India is widely seen as a victim of politics disguised as environmentalism. Here environmental risk becomes linked to country risk.

### How Hard Does It Hit?

If environmental risk can manifest itself in many and varied forms, the net effect to sponsors and bankers is less diverse. These effects are:

- increased costs for a project as changes need to be made in specifications or to finance further studies;

*(continued)*

*(continued)*

- delays caused to a scheduled completion and on-stream dates, causing cost overruns;
- unanticipated costs such as cleaning up previous pollution on the project site;
- ongoing liabilities such as future clean-up regulations.

But the most dangerous from a cash flow perspective are delays to completion incurred by environmental concerns. Anything that holds up a project's completion threatens its financing if done on a project finance basis. Moreover, such delays make bankers nervous and any further projects of a similar nature may find the margins banks want from them to be higher. . . .

Roads, for example, seemingly harmless compared to mines, can still attract powerful environmental opposition. In Poland, construction of a 2,500km $8 billion roads programme is being slowed by protests from residents' groups. And in the UK, some protesters to the governments' roads scheme have become household names.

Water too, is subject to significant environmental risks. In the US, Congressional-driven reduction of acceptable levels of contaminants in drinking water and wastewater is forcing companies to invest heavily in new technology to meet these new criteria. Federal reserves are being made available to provide cheaper loans for these companies and municipalities. But in emerging markets, this would be even more important. "As you go further down the customer food chain, political sensitivity to price generally increases. Retail tariffs in particular can be quite politically sensitive," says Tom Marshella, managing director of project/infrastructure finance bank loan ratings at Moody's in New York. . . .

### How to Avoid the Greens
There seems to be two approaches in overcoming such problems. The first relates to the direct green aspect of environmental risk and is best met by em-

ploying advanced and clean technology. This may add costs but these could pale into insignificance compared with overall costs of a delay.

Here however, the split between the developed and developing world makes a telling distinction. "You can see two levels of investor sensitivity between developed and developing countries," says Marshella at Moody's. "In the mature markets any incremental expenditure to meet the latest environmental standards will drive up costs and possibly out-price a project. But in developing markets, the prospects for growth and demand can quite often override these additional costs."

The other aspect is one of sensitivity. "Successful developers realize they have to take a wider view," says Chew at Standard & Poor's. "There is a view on the part of some developers that once a project has won the necessary permits from the relevant government departments the project is assured, all other things being equal. This is not the case. Material local opposition must be dealt with effectively and sensitively."

As a result of the cost and delays related to environmental risk, many sponsors draw no distinction between operations in the developed or developing world. "Emerging markets are toughening up environmental guidelines," says Minorco's Thompson. "Where the laws and regulations are missing or inadequate, we adopt best industry practice to minimize environmental risk."

Perhaps ABB's actions in the South Humber power project in the UK demonstrate the lengths to which some companies will go. ABB halted construction of the largest power project in western Europe for months to allow migrating birds to feed and rest on their way south. This is good public relations, but is it good business? Whatever it is, environmental risk is here to stay and sponsors and bankers will have to continue to adjust and adapt to this ever-changing beast.

***Philip Carter***
*Project Finance*

© Project Finance November 1997, Euromoney Publications. Reprinted by permission.

## Environmental Law as an Anticompetitive Tool

"Environmentally responsible" nations cannot be said to be without sin. Often such nations en-act strict local environmental laws not to save the environment, but with the principal purpose of preventing competition from a foreign enterprise.

The European Union has been accused of using this device on several occasions to protect its meat and dairy products industry, which has been battered by foreign competition. In 1993, the European Union traced an outbreak of hoof and mouth disease in Italian livestock to Croatia. Rather than banning Italian meat or Croatian meat, the Union banned meat from the entire former East bloc. Needless to say, the arbitrariness of banning meat from half a continent on the basis of a disease outbreak in a region of one small nation, especially while not banning meat from the only country where the disease had occurred, struck many producers as unfair. Eastern bloc meat was, however, cheaper. Similarly, members of the European Union banned U.S. beef because many U.S. producers enhanced their livestock through bovine growth hormones. No proof that the hormones had any adverse effect on the meat was ever offered. U.S. meat was, however, demonstrably less expensive and more popular among European consumers.

The United States has also been accused of using environmentally disguised trade barriers. The European Union has complained about a variety of U.S. taxes and fines, which they assert are disproportionately directed at European auto imports. In recent years, the United States enacted *Corporate Average Fuel Efficiency (CAFE) standards* and "gas guzzler" surtaxes ostensibly to encourage fuel conservation and reduce air pollution. At the same time, the United States enacted a luxury tax on certain high-priced vehicles. The taxes nominally apply to domestic cars as well as European autos. Interestingly, however, European auto makers pay about 90 percent of the combined gas guzzler taxes, luxury taxes, and CAFE fines, although they hold only about 4 percent of the U.S. automobile market.

A particularly amusing example of alleged "environmental" anticompetitive behavior is found in the French resort town of Grenoble. The city's leaders banned Bermuda shorts in public pools and encouraged bathers to wear bikinis and other skimpy traditional French bathing suits. They argued that the added material in the Bermuda shorts polluted their pools. Interestingly, most Bermuda shorts were foreign made.

**http://www.econet.apc.org/ciel**
*See for links and information at the site of the Center for International Environmental Law.*

# Traditional International Remedies
## The Polluter Pays: Responsibility for Pollution

In the absence of agreement, the only way a country may address its neighbor's environmental pollution is through the dispute resolution mechanisms available under international law. Binding adjudication is not common because the alleged polluter will seldom consent to jurisdiction in such cases.

An instance in which the polluter did consent to arbitration involved a Canadian smelter that was belching fumes into the United States in the 1930s. Because such consent is so rare, the case remains one of the more complete statements of the environmental obligations among nations. The opinion is also noteworthy because the legendary Professor Charles "Bull" Warren—after whom the law professor in the film *The Paper Chase* is said to have been modeled—had a hand in drafting it.

### The Trail Smelter Arbitration
*3 R. Int'l Arb. Awards 1938 (1941)*
*Trail Smelter Arbitral Tribunal*

MESSRS. HASTIE, GREENSHIELDS, AND WARREN

This Tribunal is constituted under, and its powers are derived from and limited by, the Convention between the United States of America and the Dominion of Canada signed at Ottawa, April 15, 1935. . . . The controversy is between two governments involving damage occurring or having occurred, in the territory of one of them (the United States of America) and alleged to be due to an agency situated in the territory of the other (the Dominion of Canada). As between the two countries involved,

*(continued)*

*(continued)*

each has an equal interest that if a nuisance is proved, the indemnity to damaged parties for proven damage shall be just and adequate and each has also an equal interest that unproven or unwarranted claims shall not be allowed. For, while the United States' interests may now be claimed to be injured by the operations of a Canadian corporation, it is equally possible that at some time in the future Canadian interests might be claimed to be injured by an American corporation. The Columbia River has its source in the Dominion of Canada. At a place in British Columbia named Trail, it flows past a smelter located in a gorge, where zinc and lead are smelted in large quantities. From Trail, its course is easterly and then it swings in a long curve to the international boundary line, at which point it is running in a southwesterly direction; and its course south of the boundary continues in that general direction. The distance from Trail to the boundary line is about seven miles as the crow flies or about eleven miles, following the course of the river. . . .

In 1906, a smelter was started under American auspices near the locality known as Trail, B.C. In 1936, the Consolidated Mining and Smelting Company of Canada, Limited, obtained a charter of incorporation from the Canadian authorities, and that company acquired the smelter plant at Trail as it then existed. Since that time, the Canadian company, without interruption, has operated the smelter, and from time to time has greatly added to the plant until it has become one of the best and largest equipped smelting plants on the American continent. . . . This increased production resulted in more sulphur dioxide fumes and higher concentrations being emitted into the air.

From 1925, at least, to 1937, damage occurred in the State of Washington resulting from sulphur dioxide emitted from the Trail Smelter [by adversely affecting agricultural activities]. The second question under Article III of the Convention is as follows:

In the event of the answer to the first part of the preceding question being affirmative, whether the Trail Smelter should be required to refrain from causing damage in the State of Washington in the future, and, if so, to what extent?

Damage has occurred since January 1, 1932, as fully set forth in the previous decision. To that extent, the first part of the preceding question has thus been answered in the affirmative.

As Professor Eagleton puts it (Responsibility of States in International Law 1928, p. 80): "A state owes at all times a duty to protect other states against injurious acts by individuals from within its jurisdiction." . . . But the real difficulty arises rather when it comes to determine what, *pro subjecta materie,* is deemed to constitute an injurious act.

The Tribunal . . . finds that, under the principles of international law, as well as of the law of the United States, no state has the right to use or permit the use of its territory in such a manner as to cause injury by fumes or in the territory of another or the properties or persons therein, when the case is of serious consequence and the injury is established by clear and convincing evidence.

Considering the circumstances of the case, the Tribunal holds that the Dominion of Canada is responsible in international law for the conduct of the Trail Smelter. Apart from the undertakings in the Convention, it is, therefore, the duty of the government of the Dominion of Canada to see to it that this conduct should be in conformity with the obligation of the Dominion under international law as herein determined.

**Decision.** The Tribunal held that so long as the existing conditions in the Columbia River Valley prevailed, the Trail Smelter would be required to refrain from causing any damage through fumes in the State of Washington. It further found that the indemnity for such damage should be fixed in such manner as the governments, acting under the Convention, should agree upon.

## Regulation of Products That Violate Environmental Objectives

Because international binding arbitration of environmental disputes such as in the *Trail Smelter* case are rare, a more frequent method for counterattack is for the conservation-minded nation to outlaw or inhibit import of the offending product. These regulations take two basic forms: (1) regulations against a product because the product itself violates environmental norms in the regulating country, and (2) regulations against a product because it is manufactured through a process that is environmentally objectionable. This type of counterattack, however, is somewhat restricted by the General Agreement on Tariffs and Trade (GATT), a treaty to which almost all significant commercial nations are party.

These GATT restrictions theoretically do not prevent nations from excluding products that are environmentally offensive by their very nature. In fact, it is this flexibility that some nations have manipulated to keep out other nations' meat and bathing suits. In the following case, the United States was able to keep out Canadian lobsters, because they did not meet U.S. minimum size requirements. This "nondiscriminatory internal regulation" was upheld although lobsters that reside in colder Canadian waters are naturally

smaller and therefore disproportionately affected by the regulation. One should especially focus on the tribunal's explanation of GATT restrictions and how the U.S. avoided them; the minority view is also instructive in pointing to gray areas in these GATT restrictions.

As the *Canadian Lobster* case demonstrates, states have a great deal of flexibility in excluding products that are by their own nature contrary to local environmental standards. In fact, the flexibility is so great that nations at times misuse facially neutral standards—such as "no baggy swimsuits"—to give preference to local products. But if nothing is wrong with the product itself, a country will have more difficulty excluding the product on an environmental basis.

---

### Lobsters from Canada
*1990 WL 299945*
*United States–Canada Free Trade Agreement Binational Panel*

**BACKGROUND AND FACTS**

The American Lobster is only found in U.S. and Canadian waters in the western Atlantic Ocean. It grows by shedding its external shell, a process called "molting." American lobsters molt about 20–25 times between birth and sexual maturity. Water temperature affects how often lobsters molt. In cold waters it may take a lobster up to ten years to reach sexual maturity while in warm waters, lobsters reach sexual maturity in as little as five years. Canadian waters tend to be colder than U.S. waters.

In 1989, the United States Congress passed an amendment to the Magnuson Fishery Conservation and Management Act that prohibited the transport of whole live lobsters smaller than a certain minimum size.

Canada sought relief against the United States before the Free Trade Agreement Binational Panel, alleging that the Magnuson Act was a restriction on importation of lobsters from Canada, in violation of Article XI of GATT. The United States argued that the Magnuson Act was not a "restriction on importation" but an "internal measure" subject only to GATT Article III. The United States further argued that even if Article XI applied, the Magnuson Act fell within the exception to Article XI found in Article XX(g), which permits restrictions on importation if they relate to conservation of an exhaustible natural resource.

CHAIRMAN NORWOOD, MESSRS. CLINGAN, LATIMER, AND POLLER, AND MS. WEST

**The Majority View.** The pertinent part of Article XI is set forth in paragraph 1 of that Article, and reads:

No prohibitions or restrictions other than duties, taxes or other charges . . . shall be instituted or maintained by any contracting party on the importation of any product of the territory of any other contracting party. . . .

Article III, in summary, prohibits the use of any form of [nontariff barrier] (NTB) to afford protection to domestic production. . . . This no-protection principle is supported by an explicit ban on the use of such measures in a discriminatory manner against imported products, whether imposed on them at the time they are at the border or after they have entered the commerce of the importing country. Article III sets forth the principle of nondiscrimination or equal treatment or, more precisely, "national treatment" between imported and domestic products.

Paragraph 4 of Article III expresses the no-protection principle in the following terms:

The products of the territory of any contracting party imported into the territory of any other

*(continued)*

*(continued)*

contracting party shall be accorded treatment no less favorable than accorded to like products of national origin in respect of all laws, regulations and requirements affecting their internal sale, offering for sale, purchase, transportation, distribution or use.

Article XI is the principal GATT Article containing the general ban against the use of QRs [qualitative restrictions] to limit importation. The Article itself contains exceptions, such as that for certain QRs on agricultural and fisheries products.

Article III is the principal GATT Article limiting the use of "border" and "internal" measures on imported goods. The rule of "national" treatment that it specifies to carry out the competition principle noted earlier bars a country from extending internal measures to imported goods in a way that bears more onerously on the imported products than on the like domestic products.

The language [Article XI uses] in stating the conditions on what importing countries may do to limit the importation or the internal marketing of imported goods differs in describing the state of commerce at which the measures on imported goods is aimed.

Article XI:1 is written in terms of prohibitions or restrictions . . . instituted or maintained . . . on the importation of any product. . . .

Article III:1 (as well as III:4) is drafted in terms of laws, regulations and requirements affecting the internal sale, offering for sale, purchase, transportation, distribution or use of products. . . . And Article III, the interpretative note, concerns measures "of the kind referred to in paragraph 1" that are "collected or enforced in the case of the imported product at the time or point of importation."

Although U.S. authorities are empowered under the amendment to enforce the minimum size limits at various points in the internal distribution chain, the United States said enforcement activity was expected to take place on board the lobster fishing vessels, or preferably, at the points of landings and at the lobster pounds or similar facilities where the lobsters are sorted and kept alive for further distribution.

The American authorities indicated it was feasible to verify compliance with a minimum size standard only when lobsters arrived at pounds or holding tanks and were uncrated or at later stages of distribution, particularly at restaurants or supermarkets.

While the measures could be applied at the border or internally, it was the intention, expectation, and current policy to apply the U.S. measures internally.

As between Articles XI and III, the Panel considered whether the effect on trade attributed to a measure imposed on imported products determines whether the measure is covered by one of these Articles rather than the other. . . . The trade effects on Canadian lobsters will not differ if the U.S. measures are determined to fall under one of these Articles rather than the other. Whether as Article XI measures on importation or as Article III measures on internal marketing, the U.S. limits on Canadian lobsters will have identical effects: imports of sub-sized lobsters will be zero. As noted in the following section, Article III does not distinguish between the intensity or the effect of the measures it covers. It is nearly impossible to draw lines on the continuum of the effects of regulatory measures imposed on the internal sale, transportation, and marketing of goods. Accordingly, the Panel concluded that the effect of the U.S. measures on trade between the Parties in Canadian lobsters does not determine whether Article XI or III is applicable.

In testing each of the two alternative interpretations—that Article III or that Article XI applies to the U.S. measures—the Panel took note of the treatment of certain prohibitions and restrictions that each Party imposes in its own country on marketing various products and that were cited by the Parties in the proceeding.

The import counterpart of some of these measures would presumably be permitted by one of the general exceptions listed in Article XX, for example, any that could be justified as necessary to protect human, animal, or plant life or health. But many such prohibitions or restrictions affecting imported goods clearly would not. The internal marketing counterparts of these measures therefore would not be permissible under GATT if they were to fall under Article XI. Article III, on the other hand, was structured to permit governments to impose internal regulatory measures, subject to the national treatment standard, whether or not such measures met the specific exceptions of Article XX.

*(continued)*

*(continued)*

The Panel concluded that the appropriate principle to be used in determining whether the U.S. measures were covered by Article III was the nonprotection principle of paragraph 1 of that Article.

The Panel determined that the U.S. measures imposed on live U.S. and Canadian lobsters were covered by Article III and not by Article XI. In particular, they considered that the measures, as now applied in the U.S. internal market, or as they might be imposed at the border, came within the scope of "laws, regulations requirements affecting the internal sale, offering for sale, purchase, transportation, distribution or use of products."

**The Minority View: That Article XI Is Applicable.** Some members of the Panel concluded that as long as a measure prevents a product from entering a market, it will be covered by Article XI. What is determinative is the practical effect of the measure. Therefore, some members of the Panel concluded that Article III governs measures which affect the conditions on which the imported product may be sold while Article XI measures prevent the imported product from entering the market at all. Measures couched in terms leading the reader to Article III may in truth and substance and effect be measures which the GATT signatories intended to prohibit by Article XI; that intent must be respected. In any event, it is one thing to make an exporter's competition in the importing country's market prohibitively expensive, by discriminatory requirements, but it is quite another to bar entry into the market; the 1989 amendment fits into the latter category.

In view of the effect of the 1989 amendment (effect which is exactly the intent of those drafting it:

to exclude Canadian sub-sized lobsters from the American market), and in view of the language of Article XI and of the analysis of GATT Panel precedents, some members of the Panel concluded that the 1989 amendment is prohibited by Article XI. It is a prohibition or restriction on international commerce, in effect on importation. Its intended and practical effect is to deny to Canadian, and some domestic, sub-sized lobsters the access they had to the American market until January of 1990. Taking all this into consideration, the members of the Panel who concluded that the U.S. measures were in conflict with Article XI were able to conclude only that the objectives of the 1989 amendment were both of a conservation nature and a trade restriction. Due to the fact that there was no persuasive evidence to support the assertion that the amendment's primary objective was conservation, and the limited discussion of alternatives, these members were unable to draw a conclusion that the amendment was "primarily aimed at" conservation. The United States, for example, did not address the reasons for which its conservation objectives could not be met by special marking of Canadian small lobsters, requirements that lobsters be sorted by size prior to importation into the United States, particular documentary requirements as to sub-sized lobsters of Canadian origin, increased penalties for the possession of sub-sized lobsters, more vigilant enforcement efforts, or possibly other requirements.

**Decision.** The majority of the Panel ruled that the U.S. lobster size regulations were "internal measures" and therefore did not violate GATT's prohibition against restrictions that apply only to imports. The United States was permitted to continue applying the same minimum size rules to Canadian lobsters as to U.S. lobsters.

## Regulation of Products with Environmentally Objectionable Production Processes

Seldom is any threat to the environment or to health inherent in a product itself. Rather, harm usually comes to the environment through the process used to make the product. For instance, nothing about finished steel is environmentally

harmful. But if the plant that manufactures the steel has no pollution control devices, the plant will destroy the ecosystems in bodies of water surrounding it, darken the atmosphere with gases, and contribute to acid rain. As the following case demonstrates, however, one nation cannot exclude the import of a product from another nation because its production processes violate the conservationist nation's environmental policies.

## BACKGROUND AND FACTS

In the Eastern Tropical Pacific Ocean (ETP), yellowfin tuna and dolphins often swim in close proximity to each other. In fact, fishermen in the ETP find schools of tuna by chasing dolphins and intentionally encircling them with "purse seine" nets to catch the tuna underneath. Unless the fishermen employ special procedures, this practice results in the incidental capture and killing of large numbers of dolphins.

In the Marine Mammal Protection Act (MMPA), the United States sought to dramatically reduce this incidental killing of dolphins. The Act places an absolute limit on the number of dolphins that may be incidentally killed and, through regulations, has extensive requirements on the fishing of tuna in the ETP to prevent incidental catches, including bans on purse seine nets. Section 101(a)(2) of the Act also requires the Secretary of the Treasury to ban the import of fish that have been caught with fishing technology that results in the incidental killing of dolphins.

Pursuant to Section 101(a)(2) and based on a finding that the Mexican fishing fleet was killing excessive numbers of dolphins in its ETP tuna-fishing activities, the U.S. Government imposed an embargo on imports of all yellowfin tuna from Mexico. Mexico requested that its complaint be heard by a dispute resolution panel of the General Agreement on Tariffs and Trade, alleging that Section 101(a)(2) violated GATT. Specifically, Mexico argued that Article XI of GATT applied to the MMPA provision and that the provision did not qualify for any exception under Article XX. As in the *Canadian Lobster* case, the United States took the position that Section 101(a)(2) was an "internal measure" governed under Article III.

## CHAIRMAN SZEPESI AND MESSRS. RAMSAUER AND ROSELLI

The Panel noted that Mexico had argued that the measures prohibiting imports of certain yellowfin tuna and yellowfin tuna products form Mexico imposed by the United States were quantitative restrictions on importation under Article XI, while the United States had argued that these measures were internal regulations enforced at the time or point of importation under Article III:4.

*United States Restrictions on Imports of Tuna*
30 I.L.M. 1594 (1991)
Dispute Settlement Panel,
General Agreement on Tariffs and Trade

The MMPA did not regulate tuna products as such, and in particular did not regulate the sale of tuna or tuna products. Nor did it prescribe fishing techniques that could have an effect on tuna as a product. This raised in the Panel's view the question of whether the tuna harvesting regulations could be regarded as a measure that "applies to" imported and domestic tuna within the meaning of Article III and consequently as a measure which the United States could enforce consistently with that Note in the case of imported tuna at the time or point of importation.

The text of Article III:1 refers to the application to imported or domestic *products* of "laws, regulations and requirements affecting the internal sale . . . of *products*" and "internal quantitative regulations requiring the mixture, processing or use of *products*"; it sets forth the principle that such regulations on *products* not be applied so as to afford protection to domestic production.

It was apparent to the Panel that the comparison implied was necessarily one between the measures applied to imported products and the measures applied to like domestic products.

The Panel concluded from the above considerations that [Article III] covers only those measures that are applied to the product as such. The Panel noted that the MMPA regulates the domestic harvesting of yellowfin tuna to reduce the incidental taking of dolphin, but that these regulations could not be regarded as being applied to tuna products as such because they would not directly regulate the sale of tuna and could not possibly affect tuna as a product. Therefore, the Panel found that the import prohibition on certain yellowfin tuna and certain yellowfin tuna products of Mexico and the provisions of the MMPA under which it is imposed did not constitute internal regulations covered by [Article III].

The Panel noted that under General Agreement, quantitative restrictions on imports are forbidden by Article XI:1. . . .

The Panel therefore found that the direct import prohibition on certain yellowfin tuna and certain yellowfin tuna products from Mexico and the provisions of the MMPA under which it is imposed

*(continued)*

*(continued)*

were inconsistent with Article XI:1. The Panel proceeded to examine whether Article XX(b) or Article XX(g) could justify the MMPA provisions. The Panel noted that Article XX provides that:

Subject to the requirement that such measures are not applied in a manner which would constitute a means of arbitrary or unjustifiable discrimination between countries where the same conditions prevail, or a disguised restriction on international trade, nothing in this Agreement shall be construed to prevent the adoption or enforcement by any contracting party of measures . . .

(b) necessary to protect human, animal or plant life or health; . . .
(g) relating to the conservation of exhaustible natural resources if such measures are made effective in conjunction with restrictions on domestic production or consumption.

The United States considered the prohibition of imports of certain yellowfin tuna and certain yellowfin tuna products from Mexico to be justified by Article XX(b) because they served solely the purpose of protecting dolphin life and health.

The Panel recalled the finding of a previous panel that this paragraph of Article XX was intended to allow contracting parties to impose trade restrictive measures inconsistent with the General Agreement to pursue overriding public policy goals to the extent that such inconsistencies were unavoidable. The Panel considered that if the broad interpretation of Article XX(b) suggested by the United States were accepted, each contracting party could unilaterally determine the life or health protection policies from which other contracting parties could not deviate without jeopardizing their rights under the General Agreement. The General Agreement would then no longer constitute a multilateral framework for trade among all contracting parties but would provide legal security only in respect of trade between a limited number of contracting parties with identical internal regulations.

The Panel proceeded to examine whether the prohibition on imports of certain yellowfin tuna and certain yellowfin tuna products from Mexico and the MMPA provisions under which it was imposed could be justified under the exception in Article XX(g).

The Panel noted that Article XX(g) required that the measures relating to the conservation of exhaustible natural resources be taken "in conjunction with restrictions on domestic production or consumption." A previous panel had found that a measure could only be considered to have been taken "in conjunction with" production restrictions "if it was primarily aimed at rendering effective these restrictions." A country can effectively control the production or consumption of an exhaustible natural resource only to the extent that the production or consumption is under its jurisdiction.

The Panel considered that if the extrajurisdictional interpretation of Article XX(g) suggested by the United States were accepted, each contracting party could unilaterally determine the conservation policies from which other contracting parties could not deviate without jeopardizing their rights under the General Agreement. The considerations that led the Panel to reject an extrajurisdictional application of Article XX(b) therefore apply also to Article XX(g).

On the basis of the above considerations, the Panel found that the United States direct import prohibition on certain yellowfin tuna and certain yellowfin tuna products of Mexico directly imported from Mexico, and the provisions of the MMPA under which it is imposed, could not be justified under Article XX(g).

The Panel wished to note the fact, made evident during its consideration of this case, that the provisions of the General Agreement impose few constraints on a contracting party's implementation of domestic environmental policies.

[A] contracting party is free to tax or regulate imported products and like domestic products as long as its taxes or regulations do not discriminate against imported products or afford protection to domestic producers, and a contracting party is also free to tax or regulate domestic production for environmental purposes. As a corollary to these rights, a contracting party may not restrict imports of a product merely because it originates in a country with environmental policies different from its own.

**Decision.** The Panel found that the MMPA was inconsistent with the United States' obligations under GATT. The Panel requested that the United States modify the MMPA to make it consistent with GATT. Because the United States and Mexico resolved the dispute, neither requested that the

*(continued)*

*(continued)*

Panel's decision be adopted by the full GATT Council. Accordingly, it is not technically binding, but its reasoning retains its persuasive force.

**Comment.** The U.S. Congress was not happy with the GATT decision and did not respond as the GATT Panel would have anticipated. In October 1992, it enacted the *International Dolphin Conservation Act* under which any nation cur-

rently under embargo could have it lifted by agreeing to reduce dolphin mortality and to abide by a five-year moratorium on the use of purse seine nets after 1994. If the nation agreed but later failed to comply with the moratorium, the executive branch was authorized to reimpose the embargo. The IDCA would have raised renewed challenges under GATT, but the pressures of NAFTA passage and a consumer boycott of purse-seine-netted tuna effectively led to a "voluntary" end to the dispute.

## Litigation Against Polluters in Affected Country

If the polluting foreign investor is subject to the jurisdiction of the conservationist nation's courts, it might be hailed into court there. This scenario is quite possible where the pollution directly affects the territory of the conservationist nation.

A particularly interesting example involves international emissions from a nuclear plant. The Oberste Gerichtshof of Austria—its highest court—held that Austrian landowners could sue the former Czechoslovakia in Austrian courts for the environmental effects of such emissions. Note especially the court's reliance on the absence of a valid claim under Czech law.

---

### Judgment of February 23, 1988
*39 Osterreichische Zeitschriit fur Offentliches Recht und Volkerrecht 360*
*Oberste Gerichtshof of Austria*

BACKGROUND AND FACTS
The plaintiff, an owner of real estate in Austria near the former Czechoslovakia, brought action in Austrian courts seeking to prevent the construction of a nuclear power plant in Czechoslovakia. The plaintiff alleged that the plant had not been properly licensed. Further, he alleged that the effects of radionuclides generated during the plant's normal operation—and especially in case of an accident—threatened his real estate, 115 kilometers away. Plaintiff alleged that the operation of the plant was not possible without the emissions of radioactive-contaminated water vapor and of excessive warmth.

The Court of First Instance denied plaintiff's claim, holding that it lacked *jurisdiction ratione loci*—geographic jurisdiction over the matter. On appeal, the Court of Second Instance affirmed the lower court decision on the same grounds. The Oberste Gerichtshof (Supreme Court) of Austria, however, disagreed with the courts below.

PER CURIAM
The Court of First Instance—affirmed by the Court of Second Instance—has denied its [own] *jurisdiction ratione loci* . . . but the Supreme Court is of the opinion that [the statute governing venue] of claims related to real estate] also provides *jurisdiction ratione loci* for Austrian courts over claims . . . of real estate owners affected by emissions [of a foreign state]. No treaty rules exist in the case in question with respect to Czechoslovakia.

It is unreasonable to require the claimant to pursue legal proceedings in Czechoslovakia, which obviously are not possible because there the problem under consideration is treated as a public law problem and acts *jure imperii* [official acts] cannot give rise to civil law obligations. This view is not consistent with Austrian law [under which] foreign states can be sued for acts *jure gestionis* [commercial activity] before courts [of another state]; [and the

*(continued)*

*(continued)*

question whether acts of the state are] acts *jure imperii* or *jure gestionis* is not to be determined by the national law in question but according to general international law. [Under such international law] the construction and the operation of a . . . plant for the generation of electricity are not within the scope of *jure imperii,* but are *jure gestionis* and therefore not excluded from the national [Austrian] jurisdiction. . . .

It cannot be said that legal proceedings in Austria would only lead to a judgment which is not enforcible and therefore would only have academic, and not protective, importance; although in the absence of a treaty on execution of judgments with the state in question, an execution of the judgment would presumably not be possible in Czechoslovakia, the pecuniary penalties imposed to enforce

the claim . . . could probably be enforced in Austria and a violation by the defendant of the restraining order of a court could be a legal ground for possible claims of damages by the plaintiff.

As all conditions for Austrian jurisdiction exist but the *jurisdiction ratione loci* has been rejected by the court which would have been competent according to [Austrian law], the Supreme Court . . . is competent to designate a Court of First Instance as the court having *jurisdiction ratione loci* in this case.

**Decision.** The Supreme Court of Austria reversed the finding of the Court of Second Instance that Austrian courts lacked jurisdiction over the plaintiff's claim. It remanded the matter to the trial court where the plaintiff's real estate was situated for further pursuit of the litigation.

## Litigation Against Polluters in Polluter's Home

Another traditional approach to obtaining relief against a polluter is to sue it in its home jurisdiction. In many countries, this approach is not practical: The local judges would be quite disinclined to rule against a significant local enterprise. Even in a relatively neutral forum, however, such a suit can run into significant dif-

ficulties. In *Aguinda v. Texaco, Inc.*, a U.S. court found that the victims of environmental misdeeds abroad could be sued in the United States to seek legal redress. But such a ruling depended on the demonstration that significant activities had occurred in the United States. While reading the following case, note that, as in the *Judgment of February 23, 1988,* the Court focuses on the availability of a remedy in the Ecuadorean court system.

### Aguinda v. Texaco, Inc.
*1994 WL 142006 (1994)*
*United States District Court for*
*Southern District of New York*

**BACKGROUND AND FACTS**
Plaintiffs were a number of Ecuadoran citizens residing in the tropical rain forest of Eastern Ecuador. They sought to represent a class of 30,000 Ecuadorans against Texaco, Inc., alleging that Texaco had engaged in massive environmental abuse for a period of decades, ending in 1990. The plaintiffs alleged that among the activities were large-scale disposal of inadequately treated hazardous wastes and destruction of tropical rain forest habitats. This disposal, the plaintiffs alleged, caused harm to indigenous peoples living in the rain forest, to their property, and to the stability of Amazon basin habitats. The

plaintiffs sought damages for their injuries and an injunction preventing the defendant from continuing or renewing its polluting activities.

Texaco moved to dismiss the case on the basis that the courts of the United States were an inconvenient forum for adjudicating the claims and that summary judgment was appropriate as to some of the counts.

**JUDGE BRODERICK**
Pursuit of individualized monetary relief for a large class of persons in a foreign country growing out of events implemented abroad presents

*(continued)*

*(continued)*

substantial difficulties, even though those events were partially initiated in the United States. These difficulties are sufficient to make a forum in New York inconvenient, and to cause litigation of such claims here to run counter to the goal of "just, speedy and inexpensive" judicial administration . . . provided necessary steps are taken to assure availability of an alternate forum for such claims in Ecuador. Disputes over class membership, determinations of individualized or common damages, and the need for large amounts of testimony with interpreters, perhaps often in local dialects, would make effective adjudication in New York problematic at best. Most [factors] appear to favor resolution of damage claims in Ecuador. These include access to proof, availability of witnesses, possible viewing of sites, local interest, administrative difficulties, problems of choice of law and application of foreign law.

Appropriate caution in making any final determination requires that prior to dismissal of any part of this case on *forum non conveniens* or other grounds raised by Texaco, Texaco must:

a. Execute a binding acceptance of personal jurisdiction over it in Ecuadoran courts and
b. Provide binding acceptance of such jurisdiction by any Texaco subsidiaries having assets derived from the operations in Ecuador at issue, or waiver of the corporate veil by Texaco, or
c. Post an adequate bond to cover any liability imposed by the Ecuadoran courts.

If these requisites are met, consideration may be given to (a) absolute dismissal of plaintiffs' individualized monetary and class action claims or (b) stay of litigation of such claims in this court to permit their pursuit in Ecuador.

Many of the factors discussed above which may favor dismissal of plaintiffs' individual and class action damage claims on *forum non conveniens* grounds are less applicable insofar as injunctive relief is concerned, particularly if the demand for such relief is based on allegedly initiatory events in the United States. There is no known currently ongoing litigation between the parties in Ecuador, nor is there supervision of an entity located in Ecuador, nor is there [anything] which would be disrupted were jurisdiction over such equitable claims . . . to be exercised by this court.

The existence or nonexistence of events in this country which may be related to alleged injury in Ecuador may be explored based on documents or other information received in or sent from this country, minutes or recollections of consultations conducted with management in the United States, and evidentiary support from U.S. sources for types of conduct challenged by plaintiffs. Discovery of documents within the control of the defendant and of witnesses located here or on the payroll of the defendant, together with information plaintiffs can furnish without discovery may provide significant information in those respects.

In *Sequihua v. Texaco,* Civil Action # H-93-3432 (S .D. Tex. Jan. 27, 1994), the court dismissed environmental pollution claims against Texaco also involving Ecuador on grounds of comity and *forum non conveniens.* That case differs from the one at bar as set forth in plaintiffs' complaint and supplementary papers in that in Sequihua the "challenged activity . . . occurred entirely in Ecuador," the "enforcement . . . of any judgment" was assumed to be required to be pursued in Ecuador, and relevant witnesses were expected to be solely those located in Ecuador. By contrast, decision making on the part of the defendant in the United States may or may not turn out to support some or all of plaintiffs' claims in the present case. . . .

Exploration of factual information reasonably available may, however, lead to the conclusion that extensive on-site investigation or extensive testimony to be taken in Ecuador are necessary to establish or refute plaintiffs' claims. Were that to become evident, *forum non conveniens* dismissal of equitable claims as well as those for class monetary relief might become necessary provided that the conditions described above for such dismissal were met.

Texaco moves to dismiss several claims as based on the "local action" doctrine under which actions involving specific real property, including actions for trespass, creating a nuisance on land affecting nearby properties, and similar torts must be tried where the land is located.

Further information is necessary to determine whether or not the current case falls within this category. If any injury caused by defendant's conduct is confined to specifiable real estate, the core concerns underlying the local action doctrine would be applicable. Large-scale industrial pollution in liquid form by contrast, may spread in widening circles not limited to any specific properties. . . . If discovery indicates that actionable steps were initiated in the United States, the local action concept might be inapplicable. . . .

*(continued)*

*(continued)*

Although the local action doctrine does not lead to automatic dismissal of any of plaintiffs' claims, [it] might lead to dismissal of some claims if the facts as developed show that initiation and effects of the challenged behavior of the defendant were closely confined to specific real estate. . . .

Texaco moves to dismiss count VIII alleging violation of the Alien Tort statute . . . which was originally enacted in 1789 and by its terms is applicable to private as well as governmental actors. The Alien Tort statute provides:

> The district courts shall have original jurisdiction of any civil action by an alien for a tort only, committed in violation of the law of nations or a treaty of the United States.

Plaintiffs rely on the Alien Tort statute as a source of substantive law. Ordinarily governmental abuses such as official torture are the subject of suits under the Act, but the absence of such a limitation was explicitly noted as significant in *Argentine Republic v. Hess*. . . . No violation of a treaty has been alleged. The law of nations is, by contrast, customary in nature, to be defined by the usages, solemn commitments and clearly articulated principles of the international community. Participation of the United States in formulation of such usages, commitments and principles is, of course, of particular importance—and may indeed be necessary—where the courts of the United States are asked to enforce them.

Non-treaty international law may be treated as the "sober second thought of the community" upon which, as stated by Justice (later Chief Justice) Harlan F. Stone, . . . all law ultimately rests. No single document can create it, but the unanimity of view as well as consistency with domestic law and its objectives are highly relevant. . . .

Although many authorities are relevant, perhaps the most pertinent in the present case is the Rio Declaration on Environment and Development (1992). Principle 2 on the first page of the document recognizes that states have "the sovereign right to exploit their own resources pursuant to their own environmental and developmental policies," but also have "the responsibility to ensure that activities within their jurisdiction or control do not cause damage to the environment of other States or areas beyond the limits of national jurisdiction."

The Rio Declaration may be declaratory of what it treated as pre-existing principles just as was the Declaration of Independence. Plaintiffs may or may not be able to establish international recognition of the worldwide impact from effects on tropical rain forests as a result of any conduct alleged in their papers which may have been initiated in the United States.

Environmental damage is recognized in the domestic law of the United States as subject to legal restrictions. See among numerous other provisions, the National Environmental Policy Act [and] Endangered Species Act. . . . Indeed, an entire title of the United States Code (Title 16) is devoted explicitly to conservation. The totality of these enactments bespeak an overall commitment to responsible stewardship toward the environment. . . .

Even more significant, United States laws governing hazardous wastes . . . may well prohibit the conduct alleged in the complaint if carried out in the United States. While this would not necessarily inhibit actions in the United States leading to conduct abroad permitted by foreign law, it is relevant as confirming United States' adherence to international commitments to control such wastes. This tends to support the appropriateness of permitting suit . . . if there were established misuse of hazardous waste of sufficient magnitude to amount to a violation of international law.

Decision concerning the possible applicability of [U.S. law] to this case must await additional information after further discovery focusing on events, if any, initiated or assisted in the United States which might violate international law.

Texaco seeks dismissal of the complaint on grounds of international comity, inasmuch as Ecuador, not the United States, enacts laws or regulations governing land use in that country. . . .

At this point, no conflict with Ecuadoran law appears to be present. It is unclear at this stage what impact licenses or other approvals obtained in Ecuador may have on this case. . . . An approval to proceed with an activity does not necessarily include approval of the manner in which that activity is carried out. . . .

Conduct abroad affecting the United States is widely regarded as being under some circumstances a proper subject of action under United States law in the courts of the United States as well as in the courts of the nation where such conduct is implemented. If more than merely preparatory steps are taken in the United States, if substantial effects are caused in the United States, exercise of jurisdiction may be appropriate. . . .

*(continued)*

*(continued)*

The Government of Ecuador has submitted an amicus brief in support of Texaco's motion to dismiss, arguing that exercise of jurisdiction in this case would cause a disincentive to United States firms considering investment in Ecuador:

> Ecuador needs foreign investment in order to stimulate its economy. . . . Foreign investors naturally assume that disputes relating to the development of Ecuador's natural resources are to be adjudicated by the courts of Ecuador.

Exercise of judicial jurisdiction over events initiated in the United States and carried out abroad (whether in Ecuador or elsewhere) is, however, country-neutral in nature and cannot encourage or discourage investment in any particular country, unless the court were to find that country's courts unqualified to adjudicate relevant matters— a contention made by plaintiffs with respect to Ecuador but not now under consideration and not implicated by the issues delineated in this memorandum order.

Any disincentive caused by exercise of jurisdiction here would not be to investment in Ecuador, which could offer as much protection to foreign investors as any other country, but to conduct likely to violate applicable legal norms regardless of the site of the property affected.

Developing nations such as Ecuador benefit from foreign investment but are injured by environmental pollution. As indicated by the amicus brief, in order to attract investment such countries often seek to create the most favorable climate possible—just as a municipality seeking a major athletic team must frequently offer tax and other benefits to attract the team to locate there. Any differential burden imposed by or because of the situation in any particular locale, including Ecuador, may, as pointed out by the amicus brief, discourage such investment. For example, were this court to find that Ecuadoran courts were unable to handle fairly cases concerning events there, triggering litigation at the headquarters of an investor, investment in Ecuador might be chilled. No such finding is either made or suggested here.

If, on the other hand, litigation at the home site of an investor is based upon conduct initiated at that home site irrespective of where carried out, no such negative effect can be expected. Indeed, the country seeking and benefitting from investment may be relieved by such litigation of the need to offend investors by imposing some environmental or other controls which, however desirable, might be resisted by the investors.

**Decision.** The Court reserved judgment on each of Texaco's motions, pending the results of discovery on the extent to which events giving rise to the harm occurred in the United States or were carried out in response to directives issued in the United States. Texaco did not immediately agree to Ecuadoran jurisdiction, so the damages case proceeded, pending discovery, in the United States.

An approach centered on the jurisdiction of United States courts may be effective against U.S. companies. But it seems ultimately doomed to be ineffective, because it cannot provide relief if none of the acts relating to environmentally suspect action occurred in the United States. A U.S. investor could, for example, assure that all discussion relating to a specific polluting project take place in the country with the most forgiving environmental laws. For an approach to be effective in furthering conservation, therefore, it needs to be multinational in scope.

## Inadequacies of the Traditional International Pollution-Control System

Existing international remedies can be effective in specific instances, but they are unlikely to be effective in transforming the international environmental legal system. International arbitration can proceed only if both parties have consented. Such consent is infrequent in the environmental context, however, because a nation usually does not voluntarily subject itself to a proceeding about pollution generated from its own territory. As we have seen, trade sanctions must be couched in product defects. But most environmental damage is caused by manufacturing processes and, as we saw in the U.S.–Mexico Tuna arbitration, such processes are largely exempt from regulation under GATT. Litigation in the affected conservationist nation can be effective against investors. But the affected nation must be sufficiently close to have a direct physical adverse effect. Litigation in the polluter's home country can be circumvented by having all action and decisions occur in the less conscientious nation. Accordingly, new approaches are being pursued to address the problem of global pollution.

## Emerging Problems and Solutions

In light of the perceived shortcomings of traditional legal methodologies for addressing environmental controversies, the world has been developing regional and global solutions. We survey a representative group of the more important of these approaches.

### Regional Approaches

**National Constraints on Exports.** The most regional approach to environmental protection is in national environmental regulation of exports. Even if GATT constrains a nation from excluding imports created in environmentally suspect ways, it can certainly regulate its exports. The U.S. law relating to the export of environmentally hazardous materials is an excellent case in point.

The cornerstone of U.S. environmental regulation of export of hazardous materials is the principle of prior informed consent (PIC). The export of pesticides, for example, is regulated by the U.S. Environmental Protection Agency (EPA) under the Federal Insecticide, Fungicide, and Rodenticide Act (FIFRA). FIFRA requires that before a U.S. seller can export pesticides that are not registered for use in the United States, it must obtain the prior informed consent of the purchaser and give notice to the appropriate official in the receiving country.

The restrictions of the Resource Conservation and Recovery Act (RICRA) are even more demanding on the export of hazardous waste. RICRA requires the exporter to provide notice to the EPA of any forthcoming shipment. Then the government of the receiving country must expressly accept the shipment and provide written notice to the EPA of that consent. Special manifest requirements apply to the shipment, and the exporter has annual reporting obligations to the EPA.

U.S. legislation also seeks to assure that the foreign government's consent is thoroughly informed. The Toxic Substances Control Act (TOSCA) imposes reporting and record-keeping requirements on all chemical substances. In international transactions, TOSCA requires exporters of chemicals or articles containing chemicals to notify the EPA of the export of any chemical that is or has been subject to testing under the statute. EPA must then notify the foreign government of the EPA action with respect to the chemical.

The United States has many laws regulating pesticide use within the United States, but no law exists that forbids manufacturers from exporting banned pesticides to countries with less stringent or poorly enforced laws. This creates the so-called "Circle of Poison"—U.S.-banned pesticides are exported to the Third World and used on crops, the produce of which is then exported back to the US. These pesticides then reenter the United States as residues on food products.

Legislation to break the so-called "Circle of Poison" has been debated for years in the U.S. Congress. The object of the legislation would be to replace Prior Informed Consent with a prohibition on the export of such products. U.S. exporters argue that the failure to obtain approval in the United States is frequently due to the fact that the pesticides are for tropical plants and have little use in the United States. Further, they note that the environmental risk from such pesticides is unproven, while malnutrition and starvation in the Third World is quite palpable. Finally, they point out that, since U.S. legislation would only affect U.S. companies, the bills would only increase the market share of their foreign competitors.

The following excerpt illustrates the "Circle of Poison" problem through a case study of the problem in Mexican agricultural imports to the United States.

# The "Circle of Poison" Issue

## 1. The Issue

Although considerable controversy exists concerning the exportation of pesticides, the United States continues to export banned or unregistered pesticides to Mexico. The detrimental consequences are twofold. First, pesticide exports create a "circle of poison" situation in which US banned pesticides are exported to the Third World and are used on crops whose produce is then sent back to the US. Second, considerable evidence exists concerning the harmful health effects of pesticides on agricultural workers in the Third World.

## 2. Description

The United States relies heavily on the importation of food produced from Third World countries, particularly from Mexico: 25 percent of all fresh and frozen produce in the US is imported, 50 percent of which comes from Mexico. Furthermore, these figures are increasing. From 1989 to 1990, fruit imports from Mexico increased by $100 million and by $200 million for vegetables. . . .

While the US increases its reliance on Mexican produce, Mexico has increased its reliance on pesticide imports and is currently the second largest pesticide importer in Latin America (Tansey, 56). In turn, the US chemical industry has increased its pesticide production and exportation to meet growing demand. From 1990 to 1991, production increased by 3.5% and sales reached $7.6 billion with one billion pounds of pesticides produced. Pesticide exports accounted for nearly one-third of sales, 25 percent of which were not registered by the EPA. . . . Furthermore, US customs records show that exports of chlordane, one of the most toxic pesticides ever formulated, increased tenfold between 1987 and 1990. . . . 26 pesticide ingredients banned from use in the US are exported to the Third World, six of which are used in Mexico. . . .

[F]irst, toxicity threatens US consumers in the "circle of poison" effect in which unregistered or banned pesticides are exported to Mexico and sprayed on crops whose produce is then exported back to the US. . . . The EPA ranks pesticide residues as one of the leading health problems in the US. A study conducted by the National Academy of Scientists estimates that in the next 70 years, one million additional cases of cancer in the US will be caused by pest residues. . . .

In the early 1980s, 15 percent of beans and 13 percent of peppers imported from Mexico exceeded FDA limitations for pesticide residues. . . . Currently, FDA tests on imported foods reveal that contamination by illegal pesticides account for only five percent of imports; however, contamination rates are higher for imported carrots, pineapples, rice, peas and pears. . . . Moreover, the FDA only tests one or two percent of imports . . . while the rest wind up in US grocery stores.

In June 1990, the US Senate Agricultural Committee voted to ban the export of unsafe pesticides. The panel adopted the legislation as part of the 1990 farm bill and hoped that the House of Representatives would address the issue. Strong objection to the bill came from the National Agricultural Chemicals Association, a trade group consisting of pesticide manufacturers, whose 1989 export sales totaled $2.2 billion. The bill was never enacted and, although the issue continues to be debated, it is largely ignored. . . .

Critics argue that most pesticide exports are merely unregistered in the US rather than banned. Many pesticides formulated in the US are never tested for approval because they are of no use to US agricultural needs are sent directly to countries with suitable soils or who grow produce that can utilize the chemicals. Critics also argue that, with a ban, countries will seek out other countries who are willing to supply the banned pesticides. . . .

The second consequence is the health hazards that Mexican workers face when using banned or unregistered pesticides. Since 1990, the Mexican government has made environmental standards much more strict yet does very little to enforce them. Furthermore, inspection of pesticides and pesticide residue is almost unheard of. . . .

*(continued)*

*(continued)*

Improper pesticide use has been found to cause various forms of cancer, birth defects, miscarriages, sterility, and deaths. The Third World uses 80 percent of the world's pesticides and the World Health Organization estimates that all of the 220,000 annual pesticide related deaths occur in the Third World. . . . Moreover, agricultural workers are rarely given sufficient information on the risks involved and thus do not take proper protective measures when using pesticides. As a result, pesticide poisoning is thirteen times higher for Latin American workers than for US workers. . . .

In the Culiacan Valley in Sinaloa, Mexico three thousand field workers are hospitalized each year from pesticide intoxication alone. Contrary to widespread belief, the North American Free Trade Agreement (NAFTA) has not reduced the level of pesticide use in Mexico. . . .

Reprinted courtesy of Colleen Tighe.

In certain areas, national legislation—even of a nation as large as the United States—has virtually no effect. For most environmental issues, global and regional problems require multinational solutions.

**North American Environmental Treaties.** In North America, progress toward common environmental standards has been through bilateral treaties and the North American Free Trade Agreement. Before the passage of NAFTA, the United States had negotiated bilateral agreements with Mexico regarding hazardous waste and transfrontier air pollution. It also had negotiated several treaties with Canada on a number of environmental issues, including acid rain.

NAFTA placed continental cooperation on a more permanent footing. First, in order to persuade the U.S Congress to pass the treaty, Mexico made substantial modifications in its environmental laws. Then, NAFTA's Environmental Side Agreements established the North American Commission for Environmental Cooperation (CEC), headquartered in Montreal. While the North American Free Trade Commission is normally to consider all trade disputes, including disputes with environmental implications, the CEC is to determine whether any party to NAFTA has shown a "persistent pattern of failure" to "effectively enforce its environmental law." A finding of such a pattern can result in a broad range of sanctions, including suspension of NAFTA benefits. Under the Treaty, the parties agreed to jointly finance a variety of border wastewater and water pollution projects. Finally, NAFTA creates permanent committees for Standards-Related Measures and for Sanitary and Phytosanitary Measures to harmonize the environmental laws among the nations. The objectives of this effort are to convert such regulation into acceptable standards in NAFTA countries and ultimately to remove such standards as an impediment to trade.

As we have seen, these agreements still do not permit the United States and Canada to impose their policies on less-developed Mexico. In fact in late 1995, the Commission broadly declares it has no right to investigate actions by legislatures of NAFTA countries even if those actions effectively nullify other laws. The lure of free trade was effectively employed to persuade Mexico to make its laws more protective of the environment and, for the first time, a multinational structure was created to enforce environmental standards. Enforcement of this new legal scheme in Mexico, however, is still unsatisfactory.

The Commission has not exerted decisive influence in multinational disputes. For the most part, it has conducted studies as to proposed developments in border areas. For example, in January 1998, the Commission selected a 10-member panel to review the findings of the commission study of the San Pedro River. The concept of the study was to help "guide and inform policy makers, local residents and the North American public about the conservation of this shared asset." Similar small "eco-projects" have to date been the lifeblood of the commission.

**European Union Environmental Initiatives.** The many nation-states in Europe, by their sheer numbers, require a multilateral solution. In December 1985, within the European Union the *Single European Act* made the environment an official responsibility of the EU, amending Section 13 of the Treaty of Rome with a new Title VII on "Environment." In October 1987, the European Council enacted a comprehensive environmental action program. In all, the Council of Ministers of the European Communities has adopted more than 125 different directives on environmental protection that the member states are obliged to implement through national legislation.

The European Union has also issued a "Green Paper" in its attempts to arrive at a uniform system of civil liability for damage to the environment. The proposal would standardize the principles under which firms have to pay to repair environmental damage. It specifies situations under which strict liability concepts apply and compensation mechanisms for cases in which the responsible party cannot be identified.

The member states have been dragging their feet on implementation of these Union initiatives. In February 1990, the EU commissioner in charge of environmental protection made an unusual public condemnation of the omission and negligence of member states in implementing the environmental directives. Since then the European Commission has initiated about 250 infringement procedures against members to compel implementation. Many EU members now rival the United States in the thoroughness of environmental protection schemes. Newcomers to the EU, however, have been slower to adopt a more demanding scheme. For example, many years after Spain's admission in the Union, it has yet to comply with all of the Commission's directives.

**Regional Marine Treaties.** Nations sharing a body of water have been markedly successful in enacting regional environmental cooperation schemes. This type of environmental protection agreement was pioneered in 1972 by the *London Convention for the Prevention of Marine Pollution by Dumping from Ships and Aircraft,* which prohibited the dumping of specified hazardous wastes from ships at sea and required permits for the dumping of others. The *Helsinki Convention on the Protection of the Marine Environment of the Baltic Sea Area* improved on the London Convention by providing for an effective international inspection and enforcement network. The *Barcelona Convention for the Protection of the Mediterranean Sea from Pollution* took matters further by enlarging the London Convention's list of prohibited substances. Similar convention arrangements have been concluded for the Red Sea and the Gulf of Aden, the Caribbean, the Southeast Pacific, and the South Pacific.

**Developments in Asia and the South Pacific.** Countries in Asia and the South Pacific are not renowned for successful enforcement of environmental policy. The emphasis in the region has been much more on industrial development than on reducing the environmentally adverse byproducts of that development. Indeed, as discussed below, China and India are leaders of emerging countries' resistance to global attempts to outlaw technologies that deplete the ozone layer. Further, the East Asian financial crisis of 1997 reduced even more the limited resources committed to environmental efforts.

Nevertheless, some nations have made efforts at environmental cooperation in the region. A number of countries in the region have entered into the *ASEAN Agreement on the Conservation of Nature and Natural Resources,* under which each of the parties recognize "the responsibility of ensuring that activities under their jurisdiction or control do not cause damage to the environment or the natural resources under the jurisdiction" of other nations. In addition, a number of regional environmental programs have recently been established to coordinate policy: (1) the South Asia Cooperative Environment Program (Afghanistan, Bangladesh, India, Iran, Maldives, Nepal, Pakistan, and Sri Lanka); (2) ASEAN (Singapore, Thailand, and Brunei); and (3) the South Pacific Regional Environment Program (with participation of 21 South Pacific island nations).

**Initiatives by Multilateral Agencies.** Multilateral agencies have advanced the effort by applying uniform environmental standards to projects that they finance. The World Bank, for example, has published a 460-page volume of environmental guidelines for its personnel to use in evaluating the adequacy and effectiveness of pollution control measures for industrial projects. If a country wishes to obtain financing for its projects from the World Bank or its International Finance Corporation (IFC) affiliate, the characteristics of the project must fall within accepted world environmental standards. In light of the importance of these financing sources in the Third World, the impact on new projects has been very substantial.

## Global Solutions

For global problems—and environmental pollution is inescapably global in its effect—only global solutions will do. The United Nations began its work in this arena in December 1972 when it adopted the *Stockholm Declaration on the Human Environment* and founded the *United Nations Environmental Programme* (UNEP). UNEP has now been the catalyst for the formulation and adoption of almost 30 binding multilateral instruments and ten sets of non-binding environmental guidelines and principles.

**The World Trade Organization.** As demonstrated in the preceding review of traditional environmental remedies, GATT affirmatively prevents a conservationist nation from trying to impose its policies on others through trade policy. Environmentalists are working hard to reverse this by adding provisions to GATT to be implemented in the context of the successor to GATT, the World Trade Organization.

Most developed nations favor the creation of a permanent trade and environment committee to advance and implement pro-environment proposals. The less-developed countries resist the concept strongly. Virtually every such proposal coming from an environmental committee would, in their view, adversely affect their exports into the developed world. Some structure seems inevitable, but years of discussion have created little more than commissions to further study the possibility.

One substantive proposal currently under consideration is an additional *ad valorem* tax on all imports to promote environment-friendly development in poorer nations. This proposal addresses the inability of the Third World to pay for the technology necessary to implement a cleaner environment. But poor countries are not enthusiastic about the proposal. First, paying a tax on their exports would make them less competitive with domestic products. Second, the funds would ultimately find their way back to the richer countries which manufacture the antipollution infrastructure.

The less-developed countries have offered their own suggestion: that the richer nations simply make the technology available for no charge. This sentiment caused quite a commotion in regard to the *Convention on Biological Biodiversity,* including strong opposition from the United States, the home of most the manufacturers of that equipment. The less-developed world was willing to assure that species important to biomedical research would be kept alive. But, in return, the owners of intellectual information would have to share that information. Not surprisingly, the United States, which is the home country of most firms with important biomedical information, did not support that portion of the Convention either. The crafting of provisions which left some of the more difficult questions open for another day allowed the United States to join in the Convention. But those difficult issues must be faced in the future.

Another set of proposals focus on uniform WTO accepted standards for labeling and packaging. The concept is to establish standards that protect the environment and yet prevent nations from using such standards as a trade barrier. As the following article reflects, the alliances and diplomatic exchanges on these issues are as fascinating as the issues themselves.

---

**http://www.wto.org/wto/environ/ environm.htm**
*See for environmental information on the WTO site.*

# Lessons from Cairo

The forthcoming global negotiations on trade and the environment will be daunting, for just as the recent Cairo conference dealt with values and mores, so must these ideals be applied to trade and the environment. The developing world fears—with some justification—that the North, led by the U.S., will try to impose its environmental will on the global trading system.

The Islamic fundamentalism voiced at the Cairo conference is not just an expression of religious belief but, equally important, a warning to the North that other nations have their values, too.

A basic organizing tenet for the Cairo conference was that population growth and economic development are directly linked. Some would say the linkage is inverse—the faster the population growth, the slower the developmental growth. Regardless, it is a fact that economics was one of the driving forces behind the conference.

Some of the countries of the South suspect the organizing motives of the conference and may believe the reason the North advocates population control is fear that the non-white global population will ultimately dominate the global economy or, worse, that the non-white nations will send their poor to the North, relieving population pressures in the South.

Likewise, however noble in theory a negotiation on trade and the environment might seem to its organizers (who will surely come from the North), such a negotiation will have less to do with saving the environment and more with preserving the economic status quo between the North and the South.

For while we in the North say that there has been enough degradation of the planet, it is also a fact that we have made it economically because of our earlier degradation, and we can afford to be "noble." The South takes a different view. The South has not yet matured economically. For it to do so, there will have to be more, not less, degradation of the planet. The South is not about to be ordered, hectored, lectured or negotiated into a permanent second-class economic position.

The trade-environment debate does not play very well in countries like Chad or Bangladesh, let alone China or Brazil. These latter countries of the South view our preaching on the environment as another form of imperialism. I suspect many of the southern countries at the Cairo conference regard our position on population similarly—as a form of keeping the South down.

This is the greatest challenge to the U.S. trade policymakers—to convince the South that negotiations on trade and the environment are not just disguised economic imperialism or a way of maintaining the North's control of the global economy.

## Chinese Power

All this does not make pleasant reading. Like demographic growth patterns, one can already discern with reasonable accuracy the economic powers of the next two decades. We, the U.S., possibly Europe and probably Japan will remain economic powers. But we will be equaled—if not surpassed—by China. The die is already cast. If India keeps on its recent course of market reform, it could truly take off, and if Russia finally gets its act together, its economic potential is enormous.

Within the next 20 to 25 years, we will have to share economic and political power with at least one non-Western nation—China—which we have not done post-World War II. While we have been sharing economic power with Japan, we have never had to share political power. Japan has refused to convert its economic might into political clout. The Chinese almost certainly won't be so passive.

As the Uruguay Round negotiations demonstrated, it is difficult enough to conduct negotiations just about trade. But when one adds subjective non-trade values to the negotiations, such as environmental standards, the trade-negotiating task becomes not only more difficult but exponentially more so.

This is what the Cairo conference teaches us. Global negotiations on matters touching upon

*(continued)*

**The Basel Convention.**   One of the best examples of multinational cooperation in environmental matters is the *Basel Convention on Transboundary Movements of Hazardous Wastes and Their Disposal,* which was adopted by 116 nations under the auspices of UNEP. The Basel system is not as stringent, but it is broader in scope than the U.S. law on movement of hazardous waste discussed previously.

As the volume of waste ballooned in the 1980s, a substantial trade developed in the transport of wastes from the United States and Western European countries to developing nations. Because of strict environmental restrictions on disposal in the developed countries, and low or no restrictions in developing nations, waste generators could dispose of hazardous waste at a much lower cost by simply sending it on a barge to a less-developed country. For example, Guinea Bissau entered into contracts valued at more than $600 million over five years—about the size of its entire gross national product—to receive U.S. and European garbage. The downside of this system, of course, is that unremediated hazardous wastes enter the world's ecosystem just as surely whether they are dumped in Bissau, Guinea Bissau, or in Champaign, Illinois. The emerging countries, which were realizing substantial revenues, were reluctant to change the arrangement.

The Basel Convention regulates the transport of wastes that display certain "hazardous characteristics." Transport is prohibited unless the disposer notifies the governments of receiving and transit nations of the nature and amount of wastes in a shipment. These governments must then authorize the shipment; the receiving nation must also confirm that arrangements are in place for the "environmentally sound management of the wastes in question." During shipment, the refuse must be clearly manifested with the contents of the shipment. Upon completion of disposal, the exporter must notify the receiving nation; if completion is not effected, the exporting nation must accept a return of the wastes. To prevent the development of "waste outlaw" nations, all signatories are prohibited from permitting the transport of wastes to non-signatories.

The Convention is hampered by a lack of consensus on a number of key definitional issues. No widely accepted definition of what is "hazardous" has been determined. Nor has a universal agreement on what management is sufficient to *remediate* wastes, i.e., render them harmless to the environment, been established. The difficulties in these areas are exacerbated by the substantial incentive that officials in receiving nations have in allowing unrestricted transport of refuse, which can make them less demanding than officials in developed nations. If the governing elites receiving countries—many of which are not democratic—are unenthusiastic in enforcement, the Basel Convention does not work well. UNEP and others continue to work on these difficult definitional and enforcement issues.

**The Convention on International Trade in Endangered Species.**   *The Convention on International Trade in Endangered Species of Flora and Fauna* (CITES), which was enacted about two decades ago, is an example of how well a treaty can work when it has broad political support. CITES created a system for identifying and listing endangered and threatened species. It forbids the import or export of such species unless a "scientific authority" finds that the import or export will not aggravate the species' situation. Noncompliant nations, whether parties or nonparties to the Convention, face potentially crushing multilateral trade sanctions for violations. Because of the broad support for CITES in both developed and most less-developed nations, the treaty is generally judged to be effective. The former outlaw nations have been brought to heel by overwhelming political pressure.

**The Montreal Protocol.** UNEP has also sponsored a particularly comprehensive example of a global solution to a global environmental problem in the *Montreal Protocol on Substances That Deplete the Ozone Layer,* which calls for a gradual reduction of substances feared to damage the ozone layer. The Protocol imposes a freeze on consumption and a 10 percent limit on increases in production beginning in 1990, a 20 percent reduction in both consumption and production by 1993, and a further 30 percent reduction in production by 1998. The Protocol uses the same sanction as used in CITES against violators: All signatories to the Protocol are pledged to impose trade sanctions against violators.

The Protocol assuaged the concerns of the Third World countries by permitting them greater flexibility in compliance with the Protocol than the more developed countries. In other words, the industrialized countries have to reduce their chlorofluorocarbon (CFC) levels before the emerging countries. For a period, factories in the emerging countries would have less demanding standards than those in the industrialized nations. The idea is that, over time, the production levels of chlorofluorocarbons (CFCs) in the developed world would tend to become more equal with those in the less-developed world, and, eventually, all would decline.

This inequality in treatment has created a significant political issue in the United States, as manufacturers and workers discover the difficulties of competing with foreign-based firms that can use less expensive, dirtier equipment and processes. In fact, U.S. firms in affected industries increasingly move manufacturing facilities to such lower cost nations. The future of the Montreal Protocol may rest with how industrialized nations cope with this transitional period of inequality.

**The Climate Control Convention.** Difficult as resolving the issues of the ozone layer has proved to be, agreement is even harder in the context of "global warming," addressed in the *Climate Change Convention.* After all, CFCs and halons are rather obscure chemicals that make life somewhat easier but are not critical to industrial development. But if the earth really is experiencing a global warming, resolution of such a problem requires a substantial reduction in thermal energy use. At issue are not only the internal combustion engines of automobiles and lawn mowers; most electric power in the United States is generated through burning of fossil fuels. Because energy use is central to economic growth, the less-developed countries are unlikely to agree quickly to any limitations that could restrict their economic development. The less-developed world is not alone in its opposition. The United States and the United Kingdom, which rely heavily on fossil fuels for their energy needs, have steadfastly—through both "liberal" and "conservative" governments—opposed any quantitative or temporal goals for carbon dioxide emissions. Also, the Japanese and French, who rely on nuclear power, which does not create carbon dioxide, delight in using this forum to criticize the principal critics of their nuclear programs.

To complicate matters further, global warming would not affect all nations adversely. Even though drought would occur in some currently fertile areas, on balance a warmer, moister climate would provide longer, frost-free growing seasons. According to a UNEP study, a 1.5° C temperature increase in the Central European section of the former Soviet Union would result in a 30 percent increase in its wheat yield.

Finally, scientists continue to disagree about whether the thickening blanket of greenhouse gases is, in fact, increasing world temperatures. Various theories as to the circulation of air in the atmosphere and theories about the cooling effect of other synthetic airborne materials—such as sulfate particles that impede the sunlight's penetration of the atmosphere—give significant substance to the arguments of those nations that oppose a global warming treaty. In short, a meaningful treaty is probably not a realistic prospect in the foreseeable future.

At the 1992 United Nations Rio Conference on Environment and Development, the world community took its first tentative step toward a multilateral resolution of this problem. The Convention does not resolve any of the foregoing disputes or require any measures from its parties. Rather, it establishes a framework for later discussions leading to more specific treaties on the issue. The Convention identifies harmonization of national regulation and disguised discrimination against imports as areas to be addressed.

**General Prospects for Global Environmental Solutions.** In a world where emerging public opinion strongly favors environmental protection, one should not underestimate the potential for global solutions. For example, a decade ago the differences between whaling nations and environmentalists in non-whaling nations were thought to be intractable. The force of public opinion in the whalers' own countries led to an agreement to permit international regulation. Today, commercial hunting of whales is regulated by the International Whaling Commission which meets periodically to determine how much, if any, whaling is to be allowed. From 1986 through 1992, the commission effectively banned whaling, with an increase in whale stocks that has so far saved the threatened mammals from extinction.

For foreign investors, agreements like the Montreal Protocol—if it stays in force despite political pressure—mean that their manufacturing plants in less-developed countries will need to comply with international standards at some point in the future. Further, because the Protocol also prohibits trade in CFCs between parties to the Protocol and nonparties, foreign investors that manufacture products in the Third World for export to the developed world must expect that those export markets are likely to be closed to them if their plants are located in a country that is not a party to the agreement. The bottom line for foreign investors is that differences in environmental regulations are becoming increasingly difficult to exploit.

# Chapter Summary

Environmental law is an area of rapidly increasing regulation as conservationism becomes an accepted goal of political groups across the spectrum. As this trend is internationalized through bilateral and multilateral treaties, the investor who seeks to avoid environmental protection laws runs the risk of being trapped abroad with an unusable investment.

---

## QUESTIONS AND CASE PROBLEMS

1. What would the Austrian Supreme Court have done if a private cause of action had been available in the former Czechoslovakia? How do you think the court would handle complaints about a nuclear accident such as Chernobyl?
2. How would an Austrian judgment for money damages against the former Czechoslovakian government be enforced? What type of injunctive relief would be possible?
3. If a U.S. company is presented with the opportunity to build a plant in a former communist country with less-stringent laws on carbon dioxide emissions, what factors should it take into consideration before proceeding with the project? To what extent is the long-term investment interest of the company's shareholders to be considered? Are any other issues relevant to management's consideration? Would the company's president, who bypassed this low-risk opportunity to realize profit for the shareholders because of personal political views, have fulfilled management's fiduciary obligations to the shareholders?
4. Assume that a democratically elected government, after a favorable vote in a popular referendum, launches a program to clear 150,000 acres of tropical rain forest in order to promote economic development. To carry out the will of the people, the government issues a request for proposals to international engineering firms for a contract to help clear the acreage. A number of international firms have indicated that they will bid on the project. Prepare a memo to your U.S. firm expressing your views on whether the firm should submit a bid.

5. Despite the Montreal Protocol, the nation of Livy continues to produce CFC-emitting refrigerators and to export them to nations throughout the world. A number of governments object to Livy's practices and ban its exports, pursuant to the Protocol. Livy brings an action under GATT, alleging that under the principles stated in the Mexican Tuna case, this is an attempt to impose conservationist policies on Livy. How should the GATT Panel rule?

6. The Kingdom of Carolinium has a strong commitment to the preservation of wild horse herds. The neighboring Republic of Giles Run is a major dog food manufacturer and regularly uses wild horse meat in its products. These products are exported to and marketed in Carolinium. In accordance with its principles, Carolinium enacted the Horse Conservation and Health Act (HCHA) banning the use of all horse meat in any animal or human food products. Carolinium justified the HCHA on conservationist and health grounds. The evidence for any health hazard from horse meat is limited to a few scattered cases of botulism. The Carolinium ban effectively terminated all dog food exports from Giles Run. In response, Giles Run called for the creation of a GATT panel to consider the HCHA violation of GATT. How should the GATT Panel rule?

## MANAGERIAL IMPLICATIONS

Your employer, Ortiz-Hartman Steel Limited, is a specialty U.S. steel manufacturer. Over the past several years, Ortiz-Hartman has been underbid in its specialty steel submarket by manufacturers from the Bishopric of Saul, a nation that has virtually no environmental laws. Steel plants in Saul spew pollutants into the air and the rivers. Some of the pollutants damage the property and health of Saul subjects, but no cause of action in Saul affords them relief. Other pollutants damage the environment in neighboring countries. Faced with crippling competition, some members of Ortiz-Hartman management recommend that Ortiz-Hartman build a plant in Saul and take advantage of the more forgiving pollution laws.

1. Your employer asks you to prepare a memorandum summarizing the potential liability to Ortiz-Hartman associated with building a plant in Saul under current law. In your assessment, address all possible sources of liability, even those which you consider to be unlikely. Explain the detailed reasoning for your assessments.

2. Prepare a memorandum summarizing long-term risk in light of emerging international environmental legal standards.

# Chapter Twenty-Three

# Regulating the Competitive Environment

An enterprise with great market power must be concerned with the limits that antitrust or competition laws place on extensions of that power. Such extensions include not only the introduction of products but also franchise and licensing arrangements.

Unlike other bodies of law reviewed in Part Four of this book, the general substance of competition laws is markedly similar from nation to nation. The way in which the laws are carried out, however, differs significantly from place to place.

## Historical Development of International Antitrust Law

Until World War II, antitrust law was a phenomenon largely confined to the United States. Although a number of countries, such as Germany and Canada, had laws on the books prohibiting unfair competition, those laws focused more on false advertising than on market share issues. In contrast to the U.S. approach, many nations had large, state-encouraged cartels that dominated their industrial production.

The virtues of antitrust law were first preached by the post-World War II U.S. armies of occupation. Under the somewhat persuasive influence of heavy artillery, Germany and Japan decartelized their economies. Apparently, the seeds of antitrust law took root very well in the Federal Republic of Germany, which developed a distinctive body of statutory antitrust law. This German development may, in turn, have led to the dramatic development of *competition law* in the European Union. (As noted at length in previous chapters, the Union was originally created by the Treaty of Rome, signed on March 25, 1957.) Under Articles 85 and 86 of the treaty, the signatories pledged to regulate anticompetitive actions within the Union and outlaw the abuse of dominant market power. These articles, now implemented by the Commission of the European Communities, form the bedrock upon which the highly sophisticated competition law of the European Union (EU) is based.

Indeed, even as the influence of antitrust law has declined in the United States in recent years, it has increased in importance in other countries. In the United States, the Department of Justice has been much more tolerant of business combinations than in the past, permitting large concentrations of U.S. companies. In the last decade, the Commission's Directorate-General IV (DG-IV)—the EU's version of a combination of the Federal Trade Commission and the U.S. Department of Justice in antitrust enforcement matters—has prepared numerous regulations for adoption by the European Council of Ministers and issued a host of decisions and exemptions. Competition law has also become an important activity for the European Court of Justice, which hears appeals of Commission decisions and referrals from the courts of the EU member states on competition law issues.

Although Europe tends to be the center of attention in international competition law, other nations around the world have also got into the act. In 1976, for instance, Canada amended its statutes to prohibit a broader range of anticompetitive activities and to provide a private cause of action in certain circumstances. Similarly, in 1980, South Korea—a nation scarcely out of the ranks of less-developed nations—enacted its own Monopoly Regulation and Fair Trade Act. In the early 1990s, Hungary, Poland,

Russia, Slovakia, and the Czech Republic all enacted competition laws drawn primarily from the European Union model.

The trend toward greater enforcement of competition law is not universal. Many countries have such laws on their books and simply do not enforce them. Japan, for example, has long had anti-monopoly laws, which it strengthened by increasing penalties twenty-fold in response to United States pressure in the early 1990s. In 1997, Japan increased its "trust-busting" activity by granting more power and independence to its Fair Trade Commission and reducing the number of exemptions in its Anti-Monopoly Act. Even after all of this legislative activity, however, enforcement remains limited to flagrant violations such as bid rigging and political corruption, or to relatively weak industries without significant political clout. Finally, the nations, such as Cuba and Vietnam, that still subscribe to Marxist economic theory, have no laws proscribing their state-run monopolies. But fewer and fewer nations follow Marxist economic theory. Thus, businesses today face conflicting trends; as antitrust law has become less important in domestic U.S. transactions, competition law has become more important in international transactions.

> **http://www.ipanet.net**
> *Register here and select Business Conditions:*
> *Quick Reference under Databases for links to*
> *competitive information.*

## Basic Regulatory Framework

The form of antitrust laws differs somewhat from nation to nation. Germany's competition law, the *Gesetzgegen Wettbewerbsbeschrankungen,* is highly detailed and addresses many issues in advance so as to limit the discretion of the administering agency and the courts to define and develop the law. In stark contrast, but consistent with its bureaucratic legal practice, the Korea Monopoly Regulation and Fair Trade Act is drafted in more general terms. It leaves to administrative regulations the specification of what is prohibited and how it is prohibited. Consistent with litigious tradition, antitrust laws in the United States are stated in general terms, with the details worked out in court.

Despite these differences in form, the substance of competition law is remarkably similar in its focus on two types of activity. First, competition laws tend to prohibit agreements between competitors that restrict competition. From this general principle there flows a whole range of specific prohibitions against anti-competitive clauses in licensing, franchising, and other types of agreements. Second, such laws prohibit the abuse of a dominant market position. Again, from this general principle come a variety of concepts such as bans against refusals to deal. The following analysis is structured around these two general types of prohibitions.

## Prohibitions Against Agreements to Restrict Competition

Article 85 of the Treaty of Rome is similar to Section 1 of the *Sherman Antitrust Act* in prohibiting concerted anti-competitive conduct. The Sherman Act does so in broad, unspecific language. Article 85(1) generally prohibits

agreements between undertakings [firms], decisions by associations of undertakings or concerted parties which may affect trade between the Member States of the European [Union] and which have as their object for effect the prevention, restriction, or distortion of competition within the Common Market.

Article 85(1) then lists specific forms of prohibited conduct such as direct and indirect price fixing; product limits or controls on production, markets, technical developments, or investments; the sharing of markets or supply sources; the application of dissimilar conditions to equivalent transactions with other trading partners, thereby placing them at a competitive disadvantage; and tying arrangements. Similar restrictions may be found in competition law provisions of other nations.

Prohibitions against agreements that restrict competition are ordinarily the most relevant to international transactions. As noted in Chapter Seventeen (Licensing Agreements and the Protection of Intellectual Property Rights), a principal objective of every licensor is to prevent its licensee from competing with it. Left to its own devices, the licensor would seek pledges of eternal non-competition throughout the Milky Way Galaxy. The licensor must, however, moderate its demands consistent with local competition law. Even if the licensee is unsuccessful in resisting such demands, local competition law will void provisions deemed to be excessively anti-competitive.

Local competition regulation can take many forms. For example, Chile generally prohibits the establishment of exclusive distribution systems that restrict trade. Because exclusive distribution agreements always restrict trade, this prohibition means that one must review all such arrangements with officials from the *Fiscalía Nacional Económica,* the Chilean antitrust enforcer, to obtain discretionary preclearance.

In the European Union, the restrictions on licensors are more susceptible to reasoned articulation. In the area of patent licensing, DG-IV is forgiving of some anti-competitive restrictions but not as forgiving as U.S. authorities would be, particularly with respect to products that include both patented and unpatented components. U.S. policy tends to be accepting of a patent holder's restrictions in the hope of giving greater encouragement to innovation. The *Windsurfing* decision, an important case developing this issue, involved a most American export—the California sailboard.

---

### Windsurfing International Inc. v. Commission of the E.C.

2 Eur. Ct. Rep. 611 (1986)
Court of Justice of the European Communities

**BACKGROUND AND FACTS**
Windsurfing International was a company founded by Mr. Hoyle Schweitzer, a key figure in the development of sailboards. The sailboard is an apparatus composed of a "board" (a hull made of synthetic materials equipped with a centerboard) and a "rig" (an assemblage consisting essentially of a mast, a joint for the mast, a sail, and spars) that makes it possible to combine the art of surfing with the sport of sailing. On January 1, 1973, Windsurfing International granted to Ten Cate, a Dutch firm, an exclusive license for the production and sale in Europe of sailboards incorporating Windsurfing's know-how. Ten Cate later granted sublicenses to the German firms Ostermann and Shark. In 1978, they were taken over by Windsurfing International, which then concluded licensing agreements with other German firms: Akutec, SAN, Kleppler, and Marker.

**PER CURIAM**
The first of the clauses at issue, as described by the Commission, imposed on licensees the obligation to exploit the invention only for the purpose of mounting the patented rig on certain types of board specified in the agreement, and the obligation to submit for the licensor's approval, prior to their being placed on the market, any new board types on which the licensees intended to use the rigs. . . . [U]nder the terms of those agreements any modification to a board was subject to the licensor's approval.

Windsurfing International . . . argues that . . . the purpose of the requirement was not to restrict the types of sailboards which could be manufactured by the licensees but solely to ensure that the boards were not of inferior quality. . . .

[I]t cannot be accepted without more that controls such as those provided for in the licensing agreements were compatible with Article 85. Such controls must be effected according to quality and safety criteria agreed upon in advance and on the basis of objectively verifiable criteria. If it were otherwise, the discretionary nature of those controls would in effect enable a licensor to impose his own selection of models upon the licensees, which would be contrary to Article 85. . . .

It must therefore be held that Windsurfing International's real interest lay in ensuring that there was sufficient product differentiation between its licensees' sailboards to cover the widest possible spectrum of market demand.

Insofar as Windsurfing International also seeks to justify its controls by relying on the alleged liability of a licensor under California law for accidents caused by the poor quality of a licensed product, it must be pointed out that even if such liability does exist it does not affect the question of the compatibility of such controls with Community law. . . .

The third disputed clause related to the obligation on the licensees to pay royalties on sales of components calculated on the basis of the net selling price of the product.

Insofar as Windsurfing International's agreement with SAN, Klepper, and Marker also included

*(continued)*

*(continued)*

components in the definition of the product, it must be concluded that the contested decision is incorrect in stating that the agreements contained a clause requiring the licensees to pay royalties on components on the basis of the price of a complete sailboard. The same considerations apply with still greater force to the agreement between Ten Cate and Ostermann as worded before it was taken over by Windsurfing International, which distinguished expressly between the royalties payable on the product and those payable on components.

[I]t must also be pointed out that the royalty levied on the sale of rigs on the basis of that calculation proves not to have been higher than that laid down for the sale of separate rigs in the new agreements, since the licensees acknowledged that it would be equitable to accept a higher rate of royalty once the licensor's remuneration was to be calculated on the price of the rig alone. It follows that that method of calculation did not have as its object or effect a restriction of competition in the sale of separate rigs. . . . The fourth of the clauses at issue relates to the obligation on the licensees to affix to boards manufactured and marketed in Germany a notice stating "licensed by Hoyle Schweitzer" or "licensed by Windsurfing International."

Windsurfing International considers that such a clause is not of such a nature as to distort competition because no consumer could infer from such a notice that the board was manufactured with Windsurfing International's know-how but only that Windsurfing International had issued a license to sell a complete sailboard. In any event there was nothing to prevent li-

censees from representing themselves as technically independent.

Despite Windsurfing International's contention that it was not the object of the clause to distort competition but merely to convey the information, by means of a notice affixed in a place where it was easily visible, that the production and sale of sailboards were made impossible by a license from Windsurfing International, it is nonetheless true that by requiring such a notice Windsurfing International encouraged uncertainty as to whether or not the board too was covered by the patent and thereby diminished the consumer's confidence in the licensees so as to gain a competitive advantage for itself. . . .

The sixth clause at issue provides for the obligation on the licensees to restrict production of the licensed product to a specific manufacturing plant in the Federal Republic of Germany, together with Windsurfing International's right to terminate the agreement immediately should the licensees change their production site. . . .

Insofar as Windsurfing International prohibited its licensees from also manufacturing the product in a country where it had no patent protection and so marketing that product without paying a royalty, it limited freedom of competition by means of a clause which had nothing to do with the patent.

**Decision.**   The Court of Justice of the European Communities held that, except for the obligation to pay royalties on sales of components, the Commission's decision was correct in finding that the contract clauses were invalid because they had as their object or effect a restriction on competition within the Common Market.

---

The *Windsurfing* decision evidences more than a latent European antipathy to sun and fun. It reflects a significant difference between the ways that the European Union and the United States analyze competition issues raised by patent licenses. U.S. antitrust experts tend to view enhanced profit for the patent holder as a desirable incentive to innovation. By contrast, the Europeans increasingly view the monopoly inherent in a patent as a danger to competition that should be minimized as much as possible.

The European Commission is more flexible with respect to know-how transfer agreements than with patent licenses. The rationale is that be-

cause the owner of know-how does not have any legally protectable right to its knowledge, it can rely only on secrecy. The only way to protect secrecy is through restrictive provisions prohibiting the licensee from competing against the licensor or from disclosing the know-how to any third party. If the Commission could not give the potential licensor confidence that its know-how would be kept secret, the licensor would be left with little incentive to enter into any agreement. The result would be anti-competitive since no one but the licensor would have the know-how.

The *Windsurfing* decision also illustrates how the European Commission goes about its task.

It first determines whether an agreement restricts competition in violation of Article 85(1). The Commission then analyzes whether a procompetitive justification permits it to be exempted under Article 85(3).

Franchise agreements involve peculiar considerations because the franchiser must have substantial control over the franchisee. Like other licensors, the franchiser must protect its know-how. In addition, the franchiser must assure that the franchisee is producing and marketing the product in a manner consistent with the franchiser's good name. One franchisee's poor performance can have adverse effects on the franchiser's operations internationally. Indeed, the franchiser may wish to prevent the franchisee from charging prices that are inconsistent with the pricing practices of other franchisees. The European Court of Justice has considered these unusual attributes of the franchiser–franchisee relationship and, in general, has given franchisers and franchisees great flexibility in structuring their relationships.

In Japan, until recently, distribution agreements had been an instrument for the reduction of competition. Because of established "custom and tradition," foreign companies were compelled to enter into a single, exclusive distributorship agreement for all of Japan. Obviously, the single distributor was able to exact unusually favorable terms, and the Japanese consumer was confronted with unusually high prices. In 1990, however, the Japan Fair Trade Commission ruled that companies with at least a 25 percent share of the Japanese market are prohibited from signing exclusive import distribution contracts. Thus, the trend toward greater scrutiny of licensing and distribution agreements is apparently spreading to the Far East.

**http://www.mac.doc.gov/tcc/treaty.htm**
*Select a topic under "competition."*

## Abuse of Dominant Market Position

Article 86 of the Treaty of Rome is the counterpart of Section 2 of the Sherman Act. Both provisions, and their counterparts in other national competition statutes, address the problem of monopolies and the abuse of monopoly power. To be in violation of such monopoly provisions, a company must first have a dominant market position, which is defined differently in different countries and in different industries. Second, the dominant party must be found to have abused this position.

In smaller countries, where by definition fewer entities can survive in the relevant markets, market domination tends to be more widely tolerated. Thus, in Canada, where industry is considerably more concentrated than in the United States, optimal levels of industrial concentration are likely to be relatively higher than in the United States. Moreover, cultural and historical factors are also of considerable importance. For instance, in Germany and France, refusals to deal (*refus de vente*) are closely proscribed, even if the refuser has a relatively low level of market dominance.

Among all this diversity, fundamental principles in competition law matters hold true universally. One principle is that when market dominance is being abused by a foreign entity, the local courts and regulators can be expected to respond with particular vigor. In the ensuing case, the only regret of the Australian judge was that he could not levy a higher fine.

---

BACKGROUND AND FACTS
Sony, a Japanese electronics manufacturer, sold its goods in Australia through an Australian subsidiary and a network of independent electronics dealers. Australia's Trade Practices Commission brought action against Sony's Australian subsidiary, alleging that it had used its market dominance to prevent dealers

*Trade Practices Commission v. Sony (Australia) PTY, LTD.*
*Unreported (September 14, 1990)*
*Federal Court of Australia*
*Queensland District Registry*

from engaging in competition that would reduce the retail price of Sony products to Australian consumers. The specific practice, carried out by local Sony managers Alexander Pagonis and Michael Baxter, was to withhold products from dealers who lowered prices below Sony's

*(continued)*

*(continued)*

recommended retail prices. The Court found Sony (Australia) guilty of the allegations.

JUDGE PINCUS

Here, the evidence showed the fairly vigorous attempts made to induce compliance with recommended prices and thus suppress price competition between Sony's dealers. Sony must have believed that its likely monetary gain from doing so was such as to outweigh the risks attaching to the contravention: bad publicity, legal costs and penalties. But there is no evidence upon which one could assess what the amount of that gain was thought to be, except for a remark made by Pagonis suggesting that discounting had cost Sony in Queensland a million dollars' worth of business. Were it not for the desirability of setting penalties conforming to the level found in the authorities, I should have been inclined to assess penalties at higher sums than have in fact been fixed. When one finds deliberate breaches of the price maintenance provisions of the Trade Practices Act committed by a subsidiary of one of the greatest manufacturers of electronic consumer goods, after years of attempts to enforce compliance with these provisions, one can only suspect that the penalties have not been taken very seriously. Their deterrent effect has been insufficient, it appears, to counter-balance the profit apparently derived from protecting recommended prices against the effect of competition between their dealers.

Six contraventions were found to have been committed by Sony, six by Pagonis and one by Baxter. . . . The Alsound contravention, which is specifically dealt with under the heading "First Allegation" in my reasons, consisted in its having withheld supply of goods to Alsound for a proscribed reason. Withholding was not complete but lasted for a substantial period of time, depriving Alsound of a substantial quantity of goods which it would otherwise have been able to purchase and resell. Sony sought to disguise its purposes by claiming a lack of stock.

Some information about Sony's purposes in treating Alsound, with which it had dealt for quite some years, in this fashion, is to be found in statements made by Pagonis. In discussing with the representatives of Sony the withholding of stock, Pagonis said, in effect, that this was done because of price cutting by Alsound. Pagonis said, in effect, that because the price cutting by companies such as Alsound, in particular, he was "probably heavier handed at the moment than what the other States are. . . . " This implies that the particular steps taken by Pagonis were not directly dictated by his superiors, but that he had a discretion as to his mode of enforcement of recommended prices.

Mr. Ishida has produced brief letters from other Sony personnel denying knowledge of Pagonis's activities, but that material is not of sufficient strength to rebut the inference I have mentioned.

Pagonis said, during the conversation referred to above, that:

> We ceased supply to Alsound because we found that, we believe that, it is costing us millions of dollars' worth of business a year in that particular area by cutting the hell out of Sony's price.

Mr. Uldis Sirovs has given evidence, which is uncontradicted, of a substantial drop in the value of goods supplied by Sony between the year ended 30 June 1987 and that ended 30 June 1988. Mr. Sirovs attributed the drop (about 82 percent) to nonsupply, delays in supply, and the like. It seems clear that Alsound was severely punished for its nonadherence to Sony's prices.

Of the five Photocontinental contraventions, the first three appear to me related to one another in such a way that it is convenient to treat them together. [On 28 October 1987, Mr. Pagonis] announced that he proposed to cut off supply to Photocontinental until some time in the following month and conveyed a threat that future misconduct would be visited with worse punishment. There was a withholding of supply, in fact, following on that discussion and then on 5 November Pagonis told Photocontinental that he had decided to resupply, but made statements to induce future adherence to Sony's prices.

The remaining two contraventions relating to Photocontinental were of a withholding of supply from February 1988 and an inducement of May 1988. Photocontinental was told by Pagonis that Sony would not supply video cameras "as we had sold Sony video cameras at cheaper prices than Sony's prices." The last conversation was simply another attempted inducement. I should add that it was followed by a dispute about accounts, raised by Sony as an excuse to refuse supply.

*(continued)*

*(continued)*

It is my opinion that the risk of repetition of these contraventions, or similar contraventions, on the part of Sony is not high. However, the recurrence of resale price maintenance contraventions by major (and presumably well-advised) companies, long after the enactment of the *Trade Practices Act* suggests, as I have mentioned, a need for deterrence.

In my opinion, the contraventions were deliberate; there is no reason to think that what Pagonis did was unknown to his superiors or in any sense unauthorized. Pagonis's actions and those of Baxter were, as I infer, within the scope of the discretion permitted to executives seeking to achieve compliance with Sony's recommended prices. The case is one in which Sony has been shown to have flouted the law.

Although, as I have mentioned, no evidence has been called to elucidate the circumstances in which the contraventions occurred and in particular the extent to which central management gave directions as to the details of what was to be done, I am not prepared to find against Pagonis and Baxter that they were personally responsible in any way for the formation of the strategy they were implementing; I propose then to set their penalties at one-tenth of those against Sony.

**Decision.** The Court imposed a $250,000 fine on Sony (Australia), a $25,000 fine on Mr. Pagonis, and a $12,000 fine on Mr. Baxter.

## The EU Merger Regulation

The foregoing cases and commentary describe traditional enforcement mechanisms that are familiar to U.S. businesspeople. With some exceptions, to be discussed in the following section, the parties acted and the authorities subsequently reacted. Beginning September 21, 1990, however, the Council of the European Communities enacted Regulation 4064/89, better known as the EU Merger Regulation. Under the Merger Regulation, parties to all mergers, acquisitions, joint ventures, and other business combinations having a *community dimension* must provide pretransaction notification to the Commission.

The EU Merger Regulation is administered by the Commission's Merger Task Force in rapid-fire fashion. Under the Regulation, deals "notified" to the Commission are automatically suspended for the first three weeks of the merger inquiry. During the three-week period, the Task Force intensively studies the competitive effects of the proposed transaction. It also entertains the views of third parties if they can demonstrate a sufficient interest in the proposed merger. Only rarely will the Task Force extend the suspension period; it generally renders a decision within the period.

The review begins with a determination of "community dimension" in cases of any dispute on the issue. Such a dimension exists when (1) the aggregate worldwide sales of all the firms being combined exceed 5 billion European currency units (ECUs), approximately $6.25 billion, and (2) the aggregate sales of the firms within the Union exceeds 250 million ECUs, approximately $312 million. (A European currency unit, or ECU, is a currency unit tied to the value of the currencies of the member states of the Union: Under the 1993 Treaty of Maastricht, the ECU is to be the single European currency beginning at the end of the century for a number of ECU member states.) Even if these tests are satisfied, a concentration of business interests does not have a community dimension if more than two-thirds of the aggregate community-wide profit is in only one Member State. If the proposed concentration has a "community dimension," then only the Commission is to examine the transaction; Member States cannot interfere with or contradict the Commission's findings. Otherwise, a Member State can enforce its own national competition law to mergers having only a national effect.

Once the Task Force determines that the transaction has a community dimension, it then determines whether the concentration is *compatible* with the common market. In essence, a concentration that creates or strengthens a dominant position so as to "significantly impede" effective competition within the Union is "incompatible" with the common market.

The criteria employed in assessing compatibility include market share (compatibility is presumed if joint market share in the common market does not exceed 25 percent); legal or practical barriers to entry, notice of supply, and demand in relevant markets; competition from firms outside the Union; and the structure of the markets.

In essence, the Commission undertakes a two-step analysis to determine whether an "undertaking" in a merger creates or strengthens a dominant position. First, it defines the "relevant markets" affected by the merger in terms of both product line and geography. Second, the Commission determines the effect of the merger on the market so defined. The *Varta/Bosch* case that follows illustrates the multiplicity of factors that can be considered in these two analyses.

---

### BACKGROUND AND FACTS

Varta Batterie AG and Robert Bosch GmbH sought to create a new company, Starterbatterie GmbH, to which the companies would transfer all their national and international starter battery businesses, including product-related R&D and production and distribution facilities. Varta and Bosch would then withdraw from such activities. The two venturers would control the new company jointly and share its profits.

At the time of the proposal, Varta was the most important battery producer in Germany and one of the most important battery manufacturers in the Community. It was active in every member state as a supplier to vehicle producers as well as to retailers.

Bosch was a worldwide producer of automotive parts, including starter batteries. Bosch had offered starter batteries mainly to the replacement market, in which it was well represented all over Europe. Bosch supplied the original equipment market for starter batteries mainly in Spain, through its Spanish subsidiary Femsa.

Varta and Bosch argued to the Commission that the merger did not have any relevant anticompetitive effect because the relevant product market was all starter batteries and the relevant geographical market was the entire European Community. If one viewed the markets in that way, the Varta and Bosch combination would lack a threatening market share.

### VICE-PRESIDENT BRITTAN

### IV. DECISIONS TAKEN BY THE COMMISSION DURING THE PROCEEDINGS

#### 1. The Decision to Initiate Proceedings

After examination of the notification, the Commission concluded that the notified operation

*Case No. IV/MO12*
*Varta Bosch*
*1991 O.J.L. 329*
*Commission of the European Communities*

raised serious doubts as to its compatibility with the common market. It therefore decided on 12 April 1991 to initiate proceedings pursuant to . . . Regulation (EEC) No 4064/89.

#### 2. The Statement of Objections

Following investigations carried out amongst a broad range of undertakings operating in the affected markets as competitors or customers, the Commission sent the parties . . . a Statement of Objections in which it raised objections regarding the replacement market for starter batteries in Germany and Spain.

The objections set out in the Statement of Objections may be summarized as follows:

#### (a) Relevant product market

The starter battery sector has to be divided into two distinct product markets:

- **the original equipment market, which comprises the supply of starter batteries for vehicle producers for the initial equipment of new vehicles;**
- **the replacement market, which comprises the supply of replacement batteries to the retail market for the equipment of used cars.**

In general terms the distinction between the two product markets is not mainly based on a difference in the product itself or on the function of the product. . . .

[T]he original equipment market is characterized by its specific demand side, the automobile industry. . . . In particular, supply to the original equipment market implies a steady demand of a reduced number of battery types . . . by a small number of clients. . . . As to the nature of the product, batteries for the original equipment market

*(continued)*

*(continued)*

have to correspond to the specifications required by the car manufacturers. . . . The quality and standard including zero-defect reliability of the products is prescribed and controlled by the car manufacturers. Supply to the original equipment market is generally linked to R&D cooperation for new products with the car manufacturers which enables the suppliers to follow the latest technical developments in the market. Distribution on the original equipment market means just-in-time delivery to a small number of clients.

Supply to the replacement market, on the other hand, implies strong seasonal fluctuations in demand for a larger number of battery types . . . with a variety of different distributors ranging from purchase organizations, wholesalers, car producers and department stores to ultimate dealers. As to the nature of the product, replacement batteries . . . are adapted to current standards so that the same type can be used in some cars of different producers. . . . The quality and standards are not controlled by the customers . . . nor is there any feedback or cooperation as to R&D for new products. Distribution to the sales markets requires the existence of a distribution and service network system because a number of clients require delivery to the local outlets and service. . . .

*(b) Relevant geographical markets*

The replacement markets for starter batteries in Germany and Spain are still considered as national markets. Investigation has shown sufficiently homogeneous conditions of competition in both countries, which differ appreciably from the conditions of competition in the other Member States, to establish separate geographic markets.

Two factors indicate this:

- **the market shares of the manufacturers are very different in each Member State,**
- **[t]he manufacturers are able to charge in Germany and Spain for the same types of batteries different prices to those which they charge in the other Member States.**

These differences . . . may be attributed to a range of causes. . . .

(i) Nature and characteristics of the product

Starter batteries are adapted to the specific electrical requirements of the different types of vehicles. . . . More than 400 different types of replacement batteries are currently produced in the Community. . . . The importance of sales of these different types varies in the respective Member States. The different stock of cars in the different Member States influences the battery types sold in the Member States. . . . Given the large variety in types offered in the Community, replacement batteries cannot be regarded as homogeneous products. . . .

(ii) Buyer preferences

The preferences of buyers for branded replacement starter batteries are evident in every Member State and they differ significantly in brands favoured. . . . In Germany Bosch sells [a substantial share] of its branded batteries under the "Bosch" label whereas in France and Spain it sells [a substantial share] under its "FEMSA" label. In Spain and Germany Varta sells [a substantial share] . . . of its branded batteries under the "Varta" label, whereas it sells in France [a substantial share] under its brand "Baroclem." . . .

(iii) Structure of the demand side

. . . There are substantial differences in the spread and importance of the different distribution channels present in each Member State. . . .

(iv) Supply side and barriers to entry

The concentration of supply varies considerably from one Member State to another. . . . [S]ignificant market penetration in the five largest Member States in most cases only became possible through acquisition of a national company or of an existing plant.

*(c) Market dominance*

The proposed concentration would give the new entity a dominant position in Germany and Spain, with the result that effective competition would be significantly impeded, because of the following factors:

*The German market*

The market share of the new entity would amount to 44.3. The lead of the order of (>25) over the next largest competitors would be considerable.

The other competitors are small and medium-sized battery specialists.

Varta/Bosch has greater financial strength than the most important competitors.

The new entity has leading production capacity in comparison with its nearest competitors and furthermore the existing use of capacity by its nearest competitors is already high.

*(continued)*

*(continued)*

The other large European producers on the German market have only small market shares.

### The Spanish market

The market share of the new entity would amount to 44.5.

The existence of an equally strong competitor, Tudor SA, could lead for several reasons to alignment of the behaviour of both competitors. In particular the absence of other large actual competitors able to counter any alignment of the behaviour of the main competitors on the Spanish market is noted.

## V. CHANGES AFTER SENDING THE STATEMENT OF OBJECTIONS

Since the Statement of Objections was sent, the following factual changes have occurred:

—Fiat has acquired the French battery producer CEAc, which has a market share of between 2 and 5 percent in Germany;

—The Fiat group has entered into an agreement to acquire via CEAc the German battery producer, Sonnenschein. Sonnenschein has a market share of between 5 and 10 percent in Germany, and the following commitments have been entered into by Varta:

- **Varta has informed the Commission that it will cut its cooperative links with the Deta/Mareg group of companies. It will, for this purpose, within an agreed period;**
- **terminate its licence agreement with the Deta/Mareg group and will not prolong Deta/Mareg's right to use any of Varta's property rights. . . .**
- **end any overlapping between membership of the management and supervisory board of Varta on the one hand and of the Deta/Mareg group on the other hand.**

## VI. IMPLICATIONS OF FACTUAL CHANGES AND COMMITMENTS IN THE AFFECTED MARKETS

The above mentioned concentration projects of Fiat (CEAc and Sonnenschein) and Varta's commitment constitute an important change in the market structure and have an influence on the assessment of the concentration project Varta/Bosch as far as the creation of a dominant position is concerned. They do not however influence the Commission's overall assessment of the definition of the relevant product and the relevant geographic markets. . . .

### 3. Market dominance

The abovementioned factual changes have, in contrast, an impact on the legal assessment as to whether the concentration would create a dominant position for the new entity on the German market.

### (a) Acquisitions by Fiat

. . . Due to the acquisitions of CEAc and Sonnenschein, Fiat's market share in Germany will increase from 1 to more than 10 [percent].

More important than the pure increase of market share is the substantial material change of the competitive potential that accompanies this increase.

Before the two acquisitions, Fiat/Magneti Marelli's, as well as CEAc's, market potential in Germany was largely restricted [because] Fiat and CEAc did not have a physical presence in the German market. In particular they did not have well-known German brands and they had at their disposal only a marginal distribution network. . . . Before the acquisition, Sonnenschein's market potential was even weaker than indicated by its market share because it faced considerable financial difficulties and was confronted with ecological problems. . . .

The concentration of Fiat, CEAc and Sonnenschein will create substantial synergy effects. . . . Fiat will . . . have access to a well-known German brand and to all distribution channels. By that improved market access, Fiat's financial strength and its spare capacity will be able to have, for the first time, an impact on the German market. Due to the merger of Fiat/CEAc/Sonnenschein, a strong competitor will emerge whose competitive potential will be significantly larger than the sum of the separate potential of each of the companies before the merger.

### (b) Ending the cooperation with Deta/Mareg

Ending the cooperation between Varta and Deta/Mareg will influence the competitive relationship between the two groups in the sense that Deta/Mareg will be able to become an independent operator on the German market, and to enter into effective competition with the new entity Varta/Bosch. . . .

### (c) Impact on competition

This improved access through Sonnenschein into the market will now give Fiat/CEAc the choice to use to a significant extent its financial strength and spare capacity also in the German market,

*(continued)*

*(continued)*

which it could not do before because of its restricted clientele. . . .

Furthermore, Deta/Mareg will become an independent player in the near future in the German market. . . .

**Decision.** The Commission ruled the concentration of Varta/Bosch "compatible with the common market," provided that (a) Varta terminate the license agreement with Deta/Mareg at the earliest possible termination date and any new license agreements on starter batteries would be concluded only with the consent of the Commission; and (b) Varta ensure no overlap occur in the membership of the supervisory or management boards of Varta and Deta/Mareg.

Furthermore, the Commission has broad investigative powers under the Merger Regulation, including the ability to request information, to examine or copy books and other business records, to ask "for oral explanations on the spot," and to conduct on-site investigations. Finally, the Commission also has broad powers to levy fines for noncompliance or failure to cooperate during the investigative process.

The point at which the Task Force review under Merger Regulation ends and "normal" DG-IV review under Articles 85 and 86 begins is a hazy issue. If a proposed joint venture is "concentrative"—one that will "independently and permanently perform all of the functions of an autonomous economic entity," without "coordination of the competitive behavior of the parties amongst themselves or between them and the joint venture,"—it is deemed to be subject to review under the Merger Regulation. If on the other hand, it is merely "cooperative," DG-IV is in charge. In fact, because the procedure under the Merger Regulation is so much quicker than under DG-IV, firms have strained to characterize their ventures as "concentrative" and garner review under the Regulation. Accordingly, the precedents in this area are quite inconsistent.

**http://www.parliament.the-stationery-office.co.uk/**

*Select the U.K. parliament publications database, and initiate a search for the EU Merger Regulation.*

# Distinctions of Non-U.S. Competition Law

Foreign competition law may be similar to U.S. law in substance, but it is enforced in quite a different way. The most obvious distinction, and the primary reason for the absence of much litigation under competition law outside the United States, is in the sanctions for violating the law.

## Availability of Private Causes of Action for Damages

U.S. law has been enforced principally by "private attorneys general"—private parties who have ostensibly have been injured by the antitrust violation. Such plaintiffs have been encouraged by the United States' recognition of a private cause of action for violations of antitrust rules and the award of treble damages to successful litigants. With this large pot of gold at the end of the litigation rainbow and relatively little downside exposure (U.S. litigants need not pay the other side's lawyer's fees if they lose), plaintiffs are encouraged to take their shot, and risk-averse defendants are encouraged to settle out of court before trial.

Foreign countries have no treble-damage awards but do have significant costs for unsuccessful plaintiffs; hence, they have little litigation. In fact, many countries provide no private cause of action at all. In Germany, enforcement of competition law is in the hands of the *Bundeskartellamt* (Federal Cartel Office); in Korea, the Minister for the Economic Planning Board enforces the Act. In the European Union, Article 85(2) declares null and void any agreement that violates the terms of Article 85(1) but does not provide for a private cause of action for damages.

U.S. antitrust lawyers might be somewhat bemused by the punishment meted out in South Korea. When the three largest Korean manufacturers of color televisions were conclusively found to have engaged in a price-fixing scheme, they were ordered to end the scheme and to offer a public apology to the Korean people. Because this ruling brought great dishonor to these companies in a culture in which people avoid dishonor at all costs, this punishment sufficed. Apparently, people in other societies are not sold on the American idea that litigation should be the principal avenue for the vindication of rights.

## Article 85(3) and the Rule of Reason

The analytical framework established by U.S. antitrust law distinguishes between actions that are *per se* wrong and actions to which the *rule of reason* applies. Simply put, per se violations are those that no amount of explanation can make legal, while actions subject to the rule of reason can be legal if, upon analysis, they are not found to be anti-competitive.

A raging academic dispute surrounds the issue of whether the rule of reason is an appropriate mode of analysis under EU competition laws. In theory, the European Commission's exemption system functions somewhat like the rule of reason analysis. Agreements that on their face violate the terms of Article 85(1) may nevertheless be entered into if the prospective parties to the contract can obtain an individual exemption or a negative clearance. Employing similar analysis, the Commission grants block exemptions to entire classes of contracts.

An *individual exemption* essentially allows an agreement that would otherwise violate Article 85 because it has favorable economic effects overall. For example, an individual exemption might be granted if the proposed agreement improves the production of goods or promotes technological economic progress, imposes only restrictions indispensable to such product improvement, and does not eliminate competition as to a substantial part of the products in question. This weighing of public benefit against public loss from anti-competitive activity has been adopted in the antitrust laws of each of the formerly communist nations of Central and Eastern Europe.

A *negative clearance,* on the other hand, is confirmation that the proposed agreement does not fall within Article 85(1) at all. It requires the Commission's analysis of whether, in fact, the proposed agreement will impair competition. The disadvantage of the negative clearance is

that if the facts as to competition turn out to differ from those represented on the application, the parties can nonetheless be fined.

Finally, the *block exemption* also involves a *rule of reason* analysis by the Commission. Under the terms of the block exemption, the Commission identifies the type of agreement eligible for exemptions and the types of anti-competitive provisions permitted in such agreements. In considering each provision to be included in a block-exemption contract, the Commission weighs the European Union's interest in promoting productive cooperation between parties against the costs of somewhat reduced cooperation. The three existing block exemptions are exclusive distribution, exclusive purchasing—including special arrangements for beer—and oil-and-gas franchising.

## Preapproval Procedures versus Litigation

The preceding examination of non-U.S. antitrust laws reveals another difference among the U.S. system and various foreign systems. In their exemption system and the EU Merger Regulation, Europeans have structured their system to provide for a resolution of competition law issues prior to the transaction taking place, typically through administrative action. The parties to the request may generally rely on the European Commission's negative clearance. Other non–U.S. systems have similar pre-clearance procedures on which parties can rely and which significantly reduce the amount of private litigation to enforce competition law outside the United States.

If the European Commission had to clear every potentially anti-competitive action in Europe, however, it would need a much larger staff than the 400 people who work in DG-IV. In the period from 1990 through 1994, for example, the Commission granted only 16 individual exemptions. Negative clearances are even rarer.

The Commission has nonetheless opted for a pre-clearance approach by creating *de minimis* exceptions and granting block exemptions. The de minimis exception essentially provided that Article 85(1) was not violated if (1) the parties to the agreement in question have combined gross annual revenues of less than 200 million ECUs, and (2) the products covered by the agreement do not account for more than 5 percent of the volume in the relevant market. Further, as noted previously, the EU Merger Regulation has a much higher "community dimension" threshold. Thus, with the de minimis exception, the majority of agreements within the European Union are not considered to be anti-competitive. The Commission will on occasion also issue "comfort letters" that tell companies that their anticipated transaction, if implemented as represented, is not likely to infringe competition rules.

The Commission addresses the community dimension of most business arrangements through block exemptions applicable to entire industries and/or types of agreements. The broad number of subject areas permit companies to proceed with confidence in not violating Article 85(1) as long as they follow the highly specific instructions of the Commission. The parties whose agreements in these categories precisely follow the phraseology approved by the Commission need not seek approval from the Commission in order to have their transaction considered exempt.

The great benefit of this pre-approval approach pursued by the European Union and many other governments is that the parties can consummate the transaction without risk of subsequent nullification of the transaction and fines. The pre-approval approach, however, has costs of its own. Essentially, the approach prohibits virtually everything, then exempts large areas. Businesses are burdened with trying to write agreements that fit the rigid categories of the exemptions and this exercise encompasses both a good deal of time and a

considerable amount of money in attorneys' fees. Too much emphasis is put on analyzing the conformity of contract clauses with the Commission block exemption models at the expense of considering the clauses' economic impact. Further, the approach greatly hinders innovation in fashioning contractual arrangements, which is not an insubstantial cost. After all, one of the engines of freewheeling capitalism is that different parties invent mutually beneficial arrangements that permit them to service customers better. Second, the need for preapproval of transactions by a bureaucracy introduces an element of delay that can undo many prospective alliances. Delays have not been a problem with the Merger Task Force, but they have been a serious concern in DG-IV reviews, as well as in the reviews of many less-developed agencies.

In 1997, the Commission sought to address some of these difficulties by advancing a "Green Paper" presenting possible options to change the EU competition law regulation in general and "block exemptions" in particular. Under some possibilities, block exemptions would cover clauses in a general way rather than specifying the precise language of clauses. Also, a proscribed clause would not void an exemption for the entire agreement. (Thus, the invalid clause would be severed from the rest of the valid agreement). The differences of view engendered in the European Parliament by the emerging changes in competition policy are reflected in the following article.

The United States does not have an analogous pre-approval system. The closest parallel is the re-

---

*Foreign Accents*

# Competition Policy

### [Members of the European Parliament] Demand More Flexible Exemptions for Vertical Restraints

**S**ummary: The European Parliament would like to see a much more flexible approach to the granting of block exemptions from normal competition rules for vertical agreements in the retail distribution sector. In adopting a report drafted by Marianne Thyssen (EPP, Belgium), the Parliament's plenum thus signalled on July 18 its one

major area of disagreement with the stance taken by the European Commission in its January 1997 Green Paper on Vertical Restraints and Competition Policy.

In a formal Resolution, the [Members of the European Parliament (MEPs)] called upon the Commis-

*(continued)*

view process created by the *Hart-Scott-Rodino Act,* under which certain mergers, joint venture agreements, and similar transactions must be brought before the Department of Justice (DOJ) before they are concluded. The DOJ's permission to conclude the transaction does not, however, preclude the Department from later litigating the issues, nor does it prevent any private party from bringing such a suit. In fact, in the 1990 case of *California v. American Stores Co.,* the U.S. Supreme Court held that private parties and state authorities may sue in federal court for divestiture of a merger even after it has been approved by the U.S. Department of Justice or the Federal Trade Commission. On the whole, antitrust analysis in the United States is developed in the courts in the context of litigation.

Another area in which the United States differs from European Union countries is the extent to which statutes are given extraterritorial application. This difference has engendered such international hostility that it deserves separate treatment.

## Extraterritorial Effect of Competition Laws

In an increasingly interdependent world, no country or continent operates in isolation. For example, anti-competitive behavior in Costa Rica may well have an adverse effect on the price of bananas in the United States. The basic question is whether U.S. law can or should do anything to prevent Costa Rican monopolistic action. Europeans historically have been reluctant to apply their competition law outside the Common Market. Americans have tended to apply their antitrust law to every corner of the globe.

## The U.S. Effects Test

The United States started with a limited concept of extraterritorial jurisdiction but has since developed it in a way that accords U.S. antitrust law a substantial extraterritorial effect. The issue was first examined in *American Banana Co. v. United Fruit Co.* by the great Justice Oliver Wendell Holmes and resolved in a fashion with which most Europeans would feel comfortable.

In *American Banana,* the plaintiff, a U.S. corporation, alleged that a rival U.S. corporation had caused the Costa Rican government to seize the plaintiff's banana plantation and prevent the completion of plaintiff's railway. The plaintiff argued that these acts prevented it from competing in the production and sale of bananas for export to the

United States, in violation of the Sherman Antitrust Act. Justice Holmes dismissed the complaint, interpreting the Sherman Act "as intended to be confined in its operation and effect to the territorial limits over which the lawmaker has general and legitimate powers." Because the United States could not control what happened in Costa Rica, Justice Holmes reasoned that Congress did not intend to regulate what happened there.

Justice Holmes's elegant prose did not hold for long in the United States. Court decisions after

*American Banana* tended to acknowledge the case and its reasoning but applied the ruling in odd ways. In time, this process of ignoring the decision rendered it null and opened the way for a new interpretation of the intent of Congress in the Sherman Act, the so-called U.S. *effects doctrine*, developed in the landmark case of *United States v. Aluminum Co. of America*. The Alcoa case was written by Judge Learned Hand, who many contend was the greatest federal Court of Appeals judge in American history.

---

### *U.S. v. Aluminum Co. of America*
### 148 F.2d 416 (1945)
### United States Court of Appeals for the Second Circuit

BACKGROUND AND FACTS

In 1931, a group of aluminum producers, one French, two German, one Swiss, one British, and one Canadian (Limited), formed a Swiss corporation named "Alliance." Each of the producers was a shareholder of Alliance.

In 1936, the shareholders instituted a system of royalties centered around Alliance. Each shareholder was to have a fixed free production quota for every share it held, but as its production exceeded the sum of its quotas, it was to pay a royalty, graduated in proportion to the excess, to Alliance. Alliance then dividended the royalties to the shareholders in proportion to their shares. The effect was to create a cartel that controlled aluminum supplies and therefore kept prices high. Imports into the United States were included in the quotas.

The cartel ended in 1939, when the German shareholders became enemies of the French, British, and Canadian shareholders.

JUDGE HAND

Did the agreement . . . of 1936 violate Section 1 of the [Sherman] Act? [W]e are concerned only with whether Congress chose to attach liability to the conduct outside the United States of persons not in allegiance to it. That being so, the only question open is whether Congress intended to impose the liability, and whether our own Constitution permitted it to do so: as a court of the United States, we cannot look beyond our own law. Nevertheless, it is quite true that we are not to read general words, such as those in this act without regard to the limitations customarily observed by nations upon the exercise of their powers; limitations which generally correspond

to those fixed by the "Conflict of Laws." . . . We should not impute to Congress an intent to punish all whom its courts can catch, for conduct which has no consequences within the United States. On the other hand, it is settled law . . . that any state may impose liabilities, even upon persons not within its allegiance, for conduct outside its borders that has consequences within its borders which the state reprehends; and these liabilities other states will ordinarily recognize. It may be argued that this act extends further. Two situations are possible. There may be agreements made beyond our borders not intended to affect imports, which do affect them, or which affect exports. Almost any limitation of the supply of goods in Europe, for example, or in South America, may have repercussions in the United States if there is trade between the two. Yet when one considers the international complications likely to arise from an effort in this country to treat such agreements as unlawful, it is safe to assume that Congress certainly did not intend to act to cover them. Such agreements may on the other hand intend to include imports into the United States, and yet it may appear that they have had no effect upon them. That situation might be thought to fall within the doctrine that intent may be a substitute for performance in the case of a contract made within the United States; or it might be thought to fall within the doctrine that a statute should not be interpreted to cover acts abroad which have no consequence here. We shall not choose between these alternatives; but for argument we shall assume that the act does not cover agreements, even though intended to affect imports or exports, unless its performance

*(continued)*

*(continued)*

is shown actually to have had some effect upon them. [The agreement] would clearly have been unlawful, had [it] been made within the United States; and it follows from what we have just said that [it was] unlawful, though made abroad, if [it was] intended to affect imports and did affect them. . . . The [trial] judge found that it was not the purpose of the agreement to suppress or restrain the exportation of aluminum to the United States for sale in competition with "Alcoa." By that we understand that he meant that the agreement was not specifically directed to "Alcoa," because it only applied generally to the production of the shareholders. If he meant that it was not expected that the general restriction upon production would have an effect upon imports, we cannot agree, for the change made in 1936 was deliberate and was expressly made to accomplish just that. It would have been an idle gesture, unless the shareholders had supposed that it would, or at least might, have that effect. The first of the conditions which we mentioned was therefore satisfied; the intent was to set up a quota system for imports.

[A] depressant upon production which applies generally may be assumed . . . to distribute its effect evenly upon all markets. Again, when the [shareholders of Alliance] took the trouble specif-

ically to make the depressant apply to a given market, there is reason to suppose that they expected that it would have some effect, which it could have only by lessening what would otherwise have been imported. If the motive they introduced was over-balanced in all instances by motives which induced the shareholders to import, if the United States market became so attractive that the royalties did not count at all and their expectations were in fact defeated, they to whom the facts were more accessible than to the plaintiff ought to prove it. . . .

There remains only the question whether this assumed restriction had any influence upon prices. . . . [A]n agreement to withdraw any substantial part of the supply from a market would, if carried out, have some effect upon prices, and was as unlawful as an agreement expressly to fix prices. The underlying doctrine was that all factors which contribute to determine prices, must be kept free to operate unhampered by agreements. For these reasons we think that the agreement of 1936 violated Section 1 of the [Sherman Antitrust] Act.

**Decision.**    The U.S. Court of Appeals for the Second Circuit reversed the district court decision and remanded the case to it for further proceedings consistent with its opinion.

---

Although careful to require consequences in the United States, Judge Hand, in *Alcoa,* pushed the reach of U.S. antitrust law farther toward extraterritoriality than had Justice Holmes. In subsequent cases, this trend intensified. U.S. courts interpreted the Sherman Act to require ever-decreasing "effect" on the United States before it was applicable. In addition, other courts turned to the question of whether actions by Americans affecting foreign markets could somehow satisfy the effects test.

Perhaps the crowning touch in this expansion came in *Joseph Muller Corp., Zurich v. Société Anonyme de Gérance et D'Armament,* when a Swiss corporation sued a French corporation in the United States, claiming a violation of U.S. antitrust laws, even though no U.S. companies or consumers were directly affected by any of the acts in question. Further, a Franco–Swiss treaty required that any suits between French and Swiss citizens were to be brought in the defendant's

country. Nevertheless, the U.S. trial court found the requisite effects for jurisdiction over the dispute. U.S. courts, in applying the "effects" test of *Alcoa,* effectively displaced foreign treaties and laws on the basis of minimal U.S. connections.

By the 1970s, some federal courts of appeal had grown disenchanted with the *Alcoa* test because of its failure to take into account the legitimate interests of foreign nations. They thus developed a *jurisdictional rule of reason* that took into account (1) whether the action had some effect on U.S. commerce, (2) whether the restraint was of a type and magnitude to be considered a violation of the U.S. antitrust laws, and (3) the comity interests of the foreign nation against the interests of the United States in antitrust enforcement.

Because of the international friction created by the level of intervention by U.S. courts' liberal interpretation of the Sherman Act, the U.S. Congress finally tried to clarify its intent in the

Sherman Act. In 1982, Congress adopted a strict version of the "effects" test in the *Foreign Trade Antitrust Improvements Act.* In essence, the Act provides that U.S. antitrust law does not apply to conduct unless such conduct has a "direct, substantial, and reasonably foreseeable effect on United States commerce or on the business of a person engaged in exporting goods from the United States to foreign nations."

The efforts of Congress to clarify the extraterritorial application of the Sherman Act did not end disagreement. As the following case makes clear, five of the members of the U.S. Supreme Court continue to have a rather sweeping view of the scope of the Sherman Act's applicability. Because three Justices joined Justice Scalia in his dissenting opinion, however, the resolution of this disagreement in future cases remains unclear.

---

### Hartford Fire Insurance Co., et al. v. California, et al.
#### 509 U.S. 764
#### United States Supreme Court

**BACKGROUND AND FACTS**
Nineteen of the United States and numerous private parties brought antitrust suits against U.S. insurers, U.S. and foreign reinsurers based in London, and insurance brokers. The insurers, reinsurers, and brokers were alleged to have agreed to boycott commercial general liability (CGL) insurers that refused to change the terms of their standard domestic CGL insurance policies to conform with the policies the defendant insurers wanted to sell. The plaintiff States asserted that the practical effect of the policies that the defendant insurers wanted to sell was that (1) occurrence CGL coverage would become unavailable for many risks; (2) pollution liability coverage would become almost entirely unavailable for the vast majority of casualty insurance purchasers; and (3) coverage of seepage, pollution, and property contamination risks would be limited. The U.S. District Court for the Northern District of California dismissed the suits because it refused to exercise Sherman Act jurisdiction over foreign reinsurers under principles of international comity. The Court of Appeals for the Ninth Circuit reversed this decision of the District Court.

**JUSTICE SOUTER**
[W]e take up the question . . . whether certain claims against the London reinsurers should have been dismissed as improper applications of the Sherman Act to foreign conduct. . . .

At the outset, we note that the District Court undoubtedly had jurisdiction of these Sherman Act claims. . . . Although the proposition was perhaps not always free from doubt, see *American Banana Co. v. United Fruit Co.,* . . . it is well estab-

lished by now that the Sherman Act applies to foreign conduct that was meant to produce and did in fact produce some substantial effect in the United States. (See *United States v. Aluminum Co. of America.*) Such is the conduct alleged here: that the London reinsurers engaged in unlawful conspiracies to affect the market for insurance in the United States and that their conduct in fact produced substantial effect. . . .

According to the London reinsurers, the District Court should have declined to exercise such jurisdiction under the principle of international comity. The Court of Appeals agreed that courts should look to that principle in deciding whether to exercise jurisdiction under the Sherman Act. . . . But other factors, in the court's view, including the London reinsurers' express purpose to affect United States commerce and the substantial nature of the effect produced, outweighed the supposed conflict and required the exercise of jurisdiction in this case. . . .

When it enacted the Foreign Trade Antitrust Improvements Act of 1982 . . . Congress expressed no view on the question whether a court with Sherman Act jurisdiction should ever decline to exercise such jurisdiction on grounds of international comity. . . .

We need not decide that question here, however, for even assuming that in a proper case a court may decline to exercise Sherman Act jurisdiction over foreign conduct (or, as Justice Scalia would put it, may conclude by the employment of comity analysis in the first instance that there is no jurisdiction), international comity would not counsel against exercising jurisdiction in the circumstances alleged here.

*(continued)*

*(continued)*

The only substantial question in this case is whether "there is in fact a true conflict between domestic and foreign law." . . . The London reinsurers contend that applying the Act to their conduct would conflict significantly with British law, and the British Government, appearing before us as amicus curiae, concurs. . . . They assert that Parliament has established a comprehensive regulatory regime over the London reinsurance market and that the conduct alleged here was perfectly consistent with British law and policy. But this is not to state a conflict. "[T]he fact that conduct is lawful in the state in which it took place will not, of itself, bar application of the United States antitrust laws," even where the foreign state has a strong policy to permit or encourage such conduct. . . . No conflict exists, for these purposes, "where a person subject to regulation by two states can comply with the laws of both. . . . " Since the London reinsurers do not argue that British law requires them to act in some fashion prohibited by the law of the United States . . . or claim that their compliance with the laws of both countries is otherwise impossible, we see no conflict with British law. . . . We have no need in this case to address other considerations that might inform a decision to refrain from the exercise of jurisdiction on grounds of international comity.

## JUSTICE SCALIA, DISSENTING

I dissent from the Court's ruling concerning the extraterritorial application of the Sherman Act. . . .

[V]arious British corporations and other British subjects, argue that certain of the claims against them constitute an inappropriate extraterritorial application of the Sherman Act. It is important to distinguish two distinct questions raised by this petition: whether the District Court had jurisdiction, and whether the Sherman Act reaches the extraterritorial conduct alleged here.

On the first question, I believe that the District Court had subject-matter jurisdiction over the Sherman Act claims against all the defendants. . . . The respondents asserted nonfrivolous claims under the Sherman Act, and [the U.S. judicial code] vests district courts with subject-matter jurisdiction over cases "arising under" federal statutes. . . .

The second question—the extraterritorial reach of the Sherman Act—has nothing to do with the jurisdiction of the courts. It is a question of substantive law turning on whether, in enacting the Sherman Act, Congress asserted regulatory power over the challenged conduct. . . . If a plaintiff fails to prevail on this issue, the court does not dismiss the claim for want of subject-matter jurisdiction—want of power to adjudicate; rather, it decides the claim, ruling on the merits that the plaintiff has failed to state a cause of action under the relevant statute. (See *American Banana Co. v. United Fruit Co.*)

There is, however, a type of "jurisdiction" relevant to determining the extraterritorial reach of a statute; it is known as "legislative jurisdiction," . . . or "jurisdiction to prescribe." . . . This refers to "the authority of a state to make its law applicable to persons or activities," and is quite a separate matter from "jurisdiction to adjudicate." . . . There is no doubt, of course, that Congress possesses legislative jurisdiction over the acts alleged in this complaint: Congress has broad power under [the Constitution] "[t]o regulate Commerce with foreign Nations," and this Court has repeatedly upheld its power to make laws applicable to persons or activities beyond our territorial boundaries where United States interests are affected. . . . But the question in this case is whether, and to what extent, Congress has exercised that undoubted legislative jurisdiction in enacting the Sherman Act.

Two canons of statutory construction are relevant in this inquiry. The first is the "long-standing principle of American law 'that legislation of Congress, unless a contrary intent appears, is meant to apply only within the territorial jurisdiction of the United States. . . .'" We have, however, found the presumption to be overcome with respect to our antitrust laws; it is now well established that the Sherman Act applies extraterritorially. (See *United States v. Aluminum Co. of America.*)

But if the presumption against extraterritoriality has been overcome or is otherwise inapplicable, a second canon of statutory construction becomes relevant: "[A]n act of Congress ought never to be construed to violate the law of nations if any other possible construction remains." . . . Though it clearly has constitutional authority to do so, Congress is generally presumed not to have exceeded those customary international-law limits on jurisdiction to prescribe.

Consistent with that presumption, this and other courts have frequently recognized that,

*(continued)*

*(continued)*

even where the presumption against extraterritoriality does not apply, statutes should not be interpreted to regulate foreign persons or conduct if that regulation would conflict with principles of international law. . . . "The controlling considerations" in this choice-of-law analysis were "the interacting interests of the United States and of foreign countries." . . .

The solution . . . adopted [by the Court in a maritime personal injury case] was to construe the statute "to apply only to areas and transactions in which American law would be considered operative under prevalent doctrines of international law." . . . [T]he principle was expressed in *United States v. Aluminum Co. of America* . . . the decision that established the extraterritorial reach of the Sherman Act. . . .

The "comity" [authorities] refer to is not the comity of courts, whereby judges decline to exercise jurisdiction over matters more appropriately adjudged elsewhere, but rather what might be termed "prescriptive comity": the respect sovereign nations afford each other by limiting the reach of their laws. That comity is exercised by legislatures when they enact laws, and courts assume it has been exercised when they come to interpreting the scope of laws their legislatures have enacted. . . . Comity in this sense includes the choice-of-law principles that, "in the absence of contrary congressional direction," are assumed to be incorporated into our substantive laws having extraterritorial reach. . . . Considering comity in this way is just part of determining whether the Sherman Act prohibits the conduct at issue. . . .

Under the Restatement [of Foreign Relations Law], a nation having some "basis" for jurisdiction to prescribe law should nonetheless refrain from exercising that jurisdiction "with respect to a person or activity having connections with another state when the exercise of such jurisdiction is unreasonable. . . ." The "reasonableness" inquiry turns on a number of factors including, but not limited to: "the extent to which the activity takes place within the territory [of the regulating state] . . . the connections, such as nationality, residence, or economic activity, between the regulating state and the person principally responsible for the activity to be regulated . . . the character of the activity to be regulated, the importance of regulation to the regulating state, the extent to which other states regulate such activi-

ties, and the degree to which the desirability of such regulation is generally accepted . . . the extent to which another state may have an interest in regulating the activity . . . [and] the likelihood of conflict with regulation by another state. . . ."

Rarely would these factors point more clearly against application of United States law. The activity relevant to the counts at issue here took place primarily in the United Kingdom, and the defendants in these counts are British corporations and British subjects having their principal place of business or residence outside the United States. Great Britain has established a comprehensive regulatory scheme governing the London reinsurance markets, and clearly has a heavy "interest in regulating the activity." . . . Finally, section 2(b) of the McCarran-Ferguson Act allows state regulatory statutes to override the Sherman Act in the insurance field, subject only to [a] narrow "boycott" exception . . . suggesting that "the importance of regulation to the [United States]" . . . is slight. Considering these factors, I think it unimaginable that an assertion of legislative jurisdiction by the United States would be considered reasonable, and therefore it is inappropriate to assume, in the absence of statutory indication to the contrary, that Congress has made such an assertion.

It is evident from what I have said that the Court's comity analysis, which proceeds as though the issue is whether the courts should "decline to exercise . . . jurisdiction . . . " rather than whether the Sherman Act covers this conduct, is simply misdirected. . . . If one erroneously chooses, as the Court does, to make adjudicative jurisdiction (or, more precisely, abstention) the vehicle for taking account of the needs of prescriptive comity, the Court still gets it wrong. It concludes that no "true conflict" counseling nonapplication of United States law (or rather, as it thinks, United States judicial jurisdiction) exists unless compliance with United States law would constitute a violation of another country's law. . . . That breathtakingly broad proposition . . . will bring the Sherman Act and other laws into sharp and unnecessary conflict with the legitimate interests of other countries—particularly our closest trading partners.

[T]here is clearly a conflict in this case. The petitioners here . . . were not compelled by any foreign law to take their allegedly wrongful actions, but that [does not] preclude a conflict-of-laws analysis. . . . Where applicable foreign and

*(continued)*

---

*(continued)*

domestic law provide different substantive rules of decision to govern the parties' dispute, a conflict-of-laws analysis is necessary.

**Decision.** The Supreme Court affirmed that part of the judgment of Court of Appeals which reversed the District Court's refusal to exercise jurisdiction over foreign reinsurers.

---

As the operations and investments of U.S. and foreign businesses have become increasingly enmeshed, the DOJ and the Federal Trade Commission have been obliged to develop enforcement guidelines so that businesspeople will have a better sense of when they might expect prosecution. In 1995, these Antitrust Enforcement Guidelines for International Operations were revised to express a great "interest in international cooperation" and 14 illustrative examples were set forth. The Guidelines indicate that the agencies will conduct a comity analysis before they pursue an investigation of foreign conduct, as an assurance that U.S. regulators will not go willy-nilly into other nations' jurisdiction.

Despite the expressed desire of promotion of international harmony, however, the agencies showed that they intend to be aggressive. The 1995 Guidelines cite the Hartford Fire holding to support the U.S. government view that interest balancing is a *discretionary* matter of comity. In addition, whereas in the 1988 version of the Guidelines DOJ had announced that it would only pursue export commerce cases in which U.S. consumers were also harmed, this footnote does not appear in the 1995 Guidelines.

United States courts similarly continue to be aggressive in the assertion of their jurisdiction over transactions concluded in foreign nations. In 1995, a federal judge ruled that a Danish company doing business in Great Britain could sue a British company in the United States for alleged anti-competitive conduct in Great Britain because the British company's activity would prevent the Danish company from exporting goods to the United States.

---

### *Eskofot A/S v. Du Pont (U.K.) Limited, et al. Defendants*
*872 F. Supp. 81 (1995)*
*United States District Court for the Southern District of New York*

BACKGROUND AND FACTS Eskofot A/S, a Danish company, is a large producer of equipment for the graphic arts and printing industry. It has average annual sales of approximately $75 million, $12 million of which is derived from sales in the United States. Du Pont U.K. is an English corporation and has a printing and graphic arts division in England. Its total sales in 1992 were in excess of £700,000,000, and of that amount, £50,000,000 resulted from sales outside of Britain. The defendant, Du Pont U.K. conducted no business in the United States, had no office, employees, bank accounts, books, or records there and was not licensed to do business in the United States Howson-Algraphy Division of Vickers PLC ("Howson") is the indirect predecessor of Du Pont U.K.

Eskofot brought an action under the Sherman Act against E.I. du Pont de Nemours & Company and Du Pont (U.K.) Limited. Eskofot alleged that defendants had monopolized the domestic and international market for certain printing equipment and materials. It further alleged that defendants have engaged and continue to engage in systematic, intentional conduct which restrains trade.

Eskofot and Howson began work on a new printing system in 1987 and formalized their relationship with the execution of a written agreement on November 3, 1987. In May 1989, Howson was sold to Du Pont, and its name was changed to Du-Pont-Howson Limited ("DPH"). DPH accepted the assignment of Eskofot's contract, and DPH executed two additional agreements with Eskofot relating to materials for the development of platemaking systems.

*(continued)*

*(continued)*

In 1992, Du Pont U.K. acquired DPH, and in June 1992, Du Pont U.K. notified Eskofot that it wanted to cancel the agreements. Eskofot alleged that Du Pont retained full control of Silverlith plates, processors, and chemicals and that defendants intensified their worldwide sales and marketing efforts for Silverlith. In April 1993, Eskofot instituted an action against Du Pont U.K. in England (the "English action") for breach of the consumables agreement and for damages stemming from Du Pont's alleged abuse of its dominant market position, pursuant to Article 86 of the Treaty of Rome. Four months after bringing the English action, plaintiff instituted the action in New York.

JUDGE LEISURE

Defendants maintain that the Court's jurisdiction to hear antitrust claims brought by foreign competitors derives from the Foreign Trade Antitrust Improvements Act, 15 U.S.C. S 6a (the "FTAIA") Defendants note that the FTAIA was intended to exempt from U.S. antitrust law conduct that lacks the necessary level of domestic effect. . . . Defendants contend that Eskofot's complaint pleads no facts from which the Court can conclude that defendants' conduct had a direct, substantial, and reasonably foreseeable effect in the United States. . . . Before reaching this issue, however, the Court must first decide whether the FTAIA is applicable to this case. Plaintiff argues that the FTAIA does not apply to a claim that trade, involving foreign nations, has affected the import commerce of the United States. . . . Eskofot further argues that the instant dispute relates directly to import commerce. Consequently, Eskofot concludes, this case should not be considered under the FTAIA "direct, substantial and reasonably foreseeable" standard. . . .

This Court notes that the FTAIA, by its own terms, clearly states that the provisions of the Sherman Act do not apply to conduct involving trade or commerce, "other than import trade or import commerce," with foreign nations. The implication that the Sherman Act provisions continue to apply to import trade and import commerce is unmistakable. Plaintiff contends that defendants' actions have precluded it from exporting goods into the United States. Consequently, plaintiff's pleading alleges an impact on import trade and import commerce into the United States.

Rather than the FTAIA's "direct, substantial and reasonably foreseeable" standard, the Court must determine whether the challenged conduct has, or is intended to have, any anti-competitive effect upon United States commerce. . . . Eskofot alleges that defendants' actions have had a significant anti-competitive effect upon United States commerce. Moreover, Eskofot alleges facts which, if true, amply support its contention. As a result, this Court has subject matter jurisdiction.

Eskofot alleges that both it and Du Pont always planned to market and sell, respectively, the Proff Print and Silverlith systems and their component parts in the United States. Eskofot further asserts that it would have sold its Proff Print system in the United States if it were not for defendants' conduct, and that defendants still intend to market their Silverlith system in the United States. Defendants dispute these assertions and contend that they are merely conclusory allegations that should be accorded little weight in determining whether to apply American antitrust laws.

The Court notes that, in the present posture of this action, factual questions must be resolved in favor of plaintiff. The instant allegations, for example, require a careful investigation of the records of the various parties before they can be resolved. Whether Eskofot or either of the defendants initiated research to develop the System with the expectation of selling significant quantities in the American market is very much a question of fact. Certainly Eskofot and defendants have the capacity to sell their systems in the United States, and both Du Pont and Eskofot currently sell a certain percentage of their products in the United States. Whether Du Pont or Du Pont U.K. has sold, developed plans to sell, or harbors ambitions of selling the Silverlith system in the United States are questions of fact. Resolving these questions and other factual questions in favor of the plaintiff, this Court finds that plaintiff has sufficiently demonstrated that defendants' conduct impacted the import trade of the United States.

Plaintiff must still demonstrate that it was prevented, by defendants' actions, from marketing the Proff Print system in the United States. Otherwise, it has failed to demonstrate an anti-competitive effect on United States' commerce. However, again, this Court finds that plaintiff has sufficiently

*(continued)*

*(continued)*

alleged facts which, if true, support its contention that defendants' conduct was anti-competitive.

In sum, plaintiff has alleged that: its sale of the Proff Print system in the United States was precluded by defendants' actions, defendants intend to sell Silverlith in the United States, defendants have already initiated marketing activities in the United States to facilitate future sales, and that consumers in the United States will be negatively affected by the higher prices and reduced output that flow from the emergence of a monopoly. Defendants do not convincingly dispel these concerns or transform plaintiff's factual allegations into mere speculative inferences simply by revealing that plaintiff's assertions are not quantitatively definite or that plaintiff has failed, at this stage of the action, conclusively to demonstrate its assertions. Plaintiff does not have to meet such standards, in the present posture of the instant action, and it is not apparent, as defendants urge, that any potential restraint on U.S. commerce would be de minimis.

This Court cannot conclude that no set of facts would support plaintiff's claim that defendants' conduct has had an anti-competitive effect on trade or commerce in the United States. Moreover, this Court cannot even conclude that the conduct alleged by plaintiff has not had a direct, actual, and foreseeable effect in the United States. Accordingly, this Court cannot dismiss this action for lack of subject matter jurisdiction. . . .

Defendants urge this Court to dismiss or stay the instant action on grounds of international comity and judicial efficiency. They observe that plaintiff commenced the English action in April 1993, more than four months prior to the commencement of this action. . . . Defendants advance the position that the doctrine of international comity compels deference to the decisions of a foreign court "if it is shown that the foreign court is a court of competent jurisdiction, and that the laws and public policy of the forum state and the rights of its residents will not be violated.". . . Plaintiff, however, describes a number of differences in the two actions. Du Pont is not a named defendant in the English action. In fact, Eskofot asserts that Du Pont U.K. specifically refused to provide Eskofot with any discovery from Du Pont in the English action. . . . The English action does not concern American antitrust law, nor are possible effects in the United States at issue in that litigation. The English action does not involve questions of Du Pont's relationship with Du Pont U.K., nor does it involve Du Pont's alleged attempts to exclude Eskofot from the American market for the System.

Instead, the English action asserts two claims for relief, breach of contract and violation of Article 86 of the Treaty of Rome. Eskofot asserts neither of these two claims in the action pending in the United States. Plaintiff does, however, state causes of action in the United States suit arising out of purportedly illegal mergers conducted by defendants. These mergers are not at issue in the English action. . . . This Court finds, however, that there are many important issues that will not be reached in the English action, and in addition, any outcome there will be arrived at without the participation of Du Pont, a major party in the instant action. For example, American antitrust law will not be at issue in the English action, nor will a determination by a foreign court under Article 86 of the Treaty of Rome greatly impact this Court's findings under American antitrust law. . . .

As a consequence, although the disposition of the English action may narrow the issues and redefine the controversy between the parties, this Court cannot conclude that a stay or dismissal of the instant action is compelled by international comity and judicial efficiency.

## The European Effects Test

Virtually all nations other than the United States take a more restrained approach to extraterritorial antitrust jurisdiction. Under the *territorial* theory of jurisdiction, which is widely accepted throughout the world, a nation may clearly assert jurisdiction over a merger involving a firm based in its territory. Thus, the People's Republic of Mozambique would be within its internationally recognized rights in asserting jurisdiction over a merger between a Mozambique company and a Canadian firm.

A somewhat more controversial case arises when a subsidiary of a foreign-based company seeks to engage in a transaction within the host country's jurisdiction. Although this situation does not involve questions as to jurisdiction over the subsidiary under the territorial theory, if the host country cannot also obtain authority over the foreign parent, that parent could evade the host country's competition laws merely by conducting all of its activities in the host country through a controlled subsidiary. Faced with this difficulty, the European Court of Justice devised the *single economic unit* concept, under which the Court imputes the behavior of a controlled subsidiary to the parent. As can be seen in the following case, this concept also permits the Court to consider the parent's level of market dominance in determining whether the subsidiary's actions are monopolistic. In a subsequent case, the *Philip Morris* judgment, the Court expanded this concept to find jurisdiction not only when actual voting control is acquired but also when the foreign acquirer would achieve "material influence" over an erstwhile European competitor.

---

## Europemballage Corp. v. E.C. Commission
### Common Mkt. L.R. 199 (1973)
### Court of Justice of the European Communities

### BACKGROUND AND FACTS

Continental Can Company (Continental Can), a U.S. company, acquired an 85.8 percent holding in Schmalbach-Lubeca-Werke, A.G., a West German firm. Continental Can subsequently formed Europemballage Corporation in the United States, which a few weeks later acquired 91.7 percent of a Dutch company, Thomassen & Drijver-Verblifa, in the same line of business as Schmalbach. The following day, the Commission of the European Communities instituted proceedings against Continental Can and Europemballage for breach of Article 86 of the Treaty of Rome, and it later issued a decision ordering a scheme for divestiture to be submitted to the Commission.

The parties appealed to the European Court of Justice.

### PER CURIAM

The applicant companies maintain that according to the general principles of public international law, as an undertaking with a seat outside the Community, Continental Can is not subject to the jurisdiction of the Commission or the Court of Justice; that the Commission therefore had no power to issue the challenged decision against Continental Can or to address to it the demand contained in Article 2 of the decision; and that furthermore the unlawful conduct in respect of which the Commission took proceedings was not directly attributable to Continental Can but to Europemballage.

The applicant companies cannot deny that Europemballage, set up on 20 February 1970 by Continental Can, is a subsidiary company of Continental Can. The fact that the subsidiary has its own legal personality cannot rule out the possibility that its conduct may be imputed to its parent company. This is particularly the case where the subsidiary does not determine its market behavior autonomously but mainly follows the instructions of the parent company.

It is established that Continental Can caused Europemballege to make an offer to buy to the Thomassen & Drijver-Verblifa shareholders in Holland and provided the necessary funds for this purchase. On 8 April 1970, Europemballage bought the Thomassen & Drijver-Verblifa shares and bonds offered to it on that date. Therefore this transaction on the basis of which the Commission adopted the decision in question must be attributed not only to Europemballage but also and mainly to Continental Can. Community law is applicable to such an acquisition which affects the market conditions within the Community. The fact that Continental Can does not have a seat in the territory of one of the member-States does not suffice to remove it from the jurisdiction of Community law.

The plea of lack of jurisdiction must therefore be rejected.

**Decision.** The Court of Justice of the European Communities upheld the decision of the European Commission.

---

The farthest reach of the accepted territorial jurisdiction doctrine is the principle of *objective territoriality*. Under this principle, a state may exercise jurisdiction over conduct commenced outside its territory when the act or effect of the act is physically completed inside its territory.

Many nations, however, have vigorously resisted extension of this effects test beyond physical effects in the host country to mere consequences that result within a nation, such as effects from anti-competitive conduct.

This more-restricted European effects test has meant that companies can conspire to limit competition in exports to a nation without that nation being able to claim jurisdiction over the conspiracy. For example, in Germany, each *export-kartell* unifies the marketing power of German corporations in a single industry for potent export activity outside the Common Market.

As Europeans have begun to develop their own massive multinational market, however, they have become more flexible in defining what constitutes a "physical completion" of an act within a territory. In the following case, commonly referred to as the *Wood Pulp* case, the European Court of Justice found that the European Commission could assert jurisdiction over foreign companies with *no* presence in the Union but which exported to the Union through independent distributors. The Court justified jurisdiction on the basis that the firms had engaged in price-fixing activity that was "implemented" within the Union.

## A. Ahlstrom Osakeyhtio v. E.C. Commission

*1987–88 Tfr. Binder Common Mkt. Rep.*
*(CCH) 14,491 (1988)*
*Court of Justice of the European Communities*

### BACKGROUND AND FACTS

Wood pulp is the principal raw material used in production of paper and paper board. In 1988, member states produced only a small fraction of their requirements for wood pulp. Virtually all of the product purchased in the European Union originated from producers in countries that were then not members of the Union: Finland, Sweden, Canada, and the United States.

Many of these wood pulp producers had no presence in the Union. They sold their products to independent distributors and users located in the Union.

In each of these countries, the wood pulp producers organized into associations for export. In the United States, this group was the *Pulp, Paper, and Paper Board Export Association of the United States* (known as KEA), formed under the *Webb-Pomerene Act,* which exempts associations of U.S. exporters from U.S. antitrust laws. Each of these associations engaged in discussions on pricing policy regarding exports to the Union.

The European Commission brought action against the members of the associations under the Treaty of Rome, found them guilty of anti-competitive activity under Article 85 of the Treaty, and imposed fines on them. The associations appealed to the Court of Justice, asserting that the Commission lacked jurisdiction over them.

### PRESIDENT LORD MACKENZIE STUART

All the applicants that made submissions regarding jurisdiction maintain first of all that by applying the competition rules of the Treaty to them the Commission has misconstrued the territorial scope of Article 85. They note that in its judgment of July 14, 1972, the Court of Justice did not adopt the "effects doctrine" but emphasized that the case involved conduct restricting competition within the Common Market because of the activities of subsidiaries that could be imputed to the parent companies. The applicants add that even if there is a basis in [Union] law for applying Article 85 to them, the action of applying the rule interpreted in that way would be contrary to public international law, which precludes any claim by the [Union] to regulate conduct restricting competition adopted outside the territory of the [Union] merely by reason of the economic repercussions which that conduct produces within the [Union].

The applicants which are members of the KEA further submit that the application of [Union] competition rules to them is contrary to public international law insofar as it is in breach of the principle of noninterference. They maintain that in this case the application of Article 85 harmed the interest of the United States in promoting exports by United States undertakings as recognized in the Webb-Pomerene Act of 1918, under which export associations, like the KEA, are exempt from United States antitrust laws.

Insofar as the submission concerning the infringement of Article 85 of the Treaty itself is concerned, it should be recalled that under that

*(continued)*

*(continued)*

provision all agreements between undertakings and concerted practices which may affect trade between Member States and which have as their object or effect the restriction of competition within the Common Market are prohibited.

It should be noted that the main sources of supply of wood pulp are outside the [Union]—in Canada, the United States, Sweden, and Finland—and that the market therefore has global dimensions. Where wood pulp producers established in those countries sell directly to purchasers established in the [Union] and engage in price competition in order to win orders from those customers, that constitutes competition within the Common Market.

It follows that where those producers concert on the prices to be charged to their customers in the [Union] and put that concentration into effect by selling at prices that are actually coordinated, they are taking part in concertation that has the object and effect of restricting competition with the Common Market within the meaning of Article 85 of the Treaty.

Accordingly, it must be concluded that by applying the competition rules in the Treaty in the circumstances of this case to undertakings whose registered offices are situated outside the [Union], the Commission has not made an incorrect assessment of the territorial scope of Article 85. The applicants have submitted that the decision is incompatible with public international law on the grounds that the application of the competition rules in this case was founded exclusively on the economic repercussions within the Common Market of conduct restricting competition which was adopted outside the [Union].

It should be observed that an infringement of Article 85, such as the conclusion of an agreement that has had the effect of restricting competition within the Common Market, consists of conduct made up of two elements: the formation of the agreement, decision, or concerted practice and the implementation thereof. If the applicability of prohibitions laid down under the competition law were made to depend on the place where the agreement, decision, or concerted practice was formed, the result would obviously be to give undertakings an easy means of evading those prohibitions. The decisive factor therefore is the place where it is implemented.

The producers in this case implemented their pricing agreement within the Common Market. It is immaterial in that respect whether or not they had recourse to subsidiaries, agents, subagents, or branches within the [Union] in order to make their contacts with purchasers within the [Union].

Accordingly, the [Union's] jurisdiction to apply its competition rules to such conduct is covered by the territoriality principle as universally recognized in public international law.

As regards the argument based on the infringement of the principle of non-interference, it should be pointed out that the applicants who are members of KEA have referred to a rule and the effect of those rules is that a person finds himself subject to contradictory orders as to the conduct he must adopt, each State is obliged to exercise its jurisdiction with moderation.

There is not, in this case, any contradiction between the conduct required by the United States and that required by the [Union] since the Webb-Pomerene Act merely exempts the conclusion of export cartels from the application of United States antitrust laws but does not require such cartels to be concluded.

**Decision.** The Court of Justice affirmed the Commission's imposition of fines on the foreign companies that had coordinated their pricing policies.

---

The Court in the *Wood Pulp* decision expressly declined to adopt the U.S. effects test. But the EU Merger Regulation literally applies to companies outside the Union; the definition of "community dimension" measures aggregate worldwide sales of the two merged entities, not whether the assets are located inside the Union. As long as the two foreign firms have sales in the Union in excess of 250 million ECUs and worldwide sales in excess of 5 billion ECUs, they would be caught. Does this mean that, if two large U.S. firms with significant sales to European distributors merge in the United States, they must comply with the regulation? Certainly, the *Tetra-Pak/Alja Laval* case discussed earlier suggests that such is already the case for foreign companies whose principal market is the European Union. Nonetheless, although it is a logical extension of *Wood Pulp*, such an exercise of jurisdiction would convert the "implementation" test into a thinly veiled European "effects test." This seems most unlikely in light of the historical resistance of Europe and other nations to the U.S. effects doctrine.

## Blocking Legislation

A necessary upshot of the U.S. effects doctrine is that the U.S. litigation system and anticompetitive theory are carried into foreign nations. As noted earlier, too, the U.S. system of litigation is particularly repugnant to many non-Americans. The clash triggered a rash of dueling legislation. In an antitrust action brought by the Justice Department against the uranium production industry, an American producer alleged that uranium producers outside the United States had formed a cartel to raise the price of uranium. As the producer sought discovery against foreign producers to document its charges, foreign nations cried foul. They asserted that the uranium litigation was an attempt by the United States to enforce its economic policies abroad.

In short order, Canada, Australia, France, the Netherlands, New Zealand, Switzerland, Germany, and the United Kingdom enacted *blocking legislation.* Essentially, these statutes contain provisions that block the discovery of documents located in their countries and bar the enforcement of foreign judgments there. In addition, some contain *clawback provisions,* under which the foreign companies can sue in their own country to recover against local U.S. assets all or part of the amount of an antitrust judgment rendered in the United States.

These blocking laws are tantamount to international legal warfare. Blocking legislation is still a useful tool in other contexts. For example, many nations reacted against the Cuban Democracy Act of 1992, a U.S. law that prohibits foreign subsidiaries of U.S. corporations from doing business in Cuba by forbidding those subsidiaries from obeying the Act. Then when the Clinton Administration set forth its somewhat more aggressive international antitrust stance, the threat of blocking legislation loomed once more.

---

*Foreign Accents*

---

# Business and the Law: Rebuff for US over Antitrust Stance

### Draft Guidelines on Jurisdiction Outside the Country Are Unpopular with Other Governments

The draft US guidelines on the application of its antitrust laws to anti-competitive practices outside the United States published by the Clinton administration last October have met with a frosty response from the British government. . . .

[T]he UK government's view is that by adopting an aggressive approach to the assertion of US antitrust jurisdiction abroad, rather than fostering international co-operation the guidelines seem likely only to undermine those efforts.

Friction between the US and its trading partners over the extraterritorial application of regulatory laws is nothing new. The issue has also sparked fears in the international business community

about the uncertainty and risk of conflicting legal requirements that it creates, dampening international commerce and investment.

In spite of the publication of international antitrust guidelines by previous US administrations and several attempts by the US Supreme Court—the most recent in 1993—to clarify the issue, uncertainty over the long arm of US regulatory laws remains.

The US's trading partners therefore had high hopes for the new guidelines. However, when after considerable delay they were eventually published last October, it was apparent these hopes were going to be dashed. . . .

*(continued)*

*(continued)*

Britain's response begins by reiterating that the UK and US have a shared interest in ensuring fair and open competition in international business, but then goes on to say that the guidelines nevertheless show that significant differences remain between the scope of the two countries' antitrust laws. Those differences include both the principles on which the laws are based and the approach to their enforcement.

The UK's response expresses concern that the guidelines give an impression of increasing willingness on the part of the US Justice Department and the Federal Trade Commission to take unilateral action in international cases. This is all the more worrying at a time when cooperation in enforcement of antitrust laws is supposed to be on the increase. It warns there is a risk that this approach by the US "could lead to jurisdictional conflicts which would hinder effective cooperation and enforcement to the benefit of neither party". . . .

In support of its argument that the international community increasingly recognises its approach as the correct one, the US authorities cite in the guidelines European competition laws as requiring that anti-competitive conduct under investigation should 'affect trade between member states'.

Britain disputes this. It says the European Court of Justice has made clear that there is a legitimate jurisdictional claim under European law only where the anti-competitive conduct in question was 'implemented' within the community.

It is only under the US interpretation of the effects doctrine that commercial actions not implemented within US territory are nevertheless regarded as falling within US jurisdiction, the UK says Britain is also worried by the assertion of jurisdiction by the US authorities over anti-competitive conduct that restricts US export opportunities, such as agreements between foreign companies to adopt technical standards incompatible with those covering US goods.

Britain remarks: "Such jurisdictional claims show US antitrust law being used as an instrument of trade policy to open markets perceived as closed to US exporters. The UK government regards this as an objectionable and inappropriate use of antitrust powers."

Turning to enforcement of US antitrust laws, the British government welcomes the statement that the US authorities will take principles of international comity into account. Under these principles US law would not be applied extra-territorially to foreign conduct if the balance of foreign interests in exercising jurisdiction outweighed US interests.

But the UK is concerned that the guidelines have introduced the effectiveness of foreign enforcement as a factor to be taken into account when considering under comity principles whether the US should yield jurisdiction to a foreign government.

The British government says this shows that the US will be increasingly prepared to consider unilateral action on the basis of whether foreign governments are prepared to take action or if it perceives that the remedies available in a particular jurisdiction are inadequate.

Britain objects to that because it does not give appropriate recognition in cases falling principally within the jurisdiction of foreign governments to the law and policy of those governments which may include a decision not to pursue a particular case. In particular the UK government would object to unilateral action by the US solely on the Justice Department and trade commission's assessment of the adequacy of antitrust enforcement in other countries.

The UK concludes its comments by saying that if the US maintains this approach it is likely to lead to more frequent confrontation with other sovereign states. It could also lead, in appropriate cases, to states invoking "blocking statutes" preventing such things as the disclosure of documents or information for use in US proceedings. Several countries—including the UK—already have such blocking statutes in place.

The UK says the invocation of blocking legislation by a foreign government would be an important indication of the degree of concern and should be regarded as decisive when the US is deciding whether foreign interests in exercising jurisdiction outweigh its own interests. . . .

However, companies active in the international markets which are tempted to discount the risk of running foul of US antitrust laws outside US borders should heed the case of *Eskofot v Du Pont*. . . .

***Robert Rice***
*The Financial Times*, **March 7, 1995.**

# Chapter Summary

One of the prices of business success is regulation by antitrust laws. Fears that antitrust laws would cripple U.S. enterprises in international competition led to a progressive de-emphasis on the antitrust laws in the United States during the Reagan and Bush Administrations. Actions of the Clinton Administration have not changed this direction significantly. Just when American entrepreneurs thought it was safe to monopolize, however, the European Union and other nations have begun a spirited effort to beef up their own competition laws. The body of antitrust law, thought to be dying in the U.S. context, has been reincarnated abroad.

---

## QUESTIONS AND CASE PROBLEMS

1. The Slobovian Confederation's five producers control 95 percent of the world's supply of "goom," the key ingredient in the production of goomey bears. To maximize the Slobovian standard of living, the government passed a law creating a cartel among the five producers and forbidding access to Slobovian goom by any other entity. The price of goomey bears sky-rocketed in the United States. Giggles Consolidated, a U.S. candy manufacturer, attempted to purchase a goom mine in Slobovia but was rejected by the cartel. As a result, Giggles brought an antitrust action against the cartel members in a U.S. district court. Does U.S. law apply? If the U.S. court finds for Giggles, how can U.S. courts enforce such a judgment?

2. In the case in Question 1, if a U.S. court sought to enforce U.S. laws on Slobovia's leading export, how would U.S.–Slobovian relations be affected? What if a key U.S. naval base was located in Slobovia? How well equipped are courts to conduct such relations?

3. In *Alcoa,* Judge Hand points out that even agreements to restrict trade only in Europe and South America would have anti-competitive repercussions in the United States. What additional element did he require before giving U.S. antitrust law extraterritorial effect?

4. If Judge Hand had written his decision in December 1941, at the beginning of World War II, rather than in 1945, at its successful end, would he have handed down a judgment against the national aluminum company of a principal ally of the United States? Should a decision affecting the nation's relations with an ally reflect such considerations? Do you think the U.S. role in that war affected judges' perceptions of the relative importance of U.S. law?

5. If you managed a British company, would you bring its lawsuit against another British company in business that "affects" the U.S. market under U.S. antitrust laws rather than British competition law? What advantages does a company have in alleging an antitrust conspiracy? Describe the differences between U.S. law and British law in the areas of pretrial discovery, attorneys' fees, and potential damage awards.

6. U.S. antitrust law reflects U.S. economic policy. If U.S. antitrust law resolves an economic dispute among British companies, has U.S. economic policy been extended to Britain? What are the implications of the United Kingdom's requirement that British companies use its own policy in resolving such disputes?

7. Could a European who was injured in a sailboarding accident sue Windsurfing International under California law, even if Windsurfing International could not control its licensee's products? Why did the European Court disregard these considerations? Do you think that the European Court's detailed analyses of each provision of the contracts between Windsurfing International and its licensees unduly interfere with the licensor's rights to exploit know-how? Would Windsurfing International have undue competitive advantages if it regained any one of the provisions that were voided? Would Windsurfing be better off to establish a local branch under its control rather than license its technology?

8. Did the agreement between Varta and Bosch have features that restrict competition? Did the companies violate Article 85(1)? Did their agreement have features that promote competition? How did the European Commission work out these pros and cons? How does Article 85(3) work to further competition in ambiguous circumstances?

## MANAGERIAL IMPLICATIONS

Your firm, Ellis Pets Consolidated, has developed a state-of-the-art process for producing see-through plastic hamster cages. The plastic is thin, so as not to distort the pet owner's view of the hamster, yet hard enough to resist the hamster's gnawing and quite inexpensive in a market with great price elasticity. The Ellis process is strictly know-how; on advice of patent counsel, Ellis has not sought any patent protection. Ellis has achieved a dominant share in the United States market with its line of see-through hamster cages. A large international plastics manufacturer headquartered in Lyon, France—Vivian Plastique, S.A.—wishes to license the process from Ellis to apply it to other uses.

1. Vivian sees the process as so valuable that it is willing to agree never to use the process for applications within the pet industry anywhere in the world. In fact, Vivian is willing to agree never to enter the pet industry in any way. Analyze for Ellis the enforceability of these proposed agreements by Vivian. Include in your analysis alternatives that would be preferable for Ellis.

2. The hamster cage manufacturers of Europe suddenly become aware of the threat posed by Ellis. They agree to apply concerted pressure on pet stores throughout Europe to shut Ellis out. Ellis brings an antitrust action in the U.S. District Court for the Southern District of Florida. Does the court have jurisdiction over the European hamster cage manufacturers? Will Ellis be able to enforce discovery requests in Europe?

# Treaty Establishing the European Economic Community

*Treaty of Rome 1957, as amended through 1988. 1987 Single European Act Amendments identified by SEA in brackets.\* (Selected Provisions)*

## Part One: Principles

*Article 1*
By this Treaty, the High Contracting Parties establish among themselves a EUROPEAN ECONOMIC COMMUNITY.

*Article 2*
The Community shall have as its task, by establishing a common market and progressively approximating the economic policies of Member States, to promote throughout the Community a harmonious development of economic activities, a continuous and balanced expansion, an increase in stability, an accelerated raising of the standard of living and closer relations between the States belonging to it.

*Article 3*
For the purposes set out in Article 2, the activities of the Community shall include, as provided in this Treaty and in accordance with the timetable set out therein

   (a) the elimination, as between Member States, of customs duties and of quantitative restrictions on the import and export of goods, and of all other measures having equivalent effect;

   (b) the establishment of a common customs tariff and of a common commercial policy towards third countries;

   (c) the abolition, as between Member States, of obstacles to freedom of movement for persons, services and capital;

   (d) the adoption of a common policy in the sphere of agriculture;

   (e) the adoption of a common policy in the sphere of transport;

   (f) the institution of a system ensuring that competition in the common market is not distorted;

   (g) the application of procedures by which the economic policies of Member States can be co-ordinated and disequilibria in their balances of payments remedied;

   (h) the approximation of the laws of Member States to the extent required for the proper functioning of the common market;

   (i) the creation of a European Social Fund in order to improve employment opportunities for workers and to contribute to the raising of their standard of living;

   (j) the establishment of a European Investment Bank to facilitate the economic expansion of the Community by opening up fresh resources;

   (k) the association of the overseas countries and territories in order to increase trade and to promote jointly economic and social development.

*Article 4*
1. The tasks entrusted to the Community shall be carried out by the following institutions:
   an ASSEMBLY,
   a COUNCIL,
   a COMMISSION,
   a COURT OF JUSTICE.
   Each institution shall act within the limits of the powers conferred upon it by this Treaty.
2. The Council and the Commission shall be assisted by an Economic and Social Committee acting in an advisory capacity.
3. The audit shall be carried out by a Court of Auditors acting within the limits of the powers conferred upon it by this Treaty.

*Article 5*
Member States shall take all appropriate measures, whether general or particular, to ensure fulfilment of the obligations arising out of this Treaty or resulting

\*Courtesy of European Community Information Service, Washington, D.C.

from action taken by the institutions of the Community. They shall facilitate the achievement of the Community's tasks.

They shall abstain from any measure which could jeopardise the attainment of the objectives of this Treaty.

### Article 6

1. Member States shall, in close cooperation with the institutions of the Community, coordinate their respective economic policies to the extent necessary to attain the objectives of this Treaty.
2. The institutions of the Community shall take care not to prejudice the internal and external financial stability of the Member States.

### Article 7

Within the scope of application of this Treaty, and without prejudice to any special provisions contained therein, any discrimination on grounds of nationality shall be prohibited.

The Council may, on a proposal from the Commission and in cooperation with the European Parliament, adopt, by a qualified majority, rules designed to prohibit such discrimination.

### Article 8

1. The common market shall be progressively established during a transitional period of twelve years.

    This transitional period shall be divided into three stages of four years each; the length of each stage may be altered in accordance with the provisions set out below.

    * * *

6. Nothing in the preceding paragraphs shall cause the transitional period to last more than fifteen years after the entry into force of this Treaty.
7. Save for the exceptions or derogations provided for in this Treaty, the expiry of the transitional period shall constitute the latest date by which all the rules laid down must enter into force and all the measures required for establishing the common market must be implemented.

### Article 8 A [SEA]

The Community shall adopt measures with the aim of progressively establishing the internal market over a period expiring on 31 December 1992, in accordance with the provisions of this Article and of Articles 8 D, 8 C, 28, 57(2), 59, 70(1), 83, 99, 100 A and 100 B and without prejudice to the other provisions of this Treaty.

The internal market shall comprise an area without internal frontiers in which the free movement of goods,

persons, services and capital is ensured in accordance with the provisions of this Treaty.

### Article 8 B [SEA]

The Commission shall report to the Council before 31 December 1988 and again before 31 December 1990 on the progress made towards achieving the internal market within the time limit fixed in Article 8 A.

The Council, acting by a qualified majority on a proposal from the Commission, shall determine the guidelines and conditions necessary to ensure balanced progress in all the sectors concerned.

### Article 8 C [SEA]

When drawing up its proposals with a view to achieving the objectives set out in Article 8 A, the Commission shall take into account the extent of the effort that certain economies showing differences in development will have to sustain during the period of establishment of the internal market and it may propose appropriate provisions.

If these provisions take the form of derogations, they must be of a temporary nature and must cause the least possible disturbance to the functioning of the common market.

# Part Two: Foundations of the Community

## TITLE I. FREE MOVEMENT OF GOODS

### Article 9

1. The Community shall be based upon a customs union which shall cover all trade in goods and which shall involve the prohibition between Member States of customs duties on imports and exports and of all charges having equivalent effect, and the adoption of a common customs tariff in their relations with third countries.
2. The provisions of Chapter 1, Section 1, and of Chapter 2 of this Title shall apply to products originating in Member States and to products coming from third countries which are in free circulation in Member States.

## Chapter 1. The Customs Union

*Section 1*
*Elimination of Customs Duties*
*Between Member States*
*Article 12*
Member States shall refrain from introducing between themselves any new customs duties on imports or ex-

ports or any charges having equivalent effect, and from increasing those which they already apply in their trade with each other.

## Section 2
### Setting up of the Common Customs Tariff
### Article 28 [SEA]

Any autonomous alteration or suspension of duties in the common customs tariff shall be decided by the Council acting by a qualified majority on a proposal from the Commission.

# Chapter 2. Elimination of Quantitative Restrictions Between Member States

### Article 30

Quantitative restrictions on imports and all measures having equivalent effect shall, without prejudice to the following provisions, be prohibited between Member States.

### Article 31

Member States shall refrain from introducing between themselves any new quantitative restrictions or measures having equivalent effect.

\* \* \*

### Article 32

In their trade with one another, Member States shall refrain from making more restrictive the quotas and measures having equivalent effect existing at the date of the entry into force of this Treaty.

These quotas shall be abolished by the end of the transitional period at the latest. During that period, they shall be progressively abolished

\* \* \*

### Article 34

1. Quantitative restrictions on exports, and all measures having equivalent effect, shall be prohibited between Member States.
2. Member States shall, by the end of the first stage at the latest, abolish all quantitative restrictions on exports and any measures having equivalent effect which are in existence when this Treaty enters into force.

\* \* \*

### Article 36

The provisions of Articles 30 to 34 shall not preclude prohibitions or restrictions on imports, exports or goods in transit justified on grounds of public morality, public policy or public security; the protection of

health and life of humans, animals or plants; the protection of national treasures possessing artistic, historic or archaeological value; or the protection of industrial and commercial property. Such prohibitions or restrictions shall not, however, constitute a means of arbitrary discrimination or a disguised restriction on trade between Member States.

## TITLE II. AGRICULTURE

### Article 38

1. The common market shall extend to agriculture and trade in agricultural products. "Agricultural products" means the products of the soil, of stock-farming and of fisheries and products of first-stage processing directly related to these products.

\* \* \*

4. The operation and development of the common market for agricultural products must be accompanied by the establishment of a common agricultural policy among the Member States.

### Article 39

1. The objectives of the common agricultural policy shall be:
   (a) to increase agricultural productivity by promoting technical progress and by ensuring the rational development of agricultural production and the optimum utilisation of the factors of production, in particular labour;
   (b) thus to ensure a fair standard of living for the agricultural community, in particular by increasing the individual earnings of persons engaged in agriculture;
   (c) to stabilise markets;
   (d) to assure the availability of supplies;
   (e) to ensure that supplies reach consumers at reasonable prices.
2. In working out the common agricultural policy and the special methods for its application, account shall be taken of:
   (a) the particular nature of agricultural activity, which results from the social structure of agriculture and from structural and natural disparities between the various agricultural regions;
   (b) the need to effect the appropriate adjustments by degrees;
   (c) the fact that in the Member States agriculture constitutes a sector closely linked with the economy as a whole.

### Article 40

1. Member States shall develop the common agricultural policy by degrees during the transitional

period and shall bring it into force by the end of that period at the latest.

2. In order to attain the objectives set out in Article 39 a common organisation of agricultural markets shall be established.

\* \* \*

## TITLE III. FREE MOVEMENT OF PERSONS, SERVICES, CAPITAL

## Chapter 1. Workers

*Article 48*

1. Freedom of movement for workers shall be secured within the Community by the end of the transitional period at the latest.
2. Such freedom of movement shall entail the abolition of any discrimination based on nationality between workers of the Member States as regards employment, remuneration and other conditions of work and employment.
3. It shall entail the right, subject to limitations justified on grounds of public policy, public security or public health:
   (a) to accept offers of employment actually made;
   (b) to move freely within the territory of Member States for this purpose;
   (c) to stay in a Member State for the purpose of employment in accordance with the provisions governing the employment of nationals of that State laid down by law, regulation or administrative action;
   (d) to remain in the territory of a Member State after having been employed in that State, subject to conditions which shall be embodied in implementing regulations to be drawn up by the Commission.
4. The provisions of this Article shall not apply to employment in the public service.

## Chapter 2. Right of Establishment

*Article 52*

Within the framework of the provisions set out below, restrictions on the freedom of establishment of nationals of a Member State in the territory of another Member State shall be abolished by progressive stages in the course of the transitional period. Such progressive abolition shall also apply to restrictions on the setting up of agencies, branches or subsidiaries by nationals of any Member State established in the territory of any Member State.

Freedom of establishment shall include the right to take up and pursue activities as self-employed persons and to set up and manage undertakings, in particular

companies or firms within the meaning of the second paragraph of Article 58, under the conditions laid down for its own nationals by the law of the country where such establishment is effected, subject to the provisions of the Chapter relating to capital.

*Article 57*

1. In order to make it easier for persons to take up and pursue activities as self-employed persons, the Council shall, on a proposal from the Commission and in cooperation with the European Parliament, acting unanimously during the first stage and by a qualified majority thereafter, issue directives for the mutual recognition of diplomas, certificates and other evidence of formal qualifications.

## Chapter 4. Capital

*Article 67*

1. During the transitional period and to the extent necessary to ensure the proper functioning of the common market, Member States shall progressively abolish between themselves all restrictions on the movement of capital belonging to persons resident in Member States and any discrimination based on the nationality or on the place of residence of the parties or on the place where such capital is invested.
2. Current payments connected with the movement of capital between Member States shall be freed from all restrictions by the end of the first stage at the latest.

*Article 68*

1. Member States shall, as regards the matters dealt with in this Chapter, be as liberal as possible in granting such exchange authorisations as are still necessary after the entry into force of this Treaty.
2. Where a Member State applies to the movements of capital liberalised in accordance with the provisions of this Chapter the domestic rules governing the capital market and the credit system, it shall do so in a nondiscriminatory manner.

\* \* \*

## Chapter 5. Transport

*Article 74*

The objectives of this Treaty shall, in matters governed by this Title, be pursued by Member States within the framework of a common transport policy.

\* \* \*

# Part Three: Policy of the Community

## Title I. Common Rules

## Chapter 1. Rules on Competition

*Section 1*
*Rules Applying to Undertakings*
*Article 85*

1. The following shall be prohibited as incompatible with the common market: all agreements between undertakings, decision by associations of undertakings and concerted practices which may affect trade between Member States and which have as their object or effect the prevention, restriction or distortion of competition within the common market, and in particular those which:

   (a) directly or indirectly fix purchase or selling prices or any other trading conditions;

   (b) limit or control production, markets, technical development, or investment;

   (c) share markets or sources of supply;

   (d) apply dissimilar conditions to equivalent transactions with other trading parties, thereby placing them at a competitive disadvantage;

   (e) make the conclusion of contracts subject to acceptance by the other parties of supplementary obligations which, by their nature or according to commercial usage, have no connection with the subject of such contracts.

2. Any agreements or decisions prohibited pursuant to this Article shall be automatically void.

3. The provisions of paragraph 1 may, however, be declared inapplicable in the case of:

   —any agreement or category of agreements between undertakings;

   —any decision or category of decisions by associations of undertakings;

   —any concerted practice or category of concerted practices;

   which contributes to improving the production or distribution of goods or to promoting technical or economic progress, while allowing consumers a fair share of the resulting benefit, and which does not:

   (a) impose on the undertakings concerned restrictions which are not indispensable to the attainment of these objectives;

   (b) afford such undertakings the possibility of eliminating competition in respect of a substantial part of the products in question.

*Article 86*

Any abuse by one or more undertakings of a dominant position within the common market or in a substantial part of it shall be prohibited as incompatible with the common market in so far as it may affect trade between Member States.

Such abuse may, in particular, consist in:

(a) directly or indirectly imposing unfair purchase or selling prices or other unfair trading conditions;

(b) limiting production, markets or technical development to the prejudice of consumers;

(c) applying dissimilar conditions to equivalent transactions with other trading parties, thereby placing them at a competitive disadvantage;

(d) making the conclusion of contracts subject to acceptance by the other parties of supplementary obligations which, by their nature or according to commercial usage, have no connection with the subject of such contracts.

*Article 87*

1. Within three years of the entry into force of this Treaty the Council shall, acting unanimously on a proposal from the Commission and after consulting the Assembly, adopt any appropriate regulations or directives to give effect to the principles set out in Articles 85 and 86.

   If such provisions have not been adopted within the period mentioned, they shall be laid down by the Council, acting by a qualified majority on a proposal from the Commission and after consulting the Assembly.

2. The regulations or directives referred to in paragraph 1 shall be designed in particular:

   (a) to ensure compliance with the prohibitions laid down in Article 85(1) and in Article 86 by making provisions for fines and periodic penalty payments;

   (b) to lay down detailed rules for the application of Article 85(3), taking into account the need to ensure effective supervision on the one hand, and to simplify administration to the greatest possible extent on the other;

   (c) to define, if need be, in the various branches of the economy, the scope of the provisions of Articles 85 and 86;

   (d) to define the respective functions of the Commission and of the Court of Justice in applying the provisions laid down in this paragraph;

   (e) to determine the relationship between national laws and the provisions contained in this Section or adopted pursuant to this Article.

*Article 88*

Until the entry into force of the provisions adopted in pursuance of Article 87, the authorities in Member States shall rule on the admissibility of agreements, decisions and concerted practices and on abuse of a dominant position in the common market in accordance with the law of their country and with the provisions of Article 85, in particular paragraph 3, and of Article 86.

### Article 89

1. Without prejudice to Article 88, the Commission shall, as soon as it takes up its duties, ensure the application of the principles laid down in Articles 85 and 86. On application by a Member State or on its own initiative, and in cooperation with the competent authorities in the Member States, who shall give it their assistance, the Commission shall investigate cases of suspected infringement of these principles. If it finds that there has been an infringement, it shall propose appropriate measures to bring it to an end.

2. If the infringement is not brought to an end, the Commission shall record such infringement of the principles in a reasoned decision. The Commission may publish its decision and authorise Member States to take the measures, the conditions and details of which it shall determine, needed to remedy the situation.

### Article 90

1. In the case of public undertakings and undertakings to which Member States grant special or exclusive rights, Member States shall neither enact nor maintain in force any measure contrary to the rules contained in this Treaty, in particular to those rules provided for in Article 7 and Articles 85 to 94.

2. Undertakings entrusted with the operation of services of general economic interest or having the character of a revenue-producing monopoly shall be subject to the rules contained in this Treaty, in particular to the rules on competition, in so far as the application of such rules does not obstruct the performance, in law or in fact, of the particular tasks assigned to them. The development of trade must not be affected to such an extent as would be contrary to the interests of the Community.

3. The Commission shall ensure the application of the provisions of this Article and shall, where necessary, address appropriate directives or decisions to Member States.

### Section 2
### Dumping
### Article 91

1. If, during the transitional period, the Commission, on application by a Member State or by any other interested party, finds that dumping is being practised within the common market, it shall address

recommendations to the person or persons with whom such practices originate for the purpose of putting an end to them.

Should the practices continue, the Commission shall authorise the injured Member State to take protective measures, the conditions and details of which the Commission shall determine.

2. As soon as this Treaty enters into force, products which originate in or are in free circulation in one Member State and which have been exported to another Member State shall, on reimportation, be admitted into the territory of the first-mentioned State free of all customs duties, quantitative restrictions or measures having equivalent effect. The Commission shall lay down appropriate rules for the application of this paragraph.

### Section 3
### Aids Granted by States
### Article 92

1. Save as otherwise provided in this Treaty, any aid granted by a Member State or through State resources in any form whatsoever which distorts or threatens to distort competition by favouring certain undertakings or the production of certain goods shall, in so far as it affects trade between Member States, be incompatible with the common market.

2. The following shall be compatible with the common market:
   (a) aid having a social character, granted to individual consumers, provided that such aid is granted without discrimination related to the origin of the products concerned;
   (b) aid to make good the damage caused by natural disasters or exceptional occurrences;
   (c) aid granted to the economy of certain areas of the Federal Republic of Germany affected by the division of Germany, in so far as such aid is required in order to compensate for the economic disadvantages caused by that division.

3. The following may be considered to be compatible with the common market:
   (a) aid to promote the economic development of areas where the standard of living is abnormally low or where there is serious underemployment;
   (b) aid to promote the execution of an important project of common European interest or to remedy a serious disturbance in the economy of a Member State;
   (c) aid to facilitate the development of certain economic activities or of certain economic areas, where such aid does not adversely affect trading conditions to an extent contrary to the common interest. However, the aids granted to

shipbuilding as of 1 January 1957 shall, in so far as they serve only to compensate for the absence of customs protection, be progressively reduced under the same conditions as apply to the elimination of customs duties, subject to the provisions of this Treaty concerning common commercial policy towards third countries;

(d) such other categories of aid as may be specified by decision of the Council acting by a qualified majority on a proposal from the Commission.

## Chapter 2. Tax Provisions

### Article 95

No Member State shall impose, directly or indirectly, on the products of other Member States any internal taxation of any kind in excess of that imposed directly or indirectly on similar domestic products.

Furthermore, no Member State shall impose on the products of other Member States any internal taxation of such a nature as to afford indirect protection to other products.

Member States shall, not later than at the beginning of the second stage, repeal or amend any provisions existing when this Treaty enters into force which conflict with the preceding rules.

### Article 99 [SEA]

The Council shall, acting unanimously on a proposal from the Commission and after consulting the European Parliament, adopt provisions on the harmonization of legislation concerning turnover taxes, excise duties, and other forms of indirect taxation to the extent that such harmonization is necessary to ensure the establishment and the operation of the internal market within the time-limits laid down in Article 1.

## Chapter 3. Approximation of Laws

### Article 100

The Council shall, acting unanimously on a proposal from the Commission, issue directives for the approximation of such provisions laid down by law, regulation or administrative action in Member States as directly affect the establishment or functioning of the common market.

The Assembly and the Economic and Social Committee shall be consulted in the case of directives whose implementation would, in one or more Member States, involve the amendment of legislation.

### Article 100 A [SEA]

By way of derogation from Article 100 and save where otherwise provided in this Treaty, the following provisions shall apply for the attainment of the objectives of Article 1: the Council shall, acting by a qualified majority on a proposal from the Commission after consulting the European Parliament and the Economic and Social Committee, adopt the measures for the approximation of such provisions laid down by law, regulation or administrative action in Member States as have as their object the establishment and operation of the internal market.

The first paragraph shall not apply to fiscal provisions, to those relating to the free movement of persons nor to those relating to the rights and interests of employed persons.

The Commission's proposals for the approximation of laws on health, safety, environmental protection and consumer protection will be based on a high level of protection.

If, after adoption of a harmonization measure or a decision pursuant to Article 6 by the Council acting by a qualified majority, a Member State deems it necessary to implement national provisions on grounds of major needs as referred to in Article 36, or relating to protection of the working environment and the natural environment, it shall notify the Commission thereof.

The Commission shall confirm the provisions involved after having verified that they are not a means of arbitrary discrimination or disguised restriction in trade between Member States.

By way of derogation from the procedures in Articles 169 and 170, the Commission or any Member State may bring the matter directly before the Court of Justice if it considers that another Member State is abusing the powers provided for in this Article.

The harmonization measures referred to above shall, in appropriate cases, include a safeguard clause authorizing the Member States to take, for one or more of the noneconomic reasons referred to in Article 36 of the Treaty, provisional measures subject to a Community control procedure.

### Article 100 B [SEA]

1. During 1992, the Commission shall, together with each Member State, draw up an inventory of national laws, regulations and administrative provisions which fall under Article 100 A and which have not been harmonized pursuant to that Article.

   The Council, acting in accordance with the provisions of Article 100 A, may decide that the provisions in force in a Member State must be recognized as being equivalent to those applied by another Member State.

2. The provisions of Article 100 A(4) shall apply by analogy.

3. The Commission shall draw up the inventory referred to in the first subparagraph of paragraph 1

and shall submit appropriate proposals in good time to allow the Council to act before the end of 1992.

### Article 101

Where the Commission finds that a difference between the provisions laid down by law, regulation or administrative action in Member States is distorting the conditions of competition in the common market and that the resultant distortion needs to be eliminated, it shall consult the Member States concerned. If such consultation does not result in an agreement eliminating the distortion in question, the Council shall, on a proposal from the Commission, acting unanimously during the first stage and by a qualified majority thereafter, issue the necessary directives. The Commission and the Council may take any other appropriate measures provided for in this Treaty.

### Article 102

1. Where there is reason to fear that the adoption or amendment of a provision laid down by law, regulation or administrative action may cause distortion within the meaning of Article 101, a Member State desiring to proceed therewith shall consult the Commission. After consulting the Member States, the Commission shall recommend to the States concerned such measures as may be appropriate to avoid the distortion in question.
2. If a State desiring to introduce or amend its own provisions does not comply with the recommendation addressed to it by the Commission, other Member States shall not be required, in pursuance of Article 101, to amend their own provisions in order to eliminate such distortion. If the Member State which has ignored the recommendation of the Commission causes distortion detrimental only to itself, the provisions of Article 101 shall not apply.

### TITLE II. ECONOMIC POLICY

\* \* \*

### Article 58

Companies or firms formed in accordance with the law of a Member State and having their registered office, central administration or principal place of business within the Community shall, for the purposes of this Chapter, be treated in the same way as natural persons who are nationals of Member States.

"Companies or firms" means companies or firms constituted under civil or commercial law, including cooperative societies, and other legal persons governed by public or private law, save for those which are non-profit-making.

## Chapter 3. Services

### Article 59

Within the framework of the provisions set out below, restrictions on to provide services within the Community shall be progressively freedom abolished during the transitional period in respect of nationals of Member States who are established in a State of the Community other than that of the person for whom the services are intended.

The Council may, acting by a qualified majority on a proposal from the Commission, extend the provisions of this Chapter to nationals of a third country who provide services and who are established within the Community.

## Chapter 1. Cooperation in Economic and Monetary Policy (Economic and Monetary Union)

### Article 102 A [SEA]

1. In order to ensure the convergency of economic and monetary policy which is necessary for the further development of the Community, Member States shall cooperate in accordance with the objectives of Article 104. In doing so, they shall take account of the experience acquired in cooperation in the framework of the European Monetary System and in developing the ECU, and shall respect existing powers in this field.
2. Insofar as further development in the field of economic and monetary policy necessitates institutional changes, the procedure laid down in Article 236 shall be applicable. The Commission, the Monetary Committee and the Committee of Governors of the Central Banks shall be consulted regarding institutional changes in the area of monetary policy.

\* \* \*

## Chapter 3. Balance of Payments

### Article 104

Each Member State shall pursue the economic policy needed to ensure the equilibrium of its overall balance of payments and to maintain confidence in its currency, while taking care to ensure a high level of employment and a stable level of prices.

\* \* \*

### Article 107

1. Each Member State shall treat its policy with regard to rates of exchange as a matter of common concern.

\* \* \*

TITLE III. SOCIAL POLICY

# Chapter 1. Social Provisions

### Article 117

Member States agree upon the need to promote improved working conditions and an improved standard of living for workers, so as to make possible their harmonisation while the improvement is being maintained.

They believe that such a development will ensue not only from the functioning of the common market, which will favour the harmonisation of social systems, but also from the procedures provided for in this Treaty and from the approximation of provisions laid down by law, regulation or administrative action.

### Article 118

Without prejudice to the other provisions of this Treaty and in conformity with its general objectives, the Commission shall have the task of promoting close cooperation between Member States in the social field, particularly in matters relating to:

—employment;
—labour law and working conditions;
—basic and advanced vocational training;
—social security;
—prevention of occupational accidents and diseases;
—occupational hygiene;
—the right of association, and collective bargaining between employers and workers.

To this end, the Commission shall act in close contact with Member States by making studies, delivering opinions and arranging consultations both on problems arising at national level and on those of concern to international organisations.

Before delivering the opinions provided for in this Article, the Commission shall consult the Economic and Social Committee.

The Council may, acting unanimously at the request of the Court of Justice and after consulting the Commission and the European Parliament, amend the provisions of Title III of the Statute.

### [SEA] Article 118 A [SEA]

1. Member States shall pay particular attention to encouraging improvements, especially in the working environment, as regards the health and safety of workers, and shall set as their objective the harmonization of conditions in this area, while maintaining the improvements made.

2. In order to help achieve the objective laid down in the first paragraph, the Council, acting by a quali-

fied majority on a proposal from the Commission, in cooperation with the European Parliament and after consulting the Economic and Social Committee, shall adopt, by means of directives, minimum requirements for gradual implementation, having regard to the conditions and technical rules obtaining in each of the Member States.

Such directives shall avoid imposing administrative, financial and legal constraints in a way which would hold back the creation and development of small and medium-sized undertakings.

3. The provisions adopted pursuant to this Article shall not prevent any Member State from maintaining or introducing more stringent measures for the protection of working conditions compatible with this Treaty.

### Article 118 B [SEA]

The Commission shall endeavour to develop the dialogue between management and labour at European level which could, if the two sides consider it desirable, lead to relations based on agreement.

### Article 119

Each Member State shall during the first stage ensure and subsequently maintain the application of the principle that men and women should receive equal pay for equal work.

For the purpose of this Article, "pay" means the ordinary basic or minimum wage or salary and any other consideration, whether in cash or in kind, which the worker receives, directly or indirectly, in respect of his employment from his employer.

Equal pay without discrimination based on sex means:

(a) that pay for the same work at piece rates shall be calculated on the basis of the same unit of measurement;

(b) that pay for work at time rates shall be the same for the same job.

\* \* \*

# Chapter 2. The European Social Fund

TITLE IV. THE EUROPEAN INVESTMENT BANK

### Article 129

A European Investment Bank is hereby established; it shall have legal personality.

The members of the European Investment Bank shall be the Member States.

The Statute of the European Investment Bank is laid down in a Protocol annexed to this Treaty.

### TITLE V. ECONOMIC AND SOCIAL COHESION

#### [SEA] *Article 130 A*

In order to promote its overall harmonious development, the Community shall develop and pursue its actions leading to the strengthening of its economic and social cohesion.

In particular the Community shall aim at reducing disparities between the various regions and the backwardness of the least-favoured regions.

\* \* \*

### TITLE VII. ENVIRONMENT

#### [SEA] *Article 130 R*

1. Action by the Community relating to the environment shall have the following objectives:
   (i) to preserve, protect and improve the quality of the environment;
   (ii) to contribute towards protecting human health;
   (iii) to ensure a prudent and rational utilization of natural resources.
2. Action by the Community relating to the environment shall be based on the principles that preventive action should be taken, that environmental damage should as a priority be rectified at source, and that the polluter should pay. Environmental protection requirements shall be a component of the Community's other policies.
3. In preparing its action relating to the environment, the Community shall take account of:
   (i) available scientific and technical data;
   (ii) environmental conditions in the various regions of the Community;
   (iii) the potential benefits and costs of action or of lack of action;
   (iv) the economic and social development of the Community as a whole and the balanced development of its regions.
4. The Community shall take action relating to the environment to the extent to which the objectives referred to in paragraph 1 can be attained better at Community level than at the level of the individual Member States. Without prejudice to certain measures of a Community nature, the Member States shall finance and implement the other measures.
5. Within their respective spheres of competence, the Community and the Member States shall cooperate with third countries and with the relevant international organizations. The arrangements for Community cooperation may be the subject of agreements between the Community and the third parties concerned, which shall be negotiated and concluded in accordance with Article 228.

The previous paragraph shall be without prejudice to Member States' competence to negotiate in international bodies and to conclude international agreements.

#### *Article 130 S*

The Council, acting unanimously on a proposal from the Commission and after consulting the European Parliament and the Economic and Social Committee, shall decide what action is to be taken by the Community.

The Council shall, under the conditions laid down in the preceding subparagraph, define those matters on which decisions are to be taken by a qualified majority.

#### *Article 130 T*

The protective measures adopted in common pursuant to Article 130 S shall not prevent any Member State from maintaining or introducing more stringent protective measures compatible with this Treaty.

# Part Five: Institutions of the Community

### TITLE I. PROVISIONS GOVERNING THE INSTITUTIONS

## Chapter 1. The Institutions

*Section 1*
*The Assembly*
*Article 137*

The Assembly, which shall consist of representatives of the peoples of the States brought together in the Community, shall exercise the advisory and supervisory powers which are conferred upon it by this Treaty.

*Article 138*

1. The representatives in the Assembly of the peoples of the States brought together in the Community shall be elected by direct universal suffrage.
2. The number of representatives elected in each Member State shall be as follows.

| | |
|---|---|
| Belgium | 24 |
| Denmark | 16 |
| Germany | 81 |
| Greece | 24 |
| France | 81 |
| Ireland | 15 |
| Italy | 81 |
| Luxembourg | 6 |
| Netherlands | 25 |

| | |
|---|---|
| Portugal | 24 |
| Spain | 60 |
| United Kingdom | 81 |

\* \* \*

## Article 140

The Assembly shall elect its President and its officers from among its members.

Members of the Commission may attend all meetings and shall, at their request, be heard on behalf of the Commission.

The Commission shall reply orally or in writing to questions put to it by the Assembly or by its members.

The Council shall be heard by the Assembly in accordance with the conditions laid down by the Council in its rules of procedure.

## Article 141

Save as otherwise provided in this Treaty the Assembly shall act by an absolute majority of the votes cast.

The rules of procedure shall determine the quorum.

\* \* \*

## Article 144

If a motion of censure on the activities of the Commission is tabled before it, the Assembly shall not vote thereon until at least three days after the motion has been tabled and only by open vote.

If the motion of censure is carried by a two-thirds majority of the votes cast, representing a majority of the members of the Assembly, the members of the Commission shall resign as a body. They shall continue to deal with current business until they are replaced in accordance with Article 158.

## Section 2
## The Council
## Article 145

[SEA] To ensure that the objectives set out in this Treaty are attained, the Council shall, in accordance with the provisions of this Treaty:

—ensure coordination of the general economic policies of the Member States;

—have power to take decisions;

—confer on the Commission, in the acts it adopts, powers for the implementation of the rules it lays down.

The Council may impose certain requirements in respect of the exercise of those powers. The Council may also reserve the right in specific cases to exercise implementing powers itself directly.

The requirements referred to above must be consonant with principles and rules to be laid down in advance by the Council, acting unanimously on a proposal from the Commission and after obtaining the Opinion of the European Parliament.

## Article 146
## (Article 2 of the Merger Treaty)

The Council shall consist of Representatives of the Member States. Each Government shall delegate to it one of its members.

The office of the President shall be held for a term of six months by each member of the Council in turn, in the following order of Member States: Belgium, Denmark, Germany, Greece, France, Ireland, Italy, Luxembourg, Netherlands, Portugal, Spain, United Kingdom.

\* \* \*

## Article 148

1. Save as otherwise provided in this Treaty, the Council shall act by a majority of its members.
2. Where the Council is required to act by a qualified majority, the votes of its members shall be weighted as follows:

| | |
|---|---|
| Belgium | 5 |
| Denmark | 3 |
| Germany | 10 |
| Greece | 5 |
| France | 10 |
| Ireland | 3 |
| Italy | 10 |
| Luxembourg | 2 |
| Netherlands | 5 |
| Portugal | 5 |
| Spain | 8 |
| United Kingdom | 10 |

For their adoption, acts of the Council shall require at least:

—54 votes in favour where this Treaty requires them to be adopted on a proposal from the Commission.

—54 votes in favour, cast by at least eight members, in other cases.

3. Abstentions by members present in person or represented shall not prevent the adoption by the Council of acts which require unanimity.

## Article 149 [SEA]

1. Where, in pursuance of this Treaty, the Council acts on a proposal from the Commission, unanimity shall be required for an act constituting an amendment to that proposal.

2. Where, in pursuance of this Treaty, a Council act is adopted in cooperation with the European Parliament, the following procedure shall apply:

   (a) The Council, acting by a qualified majority under the conditions of paragraph 1 above, on a proposal from the Commission and after obtaining the Opinion of the European Parliament, shall adopt a common position.

   (b) The common position of the Council shall be transmitted to the European Parliament. The Council and the Commission shall inform the Parliament fully of the reasons which led the Council to adopt its common position and also of the Commission's position.

   If, within three months of such communication, the European Parliament approves this common position or has not taken a decision within that period, the Council shall definitively adopt the act in question in accordance with the common position.

   (c) Within the period of three months referred to in paragraph 2(b), the European Parliament may, by an absolute majority of its constituent members, propose amendments to the common position of the Council. The European Parliament may also reject the common position of the Council by the same majority. The result of the proceedings shall be transmitted to the Council and the Commission.

   If the Parliament has rejected the common position of the Council, unanimity shall be required for the Council to act on a second reading.

   (d) The Commission shall, within the period of one month, reexamine the proposal, on the basis of which the Council adopted its common position, by taking into account the amendments proposed by the European Parliament.

   (e) The Council, acting by a qualified majority, shall adopt the proposal reexamined by the Commission. Unanimity shall be required for the Council to amend the reexamined Commission proposal.

   (f) The Council shall be required to act within a period of three months.

3. As long as the Council has not acted, the Commission may alter its original proposal at any time during the procedure.

\* \* \*

## Article 152

The Council may request the Commission to undertake any studies which the Council considers desirable for the attainment of the common objectives, and to submit to it any appropriate proposals.

\* \* \*

## Section 3
### The Commission
### Article 155

In order to ensure the proper functioning and development of the common market, the Commission shall:

—ensure that the provisions of this Treaty and the measures taken by the institutions pursuant thereto are applied;

—formulate recommendations or deliver opinions on matters dealt with in this Treaty, if it expressly so provides or if the Commission considers it necessary;

—have its own power of decision and participate in the shaping of measures taken by the Council and by the Assembly in the manner provided for in this Treaty;

—exercise the powers conferred on it by the Council for the implementation of the rules laid down by the latter.

\* \* \*

## Article 157

1. The Commission shall consist of 17 members, who shall be chosen on the grounds of their general competence and whose independence is beyond doubt.

   The number of members of the Commission may be altered by the Council, acting unanimously.

   Only nationals of Member States may be members of the Commission.

   The Commission must include at least one national of each of the Member States, but may not include more than two members having the nationality of the same State.

2. The members of the Commission shall, in the general interest of the Communities, be completely independent in the performance of their duties.

   In the performance of these duties, they shall neither seek nor take instructions from any Government or from any other body. They shall refrain from any action incompatible with their duties. Each Member State undertakes to respect this principle and not to seek to influence the members of the Commission in the performance of their tasks. The members of the Commission may not, during their term of office, engage in any other occupation, whether gainful or not. When entering upon their duties they shall give a solemn undertaking that, both during and after their term of office, they will respect the obligations arising therefrom and in particular their duty to behave with integrity and discretion as regards the acceptance, after they have ceased to hold office, of certain appointments or benefits. In the event of any breach of these obligations, the Court of Justice may, on application by the Council or the Commission, rule that the member concerned be, according to the circumstances, either compulsorily retired in accordance with the provisions of Article 13 or deprived of his right to a pension or other benefits in its stead.

## Article 158

The members of the Commission shall be appointed by common accord of the Governments of the Member States.

Their term of office shall be four years. It shall be renewable.

\* \* \*

## Article 160

If any member of the Commission no longer fulfils the conditions required for the performance of his duties or if he has been guilty of serious misconduct, the Court of Justice may, on application by the Council or the Commission, compulsorily retire him.

\* \* \*

## Section 4
## The Court of Justice
## Article 164

The Court of Justice shall ensure that in the interpretation and application of this Treaty and the law is observed.

## Article 165

The Court of Justice shall consist of 13 Judges.

The Court of Justice shall sit in plenary session. It may, however, form chambers, each consisting of three or five Judges, either to undertake certain preparatory inquiries or to adjudicate on particular categories of cases in accordance with rules laid down for these purposes.

Whenever the Court of Justice hears cases brought before it by a Member State or by one of the institutions of the Community or, to the extent that the chambers of the Court do not have the requisite jurisdiction under the Rules of Procedure as to give preliminary rulings on questions submitted to it pursuant to Article 177, it shall sit in plenary session.

Should the Court of Justice so request, the Council may, acting unanimously, increase the number of Judges and make the necessary adjustments to the second and third paragraphs of this Article and to the second paragraph of Article 167.

## Article 166

The Court of Justice shall be assisted by six Advocates-General.

It shall be the duty of the Advocate-General, acting with complete impartiality and independence, to make, in open court, reasoned submissions on cases brought before the Court of Justice, in order to assist the Court in the performance of the task assigned to it in Article 164.

Should the Court of Justice so request, the Council may, acting unanimously, increase the number of Advocates-General and make the necessary adjustments to the third paragraph of Article 167.

## Article 167

The Judges and Advocates-General shall be chosen from persons whose independence is beyond doubt and who possess the qualifications required for appointment to the highest judicial offices in their respective countries or who are jurisconsults of recognised competence; they shall be appointed by common accord of the Governments of the Member States for a term of six years.

Every three years there shall be a partial replacement of the Judges. Six and seven Judges shall be replaced alternately.

Every three years there shall be a partial replacement of the Advocates-General. Three Advocates-General shall be replaced alternately.

Retiring Judges and Advocates-General shall be eligible for reappointment.

The Judges shall elect the President of the Court of Justice from among their number for a term of three years. He may be reelected.

\* \* \*

## Article 168 A [SEA]

1. At the request of the Court of Justice and after consulting the Commission and the European Parliament, the Council may, acting unanimously, attach to the Court of Justice a court with jurisdiction to hear and determine at first instance, subject to a right of appeal to the Court of Justice on points of law only and in accordance with the conditions laid down by the Statute, certain classes of action or proceeding brought by natural or legal persons. That court shall not be competent to hear and determine actions brought by Member States or by Community Institutions or questions referred for a preliminary ruling under Article 177.

2. The Council, following the procedure laid down in paragraph 1, shall determine the composition of that court and adopt the necessary adjustments and additional provisions to the Statute of the Court of

Justice. Unless the Council decides otherwise, the provisions of this Treaty relating to the Court of Justice, in particular the provisions of the Protocol on the Statute of the Court of Justice, shall apply to that court.

3. The members of that court shall be chosen from persons whose independence is beyond doubt and who possess the ability required for appointment to judicial office; they shall be appointed by common accord of the Governments of the Member States for a term of six years. The membership shall be partially renewed every three years. Retiring members shall be eligible for reappointment.

4. That court shall establish its rules of procedure in agreement with the Court of Justice. Those rules shall require the unanimous approval of the Council.

### Article 169

If the Commission considers that a Member State has failed to fulfil an obligation under this Treaty, it shall deliver a reasoned opinion on the matter after giving the State concerned the opportunity to submit its observations.

If the State concerned does not comply with the opinion within the period laid down by the Commission, the latter may bring the matter before the Court of Justice.

### Article 170

A Member State which considers that another Member State has failed to fulfil an obligation under this Treaty may bring the matter before the Court of Justice. Before a Member State brings an action against another Member State for an alleged infringement of an obligation under this Treaty, it shall bring the matter before the Commission.

The Commission shall deliver a reasoned opinion after each of the States concerned has been given the opportunity to submit its own case and its observations on the other party's case both orally and in writing. If the Commission has not delivered an opinion within three months of the date on which the matter was brought before it, the absence of such opinion shall not prevent the matter from being brought before the Court of Justice.

### Article 171

If the Court of Justice finds that a Member State has failed to fulfil an obligation under this Treaty, the State shall be required to take the necessary measures to comply with the judgment of the Court of Justice.

### Article 172

Regulations made by the Council pursuant to the provisions of this Treaty may give the Court of Justice un-limited jurisdiction in regard to the penalties provided for in such regulations.

### Article 173

The Court of Justice shall review the legality of acts of the Council and the Commission other than recommendations or opinions. It shall for this purpose have jurisdiction in actions brought by a Member State, the Council or the Commission on grounds of lack of competence, infringement of an essential procedural requirement, infringement of this Treaty or of any rule of law relating to its application, or misuse of powers.

Any natural or legal person may, under the same conditions, institute proceedings against a decision addressed to that person or against a decision which, although in the form of a regulation or a decision addressed to another person, is of direct and individual concern to the former. The proceedings provided for in this Article shall be instituted within two months of the publication of the measure, or of its notification to the plaintiff, or, in the absence thereof, of the day on which it came to the knowledge of the latter, as the case may be.

### Article 174

If the action is well founded, the Court of Justice shall declare the act concerned to be void.

In the case of a regulation, however, the Court of Justice shall, if it considers this necessary, state which of the effects of the regulation which it has declared void shall be considered as definitive.

### Article 175

Should the Council or the Commission, in infringement of this Treaty, fail to act, the Member States and the other institutions of the Community may bring an action before the Court of Justice to have the infringement established. The action shall be admissible only if the institution concerned has first been called upon to act. If, within two months of being so called upon, the institution concerned has not defined its position, the action may be brought within a further period of two months.

Any natural or legal person may, under the conditions laid down in the preceding paragraphs, complain to the Court of Justice that an institution of the Community has failed to address to that person any act other than a recommendation or an opinion.

### Article 176

The institution whose act has been declared void or whose failure to act has been declared contrary to this Treaty shall be required to take the necessary measures to comply with the judgment of the Court of Justice. This obligation shall not affect any obligation which may result from the application of the second paragraph of Article 215.

### Article 177
The Court of Justice shall have jurisdiction to give preliminary rulings concerning:

(a) the interpretation of this Treaty;
(b) the validity and interpretation of acts of the institutions of the Community;
(c) the interpretation of the statutes of bodies established by an act of the Council where those statutes so provide.

Where such a question is raised before any court or tribunal of a Member State, that court or tribunal may, if it considers that a decision on the question is necessary to enable it to give judgment, request the Court of Justice to give a ruling thereon. Where any such question is raised in a case pending before a court or tribunal of a Member State, against whose decisions there is no judicial remedy under national law, that court or tribunal shall bring the matter before the Court of Justice.

### Article 178
The Court of Justice shall have jurisdiction in disputes relating to compensation for damage provided for in the second paragraph of Article 215.

### Article 179
The Court of Justice shall have jurisdiction in any dispute between the Community and its servants within the limits and under the conditions laid down in the Staff Regulations or the Conditions of Employment.

### Article 180
The Court of Justice shall, within the limits hereinafter laid down, have jurisdiction in disputes concerning:

(a) the fulfilment by Member States of obligations under the Statute of the European Investment Bank. In this connection, the Board of Directors of the Bank shall enjoy the powers conferred upon the Commission by Article 169;
(b) measures adopted by the Board of Governors of the Bank. In this connection, any Member State, the Commission or the Board of Directors of the Bank may institute proceedings under the conditions laid down in Article 173;
(c) measures adopted by the Board of Directors of the Bank. Proceedings against such measures may be instituted only by a Member State or by the Commission, under the conditions laid down in Article 173, and solely on the grounds of non-compliance with the procedure provided for in Article 21(2), (5), (6) and (7) of the Statute of the Bank.

### Article 181
The Court of Justice shall have jurisdiction to give judgment pursuant to any arbitration clause contained in the contract concluded by or on behalf of the Community, whether that contract be governed by public or private law.

### Article 182
The Court of Justice shall have jurisdiction in the dispute between Member States which relates to the subject matter of this Treaty if the dispute is submitted to it under a special agreement between the parties.

### Article 183
Save where jurisdiction is conferred on the Court of Justice by this Treaty, disputes to which the Community is a party shall not on that ground be excluded from the jurisdiction of the courts or tribunals of the Member States.

### Article 184
Notwithstanding the expiry of the period laid down in the third paragraph of Article 173, any party may, in proceedings in which a regulation of the Council or of the Commission is in issue, plead the grounds specified in the first paragraph of Article 173, in order to invoke before the Court of Justice the inapplicability of that regulation.

### Article 185
Actions brought before the Court of Justice shall not have suspensory effect. The Court of Justice may, however, if it considers that circumstances so require, order that application of the contested act be suspended.

### Article 186
The Court of Justice may in any cases before it prescribe any necessary interim measures.

### Article 187
The judgments of the Court of Justice shall be enforceable under the conditions laid down in Article 192.

\* \* \*

## Chapter 2. Provisions Common To Several Institutions

### Article 189
In order to carry out their task the Council and the Commission shall, in accordance with the provisions of this Treaty, make regulations, issue directives, take decisions, make recommendations or deliver opinions. A regulation shall have general application. It shall be binding in its entirety and directly applicable in all

Member States. A directive shall be binding, as to the result to be achieved, upon each Member State to which it is addressed, but shall leave to the national authorities the choice of form and methods. A decision shall be binding in its entirety upon those to whom it is addressed. Recommendations and opinions shall have no binding force.

\* \* \*

### Article 192

Decisions of the Council or of the Commission which impose a pecuniary obligation on persons other than States shall be enforceable.

Enforcement shall be governed by the rules of civil procedure in force in the State in the territory of which it is carried out. The order for its enforcement shall be appended in the decision, without other formality than verification of the authenticity of the decision, by the national authority which the government of each Member State shall designate for this purpose and shall make known to the Commission and to the Court of Justice. When these formalities have been completed on application by the party concerned, the latter may proceed to enforcement in accordance with the national law, by bringing the matter directly before the competent authority.

Enforcement may be suspended only by a decision of the Court of Justice. However, the courts of the country concerned shall have jurisdiction over complaints that enforcement is being carried out in an irregular manner.

## Part Six: General and Final Provisions

### Article 210

The Community shall have legal personality.

### Article 236

The Government of any Member State or the Commission may submit to the Council proposals for the amendment of this Treaty.

If the Council, after consulting the Assembly and, where appropriate, the Commission, delivers an opinion in favour of calling a conference of representatives of the Governments of the Member States, the conference shall be convened by the President of the Council for the purpose of determining by common accord the amendments to be made to this Treaty.

The amendments shall enter into force after being ratified by all the Member States in accordance with their respective constitutional requirements.

### Article 237

Any European State may apply to become a member of the Community. It shall address its application to the Council which, after consulting the Commission, shall act unanimously after receiving the assent of the European Parliament which shall act by a majority of its members.

The conditions of admission and the adjustments to this Treaty necessitated thereby shall be the subject of an agreement between the Member States and the applicant State. This agreement shall be submitted for ratification by all the Contracting States in accordance with their respective constitutional requirements.

### Article 238

The Community may conclude with a third State, a union of States or an international organisation agreements establishing an association involving reciprocal rights and obligations, common action and special procedures.

These agreements shall be concluded by the Council, acting unanimously and after receiving the assent of the European Parliament which shall act by a majority of its members.

Where such agreements call for amendments to this Treaty, these amendments shall first be adopted in accordance with the procedure laid down in Article 236.

### Article 240

This Treaty is concluded for an unlimited period.

# Maastricht Treaty on European Union

*(Selected Provisions)* 31 I.L.M. 247 (1992)
(Reprinted with permission)

## TITLE I. COMMON PROVISIONS

### Article A
By this Treaty, the High Contracting Parties establish among themselves a European Union, hereinafter called "the Union".

This Treaty marks a new stage in the process of creating an ever closer union among the peoples of Europe, in which decisions are taken as closely as possible to the citizen.

The Union shall be founded on the European Communities, supplemented by the policies and forms of cooperation established by this Treaty. Its task shall be to organize, in a manner demonstrating consistency and solidarity, relations between the Member States and between their peoples.

### Article B
The Union shall set itself the following objectives:
—to promote economic and social progress which is balanced and sustainable, in particular through the creation of an area without internal frontiers, through the strengthening of economic and social cohesion and through the establishment of economic and monetary union, ultimately including a single currency in accordance with the provisions of this Treaty;
—to assert its identity on the international scene, in particular through the implementation of a common foreign and security policy including the eventual framing of a common defence policy, which might in time lead to a common defence;
—to strengthen the protection of the rights and interests of the nationals of its Member States through the introduction of a citizenship of the Union;
—to develop close cooperation on justice and home affairs;
—to maintain in full the "acquis communautaire" and build on it with a view to considering, through the procedure referred to in Article N(2), to what extent the policies and forms of cooperation introduced by this Treaty may need to be revised with the aim of ensuring the effectiveness of the mechanisms and the institutions of the Community.

The objectives of the Union shall be achieved as provided in this Treaty and in accordance with the conditions and the timetable set out therein while respecting the principle of subsidiarity as defined in Article 3b of the Treaty establishing the European Community.

### Article C
The Union shall be served by a single institutional framework which shall ensure the consistency and the continuity of the activities carried out in order to attain its objectives while respecting and building upon the "acquis communautaire".

The Union shall in particular ensure the consistency of its external activities as a whole in the context of its external relations, security, economic and development policies. The Council and the Commission shall be responsible for ensuring such consistency. They shall ensure the implementation of these policies, each in accordance with its respective powers.

### Article D
The European Council shall provide the Union with the necessary impetus for its development and shall define the general political guidelines thereof.

The European Council shall bring together the Heads of State or of Government of the Member States and the President of the Commission. They shall be assisted by the Ministers for Foreign Affairs of the Member States and by a Member of the Commission. The European Council shall meet at least twice a year, under the chairmanship of the Head of State or of Government of the Member State which holds the Presidency of the Council.

The European Council shall submit to the European Parliament a report after each of its meetings and a yearly written report on the progress achieved by the Union.

### Article E
The European Parliament, the Council, the Commission and the Court of Justice shall exercise their powers under the conditions and for the purposes provided for, on the one hand, by the provisions of the Treaties establishing the European Communities and of the subsequent Treaties and Acts modifying and supplementing them and, on the other hand, by the other provisions of this Treaty.

### Article F
1. The Union shall respect the national identities of its Member States, whose systems of government are founded on the principles of democracy.
2. The Union shall respect fundamental rights, as guaranteed by the European Convention for the Protection of Human Rights and Fundamental Freedoms signed in Rome on 4 November 1950 and as they result from the constitutional traditions common to the Member States, as general principles of Community law.
3. The Union shall provide itself with the means necessary to attain its objectives and carry through its policies.

### TITLE II. SELECTED PROVISIONS AMENDING THE TREATY ESTABLISHING THE EUROPEAN ECONOMIC COMMUNITY WITH A VIEW TO ESTABLISHING THE EUROPEAN COMMUNITY

### Article G
The Treaty establishing the European Economic Community shall be amended in accordance with the provisions of this Article, in order to establish a European Community.
A. Throughout the Treaty:
1) The term "European Economic Community" shall be replaced by the term "European Community."
B. In Part One "Principles":
2) Article 2 shall be replaced by the following:

### Article 2
The Community shall have as its task, by establishing a common market and an economic and monetary union and by implementing the common policies or activities referred to in Articles 3 and 3a, to promote throughout the Community a harmonious and balanced development of economic activities, sustainable and non-inflationary growth respecting the environment, a high degree of convergence of economic performance, a high level of em-

ployment and of social protection, the raising of the standard of living and quality of life, and economic and social cohesion and solidarity among Member States."

3) Article 3 shall be replaced by the following:

### Article 3
For the purposes set out in Article 2, the activities of the Community shall include, as provided in this Treaty and in accordance with the timetable set out therein:
(a) the elimination, as between Member States, of customs duties and quantitative restrictions on the import and export of goods, and of all other measures having equivalent effect;
(b) a common commercial policy;
(c) an internal market characterized by the abolition, as between Member States, of obstacles to the free movement of goods, persons, services, and capital;
(d) measures concerning the entry and movement of persons in the internal market as provided for in Article 100c;
(e) a common policy in the sphere of agriculture and fisheries;
(f) a common policy in the sphere of transport;
(g) a system ensuring that competition in the internal market is not distorted;
(h) the approximation of the laws of Member States to the extent required for the functioning of the common market;
(i) a policy in the social sphere comprising a European Social Fund;
(j) the strengthening of economic and social cohesion;
(k) a policy in the sphere of the environment;
(l) the strengthening of the competitiveness of Community industry;
(m) the promotion of research and technological development;
(n) encouragement for the establishment and development of trans-European networks;
(o) a contribution to the attainment of a high level of health protection;
(p) a contribution to education and training of quality and to the flowering of the cultures of the Member States;
(q) a policy in the sphere of development cooperation;
(r) the association of the overseas countries and territories in order to increase trade and promote jointly economic and social development;
(s) a contribution to the strengthening of consumer protection;

(t)   measures in the spheres of energy, civil protection and tourism."

4)  The following Article shall be inserted:

### Article 3a

1.  For the purposes set out in Article 2, the activities of the Member States and the Community shall include, as provided in this Treaty and in accordance with the timetable set out therein, the adoption of an economic policy which is based on the close co-ordination of Member States' economic policies, on the internal market and on the definition of common objectives, and conducted in accordance with the principle of an open market economy with free competition.

2.  Concurrently with the foregoing, and as provided in this Treaty and in accordance with the timetable and the procedures set out therein, these activities shall include the irrevocable fixing of exchange rates leading to the introduction of a single currency, the ECU, and the definition and conduct of a single monetary policy and exchange rate policy the primary objective of both of which shall be to maintain price stability and, without prejudice to this objective, to support the general economic policies in the Community, in accordance with the principle of an open market economy with free competition.

3.  These activities of the Member States and the Community shall entail compliance with the following guiding principles: stable prices, sound public finances and monetary conditions and a sustainable balance of payments."

7)  The following Articles shall be inserted:

### Article 4a

A European System of Central Banks (hereinafter referred to as "ESCB") and a European Central Bank (hereinafter referred to as "ECB") shall be established in accordance with the procedures laid down in this Treaty; they shall act within the limits of the powers conferred upon them by this Treaty and by the Statute of the ESCB and of the ECB (hereinafter referred to as "Statute of the ESCB") annexed thereto. [*See* 31 I.L.M. 331 (1992)]

## Chapter 2. Monetary Policy

### Article 105

1.  The primary objective of the ESCB shall be to maintain price stability. Without prejudice to the objective of price stability, the ESCB shall support the general economic policies in the Community with a view to contributing to the achievement of the objectives of the Community as laid down in Article 2. The ESCB shall act in accordance with the principle of an open market economy with free competition, favouring an efficient allocation of resources, and in compliance with the principles set out in Article 3a.

2.  The basic tasks to be carried out through the ESCB shall be:
    —to define and implement the monetary policy of the Community;
    —to conduct foreign exchange operations consistent with the provisions of Article 109;
    —to hold and manage the official foreign reserves of the Member States;
    —to promote the smooth operation of payment systems.

3.  The third indent of paragraph 2 shall be without prejudice to the holding and management by the governments of Member States of foreign exchange working balances.

4.  The ECB shall be consulted:
    —on any proposed Community act in its fields of competence;
    —by national authorities regarding any draft legislative provision in its fields of competence, but within the limits and under the conditions set out by the Council in accordance with the procedure laid down in Article 106(6).

    The ECB may submit opinions to the appropriate Community institutions or bodies or to national authorities on matters within its fields of competence.

5.  The ESCB shall contribute to the smooth conduct of policies pursued by the competent authorities relating to the prudential supervision of credit institutions and the stability of the financial system.

6.  The Council may, acting unanimously on a proposal from the Commission and after consulting the ECB and after receiving the assent of the European Parliament, confer upon the ECB specific tasks concerning policies relating to the prudential supervision of credit institutions and other financial institutions with the exception of insurance undertakings.

### Article 105a

1.  The ECB shall have the exclusive right to authorize the issue of bank notes within the Community. The ECB and the national central banks may issue such notes. The bank notes issued by the ECB and the national central banks shall be the only such notes to have the status of legal tender within the Community.

2. Member States may issue coins subject to approval by the ECB of the volume of the issue. The Council may, acting in accordance with the procedure referred to in Article 189c and after consulting the ECB, adopt measures to harmonize the denominations and technical specifications of all coins intended for circulation to the extent necessary to permit their smooth circulation within the Community.

### Article 109f

1. At the start of the second stage, a European Monetary Institute (hereinafter referred to as "EMI") shall be established and take up its duties; it shall have legal personality and be directed and managed by a Council, consisting of a President and the Governors of the national central banks, one of whom shall be Vice-President.

\* \* \*

3. For the preparation of the third stage, the EMI shall:
   —prepare the instruments and the procedures necessary for carrying out a single monetary policy in the third stage;
   —promote the harmonization, where necessary, of the rules and practices governing the collection, compilation and distribution of statistics in the areas within its field of competence;
   —prepare the rules for operations to be undertaken by the national central banks in the framework of the ESCB;
   —promote the efficiency of cross-border payments;
   —supervise the technical preparation of ECU bank notes.

   At the latest by 31 December 1996, the EMI shall specify the regulatory, organizational and logistical framework necessary for the ESCB to perform its tasks in the third stage. This framework shall be submitted for decision to the ECB at the date of its establishment.

4. The EMI, acting by a majority of two thirds of the members of its Council may:
   —formulate opinions or recommendations on the overall orientation of monetary policy and exchange rate policy as well as on related measures introduced in each Member State;
   —submit opinions or recommendations to Governments and to the Council on policies which might affect the internal or external monetary situation in the Community and, in particular, the functioning of the European Monetary System;
   —make recommendations to the monetary authorities of the Member States concerning the conduct of their monetary policy.

5. The EMI, acting unanimously, may decide to publish its opinions and its recommendations.

### Article 109j

\* \* \*

4. If by the end of 1997 the date for the beginning of the third stage has not been set, the third stage shall start on 1 January 1999. Before 1 July 1998, the Council, meeting in the composition of Heads of State or of Government, after a repetition of the procedure provided for in paragraphs 1 and 2, with the exception of the second indent of paragraph 2, taking into account the reports referred to in paragraph 1 and the opinion of the European Parliament, shall, acting by a qualified majority and on the basis of the recommendations of the Council referred to in paragraph 2, confirm which Member States fulfil the necessary conditions for the adoption of a single currency.

# Appendix C

# United Nations Convention on Contracts for the International Sale of Goods[1]

*The States Parties to this Convention,*

*Bearing in mind* the broad objectives in the resolutions adopted by the sixth special session of the General Assembly of the United Nations on the establishment of a New International Economic Order,

*Considering* that the development of international trade on the basis of equality and mutual benefit is an important element in promoting friendly relations among States,

*Being of the opinion* that the adoption of uniform rules which govern contracts for the international sale of goods and take into account the different social, economic and legal systems would contribute to the removal of legal barriers in international trade and promote the development of international trade,

*Have agreed* as follows:

## Part One: Sphere of Application and General Provisions

### Chapter I. Sphere of Application

*Article I*

(1) This Convention applies to contracts of sale of goods between parties whose places of business are in different States:

    (a) when the States are Contracting States; or

    (b) when the rules of private international law lead to the application of the law of a Contracting State.

(2) The fact that the parties have their places of business in different States is to be disregarded whenever this fact does not appear either from the contract or from any dealings between, or from information disclosed by, the parties at any time or at the conclusion of the contract.

(3) Neither the nationality of the parties nor the civil or commercial character of the parties or of the contract is to be taken into consideration in determining the application of this Convention.

*Article 2*

This Convention does not apply to sales:

    (a) of goods bought for personal, family or household use, unless the seller, at any time before or at the conclusion of the contract, neither knew nor ought to have known that the goods were bought for any such use:

    (b) by auction;

    (c) on execution or otherwise by authority of law;

    (d) of stocks, shares, investment securities, negotiable instruments or money;

    (e) of ships, vessels, hovercraft or aircraft.

    (f) of electricity.

*Article 3*

(1) Contracts for the supply of goods to be manufactured or produced are to be considered sales unless the party who orders the goods undertakes to supply a substantial part of the materials necessary for such manufacture or production.

(2) This Convention does not apply to contracts in which the preponderant part of the obligations of the party who furnishes the goods consists in the supply of labour or other services.

*Article 4*

This Convention governs only the formation of the contract of sale and the rights and obligations of the seller and the buyer arising from such a contract. In

[1]Source of text: U.N. Document A/CONF.97/18, Annex I, English version reprinted in 52 Fed. Reg. 6264 (1987) and in 19 I.L.M. 668 (1980)

particular, except as otherwise expressly provided in this Convention, it is not concerned with:

- (a) the validity of the contract or of any of its provisions or of any usage;
- (b) the effect which the contract may have on the property in the goods sold.

### Article 5

This Convention does not apply to the liability of the seller for death or personal injury caused by the goods to any person.

### Article 6

The parties may exclude the application of this Convention or, subject to article 12, derogate from or vary the effect of any of its provisions.

## Chapter 2. General Provisions

### Article 7

(1) In the interpretation of this Convention, regard is to be had to its international character and to the need to promote uniformity in its application and the observance of good faith in international trade.

(2) Questions concerning matters governed by this Convention which are not expressly settled in it are to be settled in conformity with the general principles on which it is based or, in the absence of such principles, in conformity with the law applicable by virtue of the rules of private international law.

### Article 8

(1) For the purposes of this Convention statements made by and other conduct of a party are to be interpreted according to his intent where the other party knew or could not have been unaware what that intent was.

(2) If the preceding paragraph is not applicable, statements made by and other conduct of a party are to be interpreted according to the understanding that a reasonable person of the same kind as the other party would have had in the same circumstances.

(3) In determining the intent of a party or the understanding a reasonable person would have had, due consideration is to be given to all relevant circumstances of the case including the negotiations, any practices which the parties have established between themselves, usages and any subsequent conduct of the parties.

### Article 9

(1) The parties are bound by any usage to which they have agreed and by any practices which they have established between themselves.

(2) The parties are considered, unless otherwise agreed, to have impliedly made applicable to their contract or its formation a usage of which the parties knew or ought to have known and which in international trade is widely known to, and regularly observed by, parties to contracts of the type involved in the particular trade concerned.

### Article 10

For the purposes of this Convention:

- (a) if a party has more than one place of business, the place of business is that which has the closest relationship to the contact and its performance, having regard to the circumstances known to or contemplated by the parties at any time before or at the conclusion of the contract;
- (b) if a party does not have a place of business, reference is to be made to his habitual residence.

### Article 11

A contract of sale need not be concluded in or evidence by writing and is not subject to any other requirements as to form. It may be proved by any means, including witnesses.

### Article 12

Any provision of article 11, article 29 or Part II of this Convention that allows a contract of sale or its modification or termination by agreement or any offer, acceptance or other indication of intention to be made in any form other than in writing does not apply where any party has his place of business in a Contracting State which has made a declaration under article 96 of this Convention. The parties may not derogate from or vary the effect of this article.

### Article 13

For the purposes of this Convention 'writing' includes telegram and telex.

## Part Two: Formation of the Contract

### Article 14

(1) A proposal for concluding a contract addressed to one or more specific persons constitutes an offer if it is sufficiently definite and indicates the inten-

tion of the offeror to be bound in case of acceptance. A proposal is sufficiently definite if it indicates the goods and expressly or implicitly fixes or makes provision for determining the quantity and the price.

(2) A proposal other than one addressed to one or more specific persons is to be considered merely as an invitation to make offers, unless the contrary is clearly indicated by the person making the proposal.

### Article 15

(1) An offer becomes effective when it reaches the offeree.

(2) An offer, even if it is irrevocable, may be withdrawn if the withdrawal reaches the offeree before or at the same time as the offer.

### Article 16

(1) Until a contract is concluded an offer may be revoked if the revocation reaches the offeree before he has dispatched an acceptance.

(2) However, an offer cannot be revoked:
   (a) if it indicates, whether by stating a fixed time for acceptance or otherwise, that it is irrevocable; or
   (b) if it was reasonable for the offeree to rely on the offer as being irrevocable and the offeree has acted in reliance on the offer.

### Article 17

An offer, even if it is irrevocable, is terminated when a rejection reaches the offeror.

### Article 18

(1) A statement made by or other conduct of the offeree indicating assent to an offer is an acceptance. Silence or inactivity does not in itself amount to acceptance.

(2) An acceptance of an offer becomes effective at the moment the indication of assent reaches the offeror. An acceptance is not effective if the indication of assent does not reach the offeror within the time he has fixed or, if no time is fixed, within a reasonable time, due account being taken of the circumstances of the transaction, including the rapidity of the means of communication employed by the offeror. An oral offer must be accepted immediately unless the circumstances indicate otherwise.

(3) However, if, by virtue of the offer or as a result of practices which the parties have established between themselves or of usage, the offeree may indicate assent by performing an act, such as one relating to the dispatch of the goods or payment of the price, without notice to the offeror, the acceptance is effective at the moment the act is performed, provided that the act is performed within the period of time laid down in the preceding paragraph.

### Article 19

(1) A reply to an offer which purports to be an acceptance but contains additions, limitations or other modifications is a rejection of the offer and constitutes a counter-offer.

(2) However, a reply to an offer which purports to be an acceptance but contains additional or different terms which do not materially alter the terms of the offer constitutes an acceptance, unless the offeror, without undue delay, objects orally to the discrepancy or dispatches a notice to that effect. If he does not so object, the terms of the contract are the terms of the offer with the modifications contained in the acceptance.

(3) Additional or different terms relating, among other things, to the price, payment, quality and quantity of the goods, place and time of delivery, extent of one party's liability to the other or the settlement of disputes are considered to alter the terms of the offer materially.

### Article 20

(1) A period of time for acceptance fixed by the offeror in a telegram or a letter begins to run from the moment the telegram is handed in for dispatch or from the date shown on the letter or, if no such date is shown, from the date shown on the envelope. A period of time for acceptance fixed by the offeror by telephone, telex or other means of instantaneous communication, begins to run from the moment that the offer reaches the offeree.

(2) Official holidays or non-business days occurring during the period for acceptance are included in calculating the period. However, if a notice of acceptance cannot be delivered at the address of the offeror on the last day of the period because that day falls on an official holiday or a non-business day at the place of business of the offeror, the period is extended until the first business day which follows.

### Article 21

(1) A late acceptance is nevertheless effective as an acceptance if without delay the offeror orally so informs the offeree or dispatches a notice to that effect.

(2) If a letter or other writing containing a late acceptance shows that it has been sent in such circumstances that if its transmission had been normal it would have reached the offeror in due time, the late acceptance is effective as an acceptance unless, without delay, the offeror orally informs the offeree that he considers his offer as having lapsed or dispatches a notice to that effect.

### Article 22

An acceptance may be withdrawn if the withdrawal reaches the offeror before or at the same time as the acceptance would have become effective.

### Article 23

A contract is concluded at the moment when an acceptance of an offer becomes effective in accordance with the provisions of this Convention.

### Article 24

For the purposes of the Part of the Convention, an offer, declaration of acceptance or any other indication of intention 'reaches' the addressee when it is made orally to him or delivered by any other means to him personally, to his place of business or mailing address or, if he does not have a place of business or mailing address, to his habitual residence.

# Part Three: Sale of Goods

## Chapter 1. General Provisions

### Article 25

A breach of contract committed by one of the parties is fundamental if it results in such detriment to the other party as substantially to deprive him of what he is entitled to expect under the contract, unless the party in breach did not foresee and a reasonable person of the same kind in the same circumstances would not have foreseen such a result.

### Article 26

A declaration of avoidance of the contract is effective only if made by notice to the other party.

### Article 27

Unless otherwise expressly provided in this Part of the Convention, if any notice, request or other communication is given or made by a party in accordance with this Part and by means appropriate in the circumstances, a delay of error in the transmission of the communication or its failure to arrive does not deprive that party of the right to rely on the communication.

### Article 28

If, in accordance with the provisions of this Convention, one party is entitled to require performance of any obligation by the other party, a court is not bound to enter a judgement for specific performance unless the court would do so under its own law in respect of similar contracts of sale not governed by this Convention.

### Article 29

(1) A contract may be modified or terminated by the mere agreement of the parties.
(2) A contract in writing which contains a provision requiring any modification or termination by agreement to be in writing may not be otherwise modified or terminated by agreement. However, a party may be precluded by his conduct from asserting such a provision to the extent that the other party has relied on that conduct.

## Chapter 2. Obligations of the Seller

### Article 30

The seller must deliver the goods, hand over any documents relating to them and transfer the property in the goods, as required by the contract and this Convention.

**SECTION I. DELIVERY OF THE GOODS AND HANDING OVER OF DOCUMENTS**

### Article 31

If the seller is not bound to deliver the goods at any other particular place, his obligation to deliver consists:
(a) if the contract of sale involves carriage of the goods—in handing the goods over to the first carrier for transmission to the buyer;
(b) if, in cases, not within the preceding subparagraph, the contract relates to specific goods, or unidentified goods to be drawn from a specific stock or to be manufactured or produced, and at the time of the conclusion of the contract the parties knew that the goods were at, or were to be manufactured or produced at, a particular place—in placing the goods at the buyer's disposal at that place;
(c) in other cases—in placing the goods at the buyer's disposal at the place where the seller had his place of business at the time of the conclusion of the contract.

### Article 32

(1) If the seller, in accordance with the contract or this Convention, hands the goods over to a carrier and

if the goods are not clearly identified to the contract by markings on the goods, by shipping documents or otherwise, the seller must give the buyer notice of the consignment specifying the goods.

(2) If the seller is bound to arrange for carriage of the goods, he must make such contracts as are necessary for carriage to the place fixed by means of transportation appropriate in the circumstances and according to the usual terms for such transportation.

(3) If the seller is not bound to effect insurance in respect of the carriage of the goods, he must, at the buyer's request, provide him with all valuable information necessary to enable him to effect such insurance.

## Article 33

The seller must deliver the goods:

(a) if a date is fixed by or determinable from the contract, on that date;

(b) if a period of time is fixed by or determinable from the contract, at any time within that period unless circumstances indicate that the buyer is to choose a date; or

(c) in any other case, within a reasonable time after the conclusion of the contract.

## Article 34

If the seller is bound to hand over documents relating to the goods, he must hand them over at the time and place and in the form required by the contract. If the seller has handed over documents before that time, he may, up to that time, cure any lack of conformity in the documents, if the exercise of this right does not cause the buyer unreasonable inconvenience or unreasonable expense. However, the buyer retains any right to claim damages as provided for in this Convention.

## SECTION II. CONFORMITY OF THE GOODS AND THIRD PARTY CLAIMS

## Article 35

(1) The seller must deliver goods which are of the quantity, quality and description required by the contract and which are contained or packaged in the manner required by the contract.

(2) Except where the parties have agreed otherwise, the goods do not conform with the contract unless they:

(a) are fit for the purposes for which goods of the same description would ordinarily be used;

(b) are fit for any particular purpose expressly or impliedly made known to the seller at the time

of the conclusion of the contract, except where the circumstances show that the buyer did not rely, or that it was unreasonable for him to rely, on the seller's skill and judgement;

(c) possess the qualities of goods which the seller has held out to the buyer as a sample or model;

(d) are contained or packaged in the manner usual for such goods or, where there is no such manner, in a manner adequate to preserve and protect the goods.

(3) The seller is not liable under subparagraphs (a) to (d) of the preceding paragraph for any lack of conformity of the goods if at the time of the conclusion of the contract the buyer knew or could not have been unaware of such lack of conformity.

## Article 36

(1) The seller is liable in accordance with the contract and this Convention for any lack of conformity which exists at the time when the risk passes to the buyer, even though the lack of conformity becomes apparent only after that time.

(2) The seller is also liable for any lack of conformity which occurs after the time indicated in the preceding paragraph and which is due to a breach of any of his obligations, including a breach of any guarantee that for a period of time the goods will remain fit for their ordinary purpose or for some particular purpose or will retain specified qualities or characteristics.

## Article 37

If the seller has delivered goods before the date for delivery, he may, up to that date, deliver any missing part or make up any deficiency in the quantity of the goods delivered, or deliver goods in replacement of any nonconforming goods delivered or remedy any lack of conformity in the goods delivered, provided that the exercise of this right does not cause the buyer unreasonable inconvenience or unreasonable expense. However, the buyer retains any right to claim damages as provided for in this Convention.

## Article 38

(1) The buyer must examine the goods, or cause them to be examined, within as short a period as is practicable in the circumstances.

(2) If the contract involves carriage of the goods, examination may be deferred until after the goods have arrived at their destination.

(3) If the goods are redirected in transit or redispatched by the buyer without a reasonable opportunity for examination by him and at the time of

the conclusion of the contract the seller knew or ought to have known of the possibility of such re-direction or redispatch, examination may be deferred until after the goods have arrived at the new destination.

### Article 39

(1) The buyer loses the right to rely on a lack of conformity of the goods if he does not give notice to the seller specifying the nature of the lack of conformity within a reasonable time after he has discovered it or ought to have discovered it.

(2) In any event, the buyer loses the right to rely on a lack of conformity of the goods if he does not give the seller notice thereof at the latest within a period of two years from the date on which the goods were actually handed over to the buyer, unless this time-limit is inconsistent with a contractual period of guarantee.

### Article 40

The seller is not entitled to rely on the provisions of articles 38 and 39 if the lack of conformity relates to facts of which he knew or could not have been unaware and which he did not disclose to the buyer.

### Article 41

The seller must deliver goods which are free from any right or claim of a third party, unless the buyer agreed to take the goods subject to that right or claim. However, if such right or claim is based on industrial property or other intellectual property, the seller's obligation is governed by article 42.

### Article 42

(1) The seller must deliver goods which are free from any right or claim of a third party based on industrial property or other intellectual property, of which at the time of the conclusion of the contract the seller knew or could not have been unaware, provided that the right or claim is based on industrial property or other intellectual property:

 (a) under the law of the State where the goods will be resold or otherwise used, if it was contemplated by the parties at the time of the conclusion of the contract that the goods would be resold or otherwise used in that State; or

 (b) in any other case, under the law of the State where the buyer has his place of business.

(2) The obligation of the seller under the preceding paragraph does not extend to cases where:

 (a) at the time of the conclusion of the contract the buyer knew or could not have been unaware of the right or claim; or

 (b) the right or claim results from the seller's compliance with technical drawings, designs, formulae or other such specifications furnished by the buyer.

### Article 43

(1) The buyer loses the right to rely on the provisions of article 41 or article 42 if he does not give notice to the seller specifying the nature of the right or claim of the third party within a reasonable time after he has become aware or ought to have become aware of the right or claim.

(2) The seller is not entitled to rely on the provisions of the preceding paragraph if he knew of the right or claim of the third party and the nature of it.

### Article 44

Notwithstanding the provisions of paragraph (1) of article 39 and paragraph (1) of article 43, the buyer may reduce the price in accordance with article 50 or claim damages, except for loss of profit, if he has a reasonable excuse for his failure to give the required notice.

## SECTION III. REMEDIES FOR BREACH OF CONTRACT BY THE SELLER

### Article 45

(1) If the seller fails to perform any of his obligations under the contract or this Convention, the buyer may:

 (a) exercise the rights provided in articles 46 to 52;

 (b) claim damages as provided in articles 74 to 77.

(2) The buyer is not deprived of any right he may have to claim damages by exercising his right to other remedies.

(3) No period of grace may be granted to the seller by a court or arbitral tribunal when the buyer resorts to a remedy for breach of contract.

### Article 46

(1) The buyer may require performance by the seller of his obligations unless the buyer has resorted to a remedy which is inconsistent with this requirement.

(2) If the goods do not conform with the contract, the buyer may require delivery of substitute goods only if the lack of conformity constitutes a fundamental breach of contract and a request for substitute goods is made either in conjunction with notice given under article 39 or within a reasonable time thereafter.

(3) If the goods do not conform with the contract, the buyer may require the seller to remedy the lack of

conformity by repair, unless this is unreasonable having regard to all the circumstances. A request for repair must be made either in conjunction with notice given under article 39 or within a reasonable time thereafter.

### Article 47

(1) The buyer may fix an additional period of time of reasonable length for performance by the seller of his obligations.

(2) Unless the buyer has received notice from the seller that he will not perform within the period so fixed, the buyer may not, during that period, resort to any remedy for breach of contract. However, the buyer is not deprived thereby of any right he may have to claim damages for delay in performance.

### Article 48

(1) Subject to article 49, the seller may, even after the date for delivery, remedy at his own expense any failure to perform his obligations, if he can do so without unreasonable delay and without causing the buyer unreasonable inconvenience or uncertainty of reimbursement by the seller of expenses advanced by the buyer. However, the buyer retains any right to claim damages as provided for in this Convention.

(2) If the seller requests the buyer to make known whether he will accept performance and the buyer does not comply with the request within a reasonable time, the seller may perform within the time indicated in his request. The buyer may not, during that period of time, resort to any remedy which is inconsistent with performance by the seller.

(3) A notice by the seller that he will perform within a specified period of time is assumed to include a request, under the preceding paragraph, that the buyer make known his decision.

(4) A request or notice by the seller under paragraph (2) or (3) of this article is not effective unless received by the buyer.

### Article 49

(1) The buyer may declare the contract avoided:
  (a) if the failure by the seller to perform any of his obligations under the contract or this Convention amounts to a fundamental breach of contract; or
  (b) in case of non-delivery, if the seller does not deliver the goods within the additional period of time fixed by the buyer in accordance with paragraph (1) or article 47 or declares that he will not deliver within the period so fixed.

(2) However, in cases where the seller has delivered the goods, the buyer loses the right to declare the contract avoided unless he does so:
  (a) in respect of late delivery, within a reasonable time after he has become aware that delivery has been made;
  (b) in respect of any breach other than late delivery, within a reasonable time:
    (i) after he knew or ought to have known of the breach;
    (ii) after the expiration of any additional period of time fixed by the buyer in accordance with paragraph (1) of article 47, or after the seller has declared that he will not perform his obligations within such an additional period; or
    (iii) after the expiration of any additional period of time indicated by the seller in accordance with paragraph (2) of article 48, or after the buyer has declared that he will not accept performance.

### Article 50

If the goods do not conform with the contract and whether or not the price has already been paid, the buyer may reduce the price in the same proportion as the value that the goods actually delivered had at the time of the delivery bears to the value that conforming goods would have had at that time. However, if the seller remedies any failure to perform his obligations in accordance with article 37 or article 48 or if the buyer refuses to accept performance by the seller in accordance with those articles, the buyer may not reduce the price.

### Article 51

(1) If the seller delivers only a part of the goods or if only a part of the goods delivered is in conformity with the contract, articles 46 to 50 apply in respect of the part which is missing or which does not conform.

(2) The buyer may declare the contract avoided in its entirety only if the failure to make delivery completely or in conformity with the contract amounts to a fundamental breach of the contract.

### Article 52

(1) If the seller delivers the goods before the date fixed, the buyer may take delivery or refuse to take delivery.

(2) If the seller delivers a quantity of goods greater than that provided for in the contract, the buyer may take delivery or refuse to take delivery of the excess quantity. If the buyer takes delivery of all

or part of the excess quantity, he must pay for it at the contract rate.

# Chapter 3. Obligations of the Buyer

## Article 53

The buyer must pay the price for the goods and take delivery of them as required by the contract and this Convention.

### Section I. Payment of the Price

## Article 54

The buyer's obligation to pay the price includes taking such steps and complying with such formalities as may be required under the contract or any laws and regulations to enable payment to be made.

## Article 55

Where a contract has been validly concluded but does not expressly or implicitly fix or make provision for determining the price, the parties are considered, in the absence of any indication to the contrary, to have impliedly made reference to the price generally charged at the time of the conclusion of the contract for such goods sold under comparable circumstances in the trade concerned.

## Article 56

If the price is fixed according to the weight of the goods, in case of doubt it is to be determined by the net weight.

## Article 57

(1) If the buyer is not bound to pay the price at any other particular place, he must pay it to the seller:
   (a) at the seller's place of business; or
   (b) if the payment is to be made against the handing over of the goods or of documents, at the place where the handing over takes place.
(2) The seller must bear any increase in the expenses incidental to payment which is caused by a change in his place of business subsequent to the conclusion of the contract.

## Article 58

(1) If the buyer is not bound to pay the price at any other specific time, he must pay it when the seller places either the goods or documents controlling their disposition at the buyer's disposal in accordance with the contract and this Convention. The seller may make such payment a condition for handing over the goods or documents.

(2) If the contract involves carriage of the goods, the seller may dispatch the goods on terms whereby the goods, or documents controlling their disposition, will not be handed over to the buyer except against payment of the price.

(3) The buyer is not bound to pay the price until he has had an opportunity to examine the goods, unless the procedures for delivery or payment agreed upon by the parties are inconsistent with his having such an opportunity.

## Article 59

The buyer must pay the price on the date fixed by or determinable from the contract and this Convention without the need for any request or compliance with any formality on the part of the seller.

### Section II. Taking Delivery

## Article 60

The buyer's obligation to take delivery consists:
   (a) in doing all the acts which could reasonably be expected of him in order to enable the seller to make delivery; and
   (b) in taking over the goods.

### Section III. Remedies for Breach of Contract by the Buyer

## Article 61

(1) If the buyer fails to perform any of his obligations under the contract or this Convention, the seller may:
   (a) exercise the rights provided in articles 62 to 65;
   (b) claim damages as provided in articles 74 to 77.
(2) The seller is not deprived of any right he may have to claim damages by exercising his right to other remedies.
(3) No period of grace may be granted to the buyer by a court or arbitral tribunal when the seller resorts to a remedy for breach of contract.

## Article 62

The seller may require the buyer to pay the price, take delivery or perform his other obligations, unless the seller has resorted to a remedy which is inconsistent with this requirement.

## Article 63

(1) The seller may fix an additional period of time of reasonable length for performance by the buyer of his obligations.

(2) Unless the seller has received notice from the buyer that he will not perform within the period so fixed, the seller may not, during that period, resort to any remedy for breach of contract. However, the seller is not deprived thereby of any right he may have to claim damages for delay in performance.

*Article 64*

(1) The seller may declare the contract avoided:
   (a) if the failure by the buyer to perform any of his obligations under the contract or this Convention amounts to a fundamental breach of contract; or
   (b) if the buyer does not, within the additional period of time fixed by the seller in accordance with paragraph (1) of article 63, perform his obligation to pay the price or take delivery of the goods, or if he declares that he will not do so within the period so fixed.
(2) However, in cases where the buyer has paid the price, the seller loses the right to declare the contract avoided unless he does so:
   (a) in respect of late performance by the buyer, before the seller has become aware that performance has been rendered; or
   (b) in respect of any breach other than late performance by the buyer, within a reasonable time:
      (i) after the seller knew or ought to have known of the breach; or
      (ii) after the expiration of any additional period of time fixed by the seller in accordance with paragraph (1) of article 63, or after the buyer has declared that he will not perform his obligations within such an additional period.

*Article 65*

(1) If under the contract the buyer is to specify the form, measurement or other features of the goods and he fails to make such specification either on the date agreed upon or within a reasonable time after receipt of a request from the seller, the seller may, without prejudice to any other rights he may have, make the specification himself in accordance with the requirements of the buyer that may be known to him.
(2) If the seller makes the specification himself, he must inform the buyer of the details thereof and must fix a reasonable time within which the buyer may make a different specification. If, after receipt of such a communication, the buyer fails to do so within the time so fixed, the specification made by the seller is binding.

## Chapter 4. Passing of Risk

*Article 66*

Loss of or damage to the goods after the risk has passed to the buyer does not discharge him from his obligation to pay the price, unless the loss or damage is due to an act or omission of the seller.

*Article 67*

(1) If the contract of sale involves carriage of the goods and the seller is not bound to hand them over at a particular place, the risk passes to the buyer when the goods are handed over to the first carrier for transmission to the buyer in accordance with the contract of sale. If the seller is bound to hand the goods over to a carrier at a particular place, the risk does not pass to the buyer until the goods are handed over to the carrier at that place. The fact that the seller is authorized to retain documents controlling the disposition of the goods does not affect the passage of the risk.
(2) Nevertheless, the risk does not pass to the buyer until the goods are clearly identified to the contract, whether by markings on the goods, by shipping documents, by notice given to the buyer or otherwise.

*Article 68*

The risk in respect of goods sold in transit passes to the buyer from the time of the conclusion of the contract. However, if the circumstances so indicate, the risk is assumed by the buyer from the time the goods were handed over to the carrier who issued the documents embodying the contract of carriage. Nevertheless, if at the time of the conclusion of the contract of sale the seller knew or ought to have known that the goods had been lost or damaged and did not disclose this to the buyer, the loss or damage is at the risk of the seller.

*Article 69*

(1) In cases not within articles 67 and 68, the risk passes to the buyer when he takes over the goods or, if he does not do so in due time, from the time when the goods are placed at his disposal and he commits a breach of contract by failing to take delivery.
(2) However, if the buyer is bound to take over the goods at a place other than a place of business of the seller, the risk passes when delivery is due and the buyer is aware of the fact that the goods are placed at his disposal at that place.
(3) If the contract relates to goods not then identified, the goods are considered not to be placed at the disposal of the buyer until they are clearly identified to the contract.

### Article 70

If the seller has committed a fundamental breach of contract, articles 67, 68 and 69 do not impair the remedies available to the buyer on account of the breach.

## Chapter 5. Provisions Common to the Obligations of the Seller and of the Buyer

### Section I. Anticipatory Breach and Installment Contracts

### Article 71

(1) A party may suspend the performance of his obligations if, after the conclusion of the contract, it becomes apparent that the other party will not perform a substantial part of his obligations as a result of:

    (a) a serious deficiency in his ability to perform or in his creditworthiness; or

    (b) his conduct in preparing to perform or in performing the contract.

(2) If the seller has already dispatched the goods before the grounds described in the preceding paragraph become evident, he may prevent the handing over of the goods to the buyer even though the buyer holds a document which entitles him to obtain them. The present paragraph relates only to the rights in the goods as between the buyer and the seller.

(3) A party suspending performance, whether before or after dispatch of the goods, must immediately give notice of the suspension to the other party and must continue with performance if the other party provides adequate assurance of his performance.

### Article 72

(1) If prior to the date for performance of the contract it is clear that one of the parties will commit a fundamental breach of contract, the other party may declare the contract avoided.

(2) If time allows, the party intending to declare the contract avoided must give reasonable notice to the other party in order to permit him to provide adequate assurance of his performance.

(3) The requirements of the preceding paragraph do not apply if the other party has declared that he will not perform his obligations.

### Article 73

(1) In the case of a contract for delivery of goods by instalments, if the failure of one party to perform any of his obligations in respect of any instalment constitutes a fundamental breach of contract with respect to that instalment, the other party may declare the contract avoided with respect to that instalment.

(2) If one party's failure to perform any of his obligations in respect of any instalment gives the other party good grounds to conclude that a fundamental breach of contract will occur with respect to future instalments, he may declare the contract avoided for the future, provided that he does so within a reasonable time.

(3) A buyer who declares the contract avoided in respect of any delivery may, at the same time, declare it avoided in respect of deliveries already made or of future deliveries if, by reason of their interdependence, those deliveries could not be used for the purpose contemplated by the parties at the time of the conclusion of the contract.

### Section II. Damages

### Article 74

Damages for breach of contract by one party consist of a sum equal to the loss, including loss of profit, suffered by the other party as a consequence of the breach. Such damages may not exceed the loss which the party in breach foresaw or ought to have foreseen at the time of the conclusion of the contract, in the light of the facts and matters of which he then knew or ought to have known, as a possible consequence of the breach of contract.

### Article 75

If the contract is avoided and if, in a reasonable manner and within a reasonable time after avoidance, the buyer has bought goods in replacement or the seller has resold the goods, the party claiming damages may recover the difference between the contract price and the price in the substitute transaction as well as any further damages recoverable under article 74.

### Article 76

(1) If the contract is avoided and there is a current price for the goods, the party claiming damages may, if he has not made a purchase or resale under article 75, recover the difference between the price fixed by the contract and the current price at the time of avoidance as well as any further damages recoverable under article 74. If, however, the party claiming damages has avoided the contract after taking over the goods, the current price at the time of such taking over shall be applied instead of the current price at the time of avoidance.

(2) For the purposes of the preceding paragraph, the current price is the price prevailing at the place

where delivery of the goods should have been made or, if there is no current price at that place, the price at such other place as serves as a reasonable substitute, making due allowance for differences in the cost of transporting the goods.

## Article 77

A party who relies on a breach of contract must take such measures as are reasonable in the circumstances to mitigate the loss, including loss of profit, resulting from the breach. If he fails to take such measures, the party in breach may claim a reduction in the damages in the amount by which the loss should have been mitigated.

## Section III. Interest

## Article 78

If a party fails to pay the price or any other sum that is in arrears, the other party is entitled to interest on it, without prejudice to any claim for damages recoverable under article 74.

## Section IV. Exemptions

## Article 79

(1) A party is not liable for a failure to perform any of his obligations if he proves that the failure was due to an impediment beyond his control and that he could not reasonably be expected to have taken the impediment into account at the time of the conclusion of the contract or to have avoided or overcome it or its consequences.

(2) If the party's failure is due to the failure by a third person whom he has engaged to perform the whole or a part of the contract, that party is exempt from liability only if:
   (a) he is exempt under the preceding paragraph; and
   (b) the person whom he has so engaged would be so exempt if the provisions of that paragraph were applied to him.

(3) The exemption provided by this article has effect for the period during which the impediment exists.

(4) The party who fails to perform must give notice to the other party of the impediment and its effect on his ability to perform. If the notice is not received by the other party within a reasonable time after the party who fails to perform knew or ought to have known of the impediment, he is liable for damages resulting from such nonreceipt.

(5) Nothing in this article prevents either party from exercising any right other than to claim damages under this Convention.

## Article 80

A party may not rely on a failure of the other party to perform, to the extent that such failure was caused by the first party's act or omission.

## Section V. Effects of Avoidance

## Article 81

(1) Avoidance of the contract releases both parties from their obligations under it, subject to any damages which may be due. Avoidance does not affect any provision of the contract for the settlement of disputes or any other provision of the contract governing the rights and obligations of the parties consequent upon the avoidance of the contract.

(2) A party who has performed the contract either wholly or in part may claim restitution from the other party of whatever the first party has supplied or paid under the contract. If both parties are bound to make restitution, they must do so concurrently.

## Article 82

(1) The buyer loses the right to declare the contract avoided or to require the seller to deliver substitute goods if it is impossible for him to make restitution of the goods substantially in the condition in which he received them.

(2) The preceding paragraph does not apply:
   (a) if the impossibility of making restitution of the goods or of making restitution of the goods substantially in the condition in which the buyer received them is not due to his act or omission;
   (b) if the goods or part of the goods have perished or deteriorated as a result of the examination provided for in article 38; or
   (c) if the goods or part of the goods have been sold in the normal course of business or have been consumed or transformed by the buyer in the course of normal use before he discovered or ought to have discovered the lack of conformity.

## Article 83

A buyer who has lost the right to declare the contract avoided or to require the seller to deliver substitute goods in accordance with article 82 retains all other remedies under the contract and this Convention.

## Article 84

(1) If the seller is bound to refund the price, he must also pay interest on it, from the date on which the price was paid.

(2) The buyer must account to the seller for all benefits which he has derived from the goods or part of them:
   (a) if he must make restitution of the goods or part of them; or

(b) if it is impossible for him to make restitution of all or part of the goods or to make restitution of all or part of the goods substantially in the condition in which he received them, but he has nevertheless declared the contract avoided or required the seller to deliver substitute goods.

## Section VI. Preservation of the Goods

### Article 85

If the buyer is in delay in taking delivery of the goods or, where payment of the price and delivery of the goods are to be made concurrently, if he fails to pay the price, and the seller is either in possession of the goods or otherwise able to control their disposition, the seller must take such steps as are reasonable in the circumstances to preserve them. He is entitled to retain them until he has been reimbursed his reasonable expenses by the buyer.

### Article 86

(1) If the buyer has received the goods and intends to exercise any right under the contract or this Convention to reject them, he must take such steps to preserve them as are reasonable in the circumstances. He is entitled to retain them until he has been reimbursed his reasonable expenses by the seller.

(2) If goods dispatched to the buyer have been placed at his disposal at their destination and he exercises the right to reject them, he must take possession of them on behalf of the seller, provided that this can be done without payment of the price and without unreasonable inconvenience or unreasonable expense. This provision does not apply if the seller or a person authorized to take charge of the goods on his behalf is present at the destination. If the buyer takes possession of the goods under this paragraph, his rights and obligations are governed by the preceding paragraph.

### Article 87

A party who is bound to take steps to preserve the goods may deposit them in a warehouse of a third person at the expense of the other party provided that the expense incurred is not unreasonable.

### Article 88

(1) A party who is bound to preserve the goods in accordance with article 85 or 86 may sell them by any appropriate means if there has been an unreasonable delay by the other party in taking possession of the goods or in taking them back or in paying the price or the cost of preservation, provided that reasonable notice of the intention to sell has been given to the other party.

(2) If the goods are subject to rapid deterioration or their preservation would involve unreasonable expense, a party who is bound to preserve the goods in accordance with article 85 or 86 must take reasonable measures to sell them. To the extent possible he must give notice to the other party of his intention to sell.

(3) A party selling the goods has the right to retain out of the proceeds of sale an amount equal to the reasonable expenses of preserving the goods and of selling them. He must account to the other party for the balance.

# Part Four: Final Provisions

### Article 89

The Secretary-General of the United Nations is hereby designated as the depositary for this Convention.

### Article 90

This Convention does not prevail over any international agreement which has already been or may be entered into and which contains provisions concerning the matters governed by this Convention, provided that the parties have their places of business in States parties to such agreement.

### Article 91

(1) This Convention is open for signature at the concluding meeting of the United Nations Conference on Contracts for the International Sale of Goods and will remain open for signature by all States at the Headquarters of the United Nations, New York until 30 September 1981.

(2) This Convention is subject to ratification, acceptance or approval by the signatory States.

(3) This Convention is open for accession by all States which are not signatory States as from the date it is open for signature.

(4) Instruments of ratification, acceptance, approval and accession are to be deposited with the Secretary-General of the United Nations.

### Article 92

(1) A Contracting State may declare at the time of signature, ratification, acceptance, approval or accession that it will not be bound by Part II of this Convention or that it will not be bound by Part III of this Convention.

(2) A Contracting State which makes a declaration in accordance with the preceding paragraph in re-

spect of Part II or Part III of this Convention is not to be considered a Contracting State within paragraph (1) of article 1 of this Convention in respect of matters governed by the Part to which the declaration applies.

### Article 93

(1) If a Contracting State has two or more territorial units in which, according to its constitution, different systems of law are applicable in relation to the matters dealt with in this Convention, it may, at the time of signature, ratification, acceptance, approval or accession, declare that this Convention is to extend to all its territorial units or only to one or more of them, and may amend its declaration by submitting another declaration at any time.

(2) These declarations are to be notified to the depositary and are to state expressly the territorial units to which the Convention extends.

(3) If, by virtue of a declaration under this article, this Convention extends to one or more but not all of the territorial units of a Contracting State, and if the place of business of a party is located in that State, this place of business, for the purposes of this Convention, is considered not to be in a Contracting State, unless it is in a territorial unit to which the Convention extends.

(4) If a Contracting State makes no declaration under paragraph (1) of this article, the Convention is to extend to all territorial units of that State.

### Article 94

(1) Two or more Contracting States which have the same or closely related legal rules on matters governed by this Convention may at any time declare that the Convention is not to apply to contracts of sale or to their formation where the parties have their places of business in those States. Such declarations may be made jointly or by reciprocal unilateral declarations.

(2) A Contracting State which has the same or closely related legal rules on matters governed by this Convention as one or more non-Contracting States may at any time declare that the Convention is not to apply to contracts of sale or to their formation where the parties have their place of business in those States.

(3) If a State which is the object of a declaration under the preceding paragraph subsequently becomes a Contracting State, the declaration made will, as from the date on which the Convention enters into force in respect of the new Contracting State, have the effect of a declaration made under paragraph (1), provided that the new Contracting State joins in such declaration or makes a reciprocal unilateral declaration.

### Article 95

Any State may declare at the time of the deposit of its instrument of ratification, acceptance, approval or accession that it will not be bound by subparagraph (1)(b) of article 1 of this Convention.

### Article 96

A Contracting State whose legislation requires contracts of sale to be concluded in or evidenced by writing may at any time make a declaration in accordance with article 12 that any provision of article 11, article 29, or Part II of this Convention, that allows a contract sale or its modification or termination by agreement or any offer, acceptance, or other indication of intention to be made in any form other than in writing, does not apply where any party has his place of business in that State.

### Article 97

(1) Declarations made under this Convention at the time of signature are subject to confirmation upon ratification, acceptance or approval.

(2) Declarations and confirmations of declarations are to be in writing and be formally notified to the depositary.

(3) A declaration takes effect simultaneously with the entry into force of this Convention in respect of the State concerned. However, a declaration of which the depositary receives formal notification after such entry into force takes effect on the first day of the month following the expiration of six months after the date of its receipt by the depositary. Reciprocal unilateral declarations under article 94 takes effect on the first day of the month following the expiration of six months after the receipt of the latest declaration by the depositary.

(4) Any State which makes a declaration under this Convention may withdraw it at any time by a formal notification in writing addressed to the depositary. Such withdrawal is to take effect on the first day of the month following the expiration of six months after the date of the receipt of the notification by the depositary.

(5) A withdrawal of a declaration made under article 94 renders inoperative, as from the date on which the withdrawal takes effect, any reciprocal declaration made by another State under that article.

### Article 98

No reservations are permitted except those expressly authorized in this Convention.

*Article 99*

(1) This Convention enters into force, subject to the provisions of paragraph (6) of this article, on the first day of the month following the expiration of twelve months after the date of deposit of the tenth instrument of ratification, acceptance, approval or accession, including an instrument which contains a declaration made under article 92.

(2) When a State ratifies, accepts, approves or accedes to this Convention after the deposit of the tenth instrument of ratification, acceptance, approval or ascession, this Convention, with the exception of the Part excluded, enters into force in respect of that State, subject to the provisions of paragraph (6) of this article, on the first day of the month following the expiration of twelve months after the date of the deposit of its instrument of ratification, acceptance, approval or accession.

(3) A State which ratifies, accepts, approves or accedes to this Convention and is a party to either or both the Convention relating to a Uniform Law on the Formation of Contracts for the International Sale of Goods done at The Hague on 1 July 1964 (1964 Hague Formation Convention) and the Convention relating to a Uniform Law on the International Sale of Goods done at The Hague on 1 July 1964 (1964 Hague Sales Convention) shall at the same time denounce, as the case may be, either or both the 1964 Hague Sales Convention and the 1964 Hague Formation Convention by notifying the Government of the Netherlands to that effect.

(4) A State party to the 1964 Hague Sales Convention which ratifies, accepts, approves or accedes to the present Convention and declares or has declared under article 92 that it will not be bound by Part II of this Convention shall at the time of ratification, acceptance, approval or accession denounce the 1964 Hague Sales Convention by notifying the Government of the Netherlands to that effect.

(5) A State party to the 1964 Hague Formation Convention which ratifies, accepts, approves or accedes to the present Convention and declares or has declared under article 92 that it will not be bound by Part III of this Convention shall at the time of ratification, acceptance, approval or accession denounce the 1964 Hague Formation Convention by notifying the Government of the Netherlands to that effect.

(6) For the purpose of this article, ratifications, acceptances, approvals and accessions in respect of this Convention by States parties to the 1964 Hague Formation Convention or to the 1964 Hague Sales Convention shall not be effective until such denunciations as may be required on the part of those States in respect of the latter two Conventions have themselves become effective. The depositary of this Convention shall consult with the Government of the Netherlands, as the depositary of the 1964 Conventions, so as to ensure necessary co-ordination in this respect.

*Article 100*

(1) This Convention applies to the formation of a contract only when the proposal for concluding the contract is made on or after the date when the Convention enters into force in respect of the Contracting States referred to in subparagraph (1)(a) or the Contracting State referred to in subparagraph (1)(b) of article 1.

(2) This Convention applies only to contracts concluded on or after the date when the Convention enters into force in respect of the Contracting States referred to in subparagraph (1)(a) or the Contracting State referred to in subparagraph (1)(b) of article 1.

*Article 101*

(1) A Contracting State may denounce this Convention, or Part II or Part III of the Convention, by a formal notification in writing addressed to the depositary.

(2) The denunciation takes effect on the first day of the month following the expiration of twelve months after the notification is received by the depositary. Where a longer period for the denunciation to take effect is specified in the notification, the denunciation takes effect upon the expiration of such longer period after the notification is received by the depositary.

*DONE* at Vienna, this day of eleventh day of April, one thousand nine hundred and eighty, in a single original, of which the Arabic, Chinese, English, French, Russian and Spanish texts are equally authentic.

*IN WITNESS WHEREOF* the undersigned plenipotentiaries, being duly authorized by their respective Governments, have signed this Convention.

# Uniform Commercial Code: Selected Provisions on Risk of Loss

## Part Three: General Obligations and Construction of Contract

### § 2-319. F.O.B. and F.A.S. Terms

(1) Unless otherwise agreed, the term F.O.B. (which means "free on board") at a named place, even though used only in connection with the stated price, is a delivery term under which

   (a) when the term F.O.B. the place of shipment, the seller must at that place ship the goods in the manner provided in this Article (Section 2-504) and bear the expense and risk of putting them into the possession of the carrier; or

   (b) when the term is F.O.B. the place of destination, the seller must at his own expense and risk transport the goods to that place and there tender delivery of them in the manner provided in this Article (Section 2-503);

   (c) when under either (a) or (b) the term is also F.O.B. vessel, car or other vehicle, the seller must in addition at his own expense and risk load the goods on board. If the term is F.O.B. vessel, the buyer must name the vessel and, in an appropriate case, the seller must comply with the provisions of this Article on the form of bill of lading (Section 2-323).

(2) Unless otherwise agreed, the term F.A.S. vessel (which means "free alongside") at a named port, even though used only in connection with the stated price, is a delivery term under which seller must

   (a) at his own expense and risk deliver the goods alongside the vessel in the manner usual in that port or on a dock designated and provided by the buyer; and

   (b) obtain and tender a receipt for the goods in exchange for which the carrier is under a duty to issue a bill of lading.

(3) Unless otherwise agreed in any case falling within subsection (1)(a) or (c) or subsection (2) the buyer must seasonably give any needed instructions for making delivery, including, when the term is F.A.S. or F.O.B., the loading berth of the vessel and, in an appropriate case, its name and sailing date. The seller may treat the failure of needed instructions as a failure of cooperation under this Article (section 2-311). He may also at his option move the goods in any reasonable manner preparatory to delivery or shipment.

(4) Under the term F.O.B. vessel or F.A.S., unless otherwise agreed, the buyer must make payment against tender of the required documents and the seller may not tender nor the buyer demand delivery of the goods in substitution for the documents.

### § 2-320. C.I.F. and C. & F. Terms

(1) The term C.I.F. means that the price includes in a lump sum the cost of the goods and the insurance and freight to the named destination. The term C. & F. or C.F. means that the price so includes cost and freight to the named destination.

(2) Unless otherwise agreed and even though used only in connection with the stated price and destination, the term C.I.F. destination or its equivalent requires the seller at his own expense and risk to

   (a) put the goods into the possession of a carrier at the port for shipment and obtain a negotiable bill or bills of lading covering the entire transportation to the named destination; and

   (b) load the goods and obtain a receipt from the carrier (which may be contained in the bill of lading) showing that the freight has been paid or provided for; and

   (c) obtain a policy or certificate of insurance, including any war risk insurance, of a kind and on terms then current at the port of shipment in the usual amount, in the currency of the contract, shown to cover the same goods covered by the bill of lading and providing for payment of loss to the order of the buyer or for the account of whom it may concern; but the seller may add to the price the amount of the premium for any such war risk insurance; and

(d) prepare an invoice of the goods and procure any other documents required to effect shipment or to comply with the contract; and

(e) forward and tender with commercial promptness all the documents in due form and with any indorsement necessary to perfect the buyer's rights.

(3) Unless otherwise agreed, the term C. & F. or its equivalent has the same effect and imposes upon the seller the same obligations and risks as a C.I.F. term except the obligation as to insurance.

(4) Under the term C.I.F. or C. & F., unless otherwise agreed the buyer must make payment against tender of the required documents and the seller may not tender nor the buyer demand delivery of the goods in substitution for the documents.

## § 2-321. C.I.F. or C. & F.: "Net Landed Weights"; "Payment on Arrival"; Warranty of Condition on Arrival

Under a contract containing a term C.I.F. or C. & F.

(1) Where the price is based on or is to be adjusted according to "net landed weights," "delivered weights," "out turn" quantity or quality or the like, unless otherwise agreed the seller must reasonably estimate the price. The payment due on tender of the documents called for by the contract is the amount so estimated, but after final adjustment of the price a settlement must be made with commercial promptness.

(2) An agreement described in subsection (1) or any warranty of quality or condition of the goods on arrival places upon the seller the risk of ordinary deterioration, shrinkage and the like in transportation but has no effect on the place or time of identification to the contract for sale or delivery or on the passing of the risk of loss.

(3) Unless otherwise agreed, where the contract provides for payment on or after arrival of the goods the seller must before payment allow such preliminary inspection as is feasible; but if the goods are lost, delivery of the documents and payment are due when the goods should have arrived.

## § 2-322. Delivery "Ex-Ship"

(1) Unless otherwise agreed, a term for delivery of goods "ex-ship" (which means from the carrying vessel) or in equivalent language is not restricted to a particular ship and requires delivery from a ship which has reached a place at the named port of destination where goods of the kind are usually discharged.

(2) Under such a term, unless otherwise agreed

(a) the seller must discharge all liens arising out of the carriage and furnish the buyer with a direction which puts the carrier under a duty to deliver the goods; and

(b) the risk of loss does not pass to the buyer until the goods leave the ship's tackle or are otherwise properly unloaded.

## § 2-323. Form of Bill of Lading Required in Overseas Shipment; "Overseas"

(1) Where the contract contemplates overseas shipment and contains a term C.I.F. or C. & F. or F.O.B. vessel, the seller unless otherwise agreed must obtain a negotiable bill of lading stating that the goods have been loaded on board or, in the case of a term C.I.F. or C. & F., received for shipment.

(2) Where in a case within subsection (1) a bill of lading has been issued in a set of parts, unless otherwise agreed, if the documents are not to be sent from abroad the buyer may demand tender of the full set; otherwise only one part of the bill of lading need be tendered. Even if the agreement expressly requires a full set

(a) due tender of a single part is acceptable within the provisions of this Article on cure of improper delivery (subsection (1) of Section 2-508); and

(b) even though the full set is demanded, if the documents are sent from abroad the person tendering an incomplete set may nevertheless require payment upon furnishing an indemnity which the buyer in good faith deems adequate.

(3) A shipment by water or by air or a contract contemplating such shipment is "overseas" insofar as by usage of trade or agreement it is subject to the commercial, financing or shipping practices characteristic of international deep water commerce.

## § 2-324. "No Arrival, No Sale" Term

Under a term "no arrival, no sale" or terms of like meaning, unless otherwise agreed,

    (a) the seller must properly ship conforming goods and if they arrive by any means he must tender them on arrival but he assumes no obligation that the goods will arrive unless he has caused the non-arrival; and

    (b) where without fault of the seller the goods are in part lost or have so deteriorated as no longer to conform to the contract or arrive after the contract time, the buyer may proceed as if there had been casualty to identified goods (Section 2-613).

## § 2-325. "Letter of Credit" Term; "Confirmed Credit"

(1) Failure of the buyer seasonably to furnish an agreed letter of credit is a breach of the contract for sale.

(2) The delivery to seller of a proper letter of credit suspends the buyer's obligation to pay. If the letter of credit is dishonored, the seller may on seasonable notification to the buyer require payment directly from him.

(3) Unless otherwise agreed the term "letter of credit" or "banker's credit" in a contract for sale means an irrevocable credit issued by a financing agency of good repute and, where the shipment is overseas, of good international repute. The term "confirmed credit" means that the credit must also carry the direct obligation of such an agency which does business in the seller's financial market.

# Part Five: Performance

## § 2-503. Manner of Seller's Tender of Delivery

(1) Tender of delivery requires that the seller put and hold conforming goods at the buyer's disposition and give the buyer any notification reasonably necessary to enable him to take delivery. The manner, time and place for tender are determined by the agreement and this Article, and in particular

    (a) tender must be at a reasonable hour, and if it is of goods they must be kept available for the period reasonably necessary to enable the buyer to take possession; but

    (b) Unless otherwise agreed the buyer must furnish facilities reasonably suited to the receipt of the goods.

(2) Where the case is within the next section respecting shipment tender requires that the seller comply with its provisions.

(3) Where the seller is required to deliver at a particular destination tender requires that he comply with subsection (1) and also in any appropriate case tender documents as described in subsections (4) and (5) of this section.

(4) Where goods are in the possession of a bailee and are to be delivered without being moved

    (a) tender requires that the seller either tender a negotiable document of title covering such goods or procure acknowledgment by the bailee of the buyer's right to possession of the goods; but

    (b) tender to the buyer of a non-negotiable document of title or of a written direction to the bailee to deliver is sufficient tender unless the buyer seasonably objects, and receipt by the bailee of notification of the buyer's rights fixes those rights as against the bailee and all third persons; but risk of loss of the goods and of any failure by the bailee to honor the nonnegotiable document of title or to obey the direction remains on the seller until the buyer has had a reasonable time to present the document or direction, and a refusal by the bailee to honor the document or to obey the direction defeats the tender.

(5) Where the contract requires the seller to deliver documents

    (a) he must tender all such documents in correct form, except as provided in this Article with respect to bills of lading in a set (subsection (2) of Section 2-323); and

    (b) tender through customary banking channels is sufficient and dishonor of a draft accompanying the documents constitutes nonacceptance or rejection.

## § 2-504. Shipment by Seller

Where the seller is required or authorized to send the goods to the buyer and the contract does not require him to deliver them at a particular destination, then unless otherwise agreed he must

    (a) put the goods in the possession of such a carrier and make such a contract for their transportation as may be reasonable having regard to the nature of the goods and other circumstances of the case; and

(b) obtain and promptly deliver or tender in due form any document necessary to enable the buyer to obtain possession of the goods or otherwise required by the agreement or by usage of trade; and

(c) promptly notify the buyer of the shipment. Failure to notify the buyer under paragraph (c) or to make a proper contract under paragraph (a) is a ground for rejection only if material delay or loss ensues.

## § 2-505. Seller's Shipment Under Reservation

(1) Where the seller has identified goods to the contract by or before shipment

(a) his procurement of a negotiable bill of lading to his own order or otherwise reserves in him a security interest in the goods. His procurement of the bill to the order of a financing agency or of the buyer indicates in addition only the seller's expectation of transferring that interest to the person named.

(b) a nonnegotiable bill of lading to himself or his nominee reserves possession of the goods as security but except in a case of conditional delivery (subsection (2) of Section 2-507) a nonnegotiable bill of lading naming the buyer as consignee reserves no security interest even though the seller retains possession of the bill of lading.

(2) When shipment by the seller with reservation of a security interest is in violation of the contract for sale it constitutes an improper contract for transportation within the preceding section but impairs neither the rights given to the buyer by shipment and identification of the goods to the contract nor the seller's powers as a holder of a negotiable document.

## § 2-506. Rights of Financing Agency

(1) A financing agency by paying or purchasing for value a draft which relates to a shipment of goods acquires to the extent of the payment or purchase and in addition to its own rights under the draft and any document of title securing it any rights of the shipper in the goods including the right to stop delivery and the shipper's right to have the draft honored by the buyer.

(2) The right to reimbursement of a financing agency which has in good faith honored or purchased the draft under commitment to or authority from the buyer is not impaired by subsequent discovery of defects with reference to any relevant document which was apparently regular on its face.

## § 2-507. Effect of Seller's Tender; Delivery on Condition

(1) Tender of delivery is a condition to the buyer's duty to accept the goods and, unless otherwise agreed, to his duty to pay for them. Tender entitles the seller to acceptance of the goods and to payment according to the contract.

(2) Where payment is due and demanded on the delivery to the buyer of goods or documents of title, his right as against the seller to retain or dispose of them is conditional upon his making the payment due.

## § 2-508. Cure by Seller of Improper Tender or Delivery; Replacement

(1) Where any tender or delivery by the seller is rejected because non-conforming and the time for performance has not yet expired, the seller may seasonably notify the buyer of his intention to cure and may then within the contract time make a conforming delivery.

(2) Where the buyer rejects a non-conforming tender which the seller had reasonable grounds to believe would be acceptable with or without money allowance the seller may if he seasonably notifies the buyer have a further reasonable time to substitute a conforming tender.

## § 2-509. Risk of Loss in the Absence of Breach

(1) Where the contract requires or authorizes the seller to ship the goods by carrier

(a) if it does not require him to deliver them at a particular destination, the risk of loss passes to the buyer when the goods are duly delivered to the carrier even though the shipment is under reservation (Section 2-505); but

(b) if it does require him to deliver them at a particular destination and the goods are there duly tendered while in the possession of the carrier, the risk of loss passes to the buyer when the goods are there duly so tendered as to enable the buyer to take delivery.

(2) Where the goods are held by a bailee to be delivered without being moved, the risk of loss passes to the buyer

(a) on his receipt of a negotiable document of title covering the goods; or

(b) on acknowledgment by the bailee of the buyer's right to possession of the goods; or

(c) after his receipt of a nonnegotiable document of title or other written direction to deliver, as provided in subsection (4)(b) of Section 2-503.

(3) In any case not within subsection (1) or (2), the risk of loss passes to the buyer on his receipt of the goods if the seller is a merchant; otherwise the risk passes to the buyer on tender of delivery.

(4) The provisions of this section are subject to contrary agreement of the parties and to the provision of this Article on sale on approval (Section 2-327) and on effect of breach on risk of loss (Section 2-510).

## § 2-510. Effect of Breach on Risk of Loss

(1) Where a tender or delivery of goods so fails to conform to the contract as to give a right of rejection, the risk of their loss remains on the seller until cure or acceptance.

(2) Where the buyer rightfully revokes acceptance, he may to the extent of any deficiency in his effective insurance coverage treat the risk of loss as having rested on the seller from the beginning.

(3) Where the buyer, as to conforming goods already identified to the contract for sale, repudiates or is otherwise in breach before risk of their loss has passed to him, the seller may to the extent of any deficiency in his effective insurance coverage treat the risk of loss as resting on the buyer for a commercially reasonable time.

## § 2-513. Buyer's Right to Inspection of Goods

(1) Unless otherwise agreed and subject to subsection (3), where goods are tendered or delivered or identified to the contract for sale, the buyer has a right before payment or acceptance to inspect them at any reasonable place and time and in any reasonable manner. When the seller is required or authorized to send the goods to the buyer, the inspection may be after their arrival.

(2) Expenses of inspection must be borne by the buyer but may be recovered from the seller if the goods do not conform and are rejected.

(3) Unless otherwise agreed and subject to the provisions of this Article on C.I.F. contracts (subsection (3) of Section 2-321), the buyer is not entitled to inspect the goods before payment of the price when the contract provides

(a) for delivery "C.O.D." or on other like terms; or

(b) for payment against documents of title, except where such payment is due only after the goods are to become available for inspection.

(4) A place or method of inspection fixed by the parties is presumed to be exclusive but, unless otherwise expressly agreed, it does not postpone identification or shift the place for delivery or for passing the risk of loss. If compliance becomes impossible, inspection shall be as provided in this section unless the place or method fixed was clearly intended as an indispensable condition, failure of which avoids the contract.

## § 2-514. When Documents Deliverable on Acceptance; When on Payment

Unless otherwise agreed, documents against which a draft is drawn are to be delivered to the drawee on acceptance of the draft if it is payable more than three days after presentment; otherwise, only on payment.

*Appendix E*

# INCOTERMS (1990)*

## EXW: EX WORKS (. . . named place)

*Ex works* means that the seller fulfills his obligation to deliver when he has made the goods available at his premises (i.e. works, factory, warehouse, etc.) to the buyer. In particular, he is not responsible for loading the goods on the vehicle provided by the buyer or for clearing the goods for export, unless otherwise agreed. The buyer bears all costs and risks involved in taking the goods from the seller's premises to the desired destination. This term thus represents the minimum obligation for the seller. This term should not be used when the buyer cannot carry out directly or indirectly the export formalities. In such circumstances, the FCA term should be used.

## FCA: Free Carrier (. . . named place)

*Free Carrier* means that the seller fulfills his obligation to deliver when he has handed over the goods, cleared for export, into the charge of the carrier named by the buyer at the named place or point. If no precise point is indicated by the buyer, the seller may choose within the place or range stipulated where the carrier shall take the goods into his charge. When, according to commercial practice, the seller's assistance is required in making the contract with the carrier (such as in rail or air transport) the seller may act at the buyer's risk and expense.

This term may be used for any mode of transport, including multimodal transport.

*Carrier* means any person who, in a contract of carriage, undertakes to perform or to procure the performance of carriage by rail, road, sea, air, inland waterway or by a combination of such modes. If the buyer instructs the seller to deliver the cargo to a person, e.g. a freight forwarder who is not a carrier, the seller is deemed to have fulfilled his obligation to deliver the goods when they are in the custody of that person.

*Transport terminal* means a railway terminal, a freight station, a container terminal or yard, a multi-purpose cargo terminal or any similar receiving point.

*Container* includes any equipment used to unitise cargo, e.g. all types of containers and/or flats, whether ISO accepted or not, trailers, swap bodies, ro-ro equipment, igloos, and applies to all modes of transport.

## FAS: Free Alongside Ship (. . . named port of shipment)

*Free Alongside Ship* means that the seller fulfills his obligation to deliver when the goods have been placed alongside the vessel on the quay or in lighters at the named port of shipment. This means that the buyer has to bear all costs and risks of loss of or damage to the goods from that moment.

The FAS term requires the buyer to clear the goods for export. It should not be used when the buyer cannot carry out directly or indirectly the export formalities.

This term can only be used for sea or inland waterway transport.

## FOB: Free on Board (. . . named port of shipment)

*Free on Board* means that the seller fulfills his obligation to deliver when the goods have passed over the ship's rail at the named port of shipment. This means that the buyer has to bear all costs and risks of loss of or damage to the goods from that point.

The FOB term requires the seller to clear the goods for export. This term can only be used for sea or inland waterway transport. When the ship's rail serves no practical purpose, such as in the case of roll-on/roll-off or container traffic, the FCA term is more appropriate to use.

# CFR: Cost and Freight (. . . named port of destination)

*Cost and Freight* means that the seller must pay the costs and freight necessary to bring the goods to the named port of destination but the risk of loss of or damage to the goods, as well as any additional costs due to events occurring after the time the goods have been delivered on board the vessel, is transferred from the seller to the buyer when the goods pass the ship's rail in the port of shipment.

The CFR term requires the seller to clear the goods for export. This term can only be used for sea and inland waterway transport. When the ship's rail serves no practical purpose, such as in the case of roll-on/roll-off or container traffic, the CPT term is more appropriate to use.

# CIF: Cost, Insurance and Freight (. . . named port of destination)

*Cost, Insurance and Freight* means that the seller has the same obligations as under CFR but with the addition that he has to procure marine insurance against the buyer's risk of loss of or damage to the goods during the carriage. The seller contracts for insurance and pays the insurance premium.

The buyer should note that under the CIF term the seller is only required to obtain insurance on minimum coverage.

The CIF term requires the seller to clear the goods for export. This term can only be used for sea and inland waterway transport. When the ship's rail serves no practical purposes such as in the case of roll-on/roll-off or container traffic, the CIP term is more appropriate to use.

# CPT: Carriage Paid to (. . . named place of destination)

*Carriage Paid to* means that the seller pays the freight for the carriage of the goods to the named destination. The risk of loss of or damage to the goods, as well as any additional costs due to events occurring after the time the goods have been delivered to the carrier, is transferred from the seller to the buyer when the goods have been delivered into the custody of the carrier.

*Carrier* means any person who, in a contract of carriage, undertakes to perform or to procure the performance of carriage, by rail, road, sea, air, inland waterway or by a combination of such modes.

If subsequent carriers are used for the carriage to the agreed destination, the risk passes when the goods have been delivered to the first carrier.

The CPT term requires the seller to clear the goods for export. This term may be used for any mode of transport including multimodal transport.

# CIP: Carriage and Insurance Paid to (. . . named place of destination)

*Carriage and Insurance Paid to* (. . .) means that the seller has the same obligations as under CPT but with the addition that the seller has to procure cargo insurance against the buyer's risk of loss of or damage to the goods during the carriage. The seller contracts for insurance and pays the insurance premium.

The buyer should note that under the CIP term the seller is only required to obtain insurance on minimum coverage.

The CIP term requires the seller to clear the goods for export. This term may be used for any mode of transport including multimodal transport.

# DAF: Delivered at Frontier (. . . named place)

*Delivered at frontier* means that the seller fulfills his obligation to deliver when the goods have been made available, cleared for export, at the named point and place at the frontier, but before the customs border of the adjoining country. The term *frontier* may be used for any frontier including that of the country of export. Therefore, it is of vital importance that the frontier in question be defined precisely by always naming the point and place in the term. The term is primarily intended to be used when goods are to be carried by rail or road, but it may be used for any mode of transport.

# DES: Delivered Ex Ship (. . . named port of destination)

*Delivered Ex Ship* means that the seller fulfills his obligation to deliver when the goods have been made available to the buyer on board the ship uncleared for import at the named port of destination. The seller has to bear all the costs and risks involved in bringing the goods to the named port of destination. This term can only be used for sea or inland waterway transport.

## DEQ: Delivered Ex Quay (Duty Paid) (. . . named port of destination)

*Delivered Ex Quay (duty paid)* means that the seller fulfills his obligation to deliver when he has made the goods available to the buyer on the quay (wharf) at the named port of destination, cleared for importation. The seller has to bear all risks and costs including duties, taxes and other charges of delivering the goods thereto.

This term should not be used if the seller is unable directly or indirectly to obtain the import licence.

If the parties wish the buyer to clear the goods for importation and pay the duty the words *duty unpaid* should be used instead of *duty paid.*

If the parties wish to exclude from the seller's obligations some of the costs payable upon importation of the goods (such as value added tax (VAT)), this should be made clear by adding words to this effect: *Delivered ex quay, VAT unpaid (. . . named port of destination).*

This term can only be used for sea or inland waterway transport.

## DDU: Delivered Duty Unpaid (. . . named place of destination)

*Delivered duty unpaid* means that the seller fulfills his obligation to deliver when the goods have been made available at the named place in the country of importation. The seller has to bear the costs and risks involved in bringing the goods thereto (excluding duties, taxes and other official charges payable upon importation as well as the costs and risks of carrying out customs formalities). The buyer has to pay any additional costs and to bear any risks caused by his failure to clear the goods for import in time.

If the parties wish the seller to carry out customs formalities and bear the costs and risks resulting therefrom, this has to be made clear by adding words to this effect.

If the parties wish to include in the seller's obligations some of the costs payable upon importation of the goods (such as value added tax (VAT)), this should be made clear by adding words to this effect: *Delivered duty unpaid, VAT paid, (. . . named place of destination).*

This term may be used irrespective of the mode of transport.

## DDP: Delivered Duty Paid (. . . named place of destination)

*Delivered duty paid* means that the seller fulfils his obligation to deliver when the goods have been made available at the named place in the country of importation. The seller has to bear the risks and costs, including duties, taxes and other charges of delivering the goods thereto, cleared for importation. Whilst the EXW term represents the minimum obligation for the seller, DDP represents the maximum obligation.

This term should not be used if the seller is unable directly or indirectly to obtain the import licence.

If the parties wish the buyer to clear the goods for importation and to pay the duty, the term DDU should be used.

If the parties wish to exclude from the seller's obligations some of the costs payable upon importation of the goods (such as value added tax (VAT)), this should be made clear by adding words to this effect: *Delivered duty paid, VAT unpaid (. . . named place of destination).*

This term may be used irrespective of the mode of transport.

# Appendix F

# The General Agreement on Tariffs and Trade[1]

*55 U.N.T.S. 194 (1947)*
*(Selected Provisions)*

## Part One:

### Article I
*General Most-Favoured-Nation Treatment*

1. With respect to customs duties and charges of any kind imposed on or in connection with importation or exportation or imposed on the international transfer of payments for imports or exports, and with respect to the method of levying such duties and charges, and with respect to all rules and formalities in connection with importation and exportation, and with respect to all matters referred to in paragraphs 2 and 4 of Article III, any advantage, favour, privilege or immunity granted by any contracting party to any product originating in or destined for any other country shall be accorded immediately and unconditionally to the like product originating in or destined for the territories of all other contracting parties.

\* \* \*

### Article II
*Schedules of Concessions*

1. (a) Each contracting party shall accord to the commerce of the other contracting parties treatment no less favourable than that provided for in the appropriate Part of the appropriate Schedule annexed to this Agreement.

   (b) The products described in Part I of the Schedule relating to any contracting party, which are the products of territories of other contracting parties, shall, on their importation into the territory to which the Schedule relates, and subject to the terms, conditions or qualifications set forth in that Schedule, be exempt from ordinary customs duties in excess of those set forth and provided for therein. Such products shall also be exempt from all other duties or charges of any kind imposed on or in connection with importation in excess of those imposed on the date of this Agreement or those directly and mandatorily required to be imposed thereafter by legislation in force in the importing territory on that date.

## Part Two:

### Article III
*National Treatment on Internal Taxation and Regulation*

1. The contracting parties recognize that internal taxes and other internal charges, and laws, regulations and requirements affecting the internal sale, offering for sale, purchase, transportation, distribution or use of products, and internal quantitative regulations requiring the mixture, processing or use of products in specified amounts or proportions, should not be applied to imported or domestic products so as to afford protection to domestic production.

2. The products of the territory of any contracting party imported into the territory of any other contracting party shall not be subject, directly or indirectly, to internal taxes or other internal charges of any kind in excess of those applied, directly or indirectly, to like domestic products. Moreover, no contracting party shall otherwise apply internal taxes or other internal charges to imported or domestic products in a manner contrary to the principles set forth in paragraph 1.

\* \* \*

4. The products of the territory of any contracting party imported into the territory of any other contracting party shall be accorded treatment no less favourable than that accorded to like products of

---

[1]All references to "Contracting Parties" now refers to Members of the World Trade Organization.

national origin in respect of all laws, regulations and requirements affecting their internal sale, offering for sale, purchase, transportation, distribution or use. The provisions of this paragraph shall not prevent the application of differential internal transportation charges which are based exclusively on the economic operation of the means of transport and not on the nationality of the product.

5. No contracting party shall establish or maintain any internal quantitative regulation relating to the mixture, processing or use of products in specified amounts or proportions which requires, directly or indirectly, that any specified amount or proportion of any product which is the subject of the regulation must be supplied from domestic sources. Moreover, no contracting party shall otherwise apply internal quantitative regulations in a manner contrary to the principles set forth in paragraph 1.

* * *

7. No internal quantitative regulation relating to the mixture, processing or use of products in specified amounts or proportions shall be applied in such a manner as to allocate any such amount of proportion among external sources of supply.

8. (a) The provisions of this Article shall not apply to laws, regulations or requirements governing the procurement by governmental agencies of products purchased for governmental purposes and not with a view to commercial resale or with a view to use in the production of goods for commercial sale.

   (b) The provisions of this article shall not prevent the payment of subsidies exclusively to domestic producers, including payments to domestic producers derived from the proceeds of internal taxes or charges applied consistently with the provisions of this Article and subsidies effected through governmental purchases of domestic products.

* * *

## Article VI
### Anti-dumping and Countervailing Duties

1. The contracting parties recognize that dumping, by which products of one country are introduced into the commerce of another country at less than the normal value of the products, is to be condemned if it causes or threatens material injury to an established industry in the territory of a contracting party or materially retards the establishment of a domestic industry. For the purposes of this Article, a product is to be considered as being introduced into the commerce of an importing country at less than its normal value, if the price of the product exported from one country to another

   (a) is less than the comparable price, in the ordinary course of trade, for the like product when destined for consumption in the exporting country, or,

   (b) in the absence of such domestic price, is less than either

      (i) the highest comparable price for the like product for export to any third country in the ordinary course of trade, or

      (ii) the cost of production of the product in the country of origin plus a reasonable addition for selling cost and profit.

   Due allowance shall be made in each case for differences in conditions and terms of sale, for differences in taxation, and for other differences affecting price comparability.

2. In order to offset or prevent dumping, a contracting party may levy on any dumped product an anti-dumping duty not greater in amount than the margin of dumping in respect of such product. For the purposes of this Article, the margin of dumping is the price difference determined in accordance with the provisions of paragraph 1.

3. No countervailing duty shall be levied on any product of the territory of any contracting party imported into the territory of another contracting party in excess of an amount equal to the estimated bounty or subsidy determined to have been granted, directly or indirectly, on the manufacture, production or export of such product in the country of origin or exportation, including any special subsidy to the transportation of a particular product. The term 'countervailing duty' shall be understood to mean a special duty levied for the purpose of offsetting any bounty or subsidy bestowed, directly or indirectly, upon the manufacture, production or export of any merchandise.

4. No product of the territory of any contracting party imported into the territory of any other contracting party shall be subject to antidumping or countervailing duty by reason of the exemption of such product from duties or taxes borne by the like product when destined for consumption in the country of origin or exportation, or by reason of the refund of such duties or taxes.

5. No product of the territory of any contracting party imported into the territory of any other contracting party shall be subject to both anti-dumping and countervailing duties to compensate for the same situation of dumping or export subsidization.

6. (a) No contracting party shall levy any anti-dumping or countervailing duty on the im-

portation of any product of the territory of another contracting party unless it determines that the effect of the dumping or subsidization, as the case may be, is such as to cause or threaten material injury to an established domestic industry, or is such as to retard materially the establishment of a domestic industry.

\* \* \*

## Article VII
### Valuation for Customs Purposes

1. The contracting parties recognize the validity of the general principles of valuation set forth in the following paragraphs of this Article, and they undertake to give effect to such principles, in respect of all products subject to duties or other charges or restrictions on importation and exportation based upon or regulated in any manner by value. Moreover, they shall, upon a request by another contracting party review the operation of any of their laws or regulations relating to value for customs purposes in the light of these principles. The CONTRACTING PARTIES may request from contracting parties reports on steps taken by them in pursuance of the provisions of this Article.

2. (a) The value for customs purposes of imported merchandise should be based on the actual value of the imported merchandise on which duty is assessed, or of like merchandise, and should not be based on the value of merchandise of national origin or on arbitrary or fictitious values.

   (b) "Actual value" should be the price at which, at a time and place determined by the legislation of the country of importation, such or like merchandise is sold or offered for sale in the ordinary course of trade under fully competitive conditions. To the extent to which the price of such or like merchandise is governed by the quantity in a particular transaction, the price to be considered should uniformly be related to either (i) comparable quantities, or (ii) quantities not less favourable to importers than those in which the greater volume of the merchandise is sold in the trade between the countries of exportation and importation.

   (c) When the actual value is not ascertainable in accordance with subparagraph (b) of this paragraph, the value for customs purposes should be based on the nearest ascertainable equivalent of such value.

\* \* \*

## Article VIII
### Fees and Formalities Connected with Importation and Exportation

1. (a) All fees and charges of whatever character (other than import and export duties and other than taxes within the purview of Article III) imposed by contracting parties on or in connexion with importation or exportation shall be limited in amount to the approximate cost of services rendered and shall not represent an indirect protection to domestic products or a taxation or imports or exports for fiscal purposes.

   (b) The contracting parties recognize the need for reducing the number and diversity of fees and charges referred to in sub-paragraph (a).

   (c) The contracting parties also recognize the need for minimizing the incidence and complexity of import and export formalities and for decreasing and simplifying import and export documentation requirements.

2. A contracting party shall, upon request by another contracting party or by the CONTRACTING PARTIES, review the operation of its laws and regulations in the light of the provisions of this Article.

3. No contracting party shall impose substantial penalties for minor breaches of customs regulations or procedural requirements. In particular, no penalty in respect of any omission or mistake in customs documentation which is easily rectifiable and obviously made without fraudulent intent or gross negligence shall be greater than necessary to serve merely as a warning.

4. The provisions of this Article shall extend to fees, charges, formalities and requirements imposed by governmental authorities in connexion with importation and exportation, including those relating to:

   (a) consular transactions, such as consular invoices and certificates;

   (b) quantitative restrictions;

   (c) licensing;

   (d) exchange control;

   (e) statistical services;

   (f) documents, documentation and certification;

   (g) analysis and inspection; and

   (h) quarantine, sanitation and fumigation.

## Article IX
### Marks of Origin

1. Each contracting party shall accord to the products of the territories of other contracting parties treatment with regard to marking requirements no less favourable than the treatment accorded to like products of any third country.

2. The contracting parties recognize that, in adopting and enforcing laws and regulations relating to marks of origin, the difficulties and inconveniences which such measures may cause to the commerce and industry of exporting countries should be reduced to a minimum, due regard being had to the necessity of protecting consumers against fraudulent or misleading indications.

3. Whenever it is administratively practicable to do so, contracting parties should permit required marks of origin to be affixed at the time of importation.

4. The laws and regulations of contracting parties relating to the marking of imported products shall be such as to permit compliance without seriously damaging the products, or materially reducing their value, or unreasonably increasing their cost.

5. As a general rule, no special duty or penalty should be imposed by any contracting party for failure to comply with marking requirements prior to importation unless corrective marking is unreasonably delayed or deceptive marks have been affixed or the required marking has been intentionally omitted.

6. The contracting parties shall co-operate with each other with a view to preventing the use of trade names in such manner as to misrepresent the true origin of a product, to the detriment of such distinctive regional or geographical names of products of the territory of a contracting party as are protected by its legislation. Each contracting party shall accord full and sympathetic consideration to such requests or representations as may be made by any other contracting party regarding the application of the undertaking set forth in the preceding sentence to names of products which have been communicated to it by the other contracting party.

## Article X
### Publication and Administration of Trade Regulations

1. Laws, regulations, judicial decisions and administrative rulings of general application, made effective by any contracting party, pertaining to the classification or the valuation of products for customs purposes, or to rates of duty, taxes or other charges, or to requirements, restrictions or prohibitions on imports or exports or on the transfer of payments therefor, or affecting their sale, distribution, transportation, insurance, warehousing, inspection, exhibition, processing, mixing or other use, shall be published promptly in such a manner as to enable governments and traders to become acquainted with them. Agreements affecting international trade policy which are in force between the government or a governmental agency of any contracting party and the government or governmental agency of any other contracting party shall also be published. The provisions of this paragraph shall not require any contracting party to disclose confidential information which would impede law enforcement or otherwise be contrary to the public interest or would prejudice the legitimate commercial interests of particular enterprises, public or private.

\* \* \*

## Article XI
### General Elimination of Quantitative Restrictions

1. No prohibitions or restrictions other than duties, taxes or other charges, whether made effective through quotas, import or export licences or other measures, shall be instituted or maintained by any contracting party on the importation of any product of the territory of any other contracting party or on the exportation or sale for export of any product destined for the territory of any other contracting party.

\* \* \*

## Article XII
### Restrictions to Safeguard the Balance of Payments

1. Notwithstanding the provisions of paragraph 1 of Article XI, any contracting party, in order to safeguard its external financial position and its balance of payments, may restrict the quantity or value of merchandise permitted to be imported, subject to the provisions of the following paragraphs of this Article.

2. (a) Import restrictions instituted, maintained or intensified by a contracting party under this Article shall not exceed those necessary:
   (i) to forestall the imminent threat of, or to stop, a serious decline in its monetary reserves, or
   (ii) in the case of a contracting party with very low monetary reserves, to achieve a reasonable rate of increase in its reserves.

\* \* \*

## Article XIII
### Non-discriminatory Administration of Quantitative Restrictions

1. No prohibition or restriction shall be applied by any contracting party on the importation of any product of the territory of any other contracting party or on the exportation of any product destined for the territory of any other contracting party, unless the importation of the like product of all third countries

or the exportation of the like product to all third countries is similarly prohibited or restricted.

\* \* \*

## Article XIX
### Emergency Action on Imports of Particular Products

1. (a) If, as a result of unforeseen developments, and of the effect of the obligations incurred by a contracting party under this Agreement, including tariff concessions, any product is being imported into the territory of that contracting party in such increased quantities and under such conditions as to cause or threaten serious injury to domestic producers in that territory of like or directly competitive products, the contracting party shall be free, in respect of such product, and to the extent and for such time as may be necessary to prevent or remedy such injury, to suspend the obligation in whole or in part or to withdraw or modify the concession.

\* \* \*

2. Before any contracting party shall take action pursuant to the provisions of paragraph 1 of this Article, it shall give notice in writing to the CONTRACTING PARTIES as far in advance as may be practicable and shall afford the CONTRACTING PARTIES and those contracting parties having a substantial interest as exporters of the product concerned an opportunity to consult with it in respect of the proposed action. When such notice is given in relation to a concession with respect to a preference, the notice shall name the contracting party which has requested the action. In critical circumstances, where delay would cause damage which it would be difficult to repair, action under paragraph 1 of this Article may be taken provisionally without prior consultation, on the condition that consultation shall be effected immediately after taking such action.

\* \* \*

## Article XX
### General Exceptions

Subject to the requirement that such measures are not applied in a manner which would constitute a means of arbitrary or unjustifiable discrimination between countries where the same conditions prevail, or a disguised restriction on international trade, nothing in this Agreement shall be construed to prevent the adoption or enforcement by any contracting party of measures:

(a) necessary to protect public morals;
(b) necessary to protect human, animal or plant life or health;
(c) relating to the importation or exportation of gold or silver;
(d) necessary to secure compliance with laws or regulations which are not inconsistent with the provisions of this Agreement, including those relating to customs enforcement, the enforcement of monopolies operated under paragraph 4 of Article II and Article XVII, the protection of patents, trade marks and copyrights, and the prevention of deceptive practices;
(e) relating to the products of prison labour;
(f) imposed for the protection of national treasures of artistic, historic or archaeological value;
(g) relating to the conservation of exhaustible natural resources if such measures are made effective in conjunction with restrictions on domestic production or consumption;
(h) undertaken in pursuance of obligations under any intergovernmental commodity agreement which conforms to criteria submitted to the CONTRACTING PARTIES and not disapproved by them or which is itself so submitted and not so disapproved;
(i) involving restrictions on exports of domestic materials necessary to ensure essential quantities of such materials to a domestic processing industry during periods when the domestic price of such materials is held below the world price as PART of a governmental stabilization plan; Provided that such restrictions shall not operate to increase the exports of or the protection afforded to such domestic industry, and shall not depart from the provisions of this Agreement relating to non-discrimination;
(j) essential to the acquisition or distribution of products in general or local short supply;

\* \* \*

## Article XXII
### Consultation

1. Each contracting party shall accord sympathetic consideration to, and shall afford adequate opportunity for consultation regarding, such representations as may be made by another contracting party with respect to any matter affecting the operation of this Agreement.

\* \* \*

## Article XXIII
### Nullification or Impairment

1. If any contracting party should consider that any benefit accruing to it directly or indirectly under this Agreement is being nullified or impaired or that

the attainment of any objective of the Agreement is being impeded as the result of

(a) the failure of another contracting party to carry out its obligations under this Agreement, or

(b) the application by another contracting party of any measure, whether or not it conflicts with the provisions of this Agreement, or

(c) the existence of any other situation, the contracting party may, with a view to the satisfactory adjustment of the matter, make written representations or proposals to the other contracting party or parties which it considers to be concerned. Any contracting party thus approached shall give sympathetic consideration to the representations or proposals made to it.

2. If no satisfactory adjustment is effected between the contracting parties concerned within a reasonable time, or if the difficulty is of the type described in paragraph 1 (c) of this Article, the matter may be referred to the CONTRACTING PARTIES. The CONTRACTING PARTIES shall promptly investigate any matter so referred to them and shall make appropriate recommendations to the contracting parties which they consider to be concerned, or give a ruling on the matter, as appropriate. The CONTRACTING PARTIES may consult with contracting parties, with the Economic and Social Council of the United Nations and with any appropriate inter-governmental organization in cases where they consider such consultation necessary. If the CONTRACTING PARTIES consider that the circumstances are serious enough to justify such action, they may authorize a contracting party or parties to suspend the application to any other contracting party or parties of such concessions or other obligations under this Agreement as they determine to be appropriate in the circumstances. If the application to any contracting party of any concession or other obligation is in fact suspended, that contracting party shall then be free, not later than sixty days after such action is taken, to give written notice to the Executive Secretary to the CONTRACTING PARTIES of its intention to withdraw from this Agreement and such withdrawal shall take effect upon the sixtieth day following the day on which such notice is received by him.

# Part Three:

*Article XXIV*
*Territorial Application—Frontier Traffic—*
*Customs Unions and Free-trade Areas*

\* \* \*

4. The contracting parties recognize the desirability of increasing freedom of trade by the development, through voluntary agreements, of closer integration between the economies of the countries parties to such agreements. They also recognize that the purpose of a customs union or of a free-trade area should be to facilitate trade between the constituent territories and not to raise barriers to the trade of other contracting parties with such territories.

5. Accordingly, the provisions of this Agreement shall not prevent, as between the territories of contracting parties, the formation of a customs union or of a free-trade area or the adoption of an interim agreement necessary for the formation of a customs union or of a free-trade area; Provided that:

(a) with respect to a customs union, or an interim agreement leading to the formation of a customs union, the duties and other regulations of commerce imposed at the institution of any such union or interim agreement in respect of trade with contracting parties not parties to such union or agreement shall not on the whole be higher or more restrictive than the general incidence of the duties and regulations of commerce applicable in the constituent territories prior to the formation of such union or the adoption of such interim agreement, as the case may be;

(b) with respect to a free-trade area, or an interim agreement leading to the formation of a free-trade area, the duties and other regulations of commerce maintained in each of the constituent territories and applicable at the formation of such free-trade area or the adoption of such interim agreement to the trade of contracting parties not included in such area or not parties to such agreement shall not be higher or more restrictive than the corresponding duties and other regulations of commerce existing in the same constituent territories prior to the formation of the free-trade area, or interim agreement, as the case may be; and

\* \* \*

*Article XXVIII*
*Tariff Negotiations*

1. The contracting parties recognize that customs duties often constitute serious obstacles to trade; thus negotiations on a reciprocal and mutually advantageous basis, directed to the substantial reduction of the general level of tariffs and other charges on imports and exports and in particular to the reduction of such high tariffs as discourage the importation even of minimum quantities, and conducted with

due regard to the objectives of this Agreement and the varying needs of individual contracting parties, are of great importance to the expansion of international trade. The CONTRACTING PARTIES may therefore sponsor such negotiations from time to time.

2. (a) Negotiations under this Article may be carried out on a selective product-by-product basis or by the application of such multilateral procedures as may be accepted by the contracting parties concerned. Such negotiations may be directed towards the reduction of duties, the binding of duties at then existing levels or undertakings that individual duties or the average duties on specified categories of products shall not exceed specified levels. The binding against increase of low duties or of duty-free treatment shall, in principle, be recognized as a concession equivalent in value to the reduction of high duties.

\* \* \*

### Article XXXVII
### Commitments

1. The developed contracting parties shall to the fullest extent possible . . . (a) accord high priority to the reduction and elimination of barriers to products currently or potentially of particular export interest to less-developed contracting parties, including customs duties and other restrictions which differentiate unreasonably between such products in their primary and in their processed forms;

\* \* \*

# Agreement Establishing the World Trade Organization[1]

*General Agreement on Tariffs and Trade (Selected Provisions)*
*April 15, 1994*

*Article I*
*Establishment of the Organization*

The World Trade Organization (hereinafter referred to as "the WTO") is hereby established.

*Article II*
*Scope of the WTO*

1. The WTO shall provide the common institutional framework for the conduct of trade relations among its Members in matters related to the agreements and associated legal instruments included in the Annexes to this Agreement.

*Article III*
*Functions of the WTO*

1. The WTO shall facilitate the implementation, administration and operation, and further the objectives, of this Agreement and of the Multilateral Trade Agreements. . . .

*Article IV*
*Structure of the WTO*

1. There shall be a Ministerial Conference composed of representatives of all the Members, which shall meet at least once every two years. The Ministerial Conference shall carry out the functions of the WTO and take actions necessary to this effect. The Ministerial Conference shall have the authority to take decisions on all matters under any of the Multilateral Trade Agreements, if so requested by a Member, in accordance with the specific requirements for decision-making in this Agreement and in the relevant Multilateral Trade Agreement.
2. There shall be a General Council composed of representatives of all the Members, which shall meet as appropriate. In the intervals between meetings of the Ministerial Conference, its functions shall be conducted by the General Council. The General Council shall also carry out the functions assigned to it by this Agreement . . .
3. The General Council shall convene as appropriate to discharge the responsibilities of the Dispute Settlement Body provided for in the Dispute Settlement Understanding. The Dispute Settlement Body may have its own chairman and shall establish such rules of procedure as it deems necessary for the fulfilment of those responsibilities.
5. There shall be a Council for Trade in Goods, a Council for Trade in Services and a Council for Trade-Related Aspects of Intellectual Property Rights (hereinafter referred to as the "Council for TRIPS"), which shall operate under the general guidance of the General Council. The Council for Trade in Goods shall oversee the functioning of the Multilateral Trade Agreements in Annex 1A. The Council for Trade in Services shall oversee the functioning of the General Agreement on Trade in Services (hereinafter referred to as "GATS"). The Council for TRIPS shall oversee the functioning of the Agreement on Trade-Related Aspects of Intellectual Property Rights (hereinafter referred to as the "Agreement on TRIPS"). These Councils shall carry out the functions assigned to them by their respective agreements and by the General Council. They shall establish their respective rules of procedure subject to the approval of the General Council. Membership in these Councils shall be open to representatives of all Members. These Councils shall meet as necessary to carry out their functions.

---

[1]The Final Text of the GATT Uruguay Round Agreements as signed on April 15, 1994 at Marrakech, Morocco is available through the U.S. Government Printing Office, ISBN 0-16-045022-5.

*Article VI*
*The Secretariat*
1. There shall be a Secretariat of the WTO (hereinafter referred to as "the Secretariat") headed by a Director-General.
2. The Ministerial Conference shall appoint the Director-General and adopt regulations setting out the powers, duties, conditions of service and term of office of the Director-General.
4. The responsibilities of the Director-General and of the staff of the Secretariat shall be exclusively international in character. In the discharge of their duties, the Director-General and the staff of the Secretariat shall not seek or accept instructions from any government or any other authority external to the WTO.

*Article IX*
*Decision-Making*
1. The WTO shall continue the practice of decision-making by consensus followed under GATT 1947. Except as otherwise provided, where a decision cannot be arrived at by consensus, the matter at issue shall be decided by voting. At meetings of the Ministerial Conference and the General Council, each Member of the WTO shall have one vote. Where the European Communities exercise their right to vote, they shall have a number of votes equal to the number of their member States which are Members of the WTO. Decisions of the Ministerial Conference and the General Council shall be taken by a majority of the votes cast, unless otherwise provided in this Agreement or in the relevant Multilateral Trade Agreement.

*Article XI*
*Original Membership*
1. The contracting parties to GATT 1947 as of the date of entry into force of this Agreement, and the European Communities, which accept this Agreement and the Multilateral Trade Agreements and for which Schedules of Concessions and Commitments are annexed to GATT 1994 and for which Schedules of Specific Commitments are annexed to GATS shall become original Members of the WTO.

2. The least-developed countries recognized as such by the United Nations will only be required to undertake commitments and concessions to the extent consistent with their individual development, financial and trade needs or their administrative and institutional capabilities.

*Article XII*
*Accession*
1. Any State or separate customs territory possessing full autonomy in the conduct of its external commercial relations and of the other matters provided for in this Agreement and the Multilateral Trade Agreements may accede to this Agreement, on terms to be agreed between it and the WTO. Such accession shall apply to this Agreement and the Multilateral Trade Agreements annexed thereto.

*Article XIV*
*Acceptance, Entry into Force and Deposit*
1. This Agreement shall be open for acceptance, by signature or otherwise, by contracting parties to GATT 1947, and the European Communities, which are eligible to become original Members of the WTO in accordance with Article XI of this Agreement. Such acceptance shall apply to this Agreement and the Multilateral Trade Agreements annexed hereto.

*Article XVI*
*Miscellaneous Provisions*
1. Except as otherwise provided under this Agreement or the Multilateral Trade Agreements, the WTO shall be guided by the decisions, procedures and customary practices followed by the Contracting Parties to GATT 1947 and the bodies established in the framework of GATT 1947.
4. Each Member shall ensure the conformity of its laws, regulations and administrative procedures with its obligations as provided in the annexed Agreements.

DONE at Marrakesh this fifteenth day of April one thousand nine hundred and ninety-four, in a single copy, in the English, French and Spanish languages, each text being authentic.

# Multilateral Agreements on Trade in Goods (Selected Provisions)[1]

*General Agreement on Tariffs and Trade*
*April 15, 1994*

## General Agreement on Tariffs and Trade 1994

\* \* \*

1. The General Agreement on Tariffs and Trade 1994 ("GATT 1994") shall consist of:
   (a) the provisions in the General Agreement on Tariffs and Trade, dated 30 October 1947 . . . as amended or modified by the terms of legal instruments which have entered into force before the date of entry into force of the WTO Agreement;
   (b) the provisions of the legal instruments . . . that have entered into force under the GATT 1947 before the date of entry into force of the WTO Agreement:
      (i) protocols and certifications relating to tariff concessions;
      (iv) other decisions of the Contracting Parties to GATT 1947;
   (c) the Understandings [set forth in the Uruguay Round Agreements];
   (d) the Marrakesh Protocol to GATT 1994.
2. Explanatory Notes
   (a) The references to "contracting party" in the provisions of GATT 1994 shall be deemed to read "Member". . . .

## Understanding on Balance-of-Payments

\* \* \*

3. Members shall seek to avoid the imposition of new quantitative restrictions for balance-of-payments pur- poses unless, because of a critical balance-of-payments situation, price-based measures cannot arrest a sharp deterioration in the external payments position. In those cases in which a Member applies quantitative restrictions, it shall provide justification as to the reasons why price-based measures are not an adequate instrument to deal with the balance-of-payments situation. A Member maintaining quantitative restrictions shall indicate in successive consultations the progress made in significantly reducing the incidence and restrictive effect of such measures. It is understood that not more than one type of restrictive import measure taken for balance-of-payments purposes may be applied on the same product.
4. Members confirm that restrictive import measures taken for balance-of-payments purposes may only be applied to control the general level of imports and may not exceed what is necessary to address the balance-of-payments situation. In order to minimize any incidental protective effects, a Member shall administer restrictions in a transparent manner. The authorities of the importing Member shall provide adequate justification as to the criteria used to determine which products are subject to restriction. . . .

## Marrakesh Protocol to GATT 1994

\* \* \*

2. The tariff reductions agreed upon by each Member shall be implemented in five equal rate reductions, except as may be otherwise specified in a Member's Schedule. The first such reduction shall be made effective on the date of entry into force of the WTO Agreement, each successive reduction shall be made effective on 1 January of each of the following

---

[1]Certain complex agreements have not been included here. They include the Subsidies Agreement, the Agreement on Agriculture, the Agreement on Rules of Origin, and the Understanding on Rules and Procedures Governing the Settlement of Disputes.

years, and the final rate shall become effective no later than the date four years after the date of entry into force of the WTO Agreement, except as may be otherwise specified in that Member's Schedule.

3. The implementation of the concessions and commitments contained in the schedules annexed to this Protocol shall, upon request, be subject to multilateral examination by the Members.

# Agreement on the Application of Sanitary and Phytosanitary Measures

\* \* \*

1.1. This Agreement applies to all sanitary and phytosanitary measures which may, directly or indirectly, affect international trade.

2.1. Members have the right to take sanitary and phytosanitary measures necessary for the protection of human, animal or plant life or health, provided that such measures are not inconsistent with the provisions of this Agreement.

2.2. Members shall ensure that any sanitary or phytosanitary measure is applied only to the extent necessary to protect human, animal or plant life or health, is based on scientific principles and is not maintained without sufficient scientific evidence. . . .

2.3. Members shall ensure that their sanitary and phytosanitary measures do not arbitrarily or unjustifiably discriminate between Members where identical or similar conditions prevail, including between their own territory and that of other Members. Sanitary and phytosanitary measures shall not be applied in a manner which would constitute a disguised restriction on international trade.

5.2. In the assessment of risks, Members shall take into account available scientific evidence; relevant processes and production methods; relevant inspection, sampling and testing methods; prevalence of specific diseases or pests; existence of pest- or disease-free areas; relevant ecological and environmental conditions; and quarantine or other treatment.

# Agreement on Textiles and Clothing

\* \* \*

1.1. This Agreement sets out provisions to be applied by Members during a transition period for the integration of the textiles and clothing sector into GATT 1994.

2.1. All quantitative restrictions within bilateral agreements maintained under the MFA . . . shall . . . be notified in detail, including the restraint levels, growth rates and flexibility provisions, by the Members maintaining such restrictions to the Textiles Monitoring Body provided for [herein]. Members agree that as of the date of entry into force of the WTO Agreement, all such restrictions maintained between GATT 1947 contracting parties, and in place on the day before such entry into force, shall be governed by the provisions of this Agreement.

5.1. Members agree that circumvention by transshipment, re-routing, false declaration concerning country or place of origin, and falsification of official documents, frustrates the implementation of this Agreement to integrate the textiles and clothing sector into GATT 1994. Accordingly, Members should establish the necessary legal provisions and/or administrative procedures to address and take action against such circumvention. Members further agree that, consistent with their domestic laws and procedures, they will cooperate fully to address problems arising from circumvention.

5.6. Members agree that false declaration concerning fibre content, quantities, description or classification of merchandise also frustrates the objective of this Agreement. Where there is evidence that any such false declaration has been made for purposes of circumvention, Members agree that appropriate measures, consistent with domestic laws and procedures, should be taken against the exporters or importers involved.

# Agreement on Technical Barriers to Trade

\* \* \*

2.1. Members shall ensure that in respect of technical regulations, products imported from the territory of any Member shall be accorded treatment no less favourable than that accorded to like products of national origin and to like products originating in any other country.

2.2. Members shall ensure that technical regulations are not prepared, adopted or applied with a view to or with the effect of creating unnecessary obstacles to international trade. For this purpose, technical regulations shall not be more trade-restrictive than necessary to fulfil a legitimate objective, taking account of the risks non-fulfilment would create. Such legitimate objectives are, inter alia: national security requirements; the prevention of deceptive practices; protection of human health or safety, animal or plant life or health, or the environment. In assessing such risks, relevant elements of consideration are, inter alia: available scientific and technical information, related processing technology or intended end-uses of products.

2.3. Technical regulations shall not be maintained if the circumstances or objectives giving rise to their adoption no longer exist or if the changed circumstances or objectives can be addressed in a less trade-restrictive manner.

2.4. Where technical regulations are required and relevant international standards exist or their completion is imminent, Members shall use them, or the relevant parts of them, as a basis for their technical regulations except when such international standards or relevant parts would be an ineffective or inappropriate means for the fulfilment of the legitimate objectives pursued, for instance because of fundamental climatic or geographical factors or fundamental technological problems.

2.8. Wherever appropriate, Members shall specify technical regulations based on product requirements in terms of performance rather than design or descriptive characteristics.

2.11. Members shall ensure that all technical regulations which have been adopted are published promptly or otherwise made available in such a manner as to enable interested parties in other Members to become acquainted with them.

# Agreement on Trade-Related Investment Measures

\* \* \*

1. This Agreement applies to investment measures related to trade in goods only (referred to in this Agreement as "TRIMs").
Illustrative List of Prohibited Restrictions:

1. TRIMs that are inconsistent with the obligation of national treatment . . . include those which are mandatory or enforceable under domestic law or under administrative rulings, or compliance with which is necessary to obtain an advantage, and which require:

   (a) the purchase or use by an enterprise of products of domestic origin or from any domestic source, whether specified in terms of particular products, in terms of volume or value of products, or in terms of a proportion of volume or value of its local production; or

   (b) that an enterprise's purchases or use of imported products be limited to an amount related to the volume or value of local products that it exports.

2. TRIMs that are inconsistent with the obligation of general elimination of quantitative restrictions . . . include those which are mandatory or enforceable under domestic law or under administrative rulings, or compliance with which is necessary to obtain an advantage, and which restrict:

   (a) the importation by an enterprise of products used in or related to its local production, generally or to an amount related to the volume or value of local production that it exports;

   (b) the importation by an enterprise of products used in or related to its local production by restricting its access to foreign exchange to an amount related to the foreign exchange inflows attributable to the enterprise; or

   (c) the exportation or sale for export by an enterprise of products, whether specified in terms of particular products, in terms of volume or value of products, or in terms of a proportion of volume or value of its local production.

# GATT 1994 Antidumping Agreement

\* \* \*

2.1. For the purpose of this Agreement, a product is to be considered as being dumped, i.e. introduced into the commerce of another country at less than its normal value, if the export price of the product exported from one country to another is less than the comparable price, in the ordinary course of trade, for the like product when destined for consumption in the exporting country.

2.4. A fair comparison shall be made between the export price and the normal value. This comparison shall be made at the same level of trade, normally at the ex-factory level, and in respect of sales made at as nearly as possible the same time. Due allowance shall be made in each case, on its merits, for differences which affect price comparability, including differences in conditions and terms of sale, taxation, levels of trade, quantities, physical characteristics, and any other differences which are also demonstrated to affect price comparability.

3.4. The examination of the impact of the dumped imports on the domestic industry concerned shall include an evaluation of all relevant economic factors and indices having a bearing on the state of the industry, including actual and potential decline in sales, profits, output, market share, productivity, return on investments, or utilization of capacity; factors affecting domestic prices; the magnitude of the margin of dumping; actual and potential negative effects on cash flow, inventories, employment, wages, growth, ability to raise capital or investments. This list is not exhaustive, nor can one or several of these factors necessarily give decisive guidance.

## Agreement on Customs Valuation

\* \* \*

1. The customs value of imported goods shall be the transaction value, that is the price actually paid or payable for the goods when sold for export to the country of importation . . . provided:
   (c) that no part of the proceeds of any subsequent resale, disposal or use of the goods by the buyer will accrue directly or indirectly to the seller . . . ; and
   (d) that the buyer and seller are not related, or where the buyer and seller are related, that the transaction value is acceptable for customs purposes under the provisions of paragraph 2.
2. (a) In determining whether the transaction value is acceptable for the purposes of paragraph 1, the fact that the buyer and the seller are related . . . shall not in itself be grounds for regarding the transaction value as unacceptable. In such case the circumstances surrounding the sale shall be examined and the transaction value shall be accepted provided that the relationship did not influence the price.

## Agreement on Preshipment Inspection

\* \* \*

1.3. Preshipment inspection activities are all activities relating to the verification of the quality, the quantity, the price, including currency exchange rate and financial terms, and/or the customs classification of goods to be exported to the territory of the user Member.
2.1. User Members shall ensure that preshipment inspection activities are carried out in a nondiscriminatory manner, and that the procedures and criteria employed in the conduct of these activities are objective and are applied on an equal basis to all exporters affected by such activities. They shall ensure uniform performance of inspection by all the inspectors of the preshipment inspection entities contracted or mandated by them.
2.3. User Members shall ensure that all preshipment inspection activities, including the issuance of a Clean Report of Findings or a note of nonissuance, are performed in the customs territory from which the goods are exported or, if the inspection cannot be carried out in that customs territory given the complex nature of the products involved, or if both parties agree, in the customs territory in which the goods are manufactured.
2.4. User Members shall ensure that quantity and quality inspections are performed in accordance with the standards defined by the seller and the buyer in the purchase agreement and that, in the absence of such standards, relevant international standards apply.
2.5. User Members shall ensure that preshipment inspection activities are conducted in a transparent manner.
2.15. User Members shall ensure that preshipment inspection entities avoid unreasonable delays in inspection of shipments.

## Agreement on Import Licensing Procedures

\* \* \*

1.3. The rules for import licensing procedures shall be neutral in application and administered in a fair and equitable manner.
1.9. The foreign exchange necessary to pay for licensed imports shall be made available to license holders on the same basis as to importers of goods not requiring import licences.

## Agreement on Safeguards

\* \* \*

2.1. A Member may apply a safeguard measure to a product only if that Member has determined . . . that such product is being imported into its territory in such increased quantities, absolute or relative to domestic production, and under such conditions as to cause or threaten to cause serious injury to the domestic industry that produces like or directly competitive products.

2.2. Safeguard measures shall be applied to a product being imported irrespective of its source.

5.1. A Member shall apply safeguard measures only to the extent necessary to prevent or remedy serious injury and to facilitate adjustment. If a quantitative restriction is used, such a measure shall not reduce the quantity of imports below the level of a recent period which shall be the average of imports in the last three representative years for which statistics are available, unless clear justification is given that a different level is necessary to prevent or remedy serious injury. Members should choose measures most suitable for the achievement of these objectives.

5.2. In cases in which a quota is allocated among supplying countries, the Member applying the restrictions may seek agreement with respect to the allocation of shares in the quota with all other Members having a substantial interest in supplying the product concerned.

7.1. A Member shall apply safeguard measures only for such period of time as may be necessary to prevent or remedy serious injury and to facilitate adjustment. The period shall not exceed four years, unless it is extended. . . .

# Agreement on Government Procurement

\* \* \*

3.1. With respect to all laws, regulations, procedures and practices regarding government procurement by this Agreement, each Party shall provide immediately and unconditionally to the products, services and suppliers of other Parties offering products or services of the Parties, treatment no less favorable than:

(a) that accorded to domestic products, services and suppliers; and

(b) that accorded to products, services and suppliers of any other Party.

7.2. [Government] entities shall not provide to any supplier information with regard to a specific procurement in a manner which would have the effect of precluding competition.

8 (b). Any conditions for participation in tendering procedures shall be limited to those which are essential to ensure the firm's capability to fulfil the contract in question.

16.1. [Government] entities shall not, in the qualification and selection of suppliers, products or services, or in the evaluation of tenders and award of contracts, impose, seek or consider offsets.

19.1. Each Party shall promptly publish any law, regulation, judicial decision, administrative ruling . . . regarding government procurement. . . .

20.2. Each party shall provide non-discriminatory, timely, transparent and effective procedures enabling suppliers to challenge alleged breaches of the Agreement arising in the context of procurements which they have, or have had, an interest.

# General Agreement on Trade in Services (Selected Provisions)

*April 15, 1994*

## Article I
### Scope and Definition

1. This Agreement applies to measures by Members affecting trade in services.

## Article II
### Most-Favoured-Nation Treatment

1. With respect to any measure covered by this Agreement, each Member shall accord immediately and unconditionally to services and service suppliers of any other Member treatment no less favourable than that it accords to like services and service suppliers of any other country.

## Article III
### Transparency

1. Each Member shall publish promptly and, except in emergency situations, at the latest by the time of their entry into force, all relevant measures of general application which pertain to or affect the operation of this Agreement. International agreements pertaining to or affecting trade in services to which a Member is a signatory shall also be published.

## Article VI
### Domestic Regulation

1. In sectors where specific commitments are undertaken, each Member shall ensure that all measures of general application affecting trade in services are administered in a reasonable, objective and impartial manner. . . .

4. With a view to ensuring that measures relating to qualification requirements and procedures, technical standards and licensing requirements do not constitute unnecessary barriers to trade in services, the Council for Trade in Services shall, through appropriate bodies it may establish, develop any necessary disciplines. Such disciplines shall aim to ensure that such requirements are, inter alia:

   (a) based on objective and transparent criteria, such as competence and the ability to supply the service;
   (b) not more burdensome than necessary to ensure the quality of the service;
   (c) in the case of licensing procedures, not in themselves a restriction on the supply of the service. . . .

6. In sectors where specific commitments regarding professional services are undertaken, each Member shall provide for adequate procedures to verify the competence of professionals of any other Member.

## Article VII
### Recognition

1. For the purposes of the fulfilment, in whole or in part, of its standards or criteria for the authorization, licensing or certification of services suppliers . . . a Member may recognize the education or experience obtained, requirements met, or licenses or certifications granted in a particular country. Such recognition, which may be achieved through harmonization or otherwise, may be based upon an agreement or arrangement with the country concerned or may be accorded autonomously.

3. A Member shall not accord recognition in a manner which would constitute a means of discrimination between countries in the application of its standards or criteria for the authorization, licensing or certification of services suppliers, or a disguised restriction on trade in services.

## Article X
### Emergency Safeguard Measures

1. There shall be multilateral negotiations on the question of emergency safeguard measures based on the principle of non-discrimination. The results of such negotiations shall enter into effect on a date not later than three years from the date of entry into force of the WTO Agreement.

*Article XI*
*Payments and Transfers*

1. Except under the circumstances envisaged in Article XII, a Member shall not apply restrictions on international transfers and payments for current transactions relating to its specific commitments.

*Article XIX*
*Negotiation of Specific Commitments*

1. In pursuance of the objectives of this Agreement, Members shall enter into successive rounds of negotiations, beginning not later than five years from the date of entry into force of the WTO Agreement and periodically thereafter, with a view to achieving a progressively higher level of liberalization. Such negotiations shall be directed to the reduction or elimination of the adverse effects on trade in services of measures as a means of providing effective market access. This process shall take place with a view to promoting the interests of all participants on a mutually advantageous basis and to securing an overall balance of rights and obligations.

*Article XX*
*Schedules of Specific Commitments*

3. Schedules of specific commitments shall be annexed to this Agreement and shall form an integral part thereof.

# Agreement on Trade-Related Aspects of Intellectual Property Rights

*General Agreement on Tariffs and Trade*
*April 15, 1994*

## Part One: General Provisions and Basic Principles

*Article 3*
*National Treatment*

1.  Each Member shall accord to the nationals of other Members treatment no less favourable than that it accords to its own nationals with regard to the protection of intellectual property, subject to the exceptions already provided in, respectively, the Paris Convention (1967), the Berne Convention (1971), the Rome Convention or the Treaty on Intellectual Property in Respect of Integrated Circuits.

*Article 4*
*Most-Favoured-Nation Treatment*

With regard to the protection of intellectual property, any advantage, favour, privilege or immunity granted by a Member to the nationals of any other country shall be accorded immediately and unconditionally to the nationals of all other Members.

*Article 7*
*Objectives*

The protection and enforcement of intellectual property rights should contribute to the promotion of technological innovation and to the transfer and dissemination of technology, to the mutual advantage of producers and users of technological knowledge and in a manner conducive to social and economic welfare, and to a balance of rights and obligations.

## Part Two: Standards Concerning the Availability, Scope and Use of Intellectual Property Rights

SECTION I: COPYRIGHT AND RELATED RIGHTS

*Article 9*
*Relation to the Berne Convention*

1.  Members shall comply with . . . the Berne Convention (1971). . . .
2.  Copyright protection shall extend to expressions and not to ideas, procedures, methods of operation or mathematical concepts as such.

*Article 10*
*Computer Programs and Compilations of Data*

1.  Computer programs, whether in source or object code, shall be protected as literary works under the Berne Convention (1971).

*Article 11*
*Rental Rights*

In respect of at least computer programs and cinematographic works, a Member shall provide authors and their successors in title the right to authorize or to prohibit the commercial rental to the public of originals or copies of their copyright works. A Member shall be excepted from this obligation in respect of cinematographic works unless such rental has led to widespread copying of such works which is materially impairing the exclusive right of reproduction conferred in that

Member on authors and their successors in title. In respect of computer programs, this obligation does not apply to rentals where the program itself is not the essential object of the rental.

### Article 12
### Term of Protection

Whenever the term of protection of a work, other than a photographic work or a work of applied art, is calculated on a basis other than the life of a natural person, such term shall be no less than 50 years from the end of the calendar year of authorized publication, or, failing such authorized publication within 50 years from the making of the work, 50 years from the end of the calendar year of making.

### Article 14
### Protection of Performers, Producers of Phonograms (Sound Recordings) and Broadcasting Organizations

1. In respect of a fixation of their performance on a phonogram, performers shall have the possibility of preventing the following acts when undertaken without their authorization: the fixation of their unfixed performance and the reproduction of such fixation. Performers shall also have the possibility of preventing the following acts when undertaken without their authorization: the broadcasting by wireless means and the communication to the public of their live performance.
5. The term of the protection available under this Agreement to performers and producers of phonograms shall last at least until the end of a period of 50 years computed from the end of the calendar year in which the fixation was made or the performance took place. The term of protection granted pursuant to paragraph 3 shall last for at least 20 years from the end of the calendar year in which the broadcast took place.

### Section II: Trademarks

### Article 15
### Protectable Subject Matter

1. Any sign, or any combination of signs, capable of distinguishing the goods or services of one undertaking from those of other undertakings, shall be capable of constituting a trademark. Such signs, in particular words including personal names, letters, numerals, figurative elements and combinations of colours as well as any combination of such signs, shall be eligible for registration as trademarks. Where signs are not inherently capable of distinguishing the relevant goods or services, Members may make registrability depend on distinctiveness acquired through use. Members may require, as a condition of registration, that signs be visually perceptible.
3. Members may make registrability depend on use. However, actual use of a trademark shall not be a condition for filing an application for registration. An application shall not be refused solely on the ground that intended use has not taken place before the expiry of a period of three years from the date of application.
4. The nature of the goods or services to which a trademark is to be applied shall in no case form an obstacle to registration of the trademark.
5. Members shall publish each trademark either before it is registered or promptly after it is registered and shall afford a reasonable opportunity for petitions to cancel the registration. In addition, Members may afford an opportunity for the registration of a trademark to be opposed.

### Article 16
### Rights Conferred

1. The owner of a registered trademark shall have the exclusive right to prevent all third parties not having the owner's consent from using in the course of trade identical or similar signs for goods or services which are identical or similar to those in respect of which the trademark is registered where such use would result in a likelihood of confusion. In case of the use of an identical sign for identical goods or services, a likelihood of confusion shall be presumed. The rights described above shall not prejudice any existing prior rights, nor shall they affect the possibility of Members making rights available on the basis of use.

### Article 18
### Term of Protection

Initial registration, and each renewal of registration, of a trademark shall be for a term of no less than seven years. The registration of a trademark shall be renewable indefinitely.

### Article 19
### Requirement of Use

1. If use is required to maintain a registration, the registration may be cancelled only after an uninterrupted period of at least three years of non-use, unless valid reasons based on the existence of obstacles to such use are shown by the trademark

owner. Circumstances arising independently of the will of the owner of the trademark which constitute an obstacle to the use of the trademark, such as import restrictions on or other government requirements for goods or services protected by the trademark, shall be recognized as valid reasons for non-use.

2. When subject to the control of its owner, use of a trademark by another person shall be recognized as use of the trademark for the purpose of maintaining the registration.

## Article 20
### Other Requirements

The use of a trademark in the course of trade shall not be unjustifiably encumbered by special requirements, such as use with another trademark, use in a special form or use in a manner detrimental to its capability to distinguish the goods or services of one undertaking from those of other undertakings. This will not preclude a requirement prescribing the use of the trademark identifying the undertaking producing the goods or services along with, but without linking it to, the trademark distinguishing the specific goods or services in question of that undertaking.

## Article 21
### Licensing and Assignment

Members may determine conditions on the licensing and assignment of trademarks, it being understood that the compulsory licensing of trademarks shall not be permitted and that the owner of a registered trademark shall have the right to assign the trademark with or without the transfer of the business to which the trademark belongs.

## SECTION III: GEOGRAPHICAL INDICATIONS

## Article 22
### Protection of Geographical Indications

1. Geographical indications are, for the purposes of this Agreement, indications which identify a good as originating in the territory of a Member, or a region or locality in that territory, where a given quality, reputation or other characteristic of the good is essentially attributable to its geographical origin.

2. In respect of geographical indications, Members shall provide the legal means for interested parties to prevent: (a) the use of any means in the designation or presentation of a good that indicates or suggests that the good in question originates in a geographical area other than the true place of origin in a manner which misleads the public as to the geographical origin of the good; (b) any use which constitutes an act of unfair competition within the meaning of Article 10bis of the Paris Convention (1967).

3. A Member shall, ex officio if its legislation so permits or at the request of an interested party, refuse or invalidate the registration of a trademark which contains or consists of a geographical indication with respect to goods not originating in the territory indicated, if use of the indication in the trademark for such goods in that Member is of such a nature as to mislead the public as to the true place of origin.

4. The protection under paragraphs 1, 2 and 3 shall be applicable against a geographical indication which, although literally true as to the territory, region or locality in which the goods originate, falsely represents to the public that the goods originate in another territory.

## Article 23
### Additional Protection for Geographical Indications for Wines and Spirits

1. Each Member shall provide the legal means for interested parties to prevent use of a geographical indication identifying wines for wines not originating in the place indicated by the geographical indication in question or identifying spirits for spirits not originating in the place indicated by the geographical indication in question, even where the true origin of the goods is indicated or the geographical indication is used in translation or accompanied by expressions such as "kind," "type," "style," "imitation" or the like.

## SECTION IV: INDUSTRIAL DESIGNS

## Article 25
### Requirements for Protection

1. Members shall provide for the protection of independently created industrial designs that are new or original. Members may provide that designs are not new or original if they do not significantly differ from known designs or combinations of known design features. Members may provide that such protection shall not extend to designs dictated essentially by technical or functional considerations.

## Article 26
### Protection

1. The owner of a protected industrial design shall have the right to prevent third parties not having

the owner's consent from making, selling or importing articles bearing or embodying a design which is a copy, or substantially a copy, of the protected design, when such acts are undertaken for commercial purposes.

3. The duration of protection available shall amount to at least 10 years.

## SECTION V: PATENTS

### Article 27
### Patentable Subject Matter

1. Subject to the provisions of paragraphs 2 and 3, patents shall be available for any inventions, whether products or processes, in all fields of technology, provided that they are new, involve an inventive step and are capable of industrial application. Subject to paragraph 4 of Article 65, paragraph 8 of Article 70 and paragraph 3 of this Article, patents shall be available and patent rights enjoyable without discrimination as to the place of invention, the field of technology and whether products are imported or locally produced.

2. Members may exclude from patentability inventions, the prevention within their territory of the commercial exploitation of which is necessary to protect the public order or morality, including to protect human, animal or plant life or health or to avoid serious prejudice to the environment, provided that such exclusion is not made merely because the exploitation is prohibited by their law.

3. Members may also exclude from patentability: (a) diagnostic, therapeutic and surgical methods for the treatment of humans or animals; (b) plants and animals other than micro-organisms, and essentially biological processes for the production of plants or animals other than non- biological and microbiological processes. However, Members shall provide for the protection of plant varieties either by patents or by an effective sui generis system or by any combination thereof. The provisions of this subparagraph shall be reviewed four years after the date of entry into force of the WTO Agreement.

### Article 28
### Rights Conferred

1. A patent shall confer on its owner the following exclusive rights: (a) where the subject matter of a patent is a product, to prevent third parties not having the owner's consent from the acts of: making, using, offering for sale, selling, or importing for

these purposes that product; (b) where the subject matter of a patent is a process, to prevent third parties not having the owner's consent from the act of using the process, and from the acts of: using, offering for sale, selling, or importing for these purposes at least the product obtained directly by that process.

2. Patent owners shall also have the right to assign, or transfer by succession, the patent and to conclude licensing contracts.

### Article 29
### Conditions on Patent Applicants

1. Members shall require that an applicant for a patent shall disclose the invention in a manner sufficiently clear and complete for the invention to be carried out by a person skilled in the art and may require the applicant to indicate the best mode for carrying out the invention known to the inventor at the filing date or, where priority is claimed, at the priority date of the application.

2. Members may require an applicant for a patent to provide information concerning the applicant's corresponding foreign applications and grants.

### Article 31
### Other Use Without Authorization
### of the Right Holder

Where the law of a Member allows for other use of the subject matter of a patent without the authorization of the right holder, including use by the government or third parties authorized by the government, the following provisions shall be respected: (a) authorization of such use shall be considered on its individual merits; (b) such use may only be permitted if, prior to such use, the proposed user has made efforts to obtain authorization from the right holder on reasonable commercial terms and conditions and that such efforts have not been successful within a reasonable period of time. This requirement may be waived by a Member in the case of a national emergency or other circumstances of extreme urgency or in cases of public non-commercial use. In situations of national emergency or other circumstances of extreme urgency, the right holder shall, nevertheless, be notified as soon as reasonably practicable. . . .

### Article 32
### Revocation/Forfeiture

An opportunity for judicial review of any decision to revoke or forfeit a patent shall be available.

*Article 33*
*Term of Protection*

The term of protection available shall not end before the expiration of a period of twenty years counted from the filing date.

# Part Three: Enforcement of Intellectual Property Rights

*Article 41*

1. Members shall ensure that enforcement procedures as specified in this Part are available under their law so as to permit effective action against any act of infringement of intellectual property rights covered by this Agreement, including expeditious remedies to prevent infringements and remedies which constitute a deterrent to further infringements. These procedures shall be applied in such a manner as to avoid the creation of barriers to legitimate trade and to provide for safeguards against their abuse.
2. Procedures concerning the enforcement of intellectual property rights shall be fair and equitable. They shall not be unnecessarily complicated or costly, or entail unreasonable time-limits or unwarranted delays.
3. Decisions on the merits of a case shall preferably be in writing and reasoned. They shall be made available at least to the parties to the proceeding without undue delay. Decisions on the merits of a case shall be based only on evidence in respect of which parties were offered the opportunity to be heard.
4. Parties to a proceeding shall have an opportunity for review by a judicial authority of final administrative decisions and, subject to jurisdictional provisions in a Member's law concerning the importance of a case, of at least the legal aspects of initial judicial decisions on the merits of a case. However, there shall be no obligation to provide an opportunity for review of acquittals in criminal cases.

*Article 44*
*Injunctions*

1. The judicial authorities shall have the authority to order a party to desist from an infringement, inter alia to prevent the entry into the channels of commerce in their jurisdiction of imported goods that involve the infringement of an intellectual property right, immediately after customs clearance of such goods. Members are not obliged to accord such authority in respect of protected subject matter ac-

quired or ordered by a person prior to knowing or having reasonable grounds to know that dealing in such subject matter would entail the infringement of an intellectual property right.

*Article 45*
*Damages*

1. The judicial authorities shall have the authority to order the infringer to pay the right holder damages adequate to compensate for the injury the right holder has suffered because of an infringement of that person's intellectual property right by an infringer who knowingly, or with reasonable grounds to know, engaged in infringing activity.

*Article 48*
*Indemnification of the Defendant*

1. The judicial authorities shall have the authority to order a party at whose request measures were taken and who has abused enforcement procedures to provide to a party wrongfully enjoined or restrained adequate compensation for the injury suffered because of such abuse. The judicial authorities shall also have the authority to order the applicant to pay the defendant expenses, which may include appropriate attorney's fees.

*Article 51*
*Suspension of Release by Customs Authorities*

Members shall, in conformity with the provisions set out below, adopt procedures to enable a right holder, who has valid grounds for suspecting that the importation of counterfeit trademark or pirated copyright goods may take place, to lodge an application in writing with competent authorities, administrative or judicial, for the suspension by the customs authorities of the release into free circulation of such goods. Members may enable such an application to be made in respect of goods which involve other infringements of intellectual property rights, provided that the requirements of this Section are met. Members may also provide for corresponding procedures concerning the suspension by the customs authorities of the release of infringing goods destined for exportation from their territories.

*Article 57*
*Right of Inspection and Information*

Without prejudice to the protection of confidential information, Members shall provide the competent authorities the authority to give the right holder sufficient opportunity to have any goods detained by the customs authorities inspected in order to substantiate the right holder's claims. The competent authorities shall also have authority to give the importer an equivalent opportunity to have any such goods inspected. Where a positive determination has been made on the merits of a case, Members may provide the competent authorities the authority to inform the right holder of the names and addresses of the consignor, the importer and the consignee and of the quantity of the goods in question.

### Article 59
### Remedies

Without prejudice to other rights of action open to the right holder and subject to the right of the defendant to seek review by a judicial authority, competent authorities shall have the authority to order the destruction or disposal of infringing goods in accordance with the principles set out in Article 46. In regard to counterfeit trademark goods, the authorities shall not allow the re-exportation of the infringing goods in an unaltered state or subject them to a different customs procedure, other than in exceptional circumstances.

### Article 60
### De Minimis Imports

Members may exclude from the application of the above provisions small quantities of goods of a non-commercial nature contained in travellers' personal luggage or sent in small consignments.

## SECTION V: CRIMINAL PROCEDURES

### Article 61

Members shall provide for criminal procedures and penalties to be applied at least in cases of wilful trademark counterfeiting or copyright piracy on a commercial scale. Remedies available shall include imprisonment and/or monetary fines sufficient to provide a deterrent, consistently with the level of penalties applied for crimes of a corresponding gravity. In appropriate cases, remedies available shall also include the seizure, forfeiture and destruction of the infringing goods and of any materials and implements the predominant use of which has been in the commission of the offence. Members may provide for criminal procedures and penalties to be applied in other cases of infringement of intellectual property rights, in particular where they are committed wilfully and on a commercial scale.

# Part Seven: Institutional Arrangements

### Article 68
### Council for Trade-Related Aspects of Intellectual Property Rights

The Council for TRIPS shall monitor the operation of this Agreement and, in particular, Members' compliance with their obligations hereunder, and shall afford Members the opportunity of consulting on matters relating to the trade-related aspects of intellectual property rights.

# North American Free Trade Agreement

**Between the Government of the United States of America, the Government of Canada and the Government of the United Mexican States (Selected Provisions) Effective January 1, 1994**

## Part One: General Part

*Article 101*
*Establishment of the Free Trade Area*
The Parties to this Agreement, consistent with Article XXIV of the General Agreement on Tariffs and Trade, hereby establish a free trade area.

*Article 103*
*Relation to Other Agreements*
1. The Parties affirm their existing rights and obligations with respect to each other under the General Agreement on Tariffs and Trade and other agreements to which such Parties are party.
2. In the event of any inconsistency between this Agreement and such other agreements, this Agreement shall prevail to the extent of the inconsistency, except as otherwise provided in this Agreement.

## Part Two: Trade in Goods

*Article 301*
*National Treatment*
1. Each Party shall accord national treatment to the goods of another Party in accordance with Article III of the General Agreement on Tariffs and Trade (GATT) . . .

*Article 302*
*Tariff Elimination*
1. Except as otherwise provided in this Agreement, no Party may increase any existing customs duty, or adopt any customs duty, on an originating good.
2. Except as otherwise provided in this Agreement, each Party shall progressively eliminate its customs duties on originating goods in accordance with its Schedule. . . .

*Article 305*
*Temporary Admission of Goods*
1. Each Party shall grant duty-free temporary admission for: (a) professional equipment necessary for carrying out the business activity, trade or profession of a business person who qualifies for temporary entry . . . (b) equipment for the press or for sound or television broadcasting and cinematographic equipment, (c) goods imported for sports purposes and goods intended for display or demonstration, and (d) commercial samples and advertising films, imported from the territory of another Party, regardless of their origin and regardless of whether like, directly competitive or substitutable goods are available in the territory of the Party. . . .

*Article 306*
*Duty-Free Entry of Certain Commercial Samples and Printed Advertising Materials*
Each Party shall grant duty-free entry to commercial samples of negligible value, and to printed advertising materials, imported from the territory of another Party, regardless of their origin, but may require that: (a) such samples be imported solely for the solicitation of orders for goods, or services provided from the territory, of another Party or non-Party; or (b) such advertising materials be imported in packets that each contain no more than one copy of each such material and that neither such materials nor packets form part of a larger consignment.

*Article 307*
*Goods Re-Entered after Repair or Alteration*
1. [N]o Party may apply a customs duty to a good, regardless of its origin, that re-enters its territory after that good has been exported from its territory to the territory of another Party for repair or alteration, regardless of whether such repair or alteration could be performed in its territory.

2. [N]o Party may apply a customs duty to a good, regardless of its origin, imported temporarily from the territory of another Party for repair or alteration.

### Article 309
*Import and Export Restrictions*
1. Except as otherwise provided in this Agreement, no Party may adopt or maintain any prohibition or restriction on the importation of any good of another Party or on the exportation or sale for export of any good destined for the territory of another Party, except in accordance with Article XI of the GATT, including its interpretative notes, and to this end Article XI of the GATT and its interpretative notes, or any equivalent provision of a successor agreement to which all Parties are party, are incorporated into and made a part of this Agreement.
2. The Parties understand that the GATT rights and obligations incorporated by paragraph 1 prohibit, in any circumstances in which any other form of restriction is prohibited, export price requirements and, except as permitted in enforcement of countervailing and antidumping orders and undertakings, import price requirements.
3. In the event that a Party adopts or maintains a prohibition or restriction on the importation from or exportation to a non-Party of a good, nothing in this Agreement shall be construed to prevent the Party from: (a) limiting or prohibiting the importation from the territory of another Party of such good of that non-Party; or (b) requiring as a condition of export of such good of the Party to the territory of another Party, that the good not be re-exported to the non-Party, directly or indirectly, without being consumed in the territory of the other Party. . . .

### Article 316
*Consultations and Committee on Trade in Goods*
1. The Parties hereby establish a Committee on Trade in Goods, comprising representatives of each Party.
2. The Committee shall meet on the request of any Party or the Commission to consider any matter arising under this Chapter.

# Chapter 4. Rules of Origin

### Article 401
*Originating Goods*
Except as otherwise provided in this Chapter, a good shall originate in the territory of a Party where: (a) the good is wholly obtained or produced entirely in the territory of one or more of the Parties . . . (b) each of the non-originating materials used in the production of the good undergoes an applicable change in tariff classification set out in Annex 401 as a result of production occurring entirely in the territory of one or more of the Parties, or the good otherwise satisfies the applicable requirements of that Annex where no change in tariff classification is required, and the good satisfies all other applicable requirements of this Chapter; (c) the good is produced entirely in the territory of one or more of the Parties exclusively from originating materials; or (d) except for a good provided for in Chapters 61 through 63 of the Harmonized System, the good is produced entirely in the territory of one or more of the Parties but one or more of the non-originating materials provided for as parts under the Harmonized System that are used in the production of the good does not undergo a change in tariff classification because (i) the good was imported into the territory of a Party in an unassembled or a disassembled form but was classified as an assembled good pursuant to General Rule of Interpretation 2(a) of the Harmonized System, or (ii) the heading for the good provides for and specifically describes both the good itself and its parts and is not further subdivided into subheadings, or the subheading for the good provides for and specifically describes both the good itself and its parts, provided that the regional value content of the good, determined in accordance with Article 402, is not less than 60 percent where the transaction value method is used, or is not less than 50 percent where the net cost method is used, and that the good satisfies all other applicable requirements of this Chapter.

# Chapter 8. Emergency Action

### Article 801
*Bilateral Actions*
1. [During] the transition period only, if a good originating in the territory of a Party, as a result of the reduction or elimination of a duty provided for in this Agreement, is being imported into the territory of another Party in such increased quantities, in absolute terms, and under such conditions that the imports of the good from that Party alone constitute a substantial cause of serious injury, or threat thereof, to a domestic industry producing a like or directly competitive good, the Party into whose territory the good is being imported may, to the minimum extent necessary to remedy or prevent the injury: (a) suspend the further reduction of any rate of duty provided for under this Agreement on the good; (b) increase the rate of duty on the good to a level not to exceed the lesser of (i) the most-favored-nation (MFN) applied rate of duty in effect at the time the action is taken,

and (ii) the MFN applied rate of duty in effect on the day immediately preceding the date of entry into force of this Agreement; or (c) in the case of a duty applied to a good on a seasonal basis, increase the rate of duty to a level not to exceed the MFN applied rate of duty that was in effect on the good for the corresponding season immediately preceding the date of entry into force of this Agreement. . . .

4. The Party taking an action under this Article shall provide to the Party against whose good the action is taken mutually agreed trade liberalizing compensation in the form of concessions having substantially equivalent trade effects or equivalent to the value of the additional duties expected to result from the action. . . .

*Article 802*
*Global Actions*

1. Each Party retains its rights and obligations under Article XIX of the GATT or any safeguard agreement pursuant thereto except those regarding compensation or retaliation and exclusion from an action to the extent that such rights or obligations are inconsistent with this Article. Any Party taking an emergency action under Article XIX or any such agreement shall exclude imports of a good from each other Party from the action unless: (a) imports from a Party, considered individually, account for a substantial share of total imports; and (b) imports from a Party, considered individually, or in exceptional circumstances imports from Parties considered collectively, contribute importantly to the serious injury, or threat thereof, caused by imports.

# Part Three: Technical Barriers to Trade

*Article 904*
*Basic Rights and Obligations*

1. Each Party may, in accordance with this Agreement, adopt, maintain or apply any standards-related measure, including any such measure relating to safety, the protection of human, animal or plant life or health, the environment or consumers, and any measure to ensure its enforcement or implementation. . . .

2. Notwithstanding any other provision of this Chapter, each Party may, in pursuing its legitimate objectives of safety or the protection of human, animal or plant life or health, the environment or consumers, establish the levels of protection that it considers appropriate. . . .

4. No Party may prepare, adopt, maintain or apply any standards-related measure with a view to or with the effect of creating an unnecessary obstacle to trade between the Parties. An unnecessary obstacle to trade shall not be deemed to be created where: (a) the demonstrable purpose of the measure is to achieve a legitimate objective; and (b) the measure does not operate to exclude goods of another Party that meet that legitimate objective.

*Article 905*
*Use of International Standards*

1. Each Party shall use, as a basis for its standards-related measures, relevant international standards. . . .

2. A Party's standards-related measure that conforms to an international standard shall be presumed to be consistent with Article 904(3) and (4).

# Part Five: Investment, Services and Related Matters

*Article 1102*
*National Treatment*

1. Each Party shall accord to investors of another Party treatment no less favorable than that it accords, in like circumstances, to its own investors with respect to the establishment, acquisition, expansion, management, conduct, operation, and sale or other disposition of investments.

2. Each Party shall accord to investments of investors of another Party treatment no less favorable than that it accords, in like circumstances, to investments of its own investors with respect to the establishment, acquisition, expansion, management, conduct, operation, and sale or other disposition of investments.

3. The treatment accorded by a Party under paragraphs 1 and 2 means, with respect to a state or province, treatment no less favorable than the most favorable treatment accorded, in like circumstances, by that state or province to investors, and to investments of investors, of the Party of which it forms a part. . . .

*Article 1103*
*Most-Favored-Nation Treatment*

1. Each Party shall accord to investors of another Party treatment no less favorable than that it accords, in like circumstances, to investors of any other Party or of a non-Party with respect to the establishment, acquisition, expansion, management, conduct, operation, and sale or other disposition of investments.

2. Each Party shall accord to investments of investors of another Party treatment no less favorable than that it accords, in like circumstances, to investments of investors of any other Party or of a non-Party with respect to the establishment, acquisition, expansion, management, conduct, operation, and sale or other disposition of investments.

### Article 1106
*Performance Requirements*
1. No Party may impose or enforce any of the following requirements, or enforce any commitment or undertaking, in connection with the establishment, acquisition, expansion, management, conduct or operation of an investment of an investor of a Party or of a non-Party in its territory: (a) to export a given level or percentage of goods or services; (b) to achieve a given level or percentage of domestic content; (c) to purchase, use or accord a preference to goods produced or services provided in its territory, or to purchase goods or services from persons in its territory; (d) to relate in any way the volume or value of imports to the volume or value of exports or to the amount of foreign exchange inflows associated with such investment; (e) to restrict sales of goods or services in its territory that such investment produces or provides by relating such sales in any way to the volume or value of its exports or foreign exchange earnings; (f) to transfer technology, a production process or other proprietary knowledge to a person in its territory, except when the requirement is imposed or the commitment or undertaking is enforced by a court, administrative tribunal or competition authority to remedy an alleged violation of competition laws or to act in a manner not inconsistent with other provisions of this Agreement; or (g) to act as the exclusive supplier of the goods it produces or services it provides to a specific region or world market.

### Article 1107
*Senior Management and Boards of Directors*
1. No Party may require that an enterprise of that Party that is an investment of an investor of another Party appoint to senior management positions individuals of any particular nationality.
2. A Party may require that a majority of the board of directors, or any committee thereof, of an enterprise of that Party that is an investment of an investor of another Party, be of a particular nationality, or resident in the territory of the Party, provided that the requirement does not materially impair the ability of the investor to exercise control over its investment.

### Article 1110
*Expropriation and Compensation*
1. No Party may directly or indirectly nationalize or expropriate an investment of an investor of another Party in its territory or take a measure tantamount to nationalization or expropriation of such an investment ("expropriation"), except: (a) for a public purpose; (b) on a non-discriminatory basis; (c) in accordance with due process of law and Article 1105(1); and (d) on payment of compensation in accordance with paragraphs 2 through 6.
2. Compensation shall be equivalent to the fair market value of the expropriated investment immediately before the expropriation took place ("date of expropriation"), and shall not reflect any change in value occurring because the intended expropriation had become known earlier. Valuation criteria shall include going concern value, asset value including declared tax value of tangible property, and other criteria, as appropriate, to determine fair market value.
3. Compensation shall be paid without delay and be fully realizable.

### Article 1114
*Environmental Measures*
1. Nothing in this Chapter shall be construed to prevent a Party from adopting, maintaining or enforcing any measure otherwise consistent with this Chapter that it considers appropriate to ensure that investment activity in its territory is undertaken in a manner sensitive to environmental concerns.
2. The Parties recognize that it is inappropriate to encourage investment by relaxing domestic health, safety or environmental measures. Accordingly, a Party should not waive or otherwise derogate from, or offer to waive or otherwise derogate from, such measures as an encouragement for the establishment, acquisition, expansion or retention in its territory of an investment of an investor.

## Chapter 12. Cross-border Trade in Services

### Article 1201
*Scope and Coverage*
This Chapter does not apply to: (a) financial services, (b) air services. . . .

### Article 1202
*National Treatment*
1. Each Party shall accord to service providers of another Party treatment no less favorable than that it

accords, in like circumstances, to its own service providers.

2. The treatment accorded by a Party under paragraph 1 means, with respect to a state or province, treatment no less favorable than the most favorable treatment accorded, in like circumstances, by that state or province to service providers of the Party of which it forms a part.

*Article 1205*
*Local Presence*
No Party may require a service provider of another Party to establish or maintain a representative office or any form of enterprise, or to be resident, in its territory as a condition for the cross-border provision of a service.

# Chapter 14. Financial Services

*Article 1403*
*Establishment of Financial Institutions*
1. The Parties recognize the principle that an investor of another Party should be permitted to establish a financial institution in the territory of a Party in the juridical form chosen by such investor.
2. The Parties also recognize the principle that an investor of another Party should be permitted to participate widely in a Party's market through the ability of such investor to: (a) provide in that Party's territory a range of financial services through separate financial institutions as may be required by that Party; (b) expand geographically in that Party's territory; and (c) own financial institutions in that Party's territory without being subject to ownership requirements specific to foreign financial institutions.

*Article 1404*
*Cross-Border Trade*
1. No Party may adopt any measure restricting any type of cross-border trade in financial services by cross-border financial service providers of another Party that the Party permits on the date of entry into force of this Agreement, except to the extent set out in Section B of the Party's Schedule to Annex VII.

*Article 1405*
*National Treatment*
1. Each Party shall accord to investors of another Party treatment no less favorable than that it accords to its own investors, in like circumstances, with respect to the establishment, acquisition, expansion, management, conduct, operation, and sale or other disposition of financial institutions and investments in financial institutions in its territory.

2. Each Party shall accord to financial institutions of another Party and to investments of investors of another Party in financial institutions treatment no less favorable than that it accords to its own financial institutions and to investments of its own investors in financial institutions, in like circumstances, with respect to the establishment, acquisition, expansion, management, conduct, operation, and sale or other disposition of financial institutions and investments.

# Chapter 15. Competition Policy, Monopolies and State Enterprises

*Article 1501*
*Competition Law*
1. Each Party shall adopt or maintain measures to proscribe anti-competitive business conduct and take appropriate action with respect thereto, recognizing that such measures will enhance the fulfillment of the objectives of this Agreement. To this end the Parties shall consult from time to time about the effectiveness of measures undertaken by each Party.
2. Each Party recognizes the importance of cooperation and coordination among their authorities to further effective competition law enforcement in the free trade area. The Parties shall cooperate on issues of competition law enforcement policy, including mutual legal assistance, notification, consultation and exchange of information relating to the enforcement of competition laws and policies in the free trade area.
3. No Party may have recourse to dispute settlement under this Agreement for any matter arising under this Article.

# Chapter 16. Temporary Entry for Business Persons

*Article 1603*
*Grant of Temporary Entry*
1. Each Party shall grant temporary entry to business persons who are otherwise qualified for entry under applicable measures relating to public health and safety and national security. . . .
2. A Party may refuse to issue an immigration document authorizing employment to a business person where the temporary entry of that person might affect adversely: (a) the settlement of any labor dispute that is in progress at the place or intended place of employment; or (b) the employment of any person who is involved in such dispute. . . .

# Part Six: Intellectual Property

*Article 1701*
*Nature and Scope of Obligations*

Each Party shall provide in its territory to the nationals of another Party adequate and effective protection and enforcement of intellectual property rights, while ensuring that measures to enforce intellectual property rights do not themselves become barriers to legitimate trade.

*Article 1705*
*Copyright*

1. Each Party shall protect the works covered by the Berne Convention, including any other works that embody original expression within the meaning of that Convention. In particular: (a) all types of computer programs are literary works within the meaning of the Berne Convention and each Party shall protect them as such; and (b) compilations of data or other material, whether in machine readable or other form, which by reason of the selection or arrangement of their contents constitute intellectual creations, shall be protected as such. The protection a Party provides under subparagraph (b) shall not extend to the data or material itself, or prejudice any copyright subsisting in that data or material.

2. Each Party shall provide to authors and their successors in interest those rights enumerated in the Berne Convention . . . including the right to authorize or prohibit: (a) the importation into the Party's territory of copies of the work made without the right holder's authorization; (b) the first public distribution of the original and each copy of the work by sale, rental or otherwise; (c) the communication of a work to the public; and (d) the commercial rental of the original or a copy of a computer program.

4. Each Party shall provide that, where the term of protection of a work, other than a photographic work or a work of applied art, is to be calculated on a basis other than the life of a natural person, the term shall be not less than 50 years from the end of the calendar year of the first authorized publication of the work or, failing such authorized publication within 50 years from the making of the work, 50 years from the end of the calendar year of making.

*Article 1706*
*Sound Recordings*

2. Each Party shall provide a term of protection for sound recordings of at least 50 years from the end of the calendar year in which the fixation was made.

*Article 1708*
*Trademarks*

1. For purposes of this Agreement, a trademark consists of any sign, or any combination of signs, capable of distinguishing the goods or services of one person from those of another, including personal names, designs, letters, numerals, colors, figurative elements, or the shape of goods or of their packaging. Trademarks shall include service marks and collective marks, and may include certification marks. A Party may require, as a condition for registration, that a sign be visually perceptible.

2. Each Party shall provide to the owner of a registered trademark the right to prevent all persons not having the owner's consent from using in commerce identical or similar signs for goods or services that are identical or similar to those goods or services in respect of which the owner's trademark is registered, where such use would result in a likelihood of confusion. In the case of the use of an identical sign for identical goods or services, a likelihood of confusion shall be presumed. The rights described above shall not prejudice any prior rights, nor shall they affect the possibility of a Party making rights available on the basis of use.

3. A Party may make registrability depend on use. However, actual use of a trademark shall not be a condition for filing an application for registration. No Party may refuse an application solely on the ground that intended use has not taken place before the expiry of a period of three years from the date of application for registration. . . .

7. Each Party shall provide that the initial registration of a trademark be for a term of at least 10 years and that the registration be indefinitely renewable for terms of not less than 10 years when conditions for renewal have been met.

8. Each Party shall require the use of a trademark to maintain a registration. The registration may be canceled for the reason of non-use only after an uninterrupted period of at least two years of non-use, unless valid reasons based on the existence of obstacles to such use are shown by the trademark owner. Each Party shall recognize, as valid reasons for non-use, circumstances arising independently of the will of the trademark owner that constitute an obstacle to the use of the trademark, such as import restrictions on, or other government requirements for, goods or services identified by the trademark.

11. A Party may determine conditions on the licensing and assignment of trademarks, it being understood that the compulsory licensing of trademarks shall not be permitted and that the owner of a reg-

istered trademark shall have the right to assign its trademark with or without the transfer of the business to which the trademark belongs.

13. Each Party shall prohibit the registration as a trademark of words, at least in English, French or Spanish, that generically designate goods or services or types of goods or services to which the trademark applies.

### Article 1709
### Patents

1. [E]ach Party shall make patents available for any inventions, whether products or processes, in all fields of technology, provided that such inventions are new, result from an inventive step and are capable of industrial application. For purposes of this Article, a Party may deem the terms "inventive step" and "capable of industrial application" to be synonymous with the terms "non-obvious" and "useful," respectively.

5. Each Party shall provide that: (a) where the subject matter of a patent is a product, the patent shall confer on the patent owner the right to prevent other persons from making, using or selling the subject matter of the patent, without the patent owner's consent; and (b) where the subject matter of a patent is a process, the patent shall confer on the patent owner the right to prevent other persons from using that process and from using, selling, or importing at least the product obtained directly by that process, without the patent owner's consent.

### Article 1711
### Trade Secrets

1. Each Party shall provide the legal means for any person to prevent trade secrets from being disclosed to, acquired by, or used by others without the consent of the person lawfully in control of the information in a manner contrary to honest commercial practices, in so far as: (a) the information is secret in the sense that it is not, as a body or in the precise configuration and assembly of its components, generally known among or readily accessible to persons that normally deal with the kind of information in question; (b) the information has actual or potential commercial value because it is secret; and (c) the person lawfully in control of the information has taken reasonable steps under the circumstances to keep it secret.

2. A Party may require that to qualify for protection a trade secret must be evidenced in documents, electronic or magnetic means, optical discs, microfilms, films or other similar instruments.

3. No Party may limit the duration of protection for trade secrets, so long as the conditions in paragraph 1 exist.

### Article 1712
### Geographical Indications

1. Each Party shall provide, in respect of geographical indications, the legal means for interested persons to prevent: (a) the use of any means in the designation or presentation of a good that indicates or suggests that the good in question originates in a territory, region or locality other than the true place of origin, in a manner that misleads the public as to the geographical origin of the good; (b) any use that constitutes an act of unfair competition within the meaning of the Paris Convention.

2. Each Party shall, on its own initiative if its domestic law so permits or at the request of an interested person, refuse to register, or invalidate the registration of, a trademark containing or consisting of a geographical indication with respect to goods that do not originate in the indicated territory, region or locality, if use of the indication in the trademark for such goods is of such a nature as to mislead the public as to the geographical origin of the good.

## Chapter 22. Institutional Arrangements and Dispute Settlement Procedures

### Article 2001
### The Free Trade Commission

1. The Parties hereby establish the Free Trade Commission, comprising cabinet-level representatives of the Parties or their designees.

2. The Commission shall: (a) supervise the implementation of this Agreement . . . (c) resolve disputes that may arise regarding its interpretation or application; (d) supervise the work of all committees and working groups established under this Agreement. . . .

### Article 2005
### GATT Dispute Settlement

[D]isputes regarding any matter arising under both this Agreement and the General Agreement on Tariffs and Trade, any agreement negotiated thereunder, or any successor agreement (GATT), may be settled in either forum at the discretion of the complaining Party.

### Article 2021
### Private Rights

No Party may provide for a right of action under its domestic law against any other Party on the ground that a measure of another Party is inconsistent with this Agreement.

# Index